International GAAP® 2016

Generally Accepted Accounting Practice
under International Financial Reporting Standards

Martin Beyersdorff
Mike Bonham
Linzi Carr
Wei Li Chan
Tony Clifford
Angela Covic
Mike Davies
Pieter Dekker
Julie Dempers
Tim Denton
Marianne Dudareva
Jane Hurworth

Praveen Jindal
Ted Jones
Bernd Kremp
Dean Lockhart
Thomas Luescher
Sharon MacIntyre
Amanda Marrion
Steve Martin
Emily Moll
Richard Moore
Victoria O'Leary
Margaret Pankhurst

Christoph Piesbergen
Alexandra Poddubnaya
Michael Pratt
Inayatullah Qureshi
Tim Rogerson
Serene Seah-Tan
Anna Sirocka
Charlene Teo
Michael Varila
Tracey Waring
Jane Watson

EY
Building a better
working world

WILEY

About this book

International GAAP® 2016 has been fully revised and updated in order to:

- Explore the implementation issues arising as entities plan for the future adoption of IFRS 9 (*Financial Instruments*) and IFRS 15 (*Revenue from Contracts with Customers*), including those referred to the IFRS Transition Resource Group for Impairment of Financial Instruments and the Joint Transition Resource Group for Revenue Recognition.

- Address amended standards and new interpretations issued since the preparation of the 2015 edition.

- Explain the many other initiatives that are currently being discussed by the IASB and by the IFRS Interpretations Committee and the potential consequential changes to accounting requirements. In particular, projects on insurance contracts, leases and the conceptual framework for financial reporting may all result in significant changes to current accounting practice.

- Provide insight on the many issues relating to the practical application of IFRS, based on the extensive experience of the book's authors in dealing with recent day-to-day issues.

The book is published in three volumes. The 54 chapters – listed on pages ix to xi – are split between the three volumes as follows:

- Volume 1 - Chapters 1 to 20,
- Volume 2 - Chapters 21 to 40,
- Volume 3 - Chapters 41 to 54.

Each chapter includes a detailed list of contents and list of illustrative examples.

Each of the three volumes contains the following indexes covering all three volumes:

- an index of extracts from financial statements,
- an index of references to standards and interpretations,
- a general index.

Preface

The IASB reported earlier this year that 116 of the 140 jurisdictions they have researched require the use of IFRS for all or most listed companies and financial institutions, and a further 12 permit the use of IFRS. IFRS is clearly maturing and is now used in more countries than ever before. While there are some very large economies – China, India, Japan and the United States – that do not require IFRS for all or most of their listed companies, considerable progress has been made in these and other countries to move towards IFRS or to converge with IFRS. Although convergence between IFRS and US GAAP is no longer a primary objective of the IASB, there is a broad-based appreciation that companies around the world are best served by keeping the differences between IFRS and US GAAP to a minimum.

There have been a number of noteworthy developments regarding the governance of IFRS in the past year. In April 2015, the IFRS Foundation and the IASB presented their new mission statement, which is 'to develop International Financial Reporting Standards that bring transparency, accountability and efficiency to financial markets around the world. Our work serves the public interest by fostering trust, growth and long-term financial stability in the global economy.' The mission statement rightly puts accounting standard setting in its broader context of supporting the public interest and development of the global economy.

In July 2015, the trustees of the IFRS Foundation issued a request for views on the structure and effectiveness of the organisation. There have already been five reviews dealing with the constitution, strategy or governance of the IFRS Foundation. This is considerably more than for comparable international organisations and illustrates the fine balance that the IFRS Foundation needs to strike between its organisation as a private sector body and its public interest mission.

The existing three-tier model of the IASB, the Trustees and the Monitoring Board aims to achieve an appropriate balance between independence and accountability. Though it is structured as a private sector body, the IASB's increasing commitments to public authorities – for example, its membership of the Financial Stability Board, its link to the Monitoring Board, and memoranda of understanding with IOSCO and ESMA – have enhanced its legitimacy as a global standard setter. Although the three-tier structure was broadly supported in previous reviews of the IFRS Foundation, the Trustees are seeking views on the functioning of the structure and suggestions in the spirit of continuous improvement. In our view, the IFRS Foundation will need to continue to demonstrate to public authorities that it is able to operate an independent, yet responsive, standard-setting process within a framework of public accountability.

Michel Prada, Chairman of the Trustees of the IFRS Foundation, noted in a recent speech to the International Forum of Accounting Standard Setters that it is essential for the IFRS Foundation 'to foster trust and public confidence in its work' and that it needs 'to be inclusive in its activities and transparent in its decision-making and it also needs to be accountable'. In line with that sentiment, the current review focuses on the relevance of IFRS, consistent application of IFRS and the governance and financing of the IFRS Foundation. While past reviews have delivered incremental enhancements in governance, questions around sovereignty, democratic principles, funding, convergence and financial stability will undoubtedly also be raised in this review. In particular, we believe that the IFRS Foundation should use the responses to this consultation to develop a coherent strategy about how it can contribute constructively to and interact with other forms of reporting, such as corporate reporting, integrated reporting, sustainability reporting and reporting of alternative performance measures.

In August 2015, the IASB published its request for views *2015 Agenda Consultation*, which seeks input on the IASB's priorities from 2016 to 2020. We support the agenda consultation process as it allows the IASB to receive views from a wide range of constituents; in addition it makes the IASB's agenda setting process more transparent.

In the past year, the IASB has spent considerable time and effort on its main projects: leases, insurance contracts and the conceptual framework. The leases project is now nearing completion and is expected to be published in late 2015.

As we noted last year, the interaction between IFRS 9 and the insurance contracts project remains challenging. However, the IASB has made progress here and is expected to publish an exposure draft to accommodate insurance companies. The IASB has also made progress on the insurance contracts project itself, especially in the context of participating contracts, but more work is still to be done.

In May 2015, the IASB published its exposure draft *Conceptual Framework for Financial Reporting*. The exposure draft is more complete than the existing Conceptual Framework, as it covers in greater detail topics such as measurement, financial performance, derecognition and the reporting entity. Notably, the exposure draft also discusses the role of stewardship and prudence in financial reporting. However, important conceptual issues such as the distinction between debt and equity, the role of profit and loss versus other comprehensive income, the unit of account, non-exchange transactions and risk-sharing arrangements, may need to be further addressed. We understand the IASB will be deciding the direction of the project during the first half of 2016.

The IFRS Foundation Trustees have identified, in the 2015 review of the organisation, the consistency of application and implementation as one of the IFRS Foundation's primary strategic goals. They correctly see this in a holistic manner as requiring: clear drafting of standards, guidance that is consistent with a principle-based approach to standard setting, a responsive approach towards requests for interpretations, close co-operation with enforcers and educational efforts.

In that context, we note that the joint IASB/FASB transition resource group for revenue recognition and the IASB's transition resource group for impairment of financial instruments have provided valuable forums for identifying interpretation questions. Furthermore, the memoranda of understanding with IOSCO and ESMA, the involvement of enforcers in the IASB's processes and attendance of IASB members and staff in IFRS enforcers' discussion sessions play an important role in promoting consistency and coherence in enforcement.

Drafting accounting standards for a worldwide audience involves a particular level of complexity because constituents interpret the wording in the context of their own experience and background. Therefore we believe that a rigorous, transparent and broad-based review of standards, before they are issued, is essential in ensuring that they are clear, understandable and enforceable in practice. Such a robust review should reduce the need for transition resource groups and technical amendments shortly after issuing new standards.

The consistent application of IFRS remains essential to its credibility. We believe that *International GAAP*, now in its eleventh edition, plays an important role in ensuring consistent application. Our team of authors and reviewers hails from all parts of the world, and includes not only our global technical experts but also senior client-facing staff. This gives us an in-depth knowledge of practice in many different countries and industry sectors, enabling us to go beyond mere recitation of the requirements of standards to explaining their application in many varied situations.

****

We are deeply indebted to many of our colleagues within the global organisation of EY for their selfless assistance and support in the publication of this book. It has been a truly international effort, with valuable contributions from EY people around the globe.

Our thanks go particularly to those who reviewed, edited and assisted in the preparation of drafts, most notably: Justine Belton, Glenn Brady, Larissa Clark, Muriel Courel, Tai Danmola, Jackson Day, Gary Donald, Charles Feeney, Josh Forgione, Peter Gittens, Laure Guégan, Paul Hebditch, Guy Jones, Steve Kane, Dan Knightly, Akashi Kohno, Steinar Kvifte, Vincent de La Bachelerie, Twan van Limpt, Michiel van der Lof, James Luke, Robert McCracken, Joseph McGrath, Kerri Madden, Mark Mahar, John O'Grady, Eric Ohlund, Danita Ostling, Hedy Richards, Gerard van Santen, Tom Sciametta, Khilan Shah, Rachel Simons, Alison Spivey, Paul Sutcliffe, Leo van der Tas, Danny Trotman, Hans van der Veen, Arne Weber, Matthew Williams, Mark Woodward and Luci Wright.

Our thanks also go to everyone who directly or indirectly contributed to the book's creation, including the following members of the Financial Reporting Group in the UK: Denise Brand, Rob Carrington, Larissa Connor, Ann Gillan, Rabindra Jogarajan, Andrea Maylor, Bunmi Oluitan and Claire Taylor.

We also thank Jeremy Gugenheim for his assistance with the production technology throughout the period of writing.

London,	*Martin Beyersdorff*	*Praveen Jindal*	*Christoph Piesbergen*
October 2015	*Mike Bonham*	*Ted Jones*	*Alexandra Poddubnaya*
	Linzi Carr	*Bernd Kremp*	*Michael Pratt*
	Wei Li Chan	*Dean Lockhart*	*Inayatullah Qureshi*
	Tony Clifford	*Thomas Luescher*	*Tim Rogerson*
	Angela Covic	*Sharon MacIntyre*	*Serene Seah-Tan*
	Mike Davies	*Amanda Marrion*	*Anna Sirocka*
	Pieter Dekker	*Steve Martin*	*Charlene Teo*
	Julie Dempers	*Emily Moll*	*Michael Varila*
	Tim Denton	*Richard Moore*	*Tracey Waring*
	Marianne Dudareva	*Victoria O'Leary*	*Jane Watson*
	Jane Hurworth	*Margaret Pankhurst*	

Lists of chapters

Volume 1

The lists of chapters in volumes 2 and 3 follow overleaf.

Volume 2

The lists of chapters in volume 3 follows overleaf.

Volume 3

Abbreviations

The following abbreviations are used in this book:

Professional and regulatory bodies:

AASB	Australian Accounting Standards Board
AcSB	Accounting Standards Board of Canada
AICPA	American Institute of Certified Public Accountants
AOSSG	Asian-Oceanian Standard-Setters Group
APB	Accounting Principles Board (of the AICPA, predecessor of the FASB)
ARC	Accounting Regulatory Committee of representatives of EU Member States
ASAF	Accounting Standards Advisory Forum
ASB	Accounting Standards Board in the UK
ASBJ	Accounting Standards Board of Japan
ASU	Accounting Standards Update
CASC	China Accounting Standards Committee
CESR	Committee of European Securities Regulators, an independent committee whose members comprised senior representatives from EU securities regulators (replaced by ESMA)
CICA	Canadian Institute of Chartered Accountants
EC	European Commission
ECB	European Central Bank
ECOFIN	The Economic and Financial Affairs Council
EDTF	Enhanced Disclosure Task Force of the (FSB)
EFRAG	European Financial Reporting Advisory Group
EITF	Emerging Issues Task Force in the US
EPRA	European Public Real Estate Association
ESMA	European Securities and Markets Authority (see CESR)
EU	European Union
FAF	Financial Accounting Foundation
FASB	Financial Accounting Standards Board in the US
FCAG	Financial Crisis Advisory Group
FEE	Federation of European Accountants

FSB	Financial Stability Board (successor to the FSF)
FSF	Financial Stability Forum
G4+1	The (now disbanded) group of four plus 1, actually with six members, that comprised an informal 'think tank' of staff from the standard setters from Australia, Canada, New Zealand, UK, and USA, plus the IASC
G7	The Group of Seven Finance Ministers (successor to G8)
G8	The Group of Eight Finance Ministers
G20	The Group of Twenty Finance Ministers and Central Bank Governors
GPPC	Global Public Policy Committee of the six largest accounting networks
HKICPA	Hong Kong Institute of Certified Public Accountants
ICAI	Institute of Chartered Accountants of India
IASB	International Accounting Standards Board
IASC	International Accounting Standards Committee. The former Board of the IASC was the predecessor of the IASB
IASCF	International Accounting Standards Committee Foundation (predecessor of the IFRS Foundation)
ICAEW	Institute of Chartered Accountants in England and Wales
ICAS	Institute of Chartered Accountants of Scotland
IFAC	International Federation of Accountants
IFASS	International Forum of Accounting Standard Setters
IFRIC	The IFRS Interpretations Committee (formerly the International Financial Reporting Interpretations Committee) of the IASB
IGC	Implementation Guidance Committee on IAS 39 (now disbanded)
IOSCO	International Organisation of Securities Commissions
IPSASB	International Public Sector Accounting Standards Board
IPTF	International Practices Task Force (a task force of the SEC Regulations Committee)
ISDA	International Swaps and Derivatives Association
IVSC	International Valuation Standards Council
KASB	Korea Accounting Standards Board
RICS	Royal Institution of Chartered Surveyors
SAC	Standards Advisory Council, predecessor of the IFRS Advisory Council which provides advice to the IASB on a wide range of issues
SEC	Securities and Exchange Commission (the US securities regulator)
SIC	Standing Interpretations Committee of the IASC (replaced by IFRIC)
TEG	Technical Expert Group, an advisor to the European Commission
TRG	Joint Transition Resource Group for Revenue Recognition

Accounting related terms:

ADS	American Depositary Shares
AFS	Available-for-sale investment
ARB	Accounting Research Bulletins (issued by the AICPA)
ARS	Accounting Research Studies (issued by the APB)
ASC	Accounting Standards Codification®. The single source of authoritative US GAAP recognised by the FASB, to be applied to non-governmental entities for interim and accounting periods ending after 15 September 2009
ASU	Accounting Standards Update
CCIRS	Cross Currency Interest Rate Swap
CDO	Collateralised Debt Obligation
CGU	Cash-generating Unit
CU	Currency Unit
DD&A	Depreciation, Depletion and Amortisation
DPF	Discretionary Participation Feature
E&E	Exploration and Evaluation
EBIT	Earnings Before Interest and Taxes
EBITDA	Earnings Before Interest, Taxes, Depreciation and Amortisation
EIR	Effective Interest Rate
EPS	Earnings per Share
FAS	Financial Accounting Standards (issued by the FASB). Superseded by Accounting Standards Codification® (ASC)
FC	Foreign currency
FIFO	First-In, First-Out basis of valuation
FRS	Financial Reporting Standard (issued by the ASB)
FTA	First-time Adoption
FVLCD	Fair value less costs of disposal
FVLCS	Fair value less costs to sell (following the issue of IFRS 13, generally replaced by FVLCD)
GAAP	Generally accepted accounting practice (as it applies under IFRS), or generally accepted accounting principles (as it applies to the US)
HTM	Held-to-maturity investment
IAS	International Accounting Standard (issued by the former board of the IASC)
IBNR	Incurred but not reported claims
IFRS	International Financial Reporting Standard (issued by the IASB)
IGC Q&A	Implementation guidance to the original version of IAS 39 (issued by the IGC)

IPO	Initial Public Offering
IPR&D	In-process Research and Development
IPSAS	International Public Sector Accounting Standard
IRR	Internal Rate of Return
IRS	Interest Rate Swap
JA	Joint Arrangement
JCA	Jointly Controlled Asset
JCE	Jointly Controlled Entity
JCO	Jointly Controlled Operation
JO	Joint Operation
JV	Joint Venture
LAT	Liability Adequacy Test
LC	Local Currency
LIBOR	London Inter Bank Offered Rate
LIFO	Last-In, First-Out basis of valuation
NCI	Non-controlling Interest
NBV	Net Book Value
NPV	Net Present Value
NRV	Net Realisable Value
OCI	Other Comprehensive Income
PP&E	Property, Plant and Equipment
R&D	Research and Development
SCA	Service Concession Arrangement
SE	Structured Entity
SFAC	Statement of Financial Accounting Concepts (issued by the FASB as part of its conceptual framework project)
SFAS	Statement of Financial Accounting Standards (issued by the FASB). Superseded by Accounting Standards Codification® (ASC)
SME	Small or medium-sized entity
SPE	Special Purpose Entity
SV	Separate Vehicle
TSR	Total Shareholder Return
VIU	Value In Use
WACC	Weighted Average Cost of Capital

References to IFRSs, IASs, Interpretations and supporting documentation:

AG	Application Guidance
AV	Alternative View
B, BCZ	Basis for Conclusions on IASs
BC	Basis for Conclusions on IFRSs and IASs
DI	Draft Interpretation
DO	Dissenting Opinion
DP	Discussion Paper
ED	Exposure Draft
IE	Illustrative Examples on IFRSs and IASs
IG	Implementation Guidance
IN	Introduction to IFRSs and IASs

Authoritative literature

The content of this book takes into account all accounting standards and other relevant rules issued up to September 2015. Consequently, it covers the IASB's *Conceptual Framework for Financial Reporting* and authoritative literature listed below.

References in the main text of each chapter to the pronouncements below are generally to the versions of those pronouncements as approved and expected to be included in the Blue Book edition of the Bound Volume 2016 International Financial Reporting Standards – IFRS – Consolidated without early application – Official pronouncements applicable on 1 January 2016, to be published by the IASB.

References to those pronouncements below which have an effective date after 1 January 2016 (such as IFRS 9 – *Financial Instruments*) are to the versions of those pronouncements as denoted by the ISBN references noted below. These are expected to be included in the Red Book edition of the Bound Volume 2016 International Financial Reporting Standards – IFRS – Official pronouncements issued at 1 January 2016, to be published by the IASB.

References in the main text to pronouncements that applied only to periods beginning before 1 January 2016 are generally denoted by the last version of the Blue Book edition of the Bound Volume in which they were included. For example, IAS 27 (2012) refers to IAS 27 – *Consolidated and Separate Financial Statements*, which was included in the Blue Book edition of the Bound Volume 2012 International Financial Reporting Standards – IFRS – Consolidated without early application – Official pronouncements applicable on 1 January 2012.

US GAAP accounting standards are organised within a comprehensive FASB Accounting Standards Codification®, which is now the single source of authoritative US GAAP recognised by the FASB to be applied to non-governmental entities and has been applied in this publication.

† The standards and interpretations marked with a dagger have been withdrawn or superseded.

IASB Framework
The Conceptual Framework for Financial Reporting

International Financial Reporting Standards (2016 Bound Volume)	
IFRS 1	First-time Adoption of International Financial Reporting Standards
IFRS 2	Share-based Payment
IFRS 3	Business Combinations
IFRS 4	Insurance Contracts
IFRS 5	Non-current Assets Held for Sale and Discontinued Operations

IFRS Interpretations Committee Interpretations

Standing Interpretations Committee Interpretations

IASB Exposure Drafts

ED/2013/6	Leases
ED/2013/7	Insurance Contracts
ED/2014/3	Recognition of Deferred Tax Assets for Unrealised Losses (Proposed amendments to IAS 12)
ED/2014/4	Measuring Quoted Investments in Subsidiaries, Joint Ventures and Associates at Fair Value (Proposed amendments to IFRS 10, IFRS 12, IAS 27, IAS 28 and IAS 36 and Illustrative Examples for IFRS 13)
ED/2014/5	Classification and Measurement of Share-based Payment Transactions (proposed amendments to IFRS 2)
ED/2014/6	Disclosure Initiative (Proposed amendments to IAS 7)
ED/2015/1	Classification of Liabilities (Proposed amendments to IAS 1)
ED/2015/3	Conceptual Framework for Financial Reporting
ED/2015/4	Updating References to the Conceptual Framework (Proposed amendments to IFRS 2, IFRS 3, IFRS 4, IFRS 6, IAS 1, IAS 8, IAS 34, SIC-27 and SIC-32)
ED/2015/5	Remeasurement on a Plan Amendment, Curtailment or Settlement/Availability of a Refund from a Defined Benefit Plan (Proposed amendments to IAS 19 and IFRIC 14)
ED/2015/6	Clarifications to IFRS 15
ED/2015/7	Effective Date of Amendments to IFRS 10 and IAS 28

IFRS Interpretations Committee Exposure Drafts

DI/2012/2	Put Options Written on Non-controlling Interests	ISBN 978-1-907877-61-2

IASB Discussion Papers

DP/2014/1	Accounting for Dynamic Risk Management: a Portfolio Revaluation Approach to Macro Hedging	ISBN 978-1-909704-39-8
DP/2014/2	Reporting the Financial Effects of Rate Regulation	ISBN 978-1-909704-58-9

Other IASB publications

IFRS for SMEs	International Financial Reporting Standard (IFRS) for Small and Medium-sized Entities (SMEs)	ISBN 978-1-907026-16-4
IFRS for SMEs	International Financial Reporting Standard (IFRS) for Small and Medium-sized Entities (SMEs) – 2015 Amendments to the IFRS for SMEs (May 2015)	ISBN 978-1-909704-77-0

Chapter 41   Financial instruments: Introduction

Chapter 41   Financial instruments: Introduction

1   STANDARDS APPLYING TO FINANCIAL INSTRUMENTS

The IASB's accounting requirements for financial instruments are regarded by many as some of the more difficult to understand. There are many likely reasons for this, including the fact that it is such a broad topic encompassing some of the more complex contracts entities enter into. In addition, the requirements have been subject to a process of almost continual change over the last fifteen years or so and are dealt with in a number of different standards and other pronouncements.

The following are the standards which deal primarily with the accounting for financial instruments:

- IAS 32 – *Financial Instruments: Presentation;*
- IAS 39 – *Financial Instruments: Recognition and Measurement;*
- IFRS 7 – *Financial Instruments: Disclosures;* and
- IFRS 9 – *Financial Instruments.*

In addition a number of interpretations address the requirements of these standards, including:

- IFRIC 2 – *Members' Shares in Co-operative Entities and Similar Instruments;*
- IFRIC 9 – *Reassessment of Embedded Derivatives;*
- IFRIC 10 – *Interim Financial Reporting and Impairment;*
- IFRIC 16 – *Hedges of a Net Investment in a Foreign Operation;* and
- IFRIC 19 – *Extinguishing Financial Liabilities with Equity Instruments.*

Information about the development of the standards is set out at 1.1 to 1.4 below.

1.1   IAS 32

The original version of IAS 32 – *Financial Instruments: Disclosure and Presentation* – was published in March 1995. The presentation requirements of the standard were subject to significant review during 2002 and 2003 as part of the IASB's improvements project and a revised standard was published in December 2003. IFRS 7, which was published in August 2005, superseded the disclosure requirements in IAS 32 and the title of the latter standard was changed to reflect this. In February 2008, the IASB amended IAS 32 to change the classification of certain puttable financial instruments and instruments of limited life entities from liabilities to equity. Further amendments to IAS 32, designed to clarify its requirements for offsetting (or netting) of financial instruments, were issued in December 2011 and numerous other amendments have been made throughout the life of the standard.

The IASB recognises that the classification of financial instruments as liabilities or equity in accordance with IAS 32 presents many challenges. Consequently, it has embarked on a research project to explore whether the requirements in IAS 32 could be improved. In addition, it is looking at what improvements could be made to the presentation and disclosure requirements for financial instruments with characteristics of equity. The next formal step in this project is likely to be the publication of a discussion paper, but at the time of writing, the timing for this has yet to be determined.

1.2   IAS 39

IAS 39 was originally published in March 1999. Its origins could be found in US GAAP and at a high level there were only limited differences between the two systems. The IASC adopted a similar 'mixed attribute' model, i.e. some financial instruments were measured by reference to their historical cost and some by reference to their fair value and the main ideas embodied in IAS 39 were:

- derivatives (including some embedded within other contracts) were measured at fair value;
- many financial assets were also measured at fair value;
- non-derivative liabilities were measured at amortised cost;
- hedge accounting rules were established such that:
  - the methods of hedge accounting were defined in a way that severely curtailed existing practices in many countries;
  - hedges were tested for effectiveness; and
  - ineffectiveness was reported in profit or loss; and
- certain fair value gains and losses could be reported initially in equity before being recycled into profit or loss at a later date.

By dealing with most aspects of virtually all financial instruments, it was the longest, and by far the most complex, standard issued by the IASC. The IASC saw a consequent need to help preparers, auditors and users to understand the practical implications of IAS 39. They did this by establishing a process whereby guidance in the form of Questions and Answers (Q&A) was developed and over 200 final Q&A were published. IAS 39, like IAS 32, was subject to significant review during 2002 and 2003 as part of the IASB's improvements project and a revised standard, incorporating most of the Q&A as implementation guidance, was published in December 2003.

Many other changes have been made to IAS 39 since its original publication. These include amendments in March 2004 allowing the use of hedge accounting for certain portfolio (or macro) hedges of interest rate risk and more in June 2005 restricting the ability of entities to designate financial instruments at fair value through profit or loss. Another notable change was made during the financial crisis in October 2008, allowing entities to reclassify certain financial assets thereby reducing the use of fair value accounting (see Chapter 45 at 6). More recently, the publication of IFRS 9 will, when applied, result in most of the requirements of IAS 39 being superseded or carried forward to IFRS 9. However, as noted at 1.4 below, entities may continue to apply some or all the hedge accounting requirements of IAS 39 even after applying IFRS 9.

1.3   IFRS 7

A project principally focused on revising the then IAS 30 – *Disclosures in the Financial Statements of Banks and Similar Financial Institutions* – evolved into a comprehensive review of all disclosure requirements related to financial instruments. This resulted in the publication of IFRS 7 in August 2005, superseding IAS 30 and the disclosure requirements in IAS 32.

IFRS 7 has been subject to a number of amendments since publication. The requirements relating to liquidity risk were improved in the light of experience gained in the financial crisis; disclosures about transfers of financial assets were enhanced following an aborted attempt to revise the requirements addressing derecognition of financial assets in IAS 39; and more information about offsetting and netting agreements is now required. IFRS 9, when applied, also makes a significant number of amendments and additions to IFRS 7.

1.4   IFRS 9

In April 2009, during the financial crisis, the IASB committed itself to a comprehensive review of IAS 39. The IASB's plan split this project into the following three phases, each of which would result in the publication of requirements replacing the corresponding parts of IAS 39:

- classification of financial assets and financial liabilities;
- impairment and the effective interest method; and
- hedge accounting.

Originally, the IASB had proposed a very simplified accounting model under which all financial instruments would be measured either at amortised cost or at fair value through profit or loss. However, additional categories of financial asset were introduced allowing certain investments in debt and equity instruments to be measured at fair value with most changes in value recognised in other comprehensive income. For debt instruments, those gains and losses are subsequently recycled to profit or loss on derecognition. In addition, the accounting for financial liabilities was eventually left much the same as in IAS 39, although the IASB introduced a requirement to recognise in other comprehensive income (rather than profit or loss) gains or losses on most financial liabilities designated at fair value through profit or loss to the extent they represent changes in the instrument's credit risk. The requirements of these parts of IFRS 9 are primarily covered in Chapters 46 and 49.

During the financial crisis, a number of commentators criticised the requirements of IAS 39 for unnecessarily delaying the recognition of impairments. IAS 39 uses a so called 'incurred loss' approach whereby impairments are not recognised until there is objective evidence of the impairment having occurred. The requirements in IFRS 9 are better described as an 'expected loss' approach. In almost all circumstances, applying IFRS 9 will result in the recognition of an impairment expense sooner than would have been the case under IAS 39. Consequently, at any point in time, an entity will have accumulated a higher impairment provision (and report a lower amount of equity) than would have arisen from applying IAS 39. This part of IFRS 9 is covered in Chapter 49 at 5.

The hedge accounting phase of the project was designed to simplify hedge accounting, expand the relationships for which hedge accounting could be applied and align the accounting requirements more closely with entities' risk management practices. IFRS 9 does not itself address portfolio hedge accounting and, viewed in isolation, is much less accommodating than IAS 39. However, IFRS 9 does allow for the continued application of the portfolio fair value hedge accounting requirements of IAS 39 alongside its more general hedge accounting requirements. In addition, entities wishing to use the portfolio cash flow hedge accounting guidance in IAS 39 can continue applying the entirety of IAS 39's hedge accounting requirements but without applying any of the hedge accounting requirements of IFRS 9.

The IASB has a separate project which aims to eliminate any need for this continued application of IAS 39 (and also the so-called EU 'carve-out' – see 2 below). A discussion paper, *Accounting for Dynamic Risk Management: a Portfolio Revaluation Approach to Macro Hedging*, was published in April 2014, but the IASB has since concluded it is not yet in a position to develop its proposals into an exposure draft. Instead, the likely next step will be the publication of another discussion paper and the timing for this has yet to be determined. The hedge accounting requirements of IFRS 9 are covered in Chapter 52 and those of IAS 39 in Chapter 51.

The first version of IFRS 9 was published in November 2009 and significant amendments followed in October 2010 and November 2013 before it was finally completed in July 2014. Adoption of IFRS 9 is required for periods commencing on or after 1 January 2018. A number of constituents, primarily but not exclusively from Europe, have called for insurers to be allowed a delay in their application of IFRS 9. This is to avoid certain accounting consequences that might arise from applying IFRS 9 before a replacement for IFRS 4 – *Insurance Contracts.* Further information about this is included in Chapter 54 at 11.

During the development of IFRS 9, the IASB worked closely with its counterparts at the FASB with the aim of aligning as far as possible the financial reporting requirements for financial instruments in accordance with IFRS and US GAAP. However, only limited progress has been made to date in achieving this objective. The requirements for measuring fair values under the two bodies of GAAP are to a large extent the same and, at the time of writing, it is expected that the FASB will introduce some form of expected loss model for recognising impairments. However, there remain significant differences in other areas including the approaches to classifying and measuring financial assets and to offsetting of financial assets and financial liabilities. Important differences also remain in the area of hedge accounting.

1.5 Structure and objectives of the standards

The main text of the standards is supplemented by application guidance (which is an integral part of each standard).[1] IAS 32, IAS 39 and IFRS 9 are each supplemented by illustrative examples and IAS 39, IFRS 7 and IFRS 9 by implementation guidance. These examples and guidance accompany, but are not part of, the standards.[2]

The objective of IAS 32 is to establish principles for presenting financial instruments as liabilities or equity and for offsetting financial assets and financial liabilities *[IAS 32.2]* whilst for IAS 39 (until IFRS 9 is applied) it is to establish principles for recognising and measuring financial assets, financial liabilities and some contracts to buy or sell non-financial items. *[IAS 39.1]*. The objective of IFRS 9 is to establish principles for the financial reporting of financial assets and financial liabilities that will present relevant and useful information to users of financial statements for their assessment of the amounts, timing and uncertainty of the entity's future cash flows. *[IFRS 9.1.1]*. The objective of IFRS 7 is to require entities to provide disclosures in their financial statements that enable users to evaluate:

(a) the significance of financial instruments for the entity's financial position and performance; and

(b) the nature and extent of risks arising from financial instruments to which the entity is exposed during the period and at the reporting date, and how the entity manages those risks. *[IFRS 7.1]*.

2 ADOPTION OF IFRS IN THE EUROPEAN UNION

An endorsement mechanism has been implemented whereby only those standards and interpretations that have been adopted for application within the EU may be applied in financial statements prepared in accordance with the 'IAS Regulation'. The role of this mechanism is not to reformulate or replace IFRSs, but to oversee the adoption of new standards and interpretations, intervening only when they contain material deficiencies or have failed to cater for features specific to the EU economic or legal environments. Given the number of constituents within the EU, the potential for non-endorsement in practice provides a degree of additional leverage over the work of the IASB.

IAS 39 as endorsed for use in the EU is currently different in one important respect from the version published by the IASB. Certain text has been removed (commonly known as a 'carve-out') so that, essentially, the EU version allows the use of macro-hedge accounting in situations that the full version of IAS 39 does not.[3] The European Commission has continued to emphasise the need for the IASB and representatives of European banks to find an appropriate technical solution to allow the removal of the carve-out as rapidly as possible.[4] However, there have been only limited signs of progress on this issue and IFRS 9 will not remove the reasons for the carve-out (see 1.4 above).

Originally IFRS 9 was scheduled for fast-track endorsement so that banks could apply the first version in their 2009 financial statements. However, these plans were withdrawn and the process postponed pending completion of the entire standard. At the time of writing, it had been suggested that endorsement might occur by the end of 2015, but until that happens European companies are prohibited from adopting IFRS 9 in financial statements prepared in accordance with the IAS Regulation. It is also possible, although by no means certain, that the endorsed version of IFRS 9 will allow insurers a later mandatory effective date to avoid certain possible accounting consequences of applying IFRS 9 before a replacement for IFRS 4 is available (see 1.4 above).

3   HOW FINANCIAL INSTRUMENTS ARE DEALT WITH IN CHAPTERS 41 TO 53

The subject matter of this and the next twelve chapters is the recognition, measurement, presentation and disclosure of financial instruments as addressed in IAS 32, IAS 39, IFRS 7 and, where applied, IFRS 9. The topics covered by each, are as follows:

Chapter 41 – *Introduction*
- standards dealing with financial instruments
- European adoption

Chapter 42 – *Definitions and scope*
- key definitions
- scope and exceptions

Chapter 43 – *Derivatives and embedded derivatives*
- the defining characteristics of derivatives
- derivatives embedded within other contracts
- linked and separate transactions and 'synthetic' instruments

Chapter 44 – *Financial liabilities and equity*
- the classification of financial instruments by their issuer as financial liabilities or equity
- contracts settled by the delivery of equity instruments
- compound financial instruments (i.e. those containing both a liability and an equity component from the issuer's perspective)
- settlement of financial liabilities with equity instruments
- accounting for interest, dividends gains and losses
- treasury shares (i.e. shares held by their issuer)

Chapter 45 – *Classification (IAS 39)*
- determining the measurement category of financial assets and financial liabilities

Chapter 46 – *Classification (IFRS 9)*
- determining the measurement category of financial assets and financial liabilities

Chapter 47 – *Recognition and initial measurement*
- recognition
- initial measurement

Chapter 48 – *Subsequent measurement (IAS 39)*
- subsequent measurement and recognition of gains and losses
- amortised cost and the effective interest method
- impairment of financial assets
- the effect of foreign currencies

Chapter 49 – *Subsequent measurement (IFRS 9)*
- subsequent measurement and recognition of gains and losses
- amortised cost and the effective interest method
- impairment of financial assets
- the effect of foreign currencies

Chapter 50 – *Derecognition*
- derecognition of financial assets
- derecognition of financial liabilities

Chapter 51 – *Hedge accounting (IAS 39)*
- hedging instruments and hedged items
- types of hedging relationships
- accounting for effective hedges
- qualifying conditions for hedge accounting
- portfolio (or macro) hedging

Chapter 52 – *Hedge accounting (IFRS 9)*
- hedging instruments and hedged items
- qualifying conditions for hedge accounting
- other changes from IAS 39

Chapter 53 – *Presentation and disclosure*
- disclosure requirements of IFRS 7
- presentation of financial instruments and related transactions, gains and losses in the financial statements.

References

1 IAS 32, Application Guidance, para. before para. AG1, IAS 39, Application guidance, para. before para. AG1, IFRS 7, *Financial Instruments: Disclosure,* Appendix B, Application guidance, para. after main heading, IFRS 9, *Financial Instruments,* Appendix B, Application guidance, para. after main heading.

2 IAS 32, Illustrative Examples, para. after main heading, IAS 39, Illustrative Example, para. after main heading and Guidance on Implementing, para. before main heading Section A, IFRS 7, Guidance on implementing, para. after main heading and IFRS 9, Illustrative Example, para. after main heading and Guidance on Implementing, para. before main heading Section B.

3 Press Release IP/04/1385, *Accounting standards: Commission endorses IAS 39,* European Commission, 19 November 2004.

4 Press Release IP/05/1423, *Accounting standards: Commission endorses 'IAS 39 Fair Value Option',* European Commission, 15 November 2005.

Chapter 42   Financial instruments: Definitions and scope

List of examples

Chapter 42   Financial instruments: Definitions and scope

1   INTRODUCTION

In many cases it will be clear whether an asset, liability, equity share or other similar instrument should be accounted for in accordance with one or more of the relevant standards that apply to financial instruments. However, at the margins, determining whether these IFRSs should be applied is not so easy.

Firstly, one needs to determine whether the definition of a financial instrument is met; secondly, not all financial instruments are within the scope of each of these IFRSs – some are within the scope of other standards and some are not within the scope of any standard; and finally, certain contracts that do not meet the definition of a financial instrument are within the scope of some of these standards.

This chapter addresses these issues in three main sections covering the following broad areas:

*   application of the definitions used in IFRS, i.e. determining what a financial instrument actually is (see 2 below);
*   determining which financial instruments are within the scope of which standards (see 3 below); and
*   assessing whether a non-financial contract is to be accounted for as if it were a financial instrument (see 4 below).

IFRS 9 – *Financial Instruments* – was finalised by the IASB in July 2014. It is effective for periods beginning on or after 1 January 2018 and will replace substantially all of the requirements relating to the recognition and measurement of financial instruments in IAS 39 – *Financial Instruments: Recognition and Measurement*. Where IFRS 9 changes the definitions or its scope is different to IAS 39, this is noted in the relevant part of this chapter.

2   WHAT IS A FINANCIAL INSTRUMENT?

2.1   Definitions

The main terms used in the standards that apply to financial instruments are defined in IAS 32 – *Financial Instruments: Presentation* – as follows:

A *financial instrument* is any contract that gives rise to a financial asset of one entity and a financial liability or equity instrument of another entity.

A *financial asset* is any asset that is:

(a)   cash;

(b)   an equity instrument of another entity;

(c)   a contractual right:

   (i)   to receive cash or another financial asset from another entity; or

   (ii)   to exchange financial assets or financial liabilities with another entity under conditions that are potentially favourable to the entity; or

(d)   a contract that will or may be settled in the entity's own equity instruments and is:

   (i)   a non-derivative for which the entity is or may be obliged to receive a variable number of the entity's own equity instruments; or

   (ii)   a derivative that will or may be settled other than by the exchange of a fixed amount of cash or another financial asset for a fixed number of the entity's own equity instruments. For this purpose the entity's own equity instruments do not include certain puttable and similar financial instruments classified by exception as equity instruments (see Chapter 44 at 4.6) or instruments that are themselves contracts for the future receipt or delivery of the entity's own equity instruments.

A *financial liability* is any liability that is:

(a)   a contractual obligation:

   (i)   to deliver cash or another financial asset to another entity; or

   (ii)   to exchange financial assets or financial liabilities with another entity under conditions that are potentially unfavourable to the entity; or

(b)   a contract that will or may be settled in the entity's own equity instruments and is:

   (i)   a non-derivative for which the entity is or may be obliged to deliver a variable number of the entity's own equity instruments; or

   (ii)   a derivative that will or may be settled other than by the exchange of a fixed amount of cash or another financial asset for a fixed number of the entity's own equity instruments. For this purpose the entity's own equity instruments do not include certain puttable and similar financial instruments classified by exception as equity instruments, or instruments that are themselves contracts for the future receipt or delivery of the entity's own equity instruments.

An *equity instrument* is any contract that evidences a residual interest in the assets of an entity after deducting all of its liabilities. *[IAS 32.11].*

For the purpose of these definitions, 'entity' includes individuals, partnerships, incorporated bodies, trusts and government agencies. *[IAS 32.14].*

2.2   Applying the definitions

2.2.1   *The need for a contract*

The terms 'contract' and 'contractual' are important to the definitions and refer to 'an agreement between two or more parties that has clear economic consequences that the parties have little, if any, discretion to avoid, usually because the agreement is enforceable by law'. Such contracts may take a variety of forms and need not be in writing. *[IAS 32.13].*

The Interpretations Committee examined the question of what constitutes a contract in the context of gaming transactions. This is because, in some jurisdictions, a wager does not give rise to a contract that is enforceable under local contract law. The Interpretations Committee staff noted that a gaming transaction constitutes an agreement between two or more parties that has clear economic consequences for both. Furthermore, in most countries, gambling is heavily regulated and only parties acting within a regulated framework are licensed to operate gaming institutions, so that such entities cannot realistically fail to pay out on a good wager and therefore the gaming institution will have little or no discretion as to whether it pays out on the bet. Consequently, the Interpretations Committee agreed that a wager should be treated as a contract.[1]

Whilst this seems an entirely plausible analysis in context, it is a little difficult to reconcile with the conclusions of the Interpretations Committee and the IASB concerning the existence (or otherwise) of a contractual obligation to make payments on certain preference shares and similar securities. In those cases, terms of an instrument that effectively force the issuer to transfer cash or other financial assets to the holder although not legally required to do so (often referred to as 'economic compulsion'), are not taken into account (see Chapter 44 at 4.5.6).

A contractual right or contractual obligation to receive, deliver or exchange financial instruments is itself a financial instrument. A chain of contractual rights or contractual obligations meets the definition of a financial instrument if it will ultimately lead to the receipt or payment of cash or to the acquisition or issue of an equity instrument. *[IAS 32.AG7].*

Assets and liabilities relating to non-contractual arrangements that arise as a result of statutory requirements imposed by governments, such as income taxes or levies are not financial liabilities or financial assets because they are not contractual. *[IAS 32.AG12].* Accounting for income taxes is dealt with in more detail in another standard, IAS 12 – *Income Taxes* (see Chapter 30), while levies are covered by IFRIC 21 – *Levies* (see Chapter 27).

Similarly, constructive obligations as defined in IAS 37 – *Provisions, Contingent Liabilities and Contingent Assets* (see Chapter 27 at 3.1.1) do not arise from contracts and are therefore not financial liabilities. *[IAS 32.AG12].*

2.2.2   Simple financial instruments

Currency (or cash) is a financial asset because it represents the medium of exchange and is therefore the basis on which all transactions are measured and recognised in financial statements. A deposit of cash with a bank or similar financial institution is a financial asset because it represents the contractual right of the depositor to obtain cash from the institution or to draw a cheque or similar instrument against the balance in favour of a creditor in payment of a financial liability. *[IAS 32.AG3].*

The following common financial instruments give rise to financial assets representing a contractual right to receive cash in the future and corresponding financial liabilities representing a contractual obligation to deliver cash in the future:

(a)   trade accounts receivable and payable;

(b)   notes receivable and payable;

(c)   loans receivable and payable; and

(d)   bonds receivable and payable.

In each case, one party's contractual right to receive (or obligation to pay) cash is matched by the other party's corresponding obligation to pay (or right to receive). *[IAS 32.AG4].*

Another type of financial instrument is one for which the economic benefit to be received or given up is a financial asset other than cash. For example, a note payable in government bonds gives the holder the contractual right to receive, and the issuer the contractual obligation to deliver, government bonds, not cash. The bonds are financial assets because they represent obligations of the issuing government to pay cash. The note is, therefore, a financial asset of the note holder and a financial liability of the note issuer. *[IAS 32.AG5].*

Perpetual debt instruments (such as perpetual bonds, debentures and capital notes) normally provide the holder with the contractual right to receive payments on account of interest at fixed dates extending indefinitely, either with no right to receive a return of principal or a right to a return of principal under terms that make it very unlikely or very far in the future. For example, an entity may issue a financial instrument requiring it to make annual payments in perpetuity equal to a stated interest rate of 8% applied to a stated par or principal amount of $1,000. Assuming 8% is the market rate of interest for the instrument when issued, the issuer assumes a contractual obligation to make a stream of future interest payments having a net present value (or fair value) of $1,000 on initial recognition. The holder and issuer of the instrument have a financial asset and a financial liability, respectively. *[IAS 32.AG6].*

2.2.3   Contingent rights and obligations

The ability to exercise a contractual right or the requirement to satisfy a contractual obligation may be absolute (as in the examples at 2.2.2 above), or it may be contingent on the occurrence of a future event. A contingent right or obligation, e.g. to receive or deliver cash, meets the definition of a financial asset or a financial liability. *[IAS 32.AG8].*

For example, a financial guarantee is a contractual right of the lender to receive cash from the guarantor, and a corresponding contractual obligation of the guarantor to pay the lender, if the borrower defaults. The contractual right and obligation exist because of a past transaction or event (the assumption of the guarantee), even though the lender's ability to exercise its right and the requirement for the guarantor to perform under its obligation are both contingent on a future act of default by the borrower. *[IAS 32.AG8]*.

However, even though contingent rights and obligations can meet the definition of a financial instrument, they are not always recognised in the financial statements as such. For example, contingent rights and obligations may be insurance contracts within the scope of IFRS 4 – *Insurance Contracts* (see Chapter 54 at 3.3) or may otherwise be excluded from the scope of IAS 39 or IFRS 9, when applied (see 3 below). *[IAS 32.AG8]*.

2.2.4   Leases

A finance lease, according to the accounting model in IAS 17 – *Leases,* is regarded as primarily an entitlement to receive, and an obligation to make, a stream of payments that are substantially the same as blended payments of principal and interest under a loan agreement. The lessor accounts for its investment in the amount receivable under the lease contract rather than the leased asset itself. *[IAS 32.AG9]*. The lessee accounts for its obligation to the lessor (in addition to the leased asset).

An operating lease, on the other hand, is regarded as primarily an uncompleted contract committing the lessor to provide the use of an asset in future periods in exchange for consideration similar to a fee for a service. The lessor continues to account for the leased asset itself rather than any amount receivable in the future under the contract. *[IAS 32.AG9]*.

Accordingly, a finance lease arrangement is regarded as a financial instrument and an operating lease is not regarded as a financial instrument except as regards individual payments currently due and payable. *[IAS 32.AG9]*. Nevertheless, as discussed in more detail at 3.2 below, financial instruments arising from leases are not always accounted for under IAS 39 or IFRS 9.

The standards do not explicitly address whether an accrued liability (or receivable) under an operating lease meets the definition of a financial liability (or financial asset) before the due date for payment. However, the guidance on accounting for service concession arrangements (see 2.2.6 below) suggests that such accruals should be considered financial instruments.

2.2.5   Non-financial assets and liabilities and contracts thereon

Physical assets (such as inventories, property, plant and equipment), leased assets and intangible assets (such as patents and trademarks) are not financial assets. Control of such physical and intangible assets creates an opportunity to generate an inflow of cash or another financial asset, but it does not give rise to a present right to receive cash or another financial asset. *[IAS 32.AG10]*. For example, whilst gold bullion is highly liquid (and perhaps more liquid than many financial instruments), it gives no contractual right to receive cash or another financial asset, and so is therefore a commodity, not a financial asset. *[IAS 39.B.1, IFRS 9.B.1]*.

Assets such as prepaid expenses, for which the future economic benefit is the receipt of goods or services rather than the right to receive cash or another financial asset, are not financial assets. Similarly, items such as deferred revenue and most warranty obligations are not financial liabilities because the outflow of economic benefits associated with them is the delivery of goods and services rather than a contractual obligation to pay cash or another financial asset. *[IAS 32.AG11].*

Contracts to buy or sell non-financial items do not meet the definition of a financial instrument because the contractual right of one party to receive a non-financial asset or service and the corresponding obligation of the other party do not establish a present right or obligation of either party to receive, deliver or exchange a financial asset. For example, contracts that provide for settlement only by the receipt or delivery of a non-financial item (e.g. an option, future or forward contract on silver and many similar commodity contracts) are not financial instruments. However, as set out at 4 below, certain contracts to buy or sell non-financial items that can be settled net or by exchanging financial instruments, or in which the non-financial item is readily convertible into cash are included within the scope of IAS 32, IAS 39 and IFRS 9, essentially because they exhibit similar characteristics to financial instruments. *[IAS 32.AG20].*

In some industries, e.g. brewing and heating gas, entities distribute their products in returnable containers. Often, these entities will collect a cash deposit for each container delivered which they have an obligation to refund on return of the container. The Interpretations Committee found itself in November 2007 addressing the classification of these obligations, in particular whether they met the definition of a financial instrument.[2] It is easy to jump to the conclusion (as the Interpretations Committee did initially[3]) that such an arrangement represents a contract to exchange a non-financial item (the container) for cash and is therefore outside the scope of IAS 39. However, the Interpretations Committee recognised that this analysis holds true only if, in accounting terms, the container ceases to be an asset of the entity when the sale is made, i.e. it is derecognised. If the container is not derecognised, the entity cannot be regarded as receiving the non-financial asset because the accounting treatment regards the entity as retaining the asset. Instead, the deposit simply represents an obligation to transfer cash and is therefore a financial liability.[4]

Some contracts are commodity-linked, but do not involve settlement through the physical receipt or delivery of a commodity. Instead they specify settlement through cash payments that are determined according to a formula in the contract. For example, the principal amount of a bond may be calculated by applying the market price of oil prevailing at the maturity of the bond to a fixed quantity of oil, but is settled only in cash. Such a contract constitutes a financial instrument. *[IAS 32.AG22].*

Financial instruments also include contracts that give rise to a non-financial asset or non-financial liability in addition to a financial asset or financial liability. Such arrangements often give one party an option to exchange a financial asset for a non-financial asset. For example, an oil-linked bond may give the holder the right to receive a stream of fixed periodic interest payments and a fixed amount of cash on maturity, with the option to exchange the principal amount for a fixed quantity of oil. The desirability of exercising this option will vary over time depending on the fair value of oil relative to the exchange ratio of cash for oil (the exchange price) inherent in the bond, but the intentions of the bondholder do not affect the substance of the component assets. The financial asset of the holder and the financial liability of the issuer make the bond a financial instrument, regardless of the other types of assets and liabilities also created. *[IAS 32.AG23]*.

2.2.6 *Payments for goods and services*

Where payment on a contract involving the receipt or delivery of physical assets is deferred past the date of transfer of the asset, a financial instrument arises at the date of delivery. In other words, the sale or purchase of goods on trade credit gives rise to a financial asset (a trade receivable) and a financial liability (a trade payable) when the goods are transferred. *[IAS 32.AG21]*. This is the case even if an invoice is not issued at the time of delivery.

IAS 32 does not explain whether the same logic should apply to the delivery of other, less tangible, non-financial items, e.g. construction or other services. IFRIC 12 – *Service Concession Arrangements* – provides guidance on how operators of service concessions over public infrastructure assets should account for these arrangements. Where an operator obtains an unconditional contractual right to receive cash from the grantor in exchange for construction or other services, the accrued revenue represents a financial asset. This is the case even if payment is not due immediately and even if it is contingent on the operator ensuring that the underlying infrastructure meets specified quality or efficiency requirements (see Chapter 26 at 4.2). *[IFRIC 12.16]*.

However, should the same logic apply to the delivery of construction or other services where the revenue earned is accounted for under IAS 11 – *Construction Contracts* – or IAS 18 – *Revenue*? In these cases it is not entirely clear whether amounts recoverable on contracts or other accrued revenue that is not currently due and payable should be considered a financial asset. Whilst the guidance on accounting for service concession arrangements suggests that these assets should be regarded as financial instruments, the standards are not clear on this, at least in cases where future performance is necessary before a payment becomes due.

In July 2008 the Interpretations Committee considered a similar issue, namely the question of when trail commissions paid by an investment manager to a financial advisor should be recognised as revenue (or a liability) if no further services are to be provided. Typically, an advisor will continue to receive payments from the manager whose products were recommended by them, provided the client does not withdraw or redeem the invested funds. Similar arrangements are common in many other industries, for example telecommunications where the retailer of a mobile telephone and related contract will often receive commissions from the network operator based on the customer's telephone usage.

The Interpretations Committee staff was clear in its analysis that the advisor's contingent right to receive uncertain amounts of cash from the investment manager represented a financial asset that should be recognised as revenue immediately. Similarly, it concluded that the fund should recognise a financial liability. The staff noted, in particular, that payments do not need to be certain or fixed in amount for a financial instrument to exist.[5] However, the Interpretations Committee decided not to take the issue onto its agenda, noting the complexity of the issue, the pervasive effect of any conclusions reached and that there was diversity in practice. This diversity was, it said, caused in part by the difficulty in determining whether the entity is required to provide any future service in return for the commission, considering all relevant circumstances, and also by the fact that IAS 18 and IAS 39 or IFRS 9 have different recognition criteria and views differ on which is the relevant standard.[6]

IAS 11 and IAS 18 are replaced by IFRS 15 – *Revenue from Contracts with Customers* – with effect from 1 January 2018. Rights and obligations within the scope of IFRS 15 are not accounted for as financial instruments, other than unconditional rights to consideration in exchanges for goods and services transferred to the customer that IFRS 15 specifies as accounted for in accordance with IAS 39 or IFRS 9 (see Chapter 29 at 9.1). *[IAS 39.2(k), IFRS 9.2.1(j), IFRS 15.108].* This will provide a degree more clarity about the accounting to be followed by a supplier of goods or services. Furthermore, the consequential amendments to IFRIC 12 brought in by IFRS 15 align the IFRIC 12 guidance with IFRS 15.

2.2.7   Equity instruments

Equity instruments include non-puttable ordinary shares, some puttable and similar instruments, some types of preference shares and warrants or written call options that allow the holder to subscribe for or purchase a fixed number of non-puttable ordinary shares in the issuing entity, in exchange for a fixed amount of cash or another financial asset. *[IAS 32.AG13].* The definition of equity instruments is considered in more detail in Chapter 44 at 3.

2.2.8   Derivative financial instruments

As well as primary instruments such as receivables, payables and equity instruments, financial instruments also include derivatives such as financial options, futures and forwards, interest rate swaps and currency swaps. Derivatives normally transfer one or more of the financial risks inherent in an underlying primary instrument between the contracting parties without any need to transfer the underlying instruments themselves (either at inception of the contract or even, where cash settled, on termination). *[IAS 32.AG15, AG16].*

There are important accounting consequences for financial instruments that are considered to be derivatives, and the defining characteristics of derivatives are covered in more detail in Chapter 43 at 2.

As noted at 2.2.5 above, certain derivative contracts on non-financial items are included within the scope of IAS 32 and IAS 39, even though they are not, strictly, financial instruments as defined. These contracts are covered in more detail at 4 below.

On inception, the terms of a derivative financial instrument generally give one party a contractual right (or obligation) to exchange financial assets or financial liabilities with another party under conditions that are potentially favourable (or unfavourable). Some instruments embody both a right and an obligation to make an exchange and, as prices in financial markets change, those terms may become either favourable or unfavourable. *[IAS 32.AG16].*

A put or call option to exchange financial assets or financial liabilities gives the holder a right to obtain potential future economic benefits associated with changes in the fair value of the underlying instrument. Conversely, the writer of an option assumes an obligation to forgo such potential future economic benefits or bear potential losses associated with the underlying instrument. The contractual right (or obligation) of the holder (or writer) meets the definition of a financial asset (or liability). The financial instrument underlying an option contract may be any financial asset, including shares in other entities and interest-bearing instruments. An option may require the writer to issue a debt instrument, rather than transfer a financial asset, but the instrument underlying the option would constitute a financial asset of the holder if the option were exercised. The option-holder's right (or writer's obligation) to exchange the financial asset under potentially favourable (or unfavourable) conditions is distinct from the underlying financial asset to be exchanged upon exercise of the option. The nature of the holder's right and of the writer's obligation (which characterises such contracts as a financial instrument) are not affected by the likelihood that the option will be exercised. *[IAS 32.AG17].*

Another common type of derivative is a forward contract. For example, consider a contract in which two parties (the seller and the purchaser) promise in six months' time to exchange $1,000 cash (the purchaser will pay cash) for $1,000 face amount of fixed rate government bonds (the seller will deliver the bonds). During those six months, both parties have a contractual right and a contractual obligation to exchange financial instruments (cash in exchange for bonds). If the market price of the government bonds rises above $1,000, the conditions will be favourable to the purchaser and unfavourable to the seller, and *vice versa* if the market price falls below $1,000. The purchaser has a contractual right (a financial asset) similar to the right under a call option held and a contractual obligation (a financial liability) similar to the obligation under a put option written. The seller has a contractual right (a financial asset) similar to the right under a put option held and a contractual obligation (a financial liability) similar to the obligation under a call option written. As with options, these contractual rights and obligations constitute financial assets and financial liabilities separate and distinct from the underlying financial instruments (the bonds and cash to be exchanged). Both parties to a forward contract have an obligation to perform at the agreed time, whereas performance under an option contract occurs only if and when the holder of the option chooses to exercise it. *[IAS 32.AG18].*

Many other types of derivative also embody a right or obligation to make a future exchange, including interest rate and currency swaps, interest rate caps, collars and floors, loan commitments, note issuance facilities and letters of credit. An interest rate swap contract may be viewed as a variation of a forward contract in which the parties agree to make a series of future exchanges of cash amounts, one amount calculated with reference to a floating interest rate and the other with reference to a fixed interest rate. Futures contracts are another variation of forward contracts, differing primarily in that the contracts are standardised and traded on an exchange. *[IAS 32.AG19].*

Chapter 42

2.2.9   *Dividends payable*

As part of its project to provide authoritative accounting guidance for non-cash distributions (see Chapter 8 at 2.4.2), the Interpretations Committee found itself debating the seemingly simple question of how to account for a declared but unpaid cash dividend (or, more accurately, which standard applies to such a liability). Although there are clear indicators within IFRS that an obligation to pay a cash dividend is a financial liability,[7] the Interpretations Committee originally proposed that IAS 37 should be applied to all dividend obligations,[8] a decision that appeared to have been made more on the grounds of expediency rather than using any robust technical analysis. By the time IFRIC 17 – *Distributions of Non-cash Assets to Owners* – was published in November 2008, the Interpretations Committee had modified its position slightly. Aside from those standards dealing with the measurement of liabilities that are clearly not relevant (e.g. IAS 12), they considered that others, such as IAS 37 and IAS 39, were simply not applicable because they addressed liabilities arising only from exchange transactions, whereas IFRIC 17 dealt with non-reciprocal distributions. *[IFRIC 17.BC22]*. Instead, IFRIC 17 simply specifies the accounting treatment to be applied to distributions without linking to any individual standard. *[IFRIC 17.BC27]*. In other words, the Interpretations Committee appeared to conclude that dividends payable should not be regarded as financial liabilities.

3   SCOPE

IAS 32, IAS 39, IFRS 7 and IFRS 9 – *Financial Instruments: Disclosures* – apply to the financial statements of all entities that are prepared in accordance with International Financial Reporting Standards. *[IAS 32.4, IAS 39.2, IFRS 7.3, IFRS 9.2.1]*. In other words there are no exclusions from the presentation, recognition, measurement, or even the disclosure requirements, of these standards, even for entities that do not have publicly traded securities or those that are subsidiaries of other entities.

The standards do not, however, apply to all of an entity's financial instruments, some of which are excluded from their scope, for example insurance contracts (see Chapter 54). These exceptions are considered in more detail below. Conversely, certain contracts over non-financial items that behave in a similar way to financial instruments but do not actually fall within the definition – essentially some commodity contracts – are included within the scope of the standards and these are considered at 4 below.

3.1   Subsidiaries, associates, joint ventures and similar investments

Most interests in subsidiaries, associates, and joint ventures that are consolidated or equity accounted in consolidated financial statements are outside the scope of IAS 32, IAS 39, IFRS 7 and IFRS 9. However, such instruments should be accounted for in accordance with IAS 39 or IFRS 9 and disclosed in accordance with IFRS 7 in the following situations: *[IAS 32.4(a), IAS 39.2(a), IFRS 7.3(a), IFRS 9.2.1(a)]*

- in separate financial statements of the parent or investor if the entity chooses not to account for those investments at cost (see Chapter 8 at 2); *[IAS 27.10, IAS 27.11, IAS 28.44]*

- when investments in an associate or a joint venture held by a venture capital organisation, mutual fund, unit trust or similar entity are classified as financial instruments at fair value through profit or loss on initial recognition (see Chapter 11 at 5.3 and Chapter 45 at 2.2.2). *[IAS 28.18]*. When an entity has an investment in an associate, a portion of which is held indirectly through a venture capital organisation, mutual fund, unit trust or similar entity including an investment-linked insurance fund, the entity may elect to measure that portion of the investment in the associate at fair value through profit or loss regardless of whether the venture capital organisation, mutual fund, unit trust or similar entity has significant influence over that portion of the investment. If the election is made, the equity method should be applied to any remaining portion of the investment; *[IAS 28.19]* and

- an investment in a subsidiary by an investment entity that is measured at fair value through profit or loss using the investment entity exception (see Chapter 6 at 2.3.3). *[IFRS 10.31]*.

In January 2013, the Interpretations Committee concluded that impairments of investments in subsidiaries, associates and joint ventures accounted for at cost in the separate financial statements of the investor are dealt with by IAS 36 – *Impairment of Assets* – not IAS 39.[9]

IAS 32, IAS 39, IFRS 7 and IFRS 9 apply to most derivatives on interests in subsidiaries, associates and joint ventures, irrespective of how the investment is otherwise accounted for. However, IAS 39 and IFRS 9 do not apply to instruments containing potential voting rights that, in substance, give access to the economic benefits arising from an ownership interest which is consolidated or equity accounted (see Chapter 7 at 2.2, Chapter 11 at 4.3 and Chapter 12 at 4.2.2). *[IFRS 10.B91]*.

From the perspective of an entity issuing derivatives, the requirements of IAS 39, IFRS 9 and IFRS 7 do not apply if such derivatives meet the definition of an equity instrument of the entity. *[IAS 32.4(a), IAS 39.2(a), IFRS 7.3(a), IFRS 9.2.1(a)]*. For example, a written call option issued by a subsidiary that can be settled only by the subsidiary issuing a fixed number of its shares to the holder in exchange for a fixed amount of cash might meet the definition of equity (see 3.6 below and Chapter 44 at 5.1).

Sometimes an entity will make a strategic investment in the equity of another party. These are often made with the intention of establishing or maintaining a long-term operating relationship with the investee. Unless they are equity accounted as associates or joint ventures, these investments are within the scope of IAS 39 and IFRS 9. *[IAS 39.AG3, IFRS 9.B2.3]*.

3.2   Leases

Whilst all rights and obligations under leases to which IAS 17 applies (see Chapter 24) are within the scope of IAS 32 and IFRS 7, they are only within the scope of IAS 39 and IFRS 9 to the following extent:

- lease receivables and payables are subject to the derecognition provisions in IAS 39 and IFRS 9 (see Chapter 50);

- lease receivables are subject to the 'incurred loss' impairment provisions in IAS 39 (see Chapter 48 at 4) or the 'expected credit loss' requirements of IFRS 9 (see Chapter 49 at 5); and

- the relevant provisions of IAS 39 and IFRS 9 apply to derivatives embedded within leases (see Chapter 43 at 4 to 7).

Otherwise the applicable standard is IAS 17, not IAS 39 or IFRS 9. *[IAS 39.2(b), IFRS 9.2.1(b)].*

3.3   Insurance contracts

Although insurance contracts often satisfy the definition of a financial instrument, in general they have not, historically, been accounted for as such. In fact the IASB has been conducting a project on accounting for insurance contracts for a number of years and the first standard on the topic, IFRS 4 (which is discussed in detail in Chapter 54), was published in March 2004.

An insurance contract is defined in IFRS 4 as one under which one party (the insurer) accepts significant insurance risk from another party (the policyholder) by agreeing to compensate the policyholder if a specified uncertain future event (the insured event) adversely affects the policyholder. Insurance risk is defined as risk, other than financial risk, transferred from the holder of a contract to the issuer. Financial risk is defined as the risk of a possible future change in one or more of a specified interest rate, financial instrument price, commodity price, foreign exchange rate, index of prices or rates, credit rating or credit index or other variable, provided in the case of a non-financial variable that the variable is not specific to a party to the contract. *[IFRS 4 Appendix A].* In many cases it will be quite clear whether a contract is an insurance contract or not, although this will not always be the case and IFRS 4 contains several pages of guidance on this definition (see Chapter 54 at 3). *[IFRS 4 Appendix B].*

Insurance contracts, as defined, are generally outside the scope of IAS 32, IAS 39, IFRS 7 and IFRS 9. *[IAS 32.4(d), IAS 39.2(e), IFRS 7.3(d), IFRS 9.2.1(e)].* IAS 39 and IFRS 9 do, however, apply to derivatives that are embedded in insurance contracts if the derivative itself is not within the scope of IFRS 4. *[IFRS 4.7, IAS 39.2(e), IFRS 9.2.1(e)].* IAS 32 and IFRS 7 apply to derivatives embedded in insurance contracts if IAS 39 or IFRS 9 requires them to be accounted for separately. *[IAS 32.4(d), IFRS 7.3(d)].* Finally, financial guarantee contracts which meet the definition of an insurance contract are normally accounted for under IAS 39 and IFRS 9 and disclosed in accordance with IFRS 7 if the risk transferred is significant (see 3.4 below). *[IAS 39.AG4(a), IFRS 9.B2.5(a)].*

The application guidance makes it clear that insurers' financial instruments that are not within the scope of IFRS 4 should be accounted for under IAS 39 or IFRS 9. *[IAS 39.AG3A, IFRS 9.B2.4].*

3.3.1   Weather derivatives

Contracts which require a payment based on climatic variables (often referred to as 'weather derivatives') or on geological or other physical variables are within the scope of IAS 39 or IFRS 9 unless they meet the definition of an insurance contract. *[IAS 39.AG1, IFRS 9.B2.1]*. Generic or standardised contracts will rarely meet the definition of insurance contracts because the variable is unlikely to be specific to either party to the contract. *[IFRS 4.B18(l), IFRS 4.B19(g)]*. This is illustrated in the following example.

Example 42.1:   Rainfall contract – derivative financial instrument or insurance contract?

Company E has contracted to lease a stall at an open-air event from which it plans to sell goods to people attending the event. The event will be held at a village approximately 100 km from Capital City.

Because E is concerned that poor weather may deter people from attending the event, it enters into a contract with Financial Institution K, the terms of which are that, in return for a premium paid by E on inception of the contract, K will pay a fixed amount of money to E if, during the day of the event, it rains for more than three hours at the meteorological station in the centre of Capital City.

The non-financial variable in the contract, i.e. rainfall at the meteorological station, is not specific to E. Particularly, E will only suffer loss as a result of rainfall at the village, not at Capital City. Also, because the potential payment to be received is for a fixed amount, it might not be possible to demonstrate that E has suffered a loss for which it has been compensated. Therefore, E should account for the contract as a financial instrument under IAS 39 or IFRS 9.

3.3.2   Contracts with discretionary participation features

Financial instruments (normally taking the form of life insurance policies) which contain what are called discretionary participation features, essentially rights of the holder to receive additional benefits whose amount or timing is, contractually, at the discretion of the issuer, are accounted for under IFRS 4. *[IFRS 4 Appendix A]*. Accordingly, IAS 39 and the parts of IAS 32 dealing with the distinction between financial liabilities and equity instruments (see Chapter 44 at 3 to 7) do not apply to such contracts, although the disclosure requirements of IFRS 7 do apply. *[IAS 32.4(e), IAS 39.2(e), IFRS 9.2.1(e), IFRS 4.2(b), IFRS 7.3]*.

IAS 39 and IFRS 9 do, however, apply to derivatives that are embedded in contracts containing discretionary participation features if the derivative itself is not within the scope of IFRS 4. *[IAS 39.2(e), IFRS 9.2.1(e)]*.

3.4   Financial guarantee contracts

Where a contract meets the definition of a financial guarantee contract (see 3.4.1 below) the issuer is normally required to apply specific accounting requirements within IAS 39 or IFRS 9, which are different from those applying to other financial liabilities – essentially the contract is measured at fair value on initial recognition and this amount is amortised to profit or loss provided it is not considered probable that the guarantee will be called (see Chapter 48 at 2.8 and Chapter 49 at 2.8). There are exceptions to this general requirement and these are dealt with at 3.4.2 below.

3.4.1   *Definition of a financial guarantee contract*

A financial guarantee contract is defined as a contract that requires the issuer to make specified payments to reimburse the holder for a loss it incurs because a specified debtor fails to make payment when due in accordance with the original or modified terms of a debt instrument. *[IAS 39.9, IFRS 4 Appendix A, IFRS 9 Appendix A].*

3.4.1.A   *Reimbursement for loss incurred*

Some credit-related guarantees (or letters of credit, credit derivative default contracts or credit insurance contracts) do not, as a precondition for payment, require that the holder is exposed to, and has incurred a loss on, the failure of the debtor to make payments on the guaranteed asset when due. An example of such a guarantee is one that requires payments in response to changes in a specified credit rating or credit index. Such guarantees are not financial guarantee contracts, as defined in IAS 39 and IFRS 9, and are not insurance contracts, as defined in IFRS 4. Rather, they are derivatives and accordingly fall within the scope of IAS 39 and IFRS 9. *[IAS 39.AG4(b), IFRS 9.B2.5(b), IFRS 4.B19(f)].*

When a debtor defaults on a guaranteed loan a significant time period may elapse prior to full and final legal settlement of the loss. Because of this, certain credit protection contracts provide for the guarantor to make a payment at a fixed point after the default event using the best estimate of loss at the time. Such payments typically terminate the credit protection contract with no party having any further claim under it whilst ownership of the loan remains with the guaranteed party. In situations like this, if the final loss on the debtor exceeds the amount estimated on payment of the guarantee, the guaranteed party will suffer an overall financial loss; conversely, the guaranteed party may receive a payment under the guarantee but eventually suffer a smaller loss on the loan. Therefore such a contract will often not meet the essence of the definition of a financial guarantee. However, if the payment is designed to be a reasonable estimate of the loss actually incurred, such a feature (which is common in many conventional insurance contracts) will sometimes allow the contract to be classified as a financial guarantee contract. This will particularly be the case if such payments are agreed by both parties in order to settle the financial guarantee, as opposed to being specified as part of the original contract.

Also, such a contract should meet the definition of a guarantee if it was structured in either of the following ways:

- the contract requires the guarantor to purchase the defaulted loan for its nominal amount; or
- on settlement of the final loss, the contract provides for a further payment between the guarantor and guaranteed party for any difference between that amount and the initial loss estimate that was paid.

3.4.1.B   *Debt instrument*

Although the term 'debt instrument' is used extensively as a fundamental part of the definition of a 'financial guarantee contract', it is not defined within IAS 32, IAS 39, IFRS 9, IFRS 4 or IFRS 7. The term will typically be considered to include trade debts, overdrafts and other borrowings including mortgage loans and certain debt securities.

However, entities often provide guarantees of other items and analysing these in the context of IAS 39, IFRS 9 and IFRS 4 is not always straightforward. Consider, for example, a guarantee of a lessor's receipts under a lease. In substance, a finance lease gives rise to a loan agreement (see 2.2.4 above) and it therefore seems clear that a guarantee of payments on such a lease should be considered a financial guarantee contract.

From the perspective of the guarantor, a guarantee of a non-cancellable operating lease will give rise to a substantially similar exposure, i.e. credit risk of the lessee. Moreover, individual payments currently due and payable are recognised as financial (debt) instruments. Therefore, such guarantees would seem to meet the definition of a financial guarantee at least insofar as they relate to payments currently due and payable. It may be argued that the remainder of the contract (normally the majority) fails to meet the definition because it provides a guarantee of *future* debt instruments. However, the standard does not explicitly require the debt instrument to be accounted for as a financial instrument that is currently due and we believe a guarantee of a lessor's receipts under an operating lease could also be argued to meet the definition of a financial guarantee contract.

Where it is accepted that such a guarantee is not a financial guarantee contract, one must still examine how the related obligations should be accounted for – the contract is, after all, a financial instrument. The possibilities are a derivative financial instrument (accounted for at fair value through profit or loss under IAS 39 and IFRS 9) or an insurance contract (accounted for under IFRS 4 – commonly resulting only in disclosure of a contingent liability, assuming payment is not considered probable). The analysis depends on whether the risk transferred by the guarantee is considered financial risk or insurance risk (see 3.3 above). Credit risk sits on the cusp of the relevant definitions making the judgement a marginal one, although we believe that in many situations the arguments for treatment as an insurance contract will be credible. Of course for this to be the case the guarantee must only compensate the holder for loss in the event of default.

Other types of guarantee can add further complications – for example guarantees of pension plan contributions to funded defined benefit schemes. Where such a guarantee is in respect of discrete identifiable payments, the analysis above for operating leases seems equally applicable. However, the terms of such a guarantee might have the effect that the guaranteed amount depends on the performance of the assets within the scheme. In these cases, the guarantee seems to give rise to a transfer of financial risk (i.e. the value of the asset) in addition to credit risk, which might lend support for its treatment as a derivative.

3.4.1.C   Form and existence of contract

The application guidance to IAS 39 and IFRS 9 emphasises that, whilst financial guarantee contracts may have various legal forms (such as guarantees, some types of letters of credit, credit default contracts or insurance contracts), their accounting treatment does not depend on their legal form. [IAS 39.AG4, IFRS 9.B2.5].

In some cases guarantees arise, directly or indirectly, as a result of the operation of statute or regulation. In such situations, it is necessary to examine whether the arrangement gives rise to a contract as that term is used in IAS 32. For example, in some jurisdictions, a subsidiary may avoid filing its financial statements or having them audited if its parent and fellow subsidiaries guarantee its liabilities by entering into a deed of cross guarantee. In other jurisdictions similar relief is granted if group companies elect to make a statutory declaration of guarantee. In the first situation it would seem appropriate for the issuer to regard the deed as a contract and hence any guarantee made under it would be within the scope of IAS 39 or IFRS 9. The statutory nature of the declaration in the second situation makes the analysis more difficult. Although the substance of the arrangement is little different from the first situation, statutory obligations are not financial liabilities and are therefore outside the scope of IAS 39 or IFRS 9.

3.4.2   Issuers of financial guarantee contracts

In general, issuers of financial guarantees contracts should apply IAS 32, IAS 39 IFRS 9 and IFRS 7 to those contracts if the risk transferred is significant. *[IAS 39.AG4(a), IFRS 9.B2.5(a)]*. However, if an entity has previously asserted explicitly that it regards such contracts as insurance contracts and has used accounting applicable to insurance contracts, the issuer may elect to apply either IAS 39/IFRS 9 or IFRS 4 (see Chapter 54 at 2.2.3.D). That election may be made contract by contract, but the election for each contract is irrevocable. *[IAS 32.4(d), IAS 39.2(e), IFRS 4.4(d), IFRS 7.3(d), IFRS 9.2.1(e)]*. This concession does not extend to contracts that are similar to financial guarantee contracts but are actually derivative financial instruments (see 3.4.1.A above).

The IASB was concerned that entities other than credit insurers could elect to apply IFRS 4 to financial guarantee contracts and consequently (if their accounting policies permitted) recognise no liability on inception. Consequently, it imposed the restrictions outlined in the previous paragraph. *[IAS 39.BC23A, IFRS 9.BCZ2.12]*. The application guidance contains further information on these restrictions where it is explained that assertions that an issuer regards contracts as insurance contracts are typically found throughout the issuer's communications with customers and regulators, contracts, business documentation as well as in their financial statements. Furthermore, insurance contracts are often subject to accounting requirements that are distinct from the requirements for other types of transaction, such as contracts issued by banks or commercial companies. In such cases, an issuer's financial statements would typically include a statement that the issuer had used those accounting requirements, i.e. ones normally applied to insurance contracts. *[IAS 39.AG4A, IFRS 9.B2.6]*. Nevertheless, other companies do consider it appropriate to apply IFRS 4 rather than IAS 39 or IFRS 9 to these contracts. Rolls Royce discloses the following accounting policy in respect of guarantees that it provides.

> **Extract 42.1: Rolls Royce plc (2014)**
> **Notes to the Consolidated Financial Statements** [extract]
> 1.   **Accounting Policies** [extract]
>   **Sales Financing Support** [extract]
>
> In connection with the sale of its products, the Group will, on occasion, provide financing support for its customers. These arrangements fall into two categories: credit-based guarantees and asset-value guarantees. In accordance with the requirements of IAS 39 and IFRS 4 *Insurance Contracts*, credit-based guarantees are treated as insurance contracts. The Group considers asset-value guarantees to be non-financial liabilities and accordingly these are also treated as insurance contracts.

The IASB is addressing the question of how to account for financial guarantee contracts in its project on insurance contracts. At the time of writing, the IASB has proposed that insurers will continue to be given a similar accounting policy choice (see Chapter 54 at 11.3).[10]

Accounting for the revenue associated with financial guarantee contracts issued in connection with the sale of goods is dealt with under IAS 18 or IFRS 15 (see Chapter 28 and Chapter 29). *[IAS 39.AG4(c), IFRS 9.B2.5(c)]*.

3.4.3   Holders of financial guarantee contracts

Financial guarantee contracts held are not within the scope of IAS 39 or IFRS 9 because they are insurance contracts (see 3.3 above). *[IAS 39.IN6]*. Nor does IFRS 4 apply to insurance contracts that an entity holds (other than reinsurance contracts). *[IFRS 4.4(f)]*. Accordingly, as explained in the guidance on implementing IFRS 4, the holder of a financial guarantee contract will need to develop its accounting policy in accordance with the 'hierarchy' in IAS 8 – *Accounting Policies, Changes in Accounting Estimates and Errors*. The IAS 8 hierarchy specifies criteria to use if no IFRS applies specifically (see Chapter 3 at 4). *[IFRS 4.IG2 Example 1.11]*.

In selecting their policy, entities may initially look to the requirements of IAS 37 dealing with contingent assets (see Chapter 27 at 3.2.2), at least as far as recoveries under the contract are concerned. However, applying IAS 37 will not always be appropriate, as discussed in Chapter 48 at 4.2.2 in the context of loan impairments. In certain situations it may also be possible for the holder of a financial guarantee contract to account for it as an asset at fair value through profit or loss. This might be considered appropriate if it was acquired subsequent to the initial recognition of a guaranteed asset that had itself been classified as at fair value through profit or loss.

3.4.4   Financial guarantee contracts between entities under common control

The IASB was asked to provide an exemption from the measurement requirements of IAS 39 for guarantees issued between parents and their subsidiaries, between entities under common control and by a parent or subsidiary on behalf of a subsidiary or a parent (a similar exemption is available under US GAAP.) It was argued that the requirement to recognise these financial guarantee contracts in separate or individual financial statements would cause costs disproportionate to the likely benefits, given that intragroup transactions are eliminated on consolidation. However, to avoid the omission of material liabilities from separate or individual financial statements, the IASB decided not to create such an exemption. *[IAS 39.BC23C, IFRS 9.BCZ2.14]*.

Therefore, for example, where a parent guarantees the borrowings of a subsidiary, the guarantee should be accounted for as a standalone instrument in the parent's separate financial statements. However, for the purposes of the parent's consolidated financial statements, such guarantees are normally considered an integral part of the terms of the borrowing (see Chapter 44 at 4.8) and therefore should not be accounted for independently of the borrowing. *[IAS 32.AG29]*.

3.5   Loan commitments

Loan commitments are firm commitments to provide credit under pre-specified terms and conditions. *[IAS 39.BC15, IFRS 9.BCZ2.2]*. The term can include arrangements such as offers to individuals in respect of residential mortgage loans as well as committed borrowing facilities granted to a corporate entity.

Although they meet the definition of a derivative financial instrument (see 2.2.8 above and Chapter 43 at 2), a pragmatic decision has been taken by the IASB to simplify the accounting for holders and issuers of many loan commitments. *[IAS 39.BC16, IFRS 9.BCZ2.3]*. Accordingly, loan commitments that cannot be settled net – in practice, most loan commitments – may be excluded from most of the scope of IAS 39 and IFRS 9. They are, however, subject to the IAS 39 and IFRS 9 derecognition provisions (see Chapter 50 at 6) and are included within the scope of IFRS 7. *[IAS 39.2(h), IFRS 7.4]*. Some loan commitments, however, are within the scope of IAS 39 and IFRS 9, namely: *[IAS 39.2(h), 4, IFRS 9.2.1(g)]*

- those that are designated as financial liabilities at fair value through profit or loss (this may be appropriate if the associated risk exposures are managed on a fair value basis or because designation eliminates an accounting mismatch – see Chapter 45 at 2.2.1); *[IAS 39.4(a), IAS 39.BC17, IFRS 9.2.3(a)]*

- commitments that can be settled net in cash or by delivering or issuing another financial instrument; *[IAS 39.4(b), IAS 39.BC18, IFRS 9.2.3(b)]* and

- all those within the same class where the entity has a past practice of selling the assets resulting from its loan commitments shortly after origination. The IASB sees this as achieving net settlement. *[IAS 39.4(a), IAS 39.BC18, IFRS 9.2.3(a)]*.

In addition, commitments to provide a loan at a below-market interest rate are also within the scope of IAS 39 and IFRS 9. *[IAS 39.4(c), IFRS 9.2.3(c)]*. For these loan commitments, the standards contain specific measurement requirements which are different from those applying to other financial liabilities. Under IAS 39 they are measured at fair value on initial recognition and this amount is amortised to profit or loss, provided it is not considered an onerous contract (see Chapter 48 at 2.8 and Chapter 49 at 2.8). IFRS 9 also requires the commitments to be measured at fair value on initial recognition and subsequently amortised to profit or loss but requires the expected credit loss allowance to be used if higher and does not take into account whether there is an onerous contract or not. *[IAS 39.47(d), IFRS 9.4.2.1(d)]*. The reason for this accounting treatment is that the IASB was concerned that liabilities resulting from such commitments might not be recognised in the statement of financial position because, often, no cash consideration is received. *[IAS 39.BC20]*.

Entities applying IFRS 9 that have issued loan commitments which are not otherwise within the scope of the standard should apply the impairment requirements of IFRS 9 to those loan commitments. *[IFRS 9.2.1(g)]*.

In respect of commitments that can be settled net in cash IAS 39 and IFRS 9 contain only limited guidance on what 'net settlement' means. Clearly a fixed interest rate loan commitment that gives the lender and/or the borrower an explicit right to settle the value of the contract (taking into account changes in interest rates etc.) in cash or by delivery or issuing another financial instrument would be considered a form of net settlement and therefore a derivative. However, paying out a loan in instalments (for example, a mortgage construction loan where instalments are paid out in line with the progress of construction) is not regarded as net settlement. *[IAS 39.4(b)]*.

As a matter of fact, most loan commitments could be settled net if both parties agreed, essentially by renegotiating the terms of the contract. Of more relevance is the question of whether one party has the practical ability to settle net, e.g. because the terms of the contract allow net settlement or by the use of some market mechanism.

Where the entity has a past practice of selling the assets shortly after origination no guidance is given on what is meant by a class (although the basis for conclusions makes it clear that an entity can have more than one). *[IAS 39.BC19, IFRS 9.BCZ2.6]*. Therefore, an assessment will need to be made based on individual circumstances.

Example 42.2:   Identifying classes of loan commitment

A banking group has two main operating subsidiaries, one in country A and the other in country B. Although they share common functions (e.g. information systems) the two subsidiaries' operations are clearly distinct.

Both subsidiaries originate similar loans under loan commitments. In country A there is an active and liquid market for the assets resulting from loan commitments issued in that country. The subsidiary operating in that country has a past practice of disposing of such assets in this market shortly after origination. There is no such market in country B.

The fact that one subsidiary has a past practice of settling its loan commitments net (as the term is used in the standard) would not normally mean that the loan commitments issued in country B are required to be classified as at fair value through profit or loss.

The above example is relatively straightforward – in some circumstances it may be more difficult to define the class. However, there is no reason why an individual entity (say a subsidiary of a group) cannot have two or more classes of loan commitment, e.g. where they result in the origination of different types of asset that are clearly managed separately.

An issuer of loan commitments applying IAS 39 is required to apply IAS 37 if they are not subject to the requirements of IAS 39. *[IAS 39.2(h)]*. Particularly, a provision should be established if a loan commitment becomes an onerous contract as defined in that standard (see Chapter 27 at 6.2). HSBC has disclosed the following accounting policy in respect of onerous loan commitments.

Extract 42.2: HSBC Holdings plc (2014)

Notes on the Financial Statements [extract]

1.   Basis of preparation and significant accounting policies [extract]

(j)   Loans and advances to banks and customers [extract]

HSBC may commit to underwrite loans on fixed contractual terms for specified periods of time. [...] . Where HSBC intends to hold the loan, a provision on the loan commitment is only recorded where it is probable that HSBC will incur a loss.

Entities applying IFRS 9 would, instead of the requirements of IAS 37, apply the impairment provisions of IFRS 9. *[IFRS 9.5.5.1]*.

Any associated entitlement to fees should be accounted for in accordance with IAS 18 or IFRS 15, IAS 39 or IFRS 9 (see Chapter 28, Chapter 29, Chapter 48 at 3 and Chapter 49 at 3 respectively). No accounting requirements are specified for holders of loan commitments, but they will normally be accounted for as executory contracts – essentially, this means that fees payable will be recognised as an expense in a manner that is appropriate to the terms of the commitment. Any resulting borrowing will obviously be accounted for as a financial liability under IAS 39 or IFRS 9.

Although much of the discussion has focused on loan commitments as options to provide credit, *[IAS 39.BC15, IFRS 9.BCZ2.2]*, we believe it can be appropriate to apply the exclusion from IAS 39 or IFRS 9 to non-optional commitments to provide credit, provided the necessary conditions above are met.

The exclusion is available only for contracts to provide credit. Normally, therefore, it will be applicable only where there is a commitment to lend funds, and certainly not for all contracts that may result in the subsequent recognition of an asset or liability that is accounted for at amortised cost. Consider, for example, a contract between entities A and B that gives B the right to sell to A a transferable (but unquoted) debt security issued by entity C that B currently owns. Even if, on subsequent acquisition, A will classify the debt security within loans and receivables (see Chapter 45 at 4), the contract would not generally be considered a loan commitment as it does not involve A providing credit to B.

3.6   Equity instruments

3.6.1   *Equity instruments issued*

Financial instruments (including options and warrants) that are issued by the reporting entity and meet the definition of equity instruments in IAS 32 (see 2.1 above and Chapter 44 at 3 and 4) are outside the scope of IAS 39 and IFRS 9. *[IAS 39.2(d), IFRS 9.2.1(d)]*.

In principle, IFRS 7 applies to issued equity instruments except for those that are derivatives based on interests in subsidiaries, associates or joint ventures (see 3.1 above). *[IFRS 7.3(a)]*. However, this is of largely academic interest because IFRS 7 specifies no disclosure requirements for issued equity instruments.

In fact, the scope of IFRS 7 for these types of instrument is even more curious. Firstly, it is explained that derivatives over subsidiaries, associates and joint ventures that are equity instruments from the point of view of the issuer are excluded from the scope of IFRS 7 because equity instruments are not remeasured and hence do not expose the issuer to statement of financial position and income statement risk. Also, the disclosures about the significance of financial instruments for financial position and performance are not considered relevant for equity instruments. *[IFRS 7.BC8]*. Given the reasons quoted, it is not entirely clear why the IASB did not exclude all instruments meeting the definition of equity in IAS 32 from the scope of IFRS 7, e.g. non-puttable ordinary shares issued by the reporting entity. Secondly, it is very difficult to see how a derivative over a reporting entity's associate or joint venture could ever meet the definition of equity from the perspective of the reporting entity.

3.6.2 Equity instruments held

From the point of view of the holder, equity instruments are within the scope of IAS 39, IFRS 7 and IFRS 9 (unless they meet the exception at 3.1 above). *[IAS 39.2(d), IFRS 9.2.1(d)]*.

3.7 Business combinations

3.7.1 Contingent consideration in a business combination

3.7.1.A Payable by an acquirer

For business combinations accounted for under IFRS 3 – *Business Combinations*, contingent consideration that meets the definition of a financial instrument will be measured at fair value, with any resulting gain or loss recognised either in profit or loss or in other comprehensive income, in accordance with IAS 39 and IFRS 9 (see Chapter 9 at 7.1). *[IFRS 3.58(b)(i)]*.

Further, contingent consideration arising from an acquiree's prior business combination that an acquirer assumes in its subsequent acquisition of the acquiree does not meet the definition of contingent consideration in the acquirer's business combination. Rather, it is one of the identifiable liabilities assumed in the subsequent acquisition. Therefore, to the extent that such arrangements are financial instruments, they are within the scope of IAS 32, IAS 39, IFRS 9 and IFRS 7.[11]

3.7.1.B Receivable by a vendor

IAS 39 does not go on to explain whether the vendor should be accounting for the contingent consideration in accordance with its provisions.

In most cases the vendor will have a contractual right to receive cash or another financial asset from the purchaser and, therefore, it is hard to avoid the conclusion that the contingent consideration meets the definition of a financial asset and hence is within the scope of IAS 39 and IFRS 9, not IAS 37. IFRS 10 – *Consolidated Financial Statements* – requires consideration received on the loss of control of an entity or business to be measured at fair value, which is consistent with the treatment required by IAS 39 and IFRS 9.

3.7.2   *Contracts between an acquirer and a vendor in a business combination*

IAS 39 and IFRS 9 do not apply to forward contracts between an acquirer and a selling shareholder to buy or sell an acquiree that will result in a business combination at a future acquisition date. In order to qualify for this scope exclusion, the term of the forward contract should not exceed a reasonable period normally necessary to obtain any required approvals and to complete the transaction, for example to accommodate the completion of necessary regulatory and legal processes. *[IAS 39.2(g), BC24A, IFRS 9.2.1(f), BCZ2.39].*

It applies only when completion of the business combination is not dependent on further actions of either party. Option contracts allow one party to control the occurrence or non-occurrence of future events depending on whether the option is exercised. Consequently, option contracts that on exercise will result in the reporting entity obtaining control of another entity are within the scope of IAS 39, whether or not they are currently exercisable. *[IAS 39.BC24B, BC24C, IFRS 9.BCZ2.40, BCZ2.41].*

It was suggested that 'in-substance' or 'synthetic' forward contracts, e.g. the combination of a written put and purchased call where the strike prices, exercise dates and notional amounts are equal, or a deeply in- or out-of-the-money option, should be excluded from the scope of IAS 39 and by implication IFRS 9. However, the IASB staff did not agree with the notion that synthetic forward contracts (which do provide optionality to one or both parties) are substantially identical to forward contracts (which commit both parties). The IASB staff accepted that in normal financial instrument transactions, the economics of a synthetic forward will be favourable to one party to the contract and should therefore result in its exercise, but a similar assumption does not necessarily hold true in business combination transactions because one party may choose not to exercise the option due to other factors. Therefore, it is not possible to assert that the contracts will always result in a business combination.[12]

The acquisition of an interest in an associate represents the acquisition of a financial instrument, not an acquisition of a business. Therefore the scope exclusion should not be applied by analogy to contracts to acquire investments in associates and similar transactions. *[IAS 39.BC24D, IFRS 9.BCZ2.42].*

Another related issue is the treatment of contracts, whether options or forwards, to purchase an entity that owns a single asset such as a ship or building which does not constitute a business. The reason a contract for a business combination is normally considered to be a financial instrument seems to be because it is a contract to purchase equity instruments. Consequently, a contract to purchase all of the shares in a single asset company would also meet the definition of a financial instrument, yet on the face of it such a contract would not be excluded from the scope of IAS 39 if the asset did not represent a business. The IASB staff disagreed with this analysis and argued that such a contract should be analysed as a contract to purchase the underlying asset which would normally be outside the scope of IAS 39 or IFRS 9.[13] Although forward contracts between an acquirer and a vendor in a business combination are scoped out of IAS 39 and hence are not accounted for as derivatives, they are still within the scope of IFRS 7.

3.8 Contingent pricing of property, plant and equipment and intangible assets

IAS 32 (as currently worded) is clear that the purchase of goods on credit gives rise to a financial liability when the goods are delivered (see 2.2.6 above) and that a contingent obligation to deliver cash meets the definition of a financial liability (see 2.2.3 above). Consequently, it would seem that a financial liability arises on the outright purchase of an item of property, plant and equipment or an intangible asset, where the purchase contract requires the subsequent payment of contingent consideration, for example amounts based on the performance of the asset. Further, because there is no exemption from applying IAS 39 or IFRS 9 to such contracts, one might expect that such a liability would be accounted for in accordance with IAS 39 or IFRS 9 i.e. any measurement changes to that liability would flow through the statement of profit or loss. This would be consistent with the accounting treatment for contingent consideration arising from a business combination under IFRS 3 (see 3.7.1.A above).

However, in practice, contracts can be more complex than suggested in the previous paragraph and often give rise to situations where the purchaser can influence or control the crystallisation of the contingent payments, e.g. where the contingent payments take the form of sales-based royalties. These complexities can raise broader questions about the nature of the obligations and, like for trail commissions (see 2.2.6 above), the appropriate accounting standard to apply. In January 2011, the Interpretations Committee decided to take this issue onto its agenda and has discussed it a number of times. Initially the discussions focused on purchases of individual assets but they were later widened to cover contingent payments made under service concessions. The Interpretations Committee could not reach a consensus on whether variable payments that are dependent on the purchaser's future activity should be included in the initial measurement of any financial liability. Nevertheless, it recommended to the IASB that it amends IFRS so that, to the extent such arrangements are dealt with as financial liabilities, most remeasurements should be accounted for as adjustments to the cost of the asset.[14] However, the IASB decided not to consider this issue until further progress had been made in its project dealing with leases.[15] This issue is discussed in more detail in Chapter 17 at 4.5, Chapter 18 at 4.1.9 and Chapter 40 at 8.4.1.

Where contingent consideration arises in the event of a sale, the advent of IFRS 15 creates some uncertainty with regard to the accounting for the disposal of single assets held within a corporate entity. IFRS 15 specifies how to account for variable consideration, which can occur where entitlement to the proceeds on the disposal of an asset are contingent upon a future event (see Chapter 29). However as noted at 3.7.1.B above, IFRS 10 requires consideration received on the loss of control of a subsidiary to be measured at fair value. *[IFRS 10.B98(b)(i)].* It is therefore unclear, where a single asset held within a subsidiary is disposed of by selling the shares in the subsidiary, whether IFRS 15 or IFRS 10 should be applied.

Chapter 42

3.9   Employee benefit plans and share-based payment

Employers' rights and obligations under employee benefit plans, which are dealt with under IAS 19 – *Employee Benefits* – are excluded from the scope of IAS 32, IAS 39, IFRS 7 and IFRS 9. *[IAS 32.4(b), IAS 39.2(c), IFRS 7.3(b), IFRS 9.2.1(c)].* The Interpretations Committee noted that IAS 19 indicates that employee benefit plans include a wide range of formal and informal arrangements and concluded it was clear that the exclusion of employee benefit plans from IAS 32 (and by implication IAS 39, IFRS 7 and IFRS 9) includes all employee benefits covered by IAS 19, for example a liability for long service leave.[16]

Similarly, most financial instruments, contracts and obligations arising from share-based payment transactions, which are dealt with under IFRS 2 – *Share-based Payment* – are also excluded. However, IAS 32, IAS 39, IFRS 7 and IFRS 9 do apply to contracts to buy or sell non-financial items in share-based transactions that can be settled net (as that term is used in this context) unless they are considered to be 'normal' sales and purchases (see 4 below). *[IAS 32.4(f)(i), IAS 39.2(i), IFRS 7.3(e), IFRS 9.2.1(h)].* For example, a contract to purchase a fixed quantity of oil in exchange for issuing of a fixed number of shares that could be settled net would be excluded from the scope of IAS 32, IAS 39, IFRS 7 and IFRS 9 only if it qualified as a 'normal' purchase (which would be unlikely).

In addition, IAS 32 applies to treasury shares (see Chapter 44 at 9) that are purchased, sold, issued or cancelled in connection with employee share option plans, employee share purchase plans, and all other share-based payment arrangements. *[IAS 32.4(f)(ii)].*

3.10   Reimbursement rights in respect of provisions

Most reimbursement rights in respect of provisions arise from insurance contracts and are therefore outside the scope of IAS 39 as set out at 3.3 above. The scope of IAS 39 and IFRS 9 is also restricted so as not to apply to other financial instruments that are rights to payments to reimburse the entity for expenditure it is required to make to settle a liability that it has recognised as a provision in accordance with IAS 37 in the current or an earlier period. *[IAS 39.2(j), IFRS 9.2.1(i)].*

However, a residual interest in a decommissioning or similar fund that extends beyond a right to reimbursement, such as a contractual right to distributions once all the decommissioning has been completed or on winding up the fund, may be an equity instrument within the scope of IAS 39 and IFRS 9. *[IFRIC 5.5].*

3.11   Disposal groups classified as held for sale and discontinued operations

The disclosure requirements in IFRS 7 will not apply to financial instruments within a disposal group classified as held for sale or within a discontinued operation, except for disclosures about the measurement of those assets and liabilities (see Chapter 53 at 4) if such disclosures are not already provided in other notes to the financial statements. *[IFRS 5.5B].* However, additional disclosures about such assets (or disposal groups) may be necessary to comply with the general requirements of IAS 1 – *Presentation of Financial Statements* – particularly for financial statements to achieve a fair presentation and to disclose information about assumptions made and the sources of estimation uncertainty (see Chapter 3 at 4.1.1.A and 5.2.1 respectively). *[IAS 1.15, 125, IFRS 5.5B].*

3.12 Indemnification assets

IFRS 3 specifies the accounting treatment for 'indemnification assets', a term that is not defined but is described as follows:

> 'The seller in a business combination may contractually indemnify the acquirer for the outcome of a contingency or uncertainty related to all or part of a specific asset or liability. For example, the seller may indemnify the acquirer against losses above a specified amount on a liability arising from a particular contingency; in other words, the seller will guarantee that the acquirer's liability will not exceed a specified amount. As a result, the acquirer obtains an indemnification asset.' *[IFRS 3.27].*

An indemnification asset will normally meet the definition of a financial asset within IAS 32. In some situations the asset might be considered a right under an insurance contract (see 3.3 above) and in others it could be seen as similar to a reimbursement right (see 3.10 above). However, there will be cases where these assets are, strictly, within the scope of IAS 39 or IFRS 9, creating something of a tension with IFRS 3. This appears to be nothing more than an oversight and, in our view, entities should apply the more specific requirements of IFRS 3 when accounting for these assets which are covered in more detail in Chapter 9 at 5.6.4.

4 CONTRACTS TO BUY OR SELL COMMODITIES AND OTHER NON-FINANCIAL ITEMS

Contracts to buy or sell non-financial items do not generally meet the definition of a financial instrument (see 2.2.5 above). However, many such contracts are standardised in form and traded on organised markets in much the same way as some derivative financial instruments. The application guidance explains that a commodity futures contract, for example, may be bought and sold readily for cash because it is listed for trading on an exchange and may change hands many times. *[IAS 32.AG20].* In fact, this is not strictly true because such contracts are bilateral agreements that cannot be transferred in this way. Rather, the contract would normally be 'closed out' (rather than sold) by entering into an offsetting agreement with the original counterparty or with the exchange on which it is traded.

The ability to buy or sell such a contract for cash, the ease with which it may be bought or sold (or, more correctly, closed out), and the possibility of negotiating a cash settlement of the obligation to receive or deliver the commodity, do not alter the fundamental character of the contract in a way that creates a financial instrument. The buying and selling parties are, in effect, trading the underlying commodity or other asset. However, the IASB is of the view that there are many circumstances where they should be accounted for as if they were financial instruments. *[IAS 32.AG20].*

Accordingly, the provisions of IAS 32, IAS 39, IFRS 7 and IFRS 9 are normally applied to those contracts to buy or sell non-financial items that can be settled net in cash or another financial instrument or by exchanging financial instruments or in which the non-financial instrument is readily convertible to cash, effectively as if the contracts were financial instruments (see 4.1 below). However, there is an exception for what are commonly termed 'normal' purchases and sales or 'own use' contracts (these are considered in more detail at 4.2 below). *[IAS 32.8, IAS 39.5, IFRS 9.2.4, IFRS 7.5].*

Typically the non-financial item will be a commodity, but this is not necessarily the case. For example, an emission right, which is an intangible asset (see Chapter 17 at 11.2), is a non-financial item. Therefore these requirements would apply equally to contracts for the purchase or sale of emission rights if they could be settled net. These requirements will also be appropriate for determining whether certain commodity leases are within the scope of IAS 39 and IFRS 9.

4.1   Contracts that may be settled net

IAS 39 and IFRS 9 explain that there are various ways in which a contract to buy or sell a non-financial item can be settled net, including when: *[IAS 32.9, IAS 39.6, BC24, IFRS 9.2.6, BCZ2.18]*

(a)   the terms of the contract permit either party to settle it net;

(b)   the ability to settle the contract net is not explicit in its terms, but the entity has a practice of settling similar contracts (see 4.2.1 below) net (whether with the counterparty, by entering into offsetting contracts or by selling the contract before its exercise or lapse);

(c)   for similar contracts (see 4.2.2 below), the entity has a practice of taking delivery of the underlying and selling it within a short period after delivery for the purpose of generating a profit from short-term fluctuations in price or dealer's margin; and

(d)   the non-financial item that is the subject of the contract is readily convertible to cash (see below).

There is no further guidance in IAS 39 or IFRS 9 explaining what is meant by 'readily convertible to cash'. Typically, a non-financial item would be considered readily convertible to cash if it consists of largely fungible units and quoted spot prices are available in an active market that can absorb the quantity held by the entity without significantly affecting the price.

Whether there exists an active market for a non-financial item, particularly a physical one such as a commodity, will depend on its quality, location or other characteristics such as size or weight. For example, if a commodity is actively traded in London, this may have the effect that the same commodity located in, say, Rotterdam is considered readily convertible to cash as well as if it was located in London. However, if it were located in Siberia it might not be considered readily convertible to cash if more than a little effort were required (often because of transportation needs) for it to be readily sold.

Like loan commitments, most contracts could as a matter of fact be settled net if both parties agreed to renegotiate terms. Again we do not believe the IASB intended the possibility of such renegotiations to be considered in determining whether or not such contracts may be settled net. Of more relevance is the question of whether one party has the practical ability to settle net, e.g. in accordance with the terms of the contract or by the use of some market mechanism.

4.2 Normal sales and purchases (or own use contracts)

As indicated at 4 above, the provisions of IAS 32, IAS 39, IFRS 9 and IFRS 7 are not to be applied to those contracts to buy or sell non-financial items that can be settled net if they were entered into and continue to be held for the purpose of the receipt or delivery of the non-financial item in accordance with the entity's expected purchase, sale or usage requirements (a 'normal' purchase or sale). *[IAS 32.8, IAS 39.5, IFRS 7.5, IFRS 9.2.4].* When such a contract meets the criteria to be classified as own use, an entity cannot normally choose to apply IAS 39 or IFRS 9 to it. However, an entity applying IFRS 9 may in certain circumstances be able to designate such a contract at fair value through profit or loss (see 4.2.6 below). Further, some entities currently consider it appropriate to designate such contracts at fair value though profit or loss under IAS 39 if they contain substantive embedded derivatives – see Chapter 45 at 2.2.3. It should be noted that this is a two-part test, i.e. in order to qualify as a normal purchase or sale, the contract needs to both (a) have been entered into, and (b) continue to be held, for that purpose. Consequently, a reclassification of an instrument can be only one way. For example, if a contract that was originally entered into for the purpose of delivery ceases to be held for that purpose at a later date, it should subsequently be accounted for as a financial instrument under IAS 39 or IFRS 9. Conversely, where an entity holds a contract that was not originally held for the purpose of delivery and was accounted for under IAS 39 or IFRS 9, but subsequently its intentions change such that it is expected to be settled by delivery, the contract remains within the scope of IAS 39 or IFRS 9.

The IASB views the practice of settling net or taking delivery of the underlying and selling it within a short period after delivery as an indication that the contracts are not normal purchases or sales. Therefore, contracts to which (b) or (c) at 4.1 above apply cannot be subject to the normal purchase or sale exception. Other contracts that can be settled net are evaluated to determine whether this exception can actually apply. *[IAS 32.9, IAS 39.6, BC24, IFRS 9.2.6, BCZ2.18].*

The implications of this requirement are considered further at 4.2.1 and 4.2.2 below.

The implementation guidance illustrates the application of the exception as follows:

Example 42.3: *Determining whether a copper forward is within the scope of IAS 39 and IFRS 9*

Company XYZ enters into a fixed-price forward contract to purchase 1,000 kg of copper in accordance with its expected usage requirements. The contract permits XYZ to take physical delivery of the copper at the end of twelve months, or to pay or receive a net settlement in cash, based on the change in fair value of copper.

The contract is a derivative instrument because there is no initial net investment, the contract is based on the price of copper, and it is to be settled at a future date. However, if XYZ intends to settle the contract by taking delivery and has no history of settling similar contracts net in cash, or of taking delivery of the copper and selling it within a short period after delivery for the purpose of generating a profit from short-term fluctuations in price or dealer's margin, the contract is accounted for as an executory contract rather than as a derivative. *[IAS 39.A.1, IFRS 9.A.1].*

Sometimes a market design or process imposes a structure or intermediary that prevents the producer of a non-financial item from physically delivering it to the customer. For example, a gold miner may produce gold bars (dore) that are physically delivered to a mint for refining and, whilst remaining at the mint, the gold could be credited to either the producer's or a counterparty's 'gold account'. Where the producer enters into a contract for the sale of gold which is settled by allocating gold to the counterparty's gold account, this may constitute 'delivery' as that term is used in the standard. Accordingly, a contract that is expected to be settled in this way could potentially be considered a normal sale (although of course it would need to meet all the other requirements). However, if the gold is credited to the producer's account and the sale contract was settled net in cash, this would not constitute delivery. In these circumstances, treating the contract as a normal sale would, in effect, link a non-deliverable contract entered into with a customer with a transaction to buy or sell through an intermediary as a single synthetic arrangement, contrary to the general requirements on linking contracts discussed in Chapter 43 at 8.[17]

4.2.1   Net settlement of similar contracts

If the terms of a contract do not explicitly provide for net settlement but an entity has a practice of settling similar contracts net, that contract should be considered as capable of being settled net (see 4.1 above). Net settlement could be achieved either by entering into offsetting contracts with the original counterparty or by selling the contract before its maturity. In these circumstances the contract cannot be considered a normal sale or purchase and is accounted for in accordance with IAS 39 or IFRS 9 (see 4.1 above). *[IAS 32.9, IAS 39.6, BC24, IFRS 9.2.4, BCZ2.18].*

The standard contains no further guidance on what degree of past practice would be necessary to prevent an entity from treating similar contracts as own use. We do not believe that any net settlement automatically taints an entity's ability to apply the own use exception, for example where an entity is required to close out a number of contracts as a result of an exceptional disruption arising from external events at a production facility. However, judgement will always need to be applied based on the facts and circumstances of each individual case.

Read literally, the reference to 'similar contracts' could be particularly troublesome. For example, it is common for entities in, say, the energy sector to have a trading arm that is managed completely separately from their other operations. These trading operations commonly trade in contracts on non-financial assets, the terms of which are similar, if not identical, to those used by the entity's other operations for the purpose of physical supply. Accordingly, the standard might suggest that the normal purchase or sale exemption is unavailable to any entity that has a trading operation. However, we believe that a more appropriate interpretation is that contracts should be 'similar' as to their purpose within the business (e.g. for trading or for physical supply) not just as to their contractual terms.

4.2.2   Commodity broker-traders and similar entities

IAS 39 and IFRS 9 contain no further guidance on what degree of net settlement (or trading) is necessary to make the normal sale or purchase exemption inapplicable, but in many cases it will be reasonably clear. For example, in our view, the presumption must be that contracts entered into by a commodity broker-trader that measures its inventories at fair value less costs to sell in accordance with IAS 2 – *Inventories* (see Chapter 22 at 2) falls within the scope of IAS 39 and IFRS 9. However, there will be situations that are much less clear-cut and the application of judgement will be necessary. Factors to consider in making this assessment might include:

- how the entity manages the business and intends to profit from the contract;
- whether value is added by linking parties which are normal buyers and sellers in the value chain;
- whether the entity takes price risk;
- how the contract is settled; and
- the entity's customer base.

Again the reference in the standard to 'similar contracts' in this context may be troublesome for certain entities. However, as noted at 4.2.1 above, we believe contracts should be 'similar' as to their purpose within the business (e.g. for trading or for physical supply) not just as to their contractual terms.

4.2.3   *Written options that can be settled net*

The IASB does not believe that a written option to buy or sell a non-financial item that can be settled net can be regarded as being for the purpose of receipt or delivery in accordance with the entity's expected sale or usage requirements. Essentially, this is because the entity cannot control whether or not the purchase or sale will take place. Accordingly, IAS 32, IAS 39, IFRS 7 and IFRS 9 apply to written options that can be settled net according to the terms of the contract or where the underlying non-financial item is readily convertible to cash (see (a) and (d) at 4.1 above). *[IAS 32.10, IAS 39.7, BC24, IFRS 9.2.7, BCZ2.18].*

Example 42.4:   Determining whether a put option on an office building is within the scope of IAS 39 and IFRS 9

Company XYZ owns an office building. It enters into a put option with an investor, which expires in five years and permits it to put the building to the investor for £150 million. The current value of the building is £175 million. The option, if exercised, may be settled through physical delivery or net cash, at XYZ's option.

XYZ's accounting depends on its intention and past practice for settlement. Although the contract meets the definition of a derivative, XYZ does not account for it as a derivative if it intends to settle the contract by delivering the building in the event of exercise and there is no past practice of settling net.

The investor, however, cannot conclude that the option was entered into to meet its expected purchase, sale, or usage requirements because it does not have the ability to require delivery. The contract may be settled net and is a written option. Regardless of past practices, its intention does not affect whether settlement is by delivery or in cash. Accordingly, the investor accounts for the contract as a derivative. As noted in Chapter 43 at 2 and in Chapter 45 at 2, this will involve remeasuring the derivative to its fair value each reporting period with any associated gains and losses recognised in profit or loss.

However, if the contract were a forward contract rather than an option, required physical delivery and the investor had no past practice of settling net (either in cash or by way of taking delivery and subsequently selling within a short period), the contract would not be accounted for as a derivative. *[IAS 39.A.2, IFRS 9.A.2].*

4.2.4   Electricity and similar 'end-user' contracts

There have been problems in determining whether or not IAS 32, IAS 39, IFRS 7 and IFRS 9 apply to contracts to sell non-financial items (for example electricity or natural gas) to 'end-users' such as retail customers. The non-financial items will often be considered readily convertible to cash (see 4.1 above), at least by the supplier. Accordingly, contracts to supply such items might be considered contracts that can be settled net.

Furthermore, end-user contracts often enable the customer to purchase as much of the non-financial item as needed at a given price to satisfy its usage requirements, i.e. the supplier does not have the contractual right to control whether or not the sale will take place. This might suggest that, from the perspective of the supplier, the contract is a written option with the consequence that it could not regard it as meeting the normal sale and purchase exemption (see 4.2.3 above).

However, many argued that this was not necessarily the case, particularly in the following circumstances:

* the non-financial item is an essential item for the customer;

* the customer does not have access to a market where the non-financial item can be resold;

* the non-financial item is not easily stored in any significant amounts by the customer; and

* the supplier is the sole provider of the non-financial item for a certain period of time.

In circumstances such as these, the apparent optionality within the contract is not exercisable by the retail customer in any economic sense. The customer will purchase volumes required whether the terms in the contract are advantageous or not and would not have the practical ability to sell any excess amounts purchased. Such a contract can have both a positive value and a negative value for the supplier when compared with market conditions and therefore fails to exhibit one of the key characteristics of an option, i.e. that it has only a positive value for the holder (the customer) and only a negative value for the writer (the supplier). In many respects the positive value stems from an intangible, rather than financial, aspect of the contract, being the likelihood that the customer will exercise the option. Accordingly, it was often argued that such contracts should not be considered written options (and therefore not within the scope of IAS 39 or IFRS 9).

Even if contracts such as these are considered to be within the scope of IAS 39 or IFRS 9, it is common for the supplier to have the ability to increase the price charged at relatively short notice. Also, the customer may be able to cancel the contract without penalty and switch to another supplier. Features such as these are likely to reduce any fair value that the contract can have.

Only a small number of energy suppliers appeared to regard these contracts as falling within the scope of IAS 39 or IFRS 9, The Interpretations Committee noted that the guidance already explains what constitutes a written option, essentially confirming that in this context a written option arises where a supplier does not have the contractual right to control whether or not a sale will take place.[18]

The Interpretations Committee also noted that 'in many situations these contracts are not capable of net cash settlement' and 'would not be ... within the scope of IAS 39'. No detailed explanation was provided of why the ability of the supplier to readily realise the non-financial item for cash does not enable it to settle the contract net (as that term is used in IAS 39).[19] However, we understand the reason underlying the comment to be the inability of the counterparty to realise the non-financial item (and hence the contract) for cash. This establishes a useful principle that may be applied in similar situations, i.e. a contract is not capable of net settlement if the contract is an option and the option holder cannot readily realise the non-financial item for cash.

4.2.5 Other contracts containing volume flexibility

It is not uncommon for other sales contracts, such as those with large industrial customers, to contain volume flexibility features. For example, a supplier might enter into a contract requiring it to deliver, say, 100,000 units at a given price as well as giving the counterparty the option to purchase a further 20,000 units at the same price. The customer might well have access to markets for the non-financial item and, following the guidance of the Interpretations Committee, the supplier might consider such a contract to be within the scope of IAS 39 or IFRS 9 as it contains a written option.

However, the supplier could split the contract into two separate components for accounting purposes: a forward contract to supply 100,000 units (which may qualify as a normal sale) and a written option to supply 20,000 units (which would not). Arguments put forward include:

- the parties could easily have entered into two separate contracts, a forward contract and a written option; and

- it is appropriate to analogise to the requirements for embedded derivatives and separate a written option from the normal forward sale or purchase contract because it is not closely related (see Chapter 43 at 4 to 7).

In our view, entities may apply either of these interpretations as an accounting policy choice. The Interpretations Committee was asked to consider the appropriate treatment of such contracts and the initial view of the staff was that such contracts could not be split into two accounting units. However, after performing further research, the Interpretations Committee recognised that significant diversity exists in practice and decided not to address the issue because the IASB would consider the scope of IAS 39, including the guidance about contracts to buy or sell non-financial items, as part of the project to replace that standard.[20] However, IFRS 9 does not address these scope issues except for the application of the fair value option to non-financial items referred to at 4.2.6 below.

4.2.6 Fair value option in IFRS 9

Own use contracts are accounted for as normal sales or purchase contracts (i.e. executory contracts), with the idea that any fair value change of the contract is not relevant given that the contract is used for the entity's own use. However, participants in several industries often enter into similar contracts both for own use and for trading purposes and manage all the contracts together with derivatives on a fair value basis (so as to manage the fair value risk to close to nil). In such a situation, own use accounting leads to an accounting mismatch, as the fair value change of the derivatives and the trading positions cannot be offset against fair value changes of the own use contracts.

To eliminate the accounting mismatch, an entity could apply hedge accounting by designating own use contracts as hedged items in a fair value hedge relationship. However, hedge accounting in these circumstances is administratively burdensome and often produces less meaningful results than fair value accounting. Furthermore, entities enter into large volumes of commodity contracts and, within the large volume of contracts, some positions may naturally offset each other. An entity would therefore typically hedge on a net basis. *[IFRS 9.BCZ2.24]*.

IFRS 9, however, introduces a fair value option for own use contracts. At inception of a contract, an entity may make an irrevocable designation to measure an own use contract at fair value through profit or loss (the 'fair value option') even if it was entered into for the purpose of the receipt or delivery of a non-financial item in accordance with the entity's expected purchase, sale or usage requirement. However, such designation is only allowed if it eliminates or significantly reduces an accounting mismatch that would otherwise arise from not recognising that contract because it is excluded from the scope of IFRS 9. *[IFRS 9.2.5]*.

On transition to IFRS 9, entities can apply the fair value option on an 'all-or-nothing' basis for similar types of (already existing) own use contracts (see Chapter 52 at 10.2). *[IFRS 9.7.2.14A]*.[21]

References

1 Information for Observers (May 2007 IFRIC meeting), *Gaming Transactions*, IASB, May 2007, paras. 25 to 27 and *IFRIC Update*, July 2007.

2 Information for Observers (November 2007 IFRIC Meeting), *Deposits on returnable containers (Agenda Paper 7B)*, IASB, November 2007, paras. 1 and 2.

3 *IFRIC Update*, November 2007.

4 *IFRIC Update*, May 2008.

5 Information for Observers (July 2008 IFRIC meeting), *Accounting for Trailing Commission (Agenda Paper 6B)*, IASB, July 2008, paras. 6 and 7.

6 *IFRIC Update*, September 2008.

7 For example, IAS 32, paras. 13 and AG13 and IAS 39, para. F.2.7.

8 IFRIC D23, *Distributions of Non-cash Assets to Owners*, IASB, January 2008, paras. 9 to 11.

9 *IFRIC Update*, January 2013.

10 *Exposure Draft, Insurance Contracts*, IASB, June 2013, 7(f).

11 *IASB Update*, June 2009.

12 Information for Observers (March 2009 IASB meeting), *IAS 39 Financial Instruments: Recognition and Measurement – Scope exemption for business combination contracts (IAS 39.2(g)) (Agenda Paper 10C)*, IASB, March 2009, paras. 13 and 15.

13 Information for Observers (March 2009 IASB meeting), *IAS 39 Financial Instruments: Recognition and Measurement – Scope exemption for business combination contracts (IAS 39.2(g)) (Agenda Paper 10C)*, IASB, March 2009, paras. 9 and 10.

14 *IFRIC Update*, March 2013 and Staff Paper (March 2013 IFRIC Meeting) *Variable payments for the separate acquisition of property, plant and equipment and intangible assets.*

15 *IFRIC Update*, July 2013.

16 *IFRIC Update*, November 2005.

17 *IFRIC Update*, August 2005.

18 *IFRIC Update*, March 2007 and Information for Observers (January 2007 IFRIC meeting), *IAS 39 Financial Instruments: Recognition and Measurement – Written options in retail energy contracts (Agenda Paper 14(iv))*, IASB, January 2007, paras. 9 to 11.

19 *IFRIC Update*, March 2007 and Information for Observers (January 2007 IFRIC meeting), *IAS 39 Financial Instruments: Recognition and Measurement – Written options in retail energy contracts (Agenda Paper 14(iv))*, IASB, January 2007, para. 15.

20 *IFRIC Update*, March 2010.

21 *IASB Update*, January 2013.

Chapter 42

Chapter 43   Financial instruments: Derivatives and embedded derivatives

List of examples

Chapter 43

Chapter 43   Financial instruments: Derivatives and embedded derivatives

1   INTRODUCTION

Under IAS 39 – *Financial Instruments: Recognition and Measurement* – and IFRS 9 – *Financial Instruments*, the question of whether an instrument is a derivative or not is an important one for accounting purposes. Derivatives are normally recorded in the statement of financial position at fair value with any changes in value reported in profit or loss, although there are some exceptions, e.g. derivatives that are designated in certain effective hedge relationships (see Chapter 45 at 2.1 and Chapter 46 at 2 and 3).

For many financial instruments, it will be reasonably clear whether or not they are derivatives, but there will be more marginal cases. Accordingly, the term derivative is formally defined within IAS 39 and IFRS 9, and this definition, together with examples of derivatives, is considered further at 2 and 3 below.

IAS 39 and IFRS 9 also contain the concept of an embedded derivative which is described as a component of a hybrid or combined instrument that also includes a non-derivative host contract. In certain circumstances embedded derivatives are required to be accounted for separately as if they were freestanding derivatives. The IASB introduced this concept because it believes that entities should not be able to circumvent the accounting requirements for derivatives merely by embedding a derivative in a non-derivative financial instrument or other non-financial contract, e.g. by placing a commodity forward in a debt instrument. In other words, it is chiefly an anti-abuse measure designed to enforce 'derivative accounting' on those derivatives that are 'hidden' in other contracts. *[IAS 39.BC37, IFRS 9.BCZ4.92]*. Embedded derivatives, and the situations in which they are required to be accounted for separately, are considered in more detail at 4 to 7 below. Under IFRS 9 the concept of embedded derivatives applies to financial liabilities and non-financial items only. Embedded derivatives are not separated from financial assets within the scope of IFRS 9 and the requirements of IFRS 9 are applied to the hybrid contract as a whole.

In addition to assessing when a financial instrument or other contract should be accounted for as if it were two contracts, we consider at 8 below situations when two financial instruments should be accounted for as if they were one, together with the question of linkage (for financial reporting purposes) of transactions more generally.

This chapter does not deal with valuation of derivative financial instruments. Chapter 14 outlines the requirements of IFRS 13 – *Fair Value Measurement*, a Standard that defines fair value and provides principles-based guidance on how to measure fair value under IFRS. Additional guidance affecting the valuation of derivatives can be found in Chapter 51 at 5.3.4.A ('Discount rates for calculating the fair value of derivatives') and at 5.3.4.B ('Currency basis risk in cross-currency interest rate swaps').

2   DEFINITION OF A DERIVATIVE

A derivative is a financial instrument or other contract within the scope of IAS 39 or IFRS 9 (see Chapter 42 at 2 and 3) with all of the following characteristics:

(a)   its value changes in response to the change in a specified interest rate, financial instrument price, commodity price, foreign exchange rate, index of prices or rates, credit rating or credit index, or other variable, provided in the case of a non-financial variable that the variable is not specific to a party to the contract (sometimes called the 'underlying');

(b)   it requires no initial net investment, or an initial net investment that is smaller than would be required for other types of contracts that would be expected to have a similar response to changes in market factors; and

(c)   it is settled at a future date. *[IAS 39.9, IFRS 9 Appendix A].*

These three defining characteristics are considered further below.

2.1   Changes in value in response to changes in underlying

2.1.1   *Notional amounts*

A derivative usually has a notional amount, such as an amount of currency, number of shares or units of weight or volume, but does not require the holder or writer to invest or receive the notional amount at inception.

Example 43.1:   Notional amount of a derivative

Company XYZ, whose functional currency is the US dollar, has placed an order with a company in France for delivery in six month time. The price to be paid in six month time is €2,000,000. To hedge the exposure to currency risk, XYZ enters into a contract with an investment bank to convert US dollars to euros at a fixed exchange rate. The contract requires the investment bank to remit €2,000,000 in exchange for US dollars at a fixed exchange rate of 1.65 (US$3,300,000). The notional amount of the contract in euros terms is €2,000,000.

However, while a derivative usually has a notional amount, this is not always the case: a derivative could require a fixed payment or payment of an amount that can change (but not proportionally with a change in the underlying) as a result of some future event that is unrelated to a notional amount. For example, a contract that requires a fixed payment of €1,000 if six-month LIBOR increases by

100 basis points is a derivative, but does not have a specified notional amount (at least not in the conventional sense). *[IAS 39.AG9, IFRS 9.BA.1].* A further example is shown below.

Example 43.2:   Derivative containing no notional amount

XYZ enters into a contract that requires payment of $1,000 if ABC's share price increases by $5 or more during a six-month period; XYZ will receive $1,000 if the share price decreases by $5 or more during the same six-month period; no payment will be made if the price swing is less than $5 up or down.

The settlement amount changes with an underlying, ABC's share price, although there is no notional amount to determine the settlement amount. Instead, there is a payment provision that is based on changes in the underlying. Provided all the other characteristics of a derivative are present, which they are in this case, such an instrument is a derivative.[1]

2.1.2   Underlying variables

It follows from the definition (see 2 above) that a derivative will always have at least one underlying variable. The following underlying variables are referred to in the standard, but this is not an exhaustive list (we have provided an example for each of the underlyings):

- specified interest rate (e.g. LIBOR);
- financial instrument price (e.g. the share price of an entity);
- commodity price (e.g. the price of a barrel of oil);
- foreign exchange rate (e.g. the £/$ spot rate);
- index of prices or rates (e.g. Consumer Price Index);
- credit rating (e.g. Fitch);
- credit index (e.g. AAA rated corporate bond index); and
- non-financial variable (e.g. index of earthquake losses or of temperatures).

The application guidance explains that a contract to receive a royalty, often in exchange for the use of certain property that is not exchange-traded, where the payment is based on the volume of related sales or service revenues and accounted for under IAS 18 – *Revenue* (see Chapter 28 at 3.12) is not accounted for as a derivative. *[IAS 39.AG2, IFRS 9.B2.2].*

Derivatives that are based on sales volume are not necessarily excluded from the scope of IAS 39 (IFRS 9), especially where there is another (financial) underlying, as set out in the next example.

Example 43.3:   Derivative containing two underlyings

Company XYZ, whose functional currency is the US dollar, sells products in France denominated in euros. XYZ enters into a contract with an investment bank to convert euros to US dollars at a fixed exchange rate. The contract requires XYZ to remit euros based on its sales volume in France in exchange for US dollars at a fixed exchange rate of 1.00.

The contract has two underlying variables, the foreign exchange rate and the volume of sales, no initial net investment, and a payment provision. Therefore, as the implementation guidance explains, it is a derivative. *[IAS 39.B.8, IFRS 9.B.8].*

However, contracts that are linked to variables that might be considered non-financial, such as an entity's revenue, can sometimes cause particular interpretative problems.

2.1.3   Non-financial variables specific to one party to the contract

The definition of a derivative (see 2 above) refers to underlyings that are non-financial variables specific to one party to the contract. This reference was introduced by IFRS 4 – *Insurance Contracts* – to help determine whether or not a financial instrument is an insurance contract (see Chapter 42 at 3.3). An insurance contract is likely to contain such an underlying, for example the occurrence or non-occurrence of a fire that damages or destroys an asset of a party to the contract. Non-financial variables that are not specific to one party to the contract might include an index of earthquake losses in a particular region or an index of temperatures in a particular city. *[IAS 39.AG12A, IFRS 9.BA.5]*. Those based on climatic variables are sometimes referred to as 'weather derivatives'. *[IAS 39.AG1, IFRS 9.B2.1]*.

A change in the fair value of a non-financial asset is specific to the owner if the fair value reflects not only changes in market prices for such assets (a financial variable) but also the condition of the specific non-financial asset held (a non-financial variable). For example, if a guarantee of the residual value of a specific car exposes the guarantor to the risk of changes in the car's physical condition, the change in that residual value is specific to the owner of the car, and so would not be a derivative. *[IAS 39.AG12A, IFRS 9.BA.5]*.

Contracts with non-financial variables arise in the gaming industry where a gaming institution takes a position against a customer (rather than providing services to manage the organisation of games between two or more parties). For example, a customer will pay a stake to a bookmaker such that the bookmaker is contractually obliged to pay the customer a specified amount in the event that the bet is a winning one, e.g. if the specified horse wins a given race. The underlying variable (the outcome of the race) is clearly non-financial in nature, but it is unlikely to be specific to either party to the contract. Accordingly such contracts will typically be derivative financial instruments.[2]

It is not clear whether the reference to non-financial variables specific to one party to the contract means that all instruments with such an underlying would fail to meet the definition of a derivative or only those contracts that are insurance contracts, for which the reference was originally introduced. Until the standard is clarified, in our view, a legitimate case can be made for either view.

The Interpretations Committee considered this issue in the context of contracts indexed to an entity's revenue or EBITDA and initially came to a tentative conclusion that the exclusion was not restricted to insurance contracts.[3] However, that conclusion was later withdrawn and the Interpretations Committee referred the issue to the IASB, recommending that the standard be amended to limit the exclusion to insurance contracts.[4]

The IASB confirmed that it had intended the exclusion to apply only to contracts that are within the scope of IFRS 4[5] and in October 2007 proposed amendments to IAS 39 to reflect this view.[6] However, the proposed amendments would have resulted in a significant change to current practice with many contracts being brought into the scope of IAS 39 and inappropriately accounted for at fair value, for example:

- lease contracts with payments based on performance measures specific to the lessee;
- pharmaceutical contracts with payments based on the success rate of that drug;
- mobile phone service provider arrangements with distributors remunerated on the basis of the length of contract term agreed with the end customer;
- technology licensing agreements with payments due to the licensor based on production volumes; and
- some service concession arrangements.

In effect, entities would be required to place a fair value on their own business risk or future profit streams. The IASB staff concluded that further research into possible implications was needed and that this should be included as a separate project for a major amendment of IAS 39.[7] In October 2008, the IASB decided not to proceed with the proposed amendment in the annual improvements process, but would consider addressing the issue in a future project.[8] The existing definition of a derivative (see 2 above) was incorporated in IFRS 9 without alteration, leaving the issue unaddressed.

A further issue arises in that it is not always clear whether a variable is non-financial. This is illustrated in the following example (in this case the underlying is associated with an embedded feature which might or might not meet the definition of a derivative).

Example 43.4: Borrowing with coupons linked to revenue

Company F, a manufacturing entity, issues a debt instrument for its par value of €10m. It is repayable in ten years' time at par and an annual coupon is payable that comprises two elements: a fixed amount of 2.5% of the par value and a variable amount equating to 0.01% of F's annual revenues. Company F does not designate the instrument at fair value through profit or loss.

It is assumed that if F had instead issued a more conventional fixed rate borrowing for the same amount with the same maturity it would have been required to pay an annual coupon of 4% of the par value. Therefore, on the face of it, the debt contains an embedded feature that represents a swap with an initial fair value of zero whereby F receives a fixed amount annually (1.5% of €10m) and pays a variable amount annually (0.01% of its revenues). Question is now whether this feature represents an embedded derivative that should be separated from the host contact and accounted for separately; see embedded derivative guidance at 4 below.

It is very hard to argue that the economic characteristics and risks of this embedded feature are closely related to the debt instrument and the variable (F's revenue) is clearly specific to F. The key issue is whether F's revenue is a financial or non-financial variable and therefore whether the embedded feature meets the definition of a derivative.

It is not only contracts with payments based on revenue that can cause such problems. Some contracts may require payments based on other measures taken or derived from an entity's financial statements such as EBITDA. The Interpretations Committee considered this matter in July 2006 and concluded there was a lack of clarity within IAS 39, believed it would be unable to reach a consensus on a timely basis and tentatively decided not to address it further.[9] In January 2007, the Interpretations Committee decided to withdraw its earlier conclusion and referred the matter to the IASB.[10] However, the IASB eventually decided not to amend IAS 39 to deal with this issue.

Whilst it is tempting to regard an entity's revenue and EBITDA as financial variables, they are driven by a number of different factors many of which are clearly non-financial in nature, for example the general business risks faced by the entity. In addition, many of the drivers of EBITDA and revenue will be specific to that business, for example the location of the business, the nature of its goods or services and management actions.

Two companies that have faced this issue in practice are Gaz de France and Renault. They have issued liabilities on which coupons are linked to 'value added' (a measure of profit previously reported under French GAAP), revenue and net profit. As can be seen in the following extracts, Gaz de France, in accounting for the entire instrument at amortised cost, appears to view 'value added' as a non-financial variable, whereas Renault clearly states that its revenue-linked and net profit-linked features are considered embedded derivatives.

Extract 43.1: Gaz de France S.A. (2007)

NOTES (TO THE CONSOLIDATED FINANCIAL STATEMENTS) [extract]
A – ACCOUNTING PRINCIPLES AND EVALUATION METHODS [extract]
2 – 22.3 Loans and receivables [extract]

Gaz de France issued irredeemable securities in 1985 and 1986 as authorized by French law 83.1 of January 1, 1983, and by Law 85.695 of July 11, 1985. These securities are assessed at their amortized cost. As they do not meet the criteria of an equity instrument, they are classified as debt/financial liabilities.
Return

The return of irredeemable securities, subject to a limit of between 85% and 130% of the average bond interest rate, comprises a fixed portion equal to 63% of the French Average Bond Rate ("TMO" in the French acronym) and a variable portion calculated on the basis of the growth in Gaz de France's "value added" in the previous year (or that of the consolidated group, Group share only, if this is more favourable).

The return on irredeemable securities according to the effective interest method is treated as a borrowing cost in interest expense.

Extract 43.2: Renault SA (2014)

NOTES TO THE CONSOLIDATED FINANCIAL STATEMENT [extract]
2 – ACCOUNTING POLICIES AND SCOPE OF CONSOLIDATION [extract]
W – Financial liabilities of the Automotive segment and sales financing debts [extract]

Redeemable shares

In accordance with IAS 39, the Group considers that the variable interest on redeemable shares is an embedded derivative ...

23 – Financial liabilities and sales financing debts [extract]

Redeemable shares [extract]

The redeemable shares issued in October 1983 and April 1984 by Renault SA are subordinated perpetual shares. They earn a minimum annual return of 9% comprising a 6.75% fixed portion and a variable portion that depends on consolidated revenues and is calculated based on identical Group structure and methods. [...]

The return on Diac redeemable shares issued in 1985 comprises a fixed portion equal to the Annual Monetary Rate, and a variable portion calculated by multiplying an amount equal to 40% of the Annual Monetary Rate by the rate of increase in net consolidated profit of the Diac sub-group compared to the prior year.

In 2009 the Interpretations Committee was asked to consider the accounting treatment for an instrument that contains participation rights by which the instrument holder shares in the net income and losses of the issuer. However, the Interpretations Committee considered the issue without reconsidering the assumptions described in the request, including one that the financial liability did not contain any embedded derivatives.[11] In other words, the Interpretations Committee implicitly accepted that such a feature need not be separated but did not indicate that separation was necessarily prohibited.

In practice, we believe that an entity may make an accounting policy choice as to whether the entity's revenue, EBITDA or other measures taken or derived from the entity's financial statements, are financial or non-financial variables. Once an entity elects a particular policy, it must consistently apply that approach to all similar transactions.

2.2 Initial net investment

The second key characteristic of a derivative is that it has no initial net investment, or one that is smaller than would be required for other types of contracts that would be expected to have a similar response to changes in market factors (see 2 above). *[IAS 39.9, IFRS 9 Appendix A].*

An option contract meets the definition because the premium is less than the investment that would be required to obtain the underlying financial instrument to which the option is linked. *[IAS 39.AG11, IFRS 9.BA.3].*

The implementation guidance to the original standard suggested that the purchase of a deep in the money call option would fail to satisfy the original 'little net investment' test if the premium paid was equal *or close to* the amount required to invest in the underlying instrument.[12] However, the implementation guidance on which Example 43.8 below is based explains that a contract is not a derivative if the initial net investment *approximates* the amount that an entity otherwise would be required to invest. *[IAS 39.B.9, IFRS 9.B.9].* Currency swaps sometimes require an exchange of different currencies of equal value at inception. This does not mean that they would not meet the definition a derivative, i.e. no initial net investment or an initial investment that is smaller than would be required for other types of contracts that would be expected to have a similar response to changes in market factors, as the following example demonstrates.

Example 43.5: Currency swap – initial exchange of principal

Company A and Company B enter into a five year fixed-for-fixed currency swap on euros and US dollars. The current spot exchange rate is €1 = US$1. The five year interest rate in the US is 8%, while the five year interest rate in Europe is 6%. On initiation of the swap, A pays €2,000 to B, which in return pays US$2,000 to A. During the swap's life, A and B make periodic interest payments to each other without netting. B pays 6% per year on the €2,000 it has received (€120 per year), while A pays 8% per year on the US$2,000 it has received (US$160 per year). On termination of the swap, the two parties again exchange the original principal amounts.

The currency swap is a derivative financial instrument since the contract involves a zero initial *net* investment (an exchange of one currency for another of equal fair values), it has an underlying, and it will be settled at a future date. *[IAS 39.AG11, IFRS 9.BA.3].*

The following examples illustrate how to assess the initial net investment characteristic in various prepaid derivatives – these can provide guidance when assessing whether what appears to be a non-derivative instrument is actually a derivative.

Example 43.6:   *Prepaid interest rate swap (prepaid fixed leg)*

Company S enters into a €1,000 notional amount five year pay-fixed, receive-variable interest rate swap. The interest rate of the variable part of the swap resets on a quarterly basis to three month LIBOR. The interest rate of the fixed part of the swap is 10% per annum. At inception of the swap S prepays its fixed obligation of €500 (€1,000 × 10% × 5 years), discounted using market interest rates, while retaining the right to receive the LIBOR-based interest payments on the €1,000 over the life of the swap.

The initial net investment in the swap is significantly less than the notional amount on which the variable payments under the variable leg will be calculated and therefore requires an initial net investment that is smaller than would be required for other types of contracts that would be expected to have a similar response to changes in market conditions, such as a variable rate bond. It therefore fulfils the 'no initial net investment or an initial investment that is smaller than would be required for other types of contracts that would be expected to have similar response to change in market factors' criterion. Even though S has no future performance obligation, the ultimate settlement of the contract is at a future date and its value changes in response to changes in LIBOR. Accordingly, it is a derivative. *[IAS 39.B.4, IFRS 9.B.4]*.

Example 43.7:   *Prepaid interest rate swap (prepaid floating leg)*

Instead of the transactions in Example 43.6, Company S enters into a €1,000 notional amount five year pay-variable, receive-fixed interest rate swap. The variable leg of the swap resets on a quarterly basis to three month LIBOR. The fixed interest payments under the swap are calculated as 10% of the notional amount, i.e. €100 per year. By agreement with the counterparty, S prepays and discharges its obligation under the variable leg of the swap at inception by paying a fixed amount determined according to current market rates, while retaining the right to receive the fixed interest payments of €100 per year.

The cash inflows under the contract are equivalent to those of a financial instrument with a fixed annuity stream since S knows it will receive €100 per year over the life of the swap. Therefore, all else being equal, the initial investment in the contract should equal that of other financial instruments consisting of fixed annuities. Thus, the initial net investment in the pay-variable, receive-fixed interest rate swap is equal to the investment required in a non-derivative contract that has a similar response to changes in market conditions. For this reason, the instrument does not exhibit characteristic 'no initial net investment or an initial investment that is smaller than would be required for other types of contracts that would be expected to have similar response to changes in market factors' requirement and is therefore not a derivative. *[IAS 39.B.5, IFRS 9.B.5]*.

The conclusions in Examples 43.6 and 43.7 above are fundamentally different for what, on the face of it, appear to be very similar transactions. The key difference is that in Example 43.7 all possible cash flow variances are eliminated and, consequently, the resulting cash flows exhibit the characteristics of a simple non-derivative instrument, i.e. an amortising loan.

Example 43.8:   *Prepaid forward purchase of shares*

Company S also enters into a forward contract to purchase 100 shares in T in one year. The current share price is €50 per share and the one year forward price €55. S is required to prepay the forward contract at inception with a €5,000 payment.

The initial investment in the forward contract of €5,000 is less than the notional amount applied to the underlying, 100 shares at the forward price of €55 per share, i.e. €5,500. However, the initial net investment approximates the investment that would be required for other types of contracts that would be expected to have a similar response to changes in market factors because T's shares could be purchased at inception for the same price of €50. Accordingly, the prepaid forward does not exhibit characteristic 'no initial net investment or an initial investment that is smaller than would be required for other types of contracts that would be expected to have similar response to changes in market factors' criterion and is therefore not a derivative. *[IAS 39.B.9, IFRS 9.B.9]*.

Many derivative instruments, such as futures contracts and exchange traded written options, require margin payments. The implementation guidance explains that a margin payment is not part of the initial net investment in a derivative, but is a form of collateral for the counterparty or clearing-house and may take the form of cash, securities, or other specified assets, typically liquid assets. Consequently, they are separate assets that are accounted for separately. *[IAS 39.B.10, IFRS 9.B.10].* However, while accounted for separately, the margin call and the derivative would be presented net in the statement of financial position if the offsetting requirements of IAS 32 – *Financial Instruments: Presentation* – are met (see Chapter 53 at 7.4). In some jurisdictions, depending on the precise terms of the related contracts, margin payments may actually represent a partial settlement of a derivative.

2.3 Future settlement

The third characteristic is that settlement takes place at a future date. Sometimes, a contract will require gross cash settlement. However, as illustrated in the next example, it makes no difference whether the future settlements are gross or net.

Example 43.9:   Interest rate swap – gross or net settlement

Company ABC is considering entering into an interest rate swap with a counterparty, XYZ. The proposed terms are that ABC pays a fixed rate of 8% and receives a variable amount based on three month LIBOR, reset on a quarterly basis; the fixed and variable amounts are determined based on a €1,000 notional amount; ABC and XYZ do not exchange the notional amount and ABC pays or receives a net cash amount each quarter based on the difference between 8% and three month LIBOR. Alternatively, settlement may be on a gross basis.

The contract meets the definition of a derivative regardless of whether there is net or gross settlement because its value changes in response to changes in an underlying variable (LIBOR), there is no initial net investment and settlements occur at future dates – it makes no difference whether ABC and XYZ actually make the interest payments to each other (gross settlement) or settle on a net basis. *[IAS 39.B.3, IFRS 9.B.3].*

The definition of a derivative also includes contracts that are settled gross by delivery of the underlying item, e.g. a forward contract to purchase a fixed rate debt instrument. An entity may have a contract to buy or sell a non-financial item that can be settled net, e.g. a contract to buy or sell a commodity at a fixed price at a future date; if that contract is within the scope of IAS 39 or IFRS 9 (see Chapter 42 at 4), then the question of whether or not it meets the definition of a derivative will be assessed in the same way as for a financial instrument that may be settled gross. *[IAS 39.AG10, IFRS 9.BA.2].*

Expiry of an option at its maturity is a form of settlement even though there is no additional exchange of consideration. Therefore, even if an option is not expected to be exercised, e.g. because it is significantly 'out of the money', it can still be a derivative. *[IAS 39.B.7, IFRS 9.B.7].* Such an option will have some value, albeit small, because it still offers the opportunity for gain if it becomes 'in the money' before expiry even if such a possibility is remote – the more remote the possibility, the lower its value.

Chapter 43

3   EXAMPLES OF DERIVATIVES

3.1   Common derivatives

The following table provides examples of contracts that normally qualify as derivatives. The list is not exhaustive – any contract that has an underlying may be a derivative. Moreover, as set out in Chapter 42 at 3, even if an instrument meets the definition of a derivative, it may not fall within the scope of IAS 39 or IFRS 9.

Type of contract	Main pricing-settlement underlying variable
Interest rate swap	Interest rates
Currency swap (foreign exchange swap)	Currency rates
Commodity swap	Commodity prices
Equity swap	Equity prices (equity of another entity)
Credit swap	Credit rating, credit index, or credit price
Total return swap	Total fair value of the reference asset and interest rates
Purchased or written bond option (call or put)	Interest rates
Purchased or written currency option (call or put)	Currency rates
Purchased or written commodity option (call or put)	Commodity prices
Purchased or written stock option (call or put)	Equity prices (equity of another entity)
Interest rate futures linked to government debt (treasury futures)	Interest rates
Currency futures	Currency rates
Commodity futures	Commodity prices
Interest rate forward linked to government debt (treasury forward)	Interest rates
Currency forward	Currency rates
Commodity forward	Commodity prices
Equity forward	Equity prices (equity of another entity) [IAS 39.B.2, IFRS 9.B.2]

3.2   In-substance derivatives

The implementation guidance explains that the accounting should follow the substance of arrangements. In particular, non-derivative transactions should be aggregated and treated as a derivative when, in substance, the transactions result in a derivative. Indicators of this would include:

- they are entered into at the same time and in contemplation of one another;
- they have the same counterparty;
- they relate to the same risk; and
- there is no apparent economic need or substantive business purpose for structuring the transactions separately that could not also have been accomplished in a single transaction. *[IAS 39.B.6, IFRS 9.B.6].*

The application of this guidance is illustrated in the following example.

Example 43.10: In-substance derivative – offsetting loans

Company A makes a five year fixed rate loan to Company B, while at the same time B makes a five year variable rate loan for the same amount to A. There are no transfers of principal at inception of the two loans, since A and B have a netting agreement.

The combined contractual effect of the loans is the equivalent of an interest rate swap arrangement, i.e. there is an underlying variable, no initial net investment, and future settlement. This meets the definition of a derivative.

This would be the case even if there was no netting agreement, because the definition of a derivative instrument does not require net settlement (see Example 43.9 at 2.3 above). *[IAS 39.B.6, IFRS 9.B.6].*

The analysis above would be equally applicable if the loans were in different currencies – such an arrangement could synthesise a cross-currency interest rate swap and should be accounted for as a derivative if that is its substance.

3.3 Regular way contracts

A regular way purchase or sale is a purchase or sale of a financial asset under a contract whose terms require delivery of the asset within the time frame established generally by regulation or convention in the marketplace concerned. *[IAS 39.9, IFRS 9 Appendix A].* Such contracts give rise to a fixed price commitment between trade date and settlement date, that meets the definition of a derivative. However, because of the short duration of the commitments, they are not accounted for as derivatives but in accordance with special accounting rules. These requirements are discussed in Chapter 47 at 2.2. *[IAS 39.AG12, IFRS 9.BA.4].*

4 EMBEDDED DERIVATIVES

An embedded derivative is a component of a hybrid or combined instrument that also includes a non-derivative host contract; it has the effect that some of the cash flows of the combined instrument vary in a similar way to a stand-alone derivative. In other words, it causes some or all of the cash flows, that otherwise would be required by the contract, to be modified according to a specified interest rate, financial instrument price, commodity price, foreign exchange rate, index of prices or rates, credit rating or credit index, or other underlying variable (provided in the case of a non-financial variable that the variable is not specific to a party to the contract). *[IAS 39.10, IFRS 9.4.3.1].*

Common examples of contracts that can contain embedded derivatives include non-derivative financial instruments (especially debt instruments), leases, insurance contracts as well as contracts for the supply of goods or services. In fact, they may occur in all sorts of unsuspected locations.

Under IFRS 9 the concept of embedded derivatives applies to only financial liabilities and non-financial items. Embedded derivatives are not separated from financial assets within the scope of IFRS 9 and the requirements of IFRS 9 are applied to the hybrid contract as a whole. *[IFRS 9.4.3.2]*.

Normal sale or purchase contracts (see Chapter 42 at 4) can also contain embedded derivatives. This is an important difference from US GAAP, under which a contract for the sale or purchase of a non-financial item, that can be settled net, cannot be treated as a normal sale or purchase at all if it contains an embedded pricing feature, that is not clearly and closely related to the host contract – instead the whole contract would be accounted for as a derivative.

In the basis for conclusions to IAS 39 and IFRS 9, the IASB asserts that, in principle, *all* embedded derivatives that are not measured at fair value with gains and losses recognised in profit or loss ought to be accounted for separately, but explains that, as a practical expedient, they should not be where they are regarded as 'closely related' to their host contracts. In those cases, it is believed less likely that the derivative was embedded to achieve a desired accounting result. *[IAS 39.BC37, IFRS 9.BCZ4.92]*.

Accordingly, only where all of the following conditions are met should an embedded derivative be separated from the host contract and accounted for separately:

(a)   the economic characteristics and risks of the embedded derivative are not closely related to the economic characteristics and risks of the host contract;

(b)   a separate instrument with the same terms as the embedded derivative would meet the definition of a derivative; and

(c)   the hybrid (combined) instrument is not measured at fair value with changes in fair value recognised in profit or loss. *[IAS 39.11, IFRS 9.4.3.3]*.

If any of these conditions are not met, the embedded derivative should not be accounted for separately, *[IAS 39.11, AG33, IFRS 9.4.3.3, IFRS 9.B4.3.8]*, i.e. an entity is prohibited from separating an embedded derivative that is closely related to its host contract. The process is similar, although not identical, to that applied when separating the equity element of a compound instrument by the issuer under IAS 32 (see Chapter 44 at 6). The assessment of the closely related criterion should be made when the entity first becomes a party to a contract or in other words on initial recognition of the contract (see 7 below). *[IFRIC 9.7, IFRS 9.B4.3.1, B4.3.11]*.

The accounting treatment for a separated embedded derivative is the same as for a standalone derivative. Such an instrument (actually, in this case, a component of an instrument) will normally be recorded in the statement of financial position at fair value with all changes in value being recognised in profit or loss (see 1 above, Chapter 45 at 2.1 and Chapter 46 at 2 and 3), although there are some exceptions, e.g. embedded derivatives may be designated as a hedging instrument in an effective hedge relationship in the same way as standalone derivatives (see Chapter 51 at 2.1.1).

A derivative that is attached to a financial instrument but is contractually transferable independently of that instrument, or has a different counterparty from that instrument, is not an embedded derivative, but a separate financial instrument. *[IAS 39.10, IFRS 9.4.3.1].*

Where an entity is unable to measure an embedded derivative that is required to be separated from its host, either on acquisition or subsequently, the entire contract is designated at fair value through profit or loss. *[IAS 39.12, IAS 39.C.11, IFRS 9.4.3.6].* Even if the embedded derivative's fair value cannot be determined reliably on the basis of its terms and conditions (for example if it is based on an equity instrument, that does not have a quoted price in an active market for an identical instrument, i.e. a Level 1 input), it may be determined indirectly as the difference between hybrid (combined) instrument and the host instrument, if their fair values can be determined. *[IAS 39.13, IFRS 9.4.3.7].*

It is important to note that the requirement to separate an embedded derivative from a host contract applies to all parties to a contract e.g. the issuer of a debt instrument and the holder of the debt instrument. However, the parties might reach different accounting treatments when applying the guidance in the standard. From the issuer's perspective, the conversion option in a convertible debt instrument denominated in the functional currency of the issuer would be classified as an equity instrument, assuming it meets the conditions for classification as equity under IAS 32 (see Chapter 44), and is therefore excluded from the scope of IAS 39 or IFRS 9. From the holder's perspective under IAS 39 the conversion option is not closely related to the host debt instrument and therefore needs to be separated from the host contract (see 5.1.8 below).

5 EMBEDDED DERIVATIVES: THE MEANING OF 'CLOSELY RELATED'

The standard does not define what is meant by 'closely related'. Instead, it illustrates what was intended by providing a series of situations where the embedded derivative is, or is not, regarded as closely related to the host. Making this determination can prove very challenging, not least because the illustrations do not always seem to be consistent with each other. This guidance is considered in the remainder of this subsection.

5.1 Financial instrument hosts

Where a host contract has no stated or predetermined maturity and represents a residual interest in the net assets of an entity, its economic characteristics and risks are those of an equity instrument – therefore, an embedded derivative would need to possess equity characteristics related to the same entity to be regarded as closely related. More commonly, if the host is not an equity instrument and meets the definition of a financial instrument, then its economic characteristics and risks are those of a debt instrument. *[IAS 39.AG27, IFRS 9.B4.3.2].* The application of these principles to debt hosts is considered at 5.1.1 to 5.1.8 below and to equity hosts at 5.1.10 below; instruments that may be debt or equity hosts are considered at 5.1.9 below.

5.1.1   Foreign currency monetary items

A monetary item denominated in a currency other than an entity's functional currency is accounted for under IAS 21 – *The Effects of Changes in Foreign Exchange Rates* – with foreign currency gains and losses recognised in profit or loss. The embedded foreign currency derivative is considered closely related to a debt host and is not separated. In other words it would not be considered a functional currency monetary item and a foreign currency forward contract. This also applies where the embedded derivative in a host debt instrument provides a stream either of principal or of interest payments denominated in a foreign currency (e.g. a dual currency bond). *[IAS 39.AG33(c), IFRS 9.B4.3.8(c)].*

5.1.2   Interest rate indices

Many debt instruments contain embedded interest rate indices that can change the amount of interest that would otherwise be paid or received. One of the simplest examples would be a floating rate loan whereby interest is paid quarterly based on three month LIBOR. More complex examples might include the following:

- inverse floater – coupons are paid at a fixed rate minus LIBOR;

- levered inverse floater – as above but a multiplier greater than 1.0 is applied to the resulting coupon;

- delevered floater – coupons lag overall movements in a specified rate, e.g. coupons equal a proportion of the ten year constant maturity treasuries rate plus a fixed premium; or

- range floater – interest is paid at a fixed rate but only for each day in a given period that LIBOR is within a stated range.

In such cases the embedded derivative is closely related to the host debt instrument unless:

(a)   the combined instrument can be settled in such a way that the holder would not recover substantially all of its recognised investment; or

(b)   the embedded derivative could at least double the holder's initial rate of return on the host contract *and* could result in a rate of return that is at least twice what the market return would be for a contract with the same terms as the host contract (often referred to as the 'double-double test'). *[IAS 39.AG33(a), IFRS 9.B4.3.8(a)].*

If a holder is permitted, but not required, to settle the combined instrument in a manner such that it does not recover substantially all of its recognised investment, e.g. puttable debt, condition (a) is not satisfied and the embedded derivative is not separated. *[IAS 39.C.10, IFRS 9.C.10].* The standard does not define 'substantially all' and therefore judgement will need to be applied, considering all relevant facts and circumstances.

To meet condition (b), the embedded derivative must be able to double the initial return *and* result in a rate of return that is at least twice what would be expected for a similar contract at the time it takes effect. If it meets only one part of this condition, but not the other, the derivative is regarded as closely related to the host. Due to the requirement 'could result in a rate of return that is at least twice what the market return would be for a contract with the same terms as the host contract', the derivative embedded in a simple variable rate loan would be considered closely related to the host because the variable rate at any specific time would be a market rate.

As with all embedded derivatives, the assessment of condition (a) and (b) above is made when the entity becomes party to the contract on the basis of market conditions existing at that time (see 4 above). Important to note is, the assessment is based on the possibility of the holder not recovering its recognised investment or doubling its initial return and obtaining twice the then-market return. The likelihood of this happening is ignored in making the assessment. Therefore, even if the likelihood of this happening is low, the embedded derivative has to be separated from the host contract. The valuation of the embedded derivative would however consider the low probability of this happening, possibly resulting in a relatively low fair value at inception.

An example where the holder would not recover substantially all of its recognised investment would be a bond which becomes immediately repayable if LIBOR increases above a certain threshold, at an amount significantly lower than its issue price. A further example is set out below.

Example 43.11:   Leveraged inverse floater – not recovering substantially all of the initial investment

Company A invests in a leveraged inverse floater loan note for its par value of US$20m. Interest is payable annually and is calculated as 10% minus 2 times three month LIBOR. At the time company A invests in the loan note, three month LIBOR is 3%, giving an initial return of 4%. There is no floor imposed on the interest rate and the rate could therefore be negative if LIBOR increases above 5%. In such a case, company A would need to pay interest on its investment, which would leave it unable to recover substantially all of its recognised investment. The embedded derivative is therefore not closely related to the host contract and will be accounted for separately.

An example of condition (b) above, the 'double-double test', is set out below.

Example 43.12:   Leveraged inverse floater – 'double-double test'

Assume the same fact pattern as in Example 43.11, except that there is a floor imposed on the coupon rate so that rate could not be negative. In such a case, company A would recover substantially all of its recognised investment, meaning that no embedded derivative needs to be separated based on condition (a) above. However, before company A could conclude on whether or not an embedded derivative needs to be recognised separately, it would need to evaluate condition (b) above. The first step is to assess whether there is a possible scenario in which the initial return of the investor would at least double. If LIBOR falls to 1% or to below 1%, say 0.5%, then the interest rate on the loan note would be 9%, which is more than double the investor's initial rate of return of 4%. The first part of the condition under (b) above is therefore fulfilled.

The question is now whether 9% is twice the market return for a contract with the same terms as the host contract. With LIBOR being 0.5% this will most likely be the case, leaving both parts of condition (b) above fulfilled. The embedded derivative is therefore not closely related to the host contract and will be accounted for separately. If however, it is concluded that 9% is not twice the market return for a contract with the same terms as the host contract, then only one part of the condition under (b) above would be fulfilled and the embedded feature would be considered closely related to the host with no requirement to record it separately.

5.1.3   Term extension and similar call, put and prepayment options in debt instruments

The application guidance explains that a call, put or prepayment option embedded in a host debt instrument is closely related to the host instrument if, on each exercise date, the option's exercise price is approximately equal to the debt instrument's amortised cost or the exercise price reimburses the lender for an amount up to the approximate present value of lost interest for the remaining term of the host contract; otherwise it is not regarded as closely related. *[IAS 39.AG30(g), IFRS 9.B4.3.5(e)].* There is no elaboration on what is meant by the term 'approximately equal' and so judgement will need to be applied.

It also says that an option or automatic provision to extend the remaining term to maturity of a debt instrument is not closely related to the host unless, at the time of the extension, there is a concurrent adjustment to the approximate current market rate of interest. *[IAS 39.AG30(c), IFRS 9.B4.3.5(b)].* The current market rate of interest would take into consideration the credit risk of the issuer. Taken in isolation, the above two paragraphs appear reasonably straightforward to apply. However, in some situations, they are contradictory as set out in the following example.

Example 43.13:   Extension and prepayment options

Company Z borrows €1,000 from Bank A on which it is required to pay €50 per annum interest. Under the terms of the borrowing agreement, Z is required to repay €1,000 in three years' time unless, at repayment date, it exercises an option to extend the term of the borrowing for a further two years. If this option is exercised €50 interest per annum is payable for the additional term.

Company Z also borrows €1,000 from Bank B on which it is required to pay €50 per annum interest. Under the terms of this borrowing agreement, Z is required to repay €1,000 in five years' time unless, at the end of three years, it exercises an option to redeem the borrowing for €1,000.

It can be seen that in all practical respects these two instruments are identical – the only difference is the way in which the terms of the embedded options are expressed. In the first case the guidance indicates that the (term extension) option is not closely related to the debt as there is no concurrent adjustment to market interest rates. However, in the second case the (prepayment) option *is* considered closely related provided the amortised cost of the liability would be approximately €1,000, the exercise price of the settlement option, at the end of year three (which it should be).

As set out at 6.2 below, an embedded option-based derivative should be separated from its host contract on the basis of the stated terms of the option feature. However, in situations similar to the one described above, there is significant diversity in practice and we are aware of at least two ways in which entities have dealt with this contradiction in practice. Some entities have looked to the wording in the contract so that what is described as an extension option (or a prepayment option) is evaluated in accordance with the guidance for extension options (or prepayment options). Other entities have determined the most likely outcome of the hybrid instrument based on conditions at initial recognition and the alternative outcome is regarded as the 'option'. Under this latter approach, if Company Z in the example above considered it was likely to repay its loans from Bank A and Bank B after three years, both loans would be regarded as having a two-year extension option. The first approach is based on the contractual terms, while the second approach is substance-based.

Another complication is that, viewed as a separate instrument, a term extension option is effectively a loan commitment. As loan commitments are generally outside the scope of IAS 39 (see Chapter 42 at 3), some would argue they do not meet the definition of a derivative (see 2 above). Accordingly, when embedded in a host debt instrument, a loan commitment would not be separated as an embedded derivative or, alternatively, would be separated and accounted for as a loan commitment.[13]

The Interpretations Committee discussed both of the above contradictions in March 2012, noting significant diversity in practice and recommended that the IASB consider this issue when it redeliberated the classification and measurement requirements of financial liabilities under IFRS 9. The Committee decided that if the Board did not address this issue as part of its redeliberations, then the Committee would revisit this issue and consider whether guidance should be provided to clarify the accounting for the issuer of a fixed-rate-debt instrument that includes a term-extending option.[14] This issue remains unaddressed in IFRS 9 with no indication from the Interpretations Committee about bringing it back onto its agenda. Preparers of financial statements are therefore left to apply their own judgement considering all the facts and circumstances.

For put, call and prepayment options, there is a further complication that the determination as to whether or not the option is closely related depends on the amortised cost of the instrument. It is not clear whether this reference is to the amortised cost of the host instrument, on the assumption that the option is separated, or to the amortised cost of the entire instrument on the assumption that the option is not separated. As can be seen in Chapter 48 at 3.2 and Chapter 49 at 3.2, the existence of such options can affect the amortised cost, especially for a portfolio of instruments. Although one trade body has published guidance explaining that where early repayment fees are included in the calculation of effective interest, the prepayment option is likely to be closely related to the loan,[15] entities are largely left to apply their own judgement to assess which appears the most appropriate in the specific circumstances.

Prepayment options are also considered closely related to the host debt instrument if the exercise price reimburses the lender for an amount up to the approximate present value of lost interest for the remaining term of the host contract. For these purposes, lost interest is the product of the principal amount prepaid multiplied by the interest rate differential, i.e. the excess of the effective interest rate of the host contract over the effective interest rate that the entity would receive at the prepayment date if it reinvested the principal amount prepaid in a similar contract for the remaining term of the host contract. *[IAS 39.AG30(g)(ii), IFRS 9.B4.3.5(e)(ii)].* In other words, in order for the prepayment option to be considered closely related to the host, the exercise price of the prepayment option would need to compensate the lender for loss of interest by reducing the economic loss from that which would be incurred on reinvestment. *[IAS 39.BC40C, IFRS 9.BCZ4.97].*

From the perspective of the issuer of a convertible debt instrument with an embedded call or put option, the assessment of whether the option is closely related to the host debt instrument is made before separating the equity element in accordance with IAS 32. *[IAS 39.AG30(g), IFRS 9.B4.3.5(e)]*. This provides a specific relaxation from the general guidance on prepayment options above because, for accounting purposes, separate accounting for the equity component results in a discount on recognition of the liability component (see Chapter 44 at 6.2), which means that the amortised cost and exercise price are unlikely to approximate to each other for much of the term of the instrument.

An embedded prepayment option in an interest-only or principal-only strip is regarded as closely related to the host contract provided the host contract (i) initially resulted from separating the right to receive contractual cash flows of a financial instrument that, in and of itself, did not contain an embedded derivative, and (ii) does not contain any terms not present in the original host debt contract. *[IAS 39.AG33(e), IFRS 9.B4.3.8(e)]*. Again this is a specific relaxation from the general guidance on prepayment options above.

If an entity issues a debt instrument and the holder writes a call option on the debt instrument to a third party, the issuer regards the call option as extending the term to maturity of the debt instrument, provided it can be required to participate in or facilitate the remarketing of the debt instrument as a result of the call option being exercised. *[IAS 39.AG30(c), IFRS 9.B4.3.5(b)]*. Such a component is presumably considered to represent part of a hybrid financial instrument contract rather than a separate instrument in its own right (see 4 above).

5.1.4   *Interest rate floors and caps*

An embedded floor or cap on the interest rate on a debt instrument is closely related to the host debt instrument, provided the cap is at or above the market rate of interest, and the floor is at or below the market rate of interest, when the instrument is issued (in other words it needs to be at- or out-of-the-money), and the cap or floor is not leveraged in relation to the host instrument. *[IAS 39.AG33(b), IFRS 9.B4.3.8(b)]*.

The standard does not clarify what is meant by 'market rate of interest', or whether the cap (floor) should be considered as a single derivative or a series of caplets (floorlets) to be evaluated separately. Where the cap (floor) is at a constant amount throughout the term of the debt, historically entities have often compared the cap (floor) rate with the current spot floating rate at inception of the contract to determine whether the embedded derivative is closely related. However, in the current extremely low interest rate environment of many economies, floors are more commonly being set at higher rates than current spot rates. As a result, entities are starting to evaluate whether more sophisticated approaches to evaluate these features are more appropriate, e.g. by comparing the average forward rate over the life of the bond with the floor rate or by comparing the forward rate at each interest reset date with each floorlet rate. We do not believe it is necessary for both a cap *and* a floor to be present to be considered closely related. For example, a cap (or floor) on the coupon paid on a debt instrument without a corresponding floor (or cap) could be regarded as closely related to the host, provided it was above (or below) the market rate of interest on origination.

5.1.5   Inflation-linked debt instruments

It is quite common for some entities (and governments) to issue inflation-linked debt instruments, i.e. where interest and/or principal payments are linked to, say, a consumer price index. The only guidance in IAS 39 and IFRS 9 relating to embedded inflation-linked features is provided in the context of leases (see 5.3.2 below). If that guidance is accepted as applying to finance leases, it should also apply to debt instruments because finance leases result in assets and liabilities that are, in substance, no different to debt instruments (see Chapter 42 at 2.2.4). Further, in much finance theory, either real (applied to current prices) or nominal (applied to inflation adjusted prices) interest rates are used, suggesting a strong link between inflation and interest rates. Finally, a government or central bank will generally raise short-term interest rates as inflation rises and reduce rates as inflation recedes, which also suggests a close relationship between the two.

Therefore, we believe it would often be appropriate to treat the embedded derivative in inflation-linked debt as similar to an interest rate index and refer to the guidance at 5.1.2 above to determine whether the index is regarded as closely related to the debt. Typically, the index will be closely related to the debt where it is based on inflation in an economic environment in which the bond is issued/denominated, it is not significantly leveraged in relation to the debt and there is a sufficiently low risk of the investor not recovering its initial investment (only sometimes do such instruments provide an absolute guarantee that the principal will not be lost, although this situation will normally only arise if, over the life of the instrument, cumulative inflation is negative). However, some may argue that even if there is a very small risk of the initial investment not being recovered, the embedded derivative should be separated.

The staff of the Interpretations Committee has expressed a view that it would be appropriate to treat the embedded derivative in inflation-linked debt as closely related in economic environments where interest rates are mainly set so as to meet inflation targets, as evidenced by strong long-run correlation between nominal interest rates and inflation. In such jurisdictions they considered the characteristics and risks of the inflation embedded derivative to be closely related to the host debt contract.[16] Further, in debating the application of the effective interest method to such instruments (see Chapter 48 at 3.6 and Chapter 49 at 3.6) they have implicitly acknowledged that these instruments do not necessarily contain embedded derivatives requiring separation.

5.1.6   Commodity- and equity-linked interest and principal payments

Equity-indexed or commodity-indexed interest or principal payments embedded in a host debt instrument, i.e. where the amount of interest or principal is indexed to the value of an equity instrument or commodity (e.g. gold), are not closely related to the host debt instrument because the risks inherent in the embedded derivative are dissimilar to those of the host. *[IAS 39.AG30(d)-(e), IFRS 9.B4.3.5(c)-(d)].* This is illustrated in the following example.

Example 43.14:   Bond linked to commodity price

A mining company issues a ten year debt instrument for its par value of US$15m. Interest is payable annually and consists of guaranteed interest of 5% per annum and contingent interest of 0.5% if the price of commodity A increases above US$300 in the relevant year, 1% if the price of commodity A increases above US$400 in the relevant year or 1.5% if the price of commodity A increases above US$500 in the relevant year. The mining company could have issued the bond without the contingent interest rate feature at a rate of 6%.

The commodity price feature is a swap contract to receive 1% fixed interest and pay a variable amount of interest depending on the price of commodity A. This feature is not closely related to the debt host contract and therefore must be separated as an embedded derivative.

Another example of such an instrument is given in Example 45.1 in Chapter 45 at 3.1.

A common type of transaction is where refiners of commodities enter into purchase contracts for mineral ores, whereby the price is adjusted subsequent to delivery, based on the quoted market price of the refined commodity extracted from the ore. These arrangements, often called provisionally-priced contracts, can provide the refiner with a hedge of the fair value of its inventories and/or related sales proceeds which vary depending on subsequent changes in quoted commodity prices. Like the debt instruments noted above, any payable (or receivable) recognised at the time of delivery will contain an embedded commodity derivative. BHP Billiton supplies products on these terms and explains its accounting policy as follows.

Extract 43.3: BHP Billiton (2014)
Notes to Financial Statements [extract]
1   Accounting policies [extract]
Sales revenue [extract]

For certain commodities, the sales price is determined on a provisional basis at the date of sale and adjustments to the sales price subsequently occurs based on movements in quoted market or contractual prices up to the date of final pricing. The period between provisional invoicing and final pricing is typically between 60 and 120 days. Revenue on provisionally priced sales is recognised based on the estimated fair value of the total consideration receivable. The revenue adjustment mechanism embedded within provisionally priced sales arrangements has the character of a commodity derivative. Accordingly, the fair value of the final sales price adjustment is re-estimated continuously and changes in fair value are recognised as an adjustment to revenue. In all cases, fair value is estimated by reference to forward market prices.

However, it would not normally be regarded as necessary to account separately for such an embedded derivative prior to delivery of the non-financial item. This is because, until delivery occurs, the contract is considered executory and the pricing feature would be considered closely related to the commodity being delivered (see 5.2.2 below).

5.1.7   Credit-linked notes

Credit derivatives are sometimes embedded in a host debt instrument whereby one party (the 'beneficiary') transfers the credit risk of a particular reference asset, which it may not own, to another party (the 'guarantor'). Such credit derivatives allow the guarantor to assume the credit risk associated with the reference asset without directly owning it.

Whilst the economic characteristics of a debt instrument will include credit risk, should the embedded derivative be a credit derivative linked to the credit standing of an entity other than the issuer, it would not normally be regarded as closely related to the host debt instrument if the issuer were not required, through the terms of the financial instrument, to own the reference asset. *[IAS 39.AG30(h), IFRS 9.B4.3.5(f)].*

For example, an entity (commonly a structured entity) may issue various tranches of debt instruments that are referenced to a group of assets, such as a portfolio of bonds, mortgages or trade receivables, and the credit exposure from those assets is allocated to the debt instruments using a so called 'waterfall' feature. The waterfall feature itself does not normally result in the separation of an embedded credit derivative; it is the location or ownership of the reference assets that is most important to the assessment.[17] If the entity is required to hold the reference assets, the credit risk embedded in the debt instruments is considered closely related. However, if the issuer of the debt instruments held a credit derivative over the reference assets rather than the assets themselves, the embedded credit derivative would not be regarded as closely related.

Bradford and Bingley has separately accounted for derivatives embedded within a number of its collateralised debt obligation investments as explained below.

Extract 43.4: Bradford and Bingley plc (2007)

Notes to the Financial Statements [extract]
1.   **Principal accounting policies** [extract]
(n)   **Derivative financial instruments and hedge accounting** [extract]

The Group recognises that its holding of synthetic CDOs (where the SPV issuing the CDO contains a credit derivative) contains an embedded derivative if the CDO's originator does not hold the reference assets on its balance sheet or if the sponsor of the CDO is not required to hold the reference assets on its own balance sheet. Consequently, the fair value of the credit derivative contract is separated from the host synthetic CDO with changes in its fair value recognised within 'fair value movements'.

5.1.8   Convertible and exchangeable debt instruments

An equity conversion feature, embedded in a convertible debt instrument, is not closely related to the host debt instrument from the perspective of the holder of the instrument (from the issuer's perspective, the equity conversion option is often an equity instrument and excluded from the scope of IAS 39 – see Chapter 44 at 6.2). *[IAS 39.AG30(f), C.3].*

Where IFRS 9 is applied, the embedded derivative is not separated from financial assets within the scope of the standard and the requirements of the standard are applied to the hybrid contract as a whole. *[IFRS 9.4.3.2].*

In some instances, venture capital entities provide subordinated loans on terms that entitled them to receive shares if and when the borrowing entity lists its shares on a stock exchange, as illustrated in the following example.

Example 43.15:   Equity kicker

A venture capital investor, Company V, provides a subordinated loan to Company A and agrees that in addition to interest and repayment of principal, if A lists its shares on a stock exchange, V will be entitled to receive shares in A free of charge or at a very low price (an 'equity kicker'). As a result of this feature, interest on the loan is lower than it would otherwise be. The loan is not measured at fair value with changes in fair value recognised in profit or loss.

The economic characteristics and risks of an equity return are not closely related to those of the host debt instrument. The equity kicker meets the definition of a derivative because it has a value that changes in response to the change in the price of A's shares, requires only a relatively small initial net investment, and is settled at a future date. It does not matter that the right to receive shares is contingent upon the borrower's future listing *[IAS 39.C.4, IFRS 9.C.4]* (although the probability of this event occurring will influence the fair value of the embedded derivative).

Similarly, the derivative embedded in a bond that is convertible (or exchangeable) into equity shares of a third party will not be closely related to the host debt instrument – in this case, either from the point of view of the holder or of the issuer.

5.1.9   *Puttable instruments*

Another example of a hybrid contract is a financial instrument that gives the holder a right to put it back to the issuer in exchange for an amount that varies on the basis of the change in an equity or commodity price or index (a 'puttable instrument'). Where the host is a debt instrument, the embedded derivative, the indexed principal payment, cannot be regarded as closely related to that debt instrument. Because the principal payment can increase and decrease, the embedded derivative is a non-option derivative whose value is indexed to the underlying variable (see 6.1 below). *[IAS 39.AG30(a), AG31, IFRS 9.B4.3.5(a), B4.3.6]*.

From the perspective of the issuer of a puttable instrument, that can be put back at any time for cash equal to a proportionate share of the net asset value of an entity (such as units of an open-ended mutual fund or some unit-linked investment products), the effect of the issuer separating an embedded derivative and accounting for each component is to measure the combined instrument at the redemption amount, that would be payable at the end of the reporting period if the holder were to exercise its right to put the instrument back to the issuer. *[IAS 39.AG32, IFRS 9.B4.3.7]*.

IAS 39 is not entirely clear whether a similar treatment should apply to the holder of such an instrument. If it did, it would mean that all changes in the fair value of an entity's investment in a unit trust would be recognised in profit or loss, even if it were classified as available-for-sale. However, to the extent that anyone has a residual interest in the net assets of a unit trust, it is the unit-holders. Consequently, a more intuitive view of the investment might be as an equity instrument host with an embedded put option, exercisable at net asset value. Further, because net asset value will approximate fair value, the embedded derivative would have little or no value. A related issue has been considered by the Interpretations Committee, namely the treatment by the holder of instruments, that are puttable at an amount other than fair value (for example a proportion of the book value of net assets determined under IFRS or local GAAP) but which otherwise have characteristics and risks that are similar to an equity instrument, such as discretionary distributions. Although the Interpretations Committee did not take the issue onto its agenda, it indicated that the requirement for the issuer to apply IAS 32 and the holder to apply IAS 39 means that their respective accounting treatments need not necessarily be symmetrical. Accordingly, it may be appropriate for the holder to regard the host as an equity, not debt, instrument. Of course, in this case, the put option would have a non-zero fair value and should be accounted for separately as an embedded derivative.[18]

Further support for this can be found in the definition of loans and receivables: IAS 39 explains that an interest in a pool of assets that are not loans or receivables (such as an interest in a mutual fund) is not considered to be a loan or receivable (see Chapter 45 at 4). *[IAS 39.9]*. This also suggests the host might validly be considered an equity instrument from the point of view of the holder.

Therefore, we believe entities can account for unit trust and similar investments under IAS 39 as available-for-sale equity investments whilst recognising fair value gains and losses in equity. Where IFRS 9 is applied, the requirements of the standard are applied to the instrument as a whole, resulting in such investments in puttable instruments being recognised at fair value through profit or loss in their entirety. *[IFRS 9.4.3.2]*.

5.1.10 Callable equity instruments

An equity instrument containing an embedded call option enabling the issuer to reacquire that equity instrument at a specified price is not closely related to the host equity instrument from the perspective of the holder under IAS 39. *[IAS 39.AG30(b)]*.

Where IFRS 9 is applied, embedded derivatives are not separated from financial assets within the scope of the standard and the requirements of IFRS 9 are applied to the hybrid contract as a whole. *[IFRS 9.4.3.2]*.

5.2 Contracts for the sale of goods or services

5.2.1 Foreign currency derivatives

An embedded foreign currency derivative in a contract that is not a financial instrument is closely related to the host contract provided it is not leveraged, does not contain an option feature and requires payments denominated in one of the following currencies:

(i)   the functional currency of any substantial party to the contract – see 5.2.1.A below;

(ii) the currency in which the price of the related good or service that is acquired or delivered is routinely denominated in commercial transactions around the world (such as the US dollar for crude oil transactions) – see 5.2.1.B below; or

(iii) a currency that is commonly used in contracts to purchase or sell non-financial items in the economic environment in which the transaction takes place (e.g. a relatively stable and liquid currency that is commonly used in local business transactions or external trade) – see 5.2.1.C below.

Therefore, in such cases the embedded foreign currency derivative is not accounted for separately from the host contract. *[IAS 39.AG33(d), IFRS 9.B4.3.8(d)]*. An example would be a contract for the purchase or sale of a non-financial item, where the price is denominated in a foreign currency that meets one of the three criteria outlined above.

5.2.1.A Functional currency of counterparty

In principle, the assessment of exception (i) above is straightforward. In practice, however, the functional currency of the counterparty to a contract will not always be known with certainty and, in some cases, can be a somewhat subjective assessment even for the counterparty's management (assuming the counterparty is a corporate entity) – see Chapter 15 at 4. Consequently, entities will need to demonstrate they have taken appropriate steps to make a reasonable judgement as to their counterparties' functional currencies. Where available, a counterparty's financial statements will provide evidence of its functional currency. Otherwise, it would often be appropriate to assume that an entity operating in a single country has that country's currency as its functional currency, although if there were indicators to the contrary these would have to be taken into account.

Another practical problem that arises in applying this exception is identifying which parties to a contract are 'substantial'. Neither IAS 39 nor IFRS 9 provide any further guidance, but it is generally considered that such a party should be one that is acting as principal to the contract. Therefore if, as part of a contract, a parent provides a performance guarantee in respect of services to be provided by its operating subsidiary, the parent may be seen to be the substantial party to the contract and not the subsidiary, where the subsidiary is acting as an agent. However, if the guarantee is not expected to be called upon, the parent would not normally be considered a substantial party to the contract. Particular care is necessary when assessing a contract under which one party subcontracts an element of the work to another entity under common control, say a fellow subsidiary with a different functional currency, although in most cases it will only be the primary contractor that is considered a substantial party.

5.2.1.B   Routinely denominated in commercial transactions

For the purposes of exception (ii) above, the currency must be used for similar transactions all around the world, not just in one local area. For example, if cross-border transactions in natural gas in North America are routinely denominated in US dollars and such transactions are routinely denominated in euros in Europe, neither the US dollar nor the euro is a currency in which the good or service is routinely denominated in international commerce. *[IAS 39.C.9, IFRS 9.C.9].* Accordingly, the number of items to which this will apply will be limited – in practice it will be mainly commodities that are traded in, say, US dollars throughout much of the world. Examples include crude oil, jet fuel, certain base metals (including aluminium, copper and nickel) and some precious metals (including gold, silver and platinum). One other notable item might be wide-bodied aircraft where it appears that Boeing and Airbus, the two major manufacturers, routinely denominate sales in US dollars.

In September 2014 the Interpretations Committee received a request relating to the routinely denominated criterion. They were asked to consider whether a licensing agreement denominated in a currency, in which commercial transactions of that type were routinely denominated around the world, held an embedded foreign currency derivative that was closely related to the economic characteristics of the host contract.

The Interpretations Committee noted that the issue related to a contract for a specific type of item and observed that an assessment of routinely denominated criterion is based on evidence of whether or not such commercial transactions are denominated in that currency all around the world and not merely in one local area. They further observed that the assessment of the routinely denominated criterion is a question of fact and is based on an assessment of available evidence.

5.2.1.C   Commonly used currencies

The IASB noted that the requirement to separate embedded foreign currency derivatives may be burdensome for entities that operate in economies in which business contracts denominated in a foreign currency are common. For example, entities domiciled in small countries may find it convenient to denominate business contracts with entities from other small countries in an internationally liquid currency (such as the US dollar, euro or yen) rather than the local currency of any party to the transaction. Also, an entity operating in a hyperinflationary economy may use a price list in a hard currency to protect against inflation, for example an entity that has a foreign operation in a hyperinflationary economy that denominates local contracts in the functional currency of the parent. *[IAS 39.BC39, IFRS 9.BCZ4.94].*

Unfortunately, however, the assessment of whether or not a particular currency meets this requirement in a particular situation has not been straightforward in practice and this question reached the attention of the Interpretations Committee in May 2007. After debating the matter in four consecutive meetings and initially deciding not to deal with the topic because any guidance it could provide would be more in the nature of application guidance, it asked the IASB to amend IAS 39 to clarify the wording and meaning of the standard.[19]

During its debates, the Interpretations Committee did note that entities should:[20]

* identify where the transaction takes place.

    This is not as straightforward as it might seem. For example, consider a Polish company that manufactures components in Poland and exports them to a third party in the Czech Republic. Should the sale of components be regarded as a transaction occurring in Poland or in the Czech Republic?[21] It is likely that the Polish company would regard it as occurring in Poland and the Czech entity in the Czech Republic, but this is not entirely beyond debate; and

* identify currencies that are commonly used in the economic environment in which the transaction takes place.

    Entities need to address what the population of transactions in the economic environment is. Some might suggest that transactions to which (i) or (ii) above apply should be excluded, although this is not a view shared by the staff of the Interpretations Committee which considered that all transactions should be included.[22]

    Entities should also consider what an economic environment is. The guidance, on which Example 43.16 below is based, implies that a country could be an economic environment. The references to local business transactions and to external trade in (iii) above suggest that other examples of economic environment are the external trade or internal trade environment of the country in which the transaction takes place. The question remains as to whether there could be other economic environments, for example the luxury goods market in a country. Depending on the view taken, a different treatment could arise.[23] In considering the issue subsequently, the IASB staff noted their understanding that all of these views (and possibly more, such as the internal or external trade of a specific company) were being applied in practice.[24]

The Interpretations Committee had also been asked to provide guidance on how to interpret the term 'common', but understandably was reluctant to do so.[25] The IASB staff noted that there is no guidance as to the quantum of transactions or value that would need to be denominated in a foreign currency to conclude that the currency was commonly used and that a related matter is whether 'common' should be considered in the context of a particular entity, of an industry, or of a country.[26]

The IASB staff noted other related interpretive questions raised by constituents including the following:[27]

- what evidence does an entity require to support the notion that the use of a currency is common?

- does the reporting entity need to investigate published statistics?

- if the reporting entity has to look for statistics, what percentage of business needs to be conducted in that currency to assert that use of the currency is common?

- whether the consideration that a currency is commonly used should exclude from the population set those transactions falling under (i) or (ii) above.

They concluded that there are a variety of views on the appropriate interpretation of this guidance and, consequently, that there is significant diversity in practice.[28]

In response to this analysis, the IASB decided to amend IAS 39 as part of its second annual improvements process, which resulted in proposed amendments being published in August 2008. It was noted that the guidance is intended to prohibit the separation of embedded foreign currency derivatives if the embedded derivatives are 'integral' to the contractual arrangement. This is likely to be the case if the foreign currency has one or more of the characteristics of a functional currency set out in paragraph 9 of IAS 21 (see Chapter 15 at 4.1). Accordingly, it was proposed that IAS 39 be amended to state that a currency that has one or more of those characteristics is integral to the contract.[29]

The IASB indicated that under these proposals, contracts denominated in the following foreign currencies would likely be considered integral to the contractual arrangement:[30]

- the functional currency of any substantial party to that contract;

- the currency in which the price of the related good or service that is acquired or delivered is routinely denominated in commercial transactions around the world (such as the US dollar for crude oil transactions);

- a local currency of any substantial party to that contract;

- a liquid international currency used by parties domiciled in small countries, as a convenient means of exchange;

- a hard currency used by an entity operating in a hyperinflationary economy to protect against inflation; and

- a foreign currency commonly used in local business transactions, for example when monetary amounts are viewed by the general population not in terms of the local currency but in terms of another related currency.

Aside from the examples in the first two bullets noted above, which follow from the exceptions discussed at 5.2.1.A and 5.2.1.B above, it was unclear to us why most of the other examples would follow from the proposed amendment to the standard. A number of concerns were raised by respondents to the exposure draft and in January 2009 it was concluded that this amendment could not be completed in time for inclusion in the second annual improvements process so redeliberations were deferred.[31] In June 2009 the IASB stated that it remained committed to making such an amendment and indicated that an exposure draft of revised proposals may be published later in the year.[32] However, in January 2010 the Interpretations Committee formally removed the issue from the annual improvements project in the light of the IASB's accelerated project to replace IAS 39.[33] The guidance in IAS 39 in respect of that matter was incorporated in IFRS 9 without alteration, leaving the issue unaddressed.

5.2.1.D   Examples and other practical issues

The application of the guidance above is illustrated in the examples below.

Example 43.16:   Oil contract denominated in Swiss francs

A Norwegian company agrees to sell oil to a company in France. The oil contract is denominated in Swiss francs, although oil contracts are routinely denominated in US dollars in international commerce and Norwegian krone are commonly used in contracts to purchase or sell non-financial items in Norway. Neither company carries out any significant activities in Swiss francs.

The Norwegian company should regard the supply contract as a host contract with an embedded foreign currency forward to purchase Swiss francs. The French company should regard it as a host contract with an embedded foreign currency forward to sell Swiss francs. *[IAS 39.C.7, IFRS 9.C.7].*

The implementation guidance on which this example is based does not state in which currency the host contract should be denominated (this will also be the currency of the second leg of the embedded forward contract). The currency should be chosen so that the host does not contain an embedded derivative requiring separation. In theory, therefore, it could be Norwegian krone or euro (the functional currencies of the parties to the contract) or US dollars (the currency in which oil contracts are routinely denominated in international commerce). Typically, however, an entity will use its own functional currency to define the terms of the host contract and embedded derivative.

A second issue arises where the terms of the contract require delivery and payment on different dates. For example, assume the contract was entered into on 1 January, with delivery scheduled for 30 June and payment required by 30 September. Should the embedded derivative be considered a six-month forward contract maturing on 30 June, or a nine-month forward contract maturing on 30 September? Conceptually at least, the latter approach seems more satisfactory, for example because it does not introduce into the notional terms cash flows at a point in time (i.e. on delivery) when none exist in the combined contract. In practice, however, the former approach is used far more often and is not without technical merit. For example, it avoids the recognition of an embedded foreign currency derivative between the delivery and payment dates on what would be a foreign currency denominated monetary item, something that is prohibited by IAS 39 and IFRS 9 (see 5.1.1 above).

Example 43.17:   Oil contract, denominated in US dollars and containing a leveraged
foreign exchange payment

Company A, whose functional currency is the euro, enters into a contract with Company B, whose functional currency is the Norwegian Krone, to purchase oil in six months for US$1,000. The host oil contract will be settled by making and taking delivery in the normal course of business and is not accounted for as a financial instrument because it qualifies as a normal sale or contract (see Chapter 42 at 4). The oil contract includes a leveraged foreign exchange provision whereby the parties, in addition to the provision of, and payment for, oil will exchange an amount equal to the fluctuation in the exchange rate of the US dollar and Norwegian Krone applied to a notional amount of US$100,000.

The payment of US$1,000 under the host oil contract can be viewed as a foreign currency derivative because the dollar is neither Company A nor B's functional currency. However, it would not be separated as the US dollar is the currency in which crude oil transactions are routinely denominated in international commerce.

The leveraged foreign exchange provision is in addition to the required payment for the oil transaction. It is unrelated to the host oil contract and is therefore separated and accounted for as an embedded derivative. *[IAS 39.C.8, IFRS 9.C.8]*.

In practice, all but the simplest contracts will contain other terms and features that can often make it much more difficult to isolate the precise terms of the embedded foreign currency derivative (and the host). For example, a clause may allow a purchaser to terminate the contract in return for making a specified compensation payment to the supplier – the standard offers little guidance as to whether such a feature should be included within the terms of the host, of the embedded foreign currency derivative or, possibly, of both. Other problematic terms can include options to defer the specified delivery date and options to order additional goods or services.

5.2.2   Inputs, ingredients, substitutes and other proxy pricing mechanisms

It is common for the pricing of contracts for the supply of goods, services or other non-financial items to be determined by reference to the price of inputs to, ingredients used to generate, or substitutes for the non-financial item, especially where the non-financial item is not itself quoted in an active market. For example, a provider of call centre services may determine that a large proportion of the costs of providing the service will be employee costs in a particular country. Accordingly, it may seek to link the price in a long-term contract to supply its services to the relevant wage index, effectively to provide an economic hedge of its exposure to changes in employee costs. Similarly, the producer of goods may index the price of its product to the market value of commodities that are used in the production process.

The standard contains little or no detailed guidance for determining whether or not such pricing features should be considered closely related to the host contract. However, the general requirement of the standard to assess the economic characteristics and risks would suggest that where a good link to the inputs can be established, such features will normally be considered closely related to the host, unless they were significantly leveraged.

Other proxy pricing mechanisms may arise in long-term supply agreements for commodities where there is no active market in the commodity. For example, in the 1980s, when natural gas first started to be extracted from the North Sea in significant volumes, there was no active market for that gas and thus no market price on which to base the price of long-term contracts. Because of this, suppliers and customers were willing to enter into such contracts where the price was indexed to the market price of other commodities such as crude oil that could potentially be used as a substitute for gas. For contracts entered into before the development of an active gas market, such features would normally be considered closely related, especially if similar pricing mechanisms were commonly used by other participants in the market.

Where there is an active market price for the non-financial items being supplied under the contract, different considerations apply. The use of the proxy pricing mechanism is a strong indication that the entity has entered into a speculative position and we would not normally consider such features to be closely related to the host. The separation of these types of embedded derivatives can be seen in the following extract from BP's financial statements.

Extract 43.5: BP p.l.c. (2014)

Notes on financial statements [extract]
28.   Derivative financial instruments [extract]
Embedded derivatives [extract]

The group is a party to certain natural gas contracts containing embedded derivatives. Prior to the development of an active gas trading market, UK gas contracts were priced using a basket of available price indices, primarily relating to oil products, power and inflation. After the development of an active UK gas market, certain contracts were entered into or renegotiated using pricing formulae not directly related to gas prices, for example, oil product and power prices. In these circumstances, pricing formulae have been determined to be derivatives, embedded within the overall contractual arrangements that are not clearly and closely related to the underlying commodity. The resulting fair value relating to these contracts is recognized on the balance sheet with gains or losses recognized in the income statement.

5.2.3   *Inflation-linked features*

Apart from that related to leases (see 5.3.2 below), there is no reference in the guidance to contracts containing payments that are linked to inflation. Many types of contracts contain inflation-linked payments and it would appear sensible to apply the guidance in respect of leases to these contracts. Consider, for example, a long-term agreement to supply services under which payments increase by reference to a general price index and are not leveraged in any way. In cases such as this, the embedded inflation-linked derivative would normally be considered closely related to the host provided the index related to a measure of inflation in an appropriate economic environment, such as the one in which the services were being supplied.

5.2.4   *Floors and caps*

Similar to debt instruments (see 5.1.4 above), provisions within a contract to purchase or sell an asset (e.g. a commodity) that establishes a cap and a floor on the price to be paid or received for the asset are closely related to the host contract if both the cap and floor were out-of-the-money at inception and are not leveraged. *[IAS 39.AG33(b), IFRS 9.B4.3.8(b)].*

5.2.5   Fund performance fees

In the investment management industry, it is common for a fund manager to receive a fee based on the performance of the assets managed in addition to a base fee. For example, if a fund's net asset value increases over its accounting year, the manager may be entitled to a percentage of that increase. The contract for providing investment management services to the fund clearly contains an embedded derivative (the underlying is the value of the fund's assets). However, whilst not addressed explicitly in the standard, we would normally consider it appropriate to regard such features as closely related to the host contract.

5.3   Leases

5.3.1   Foreign currency derivatives

A finance lease payable or receivable is accounted for as a financial instrument, albeit one that is not subject to all of the measurement requirements of IAS 39 or IFRS 9 (see Chapter 42 at 2.2.4). Therefore, a finance lease denominated in a foreign currency will not generally be considered to contain an embedded foreign currency derivative requiring separation, because the payable or receivable is a monetary item within the scope of IAS 21.

However, an operating lease is accounted for as an executory contract. Accordingly, where the lease payments are denominated in a foreign currency, the analysis at 5.2.1.A is applicable and it may be necessary to separate an embedded derivative. See Example 43.18 at 6.1 below for an example of a foreign exchange currency derivative requiring separation from a (hybrid) lease contract.

5.3.2   Inflation-linked features

An embedded derivative in a lease is considered closely related to the host if it is an inflation-related index such as an index of lease payments to a consumer price index, provided that the lease is not leveraged and the index relates to inflation in the entity's own economic environment. *[IAS 39.AG33(f)(i), IFRS 9.B4.3.8(f)(i)].*

5.3.3   Contingent rentals based on related sales

Where a lease requires contingent rentals based on related sales, that embedded derivative is considered to be closely related to the host lease. *[IAS 39.AG33(f)(ii), IFRS 9.B4.3.8(f)(ii)].*

5.3.4   Contingent rentals based on variable interest rates

If a derivative embedded within a lease arises from contingent rentals based on variable interest rates, it is considered closely related. *[IAS 39.AG33(f)(iii), IFRS 9.B4.3.8(f)(iii)].*

5.4   Insurance contracts

The guidance at 5.1.2 to 5.1.4, 5.1.6 and 5.2.1 above also applies to insurance contracts. IFRS 4 added two further illustrations to IAS 39 and IFRS 9 that deal primarily with insurance contracts.

A unit-linking feature embedded in a host financial instrument, or host insurance contract, is closely related to the host if the unit-denominated payments are measured at current unit values that reflect the fair values of the assets of the fund. A unit-linking feature is a contractual term that requires payments denominated in units of an internal or external investment fund. *[IAS 39.AG33(g), IFRS 9.B4.3.8(g)].*

A derivative embedded in an insurance contract is closely related to the host if the embedded derivative and host are so interdependent that the embedded derivative cannot be measured separately, i.e. without considering the host contract. *[IAS 39.AG33(h), IFRS 9.B4.3.8(h)].*

Derivatives embedded within insurance contracts are covered in more detail in Chapter 54 at 4.

6 IDENTIFYING THE TERMS OF EMBEDDED DERIVATIVES AND HOST CONTRACTS

The IASB has provided only limited guidance on determining the terms of a separated embedded derivative and host contract. Accordingly, entities may find this aspect of the embedded derivative requirements particularly difficult to implement. In addition to the guidance set out below, Examples 43.16 and 43.17 above also identify the terms of an embedded derivative requiring separation.

6.1 Embedded non-option derivatives

IAS 39 and IFRS 9 do not define the term 'non-option derivative' but suggests that it includes forwards, swaps and similar contracts. An embedded derivative of this type should be separated from its host contract on the basis of its stated or implied substantive terms, so as to result in it having a fair value of zero at initial recognition. *[IAS 39.AG28, IFRS 9.B4.3.3].*

The IASB has provided implementation guidance on separating non-option derivatives in the situation where the host is a debt instrument. It is explained that, in the absence of implied or stated terms, judgement will be necessary to identify the terms of the host (e.g. whether it should be a fixed rate, variable rate or zero coupon instrument) and the embedded derivative. However, an embedded derivative that is not already clearly present in the hybrid should not be separated, i.e. a cash flow that does not exist cannot be created. *[IAS 39.C.1, IFRS 9.C.1].*

For example, if a five year debt instrument has fixed annual interest payments of £40 and a principal payment at maturity of £1,000 multiplied by the change in an equity price index, it would be inappropriate to identify a floating rate host and an embedded equity swap that has an offsetting floating rate leg. The host should be a fixed rate debt instrument that pays £40 annually because there are no floating interest rate cash flows in the hybrid instrument. *[IAS 39.C.1, IFRS 9.C.1].*

Further, as noted above, the terms of the embedded derivative should be determined so that it has a fair value of zero on inception of the hybrid instrument. It is explained that if an embedded non-option derivative could be separated on other terms, a single hybrid instrument could be decomposed into an infinite variety of combinations of host debt instruments and embedded derivatives. This might be achieved, for example, by separating embedded derivatives with terms that create leverage, asymmetry or some other risk exposure not already present in the hybrid instrument. *[IAS 39.C.1, IFRS 9.C.1]*.

Finally, it is explained that the terms of the embedded derivative should be identified based on the conditions existing when the financial instrument was issued *[IAS 39.C.1, IFRS 9.C.1]* or following the application of IFRIC 9 – *Reassessment of Embedded Derivatives* – or the IFRS 9 equivalent guidance (see 7.1 below), when a contract is required to be reassessed.

The following example illustrates how a foreign currency derivative embedded in a (hybrid) lease contract, that is not closely related, could be separated.

Example 43.18:   Separation of embedded derivative from lease

Company X has Indian Rupees (INR) as its functional currency. On 1 January 2016 Company X entered into a nine month lease over an item of PP&E which required payments of US$100,000 on 31 March 2016, 30 June 2016 and 30 September 2016. The functional currency of the lessor is not US dollars; the price of such leases is not routinely denominated in US dollars and US dollars is not a currency that is commonly used in the economic environment in which the lease took place (see 5.3.1 above). Accordingly the embedded foreign currency derivative is not closely related to the lease.

On 1 January 2016 the spot exchange rate was 40 and the forward exchange rates for settlement on 31 March 2016, 30 June 2016 and 30 September 2016 were 41, 42 and 43 respectively. The terms of the embedded derivative could be determined as follows:

31 March 2016	Pay US$100,000	Receive INR4,100,000
30 June 2016	Pay US$100,000	Receive INR4,200,000
30 September 2016	Pay US$100,000	Receive INR4,300,000

Given the terms of the embedded derivative above, the host contract will be a nine month lease over the same PP&E as the hybrid lease contract, commencing 1 January 2016 and with scheduled payments of INR 4,100,000, INR 4,200,000 and INR 4,300,000 on 31 March 2016, 30 June 2016 and 30 September 2016. It can be seen that this host after separation of the foreign currency derivative, an INR denominated lease, does not contain an embedded derivative requiring separation and the combined terms of the two components sum to the terms of the hybrid contract. IAS 17 – *Leases* – will be applicable to this lease (see Chapter 24).

6.2   Embedded option-based derivative

As for non-option derivatives, IAS 39 and IFRS 9 do not define the term 'option-based derivative' but suggests that it includes puts, calls, caps, floors and swaptions. An embedded derivative of this type should be separated from its host contract on the basis of the stated terms of the option feature. *[IAS 39.AG28, IFRS 9.B4.3.3]*.

The implementation guidance explains that the economic nature of an option-based derivative is fundamentally different from a non-option derivative and depends critically on the strike price (or strike rate) specified for the option feature in the hybrid instrument. Therefore, the separation of such a derivative should be based on the stated terms of the option feature documented in the hybrid instrument. Consequently, in contrast to the position for non-option derivatives (see 6.1 above), an embedded option-based derivative would not normally have a fair value of zero. *[IAS 39.C.2, IFRS 9.C.2]*.

In fact, if the terms of an embedded option-based derivative were identified so as to result in it having a fair value of zero, the implied strike price would generally result in the option being infinitely out-of-the-money, i.e. it would have a zero probability of the option feature being exercised. However, since the probability of the option feature in a hybrid instrument being exercised generally is not zero, this would be inconsistent with the likely economic behaviour of the hybrid. *[IAS39.C.2, IFRS 9.C.2].*

Similarly, if the terms were identified so as to achieve an intrinsic value of zero, the strike price would equal the price of the underlying at initial recognition. In this case, the fair value of the option would consist only of time value. However, this may also be inconsistent with the likely economic behaviour of the hybrid, including the probability of the option feature being exercised, unless the agreed strike price was indeed equal to the price of the underlying at initial recognition. *[IAS 39.C.2, IFRS 9.C.2].*

6.3 Nature of a financial instrument host

If a contract consists of equity- and debt-like features, it must be determined whether the host contract is debt or equity. The classification of the host will form the basis for the 'closely related' assessment and therefore will drive whether embedded derivative features need to be separated from the host contract. For some hybrid instruments this assessment will be straightforward, for others a significant amount of judgement might be required.

Consistent with the 'closely related' assessment (see 5 above), it is suggested that, where a financial instrument contains an embedded derivative, the host should be considered as a debt instrument 'if the hybrid instrument has a stated maturity, i.e. it does not meet the definition of an equity instrument'. *[IAS 39.C.5].*

The implementation guidance illustrates this by way of an example, the substance of which is reproduced below.

Example 43.19: Equity-linked debt

Company A purchases a five year 'debt' instrument issued by Company B with a principal of £1,000, indexed to Company C's share price. At maturity, A will receive the principal plus or minus the change in the fair value of 100 of C's shares and no interest payments are made before maturity. On the date of acquisition, the purchase price is £1,000 and C's share price is £12. A classifies the instrument as available-for-sale.

The instrument is a hybrid instrument with an embedded derivative because of the equity-indexed principal and the host is a debt instrument (see above). The host is a zero coupon debt paying £1,200 at maturity. The embedded non-option derivative (a forward contract to purchase 100 shares of C for an amount equal to the forward price of C's shares at inception of the arrangement) is separated and will have an initial fair value of zero. *[IAS 39.C.5].*

A financial instrument can give rise to a residual interest in the net assets of an entity, even though IAS 32 prevents the issuing entity from classifying the instrument as equity. Where such an instrument contains an embedded derivative that requires separation, it may be appropriate to classify the host as equity rather than debt from the holder's perspective. This will commonly be the case for an investment in a unit trust (see 5.1.9 above) and may be appropriate for some structured investments which can, in substance, give rise to a residual interest in the net assets of an entity.

The treatment by the holder of equity-like instruments (say ordinary shares) that are puttable at an amount other than fair value (for example a proportion of the book value of net assets determined under IFRS or local GAAP) was discussed by the Interpretations Committee. Whilst deciding not to issue application guidance it noted the approach the holder (as opposed to the issuer) of such a financial instrument should take as follows:[34]

- Step 1 – identify embedded derivatives;
- Step 2 – determine whether the remaining instrument (i.e. the host) is a debt or an equity instrument; and
- Step 3 – determine whether the characteristics and risks of any identified embedded derivatives are closely related to those of its host contract.

Therefore, the holder would first identify the put option as an embedded derivative (the right to exchange the underlying equity instrument for a variable amount of cash); secondly it would identify the remainder as an equity instrument; and finally determine that the two were not closely related.[35]

Host contracts that are financial instruments should be accounted for under IAS 39. Otherwise, they are accounted for in accordance with other appropriate standards. This does not necessarily mean that the embedded derivative and host should be presented separately (or together) on the face of the financial statements (see Chapter 53 at 7.4.3). *[IAS 39.11, IFRS 9.4.3.4].*

Where IFRS 9 is applied, the question whether the host is a debt or equity instrument is, from the perspective of the holder of the instrument, of no relevance because embedded derivatives are not separated from financial assets within the scope of the standard and the requirements of the standard are applied to the hybrid contract as a whole. *[IFRS 9.4.3.2].*

How challenging and judgemental the identification of the host contract and the subsequent classification as debt or equity can be, is evidenced by a request received by the Interpretations Committee, to clarify the classification by the holder of a hybrid financial instrument with a revolving maturity option, an early settlement option and a suspension of interest payments option (all at the option of the issuer). The request was discussed during the March 2014 and July 2014 meetings. Specifically, the question raised was whether the host instrument should be classified as equity or as a debt instrument under IAS 39.[36]

The main features of the instrument under consideration were:

- A 30 year maturity.
- Interest feature:
    - fixed rate (government bond plus a spread);
    - the spread is stepped up after the start of the early settlement option;
    - the benchmark interest is reset every 10 years.

- Options of the issuer:
  - revolving maturity option every 30 years (option to extend the maturity every 30 years);
  - early settlement option after 10 years;
  - suspension of interest payment option in the event that dividends on ordinary shares are not distributed.

The issuer explained in its submission that if the host contract is classified before identifying any embedded derivatives, then the host could be classified as an equity instrument. This is because the instrument represents the residual interest in the net assets of the issuer, has no stated maturity and accordingly meets the definition of an equity instrument in IAS 32. On the other hand, if the host is to be classified after identifying embedded derivative features, then the host would be classified as a debt instrument. This is because it can be only regarded as equity under the assumption that the issuer will not exercise the early settlement option but will certainly exercise the revolving maturity option and this assumption may be inconsistent with the market participant's or investor's view. The Interpretations Committee observed that the issue is not widespread and noted that the financial instrument described in the submission is specific and it would not be appropriate to provide guidance on this particular issue and therefore decided not to add this issue to its agenda.

6.4 Multiple embedded derivatives

Generally, multiple embedded derivatives in a single instrument should be treated as a single compound embedded derivative. However, embedded derivatives that are classified as equity are accounted for separately from those classified as assets or liabilities (see Chapter 44 at 6). In addition, derivatives embedded in a single instrument that relate to different risk exposures and are readily separable and independent of each other, should be accounted for separately from each other. [IAS 39.AG29, IFRS 9.B4.3.4].

For example, if a debt instrument has a principal amount related to an equity index and that amount doubles if the equity index exceeds a certain level, it is not appropriate to separate both a forward and an option on the equity index because those derivative features relate to the same risk exposure. Instead, the forward and option elements are treated as a single compound embedded derivative. For the same reason, an embedded floor or cap on interest rates should not be separated into a series of 'floorlets' or 'caplets' (i.e. single interest rate options).[37]

If a hybrid instrument contains both a put option and a written call option that require separation, e.g. callable debt with a put to the holder, those options are treated as a single embedded derivative because they are not independent of each other. Furthermore, if an investor holds callable convertible debt, which can be called by the issuer, for which separation of the call option is required, it is not appropriate to separate an equity conversion option and a written call option on the debt instrument separately because the two embedded derivative features should not be valued independently of each other.[38]

On the other hand, if a hybrid debt instrument contains, for example, two options that give the holder a right to choose both the interest rate index on which interest payments are determined and the currency in which the principal is repaid, those two options may qualify for separation as two separate embedded derivatives since they relate to different risk exposures and are readily separable and independent of each other.[39]

7   REASSESSMENT OF EMBEDDED DERIVATIVES

It is clear that, on initial recognition, a contract should be reviewed to assess whether it contains one or more embedded derivatives requiring separation. However, IAS 39 is largely silent on whether this initial assessment should be revisited throughout the life of the contract. *[IFRIC 9.BC3, IFRS 9.BCZ4.99].*

Consider, for example, an entity that enters into a purchase contract denominated in US dollars. If, at the time the contract is entered into, US dollars are commonly used in the economic environment in which the transaction takes place, the contract will not contain an embedded foreign currency derivative requiring separation. Subsequently, however, the economic environment may change such that transactions are now commonly denominated in euros, rather than US dollars. Countries joining the European Union may encounter just such a scenario.

Clearly, in this situation, an embedded foreign currency derivative would be separated from any new US dollar denominated purchase contracts, assuming they would not otherwise be considered closely related. However, should the entity separately account for derivatives embedded within its existing US dollar denominated contracts that were outstanding prior to the change in the market?

Conversely, the entity may have identified, and separately accounted for, embedded foreign currency derivatives in contracts denominated in euros that were entered into before the economic environment changed. Does the change in economic circumstances mean that the embedded derivative should now be considered closely related and not separately accounted for as a derivative? *[IFRIC 9.BC4, BC5, IFRS 9.BCZ4.100-101].*

In practice, there appeared to be differing views developing on this issue. Therefore, without further guidance, the IFRIC considered it quite possible that inconsistent practice would develop. *[IFRIC 9.BC3].* Accordingly it decided to take the issue onto its agenda and, in March 2006, published IFRIC 9. Note that IFRS 9 supersedes IFRIC 9 upon adoption. However, the IASB incorporated into IFRS 9 the main requirements previously set out in IFRIC 9.

7.1   IFRIC 9

IFRIC 9 and the equivalent guidance in IFRS 9 confirm that entities should assess whether an embedded derivative is required to be separated from the host contract and accounted for as a derivative when the entity first becomes a party to the contract and explains that subsequent reassessment is generally prohibited. *[IFRIC 9.7, IFRS 9.B4.3.11].*

There are two exceptions under IAS 39 and one exception under IFRS 9 to this prohibition:

(a) where there is a change in the terms of a contract that significantly modifies the cash flows that otherwise would be required under it, in which case an assessment is required by both Standards.

In order to determine whether a modification to cash flows is significant, an entity should consider the extent to which the expected future cash flows associated with the embedded derivative, the host contract or both have changed and whether the change is significant relative to the previously expected cash flows on the contract; *[IFRIC 9.7, IFRS 9.B4.3.11]* and

(b) a reclassification of a financial asset out of the fair value through profit or loss category under IAS 39 (see Chapter 45 at 6.1.1), in which case an assessment is also required. *[IFRIC 9.7].*

In this case, the assessment of whether an embedded derivative is required to be accounted for separately from the host contract should be made on the basis of the circumstances that existed on the later date of:

(i) when the entity first became a party to the contract; and

(ii) a change in the terms of the contract that significantly modified the cash flows that otherwise would have been required.

For the purpose of this assessment, the fact that the financial asset had previously been classified at fair value through profit or loss (condition (c) at 4 above) does not mean an embedded derivative should not be separated.

If an entity is unable to make this assessment or is unable to measure separately the embedded derivative, reclassification is prohibited and the hybrid (combined) contract should remain classified as at fair value through profit or loss in its entirety. *[IFRIC 9.7A, IAS 39.12].*

7.2 Acquisition of contracts

IAS 39 and IFRS 9 require an entity to assess whether an embedded derivative needs to be separated from the host contract and accounted for as a derivative when it first becomes a party to that contract. Therefore, if an entity purchases a contract that contains an embedded derivative, it assesses whether the embedded derivative needs to be separated and accounted for as a derivative on the basis of conditions at the date it acquires it, not the date the original contract was established. *[IFRIC 9.BC10, IFRS 9.BCZ4.106].*

For example, consider an entity that purchases a debt instrument containing an embedded prepayment, put or call option some time after it was issued. In this case, the assessment of whether the exercise price of the option is approximately equal to the instrument's amortised cost (see 5.1.3 above) will be based on the amortised cost of the acquirer (taking into account any premium or discount paid as a result of changes in value since origination), not that of the issuer or original holder.

7.3   Business combinations

From the point of view of a consolidated entity, the acquisition of a contract within a business combination accounted for using the acquisition method under IFRS 3 – *Business Combinations* – is hardly different from the acquisition of a contract in general. Consequently, an assessment of the acquiree's contracts should be made on the date of acquisition as if the contracts themselves had been acquired. *[IFRS 3.15, 16(c)].*

Neither IFRIC 9, IFRS 3, nor the guidance on reassessment of embedded derivatives in IFRS 9 applies to a combination of entities or businesses under common control or the formation of a joint venture. *[IFRIC 9.5, IFRS 3.2, IFRS 9.B4.3.12].* However, in our view, if the acquisition method is applied to such arrangements, the requirements set out in IFRS 3 should be followed.

7.4   Remeasurement issues arising from reassessment

IFRIC 9 and IFRS 9 do not address remeasurement issues arising from a reassessment of embedded derivatives. *[IFRIC 9.4].* One of the reasons cited by the Interpretations Committee for prohibiting reassessment in general was the difficulty in determining the accounting treatment following a reassessment, which is explained in the following terms.

Assume that an entity, when it first became party to a contract, separately recognised a host asset, say a loan or receivable, and an embedded derivative liability. If the entity were required to reassess whether the embedded derivative was to be accounted for separately and if the entity concluded some time after becoming a party to the contract that the derivative was no longer required to be separated, then questions of recognition and measurement would arise. In the above circumstances, the entity could: *[IFRIC 9.BC9, IFRS 9.BCZ4.105]*

(a)   remove the derivative from its statement of financial position and recognise in profit or loss a corresponding gain or loss. This would lead to recognition of a gain or loss even though there had been no transaction and no change in the value of the total contract or its components;

(b)   leave the derivative as a separate item in the statement of financial position. The issue would then arise as to when the item is to be removed from the statement of financial position. Should it be amortised (and, if so, how would the amortisation affect the effective interest rate of the asset), or should it be derecognised only when the asset is derecognised?

(c)   combine the derivative (which is recognised at fair value) with the asset (which is recognised at amortised cost). This would alter both the carrying amount of the asset and its effective interest rate even though there had been no change in the economics of the whole contract. In some cases, it could also result in a negative effective interest rate.

IFRIC 9 states that subsequent reassessment is appropriate only when there has been a change in the terms of the contract that 'significantly' modifies the cash flows, accordingly the above issues are not expected to arise. *[IFRIC 9.BC9, IFRS 9.BCZ4.105].*

8   LINKED AND SEPARATE TRANSACTIONS AND 'SYNTHETIC' INSTRUMENTS

A derivative that is attached to a financial instrument, but is contractually transferable independently of that instrument, or has a different counterparty from that instrument, is not an embedded derivative, but a separate financial instrument. *[IAS 39.10, IFRS 9.4.3.1]*. This is also the case where a synthetic instrument is created by using derivatives to 'alter' the nature of a non-derivative instrument, as illustrated in the following example:

Example 43.20:   Investment in synthetic fixed-rate debt

Company A acquires a five year floating rate debt instrument issued by Company B. At the same time, it enters into a five year pay-variable, receive-fixed interest rate swap with Bank C. A considers the combination of the two instruments to be a synthetic fixed rate bond and, since it has the positive intent and ability to hold them to maturity, wants to classify them as a held-to-maturity investment (see Chapter 45 at 3).

Embedded derivatives are terms and conditions that are *included in* non-derivative host contracts and it is generally inappropriate to treat two or more separate financial instruments as a single combined, or synthetic, instrument. Each of the financial instruments has its own terms and conditions and may be transferred or settled separately. Therefore, the debt instrument and the swap must be classified separately. *[IAS 39.C.6, IFRS 9.C.6]*.

It is asserted that these transactions differ from those discussed at 3.2 above because those had no substance apart from the resulting interest rate swap. *[IAS 39.C.6, IFRS 9.C.6]*. Although some might argue that the substance of the two transactions above is the resulting synthetic fixed rate debt instrument, this interpretation is clearly not allowed under the standard.

Interestingly, the guidance does not address a much more common situation whereby a company both borrows from, and transacts a related derivative with, the same counterparty – typically the borrowing will be floating rate and the derivative a perfectly matched pay-fixed, receive-floating interest rate swap.

In fact, the subject of linking transactions for accounting purposes is a difficult one, especially in the context of financial instruments. The IASB's *Conceptual Framework* specifies that transactions should be reported in accordance with their substance and economic reality and not merely their legal form *[Framework.4.6]* and linking transactions can be seen as dealing with the question of how to interpret this principle.

IAS 32, IAS 39 and IFRS 9 deal with the subject in a piecemeal way. For example, in addition to the synthetic instrument illustration above:

- two or more non-derivative contracts that are, 'in substance', no more than a single derivative are treated as a single derivative (see 3.2 above);

- derivatives that are 'attached' to a non-derivative financial instrument may sometimes be regarded as part of a single combined instrument (see 4 above);

- in classifying an instrument in consolidated financial statements as equity or a financial liability, all terms and conditions agreed between members of the group and holders of the instrument are considered (see Chapter 44 at 4.8); and

- determining the appropriate accounting treatment for a transaction that involves the transfer of some or all rights associated with financial assets, without the sale of the assets themselves, inevitably involves linking separate contracts to assess whether the transaction results in derecognition of the assets. For example, there might be one contract defining the continued ownership of the asset and another obliging the owner to transfer the rights associated with the asset to a third party (see Chapter 47 at 3, Chapter 48 at 2 and Chapter 49 at 2).

The Interpretations Committee first considered the subject of linkage in 2002 and has, in the past, made certain recommendations to the IASB. In fact, the requirement to take account of linked terms when classifying instruments as debt or equity in consolidated financial statements was introduced into IAS 32 in December 2003 following the Interpretations Committee's deliberations. In spite of agreeing proposed indicators for when transactions should be linked, and proposed guidance on accounting for linked transactions, these have never been published as an interpretation or standard.[40]

In August 2013 the Interpretations Committee received a request to clarify whether three different transactions should be accounted for separately or be aggregated and treated as a single derivative. The Committee decided not to add this issue to its agenda but noted that in order to determine whether to aggregate and account for the three transactions as a single derivative, reference should be made to B.6 (see 3.2 above) and C.6 (see Example 43.20 above) of the Implementation Guidance to IAS 39 and paragraph AG39 of IAS 32. The Interpretations Committee noted that the application of the guidance in paragraph IG B.6 of IAS 39 requires judgement and that the indicators in that paragraph may help an entity to determine the substance of the transaction, but that the presence or absence of any single specific indicator alone may not be conclusive.[41]

Consequently, in considering the borrowing and swap situation above, we are left principally with the guidance in IAS 39 and IFRS 9. It is likely that the swap and the loan have their own terms and conditions and may be transferred or settled independently of each other. Therefore, the principles in Example 43.20 above would suggest separate accounting for the two instruments. Applying the guidance at 3.2 above (aggregating non-derivative transactions and treating them as a derivative) would also suggest separate accounting in most cases. Even though the instruments are transacted with the same counterparty, there will normally be a substantive business purpose for transacting the instruments separately.

It seems clear that in situations involving two separate legal contracts, the IASB has set the bar very high for regarding transactions as linked and, in most cases, the two instruments will be regarded as separate for accounting purposes. However, in rare situations the linkage between those contracts (normally itself contractual) may be such that for accounting purposes those contracts cannot be regarded as existing independently of each other.

References

1 IGC Q&A 10-6.
2 *IFRIC Update*, July 2007.
3 *IFRIC Update*, July 2006.
4 *IFRIC Update*, January 2007.
5 *IASB Update*, February 2007.
6 Exposure Draft, *Improvements to International Financial Reporting Standards*, IASB, October 2007.
7 Information for Observers (20 February 2008 IASB meeting), *ED Annual improvements process – Comment analysis: Summary of preliminary analysis and project plan*, IASB, February 2008, Appendix 2.
8 *IASB Update*, October 2008.
9 *IFRIC Update*, July 2006.
10 *IFRIC Update*, January 2007.
11 *IFRIC Update*, May 2009.
12 IGC Q&A 10-10.
13 Staff paper, *Term-extending options in fixed rate debt instruments*, IFRS Interpretations Committee, March 2012.
14 *IFRIC Update*, March 2012.
15 *Implementation of International Accounting Standards*, British Bankers' Association, July 2004, para. 10.
16 Information for Observers of March 2006 IFRIC meeting, *Hedging Inflation Risk (Agenda Paper 12)*, IASB, March 2006, para. 32.
17 Information for Observers (December 2008 IASB meeting), *Clarification of accounting for investments in collateralised debt obligations (Agenda Paper 6E)*, IASB, December 2008 and *Q&As on accounting for some collateralised debts obligations (CDOs) – prepared by staff of the IASB*, IASB, February 2009.
18 *IFRIC Update*, January 2007 and Information for Observers (November 2006 IFRIC meeting), *Financial Instruments puttable at an amount other than Fair Value (Agenda Paper 12(ii))*, IASB, November 2006.
19 *IFRIC Update*, May 2007, July 2007, September 2007 and November 2007.
20 *IFRIC Update*, May 2007.
21 Information for Observers (May 2007 IFRIC meeting), *IAS 39: Financial Instruments: Recognition and Measurement AG33(d)(iii) of IAS 39 (Agenda Paper 11(v))*, IASB, May 2007, paras. 12 to 14.
22 Information for Observers, paras. 18 to 19.
23 Information for Observers, paras. 20 to 28.
24 Information for Observers (December 2007 IASB meeting), *Application of paragraph AG33(d)(iii) – Bifurcation of embedded foreign currency derivative (Agenda Paper 3C)*, IASB, December 2007, para. 11.
25 Information for Observers (May 2007 IFRIC meeting), *IAS 39: Financial Instruments: Recognition and Measurement AG33(d)(iii) of IAS 39 (Agenda Paper 11(v))*, IASB, May 2007, para. 44.
26 Information for Observers (December 2007 IASB meeting), *Application of paragraph AG33(d)(iii) – Bifurcation of embedded foreign currency derivative (Agenda Paper 3C)*, IASB, December 2007, paras. 12 and 13.
27 Information for Observers, para. 14.
28 Information for Observers, para. 15.
29 Information for Observers, Appendix 1, *IASB Update*, December 2007 and Exposure Draft, *Improvements to IFRSs*, IASB, August 2008, IAS 39, para. AG33(d)(iii).
30 Exposure Draft, *Improvements to IFRSs*, IASB, August 2008, IAS 39, para. BC19.
31 *IASB Update*, January 2009 and Information for Observers (January 2009 IASB Meeting), *Annual Improvements 2009 – Comment Analysis, (Agenda Paper 6A)*, IASB, January 2009, para. 11(c) and Appendix 2.
32 *IASB Update*, June 2009 and IASB Staff Paper (June 2009 IASB Meeting), *Financial Instruments: Recognition and Measurement – Sweep Issues (Agenda Paper 3G)*, IASB, January 2009, paras. 10, 11 and 14.
33 *IFRIC Update*, January 2010.
34 Information for Observers (November 2006 IFRIC meeting), *Financial Instruments puttable at an amount other than Fair Value (Agenda Paper 12(ii))*, IASB, November 2006, para. 29.
35 Information for Observers, paras. 30 to 41.
36 *IFRIC Update*, March 2014.
37 IGC Q&A 23-8.
38 IGC Q&A 23-8.
39 IGC Q&A 23-8.
40 *IFRIC Update*, April 2002, July 2002 and February 2003 and *IASB Update*, October 2002.
41 *IFRIC Update*, March 2014.

Chapter 43

Chapter 44   Financial instruments: Financial liabilities and equity

Chapter 44

List of examples

Chapter 44

Chapter 44   Financial instruments: Financial liabilities and equity

1   INTRODUCTION

1.1   Background

The accounting treatment of liabilities (such as loans or bonds) and equity instruments (such as shares, stock or warrants) by their issuer was not historically regarded as presenting significant problems. Essentially the accounting was dictated by the legal form of the instrument, since the traditional distinction between equity and liabilities is clear. The issue of equity creates an ownership interest in a company, remunerated by dividends, which are accounted for as a distribution of retained profit, not a charge made in arriving at the result for a particular period. Liabilities, such as loan finance, on the other hand, are remunerated by interest, which is charged to profit or loss as an expense. In general, lenders rank before shareholders in priority of claims over the assets of the company, although in practice there may also be differential rights between different categories of lenders and classes of shareholders. The two forms of finance often have different tax implications, both for the investor and the investee.

In economic terms, however, the distinction between share and loan capital can be far less clear-cut than the legal categorisation would suggest. For example, a redeemable preference share could be considered to be, in substance, much more like a liability than equity. Conversely, many would argue that a bond which can never be repaid but which will be mandatorily converted into ordinary shares deserves to be thought of as being more in the nature of equity than of debt, even before conversion has occurred.

The ambiguous economic nature of such instruments has encouraged the development of a number of complex forms of finance which exhibit characteristics of both equity and debt. The 'holy grail' is generally to devise an instrument regarded as a liability by the tax authorities (such that the costs of servicing it are tax-deductible) but treated as equity for accounting and/or regulatory purposes (so that the instrument is not considered as a component of net borrowings).

The accounting classification of an instrument as a liability or equity is much more than a matter of allocation – i.e. where particular amounts are shown in the financial statements. The increasing requirement of IFRS for certain liabilities, in particular derivatives, to be carried at fair value means that the classification of an item as a liability can introduce significant volatility into reported results, that would not arise if the item were classified as an equity instrument. This is due to the fact that changes in the fair value of an equity instrument are not recognised in the financial statements. *[IAS 32.36]*.

Moreover, the extent to which an entity funds its operations through debt or equity is regarded as highly significant not only by investors, but also by other users of financial statements such as regulators and tax authorities. This means that the question of whether a particular instrument is a liability or equity raises issues of much greater and wider sensitivity than the mere matter of financial statement classification.

1.2   Development of IFRS on classification of liabilities and equity

Under IFRS, the classification of items as liabilities or equity is dealt with mainly in IAS 32 – *Financial Instruments: Presentation* – with some cross-reference to IAS 39 – *Financial Instruments: Recognition and Measurement* – or, where applicable, IFRS 9 – *Financial Instruments.*

IAS 32 was originally issued in March 1995 and subsequently amended in 1998 and 2000 as the result of the issue of, and subsequent changes to, IAS 39. However, in December 2003, the previous version of IAS 32 was withdrawn and superseded by a new version, which has itself been amended by subsequent new pronouncements, most notably IFRS 7 – *Financial Instruments: Disclosures* (see Chapter 53) and the amendment to IAS 32 – *Puttable Financial Instruments and Obligations Arising on Liquidation.*

The main text of IAS 32 is supplemented by application guidance (which is an integral part of the standard),[1] and by illustrative examples (which accompany, but are not part of, the standard).[2]

The Interpretations Committee has issued two interpretations of IAS 32 discussed in this chapter:

- IFRIC 2 – *Members' Shares in Co-operative Entities and Similar Instruments* (see 4.6.6 below); and

- IFRIC 19 – *Extinguishing Financial Liabilities with Equity Instruments* (see 7 below).

A joint attempt of the IASB and the FASB to develop a new model, in which classification of an instrument was based on whether the instrument would be settled with assets or with equity instruments of the issuer, was suspended in October 2010 due to significant challenges raised by a small group of external reviewers of a draft exposure draft.

In May 2015 the IASB published Exposure Draft ED/2015/3 – *Conceptual Framework for Financial Reporting.* Amongst other topics this proposes to refine the definition of assets and liabilities (see Chapter 2 at 3.3). The exposure draft proposes to define a liability as an entity's present obligation to transfer an economic resource as a result of a past event if the entity has no practical ability to avoid the transfer. The amount of the transfer is determined by reference to benefits that the entity has received, or activities that it has conducted, in the past. The exposure draft retains the existing definition of equity – that it is the residual interest in the assets of an entity after deducting all its liabilities.

In October 2014 the IASB also resumed the *Financial Instruments with Characteristics of Equity Research Project* to explore further how to distinguish liabilities from equity claims.

2   OBJECTIVE AND SCOPE

2.1   Objective

The objective of IAS 32 is 'to establish principles for presenting financial instruments as liabilities or equity and for offsetting financial assets and financial liabilities.' *[IAS 32.2]*. The standard, and its associated IFRIC interpretations, address:

- the classification of financial instruments, by their issuer, into financial assets, financial liabilities and equity instruments (see 3 to 6 below);

- settling a financial liability with an equity instrument (see 7 below);

- the classification of interest, dividends, losses and gains (see 8 below);

- treasury shares – i.e. an entity's own equity instruments held by the entity (see 9 below);

- forward contracts or options for the receipt or delivery of the entity's own equity instruments (see 11 below); and

- the circumstances in which financial assets and financial liabilities should be offset (see Chapter 53 at 7.4.1).

The principles in IAS 32 complement the principles for recognising and measuring financial assets and financial liabilities in IAS 39, or where applicable IFRS 9, and for disclosing information about them in IFRS 7. *[IAS 32.3]*.

2.2   Scope

The scope of IAS 32 is discussed in detail in Chapter 42 at 3.

3   DEFINITIONS

The following definitions in IAS 32 are relevant to the issues discussed in this chapter. Further general discussion on the meaning and implications of the definitions may be found in Chapter 42 at 2.

A *financial instrument* is any contract that gives rise to a financial asset of one entity and a financial liability or equity instrument of another entity. *[IAS 32.11]*.

A *financial asset* is any asset that is:

(a)   cash;

(b)   an equity instrument of another entity;

(c)   a contractual right:

   (i)   to receive cash or another financial asset from another entity; or

   (ii)   to exchange financial assets or financial liabilities with another entity under conditions that are potentially favourable to the entity; or

(d)   a contract that will or may be settled in the entity's own equity instruments and is:

   (i)   a non-derivative for which the entity is or may be obliged to receive a variable number of the entity's own equity instruments; or

   (ii)   a derivative that will or may be settled other than by the exchange of a fixed amount of cash or another financial asset for a fixed number of the entity's own equity instruments. For this purpose the entity's own equity instruments do not include:

   - puttable financial instruments classified as equity instruments in accordance with paragraphs 16A and 16B of the standard (see 4.6.2 below),

   - instruments that impose on the entity an obligation to deliver to another party a *pro rata* share of the net assets of the entity only on liquidation and are classified as equity in accordance with paragraphs 16C and 16D of the standard (see 4.6.3 below), or

   - instruments that are contracts for the future receipt or delivery of the entity's own equity instruments. *[IAS 32.11]*.

A *financial liability* is any liability that is:

(a)   a contractual obligation:

   (i)   to deliver cash or another financial asset to another entity; or

   (ii)   to exchange financial assets or financial liabilities with another entity under conditions that are potentially unfavourable to the entity; or

(b)   a contract that will or may be settled in the entity's own equity instruments and is:

   (i)   a non-derivative for which the entity is or may be obliged to deliver a variable number of the entity's own equity instruments; or

   (ii)   a derivative that will or may be settled other than by the exchange of a fixed amount of cash or another financial asset for a fixed number of the entity's own equity instruments. For this purpose, rights, options or warrants to acquire a fixed number of the entity's own equity instruments for a fixed amount of any currency are equity instruments if the entity offers the rights, options or warrants *pro rata* to all of its existing owners of the same class of its own non-derivative equity instruments. Also, for these purposes the entity's own equity instruments do not include:

- puttable financial instruments classified as equity instruments in accordance with paragraphs 16A and 16B of the standard (see 4.6.2 below),

- instruments that impose on the entity an obligation to deliver to another party a *pro rata* share of the net assets of the entity only on liquidation and are classified as equity in accordance with paragraphs 16C and 16D of the standard (see 4.6.3 below),

- or instruments that are contracts for the future receipt or delivery of the entity's own equity instruments. *[IAS 32.11]*.

As an exception to the general definition of a financial liability, an instrument that meets the definition of a financial liability is nevertheless classified as an equity instrument if it has all the features and meets the conditions in paragraphs 16A or 16B (see 4.6.2 below) or paragraphs 16C and 16D of the standard (see 4.6.3 below). *[IAS 32.11]*.

A *puttable instrument* is a financial instrument that gives the holder the right to put the instrument back to the issuer for cash or another financial asset or is automatically put back to the issuer on the occurrence of an uncertain future event or the death or retirement of the holder. *[IAS 32.11]*.

An *equity instrument* is any contract that evidences a residual interest in the assets of an entity after deducting all of its liabilities. *[IAS 32.11]*.

A *derivative* is a financial instrument or other contract within the scope of IAS 39 (see Chapter 43 at 2) with all three of the following characteristics:

- its value changes in response to the change in a specified interest rate, financial instrument price, commodity price, foreign exchange rate, index of prices or rates, credit rating or credit index, or other variable, provided in the case of a non-financial variable that the variable is not specific to a party of the contract (sometimes called the 'underlying');

- it requires no initial net investment or an initial net investment that is smaller than would be required for other types of contracts that would be expected to have a similar response to changes in market factors; and

- it is settled at a future date. *[IAS 39.9]*.

Fair value is the price that would be received to sell an asset or paid to transfer a liability in an orderly transaction between market participants at the measurement date. *[IAS 32.11]*. This is the same definition as used in IFRS 13 – *Fair Value Measurement* (see Chapter 14 at 3).

In these definitions (and throughout IAS 32 and the discussion in this chapter):

- *Contract* and *contractual* refer to an agreement between two or more parties that has clear economic consequences that the parties have little, if any, discretion to avoid, usually because the agreement is enforceable by law. Contracts, and thus financial instruments, may take a variety of forms and need not be in writing; *[IAS 32.13]*.

- *Entity* includes individuals, partnerships, incorporated bodies, trusts and government agencies. *[IAS 32.14]*.

Chapter 44

4   CLASSIFICATION OF INSTRUMENTS

The most important issue dealt with by IAS 32 is the classification of financial instruments (or their components) by their issuer as financial liabilities, financial assets or equity instruments, including non-controlling interests. The rule in IAS 32 for classification of items as financial liabilities or equity is essentially simple. An issuer of a financial instrument must classify the instrument (or its component parts) on initial recognition as a financial liability, a financial asset or an equity instrument in accordance with the substance of the contractual arrangement and the definitions of a financial liability, a financial asset and an equity instrument (see 3 above). *[IAS 32.15].* The application of this principle in practice, however, is often far from straightforward.

IAS 32 considers the question of whether a transaction is a financial liability or an equity instrument at two levels. First it examines whether an individual instrument (or class of instruments) issued by the entity is a financial liability or equity. This is principally discussed in this Section , although some of the provisions discussed at 5 and 6 below may also be relevant.

Second, where an entity settles a transaction using instruments issued by it that, when considered in isolation, would be classified as equity, IAS 32 requires the entity to consider whether the transaction considered as a whole is in fact a financial liability. This will typically be the case where a transaction is settled by issuing a variable number of equity instruments equal to an agreed value. This is principally discussed at 5 and 6 below, although some of the provisions discussed in this Section 4 may also be relevant.

The appropriate classification is made on initial recognition of the instrument and, in general, not changed subsequently (see 4.9 below on reclassification of instruments).

4.1   Definition of equity instrument

Application of the basic definitions in IAS 32 means that an instrument is an equity instrument only if both the following conditions are met:

- The instrument includes no contractual obligation either:
  - to deliver cash or another financial asset to another entity; or
  - to exchange financial assets or financial liabilities with another entity under conditions that are potentially unfavourable to the issuer.
- If the instrument will, or may, be settled in the issuer's own equity instruments, it is either:
  - a non-derivative that includes no contractual obligation for the issuer to deliver a variable number of its own equity instruments; or
  - a derivative that will be settled only by the issuer exchanging a fixed amount of cash or another financial asset for a fixed number of its own equity instruments. For this purpose the issuer's own equity instruments do not include instruments that have all the features and meet the conditions described in paragraphs 16A and 16B (see 4.6.2 below) or paragraphs 16C and 16D (see 4.6.3 below) of IAS 32 or instruments that are contracts for the future receipt or delivery of the issuer's own equity instruments. *[IAS 32.16].*

As a pragmatic exception to these basic criteria, an instrument that would otherwise meet the definition of a financial liability is nevertheless classified as an equity instrument if it is either:

- a puttable instrument with all the features, and meeting the conditions described, in paragraphs 16A and 16B of IAS 32 (see 4.6.2 below); or

- an instrument entitling the holder to a pro-rata share of assets on a liquidation with all the features, and meeting all the conditions, described in paragraphs 16C and 16D of IAS 32. *[IAS 32.16]*. This is discussed further at 4.6.3 below.

Broadly speaking, apart from this exemption, an instrument can only be classified as equity under IAS 32 if the issuer has an unconditional right to avoid delivering cash or another financial instrument (see 4.2 below) or, if it is settled through own equity instruments, it is for an exchange of a fixed amount of cash for a fixed number of the entity's own equity instruments. In all other cases it would be classified as a financial liability.

4.2 Contractual obligation to deliver cash or other financial assets

It is apparent from 4.1 above that a critical feature in differentiating a financial liability from an equity instrument is the existence of a contractual obligation of one party to the financial instrument (the issuer) either:

- to deliver cash or another financial asset to the other party (the holder); or

- to exchange financial assets or financial liabilities with the holder under conditions that are potentially unfavourable to the issuer. *[IAS 32.17]*.

IAS 32 focuses on the contractual rights and obligations arising from the terms of an instrument, rather than on the probability of those rights and obligations leading to an outflow of cash or other resources from the entity, as would be the case for a provision accounted for under IAS 37 – *Provisions, Contingent Liabilities and Contingent Assets* (see Chapter 27). Thus, IAS 32 may well:

- classify as equity: an instrument that is virtually certain to result in regular cash payments by the entity, but

- treat as a liability: an instrument which

  - gives its holder a right to receive cash rather than equity which no rational holder would exercise, or

  - exposes the issuer to a liability to repay the instrument contingent on an external event so remote that no liability would be recognised if IAS 37 rather than IAS 32 were the applicable standard.

The holder of an equity instrument (e.g. a non-puttable share) is entitled to receive a *pro rata* share of any dividends or other distributions of equity that are made. However, since the issuer does not have a contractual obligation to make such distributions (because it cannot be required to deliver cash or another financial asset to another party), the instrument is not a financial liability of the issuer. *[IAS 32.17]*. The price or value of such an instrument may well reflect a general expectation by market participants that distributions will be made on a regular basis, but, under

IAS 32, the absence of a contractual obligation requires the instrument to be classified as equity.

IAS 32 requires the issuer of a financial instrument to classify a financial instrument by reference to its substance rather than its legal form, although it is conceded that substance and form are 'commonly', but not always, the same. Typical examples of instruments that are equity in legal form but liabilities in substance are certain types of preference share (see 4.5 below) and certain units in open-ended funds, unit trusts and similar entities (see 4.6 below). *[IAS 32.18]*. Conversely, a number of entities have issued instruments which behave in most practical respects as perpetual (or even redeemable) debt, but which IAS 32 requires to be classified as equity (see 4.5 below). IAS 32 further clarifies that a financial instrument is an equity instrument, and not a financial liability, not merely if the issuer has no legal obligation to deliver cash or other financial assets to the holder at the reporting date, but only if it has an unconditional right to avoid doing so in all future circumstances other than an unforeseen liquidation. Thus, a financial instrument (other than one classified as equity under the exceptions discussed at 4.6 below) is classified as a financial liability even if:

- the issuer's ability to discharge its obligations under the instrument is restricted (e.g. by a lack of funds, the need to obtain regulatory approval to make payments on the instrument, or a shortfall of distributable profits, or other statutory restriction); *[IAS 32.19, AG25]* or

- the holder has to perform some action (e.g. formally exercise a redemption right) in order for the issuer to become obliged to transfer cash or other financial assets. *[IAS 32.19]*.

4.2.1   Relationship between an entity and its members

The unconditional right of the entity to avoid delivering cash or another financial asset in settlement of an obligation is crucial in differentiating a financial liability from an equity instrument. In our view, the role of the entity's shareholders is critical in determining the classification of financial instruments when the shareholders can decide whether the entity delivers cash or another financial asset. It is therefore important to understand the relationship between the entity and its members. Shareholders can make decisions as part of the corporate governance decision making process of the entity (generally exercised in a general meeting), or separate from the entity's corporate governance decision making process in their capacity as holders of particular instruments.

In some entities, the right to declare dividends and/or redeem capital is reserved for the members of the entity in general meeting, as a matter either of the entity's own constitution or of general legislation in the jurisdiction concerned. The effect of such a right may be that the members can require payment of a dividend irrespective of the wishes of management. Even where management has the right to prevent a payment declared by the members, the members will generally have the right to appoint the management, and can therefore appoint management that will not oppose an equity distribution declared by the members.

This raises the question whether an entity whose members have such rights should classify all its distributable retained earnings as a liability, on the grounds that the members could require earnings to be distributed as dividend, or capital to be repaid, at any time. In our view this is not appropriate, since an action reserved to the entity's shareholders in general meeting, is effectively an action of the entity itself. It is therefore at the discretion of the entity itself (as represented by the members in general meeting) that retained earnings are paid out as a dividend. Accordingly, in our view, such earnings are classified as equity, and not as a financial liability, until they become a legal liability of the entity.

If on the other hand, decisions by the shareholders are not made as part of the entity's corporate governance decision making process, but made in their capacity as holders of particular instruments, it is our view that the shareholders should be considered to be separate from the entity. The entity therefore would not have an unconditional right to avoid delivering cash or another financial asset and would have to classify the financial instrument as a financial liability.

This issue was brought to the Interpretations Committee in January 2010. The Interpretations Committee identified that diversity may exist in practice in assessing whether an entity has an unconditional right to avoid delivering cash if the contractual obligation is at the ultimate discretion of the issuer's shareholders, and consequently whether a financial instrument should be classified as a financial liability or equity. However, the Interpretations Committee concluded that the Board's then current project on financial instruments with characteristics of equity was expected to address the distinction between equity and non-equity instruments on a timely basis, and that the Interpretations Committee would therefore not add this to its agenda. In October 2010 the project was suspended but was restarted in October 2014 (see 12 below).

4.2.2 *Implied contractual obligation to deliver cash or other financial assets*

A financial instrument that does not explicitly establish a contractual obligation to deliver cash or another financial asset may nevertheless establish an obligation indirectly through its terms and conditions, *[IAS 32.20]*, as illustrated by Example 44.1.

Example 44.1: *Financial instrument with non-financial obligation that must be settled if, and only if, the entity fails to redeem the instrument*

The reporting entity borrows €1 million from its bank for five years on terms that, at the end of five years, the entity must deliver its head office building to the bank but may instead repay the loan at €1 million plus rolled-up interest at market rates.

IAS 32 states that a financial instrument, such as that in Example 44.1 above, containing a non-financial obligation that can be avoided only by making a transfer of cash or another financial asset is a financial liability. *[IAS 32.20]*. In effect, IAS 32's analysis relies on the concept of economic compulsion (i.e. the idea that no entity would rationally surrender a core asset probably worth more than €1 million in order to avoid paying €1 million cash).

Whilst this seems intuitively sensible, it is inconsistent with the definition of 'financial liability' at 3 above, which refers merely to an obligation to deliver cash or another financial asset or to exchange financial instruments on potentially unfavourable terms – there is no reference to an obligation that can be avoided only by a transfer of other non-financial assets. Indeed, as discussed at 4.5 below, IAS 32's classification of preference shares and certain similar types of capital instrument, payments on which are contractually discretionary but economically compulsory, rests on a strict analysis of whether a contractual obligation exists.

4.3   Contingent settlement provisions

Some financial instruments may require the entity to deliver cash or another financial asset, or otherwise to settle it in such a way that it would be classified as a financial liability, in the event of the occurrence or non-occurrence of uncertain future events (or on the outcome of uncertain circumstances), that are beyond the control of both the issuer and the holder of the instrument. These might include:

*   a change in a stock market index or a consumer price index;
*   changes in interest rates;
*   changes in tax law; or
*   the issuer's future revenues, net income or debt-to-equity ratio. *[IAS 32.25].*

IAS 32 provides that, since the issuer of such an instrument does not have the unconditional right to avoid delivering cash or another financial asset (or otherwise to settle it in such a way that it would be a financial liability), the instrument is a financial liability of the issuer unless:

*   the part of the contingent settlement provision that could require settlement in cash or another financial asset (or otherwise in such a way that it would be a financial liability) is not genuine (see 4.3.1 below);
*   the issuer can be required to settle the obligation in cash or another financial asset (or otherwise to settle it in such a way that it would be a financial liability) only in the event of liquidation of the issuer (see 4.3.2 below); or
*   the instrument is classified as equity under the exceptions discussed at 4.6 below. *[IAS 32.25].*

Whether or not the contingency is within the control of the issuer is therefore an important consideration when classifying financial instruments with contingent settlement provisions as either financial liabilities or equity (see 4.3.4 below).

It is interesting that 'future revenues, net income or debt-to-equity ratio' are given as examples of contingencies beyond the control of both the issuer and the holder of the instrument, since, in some cases, these matters are within the control of the entity. For example, if a payment under a financial instrument is contingent upon revenue rising above a certain level, the entity could avoid the payment by ceasing to trade before revenue reaches that level. Indeed, IAS 37 argues that certain expenses (such as legally required maintenance costs) that an entity is certain to incur if it continues to trade are not liabilities until they become legally due, because the entity could avoid them by ceasing to trade by that date. As in 4.2.2 above, the analysis in IAS 32 appears to be relying on the concept of 'economic compulsion' (i.e. the entity would not rationally cease its activities merely in order to avoid making a contingent payment), even though this does not feature in the definition of 'contingent liability' in IAS 37, or indeed in the classification of many instruments under IAS 32.

4.3.1   Contingencies that are 'not genuine'

A requirement to settle an instrument in cash or another financial asset (or otherwise in such a way that it would be a financial liability) is not genuine (see 4.3 above) if the requirement would arise 'only on the occurrence of an event that is extremely rare, highly abnormal and very unlikely to occur'. *[IAS 32.AG28]*.

Similarly, if the terms of an instrument provide for its settlement in a fixed number of the entity's equity instruments, but there are circumstances, beyond the entity's control, in which such settlement may be contractually precluded, and settlement in cash or other assets required instead, those circumstances can be ignored if there is 'no genuine possibility' that they will occur. In other words, the instrument continues to be regarded as an equity instrument and not as a financial liability. *[IAS 32.AG28]*.

Guidance in IAS 32 on the meaning of 'not genuine' in this context is unfortunately restricted to the thesaurus of synonyms ('extremely rare, highly abnormal and very unlikely to occur') above. It is, however, helpful to consider the changes made when in 2003 SIC-5 – *Classification of Financial Instruments – Contingent Settlement Provisions*[3] – was withdrawn, and its substance incorporated in these provisions of IAS 32. SIC-5 had previously required redemption terms to be ignored if they were 'remote'. Examples given by SIC-5 were where the issue of shares is contingent merely on formal approval by the authorities, or where cash settlement is triggered by an index reaching an 'extreme' level relative to its level at the time of initial recognition of the instrument.[4]

IAS 32 deliberately did not reproduce the reference to, or the examples of, 'remote' events in SIC-5. In the Basis for Conclusions to IAS 32 the IASB states that it does not believe it is appropriate to disregard events that are merely 'remote'. *[IAS 32.BC17]*. Thus it is clear that, under the revised version of IAS 32, it is not appropriate to disregard a redemption term that is triggered only when an index reaches an extreme level. This suggests that it is not open to an entity to argue (for example) that a bond that is redeemed in cash only if the entity's share price falls below, or fails to reach, a certain level can be treated as an equity instrument on the grounds that there is no genuine possibility that the share price will perform in that way.

In general, terms are included in a contract for an economic purpose and therefore are genuine. The current reference in IAS 32 to terms that are 'not genuine' is presumably intended to deal with clauses inserted into the terms of financial instruments for some legal or tax reason (e.g. so as to make conversion technically 'conditional' rather than mandatory) but having no real economic purpose or consequence.

An example of a clause that has caused some debate on this point is a 'regulatory change' clause, generally found in the terms of capital instruments issued by financial institutions such as banks and insurance companies. Such entities are generally required by local regulators to maintain certain minimum levels of equity or

Chapter 44

highly subordinated debt (generally referred to as regulatory capital) in order to be allowed to do business.

A 'regulatory change' clause will typically require an instrument which, at the date of issue, is classified as regulatory capital to be repaid in the event that it ceases to be so classified. The practice so far of the regulators in many markets has been to make changes to a regulatory classification with prospective effect only, such that any instruments already in issue continue to be regarded as regulatory capital even though they would not be under the new rules.

This has led some to question whether a 'regulatory change' clause can be regarded as a contingent settlement provision which is 'not genuine'.[5] This is ultimately a matter for the judgement of entities and their auditors in the context of the relevant regulatory environment(s). This judgement has not been made easier by the greater unpredictability of the markets (and therefore of regulators' responses to it) since the last financial crisis.

4.3.2   *Liabilities that arise only on liquidation*

As noted in 4.3 above, IAS 32 provides that a contingent settlement provision that comes into play only on liquidation of the issuer may be ignored in determining whether or not a financial instrument is a financial liability. IAS 32 refers specifically to 'liquidation'. In other words, if an instrument provides for redemption on the occurrence of events that are a possible precursor of liquidation (e.g. extreme insolvency, the financial statements not being prepared on a going concern basis, or the entity being placed under the protection of Chapter 11 of the United States Bankruptcy Code) but falling short of formal liquidation, the instrument must be treated as a financial liability.

4.3.3   *Liabilities that arise only on a change of control*

A number of entities have issued instruments on terms that require the issuing entity to transfer cash or other financial assets only in the event of a change in control of the issuing entity. This raises the question of whether such an event is outside the control of the issuing entity, with the effect than any instrument containing such a provision would be classified as a liability to the extent of any obligations arising on a change of control.

This issue is far from straightforward. As noted at 4.2.1 above, it is our view that, where the power to make a decision is reserved for the members of an entity in general meeting, for the purposes of such a decision, the members and the entity are one and the same. Therefore, we consider that any change of control requiring the approval of the members in general meeting should be regarded as within the control of the entity.

Conversely, in our view, a change of control is not within the control of the entity where it can be effected by one or more individual shareholders without reference to the members in general meeting, for example where a shareholder holding 40% of the ordinary equity sells its shares to another party already owning 30%.

However, we recognise that such a distinction is not as clear-cut as might at first sight appear, and indeed in some situations may give rise to what could be regarded as a purely form-based distinction, as illustrated by Example 44.2 below.

Example 44.2:   Change of control

X plc is owned by:

• two wealthy individuals A and B, who own, respectively, 48% and 42% of X's equity, together with

• a number of private individuals with small shareholdings totalling 10% of the equity.

In practical terms, if A and B agree that B will sell his shares to A, thus giving A a 90% controlling stake in the entity, it makes very little difference whether this is achieved by a private sale treaty between A and B or a general meeting of the company (at which A and B would be able to cast 90% of available votes in favour of the transaction).

In a situation such as that in Example 44.2 it would seem strange to say that a sale by private treaty is not within the control of X plc, but a sale agreed in general meeting is, when in either case all that matters is the intentions of A and B.

In our view, this is an area on which it would be useful for the IASB or the Interpretations Committee to issue guidance. It may be that such guidance would need to be based on 'rules' rather than principles.

4.3.4   Some typical contingent settlement provisions

The matrix below gives a number of contingent settlement provisions that we have encountered in practice – some common, some rather esoteric – together with our view as to whether they should be regarded as outside the control of the reporting entity. If a contingent settlement provision is regarded as outside the control of the issuing entity, the instrument will be classified as a liability by the issuer. If a contingent settlement provision is regarded as within the control of the reporting entity, the instrument will be classified as equity, provided that it has no other features requiring its classification as a liability and that the contingent settlement event is also outside the control of the holder.

Contingent settlement event	Within the issuer's control?
Issuer makes a distribution on ordinary shares.	Yes. Dividends on ordinary shares are discretionary (see also 4.2 above).
Upon the successful takeover of the issuer (i.e. a 'control event').	It depends. See 4.3.3 above.
Event of default under any of the issuer's debt facilities.	No.
Appointment of a receiver, administrator, entering a scheme of arrangement, or compromise agreement with creditors.	No. Whether this leads to the instrument being classified as equity or liability will depend on the respective requirements in each jurisdiction. In cases when these events do not necessarily result in liquidation of the issuer, this leads to classification as a liability, due to the requirement to ignore settlement provisions arising only on liquidation (see 4.3.2 above).

Chapter 44

Contingent settlement event	Within the issuer's control?
Upon commencement of proceedings for the winding up of the issuer.	No, but this does not lead to classification as a liability due to the requirement to ignore settlement provisions arising only on liquidation (see 4.3.2 above).
Incurring a fine exceeding a given amount, or commencement of an investigation of the issuer by, a government agency or a financial regulator.	No.
A change in accounting, taxation, or regulatory regime which is expected to adversely affect the financial position of the issuer.	No.
Suspension of listing of the issuer's shares from trading on the stock exchange for more than a certain number of days.	Probably not, but it will depend on the jurisdiction and whether the reasons for suspension are always within the control of the entity.
Commencement of war or armed conflict.	No.
Issue of a subordinated security that ranks equally or in priority to the securities.	Yes.
Issue of an IPO prospectus prior to the conversion date.	Yes.
Execution of an effective IPO.	No. The execution of a successful IPO is not within the control of the issuer.
Disposal of all or substantially all of the issuer's business undertaking or assets.	Yes.
Change in credit rating of the issuer.	No.

4.4   Examples of equity instruments

4.4.1   Issued instruments

Under the criteria above, equity instruments under IAS 32 will include non-puttable common (ordinary) shares and some types of preference share (see 4.5 below). [IAS 32.AG13].

Whilst non-puttable shares are typically equity, an issuer of non-puttable ordinary shares nevertheless assumes a liability when it formally acts to make a distribution and becomes legally obliged to the shareholders to do so. This may be the case following the declaration of a dividend, or when, on a winding up, any assets remaining after discharging the entity's liabilities become distributable to shareholders. [IAS 32.AG13]. For example, if an entity has issued €100 million of equity instruments on which it declares a dividend of €2 million, it recognises a liability of only €2 million. Whether or not a liability arises on declaration of a dividend will depend on local legislation or the terms of the instruments or both.

IAS 32 also treats as equity instruments some puttable instruments (see 4.6.2 below) and some instruments that impose an obligation on the issuer to deliver a *pro rata* share of net assets only on liquidation (see 4.6.3 below) that would otherwise be classified as financial liabilities. However, a contract that is required to be settled by the entity receiving or delivering either of these types of 'deemed' equity instrument is a financial asset or financial liability, even when it involves the exchange of a fixed amount of cash or other financial assets for a fixed number of such instruments. *[IAS 32.22A, AG13].*

4.4.2   Contracts to issue equity instruments

A contract settled using equity instruments is not necessarily itself regarded as an equity instrument. The classification of contracts settled using issued equity instruments is discussed further at 5 below.

Warrants or written call options that allow the holder to subscribe for or purchase a fixed number of non-puttable common (ordinary) shares in the issuing entity in exchange for a fixed amount of cash or another financial asset, or the fixed stated principal of a bond, are classified as equity instruments. *[IAS 32.22, AG13].* The meaning of a 'fixed' amount of cash is not as self-evident as it might appear and is discussed further at 5.2.3 below. The meaning of the 'fixed stated principal' of a bond is discussed further at 6.3.2.A below.

Conversely, an instrument is a financial liability (or financial asset) of the issuer if it gives the holder the right to obtain:

- a variable number of non-puttable common (ordinary) shares in the issuing entity in exchange for a fixed amount of cash or another financial asset; *[IAS 32.21]* or

- a fixed number of non-puttable common (ordinary) shares in the issuing entity in exchange for a variable amount of cash or another financial asset. *[IAS 32.24].*

An obligation for the entity to issue or purchase a fixed number of its own equity instruments in exchange for a fixed amount of cash or another financial asset is classified as an equity instrument of the entity. However, if such a contract contains an obligation – or even a potential obligation – for the entity to pay cash or another financial asset, it gives rise to a liability for the present value of the redemption amount (which results in a reduction of equity, not an expense – see 5.3 below). *[IAS 32.23, AG13].*

A purchased call option or other similar contract acquired by an entity that gives it the right to reacquire a fixed number of its own equity instruments in exchange for delivering a fixed amount of cash or another financial asset is not a financial asset of the entity. Rather, it is classified as an equity instrument, and any consideration paid for such a contract is therefore deducted from equity (see 11.2.1 below). *[IAS 32.22, AG14].* This requirement refers only to contracts which require the entity to settle gross (i.e. the entity pays cash in exchange for its own shares). Contracts which can be net settled (i.e. the party for whom the contract is loss-making delivers cash or shares equal to the fair value of the contract to the other party) are generally treated as financial assets or financial liabilities. This is discussed in more detail at 11 below.

4.5   Preference shares and similar instruments

Whilst some of the discussion below (and the guidance in IAS 32) is, for convenience, framed in terms of 'preference shares', it should be applied equally to any financial instrument, however described, with similar characteristics. In practice, many such instruments are not described as shares (possibly to avoid weakening any argument that, for fiscal purposes, they are tax-deductible debt rather than non-deductible equity).

Preference shares may be issued with various rights. In determining whether a preference share is a financial liability or an equity instrument, IAS 32 requires an issuer to assess the particular rights attaching to the share to determine whether it exhibits the fundamental characteristic of a financial liability. *[IAS 32.AG25].*

IAS 32 does this in part by drawing a distinction between:

- instruments mandatorily redeemable or redeemable at the holder's option (see 4.5.1 below);

- other instruments – i.e. those redeemable only at the issuer's option or not redeemable (see 4.5.2 to 4.5.4 below).

4.5.1   *Instruments redeemable mandatorily or at the holder's option*

A preference share (or other instrument) that:

- provides for mandatory redemption by the issuer for a fixed or determinable amount at a fixed or determinable future date; or

- gives the holder the right to require the issuer to redeem the instrument at or after a particular date for a fixed or determinable amount,

contains a financial liability, since the issuer has an obligation, or potential obligation, to transfer cash or other financial assets to the holder. This obligation is not negated by the potential inability of an issuer to redeem a preference share when contractually required to do so, whether because of a lack of funds, a statutory restriction or insufficient profits or reserves. *[IAS 32.18(a), AG25].*

It is more correct to say (in the words of the application guidance) that an instrument 'contains' a financial liability than to say (as the main body of the standard does) that it 'is' a financial liability. For example, if a preference share is issued on terms that it is redeemable at the holder's option but dividends are paid entirely at the issuer's discretion, it is only the amount payable on redemption that is a liability. This would lead to a 'split accounting' treatment (see 6 below), whereby, at issue, the net present value of the amount payable on redemption would be classified as a liability and the balance of the issue proceeds as equity. *[IAS 32.AG37].*

Non-discretionary dividends, on the other hand, establish an additional liability component. In such a case there is a contractual obligation to pay cash in respect of both the redemption of the principal and the required dividend payments up to the redemption of the instrument. The liability would be recognised at an amount equal to the present value of both the redemption amount and the non-discretionary dividends. Assuming that the dividends were set at market rate, which is generally the case, this would typically result in an overall liability classification of the whole instrument. While dividend payments might be set at a fixed percentage of the nominal value, this does not need to be the case. Any non-discretionary obligation to pay dividends creates a liability that needs to be recorded on initial recognition of the instrument. If an entity has an obligation that is non-discretionary, for example to pay out a percentage of it profits, then that gives rise to a financial liability (see Chapter 43 at 2.1.3 for discussions around embedded derivatives and non-financial variables specific to one party to the contract).

4.5.2   *Instruments redeemable only at the issuer's option or not redeemable*

A preference share (or other instrument) redeemable in cash only at the option of the issuer does not satisfy the definition of a financial liability in IAS 32, because the issuer does not have a present or future obligation to transfer financial assets to the shareholders. In this case, redemption of the shares is solely at the discretion of the issuer. An obligation may arise, however, when the issuer of the shares exercises its option, usually by formally notifying the shareholders of an intention to redeem the shares. *[IAS 32.AG25].*

Likewise, where preference shares are non-redeemable, there is clearly no financial liability in respect of the 'principal' amount of the shares. In reality there may be little distinction between shares redeemable at the issuer's option and non-redeemable shares, given that in many jurisdictions an entity can 'repurchase' its 'irredeemable' shares subject to no greater restrictions than would apply to a 'redemption' of 'redeemable' shares.

Ultimately, the classification of preference shares redeemable only at the issuer's option or not redeemable according to their terms must be determined by the other rights that attach to them. IAS 32 requires the classification to be based on an assessment of the substance of the contractual arrangements and the definitions of a financial liability and an equity instrument. *[IAS 32.AG26].*

If the share does establish a contractual right to a dividend, subject only to restrictions on payment of dividends in the relevant jurisdiction, it contains a financial liability in respect of the dividends. This would lead to a 'split accounting' treatment (see 6 below), whereby the net present value of the right to receive dividends would be shown as a liability and the balance of the issue proceeds as equity. Where the dividends are set at a market rate at the date of issue, it is likely that the issue proceeds would be equivalent to the fair value (at the date of issue) of dividends payable in perpetuity, so that the entire proceeds would be classified as a financial liability.

However, when redemption of the preference shares and distributions to holders of the preference shares, whether cumulative or non-cumulative, are at the discretion of the issuer, the shares are equity instruments. The classification of preference share distributions as an equity component or a financial liability component is not affected by, for example:

- a history of making distributions;
- an intention to make distributions in the future;
- a possible negative impact on the price of ordinary shares of the issuer if distributions are not made (because of restrictions on paying dividends on the ordinary shares if dividends are not paid on the preference shares – see 4.5.3 below);
- the amount of the issuer's reserves;
- an issuer's expectation of a profit or loss for a period; or
- an ability or inability of the issuer to influence the amount of its profit or loss for the period. *[IAS 32.AG26].*

The treatment of non-redeemable preference shares or other instruments with preferred rights under IAS 32 is a particularly difficult issue, since such shares often

Chapter 44

inhabit the border territory between financial liabilities and equity instruments. However, the starting point is that a non-redeemable preference share whose dividend rights are simply that a dividend (whether of a fixed, capped or discretionary amount) will be paid at the issuing entity's sole discretion, is equivalent to an ordinary equity share and therefore appropriately characterised as equity.

4.5.3   Instruments with a 'dividend blocker' or a 'dividend pusher' clause

4.5.3.A   Instruments with a 'dividend blocker'

A number of entities have issued non-redeemable instruments (or instruments redeemable only at the issuer's option) with the following broad terms:

- a discretionary annual coupon or dividend will be paid up to a capped maximum amount; and

- unless a full discretionary coupon or dividend is paid to holders of the instrument, no dividend can be paid to ordinary shareholders.

This restriction on dividend payments to ordinary shareholders is colloquially referred to as a 'dividend blocker' clause. Because payments of annual coupons or dividends are at the discretion of the issuer and the instrument is non-redeemable, the issuer has an unconditional right to avoid delivering cash or another financial asset. This is not negated by the fact that the issuer cannot pay dividends to ordinary shareholders if no coupon or dividend is paid to the holder of the instruments. The instrument is therefore classified as equity in its entirety.

The economic reality is that many entities that issue such instruments are able to do so at a cost not significantly higher than that of callable perpetual debt. This indicates that the financial markets regard 'dividend blocker' clauses as providing investors with reasonable security of receiving their 'discretionary' coupon or dividend, given the adverse economic consequences for the entity of not paying it (if sufficiently solvent to do so), namely:

- the disaffection of ordinary shareholders who could not receive any dividends; and

- the fact that the entity would find it very difficult to raise any similar finance again.

These factors could admit an argument that such instruments are equivalent to perpetual debt, which give rise to a financial liability of the issuer (see 4.7 below), in all respects, except that the holder has no right to sue for non-payment of the discretionary dividend. However, the analysis in IAS 32 is based on the implicit counter-argument that the position of a holder of an instrument, all payments on which are discretionary, is equivalent to that of an ordinary shareholder. Ordinary shares do not cease to be equity instruments simply because an entity that failed to pay dividends to its ordinary shareholders, when clearly able to do so, would be subject to adverse economic pressures from those shareholders, and might find it very difficult to raise additional share capital.

However it is worth noting that, as mentioned in 1.2 above, the Exposure Draft ED/2015/3 – *Conceptual Framework for Financial Reporting* – includes a proposed new definition of liability as a present obligation of an entity to transfer an economic resource as a result of past events where the entity has no practical ability to avoid the transfer. If adopted, this definition could result in instruments with 'dividend blockers' being classified as financial liabilities on the grounds that the entity has no practical ability to avoid the transfer.

Aviva has issued instruments with 'dividend blocker' clauses that are accounted for as equity instruments (see, in particular, the final sentences of the extract).

Extract 44.1: Aviva plc (2014)

Notes to the consolidated financial statements [extract]

35   Direct capital instruments and fixed rate tier 1 notes [extract]

Notional amount	**2014**	2013
	£m	£m
Issued November 2004		
5.9021% £500 million direct capital instrument	**500**	500
4.7291% €700 million direct capital instrument	**–**	490
	500	990
Issued May 2012		
8.25% US $650 million fixed rate tier 1 notes	**392**	392
	892	1,382

The euro and sterling direct capital instruments (the DCIs) were issued on 25 November 2004 and qualify as Innovative Tier 1 capital, as defined by the PRA in GENPRU Annex 1 'Capital Resources'. On 28 November 2014 the Company exercised its option to redeem the euro DCI on its first redemption date. The remaining sterling DCI has no fixed redemption date but the Company may, at its sole option, redeem all (but not part) of the principal amount on 27 July 2020, at which date the interest rate changes to a variable rate, or on any respective coupon payment date thereafter. [...]

No interest will accrue on any deferred coupon. Deferred coupons will be satisfied by the issue and sale of ordinary shares in the Company at their prevailing market value, to a sum as near as practicable to (and at least equal to) the relevant deferred coupons. In the event of any coupon deferral, the Company will not declare or pay any dividend on its ordinary or preference share capital.

These instruments have been treated as equity. Please refer to accounting policy AE.

4.5.3.B   Instruments with a 'dividend pusher'

A variation of the financial instrument discussed under 4.5.3.A above is one with a so called 'dividend pusher' clause which, in practice, often comes with the following broad terms:

- a discretionary annual coupon or dividend will be paid up to a capped maximum amount;
- payment of the annual coupon or dividend is required if the entity pays dividends to ordinary shareholders; and
- the instrument is non-redeemable (or redeemable only at the issuer's option).

The annual coupons or dividends are at the discretion of the issuer and the instrument is non-redeemable, indicating an unconditional right of the issuer to avoid delivering cash or another financial asset to the holder of the instrument. Whether the 'dividend pusher' clause introduces a contractual obligation to deliver cash or another financial asset depends on whether the payments of dividends to ordinary shareholders (referenced in the dividend pusher clause) are themselves discretionary. In general, payments of dividends to ordinary shareholders are at the discretion of the issuer of those shares. The 'dividend pusher' clause therefore does not introduce a contractual obligation, meaning that the issuer has an unconditional right to avoid delivering cash or another financial asset. Thus the instrument is classified as equity in its entirety.

4.5.4   Perpetual instruments with a 'step-up' clause

Some perpetual instruments are issued on terms that they are not required to be redeemed. However, if they are not redeemed on or before a given future date, any coupon or dividend paid after that date is increased, usually to a level that would give rise to a cost of finance higher than the entity would normally expect to incur. This effectively compels the issuer to redeem the instrument before the increase occurs. A provision for such an increase in the coupon or dividend is colloquially referred to as a 'step-up' clause. A 'step-up' clause is often combined with a 'dividend-blocker' or 'dividend pusher' clause (see 4.5.3.A and 4.5.3.B above).

Paragraph 22 of the version of IAS 32 in issue before its revision in December 2003 (see 1.2 above) specifically addressed 'step-up' clauses as follows:

> 'A preferred share that does not provide for mandatory redemption or redemption at the option of the holder may have a contractually provided accelerating dividend such that, within the foreseeable future, the dividend yield is scheduled to be so high that the issuer would be economically compelled to redeem the instrument.'[6]

The Basis for Conclusions to the current version of IAS 32 indicates that this example was removed because it was insufficiently clear, but there was no intention to alter the general principle of IAS 32 that an instrument that does not explicitly establish an obligation to deliver cash or other financial assets may establish an obligation indirectly through its terms and conditions (see 4.2.3 above). *[IAS 32.BC9].*

This has led some to suggest that any instrument with a 'step-up' clause contains a financial liability. In our view, however, this is to misunderstand the reason for the IASB's decision to delete the old paragraph 22. The 'confusion' caused by the paragraph was that the existence of a step-up clause is in fact irrelevant to the analysis required by IAS 32. If an instrument, whether redeemable or not, contains a contractual obligation to pay a coupon or dividend, it is a liability, irrespective of the 'step-up' clause. However, if the coupon or dividend, both before and after the step-up date, is wholly discretionary, then the instrument is, absent other contractual terms that make it a liability, an equity instrument, again irrespective of the step-up clause (see 4.5.1 and 4.5.2 above).

This analysis was confirmed by the Interpretations Committee in March 2006 in its discussion of the classification of an instrument that included a 'step-up' dividend clause that would increase the dividend at a pre-determined date in the future. The Interpretations Committee agreed that this instrument included no contractual obligation ever to pay the dividends or to call the instrument and that therefore it should be classified as equity under IAS 32.[7]

4.5.5 Relative subordination

Some have argued that instruments with 'dividend-blocker', 'dividend-pusher' or 'step-up' clauses (see 4.5.3 and 4.5.4 above) do not meet the definition of an equity instrument. Those that take this view point out that paragraph 11 of IAS 32 defines an equity instrument as 'any contract that evidences a residual interest in the assets of an entity after deducting all of its liabilities' (see 3 above) – whereas many instruments of the type described in 4.5.3 and 4.5.4 above are typically entitled only to a return of the amount originally subscribed on a winding up, rather than to any 'residual interest' in the assets. However, such an instrument does not meet the definition of a liability either, for all the reasons set out above.

Moreover, as noted at 4.1 above, IAS 32 paragraph 16 indicates that, in applying the definition in paragraph 11, an entity concludes that an instrument is equity if and only if the criteria in paragraph 16 are met. In other words, an instrument is equity if it satisfies the criteria of paragraph 16, whatever construction might be placed on paragraph 11.

In March 2006, the Interpretations Committee considered various issues relating to the classification of instruments under IAS 32, and agreed that IAS 32 was clear that the relative subordination on liquidation of a financial instrument was not relevant to its classification under IAS 32, even where the instrument ranks above an instrument classified as a liability.[8] This supports the view that an instrument can be classified as equity even if there are restrictions on participation by its holder in a liquidation or on winding up.

However, in February 2008, the IASB issued an amendment to IAS 32 (see 1.2 above) which, in very specific circumstances, requires the relative subordination of an instrument to be taken into account in determining its classification as debt or equity (see 4.6 below).

4.5.6 Economic compulsion

The discussion in 4.5.1 to 4.5.5 above illustrates that, while IAS 32 requires the issuer of a financial instrument to classify a financial instrument by reference to its substance rather than its legal form, in reality the substance is determined, if not by the legal *form*, then certainly by the precise legal *rights* of the holder of the financial instrument concerned. Ultimately, the key determinant of whether an instrument is a financial liability or an equity instrument of the issuer is whether the terms of the instrument give the holder a contractual right to receive cash or other financial assets which can be sued for at law, subject only to restrictions outside the terms of the instrument (e.g. statutory dividend controls).

By contrast, terms of an instrument that effectively force the issuer to transfer cash or other financial assets to the holder although not legally required to do so (often referred to as 'economic compulsion'), are not taken into account.

This emphasis on legal and contractual rights also helps to clarify the apparent inconsistency in the requirement of IAS 32 to take account of 'economic compulsion' in categorising financial instruments such as that in Example 44.1 at 4.2.2 above but to ignore the 'economic compulsion' to pay a discretionary dividend. The difference is that, in Example 44.1, if the issuer fails to deliver cash, it suffers an adverse consequence (i.e. the obligation to deliver another, probably more valuable, asset) *under the terms of the instrument*. By contrast, if an issuer of a discretionary instrument with a 'dividend blocker' clause (see 4.5.3.A above) fails to pay any discretionary coupon or dividend, it suffers an adverse consequence (i.e. damage to its financial reputation) arising from external economic factors rather than from the holder's rights under the terms of the share. This analysis is reinforced by the fact that the matters which IAS 32 specifically requires to be ignored in assessing whether a non-redeemable share is a liability or equity (see 4.5.2 above) are all external economic factors and pressures, and do not arise from any legal rights or obligations inherent in the instrument itself.

In response to a submission for a possible agenda item, in March 2006 the Interpretations Committee discussed the role of contractual and economic obligations in the classification of financial instruments under IAS 32.

The Interpretations Committee agreed that IAS 32 is clear that, in order for an instrument to be classified as a liability, a contractual obligation must be established (either explicitly or indirectly) through the terms and conditions of the instrument. Economic compulsion, by itself, would not result in a financial instrument being classified as a liability.

The Interpretations Committee also noted that IAS 32 restricts the role of 'substance' to consideration of the contractual terms of an instrument, and that anything outside the contractual terms is not considered for the purpose of assessing whether an instrument should be classified as a liability under IAS 32.[9]

4.5.7   'Linked' instruments

An entity may issue an instrument (the 'base' instrument) that requires a payment to be made if, and only if, a payment is made on another instrument issued by the entity (the 'linked' instrument). An example of such an instrument would be a perpetual instrument with a 'dividend blocker' clause (see 4.5.3.A above), on which the issuing entity is required to pay a coupon only if it pays a dividend to ordinary shareholders. Absent other terms requiring the perpetual instrument to be classified as a liability, it is classified as equity on the basis that the event that triggers a contractual obligation to make a payment (i.e. payment of an ordinary dividend) is itself not a contractual obligation.

If, however, where payments on the linked instrument are contractually mandatory (such that the linked instrument contains a liability), it is obvious that the base instrument must also contain a liability. This is due to the fact that, in this case, the event that triggers a contractual obligation to make a payment on the base instrument (i.e. a payment on the linked instrument) is a contractual obligation that the issuing entity cannot avoid. This analysis was confirmed by the Interpretations Committee in March 2006 following discussion of linked instruments with similar terms to these.[10]

This issue had arisen in practice in the context that the linked instrument was often very small and callable by the issuer, but on terms that required its classification as a liability under IAS 32. This would allow the issuer, with no real difficulty, to redeem the linked instrument at will and thus convert the base instrument from a liability to equity at any time. This had led some to argue that only the linked instrument should be classified as a liability.

4.5.8   'Change of control', 'taxation change' and 'regulatory change' clauses

A number of entities have issued instruments with 'dividend blocker', 'dividend pusher' and 'step-up' clauses (see 4.5.3 and 4.5.4 above), which would otherwise have been treated as equity by IAS 32, but have wished to account for them as liabilities, perhaps because they can then be hedged in a way that allows hedge accounting to be applied (see 10 below). Methods of achieving this have included the use of a *de minimis* linked liability instrument, or the inclusion of a clause requiring the repayment of the instrument in the event of a change of control. This raises the question of whether a change of control is within the control of the entity (such that the instrument is equity) or not (such that the instrument is debt), which is discussed in more detail at 4.3.3 above.

Another common method of converting an instrument that would otherwise be classified by IAS 32 as equity into debt is to add a clause requiring repayment of the instrument in the event of a fiscal or regulatory change (that in reality may be a remote possibility) – see 4.3.1 above.

4.6   Puttable instruments and instruments repayable only on liquidation

4.6.1   The issue

A 'puttable instrument' is essentially a financial instrument that gives the holder the right to put the instrument back to the issuer for cash or another financial asset (see 3 above). Prior to its amendment in February 2008 (see 1.2 above), IAS 32 classified any puttable instrument as a financial liability, including instruments the legal form of which gives the holder a right to a residual interest in the assets of the issuer.

This classification produced what some regarded as an inappropriate result in the financial statements of entities such as open-ended mutual funds, unit trusts, partnerships and some co-operative entities. Such entities often provide their unit holders or members with a right to redeem their interests in the issuer at any time for cash. Under IAS 32, prior to the February 2008 amendment, an entity whose holders had such rights might report net assets of nil, or even negative net assets, since what would, in normal usage, have been regarded as its 'equity' (i.e. assets less external borrowings) was classified as a financial liability.

For example, the owners of some co-operatives and professional partnerships are entitled to have their ownership interests repurchased at fair value. However, such entities typically do not reflect that fair value in their financial statements, because a significant part of the value may be represented by property accounted for at cost rather than fair value or by internally generated goodwill which cannot be recognised in financial statements prepared under IFRS.

Clearly, if such an entity were to recognise a liability for the right of its owners to be bought out at fair value, it would show net liabilities, which would increase (creating accounting losses) the more the fair value of the entity increases, and decrease (creating accounting profits) the more the fair value decreases. Moreover, any distributions to the owners of such entities would be shown as a charge to, rather than a distribution of, profit.

Similar concerns were raised in relation to limited-life entities. In some jurisdictions, certain types of entity are required to be wound up after a certain period of time, either automatically, or unless the members resolve otherwise. Some entities may also have a limited life under their own governing charter, or equivalent document. For example:

• a collective investment fund might be required to be liquidated on, say, the tenth anniversary of its foundation; or

• a partnership might be required to be dissolved on the death or retirement of a partner.

Such an entity arguably had no equity under IAS 32 prior to the February 2008 amendment, since its limited life imposes an obligation, outside the entity's control, to distribute all its assets. Again, some questioned whether it was very meaningful to show such an entity as having no equity.

In order to deal with these concerns, IAS 32 was amended in February 2008. In the meantime, the Interpretations Committee had published IFRIC 2 which addresses the narrower issue of the classification of certain types of puttable instrument typically issued by co-operative entities (see 4.6.6 below).

The effect of the amended standard is that certain narrowly-defined categories of puttable instruments (see 4.6.2 below) and instruments repayable on a pre-determined liquidation (see 4.6.3 below) are classified as equity, notwithstanding that they have features that would otherwise require their classification as financial liabilities.

Moreover, as discussed further at 4.6.5 below, one of the criteria for classifying such an instrument as equity, is that it is the most subordinated instrument issued by the reporting entity. This represents a significant, and controversial, departure from the normal approach of IAS 32 that the classification of an instrument should be determined only by reference to the contractual terms of that instrument, rather than those of other instruments in issue. This may mean that two entities may classify an identical instrument differently, if it is the most subordinated instrument of one entity but not of the other. It may also mean that the same entity may classify the same instrument differently at different reporting dates.

It was essentially these departures from the normal requirements of IAS 32 that led two members of the IASB (Mary Barth and Robert Garnett) to dissent from the amendment. In their view, it is not based on a clear principle, but comprises 'several paragraphs of detailed rules crafted to achieve a desired accounting result ... [and] ... to minimise structuring opportunities'.[11]

Where the exceptions in 4.6.2 and 4.6.3 below do not apply, IAS 32 takes the view that the effect of the holder's option to put the instrument back to the issuer for cash or another financial asset is that the puttable instrument meets the definition of a financial liability *[IAS 32.18(b)]* (see 3 above).

The IASB believes that the accounting treatment required by IAS 32 for instruments not subject to the exceptions in 4.6.2 and 4.6.3 below is appropriate, but points out that the classification of members' interests in such entities as a financial liability does not preclude:

- the use of captions such as 'net asset value attributable to unitholders' and 'change in net asset value attributable to unitholders' on the face of the financial statements of an entity that has no equity capital (such as some mutual funds and unit trusts); or

- the use of additional disclosure to show that total members' interests comprise items such as reserves that meet the definition of equity and puttable instruments that do not. *[IAS 32.18(b), BC7-BC8].*

The illustrative examples appended to IAS 32 give specimen disclosures to be used in such cases – see Chapter 53 at 7.4.

4.6.2   Puttable instruments

As noted above, a puttable financial instrument includes a contractual obligation for the issuer to repurchase or redeem that instrument for cash or another financial asset on exercise of the put. IAS 32 classifies a puttable instrument as an equity instrument if it has all of the following features: *[IAS 32.16A-B]*

(a)   It entitles the holder to a *pro rata* share of the entity's net assets in the event of the entity's liquidation. The entity's net assets are those assets that remain after deducting all other claims on its assets. A *pro rata* share is determined by:

    (i)   dividing the entity's net assets on liquidation into units of equal amount; and

    (ii)   multiplying that amount by the number of the units held by the financial instrument holder.

(b)   The instrument is in the class of instruments that is subordinate to all other classes of instruments. To be in such a class the instrument:

    (i)   has no priority over other claims to the assets of the entity on liquidation; and

    (ii)   does not need to be converted into another instrument before it is in the class of instruments that is subordinate to all other classes of instruments.

(c)   All financial instruments in the class of instruments that is subordinate to all other classes of instruments have identical features. For example, they must all be puttable, and the formula or other method used to calculate the repurchase or redemption price is the same for all instruments in that class.

(d)   Apart from the contractual obligation for the issuer to repurchase or redeem the instrument for cash or another financial asset, the instrument does not include any contractual obligation to deliver cash or another financial asset to another entity, or to exchange financial assets or financial liabilities with another entity under conditions that are potentially unfavourable to the entity, and it is not a contract that will or may be settled in the entity's own equity instruments as set out in subparagraph (b) of the definition of a financial liability (see 3 above).

Chapter 44

(e)   The total expected cash flows attributable to the instrument over the life of the instrument are based substantially on the profit or loss, the change in the recognised net assets, or the change in the fair value of the recognised and unrecognised net assets of the entity over the life of the instrument (excluding any effects of the instrument). *[IAS 32.16A]*. Profit or loss and the change in recognised net assets must be determined in accordance with relevant IFRSs. *[IAS 32.AG14E]*.

(f)   In addition to the instrument having all the features in (a) to (e) above, the issuer must have no other financial instrument or contract that has:

   (i)   total cash flows based substantially on the profit or loss, the change in the recognised net assets or the change in the fair value of the recognised and unrecognised net assets of the entity (excluding any effects of such instrument or contract); and

   (ii)   the effect of substantially restricting or fixing the residual return to the puttable instrument holders.

In applying this condition, the entity should not consider non-financial contracts with a holder of an instrument described in (a) to (e) above that have contractual terms and conditions that are similar to the contractual terms and conditions of an equivalent contract that might occur between a non-instrument holder and the issuing entity. If the entity cannot determine that this condition is met, it should not classify the puttable instrument as an equity instrument. *[IAS 32.16B]*.

Some of these criteria raise issues of interpretation, which are addressed at 4.6.4 below.

4.6.3   *Instruments entitling the holder to a pro rata share of net assets only on liquidation*

Some financial instruments include a contractual obligation for the issuing entity to deliver to another entity a *pro rata* share of its net assets only on liquidation. The obligation arises because liquidation either is certain to occur and outside the control of the entity (for example, a limited life entity) or is uncertain to occur but is at the option of the instrument holder. IAS 32 classifies such an instrument as an equity instrument if it has all of the following features: *[IAS 32.16C-D]*

(a)   It entitles the holder to a *pro rata* share of the entity's net assets in the event of the entity's liquidation. The entity's net assets are those assets that remain after deducting all other claims on its assets. A *pro rata* share is determined by:

   (i)   dividing the net assets of the entity on liquidation into units of equal amount; and

   (ii)   multiplying that amount by the number of the units held by the financial instrument holder.

(b)   The instrument is in the class of instruments that is subordinate to all other classes of instruments. To be in such a class the instrument:

   (i)   has no priority over other claims to the assets of the entity on liquidation; and

   (ii)   does not need to be converted into another instrument before it is in the class of instruments that is subordinate to all other classes of instruments.

(c)   All financial instruments in the class of instruments that is subordinate to all other classes of instruments must have an identical contractual obligation for the issuing entity to deliver a *pro rata* share of its net assets on liquidation. *[IAS 32.16C].*

(d)   In addition to the instrument having all the features in (a) to (c) above, the issuer must have no other financial instrument or contract that has:

   (i)   total cash flows based substantially on the profit or loss, the change in the recognised net assets or the change in the fair value of the recognised and unrecognised net assets of the entity (excluding any effects of such instrument or contract); and

   (ii)   the effect of substantially restricting or fixing the residual return to the instrument holders.

   For the purposes of applying this condition, the entity should not consider non-financial contracts with a holder of an instrument described in (a) to (c) above that have contractual terms and conditions that are similar to the contractual terms and conditions of an equivalent contract that might occur between a non-instrument holder and the issuing entity. If the entity cannot determine that this condition is met, it should not classify the instrument as an equity instrument. *[IAS 32.16D].*

Some of these criteria raise some issues of interpretation, which are addressed at 4.6.4 below.

Some of the criteria for classifying as equity financial instruments that entitle the holder to a *pro rata* share of assets only on liquidation are similar to those (in 4.6.2 above) for classifying certain puttable instruments as equity. The difference between these criteria and those for puttable instruments are:

• there is no requirement for there to be no contractual obligations other than those arising on liquidation;

• there is no requirement to consider the expected total cash flows throughout the life of the instrument; and

• the only feature that must be identical among the instruments in the class is the obligation for the issuing entity to deliver to the holder a *pro rata* share of its net assets on liquidation.

The reason for the more relaxed criteria in this case is that the IASB took the view that, given that the only obligation in this case arises on liquidation, there was no need to consider obligations other than those on liquidation. However, the IASB notes that, if an instrument does contain other obligations, these may need to be accounted for separately under IAS 32. *[IAS 32.BC67].*

Chapter 44

4.6.4   Clarification of the exemptions in 4.6.2 and 4.6.3 above

The conditions for treating certain types of puttable instruments (see 4.6.2 above) and instruments repaying a *pro rata* share of net assets on liquidation (see 4.6.3 above) as equity are complex. IAS 32 provides some clarification in respect of the following matters:

- instruments issued by a subsidiary (see 4.6.4.A below);

- determining the level of subordination of an instrument (see condition (b) under 4.6.2 and 4.6.3 above), (see 4.6.4.B below);

- the meaning of 'no obligation to deliver cash or another financial asset' (see condition (d) under 4.6.2 above) in respect of instruments with a requirement to distribute a minimum proportion of profit to shareholders (see 4.6.4.D below);

- other instruments that substantially fix or restrict the residual return to the holder of an instrument (see condition (f)(ii) in 4.6.2 above and condition (d)(ii) in 4.6.3 above), (see 4.6.4.E below); and

- transactions entered into by an instrument holder other than as owner of the entity (see 4.6.4.F below).

One matter on which IAS 32 does not provide further clarification is the meaning of 'identical features' (see condition (c) under 4.6.2 above). This is dealt with in 4.6.4.C below.

4.6.4.A   Instruments issued by a subsidiary

A subsidiary may issue an instrument that falls to be classified as equity in its separate financial statements under one of the exceptions summarised in 4.6.2 and 4.6.3 above. However, in the consolidated financial statements of the subsidiary's parent such an instrument is not recorded as a non-controlling interest, but as a financial liability. *[IAS 32.AG29A].* This reflects the fact that the exceptions in 4.6.2 and 4.6.3 above are both subject to the condition that the instrument concerned is the most subordinated instrument issued by the reporting entity. The IASB took the view that a non-controlling interest, by its nature, can never be regarded as the residual ownership interest in the consolidated financial statements. *[IAS 32.BC68].*

4.6.4.B   Relative subordination of the instrument

The exceptions in 4.6.2 and 4.6.3 above are both subject to the criterion – condition (b) – that the instrument concerned is the most subordinated instrument issued by the reporting entity. As noted at 4.6.1 above, this represents a departure from the normal principle of IAS 32 that the classification of an issued instrument as a financial liability or equity should be determined by reference only to the contractual terms of that instrument.

In order to determine whether an instrument is in the most subordinate class, the entity calculates the instrument's claim on a liquidation as at the date when it classifies the instrument. The entity reassesses the classification if there is a change in relevant circumstances (for example, if it issues or redeems another financial instrument). *[IAS 32.AG14B].* This is discussed further at 4.6.5 below.

An instrument that has a preferential right on liquidation of the entity is not regarded as an instrument with an entitlement to a *pro rata* share of the net assets of the entity. An example might be an instrument that entitles the holder to a fixed dividend on liquidation, in addition to a share of the entity's net assets, when other instruments in the subordinate class with a right to a *pro rata* share of the net assets of the entity do not have the same right on liquidation. *[IAS 32.AG14C].*

If an entity has only one class of financial instruments, that class is treated as if it were subordinate to all other classes. *[IAS 32.AG14D].*

In our view, the test of whether the instrument is the most subordinated has to be applied according to the legal rights of the various classes of instrument, even where what is legally the most subordinated instrument in issue is entitled to the return of only a nominal sum on liquidation which may be dwarfed by the entitlement of other classes of shares.

It should be noted, however, that the requirement for a puttable instrument to be in the most subordinate class of instruments issued by an entity does not preclude other, non-puttable, instruments from being classified as equity at the same time. In an agenda decision issued in March 2009, the Interpretations Committee noted that a financial instrument is first classified as a liability or equity instrument in accordance with the general requirements of IAS 32. That classification is not affected by the existence of puttable instruments.[12] Thus, for example, founders' shares in an investment fund, which are entitled only to the return of their par value on liquidation, would be classified as equity even if less subordinate than a class of puttable shares which also qualify for equity classification. Conversely, if the founders' shares were the most subordinate instruments, the puttable shares would have to be classified as liabilities.

4.6.4.C   Meaning of 'identical features'

Condition (c) under 4.6.2 above requires that 'all financial instruments in the class of instruments that is subordinate to all other classes of instruments have identical features. For example, they must all be puttable, and the formula or other method used to calculate the repurchase or redemption price is the same for all instruments in that class'. The word 'identical' does not normally need much further explanation in the English language. Nevertheless, some have questioned how literally the word must be interpreted in this case.

Consider, for example, an investment fund that issues several types of puttable shares, each equally subordinate, having identical redemption and dividend rights, but different minimum subscription thresholds and subscription fees. Do all these instruments have identical features for the purpose of this exemption? In our view the condition referred to above is primarily designed to ensure that the redemption rights of the shares do not differ. Accordingly, terms that take effect before the shares are issued (as in the example above), or are not financial, should not cause instruments to fail the 'identical features' test. Examples of features which are not financial might include rights to information or management powers. In our opinion, instruments with different features of this kind will not necessarily fail the 'identical features' test, provided such features do not have the potential to impact the redemption rights of the instruments.

Chapter 44

4.6.4.D   *No obligation to deliver cash or another financial asset*

One of the conditions for classifying a financial instrument as equity under 4.6.2 above is that the instrument does not include any contractual obligation to deliver cash or another financial asset to another entity, or to exchange financial assets or financial liabilities with another entity under conditions that are potentially unfavourable to the entity.

Some entities, particularly ones with limited lives, are required by their constitution to distribute a minimum proportion of profits to shareholders or partners each year. Subject to the matters discussed at 4.2 above, such a requirement will normally result in the puttable instrument being considered a liability. It might be argued, firstly, that no obligation arises in these circumstances until profits are made, and secondly that such distributions only represent advance payments of the residual interest in the entity and so are consistent with equity classification. However, the IASB discussed this issue while developing the 2008 amendment and concluded that a contractual obligation existed, the measurement of which was uncertain. Nevertheless, the IASB declined to provide further guidance on this issue as they considered that it would have implications for other projects.

In May 2010 the Interpretations Committee considered a request to clarify whether puttable income trust units, that include contractual provisions to make distributions on a pro-rata basis, can be classified as equity. The submission to the Interpretations Committee argued that such pro-rata obligations should not prevent the instrument from being classified as equity, by analogy to the *Classification of Rights Issues* amendment to IAS 32 (October 2009). The Interpretations Committee decided not to propose any amendment to IAS 32 to deal with this issue, making it fairly clear in the process that they did not believe such an instrument would qualify to be classified as equity.

4.6.4.E   *Instruments that substantially fix or restrict the residual return to the holder of an instrument*

A condition for classifying a financial instrument as equity under 4.6.2 or 4.6.3 above is that the issuing entity has no other financial instrument or contract that has:

- total cash flows based substantially on the profit or loss, the change in the recognised net assets or the change in the fair value of the recognised and unrecognised net assets of the entity; and
- the effect of substantially restricting or fixing the residual return.

IAS 32 notes that the following instruments, when entered into on normal commercial terms with unrelated parties, are unlikely to prevent instruments that otherwise meet the criteria in 4.6.2 or 4.6.3 above from being classified as equity:

- instruments with total cash flows substantially based on specific assets of the entity;
- instruments with total cash flows based on a percentage of revenue;
- contracts designed to reward individual employees for services rendered to the entity; and
- contracts requiring the payment of an insignificant percentage of profit for services rendered or goods provided. *[IAS 32.AG14J].*

4.6.4.F   Transactions entered into by an instrument holder other than as owner of the entity

IAS 32 observes that the holder of a financial instrument subject to one of the exceptions in 4.6.2 or 4.6.3 above may enter into transactions with the entity in a role other than that of an owner. For example, an instrument holder also may be an employee of the entity. IAS 32 requires that only the cash flows and the contractual terms and conditions of the instrument that relate to the instrument holder as an owner of the entity be considered when assessing whether the instrument should be classified as equity under conditions (a) to (e) in 4.6.2 above or conditions (a) to (c) in 4.6.3 above. *[IAS 32.AG14F]*.

An example might be a limited partnership that has limited and general partners. Some general partners may provide a guarantee to the entity and be remunerated for providing that guarantee. In such situations, the guarantee and the associated cash flows relate to the instrument holders in their role as guarantors and not in their roles as owners of the entity. Therefore, such a guarantee and the associated cash flows would not result in the general partners being considered subordinate to the limited partners, and would be disregarded when assessing whether the contractual terms of the limited partnership instruments and the general partnership instruments are identical. *[IAS 32.AG14G]*.

Another example might be a profit or loss sharing arrangement that allocates profit or loss to the instrument holders on the basis of services rendered or business generated during the current and previous years. Such arrangements are regarded as transactions with instrument holders in their role as non-owners and should not be considered when assessing the criteria in conditions (a) to (e) in 4.6.2 above or conditions (a) to (c) in 4.6.3 above. By contrast, profit or loss sharing arrangements, that allocate profit or loss to instrument holders based on the nominal amount of their instruments relative to others in the class, represent transactions with the instrument holders in their roles as owners and should be considered when assessing the criteria in conditions (a) to (e) in 4.6.2 above or conditions (a) to (c) in 4.6.3 above. *[IAS 32.AG14H]*.

IAS 32 notes that, in order for a transaction with an owner to be assessed as being undertaken in that person's capacity as a non-owner, the cash flows and contractual terms and conditions of the transaction must be similar to those of an equivalent transaction that might occur between a non-instrument holder and the issuing entity. *[IAS 32.AG14I]*.

4.6.5   Reclassification of puttable instruments and instruments imposing an obligation only on liquidation

As noted in 4.6.4.B above, IAS 32 requires the entity to continually reassess the classification of such an instrument. The entity classifies a financial instrument as an equity instrument from the date on which it has all the features and meets the conditions set out in 4.6.2 or 4.6.3 above, and reclassifies the instrument from the date on which it ceases to have all those features or meet all those conditions.

For example, if an entity redeems all its issued non-puttable instruments, any puttable instruments that remain outstanding and that have all of the features and meet all the conditions in 4.6.2 above, are reclassified as equity instruments from the date of redemption of the non-puttable instruments. *[IAS 32.16E]*.

Where an instrument, previously classified as an equity instrument, is reclassified as a financial liability, the financial liability is measured at fair value at the date of reclassification, with any difference between the carrying value of the equity instrument and the fair value of the financial liability at the date of reclassification being recognised in equity. *[IAS 32.16F(a)]*.

Where an instrument, previously classified as a financial liability, is reclassified as an equity instrument, the equity instrument is measured at the carrying value of the financial liability at the date of reclassification. *[IAS 32.16F(b)]*.

4.6.6　IFRIC 2

The issue that ultimately led to the publication of IFRIC 2 was the appropriate accounting treatment for the members' contributed capital of a co-operative entity, the members of which are entitled to ask for the return of their investment. However, the scope of IFRIC 2 is not confined to co-operative entities, and extends to any entity whose members may ask for a return of their capital. *[IFRIC 2.1-4]*.

IFRIC 2 states that the contractual right of the holder of a financial instrument to request redemption does not, in itself, require that financial instrument to be classified as a financial liability. Rather, the entity must consider all of the terms and conditions of the financial instrument in determining its classification as a financial liability or equity. Those terms and conditions include relevant local laws, regulations and the entity's governing charter in effect at the date of classification, but not expected future amendments to those laws, regulations or charter. *[IFRIC 2.5]*.

Accordingly, IFRIC 2 provides that an instrument, that would be classified as equity if the holder did not have the right to request redemption, should be classified as an equity instrument where:

- the entity has the unconditional right to refuse redemption;
- local law, regulation or the entity's governing charter imposes an unconditional prohibition on redemption; or
- the members' shares meet the criteria in 4.6.2 or 4.6.3 above for classification as equity. *[IFRIC 2.6-8]*.

IFRIC 2 distinguishes between those prohibitions on redemption in local law, regulation or the entity's governing charter that are 'unconditional' (i.e. they apply at any time) and those which prohibit redemption only when certain conditions – such as liquidity constraints – are met or not met. Prohibitions that apply only in certain circumstances are ignored and therefore would not result in equity classification. *[IFRIC 2.8]*. This is consistent with the fact that under IAS 32 the classification of an instrument as debt or equity is not influenced by considerations of liquidity (see 4.2 above).

In some cases, there may be a partial prohibition on redemption. For example, redemption may be prohibited where its effect would be to reduce the number of members' shares or the amount of paid-in capital below a certain minimum. In such cases, only the amount subject to a prohibition on redemption is treated as equity, unless:

- the entity has the unconditional right to refuse redemption as described above; or

- the members' shares meet the criteria in 4.6.2 or 4.6.3 above for classification as equity.

If the minimum number of members' shares or amount of paid-in capital changes, an appropriate transfer is made between financial liabilities and equity. *[IFRIC 2.9]*.

Any financial liability for the redemption of instruments not classified as equity is measured at fair value. In the case of members' shares with a redemption feature, the entity measures the fair value of the financial liability for redemption at no less than the maximum amount payable under the redemption provisions of its governing charter or applicable law, discounted from the first date that the amount could be required to be paid. *[IFRIC 2.10]*.

In accordance with the general provisions of IAS 32 regarding interest and dividends (see 8 below), distributions to holders of equity instruments are recognised directly in equity, net of any income tax benefits. Interest, dividends and other returns relating to financial instruments classified as financial liabilities are expenses, regardless of whether those amounts paid are legally characterised as dividends, interest or otherwise. *[IFRIC 2.11]*.

IFRIC 2 clarifies that, where members act as customers of the entity (for example, where it is a bank and members have current or deposit accounts or similar contracts with the bank), such accounts and contracts are financial liabilities of the entity. *[IFRIC 2.6]*.

4.7 Perpetual debt

'Perpetual debt' instruments are those that provide the holder with the contractual right to receive payments on account of interest at fixed dates extending into the indefinite future, either with no right to receive a return of principal or a right to a return of principal under terms that make it very unlikely or very far in the future. However, this does not mean that 'perpetual debt' is to be classified as equity, since the issue proceeds will typically represent the net present value of the liability for interest payments.

For example, an entity may issue a financial instrument requiring it to make annual payments in perpetuity equal to a stated interest rate of 8% applied to a stated par or principal amount of €1 million. Assuming 8% to be the market rate of interest for the instrument when issued, the issuer assumes a contractual obligation to make a stream of future interest payments having a fair value (present value) of €1 million. Thus perpetual debt gives rise to a financial liability of the issuer. *[IAS 32.AG6]*.

4.8 Differences of classification between consolidated and single entity financial statements

4.8.1 Consolidated financial statements

In consolidated financial statements, IAS 32 requires an entity to present non-controlling interests (i.e. the interests of other parties in the equity and income of its subsidiaries) within equity, in accordance with IAS 1 – *Presentation of Financial*

Statements (see Chapter 3 at 3.1.5) and IFRS 10 – *Consolidated Financial Statements* (see Chapter 7 at 4 and Chapter 9 at 8). *[IAS 32.AG29]*.

When classifying a financial instrument (or a component of it) in consolidated financial statements, an entity must consider all the terms and conditions agreed between all members of the group and the holders of the instrument in determining whether the group as a whole has an obligation to deliver cash or another financial asset in respect of the instrument or to settle it in a manner that results in its classification as a financial liability. *[IAS 32.AG29]*.

For example, a subsidiary in a group may issue a financial instrument and a parent or other group entity may then agree additional terms directly with the holders of the instrument so as to guarantee some or all of the payments to be made under the instrument. The effect of this is that the subsidiary may have discretion over distributions or redemption, but the group as a whole does not. *[IAS 32.AG29]*.

Accordingly, the subsidiary may appropriately classify the instrument without regard to these additional terms in its individual financial statements. For the purposes of the consolidated financial statements, however, the effect of the other agreements between members of the group and the holders of the instrument is to create an obligation or settlement provision, so that the instrument (or the component of it that is subject to the obligation) is classified as a financial liability. *[IAS 32.AG29]*.

Thus it is quite possible for a financial instrument to be classified as an equity instrument in the financial statements of the issuing subsidiary but as a financial liability in the financial statements of the group.

4.8.2   *Single entity financial statements*

The converse of the discussion in 4.8.1 above is that it is not uncommon for instruments that are classified as equity in the consolidated financial statements to give rise to liabilities and embedded derivatives in the financial statements of individual members of the group.

This is because a group wishing to raise finance for its operations will generally do so through a group entity specialising in finance-raising, which will then on-lend the proceeds of the finance raised to the relevant operating subsidiaries. The terms of the intragroup on-lending transactions will often be such that finance which constitutes equity from the perspective of group as a whole may be a liability in the individual financial statements of the finance-raising entity itself.

For example, the finance-raising entity might issue an irredeemable instrument with a 'dividend blocker' clause (see 4.5.3.A above), under the terms of which that entity is not required to make any payments to the holder unless the ultimate parent entity of the group pays a dividend to ordinary shareholders. Absent any other terms requiring its classification, in whole or in part, as a liability under IAS 32, the instrument will be treated as equity in the consolidated financial statements, since payments under the instrument are contingent on an event within the control of the group (payment of a dividend by the parent entity). In the finance-raising entity's single entity financial statements, however, the instrument should be classified as a liability, because the subsidiary cannot control the dividend policy of its parent and could therefore be forced to make payments to the holder of the instrument as a consequence of its parent entity paying a dividend.

Another common example is that a group may issue a convertible bond which is actually structured as a series of transactions along the following lines:

- a finance-raising subsidiary issues a bond, giving the holder a right to receive fixed, non-discretionary interest payments, which converts into preference shares of that subsidiary; and

- at the time that this conversion occurs, the parent entity is required to acquire the preference shares of the subsidiary from the holder (i.e. the previous bondholder) in exchange for equity of the parent.

Absent any other terms requiring classification as a liability under IAS 32, the instrument will be treated as a compound instrument, consisting of a liability and an equity component (see 6 below) in the consolidated financial statements. The instrument as a whole might be classified as a liability in the subsidiaries financial statements, if (for example) the preference shares issued on conversion by the subsidiary have terms that require them to be classified as a liability by IAS 32. In that case, the subsidiary will have issued an instrument that the holder can exchange either for cash or for a debt instrument.

From the subsidiary's perspective, therefore, there is no equity component to the instrument and the overall instrument would be classified as a liability that, under the general rules of IAS 39, must be recorded at fair value on initial recognition, which will typically be lower than the proceeds received. This is because the pricing of the instrument as a whole considers the conversion option that the holder receives, so that the interest is typically paid at a rate below the rate that would apply to a liability without a conversion option. In other words, the holder of the instrument 'pays' for the conversion option through a reduced entitlement to interest.

The group accounts reflect the difference between the proceeds of issue and the fair value of the liability component as the equity component (see 6 below). In the financial statements of the issuing subsidiary, the most appropriate accounting treatment, in our view, would be to treat this difference as an equity contribution by the parent, reflecting the fact that the subsidiary can borrow on a reduced interest basis due to the conversion option issued by the parent. Moreover, in the period prior to conversion, the parent is required to account for its contingent forward contract to acquire the preference shares in the finance company.

4.9 Reclassification of instruments

It happens from time to time that the terms of a financial instrument are modified in such a way that an instrument that was an equity instrument at the original date of issue would be classified as a financial liability if issued at the date of modification, or *vice versa*. Alternatively, the terms of the instrument may remain unaltered, but external circumstances may change. For example,

- an instrument might have been issued subject to a contingent settlement provision (see 4.3 above) that, at the date of issue, was within the control of the issuer, but ceases to be so at a later date,

- an instrument might have been issued subject to a contingent settlement provision (see 4.3 above) that, at the date of issue, was not considered genuine, but becomes so at a later date, or

- an instrument might have been issued requiring interest payments to be made when contractually mandatory interest payments are made on another instrument issued by the entity, the 'linked' instrument (see 4.5.7 above), but this linked instrument is later repaid by the entity.

Such situations raise the question of whether such changes of terms or circumstances should lead to reclassification of the instruments affected in the financial statements and, if so, how the reclassification should be accounted for.

4.9.1   Change of terms

IAS 32 gives no guidance as to whether reclassification is required, permitted or prohibited. The requirement of IAS 32 paragraph 15 that an instrument be classified 'on initial recognition' (see 4 above) could be read as implying that classification occurs only on initial recognition and is not subsequently revisited.

However, we do not consider this an appropriate analysis. A change in the terms of an instrument is equivalent to the issue of a new instrument in settlement of the original instrument. Such an exchange transaction would be accounted for by derecognising the settled instrument and recognising (and classifying as a financial liability or equity) the new replacement instrument. This analysis has been confirmed by an agenda decision of the Interpretations Committee (see 4.9.1.A below). In our view, it would be inappropriate to apply a different accounting treatment to a change in the terms of the original instrument which has the same economic result.

4.9.1.A   Equity instrument to financial liability

At its meeting in November 2006, the Interpretations Committee considered a situation in which an amendment to the contractual terms of an equity instrument resulted in the instrument being classified as a financial liability. Two issues were discussed:

- the measurement of the financial liability at the date of the amendment to the terms; and

- the treatment of any difference between the carrying amount of the previously recognised equity instrument and the amount of the financial liability recognised.

The Interpretations Committee decided not to add this issue to its agenda because, in its view, the accounting treatment is clear. The financial liability is initially recognised at fair value under the general provisions of IAS 39 (see Chapter 47 at 3). Any difference between the carrying amount of the liability and that of the previously recognised equity instrument is recognised is equity in accordance with the general principle of IAS 32 (see 8 below) that no gain or loss is recognised in profit or loss on the purchase, sale, issue or cancellation of an entity's own equity instruments.[13]

4.9.1.B   Financial liability to equity instrument

In the converse situation where the terms of a financial liability are changed such that the instrument then meets the definition of an equity instrument, we believe, as above, that the instrument should be reclassified to equity. That situation is analogous to a debt-for-equity swap as discussed at 7 below and, therefore, should be accounted for in accordance with IFRIC 19, where that interpretation applies. The most likely situation in which IFRIC 19 would not apply would be in a transaction with shareholders in their capacity as shareholders, as discussed at 7.3 below.

4.9.2   Change of circumstances

The nature and risk profile of a financial instrument may change as a result of a change in circumstances. Such a change may occur simply as the result of the passage of time. For example, in 2015 an entity might issue a bond mandatorily convertible at the end of 2018. The conversion terms are that the holder will receive a number of the issuer's equity shares, being the lower of 100 shares or a number of shares determined according to a formula based on the share price at 31 December 2015.

At the date of issue, this instrument is a financial liability since it involves an obligation to deliver a variable number of equity instruments. At 31 December 2015, however, the number of shares to be delivered on conversion can be determined and becomes fixed. Accordingly, if considered as at 31 December 2015 and later, the instrument is an equity instrument (absent any other terms requiring its continued classification as financial liability).

In our view, the liability component of the bond representing the obligation to deliver a variable number of equity instruments on 31 December 2018 expires on 31 December 2015. This liability component must therefore be derecognised (see Chapter 50 at 6), to be replaced with an equity component (see the discussion at 7 below of the appropriate accounting treatment in such circumstances).

Changes of circumstances for reasons other than the passage of time are more challenging. For example, an entity might issue a convertible bond denominated in its functional currency at that time. Such a bond would have an equity component (see 6 below). Subsequently, the entity's functional currency changes but the bond remains outstanding, now denominated in a currency other than the entity's functional currency. If a bond with these terms were issued after the change in functional currency, it would be classified in its entirety as a financial liability, since the principal of the bond would not be a 'fixed' amount by reference to the entity's functional currency (see 5.2.3 below). This raises the question of whether the equity component of the bond should be reclassified as a financial liability on the change in functional currency.

Chapter 44

In our view, there are arguments both for and against reclassification. As the arguments for reclassification are to some extent a rebuttal of those against reclassification, we discuss the latter first.

4.9.2.A   Arguments against reclassification

The principal arguments against reclassification are:

(a)   The requirement of paragraph 15 of IAS 32 to classify an instrument as a financial liability or equity 'on initial recognition' (see 4 above) could be read as implying that such classification occurs only on initial recognition and is not subsequently revisited.

(b)   Paragraphs IG35 and IG36 of the implementation guidance to IFRS 1 – *First-time Adoption of International Financial Reporting Standards* – require a compound instrument to be analysed into its components, based on the substance of the contractual arrangement, as at the date on which the instrument first satisfied the recognition criteria in IAS 32. Changes to the terms of the instrument after that date are taken into account on first-time adoption, but changes in circumstances are not.

This could be construed as establishing a more general principle that changes in the terms of instruments should be accounted for but changes in circumstances should not.

(c)   IFRIC 9 – *Reassessment of Embedded Derivatives* (see Chapter 43 at 7.1) clarifies that the assessment required by IAS 39 of whether or not an embedded derivative is required to be separated from its host contract is undertaken when the entity first becomes party to the contract, and is not revisited in the light of any subsequently changing circumstances. IFRIC 9 gives a change in functional currency as a specific example of a change in circumstance that does not lead to a reassessment.

(d)   IFRIC 2 and the provisions of IAS 32 requiring certain types of puttable and redeemable instrument to be classified as equity (see 4.6 above) each require accounting recognition to be given to some changes in the classification of a financial instrument as the result of changing circumstances. This implies that, absent such specific guidance, the 'default' position would be that there should be no accounting consequences, an inference reinforced by the requirement that the provisions of IAS 32 requiring certain types of puttable and redeemable instrument to be classified as equity must not be applied by analogy to other transactions.

4.9.2.B   Arguments for reclassification

The principal arguments in favour of reclassification are:

(a)   The definitions of financial liability and equity both use the present tense, implying that the definitions are to be applied at each reporting date, absent any more specific provision against doing so.

This is consistent with our view that some transactions falling within the scope of IFRS 2 – *Share-based Payment* – should be reclassified from equity-settled to cash-settled and *vice versa* in the light of changing circumstances (see Chapter 31 at 10.2.3). However, it could be argued that such an analogy is inappropriate given the significant differences between the definitions of equity and financial liability in IAS 32 and those of equity-settled and cash-settled share-based payment transaction in IFRS 2 (see 5.1.1 below).

(b)   The provisions of IFRS 1 referred to in (b) under 4.9.2.A above are contained in implementation guidance, which is not part of the standard. Moreover, it refers only to compound financial instruments, and appears to be implicitly addressing changes in market interest rates that might alter the arithmetical split of the instrument into its financial liability and equity components (see 6 below), rather than more general changes in circumstances.

(c)   The fact that IFRIC 9 (see (c) under 4.9.2.A above) was issued after IFRS 1, and again addresses a specific issue, indicates that a general prohibition on reassessment should not be inferred from IFRS 1. Had the Interpretations Committee wished to clarify that this was the case, they could easily have done so in IFRIC 9, which, moreover, is stated as being an interpretation of IAS 39, IFRS 1 and IFRS 3 – *Business Combinations* – not IAS 32.

However, it is equally difficult to argue that there is an implied 'default' requirement for reclassification, given the specific requirement for reclassification of certain puttable and redeemable instruments on a change in circumstances referred to in (d) in 4.9.2.A above.

What emerges from the analysis above is a lack of definitive general guidance as to whether reclassification of an instrument is permitted, required or prohibited. Accordingly, we believe that in some circumstances, such as a change in the entity's functional currency, the entity may choose, as a matter of accounting policy, either to reclassify or not to reclassify an instrument following that change of circumstances which, had it occurred before initial recognition of the instrument, would have changed its classification. The policy adopted should, in our view, be followed consistently in respect of all changes of circumstances of a similar nature.

However, some changes in circumstances can be more fundamental to the nature of the contract. For example the change in circumstances could lead to the instruments delivered under a contract ceasing to be equity instruments of the reporting entity. This situation could arise where a parent had entered into a derivative involving delivery of the equity instruments of a subsidiary and subsequently loses control of that subsidiary. Here the former subsidiary's equity instruments would now represent financial assets rather than non-controlling interests (equity) of the group. In these circumstances, it may be more difficult to argue that not reclassifying the derivative contract is appropriate.

5   CONTRACTS SETTLED BY DELIVERY OF THE ENTITY'S OWN EQUITY INSTRUMENTS

This Section deals with contracts, other than those within the scope of IFRS 2 (see Chapter 31), settled in equity instruments issued by the settler. Throughout the discussion in Section 5, 'equity instrument(s)' excludes certain puttable and redeemable instruments classified as equity under the exceptions discussed at 4.6.2 and 4.6.3 above (any contract involving the receipt or delivery of such instruments is a financial asset or liability – see 4.1 above).

Chapter 44

In order for an instrument to be classified as an equity instrument under IAS 32, it is not sufficient that it involves the reporting entity delivering or receiving its own equity (as opposed to cash or another financial asset). The number of equity instruments delivered, and the consideration for them, must be fixed – the so called 'fixed for fixed' requirement. Contracts that will be settled other than by delivery of a fixed number of shares for a fixed amount of cash do not generally meet the definition of equity. The IASB considered that to treat any transaction settled in the entity's own shares as an equity instrument would not deal adequately with transactions in which an entity is using its own shares as 'currency' – for example, where it has an obligation to pay a fixed or determinable amount that is settled in a variable number of its own shares. *[IAS 32.BC21]*. In such transactions the counterparty bears no share price risk, and is therefore not in the same position as a 'true' equity shareholder.

Where such a contract is not classified as an equity instrument by IAS 32, it will be accounted for in accordance with the general provisions of IAS 39 or, where applicable, IFRS 9 as either a financial liability or a derivative.

Broadly speaking:

- a non-derivative contract involving the issue of a fixed number of own equity instruments is an equity instrument (see 5.1 below);

- a non-derivative contract involving the issue of a variable number of own equity instruments is a financial liability (see 5.2.1 below);

- a derivative contract involving the sale or purchase of a fixed number of own equity instruments for a fixed amount of cash or other financial assets is an equity instrument (see 5.1 below);

- a derivative contract for the purchase by an entity of its own equity instruments, even if for a fixed amount of cash or other financial assets (and therefore an equity instrument) may give rise to a financial liability in respect of the cash or other financial assets to be paid. However, the initial recognition of the liability results in a reduction in equity and not in an expense (see 5.3 below). In other words, whilst there is a liability to pay cash under the contract, the contract itself is an equity instrument (and is therefore not subject to periodic remeasurement to fair value);

- a derivative contract involving the delivery or receipt of:

  - a fixed number of own equity instruments for a variable amount of cash or other financial assets;

  - a variable number of own equity instruments for a variable amount of cash or other financial assets; or

  - an amount of cash or own equity instruments with a fair value equivalent to the difference between a fixed number of own equity instruments and a fixed amount of cash or other financial assets (i.e. a net-settled derivative contract)

  is a financial asset or financial liability (see 5.2 below); and

- a derivative financial instrument with settlement options is a financial asset or liability, unless all possible settlement options would result in classification as equity (see 5.2.8 below).

There are some difficulties of interpretation surrounding the treatment of certain contracts to issue equity (see 5.4 below).

In undertaking the analysis required by IAS 32, it is sometimes helpful, where the detailed guidance in the standard is not entirely clear, to consider whether the instrument or contract under discussion exposes the holder or the issuer to the risk of movements in the fair value of the issuer's equity. If the holder is at risk to the same degree as equity investors in the entity, it is likely that the instrument or contract should be classified as equity. If, however, the entity bears the risk of movements in the fair value of the entity's equity, or the holder bears some risk, but less than that borne by equity investors in the entity, it is likely that the contract should be classified, at least in part, as a liability.

5.1 Contracts accounted for as equity instruments

A contract that will be settled by the entity delivering or receiving a fixed number of its own equity instruments in exchange for a fixed amount of cash (see 5 above) or another financial asset is an equity instrument, although a liability may be recorded for any cash payable, by the entity on settlement of the contract. An example would be an issued share option that gives the counterparty a right to buy a fixed number of the entity's shares for a fixed price or for a fixed stated principal amount of a bond (see 6.3.2.A below). *[IAS 32.22]*.

The fair value of such a contract may change due to variations in market interest rates and the share price. However, provided that such changes in fair value do not affect the amount of cash or other financial assets to be paid or received, or the number of equity instruments to be received or delivered, on settlement of the contract, the contract is an equity instrument and accounted for as such. *[IAS 32.22]*.

Any consideration received (such as the premium received for a written option or warrant on the entity's own shares) is added directly to equity. Any consideration paid (such as the premium paid for a purchased option) is deducted directly from equity. Changes in the fair value of an equity instrument are not recognised in financial statements. *[IAS 32.22, AG27(a)]*. This is consistent with the treatment of equity under the *Conceptual Framework* (and as defined in IAS 32 – see 3 above) as a residual after deducting total liabilities from total assets rather than an item 'in its own right'.

IAS 32 requires some types of puttable instruments (see 4.6.2 above) and instruments that impose an obligation to deliver a *pro rata* share of net assets only on liquidation (see 4.6.3 above) to be treated as equity instruments. However, a contract that is required to be settled by the entity receiving or delivering either of these types of equity instrument is a financial asset or financial liability, even when it involves the exchange of a fixed amount of cash or other financial assets for a fixed number of such instruments. *[IAS 32.22A, AG13]*.

Chapter 44

5.1.1   *Comparison with IFRS 2 – Share-based Payment*

The approach in IAS 32 differs from that in IFRS 2. IFRS 2 essentially treats any transaction that falls within its scope and can be settled only in shares (or other equity instruments) as an equity instrument, regardless of whether the number of shares to be delivered is fixed or variable (see Chapter 31 at 1.4.1). The two standards also differ as regards to:

- the classification of financial instruments that can be settled at the issuer's option in either equity instruments or cash (or other financial assets). Broadly, IFRS 2 requires the classification to be based on the likely outcome, whereas IAS 32 focuses on the strict legal obligations imposed by the contract; and

- the definition of equity instrument. IFRS 2 refers to the exchange of a 'fixed or determinable' amount of cash, whereas IAS 32 refers to the exchange of a 'fixed' amount of cash. This means that written options to issue own equity with a foreign currency strike price are typically equity instruments under IFRS 2, but financial assets or liabilities under IAS 32, subject to the limited exception for short-term rights issues (see 5.2.3.A below).

The IASB offers some (pragmatic rather than conceptual) explanation for these differences in the Basis for Conclusions to IFRS 2. First, it is argued that to apply IAS 32 to share option plans would mean that a variable share option plan (i.e. one where the number of shares varied according to performance) would give rise to more volatile (and typically greater) cost than a fixed plan (i.e. one where the number of shares to be awarded is fixed from the start), even if the same number of shares was ultimately delivered under each plan, which would have 'undesirable consequences'. *[IFRS 2.BC109].* This serves only to beg the question of why it is not equally 'undesirable' for the same result to arise in accounting for share-settled contracts within the scope of IAS 32 rather than IFRS 2. Second, it is noted that this is just one of several inconsistencies between IFRS 2 and IAS 32 which will be addressed in the round as part of the IASB's review of accounting for debt and equity. *[IFRS 2.BC110].* As discussed further at 12 below, this review remains somewhat more distant than was probably envisaged when IFRS 2 was issued in 2004.

5.1.2   *Number of equity instruments issued adjusted for capital restructuring or other event*

Entities, particularly larger listed companies, routinely restructure their equity capital. This may take many forms, including:

- structural changes in the issuer's ordinary shares (such as a share split, a share consolidation or a reclassification of the outstanding ordinary shares of the issuer);

- a repurchase of shares;

- a distribution of reserves or premiums, by way of extraordinary dividend;

- a payment of a dividend, or extraordinary dividend, in shares; or

- a bonus share or rights issue to existing shareholders.

Accordingly, contracts for the purchase or delivery of an entity's own equity often provide that the number of shares specified in the contract is modified in the event of such a restructuring. This provides protection to both the holder of the contract and to existing shareholders, by ensuring that their relative rights remain the same before and after the restructuring. For example, an entity with shares with a nominal (par) value of €1 might enter into an agreement that requires it to issue '100 shares'. If, before execution of that agreement, the entity has split each €1 share into ten €0.10 shares, it must issue 1,000, not 100, shares in order to give effect to the intention of the contract.

Such adjustment formulae are most commonly seen in the terms of convertible instruments (see 6 below for convertible instrument classification), so that the number of shares into which the bonds eventually convert will take account of any capital restructuring between issue and conversion of the bond, with the broad intention of putting the holders of the bond in the same position with respect to other equity holders before and after the restructuring. In addition, the terms of many convertible instruments provide for similar adjustment upon the occurrence of other actions or events which would affect the position of the convertible bondholders relative to other equity holders. Such actions or events may include, for example:

- the payment of ordinary dividends;
- an issue of equity at less than current market value;
- the repurchase of equity at more than current market value;
- the issue of further convertible securities at less than fair market value; or
- the acquisition of assets in exchange for equity at more than fair market value.

This raises the question of whether a contract with any such terms can be classified as equity under IAS 32, since the number of shares ultimately issued on conversion is not fixed at the outset, but may vary depending on whether a restructuring or other event occurs before conversion. In our view, an adjustment to the number of equity instruments issued in such circumstances should not be considered to result in the issue of a variable number of shares, where its purpose is to ensure that the bondholder's equity interest is not diluted or augmented. In other words, if the adjustment attempts to put the holders of the instruments into the same economic position relative to ordinary shareholders after the restructuring as they were in before the restructuring, then the fixed for fixed criterion is still met. We consider that the potential dilution or augmentation in the bondholder's equity interest which is to be adjusted for should be determined in comparison to the effect of the event on the other equity holders in aggregate. Thus, if shares are issued to new shareholders at a discount, the dilution suffered by the bondholders should be calculated by reference to the total number of shares in existence following the new issue.

The effect of such an adjustment is that the risks and rewards of the bondholder are more closely aligned to those of a holder of ordinary shares. IAS 32 generally treats contracts involving a variable number of equity instruments as a financial liability because the effect of the variability is that the counterparty is not exposed to any movement in the fair value of the equity instruments between the inception and execution of the contract. In this case, however, the variability is introduced so as to ensure that the counterparty remains exposed to any movement in the fair value of the equity instruments, and maintains the same interest in the equity relative to other shareholders.

The same question arises in circumstances where a convertible bond is convertible into a fixed percentage of equity. This is discussed under 6.6.6 below.

The Interpretations Committee considered a number of 'fixed for fixed' issues raised by constituents at its November 2009 meeting. However, the Interpretations Committee concluded that the Board's project *Financial Instruments with Characteristics of Equity* was expected to address issues relating to the fixed for fixed condition, and that the Interpretations Committee would therefore not add this to its agenda. As discussed further at 12 below, work on this project was suspended between October 2010 and October 2014, but has now restarted.

5.1.3   *Stepped up exercise price*

Another type of adjustment which is commonly found is where an entity issues subscription shares that have a stepped exercise price, which is fixed at inception and increases with the passage of time. Such subscription shares are typically issued as bonus shares on a *pro rata* basis to existing shareholders and give the holder the right (but not the obligation) to subscribe for a certain number of ordinary shares, at a certain price and at a certain time in the future. Our view is that subscription shares that have a stepped exercise price meet the 'fixed for fixed' condition only if the exercise prices are fixed at inception and for the entire term of the instrument, such that at any point in time the exercise price is pre-determined at the issuance of the subscription shares. If the exercise price per share is linked to an index of any kind, the 'fixed for fixed' condition is not met and the contract to issue the shares would not be classified as an equity instrument.

5.1.4   *Exchange of fixed amounts of equity (equity for equity)*

As discussed above, IAS 32 requires a contract settled in own equity to be classified as equity if, *inter alia*, it involves the exchange of a fixed amount of cash (or other financial assets) for a fixed amount of equity. This begs the question of how to classify a contract that provides for the exchange of a fixed amount of one class of the entity's equity for a fixed amount of another class. Examples might be:

- a warrant allowing the holder of a preference share classified as equity (see 4.5 above) to exchange it for an ordinary equity share;

- in consolidated financial statements, an option for a shareholder of a partly-owned subsidiary (classified within equity in the consolidated financial statements) to exchange a fixed number of shares in the subsidiary for a fixed number of shares in the parent.

One view might be that, as such a contract does not fall within the definition of an 'equity instrument' in accordance with IAS 32 it must therefore be accounted for as a derivative. The contrary view would be that the contract is so clearly an equity instrument that it should be accounted for as such. Those who hold this view would argue that the absence of any reference to such 'fixed equity for fixed equity' contracts in IAS 32 does not reflect a conscious decision by the IASB, but rather indicates that the IASB never considered such contracts at all.

A third view might be that the analysis may depend upon the specific terms of the equity instruments. For example, if the equity instrument being exchanged has debt-like features (e.g. it pays regular, but discretionary, coupons), and is denominated in the same currency as the entity's functional currency, the contract would be classified as equity, but if it were denominated in a different currency, the contact would, for the reasons discussed at 5.2.2 below, be classified as a derivative.

5.2 Contracts accounted for as financial assets or financial liabilities

5.2.1 Variable number of equity instruments

An entity may have a contractual right or obligation to receive or deliver a number of its own shares or other equity instruments that varies so that the fair value of the entity's own equity instruments to be received or delivered equals the amount of the contractual right or obligation.

The right or obligation may be for:

- a fixed amount – e.g. as many shares as are worth £100; or
- an amount that fluctuates in part or in full in response to changes in a variable other than the market price of the entity's own equity instruments, such as movements in interest rates, commodity prices, or the price of a financial instrument – e.g. as many shares as are worth:
  - 100 ounces of gold;
  - £100 plus interest at LIBOR plus 200 basis points;
  - 100 government bonds; or
  - 100 shares in a particular entity.

Such a contract is a financial asset or liability. Even though the contract must, or may, be settled through receipt or delivery of the entity's own equity instruments, the number of own equity instruments required to settle the contract will vary. The contract will therefore not fulfil the requirements of an equity instrument, and is therefore a financial asset or financial liability. *[IAS 32.21, AG27(d)]*.

5.2.2 Fixed number of equity instruments for variable consideration

A contract that will be settled by the entity delivering or receiving a fixed number of its own equity instruments in exchange for a variable amount of cash or another financial asset is a financial asset or financial liability. An example is a contract for the entity to deliver 100 of its own equity instruments in return for an amount of cash calculated to equal the value of 100 ounces of gold, *[IAS 32.24]*, or 100 specified government bonds. As discussed at 5.2.3 below, it would also include a contract for the entity to deliver 100 of its own equity instruments in return for a fixed amount of cash denominated in a currency other than its own functional currency.

Chapter 44

5.2.3   *Fixed amount of cash (or other financial assets) denominated in a currency other than the entity's functional currency*

Some contracts require an entity to issue a fixed number of equity instruments in exchange for a fixed amount of cash denominated in a currency other than the entity's functional currency. Such contracts raise a problem of interpretation illustrated by the example in paragraph 24 of IAS 32 (referred to in 5.2.1 above) of a contract being a financial asset or financial liability where the reporting entity is required 'to deliver 100 of its own equity instruments in return for an amount of cash calculated to equal the value of 100 ounces of gold'. If one substitutes '100 US dollars' for '100 ounces of gold', the latent problem becomes apparent.

Suppose a UK entity (with the pound sterling as its functional currency) issues a £100 bond convertible into a fixed number of its equity shares. As discussed in more detail at 6 below, IAS 32 requires this to be accounted for by splitting it into a liability component (the obligation to pay interest and repay principal) and an equity component (the holder's right to convert into equity). In this case the equity component is the right to convert the fixed stated £100 principal of the bond (see 6.3.2.A below) into a fixed number of shares.

Suppose instead, however, that the UK entity (with the pound sterling as its functional currency) issues a 100 US dollar bond convertible into a fixed number of its shares. The conversion feature effectively gives the bondholder the right to acquire a fixed number of shares for a fixed stated principal (see 6.3.2.A below) of $100 – is this a 'fixed amount' of cash, or is it to be regarded as being just as variable, in terms of its conversion into the functional currency of the pound sterling, as 100 ounces of gold?

If the conclusion is that $100 is a fixed amount of cash, the conversion right is accounted for as an equity component of the bond – in other words a value is assigned to it on initial recognition and it is not subsequently remeasured (see 6.2.1 below). If, on the other hand, the conclusion is that $100 is not a fixed amount of cash, then the conversion right (as an embedded derivative not regarded by IAS 39 as closely related to the host contract – see Chapter 43 at 4) is accounted for as a separate derivative financial liability, introducing potentially significant volatility into the financial statements.

There is no obvious answer to this. A contention that the $100 is a 'fixed amount' of cash is hard to reconcile with the fact that a contract to issue shares for 'as many pounds sterling as are worth $100' would clearly involve the issue of a fixed number of shares for a variable amount of cash and would therefore not be an equity instrument.

The Interpretations Committee considered this issue at its meeting in April 2005. The Committee noted that although this matter was not directly addressed in IAS 32, it was clear that, when the question is considered in conjunction with guidance in other Standards, particularly IAS 39, any obligation denominated in a foreign currency represents a variable amount of cash. Consequently, the Committee concluded that a contract settled by an entity delivering a fixed number of its own equity instruments in exchange for a fixed amount of foreign currency should be classified as a liability.[14]

5.2.3.A Rights issues with a price fixed in a currency other than the entity's functional currency

In July 2009, as a result of a recommendation from the Interpretations Committee, the IASB reconsidered this matter in the specific context of rights issues (options to purchase additional shares at a fixed price) where the price is denominated in a currency other than the entity's functional currency. The IASB was advised that the Interpretations Committee's conclusion was being applied to rights issues, with the result that the rights were being accounted for as derivative liabilities with changes in fair value being recognised in profit or loss. HSBC explained that such accounting would result in the recognition of a loss of $4.7 billion in the first quarter of 2009.

Extract 44.2: HSBC Holdings plc (2009)

Interim Management Statement Q1 2009 [extract]

Accounting impact of HSBC's Rights Issue [extract]

On 2 March 2009, HSBC announced a 5 for 12 Rights Issue of 5,060 million new ordinary shares at 254 pence per share, which was authorised by the shareholders in a general meeting on 19 March 2009. The offer period commenced on 20 March 2009, and closed for acceptance on 3 April 2009. Under IFRSs, the offer of rights is treated as a derivative because substantially all of the issue was denominated in currencies other than the Company's functional currency of US dollars, and accordingly HSBC was not able to demonstrate that it was issuing a fixed number of shares for a fixed amount of US dollars, which is the criterion under IFRSs for HSBC to account for the offer of rights in shareholders' equity. The derivative liability was measured at inception of the offer as the difference between the share price at that date and the rights price, with a corresponding debit to shareholders' equity. The revaluation of this derivative liability over the offer period, arising from an increase in the share price, has resulted in the recognition of a loss in the income statement of US$4.7 billion. The derivative liability expired on acceptance of the offer, and the closing balance was credited to shareholders' equity. Accordingly, there is no overall impact on the Group's shareholders' equity, capital position or distributable reserves.

Consequently, in October 2009, the IASB made a limited amendment to IAS 32 so as to require a rights issue granted *pro rata* to an entity's existing shareholders for a fixed amount of cash to be classified as equity, regardless of the currency in which the exercise price is denominated. *[IAS 32.11]*.

This amendment does not apply to other instruments that grant the holder the right to purchase the entity's own equity instruments, such as the conversion feature in a convertible bond. It also does not apply to long-dated foreign currency rights issues, which are therefore classified as financial liabilities if the strike price is denominated in a foreign currency. The reason for the restricted scope of the amendment is that the IASB countenanced an exception to the 'fixed for fixed' concept in IAS 32 for short-dated rights issues only because the rights are distributed *pro rata* to existing shareholders, and can therefore be seen as a transaction with owners in their capacity as such. *[IAS 32BC4I]*. The IASB does not consider long-dated transactions as primarily transactions with owners in their capacity as owners. *[IAS 32.BC4K]*.

5.2.4   *Instrument with equity settlement alternative of significantly higher value than cash settlement alternative*

A financial instrument is also a financial liability if it provides that on settlement the entity will deliver either:

(a)   cash or another financial asset; or

(b)   a number of its own shares whose value is determined to exceed substantially the value of the cash or other financial asset.

IAS 32 explains that, although the entity does not have an explicit contractual obligation to deliver cash or another financial asset, the value of the share settlement alternative is such that the entity will settle in cash. In any event, the holder has in substance been guaranteed receipt of an amount that is at least equal to the cash settlement option. *[IAS 32.20].*

5.2.5   *Fixed number of equity instruments with variable value*

A contract is a financial asset or financial liability if it is to be settled in a fixed number of shares, the value of which will be varied (e.g. by modification of the rights attaching to them) so as to be equal to a fixed amount or an amount based on changes in an underlying variable. *[IAS 32.AG27(d)].*

5.2.6   *Fixed amount of cash determined by reference to share price*

An entity might enter into an option or forward contract to sell a fixed number of equity shares for a fixed price, where the price is determined by reference to the share price. For example, it might contract to sell 100 shares for £10 each if the share price is between £0 and £10, and for £15 each if the price is higher than £10. Considered as a whole, the contract provides for the exchange of a fixed number of equity instruments for a variable amount of cash, and is therefore a derivative financial liability.

5.2.7   *Net-settled contracts over own equity*

The value of a contract over an entity's own equity instruments at the date of settlement is the difference between the value of the fixed number of equity instruments to be delivered by one party and the fixed amount of cash (or other financial assets) to be delivered by the other party. If such a contract allows for net settlement, it can then be settled by a transfer (of cash, other financial assets, or the entity's own equity) of a fair value equal to this difference. It is inherent in the general definition of an equity instrument in IAS 32 that a contract settled by a single net payment (generally referred to as net cash-settled or net equity-settled as the case may be) is a financial asset or financial liability and not an equity instrument. This is notwithstanding the fact that an economically equivalent contract settled gross (i.e. by physical delivery of the equity instruments in exchange for cash or other financial assets) would be treated as an equity instrument.

5.2.8   *Derivative financial instruments with settlement options*

A derivative financial instrument may have settlement options, whereby it gives one or other party a choice over how it is settled (e.g. the issuer or the holder can choose settlement net in cash, net in shares, or by exchanging shares for cash). A derivative that gives one party a choice of settlement options is required to be treated as a financial asset or a financial liability, unless all possible settlement alternatives would result in it being an equity instrument. *[IAS 32.26]*. An example of a derivative financial instrument with a settlement option that is a financial liability is a share option that the issuer can decide to settle net in cash or by exchanging its own shares for cash. *[IAS 32.27]*.

These provisions will apply mostly to contracts involving the sale or purchase by an entity of its own equity instruments. However, they will also be relevant to those contracts to buy or sell a non-financial item in exchange for the entity's own equity instruments that are within the scope of IAS 32 (rather than IFRS 2) because they can be settled either by delivery of the non-financial item or net in cash or another financial instrument. Such contracts are financial assets or financial liabilities and not equity instruments. *[IAS 32.27]*.

5.3 Liabilities arising from gross-settled contracts for the purchase of the entity's own equity instruments

The following discussion in 5.3 relates only to contracts that must be settled by the counterparty delivering equity instruments (other than those classified as such under the exceptions discussed at 4.6 above) and the entity paying cash (gross-settled contracts). Contracts which can be settled net (i.e. by payment of the difference between the fair value, at the time of settlement, of the equity instruments and that of the consideration given) are accounted for as financial assets or financial liabilities *[IAS 32.AG27(c)]* (see 5.2.8 above and 11 below).

IAS 32 requires some types of puttable instruments (see 4.6.2 above) and instruments that impose an obligation to deliver a *pro rata* share of net assets only on liquidation (see 4.6.3 above) to be treated as equity instruments. However, a contract that is required to be settled by the entity receiving or delivering either of these types of equity instrument is a financial asset or financial liability, even when it involves the exchange of a fixed amount of cash or other financial assets for a fixed number of such instruments. *[IAS 32.22A, AG27]*.

Entering into a gross-settled contract for the purchase of own equity instruments gives rise to a financial liability in respect of the obligation to pay the purchase or redemption price, *[IAS 32.23, AG27(a)-(b)]*, (but resulting, on initial recognition, in a reduction of equity rather than an expense). This treatment is intended to reflect the idea that a forward contract or written option to repurchase an equity share gives rise to a liability similar to that contained within a redeemable share (see 4.5 above). *[IAS 32.BC12]*.

This is the case even if:

- the contract is an equity instrument;
- the contract is a written put option (i.e. a contract that gives the counterparty the right to require the entity to buy its own shares) rather than a forward contract (i.e. a firm commitment by the entity to purchase its own shares); or
- the number of shares subject to the contract is not fixed. *[IAS 32.23, AG27(a)-(b)]*.

Chapter 44

The final bullet point above might refer to a put option written by the entity whereby the counterparty can require the entity to purchase between 1,000 and 5,000 of its own equity shares at €2 per share. In other words, the entity cannot avoid recognising a liability for the contract on the argument that it does not know exactly how many of its own shares it will be compelled to purchase.

When such a liability first arises it must be recognised, in accordance with IAS 39, at its fair value, i.e. the net present value of the redemption amount. Subsequently, the financial liability is measured in accordance with IAS 39 or, where applicable, IFRS 9 (see Chapter 47). *[IAS 32.23, AG27(b)]*. IAS 32 offers no guidance as to how this is to be calculated when, as might be the case with respect to a written put option such as that described in the previous paragraph, the number of shares to be purchased and/or the date of purchase is not known.

In our view, it would be consistent with the requirement of IFRS 13 that liabilities with a demand feature such as a demand bank deposit should be measured at the amount payable on demand *[IFRS 13.47]* (see Chapter 14 at 11.5) to adopt a 'worst case' approach. In other words, it should be assumed that the purchase will take place on the earliest possible date for the maximum number of shares. This is also consistent with IAS 32's emphasis, in the general discussion of the differences between liabilities and equity instruments, on a liability arising except to the extent that an entity has an 'unconditional' right to avoid delivering cash or other financial assets (see 4.2 above).

The treatment proposed in the previous paragraph would lead to a different accounting treatment for written 'American' put options (i.e. those that can be exercised at any time during a period ending on a future date) and written 'European' put options (i.e. those that can be exercised only at a given future date). In the case of an American option, a liability would be recorded immediately for the full potential liability. In the case of a European option, a liability would be recorded for the net present value of the full potential liability, on which interest would be accrued until the date of potential exercise. If this interpretation is correct, it has the effect that:

- a gross-settled written American put option that is an equity instrument has no effect on profit or loss (because the full amount payable on settlement would be charged to equity on inception of the contract); but

- a gross-settled European put option that is an equity instrument does affect profit or loss (because the net present value of the amount payable on settlement would be charged to equity on inception of the contract and accrued to the full settlement amount through profit or loss).

If the contract expires without delivery of the shares, the carrying amount of the financial liability is reclassified to equity. This has the rather curious effect that a share purchase contract that expires unexercised (and therefore has no impact on the entity's net assets, other than the receipt or payment of the option premium) can nevertheless give rise to a loss to the extent that interest has been recognised on the liability between initial recognition and its transfer to equity (see Example 44.21 at 11.3.2 below).

5.3.1 Contracts to purchase own equity during 'closed' or 'prohibited' periods

Financial markets often impose restrictions on an entity trading in its own listed securities for a given period (sometimes referred to as a 'closed' or 'prohibited' period) in the run-up to the announcement of its financial results for a period. However, an entity may well wish to continue to purchase its own listed equity throughout the closed period, for example as part of an ongoing share-buyback programme.

One method of achieving this may be for the entity, in advance of the closed period, to enter into a contract with a counterparty (such as a broker) whereby the counterparty purchases shares in the entity, which the entity is then obliged to acquire from the counterparty. Such a contract will give rise to a financial liability for the entity from the day on which it is entered into. As discussed above, this would initially be recorded at the net present value of the amount to be paid, with the unwinding of the discount on that liability recorded as a finance charge in profit or loss.

In addition, if the contract is for the purchase of a fixed number of shares for their market price (as opposed to the exchange of a fixed amount of cash for as many shares as are worth that amount), it will be necessary to remeasure the liability to reflect movements in the share price.

5.3.2 Contracts to acquire non-controlling interests

IFRS 10 requires non-controlling interests to be shown within equity in consolidated financial statements (see Chapter 7 at 4.3). Accordingly, the requirements of IAS 32 relating to contracts over own equity instruments also generally apply, in consolidated financial statements, to forward contracts and put and call options over non-controlling interests.

This analysis was confirmed by the Interpretations Committee in November 2006, when it considered a request to clarify the accounting treatment of contracts to acquire non-controlling interests that are put in place at the time of a business combination. It is arguable that such contracts are more appropriately accounted for under the provisions of IFRS 3 relating to deferred consideration. It may also be the case that such contracts have the effect that, while there is a non-controlling interest as a matter of law, the relevant subsidiary is nevertheless regarded by IFRS 10 as wholly-owned, in which case the acquirer also recognises a financial liability for the price payable to the non-controlling interest. A further discussion of these issues may be found in Chapter 7 at 5.

The Interpretations Committee agreed that there was likely to be divergence in practice in how the related equity is classified, but did not believe that it could reach a consensus on this matter on a timely basis. Accordingly, the Interpretations Committee decided not to add this item to its agenda.

However, the Interpretations Committee noted that the requirements of IAS 32 relating to the purchase of own equity apply to the purchase of a minority interest. After initial recognition any liability, to which IFRS 3 is not being applied, will be accounted for in accordance with IAS 39. The parent will reclassify the liability to equity if a put expires unexercised.[15] Whilst this comment was made in the context of the original version of IFRS 3 (issued in 2004), it would be equally applicable where the current version (issued in 2008) is applied.

5.3.2.A   Possible future developments – written put options over non-controlling interests

For possible future developments in respect of written put options over non-controlling interests see Chapter 7 at 5.5.

5.4   Gross-settled contracts for the sale or issue of the entity's own equity instruments

The following discussion in 5.4 relates only to contracts which must be settled by the entity delivering its own equity instruments (other than those classified as such under the exceptions discussed at 4.6 above) and the counterparty paying cash (gross-settled contracts). Contracts which can be settled net (i.e. by payment of the difference between the fair value, at the time of purchase, of the shares and that of the consideration given) are accounted as financial assets or financial liabilities (see 5.2.7). *[IAS 32.AG27(c)].*

IAS 32 requires some types of puttable instruments (see 4.6.2 above) and instruments that impose an obligation to deliver a *pro rata* share of net assets only on liquidation (see 4.6.3 above) to be treated as equity instruments. However, a contract that is required to be settled by the entity receiving or delivering either of these types of equity instrument is a financial asset or financial liability, even when it involves the exchange of a fixed amount of cash or other financial assets for a fixed number of such instruments. *[IAS 32.22A, AG27].*

If an entity enters into a gross-settled contract to sell its own equity instruments, the contract is economically the 'mirror image' of a contract for the purchase of own equity. However, there is no provision in IAS 32 that the contract gives rise to a financial asset in respect of the cash to be received from the counterparty, as compared to the specific provision that a contract to purchase own equity gives rise to a financial liability in respect of the cash to be paid to the counterparty (see 5.3 above). Consequently, it appears that such contracts give rise to no accounting entries until settlement. This analysis is confirmed by an illustrative example to IAS 32 (see Example 44.16 at 11.1.2 below).

Contracts for the sale or issue of own equity arise in situations such as those in Examples 44.3 and 44.4 below.

Example 44.3:   Share issue payable in fixed instalments

A government intends to privatise a nationalised industry with a functional currency of euro through an initial public offering (IPO) at €5 per share. In order to encourage widespread share ownership, the terms of the issue are that shares are issued on 1 January 2015, but subscribers to the IPO are required to pay only €3 per share on 1 January 2015 followed by two further instalments of €1 per share on 1 January 2016 and 1 January 2017.

Example 44.4:   Right to call for additional equity capital

A start-up technology entity with a functional currency of UK pounds sterling is unsure of its working capital requirements for the first few years of its operations. It therefore enters into an agreement with its major shareholders whereby it can require those shareholders to contribute an additional £2 per share at any time during the next seven years.

One view might be that the situation in Example 44.3 is not a contract for the future issue of equity – the share has already been issued, and so it would be quite appropriate to record a receivable for the deferred subscription payments. The accounting standard *IFRS for Small and Medium-Sized Entities* indicates that a receivable should be recognised only for shares that have been issued, but that such a receivable should be recognised as a deduction from equity, not as an asset.[16] The standard states that this proposal is derived from IAS 32[17] – an assertion difficult to reconcile with the discussion above. Interestingly, an early IASB staff draft of the exposure draft of *IFRS for Small and Medium-Sized Entities* (as made available on the IASB's website as at September 2006) admitted, with perhaps unintended candour, that this treatment is 'not in any standard'![18] In our view, current IFRS requires any receivable recognised in respect of an issued share to be shown as an asset.

On the other hand, it is clear from IAS 32 that no receivable would be recognised if the arrangement provided for the entity actually to issue further shares (*pro rata* to the shares initially issued) for €1 on 1 January 2016 and 1 January 2017.

6   COMPOUND FINANCIAL INSTRUMENTS

6.1   Background

While many financial instruments are either a liability or equity in their entirety, that is not true for all financial instruments issued by an entity. Some, referred to as compound instruments in IAS 32, contain both elements. A compound financial instrument is a non-derivative financial instrument that, from the issuer's perspective, contains both a liability and an equity component. *[IAS 32.28, AG30].* Examples include:

- A bond, in the same currency as the functional currency of the issuing entity, convertible into a fixed number of equity instruments, which effectively comprises:
    - a financial liability (the issuer's obligation to pay interest and, potentially, to redeem the bond in cash); and
    - an equity instrument (the holder's right to call for shares of the issuer).

    IAS 32 states that the economic effect of issuing such an instrument is substantially the same as simultaneously issuing a debt instrument with an early settlement provision and warrants to purchase ordinary shares, or issuing a debt instrument with detachable share purchase warrants. *[IAS 32.29].* However, this analysis is questionable in the sense that, if a company did issue such instruments separately, it is extremely unlikely that one would lapse as the result of the exercise of the other (as happens on the conversion or redemption of a convertible bond);

- A mandatorily redeemable preference share with dividends paid at the issuer's discretion, which effectively comprises:
    - a financial liability (the issuer's obligation to redeem the shares in cash); and
    - an equity instrument (the holder's right to receive dividends if declared). *[IAS 32.AG37].*

IAS 32 requires the issuer of a non-derivative financial instrument to evaluate the terms of the financial instrument to determine whether it contains both a liability and an equity component. This evaluation is based on the contractual terms of the financial instruments, the substance of the arrangement and the definition of a financial liability, financial asset and an equity instrument. If such components are identified, they must be accounted for separately as financial liabilities, financial assets or equity, *[IAS 32.28]*, and the liability and equity components shown separately in the statement of financial position. *[IAS 32.29]*.

This treatment, commonly referred to as 'split accounting', is discussed in more detail in 6.2 to 6.6 below. For simplicity, the discussion below (like that in IAS 32 itself) is framed in terms of convertible bonds, by far the most common form of compound financial instrument, but is equally applicable to other types of compound instrument, such as preference shares with different contractual terms in respect of dividends and re-payments of principal (see 4.5 above).

6.1.1   *Treatment by holder and issuer contrasted*

'Split accounting' is to be applied only by the issuer of a compound financial instrument. The accounting treatment by the holder is dealt with in IAS 39 or, where applicable, IFRS 9 and is significantly different. *[IAS 32.AG30]*. In particular:

- In the issuer's financial statements, under IAS 32:
  - on initial recognition of the instrument, the fair value of the liability component is calculated first and the equity component is treated as a residual; and
  - the equity component is never remeasured after initial recognition.
- In the holder's financial statements, under IAS 39 (see Chapter 43 at 4 and Chapter 47 at 2 and 3):
  - on initial recognition of the instrument, the conversion option is a derivative financial asset, the fair value of which is calculated first, with the loan treated as a residual amount; and
  - the derivative financial asset is likely to be constantly remeasured at fair value.
- In the holder's financial statements, under IFRS 9:
  - the instrument fails the criteria for measurement at amortised cost (in particular the 'contractual cash flow characteristics test') and is therefore carried at fair value through profit or loss (see Chapter 46 at 5).

6.2   Initial recognition – 'split accounting'

On initial recognition of a compound instrument such as a convertible bond, IAS 32 requires the issuer to:

(a)   identify the various components of the instrument;

(b)   determine the fair value of the liability component (see below); and

(c)   determine the equity component as a residual amount, essentially the issue proceeds of the instrument less the liability component determined in (b) above.

The liability component of a convertible bond should be measured first, at the fair value of a similar liability that does not have an associated equity conversion feature, but including any embedded non-equity derivative features, such as an issuer's or holder's right to require early redemption of the bond, if any such terms are included.

In practical terms, this will be done by determining the net present value of all potential contractually determined future cash flows under the instrument, discounted at the rate of interest applied by the market at the time of issue to instruments of comparable credit status and providing substantially the same cash flows, on the same terms, but without the conversion option. The fair value of any embedded non-equity derivative features is then determined and 'included in the liability component' – see, however, the further discussion of this point at 6.4.2 below. *[IAS 32.31].*

Thereafter the liability component is accounted for in accordance with the requirements of IAS 39, or – where applicable – IFRS 9, for the measurement of financial liabilities (see Chapters 47). *[IAS 32.31-32].*

IAS 32 notes that:

- the equity component of a convertible bond is an embedded option to convert the liability into equity of the issuer;
- the fair value of the option comprises its time value and its intrinsic value, if any; and
- this option has value on initial recognition even when it is out of the money. *[IAS 32.AG31(b)].*

However, not all these features are directly relevant to the accounting treatment, since the equity component is not (other than by coincidence) recorded at its fair value. Instead, in accordance with the general definition of equity as a residual, the equity component of the bond is simply the difference between the fair value of the compound instrument (total issue proceeds of the bond) and the liability component as determined above. Because of this 'residual' treatment, IAS 32 does not address the issue of how, or whether, the issue proceeds are to be allocated where more than one equity component is identified. It is important to note, that the equity component will not be remeasured subsequently.

The methodology of 'split-accounting' in IAS 32 has the effect that the sum of the carrying amounts assigned to the liability and equity components on initial recognition is always equal to the fair value that would be ascribed to the instrument as a whole. No gain or loss arises from the initial recognition of the separate components of the instrument. *[IAS 32.31].*

This treatment is illustrated in Examples 44.5 and 44.9 below.

Example 44.5:   Convertible bond – basic 'split accounting'[19]

An entity, whose functional currency is the Euro, issues 2,000 convertible bonds. The bonds have a three-year term, and are issued at par with a face value of €1,000 per bond, giving total proceeds of €2,000,000. Interest is payable annually in arrears at a nominal annual interest rate of 6% (i.e. €120,000 per annum). Each bond is convertible at any time up to maturity into 250 ordinary shares. When the bonds are issued, the prevailing market interest rate for similar debt without conversion options is 9% per annum. The entity incurs issue costs of €100,000.

The economic components of this instrument are:

- a liability component, being a discounted fixed rate debt, perhaps with an imputed holder's put option (due to the holder's right to convert at any time), and

- an equity component, representing the holder's right to convert at any time before maturity. In effect this is a written call option (from the issuer's perspective) on American terms (i.e. it can be exercised at any time until maturity of the bond).

The practical problem with this analysis is that it is not clear what is the strike price of the holder's options to put the debt and call for shares, specifically whether it is the €2,000,000 face value of the bonds or the discounted amount at which they are recorded until maturity. Perhaps for this reason, IAS 32 does not require the true fair values of these components to be calculated.

Instead the liability component is measured first at the net present value of the maximum potential cash payments that the issuer could be required to make. The difference between the proceeds of the bond issue and the calculated fair value of the liability is assigned to the equity component. The net present value (NPV) of the liability component is calculated as €1,848,122, using a discount rate of 9%, the market interest rate for similar bonds having no conversion rights, as shown.

Year	Cash flow	€	Discount factor (at 9%)	NPV of cash flow €
1	Interest	120,000	$1/1.09$	110,092
2	Interest	120,000	$1/1.09^2$	101,001
3	Interest and principal	2,120,000	$1/1.09^3$	1,637,029
		Total liability component		1,848,122
		Total equity component (balance)		151,878
		Total proceeds		2,000,000

It is next necessary to deal with the issue costs of €100,000. In accordance with the requirements of IAS 32 for such costs (see 8.1 below), these would be allocated to the liability and equity components on a *pro rata* basis. This would give the following allocation of the net issue proceeds.

	Liability component €	Equity component €	Total €
Gross proceeds (allocated as above)	1,848,122	151,878	2,000,000
Issue costs (allocated *pro rata* to gross proceeds)	(92,406)	(7,594)	(100,000)
Net proceeds	1,755,716	144,284	1,900,000

The €144,284 credited to equity is not subsequently remeasured (see 6.2.1 below). On the assumption that the liability is not classified as at fair value through profit or loss, the €1,755,716 liability component would be accounted for under the effective interest rate method. It should be borne in mind that, after taking account of the issue costs, the effective interest rate is not the 9% used to determine the gross value of the liability component, but 10.998%, as shown below.

Year	Liability b/f €	Interest at 10.998% €	Cash paid €	Liability c/f €
1	1,755,716	193,094	(120,000)	1,828,810
2	1,828,810	201,134	(120,000)	1,909,944
3	1,909,944	210,056	(2,120,000)	–
	Total finance cost	604,284		

The total finance cost can be proved as follows:

	€
Cash interest	360,000
Gross issue proceeds originally allocated to equity component	151,878
Issue costs allocated to liability component	92,406
	604,284

6.2.1   Accounting for the equity component

On initial recognition of a compound financial instrument, the equity component (i.e. the €144,284 identified in Example 44.5 above) is credited direct to equity and is not subsequently remeasured. IAS 32 does not prescribe:

- whether the credit should be to a separate component of equity (although a transitional provision relating to the February 2008 amendment of IAS 32 suggests that there is such a requirement); or
- if the entity chooses to treat it as such, how it should be described.

This ensures that there is no conflict between, on the one hand, the basic requirement of IAS 32 that there should be a credit in equity and, on the other, the legal requirements of various jurisdictions as to exactly how that credit should be allocated within equity.

After initial recognition, the classification of the liability and equity components of a convertible instrument is not revised, for example as a result of a change in the likelihood that a conversion option will be exercised, even when exercise of the option may appear to have become economically advantageous to some holders. IAS 32 points out that holders may not always act in the way that might be expected because, for example, the tax consequences resulting from conversion may differ among holders. Furthermore, the likelihood of conversion will change from time to time. The entity's contractual obligation to make future payments remains outstanding until it is extinguished through conversion, maturity of the instrument or some other transaction. *[IAS 32.30]*.

The amount originally credited to equity is subsequently neither remeasured nor reclassified to profit or loss. Thus, as illustrated by Example 43.5 above, the effective interest rate shown in profit or loss for a simple convertible bond will be equivalent to the rate that would have been paid for non-convertible debt. In effect, the dilution of shareholder value represented by the embedded conversion right is shown as an interest expense.

However, on conversion of a convertible instrument, it may be appropriate to transfer the equity component within equity (see 6.3.1 below).

6.2.2   Temporary differences arising from split accounting

In many jurisdictions it is only the cash interest paid, and sometimes also the issue costs, that are deductible for tax purposes, rather than the full amount of the finance cost charged under IAS 32. Moreover, some of these costs may be deductible in periods different from those in which they are recognised in the financial statements. These factors will give rise to temporary differences between the carrying value of the liability component of the bond and its tax base, giving rise to deferred tax required to be accounted for under IAS 12 – *Income Taxes* (see Chapter 30, particularly at 6.1.2 and 7.2.8).

6.3   Conversion, early repurchase and modification

6.3.1   *Conversion at maturity*

On conversion of a convertible instrument at maturity, IAS 32 requires the entity to derecognise the liability component and recognise it as equity. There is no gain or loss on conversion at maturity. *[IAS 32.AG32].*

Thus, for example, if the bond in Example 44.5 above were converted at maturity, the accounting entry required by IAS 32 would be:

	€	€
Liability	2,000,000	
Equity		2,000,000

The precise allocation of the credit to equity (e.g. as between share capital, additional paid-in capital, share premium, other reserves and so on) would be a matter of local legislation. In addition, IAS 32 permits the €144,284 originally allocated to the equity component in Example 44.5 above to be reallocated within equity. *[IAS 32.AG32].*

6.3.2   *Conversion before maturity*

6.3.2.A   *'Fixed stated principal' of a bond*

The consideration given for the issue of equity instruments on conversion of a bond is the discharge by the holder of the issuer from the liability to pay any further interest or principal payments on the bond. If conversion can take place only at maturity, the amount of the liability transferred to equity on conversion will always (in Example 44.5 at 6.2 above) be €2,000,000. Hence, the conversion right involves the delivery of a fixed number of shares for the waiver of the right to receive a fixed amount of cash and so is clearly an equity instrument.

However, the bond in Example 44.5 allows conversion at some point before the full term. Therefore, conversion might occur at the end of year 2, when the carrying value of the bonds would have been accreted to only €1,909,944. Hence, the carrying amount of the liability that is forgiven on conversion can vary depending on when conversion occurs. This begs the question as to whether the conversion right now involves the delivery of a fixed number of shares for the waiver of the right to receive a *variable* amount of cash, suggesting that it is no longer an equity instrument.

It is for this reason, in our view, that IAS 32 defines as an equity instrument one that involves the exchange of a fixed number of shares for the 'fixed stated principal' rather than the 'carrying amount' of a bond. *[IAS 32.22].* In other words, IAS 32 regards the 'fixed stated principal' of the bond in Example 44.5 as a constant €2,000,000. The intention is to clarify that the variation in the carrying amount of the bond during its term does not preclude the conversion right from being classified as an equity instrument.

6.3.2.B   Accounting treatment

IAS 32 refers to the treatment summarised in 6.3.1 above being applied on conversion 'at maturity'. This begs the question of the treatment required if a holder converts prior to maturity (as would have been possible under the terms of the bond in Example 44.5).

As noted in 6.3.2.A above, IAS 32 concludes that the equity component of the bond is an equity instrument on the grounds that it represents the holder's right to call for a fixed number of shares for fixed consideration, in the form of the 'fixed stated principal' of the bond.

It could be argued that the logical implication of this is that, on a holder's early conversion of the bond in Example 44.5 above, the issuer should immediately recognise a finance cost for the difference between the then carrying amount of the liability component of the bond and the fixed stated principal of €2,000,000. This would create a liability of €2,000,000 immediately before conversion, so as to acknowledge that the strike price under the holder's call option is the waiver of the right to receive a fixed stated principal of €2,000,000, rather than whatever the carrying value of the bond happens to be at the time.

However, we take the view, supported by general practice, that all that is required is to transfer to equity the carrying value of the liability at the date of conversion, as calculated after accrual of finance costs on a continuous basis, rather than at the amount shown in the most recently published financial statements. In such a case, the consideration for the issue of equity instruments is the release, by the bondholder, of the issuer from its liability to make future contractual payments under the bond, measured at the net present value of those payments.

IFRIC 19 (which generally applies to debt for equity swaps) does not apply to the conversion of a convertible instrument in accordance with its original terms (see 7 below).

6.3.2.C   Treatment of embedded derivatives on conversion

IAS 32 does not specifically address the treatment of any separated non-equity embedded derivatives outstanding at the time of conversion. The issue of principle is that, when a holder exercises its right to convert, it is effectively requiring the issuer to issue equity in consideration for the bondholder ceding its rights. These may include any right to receive future payments of principal and/or interest or to require early repayment of the bond. It seems entirely appropriate that any amounts carried in respect of such rights, including those reflected in the carrying amount of separated embedded derivatives, should be transferred to equity on conversion.

Where, however, conversion has the effect of removing an issuer's right (for example, to compel early redemption or conversion), this could be seen as a loss to the issuer rather than as consideration given by the holder for an issue of equity. In our view, however, the loss of such a right by the issuer on conversion by the holder simply represents a reduction in the proceeds received for the issue of equity, and should therefore by accounted for as a charge to equity (see also 8.1 below).

6.3.3   *Early redemption or repurchase*

It is not uncommon for the issuer of a convertible bond to redeem or repurchase it before the end of its full term, either through exercise of rights inherent in the bond, such as an embedded issuer call option, or through subsequent negotiation with bondholders.

IAS 32 contains guidance for the accounting treatment of an early redemption or repurchase of compound instruments following a tender offer to bondholders (see 6.3.3.A below).

It is not entirely clear whether this guidance applies only to redemption pursuant to a subsequent negotiation with bondholders, or whether it also applies where redemption occurs through exercise of a right inherent in the original terms of the bond. We therefore believe an entity has an accounting policy choice if redemption is based on a right inherent in original terms of the bond, such as an embedded issuer call option at par that was allocated to the liability component and considered to be clearly and closely related to the host contract (see 6.3.3.B below).

6.3.3.A   *Early repurchase through negotiation with bondholders*

When an entity extinguishes a convertible instrument before maturity through an early redemption or repurchase in which the original conversion privileges are unchanged, IAS 32 requires the entity to allocate the consideration paid and any transaction costs for the repurchase or redemption to the liability and equity components of the instrument at the date of the transaction. *[IAS 32.AG33]*.

It is not entirely clear what is meant by a 'redemption or repurchase in which the original conversion privileges are unchanged'. However, we assume that it is intended to imply that the repurchase must occur without modification of the original terms of the compound instrument, and at a price representing a fair value for the instrument on its original terms. A repurchase based on a modification of the original terms of the instrument, or at a price implying a modification of them, should presumably be dealt with according to the provisions of IAS 32 for the modification of a compound instrument (see 6.3.4 below) or those in IAS 39 for the exchange and modification of debt (see Chapter 50 at 6.2).

The method used for allocating the consideration paid and transaction costs to the separate components should be consistent with that used in the original allocation to the separate components of the proceeds received by the entity when the convertible instrument was issued (see 6.2 above). *[IAS 32.AG33]*.

The issuer is therefore required to:

- determine the fair value of the liability component and allocate this part of the purchase price to the liability component;
- allocate the remainder of the purchase price to the equity component; and
- allocate the transaction costs between the liability and equity component on a *pro rata* basis.

Once this allocation of the consideration has been made:

- the difference between the consideration allocated to the liability component and the carrying amount of the liability is recognised in profit or loss; and

- the amount of consideration relating to the equity component is recognised in equity. *[IAS 32.AG34].*

The treatment of a negotiated repurchase at fair value of a convertible instrument is illustrated by Example 44.6 below, which is based on an illustrative example in IAS 32.[20]

Example 44.6:   Early repurchase of convertible instrument

For simplicity this example:

- assumes that at inception the face amount of the instrument was equal to the carrying amount of its liability and equity components in the financial statements – i.e. there was no premium or discount on issue; and

- ignores transaction costs and tax.

On 1 January 2011, an entity issued a convertible bond with a face value of €100 million maturing on 31 December 2020, at which point the holder may opt for repayment of €100 million or conversion into 4 million shares. Interest is paid half-yearly in arrears at a nominal annual interest rate of 10% (i.e. €5m per half year). At the date of issue, the entity could have issued non-convertible debt with a ten-year term bearing interest at 11%. On issue, the carrying amount of the bond was allocated as follows:

	€m
Present value of the principal – €100m payable at the end of ten years[1]	34.3
Present value of the interest – 20 6-monthly payments of €5m[2]	59.7
Total liability component	94.0
Equity component (balance)	6.0
Proceeds of the bond issue	100.0

The amounts above are discounted using a semi-annual rate of 5.5% (11%/2) as follows:

1   $€100m/1.055^{20}$

2   $€5m \times (1/1.055 + 1/1.055^2 + 1/1.055^3 + ... 1/1.055^{20})$

On 1 January 2016, the entity makes a tender offer to the holder of the bond to repurchase the bond at its then fair value of €170 million, which the holder accepts. At the date of repurchase, the entity could have issued non-convertible debt with a five-year term with interest payable half-yearly in arrears at an annual coupon interest rate of 8%.

At the time of repurchase, the carrying amount of the liability component of the bond, discounted at the original semi-annual rate of 5.5% is as follows.

	€m
Present value of the principal – €100m payable at the end of five years[1]	58.5
Present value of the interest – 10 6-monthly payments of €5m[2]	37.7
Carrying value of liability component	96.2

1   $€100m/1.055^{10}$

2   $€5m \times (1/1.055 + 1/1.055^2 + 1/1.055^3 + ... 1/1.055^{10})$

The fair value of the liability component of the bond, discounted at the current semi-annual rate of 4% (8%/2) is as follows.

	€m
Present value of the principal – €100m payable at the end of five years[1]	67.6
Present value of the interest – 10 6-monthly payments of €5m[2]	40.5
Fair value of liability component	108.1

1    $€100m/1.04^{10}$
2    $€5m \times (1/1.04 + 1/1.04^2 + 1/1.04^3 + \ldots 1/1.04^{10})$

The fair value calculation indicates that, of the repurchase price of €170 million, €108.1 million is to be treated as redeeming the liability component of the bond, and the balance of €61.9 million as redeeming the equity component. This gives rise to the accounting entry:

	€m	€m
Liability component of bond	96.2	
Equity	61.9	
Debt settlement expense (profit or loss)	11.9	
Cash		170.0

The debt settlement expense represents the difference between the carrying value of the debt component (€96.2m) and its fair value (€108.1m).

Any costs of the repurchase would have been allocated between profit or loss and equity in proportion to the fair value of the liability and equity components at the time of redemption.

6.3.3.B   *Early repurchase through exercising an embedded call option*

It is not entirely clear whether the guidance in 6.3.3.A above applies only on early redemption or repurchase to a subsequent negotiation with bondholders, or whether it also applies where redemption occurs through exercise of rights inherent in the terms of the bond (for example an issuer call option at par allocated to the liability component and considered to be clearly and closely related to the host contract).

One way of accounting for such redemptions would be by applying the accounting treatment as discussed under 6.3.3.A above.

If, however, this early repayment option was determined, on initial recognition of the convertible bond, to be clearly and closely related to the liability host contract (see 6.4.2.A below), then it might be argued that the general measurement rules of IAS 39 apply. In such a case the liability (including the embedded call option) would be measured at amortised cost (assuming that it was not designated at fair value through profit or loss on initial recognition). Accounting under the amortised cost method is based on an effective interest rate, calculated initially based on expected future cash flows. Any change in those expected cash flows is reflected in the carrying amount of the financial instrument, by computing the present value of the revised estimated future cash flows at the instrument's original effective interest rate, with any difference from the previous amortised cost carrying amount recorded in profit or loss. [IAS 39.AG8].

A change in the expected repayment date would therefore require the amortised cost of the financial liability component to be remeasured. This treatment has the effect that the overall repayment amount at par is allocated to the liability portion of the compound instrument.

6.3.4   Modification

An entity may amend the terms of a convertible instrument to induce early conversion, for example by offering a more favourable conversion ratio or paying other additional consideration in the event of conversion before a specified date. The difference, at the date the terms are amended, between:

- the fair value of the consideration the holder receives on conversion of the instrument under the revised terms: and

- the fair value of the consideration the holder would have received under the original terms

is recognised as a loss in profit or loss. *[IAS 32.AG35].* IAS 32 illustrates this treatment, as shown in Example 44.7 below. *[IAS 32.IE47-50].*

Example 44.7:   Modification of terms of bond to induce early conversion

Suppose that the entity in Example 44.6 at 6.3.3.A above wished, on 1 January 2016, to induce the bondholder to convert the bond early. The original terms of the bond allowed for conversion into 4 million shares. The entity offers the bondholder the right to convert into 5 million shares during the period 1 January-29 February 2016. The market value of the entity's shares is €40 per share.

The enhanced conversion terms offer the bondholder the right to receive an additional 1 million shares. Accordingly, the entity recognises a cost of €40m (1m shares × share price €40/share) in profit or loss.

6.4   The components of a compound instrument

6.4.1   Determining the components of a financial instrument

The most difficult aspect of 'split accounting' is often the initial assessment of whether the instrument consists of different components and if it does, what the various components of the instrument actually are. In the examples above, it is fairly clear that the instruments consist of different components and what the various components are. However, in some instruments the analysis is far from straightforward, as illustrated by Example 44.8 below.

Example 44.8:   Analysis of compound financial instrument into components

An entity issues a bond for €100, paying an annual cash coupon of 5% on the issue price and mandatorily convertible after five years on the following terms. If, at the date of conversion, the entity's share price is €1.25 or higher, the holder will receive 80 shares. If the entity's share price is €1.00 or lower, the holder will receive 100 shares. If the entity's share price is in the range €1.00 to €1.25, the holder will receive such number of shares (between 80 and 100) as have a fair value of €100.

Any analysis must begin by determining whether the bond as whole is a non-derivative instrument. This is the case, since the issuing entity receives full consideration for its issue. The next step is to assess whether the instrument consists of different components and, if it does, to break the instrument down into these components so as to identify any equity components in the whole.

The difficulty of this assessment is evidenced by two requests received by the Interpretations Committee to address the accounting for two instruments with substantially the same features as the one in Example 44.8 above but with an

Chapter 44

additional early settlement option for the issuer, to settle the instrument at any time by delivering a maximum (fixed) number of shares (see 6.6.3.A below).[21] While the request focused only on the additional early settlement option, and not on the classification of the 'basic' instrument (an instrument with the features described in Example 44.8 above), the accounting treatment of the 'basic instrument' was added to the Interpretations Committee's agenda. It was discussed during the January 2014 and May 2014 Interpretations Committee meetings.[22]

Four alternative views with significantly different accounting outcomes, ranging from classifying the whole financial instrument as a financial liability to various combinations of financial liabilities, equity instruments and/or derivative financial liabilities, were considered by the Interpretations Committee. In the end the Interpretations Committee noted that:

- the issuer's obligation to deliver a variable number of the entity's own equity instruments is a non-derivative that meets the definition of a financial liability in paragraph 11(b)(i) of IAS 32 in its entirety (see 3 and 4.1 above); and

- the definition of a liability in IAS 32 does not have any limits or thresholds regarding the degree of variability that is required.

Therefore, the contractual substance of the instrument is a single obligation to deliver a variable number of equity instruments at maturity, with the variation based on the value of those equity instruments. The Interpretations Committee noted further that such a single obligation to deliver a variable number of own equity instruments cannot be subdivided into components for the purposes of evaluating whether the instrument contains a component that meets the definition of equity. Even though the number of equity instruments to be delivered is limited and guaranteed by the cap and the floor, the overall number of equity instruments that the issuer is obliged to deliver is not fixed and therefore the entire obligation meets the definition of a financial liability.

The Interpretations Committee noted that the cap and the floor are embedded derivative features, whose values change in response to the price of the issuer's equity shares. Therefore, assuming that the issuer has not elected to designate the entire instrument under the fair value option, the issuer must separate those features and account for the embedded derivative features separately from the host liability contract, at fair value through profit or loss in accordance with IAS 39 (or IFRS 9) (see Chapter 43 at 4 and 5).

The fact that the issue was submitted to the Interpretations Committee in the first place together with the fact that four possible accounting views were drawn up under the guidance of IAS 32, evidences how difficult and judgemental any analysis of increasingly complex instruments can be under the provisions of IAS 32.

6.4.2   Compound instruments with embedded derivatives

As noted above, in order to qualify for split accounting, a financial instrument, when considered as whole, must be a non-derivative instrument. However, one or more of its identified components may well be embedded derivatives. Indeed, the conversion right in any convertible bond represents a holder's call option whereby the entity can be required to issue a fixed number of shares for a fixed consideration (the 'fixed stated principal' of the bond – see 6.3.2.A above), which is accordingly identified as an equity component.

A bond may well contain other (non-equity) derivatives, such as options for either the issuer or the holder to require early repayment or conversion or to extend the period until conversion. The detailed guidance in IAS 32 (see 6.2 above) requires 'the fair value of any embedded non-equity derivative features to be determined and included in the liability component' when split accounting is applied. *[IAS 32.31]*. They are then subject to the normal requirement of IAS 39 for embedded derivatives to be accounted for separately if they are not considered to be closely related to the host contract (see Chapter 43 at 4).

The issuer of a compound financial instrument with other embedded derivatives is therefore required to go through the following steps:

- First step: determine the fair value of the liability component that does not have an associated equity conversion feature but including any embedded non-equity derivatives features;

- Second step: determine the equity component as a residual amount by deducting the fair value of the liability component, including any embedded non-equity derivative features, from the fair value of the compound instrument (essentially its issue proceed); and

- Third step: assess whether the embedded non-equity derivative features are closely related to the host liability component. Any not closely related embedded non-equity derivative features are accounted for separately and therefore separated from the host liability component (see Chapter 43 at 4 and 5).

Note, on initial recognition, the sum of the initial carrying amounts of the various components, determined as indicated above, must equal the overall fair value of the compound instrument.

6.4.2.A   Issuer call option – 'closely related' embedded derivatives

Example 44.9:   Convertible bond – split accounting with multiple embedded derivative features[23]

The proceeds received on the issue of a convertible bond, callable at par, are £60 million, which equals the nominal amount of the convertible bond. The value of a similar bond without a call or equity conversion option is £57 million. Based on an option-pricing model, it is determined that the value to the entity of the embedded call feature in a similar bond without an equity conversion option is £2 million. In this case, the value is allocated to the liability component so as to reduce the liability component to £55 million (£57m – £2m) and the value allocated to the equity component is £5 million (£60m – £55m). Because IAS 39 requires the embedded derivative assessment to be done before separating the equity component and the call option is at par, the option is considered to be clearly and closely related and therefore not separated from the liability host contract.

Where (as is often the case) a convertible bond is callable at par, the call option would not be a separable derivative. IAS 39 and IFRS 9 states that a call option is generally closely related to the host debt contract if the exercise price is approximately equal to the amortised cost of the host on each exercise (which would not, *prima facie* be the case). However, as an exemption to the general rule,

IAS 39 (or, where applicable, IFRS 9) requires this assessment to be made in respect of any embedded call, put or prepayment option in a convertible bond before separating the equity component. *[IAS 39.AG30(g), IFRS 9.B4.3.5(e)]*. This has the effect that an issuer's call over a convertible bond at par is effectively deemed to be equal to amortised cost for the duration of the instrument. This is discussed further in Chapter 43 at 5.

6.4.2.B   *Issuer call option – 'not closely related' embedded derivatives*

If a non-equity embedded derivative is considered not to be closely related to the host contract then it should be accounted for separately. If, in Example 44.9 above, the issuer call option were at an amount that was not approximately equal to amortised cost, and not intended to reimburse the approximate present value of lost interest (see Chapter 43 at 5), say at par plus £5 million, then the call option would not be considered clearly and closely related and therefore should be accounted for separately. The issuer in Example 44.9 would therefore record a derivative financial asset at its fair value of £2 million, assuming it would have the same fair value as in Example 44.9, a liability component of £57 million and an equity component of £5 million. The call option would subsequently be remeasured at fair value through profit or loss.

There are cases where over-enthusiastic trawling for embedded derivatives may dredge up results so counter-intuitive that it is hard to believe that they were really intended by the IASB, as illustrated by Example 44.10 below.

Example 44.10:   Foreign currency denominated equity instrument with issuer's redemption right

An entity with a functional currency of pounds sterling issues a euro-denominated capital instrument for €145 million (equivalent to £100 million at the date of issue). Coupons on the instrument are paid entirely at the entity's discretion. The entity has the right, but not the obligation, in certain circumstances to redeem the instrument (in Euros) for an amount equal to the original issue proceeds.

Taken as a whole, this is an equity instrument, because it gives rise to no obligation to transfer cash or other financial assets to the holder. However, the issuer's right to redeem, if considered in isolation is not an equity instrument, but a financial asset (a call option over own equity), since it is a derivative involving the purchase of a fixed number of equity instruments for €145 million which, although fixed in euros, is variable when translated into sterling. Suppose that the fair value of the call option, at the date of issue was £15 million.

This analysis would result in the following accounting entry on issue of the instrument:

	£m	£m
Cash	100	
Call option (statement of financial position)	15	
Equity		115

In our view, it would be inappropriate to show an increase in net assets of £115 million, when the only real transaction has been the raising of £100 million of equity for cash. In this particular case, this treatment is, in our view, not required since paragraph 28 of IAS 32 requires split accounting to be applied only where an instrument is determined to contain 'both a liability and an equity component'. In this case, there is no liability component, since the embedded derivative that has potentially been identified is, and can only ever be, an asset; accordingly, 'split accounting' is not required.

6.5   Other issues

The following issues discussed earlier in this chapter are of particular relevance to convertible bonds:

*   the Interpretations Committee's conclusion that a fixed amount of cash denominated in a currency other than the entity's functional currency is not a 'fixed amount' of cash (see 5.2.3 above and 6.6.4 and 6.6.4.A below); and

*   the treatment of instruments settled with equity instruments the number of which varies to reflect major capital restructurings before settlement (see 5.1.2 above).

These and other issues noted at various points above reinforce an increasing concern that the 'split accounting' rules in IAS 32 are implicitly based on a bond with terms much more straightforward than those of many – if not most – bonds currently in issue. See 12 below for possible future developments.

6.6   Common forms of convertible bonds

6.6.1   *Functional currency bond convertible into a fixed number of shares*

The most common form of convertible bond, a functional currency bond convertible into a fixed number of own equity instruments at the discretion of the holder, is discussed in Example 44.5 at 6.2 above.

6.6.2   *Contingent convertible bond*

A contingent convertible bond is a bond that is convertible, at the option of the holder, only on the occurrence of a contingent event outside of the control of the holder or the issuer. If the contingent event occurs then the holder has the option, but not the obligation, to convert. If the contingent event does not occur, then the bond will be settled in cash at maturity.

The fact that conversion is only contingent does not mean the instrument has no equity component. If, on occurrence of the contingent event, exercise of the conversion option would result in the exchange of a fixed number of the issuer's own equity instruments for a fixed amount of cash (in the functional currency of the issuing entity), the conversion option would meet the definition of an equity instrument under IAS 32 and the overall instrument would be treated as a compound instrument.

6.6.3   *Mandatorily convertible bond*

A mandatorily convertible bond is an instrument that, at a certain time in the future, converts into shares of the issuing entity, rather than the conversion being at the option of either the holder or the issuer of the bond. The classification of a mandatorily convertible bond on initial recognition as debt or equity depends on:

*   how the convertible bond will be settled; and

*   whether the issuer is required to pay interest up to the point of conversion.

If the fixed stated principal will be settled through delivery of a fixed number of the issuer's own shares, and the principal of the convertible bond is in the same currency as the functional currency of the issuing entity, then this feature of the bond is an equity instrument and accounted for as such (see 4.1 and 5.2.3 above). If interest on the bond is payable only at the discretion of the entity, then there is no liability component, and the entire bond is classified as an equity instrument. If, however, the entity is required to pay interest, the obligation to pay interest establishes a liability component, which is measured at the present value of the required interest payments.

If settlement can only occur through the delivery of a variable number of the issuer's own shares, calculated so that the fair value of these shares issued equals the principal amount (see 5.2.1 above), and the entity is required to pay interest then the entire bond is classified as a financial liability.

Example 44.11: Mandatorily convertible bond classified as equity

An entity, with a functional currency of Euro, issues 2,000 convertible bonds with a nominal value of €1,000 per bond, giving total proceeds of €2,000,000. The bonds have a three-year term, and interest is payable, at the discretion of the entity, annually in arrears at a nominal annual interest rate of 6% (i.e. €120,000 per annum). At maturity of the bond each bond converts into 250 ordinary shares. Because the conversion option meets the definition of an equity instrument and payment of interest is at the discretion of the entity, the entire instrument is classified as an equity instrument. The entity records the following accounting entry.

	€	€
Cash	2,000,000	
Equity		2,000,000

Example 44.12: Mandatorily convertible bond classified as a compound instrument

Assume the same fact pattern as in Example 44.11 above, except that the entity has an obligation to pay interest annually in arrears at a nominal annual interest rate of 6% (i.e. €120,000 per annum). The obligation to pay interest over three years represents a liability of the issuing entity at the net present value, using a discount rate of 9%, which is the market interest rate.

Year	Cash flow	€	Discount factor (at 9%)	NPV of cash flow €
1	Interest	120,000	$1/1.09$	110,092
2	Interest	120,000	$1/1.09^2$	101,001
3	Interest	120,000	$1/1.09^3$	92,662
		Total liability component		303,755
		Total equity component (balance)		1,696,245
		Total proceeds		2,000,000

The entity records the following accounting entry.

	€	€
Cash	2,000,000	
Equity		1,696,245
Liability		303,755

6.6.3.A   Bond which is mandatorily convertible into a variable number of shares with an option for the issuer to settle early for a maximum number of shares

At its meeting in July 2013, the Interpretations Committee considered the IAS 32 classification for a financial instrument that is mandatorily convertible into a variable number of shares, subject to a cap and floor, but with an issuer option to settle by delivering the maximum (fixed) number of shares.[24] This is a financial instrument with essentially the same features as the one described in Example 44.8 above, but with an additional option for the issuer to settle the instrument at any time before maturity (see 6.4 above for IAS 32 classification considerations for the 'basic financial instrument', ignoring the early settlement option). If the issuer chooses to exercise its early settlement option, it must deliver the maximum number of shares specified in the contract (e.g. 100 shares in Example 44.8) and pay in cash all of the interest that would have been payable if the instrument had remained outstanding until its maturity date (a so called 'make-whole provision').

Applying the IAS 32 definitions of a financial liability and of an equity instrument to such a financial instrument would result in accounting for it as a compound instrument (i.e. a financial instrument consisting of an equity element and a financial liability element). IAS 32 states that a non-derivative financial instrument is an equity instrument if the instrument will be settled in the issuer's own equity instruments and includes no contractual obligation for the issuer to deliver a variable number of its own equity instruments. *[IAS 32.11(b)(i)].* With the early settlement option, the issuer has the right to avoid delivering a variable number of shares. A portion of the financial instrument would therefore meet the definition of equity and would be accounted for as such. The interest payments on the instrument, on the other hand, impose a contractual obligation on the issuer to deliver cash in all cases and therefore meet the definition of a financial liability and would be accounted for as such.

However, this analysis ignores the fact that in exercising the early settlement option, the issuer must deliver at an earlier time a potentially greater number of its own shares, plus all the interest in cash which would have been payable over the instrument's life. The issuer can avoid delivering a variable number of its own shares but only by giving away a potentially larger amount of economic value. The question asked of the Interpretations Committee was whether such an early settlement option should be considered when classifying the financial instrument under IAS 32.

In its analysis, the Interpretations Committee noted that the definitions of financial asset, financial liability and equity instrument in IAS 32 are based on the financial instrument's contractual rights and contractual obligations.[25] However, IAS 32 requires the issuer of a financial instrument to classify the instrument in accordance with the substance of the contractual arrangement. *[IAS 32.15].* An issuer cannot assume that a financial instrument (or any component) meets the definition of an equity instrument simply because the issuer has the contractual right to settle the financial instrument by delivering a fixed number of equity instruments. The issuer would need to consider whether the early settlement option is substantive and, if it was concluded that it lacks substance, then it should be ignored for the classification assessment of the instrument.

It was noted that the guidance in paragraph 20(b) of IAS 32 is relevant because it provides an example of a situation in which one of an instrument's settlement alternatives is excluded from the classification assessment. Specifically, the example in that paragraph describes an instrument that the issuer will settle by delivering either cash or its own shares, and states that one of the settlement alternatives should be excluded from the classification assessment in some circumstances (see 5.2.4 above).

To determine whether the early settlement option is substantive, the issuer would need to understand whether there are actual economic or business reasons that would lead the issuer to exercise the option. In making that assessment, the issuer could consider whether the instrument would have been priced differently if the issuer's early settlement option had not been included in the contractual terms. The Interpretations Committee also noted that factors such as the term of the instrument, the width of the range between the cap and the floor, the issuer's share price and the volatility of the share price could be relevant to the assessment of whether the issuer's early settlement option is substantive. For example, the early settlement option may be less likely to have substance – especially if the instrument is short-lived – if the range between the cap and the floor is wide and the current share price would equate to the delivery of a number of shares that is close to the floor. That is because the issuer may have to deliver significantly more shares to settle early than it may otherwise be obliged to deliver at maturity. The Interpretations Committee considered that in light of its analysis of the existing IFRS requirements, it would not add this issue to its agenda.

6.6.3.B   *Bond which is mandatorily convertible into a variable number of shares upon a contingent 'non-viability' event*

Since the financial crisis, regulators have been looking to strengthen the capital base of financial institutions, particularly in the banking sector. Rising requirements for capital adequacy have resulted in banks looking into new forms of capital instruments. One form of such capital instruments are financial instruments that convert into a variable number of the issuer's own ordinary shares if the institution breaches a minimum regulatory requirement. This type of contingent event is called a 'non-viability' event.

While the exact terms of these instruments vary in practice, they do generally come with the following key features:

- no stated maturity but the issuer can call the instrument for the par amount of cash;

- while the instrument has a stated interest rate (e.g. 5%), payment of interest is at the discretion of the issuer;

- if the issuer breaches a minimum regulatory requirement (e.g. 'Tier 1 Capital ratio'), the instrument mandatorily converts into a variable number of the issuer's own ordinary shares. The number of shares delivered would depend on the current share price, i.e. the issuer must deliver as many shares as are worth the par amount of the instrument at conversion.

In July 2013 the Interpretations Committee considered a request to clarify the accounting for such instruments.[26] In its tentative agenda decision, the Committee noted that the instrument is a compound instrument that is composed of the following two components:

- a liability component, which reflects the issuer's obligation to deliver a variable number of its own equity instruments if the contingent non-viability event occurs; and
- an equity component, which reflects the issuer's discretion to pay interest.

To measure the liability component, the Interpretations Committee noted that the issuer must consider the fact that the contingent non-viability event could occur immediately because it is beyond the control of the issuer. Hence the liability component must be measured at the full amount that the issuer could be required to pay immediately. The equity component would be measured as a residual and thus would be measured at zero, because the instrument is issued at par and the value of the variable number of shares that will be delivered on conversion is equal to that fixed par amount.

The Interpretations Committee received 12 comment letters on the tentative agenda decision, many accepting that the Interpretation Committee's view is one way of analysing the financial instrument under IAS 32, but generally expressing the view that the relevant guidance in IAS 32 is unclear and that equally valid arguments could be made for other views. For instance, one view discussed at the time was that, when measuring the liability component, the issuer should consider the expected timing of the contingent non-viability event occurring and discount the liability accordingly. Therefore, if the issuer believed that the contingency would not occur in the near-term, the liability component would be recognised at an amount of less than par. The comments provided focused in particular on (a) the measurement of the liability component and (b) whether interest paid on the instrument, if any, would need to be recognised in equity or as interest in profit or loss. Based on the comments received, the Interpretations Committee decided, after further discussions in its January 2014 meeting, not to add this issue to its agenda and noted that the scope of the issues raised in the submission was too broad to be addressed in an efficient manner.[27] There is therefore the potential for diversity in practice until this issue is clarified by the IASB. This is illustrated by the following example:

Example 44.13:   Convertible bond mandatorily convertible upon 'non-viability' event

A bank issues €100 million of contingent convertible bonds. The bonds notionally pay fixed interest of 7% annually however interest payments are at the sole discretion of the issuer providing that no dividend is paid on the ordinary shares of the issuer. The bonds are perpetual, but the issuer has the right to call the shares after five years and on every succeeding fifth anniversary thereafter.

The instrument is immediately converted into ordinary shares with a fair value equal to the par value of the bonds upon either:

- the bank's fully loaded Common Equity Tier 1 (CET 1) ratio falling below 7%; or
- the local regulator declaring a non-viability event.

The instrument has both debt features, such as the contingent settlement provision which requires settlement in a variable number of shares upon a non-viability event, and equity features, such as the perpetual nature of the instrument and the discretionary interest payments. As discussed above there are a number of views that could be taken on how to classify this instrument.

Chapter 44

Based on the Interpretations Committee's discussion, the view could be taken that the bonds are a compound instrument and that because the contingent settlement provision might be activated immediately, a liability for the par amount of the bond should be recorded. The equity component of the instrument representing the discretionary interest payments would therefore have no value.

However this could be viewed as odd given that there is usually no expectation that a trigger event will occur when the instrument is first issued. As such it might be considered to be more reasonable to estimate when a trigger event is most likely to occur and calculate the liability component on that basis with the residual amount being classified as equity.

There is a further argument that the whole instrument falls within the definition of a liability rather than a compound instrument as the entity may be required to deliver a variable number of shares for a non-derivative instrument. *[IAS 32.11(b)(i)]*.

The conversion trigger itself is not a separable embedded derivative as redemption at amortised cost is regarded as being closely related to the host contract. This is the case even if the debt and equity components of the instrument are separated, as the evaluation of the embedded derivative has to be performed prior to the separation of the equity component. *[IAS 39.AG30(g)]*.

Similarly the call option exercisable to extend the term of the instrument is not a separable embedded derivative as the option is at par and so is also closely related.

Any discretionary interest payments would be classified depending on whether the host is classified as a liability, in which case the payments would be interest, or as a compound instrument, in which case payments would be dividends.

A further complication arises with the recent introduction of bank resolution regimes, such as the European Union's Banking Recovery and Resolution Directive (BRRD). These regimes subject certain financial instruments to bail-in, where banking regulators have the power to write down an instrument or convert it into another CET 1 instrument at their discretion.

As the right to convert the instrument is at the option of the regulator and not the issuer it is arguable that the instrument cannot be classified as equity. The exception for settlement in case of liquidation (see 4.3.2 above) does not apply here as the regulator is likely to invoke the resolution tool well before liquidation occurs. Also IFRIC 2 specifies that local law and regulations in effect at the classification date together with the terms contained in the instrument's documentation constitute the terms and conditions of the instrument. *[IFRIC 2.BC10]*.

The main conclusion to be drawn from examples such as these is that the provisions of IAS 32, which were originally drafted in the mid 1990s to deal with 'traditional' convertible instruments, are not always adequate for dealing with the increasingly complex range of instruments available in the financial markets.

6.6.4   Foreign currency convertible bond

If an entity issues a bond in a currency other than its functional currency, the conversion option will not meet the definition of equity in IAS 32, even if the bond is convertible into a fixed number of shares. This is because a fixed amount of foreign currency (a currency different to the functional currency of the bond) is not a fixed amount of cash (see 5.2.3 above). A foreign currency convertible bond is therefore classified as a financial liability under IAS 32, and then measured under the requirements of IAS 39. An equity conversion option embedded in a financial liability is not considered by IAS 39 to be clearly and closely related to the host contract, and should be accounted for as a separate derivative financial instrument measured at fair value through profit or loss.

6.6.4.A   *Instrument issued by foreign subsidiary convertible into equity of parent*

The Interpretations Committee's conclusion that (other than in the context of certain rights issues – see 5.2.3.A above) a fixed amount of cash denominated in a currency other than the entity's functional currency is not a 'fixed amount' of cash (see 5.2.3 above) leads to the rather counter-intuitive result that the classification of certain instruments in consolidated financial statements depends on the functional currency of the issuing entity.

If, in the example in 5.2.3 above, the UK entity's US subsidiary (with a functional currency of US dollars) issued the same $100 bond convertible into its own equity, convertible in turn into the UK parent's equity, the conversion right would (from the perspective of the US subsidiary) involve the issue of a fixed number of shares for a fixed amount of cash and thus be an equity instrument. Moreover, this classification would not change on consolidation since IFRS has no concept of a group functional currency (see Chapter 15).

The Interpretations Committee discussed this issue at its meetings in July and November 2006. Specifically, it was asked to consider whether the fixed stated principal of the convertible instrument exchanged for equity of the parent on conversion can be considered 'fixed' if it is denominated in the functional currency of either the issuer of the exchangeable financial instruments (i.e. the US subsidiary in the example above) or the issuer of the equity instruments (i.e. the UK parent in the example).

The Interpretations Committee noted that a group does not have a functional currency. It therefore discussed whether it should add a project to its agenda to address which currency should be the reference point in determining whether the embedded conversion options are denominated in a foreign currency. The Interpretations Committee believed that the issue was sufficiently narrow that it was not expected to have widespread relevance in practice. The Interpretations Committee, therefore, decided not to take the issue onto its agenda.[28]

In our view, given the absence of specific guidance, an entity may, as a matter of accounting policy, determine the classification, in its consolidated financial statements, of an instrument issued by a subsidiary by reference either to that subsidiary's own functional currency or to the functional currency of the parent into whose equity the bond is convertible.

The effect of this policy choice will be that, where the debt is denominated in a currency other than the designated reference functional currency, the consolidated financial statements contain no equity component. This policy, and its consequences under IAS 32, must be applied consistently, as illustrated by Example 44.14 below.

Example 44.14:   Convertible bond issued by a subsidiary with a functional currency different to that of the parent

Suppose that a UK entity with a functional currency of the pound sterling (GBP) has a US trading subsidiary with a functional currency of the US dollar (USD). The US subsidiary issues a bond convertible, at the holder's option, into equity of the UK parent.

If the parent's functional currency (GBP) is the reference currency, the accounting treatment of the holder's conversion right in the consolidated financial statements will be as follows:

- if the fixed stated principal of the bond is denominated in GBP: equity (stated principal of bond is fixed by reference to GBP); but

- if the fixed stated principal of the bond is denominated in a currency other than GBP: derivative (stated principal of bond is variable by reference to GBP).

If, however, the subsidiary's functional currency (USD) is the reference currency, a converse analysis applies, and the accounting treatment of the holder's conversion right in the consolidated financial statements will be as follows:

- if the fixed stated principal of the bond is denominated in USD: equity (stated principal of bond is fixed by reference to USD); but

- if the fixed stated principal of the bond is denominated in a currency other than USD: derivative (stated principal of bond is variable by reference to USD).

It may be that the Interpretations Committee's reluctance to issue guidance on this matter was influenced by the more subtle point that, in most cases, the issuing entity will not be, as in Example 44.14 above, a trading subsidiary, but rather a subsidiary created only for the purposes of the bond issue. IAS 21 – *The Effects of Changes in Foreign Exchange Rates* – suggests that the functional currency of such a 'single transaction' entity is the same as that of the parent for whose equity the bond will be exchanged, irrespective of the currency in which the bond is denominated (see Chapter 15 at 4). In short, the Interpretations Committee was perhaps hinting that the real problem may be the misapplication of IAS 21 in the financial statements of the issuing subsidiary rather than the interpretation of IAS 32.

6.6.5   Convertibles with cash settlement at the option of the issuer

As discussed as 5.2.8 above, IAS 32 requires a derivative with two or more settlement options to be treated as a financial asset or a financial liability unless all possible settlement alternatives would result in it being an equity instrument. Many convertible bonds currently in issue contain a provision whereby, if the holder exercises its conversion option, the issuer may instead pay cash equal to the fair value of the shares that it would otherwise have been required to deliver. This is to allow for unforeseen circumstances, such as an inability to issue the necessary number of shares to effect conversion at the appropriate time.

Where a bond has such a term, the conversion right is a derivative (in effect, a written call option over the issuer's own shares) which may potentially be settled in cash, such that there is a settlement alternative that does not result in it being an equity instrument. This means that the 'equity component' of a bond with an issuer cash settlement option is not in fact an equity instrument, but a financial liability. The financial reporting implication of this is that the conversion right must be accounted for as a derivative at fair value, with changes in value included in profit or loss – in other words the financial statements will reflect gains and losses based on the movement of the reporting entity's own share price.

6.6.6 Bond convertible into fixed percentage of equity

The terms of a convertible bond may allow conversion into a fixed percentage of outstanding shares of the issuer at the time of the conversion, so that the absolute number of shares to be issued is not fixed and is not known until conversion occurs. This raises the question of whether such a clause violates the 'fixed for fixed' criterion, or whether it can be seen as an anti-dilutive mechanism to keep the holder in the same economic position relative to other shareholders at all times (similarly to bonds whose conversion ratio is adjusted for changes in share capital, as discussed under 5.1.2 above).

Our view is that such a conversion option cannot normally be classified as equity, because the entity's capital structure could change in ways that put the convertible bond holder into a better economic position relative to other shareholders.

7 SETTLEMENT OF FINANCIAL LIABILITY WITH EQUITY INSTRUMENT

Neither IAS 32 nor IAS 39 specifically addresses the accounting treatment to be adopted where an entity issues non-convertible debt, but subsequently enters into an agreement with the debt holder to discharge all or part of the liability in exchange for an issue of equity. These transactions, which are sometimes referred to as 'debt for equity swaps', most often occur when the entity is in financial difficulties and became widespread, particularly among highly leveraged entities, following the financial crisis.

The Interpretations Committee noted that divergent accounting treatments for such transactions were being applied and decided to address this by developing an interpretation. As a result, IFRIC 19 was published in November 2009. *[IFRIC 19.1].*

7.1 Scope and effective date of IFRIC 19

IFRIC 19 addresses the accounting by an entity when the terms of a financial liability are renegotiated and result in the entity issuing equity instruments to a creditor to extinguish all or part of the financial liability. It does not address the accounting by the creditor. *[IFRIC 19.2].*

Further, the interpretation does not apply to transactions in situations where: *[IFRIC 19.3]*

- the creditor is also a direct or indirect shareholder and is acting in its capacity as a direct or indirect existing shareholder (see 7.3 below);

- the creditor and the entity are controlled by the same party or parties before and after the transaction and the substance of the transaction includes an equity distribution by, or contribution to, the entity (see 7.3 below); or

- the extinguishment of the financial liability by issuing equity shares is in accordance with the original terms of the financial liability. This will most commonly arise on conversion of a convertible bond that has been subject to 'split accounting', the accounting for which is covered at 6 above.

7.2   Requirements of IFRIC 19

Equity instruments issued to a creditor to extinguish all or part of a financial liability are treated as consideration paid and should normally be measured at their fair value at the date of extinguishment. However, if that fair value cannot be reliably measured, the equity instruments should be measured to reflect the fair value of the financial liability extinguished. The difference between the carrying amount of the financial liability and the consideration paid (including the equity instruments issued) should be recognised in profit or loss and should be disclosed separately. *[IFRIC 19.5-7, 9, 11].*

These requirements are illustrated in the following simple example.

Example 44.15:   Discharge of liability for fresh issue of equity

During 2009 an entity issued £100 million bonds due to be repaid in 2019. By 2016 the entity is in some financial difficulty and reaches an agreement with the holders of the bonds whereby they will accept equity shares in the entity in full and final settlement of all amounts due under the bonds. On the date the agreement concludes, the carrying amount of the bonds is £99 million and the fair value of the equity shares issued is £60 million.

In this situation the entity would measure the equity instruments issued at their fair value of £60 million and recognise a profit on extinguishment of £39 million [£99 million – £60 million].

Debt for equity swaps often take place in situations when the terms of the financial liability such as covenants are breached and the liability has become, or will become, repayable on demand. Normally, the fair value of a financial liability with a demand feature is required by IFRS 13 to be measured at no less than the amount payable on demand, discounted from the first date that the amount could be required to be paid (see Chapter 14 at 11.5). However, in the IASB's view, the fact that a debt for equity swap has occurred indicates that the demand feature is no longer substantive. Consequently, where the fair value of the equity instruments issued is based on the fair value of the liability extinguished, this particular aspect of IFRS 13 is not applied. *[IFRIC 19.7, BC22].*

If only part of the financial liability is extinguished, some of the consideration paid might relate to a modification of the terms of the liability that remains outstanding. If so, the consideration paid should be allocated between the part of the liability extinguished and the part of the liability that remains outstanding. All relevant facts and circumstances relating to the transaction should be considered in making this allocation. *[IFRIC 19.8].* Any consideration so allocated forms part of the assessment of whether the terms of that remaining liability have been substantially modified. If the remaining liability has been substantially modified, the modification should be accounted for as an extinguishment of the original liability and the recognition of a new liability in accordance with IAS 39 (see Chapter 50 at 6.2). *[IFRIC 19.10].*

7.3   Debt for equity swaps with shareholders

As noted at 7.1 above, a debt for equity swap is outside the scope of IFRIC 19 when the creditor is a shareholder acting in its capacity as such, or where the entity and the creditor are under common control and the substance of the transaction includes a distribution by, or capital contribution to, the entity.

In our view, such transactions may be accounted for either in a manner similar to that required by IFRIC 19 or by recording the equity instruments issued at the carrying amount of the financial liability extinguished so that no profit or loss is recognised. This latter method was in fact commonly applied to debt for equity swaps before the publication of IFRIC 19.

8   INTEREST, DIVIDENDS, GAINS AND LOSSES

The basic principle of IAS 32 is that inflows and outflows of cash (and other assets) associated with equity instruments are recognised in equity and the net impact of inflows and outflows of cash (and other assets) associated with financial liabilities is ultimately recognised in profit or loss. Accordingly, IAS 32 requires:

- interest, dividends, losses and gains relating to a financial instrument or a component that is a financial liability to be recognised as income or expense in profit or loss;

- distributions to holders of an equity instrument to be debited directly to equity; and

- the transaction costs of an equity transaction to be accounted for as a deduction from equity, other than the costs of issuing an equity instrument that are directly attributable to the acquisition of a business (which are accounted for under IFRS 3 – see Chapter 9). *[IAS 32.35]*.

The treatment of the costs and gains associated with instruments is determined by their classification in the financial statements under IAS 32, and not by their legal form. Thus dividends paid on shares classified as financial liabilities (see 4.5 above) will be recognised as an expense in profit or loss, not as an appropriation of equity.

The basic principle summarised above also applies to compound instruments and requires any payments in relation to the equity component to be recorded in equity and any payments in relation to the liability component to be recorded in profit or loss. (As discussed at 6.6.3.B above, it is not clear whether this basic principle also applies when the full amount of the issuance proceeds of a compound instrument is allocated to the liability.) A mandatorily redeemable preference share with dividends paid at the discretion of the entity results in the classification of a liability equal to the net present value of the redemption amount and an equity classification equal to the excess of the proceeds over the liability component (the net present value of the redemption amount) (see 4.5.1 above). Because the redemption obligation is classified as a liability, the unwinding of the discount on this component is recorded and classified as an interest expense. Any dividends paid, on the other hand, relate to the equity component and are therefore recorded as a distribution of profit. *[IAS 32.AG37]*.

Gains and losses associated with redemptions or refinancings of financial liabilities are recognised in profit or loss, whereas redemptions or refinancings of equity instruments are recognised as changes in equity. *[IAS 32.36]*.

Similarly, gains and losses related to changes in the carrying amount of a financial liability are recognised as income or expense in profit or loss, even when they relate to an instrument that includes a right to the residual interest in the assets of the entity in exchange for cash or another financial asset (see 4.6 above). However, IAS 32 notes that IAS 1 requires any gain or loss arising from the remeasurement of such an instrument to be shown separately in the statement of comprehensive income, where it is relevant in explaining the entity's performance. *[IAS 32.41]*.

Changes in the fair value of an instrument that meets the definition of an equity instrument are not recognised in the financial statements. *[IAS 32.36]*.

IAS 32 permits dividends classified as an expense (i.e. because they relate to an instrument, or component of an instrument, that is legally a share but classified as a financial liability under IAS 32) to be presented in the statement of comprehensive income or separate income statement (if presented), either with interest on other liabilities or as a separate item. The standard notes that, in some circumstances, separate disclosure is desirable, because of the differences between interest and dividends with respect to matters such as tax deductibility. Disclosure of interest and dividends is required by IAS 1 (see Chapter 3) and IFRS 7 (see Chapter 53). *[IAS 32.40]*.

8.1   Transaction costs of equity transactions

An entity typically incurs various costs in issuing or acquiring its own equity instruments, such as registration and other regulatory fees, amounts paid to legal, accounting and other professional advisers, printing costs and stamp duties. The transaction costs of an equity transaction are accounted for as a deduction from equity, but only to the extent they are *incremental costs directly attributable* to the equity transaction that otherwise would have been avoided. The costs of an equity transaction that is abandoned are recognised as an expense. *[IAS 32.37]*.

IAS 32 requires that only the costs of 'issuing or acquiring' equity are recognised in equity. Accordingly, it seems clear that the costs of listing shares already in issue should not be set off against equity, but recognised as an expense.

The standard also requires that transaction costs that relate jointly to more than one transaction (for example, costs of a concurrent offering of some shares and a stock exchange listing of other shares) are allocated to those transactions using a basis of allocation that is rational and consistent with similar transactions. *[IAS 32.38]*. In its agenda decision of September 2008, the Interpretations Committee declined to provide further guidance on the extent of the transaction costs to be accounted for as a deduction from equity and how to allocate costs that relate jointly to more than one transaction, believing existing guidance to be adequate.

However, the Interpretations Committee noted that the terms 'incremental' and 'directly attributable' are used with similar but not identical meanings in many Standards and Interpretations, leading to diversity in practice. It therefore recommended that the IASB develop common definitions for both terms to be added to the Glossary as part of the annual improvements process. However, the IASB did not propose any such amendments in the next exposure draft published in August 2009.

It may well be that, in an initial public offering ('IPO'), for example, an entity simultaneously lists its existing equity and additional newly-issued equity. In that situation the total costs of the IPO should, in our view, be allocated between the newly issued shares and the existing shares on a rational basis (e.g. by reference to the ratio of the number of new shares to the number of total shares), with only the proportion relating to the issue of new shares being deducted from equity.

Transaction costs that relate to the issue of a compound financial instrument are allocated to the liability and equity components of the instrument in proportion to the allocation of proceeds (see Example 44.5 at 6.2 above). *[IAS 32.37].*

IAS 32 does not specifically address the treatment of transaction costs incurred to acquire a non-controlling interest in a subsidiary, or dispose of such an interest without loss of control in the consolidated financial statements of the parent entity. IFRS 10 indicates that 'changes in a parent's ownership interest in a subsidiary that do not result in the parent losing control of the subsidiary are equity transactions'. *[IFRS 10.23].* Accordingly, we believe that the costs of such transactions should be deducted from equity in accordance with the principles described above.

IAS 32 and IFRS 10 do not specify whether such costs should be allocated to the parent's equity or to the non-controlling interest, to the extent it is still reflected in the statement of financial position. In our view, this is a matter of choice based on the facts and circumstances surrounding the transaction, and any local legal requirements. On any subsequent disposal of the subsidiary involving loss of control, the transaction costs previously recognised in equity should not be reclassified from equity to profit or loss, since they represent transactions with owners in their capacity as owners rather than components of other comprehensive income. *[IAS 1.106, 109].*

The amount of transaction costs accounted for as a deduction from equity in the period is required to be disclosed separately under IAS 1 (see Chapter 3 at 3.3) and IFRS 7 (see Chapter 53 at 7.3).

8.2   Tax effects of equity transactions

As originally issued, IAS 32 required distributions to shareholders and transaction costs of equity instruments to be shown net of any tax benefit. *Annual Improvements to IFRSs 2009-2011 Cycle* issued in May 2012 amended IAS 32 so as to remove the reference to income tax benefit from IAS 32. This means that all tax effects of equity transactions are allocated in accordance with the general principles of IAS 12.

Unfortunately, it is not entirely clear how IAS 12 requires the tax effects of certain equity transactions to be dealt with and different views can be taken whether tax benefits in respect of distributions are to be recognised in equity or profit or loss (see Chapter 30 at 10.3.5).

Chapter 44

9 TREASURY SHARES

Treasury shares are shares issued by an entity that are held by the entity. *[IAS 32.33]*. In consolidated financial statements, this will include shares issued by any group entity that are held by that entity or by any other members of the consolidated group. They will also include shares held by an employee benefit trust that is consolidated or treated as an extension of the reporting entity. Treasury shares will generally not include shares in a group entity held by any associates or the entity's pension fund. However, IAS 1 requires disclosure of own shares held by subsidiaries or associates *[IAS 1.79(a)(vi)]* and IAS 19 – *Employee Benefits* – requires disclosure of own shares held by defined benefit plans. *[IAS 19.143]*. Holdings of treasury shares may arise in a number of ways. For example:

- The entity holds the shares as the result of a direct transaction, such as a market purchase, or a buy-back of shares from shareholders as a whole, or a particular group of shareholders;

- The entity is in the financial services sector with a market-making operation that buys and sells its own shares along with those of other listed entities in the normal course of business, or holds them in order to 'hedge' issued derivatives;

- In consolidated financial statements:

    - the shares were purchased by another entity which subsequently became a subsidiary of the reporting entity, either through acquisition or changes in financial reporting requirements;

    - the shares have been purchased by an entity that is a consolidated SPE of the reporting entity.

The circumstances in which an entity is permitted to hold treasury shares are a matter for legislation in the jurisdiction concerned.

Treasury shares do not include own shares held by an entity on behalf of others, such as when a financial institution holds its own equity on behalf of a client. In such cases, there is an agency relationship and as a result those holdings are not included in the entity's statement of financial position, either as assets or as a deduction from equity. *[IAS 32.AG36]*.

If an entity reacquires its own equity instruments, IAS 32 requires those instruments to be deducted from equity. They are not recognised as financial assets, regardless of the reason for which they are reacquired. No gain or loss is recognised in profit or loss on the purchase, sale, issue or cancellation of an entity's own equity instruments. Accordingly, any consideration paid or received in connection with treasury share must be recognised directly in equity. *[IAS 32.33, AG36]*.

IAS 1 requires the amount of treasury shares to be disclosed separately either on the face of the statement of financial position or in the notes (see Chapter 3 at 3.1.6). In addition IAS 24 – *Related Party Disclosures* – requires an entity to make disclosures where it reacquires its own equity instruments from related parties (see Chapter 36 at 2.5). *[IAS 32.34]*. There is a similar requirement in IFRS 7 (see Chapter 53 at 7.3).

As in the case of the requirements for the treatment of the equity component of a compound financial instrument (see 6 above), IAS 32 does not prescribe precisely what components of equity should be adjusted as the result of a treasury share transaction. This may have been to ensure that there was no conflict between, on the one hand, the basic requirement of IAS 32 that there should be an adjustment to equity and, on the other hand, the legal requirements of various jurisdictions as to exactly how that adjustment should be allocated within equity.

9.1   Transactions in own shares not at fair value

The requirement of IAS 32 that no profits or losses should ever be recognised on transactions in own equity instruments differs from the approach taken in IFRS 2. If an employee share award is characterised as an equity instrument under IFRS 2 (a 'share-settled' award) and settled in cash (or other assets) at more than its fair value, the excess of the consideration over the fair value is recognised as an expense (see Chapter 31).

It is not clear whether or not the IASB specifically considered transactions in own equity other than at fair value in the context of IAS 32, particularly since the relevant provisions of IAS 32 essentially reproduce requirements previously contained in SIC-16 – *Share Capital – Reacquired Own Equity Instruments (Treasury Shares)* – which was implicitly addressing market purchases and sales at fair value. In other words, the provision can be seen merely as clarifying that, if an entity buys one of its own shares in the market for £10 which it later reissues in the market at £12 or £7, it has not made, respectively, a profit of £2 or a loss of £3.

This is slightly different to the situation where an entity purchases an equity instrument for more than its fair value – i.e. if the original purchase had been for £11 when the market price was £10. Such a transaction could occur, for example where the entity wishes to rid itself of a troublesome shareholder or group of shareholders. In this case, the entity might have to offer a premium specific to the holder over and above the 'true' fair value of the equity instruments concerned. There could be an argument that such a transaction does not fall within the type of transaction envisaged by the rules for treasury shares, such that the holder-specific premium should be accounted for in profit or loss, not equity. Alternatively, it might be argued that, in the specific circumstances, the amount paid is the fair value of the particular shares concerned.

A transaction in which the entity issues shares (or reissues treasury shares) for cash or other assets with a fair value lower than the fair value of the shares would *prima facie* fall within the scope of IFRS 2, requiring the shortfall to be accounted for under IFRS 2 (see Chapter 31 at 2.2.2.C).

10   'HEDGING' OF INSTRUMENTS CLASSIFIED AS EQUITY

A consequence of the requirement, discussed in 4.5.2 to 4.5.6 above, to treat discretionary instruments with certain debt-like characteristics as equity is that the issuer will not be able to adopt hedge accounting in respect of any instrument taken out as a hedge of the instrument (e.g. a receive fixed, pay floating interest rate swap taken out to hedge a fixed rate discretionary dividend on non-redeemable shares). This is because IAS 39 does not recognise a hedge of own equity as a valid hedging relationship (see Chapter 51 and 52).

Accordingly, if an issuer of an equity instrument bearing a fixed-rate discretionary coupon or dividend enters into an interest rate swap to hedge its cash outflows, the swap will be accounted for under the normal rules for derivatives not forming part of a hedging relationship – i.e. at fair value with all value changes recognised in profit or loss (see Chapters 45, 46 and 47). Although, economically speaking, any such gains and losses are offset by equal gains and losses (due to interest rate movements) on the shares, the latter, like all movements in the fair value of own equity, are ignored for financial reporting purposes under IFRS.

11   DERIVATIVES OVER OWN EQUITY INSTRUMENTS

IAS 32 provides a number of detailed examples of the accounting treatment required, under the provisions of revised IAS 32 and IAS 39, to be adopted by an entity for derivative contracts over its own equity instruments. Examples are given of each of the main possible permutations, namely:

- a forward purchase (see 11.1.1 below);
- a forward sale (see 11.1.2 below);
- a purchased call option (see 11.2.1 below);
- a written call option (see 11.2.2 below);
- a purchased put option (see 11.3.1 below); and
- a written put option (see 11.3.2 below).

All such contracts can be either:

(a)   net cash-settled (i.e. the contract provides that the parties will compare the fair value of the shares to be delivered by the seller to the amount of cash payable by the buyer and make a cash payment between themselves for the difference);

(b)   net share-settled (i.e. the contract provides that the parties will compare the fair value of the shares to be delivered by the seller to the amount of cash payable by the buyer and make a transfer between themselves of as many of the entity's shares as have a fair value equal to the difference);

(c)   gross settled (i.e. the contract provides that the seller will deliver shares to the buyer in exchange for cash); or

(d)   subject to various settlement options, whereby the manner of settlement is not predetermined, and instead one or other party can choose the manner of settlement (i.e. gross, net cash or net shares).

The examples consider the above settlement options in turn for the main possible permutations of derivatives over own equity instruments.

All derivative contracts over own equity, where settlement is not exclusively by an exchange of a fixed number of shares for a fixed amount of cash, do not meet the definition of equity instruments in IAS 32 and are, in general, treated as derivative financial assets or liabilities (see 5.2.8 above). IAS 39, or where applicable IFRS 9, requires such contracts to be accounted for at fair value through profit or loss (see Chapter 47). Exemption to this rule applies to forward purchases and written put options with an option to settle gross (see 11.1.1.D and 11.3.2.D below).

11.1   Forward contracts

11.1.1   Forward purchase

In a forward purchase transaction, the entity and a counterparty agree that on a given future date the counterparty will sell a given number of the entity's shares to the entity. Such a contract is illustrated in Example 44.16 below. *[IAS 32.IE2-6]*.

Example 44.16:   Forward purchase of shares

The reporting entity (A), which has a functional currency of Euro and a year end of 31 December, and another party (B) enter into a forward contract for the purchase of A's shares by A, for which the following are the major assumptions.

Contract date	1 February 2016
Maturity date	31 January 2017
Fixed forward price to be paid on 31 January 2017	€104
Present value of forward price on 1 February 2016	€100
Number of shares under contract	1,000
Market price per share on 1 February 2016	€100
Market price per share on 31 December 2016	€110
Market price per share on 31 January 2017	€106
Fair value of forward to A on 1 February 2016	€0
Fair value of forward to A on 31 December 2016	€6,300
Fair value of forward to A on 31 January 2017	€2,000

For simplicity, it is assumed that no dividends are paid on the underlying shares (i.e. the 'carry return' is zero) so that the present value of the forward price equals the spot price when the fair value of the forward contract is zero. The fair value of the forward has been computed as the difference between the market share price and the present value of the fixed forward price. At settlement date this is €2,000 representing 1,000 shares at €2, being the difference between the market price of €106 and the contract price of €104.

A   Net cash settlement

If the contract is entered into as net cash-settled on 1 February 2016, settlement on 31 January 2017 will take the form of receipt or delivery by A of a cash payment for the difference between the fair value of 1,000 of A's own shares, at 31 January 2017, and €104,000 (i.e. 1,000 shares at the forward price of €104 per share). Since IAS 32 classifies such contracts as derivative financial assets or liabilities (see 11 and 5.2.7 above), which are carried at fair value through profit or loss under IAS 39 (IFRS 9), A records the following accounting entries:

	€	€
1 February 2016		
No entry is required because the fair value of the contract is zero at inception and no cash is paid or received		
31 December 2016		
Forward contract (statement of financial position)	6,300	
Gain on forward (profit or loss)		6,300
To record movement in fair value of forward from zero to €6,300		
31 January 2017		
Loss on forward (profit or loss)	4,300	
Forward contract (statement of financial position)		4,300
To record movement in fair value of forward from €6,300 to €2,000		
Cash	2,000	
Forward contract (statement of financial position)		2,000
To record settlement of forward by payment of €2,000 by B to A		

B   Net share settlement

If the contract is entered into as net share-settled on 1 February 2016, settlement on 31 January 2017 will take the form of receipt or delivery by A of as many of A's shares as have a fair value equal to the difference between the fair value, at 31 January 2017, of 1,000 of A's own shares and €104,000 (i.e. 1,000 shares at the forward price of €104 per share). Because IAS 32 classifies such contracts as derivative financial assets or liabilities (see 11 and 5.2.7 above), which are carried at fair value through profit or loss under IAS 39 (or IFRS 9), A records the following accounting entries:

	€	€
1 February 2016		
No entry is required because the fair value of the contract is zero at inception and no cash is paid or received		
31 December 2016		
Forward contract (statement of financial position)	6,300	
Gain on forward (profit or loss)		6,300
To record movement in fair value of forward from zero to €6,300		
31 January 2017		
Loss on forward (profit or loss)	4,300	
Forward contract (statement of financial position)		4,300
To record movement in fair value of forward from €6,300 to €2,000		
Equity	2,000	
Forward contract (statement of financial position)		2,000

To record net settlement of forward by transfer of €2,000 worth of A's shares (€2000/106=18.9 shares) by B to A. This is shown as a deduction from equity in accordance with IAS 32's requirements for treasury shares (see 9 above).

C Gross settlement

If the contract is entered into as gross-settled on 1 February 2016, settlement on 31 January 2017 will take the form of receipt of 1,000 own shares by A in exchange for a payment of €104,000 to B. IAS 32 classifies this derivative contract as an equity instrument giving rise to a financial liability for the present value of the purchase price amount payable in one year's time (see 5.3 above). On the assumption that A accounts for this liability under the effective interest method in IAS 39 (or IFRS 9), A records the following accounting entries:

	€	€
1 February 2016		
Equity	100,000	
Liability for forward contract (statement of financial position)		100,000

To record net present value of liability on forward contract

	€	€
31 December 2016		
Interest expense	3,660	
Liability for forward contract (statement of financial position)		3,660

To accrue interest, under the effective interest rate method, on the liability to settle forward contract

	€	€
31 January 2017		
Interest expense	340	
Liability for forward contract (statement of financial position)		340

To accrue further interest, under the effective interest rate method, on the liability to settle forward contract

	€	€
Liability for forward contract (statement of financial position)	104,000	
Cash		104,000

To record settlement of the liability in cash

D Settlement options

If there are settlement options (such as net in cash, net in shares or by an exchange of a fixed amount of cash for a fixed number of shares), the forward contract is a financial asset or a financial liability – see 5.2.7 above. The contract does not meet the definition of an equity instrument, because it can be settled otherwise than by delivery of a fixed amount of cash for a fixed number of equity instruments. If one of the settlement alternatives is gross settlement by an exchange of cash for shares, A recognises a liability for the obligation to deliver cash. Otherwise, A accounts for the forward contract as a derivative.

The implementation guidance to IAS 32 states that A should recognise a liability 'if one of the settlement alternatives is to exchange cash for shares'. As drafted, this applies whether the choice of settlement rests with A or B. This seems curious since, where A has the choice of settlement, there would be no obligation for A to settle gross. We assume that the example is written on the presumption that the choice of settlement would normally rest with the counterparty rather than the entity. Paragraph 23 in the main body of the standard is clear that an equity contract gives rise to a liability for the purchase price of the shares only where there is an obligation for the entity to purchase its own equity. Accordingly, in our view, where the choice of settlement rests only with the entity, it is acceptable to record no liability, and to account for the contract as a derivative.

11.1.2   Forward sale

In a forward sale transaction, the entity and a counterparty agree that on a given future date the entity will sell (or issue) a given number of the entity's shares to the counterparty. Such a contract is illustrated in Example 44.17 below. *[IAS 32.IE7-11].*

Example 44.17:   Forward sale of shares

The reporting entity (A), which has a functional currency of Euro and a year end of 31 December, and another party (B) enter into a forward contract for the purchase of A's shares by B, for which the following are the major assumptions.

Contract date	1 February 2016
Maturity date	31 January 2017
Fixed forward price to be paid on 31 January 2017	€104
Present value of forward price on 1 February 2016	€100
Number of shares under contract	1,000
Market price per share on 1 February 2016	€100
Market price per share on 31 December 2016	€110
Market price per share on 31 January 2017	€106
Fair value of forward to A on 1 February 2016	€0
Fair value of forward to A on 31 December 2016	€(6,300)
Fair value of forward to A on 31 January 2017	€(2,000)

For simplicity, it is assumed that no dividends are paid on the underlying shares (i.e. the 'carry return' is zero) so that the present value of the forward price equals the spot price when the fair value of the forward contract is zero. The fair value of the forward has been computed as the difference between the market share price and the present value of the fixed forward price. At settlement date this is negative €2,000 representing 1,000 shares at €2, being the difference between the market price of €106 and the contract price of €104.

A   *Net cash settlement*

If the contract is entered into as net cash-settled on 1 February 2016, settlement on 31 January 2017 will take the form of receipt or delivery by A of a cash payment for the difference between the fair value of 1,000 of A's own shares, at 31 January 2017, and €104,000 (i.e. 1,000 shares at the forward price of €104 per share). Since IAS 32 classifies such contracts as derivative financial assets or liabilities (see 11 and 5.2.7 above), which are carried at fair value through profit or loss under IAS 39 (or IFRS 9), A records the following accounting entries:

	€	€

1 February 2016

No entry is required because the fair value of the contract is zero at inception and no cash is paid or received.

31 December 2016

	€	€
Loss on forward (profit or loss)	6,300	
Forward contract (statement of financial position)		6,300

To record movement in fair value of forward from zero to €(6,300)

31 January 2017

	€	€
Forward contract (statement of financial position)	4,300	
Gain on forward (profit or loss)		4,300

To record movement in fair value of forward from €(6,300) to €(2,000)

Forward contract (statement of financial position)	2,000	
Cash		2,000

To record net settlement of forward by payment of €2,000 cash by A to B

B Net share settlement

If the contract is entered into as net share-settled on 1 February 2016, settlement on 31 January 2017 will take the form of receipt or delivery by A of a payment of as many of A's shares as have a fair value equal to the difference between the fair value, at 31 January 2017, of 1,000 of A's own shares and €104,000 (i.e. 1,000 shares at the forward price of €104 per share). As IAS 32 classifies such contracts as derivative financial assets or liabilities (see 11 and 5.2.7 above), which are carried at fair value through profit or loss under IAS 39 (or IFRS 9), A records the following accounting entries:

	€	€

1 February 2016

No entry is required because the fair value of the contract is zero at inception

31 December 2016

Loss on forward (profit or loss)	6,300	
Forward contract (statement of financial position)		6,300

To record movement in fair value of forward from zero to €(6,300)

31 January 2017

Forward contract (statement of financial position)	4,300	
Gain on forward (profit or loss)		4,300

To record movement in fair value of forward from €(6,300) to €(2,000)

Forward contract (statement of financial position)	2,000	
Equity		2,000

To record net settlement of forward by delivery of €2,000 worth of A's shares to B (€2000/106=18.9 shares)

C Gross settlement

If the contract is entered into as gross-settled on 1 February 2016, settlement on 31 January 2017 will take the form of delivery of 1,000 own shares by A to B in exchange for a payment of €104,000. IAS 32 classifies this derivative contract as an equity instrument (see 5.4 above) and therefore no entries are recorded other than on settlement on the contract. While a forward sale is economically a 'mirror' of a forward purchase and both are classified as equity instruments, the accounting impact is different. A forward sale does not result in any accounting entries until the shares are finally issued/delivered, while a forward purchase establishes an obligation to pay the settlement amount and therefore meets the definition of a financial liability which needs to be recorded upon entering the contract (see part C of Example 44.16 above).

	€	€

31 January 2017

Cash	104,000	
Equity		104,000

To record settlement of forward contract through delivery of 1,000 shares for the payment of €104,000

D   *Settlement options*

If there are settlement options (such as net in cash, net in shares or by an exchange of cash and shares), the forward contract is a financial asset or a financial liability – see 5.2.8 above. A accounts for the forward contract as a derivative (as in A and B above), with the accounting entry made on settlement determined by the manner of settlement (i.e. equity or cash).

11.1.3   'Back-to-back' forward contracts

The accounting treatment in 11.1.1 and 11.1.2 above produces rather strange results when applied to 'back-to-back' forward contracts, such as might be entered into by a financial institution with two different clients. Example 44.18 below illustrates the point.

Example 44.18:   'Back-to-back' forward contracts

Suppose that a bank entered into the forward purchase contract in Example 44.16 above with a client and laid off its risk by entering into the reciprocal forward sale contract in Example 44.17 above with a second client. If both contracts are required to be settled gross, the overall effect of the accounting entries required to be made by the bank (assuming that the bank was the reporting entity in Examples 44.16 and 44.17) can be summarised as set out below. Note that these are not the actual entries that would be made, but the arithmetical sum of all the entries:

	€	€
Profit or loss (interest expense on liability for purchase contract)	4,000	
Equity (€104,000 on sale less €100,000 on purchase)		4,000

If the purchase contract is required to be settled gross, but the sale contract net in cash, the required accounting entries (again, not the actual entries, but the arithmetical sum of all the entries) can be summarised as:

	€	€
Profit or loss (loss on sale contract €2,000 plus interest on liability for purchase contract €4,000)	6,000	
Equity (purchase contract)	100,000	
Cash (€104,000 on purchase, €2,000 on sale)		106,000

If the purchase contract is required to be settled net in cash, but the sale contract gross, the required accounting entries (again, not the actual entries, but the arithmetical sum of all the entries) can be summarised as:

	€	€
Cash (€104,000 in on sale, €2,000 in on purchase)	106,000	
Profit or loss (gain on purchase contract)		2,000
Equity (sale contract)		104,000

If both contracts are net settled, no net gain or loss arises.

Some might argue that this exposes a flaw in the requirements of IAS 32. Self-evidently, these contracts are matched and should therefore, if both run to term, give rise to no economic profit or loss, irrespective of how they are settled. However, IAS 32 requires three different results to be shown depending on whether both contracts are settled gross, or one gross and the other net. This is less understandable in the case where both contracts are settled gross. However, in cases where one contract is settled net and that contract gives rise to an initial receipt or payment of cash, then some difference is bound to occur due to interest effects.

11.2 Call options

11.2.1 Purchased call option

In a purchased call option, the entity pays a counterparty for the right, but not the obligation, to purchase a given number of its own equity instruments from the counterparty for a fixed price at a future date. The accounting for such a contract is illustrated in Example 44.19 below. *[IAS 32.IE12-16]*.

Example 44.19: Purchased call option on shares

The reporting entity (A), which has a functional currency of Euro and a year end of 31 December, purchases a call option over its own shares from another party (B), for which the following are the major assumptions.

Contract date	1 February 2016
Exercise date (European terms – i.e. can be exercised only on maturity)	31 January 2017
Fixed exercise price to be paid on 31 January 2017	€102
Number of shares under contract	1,000
Market price per share on 1 February 2016	€100
Market price per share on 31 December 2016	€104
Market price per share on 31 January 2017	€104
Fair value of option to A on 1 February 2016	€5,000
Fair value of option to A on 31 December 2016	€3,000
Fair value of option to A on 31 January 2017	€2,000

The fair value of the option would be computed using an option pricing model and would be a function of a number of factors, principally the market value of the shares, the exercise price, and the time value of money.

A   Net cash settlement

If the contract is entered into as net cash-settled on 1 February 2016, then A can, on the exercise date 31 January 2017, require B to make a cash payment to A for the excess, if any, of the fair value of 1,000 of A's own shares, as of 31 January 2017, over €102,000 (i.e. 1,000 shares at the option price of €102 per share). Since IAS 32 classifies such contracts as derivative financial assets (see 11 and 5.2.7 above), which are carried at fair value through profit or loss under IAS 39 (or IFRS 9), A records the following accounting entries:

	€	€
1 February 2016		
Call option asset	5,000	
Cash		5,000

Payment of option premium (equal to fair value of option) to B

	€	€
31 December 2016		
Loss on option (profit or loss)	2,000	
Call option asset		2,000

To record movement in fair value of option from €5,000 to €3,000

31 January 2017

	€	€
Loss on option (profit or loss)	1,000	
Call option asset		1,000

To record movement in fair value of option from €3,000 to €2,000

Cash	2,000	
Call option asset		2,000

To record net settlement of option by payment of €2,000 cash by B to A

B   Net share settlement

If the contract is entered into as net share-settled on 1 February 2016, then A can, on the exercise date 31 January 2017, require B to deliver to A as many of A's own shares as have a fair value equal to any excess of 1,000 of A's own shares fair value, as of 31 January 2017 over €102,000 (i.e. 1,000 shares at the option price of €102 per share). Since IAS 32 classifies such contracts as derivative financial assets (see 11 and 5.2.7 above), which are carried at fair value through profit or loss under IAS 39 (or IFRS 9), A records the following accounting entries.

1 February 2016

	€	€
Call option asset	5,000	
Cash		5,000

Payment of option premium (equal to fair value of option) to B

31 December 2016

Loss on option (profit or loss)	2,000	
Call option asset		2,000

To record movement in fair value of option from €5,000 to €3,000

31 January 2017

Loss on option (profit or loss)	1,000	
Call option asset		1,000

To record movement in fair value of option €3,000 to €2,000

Equity	2,000	
Call option asset		2,000

To record net settlement of option by transfer of €2,000 worth of A's shares by B to A. This is shown as a deduction from equity in accordance with IAS 32's requirements for treasury shares (see 9 above).

C   Gross settlement

If the contract is entered into as gross-settled, on 1 February 2016, then A can, on the exercise date 31 January 2017, require B to deliver 1,000 of A's shares in return for a payment by A of €102,000. IAS 32 classifies such a derivative contract as an equity instrument (see 5.4 above); therefore no entries are recorded, other than to record the cash flows arising under the contract:

1 February 2016

	€	€
Equity	5,000	
Cash		5,000

Payment of option premium (equal to fair value of option) to B

31 January 2017

Equity	102,000	
Cash		102,000

To record gross settlement of option by payment of €102,000 cash to B in exchange for 1,000 own shares.

If the option had lapsed unexercised, because the market price of A's shares had fallen below €102 as at 31 January 2017, the €5,000 premium would remain in equity, even though it is, from an economic perspective, clearly a loss rather than an amount paid to repurchase A's own shares. This is because IFRS regards any holder of an instrument classified as equity under IAS 32 as an 'owner'.

In contrast to the treatment of a gross-settled forward purchase (see 11.1.1 above) and a gross-settled written put option (see 11.3.2 below), which also require a gross outflow of cash on settlement, there is no requirement to record a liability at the outset of the contract on which interest is accrued during the period of the contract. This is because:

- in a gross-settled forward purchase or written put option, the entity can be required to make a payment of cash, but

- in a purchased call option, there is no liability, since the entity has no obligation to exercise its right to call for the shares even if the option is 'in the money' and it is in the entity's interest to do so.

D   Settlement options

If there are different settlement options (such as net in cash, net in shares or by an exchange of cash and shares), the option is a financial asset. A accounts for the forward contract as a derivative (as in A and B above), with the accounting entry made on settlement determined by the manner of settlement (i.e. equity or cash).

11.2.2   Written call option

In a written call option, the entity receives a payment from a counterparty for granting to the counterparty the right, but not the obligation, to purchase a given number of the entity's own equity instruments from the entity for a fixed price at a future date. The accounting for such a contract is illustrated in Example 44.20 below. *[IAS 32.IE17-21]*.

Example 44.20:   Written call option on shares

The reporting entity (A), which has a functional currency of Euro and a year end of 31 December, writes a call option over its own shares with another party (B), for which the following are the major assumptions.

Contract date	1 February 2016
Exercise date (European terms – i.e. can be exercised only on maturity)	31 January 2017
Fixed exercise price to be paid on 31 January 2017	€102
Number of shares under contract	1,000
Market price per share on 1 February 2016	€100
Market price per share on 31 December 2016	€104
Market price per share on 31 January 2017	€104
Fair value of option to A on 1 February 2016	€(5,000)
Fair value of option to A on 31 December 2016	€(3,000)
Fair value of option to A on 31 January 2017	€(2,000)

The fair value of the option would be computed using an option pricing model and would be a function of a number of factors, principally the market value of the shares, the exercise price, and the time value of money.

A   *Net cash settlement*

If the contract is entered into as net cash-settled on 1 February 2016, then B can, on the exercise date 31 January 2017, require A to make a cash payment to B for the excess, if any, of the fair value of 1,000 of A's own shares, as of 31 January 2017, over €102,000 (i.e. 1,000 shares at the option price of €102 per share). Since IAS 32 classifies such contracts as derivative financial liabilities (see 11 and 5.2.7 above), which are carried at fair value through profit or loss under IAS 39 (or IFRS 9), A records the following accounting entries:

	€	€
1 February 2016		
Cash	5,000	
Call option liability		5,000
Receipt of option premium (equal to fair value of option) from B		
31 December 2016		
Call option liability	2,000	
Gain on option (profit or loss)		2,000
To record movement in fair value of option from €(5,000) to €(3,000)		
31 January 2017		
Call option liability	1,000	
Gain on option (profit or loss)		1,000
To record movement in fair value of option from €(3,000) to €(2,000)		
Call option liability	2,000	
Cash		2,000
To record net settlement of option by payment of €2,000 cash to B		

B   *Net share settlement*

If the contract is entered into as net share-settled on 1 February 2016, then B can, on the exercise date 31 January 2017, require A to deliver to B as many of A's own shares as have a fair value equal to any excess of 1,000 of A's own shares, as of 31 January 2017, over €102,000 (i.e. 1000 shares at the option price of €102 per share). Since IAS 32 classifies such contracts as derivative financial liabilities (see 11 and 5.2.7 above), which are carried at fair value through profit or loss under IAS 39 (or IFRS 9), A records the following accounting entries.

	€	€
1 February 2016		
Cash	5,000	
Call option liability		5,000
Receipt of option premium (equal to fair value of option) from B		
31 December 2016		
Call option liability	2,000	
Gain on option (profit or loss)		2,000
To record movement in fair value of option from €(5,000) to €(3,000)		

31 January 2017	1,000	
Call option liability		1,000
Gain on option (profit or loss)		

To record movement in fair value of option from €(3,000) to €(2,000)

Call option liability	2,000	
Equity		2,000

To record net settlement of option by issue of €2,000 worth of A's shares to B

C Gross settlement

If the contract is entered into as gross-settled, on 1 February 2016, then B can, on the exercise date 31 January 2017, require A to deliver 1,000 of A's shares in return for a payment by B of €102,000. IAS 32 classifies this derivative contract as an equity instrument (see 5.4 above); therefore no entries are recorded, other than to record the cash flows arising under the contract:

	€	€
1 February 2016		
Cash	5,000	
Equity		5,000

Receipt of option premium (equal to fair value of option) to B

31 January 2017		
Cash	102,000	
Equity		102,000

To record gross settlement of option by receipt of €102,000 cash from B in exchange for 1,000 of A's own shares.

If the option had lapsed unexercised, because the market price of A's shares had fallen below €102 as at 31 January 2017, the €5,000 premium would remain in equity, even though it is, from an economic perspective, clearly a gain rather than an amount received from an owner. This is because IFRS regards any holder of an instrument classified as equity under IAS 32 as an 'owner'.

D Settlement options

If there are different settlement options (such as net in cash, net in shares or by an exchange of cash and shares), the option is a financial liability. A accounts for the forward contract as a derivative (as in A and B above), with the accounting entry made on settlement determined by the manner of settlement (i.e. equity or cash).

11.3 Put options

11.3.1 Purchased put option

In a purchased put option, the entity makes a payment to a counterparty for the right, but not the obligation, to require the counterparty to purchase a given number of the entity's own equity instruments from the entity for a fixed price at a future date. The accounting for such a contract is illustrated in Example 44.21 below. *[IAS 32.IE22-26].*

Example 44.21:   Purchased put option on shares

The reporting entity (A), which has a functional currency of Euro and a year end of 31 December, purchases a put option over its own shares from another party (B), for which the following are the major assumptions.

Contract date	1 February 2016
Exercise date (European terms – i.e. can be exercised only on maturity)	31 January 2017
Fixed exercise price to be paid on 31 January 2017	€98
Number of shares under contract	1,000
Market price per share on 1 February 2016	€100
Market price per share on 31 December 2016	€95
Market price per share on 31 January 2017	€95
Fair value of option to A on 1 February 2016	€5,000
Fair value of option to A on 31 December 2016	€4,000
Fair value of option to A on 31 January 2017	€3,000

The fair value of the option would be computed using an option pricing model and would be a function of number of factors, principally the market value of the shares, the exercise price, and the time value of money.

A   Net cash settlement

If the contract is entered into as net cash-settled on 1 February 2016, then A can, on the exercise date 31 January 2017, require B to make a cash payment to A for the excess, if any, of €98,000 (i.e. 1,000 shares at the option price of €98 per share) over the fair value of 1,000 of A's own shares, as of 31 January 2017. Because IAS 32 classifies such contracts as derivative financial liabilities (see 11 and 5.2.7 above), which are carried at fair value through profit or loss under IAS 39 (or IFRS 9), A records the following accounting entries.

	€	€
1 February 2016		
Put option asset	5,000	
Cash		5,000

Payment of option premium (equal to fair value of option) to B

	€	€
31 December 2016		
Loss on option (profit or loss)	1,000	
Put option asset		1,000

To record movement in fair value of option from €5,000 to €4,000

	€	€
31 January 2017		
Loss on option (profit or loss)	1,000	
Put option asset		1,000

To record movement in fair value of option from €4,000 to €3,000

	€	€
Cash	3,000	
Put option asset		3,000

To record net settlement of option by receipt of €3,000 cash from B

B   Net share settlement

If the contract is entered into as net share-settled on 1 February 2016, then A can, on the exercise date 31 January 2017, require B to deliver to A as many of A's own shares as have a fair value equal to any excess of €98,000 (i.e. 1,000 shares at the option price of €98 per share) over the fair value of 1,000 of A's own shares, as of 31 January 2017. Because IAS 32 classifies such contracts as derivative financial assets (see 11 and 5.2.7 above), which are carried at fair value through profit or loss under IAS 39 (or IFRS 9), A records the following accounting entries.

	€	€
1 February 2016		
Put option asset	5,000	
Cash		5,000

Payment of option premium (equal to fair value of option) to B

31 December 2016		
Loss on option (profit or loss)	1,000	
Put option asset		1,000

To record movement in fair value of option from €5,000 to €4,000

31 January 2017		
Loss on option (profit or loss)	1,000	
Put option asset		1,000

To record movement in fair value of option from €4,000 to €3,000

Equity	3,000	
Put option asset		3,000

To record net settlement of option by receipt of €3,000 worth of A's shares from B. This is shown as a deduction from equity in accordance with IAS 32's requirements for treasury shares (see 9 above).

C   *Gross settlement*

If the contract is entered into as gross-settled, on 1 February 2016, then A can, on the exercise date 31 January 2017, require B to take delivery 1,000 of A's shares in return for a payment by B of €98,000. IAS 32 classifies this derivative contract as an equity instrument (see 5.4 above); therefore no entries are recorded, other than to record the cash flows arising under the contract:

	€	€
1 February 2016		
Equity	5,000	
Cash		5,000

Payment of option premium (equal to fair value of option) to B

31 January 2017		
Cash	98,000	
Equity		98,000

To record gross settlement of option by delivery of 1,000 own shares to B in exchange for €98,000.

If the option had lapsed unexercised, because the market price of A's shares had risen above €98 as at 31 January 2017, the €5,000 premium would remain in equity, even though it is, from an economic perspective, clearly a loss rather than an amount paid to repurchase A's own shares.

D   Settlement options

If there are different settlement options (such as net in cash, net in shares or by an exchange of cash and shares), the option is a financial asset. A accounts for the forward contract as a derivative (as in A and B above), with the accounting entry made on settlement determined by the manner of settlement (i.e. equity or cash).

11.3.2   Written put option

In a written put option, the entity receives a payment from a counterparty for granting to the counterparty the right, but not the obligation, to sell a given number of the entity's own equity instruments to the entity for a fixed price at a future date. The accounting for such a contract is illustrated in Example 44.22 below. *[IAS 32.IE27-31].*

Example 44.22:   Written put option on own shares

The reporting entity (A), which has a functional currency of Euros and a year end of 31 December, writes a put option over its own shares with another party (B), for which the following are the major assumptions.

Contract date	1 February 2016
Exercise date (European terms – i.e. can be exercised only on maturity)	31 January 2017
Fixed exercise price to be paid on 31 January 2017	€98
Number of shares under contract	1,000
Market price per share on 1 February 2016	€100
Market price per share on 31 December 2016	€95
Market price per share on 31 January 2017	€95
Fair value of option to A on 1 February 2016	€(5,000)
Fair value of option to A on 31 December 2016	€(4,000)
Fair value of option to A on 31 January 2017	€(3,000)

The fair value of the option would be computed using an option pricing model and would be a function of a number of factors, principally the market value of the shares, the exercise price, and the time value of money.

A   Net cash settlement

If the contract is entered into as net cash-settled on 1 February 2016, then B can, on the exercise date 31 January 2017, require A to make a cash payment to B for the excess, if any, of €98,000 (i.e. 1,000 shares at the option price of €98 per share) over the fair value of 1,000 of A's own shares, as of 31 January 2017. Because IAS 32 classifies such contracts as derivative financial liabilities (see 11 and 5.2.7 above), which are carried at fair value through profit or loss under IAS 39 (or IFRS 9), A records the following accounting entries.

	€	€
1 February 2016		
Cash	5,000	
Put option liability		5,000

Receipt of option premium (equal to fair value of option) from B

	€	€
31 December 2016		
Put option liability	1,000	
Gain on option (profit or loss)		1,000

To record movement in fair value of option from €(5,000) to €(4,000)

31 January 2017

Put option liability	1,000	
Gain on option (profit or loss)		1,000

To record movement in fair value of option from €(4,000) to €(3,000)

Put option liability	3,000	
Cash		3,000

To record net settlement of option by payment of €3,000 cash to B

B   Net share settlement

If the contract is entered into as net share-settled on 1 February 2016, then B can, on the exercise date 31 January 2017, require A to deliver to B as many of A's own shares as have a fair value equal to any excess of €98,000 (i.e. 1,000 shares at the option price of €98 per share) over the fair value of 1,000 of A's own shares, as of 31 January 2017. Because IAS 32 classifies such contracts as derivative financial assets (see 11 and 5.2.7 above), which are carried at fair value through profit or loss under IAS 39 (or IFRS 9), A records the following accounting entries.

	€	€
1 February 2016		
Cash	5,000	
Put option liability		5,000

Receipt of option premium (equal to fair value of option) from B

31 December 2016

Put option liability	1,000	
Gain on option (profit or loss)		1,000

To record movement in fair value of option from €(5,000) to €(4,000)

31 January 2017

Put option liability	1,000	
Gain on option (profit or loss)		1,000

To record movement in fair value of option from €(4,000) to €(3,000)

Put option liability	3,000	
Equity		3,000

To record net settlement of option by issue of €3,000 worth of own shares to B

C   Gross settlement

If the contract is entered into as gross-settled on 1 February 2016, then B can, on the exercise date 31 January 2017, require A to take delivery of 1,000 of A's own shares in return for a payment by A of €98,000. IAS 32 classifies this derivative contract as an equity instrument giving rise to a financial liability for the present value of the purchase price amount payable in one year's time (see 5.3 above). On the assumption that A accounts for this liability under the effective interest method in IAS 39 (or IFRS 9), A records the following accounting entries.

	€	€
1 February 2016		
Cash	5,000	
Equity		5,000

Receipt of option premium (equal to fair value of option) from B

Equity	95,000	
Liability (net present value of €98,000 potentially payable under option)		95,000

Recording of potential liability to settle option

31 December 2016

Interest (profit or loss)	2,750	
Liability		2,750

To accrue interest, under the effective interest rate method, on the liability

31 January 2017

Interest expense (profit or loss)	250	
Liability		250

To accrue further interest, under the effective interest rate method, on the liability

Liability	98,000	
Cash		98,000

To record gross settlement of option by delivery of by B of 1,000 shares in A in exchange for €98,000

If the option had lapsed unexercised, because the market price of A's shares had risen above €98 as at 31 January 2017, the premium of €5,000 would remain in equity and the liability of €98,000 would be reclassified to equity. The economic consequence is clearly that A has made a profit of €5,000 – the premium that it received from B, for which it has ultimately had to give nothing in return. However the overall effect of the treatment that would be required by IAS 32 can be summarised as follows:

	€	€
Cash	5,000	
Profit or loss (interest on potential liability to pay cash)	3,000	
Equity (€98,000 carrying amount of liability transferred at date of lapse less €90,000 debited on 1 February 2016)		8,000

To record a loss on a transaction that makes a profit might seem a distortion of economic reality; but in this case is a consequence of applying the *Conceptual Framework*.

D   *Settlement options*

If there are different settlement options (such as net in cash, net in shares or by an exchange of cash and shares), the option is a financial liability. A accounts for the forward contract as a derivative (as in A and B above), with the accounting entry made on settlement determined by the manner of settlement (i.e. equity or cash). If one of the settlement alternatives is to exchange cash for shares, A recognises a liability for the obligation to deliver cash (as in C above). Otherwise, Entity A accounts for the put option as a derivative liability.

The implementation guidance to IAS 32 states that A should recognise a liability 'if one of the settlement alternatives is to exchange cash for shares'. *[IAS 32.IE31]*. As drafted, this applies whether the choice of settlement rests with A or B. This seems curious since, where A has the choice of settlement, there would be no obligation for A to settle gross. We assume that the example is written on the presumption that the choice of settlement of an option would normally rest with the buyer rather than the writer of the option. Paragraph 23 in the main body of the standard is clear that an equity contract gives rise to a liability for the purchase price of the shares only where there is an obligation for the entity to purchase its own equity (see 5.3 above). Accordingly, in our view, where the choice of settlement rests only with the entity, it is acceptable to record no liability, and to account for the contract as a derivative.

12   POSSIBLE FUTURE DEVELOPMENTS

An increasing number of commentators have begun to question whether the current criteria used to distinguish equity from financial liabilities, both under IFRS and US GAAP, are entirely satisfactory. In an agenda paper for the IASB board meeting in January 2007, the IASB staff highlighted the following broad categories of implementation issue arising from IAS 32:

- *Issues arising from specific rules in the standard*

  The specific provisions in IAS 32 were written with particular types of capital instrument in mind. Where these rules are applied to instruments that differ from those for which they were written, the result may be a classification of an item as debt or equity that does not faithfully represent the underlying instrument.

- *Counter-intuitive results*

  The classification of an instrument under IAS 32 can produce results that conflict with the generally-held perception of how the instrument should be faithfully represented. An example is the treatment of certain puttable instruments, which was the subject of the amendment to IAS 32 in February 2008 discussed at 4.6.2 and 4.6.3 above.

- *Conflicts with the conceptual framework*

  Some provisions of IAS 32 conflict with the IASB's own conceptual framework. For example, IAS 32 requires some contracts over the entity's own equity, which are to be executed at a future date, to be accounted for as if they had been executed on inception of the contract. This contrasts with the required treatment under IFRS of nearly all other executory contracts, such as purchase orders and contracts of employment, for which no liability is recorded, except to the extent that the contract is onerous.

The IASB staff noted that the first of these issues could potentially be resolved by a more principles-based revision to the drafting of IAS 32, whilst the other two issues raised more fundamental questions about the whole approach of the standard.[29]

The Memorandum of Understanding published by the IASB and the FASB in February 2006 set as one of its goals for 2008 'to have issued one or more due process documents relating to a proposed standard' on the distinction between liabilities and equity. The IASB fulfilled that commitment by publishing a discussion paper in February 2008. Following receipt of comments on the discussion paper, the IASB and the FASB ('the Boards') began further deliberations and developed a draft exposure draft. In May 2010 this was distributed to a small group of external reviewers, who raised significant challenges. The reviewers felt that the proposed approach lacked clear principles, and could produce inconsistent results when applied to broadly similar instruments. In particular, many reviewers felt that the 'specified for specified' criterion was unclear and just as prone to interpretative difficulties as the 'fixed for fixed' criterion in IAS 32.

At a joint meeting in October 2010, the Boards suspended the project, acknowledging that they did not have the time necessary to deliberate the key issues. In October 2014 the IASB decided to resume the *Financial Instruments with Characteristics of Equity*

Chapter 44

Research Project (FICE), to explore further how to distinguish liabilities from equity claims. The relaunched project is in a very early state.

In May 2015 the IASB published Exposure Draft ED/2015/3 – *Conceptual Framework for Financial Reporting*. Amongst other topics this proposes to refine the definition of assets and liabilities and to develop principles and guidance to help support the classification of assets, liabilities and equity whilst retaining the existing definition of equity. The proposed definition of liability is discussed in Chapter 2 at 3.3. However it is worth noting that the proposed definition of liability as a present obligation of the entity to transfer an economic resource as a result of a past event if the entity has no practical ability to avoid the transfer may, if incorporated into FICE, result in instruments with 'dividend blocker' arrangements being classified as financial liabilities rather than equity (see 4.5.3).

References

1 IAS 32, Application Guidance, para. after main heading.
2 IAS 32, Illustrative Examples, para. after main heading.
3 SIC-5, *Classification of Financial Instruments – Contingent Settlement Provisions*, SIC, May 1998 (superseded December 2003).
4 SIC-5, para. 9.
5 *Agenda item 12B*, Information for Observers, IASB meeting, January 2007, para. 39.
6 IAS 32, (pre-2003 version – issued March 1995 and revised December 1998 and October 2000), para. 22.
7 *IFRIC Update*, March 2006.
8 *IFRIC Update*, March 2006.
9 *IFRIC Update*, March 2006.
10 *IFRIC Update*, March 2006.
11 *Amendments to IAS 32 Financial Instruments: Presentation and IAS 1 Presentation of Financial Statements – Puttable Instruments and Obligations Arising on Liquidation*, IASB, February 2008, paras. DO1 – DO6.
12 *IFRIC Update*, March 2009.
13 *IFRIC Update*, November 2006.
14 *IFRIC Update*, April 2005.

15 *IFRIC Update*, November 2006.
16 *IFRS for Small and Medium-Sized Entities*, IASB, July 2009, para. 21.2.
17 IFRS for SMEs, Derivation Table.
18 IASB staff draft of proposed exposure draft *International Financial Reporting Standard for Small and Medium-Sized Entities* (as made available on the IASB's website as at September 2006) paras. 22.2-22.4.
19 Based on Example 9 in IAS 32.IE34-IE36.
20 Based on example in IAS 32 (2.08), paras. IE39-IE46.
21 *IFRIC Update*, July 2013.
22 *IFRIC Update*, May 2014 and January 2014.
23 Based on Example 10 in IAS 32, paras. IE37-IE38.
24 *IFRIC Update*, July 2013.
25 *IFRIC Update*, January 2014.
26 *IFRIC Update*, July 2013.
27 *IFRIC Update*, January 2014.
28 *IFRIC Update*, July 2006.
29 *Overview of IAS 32 (Agenda paper 12B)*, Information for Observers, IASB meeting, January 2007, para. 48.

Chapter 45   Financial instruments: Classification (IAS 39)

List of examples

Chapter 45   Financial instruments: Classification (IAS 39)

1   INTRODUCTION

Under IAS 39 – *Financial Instruments: Recognition and Measurement* – the accounting treatment of a particular financial instrument (e.g. whether it is carried at historical cost, fair value or some other amount and whether any remeasurement gains are reported immediately in profit or loss or in other comprehensive income) will depend to some extent on some or all of the following factors:

- the purpose for which it is held, for example trading, long-term investment or hedging;

- its contractual characteristics, for example whether it is a derivative, an equity security or a debt instrument;

- whether the instrument is listed on an exchange;

- the industry in which the reporting entity operates; and

- an accounting policy or similar choice of the reporting entity.

Four categories of financial asset are set out in IAS 39. In summary, the definitions of these are as follows: [IAS 39.9]

- *Financial assets at fair value through profit or loss* – financial assets that are either defined as held for trading (see 2.1 below), or are designated as such on initial recognition;

- *Held-to-maturity investments* – non-derivative financial assets with fixed or determinable payments and fixed maturity, other than loans and receivables, for which there is a positive intention and ability to hold to maturity and which have not been designated 'at fair value through profit or loss' or as 'available-for-sale';

- *Loans and receivables* – non-derivative financial assets with fixed or determinable payments that are not quoted in an active market, do not qualify as 'trading' assets, have not been designated 'at fair value through profit or loss' or as 'available-for-sale'; and

- *Available-for-sale financial assets* – non-derivative financial assets that are designated as 'available-for-sale' or are not classified as 'loans and receivables', 'held-to-maturity investments' or 'at fair value through profit or loss'.

There are also two main categories of financial liabilities dealt with: *[IAS 39.9]*

- *Financial liabilities at fair value through profit or loss* – financial liabilities that are either classified as *held for trading* or are designated as such on initial recognition; and

- *Other financial liabilities* – not explicitly defined, but are those that are neither held for trading nor designated 'at fair value through profit or loss'.

In addition, IAS 39 specifies the accounting treatment for liabilities arising from certain financial guarantee contracts (see Chapter 42 at 3.4 and Chapter 48 at 2.8) and commitments to provide loans at below market rates of interest (see Chapter 42 at 3.5 and Chapter 48 at 2.8).

The definitions summarised above are covered in more detail in the remainder of this chapter.

2   ASSETS AND LIABILITIES AT FAIR VALUE THROUGH PROFIT OR LOSS

This category comprises instruments that are defined as 'held for trading' (including derivatives which are not designated effective hedging instruments) and those that are designated as at fair value through profit or loss – often referred to as those to which the 'fair value option' is applied. Whilst trading instruments are encompassed within this category, they are not a separate category. *[IAS 39.BC81]*. Contingent consideration that is payable (or receivable) in respect of a business combination is also included within this category where it meets the definition of a financial liability (or financial asset). *[IFRS 3.58]*.

Designation under the fair value option must take place on initial recognition of the instrument (subject to certain exemptions on first-time adoption of IFRS – see Chapter 5 at 5.11.2) and may not be revoked subsequently, i.e. a designated instrument will be included in this category from when it is first recognised until it is derecognised.

It will come as no surprise that the basic accounting requirement for all instruments included in this category is that they are recorded on the statement of financial position at fair value and any changes in value are reported in profit or loss (see Chapter 48 at 2.1).

2.1   Assets and liabilities held for trading

Assets and liabilities held for trading are defined as those that:

- are acquired or incurred principally for the purpose of sale or repurchase in the near term;

- on initial recognition are part of a portfolio of identified financial instruments that are managed together and for which there is evidence of a recent actual pattern of short-term profit-taking; or

- are derivatives (except for those that are financial guarantee contracts – see Chapter 42 at 3.4 – or are designated effective hedging instruments – see Chapter 51 at 2.1.1). The definition of a derivative is covered in Chapter 43 at 2. *[IAS 39.9].*

It follows that if an entity originates a loan with an intention of syndicating it, but fails to find sufficient commitments from other participants and tries to sell the surplus loan amount to other parties in the near term rather than holding it for the foreseeable future (a failed loan syndication), the surplus loan amount should be classified as held for trading.[1]

It is explained that trading generally reflects active and frequent buying and selling, and financial instruments held for trading are normally used with the objective of generating a profit from short-term fluctuations in price or a dealer's margin. *[IAS 39.AG14].* This is obviously not always true because, for example, many derivatives will be held for hedging or risk management purposes yet by default they are included in this category (unless the entity chooses to designate them as hedges and is successful in achieving hedge accounting as set out in Chapter 51 at 5).

In addition to derivatives, that are not accounted for as hedging instruments, financial liabilities held for trading include:

(a)   obligations to deliver financial assets borrowed by a short seller (i.e. an entity that sells financial assets it has borrowed and does not yet own);

(b)   financial liabilities that are incurred with an intention to repurchase them in the near term, such as quoted debt instruments that the issuer may buy back in the near term depending on changes in fair value; and

(c)   financial liabilities that are part of a portfolio of identified financial instruments that are managed together and for which there is evidence of a recent pattern of short-term profit-taking. *[IAS 39.AG15].*

However, the fact that a liability is used merely to fund trading activities does not in itself make that liability one that is held for trading. *[IAS 39.AG15].*

The term 'portfolio' is not explicitly defined in IAS 39, but the context in which it is used suggests that a portfolio is a collection of financial assets or financial liabilities that are managed as part of the same group. If there is evidence of a recent actual pattern of short-term profit taking on financial instruments included in such a portfolio, those financial instruments qualify as held for trading even though an individual financial instrument may, in fact, be held for a longer period of time. *[IAS 39.B.11].*

Evidence of a recent actual pattern of short-term profit taking may be established based on an evaluation of management intentions and past practice, including the level of turnover in the portfolio, whether performance is measured based on short-term profits and the average holding period (e.g. see Example 45.5 at 5 below).

Chapter 45

2.2   Instruments designated at fair value through profit or loss

One of the reasons for the fair value option is to simplify the application of IAS 39 by mitigating some of the anomalies that result from its mixed model approach. For example, it eliminates:

- the need for hedge accounting for hedges of fair value exposures when there are natural offsets, and thereby eliminates the related burden of designating hedges, tracking and analysing hedge effectiveness;
- the burden of separating embedded derivatives; and
- problems arising from a mixed-measurement model where financial assets are measured at fair value and related financial liabilities are measured at amortised cost.

In particular, it eliminates volatility in profit or loss and equity that results when matched positions of financial assets and financial liabilities are not measured consistently. It also de-emphasises interpretative issues around whether a financial instrument should be classified as held for trading. *[IAS 39.BC74A].*

An entity may designate a financial asset or financial liability at fair value through profit or loss only in either of the following circumstances: (a) when doing so results in more relevant information, because either:

- it eliminates or significantly reduces a measurement or recognition inconsistency (sometimes referred to as 'an accounting mismatch') that would otherwise arise; or
- a group of financial assets, financial liabilities or both is managed and its performance is evaluated on a fair value basis;

or (b) if it contains an embedded derivative that meets particular conditions. These are discussed further at 2.2.1 to 2.2.3 below.

Investments in unquoted equity instruments that do not have a quoted market price in an active market, and whose fair value cannot be reliably measured, cannot be designated at fair value through profit or loss. *[IAS 39.9, 11A, AG4B].*

The decision to designate a financial asset or financial liability as at fair value through profit or loss is similar to an accounting policy choice (although, unlike an accounting policy choice, it is not required in all cases to be applied consistently to all similar transactions). In other words, an entity can freely choose, when the relevant criteria are met, which of its financial assets and liabilities are to be designated without having to designate all similar instruments. *[IAS 39.AG4C].* However, an entity that designates a financial instrument as at fair value through profit or loss on the basis that it is part of a group of financial instruments that is managed and its performance is evaluated on a fair value basis should also designate all *eligible* financial instruments within that same group. New instruments that will become part of that group should also be designated at fair value through profit or loss. A similar, but separate, group of financial instruments does not need to be designated at fair value profit or loss in a similar manner.

As noted earlier, the designation of a financial instrument at fair value through profit or loss must take place on initial recognition of the instrument (subject to certain exemptions on first-time adoption of IFRS – see Chapter 5 at 5.11.2) and may not be revoked subsequently. Accordingly, when making the designation decision, reporting entities, which use the designation in lieu of hedge accounting, need to make the decision about whether or not to economically hedge the instrument on or before the time of acquisition or issuance, and also evaluate whether they intend to economically hedge the instrument until derecognition. Designating a financial instrument under the fair value option is likely to lead to unnecessary earnings volatility if the economic hedge is not intended to last until derecognition.

The fair value option cannot be applied to a portion or component of a financial instrument, e.g. changes in the fair value of a debt instrument attributable to one risk such as changes in a benchmark interest rate, but not credit risk. Further, it cannot be applied to proportions of an instrument. However, if an entity simultaneously issues two or more identical financial instruments, it is not precluded from designating only some of those instruments as being subject to the fair value option (e.g. if doing so achieves a significant reduction in an accounting mismatch). Therefore, if an entity issued a bond totalling US$100 million in the form of 100 certificates each of US$1 million, the entity could designate 10 specified certificates if to do so would meet at least one of the criteria noted above. *[IAS 39.BC85, BC86, BC86A].*

2.2.1 Designation eliminates or significantly reduces a measurement or recognition inconsistency (accounting mismatch) that would otherwise arise

The notion of an accounting mismatch necessarily involves two propositions. First, that an entity has particular assets and liabilities that are measured, or on which gains and losses are recognised, on different bases; second, that there is a perceived economic relationship between those assets and liabilities. *[IAS 39.9, BC75].*

For example, a financial asset might otherwise be classified as available-for-sale (with most changes in fair value recognised directly in equity) and a liability that is considered related would be measured at amortised cost (with changes in fair value not recognised). In such circumstances, the entity may conclude that its financial statements would provide more relevant information if both the asset and the liability were classified as at fair value through profit or loss. *[IAS 39.AG4D].* It should be noted in this case that it does not matter that there is unlikely to be a significant accounting mismatch in profit or loss – the fact that the mismatch arises only in the statement of financial position does not prevent the use of the fair value option.

IAS 39 gives the following examples of situations in which designation at fair value through profit or loss might eliminate or significantly reduce an accounting mismatch and produce more relevant information: *[IAS 39.AG4E, AG4F]*

(a) An entity has liabilities whose cash flows are contractually based on the performance of assets that would otherwise be classified as available for sale. For example, an insurer may have liabilities containing a discretionary participation feature that pay benefits based on realised and/or unrealised investment returns of a specified pool of the insurer's assets. If the measurement of those liabilities reflects current market prices, classifying the assets as at fair value through profit or loss means that changes in the fair value of the financial assets are recognised in profit or loss in the same period as related changes in the value of the liabilities.

(b) An entity has liabilities under insurance contracts whose measurement incorporates current information (as permitted by IFRS 4 – *Insurance Contracts*), and financial assets it considers related that would otherwise be classified as available for sale or measured at amortised cost.

(c) An entity has financial assets, financial liabilities or both that share a risk, such as interest rate risk, that gives rise to opposite changes in fair value that tend to offset each other. However, only some of the instruments would be measured at fair value through profit or loss (i.e. derivatives or those classified as held for trading). It may also be the case that the requirements for hedge accounting are not met, for example because the requirements for effectiveness are not met (see Chapter 51 at 5.3).

(d) An entity has financial assets, financial liabilities or both that share a risk, such as interest rate risk, that gives rise to opposite changes in fair value that tend to offset each other and the entity does not qualify for hedge accounting because none of the instruments is a derivative. Furthermore, in the absence of hedge accounting there is a significant inconsistency in the recognition of gains and losses. For example:

(i) the entity has financed a portfolio of fixed rate assets that would otherwise be classified as available-for-sale with fixed rate debentures, the changes in the fair value of which tend to offset each other. Reporting both the assets and the debentures at fair value through profit or loss corrects the inconsistency that would otherwise arise from measuring the assets at fair value with changes reported in equity and the debentures at amortised cost; or

(ii) the entity has financed a specified group of loans by issuing traded bonds, the changes in the fair value of which tend to offset each other. If, in addition, the entity regularly buys and sells the bonds but rarely, if ever, buys and sells the loans, reporting both the loans and the bonds at fair value through profit or loss eliminates the inconsistency in the timing of recognition of gains and losses that would otherwise result from measuring them both at amortised cost and recognising a gain or loss each time a bond is repurchased.

For practical purposes, an entity need not acquire all the assets and incur all the liabilities giving rise to the measurement or recognition inconsistency at exactly the same time. A reasonable delay is permitted provided that each transaction is designated as at fair value through profit or loss at its initial recognition and, at that time, any remaining transactions are expected to occur. *[IAS 39.AG4F].*

It is emphasised that it would not be acceptable to designate only some of the financial assets and financial liabilities giving rise to the inconsistency as at fair value through profit or loss if to do so would not eliminate or significantly reduce the inconsistency and would therefore not result in more relevant information. However, it would be acceptable to designate only some of a number of similar financial assets or similar financial liabilities if doing so does achieve a significant reduction (and possibly a greater reduction than other allowable designations) in the inconsistency. *[IAS 39.AG4G].*

For example, assume an entity has a number of similar financial liabilities totalling €100 and a number of similar financial assets totalling €50, but these are measured on a different basis. The entity may significantly reduce the measurement inconsistency by designating at initial recognition all of the assets but only some of the liabilities (for example, individual liabilities with a combined total of €45) as at fair value through profit or loss. However, because designation as at fair value through profit or loss can be applied only to the whole of a financial instrument, the entity in this example must designate one or more liabilities in their entirety. It could not designate either a component of a liability (e.g. changes in value attributable to only one risk, such as changes in a benchmark interest rate) or a proportion (i.e. percentage) of a liability. *[IAS 39.AG4G].*

The standard does not provide detailed prescriptive guidance about when the fair value option could be applied to eliminate an accounting mismatch. Therefore an entity is not required to demonstrate that particular assets and liabilities are managed together, that a management strategy is effective in reducing risk, e.g. by performing effectiveness tests similar to those required for hedge accounting, or that other ways of overcoming the inconsistency are unavailable. Rather, the IASB concluded that financial reporting was best served by providing entities with the opportunity to eliminate perceived accounting mismatches whenever that results in more relevant information. *[IAS 39.BC75A, BC75B].*

Although not explicitly stated, one of the items giving rise to the mismatch may, at least in principle, be non-financial. For example, investment properties accounted for using the fair value model in IAS 40 – *Investment Property* (see Chapter 19 at 6) are commonly financed with fixed rate borrowings and if it were possible to demonstrate a sufficiently high correlation between the values of these items, the borrowings could be designated as at fair value through profit or loss. However, the value of a property will depend to some extent on rent, location, maintenance and other factors which can make it difficult to do this. Nevertheless, CESR has reported that, based on the specific evidence available in a particular case, one of its enforcement agencies has accepted this treatment.[2]

Chapter 45

2.2.2 *A group of financial assets, financial liabilities or both is managed and its performance is evaluated on a fair value basis*

The second situation in which the fair value option may be used is where a group of financial assets, financial liabilities or both is managed, and its performance evaluated, on a fair value basis. In order to meet this condition, it is necessary for the group of instruments to be managed in accordance with a documented risk management or investment strategy and for information, prepared on a fair value basis, about the group of instruments to be provided internally to the entity's key management personnel (as defined in IAS 24 – *Related Party Disclosures* – see Chapter 36 at 2.2.1.D), for example the entity's board of directors and chief executive officer. *[IAS 39.9].*

It is explained that if an entity manages and evaluates the performance of a group of financial assets, financial liabilities or both in such a way, measuring that group at fair value through profit or loss results in more relevant information. The focus in this instance is on the way the entity manages and evaluates performance, rather than on the nature of its financial instruments. *[IAS 39.AG4H].* Accordingly, subject to the requirement of designation at initial recognition, an entity that designates financial instruments as at fair value through profit or loss on the basis of this condition should so designate all eligible financial instruments that are managed and evaluated together. *[IAS 39.AG4J].*

An entity's documentation of its strategy need not be extensive (e.g. it need not be in the level of detail required for hedge accounting) but should be sufficient to demonstrate that using the fair value option is consistent with the entity's risk management or investment strategy. Such documentation is not required for each individual item, but may be on a portfolio basis. The IASB notes that in many cases, the entity's existing documentation, as approved by its key management personnel, should be sufficient for this purpose. For example, if the performance management system for a department (as approved by the entity's key management personnel) clearly demonstrates that its performance is evaluated on a total return basis, no further documentation is required. *[IAS 39.AG4K, BC76B].*

The IASB made it clear in its basis for conclusions that in looking to an entity's documented risk management or investment strategy, it makes no judgement on what an entity's strategy should be. However, the IASB believes that users, in making economic decisions, would find useful a description both of the chosen strategy and of how designation at fair value through profit or loss is consistent with that strategy. Accordingly, IFRS 7 – *Financial Instruments: Disclosures* – requires these to be disclosed (see Chapter 53 at 4.1). *[IAS 39.BC76B].*

The following examples show when this condition could be met. In all cases, an entity may use this condition to designate financial assets or financial liabilities as at fair value through profit or loss only if it meets the principle above:

(a)   The entity (or component of an entity) is a venture capital organisation, mutual fund, unit trust or similar entity whose business is investing in financial assets with a view to profiting from their total return in the form of interest or dividends and changes in fair value. IAS 28 – *Investments in*

Associates and Joint Ventures – allows investments in associates and joint ventures to be measured at fair value through profit or loss in accordance with IAS 39. Such an entity may apply the same accounting policy to other investments managed on a total return basis but over which its influence is insufficient for them to be within the scope of IAS 28.

(b) The entity has financial assets and financial liabilities that share one or more risks and those risks are managed and evaluated on a fair value basis in accordance with a documented policy of asset and liability management. An example could be an entity that has issued 'structured products' containing multiple embedded derivatives and manages the resulting risks on a fair value basis using a mix of derivative and non-derivative financial instruments. A similar example could be an entity that originates fixed interest rate loans and manages the resulting benchmark interest rate risk using a mix of derivative and non-derivative financial instruments.

(c) The entity is an insurer that holds a portfolio of financial assets, manages that portfolio so as to maximise its total return (i.e. interest or dividends and changes in fair value) and evaluates its performance on that basis. The portfolio may be held to back specific liabilities, equity or both. If the portfolio is held to back specific liabilities, this condition may be met for the assets regardless of whether the insurer also manages and evaluates the liabilities on a fair value basis. It may also be met when the insurer's objective is to maximise total return on the assets over the longer term even if amounts paid to holders of participating contracts depend on other factors such as the amount of gains realised in a shorter period (e.g. a year) or are subject to the insurer's discretion. *[IAS 39.AG4I]*.

2.2.3 Instruments containing embedded derivatives

If a contract contains one or more embedded derivatives, an entity may designate the entire hybrid (or combined) contract as a financial asset or financial liability at fair value through profit or loss unless:

(a) the embedded derivative(s) does not significantly modify the cash flows that otherwise would be required by the contract; or

(b) it is clear with little or no analysis when a similar hybrid (combined) instrument is first considered that separation of the embedded derivative(s) is prohibited, such as a prepayment option embedded in a loan that permits the holder to prepay the loan for approximately its amortised cost. *[IAS 39.11A]*.

As discussed in Chapter 43 at 4 to 6, when an entity becomes a party to a hybrid (combined) instrument that contains one or more embedded derivatives, it is required to identify any such embedded derivative, assess whether it is required to be separated from the host contract and, if so, measure it at fair value at initial recognition and subsequently. These requirements can be more complex, or result in less reliable measures, than measuring the entire instrument at fair value through profit or loss. For that reason the entire instrument is normally permitted to be designated as at fair value through profit or loss. *[IAS 39.AG33A]*.

Chapter 45

Such designation may be used whether the entity is required to, or prohibited from, separating the embedded derivative from the host contract, except for those situations in (a) or (b) above – this is because doing so would not reduce complexity or increase reliability. [IAS 39.AG33B].

Little further guidance is given on what instruments might fall within (a) and (b). The basis for conclusions explains that, at one extreme, the terms of a prepayment option in an ordinary residential mortgage is likely to mean that the fair value option is unavailable to such a mortgage (unless it met one of the conditions in 2.2.1 and 2.2.2 above). At the other, it is likely to be available for 'structured products' that contain several embedded derivatives which are typically hedged with derivatives that offset all (or nearly all) of the risks they contain irrespective of the accounting treatment applied to the embedded derivatives. [IAS 39.BC77A, BC77B].

Essentially, the IASB explains, the standard seeks to strike a balance between reducing the costs of complying with the embedded derivatives provisions and the need to respond to concerns expressed regarding possible inappropriate use of the fair value option. Allowing the fair value option to be used for any instrument with an embedded derivative would make other restrictions on the use of the option ineffective, because many financial instruments include an embedded derivative. In contrast, limiting the use of the fair value option to situations in which the embedded derivative must otherwise be separated would not significantly reduce the costs of compliance and could result in less reliable measures being included in the financial statements. [IAS 39.BC78].

Taken at face value, IAS 39 might allow the fair value option to be applied to any contract containing a substantive embedded derivative, such as a lease accounted for under IAS 17 – *Leases* – or a pension arrangement accounted for under IAS 19 – *Employee Benefits*. In May 2007, the Interpretations Committee tentatively concluded that it could be applied only to a contract that would otherwise be within the scope of IAS 39.[3] However, the Interpretations Committee did not finalise its conclusion as it had become apparent that a number of entities had taken a different view, at least as regards commodity contracts that qualify as normal purchases or sales (see Chapter 42 at 4). After much discussion the Interpretations Committee, in November 2007, referred the matter to the IASB.[4]

As part of its second annual improvements process the IASB, in August 2008, proposed to amend IAS 39 so that the fair value option could be applied only to financial instruments within the scope of IAS 39.[5] However, a number of concerns were raised by respondents and, in January 2009, the IASB concluded this amendment could not be completed in time, redeliberations were deferred and in January 2010 the Interpretations Committee decided to remove the issue from the annual improvements project given the IASB's accelerated project to replace IAS 39.[6]

It would be unusual for entities to apply the fair value option to non-financial contracts containing embedded derivatives. In our experience, the one exception to this is in respect of contracts to buy or sell a non-financial item (such as a commodity) that can be settled net but are not within the scope of IAS 39 because they are considered 'normal' sale or purchase contracts (see Chapter 42 at 4). Where such contracts contain a substantive embedded derivative, some entities do designate such contracts as at fair value through profit or loss.

3 HELD-TO-MATURITY INVESTMENTS

As noted at 1 above, the held-to-maturity category comprises non-derivative financial assets with fixed or determinable payments and fixed maturity, other than loans and receivables, for which there is a positive intention and ability to hold to maturity and which have not been designated at fair value through profit or loss or as available-for-sale. *[IAS 39.9]*.

This category is viewed as an exception to be used only in limited circumstances. *[IAS 39.AG20]*. Consequently, its use is restricted by a number of detailed conditions, largely designed to test whether there is a genuine intention and ability to hold such investments to maturity. To further restrict the use of this category, hedge accounting cannot be used if interest rate or prepayment risk associated with held-to-maturity investments is hedged, *[IAS 39.79]*, for example by using a pay-fixed, receive-floating rate interest rate swap to hedge an investment that pays a fixed rate of interest (see Chapter 51 at 2.2.6). The reason for this is that designation of an investment as held to maturity requires an intention to hold to maturity regardless of changes in the fair value or cash flows due to changes in interest rates.

In theory, investments are not *designated* as held-to-maturity – they *must* be included in this category if they meet the appropriate conditions. In practice, however, because it is relatively easy for an entity to selectively fail any of the conditions, it is in effect a voluntary classification.

3.1 Instruments that may or may not be classified as held-to-maturity

Only assets with fixed or determinable payments and fixed maturity can be included in this category (see 1 and 3 above). Most equity instruments cannot be held to maturity because they have an indefinite life (such as ordinary shares) or because the amounts the holder may receive can vary in a manner that is not predetermined (such as share options, warrants and rights). A debt instrument with a variable interest rate generally can satisfy this condition. *[IAS 39.AG17]*.

A perpetual debt instrument on which interest payments are made for an indefinite period cannot be classified as held-to-maturity because there is no maturity date. *[IAS 39.AG17]*. However, there is no reason why what is in legal form a perpetual debt instrument but requires fixed or determinable payments for only a limited period cannot be classified as held-to-maturity. In effect, the instrument matures at the date of the last contractual payment and the amount invested is recovered through fixed or determinable payments and the rights in liquidation have no fair value (see Example 48.14 in Chapter 48 at 3.4).

A financial asset that is callable by the issuer satisfies the criteria for a held-to-maturity investment if the holder intends, and is able, to hold it until it is called, or until maturity, and if the holder would recover substantially all of its carrying amount. The call option, if exercised, simply accelerates the investment's maturity. However, if the investment is callable on a basis that the holder would not recover substantially all of its carrying amount, it cannot be classified as held-to-maturity. Any premium paid and capitalised transaction costs should be considered in determining whether the carrying amount would be substantially recovered. *[IAS 39.AG18]*.

A financial asset that is puttable (the holder has the right to require the issuer to repay or redeem the instrument before maturity) cannot be classified as held-to-maturity. Paying for a put feature is considered inconsistent with expressing an intention of holding such an instrument to maturity. *[IAS 39.AG19]*.

The reference to 'fixed or determinable payments and fixed maturity' in the definition means a contractual arrangement that defines the amounts and dates of payments to the holder, such as interest and principal payments. The likelihood of default is not a consideration in qualifying for this category, provided there is an intention and ability, considering the credit condition existing at the acquisition date, to hold the investment to maturity. Even if there is a significant risk of non-payment of interest and principal, for example a bond with a very low credit rating, the contractual payments on the bond may well be fixed or determinable. *[IAS 39.AG17]*.

Investments in funds where the payout in dividends and on liquidation is based on the performance of the fund would not satisfy the conditions for this category. Similarly, investments in subordinated notes for which the payout is dependent on residual cash flows would normally not satisfy the conditions for this category.

Where a combined instrument contains a host contract and an embedded derivative (see Chapter 43 at 4), the host may be classified as held-to-maturity if it has fixed or determinable payments and no other conditions are breached. This is illustrated in the following examples.

Example 45.1:   Note with index-linked principal

Company A purchases a five year interest free equity-index-linked note, with an original issue price of €10, for its market price of €12. At maturity, the note requires payment of the original issue price of €10 plus a supplemental redemption amount that depends on whether a specified stock price index exceeds a predetermined level at the maturity date. If the stock index does not exceed the predetermined level, no supplemental redemption amount is paid. If it does, the supplemental redemption amount equals the product of €1.15 and the difference between the level of the stock index at maturity and original issuance divided by the level at original issuance. A has the positive intention and ability to hold the note to maturity.

The note can be classified as a held-to-maturity investment because it has a fixed payment of €10 and fixed maturity and there is the positive intention and ability to hold it to maturity. However, the equity index feature is a call option not closely related to the debt host which must be separated as an embedded derivative (see Chapter 43 at 5.1.6). The purchase price (initial fair value) of €12 is allocated between the host debt instrument and the embedded derivative – the latter will have a non-zero fair value because it is an option-based derivative. *[IAS 39.B.13]*.

Example 45.2: Note with index-linked interest

Subsequently, A purchases a note with a fixed payment at a fixed maturity date and interest payments that are indexed to the price of a commodity or equity. There is an intention and ability to hold the note to maturity.

Again the note can be classified as held-to-maturity because it has a fixed payment and fixed maturity. However, the commodity-indexed or equity-indexed interest payments result in an embedded derivative that is separated and accounted for as a derivative. *[IAS 39.B.14]*.

It is possible for the terms of the embedded derivative to breach other conditions for classifying the host as held-to-maturity. For example, an investment in a convertible bond that can be converted *before* maturity generally cannot be classified as held-to-maturity. The embedded conversion feature allows the investor to settle the host investment before maturity and, as noted above, paying for such a conversion feature would be inconsistent with an intention to hold the host to maturity. *[IAS 39.C.3]*.

3.2 Positive intention and ability to hold to maturity

An entity should assess its intention and ability to hold these instruments to maturity when they are initially acquired and also at the end of each subsequent reporting period. *[IAS 39.AG25]*.

If any one of the following criteria is met, a positive intention to hold an investment to maturity is deemed not to exist (and the asset cannot be classified as such):

- the intention to hold the investment is for only an undefined period;
- the holder stands ready to sell the financial asset in response to changes in market interest rates or risks, liquidity needs, changes in the availability of and the yield on alternative investments, changes in financing sources and terms, or changes in foreign currency risk (although this does not apply to situations that are non-recurring and could not have been reasonably anticipated); or
- the issuer has a right to settle the financial asset at an amount significantly below its amortised cost. *[IAS 39.AG16]*.

Further, an investor is deemed not to have a demonstrated ability to hold an investment to maturity if:

- it does not have the financial resources available to continue to finance the investment until maturity; or
- it is subject to an existing legal or other constraint that could frustrate its intention to hold the financial asset to maturity (although an issuer's call option does not necessarily frustrate this intention – see 3.1 above). *[IAS 39.AG23]*.

The intention and ability to hold debt instruments to maturity is not necessarily constrained if those instruments have been pledged as collateral or are subject to a repurchase or securities lending agreements. However, an entity would not have the positive intention and ability to hold the debt instruments until maturity if it did not expect to be able to maintain or recover access to the instruments. *[IAS 39.B.18]*.

The standard also suggests that circumstances other than those described above can indicate that an entity does not have a positive intention or ability to hold an investment to maturity, *[IAS 39.AG24]* but gives no indication of what these other circumstances might be.

3.3   The tainting provisions

When an entity's actions cast doubt on its intention or ability to hold such investments to maturity, the use of amortised cost for held-to-maturity assets is precluded for 'a reasonable period of time'. *[IAS 39.AG20]*. Consequently, no investment should be classified as held-to-maturity if, during either the current financial year or the two preceding financial years, the reporting entity has sold or reclassified more than an insignificant (in relation to the total) amount of such investments before maturity other than by those effected:

(a)   close enough to maturity or call date (e.g. less than three months before maturity) so that changes in the market rate of interest did not have a significant effect on the investment's fair value;

(b)   after substantially all of the investment's original principal had been collected through scheduled payments or prepayments; or

(c)   due to an isolated non-recurring event that is beyond the holder's control and could not have been reasonably anticipated by the holder. *[IAS 39.9]*.

Therefore, if an entity makes any 'not insignificant' sale or reclassification of a held-to-maturity investment that does not fall within (a) to (c) above, the entire remaining portfolio of such investments will have to be reclassified as available-for-sale (see 5 and 6.3 below) and will be remeasured to fair value for at least the following two financial years. The nature of this 'punishment' is unique within accounting standards and has become known as the 'tainting' or, by rugby followers, the 'sin-bin' provisions.

The standard neither defines nor provides further guidance on how 'an insignificant amount' should be interpreted. Accordingly, reporting entities should make the assessment based on the facts and circumstances in each particular situation.

The guidance to the original version of IAS 39 explained that conditions (a) and (b) relate to situations in which an entity is expected to be indifferent whether to hold or sell a financial asset because movements in interest rates after substantially all of the original principal has been collected or when the instrument is close to maturity will not have a significant impact on its fair value. Accordingly, such a sale should not affect profit or loss and no price volatility would be expected during the remaining period to maturity.

It went on to say that if a financial asset is sold less than three months prior to maturity, that would generally qualify for this exception because the impact on the instrument's fair value of a difference between the stated interest rate and the market rate would generally be small for an instrument that matures in three months relative to an instrument that matures in several years. If sold after 90% or more of its original principal has been collected through scheduled payments or prepayments, condition (b) would generally be met. However, if only, say, 10% of the original principal has been collected, then that condition is clearly not met.[7]

The conditions must be applied to all held-to-maturity investments in aggregate and not to separate sub-categories of such assets (e.g. US dollar and euro denominated investments). *[IAS 39.B.20].* In consolidated financial statements they must be applied to all investments classified as held-to-maturity in those financial statements, even if they are held by different entities within the group, in different countries or in different legal or economic environments. *[IAS 39.B.21].*

Example 45.3:   Application of tainting provisions

On a number of occasions during 2015, B, a company with a calendar year-end, sells certain securities from its held-to-maturity portfolio to realise a large appreciation in their value. The value of the securities sold, in relation to the total carrying amount of the portfolio, is considered to be insignificant with respect to the individual sale transactions.

Periodic sales may raise doubt over B's intention to hold new investments to maturity. Such periodic sales should be evaluated on a cumulative basis in assessing whether or not the sales are more than insignificant. Assuming that the cumulative amount was considered significant, the application of the tainting provisions means that the rest of the held-to-maturity portfolio would need to be reclassified to available-for-sale during 2015. B would also be prohibited from reclassifying any new investments as held-to-maturity during 2016 and 2017 (i.e. two full years). Accordingly, the earliest date B could subsequently use the held-to-maturity classification is 1 January 2018.

A 'disaster scenario' that is only remotely possible, such as a run on a bank or a similar situation affecting an insurer, is not anticipated in deciding whether there is positive intention and ability to hold an investment to maturity. *[IAS 39.AG21].* Consequently, a sale triggered by such a scenario would not contradict the reporting entity's intention to hold a financial asset to maturity.

The standard also explains that sales before maturity may satisfy condition (c) above 'an isolated non-recurring event that is beyond the holder's control and could not have been reasonably anticipated' – and therefore not trigger the tainting provisions – if they are attributable to:

- a significant deterioration in the issuer's creditworthiness (see 3.3.1 below);

- a change in tax law that eliminates or significantly reduces the tax-exempt status of interest on the held-to-maturity investment, but not a change in tax law that revises the marginal tax rates applicable to interest income;

- a major business combination or major disposition, such as the sale of a segment, that necessitates the sale or transfer of held-to-maturity investments to maintain the holder's existing interest rate risk position or credit risk policy. Although the business combination itself is an event within the holder's control, the changes to its investment portfolio to maintain its interest rate risk position or credit risk policy may be consequential rather than anticipated;

- a change in statutory or regulatory requirements significantly modifying either what constitutes a permissible investment or the maximum level of particular types of investments, thereby causing disposal of a held-to-maturity investment;

- a significant increase in the industry's regulatory capital requirements that causes a downsizing by selling held-to-maturity investments; or

- a significant increase in the risk weights of held-to-maturity investments used for regulatory risk-based capital purposes. *[IAS 39.AG22].*

Chapter 45

3.3.1   Deterioration in issuer's creditworthiness

A sale following a downgrade in a credit rating by an external rating agency would not necessarily raise a question about the entity's intention to hold other investments to maturity if the downgrade provides evidence of a significant deterioration in the issuer's creditworthiness judged by reference to the credit rating at initial recognition. *[IAS 39.AG22]*. However, the rating downgrade must not have been reasonably anticipated when the investment was classified as held-to-maturity. A credit downgrade of a notch within a class or from one rating class to the immediately lower rating class could often be regarded as reasonably anticipated. *[IAS 39.B.15]*.

Similarly, where internal ratings are used for assessing exposures, changes in those ratings may help to identify issuers for which there has been a significant deterioration in creditworthiness, provided the approach to assigning ratings and changes therein give a consistent, reliable and objective measure of the credit quality of the issuers. *[IAS 39.AG22]*.

In our view, there should be a clear link between the downgrade and the sale for it to meet condition (c) at 3.3 above. If an extended period of time has elapsed between the two events, this will call into question whether the sale is actually due to the credit downgrade.

If there is evidence that a financial asset is impaired (see Chapter 48 at 4), for example a rating downgrade in combination with other information, the deterioration in creditworthiness is often regarded as significant. *[IAS 39.AG22, B.15]*.

Following the European sovereign debt crisis, a number of entities have considered disposing of certain of their held-to-maturity investments, particularly bonds issued by the weaker eurozone governments. The requirements above apply equally to government bonds as they do to other held-to-maturity investments.

In situations where a reporting entity decides to sell some, but not all, instruments issued by a single issuer who has subsequently suffered a significant deterioration in creditworthiness, significant judgement is required to assess whether the entity's intention and ability to hold some investments remains demonstrable.

3.3.2   Major business combinations or disposals

The implementation guidance makes it clear that condition (c) at 3.3 above does not extend to an unsolicited tender offer on economically favourable terms. *[IAS 39.B.19]*.

3.3.3   Significant changes in statutory or regulatory requirements

Sales of held-to-maturity investments in response to an unanticipated significant increase by the regulator in the *industry's* capital requirements may not necessarily raise a question about the intention to hold other investments to maturity. However, in some countries, regulators may set *entity-specific* capital requirements based on an assessment of the risk in that particular entity. In such scenarios, it will normally be difficult to demonstrate that the regulator's decision could not have been reasonably anticipated by the particular reporting entity.

Consequently, any sales in response to the regulator's action *will* raise doubt over the intention to hold other financial assets to maturity unless it can be demonstrated that the sales fulfil condition (c) at 3.3 above. In other words, they should result from an increase in capital requirements which is an isolated non-recurring event that is beyond the entity's control and could not have been reasonably anticipated. *[IAS 39.B.17].*

3.3.4 Change of management

A change in management is not identified as an exception and the guidance explains that sales in response to such a change would call into question the intention to hold investments to maturity. *[IAS 39.B.16].*

Example 45.4:   Change of management

A company has a portfolio of financial assets that is classified as held-to-maturity. In the current period, at the direction of the board of directors, the senior management team has been replaced. The new management wishes to sell a portion of the held-to-maturity financial assets in order to carry out an expansion strategy designated and approved by the board.

Although the previous management team had been in place since the company's formation and had never before undergone a major restructuring, the sale nevertheless calls into question the company's intention to hold remaining held-to-maturity financial assets to maturity and the company may be prohibited from using the held-to-maturity classification if the amounts involved are not insignificant. *[IAS 39.B.16].*

4   LOANS AND RECEIVABLES

At noted at 1 above, the loans and receivables category comprises non-derivative financial assets with fixed or determinable payments that are not quoted in an active market, do not qualify as 'trading' assets, have not been designated at fair value through profit or loss or as available-for-sale. In addition, the category cannot include financial assets for which the holder may not recover substantially all of its initial investment for reasons other than the issuer's credit deterioration. *[IAS 39.9].*

For most entities this category includes trade receivables, other debtors and bank deposits; for banks and similar financial institutions it will constitute a significant proportion of their non-trading assets, in particular loans and advances to customers. *[IAS 39.AG26].*

A loan asset need not be originated by the entity. For example, if an entity purchases a portfolio of loans they may be included within this category if they meet the relevant conditions. *[IAS 39.BC28].*

An asset with terms such that the holder may not recover substantially all of its initial investment (other than because of credit deterioration), for example a fixed rate interest-only strip created in a securitisation and subject to prepayment risk, should not be classified within loans and receivables. The IASB believes such instruments should be recorded at fair value, *[IAS 39.9, BC29],* probably because that value can be more volatile than that of other loans and receivables.

As noted above, instruments 'quoted in an active market' are prohibited from being included within this category and must therefore be included in one of the other three categories of financial asset. *[IAS 39.9]*. 'Quoted in an active market' means that prices are readily available in a market accessible by the reporting entity, where orderly transactions take place with sufficient frequency and volume to provide pricing information on an ongoing basis. Such quoted prices would normally be representative of fair value because they are based on current information that reflects market participants' assumptions. *[IFRS 13 Appendix A, 15-20, B34]*.

Provided there is no intention to sell the instrument immediately or in the short term, where a bank makes a term deposit with a central or other bank it is classified within loans and receivables even if the proof of deposit is negotiable, i.e. the deposit is capable of being sold. If there was such an intention to sell, the deposit would be a trading asset. *[IAS 39.B.23]*.

Non-derivative instruments that have the legal form of equities, such as preference shares, but which under IAS 32 – *Financial Instruments: Presentation* – would be classified as liabilities in the financial statements of the issuer and have fixed or determinable payments and fixed maturity (see Chapter 44 at 4.2) can potentially be classified within loans and receivables, provided the instrument is not quoted in an active market and the definition is otherwise met. However if, under IAS 32, an instrument would be classified as equity in the financial statements of the issuer, it could not be classified within loans and receivables by the holder. *[IAS 39.B.22]*.

The standard explains that an interest acquired in a pool of assets that are not loans or receivables (for example, an interest in a mutual fund or a similar fund) is not a loan or receivable. *[IAS 39.9]*. We believe this was added to clarify the treatment of investments in mutual funds, unit trusts and similar funds – this issue is dealt with in more detail in Chapter 43 at 5.1.9.

The principal difference between loans and receivables and held-to-maturity investments is that loans and receivables are not subject to the tainting provisions (see 3.3 above). Consequently, loans and receivables that are not held for trading may be measured at amortised cost even if an entity does not have the positive intention and ability to hold the loan asset until maturity. *[IAS 39.BC25]*. However, if financial assets classified as loans and receivables are subsequently sold within a short period after origination, it may call into question whether the newly originated or acquired assets are held for trading and should therefore be measured at fair value through profit or loss. Financial assets that do not meet the definition of loans and receivables, e.g. because they are quoted in an active market, may be classified as held-to-maturity investments if they meet the relevant conditions. *[IAS 39.AG26]*. However, it is important to recognise another major difference between the two classes of instrument, namely the significant restrictions on applying hedge accounting when the hedged item is a held-to-maturity investment (see Chapter 51 at 2.2.6).

On initial recognition a financial asset that would otherwise be classified as a loan or receivable may, at the entity's discretion, be designated as available-for-sale, or potentially designated at fair value through profit or loss under the fair value option, if the relevant criteria are met (see 5 below and 2.2 above respectively). *[IAS 39.9]*.

5 AVAILABLE-FOR-SALE ASSETS

Unless designated into this category (see 4 above), a financial asset is classified as available-for-sale if it does not properly belong in one of the three other categories of financial assets – at fair value through profit or loss, held-to-maturity or loans and receivables. In many respects available-for-sale is a 'default' classification.

This category normally includes equity and quoted debt securities not classified or designated at fair value through profit or loss, other than quoted debt securities held-to-maturity.

The main interpretative issue an entity is likely to experience in respect of this classification is whether a portfolio of investments can properly be regarded as available-for-sale rather than trading. The implementation guidance provides the following example to assist in making this judgement.

Example 45.5: Portfolio balancing

Company A has an investment portfolio of debt and equity instruments. The documented portfolio management guidelines specify that the equity exposure of the portfolio should be limited to between 30% and 50% of total portfolio value. The investment manager of the portfolio is authorised to balance the portfolio within the designated guidelines by buying and selling equity and debt instruments. The instruments should be classified as trading or available-for-sale depending on Company A's intent and past practice.

If the portfolio manager is authorised to buy and sell instruments to balance the risks in a portfolio, but there is no intention to trade and there is no past practice of trading for short-term profit, the instruments can be classified as available-for-sale. If instruments are bought and sold to generate short-term profits, the financial instruments in the portfolio should be classified as held for trading. *[IAS 39.B.12]*.

6 RECLASSIFICATIONS

This section deals with the situations in which financial instruments should or may be reclassified from one category to another. Accounting for the subsequent measurement of reclassified instruments is dealt with in Chapter 48 at 2.7 and the related disclosure requirements are covered in Chapter 53 at 4.4.5.

6.1 Reclassifications to or from fair value through profit or loss

To impose discipline on an entity's ability to designate items at fair value through profit or loss, financial instruments cannot generally be reclassified into or out of this category subsequent to initial recognition. *[IAS 39.50, BC73]*.

Accordingly, if an entity starts to trade (as set out at 2.1 above) a portfolio of, say, available-for-sale investments all newly acquired investments will be classified as trading, but the legacy investments will continue to be classified as available-for-sale. *[IAS 39.50]*.

However, there are a limited number of exceptions to this prohibition which are discussed below.

6.1.1 Reclassifications from held for trading

IAS 39 allows a non-derivative financial asset classified as held for trading to be reclassified out of the fair value through profit or loss category, in certain circumstances. Such a reclassification is conditional on the asset no longer being held for the purpose of sale in the near term (notwithstanding that it may have been acquired or incurred principally for this purpose) and is subject to further conditions which are considered at 6.1.1.A and 6.1.1.B below. *[IAS 39.50(c)]*. Derivatives and financial instruments designated at fair value through profit or loss on initial recognition may not be reclassified. *[IAS 39.50(a), (b)]*.

Hybrid (combined) financial assets reclassified out of the held for trading classification are required to be reassessed for bifurcation into a host contract and an embedded derivative upon reclassification (see Chapter 43 at 7.1). *[IFRIC 9.7]*.

Any such reclassification of a financial asset can now take effect only from the date when the reclassification is made. *[IAS 39.103H, 103I]*. In other words, a reclassification from the held for trading classification cannot be applied retrospectively.

6.1.1.A   Reclassifications to loans and receivables

In order to be reclassified to loans and receivables, a financial asset meeting the condition described at 6.1.1 above would need to have met the definition of loans and receivables (if the financial asset had not been required to be classified as held for trading at initial recognition) and at the date of reclassification the reporting entity should have the intention and ability to hold it for the foreseeable future or until maturity. *[IAS 39.50D]*.

As set out at 1 and 4 above, a financial asset that is quoted in an active market does not meet the definition of loans and receivables. It is not clear whether an asset would need to have met the definition of loans and receivables at the date of (a) initial recognition, or (b) reclassification, in order to qualify for reclassification. This can make a significant difference because, for example, the turbulence in the financial markets in the second half of 2008 meant that many financial assets had ceased to be quoted in an active market (which was the period many entities were seeking to reclassify them). In our opinion, both interpretations are acceptable as an accounting policy choice, and both have been seen in practice. The interpretation chosen should be applied consistently to all similar reclassifications. The following extracts show that HSBC selected the first approach and Deutsche Bank the second.

Extract 45.1: HSBC Holdings plc (2012)

Notes on the Financial Statements [extract]
2   Summary of significant accounting policies [extract]
(e)   Reclassification of financial assets [extract]

Non-derivative financial assets (other than those designated at fair value through profit or loss upon initial recognition) may be reclassified out of the fair value through profit or loss category in the following circumstances:

– financial assets that would have met the definition of loans and receivables at initial recognition (if the financial asset had not been required to be classified as held for trading) may be reclassified out of the fair value through profit or loss category if there is the intention and ability to hold the financial asset for the foreseeable future or until maturity; and

– financial assets (except financial assets that would have met the definition of loans and receivables at initial recognition) may be reclassified out of the fair value through profit or loss category and into another category in rare circumstances.

Extract 45.2: Deutsche Bank Aktiengesellschaft (2012)

Notes to the Consolidated Financial Statements [extract]
01 – Significant Accounting Policies [extract]
Financial Assets and Liabilities [extract]
Reclassification of Financial Assets [extract]

The Group may reclassify certain financial assets out of the financial assets at fair value through profit or loss classification (trading assets) and the AFS classification into the loans classification. For assets to be reclassified there must be a clear change in management intent with respect to the assets since initial recognition and the financial asset must meet the definition of a loan at the reclassification date. Additionally, there must be an intent and ability to hold the asset for the foreseeable future at the reclassification date. There is no single specific period that defines foreseeable future. Rather, it is a matter requiring management judgment. In exercising this judgment, the Group established the following minimum requirements for what constitutes foreseeable future. At the time of reclassification,

– there must be no intent to dispose of the asset through sale or securitization within one year and no internal or external requirement that would restrict the Group's ability to hold or require sale; and
– the business plan going forward should not be to profit from short-term movements in price.

Financial assets proposed for reclassification which meet these criteria are considered based on the facts and circumstances of each financial asset under consideration. A positive management assertion is required after taking into account the ability and plausibility to execute the strategy to hold.

In addition to the above criteria the Group also requires that persuasive evidence exists to assert that the expected repayment of the asset exceeds the estimated fair value and the returns on the asset will be optimized by holding it for the foreseeable future.

Foreseeable future is not a defined term and it may vary in duration depending on circumstances. Consequently, entities will need to apply judgement whenever considering such a reclassification. In our view, it would be acceptable to use twelve months as a guide. This approach has been used by a number of banks as illustrated in the following extract from RBS and Extract 45.2 above from Deutsche Bank.

Extract 45.3: The Royal Bank of Scotland Group plc (2012)

Accounting policies [extract]
15.   Financial assets [extract]

Reclassifications – held-for-trading and available-for-sale financial assets that meet the definition of loans and receivables (non-derivative financial assets with fixed or determinable payments that are not quoted in an active market) may be reclassified to loans and receivables if the Group has the intention and ability to hold the financial asset for the foreseeable future or until maturity. The Group typically regards the foreseeable future as twelve months from the date of reclassification. Additionally, held-for-trading financial assets that do not meet the definition of loans and receivables may, in rare circumstances, be transferred to available-for-sale financial assets or to held-to-maturity investments.

An entity cannot normally assert it intends to hold a financial asset for the foreseeable future unless it has an expectation that it will not consider any offers to sell. In our opinion, an entity prepared to sell a financial asset on receipt of a reasonable offer does not have an intention to hold it for the foreseeable future.

A reporting entity assesses its intention to hold a financial asset for the foreseeable future at the date of potential reclassification and ordinarily it does not need to revisit this. However, an entity may subsequently change its intentions towards a reclassified financial asset and dispose of it. In these circumstances, one would need

Chapter 45

to examine carefully the circumstances surrounding the sale to determine whether the original reclassification was appropriate, especially if the sale took place a relatively short time after reclassification. Such disposals may cast doubt about an entity's assertion that it has the intention to hold for the foreseeable future other assets that it wishes to reclassify. Nevertheless, such disposals do not necessarily mean the reclassification represents an accounting error.

6.1.1.B   *Reclassifications in rare circumstances*

In addition to those reclassifications from held for trading to loans and receivables discussed at 6.1.1.A above, an entity may, in rare circumstances, reclassify non-derivative financial assets meeting the condition described at 6.1.1 above as available-for-sale financial assets or held-to-maturity investments. *[IAS 39.50B]*. These assets can include investments in equity instruments and debt instruments that are quoted in an active market.

The standard does not expand on what is meant by rare circumstances and entities will need to exercise judgement in determining what they consider them to be. However, the IASB noted that rare circumstances arise from a single event that is unusual and highly unlikely to recur in the near term. *[IAS 39.BC104D]*. Furthermore, an October 2008 press release stated that the deterioration of the world's financial markets that had occurred during the third quarter of 2008 was a possible example and quoted the IASB's Chairman as referring to 'the rare circumstances of the current credit crisis' which provided some context for entities making this judgement.[8]

6.1.2   Re-designation and de-designation of derivatives as hedging instruments

Entities are not prohibited from (a) designating a derivative as a hedging instrument in a cash flow hedge or hedge of a net investment if it was previously classified as trading nor (b) revoking the designation of an effective cash flow hedge or hedge of a net investment involving a derivative – these are not regarded as reclassifications. *[IAS 39.50A]*.

6.1.3   Changes in accounting policy for insurance contracts

When an insurer changes its accounting policies for insurance liabilities, it is permitted (but not required) to change its accounting policy for some or all of its financial assets and reclassify them as at fair value through profit or loss (see Chapter 54 at 8.4) *[IFRS 4.45]*. IAS 39 makes it clear that this change in accounting policy is not a prohibited reclassification. *[IAS 39.50A]*.

6.2   Reclassifications between available-for-sale financial assets and loans and receivables

A financial asset classified as available-for-sale that would have met the definition of loans and receivables (if it had not been designated as available for sale) may be reclassified to loans and receivables if the entity has the intention and ability to hold the financial asset for the foreseeable future or until maturity. *[IAS 39.50E]*. Any such reclassification of a financial asset can now take effect only from the date when the reclassification is made. *[IAS 39.103H, 103I]*. In other words, reclassifications cannot be applied retrospectively.

Similar to the situation for reclassifications from held for trading to loans and receivables (see 6.1.1.A above), it is not clear whether an asset would need to have met the definition of loans and receivables at the date of (a) initial recognition, or (b) reclassification in order to qualify for reclassification. Again, either interpretation is, in our opinion, an acceptable accounting policy choice. The interpretation chosen should be applied consistently to all similar reclassifications. In contrast to the position taken on reclassifications from held for trading, one of CESR's enforcement agencies has accepted reclassifications from available-for-sale based on an assessment at the date of reclassification.[9]

IAS 39 neither requires nor prohibits reclassification of financial assets from loans and receivables to available-for-sale financial assets, for example if a debt instrument becomes quoted in an active market after initial recognition (or after reclassification to loans and receivables) and the market is expected to remain active. In our opinion, it is acceptable, although not required, for an entity to adopt an accounting policy of reclassifying such instruments as available-for-sale in these circumstances, provided the policy is applied consistently. Of course, this would require the reporting entity to continually monitor the existence or otherwise of an active market for its financial assets.

6.3 Reclassifications between held-to-maturity investments and available for sale financial assets

Reclassifications between held-to-maturity investments and available-for-sale assets are permitted. An investment will be reclassified as available-for-sale if, as a result of a change in intention or ability, it fails to meet the requirements for classification as held-to-maturity. *[IAS 39.51]*. If the tainting provisions (see 3.3 above) are triggered, any remaining held-to-maturity investments should also be reclassified as available-for-sale. *[IAS 39.52]*. Similarly, if, as a result of a change in intention or ability or because the tainting period has passed, it becomes appropriate to regard an available-for-sale asset as held-to-maturity, it should be reclassified accordingly. *[IAS 39.54]*.

6.4 Prohibited reclassifications

As noted in 6.1.1 above, derivatives and financial instruments designated at fair value through profit or loss may not be reclassified. Further, reclassifying any financial instrument into the fair value through profit or loss category after initial recognition is prohibited *[IAS 39.50]*. Despite this, paragraph 12 of IAS 39 appears to allow for one exception when an entity is unable to separately measure a separated embedded derivative from its host contract at the end of a subsequent financial reporting period. In such a scenario the standard requires the reporting entity to designate the entire hybrid (combined) contract as at fair value through profit or loss.

Reclassifications of financial liabilities are not allowed. *[IAS 39.50]*. This prohibition extends to loan commitments classified at fair value through profit or loss because they will either be derivatives or will be financial liabilities designated at fair value through profit or loss.

Chapter 45

7   CLASSIFICATION OF FINANCIAL INSTRUMENTS IN A BUSINESS COMBINATION

From the perspective of an acquirer applying the acquisition method of accounting to a business combination, IFRS 3 – *Business Combinations* – views the business combination as giving rise to the initial recognition by the acquirer of the acquiree's financial instruments. *[IFRS 3.15, 16(a)].* Therefore all financial instruments should be classified by reference to the acquirer's circumstances and intention towards those financial instruments and any designation made when the business combination occurs. In other words, an entity classifies the acquired financial instruments at the acquisition date (i.e. the moment of initial recognition from the acquirer's perspective) by applying the classification requirements, without regards to how they were previously classified by the acquiree.

In rare cases, the pooling of interests method may be used for a business combination, for example in a transaction involving entities under common control (see Chapter 10 at 3.1 and 3.3). In such cases the basis of preparation involves an assumption that the acquired entities were always part of the same reporting entity and therefore it would be appropriate to look to the classification of the financial instruments in the financial statements of the acquired entity.

8   FUTURE DEVELOPMENTS

IAS 39 will be superseded by IFRS 9 – *Financial Instruments* – which is effective for periods commencing on or after 1 January 2018. Classification of financial instruments in accordance with IFRS 9 is covered in Chapter 46.

References

1 *IFRIC Update*, May 2009.
2 *2nd extract from EECS's database of enforcement decisions*, CESR, December 2007, Decision Ref. EECS/1207-06.
3 *IFRIC Update*, May 2007.
4 *IFRIC Update*, July 2007, September 2007 and November 2007.
5 Exposure Draft, *Improvements to IFRSs*, IASB, August 2008, IAS 39, para. 11A.
6 *IASB Update*, January 2009, Information for Observers (January 2009 IASB Meeting), *Annual Improvements 2009 – Comment Analysis*, (Agenda Paper 6A), IASB, January 2009, para. 11(c) and Appendix 2, and *IFRIC Update*, January 2010.
7 IGC Q&A 83-1.
8 Press Release, *IASB amendments permit reclassification of financial instruments*, IASB, October 2008.
9 *5th extract from EECS's database of enforcement decisions*, CESR, March 2009, Decision Ref. EECS/0209-01.

Chapter 46   Financial instruments: Classification (IFRS 9)

Chapter 46

List of examples

Chapter 46

Chapter 46   Financial instruments: Classification (IFRS 9)

1   INTRODUCTION

On 24 July 2014, the International Accounting Standards Board (the IASB or the Board) published the consolidated version of IFRS 9 – *Financial Instruments* (IFRS 9 or the standard) including the revised classification requirements for financial assets. Classification determines how financial instruments are accounted for in the financial statements and, in particular, how they are measured on an ongoing basis.

The more principle-based approach of IFRS 9 will require careful use of judgment in its application. Some fact patterns have no simple and distinct outcome and we highlight in this chapter the factors that need to be considered in arriving at a conclusion. Further issues and questions are likely to be raised during the course of implementation.

2   CLASSIFYING FINANCIAL ASSETS: AN OVERVIEW

IFRS 9 has the following measurement categories for financial assets:

- Debt instruments at amortised cost.
- Debt instruments at fair value through other comprehensive income with cumulative gains and losses reclassified to profit or loss upon derecognition.
- Debt instruments, derivatives and equity instruments at fair value through profit or loss.
- Equity instruments designated as measured at fair value through other comprehensive income with gains and losses remaining in other comprehensive income, i.e. without recycling to profit or loss upon derecognition.

Apart from some options which are described in more detail at 7 and 8 below, the classification is based on both the entity's business model for managing the financial assets and the contractual cash flow characteristics of the financial assets. *[IFRS 9.4.1.1].* The synopsis below illustrates the thought process on which the classification of financial assets is based:

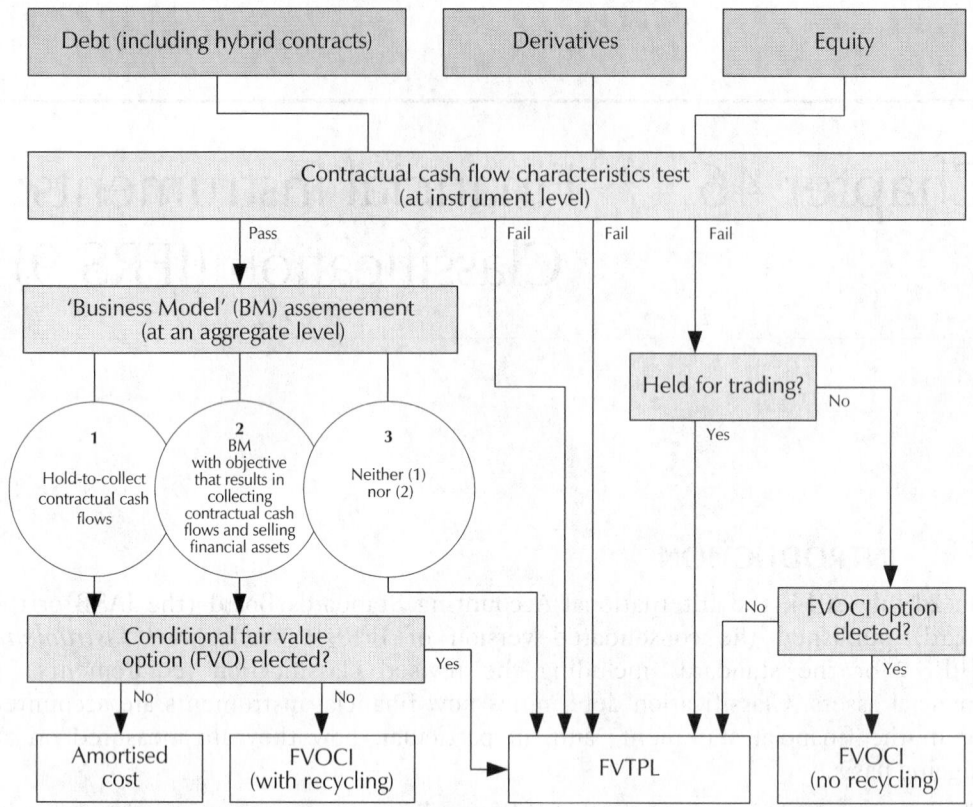

The following matrix summarises the outcome of the thought process depicted in the synopsis above:

		Contractual cash flow characteristics test	
		Pass	**Fail**
Business model	Held within a business model whose objective is to hold financial assets in order to collect contractual cash flows	Amortised cost	FVTPL[1]
	Held within a business model whose objective is achieved by both collecting contractual cash flows and selling financial assets	FVOCI[2] (debt)	FVTPL
	Financial assets which are neither held at amortised cost nor at fair value through other comprehensive income	FVTPL	FVTPL
Options	Conditional fair value option is elected	FVTPL	n/a[3]
	Option elected to present changes in fair value of an equity instrument not held for trading in OCI	n/a[4]	FVOCI (equity)

[1]   Fair value through profit or loss
[2]   Fair value through other comprehensive income

3   Financial assets which fail the contractual cash flow characteristics test are measured at fair value
      through profit or loss
4   Only debt instruments can pass the contractual cash flow characteristics test. The fair value through
      other comprehensive income option does not apply to those instruments

Measurement is covered in Chapter 49, particularly at 2.1 (financial assets measured at fair value through profit or loss), 2.2 (equity investments designated at fair value through other comprehensive income), 2.3 (debt instruments measured at fair value through other comprehensive income) and 2.4 (financial assets measured at amortised cost). This includes the effective interest method and expected credit loss impairment model for financial assets measured at amortised cost and fair value through other comprehensive income. Fair value is determined in accordance with IFRS 13 – *Fair Value Measurement* – see Chapter 14.

2.1   Debt instruments

A debt instrument is normally measured at amortised cost if both of the following conditions are met: *[IFRS 9.4.1.2]*

(a)   the asset is held within a business model whose objective is to hold assets in order to collect contractual cash flows; and

(b)   the contractual terms of the financial asset give rise on specified dates to cash flows that are solely payments of principal and interest on the principal amount outstanding.

A debt instrument is normally measured at fair value through other comprehensive income if both of the following conditions are met: *[IFRS 9.4.1.2A]*

(a)   the asset is held within a business model in which assets are managed to achieve a particular objective by both collecting contractual cash flows and selling financial assets; and

(b)   the contractual terms of the financial asset give rise on specified dates to cash flows that are solely payments of principal and interest on the principal amount outstanding.

The application of these conditions (the 'business model' assessment and 'contractual cash flow characteristics' test) is covered in more detail at 5 and 6 below, respectively.

The above requirements should be applied to an entire financial asset, even if it contains an embedded derivative. *[IFRS 9.4.3.2].* That is, in contrast with the requirements of IAS 39 – *Financial Instruments: Recognition and Measurement*, a derivative embedded within a hybrid (combined) contract containing a financial asset host should not be accounted for separately.

The application of these requirements to debt instruments means that, apart from the exceptions described in section 6.4 below, only relatively simple 'plain vanilla' debt instruments qualify to be measured at amortised cost or at fair value through other comprehensive income. Debt instruments that are neither measured at amortised cost nor at fair value though other comprehensive income are measured at fair value through profit or loss. As will be shown at 5.4 below, this includes instruments that are held for trading (see 4 below).

Chapter 46

A debt instrument which is not measured at amortised cost or at fair value through other comprehensive income must be measured at fair value through profit or loss. *[IFRS 9.4.1.4].*

Notwithstanding the criteria for debt instruments to be classified at amortised cost or at fair value through other comprehensive income, as described above, an entity may irrevocably designate a debt instrument as measured at fair value through profit or loss at initial recognition. This is allowed if doing so eliminates or significantly reduces a measurement or recognition inconsistency (sometimes referred to as an 'accounting mismatch'). Such mismatches would otherwise arise from measuring assets or liabilities or recognising the gains and losses on them on different bases. *[IFRS 9.4.1.5].* This is covered further at 7 below.

In its Basis for Conclusions, the IASB noted that the fair value through other comprehensive income measurement category is intended for debt instruments for which both amortised cost information and fair value information are relevant and useful. This will be the case if their performance is affected by both the collection of contractual cash flows and the realisation of fair values through sales. *[IFRS 9.BC4.150].*

The fair value through other comprehensive income measurement category may also help some insurers achieve consistency of measurement for assets held to back insurance liabilities under the new IFRS 4 – *Insurance Contracts* – insurance contracts model. It should also help to addresses concerns raised by preparers who expect to sell financial assets in greater volume than would be consistent with a business model whose objective is to hold financial assets to collect contractual cash flows and would, without this category, have to record such assets at fair value through profit or loss.

The fair value through other comprehensive income category differs from the available-for-sale category in IAS 39 in several aspects. First, the available-for-sale category for debt instruments was essentially a residual classification and an unrestricted election. The fair value through other comprehensive income classification under IFRS 9 reflects a business model evidenced by facts and circumstances and is neither a residual nor an election. Second, financial assets measured at fair value through other comprehensive income will be subject to the same impairment model as those measured at amortised cost. Accordingly, although the assets are recorded at fair value, the profit or loss treatment will be the same as for an amortised cost asset, with the difference between amortised cost and fair value recorded in other comprehensive income. Third, only relatively simple debt instruments will qualify for measurement at fair value through other comprehensive income as they will also need to pass the contractual cash flow characteristics test.

2.2   Equity instruments and derivatives

Equity instruments and derivatives are normally measured at fair value through profit or loss. *[IFRS 9.5.7.1].* However, on initial recognition, an entity may make an irrevocable election (on an instrument-by-instrument basis) to present in other comprehensive income subsequent changes in the fair value of an investment in an equity instrument within the scope of IFRS 9. This option applies to instruments that are neither held for trading (see 4 below) nor contingent consideration recognised by an acquirer in a business combination to which IFRS 3 – *Business*

Combinations – applies. *[IFRS 9.5.7.1(b), 5.7.5].* For the purpose of this election, the term equity instrument uses the definition in IAS 32 – *Financial Instruments: Presentation*. The use of this election is covered further at 8 below.

Although most gains and losses on investments in equity instruments designated at fair value through other comprehensive income will be recognised in other comprehensive income, dividends will normally be recognised in profit or loss. *[IFRS 9.5.7.6].* However, the IASB noted that dividends could sometimes represent a return of investment instead of a return on investment. Consequently, the IASB decided that dividends that clearly represent a recovery of part of the cost of the investment are not recognised in profit or loss. *[IFRS 9.BC5.25(a)].* Meanwhile, gains or losses recognised in other comprehensive income are never reclassified from equity to profit or loss on derecognition of the asset, and consequently, there is no need to review such investments for possible impairment.

Determining when a dividend does or does not clearly represent a recovery of cost could prove somewhat judgemental in practice, especially as the standard contains no further explanatory guidance. Also, because it is an exception to a principle, it could open up the possibility of structuring transactions to convert fair value gains into dividends through the use of intermediate holding vehicles.

3 CLASSIFYING FINANCIAL LIABILITIES

The classification of financial liabilities does not follow the approach used for the classification of financial assets; rather it remains broadly the same as under IAS 39. Financial liabilities are measured either at fair value through profit or loss or at amortised cost.

In addition, IFRS 9 specifies the accounting treatment for liabilities arising from certain financial guarantee contracts (see Chapter 42 at 3.4 and Chapter 49 at 2.8) and commitments to provide loans at below market rates of interest (see Chapter 42 at 3.5 and Chapter 49 at 2.8).

Financial liabilities are measured at fair value through profit or loss when they meet the definition of held for trading (see 4 below), *[IFRS 9 Appendix A],* or when they are designated as such on initial recognition. Designation at fair value through profit or loss is permitted when either: *[IFRS 9.4.2.2]*

(a) it eliminates or significantly reduces a measurement or recognition inconsistency (sometimes referred to as an 'accounting mismatch'). Such mismatches would otherwise arise from measuring assets or liabilities or recognising the gains and losses on them on different bases;

(b) a group of financial liabilities or financial assets and financial liabilities is managed and its performance is evaluated on a fair value basis in accordance with a documented risk management or investment strategy, and information is provided internally on that basis to the entity's key management personnel (as defined in IAS 24 – *Related Party Disclosures* – see Chapter 36 at 2.2.1.D); or

(c) a financial liability contains one or more embedded derivatives that meet certain conditions. *[IFRS 9.4.3.5].*

Chapter 46

However, for financial liabilities designated as at fair value through profit or loss, the element of gains or losses attributable to changes in credit risk should normally be recognised in other comprehensive income with the remainder recognised in profit or loss. *[IFRS 9.5.7.7].* These amounts recognised in other comprehensive income are not recycled to profit or loss if the liability is ever repurchased. This is discussed in further detail in Chapter 49 at 2.1.

All other financial liabilities are generally classified as subsequently measured at amortised cost using the effective interest method. *[IFRS 9.4.2.1].*

The definition of held for trading is dealt with at 4 below and designation at fair value through profit or loss is covered further at 7 below.

In contrast to the treatment for hybrid contracts with financial assets hosts, derivatives embedded within a financial liability host within the scope of IFRS 9 will often be separately accounted for, in the same manner as under IAS 39. That is, they must be separated if they are not closely related to the host contract, they meet the definition of a derivative, and the hybrid contract is not measured at fair value through profit or loss (see Chapter 43 at 4). Where an embedded derivative is separated from a financial liability host, the requirements of IFRS 9 dealing with classification of financial instruments should be applied separately to each of the host liability and the embedded derivative.

4   FINANCIAL ASSETS AND FINANCIAL LIABILITIES HELD FOR TRADING

The fact that a financial instrument is held for trading is important for its classification. For financial assets that are debt instruments, held for trading is a business model objective that results in measurement at fair value through profit or loss, as indicated at 2.1 above and further covered in more detail at 5.4 below. Whether or not an asset is held for trading is also relevant for the option to designate an equity instrument as measured at fair value through other comprehensive income (see 2.2 above). Similar to financial assets, if a financial liability is held for trading it is classified as measured at fair value through profit or loss (see 3 above).

Financial assets and liabilities held for trading are defined as those that: *[IFRS 9 Appendix A]*

- are acquired or incurred principally for the purpose of sale or repurchase in the near term;

- on initial recognition are part of a portfolio of identified financial instruments that are managed together and for which there is evidence of a recent actual pattern of short-term profit-taking; or

- are derivatives (except for those that are financial guarantee contracts – see Chapter 42 at 3.4 – or are designated effective hedging instruments – see Chapter 51 at 2.1.1 and 52 at 4).

It follows from the definition that if an entity originates a loan with an intention of syndicating it, the amount of the loan to be syndicated should be classified as held for trading, even if the bank fails to find sufficient commitments from other participants (a so-called 'failed' loan syndication).

The term 'portfolio' in the definition of held for trading is not explicitly defined in IFRS 9, but the context in which it is used suggests that a portfolio is a group of financial assets and/or financial liabilities that are managed as part of that group. If there is evidence of a recent actual pattern of short-term profit taking on financial instruments included in such a portfolio, those financial instruments qualify as held for trading even though an individual financial instrument may, in fact, be held for a longer period of time. *[IFRS 9.IG B.11].*

A financial asset or liability held for trading will always be measured at fair value through profit or loss.

Trading generally reflects active and frequent buying and selling, and financial instruments held for trading are normally used with the objective of generating a profit from short-term fluctuations in price or a dealer's margin. *[IFRS 9.BA.6].*

In addition to derivatives that are not accounted for as hedging instruments, financial liabilities held for trading include:

(a) obligations to deliver financial assets borrowed by a short seller (i.e. an entity that sells financial assets it has borrowed and does not yet own);

(b) financial liabilities that are incurred with an intention to repurchase them in the near term, such as quoted debt instruments that the issuer may buy back in the near term depending on changes in fair value; and

(c) financial liabilities that are part of a portfolio of identified financial instruments that are managed together and for which there is evidence of a recent pattern of short-term profit-taking. *[IFRS 9.BA.7].* However, the fact that a liability is used merely to fund trading activities does not in itself make that liability one that is held for trading. *[IFRS 9.BA.8].*

5 FINANCIAL ASSETS: THE 'BUSINESS MODEL' ASSESSMENT

The business model assessment is one of the two steps to classify financial assets. An entity's business model reflects how it manages its financial assets in order to generate cash flows; its business model determines whether cash flows will result from collecting contractual cash flows, selling the financial assets or both. This assessment is performed on the basis of scenarios that the entity reasonably expects to occur. This means, the assessment excludes so-called 'worst case' or 'stress case' scenarios. For example, an entity expects that it will sell a particular portfolio of financial assets only in a stress case scenario. If so, this scenario would not affect the entity's assessment of the business model for those assets if the entity does not reasonably expect it to occur. *[IFRS 9.B4.1.2A].*

If cash flows are realised in a way that is different from the entity's expectations at the date that the entity assessed the business model (for example, if the entity sells more or fewer financial assets than it expected when it classified the assets), this does not give rise to a prior period error in the entity's financial statements (as defined in IAS 8 – *Accounting Policies, Changes in Accounting Estimates and Errors*

Chapter 46

– see Chapter 3 at 4.6) nor does it change the classification of the remaining financial assets held in that business model (i.e. those assets that the entity recognised in prior periods and still holds), as long as the entity considered all relevant and objective information that was available at the time that it made the business model assessment. However, when an entity assesses the business model for newly originated or newly purchased financial assets, it must consider information about how cash flows were realised in the past, along with all other relevant information. This means that there is no 'tainting' concept, as in the treatment of held to maturity financial assets under IAS 39, but if there is a change in the way that cash flows are realised then this will affect the classification of new assets when first recognised in the future. (See also 9 below for guidance on reclassifications.) [IFRS 9.B4.1.2A].

An entity's business model for managing the financial assets is a matter of fact and typically observable through particular activities that the entity undertakes to achieve its objectives. An entity will need to use judgment when it assesses its business model for managing financial assets and that assessment is not determined by a single factor or activity. Rather, the entity must consider all relevant and objective evidence that is available at the date of the assessment. Such relevant and objective evidence includes, but is not limited to: [IFRS 9.B4.1.2B]

(a) how the performance of the business model and the financial assets held within that business model are evaluated and reported to the entity's key management personnel;

(b) the risks that affect the performance of the business model (and the financial assets held within) and, in particular, the way those risks are managed; and

(c) how managers of the business are compensated (for example, whether the compensation is based on the fair value of the assets managed or the contractual cash flows collected).

In addition to these three forms of evidence, in most circumstances the expected frequency, value and timing of sales are important aspects of the assessment. These are covered in more detail in 5.2.1 below.

5.1   The level at which the business model assessment is applied

The business model assessment should be performed on the basis of the entity's business model as determined by the entity's key management personnel (as defined in IAS 24 – see Chapter 36 at 2.2.1.D). [IFRS 9.B4.1.1].

An entity's business model is determined at a level that reflects how groups of financial assets are managed together to achieve a particular business objective. This does not need to be the reporting entity level. The entity's business model does not depend on management's intentions for an individual instrument. Accordingly, this condition is not an instrument-by-instrument approach to classification and should be determined on a higher level of aggregation. However, a single entity may have more than one business model for managing its financial instruments (for example, one portfolio that it manages in order to collect contractual cash flows and another portfolio that it manages in order to trade to realise fair value changes). [IFRS 9.B4.1.2].

Similarly, in some circumstances, it may be appropriate to split a portfolio of financial assets into sub-portfolios to reflect how an entity manages them. *[IFRS 9.B4.1.2]*. Those portfolios would be split and treated as separate portfolios, provided the assets belonging to each sub-portfolio are defined. A sub-portfolio approach would not be appropriate in cases where an entity is not able to define which assets would be held to collect contractual cash flows and which assets would potentially be sold. It is clear that judgement will need to be applied when determining the level of aggregation to which the business model assessment should be applied. Splitting a portfolio into two sub-portfolios might allow an entity to achieve amortised cost accounting for most of the assets within the portfolio, even if it is required to sell a certain volume of assets. The entity could define the assets it intends (or is required) to sell as one sub-portfolio while it defines the assets it intends to keep as another.

5.2 Hold to collect contractual cash flows

A financial asset which is held within a business model whose objective is to hold assets in order to collect contractual cash flows is measured at amortised cost (provided the asset also meets the contractual cash flow characteristics test). *[IFRS 9.4.1.2]*. An entity manages such assets to realise cash flows by collecting contractual payments over the life of the instrument instead of managing the overall return on the portfolio by both holding and selling assets. *[IFRS 9.B4.1.2C]*.

5.2.1 Impact of sales on the assessment

In determining whether cash flows are going to be realised by collecting the financial assets' contractual cash flows, it is necessary to consider the frequency, value and timing of sales in prior periods, whether the sales were of assets close to their maturity, the reasons for those sales, and expectations about future sales activity. However, the standard states that sales, in themselves, do not determine the business model and therefore cannot be considered in isolation. It goes on to say that, instead, information about past sales and expectations about future sales provide evidence related to how the entity's stated objective for managing the financial assets is achieved and, specifically, how cash flows are realised. An entity must consider information about past sales within the context of the reasons for those sales and the conditions that existed at that time as compared to current conditions. *[IFRS 9.B4.1.2C]*.

The standard is slightly cryptic concerning the role of sales. When it says that 'sales in themselves do not determine the business model', the emphasis seems to be on past sales. Given the guidance in the standard, the magnitude and frequency of sales is certainly very important evidence in determining an entity's business models. However, the key point is that the standard requires the consideration of *expected* future sales while past sales are of relevance only as a source of evidence. Unlike the held-to-maturity classification under IAS 39, there is no concept of tainting, whereby assets are reclassified if sales activity differs from what was originally expected.

Although the objective of an entity's business model may be to hold financial assets in order to collect contractual cash flows, the entity need not hold all of those instruments until maturity. Thus an entity's business model can be to hold financial assets to collect contractual cash flows even when some sales of financial assets occur or are expected to occur in the future. *[IFRS 9.B4.1.3]*.

The following scenarios might be consistent with a hold to collect business model:

- The business model may be to hold assets to collect contractual cash flows even if the entity sells financial assets when there is an increase in the assets' credit risk. To determine whether there has been an increase in the assets' credit risk, the entity considers reasonable and supportable information, including forward looking information. Irrespective of their frequency and value, sales due to an increase in the assets' credit risk are not inconsistent with a business model whose objective is to hold financial assets to collect contractual cash flows because the credit quality of financial assets is relevant to the entity's ability to collect contractual cash flows. Credit risk management activities that are aimed at mitigating potential credit losses due to credit deterioration are integral to such a business model. Selling a financial asset because it no longer meets the credit criteria specified in the entity's documented investment policy is an example of a sale that has occurred due to an increase in credit risk. However, in the absence of such a policy, the entity may be able to demonstrate in other ways that the sale occurred due to an increase in credit risk. *[IFRS 9.B4.1.3A]*.

- Sales that occur for other reasons, such as sales made to manage credit concentration risk (without an increase in the assets' credit risk), may also be consistent with a business model whose objective is to hold financial assets in order to collect contractual cash flows. However, such sales are likely to be consistent with a business model whose objective is to hold financial assets in order to collect contractual cash flows only if those sales are infrequent (even if significant in value) or insignificant in value both individually and in aggregate (even if frequent). *[IFRS 9.B4.1.3B]*.

- In addition, sales may be consistent with the objective of holding financial assets in order to collect contractual cash flows if the sales are made close to the maturity of the financial assets and the proceeds from the sales approximate the collection of the remaining contractual cash flows. *[IFRS 9.B4.1.3B]*. How an entity defines 'close' and 'approximate' will be a matter of judgment.

If more than an infrequent number of sales are made out of a portfolio and those sales are more than insignificant in value (either individually or in aggregate), the entity needs to assess whether and how such sales are consistent with an objective of collecting contractual cash flows. An increase in the frequency or value of sales in a particular period is not necessarily inconsistent with an objective to hold financial assets in order to collect contractual cash flows, if an entity can explain the reasons for those sales and demonstrate why those sales do not reflect a change in the entity's business model and, hence, sales will in future be lower in frequency or value. *[IFRS 9.B4.1.3B]*. This assessment is about expectations and not about intent. For instance, the fact that it is not the entity's objective to realise fair value gains or losses is not sufficient in itself to be able to conclude that measurement at amortised cost is appropriate.

Furthermore, whether a third party (such as a banking regulator in the case of some liquidity portfolios held by banks) imposes the requirement to sell the financial assets, or that activity is at the entity's discretion, is not relevant to the business model assessment. *[IFRS 9.B4.1.3B].*

In contrast, if an entity manages a portfolio of financial assets with the objective of realising cash flows through the sale of the assets, the assets would not be held under a hold to collect business model. For example, an entity might actively manage a portfolio of assets in order to realise fair value changes arising from changes in credit spreads and yield curves. In this case, the entity's business model is not to hold those assets to collect the contractual cash flows. Rather, the entity's objective results in active buying and selling with the entity managing the instruments to realise fair value gains.

IFRS 9 does not explain how 'infrequent' and 'insignificant in value' should be interpreted in practice. Overall, those thresholds could lead to diversity in application, although it is an area where we expect that consensus and best practices will emerge over time.

The overarching principle is whether the entity's key management personnel have made a decision that, collecting contractual cash flows but not selling financial assets is integral to achieving the objective of the business model. *[IFRS 9.B4.1.2C, B4.1.4A].* Under that objective, an entity will not normally expect that sales will be more than infrequent and more than insignificant in value.

Many organisations hold portfolios of financial assets for liquidity purposes. Assets in those portfolios are regularly sold because sales are required by a regulator to demonstrate liquidity, because the entity needs to cover everyday liquidity needs or because the entity tries to maximise the yield of the portfolio. It follows that such portfolios (except those that may be sold only in stress case scenarios) would probably not be measured at amortised cost (see also 5.5 below).

With reference to what should we measure 'insignificant in value'? One possibility is to interpret it as a portion of the value of the portfolio. But it is important to note that the standard requires that sales need to be insignificant in value both individually and in aggregate. *[IFRS 9.B4.1.3B].* Also, the standard is not explicit as to whether any test of insignificance should be performed period by period, or by taking into account sales over the entire life of the portfolio. However, if a period by period approach were to be used, the determination of whether sales are insignificant in value would depend on the length of the period, which means that two entities with identical portfolios but with different lengths of the reporting period would arrive at different assessments. Further, if a bank holds a portfolio of bonds with an average maturity of 20 years, sales of, say, 5% each year would mean that a considerable portion of the portfolio will have been sold before it matures, which would not seem to be consistent with a business model of holding to collect.

Another approach would be to assess whether the value is insignificant in the light of whether the business model is suitable for applying an internal rate of return accounting approach, that is, whether amortised cost information is a relevant representation of the cash flows from the portfolio. An entity could perhaps compare the fair value gains and losses, which it expects to realise through sales with the expected interest income, to determine whether it is more than insignificant. This would suggest that a larger value of sales might be regarded as less significant if the assets pay a floating rate of interest or there is expected to be little change in interest rates, so that fair value gains and losses are expected to be small. Using this approach, it may be misleading to consider net realised gains or losses, if gains and losses are expected to be significant on a gross basis.

It will be important to observe what practices emerge as the standard is implemented.

5.2.2   *Transferred financial assets that are not derecognised*

There are a number of circumstances where an entity may sell a financial asset but those assets will remain on the selling entity's statement of financial position. For example, a bank may enter into a 'repo' transaction whereby it sells a debt security and at the same time agrees to repurchase it at a fixed price. Similarly, a manufacturer may sell trade receivables as part of a factoring programme and provide a guarantee to the buyer to compensate it for any defaults by the debtors. In each case, the seller retains substantially all risks and rewards of the assets and the financial assets would not be derecognised in line with the requirements of IFRS 9.

The inevitable question that arises in these circumstances is whether these transactions should be regarded as sales when applying the business model assessment. In this context, IFRS 9 contains in example 3 of paragraph B4.1.4 only one passing reference to derecognition, but it does suggest that it is the accounting treatment and not the legal form of a transaction that determines whether the entity has ceased to hold an asset to collect contractual cash flows. Application of such an approach would give an intuitively correct answer for repo transactions, in which the seller is required to repurchase the asset at an agreed future date and price, and which are, in substance, secured financing transactions rather than sales. However, as the IASB did not provide the basis for the treatment in the example quoted above, it is not clear if accounting derecognition should always be the basis for the assessment. For instance, if a loan is sold under an agreement by which the seller will indemnify the purchaser for any credit losses (for instance if it is factored with recourse) and so the asset is not derecognised, it is not clear whether there has been a sale for the purposes of the IFRS 9 business model assessment, given that the transferor will never retake possession of the asset. We therefore believe that, except for repos, an entity has an accounting policy choice of whether it considers the legal form of the sale or the economic substance of the transaction when analysing sales within a portfolio.

5.3   Hold to collect contractual cash flows and selling financial assets

The fair value through other comprehensive income measurement category is a mandatory category for portfolios of financial assets that are held within a business model whose objective is achieved by both collecting contractual cash flows and selling financial assets (provided the asset also meets the contractual cash flow test). *[IFRS 9.4.1.2A].*

In this type of business model, the entity's key management personnel has made a decision that both collecting contractual cash flows and selling are fundamental to achieving the objective of the business model. There are various objectives that may be consistent with this type of business model. For example, the objective of the business model may be to manage everyday liquidity needs, to maintain a particular interest yield profile or to match the duration of the financial assets to the duration of the liabilities that those assets are funding. To achieve these objectives, the entity will both collect contractual cash flows and sell the financial assets. *[IFRS 9.B4.1.4A]*.

Compared to the business model with an objective to hold financial assets to collect contractual cash flows, this business model will typically involve greater frequency and value of sales. This is because selling financial assets is integral to achieving the business model's objective rather than only incidental to it. There is no threshold for the frequency or value of sales that can or must occur in this business model. *[IFRS 9.B4.1.4B]*.

As set out in the standard, the fair value through other comprehensive income is a defined category and is neither a residual nor an election. However, in practice, entities may identify those debt instruments which are held to collect contractual cash flows (see 5.2 above), those which are held for trading, those managed on a fair value basis (see 5.4 below) and those for which the entity applies the fair value option to avoid a measurement mismatch, (see 7.1 below), and then measure the remaining debt instruments at fair value through other comprehensive income. As a consequence, the fair value through other comprehensive income category might, in effect, be used as a residual, just because it is far easier to articulate business models that would be classified at amortised cost or at fair value through profit or loss.

5.4 Other business models

IFRS 9 requires financial assets to be measured at fair value through profit or loss if they are not held within either a business model whose objective is to hold assets to collect contractual cash flows or within a business model whose objective is achieved by both collecting contractual cash flows and selling financial assets. A business model that results in measurement at fair value through profit or loss is where the financial assets are held for trading (see section 4 above). Another is where the financial assets are managed on a fair value basis (see Example 46.14 below).

When the standard explains what it means by a portfolio of financial assets that is managed and whose performance is evaluated on a fair value basis it refers to the requirements for designating financial liabilities as measured at fair value through profit or loss. *[IFRS 9.B4.1.6]*. In order to be considered to be managed on a fair value basis, the portfolio needs to be managed in accordance with a documented risk management or investment strategy and for information, prepared on a fair value basis, about the group of instruments to be provided internally to the entity's key management personnel (this is as defined in IAS 24 see Chapter 36 at 2.2.1.D), for example the entity's board of directors and chief executive officer. *[IFRS 9.4.2.2(b)]*. Further, it is explained that if an entity manages and evaluates the performance of a group of financial assets, measuring that group at fair value through profit or loss results in more relevant information. *[IFRS 9B.1.33]*. Documentation of the entity's strategy need not be extensive but should be sufficient to demonstrate that the classification at fair value through profit or loss is consistent with the entity's risk management or investment strategy. *[IFRS 9B.1.35]*.

In each case, the entity manages the financial assets with the objective of realising cash flows through the sale of the assets. The entity makes decisions based on the assets' fair values and manages the assets to realise those fair values. As a consequence, the entity's objective will typically result in active buying and selling. Even though the entity will collect contractual cash flows while it holds financial assets in the fair value through profit or loss category, this is only incidental and not integral to achieving the business model's objective. *[IFRS 9.B4.1.5, B4.1.6]*.

5.5   Applying the business model test in practice

The application of the business model test is illustrated through a number of examples.

Example 46.1:   The level at which the business model assessment should be applied

A global banking group operates two business lines, retail banking and investment banking. These businesses both operate in the same five locations by means of separate subsidiaries. Each subsidiary has its own Board of Directors that is responsible for carrying out the strategic objectives as set by the group's Board of Directors.

The financial assets held by the investment banking business are measured at fair value through profit or loss in line with the group's strategy, which defines the business model, to actively trade these financial assets. Within the retail banking business, four of the five subsidiaries hold debt securities in line with the group's objective to collect contractual cash flows. However, the fifth subsidiary holds a portfolio of debt securities that it expects to sell before maturity. These assets are not held for trading, but individual assets are sold if the portfolio manager believes he or she can reinvest the funds in assets with a higher yield. As a result, a more than infrequent number of sales that are significant in value are anticipated for this portfolio and it is unlikely that this portfolio would meet the amortised cost criteria if it were assessed on its own.

The bank will need to exercise judgement to determine the appropriate level at which to assess its business model(s). Hence, different conclusions are possible depending on the facts and circumstances.

This does not mean that the bank has an accounting policy choice, but it is, rather, a matter of fact that can be observed by the way the organisation is structured and managed. In many organisations, key management personnel may determine the overall strategy and then delegate their authority for executing the strategy to others. The combination of the overall strategy and the effect of the delegated authority are among the factors that can be considered in the determination of business models.

In the specified fact pattern, the determining factor is whether the fifth subsidiary is managed independently from the other four subsidiaries (and performance is assessed and management is compensated accordingly). If it is separately managed, the number of business models is three (i.e. investment banking, one business model for the first four subsidiaries and a third business model for the fifth subsidiary). If not, the number of business models is two (i.e. one for retail banking and one for investment banking). In the case of two business models, all of the debt securities held by the retail banking business would be accounted for at fair value through other comprehensive income, unless the sales activity of the fifth subsidiary is not significant to the bank.

Example 46.2:   *Splitting portfolios*

Entity A has debt instruments worth CU100, comprising notes with maturities of three to five years. Until the adoption of IFRS 9, all of these debt instruments were classified as available-for-sale under IAS 39. CU10 of the portfolio is sold and reinvested at least once a year, while the remaining CU90 investments are typically held to near their maturity. First, the entity needs to use judgement to determine whether it has:

(a) Two business models: (i) CU90 debt instruments held to near their maturity; and (ii) CU10 debt instruments which are actively bought and sold, provided those assets can be separately identified, or

(b) One business model applied to the overall portfolio of CU100 debt investments

If scenario (a) above is considered more appropriate, the entity could achieve amortised cost classification for a majority of the debt instruments and would probably need to account for the remaining debt instruments at fair value through profit or loss or fair value through other comprehensive income. This is more likely to be the case where there is clearly a different management objective for the two groups of assets and their performance is measured, and management is compensated, accordingly.

Alternatively, if scenario (b) is considered more appropriate, the entity needs to determine whether the level of expected sales and repurchases is more than infrequent and is significant in value, requiring the whole portfolio to be measured at fair value through profit or loss or fair value through other comprehensive income (see 5.2.1 above). Whether the assets are required to be measured at fair value through profit or loss instead of fair value through other comprehensive income depends on whether the portfolio is managed on a fair value basis and fair value information is primarily used to assess asset's performance and to make decisions.

Example 46.3:   *Credit risk management activities*

An entity holds investments to collect their contractual cash flows. The funding needs of the entity are predictable and the maturity of its financial assets is matched to its estimated funding needs.

The entity performs credit risk management activities with the objective of maintaining the credit risk of the portfolio within defined risk limits. In the past, sales have typically occurred when the financial assets' credit risk has increased such that the assets no longer meet the entity's documented investment policy.

Reports to key management personnel focus on the credit quality of the financial assets and the contractual return. The entity also monitors fair values of the financial assets, among other information.

Irrespective of their frequency and value, sales due to an increase in the assets' credit risk are not inconsistent with a business model whose objective is to hold financial assets to collect contractual cash flows, because the credit quality of financial assets is relevant to the entity's ability to collect contractual cash flows.

Credit risk management activities that are aimed at avoiding potential credit losses due to credit deterioration are integral to such a business model. Selling a financial asset because it no longer meets the credit criteria specified in the entity's documented investment policy is an example of a sale that has occurred due to an increase in credit risk. However, this conclusion cannot be extended to sales to avoid excessive credit concentration (see also Example 46.4 below).

Although the entity considers, among other information, the financial assets' fair values from a liquidity perspective (i.e. the cash amount that would be realised if the entity needs to sell assets), the entity's objective is to hold the financial assets in order to collect the contractual cash flows.

Therefore, under the fact pattern specified, the entity will still be able to measure the portfolio at amortised cost.

In the absence of a documented investment or similar policy, the entity may be able to demonstrate in other ways that a sale only occurred due to an increase in credit risk. *[IFRS 9.B4.1.4 Example 1].*

Chapter 46

Example 46.4:   Sales to manage concentration risk

An entity sells financial assets to manage the concentration of the entity's credit risk to a particular obligor, country or industrial sector, without an increase in the assets' credit risk.

Such sales may be consistent with a business model whose objective is to hold financial assets in order to collect contractual cash flows, but only to the extent that they are infrequent (even if significant in value) or insignificant in value both individually and in aggregate (even if frequent). That means such sales are treated no differently than sales for any other reason. Thus, such sales are more likely to be consistent with a business model whose objective is to hold financial assets in order to collect contractual cash flows and to sell financial assets. *[IFRS 9.B4.1.3B].*

Example 46.5:   Credit-impaired financial assets in a hold to collect business model

An entity's business model is to purchase portfolios of financial assets, such as loans. Those portfolios may or may not include financial assets that are credit-impaired, that is, there have already been one or more events that have had a detrimental impact on future cash flows. If payment on the loans is not made on a timely basis, the entity attempts to realise the contractual cash flows through various means – for example, by making contact with the debtor by mail, telephone or other methods. The entity's objective is to collect contractual cash flows and the entity does not manage any of the loans in this portfolio with an objective of realising cash flows by selling them.

The objective of the entity's business model is to hold the financial assets in order to collect the contractual cash flows. *IFRS 9.B4.1.4 Example 2].*

Example 46.6:   Hedging activities in a hold to collect business model

A bank holds a portfolio of variable rate loans and enters into interest rate swaps to change the interest rate on particular loans in the portfolio from a floating interest rate to a fixed interest rate.

The fact that the entity has entered into derivatives to modify the cash flows of the portfolio does not in itself change the entity's business model. *[IFRS 9.B4.1.4 Example 2].*

Example 46.7:   Securitisation

An entity has a business model with the objective of originating loans to customers and subsequently to sell those loans to a securitisation vehicle. The securitisation vehicle issues instruments to investors. The originating entity controls the securitisation vehicle and thus consolidates it. The securitisation vehicle collects the contractual cash flows from the loans and passes them on to its investors.

It is assumed for the purposes of this example that the loans continue to be recognised in the consolidated statement of financial position because they are recognised by the securitisation vehicle.

The consolidated group originated the loans with the objective of holding them to collect the contractual cash flows and, therefore, measures them at amortised cost.

However, the originating entity has an objective of realising cash flows on the loan portfolio by selling the loans to the securitisation vehicle, so for the purposes of its separate financial statements it would not be considered to be managing this portfolio in order to collect the contractual cash flows, but to sell them. The loans would probably need to be recorded at fair value through profit or loss as long as they continue to be recognised. *[IFRS 9.B4.1.4 Example 3].* The same conclusion would be drawn for the consolidated group if the securitisation vehicle is not consolidated but the originating entity is unable to derecognise the assets.

Example 46.8:   Liquidity portfolio for stress case scenarios

A financial institution holds financial assets to meet liquidity needs in a 'stress case' scenario (e.g. a run on the bank's deposits). The entity does not anticipate selling these assets except in such a scenario. The entity monitors the credit quality of the financial assets and its objective in managing the financial assets is to collect the contractual cash flows. The entity evaluates the performance of the assets on the basis of interest revenue earned and credit losses realised.

However, the entity also monitors the fair value of the financial assets from a liquidity perspective to ensure that the cash amount that would be realised if the entity needed to sell the assets in a stress case scenario would be sufficient to meet the entity's liquidity needs. Periodically, the entity makes sales that are insignificant in value to demonstrate liquidity.

The objective of the entity's business model is to hold the financial assets to collect contractual cash flows.

The analysis would not change even if during a previous stress case scenario the entity made sales that were significant in value in order to meet its liquidity needs. Similarly, recurring sales activity that is insignificant in value is not inconsistent with holding financial assets to collect contractual cash flows.

However, the assessment would change if the entity periodically sells debt instruments that are significant in value to demonstrate liquidity, or if the entity sells the debt instruments to cover everyday liquidity needs. See Examples 46.9 and 46.10 below. *[IFRS 9.B4.1.4 Example 4]*.

Example 46.9:   Anticipated capital expenditure

A non-financial entity anticipates capital expenditure in a few years. The entity invests its excess cash in short-term and long-term financial assets so that it can fund the expenditure when the need arises. Many of the financial assets have contractual lives that exceed the entity's anticipated investment period. Therefore the entity will need to sell some of the assets before maturity to meet those funding needs.

The objective of the business model is achieved by both collecting contractual cash flows and selling financial assets.

In contrast, consider an entity that anticipates a cash outflow in five years to fund capital expenditures and invests excess cash in short-term financial assets. When the investments mature, the entity reinvests the cash into new short-term financial assets. The entity maintains this strategy until the funds are needed, at which time the entity uses the proceeds from the maturing financial assets to fund the capital expenditures. Only insignificant sales occur before maturity (unless there is an increase in credit risk). The objective of such a business model is to hold financial assets in order to collect contractual cash flows. *[IFRS 9.B4.1.4C Example 5]*.

Example 46.10:   Liquidity portfolio for every day liquidity needs

A financial institution holds financial assets to meet its everyday liquidity needs. In the past, this has resulted in frequent sales activity and such sales have been significant in value. This activity is expected to continue in the future as everyday liquidity needs can rarely be forecast with any accuracy.

The objective of the business model is meeting everyday liquidity needs. The entity achieves those objectives by both collecting contractual cash flows and selling financial assets. This means that both collecting contractual cash flows and selling financial assets are integral to achieving the business model's objective and the financial assets are measured at fair value through other comprehensive income. The frequent and significant sales activity does not mean that the portfolio is held for trading because under the business model objective above, assets are not sold with the intention of short-term profit taking. *[IFRS 9.B4.1.4 Example 4]*.

Example 46.11:   Opportunistic portfolio management

A financial institution holds a portfolio of financial assets. The entity actively manages the return on the portfolio on an opportunistic basis trying to increase the return, without a clear intention of holding the financial assets to collect contractual cash flows (although it might end up holding the assets if no other investment opportunities arise). That return consists of collecting contractual payments as well as gains and losses from the sale of financial assets.

As a result, the entity holds financial assets to collect contractual cash flows and sells financial assets to reinvest in higher yielding financial assets. In the past, this strategy has resulted in frequent sales activity and such sales have been significant in value. It is expected that the sales activity will continue in the future.

The entity achieves the objective stated above by both collecting contractual cash flows and selling financial assets. Both collecting contractual cash flows and selling financial assets are integral to achieving the business model's objective and, thus, the financial assets are measured at fair value through other comprehensive income. *[IFRS 9.B4.1.4C Example 6].*

In some cases, entities may manage a portfolio to manage its yield. In such cases, the portfolio manager may be remunerated based on the overall yield of the portfolio and fair value gains or losses may not be considered in his or her remuneration. Furthermore, management's documented strategy and defined key performance indicators may emphasise optimising long-term yield rather than fair value gains or losses and accordingly, the entity's management reporting focuses on yield rather than fair value of the debt instruments within the portfolio. However, in our view, the fact that it is not the entity's objective to realise fair value gains or losses is not sufficient in itself to be able to conclude that measurement at amortised cost is appropriate as the business model objective is not only holding financial assets to collect contractual cash flows but also results in sales which are more than infrequent and significant in value. Thus, such a portfolio would be measured at fair value through other comprehensive income.

Example 46.12:   *Replication portfolios*

Fact pattern 1: Insurance company

An insurer holds financial assets in order to fund insurance contract liabilities. The insurer uses the proceeds from the contractual cash flows on the financial assets to settle insurance contract liabilities as they come due. To ensure that the contractual cash flows from the financial assets are sufficient to settle those liabilities, the insurer undertakes significant buying and selling activity on a regular basis to rebalance its portfolio of assets and to meet cash flow needs as they arise.

The objective of the business model is to fund the insurance contract liabilities. To achieve this objective, the entity collects contractual cash flows as they come due and sells financial assets to maintain the desired profile of the asset portfolio. Thus, both collecting contractual cash flows and selling financial assets are integral to achieving the business model's objective and it follows that the financial assets are measured at fair value through other comprehensive income. *[IFRS 9.B4.1.4C Example 7].*

Fact pattern 2: Bank

A bank allocates investments into maturity bands to match the expected duration of customers' time deposits. The invested assets have a similar maturity profile and amount to the corresponding deposits. The target ratio of assets to deposits for each maturity band has pre-determined minimum and maximum levels. For example, if the ratio exceeds the maximum level because of an unexpected withdrawal of deposits, the bank will sell some assets to reduce the ratio. The choice of assets to be sold would be based on those that would generate the highest profit or incur the lowest loss.

Meanwhile, new assets will be acquired when necessary (i.e. when the ratio of assets to deposits falls below the pre-determined minimum level). The expected repayment profile of the deposits would be updated on a quarterly basis, based on changes in customer behaviour. Under IAS 39, these assets were classified as available-for-sale and there has been no history of active trading.

The question is whether adjusting the assets/deposits ratio by selling assets to correspond with a change in the expected repayment profile of the deposits would mean that the business model is inconsistent with the objective of holding to collect the contractual cash flows. In these circumstances, an analogy can be drawn to the insurance company above.

If the bank has a good track record of forecasting its deposit repayments, so that sales are expected to be infrequent, it is possible that the objective of the business model is to hold the investments to collect contractual cash flows. But, if significant sales take place each year, it is likely to be difficult to rationalise such practice with this objective. Due consideration will also need to be given to the magnitude of sales and the reasons for the sales.

Example 46.13: Loans that are to be sub-participated

An entity originates loans so that it holds part of the portfolio to maturity, but 'sub-participates' a portion of the loans to other banks, so that it transfers substantially all the risks and rewards and so achieves derecognition. The question arises whether, for the purposes of application of IFRS 9, the entity has one business model or two.

The entity could consider the activities of lending to hold and lending to sell or sub-participate as two separate business models, requiring different skills and processes. Whilst the financial assets resulting from the former would typically qualify for amortised cost measurement, those from the latter would probably not and would, therefore, most likely need to be measured at fair value through profit or loss. This split approach is likely to be acceptable as long as the entity is able to forecast with reasonable confidence that it will indeed hold the assets (or the proportion of a group of identical assets) that it determines to be measured at amortised cost.

If a loan is assessed, in part, to be sold or sub-participated, this raises the additional issue of whether a single financial asset can be classified into two separate business models. As it is already common under IAS 39 for loans to be classified in part as held for trading and in part at amortised cost, it is likely that this practice will continue under IFRS 9.

In some cases, an entity may fail to achieve the intended disposal, having previously classified a portion of a loan at fair value through profit or loss because of the intention to sell.

The standard requires classification to be determined in accordance with the business model applicable at the point of initial recognition of the asset. In this example, the fact that the entity fails to achieve an intended disposal does not trigger a reclassification in accordance with the standard as the threshold for reclassification is a very high hurdle. Therefore, loans or portions of loans that the entity fails to dispose of would continue to be recorded at fair value through profit or loss.

Example 46.14: Portfolio managed on a fair value basis

An entity manages a portfolio and measures its performance on a fair value basis and makes decisions based on the fair value of the financial assets. Such an objective typically results in frequent sales and purchases of financial assets.

A portfolio of financial assets that is managed and whose performance is evaluated on a fair value basis is neither held to collect contractual cash flows nor held both to collect contractual cash flows and to sell financial assets. In addition, a portfolio of financial assets that meets the definition of held for trading is not held to collect contractual cash flows or held both to collect contractual cash flows and to sell financial assets. The entity is primarily focused on fair value information and uses that information to assess the assets' performance and to make decisions.

Even though the entity will collect contractual cash flows while it holds financial assets in the fair value through profit or loss category, this is only incidental and not integral to achieving the business model's objective. Consequently, such portfolios of financial assets must be measured at fair value through profit or loss.

6 CHARACTERISTICS OF THE CONTRACTUAL CASH FLOWS OF THE INSTRUMENT

The assessment of the characteristics of a financial asset's contractual cash flows aims to identify whether they are 'solely payments of principal and interest on the principal amount outstanding'. Hence, the assessment is colloquially referred to as the 'SPPI test'.

The contractual cash flow characteristics test is designed to screen out financial assets on which the application of the effective interest method either is not viable from a pure mechanical standpoint or does not provide useful information about the uncertainty, timing and amount of the financial asset's contractual cash flows.

Because the effective interest method is essentially an allocation mechanism that spreads interest revenue or expense over time, amortised cost is only appropriate for simple cash flows that have low variability such as those of traditional unleveraged loans and receivables, and 'plain vanilla' debt instruments. Accordingly, the contractual cash flow characteristics test is based on the premise that it is only when the variability in the contractual cash flows arises to maintain the holder's return in line with a 'basic lending arrangement' that the application of effective interest method provides useful information. *[IFRS 9.BC4.23,158,171,172]*.

In this context, the term 'basic lending arrangement' is used broadly to capture both originated and acquired financial assets, the lender or the holder of which is looking to earn a return that compensates primarily for the time value of money and credit risk. However, such an arrangement can also include other elements that provide consideration for other basic lending risks such as liquidity risks, costs associated with holding the financial asset for a period of time (e.g. servicing or administrative costs) and a profit margin. *[IFRS 9.B4.1.7A, BC4.182(b)]*.

In contrast, contractual terms that introduce a more than *de minimis* exposure (see section 6.4.1 below) to risks or volatility in the contractual cash flows that is unrelated to a basic lending arrangement, such as exposure to changes in equity prices or commodity prices, do not give rise to contractual cash flows that are solely payments of principal and interest on the principal amount outstanding. *[IFRS 9.B4.1.7A, B4.1.18]*.

The IASB noted that it believes that amortised cost would provide relevant and useful information as long as the contractual cash flows do not introduce risks or volatility that are inconsistent with a basic lending arrangement. *[IFRS 9.BC4.180]*.

The following sections cover the main aspects of the contractual cash flow characteristics test, starting with the meaning of the terms 'principal' and 'interest' in sections 6.1 and 6.2, and discusses instruments that normally pass the test at 6.3. So called 'modified' contractual cash flows and their effect on the contractual cash flow characteristics test are dealt with in section 6.4. Contractually linked instruments are separately covered in section 6.5.

6.1   The meaning of 'principal'

'Principal' is not a defined term in IFRS 9. However, the standard states that, for the purposes of applying the contractual cash flow characteristics test, the principal is 'the fair value of the asset at initial recognition' and that it may change over the life of the financial asset (for example, if there are repayments of principal). *[IFRS 9.4.1.3(a), B4.1.7B]*.

The IASB believes that this usage reflects the economics of the financial asset from the perspective of the current holder; in other words, the entity would assess the contractual cash flow characteristics by comparing the contractual cash flows to the amount that it actually invested. *[IFRS 9.BC4.182(a)]*.

For example: Entity A issued a bond with a contractually stated principal of CU1,000. The bond was originally issued at CU990. Because interest rates have risen sharply since the bond was originally issued, Entity B, the current holder of the bond, acquired the bond in the secondary market for CU975. From the perspective of entity B, the principal amount is CU975.

The principal is, therefore, not necessarily the contractual par amount, nor (when the holder has acquired the asset subsequent to its origination) is it necessarily the amount that was advanced to the debtor when the instrument was originally issued.

The description of 'principal' as the fair value of an instrument on initial recognition avoids a concern that any financial asset acquired or issued at a substantial discount would be leveraged and hence would not have economic characteristics of interest.

A clear understanding of what the standard means by 'principal' is also necessary for the appropriate and consistent application of the contractual cash flow characteristics test to prepayable financial assets (see section 6.4.4 below).

6.2   The meaning of 'interest'

IFRS 9 states that the most significant elements of interest within a basic lending arrangement are typically the consideration for the time value of money and credit risk. In addition, interest may also include consideration for other basic lending risks (for example, liquidity risk) and costs (for example, administrative costs) associated with holding the financial asset for a particular period of time. Furthermore, interest may include a profit margin that is consistent with a basic lending arrangement.

In extreme economic circumstances, interest can be negative if, for example, the holder of a financial asset effectively pays a fee for the safekeeping of its money for a particular period of time and that fee exceeds the consideration the holder receives for the time value of money, credit risk and other basic lending risks and costs.

Contractual terms that introduce exposure to risks or volatility in the contractual cash flows that is unrelated to a basic lending arrangement, such as exposure to changes in equity prices or commodity prices, do not give rise to contractual cash flows that are solely payments of principal and interest on the principal amount outstanding. An originated or a purchased financial asset can be a basic lending arrangement irrespective of whether it is a loan in its legal form. *[IFRS 9.4.1.3(b), B4.1.7A].*

The IASB notes that the assessment of interest focuses on what the entity is being compensated for (i.e. whether the entity is receiving consideration for basic lending risks, costs and a profit margin or is being compensated for something else), instead of how much the entity receives for a particular element. For example, the Board acknowledges that different entities may price the credit risk element differently. *[IFRS 9.BC4.182(b)].* Although two entities may receive different amounts for the same element of interest, e.g. credit risk, they could both conclude that their consideration for credit risk is appropriate within a basic lending arrangement.

Time value of money is the element of interest that provides consideration for only the passage of time. That is, the time value of money element does not provide consideration for other risks or costs associated with holding the financial asset. To make this assessment, an entity applies judgement and considers relevant factors such as the currency in which the financial asset is denominated, and the period for which the interest rate is set. *[IFRS 9.B4.1.9A].*

Chapter 46

The IASB also notes that, as a general proposition, the market in which the transaction occurs is relevant to the assessment of the time value of money element. For example, in Europe, it is common to reference interest rates to LIBOR and in the United States it is common to reference interest rates to the prime rate. However, a particular interest rate does not necessarily reflect consideration for only the time value of money merely because that rate is considered 'normal' in a particular market. For example, if an interest rate is reset every year but the reference rate is always a 15-year rate, it would be difficult for an entity to conclude that such a rate provides consideration for only the passage of time, even if such pricing is commonly used in that particular market. Accordingly the IASB believes that an entity must apply judgement to conclude whether the stated time value of money element meets the objective of providing consideration for only the passage of time. *[IFRS 9.BC4.178].*

It could be argued that the standard is not entirely clear as to the status of benchmark rates such as LIBOR. For such rates, the consideration for credit risk is neither fixed, nor varies over time to reflect the specific credit risk of the obligor, but instead varies to reflect the credit risks associated with a class of borrowers. However, this seems to be a purist approach and given that LIBOR is widely used as a benchmark rate in capital markets and is cited in the standard as an example of a rate that would satisfy the criteria of the cash flow characteristics test, it would seem that this is not an issue.

6.3   Contractual features that normally pass the test

The most common instruments that normally pass the test are plain vanilla debt instruments which are acquired at par, have a fixed maturity and pay interest that is fixed at inception. Instruments that pay variable interest also normally pass the test, although further consideration is required in that case (see 6.4.4 below).

There are several features that are common in many financial assets and which would not usually cause the cash flow characteristics test to be failed. This section describes some of those features and instruments that are normally unproblematic but also highlights cases they might result in an asset failing the contractual cash flow characteristics test. Section 6.4 below describes features that are more complex and need more consideration.

6.3.1   *Conventional subordination features*

In many lending transaction the instrument is ranked relative to amounts owed by the borrower to its other creditors. An instrument that is subordinated to other instruments may be considered to have contractual cash flows that are payments of principal and interest on the principal amount outstanding if the debtor's non-payment arises only on a breach of contract and the holder has a contractual right to unpaid amounts of principal and interest on the principal amount outstanding even in the event of the debtor's bankruptcy.

For example, a trade receivable that ranks its creditor as a general creditor would qualify as having payments of principal and interest on the principal amount outstanding. This is the case even if the debtor has issued loans that are collateralised, which in the event of bankruptcy would give that loan holder priority over the claims of the general creditor in respect of the collateral but does not affect the contractual right of the general creditor to unpaid principal and other amounts due. *[IFRS 9.B4.1.19].*

On the other hand, if the subordination feature limits the contractual cash flows in any other way or introduces any kind of leverage, the instrument would fail the contractual cash flow characteristics test.

6.3.2   *Full recourse loans secured by collateral*

The fact that a full recourse loan is collateralised does not in itself affect the analysis of whether the contractual cash flows are solely payments of principal and interest on the principal amount outstanding. *[IFRS 9.B4.1.13 Instrument D].* However, a full recourse loan may, in substance, be non-recourse if the borrower has limited other assets, in which case an entity would need to assess the particular underlying assets (i.e. the collateral) to determine whether or not the contractual cash flows of the loan are payments of principal and interest on the principal amount outstanding. *[IFRS 9.B4.1.17].* The contractual cash flows may be limited to the value of the collateral which is most likely inconsistent with payments representing principal and interest in which case the loan fails the contractual cash flow characteristics test (see also Example 46.22 below).

6.3.3   *Bonds with a capped or floored interest rate*

Some bonds may have a stated maturity date but pay a variable market interest rate that is subject to a cap or a floor. The contractual cash flows of such instrument could be seen as being an instrument that has a fixed interest rate and an instrument that has a variable interest rate.

These both represent payments of principal and interest on the principal amount outstanding as long as the interest reflects consideration for the time value of money, for the credit risk associated with the instrument during the term of the instrument and for other basic lending risks and costs, as well as a profit margin.

Therefore, such an instrument can have cash flows that are solely payments of principal and interest on the principal amount outstanding. A feature such as an interest rate cap or floor may reduce cash flow variability by setting a limit on a variable interest rate or increase the cash flow variability because a fixed rate becomes variable. *[IFRS 9.B4.1.13 Instrument C].*

There would appear to be no requirement to determine whether or not the cap or floor is in the money on initial recognition, as is required by the test in IAS 39 to assess whether there is a separable embedded derivative.

We assume that a variable rate debt instrument that is subject to both a cap and a floor (known as a collar) would also satisfy the contractual characteristics test for the same reasons.

6.3.4   *Lender has discretion to change the interest rate*

In some instances, the lender may have the right to unilaterally adjust the interest rates of its loans in accordance with its own business policy. However, should the borrower disagree with the new rate, it has the right to terminate the contract and prepay the loan at par.

Such a feature does not *per se* result in the loans failing the contractual cash flow characteristic test. However, whether the loan passes the test depends on facts and circumstances which require assessment on a case-by-case basis, specifically whether interest represents considerations for the time value of money, credit risk and other basic lending risk and costs, as well as a profit margin. Aspects relevant to this assessment may include but are not limited to:

- whether this feature represents common lending practice in the jurisdiction or not; and

- whether the change in interest rate applies to all similar loans, including new loans and the ones in issue, or only to one or certain individual borrowers (this excludes changes in interest rates due to changes in the credit spread of the borrower).

Note that in practice the bank is likely to be restricted as to how much it can increase the interest rate, since if it is too high the borrower will be motivated to prepay and the bank is unlikely to remain competitive.

6.3.5   *Unleveraged inflation-linked bonds*

For some financial instruments, payments of principal and interest on the principal amount outstanding are linked to an inflation index of the currency in which the instrument is issued. The inflation link is not leveraged and the principal is protected. Linking payments of principal and interest on the principal amount outstanding to an unleveraged inflation index resets the time value of money to a current level. In other words, the interest rate on the instrument reflects 'real' interest. Thus, the interest amounts are consideration for the time value of money on the principal amount outstanding.

However, if the interest payments were indexed to another variable such as the debtor's performance (e.g. the debtor's net income) or an equity index, the contractual cash flows are not payments of principal and interest on the principal amount outstanding (unless it can be demonstrated that the indexing to the debtor's performance results in an adjustment that only compensates the holder for changes in the credit risk of the instrument, such that contractual cash flows will represent only payments for principal and interest). That is because the contractual cash flows reflect a return that is inconsistent with a basic lending arrangement (see 6 above). *[IFRS 9.B4.1.13 Instrument A]*.

The reason that the principal has to be protected is that the holder might not get repaid the principal amount (if, for instance inflation is less than anticipated, the instrument would fail the contractual cash flow characteristics test).

Example 46.15: Unleveraged inflation linked bond

Entity A invests in euro-denominated bonds with a fixed maturity issued by Entity B. Interest on the bond is linked directly to the inflation index of Eurozone Country C, which is Entity B's principal place of business. The question arises whether Entity A can measure the euro bonds at amortised cost or fair value through other comprehensive income given that interest is not linked to the inflation index of the entire Eurozone area.

The bond is denominated in euros and Eurozone Country C is part of the Eurozone, therefore, we consider the inflation link to be acceptable. The inflation index reflects the inflation rate of the currency in which the bond is issued since it is the inflation index of Entity B's economic environment, and the euro is the currency for that economic environment.

By linking the inflation index to the inflation rate of Eurozone Country C, Entity B is reflecting 'real' interest for the economic environment in which it operates. Hence, in these circumstances, Entity A may regard the interest as consideration for the time of value of money and credit risk associated with the principal amount outstanding on the bond.

6.4 Contractual features that may affect the classification

Sometimes, contractual provisions may affect the cash flows of an instrument such that they do not give rise to only a straightforward repayment of principal and interest. An entity is required to carefully assess those features in order to conclude whether or not the instrument passes the contractual cash flow characteristics test. It is important to note that the standard grants an exception for all features that are non-genuine or have only a *de minimis* impact, and can be disregarded when making the assessment (see 6.4.1 below).

Furthermore, the standard allows the time value of money element of interest to be what is referred to as 'modified' but only when the resulting cash flows could not be significantly different from an instrument that has an unmodified time value of money element (see 6.4.2 below). It also allows regulated interest rates as long as they provide consideration that is broadly consistent with the passage of time and do not introduce risks that are inconsistent with a basic lending arrangement (see 6.4.3 below).

An instrument may have other features that change the timing or amount of contractual cash flows which need to be assessed whether they represent payments of principal and interest on the principal outstanding. Examples of such features are variable interest rates, interest rates that step up, prepayment and extension options (see 6.4.4 below).

Lastly, there are features that most likely result in an instrument failing the contractual cash flow characteristics test because they introduce cash flow volatility caused by risks that are inconsistent with a basic lending arrangement (see 6.4.5).

6.4.1 De minimis and non-genuine features

A contractual cash flow characteristic does not affect the classification of the financial asset if it could have only a *de minimis* effect on the contractual cash flows of the financial asset.

In addition, if a contractual cash flow characteristic could have an effect on the contractual cash flows that is more than *de minimis* (either in a single reporting period or cumulatively) but that cash flow characteristic is not genuine, it does not affect the classification of a financial asset. A cash flow characteristic is not genuine

Chapter 46

if it affects the instrument's contractual cash flows only on the occurrence of an event that is extremely rare, highly abnormal and very unlikely to occur. *[IFRS 9.B4.1.18].*

Although the '*de minimis*' and 'non-genuine' thresholds are a high hurdle, allowing entities to disregard such features will result in more debt instruments qualifying for the amortised cost or fair value through other comprehensive income measurement categories than in previous versions of IFRS 9. The terms will need to be interpreted by preparers in analysing the impact of the clarified contractual cash flow characteristics test on the debt instruments they hold.

6.4.1.A   De minimis features

The standard does not prescribe whether a qualitative or a quantitative analysis should be performed to determine whether a feature is *de minimis* or not. While *de minimis* is not defined in IFRS 9, one dictionary definition is 'too trivial to merit consideration'. Implicit in this definition is that if an entity has to consider whether an impact is *de minimis*, whether quantitatively or qualitatively, would imply that it is not.

The *de minimis* threshold concerns the magnitude of the possible effects of the contractual cash flow characteristic. To be considered *de minimis*, the impact of the feature on the cash flows of the financial asset must be expected to be *de minimis* in each reporting period and cumulatively over the life of the financial asset.

6.4.1.B   Non-genuine features

Non-genuine features, as used in this context, are contingent features. A cash flow characteristic is not genuine if it affects the instrument's contractual cash flows only on the occurrence of an event that is extremely rare, highly abnormal and very unlikely to occur. This means, although the feature can potentially lead to cash flows which are not solely payments of principal and interest, and those cash flows may even be significant, the instrument would still qualify for amortised cost or fair value through other comprehensive income measurement, depending on the business model. (See also Chapter 44 at 4.3.1).

In our view, terms are included in a contract for an economic purpose and therefore are, in general, genuine. The threshold 'not genuine' is presumably intended to deal with clauses inserted into the terms of financial instruments for some legal or tax reason but having no real economic purpose or consequence.

An example of a clause that has caused some debate in the context of IAS 32.AG28 which uses the term non-genuine is a 'regulatory change' clause, generally found in the terms of capital instruments issued by financial institutions such as banks and insurance companies. Such entities are generally required by local regulators to maintain certain minimum levels of equity or highly subordinated debt (generally referred to as regulatory capital) in order to be allowed to do business.

A 'regulatory change' clause will typically require an instrument which, at the date of issue, is classified as regulatory capital to be repaid in the event that it ceases to be so classified. The practice so far of the regulators in many markets has been to make changes to a regulatory classification with prospective effect only, such that any instruments already in issue continue to be regarded as regulatory capital even though they would not be under the new rules.

This has led some to question whether a 'regulatory change' clause can be regarded as a contingent settlement provision which is 'not genuine'. This is ultimately a matter for the judgement of entities in the context of the relevant regulatory environment(s). This judgement has not been made easier by the greater unpredictability of the markets (and therefore of regulators' responses to it) in the recent financial crisis. However, as the clause was inserted to provide regulators with flexibility in their actions, even if they do not normally exercise that flexibility, it would be difficult to argue that it is 'non-genuine'.

Disregarding non-genuine features also means that the classification requirements of IFRS 9 cannot be overridden by introducing a contractual non-genuine cash flow characteristic in order to achieve a specific accounting outcome.

6.4.2 Contractual features that modify the consideration for the time value of money

In some cases, the time value of money element may be what the standard describes as 'modified' and so 'imperfect'. It cites, as an example, instances where the tenor of the interest rate does not correspond with the frequency with which it resets. In such cases, an entity must assess the modification to determine whether the contractual cash flows represent solely payments of principal and interest on the principal outstanding. In some circumstances, the entity may be able to make that determination by performing a qualitative assessment whereas, in other circumstances, it may be necessary to perform a quantitative analysis. *[IFRS 9.B4.1.9B].*

The objective of a quantitative assessment is to determine whether or not the contractual (undiscounted) cash flows could be significantly different from the (undiscounted) cash flows that would arise if the time value of money element was not modified (referred to as 'the benchmark' cash flows).

For example, if the financial asset under assessment contains a variable interest rate that is reset every month to a one-year interest rate, the entity compares that financial asset to a financial instrument with identical contractual terms and credit risk, except the variable interest rate is reset monthly to a one-month interest rate. If the modified time value of money element could result in contractual (undiscounted) cash flows that are significantly different from the (undiscounted) benchmark cash flows, the financial asset fails the contractual cash flow characteristics test. To make this determination, the entity must consider the effect of the modified time value of money element in each reporting period and cumulatively over the life of the financial instrument. The reason for the interest rate being set this way is not relevant to the analysis. If it is clear, with little or no analysis, whether the contractual (undiscounted) cash flows on the financial asset under the assessment could (or could not) be significantly different from the (undiscounted) benchmark cash flows, an entity need not perform a detailed assessment. *[IFRS 9.B4.1.9C].*

Chapter 46

The following table lists examples of modifications of the consideration for the time value of money which possibly meet the contractual cash flow characteristics test, depending on the outcome of the assessment described above.

Example 46.16: Examples of a modified time value of money component

Modification	Fact pattern
1 Average interest rate	The stated coupon on a debt instrument is referenced to an average of benchmark interest rates for a specified period. For example, 3-month Euribor rate determined as an average of 3-month rates during the previous quarter.
2 Lagging interest rate	The stated interest rate is referenced to lagging interest rates. For example, 6-month Euribor rate set for a 6 month period, but where the rate is fixed 2 months before the start of the interest period.
3 Tenor mismatch	The stated interest rate is reset to a reference interest rate but the frequency of rest does not match the tenor of the reference rate. For example, the interest rate on a retail mortgage is reset semi-annually based on three-month Libor.
4 Combination of the above	The stated interest rate is reset monthly to an average 12-month reference rate. The interest rate is fixed based on the average rate one month before the start of the interest period.

Time value of money does not include credit risk, so it is important to exclude it from the assessment. The standard suggests this is done by comparing the instrument with a benchmark instrument with the same credit risk, but presumably the comparison could be against an instrument with a different credit risk, as long as the effect of the difference can be excluded. *[IFRS 9.B4.1.9C]*.

When assessing a modified time value of money element, an entity must consider factors that could affect future contractual cash flows. In making the assessment, it must consider every interest rate scenario that is reasonably possible instead of every scenario that could possibly arise. This requirement is illustrated in Example 46.18 below.

If an entity concludes that the contractual (undiscounted) cash flows could be significantly different from the (undiscounted) benchmark cash flows, the financial asset does not pass the contractual cash flows characteristics test and therefore cannot be measured at amortised cost or fair value through other comprehensive income. *[IFRS 9.B4.1.9D]*.

The following examples illustrate instruments with a modified time value of money element and how the benchmark test is applied to them.

Example 46.17: Interest rate period selected at the discretion of the borrower

An entity holds an instrument that is a variable interest rate instrument with a stated maturity date that permits the borrower to choose the market interest rate on an ongoing basis. For example, at each interest rate reset date, the borrower can choose to pay three-month LIBOR for a three-month term or one-month LIBOR for a one-month term.

The contractual cash flows are solely payments of principal and interest on the principal amount outstanding as long as the interest paid over the life of the instrument reflects consideration for basic lending risks and costs as well as a profit margin. Basic lending risks and costs include consideration for the time value of money, for the credit risk associated with the instrument and for other basic lending risks and costs. The fact that the LIBOR interest rate is reset during the life of the instrument does not in itself disqualify the instrument.

However, if the borrower is able to choose to pay a one-month interest rate that is reset every three months, the interest rate is reset with a frequency that does not match the tenor of the interest rate. Therefore the time value of money element is modified. That is because the interest payable in each period is disconnected from the interest period.

In such cases, the entity must qualitatively or quantitatively assess the contractual cash flows against the cash flows of a benchmark instrument to determine whether the mismatch between the two sets of cash flows could be significantly different. The benchmark instrument is identical in all respects except that the tenor of the interest rate matches the interest period. If the analysis results in the conclusion that the two sets of cash flows could be significantly different, payments would not represent principal and interest on the principal amount outstanding.

The same analysis would apply if the borrower is able to choose between the lender's various published interest rates (e.g. the borrower can choose between the lender's published one-month variable interest rate and the lender's published three-month variable interest rate). *[IFRS 9.B4.1.13 Instrument B].*

Example 46.18:   Five-year constant maturity bond

Some bonds pay what is called a constant maturity interest rate. For example, an instrument with an original five-year maturity may pay a variable rate that is reset semi-annually but always reflects a five year rate. In such cases, the time value of money element is modified. The entity must determine whether the instrument's cash flows could be significantly different from those on a bond with a similar maturity, credit risk and interest rate reset frequency, but that that pays a semi-annual rate of interest.

In making this assessment, the entity cannot conclude that the contractual cash flows are solely payments of principal and interest on the principal amount outstanding, simply because the interest rate curve at the time of the assessment is such that the difference between a five-year interest rate and a semi-annual interest rate is not significant. Rather, the entity must also consider whether the relationship between the five-year interest rate and the semi-annual interest rate could change over the life of the instrument such that the contractual (undiscounted) cash flows over the life of the instrument could be significantly different from the (undiscounted) benchmark cash flows. *[IFRS 9.B4.1.9D].*

In this example, if the entity considers future developments, it is unlikely that it can conclude that the contractual cash flows could not be significantly different from the benchmark cash flows, considering the magnitude of the mismatch between the interest rate tenor and reset frequency. The bond will always pay a five year rate even though, except at the outset, this exceeds the instrument's remaining life. Therefore, the instrument is not likely to meet the contractual cash flow characteristics test.

6.4.3   Regulated interest rates

In some jurisdictions, the government or a regulatory authority sets interest rates. For example, such government regulation of interest rates may be part of a broad macroeconomic policy or it may be introduced to encourage entities to invest in a particular sector of the economy. In some of these cases, the objective of the time value of money element is not to provide consideration for only the passage of time. However, the Board notes that the rates are set for public policy reasons and thus are not subject to structuring to achieve a particular accounting result. *[IFRS 9.BC4.180].* Consequently, as a concession, a regulated interest rate is considered by the IASB to serve as a proxy for the time value of money element for the purpose of applying the contractual cash flow characteristics test if that regulated interest rate:

- provides consideration that is broadly consistent with the passage of time, and

- does not provide exposure to risks or volatility in the contractual cash flows that are inconsistent with a basic lending arrangement. *[IFRS 9.B4.1.9E].*

As the standard does not establish criteria to determine whether a regulated rate provides consideration that is 'broadly consistent' with the passage of time, consensus needs to be established on how this concession is applied in practice. However, in the Basis for Conclusions, the board implies that the particular instrument described in the following example would satisfy the two criteria above.

Example 46.19:   Regulated interest rates –'Livret A'

In France the interest rate on 'Livret A' savings products issued by retail banks is determined by the central bank and the government according to a formula that reflects protection against inflation and an adequate remuneration to provide incentive for investment. The legislation requires a particular portion of the amounts collected by the retail banks to be lent to a governmental agency that uses the proceeds for social programmes. The IASB noted that the time value element of interest on these accounts may not provide consideration for only the passage of time; however the IASB believes that amortised cost would provide relevant and useful information as long as the contractual cash flows do not introduce risks or volatility that are inconsistent with a basic lending arrangement. *[IFRS 9.BC4.180].*

6.4.4   Other contractual features that change the timing or amount of contractual cash flows

Some financial assets contain contractual provisions that change the timing or amount of contractual cash flows. For example, the asset may be prepaid before maturity or its term may be extended. In such cases, the entity must determine whether the contractual cash flows that could arise over the life of the instrument due to those contractual provisions are solely payments of principal and interest on the principal amount outstanding.

To make this determination, the entity must assess the contractual cash flows that could arise both before, and after, the change in contractual cash flows. The entity may also need to assess the nature of any contingent event (i.e. the trigger) that would change the timing or amount of contractual cash flows. While the nature of the contingent event in itself is not a determinative factor in assessing whether the contractual cash flows are solely payments of principal and interest, it may be an indicator.

For example, compare a financial instrument with an interest rate that is reset to a higher rate if the debtor misses a particular number of payments to a financial instrument with an interest rate that is reset to a higher rate if a specified equity index reaches a particular level. It is more likely in the former case that the contractual cash flows over the life of the instrument will be solely payments of principal and interest on the principal amount outstanding, because of the relationship between missed payments and an increase in credit risk. In contrast, in the latter case, the contingent event introduces equity price risk which is not a basic lending risk. *[IFRS 9.B4.1.10].*

The following are examples of contractual terms that result in contractual cash flows that are solely payments of principal and interest on the principal amount outstanding: *[IFRS 9.B4.1.11]*

(a)   a variable interest rate that is consideration for the time value of money and for the credit risk associated with the principal amount outstanding during a particular period of time (the consideration for credit risk may be determined at initial recognition only, and so may be fixed) and other basic lending risks and costs, as well as a profit margin (which are also likely to be fixed);

(b) a contractual term that permits the issuer (i.e. the debtor) to prepay a debt instrument or permits the holder (i.e. the creditor) to put a debt instrument back to the issuer before maturity and the prepayment amount substantially represents unpaid amounts of principal and interest on the principal amount outstanding, which may include reasonable additional compensation for the early termination of the contract; and

(c) a contractual term that permits the issuer or holder to extend the contractual term of a debt instrument (i.e. an extension option) and the terms of the extension option result in contractual cash flows during the extension period that are solely payments of principal and interest on the principal amount outstanding, which may include reasonable additional compensation for the extension of the contract.

Unfortunately, neither the standard itself nor the Basis for Conclusions specify what the IASB meant by 'reasonable additional compensation'. It seems reasonable to include direct or indirect costs attributable to early termination or extension, ranging from costs for the additional paper work to costs for adjusting a bank's hedging relationships.

The compensation for lost interest in case of early termination requires more judgment. If a borrower prepays because market interest rates have fallen, the bank may only be able to invest the prepaid amount at the new lower market rate. Therefore, the bank might charge the customer the present value of the interest differential between the original rate of the loan and the new market rate for the original remaining maturity of the loan. In addition, the bank may not be able to immediately reinvest the money and has to deposit it on its account with the central bank where it earns only little or no interest (or in some jurisdiction even incurs negative interest). Reasonable additional compensation might include compensation for lost interest for this period as well. However, this period may only include a limited number of days and certainly not the original remaining maturity of the loan.

The strict application of the definition of principal in 6.1 above would mean that debt instruments originated or acquired at a premium or discount, and which are prepayable at par, have to be measured at fair value through profit or loss. This is because, if the issuer prepays, the holder may receive a gain that is less than or in excess of a basic lending return. The IASB, however, decided to provide a narrow scope exception. Financial assets originated or acquired at a premium or discount that would otherwise have cash flows that are principal and interest, except for the effect of a prepayment option, are deemed to meet the above conditions, but only so long as: *[IFRS 9.B4.1.12]*

(a) the prepayment amount substantially represents the contractual par amount and accrued (but unpaid) interest, which may include reasonable additional compensation for the early termination of the contract; and

(b) the fair value of the prepayment feature on initial recognition of the financial asset is insignificant.

The conditions described above apply regardless of whether (i) the prepayment provision is exercisable by the issuer or by the holder; (ii) the prepayment provision is voluntary or mandatory; or (iii) the prepayment feature is contingent.

Chapter 46

Because the prepayment amount may include reasonable additional compensation for the early termination of the contract, the treatment of prepayment options under IFRS 9 is different from that under IAS 39. Under the latter, a prepayment feature is considered 'closely related' (and so is not treated as an embedded derivative that is required to be separated) only if it is prepayable at approximately the amortised cost.

Notwithstanding the above, this exception would allow some financial assets that otherwise do not have contractual cash flows that are solely payments of principal and interest to be measured at amortised cost or fair value through other comprehensive income (subject to the assessment of the business model in which they are held). In particular, the IASB observed that this exception will apply to many purchased credit-impaired financial assets with contractual prepayment features. If such an asset was purchased at a deep discount, the contractual cash flows would not be solely payments of principal and interest if, contractually, the asset could be repaid immediately at the par amount. However, that contractual prepayment feature would have an insignificant fair value if it is very unlikely that prepayment will occur. *[IFRS 9.BC4.193]*. Prepayment might be very unlikely because the debtor of a credit-impaired financial asset might not have the ability to prepay the financial asset.

Similarly, the IASB observed that this exception will apply to some prepayable financial assets that are originated at below-market interest rates. For example, this scenario may arise when an entity sells an item (for example, an automobile) and, as a marketing incentive, provides financing to the customer at an interest rate that is below the prevailing market rate. At initial recognition the entity would measure the financial asset at fair value and, as a result of the below-market interest rate, the fair value would be at a discount to the contractual par amount. The IASB observed that in that case a contractual prepayment feature would likely have an insignificant fair value because it is unlikely that the customer will choose to prepay; in particular, because the interest rate is below-market and thus the financing is advantageous. *[IFRS 9.BC4.194]*.

For instruments that are initially recognised at a discount, the fair value of the prepayment option will usually be insignificant, because the discount is a function of either an increased credit risk of the borrower (as in the first example above) or a below-market interest rate (as in the second example), and in each case the prepayment option is unlikely to be exercised and so will have little fair value. For instruments that are initially recognised at a premium, because the coupon rate is above the current market rate, the application of this guidance is more difficult. While the prepayment option will likely have a more than insignificant fair value, this will usually also be reflected in the fair value at which the asset is acquired. For instance, an investor is unlikely to pay above par for a bond that pays an above market rate of interest if it can be prepaid at par at any time. It would seem that in order for the prepayment option to be relevant for the asset's classification, it would need to be constrained. An example would be a bond that pays an above market rate of interest, with a remaining maturity of five years and that can be prepaid but only after three years. Hence the bond will have an initial fair value greater than par due to the above market rate for the first two years, while the prepayment option will have a significant fair value since it is expected to be exercised in three years' time.

In contrast, an instrument which is prepayable at fair value does not fall under the exception stated above. For such an instrument, the prepayment feature does not only affect the time value of money component. If the fair value of the instrument were to be below par on prepayment due to an increase in interest rates, then the lender may receive less than the instrument's amortised cost and is not *reimbursed* for the present value of lost interest, since the effective interest rate is less than the market rate. The return of such an instrument could therefore be different from a basic lending return. Such a prepayment feature has to be assessed similar to other features which could lead to a cash flow that is neither principal nor interest. See Example 46.29 at 6.4.5 below.

An additional issue might arise for variable rate instruments acquired at a significant discount or premium. For example, a variable rate asset acquired at a deep discount includes some leverage (see section 6.4.5 below) because the variable interest is based on the nominal amount whereas the principal is the fair value on initial recognition by the acquirer. Such an instrument would appear to fail the contractual cash flow characteristics test. However, it is unclear if this was the IASB's intention.

The following examples illustrate further instruments with contractual features that modify the timing and amount of contractual cash flows such that the instruments pass the contractual cash flows characteristics test. Some examples include possible changes to the fact pattern which may change that assessment.

Example 46.20: Debt covenants

A loan agreement contains a covenant whereby the contractual spread above the benchmark rate will increase if the borrower's earnings before interest, tax, depreciation and amortisation (EBITDA) or its debt-to-equity ratio deteriorate by a specified amount by a specified date.

Whether this instrument passes the contractual cash flow characteristics test depends on the specific terms. The loan would pass the contractual cash flow characteristics test if the covenant serves to compensate the lender for taking on a higher credit or liquidity risks.

However, if the covenant results in more than just credit or liquidity protection, or provides for an increase in the rate of return which is not considered appropriate under a basic lending arrangement, the instrument will fail the test. For example, an increase in interest rate to reflect an increase in EBITDA would not satisfy the criteria.

Example 46.21: Auction Rate Securities (ARSs)

ARSs have long-term maturity dates but their interest rate resets more frequently based on the outcome of an auction. As a result of the auction process, the interest rates are short-term and the instruments are treated like short-term investments.

In the event that an auction fails (i.e. there are insufficient buyers of the bond to establish a new rate), the rate resets to a penalty rate. The penalty rate is established at inception and does not necessarily reflect the market rate when the auction fails. It is often intended to compensate the holder for the instrument's lack of liquidity as demonstrated by the auction failure. The auction process for many such securities failed during the financial crisis.

The classification at initial recognition should be based on the contractual terms over the life of the instrument. Although the presumption on acquisition may have been that the auctions were

Chapter 46

not expected to fail, the potential penalty rate should still be taken into account in the assessment of the instrument's characteristics at initial recognition. If the penalty rate could be considered to compensate the holder for the longer-term credit risk of the instrument following the auction failure as a result of a reduction in market liquidity, it may be possible that the penalty rate reflects interest. However, as such instruments usually have multiple issues with different penalty rates, each different case would need to be carefully evaluated before a conclusion could be reached.

6.4.5   Contractual features that normally do not represent payments of principal and interest

In some cases, financial assets may have contractual cash flows that are not solely payments of principal and interest. *[IFRS 9.B4.1.14]*. Unless such a feature is *de minimis* or non-genuine, the instrument would fail the contractual cash flow characteristics test. *[IFRS 9.B4.1.18]*. Examples of such instruments with contractual cash flows that may not represent solely payments of principal and interest include instruments subject to leverage and instruments that represent investments in particular assets or cash flows.

Leverage is a contractual cash flow characteristic of some financial assets. It increases the variability of the contractual cash flows with the result that they do not have the economic characteristics of just principal and interest. Stand-alone option, forward and swap contracts are examples of financial assets that include such leverage. Thus, such contracts fail the contractual characteristics test and cannot be measured at amortised cost or fair value through other comprehensive income. *[IFRS 9.B4.1.9]*.

A financial asset may have contractual cash flows that are described as principal and interest but those cash flows do not, in economic substance, represent the payment of principal and interest on the principal amount outstanding. *[IFRS 9.B4.1.15]*. For example, under some contractual arrangements, a creditor's claim is limited to specified assets of the debtor or the cash flows from specified assets (described in the standard as a 'non-recourse' financial asset). Another example given in the standard is contractual terms stipulating that the financial asset's cash flows increase as more automobiles use a particular toll road. Those contractual cash flows are inconsistent with a basic lending arrangement. *[IFRS 9.B4.1.16]*. As a result, the instrument would not pass the contractual cash flow characteristics test unless such a feature is *de minimis* or non-genuine. *[IFRS 9.B4.1.18]*.

However, the fact that a financial asset is non-recourse does not in itself necessarily preclude the financial asset from passing the contractual cash flow characteristics test (see also section 6.3.2 above). Furthermore, conventional subordination features do not preclude an asset from passing the test (see 6.3.1 above).

The following examples illustrate instruments which normally fail the contractual cash flow characteristics test because their cash flows are not solely payments of principal and interest on the principal amount outstanding.

Example 46.22:   Non-recourse loans

Under some contractual arrangements, a creditor's claim is limited to specified assets of the debtor or the cash flows from specified assets (described in the standard as a 'non-recourse' financial asset). *[IFRS 9.B4.1.16]*. In such cases, the contractual cash flows may reflect a return that is inconsistent with a basic lending arrangement; e.g. if the contractual terms stipulate that the financial asset's return effectively varies on the basis of the performance of an underlying asset, the contractual cash flows do not represent the payment of principal and interest on the principal amount outstanding.

However, the fact that a financial asset is non-recourse does not in itself necessarily preclude the financial asset from passing the contractual cash flow characteristics test. In such situations, the creditor is required to assess ('look through to') the particular underlying assets or cash flows to determine whether the contractual cash flows of the financial asset being classified are payments of principal and interest on the principal amount outstanding. If the terms of the financial asset give rise to any other cash flows or limit the cash flows in a manner inconsistent with payments representing principal and interest, the financial asset fails the contractual cash flow characteristics test. Whether the underlying assets are financial assets or non-financial assets does not in itself affect this assessment. *[IFRS 9.B4.1.17].*

Non-recourse loans need careful consideration and many instruments that are non-recourse will fail the test. The following examples illustrate how the guidance above might be applied to non-recourse instruments that are common in practice and under which circumstances those instruments pass the contractual cash flow characteristics test:

(a) Project finance loans

Where a loan is given for the construction and maintenance of a toll road and the payments of cash flows to the lender are reduced or cancelled if less than a certain number of vehicles travel on that road, the loan is unlikely to pass the contractual cash flow characteristics test. Similarly, a loan with cash flows specifically referenced to the performance of an underlying business will not pass the test.

In other cases, where there is no such reference and there is adequate equity in the project to absorb losses before affecting the ability to meet payments on the loan, it may well pass the contractual cash flow characteristics test.

(b) Loans to a special purpose entity (SPE)

Where a loan is provided to an SPE that funds the acquisition of other assets, whether that loan passes the cash flow characteristics test will depend on the specific circumstances of the arrangement.

If the assets of the SPE are all debt instruments which would themselves pass the cash flow characteristics test, the loan to the SPE might well pass it too. Further, if, the SPE uses the loan from the entity to fund investments in assets which will not themselves pass the cash flow characteristics test, such as equity securities or non-financial assets, but the SPE has sufficient equity to cover the losses on its investments, the loan may again pass the contractual cash flow characteristics test. However, if the loan is the only source of finance to the SPE so that it absorbs any losses from the equity securities, it would not pass the cash flow characteristics test. Whether the loan is legally non-recourse does not matter in this scenario because the SPE has limited other assets to which the lender can have recourse.

(c) Mortgages

There are many different types of mortgage loans and some are structured so that in the event of default the lender has legal recourse only to the property provided as collateral and not to the borrower. This type of arrangement is common in some states of the USA. Other mortgages may, in substance, be non-recourse if the borrower has limited other assets.

In general, we do not believe that IFRS 9 was intended to require all normal collateralised loans such as mortgages to be accounted for at fair value through profit or loss. Consequently, if a loan is granted at a rate of interest that compensates the lender for the time value of money and for the credit risk associated with the principal amount, it would in our view usually pass the cash flow characteristics test, whether or not it is legally non-recourse.

However, at inception, if the expected repayment of a loan is primarily driven by future movements in the value of the collateral so that the loan is, in substance, an investment in the real estate market, then measurement at amortised cost or fair value through other comprehensive income classification would most likely be inappropriate.

Chapter 46

Example 46.23:   Dual currency instruments

For some financial assets the interest payments are denominated in a currency that is different from the principal of the financial asset. IFRS 9 requires the assessment of 'whether contractual cash flows are solely payments of principal and interest on the principal outstanding for the currency in which the financial asset is denominated'. *[IFRS 9.B4.1.8].*

This implies that any instrument in which interest is calculated based on a principal amount other than that payable on maturity will not pass the contractual cash flow characteristics test. For instance, if *variable* interest payments are computed based on a fixed principal amount in another currency, e.g. US dollars, although repayment of the principal is in sterling, the financial asset is not considered to have cash flows that are solely payments of principal and interest.

However, there may be instances where interest is denominated in a currency that is different from the principal currency, but the contractual cash flows could possibly constitute solely payments of principal and interest. For example, the principal amount of the bond is denominated (and redeemed at a fixed maturity) in Canadian dollars (CAD). Interest payments are fixed in Indian Rupees (INR) at inception based on the market interest rates and foreign exchange spot and forward rates at that time.

While not explicit in the standard, in our view, if the bond can be separated into two components that, on their own, would meet the cash flow characteristics test, then the combined instrument would do so. That is, if the bond can be viewed as the combination of a zero-coupon bond denominated in CAD and a stream of fixed payments denominated in INR, and if both instruments can be analysed as a stream of cash flows that are solely payments of principal and interest, then the sum of the two would do so as well.

The defining criterion is the fact that the interest payments have been fixed at inception and there is no exposure to changes in cash flows in the currency of denomination of the cash flows.

Example 46.24:   Convertible debt

An entity holds a bond that is convertible into equity instruments of the issuer.

The holder would analyse the convertible bond in its entirety, since IFRS 9 does not separate embedded derivatives from financial assets.

The contractual cash flows are not payments of principal and interest on the principal amount outstanding because they reflect a return that is inconsistent with a basic lending arrangement (see 6 above) i.e. the return is also linked to the value of the equity of the issuer. *[IFRS 9.B4.1.14 Instrument F].*

The assessment would change if the issuer were to use its own shares as 'currency'. That is, if the bond is convertible into a variable number of shares with a fair value equal to unpaid amounts of principal and interest on the principal amount outstanding. In this case, the bond might satisfy the contractual cash flow characteristics test and would be derecognised on conversion. However, such conversion features are often capped because, otherwise, the issuer could be required to deliver a potentially unlimited amount of shares. The existence of such a cap, if genuine, would result in the failure of the test.

Example 46.25:   Inverse floater

An entity holds a loan that pays an inverse floating interest rate (i.e. the interest rate has an inverse relationship to market interest rates, such as 6% minus 2 times LIBOR).

The contractual cash flows are not solely payments of principal and interest on the principal amount outstanding because an inverse floating rate does not represent consideration for the time value of money. *[IFRS 9.B4.1.14 Instrument G].*

Example 46.26:   Perpetual instruments with potentially deferrable coupons

An entity holds a perpetual instrument but the issuer may call the instrument at any time, paying the holder the par amount plus accrued interest due.

The instrument pays interest but payment of interest cannot be made unless the issuer is able to remain solvent immediately afterwards. There are two scenarios.

Scenario a) interest is accrued on the deferred amounts.

The contractual cash flows could be payments of principal and interest on the principal amount outstanding.

An example in the standard states that the fact that the instrument is perpetual does not in itself mean that the contractual cash flows are not payments of principal and interest on the principal amount outstanding. In effect, a perpetual instrument has continuous (multiple) extension options. Such options may result in contractual cash flows that are payments of principal and interest on the principal amount outstanding if interest payments are mandatory and must be paid in perpetuity.

Some may find it strange that the instrument is deemed to satisfy the contractual cash flow characteristics test even though the principal will never actually be paid. Also, the fact that the instrument is callable does not mean that the contractual cash flows are not payments of principal and interest on the principal amount outstanding, unless it is callable at an amount that does not substantially reflect payment of outstanding principal and interest on that principal amount outstanding. Even if the callable amount includes an amount that reasonably compensates the holder for the early termination of the instrument, the contractual cash flows could be payments of principal and interest on the principal amount outstanding. (See section 6.4.4).

Scenario a) deferred interest does not accrue additional interest.

The contractual cash flows are not payments of principal and interest on the principal amount outstanding. This is because the issuer may be required to defer interest payments and additional interest does not accrue on those deferred interest amounts. As a result, interest amounts are not consideration for the time value of money on the principal amount outstanding.

Note that, in this example, the holder is not entitled to assess whether it is probable that interest may ever be deferred. As long as the feature is genuine, the deferral of interest must be taken into account in assessing whether interest amounts are consideration for the time value of money on the principal outstanding. *[IFRS 9.B4.1.14 Instrument H]*.

Example 46.27: Write-down or conversion imposed by regulator

Scenario a) the provision is not a contractual feature

A regulated bank issues an instrument with a stated maturity date. The instrument pays a fixed interest rate and all contractual cash flows are non-discretionary.

However, the issuer is subject to legislation that permits or requires a national resolution authority to impose losses on holders of particular instruments, including the above mentioned instrument, in particular circumstances. For example, the national resolution authority has the power to write down the par amount of such an instrument or to convert it into a fixed number of the issuer's ordinary shares if the national resolution authority determines that the issuer is having severe financial difficulties, needs additional regulatory capital or is failing.

The holder would analyse the contractual terms of the financial instrument to determine whether they give rise to cash flows that are solely payments of principal and interest on the principal amount outstanding and thus are consistent with a basic lending arrangement.

According to the standard, this analysis would not consider the write-down or conversion that arise only as a result of the national resolution authority's power under statutory law to impose losses on the holders of such an instrument. That is because that power is not a contractual term of the financial instrument.

Although this example makes use of a principle that is widely applied, we note that it is not consistent with the position taken in IFRIC 2 – *Members' Shares in Co-operative Entities and Similar Instruments*, which requires an entity to include 'relevant local laws, regulations and the entity's governing charter in effect at the date of classification' when classifying a financial instrument as a liability or equity.

Chapter 46

Scenario b) the provision is a contractual feature

The contractual terms of the financial instrument permit or require the issuer or another entity to impose losses on the holder (e.g. by writing down the par amount or by converting the instrument into a fixed number of the issuer's ordinary shares), if the issuer fails to meet particular regulatory capital requirements (a non-viability event).

Provided the 'non-viability' provision is genuine, which will normally be the case, the instrument will fail the contractual cash flow characteristics test even if the probability is remote that such a loss will be imposed. *[IFRS 9.B4.1.13 Instrument E].*

Example 46.28:   Multiple of a benchmark interest rate

An entity holds an instrument for which the interest rate is quoted as a multiple of a benchmark interest rate (e.g. 2 times 3-month EURIBOR for a 3-month term).

Such features introduce leverage and the standard is explicit that leverage increases the variability of the contractual cash flows, resulting in them not having the economic characteristics of interest. As a result, such instruments would need to be measured at fair value through profit or loss. *[IFRS 9.B4.1.9].*

Example 46.29:   Fixed rate bond prepayable by the issuer at fair value

A company acquires a bond which requires the issuer to pay a fixed rate of interest and repay the principal on a fixed date. However, the issuer has the right to prepay (or call) the bond before maturity, although the amount the issuer must pay is the fair value of the bond at the time of prepayment, i.e. the fair value of the contractual interest and principal payments that remain outstanding at the point of exercise. For example, if the bond has a term of five years and the call option is exercised at the end of the second year, the fair value would be calculated by discounting the principal and interest payments due over the remaining three years at the current market interest rate for a three-year bond with similar characteristics.

The exercise price represents the fair value of unpaid amounts of principal and interest on the principal amount outstanding at the date of exercise, albeit discounted at the current market interest rate rather than the original market interest rate.

The fact that the exercise price is the fair value could be interpreted as providing reasonable additional compensation to the holder for early termination in a scenario, although this holds true only where the market rate has fallen since the issue of the bond. If interest rates rise, the holder will not receive additional compensation for early termination and will receive less than the principal amount. In these circumstances, due to the negative compensation, the bond holder would not be receiving principal and interest.

In cases where the prepayment amount is set so that there is a 'floor' equal to the par amount, i.e. the prepayment amount received by the holder cannot be less than the par amount of the bond, the prepayment amount could possibly be regarded as representing unpaid amounts of principal and interest.

Example 46.30:   Investment in open-ended money market or debt funds

In an open-ended fund, new investors are accepted by the fund after inception and existing investors have the option of leaving the fund at any time. The price at which new entrants invest in the fund or leavers exit the fund is normally based on the fair value of the fund's assets. Given that investors enter and exit the fund at a price based on fair value, the cash flows of an investment in such a fund are not solely payments of principal and interest.

In addition, such investments would not normally qualify for the option for equity instruments, to present gains and losses in other comprehensive income, as they do not normally meet the definition of an equity instrument from the perspective of the fund (i.e. the issuer). See also 8 below.

6.5   Contractually linked instruments

In some types of transactions, an entity may prioritise payments to the holders of financial assets using multiple contractually linked instruments that create concentrations of credit risk (known as tranches). Each tranche has a subordination ranking that specifies the order in which any cash flows generated by the issuer are allocated to the tranche. In such situations, the holders of a tranche have the right to payments of principal and interest on the principal amount outstanding only if the issuer generates sufficient cash flows to satisfy higher ranking tranches. *[IFRS 9.B4.1.20]*. As this guidance should be applied to 'multiple contractually linked instruments' an investment in a single tranche securitisation would not be assessed under this test. Also the Basis for Conclusions refers to classic waterfall structures with different tranches, rather than a single tranche. *[IFRS 9.BC4.26]*.

These types of arrangements can concentrate credit risk into certain tranches of a structure. Essentially such investments contained leveraged credit risk and accordingly, the IASB believes that measuring such investments at amortised cost or fair value through other comprehensive income may be inappropriate in certain circumstances. Where a structure has in issue only a single tranche, it may be more appropriate to view an investment in that tranche as a non-recourse loan (see 6.4.5 above) rather than a contractually linked instrument.

In multi-tranche transactions that concentrate credit risk in the way described above, a tranche is considered to have cash flow characteristics that are payments of principal and interest on the principal amount outstanding only if the following three criteria are met: *[IFRS 9.B4.1.21]*

(a)   the contractual terms of the tranche being assessed for classification (without looking through to the underlying pool of financial instruments) give rise to cash flows that are solely payments of principal and interest on the principal amount outstanding (e.g. the interest rate on the tranche is not linked to a commodity index).

(b)   the underlying pool of financial instruments must contain one or more instruments that have contractual cash flows that are solely payments of principal and interest on the principal amount outstanding (the primary instruments) and any other instruments in the underlying pool must either: *[IFRS 9.B4.1.23-25]*

(i)   reduce the cash flow variability of the primary instruments in the pool and, when combined with the primary instruments in the pool, result in cash flows that are solely payments of principal and interest on the principal amount outstanding, or

(ii)   align the cash flows of the tranches with the cash flows of the underlying primary instruments in the pool to address differences in and only in:

• whether the interest rate is fixed or floating;

• the currency in which the cash flows are denominated, including inflation in that currency; or

• the timing of the cash flows.

For these purposes, when identifying the underlying pool of financial instruments, the holder should 'look through' the structure until it can

Chapter 46

identify an underlying pool of instruments that are creating (rather than passing through) the cash flows. *[IFRS 9.B4.1.22]*.

(c)   the exposure to credit risk in the underlying pool of financial instruments inherent in the tranche is equal to, or lower than, the exposure to credit risk of all of the underlying pool of instruments (for example, the credit rating of the tranche is equal to or higher than the credit rating that would apply to a single borrowing that funded the underlying pool).

If the holder cannot assess whether a financial asset meets criteria (a) to (c) above at initial recognition, the tranche must be measured at fair value through profit or loss. *[IFRS 9.B4.1.26]*.

In practice it may be difficult for the holder to perform the look-through test because the underlying reference assets of a collateralised debt obligation (CDO) may not all have been acquired at the time of investment. In such circumstances, the holder will need to consider, amongst other things, the intended objectives of the CDO as well as the manager's investment mandate before determining whether the investment qualifies for measurement at amortised cost or fair value through other comprehensive income. If after this consideration the holder is able to conclude that all the underlying reference assets of the CDO will always have contractual cash flows that are solely payments of principal and interest on the principal amount outstanding, the interest in the CDO can qualify for measurement at amortised cost or fair value through other comprehensive income. Otherwise, the investment in the CDO must be accounted for at fair value through profit or loss because it fails the contractual cash flow characteristics test, unless the effect is *de minimis*.

If the underlying pool of instruments can change after initial recognition in a way that does not meet conditions (a) and (b) above, the tranche must be measured at fair value through profit or loss. However, if the underlying pool includes instruments that are collateralised by assets that do not meet the conditions above (as will often be the case), the ability to take possession of such assets is disregarded for the purposes of applying this paragraph, unless (which will be rare) the entity acquired the tranche with the intention of controlling the collateral. *[IFRS 9.B4.1.26]*.

The IASB noted that a key principle underlying the contractual cash flow provisions for contractually linked instruments was that an entity should not be disadvantaged simply by holding an asset indirectly if the underlying asset has cash flows that are solely principal and interest, and the holding is not subject to more-than-insignificant leverage or a concentration of credit risk relative to the underlying assets.

Accordingly, the IASB clarified that a tranche may have contractual cash flows that are solely payments of principal and interest even if the tranche is prepayable in the event that the underlying pool of financial instruments is prepaid. The Board noted that because the underlying pool of assets must have contractual cash flows that are solely payments of principal and interest, then, by extension, any prepayment features in those underlying financial assets are also required to be solely payments of principal and interest. *[IFRS 9.BC4.206(a)]*.

The Board's clarification that a prepayment feature in the underlying pool of assets does not necessarily prevent a tranche from meeting the contractual cash flow characteristics test is helpful. But, unless the underlying pool can only be acquired at origination, it may be very difficult to 'look through' to the underlying pool to determine if its prepayment features would themselves be solely payments of principal and interest. This is because the information will often not be available to determine whether the assets were acquired at a premium or discount, and whether the fair value of any prepayment feature was insignificant on acquisition (see 6.4.4 above).

While some contractually linked instruments may pass the contractual cash flow characteristics test and consequently may be measured at amortised cost or fair value through other comprehensive income, the contractual cash flows of the individual tranches are normally based on a pre-defined waterfall structure (i.e. principal and interest are first paid on the most senior tranche and then successively paid on more junior tranches). Accordingly, one could argue that more junior tranches could never suffer a credit loss because the contractually defined cash flows under the waterfall structure are always equal to the cash flows that an entity expects to receive, and so would never be regarded as impaired. This is, because Appendix A of IFRS 9 defines 'credit loss' as 'the difference between all contractual cash flows that are due to an entity in accordance with the contract and all the cash flows that the entity expects to receive, discounted at the original effective interest rate'.

However, consistent with treating these assets as having passed the contractual cash flow characteristics test, we believe that the impairment requirements of IFRS 9 (see Chapter 49 at 5) apply to such tranches if they are measured at amortised cost or fair value through other comprehensive income. Instead of the cash flows determined under the waterfall structure, an entity needs to consider deemed principal and interest payments as contractual cash flows when calculating expected credit losses.

6.5.1 Assessing the characteristics of the underlying pool

For the purposes of criterion (b) at 6.5 above, the underlying pool may contain financial instruments such as interest rate swaps. In order for these instruments not to preclude the use of amortised cost or fair value through other comprehensive income accounting for holders of a tranche, they must reduce the variability of cash flows, or align the cash flows of the tranches with the cash flows of the underlying pool of the primary instruments. Accordingly, an underlying pool that contains government bonds and an instrument that swaps government credit risk for (riskier) corporate credit risk would not have cash flows that represent solely principal and interest on the principal amount outstanding. *[IFRS 9.BC4.35(d)].*

If the underlying pool of financial instruments contained a purchased credit default swap, this would not prejudice the use of amortised cost or fair value through other comprehensive income accounting provided it paid out only to compensate for the loss of principal and interest, although in practice it is far more common for underlying pools to contain written rather than purchased credit default swaps. As a consequence, it may well be possible to obtain amortised cost or fair value through other comprehensive income accounting treatment for the more senior investments in 'cash' CDOs, i.e. those where the underlying pool comprises the reference debt instruments. However, tranches of 'synthetic' CDOs for which the risk exposure of the tranches is generated by derivatives, would not pass the contractual characteristics test.

6.5.2   Assessing the exposure to credit risk in the tranche held

IFRS 9 does not prescribe a method for comparing the exposure to credit risk in the tranche held to that of the underlying pool of financial instruments.

For the more senior and junior tranches, it may become obvious with relatively little analysis whether the tranche is more or less risky than the underlying assets. In some cases, it might be possible to compare the credit rating allocated to the tranche as compared with that for the underlying pool of financial instruments, provided they are all rated.

However, in some circumstances involving complex securitisation structures, a more detailed assessment may be required. For example, it might be appropriate to prepare an analysis that involves developing various credit loss scenarios for the underlying pool of financial instruments, computing the probability weighted outcomes of those scenarios, determining the probability weighted effect on the tranche held, and comparing the relative variability of the tranche held with that of the underlying assets, which is shown in the following example.

Example 46.31:   Assessing the exposure to credit risk in the tranche held

Bank A is the sponsor of a securitisation vehicle (the SPE) and holds the junior notes issued by the SPE. The SPE's assets consist of a portfolio of residential mortgages that were originated and transferred to the SPE by Bank A. The SPE does not hold any derivatives. A number of other banks invest in the mezzanine, senior and super senior tranches of notes issued by the SPE. None of the banks has any further involvement with the SPE and all banks have assessed that the SPE is not required to be consolidated in their respective financial statements. The total notional amount of mortgage assets and notes issued is CU 1,000.

The following table shows a range of expected credit losses for the portfolio of mortgages as at inception and the estimated probability that those scenarios will occur.

	Loss	Estimated probability of loss	Estimated weighted average loss
	CU	%	CU
Scenario I	40	10%	4
Scenario II	70	25%	18
Scenario III	110	30%	33
Scenario IV	180	25%	45
Scenario V	230	10%	23
Weighted average loss expectancy			**123**

The probability weighted expected losses of the underlying assets represent therefore 12.3%.

The following table illustrates how an entity may compare the credit risk of the tranche with that of the underlying pool of financial instruments:

Tranche		Super senior	Senior	Mezzanine	Junior	**Total**
Notional amount (A)		630	200	90	80	**1,000**
	Probability	Probability weighted expected losses of the tranches*				
Scenario I	10%	–	–	–	4	**4**
Scenario II	25%	–	–	–	18	**18**
Scenario III	30%	–	–	9	24	**33**
Scenario IV	25%	–	2	23	20	**45**
Scenario V	10%	–	6	9	8	**23**
Expected loss by tranche (B)		–	8	41	74	**123**
Expected loss % by tranche (B)/(A)		0.0%	4.0%	45.6%	92.5%	**12.3%**
Credit risk of tranche is less than the credit risk of the underlying assets?		Yes	Yes	No	No	
Tranche passes the contractual cash flow characteristic test		Yes	Yes	No	No	

* For each scenario, expected losses are first allocated to the junior tranches and progressively to the more senior tranches until all expected losses are absorbed. For example, in Scenario IV, the loss of CU180 would be absorbed by the Junior tranche (CU 80), mezzanine tranche (CU 90) and senior tranche (CU 10). The probability weight of 25% for Scenario IV is then applied to the expected losses allocated to each tranche.

The junior notes have an expected loss which is, in percentage terms, greater than the overall expected loss on the underlying portfolio. Therefore, these notes must be accounted for at fair value through profit or loss. Similarly, the mezzanine notes have a greater expected loss than the underlying pool and would not pass the contractual cash flow characteristics test.

The expected losses on the senior notes and the super senior notes are lower than the overall expected loss on the underlying pool of instruments and may qualify for amortised cost or fair value through other comprehensive income treatment, provided all other IFRS 9 requirements are met and the instruments are not held for trading.

In this example, it might have been possible to come to the same conclusion without a numerical calculation for the junior and super senior tranches, but the technique is helpful to determine the treatment of the intermediary notes. In practice, it may also be necessary to apply judgment through a qualitative assessment of specific facts and circumstances.

7 DESIGNATION AT FAIR VALUE THROUGH PROFIT OR LOSS

Financial assets or financial liabilities may be designated as measured at fair value through profit or loss at initial recognition if doing so eliminates or significantly reduces a measurement or recognition inconsistency (sometimes referred to as an 'accounting mismatch') that would otherwise arise. *[IFRS 9.4.1.5, 4.2.2(a)].*

Financial liabilities may also be designated at fair value through profit or loss where a group of financial liabilities or financial assets and financial liabilities is managed and its performance is evaluated on a fair value basis. *[IFRS 9.4.2.2(b)].* Financial assets that are managed on a fair value basis will always be classified at fair value through profit or loss (see 5.4 above), hence, a designation option is not needed.

Chapter 46

Designation at fair value through profit or loss in the two situations described above is permitted provided doing so results in the financial statements presenting more relevant information. *[IFRS 9.B4.1.27]*. Such a designation can be made only at initial recognition and cannot be revoked subsequently.

In addition, a hybrid contract with a host that is not an asset within the scope of IFRS 9 that contains one or more embedded derivatives meeting particular conditions may be designated, in its entirety, at fair value through profit or loss. *[IFRS 9.4.3.5]*. These conditions are discussed in detail at 7.3 below.

The decision to designate a financial asset or financial liability as measured at fair value through profit or loss is similar to an accounting policy choice, although, unlike an accounting policy choice, it is not required in all cases to be applied consistently to all similar transactions. However, for a group of financial assets and financial liabilities that is managed and its performance is evaluated on a fair value basis, all eligible financial liabilities that are managed together should be designated. *[IFRS 9.B4.1.36]*. When an entity has such a choice, IAS 8 requires the chosen policy to result in the financial statements providing reliable and more relevant information about the effects of transactions, other events and conditions on the entity's financial position, financial performance or cash flows. For example, in designating a financial liability at fair value through profit or loss, an entity needs to demonstrate that it falls within at least one of the circumstances set out above. *[IFRS 9.B4.1.28]*.

The fair value option cannot be applied to a portion or component of a financial instrument, e.g. changes in the fair value of a debt instrument attributable to one risk such as changes in a benchmark interest rate, but not credit risk. Further, it cannot be applied to proportions of an instrument. However, if an entity simultaneously issues two or more identical financial instruments, it is not precluded from designating only some of those instruments as being subject to the fair value option (e.g. if doing so achieves a significant reduction in an accounting mismatch). Therefore, if an entity issued a bond totalling US$100 million in the form of 100 certificates each of US$1 million, the entity could designate 10 specified certificates if to do so would meet at least one of the criteria noted above. *[IFRS 9.BCZ4.74-BCZ4.76]*.

The conditions in which financial instruments may be designated at fair value through profit or loss are discussed further at 7.1 to 7.3 below.

7.1 Designation eliminates or significantly reduces a measurement or recognition inconsistency (accounting mismatch) that would otherwise arise

The notion of an accounting mismatch necessarily involves two propositions. First, that an entity has particular assets and liabilities that are measured, or on which gains and losses are recognised, on different bases; and second, that there is a perceived economic relationship between those assets and liabilities. *[IFRS 9.BCZ4.61]*.

For example, absent any designation, a financial asset might be classified as subsequently measured at fair value and a liability the entity considers related would be subsequently measured at amortised cost (with changes in fair value not recognised). In such circumstances, an entity may conclude that its financial statements would provide more relevant information if both the asset and the liability were measured as at fair value through profit or loss. *[IFRS 9.B4.1.29]*.

IFRS 9 gives the following examples of situations in which designation of a financial asset or financial liability as measured at fair value through profit or loss might eliminate or significantly reduce an accounting mismatch and produce more relevant information: *[IFRS 9.B4.1.30]*

(a) an entity has liabilities under insurance contracts whose measurement incorporates current information (as permitted by IFRS 4), and financial assets it considers related that would otherwise be measured at fair value through other comprehensive income or amortised cost;

(b) an entity has financial assets, financial liabilities or both that share a risk, such as interest rate risk, that gives rise to changes in fair value that tend to offset each other. However, only some of the instruments would be measured at fair value through profit or loss (e.g. derivatives or those classified as held for trading). It may also be the case that the requirements for hedge accounting are not met, for example because the requirements for effectiveness are not met;

(c) an entity has financial assets, financial liabilities or both that share a risk, such as interest rate risk, that gives rise to changes in fair value that tend to offset each other and the entity does not use hedge accounting. This could be for different reasons, for example, because items giving rise to the accounting mismatch would not qualify for hedge accounting or because the entity does not want to use hedge accounting because of operational complexity. Furthermore, in the absence of hedge accounting there is a significant inconsistency in the recognition of gains and losses. For example, the entity has financed a specified group of loans by issuing traded bonds, the changes in the fair value of which tend to offset each other. If, in addition, the entity regularly buys and sells the bonds but rarely, if ever, buys and sells the loans, reporting both the loans and the bonds at fair value through profit or loss eliminates the inconsistency in the timing of recognition of gains and losses that would otherwise result from measuring them both at amortised cost and recognising a gain or loss each time a bond is repurchased.

For practical purposes, an entity need not acquire all the assets and incur all the liabilities giving rise to the measurement or recognition inconsistency at exactly the same time. A reasonable delay is permitted provided that each transaction is designated as at fair value through profit or loss at its initial recognition and, at that time, any remaining transactions are expected to occur. *[IFRS 9.B4.1.31]*.

It would not be acceptable to designate only some of the financial assets giving rise to the inconsistency as at fair value through profit or loss if to do so would not eliminate or significantly reduce the inconsistency and would therefore not result in more relevant information. However, it would be acceptable to designate only some of a number of similar financial assets if doing so does achieve a significant reduction (and possibly a greater reduction than other allowable designations) in the inconsistency. *[IFRS 9.B4.1.32]*.

For example, assume an entity has a number of similar financial assets totalling €100 and a number of similar financial liabilities totalling €50, but these are measured on a different basis. The entity may significantly reduce the measurement inconsistency by designating at initial recognition all of the liabilities but only some of the assets (for example, individual assets with a combined total of €45) as at fair value through profit or loss. However, because designation as at fair value through profit or loss can be applied only to the whole of a financial instrument, the entity in this example must designate one or more assets in their entirety. It could not designate either a component of an asset (e.g. changes in value attributable to only one risk, such as changes in a benchmark interest rate) or a proportion (i.e. percentage) of an asset. *[IFRS 9.B4.1.32]*.

7.2   A group of financial liabilities or financial assets and financial liabilities is managed and its performance is evaluated on a fair value basis

The second situation in which the fair value option may be used (for financial liabilities) is where a group of financial liabilities or financial assets and financial liabilities is managed, and its performance evaluated, on a fair value basis. In order to meet this condition, it is necessary for the group of instruments to be managed in accordance with a documented risk management or investment strategy and for information, prepared on a fair value basis, about the group of instruments to be provided internally to the entity's key management personnel (as defined in IAS 24 – see Chapter 36 at 2.2.1.D), for example the entity's board of directors and chief executive officer. *[IFRS 9.4.2.2(b)]*.

If an entity manages and evaluates the performance of a group of financial liabilities or financial assets and financial liabilities in such a way, measuring that group at fair value through profit or loss results in more relevant information. The focus in this instance is on the way the entity manages and evaluates performance, rather than on the nature of its financial instruments. *[IFRS 9.B4.1.33]*. Accordingly, subject to the requirement of designation at initial recognition, an entity that designates financial instruments as at fair value through profit or loss on the basis of this condition should so designate all eligible financial instruments that are managed and evaluated together. *[IFRS 9.B4.1.35]*.

An entity may designate financial liabilities as at fair value through profit or loss if it has financial assets and financial liabilities that share one or more risks and those risks are managed and evaluated on a fair value basis in accordance with a documented policy of asset and liability management. For example, the entity may issue 'structured products' containing multiple embedded derivatives and manage the resulting risks on a fair value basis using a mix of derivative and non-derivative financial instruments. *[IFRS 9.B4.1.34]*.

An entity's documentation of its strategy need not be extensive (e.g. it need not be in the level of detail required for hedge accounting) but should be sufficient to demonstrate that using the fair value option is consistent with the entity's risk management or investment strategy. Such documentation is not required for each individual item, but may be on a portfolio basis. The IASB notes that in many cases, the entity's existing documentation, as approved by its key management personnel, should be sufficient for this purpose. For example, if the performance management system for a department (as approved by the entity's key management personnel) clearly demonstrates that its performance is evaluated on a total return basis, no further documentation is required. *[IFRS 9.B4.1.36]*.

The IASB made it clear in its basis for conclusions that in looking to an entity's documented risk management or investment strategy, it makes no judgement on what an entity's strategy should be. However, the IASB believes that users, in making economic decisions, would find useful a description both of the chosen strategy and of how designation at fair value through profit or loss is consistent with that strategy. Accordingly, IFRS 7 – *Financial Instruments: Disclosures* – requires these to be disclosed (see Chapter 53 at 4.1). *[IFRS 9.BCZ4.66]*.

7.3 Hybrid contracts with a host that is not a financial asset within the scope of IFRS 9

If a contract contains one or more embedded derivatives, and the host is not a financial asset within the scope of IFRS 9, an entity may designate the entire hybrid contract as at fair value through profit or loss unless:

(a) the embedded derivative does not significantly modify the cash flows that otherwise would be required by the contract; or

(b) it is clear with little or no analysis when a similar hybrid (combined) instrument is first considered that separation of the embedded derivative(s) is prohibited, such as a prepayment option embedded in a loan that permits the holder to prepay the loan for approximately its amortised cost. *[IFRS 9.4.3.5]*.

As discussed in Chapter 43 at 4 to 6, when an entity becomes a party to a hybrid financial instrument that contains one or more embedded derivatives and the host is not a financial asset within the scope of IFRS 9, the entity is required to identify any such embedded derivative, assess whether it is required to be separated from the host contract and, if so, measure it at fair value at initial recognition and subsequently. These requirements can be more complex, or result in less reliable measures, than measuring the entire instrument at fair value through profit or loss. For that reason the entire instrument is normally permitted to be designated as at fair value through profit or loss. *[IFRS 9.B4.3.9]*.

Such designation may be used whether the entity is required to, or prohibited from, separating the embedded derivative from the host contract, except for those situations in (a) or (b) above – this is because doing so would not reduce complexity or increase reliability. *[IFRS 9.B4.3.10]*.

Little further guidance is given on what instruments might fall within (a) and (b) above. The basis for conclusions explains that, at one extreme, the terms of a prepayment option in an ordinary residential mortgage is likely to mean that the fair value option is unavailable to such a mortgage (unless it met one of the conditions in 7.1 and 7.2 above). At the other, it is likely to be available for 'structured products' that contain several embedded derivatives which are typically hedged with derivatives that offset all (or nearly all) of the risks they contain irrespective of the accounting treatment applied to the embedded derivatives. *[IFRS 9.BCZ4.68-BCZ4.70]*.

Essentially, the IASB explains, the standard seeks to strike a balance between reducing the costs of complying with the embedded derivatives provisions and the need to respond to concerns expressed regarding possible inappropriate use of the fair value option. Allowing the fair value option to be used for any instrument with an embedded derivative would make other restrictions on the use of the option ineffective, because many financial instruments include an embedded derivative. In contrast, limiting the use of the fair value option to situations in which the embedded derivative must otherwise be separated would not significantly reduce the costs of compliance and could result in less reliable measures being included in the financial statements. *[IFRS 9.BCZ4.70]*.

8   DESIGNATION OF NON-DERIVATIVE EQUITY INVESTMENTS AT FAIR VALUE THROUGH OTHER COMPREHENSIVE INCOME

An entity may acquire an investment in an equity instrument that is not held for trading. At initial recognition, the entity may make an irrevocable election (on an instrument-by-instrument basis) to present in other comprehensive income subsequent changes in the fair value of such an investment. *[IFRS 9.5.7.5, B5.7.1]*. For this purpose, the term equity instrument uses the definition in IAS 32, application of which for issuers is dealt with in detail in Chapter 44.

In particular circumstances a puttable instrument (or an instrument that imposes on the entity an obligation to deliver to another party a *pro rata* share of the net assets of the entity only on liquidation) is classified by the issuer as if it were an equity instrument. This is by virtue of an exception to the general definitions of financial liabilities and equity instruments. However, such instruments do not actually meet the definition of an equity instrument and therefore the related asset cannot be designated at fair value through other comprehensive income by the holder. *[IFRS 9.BC5.21]*.

Under IFRS 9 and IAS 39, all derivatives are deemed to be held for trading. Consequently, this election cannot be applied to a derivative such as a warrant that is classified as equity by the issuer. However, it could be applied to investments in preference shares, 'dividend stoppers' and similar instruments (see Chapter 44 at 4.5) provided they are classified as equity by the issuer.

The IASB had originally intended this accounting treatment to be available only for those equity instruments that represented a 'strategic investment'. These might include investments held for non-contractual benefits rather than primarily for increases in the value of the investment, for example where there is a requirement to hold such an investment if an entity sells its products in a particular country. However, the Board concluded that it would be difficult, and perhaps impossible, to develop a clear and robust principle that would identify investments that are different enough to justify a different presentation requirement and abandoned this restriction. *[IFRS 9.BC5.25 (c)]*.

The subsequent measurement of instruments designated in this way, including recognition of dividends, is summarised at 2 above and covered in detail in Chapter 49, particularly at 2.2.

The example below illustrates the requirements for the designation of a non-derivative equity investment at fair value through other comprehensive income, specifically, the requirement that the instrument meets the definition of an equity instrument in accordance with IAS 32.

Example 46.32: Callable, perpetual 'Tier 1' debt instrument

Consider the example where entity A invests in a perpetual Tier 1 debt instrument, which is redeemable at the option of the issuer (entity B). The instrument carries a fixed coupon that is deferred if entity B does not pay a dividend to its ordinary shareholders. If a coupon is not paid it will not accrue additional interest. The instrument does not have a maturity date, however, the coupon steps up to a higher level 20 years after issue and entity B has the right to purchase the instrument after that date for its nominal amount and any unpaid interest.

Under IFRS 9, such an instrument would not be eligible for amortised cost accounting by the holder. However, given that Entity B does not have a contractual obligation to pay cash, the instrument will qualify for classification at fair value through other comprehensive income, as it meets the definition of equity from the perspective of the issuer in accordance with IAS 32.

IFRS 7 requires disclosure of the fair value at the reporting date of each investment in equity instruments designated as fair value through other comprehensive income. The standard is specific that this is required for each such investment, if material. If an entity designated investments in equity instruments to be measured at fair value through other comprehensive income, it shall identify those investments and disclose, among other information, the fair value for each such investment at the end of the reporting period. *[IFRS 7.11A]*.

The disclosure requirement may be onerous if an entity makes significant use of the fair value through other comprehensive income option and this may act as a disincentive for its use, so entities will need to be careful when making the choices available within the standard. A further question is whether it is necessary to provide disclosures at length if each individual instrument is immaterial. We believe that the concept of materiality will need to be applied, such that the disclosures required are provided separately for investments that are themselves material and aggregated disclosures may suffice for immaterial items.

9 RECLASSIFICATION OF FINANCIAL ASSETS

In certain rare circumstances, non-derivative debt assets are required to be reclassified between the amortised cost, fair value through other comprehensive income and fair value through profit or loss categories. More specifically, when (and only when) an entity changes its business model for managing financial assets, it should reclassify all affected financial assets in accordance with the requirements set out at 5 above. *[IFRS 9.4.4.1]*. The reclassification should be applied prospectively from the 'reclassification date', *[IFRS 9.5.6.1]*, which is defined as:

> 'The first day of the first reporting period following the change in business model that results in an entity reclassifying financial assets.' *[IFRS 9 Appendix A]*.

Accordingly, any previously recognised gains, losses or interest should not be restated. *[IFRS 9.5.6.1]*.

In our view, the reference to reporting period includes interim periods for which the entity prepares an interim report. For example, an entity with a reporting date of 31 December might determine that there is a change in its business model in August 2016. If the entity prepares and publishes quarterly reports in accordance with IAS 34 – *Interim Financial Reporting,* the reclassification date would be 1 October 2016. However, if the entity prepares only half-yearly interim reports or no interim reports at all, the reclassification date would be 1 January 2017.

Changes in the business model for managing financial assets are expected to be very infrequent. They must be determined by an entity's senior management as a result of external or internal changes and must be significant to the entity's operations and demonstrable to external parties. Accordingly, a change in the objective of an entity's business model will occur only when an entity either begins or ceases to carry on an activity that is significant to its operations, and generally that will be the case only when the entity has acquired or disposed of a business line. Examples of a change in business model include the following: *[IFRS 9.B4.4.1]*

(a)   An entity has a portfolio of commercial loans that it holds to sell in the short term. The entity acquires a company that manages commercial loans and has a business model that holds the loans in order to collect the contractual cash flows. The portfolio of commercial loans is no longer for sale, and the portfolio is now managed together with the acquired commercial loans and all are held to collect the contractual cash flows.

(b)   A financial services firm decides to shut down its retail mortgage business. That business no longer accepts new business and the financial services firm is actively marketing its mortgage loan portfolio for sale.

A change in the objective of an entity's business model must be effected before the reclassification date. For example, if a financial services firm decides on 15 February to shut down its retail mortgage business and hence must reclassify all affected financial assets on 1 April (i.e. the first day of the entity's next reporting period, assuming it reports quarterly), the entity must not accept new retail mortgage business or otherwise engage in activities consistent with its former business model after 15 February. *[IFRS 9.B4.4.2].*

The following are not considered to be changes in business model: *[IFRS 9.B4.4.3]*

(a)   a change in intention related to particular financial assets (even in circumstances of significant changes in market conditions);

(b)   a temporary disappearance of a particular market for financial assets;

(c)   a transfer of financial assets between parts of the entity with different business models.

Example 46.33:   Change in the way a portfolio is managed

An entity's business model objective for a portfolio meets the criteria for amortised cost measurement but, subsequently, the entity changes the way it manages the assets.

Having determined that the objective for a portfolio originally met the business model test to be classified at amortised cost, if the entity subsequently changes the way it manages the assets (which results in a more than an infrequent number of sales), so that the business model would no longer qualify for amortised cost accounting, the question of how the entity should measure the existing assets and any newly acquired assets then arises.

Although more than an infrequent number of sales have occurred, unless there has been a fundamental change in the entity's business model, the requirements of the standard regarding reclassification are unlikely to be triggered. Changes in the business model for managing financial assets that trigger reclassification of financial assets must be significant to the entity's operations and demonstrable to external parties. They are expected to be very infrequent.

Assuming that the assets are not reclassified, it is likely that the entity will have to divide the portfolio into two sub-portfolios going forward – one for the old assets and one for any new assets acquired.

Financial assets previously held will remain at amortised cost. New financial assets acquired will be measured at fair value through profit or loss or at fair value through other comprehensive income. Whether the assets are measured at fair value through profit or loss or at fair value through other comprehensive income depends on the business model and the characteristics of the assets.

Unlike a change in business model, the contractual terms of a financial asset are known at initial recognition. However, the contractual cash flows may vary over that asset's life based on its original contractual terms. Because an entity classifies a financial asset at initial recognition on the basis of the contractual terms over the life of the instrument, reclassification on the basis of a financial asset's contractual cash flows is not permitted, unless the asset is sufficiently modified that it is derecognised. *[IFRS 9.BC4.117]*.

For instance, no reclassification is permitted or required if the conversion option of a convertible bond lapses. If, however, a convertible bond is converted into shares, the shares represent a new financial asset to be recognised by the entity. The entity would then need to determine the classification category for the new equity investment.

A related question to the above is to what extent the contractual cash flow characteristics test influences the test of whether a financial asset is sufficiently modified such that it is derecognised. It has been suggested that a modification which would result in the asset failing the contractual cash flow characteristics test is a 'substantial modification' that would result in derecognition of the asset (see also Chapter 50 at 3.4). That is because an asset that is measured at fair value through profit or loss is substantially different to an asset measured at amortised cost or fair value through other comprehensive income. However, given that it is possible to fail the contractual cash flow characteristics test because of a feature that has an impact on cash flows that is only marginally more than *de minimis*, it is difficult to argue that any modification which would result in the asset failing the contractual cash flow characteristics test is necessarily 'substantial'. Similarly, there are modifications that are undoubtedly substantial (such as a change of currency) which would not in themselves prevent an asset from passing the contractual cash flows test.

Nevertheless, whether or not a modified asset would still meet the contractual cash flow characteristics test or not could be a helpful indicator for the derecognition assessment.

10   EFFECTIVE DATE AND TRANSITION

This section covers the requirements that are applicable when an entity, which had not previously applied the November 2009 (IFRS 9(2009)), October 2010 or November 2013 version of IFRS 9, applies the final version.

Previous versions of IFRS 9 are no longer available for early adoption. Consequently, the requirements that are applicable in those situations are not covered in this publication, but are described in earlier editions.

10.1   Effective date

IFRS 9 is mandatorily applicable for periods beginning on or after 1 January 2018. Early application is permitted, although early application may be subject to approval or endorsement by the local jurisdiction. If the standard is applied early that fact should be disclosed. *[IFRS 9.7.1.1].*

IFRS 9 allows an entity to early apply the 'own credit' requirements for non-derivative financial liabilities available for early application before the remainder of the standard is applied. These provisions require an entity to present in other comprehensive income the fair value gains and losses attributable to changes in the entity's own credit risk for non-derivative financial liabilities designated as measured at fair value through profit or loss (see Chapter 49 at 2.1). This would mean that, before the mandatory effective date of IFRS 9, entities could elect to change only their accounting policy for own credit risk while continuing to account for their financial instruments in accordance with IAS 39. If an entity chooses to early apply only those provisions, it shall disclose that fact and provide on an ongoing basis the related disclosures (see Chapter 53 at 8.1). *[IFRS 9.7.1.2].*

10.2   Transition provisions

IFRS 9 contains a general requirement that it should be applied retrospectively, although it also specifies a number of exceptions which are considered in the rest of this section. *[IFRS 9.7.2.1].* The transition to IFRS 9 also requires additional disclosures which are described in Chapter 53 at 8.1.

10.2.1   *Date of initial application*

A number of the transition provisions refer to the 'date of initial application'. This is the date when an entity first applies the requirements of IFRS 9, which is the beginning of the period in which it first reports under IFRS 9, not the earliest period for which comparative figures are amended. *[IFRS 9.7.2.2].*

10.2.2   *Applying the 'business model' assessment*

Entities should make the business model assessment (see section 5 above) on the basis of the facts and circumstances that exist at the date of initial application. The resulting classification should be applied retrospectively, irrespective of the entity's business model in prior reporting periods. *[IFRS 9.7.2.3].* For these purposes, an entity should determine whether financial assets meet the definition of held for trading as if they had been acquired at the date of initial application. *[IFRS 9.B7.2.1].*

The following examples illustrate two practical issues which an entity may need to consider when applying the business model assessment at the date of initial application of IFRS 9.

Example 46.34: Loans previously reclassified from trading under IAS 39

At the date of initial application of IFRS 9, a bank holds a portfolio of loans that it intends to sell as soon as possible, but is currently unable to do so due to illiquidity in the market. The bank had taken advantage of the October 2008 amendments to IAS 39 and because it had the intention and ability to hold the assets for the foreseeable future had reclassified this portfolio from trading to loans and receivables.

An entity applying IFRS 9 for the first time should apply the business model assessment at the date of initial application. Given management's intention to sell the assets as soon as possible, the presumption would be that the portfolio should be classified as at fair value through profit or loss. It does not matter that the bank may have to hold the portfolio for the foreseeable future due to the market's illiquidity. The standard is clear that the entity's objective should be to hold the assets to collect the contractual cash flows to qualify for amortised cost classification. Such a portfolio would not meet the fair value through other comprehensive income criteria either if the intention is to sell all of the financial assets in the near term.

Example 46.35: Loans held within a business intended for disposal

An international bank has a variety of businesses each of which is managed separately. Before the date of initial application of IFRS 9, the bank makes a strategic decision to dispose of its auto finance business, which originates loans. The portfolio of loans is held under a business model whose objective is to collect their contractual cash flows. The bank intends to dispose of the entire business, including personnel, IT systems and buildings, and not merely a portfolio of loans.

There is no 'right' answer in respect of these facts and circumstances. Arguments can be articulated to support either classification of the loans at amortised cost or at fair value through profit or loss.

Proponents of amortised cost classification would argue that, at the date of initial application, even though the bank intends to sell the business at some point in the future, the loans are still held within a business model whose objective is to hold them to collect their contractual cash flows. That objective continues regardless of whether the bank intends or is able to sell the business. In addition, some of the loans may be fully collected even before the business is sold. Therefore, based on facts and circumstances at the date of initial application, the loans are considered to be held within a business model whose objective is to hold them to collect their contractual cash flows.

On the other hand, proponents of fair value through profit or loss classification would argue that on the date of initial application, the expectation is that the bank will dispose the loans rather than hold them to collect their contractual cash flows. Therefore, from the bank's perspective, the loans are no longer held within a business model whose objective is to hold assets to collect their contractual cash flows.

Due to the diversity in views and the fact that this is a prevailing issue as a result of both regulatory and government initiatives to require banks to dispose of non-core business activities or selected businesses, this is an area where further guidance from the IASB or Interpretations Committee would be welcome.

10.2.3 Applying the contractual characteristics test

For existing IFRS reporters, there are no transition provisions relating to the application of the contractual cash flow characteristics test. Accordingly, the contractual cash flow characteristics of an asset should be assessed based on conditions at the date of initial recognition, not at the date of initial application. This is likely to have the most effect when assessing contractually linked instruments (see 6.5 above) because their characteristics may have changed significantly between the date of initial recognition and the date of initial application.

Chapter 46

At the date of initial application, it may be impracticable (as defined in IAS 8) for an entity to assess a modified time value of money element as described in section 6.4.2 above on the basis of the facts and circumstances that existed at the initial recognition of the financial asset. In such instances, the entity must assess the contractual cash flow characteristics of that financial asset on the basis of the facts and circumstances that existed at the initial recognition of the financial asset. This is done without taking into account the requirements related to the modification of the time value of money element as set out in section 6.4.2 above. *[IFRS 9.7.2.4]*. This means that, in such cases, the entity would apply the assessment of the asset's contractual cash flows characteristics as set out in the original requirements issued in IFRS 9 (2009); i.e. without the notion of a modified economic relationship. *[IFRS 9.BC7.55]*. As a result, the asset would most likely be classified as measured at fair value though profit or loss.

At the date of initial application, it may be impracticable (as defined in IAS 8) for an entity to assess whether the fair value of a prepayment feature was insignificant, as described in section 6.4.4 above, on the basis of the facts and circumstances that existed at the initial recognition of the financial asset. If this is the case, an entity shall assess the contractual cash flow characteristics of that financial asset on the basis of the facts and circumstances that existed at the initial recognition of the financial asset. The entity would not take into account the exception for prepayment features. *[IFRS 9.7.2.5]*. This means that the asset would be classified as measured at fair value though profit or loss.

For contractually linked instruments, on initial application of the standard, the look-through assessment should be performed as at the date that the reporting entity (i.e. the investor in the tranche) initially recognised the contractually linked instrument. It is inappropriate to make the risk assessment based on the circumstances existing either at the date that the arrangement was first established or the date of initial application of IFRS 9.

The situation is slightly different for first-time adopters of IFRS, who are required to apply the contractual characteristics test to previously acquired assets on the basis of the facts and circumstances that exist at the date of transition to IFRSs (or the beginning of the first IFRS reporting period for entities that choose not to apply IFRS 9 in comparative periods). *[IFRS 1.B8, E1]*.

10.2.4   Making and revoking designations

On application of IFRS 9, entities are required to revisit designations previously made in accordance with IAS 39 and are given an opportunity to make designations in accordance with IFRS 9. More specifically, at the date of initial application:

(a)   any previous designation of a financial asset as measured at fair value through profit or loss may be revoked in any case, but must be revoked if such designation does not, or no longer eliminates or significantly reduces an accounting mismatch;

(b)   a financial asset or a financial liability may be designated as measured at fair value through profit or loss if such designation would now eliminate or significantly reduce an accounting mismatch;

(c)   any previous designation of a financial liability as measured at fair value through profit or loss that was made on the basis that it eliminated or significantly reduced an accounting mismatch may be revoked in any case, but must be revoked if such designation no longer eliminates or significantly reduces an accounting mismatch;

(d)   any investment in a non-derivative equity instrument that is not held for trading may be designated as at fair value through other comprehensive income.

Such designations and revocations should be made on the basis of the facts and circumstances that exist at the date of initial application and that classification should be applied retrospectively. *[IFRS 9.7.2.8-10]*. For the purposes of (d), an entity should determine whether equity investments meet the definition of held for trading as if they had been acquired at the date of initial application. *[IFRS 9.B7.2.1]*.

At the date of initial application, an entity shall determine whether the own credit requirements of IFRS 9 would create or enlarge an accounting mismatch in profit or loss on the basis of the facts and circumstances that exist at the date of initial application. Those requirements shall be applied retrospectively on the basis of that determination. *[IFRS 9.7.2.14]*.

10.2.5   *Restatement of comparatives*

Notwithstanding the general requirement to apply the standard retrospectively, an entity that adopts the classification and measurement requirements of IFRS 9 (which include the requirements related to amortised cost measurement for financial assets and expected credit losses as described in Chapter 49) shall provide the disclosures set out in IFRS 7 as described in Chapter 53 at 8.1, but need not restate prior periods. An entity may restate prior periods if, and only if, it is possible without the use of hindsight. *[IFRS 9.7.2.15]*.

Where prior periods are not restated, any difference between the previous reported carrying amounts and the new carrying amounts of financial assets and liabilities at the beginning of the annual reporting period that includes the date of initial application should be recognised in the opening retained earnings (or other component of equity, as appropriate) of the annual reporting period that includes the date of initial application. However, if an entity restates prior periods, the restated financial statements must reflect all of the requirements in IFRS 9. *[IFRS 9.7.2.15]*.

Where interim financial reports are prepared in accordance with IAS 34, the requirements in IFRS 9 need not be applied to interim periods prior to the date of initial application, if it is impracticable to do so. *[IFRS 9.7.2.16]*.

Entities adopting IFRS 9 in 2015 and onwards are required to provide additional disclosures showing the changes, as at the date of initial application, in the classification of financial assets and financial liabilities upon transition from the classification and measurement requirements of IAS 39 to those of IFRS 9. These disclosures are required even if an entity chooses to restate the comparative figures for the effect of applying IFRS 9 (see Chapter 53 at 8.1).

10.2.6   Financial instruments derecognised prior to the date of initial application

If an entity decides to restate prior periods or chooses to apply IFRS 9 from other than the beginning of an annual reporting period, it should not apply the standard to financial assets or financial liabilities that have already been derecognised at the date of initial application. *[IFRS 9.7.2.1]*. In other words, following the application of IFRS 9, to the extent those financial assets or financial liabilities were held during any period presented prior to the date of initial application, they will be accounted for under IAS 39.

When the reporting entity elects to restate comparative information or, for example, chooses to apply IFRS 9 from the beginning of an interim reporting period, the effect of derecognition could potentially be confusing for users of the financial statements, Therefore, it may require careful explanation. This is because the information for reporting periods prior to the date of initial application would be prepared on a mixed basis, partially under IFRS 9 (for those financial instruments not derecognised before that date) and partially under IAS 39 (for those financial instruments which have been derecognised prior to that date), reducing the consistency of the information provided.

10.2.7   Transition adjustments and measurement of financial assets and liabilities

10.2.7.A   Hybrid financial assets

A hybrid financial asset that is measured at fair value through profit or loss in accordance with IFRS 9, may previously have been accounted for as a host financial asset and a separate embedded derivative in accordance with IAS 39. In these circumstances, if the entity restates prior periods and the fair value of the hybrid contract had not been determined in those comparative reporting periods, at the end of each comparative reporting period the fair value of the hybrid contract is deemed to be the sum of the fair values of the components (i.e. the non-derivative host and the embedded derivative). *[IFRS 9.7.2.6]*.

At the date of initial application, any difference between the fair value of the entire hybrid contract at the date of initial application and the sum of the fair values of the components of the hybrid contract at the date of initial application should be recognised in the opening retained earnings (or other component of equity, as appropriate) of the reporting period of initial application. *[IFRS 9.7.2.7]*.

IFRS 9 abolishes the separation of embedded derivatives from financial assets required by IAS 39. Under IFRS 9, most financial assets with separable embedded derivatives would be required to be classified in their entirety as at fair value through profit or loss. For example, a loan might contain a profit participation feature that provides the lender with an additional return based on a share of profits of the borrower. However, in some cases, it might be possible to renegotiate the transaction as two separate instruments before the transition to IFRS 9 – one instrument being a loan, the host instrument (which could be recorded at amortised cost or fair value through other comprehensive income) and the other being the profit-sharing derivative (to be recorded at fair value through profit or loss). This would only be possible, we believe, if after the renegotiation, the two new instruments are in substance separate financial instruments. Indicators that this is the case would include:

- each instrument can be closed out or transferred separately, which will be a test of commercial practicality as well as legal possibility; or

- there are no clauses that have the effect that the cash flows on one instrument will affect those on the other, except for typical master netting arrangements.

The case for recognising the contracts as two separate financial instruments would be strengthened if the two new contracts were entered into at prevailing market prices, so that the original compound instrument is derecognised in under IAS 39 and a gain or loss is recognised when the two new instruments are first recorded at their fair values.

10.2.7.B   *Financial assets and liabilities measured at amortised cost*

It may be impracticable to apply retrospectively the effective interest method to a financial asset or liability that is measured at amortised cost on transition to IFRS 9, e.g. if it was previously classified at fair value through profit or loss. In those circumstances, the fair value of the financial asset or liability at the end of each comparative period should be treated as its gross carrying amount or amortised cost, respectively. Also, the fair value of the financial asset or financial liability at the date of initial application should be treated as its new gross carrying amount or amortised cost, respectively, at that date. *[IFRS 9.7.2.11].*

Aside from this exception, the effective interest method should be applied retrospectively. This means that for any financial asset reclassified in accordance with the October 2008 amendments to IAS 39, for example from trading to loans and receivables or available-for-sale, the effective interest method should be applied based on the original cost of the asset, not the amounts determined on reclassification. This is because retrospective application means that an entity presents its financial statements as if it had always applied IFRS 9. However, the standard does not have the same reclassification requirements as IAS 39. Hence, the entity has to go back to the date of initial recognition of the financial instrument in order to determine the accounting treatment.

10.2.7.C   *Unquoted equity investments*

An investment in an unquoted equity instrument (or a derivative that is linked to and must be settled by delivery of such an unquoted equity instrument) might previously have been measured at cost in accordance with IAS 39. In those circumstances the instrument should be measured at fair value at the date of initial application of IFRS 9. Any difference between the previous carrying amount and fair value should be recognised in the opening retained earnings (or other component of equity, as appropriate) of the reporting period that includes the date of initial application. *[IFRS 9.7.2.12-13].* This means that that previous periods cannot be restated. The Board explains that this is because as an entity would not have previously determined the fair value of an investment in an unquoted equity instrument and it will not now have the necessary information to determine fair value retrospectively without using hindsight. *[IFRS 9.BC7.15].*

Chapter 46

Chapter 47 Financial instruments: Recognition and initial measurement

Chapter 47

List of examples

Chapter 47   Financial instruments: Recognition and initial measurement

1   INTRODUCTION

The introduction to Chapter 41 provides a general background to the development of accounting for financial instruments. Chapter 42 deals with what qualifies as financial assets and financial liabilities and other contracts that are treated as if they were financial instruments.

This chapter deals with the question of when financial instruments should be recognised in financial statements and their initial measurement under IAS 39 – *Financial Instruments: Recognition and Measurement*, or IFRS 9 – *Financial Instruments* – when applied.

Initial measurement is normally based on the fair value of an instrument and most, but not all, of the detailed requirements of IFRS governing fair values are dealt with in IFRS 13 – *Fair Value Measurement* – which is covered in Chapter 14. IAS 39 (IFRS 9) also contains some requirements addressing fair value measurements of financial instruments and these are covered at 3.2 below.

2   RECOGNITION (IAS 39 AND IFRS 9)

2.1   General requirements

IAS 39 and, when applied, IFRS 9, provide that an entity must recognise a financial asset or a financial liability on its statement of financial position when, and only when, the entity becomes a party to the contractual provisions of the instrument. *[IAS 39.14, IFRS 9.3.1.1].* Before that, the entity does not have contractual rights or contractual obligations. Hence, there is no financial asset or a financial liability, as defined in IAS 32 – *Financial Instruments: Presentation*, to recognise. IAS 39 (IFRS 9) provides a practical exception to the application of this general principle for 'regular way' purchases of financial assets (see 2.2 below). IAS 39 (IFRS 9) gives the following examples of the more general application of this principle.

2.1.1   Receivables and payables

Unconditional receivables and payables are recognised as assets or liabilities when the entity becomes a party to the contract and, as a consequence, has a legal right to receive or a legal obligation to pay cash. *[IAS 39.AG35(a), IFRS 9.B3.1.2(a)].*

2.1.2   Firm commitments to purchase or sell goods or services

Under IFRS, assets to be acquired and liabilities to be incurred as a result of a firm commitment to purchase or sell goods or services are generally not recognised until at least one of the parties has performed under the agreement. For example, an entity that receives a firm order for goods or services does not generally recognise an asset for the consideration receivable (and the entity that places the order does not generally recognise a liability for the consideration to be paid) at the time of the commitment, but instead delays recognition until the ordered goods or services have been shipped, delivered or rendered. *[IAS 39.AG35(b), IFRS 9.B3.1.2(b)].*

This accounting applies on the assumption that the firm commitment to buy or sell non-financial items is not treated as if it were a derivative (see Chapter 42 at 4) nor designated as a hedged item in a fair value hedge (see Chapter 51 at 4.1 and Chapter 52 at 8). Where the firm commitment is treated as a derivative or designated as a hedged item in a fair value hedge, it would be recognised as an asset or liability before delivery.

2.1.3   Forward contracts

A forward contract is a contract which obliges one party to the contract to buy, and the other party to sell, the asset that is the subject of the contract for a fixed price at a future date.

A forward contract within the scope of IAS 39 (IFRS 9) is recognised as an asset or a liability at commitment date, rather than on settlement. When an entity becomes a party to a forward contract, the fair values of the right and obligation are often equal, so that the net fair value of the forward at inception is zero. If the net fair value of the right and obligation is not zero, the contract is recognised as an asset or liability. *[IAS 39.AG35(c), IFRS 9.B3.1.2(c)].*

2.1.4   Option contracts

An option contract is a contract which gives one party to the contract the right, but not the obligation, to buy from, or sell to, the other party to the contract the asset that is the subject of the contract for a fixed price at a future date (or during a period of time). An option giving the right to buy an asset is referred to as a 'call' option and one giving the right to sell as a 'put' option. An option is referred to as a 'bought' or 'purchased' option from the perspective of the party with the right to buy or sell (the 'holder') and as a 'written' option from the perspective of the party with the potential obligation to buy or sell. An option is referred to as 'in the money' when it would be in the holder's interest to exercise it and as 'out of the money' when it would not be in the holder's interest to exercise it.

Under IAS 39 (IFRS 9) an option is:

- 'deeply in the money' when it is so far in the money that it is highly unlikely to go out of the money before expiry; *[IAS 39.AG40(d), IFRS 9.B3.2.5(d)]* and

- 'deeply out of the money' when it is so far out of the money that it is highly unlikely to become in the money before expiry. *[IAS 39.AG39(c), IFRS 9.B3.2.4(c)].*

IAS 39 does not elaborate on what it means by 'highly unlikely' in this context, although the implementation guidance clarifies that 'highly probable' (in the context of a 'highly probable forecast transaction' subject to a hedge) indicates a much greater likelihood of happening than the term 'more likely than not'. *[IAS 39.F.3.7].*

Option contracts that are within the scope of IAS 39 (IFRS 9) are recognised as assets or liabilities when the holder or writer becomes a party to the contract. *[IAS 39.AG35(d), IFRS 9.B3.1.2(d)].*

2.1.5 Planned future transactions (forecast transactions)

Planned future transactions, no matter how likely, are not assets and liabilities because the entity has not become a party to a contract. They are therefore not recognised under IAS 39 (IFRS 9). *[IAS 39.AG35(e), IFRS 9.B3.1.2(e)].* However, transactions that have been entered into as a hedge of certain 'highly probable' future transactions are recognised under IAS 39 (IFRS 9) – this raises the issue of the accounting treatment of any gains or losses arising on such hedging transactions (see Chapter 51 at 4.2 and Chapter 52 at 8).

2.1.6 Treatment by transferee of transfers of financial assets not qualifying for derecognition by transferor (symmetry of recognition and derecognition of transferred assets)

IAS 39 (IFRS 9) states that, where a financial asset is transferred from one party to another in circumstances where the transferor does not derecognise the asset, the transferee should not recognise the transferred asset. Instead, the transferee derecognises the cash or other consideration paid and recognises a receivable from the transferor. If the transferor has both a right and an obligation to reacquire control of the entire transferred asset for a fixed amount (such as under a repurchase agreement – see Chapter 50 at 4.1), the transferee may account for its receivable as a loan or receivable. *[IAS 39.AG34, AG50, IFRS 9.B3.1.1, B3.2.15].*

Underlying this requirement appears to be a concern that more than one party cannot satisfy the criteria in IAS 39 (IFRS 9) for recognition of the same financial asset at the same time. In fact, however, this principle may not hold in all circumstances, since it is common for the same assets to be simultaneously recognised by more than one entity – for example if the transferor adopts settlement date accounting and the transferee trade date accounting (see 2.2 below).

2.2 'Regular way' transactions

A *regular way purchase or sale* is defined as a purchase or sale of a financial asset under a contract whose terms require delivery of the asset within the time frame established generally by regulation or convention in the marketplace concerned. *[IAS 39.9, IFRS 9 Appendix A].* A contract that can be settled by net settlement (i.e. payment or receipt of cash or other financial assets equivalent to the change in value of the contract) is not a regular way transaction, but a derivative accounted for in accordance with the requirements of IAS 39 (IFRS 9) in respect of derivatives (see Chapter 48 at 2.1 and Chapter 49 at 2.1). *[IAS 39.AG54, IFRS 9.B3.1.4].*

Many financial markets provide a mechanism whereby all transactions in certain financial instruments (particularly quoted equities and bonds) entered into on a particular date are settled a fixed number of days after that date. The date on which the agreement is entered into is called the 'trade date' and the date on which it is settled by delivery of the assets that are the subject of the agreement is called the 'settlement date'. *[IAS 39.AG55, 56, IFRS 9.B3.1.5, B3.1.6].*

One effect of this system is that, while legal title to the assets that are the subject of the transaction passes only on or after settlement date, the buyer is effectively exposed to the risks and rewards of ownership of the assets from trade date. For example, suppose that an entity enters into a contract to purchase a financial asset and later, but before settlement date, decides that it no longer requires that asset and therefore enters into a second contract to sell the asset immediately after it is received. The price of the second contract will be influenced, *inter alia*, by movements in the market value of the asset between the trade date of the first contract and that of the second, so that the entity will make a gain or incur a loss just as if it had actually owned the asset in that period.

Absent any special provisions, the accounting analysis for such transactions under IAS 39 (IFRS 9) would be that, between trade date and settlement date, an entity has a forward contract to purchase an asset (see 2.1.3 above) which, in common with all derivatives, should be recorded at fair value, with all changes in fair value recognised in profit or loss (see Chapter 48 at 2.1 and Chapter 49 at 2.1), unless the special rules for hedge accounting apply (see Chapter 51 and 52). This would not only be somewhat onerous but would also have the effect that changes in a financial asset's fair value between trade date and settlement date would be recognised in profit or loss, even though the asset itself is not measured at fair value through profit or loss.

To avoid this, IAS 39 (IFRS 9) permits assets subject to regular way transactions to be recognised, or derecognised, either as at the trade date ('trade date accounting') or as at the settlement date ('settlement date accounting'). *[IAS 39.38, IAS 39.AG55, AG56, IFRS 9.B3.1.3, B3.1.5, B3.1.6].* Whichever method is used, it is applied consistently and symmetrically (i.e. to acquisitions and disposals) to each of the main categories of financial asset identified by IAS 39 – i.e. held for trading, designated at fair value through profit or loss, held-to-maturity, loans and receivables and available-for-sale (see Chapter 45) *[IAS 39.AG53]* – or, when applied, by IFRS 9 – i.e. *mandatorily* measured at amortised cost, at fair value through other comprehensive income (FVOCI) or at fair value through profit or loss or *designated* as measured at fair value through profit or loss or at FVOCI (equity investments only) (see Chapter 46). *[IFRS 9.B3.1.3].*

The above requirements apply only to transactions in financial assets. IAS 39 does not contain any specific requirements about trade date accounting and settlement date accounting for transactions in financial instruments that are classified as financial liabilities. Therefore, the general recognition and derecognition requirements for financial liabilities in IAS 39 (IFRS 9) normally apply. *[IAS 39.B.32, IFRS 9.B.32].* Therefore, financial liabilities are normally recognised on the date the entity 'becomes a party to the contractual provisions of the instrument' (see 2.1 above) and are derecognised only when they are extinguished, i.e. when the obligation specified in the contract is discharged, cancelled or expires (see Chapter 50 at 6).

In January 2007, the IFRS Interpretations Committee addressed the accounting for short sales of securities when the transaction terms require delivery of the securities within the time frame established generally by regulation or convention in the marketplace concerned. Constituents explained that in practice, many entities apply trade date accounting to such transactions. Specifically, industry practice recognised the short sales as financial liabilities at fair value with changes in fair value recognised in profit or loss. Profit or loss would be the same as if short sales were accounted for as derivatives, but the securities are presented differently on the statement of financial position. Those constituents argued that a short sale is created by a transaction in a financial asset and hence the implementation guidance noted in the previous paragraph is not relevant.

The Committee acknowledged that requiring entities to account for short positions as derivatives may create considerable practical problems for their accounting systems and controls with little, if any, improvement to the quality of financial information presented. For these reasons, and because there is little diversity in practice, the Committee decided not to take the issue onto its agenda and thus industry practice remains prevalent.[1]

2.2.1 Trade date accounting

As noted above, the trade date is the date on which an entity commits itself to purchase or sell an asset. Trade date accounting requires:

(a) in respect of an asset to be bought: recognition on the trade date of the asset and the liability to pay for it, which means that during the period between trade date and settlement date, the entity accounts for the asset as if it already owned it; and

(b) in respect of an asset to be sold: derecognition on the trade date of the asset, together with recognition of any gain or loss on disposal and the recognition of a receivable from the buyer for payment.

IAS 39 (IFRS 9) notes that, generally, interest does not start to accrue on the asset and corresponding liability until the settlement date when title passes. *[IAS 39.AG55, IFRS 9.B3.1.5].* However, this is in fact not necessarily the case – see 2.2.2.A below.

2.2.2 Settlement date accounting

As noted above, the settlement date is the date that an asset is delivered to or by an entity. Settlement date accounting requires:

(a) in respect of an asset to be bought: the recognition of the asset on the settlement date (i.e. the date it is received by the entity). Any change in the fair value of the asset to be received during the period between the trade

Chapter 47

date and the settlement date is accounted for in the same way as the acquired asset. In other words: *[IAS 39.57, IAS 39.AG56, IFRS 9.5.7.4, IFRS 9.B3.1.6]*

- for assets carried at cost or amortised cost, the change in fair value is not recognised (other than impairment losses);

- for assets classified as financial assets at fair value through profit or loss, the change in fair value is recognised in profit or loss; and

- for available-for-sale assets (IAS 39) and financial assets measured at FVOCI (IFRS 9), the change in fair value is recognised in other comprehensive income (OCI).

(b) in respect of an asset to be sold: derecognition of the asset, recognition of any gain or loss on disposal and the recognition of a receivable from the buyer for payment on the settlement date (i.e. the date it is delivered by the entity). *[IAS 39.AG56, IFRS 9.B3.1.6]*. A change in the fair value of the asset between trade date and settlement date is not recorded in the financial statements because the seller's right to changes in the fair value ceases on the trade date. *[IAS 39.D.2.2, IFRS 9.D.2.2]*.

2.2.3 *Illustrative examples*

Examples 47.1 and 47.2 below (which are based on those in the implementation guidance appended to IAS 39) (IFRS 9) illustrate the application of trade date and settlement date accounting to the various categories of financial asset identified by IAS 39 (IFRS 9). *[IAS 39.D.2.1, D.2.2, IFRS 9.D.2.1, D.2.2]*. The accounting treatment for these categories of asset is discussed in more detail in Chapter 45 and Chapter 46.

Example 47.1:   Trade date and settlement date accounting – regular way purchase

On 29 December 2016 (trade date), an entity commits itself to purchase a financial asset for €1,000, which is its fair value on trade date. On 31 December 2016 (financial year-end) and on 4 January 2017 (settlement date) the fair value of the asset is €1,002 and €1,003, respectively. The accounting entries required to be recorded for the transaction will depend on how it is classified and whether trade date or settlement date accounting is used, as shown in the tables below:

A   Financial asset accounted for at amortised cost

	Trade date accounting			Settlement date accounting	
	€	€		€	€
29 December 2016					
Financial asset	1,000				
Liability to counterparty		1,000			
To record liability to purchase asset			*No accounting entries*		
31 December 2016					
No accounting entries			*No accounting entries*		
4 January 2017					
Liability to counterparty	1,000		Financial asset	1,000	
Cash		1,000	Cash		1,000
To record settlement of liability			*To record purchase of asset*		

B   Financial asset accounted for at fair value through profit or loss

	Trade date accounting			*Settlement date accounting*		
		€	€		€	€
29 December 2016						
	Financial asset	1,000				
	Liability to counterparty		1,000			
	To record liability to purchase asset			*No accounting entries*		
31 December 2016						
	Financial Asset	2		Receivable	2	
	Income statement		2	Income statement		2
	To record change in fair value of asset			*To record change in fair value of contract*		
4 January 2017						
	Liability to counterparty	1,000		Financial asset	1,003	
	Cash		1,000	Cash		1,000
	Financial asset	1		Receivable		2
	Income statement		1	Income statement		1
	To record settlement of liability and change in fair value of asset			*To record change in fair value and settlement of contract*		

C   Financial asset accounted for as available-for-sale*

	Trade date accounting			*Settlement date accounting*		
		€	€		€	€
29 December 2016						
	Financial asset	1,000				
	Liability to counterparty		1,000			
	To record liability to purchase asset			*No accounting entries*		
31 December 2016						
	Financial Asset	2		Receivable	2	
	OCI		2	OCI		2
	To record change in fair value of asset			*To record change in fair value of contract*		
4 January 2017						
	Liability to counterparty	1,000		Financial asset	1,003	
	Cash		1,000	Cash		1,000
	Financial asset	1		Receivable		2
	OCI		1	OCI		1
	To record settlement of liability and change in fair value of asset			*To record purchase and change in fair value of asset*		

*   When IFRS 9 is applied, the same analysis will apply to equity investments and debt instruments measured at FVOCI.

As illustrated above, for a regular way purchase, the key difference between trade date and settlement date accounting is the timing of recognition of a financial asset. Regardless of the method used, the impact on net profit or loss and net assets is the same.

Example 47.2:   Trade date and settlement date accounting – regular way sale

On 29 December 2016 (trade date) an entity enters into a contract to sell a financial asset for its then current fair value of €1,010. The asset was acquired one year earlier for €1,000 and its amortised cost is €1,000. On 31 December 2016 (financial year-end), the fair value of the asset is €1,012. On 4 January 2017 (settlement date), the fair value is €1,013. The amounts to be recorded will depend on how the asset is classified and whether trade date or settlement date accounting is used as shown in the tables below (any interest that might have accrued on the asset is disregarded).

A change in the fair value of a financial asset that is sold on a regular way basis is not recorded in the financial statements between trade date and settlement date, even if the entity applies settlement date accounting, because the seller's right to changes in the fair value ceases on the trade date.

A   Financial asset accounted for at amortised cost

	Trade date accounting			*Settlement date accounting*		
		€	€		€	€
Before 29 December 2016 (cumulative net entries)						
	Financial asset	1,000		Financial asset	1,000	
	Cash		1,000	Cash		1,000
	To record acquisition of the asset a year earlier			*To record acquisition of the asset a year earlier*		
29 December 2016						
	Receivable from counterparty	1,010				
	Financial asset		1,000			
	Gain on disposal (income statement)		10			
	To record disposal of asset			*No accounting entries*		
4 January 2017						
	Cash	1,010		Cash	1,010	
	Receivable from counterparty		1,010	Financial asset		1,000
				Gain on disposal (income statement)		10
	To record settlement of sale contract			*To record disposal of asset*		

B   Financial asset accounted for at fair value through profit or loss

	Trade date accounting			*Settlement date accounting*		
		€	€		€	€
Before 29 December 2016 (cumulative net entries)						
	Financial asset	1,010		Financial asset	1,010	
	Cash		1,000	Cash		1,000
	Income statement		10	Income statement		10
	To record acquisition and net change in fair value up to date			*To record acquisition and net change in fair value up to date*		

29 December 2016

Receivable from counterparty	1,010				
Financial asset		1,010			
To record disposal of asset			*No accounting entries*		

4 January 2017

Cash	1,010		Cash	1,010	
Receivable from counterparty		1,010	Financial asset		1,010
To record settlement of sale contract			*To record disposal of asset*		

C   Financial asset accounted for as available-for-sale*

Trade date accounting			*Settlement date accounting*		
	€	€		€	€

Before 29 December 2016 (cumulative net entries)

Financial asset	1,010		Financial asset	1,010	
Cash		1,000	Cash		1,000
OCI		10	OCI		10

Trade date accounting			*Settlement date accounting*		
	€	€		€	€

29 December 2016

Receivable from counterparty	1,010				
Financial asset		1,010			
** OCI	10				
Gain on sale (income statement)		10			
To record disposal of asset			*No accounting entries*		

4 January 2017

Cash	1,010		Cash	1,010	
Receivable from counterparty		1,010	Financial asset		1,010
**			OCI	10	
			Gain on sale (income statement)		10
To record settlement of sale contract			*To record disposal of asset*		

*   When IFRS 9 is applied, the same analysis will apply to debt instruments measured at FVOCI. The same is the case for equity investments designated as measured at FVOCI, except that for those instruments, IFRS 9 does not permit 'recycling' (i.e. transfers) of cumulative gains and losses from OCI to profit or loss. However, an entity may transfer the cumulative gains and losses within equity (e.g. from accumulated OCI to retained earnings).

**   The transfers from OCI to profit or loss (retained earnings) represent the 'recycling' of cumulative gains and losses required by IAS 39 on disposal of an available-for-sale asset (see Chapter 48 at 2.4) (or a debt instrument accounted for at FVOCI if the entity applies IFRS 9). Disposal is regarded as occurring on trade date when trade date accounting applies and on settlement date when settlement date accounting applies.

As illustrated above, for a regular way sale the key differences between trade date and settlement date accounting relate to the timing of derecognition of a financial asset and the timing of recognition of any gain or loss arising from the disposal of the financial asset. Irrespective of the method used, the impact on net profit or loss or net assets is the same.

2.2.3.A   Exchanges of non-cash financial assets

The implementation guidance to IAS 39 (IFRS 9) addresses the situation in which an entity enters into a regular way transaction whereby it commits to sell a non-cash financial asset in exchange for another non-cash financial asset.

This raises the question of whether, if the entity applies settlement date accounting to the asset to be delivered, it should recognise any change in the fair value of the financial asset to be received arising between trade date and settlement date. A further issue is that the asset being bought may be in a category of asset to which trade date accounting is applied.

The implementation guidance essentially requires the buying and selling legs of the exchange transaction to be accounted for independently, as illustrated by the following example [IAS 39.D.2.3, IFRS 9.D.2.3].

Example 47.3:   Trade date and settlement date accounting – exchange of non-cash financial assets

On 29 December 2016 (trade date), an entity enters into a contract to sell Note Receivable A, which is carried at amortised cost, in exchange for Bond B, which will be classified as held for trading and measured at fair value. Both assets have a fair value of €1,010 on 29 December 2016, while the amortised cost of Note Receivable A is €1,000. The entity uses settlement date accounting for loans and receivables and trade date accounting for assets held for trading.

On 31 December 2016 (financial year-end), the fair value of Note Receivable A is €1,012 and the fair value of Bond B is €1,009. On 4 January 2017 (settlement date), the fair value of Note Receivable A is €1,013 and the fair value of Bond B is €1,007.

The following entries are made:

	€	€
29 December 2016		
Bond B	1,010	
Liability to counterparty		1,010
To record purchase of Bond B (trade date accounting)		
31 December 2016		
Loss on Bond B (income statement)	1	
Bond B		1
To record change in fair value of Bond B		
4 January 2017		
Liability to counterparty	1,010	
Note Receivable A		1,000
Gain on disposal (income statement)		10
To record disposal of receivable A (settlement date accounting)		
Loss on Bond B (income statement)	2	
Bond B		2
To record change in fair value of Bond B		

The simultaneous recognition, between 29 December and 4 January, of both the asset being bought and the asset being given in consideration may seem counter-intuitive. However, it is no different from the accounting treatment of any purchase of goods for credit which results, in the period between delivery of, and payment for, the goods, in the simultaneous recognition of the goods, the liability to pay the supplier and the cash that will be used to do so.

3 INITIAL MEASUREMENT (IAS 39 AND IFRS 9)

3.1 General requirements

On initial recognition, financial assets and financial liabilities at fair value through profit or loss are normally measured at their fair value on the date they are initially recognised. The initial measurement of other financial instruments is also based on their fair value, but adjusted in respect of any transaction costs that are incremental and directly attributable to the acquisition or issue of the instrument. *[IAS 39.43].* Where IFRS 15 – *Revenue from Contracts with Customers* – is applied, IAS 39 and IFRS 9 specifically exclude from this requirement trade receivables that do not have a significant financing component. Such trade receivables should be measured at initial recognition at their transaction price net of transaction costs as defined by IFRS 15. *[IAS 39.43, 44A, IFRS 9.5.1.1, 5.1.3].*

3.2 Initial fair value and 'day 1' profits

IAS 39 (IFRS 9) and IFRS 13 acknowledge that the best evidence of the fair value of a financial instrument on initial recognition is normally the transaction price (i.e. the fair value of the consideration given or received), although this will not necessarily be the case in all circumstances (see Chapter 14 at 13.1.1). *[IAS 39.AG64, IFRS 9.B5.1.1, IFRS 13.58].* Although IFRS 13 specifies how to measure fair value, IAS 39 (IFRS 9) contains restrictions on recognising differences between the transaction price and the initial fair value as measured under IFRS 13, often called day 1 profits, which apply in addition to the requirements of IFRS 13 (see Chapter 14 at 13.2). *[IFRS 13.60, BC138].*

If an entity determines that the fair value on initial recognition differs from the transaction price, the difference is recognised as a gain or loss only if the fair value is based on a quoted price in an active market for an identical asset or liability (i.e. a Level 1 input) or based on a valuation technique that uses only data from observable markets. Otherwise, the difference is deferred and recognised as a gain or loss only to the extent that it arises from a change in a factor (including time) that market participants would take into account when pricing the asset or liability. *[IAS 39.43A, AG76, IFRS 9.5.1.1A, B5.1.2A].* The subsequent measurement and the subsequent recognition of gains and losses should be consistent with the requirements of IAS 39 (IFRS 9) that are covered in detail in Chapter 48 and Chapter 49. *[IAS 39.AG76A, IFRS 9.B5.2.2A].*

Therefore, entities that trade in financial instruments are prevented from immediately recognising a profit on the initial recognition of many financial instruments that are not quoted in active markets. Consequently, locked-in profits will emerge over the life of the financial instruments, although precisely how they should emerge is not at all clear. The IASB was asked to clarify that straight-line amortisation was an appropriate method of recognising the day 1 profits but decided not to do so. Somewhat unhelpfully, it stated (without further explanation) that although straight-line amortisation may be an appropriate method in some cases, it will not be appropriate in others. *[IAS 39.BC222(v)(ii)].*

3.2.1 Interest-free and low-interest long-term loans

As noted in 3.2 above, the fair value of a financial instrument on initial recognition is normally the transaction price. IAS 39 (IFRS 9) explains further that if part of the consideration given or received was for something other than the financial instrument, the entity should measure the fair value of the financial instrument in accordance with IFRS 13. For example, the fair value of a long-term loan or receivable that carries no interest could be estimated as the present value of all future cash receipts discounted using the prevailing market rate(s) of interest for instruments that are similar as to currency, term, type of interest rate, credit risk and other factors. Any additional amount advanced is an expense or a reduction of income unless it qualifies for recognition as some other type of asset. IFRS 13 requires the application of a similar approach in such circumstances. *[IAS 39.AG64, IFRS 9.B5.1.1, IFRS 13.60].* For example, an entity may provide an interest free loan to a supplier in order to receive a discount on goods or services purchased in the future and the difference between the fair value and the amount advanced might well be recognised as an asset, for example under IAS 38 – *Intangible Assets* – if the entity obtains a contractual right to the discounted supplies.

Similar issues often arise from transactions between entities under common control. In fact, IFRS 13 suggests a related party transaction may indicate that the transaction price is not the same as the fair value of an asset or liability (see Chapter 14 at 13.3). For example, parents sometimes lend money to subsidiaries on an interest-free or low-interest basis where the loan is not repayable on demand. Where, in its separate financial statements, the parent (or subsidiary) is required to record a receivable (or payable) on initial recognition at a fair value that is lower than cost, the additional consideration will normally represent an additional investment in the subsidiary (or equity contribution from the parent).

Another example is a loan received from a government that has a below-market rate of interest which should be recognised and initially measured at fair value in accordance with IAS 39 (IFRS 9). The benefit of the below-market rate loan, i.e. the excess of the consideration received over the initial carrying amount of the loan, should be accounted for as a government grant. *[IAS 20.10A].* The treatment of government grants is discussed further in Chapter 25.

If a financial instrument is recognised where the terms are 'off-market' (i.e. the consideration given or received does not equal the instrument's fair value) but instead a fee is paid or received in compensation, the instrument should be recognised at its fair value that includes an adjustment for the fee received or paid. *[IAS 39.AG65, IFRS 9.B5.1.2].*

Example 47.4: *Off-market loan with origination fee*

Bank J lends $1,000 to Company K. The loan carries interest at 5% and is repayable in full in five years' time, even though the market rate for similar loans is 8%. To compensate J for the below market rate of interest, K pays J an origination fee of $120. There are no other directly related payments by either party.

The loan is recorded at its fair value of $880 (in this example, assumed to be the net present value of $50 interest payable annually for five years and $1,000 principal repaid after five years, all discounted at 8%). This equals the net amount of cash exchanged ($1,000 loan less $120 origination fee) and hence no gain or loss is recognised on initial recognition of the loan.

Example 47.4 has been extrapolated from the example in IAS 39.AG65 and IFRS 9.B5.1.2.

Applying the requirements of IAS 39 (IFRS 9) to the simple fact pattern provided by the IASB is a relatively straightforward exercise. In practice, however, it may be more difficult to identify those fees that are required by IAS 39 (IFRS 9) to be treated as part of the financial instrument and those that should be dealt with in another way, for example under IAS 18 – *Revenue* (IFRS 15). In particular it may be difficult to determine the extent to which fees associated with a financial instrument that is not quoted in an active market represent compensation for off-market terms or for the genuine provision of services.

3.2.2 Measurement of financial instruments following modification of contractual terms that leads to initial recognition of a new instrument

An entity may agree (with the holder or the issuer) to modify the terms of an instrument that it already recognises in its financial statements as a financial asset, a financial liability or an equity instrument. In such a scenario, an entity needs to consider whether the modification of the terms triggers derecognition of the existing instrument and recognition of a new instrument (see Chapter 50 at 3.4.1). If so, the new instrument would be initially measured at fair value in accordance with the general requirements discussed at 3.1 above.

For example, when the contractual terms of an issued equity instrument are modified such that it is subsequently reclassified as a financial liability, it should be measured at its fair value on the date it is initially recognised *as a financial liability*, with any difference between this amount and the amount recorded in equity being taken to equity. This follows IAS 32 which prohibits the recognition of gains or losses on the purchase, issue, or cancellation of an entity's own equity instrument.[2]

Example 47.5: *Changes in the contractual terms of an existing equity instrument*

On 1 January 2015, Company L issues a fixed rate cumulative perpetual instrument with a face value of £10 million at par. Dividends on the instrument are cumulative but discretionary and therefore it is initially classified as equity. On 1 January 2016, L adds a new clause to the instrument so that if L is subject to a change of control, L will be required to redeem the instrument at an amount equal to the face value plus any accumulated unpaid dividends. This results in a reclassification of the instrument from equity to liability. The fair value of the instrument on 1 January 2016 is £12 million.

Upon reclassification, L should recognise the financial liability at its then fair value of £12 million and the difference of £2 million is recognised in equity (e.g. retained earnings).

Chapter 47

The accounting for a modification of a financial asset (or financial liability) that results in the recognition of a new financial asset (or financial liability) is dealt with in more detail in Chapter 50 at 3.4 and 6.2.

3.2.3   Financial guarantee contracts and off-market loan commitments

The requirement to measure financial instruments at fair value on initial recognition also applies to issued financial guarantee contracts that are within the scope of IAS 39 (IFRS 9) as well as to commitments to provide a loan at a below-market interest rate (see Chapter 42 at 3.4 and 3.5).

When issued to an unrelated party in a stand-alone arm's length transaction, the fair value of a financial guarantee contract at inception is likely to equal the premium received, unless there is evidence to the contrary. *[IAS 39.AG4(a)]*. There is likely to be such evidence where, say, a parent provided to a bank a financial guarantee in respect of its subsidiary's borrowings and charged no fee.

When an off-market loan is provided to an entity's subsidiary (see 3.2.1 above), a 'spare debit' arises in the separate financial statements of the parent as a result of the recognition of the loan at fair value. The same situation can arise when a parent provides a subsidiary with an off-market loan commitment. Again, it is normally appropriate to treat this difference as an additional cost of investment in the subsidiary (and as an equity contribution from the parent in the accounts of the subsidiary).

3.2.4   Loans and receivables acquired in a business combination

Consistent with IAS 39 (IFRS 9) and IFRS 13, IFRS 3 – *Business Combinations* – requires financial assets acquired in a business combination to be measured by the acquirer on initial recognition at their fair value. *[IFRS 3.18, IFRS 3.36]*.

IFRS 3 contains application guidance explaining that an acquirer should not recognise a separate valuation allowance (i.e. bad debt provision) in respect of loans and receivables for contractual cash flows that are deemed to be uncollectible at the acquisition date. This is because the effects of uncertainty about future cash flows are included in the fair value measure (see Chapter 9 at 5.5.5 and Chapter 49 at 5.6.3). *[IFRS 3.B41]*.

3.3   Transaction costs

As noted at 3.1 above, the initial carrying amount of an instrument that is not classified at fair value through profit or loss should be adjusted for transaction costs. Consequently, these costs are included in the calculation of the effective interest rate, in effect reducing (increasing) the amount of interest income (expense) recognised over the life of the instrument (for interest-bearing items) or affecting the amount of profit or loss on disposal or impairment (for investments in equity securities). For available-for-sale instruments or financial instruments that are measured at fair value through other comprehensive income, transaction costs are recognised in other comprehensive income as part of the change in fair value at the next remeasurement. *[IAS 39.IG E.1.1, IFRS 9.IG E.1.1]*. Transaction costs relating to the acquisition or incurrence of financial instruments at fair value through profit or loss are recognised in profit or loss as they are incurred.

Transaction costs are defined as incremental costs that are directly attributable to the acquisition, issue or disposal of a financial asset or liability. An incremental cost is one that would not have been incurred had the financial instrument not been acquired, issued or disposed of. *[IAS 39.9, IFRS 9 Appendix A].* Expenses that would be incurred on the subsequent transfer or disposal of a financial instrument are not transaction costs. *[IAS 39.E.1.1, IFRS 9.E.1.1].*

Example 47.6:   *Transaction costs – initial measurement*

Company A acquires an equity security that will be classified as available-for-sale (or, if IFRS 9 is applied, measured at fair value through other comprehensive income). The security has a fair value of £100 and this is the amount A is required to pay. In addition, A also pays a purchase commission of £2. If the asset was to be sold, a sales commission of £3 would be payable.

The initial measurement of the asset is £102, i.e. the sum of its initial fair value and the purchase commission. The commission payable on sale is not considered for this purpose. *[IAS 39.AG67, IFRS 9.B5.2.2].* If A had a reporting date immediately after the purchase of this security it would measure the security at £100 and recognise a loss of £2 in other comprehensive income.

Transaction costs include fees and commissions paid to agents (including employees acting as selling agents), advisers, brokers, and dealers. They also include levies by regulatory agencies and securities exchanges, transfer taxes and duties. Debt premiums or discounts, financing costs and allocations of internal administrative or holding costs are not transaction costs. *[IAS 39.AG13, IFRS 9.B5.4.8].*

Treating internal costs as transaction costs could open up a number of possibilities for abuse by allowing entities to defer expenses inappropriately. However, it is made clear that internal costs should be treated as transaction costs only if they are incremental and directly attributable to the acquisition, issue or disposal of a financial asset or financial liability. *[IAS 39.BC222(d)].* Therefore, it will be rare for internal costs (other than, say, commissions paid to sales staff in respect of a product sold that results in the origination or issuance of a financial instrument) to be treated as transaction costs.

3.4   Embedded derivatives and financial instrument hosts

In Chapter 43 at 6, it was explained that, in accordance with IAS 39 for financial assets and financial liabilities and as required by IFRS 9 for financial liabilities, the terms of an embedded derivative that is required to be separated and the associated host should be determined so that the derivative is initially recorded at its fair value and the host as the residual (at least for an optional derivative – a non-option embedded derivative will have a fair value and initial carrying amount of zero). *[IAS 39.AG28, IFRS 9.B4.3.3].* Separation does not apply to embedded derivatives with financial asset hosts under IFRS 9.

The standard does not clarify what it is that entities are meant to be determining the residual of. In two separate instances, the implementation guidance suggests that a host financial instrument should be recognised as the residual of the *purchase price* after adjusting for the fair value of the embedded derivative. *[IAS 39.C.3, C.5].* This does not correctly reflect the requirements of IAS 39 (IFRS 9) (which require measurement to be based on the instrument's fair value, not its purchase price – see 3.1 above) but this could be seen as little more than an oversight on the part of the IASB. We suspect the IASB's

Chapter 47

most likely intention was that the host should initially be measured based on the residual of the *fair value* of the hybrid instrument (which, admittedly, will normally equal its purchase price) adjusted for any transaction costs and also after adjusting for the fair value of the embedded derivative.

3.5   Regular way transactions

When settlement date accounting is used for 'regular way' transactions (see 2.2.2 above) and those transactions result in the recognition of assets that are subsequently measured at amortised cost or (very rarely) at cost, there is an exception to the general requirement to measure the asset on initial recognition at its fair value (see 3.1 above).

In such circumstances, rather than being initially measured by reference to their fair value on the date they are first recognised, i.e. settlement date, these financial instruments are initially measured by reference to their fair value on the trade date. *[IAS 39.44, IFRS 9.5.1.2].*

In practice, the difference will rarely be significant because of the short time scale involved between trade date and settlement date. It is because of this short duration that regular way transactions are not recognised as derivative financial instruments, but accounted for as set out at 2.2 above. *[IAS 39.AG12, IFRS 9.BA.4].*

3.6   Assets and liabilities arising from loan commitments

Loan commitments are a form of derivative financial instrument, although for pragmatic reasons the IASB decided that certain loan commitments could be excluded from the recognition requirements of IAS 39 (IFRS 9) (see Chapter 42 at 3.5).

IAS 39 requires an issuer of loan commitments not within the scope of the recognition requirements of the Standard to apply IAS 37 – *Provisions, Contingent Liabilities and Contingent Assets* – to such loan commitments (see Chapter 27). *[IAS 39.2(h)].* However, IFRS 9 requires an issuer to apply the impairment rules of IFRS 9 (see Chapter 49) to such loan commitments. *[IFRS 9.2.1(g)].*

The exclusion of loan commitments from the recognition requirements creates a degree of confusion over how assets and liabilities arising from such arrangements should be measured on initial recognition, as illustrated in the following example.

Example 47.7:   Drawdown under a committed borrowing facility (IAS 39)

Company H obtains from Bank Q a committed facility allowing it to borrow up to €10,000 at any time over the following five years, provided certain covenants specified in the facility agreement are not breached. Interest on any drawdowns is payable at LIBOR plus a fixed margin, representing Q's initial assessment of H's credit risk. Any such borrowings can be repaid at any time at the option of H, but must be repaid by the end of five years unless the facility is renegotiated and extended. They also become repayable immediately in the event that H breaches the covenants. For the purposes of this illustration, any other amounts payable by H to Q (such as non-utilisation fees) have been ignored.

Both H and Q choose to exclude the commitment from the requirements of IAS 39 and any asset or liability arising from drawdowns under the facility will be classified within loans and receivables by Q and within other liabilities by H. Q applies IAS 37 and assesses whether the facility is an onerous contract (e.g. by assessing the probability of H's default following a future drawdown). If it were, Q would recognise a provision.

After one year, no drawdowns have been made and H's credit risk has increased (although it has not breached any of the covenants, there is no expectation of default and there are no other reasons to consider it an onerous contract as defined in IAS 37). As a result of this change in credit risk, the fair value of the facility is, say, €200 (positive value to H, negative value to Q). Because the commitment is not recognised under IAS 39 and because it is not onerous, nothing is recognised in the accounts of either Q or H in respect of the facility.

Shortly afterwards H draws down the maximum €10,000 available under the facility. Because of the change in credit risk the drawdown results in the recognition of an asset (liability) by Q (H) that has a fair value at that date of, say, €9,800.

The €200 difference between the €9,800 fair value of the financial instrument created and the €10,000 cash transferred effectively represents the change in fair value of the commitment arising from the change in H's credit risk.

Should Q (H) initially measure the resulting asset (liability) at its €9,800 fair value or at €10,000, being the amount of cash actually exchanged? If it is recognised at €9,800, how is the 'spare' €200 accounted for, particularly does Q (H) recognise it as a loss (profit)?

The general requirement noted at 3.1 above would imply that the asset (liability) should initially be measured at €9,800. Consequently a loss (profit) of €200 would be recognised – this is because the spare €200 does not represent any other asset or liability arising from the transaction.

However, the Basis for Conclusions on IAS 39 (IFRS 9), explains that the effect of the loan commitment exception is that, consistent with the likely measurement basis of the resulting loan, the fair value of these commitments from changes in market interest rates or credit spreads will not be recognised or measured. *[IAS 39.BC16, IFRS 9.BCZ2.3].* This is exactly what the 'spare' €200 represents so, in accordance with the underlying rationale and objective of allowing loan commitments to be excluded from the scope of IAS 39 (IFRS 9), it seems appropriate to initially measure the asset or liability arising in this case at €10,000.

Such treatment is also consistent with that for similar assets arising from regular way transactions recognised using settlement date accounting (see 3.5 above). This is relevant because the IASB introduced the loan commitment exception as a result of issues identified by the IGC and the only solution the IGC could identify at the time involved treating loan commitments as regular way transactions and using settlement date accounting.[3]

If, in the above example, Q (H) accounted for the loan commitment at fair value through profit or loss this issue would not arise. At the time the loan was drawn down the commitment would have already been recognised as a €200 liability (asset) and an equivalent loss (profit) would have been recorded in profit or loss. The loan would then be recognised at its fair value of €9,800 and the €200 balance of the cash movement over this amount would be treated as the settlement of the loan commitment liability (asset previously recognised). Therefore, no further gain or loss would need to be recognised at this point. Until the loan is recognised, the same mechanics apply for IAS 39 and IFRS 9. Under both standards, the loan is recognised at its fair value, but after that, it is subject to either the impairment rules of IAS 39 or the impairment rules of IFRS 9. The latter require recording of the12-month or lifetime expected loss at the first reporting date after the loan is recognised (see Chapter 49).

Chapter 47

References

1 *IFRIC Update*, January 2007.
2 *IFRIC Update*, November 2006.

3 IAS 39 Implementation Guidance Committee (IGC), Q&A 30-1, July 2001.

Chapter 48   Financial instruments: Subsequent measurement (IAS 39)

Chapter 48

List of examples

Chapter 48

Chapter 48   Financial instruments: Subsequent measurement (IAS 39)

1   INTRODUCTION

Chapter 47 deals with when financial instruments should be recognised in financial statements and their initial measurement.

For entities continuing to apply IAS 39 – *Financial Instruments: Recognition and Measurement*, this chapter deals with the subsequent measurement requirements of the standard. This includes the requirements relating to amortised cost and the effective interest method, impairment, and foreign currency considerations. The related question of when a previously recognised financial instrument should be derecognised from financial statements is dealt with in Chapter 50.

Most, but not all, of the detailed requirements of IFRS governing the measurement of fair values are dealt with in IFRS 13 – *Fair Value Measurement* – which is covered in Chapter 14. IAS 39 also contains some requirements addressing fair value measurements of financial instruments and these are covered at 2.6 below.

2   SUBSEQUENT MEASUREMENT AND RECOGNITION OF GAINS AND LOSSES

As set out in Chapter 45, IAS 39 requires financial assets to be classified into one of the following four categories: *[IAS 39.45]*

- at fair value through profit or loss;
- held-to-maturity investments;
- loans and receivables; and
- available-for-sale assets.

Financial liabilities that are within the scope of IAS 39 are classified either at fair value through profit or loss or as other financial liabilities.

Following the initial recognition of financial assets and financial liabilities, their subsequent accounting treatment depends principally on the classification of the instrument, although there are a small number of exceptions. *[IAS 39.46, 47]*. These requirements are summarised in the following table and are considered in more detail in the remainder of this section.

Classification	Instrument type	Statement of financial position	Fair value gains and losses	Interest and dividends	Impairment	Foreign exchange
At fair value through profit or loss (including derivatives that are not designated in effective hedges)	Debt, Equity or Derivative	Fair value	Profit or loss*	Profit or loss*	Profit or loss* (assets)	Profit or loss*
	Equity or equity derivative: not reliably measurable	Cost	–	Profit or loss: dividends receivable	Profit or loss (assets)	–
Held-to-maturity investments	Debt	Amortised cost	–	Profit or loss: effective interest rate	Profit or loss	Profit or loss
Loans and receivables	Debt	Amortised cost	–	Profit or loss: effective interest rate	Profit or loss	Profit or loss
Available-for-sale assets	Debt	Fair value	Other comprehensive income†	Profit or loss: effective interest rate	Profit or loss	Profit or loss
	Equity	Fair value	Other comprehensive income†	Profit or loss: dividends receivable	Profit or loss	Other comprehensive income†
	Equity: not reliably measurable	Cost	–	Profit or loss: dividends receivable	Profit or loss	–
Other financial liabilities	Debt	Amortised cost	–	Profit or loss: effective interest rate	–	Profit or loss

* Little guidance is given on how gains and losses should be disaggregated – see Chapter 53 at 7.1.1.
† Reclassified from equity to profit or loss on disposal or impairment.

In addition, IAS 39 sets out the accounting treatment for certain financial guarantee contracts (see Chapter 42 at 3.4) and commitments to provide a loan at a below market interest rate (see Chapter 42 at 3.5).

2.1 Financial assets and financial liabilities at fair value through profit or loss

After initial recognition, financial assets and financial liabilities that are classified at fair value through profit or loss (including derivatives that are not designated in effective hedging relationships) should, in general, be measured at fair value, with no deduction for sale or disposal costs. Associated gains and losses are recognised in profit or loss. *[IAS 39.46, 55(a)]*.

Investments in equity instruments whose fair value cannot be reliably measured and derivatives that are linked to, and must be settled by delivery of, such instruments (see 2.6 below) are measured at cost less (for assets) any impairment (see 4.4 below). *[IAS 39.46(c), 47(a)]*. If a reliable measure of fair value subsequently becomes available, the instrument should be remeasured at that fair value, and the gain or loss recognised in profit or loss. *[IAS 39.53]*. If a reliable measure ceases to be available, it should thereafter be measured at 'cost', which is deemed to be the fair value carrying amount on that date. *[IAS 39.54]*.

The standard points out that if the fair value of a financial asset falls below zero it becomes a financial liability (assuming it is measured at fair value). *[IAS 39.AG66]*. The only real alternative would be treatment as a negative asset which would not be sensible. Although not explained in the standard, if the fair value of a financial liability becomes positive it is safe to assume that it becomes a financial asset not a negative liability.

2.2 Held-to-maturity investments

The basic requirement for held-to-maturity investments is that they are measured at amortised cost using the effective interest method, although they are also subject to review for impairment. *[IAS 39.46(b)]*. Gains and losses are recognised in profit or loss when the instrument is derecognised or impaired, as well as through the amortisation process. *[IAS 39.56]*.

The effective interest method of accounting is dealt with at 3 below and the impairment requirements of IAS 39 at 4 below.

2.3 Loans and receivables

Loans and receivables are also measured at amortised cost using the effective interest method and are subject to review for impairment with gains and losses recognised in profit or loss when the instrument is derecognised or impaired, as well as through the amortisation process. *[IAS 39.46(a), 56]*. However, in contrast to the treatment for held-to-maturity investments, this method of accounting applies to *all* loans and receivables without regard to whether they are intended to be held until maturity. *[IAS 39.AG68]*.

2.4 Available-for-sale assets

Accounting for available-for-sale assets is slightly more complex. They should, in general, be measured at fair value, with no deduction for sale or disposal costs. *[IAS 39.46]*. Gains and losses arising from changes in fair value (after adjusting for interest accruals, dividends receivable and foreign exchange gains and losses on monetary items) are initially recognised in other comprehensive income. When an asset is derecognised, often by way of sale, or is impaired, the cumulative gain or loss recognised in other comprehensive income is reclassified from equity to profit or loss. *[IAS 39.55(b)]*.

For example, consider an equity security that is purchased for its fair value of €100, has a fair value of €120 at the end of the year and is sold subsequent to the year-end for €130. In the first year a gain of €20 is recognised in other comprehensive income as a result of remeasuring the security at its fair value. In the second year a profit of €30 is recognised in profit or loss. This profit of €30 effectively represents the €10 difference between the proceeds received (€130) and the previous carrying amount

Chapter 48

of the asset (€120) and the reclassification of the €20 gain from equity. However, the implementation guidance to IAS 1 – *Presentation of Financial Statements* – illustrates that, in principle, the asset should continue to be remeasured at its fair value until the time of disposal. Therefore in the second year a gain of €10 should be recognised in other comprehensive income followed by a reclassification from equity to profit or loss of €30. *[IAS 1.IG7-9]*.

Where appropriate, interest receivable on available-for-sale assets is recognised in profit or loss using the effective interest method (see 3 below), and dividends receivable are recognised in profit or loss when a right to receive payment is established (see Chapter 28 at 3.12). Impairment and foreign currency retranslation are covered in more detail at 4 and 5 below respectively. *[IAS 39.55(b)]*. However, it should be remembered that foreign exchange gains and losses arising on monetary available-for-sale assets, such as investments in debt securities, should normally be recognised in profit or loss, not in other comprehensive income (the only exceptions being if it is designated as the hedging instrument in a cash flow hedge or hedge of a net investment – see Chapter 51).

The accounting requirements for available-for-sale assets are further illustrated in the examples below.

Example 48.1:   Gain or loss on available-for-sale shares in takeover target

Company S holds a small number of shares in Company T. The shares are classified as available-for-sale. On 20 December 2016, the fair value of the shares is $120 and the cumulative gain recognised in other comprehensive income is $20. On the same day, Company U, a large public company, acquires T. As a result, S receives shares in U in exchange for those it had in T of equal fair value.

The transaction qualifies for derecognition (see Chapter 50), therefore the cumulative gain of $20 that has been recognised in other comprehensive income should now be reclassified to profit or loss. *[IAS 39.E.3.1]*.

Example 48.2:   Available-for-sale asset – determination of interest

A company acquires a zero coupon bond at the end of 2016 for £760, its fair value, which matures at the beginning of 2020 at £1,000. It is classified as an available-for-sale asset and, accordingly, associated fair value gains and losses are recognised in other comprehensive income. Its fair value at the end of 2017, 2018 and 2019 is £850, £950 and £1,000 respectively and it can be determined that the effective interest rate is 9.6% (the effective interest method is discussed in more detail at 3 below).

The financial statements would therefore include the accounting entries set out in the following table (amortised cost is memorandum information used to determine interest).

Year	Amortised cost at start of year £		Interest – profit or loss £		Gains and losses – other comprehensive income £		Cash flow £	Fair value B/S £
2016	–		–		–		–	760
2017	760		73	*[=760 × 9.6%]*	17	*[=850 – {760 + 73}]*	–	850
2018	833	*[=760 + 73]*	80	*[=833 × 9.6%]*	20	*[=950 – {850 + 80}]*	–	950
2019	913	*[=833 + 80]*	87	*[=913 × 9.6%]*	(37)	*[=1,000 – {950 + 87}]*	–	1,000
2020	1,000	*[=913 + 87]*	–		–		1,000	–

The standard does not specify the cost formula to be used for fungible (i.e. substitutable) available-for-sale assets (or, indeed, for any other fungible financial instrument), for example equity shares issued by a single entity that are identical except perhaps for a serial number or similar identifier. This is in contrast to, say, IAS 2 – *Inventories* – which specifies the use of a weighted average cost or FIFO (first-in, first-out) basis in most circumstances. *[IAS 2.25]*.

On a theoretical level, an asset-by-asset approach is arguably the most technically pure. This would, for example, prevent the offsetting of an impairment arising on one asset against an unrealised gain on another. However, it could also allow entities to manipulate their earnings. For example, when selling an asset an entity could choose to sell one with a low (or high) cost base in order to maximise (minimise) the profit on disposal. In practice, average cost bases are typically used (perhaps applied to individual portfolios within the entity), although others may be acceptable provided they are applied consistently (e.g. both to disposals and impairment).

The financial statements of UBS disclose that it uses an average cost method.

Extract 48.1: UBS AG (2014)

Notes to the UBS AG consolidated financial statements [extract]

Note 1   Summary of significant accounting policies [extract]

9)   Financial investments available-for-sale [extract]

Financial investments available-for-sale are recognized initially at fair value less transaction costs and are measured subsequently at fair value. Unrealized gains or losses are reported in *Other comprehensive income* within *Equity*, net of applicable income taxes, until such investments are sold, collected or otherwise disposed of, or until any such investment is determined to be impaired. [...]

On disposal of an investment, any related accumulated unrealized gains or losses included in *Equity* are transferred to the income statement and reported in *Other income*. *Gains* or losses on disposal are determined using the average cost method.

Available-for-sale equity investments whose fair value cannot be reliably measured (see 2.6 below) are measured at cost less any impairment (see 4.4 below). *[IAS 39.46(c)]*. If a reliable measure of fair value subsequently becomes available, the asset should be remeasured at that fair value, and the gain or loss recognised in other comprehensive income (provided it is not impaired). *[IAS 39.53, 55(b)]*. If a reliable measure ceases to be available, it should thereafter be measured at 'cost', which is deemed to be the fair value carrying amount on that date. Any gain or loss previously recognised in other comprehensive income should remain in equity until the asset has been sold, otherwise disposed of or impaired, at which time it should be reclassified to profit or loss. *[IAS 39.54(b)]*.

2.5   Other financial liabilities

Other financial liabilities, as that term is used in Chapter 45, are measured at amortised cost using the effective interest method with gains and losses recognised in profit or loss when the instrument is derecognised as well as through the amortisation process. *[IAS 39.47, 56]*.

Chapter 48

2.6   Unquoted equity instruments and related derivatives

IAS 39 has special accounting requirements for certain equity instruments that do not have a quoted market price in an active market and derivatives that are linked to, and must be settled by delivery of, such unquoted equity instruments. Specifically, they should be measured at cost, less impairment, if their fair value cannot be reliably measured (this guidance does not replace, but rather supplements, the fair value requirements in IFRS 13).

The fair value of these instruments is deemed to be reliably measurable if: *[IAS 39.AG80]*

- the variability in the range of reasonable fair value estimates is not significant for that instrument; or

- the probabilities of the various estimates within the range can be reasonably assessed and used in estimating fair value.

IAS 39 explains that there are many situations in which the variability in the range of reasonable fair value estimates of such investments is likely not to be significant and that, normally, it is possible to estimate the fair value of a financial asset that has been acquired from a third party. However, if the range of reasonable fair value estimates is significant and the probabilities of the various estimates cannot be reasonably assessed, such instruments are precluded from fair value measurement. *[IAS 39.AG81]*.

It is not stated explicitly that the fair value of any other type of financial instrument is deemed to be reliably measurable, although in our view, it should be. There was such a statement in the original standard[1] and the original implementation guidance contained the following example to illustrate the point.

Example 48.3:   Complex stand-alone derivative – no unquoted equity underlying

Company Z acquires a complex stand-alone derivative that is based on several underlying variables, including commodity prices, interest rates, and credit indices. There is no active market or other price quotation for the derivative and no active markets for some of its underlying variables.

The presumption that the derivative's fair value can be reliably determined cannot be overcome because it is not linked to, or required to be settled by delivery of, an unquoted equity instrument. It cannot, therefore, be carried at cost.[2]

However, the Interpretations Committee has addressed this in the context of certain principal-to-principal derivatives designed to fix the price of supply of electricity. Here, valuation issues include the fact that the derivative can have a variable notional amount (often depending on one party's usage requirements) and that the term of the derivative may extend well beyond the period for which there is any observable market data. The Interpretations Committee confirmed that the only exception in IAS 39 from the requirement to fair value derivatives after initial recognition relates to instruments that are linked to, and must be settled by delivery of, unquoted equity instruments.[3]

Where a financial instrument contains an embedded derivative whose fair value cannot be reliably measured (see Chapter 43 at 4) the relaxation may apply to the hybrid (or combined) contract in its entirety if it contains a link to an unquoted equity instrument and the equity component of the hybrid instrument is sufficiently significant to preclude the reliable estimation of the fair value of the hybrid contract. The following example illustrates this situation.

Example 48.4:   Embedded derivative cannot be reliably measured

A company enters into a contract containing an embedded derivative that requires separation. However, the derivative cannot be reliably measured because it will be settled by delivery of an unquoted equity instrument whose fair value cannot be reliably measured. An example of such an instrument might be a convertible bond issued by a company whose shares are unquoted.

The entire combined contract is designated as a financial instrument at fair value through profit or loss (see Chapter 43 at 4). If the fair value of the combined instrument can be reliably measured, it is measured at fair value. However, the equity component of the combined instrument may be sufficiently significant to preclude the reliable estimation of its fair value. In this case, the combined contract is measured at cost less impairment. *[IAS 39.C.11].*[4]

2.7   Reclassifications of financial assets

As set out in Chapter 45 at 6, the standard restricts the scope for reclassifying instruments between the main categories, although IAS 39 allows reclassifications in certain circumstances. This section deals with the measurement of those financial instruments subsequent to their reclassification.

2.7.1   Reclassifications from held-for-trading

The circumstances in which a financial asset may be reclassified out of the held for trading category are discussed in Chapter 45 at 6.1.1. The financial asset should be reclassified at its fair value on the date of reclassification and this fair value becomes its new cost or amortised cost, as applicable. Any gain or loss previously recognised in profit or loss should not be reversed. *[IAS 39.50C, 50F].* If an embedded derivative is required to be separated from the reclassified financial asset (see Chapter 43 at 7.1), the initial carrying amount of the non-derivative host financial asset will be the fair value of the hybrid instrument at the date of reclassification adjusted by the fair value of the embedded derivative.

Thereafter, the appropriate measurement requirements within IAS 39 should be applied to the asset based on its new classification. For example, financial assets reclassified as loans and receivables will be measured at amortised cost using the effective interest method. However, where the effective interest method is applied, there is one difference in the way revisions to estimated cash flows are dealt with – this difference is discussed at 3.2.2 below.

2.7.2   Reclassifications from available-for-sale to loans and receivables

The circumstances in which a financial asset may be reclassified from the available-for-sale category to loans and receivables are discussed in Chapter 45 at 6.2. The financial asset should be reclassified at its fair value on the date of reclassification and this fair value becomes its new amortised cost. *[IAS 39.50F].* Thereafter, the financial asset will be measured at amortised cost using the effective interest method. However, similar to financial assets transferred out of the held for trading category (see 2.7.1 above), there is a difference in the way the effective interest method should be applied – see 3.2.2 below.

Any gain or loss previously recognised in other comprehensive income prior to reclassification should be amortised over the remaining life of the investment using the effective interest method. Similarly, any difference between the new amortised

Chapter 48

cost and maturity amount should be amortised, akin to the amortisation of a premium or discount. If the asset subsequently becomes impaired, any gain or loss remaining in equity should be reclassified to profit or loss. *[IAS 39.50F, 54]*. Further, to ensure the appropriate amount is reclassified from equity to profit or loss, the amount related to the impairment of the financial asset will normally need to be assessed on an individual basis, as it was prior to reclassification, as well as on a collective basis where appropriate.

2.7.3   Reclassifications between held-to-maturity investments and available-for-sale financial assets

Where a held-to-maturity investment is reclassified as available-for-sale (for example as a result of triggering the 'tainting' provisions – see Chapter 45 at 3.3), the asset should be remeasured to fair value and any associated gain or loss recognised in other comprehensive income. *[IAS 39.51, 52]*.

If an available-for-sale asset is reclassified as held-to-maturity, the fair value carrying amount of the financial asset on that date becomes its new amortised cost. Any previous gain or loss on that asset that has been recognised in other comprehensive income should be amortised over the remaining life of the investment using the effective interest method. Any difference between the new amortised cost and maturity amount should be similarly amortised, akin to the amortisation of a premium or discount. *[IAS 39.54(a)]*.

Example 48.5:   Debt instrument reclassified as held-to-maturity

Company Y acquires a debt instrument that it classifies as available-for-sale. The purchase price equals the fair value of the instrument, £110. Its terms are such that it pays a fixed coupon for ten years and a principal payment of £100. Subsequently, when the fair value of the instrument is £120, a gain of £12 has been recognised in other comprehensive income, and £2 of the initial cost has been amortised to profit or loss, Y reclassifies the debt instrument as held-to-maturity.

The £120 fair value carrying amount becomes the new amortised cost of the instrument thereby giving rise to an effective premium of £20 that is amortised over the remaining term to maturity using the effective interest method. In addition, the £12 gain within equity is also amortised to profit or loss over the remaining period to maturity.

In effect, interest income should be broadly the same as if the instrument had not been reclassified (or had always been classified as held-to-maturity).

If the asset subsequently becomes impaired, any gain or loss remaining in equity should be reclassified to profit or loss. *[IAS 39.54(a)]*.

2.8   Financial guarantees and commitments to provide a loan at a below-market interest rate

Financial guarantees issued and commitments made to provide a loan at a below-market interest rate should be measured on initial recognition at their (negative) fair value and subsequently at the higher of:

- the amount recognised under IAS 37 – *Provisions, Contingent Liabilities and Contingent Assets* (Chapter 27); and

- the amount initially recognised less, where appropriate, cumulative amortisation recognised in accordance with IAS 18 – *Revenue* (or, when adopted, the principles of IFRS 15 – *Revenue from Contracts with Customers*) (Chapters 28 and 29).

This assumes that the instrument is not classified at fair value through profit or loss (in which case 2.1 above applies) and, in the case of a financial guarantee contract, it does not arise from a 'failed derecognition' transaction (see 2.9.3 below). *[IAS 39.47(c), 47(d), AG4(a)].*

In assessing whether a provision should be recognised for financial guarantee contracts, entities need to determine whether groups of similar contracts should be assessed on an individual or a portfolio basis. IAS 37 itself explains that the measurement of a provision involving a large population of items should be determined on a portfolio basis using an expected value method *[IAS 37.39]* (a treatment the IASB has previously implied could be adopted for guarantees[5]) and in our experience some form of portfolio approach is commonly adopted in practice. However, the FASB published requirements applying to insurers writing financial guarantee contracts, which require provisions to be recognised and measured on a contract-by-contract basis.[6] In our view, selection of an accounting policy that is consistent with US GAAP rather than applying a portfolio approach could also be appropriate.

2.9   Exceptions to the general principles

2.9.1   Hedging relationships

Financial assets and financial liabilities that are designated as hedged items are subject to measurement under the hedge accounting requirements of IAS 39 *[IAS 39.46, 47, 56]* and these can over-ride the general accounting requirements discussed above. Also, financial instruments may be designated as hedging instruments (in hedges of foreign currency risk), which can affect whether exchange gains and losses are recognised in profit or loss or in other comprehensive income. *[IAS 39.72, 95, 102].* Hedge accounting is covered in Chapter 51.

2.9.2   Regular way transactions

Where settlement date accounting is used for regular way transactions (see Chapter 47 at 2.2.2), any change in the fair value of the asset to be received arising between trade date and settlement date is not recognised for those assets that will be measured at cost or amortised cost. For assets that will be recorded at fair value, such changes in value are recognised:

- in profit or loss for assets to be classified at fair value through profit or loss; and
- in other comprehensive income (except for impairments and certain foreign exchange gains and losses as above) for available-for-sale assets. *[IAS 39.55, 57].*

On disposal, changes in value of such assets between trade date and settlement date are not recognised because the right to changes in fair value ceases on the trade date. *[IAS 39.D.2.2].* This is illustrated in Chapter 47 at 2.2.3.

2.9.3   Liabilities arising from 'failed derecognition' transactions

There are special requirements for financial liabilities (including financial guarantee contracts) that arise when transfers of financial assets do not qualify for derecognition, or are accounted for using the continuing involvement approach. *[IAS 39.47(b)].* These are dealt with in Chapter 50 at 5.3.

Chapter 48

3   AMORTISED COST AND THE EFFECTIVE INTEREST METHOD

IAS 39 contains three key definitions relating to this method of accounting, which are set out below.

The *amortised cost* of a financial instrument is defined as the amount at which it was measured at initial recognition minus principal repayments, plus or minus the cumulative amortisation using the 'effective interest method' of any difference between that initial amount and the maturity amount, and minus any loss allowance. The *effective interest method* is a method of calculating the amortised cost of a financial instrument (or group of instruments) and of allocating the interest income or expense over the relevant period. *[IAS 39.9]*.

The *effective interest rate* is the rate that exactly discounts estimated future cash payments or receipts over the expected life of the instrument or, when appropriate, a shorter period, to the instrument's net carrying amount. The calculation of the effective interest rate should include all fees and points paid or received between the contracting parties to the extent they are an integral part of the effective interest rate. The definition refers to IAS 18 for further guidance on what should and should not be considered integral (see Chapter 28 at 5.2.3.A). The calculation should also include transaction costs, and all other premiums or discounts, but not the effect of future credit losses. *[IAS 39.9]*. Transaction costs expected to be incurred on transfer or disposal of a financial instrument are not included in the measurement of the financial instrument. *[IAS 39.E.1.1]*.

It is important to note that the effective interest rate is normally based on estimated, not contractual, cash flows and there is a presumption that the cash flows and the expected life of a group of similar financial instruments can be estimated reliably. However, in those rare cases when it is not possible to estimate reliably the cash flows or the expected life of a financial instrument (or group of instruments), the contractual cash flows over the full contractual term of the financial instrument (or group of instruments) should be used. *[IAS 39.9]*.

For consistency with the estimated cash flows approach, the effective interest rate should be calculated over the expected life of the instrument or, when applicable, a shorter period. Generally, the expected life of the instrument should be used although a shorter period is used if this is the period to which the fee, transaction costs, discount or premium relates. This will be the case when the related variable (e.g. interest rates) is re-priced to market rates before the expected maturity of the instrument. In such a case, the appropriate amortisation period is the period to the next such re-pricing date. *[IAS 39.9, AG6, BC35]*. The application of this requirement is considered in more detail at 3.3 and 3.6 below.

As set out in Chapter 44 at 6, an issued compound financial instrument such as a convertible bond is accounted for as a financial liability component and an equity component. In accounting for the financial liability at amortised cost, the expected cash flows should be those of the liability component only and the estimate should not take account of the bond being converted.

3.1   Fixed interest, fixed term instruments

The effective interest method is most easily applied to instruments that have fixed payments and a fixed term. The following examples (as well as Example 48.2 at 2.4 above) illustrate this.

Example 48.6:   Effective interest method –
amortisation of premium or discount on acquisition

At the end of 2015, a company purchases a debt instrument with five years remaining to maturity for its fair value of US$1,000 (including transaction costs). The instrument has a principal amount of US$1,250 and carries fixed interest of 4.7% payable annually (US$1,250 × 4.7% = US$59 per year). In order to allocate interest receipts and the initial discount over the term of the instrument at a constant rate on the carrying amount, it can be shown that interest needs to be accrued at the rate of 10% annually. The table below provides information about the amortised cost, interest income, and cash flows of the debt instrument in each reporting period.[7] *[IAS 39.B.26]*.

Year	(a) Amortised cost at start of year (US$)	(b = a × 10%) Interest income (US$)	(c) Cash flows (US$)	(d = a + b − c) Amortised cost at end of year (US$)
2016	1,000	100	59	1,041
2017	1,041	104	59	1,086
2018	1,086	109	59	1,136
2019	1,136	113	59	1,190
2020	1,190	119	1,250 + 59	–

Example 48.7:   Effective interest method – stepped interest rates

On 1 January 2016, Company A acquires a debt instrument for its fair value of £1,250 (including transaction costs). The principal amount is £1,250 which is repayable on 31 December 2020. The rate of interest is specified in the debt agreement as a percentage of the principal amount as follows: 6% in 2016 (£75), 8% in 2017 (£100), 10% in 2018 (£125), 12% in 2019 (£150) and 16.4% in 2020 (£205). It can be shown that the interest rate that exactly discounts the stream of future cash payments to maturity is 10%. In each period, the amortised cost at the beginning of the period is multiplied by the effective interest rate of 10% and added to the amortised cost. Any cash payments in the period are deducted from the resulting balance. Accordingly, the amortised cost, interest income and cash flows of the debt instrument in each period are as follows:

Year	(a) Amortised cost at start of year (£)	(b = a × 10%) Interest income (£)	(c) Cash flows (£)	(d = a + b − c) Amortised cost at end of year (£)
2016	1,250	125	75	1,300
2017	1,300	130	100	1,330
2018	1,330	133	125	1,338
2019	1,338	134	150	1,322
2020	1,322	133	1,250 + 205	–

It can be seen that, although the instrument is issued for £1,250 and has a maturity amount of £1,250, its amortised cost does not equal £1,250 at each reporting date. *[IAS 39.B.27]*.

Methods for determining the effective interest rate for a given set of cash flows (as in the examples above) include simple trial and error techniques as well as more

Chapter 48

methodical iterative algorithms. Alternatively, many spreadsheet applications contain 'goal-seek' or similar functions that can also be used to derive effective interest rates.

3.2   Prepayment, call and similar options

When calculating the effective interest rate, all contractual terms of the financial instrument, for example prepayment, call and similar options, should be considered. *[IAS 39.9]*. The following simple example illustrates how this principle is applied.

Example 48.8:   Effective interest rate – embedded prepayment options

Bank ABC originates 1,000 ten year loans of £10,000 with 10% stated interest. Prepayments are probable and it is possible to reasonably estimate their timing and amount. ABC determines that the effective interest rate including loan origination fees received by ABC is 10.2% based on the *contractual* payment terms of the loans as the fees received reduce the initial carrying amount.

However, if the *expected* prepayments were considered, the effective interest rate would be 10.4% since the difference between the initial amount and maturity amount is amortised over a shorter period.

The effective interest rate that should be used by ABC for this portfolio is 10.4%.[8]

3.2.1   Revisions to estimated cash flows

The standard contains an explanation of how changes to estimates of payments or receipts (e.g. because of a reassessment of the extent to which prepayments will occur) should be dealt with.

When estimates change, the carrying amount of the financial instrument (or group of instruments) should be adjusted to reflect actual and revised estimated cash flows. More precisely, the carrying amount should be calculated by computing the present value of estimated future cash flows at the instrument's original effective interest rate or, if the instrument has been designated as the hedged item in a fair value hedge, the revised effective interest rate. Any consequent adjustment should be recognised immediately in profit or loss. *[IAS 39.AG8]*.

The IASB considers this approach to have the practical advantage that it does not require recalculation of the effective interest rate, i.e. an entity simply recognises the remaining cash flows at the original rate. Consequently, a possible conflict with the requirement to discount estimated cash flows using the original effective interest rate when assessing impairment is avoided. *[IAS 39.BC36]*.

This requirement is illustrated in the following example taken from the implementation guidance.

Example 48.9:   Effective interest method – revision of estimates

At the end of 2015, a company purchases in a quoted market a debt instrument with the same terms as the instrument in Example 48.6 at 3.1 above, except that the contract also specifies that the borrower has an option to prepay the instrument and that no penalty will be charged for prepayment (i.e. any prepayment will be made at the principal amount of US$1,250 or a proportion thereof).

At inception, there is an expectation that the borrower will not prepay and so the information about the instrument's effective interest rate, amortised cost, interest income and cash flows in each reporting period would be the same as that in Example 48.6.

On the first day of 2018, the investor revises its estimate of cash flows. It now expects that 50% of the principal will be prepaid at the end of 2018 and the remaining 50% at the end of 2020. Therefore, the opening balance of the debt instrument in 2018 is adjusted to an amount calculated by discounting the amounts expected to be received in 2018 and subsequent years using the original effective interest rate (10%). This results in a revised balance of US$1,138. The adjustment of US$52 (US$1,138 – US$1,086) is recorded in profit or loss in 2018.

The table below provides information about the amortised cost, interest income and cash flows as they would be adjusted taking into account this change in estimate.

Year	(a) Amortised cost at start of year (US$)	(b = a × 10%) Interest and similar income* (US$)	(c) Cash flows (US$)	(d = a + b – c) Amortised cost at end of year (US$)
2016	1,000	100	59	1,041
2017	1,041	104	59	1,086
2018	1,086	114 + 52	625 + 59	568
2019	568	57	30	595
2020	595	60	625 + 30	–

*the standard and related guidance do not state whether the catch-up adjustment (US$52 in 2018 in this case) should be classified as interest income or as some other income or expense, simply that it should be recognised in profit or loss.

This amortised cost calculation would be applicable whether the instruments were classified as held-to-maturity or available-for-sale. *[IAS 39.B.26]*.

3.2.2 Special requirements for financial assets reclassified in accordance with IAS 39

Special rules apply to the application of the effective interest method where a financial asset is reclassified into the loans and receivables category in accordance with IAS 39 (see 2.7.1 and 2.7.2 above and Chapter 45 at 6.1 and 6.2). In such cases, where the estimates of future cash receipts are subsequently increased as a result of their increased recoverability, the effect of that increase should be recognised as an adjustment to the effective interest rate from the date of the change in estimate rather than as an adjustment to the carrying amount of the asset at the date of the change in estimate. *[IAS 39.AG8]*.

3.2.3 Interaction with the requirements for embedded derivatives

As set out in Chapter 43 at 5.1, certain debt instruments containing terms such as prepayment options are required by IAS 39 to be accounted for as two separate contracts, i.e. a host debt instrument and an embedded derivative. Although not explained in the standard, the terms accounted for separately as an embedded derivative should not be taken into account in applying the effective interest method to the host. If a prepayment option, say, were accounted for as an embedded derivative at fair value, it would effectively be accounted for twice if it was also taken into account in determining the effective interest rate of the host.

In Example 48.9 above, which is based on the implementation guidance to IAS 39, it is not clear why the prepayment option has *not* been separately accounted for as an embedded derivative. The exercise price is US$1,250 and the option may be exercised at any time, yet the amortised cost is initially only US$1,000. Therefore, unless these two figures were considered approximately equal, the option would not be regarded as closely related to the host under IAS 39 (see Chapter 43 at 5).

Chapter 48

We find it hard to believe that the IASB considers two numbers, one of which is 25% larger than the other, to be approximately equal. More likely, the requirements regarding embedded derivatives were overlooked when developing the above example as it is intended, primarily, to illustrate the accounting requirements when estimates of cash flows are revised.

This actually raises other questions with regards to the issue of whether prepayment and similar options should be regarded as closely related to the host instrument. In assessing whether the exercise price is approximately equal to the amortised cost at each exercise date, should one consider the amortised cost of the hybrid on the assumption the option is regarded as closely related, or the amortised cost of the host on the assumption that it is not? This conundrum is illustrated in the following simple example (which also provides further illustrations of the application of the effective interest method to instruments containing prepayment options).

Example 48.10:   Embedded prepayment option

Company P borrows €1,000 on terms that require it to pay annual fixed rate coupons of €80 and €1,000 principal at the end of ten years. The terms of the instrument also allow P to redeem the debt after seven years by paying the principal of €1,000 and a penalty of €100.

The debt instrument can be considered to comprise the following two components:

- a host debt instrument requiring ten annual payments of €80 followed by a €1,000 payment of principal; and

- an embedded prepayment option, exercisable only at the end of seven years with an exercise price of €1,100.

If, at inception, the prepayment option was expected *not* to be exercised, the effective interest rate of the *hybrid* would be 8%. This is the rate that would discount the expected cash flows of €80 per year for ten years plus €1,000 at the end of ten years to the initial carrying amount of €1,000. The table below provides information about the amortised cost, interest income and cash flows using this assumption.

Year	(a) Amortised cost at start of year (€)	(b = a × 8%) Interest and similar income (€)	(c) Cash flows (€)	(d = a + b − c) Amortised cost at end of year (€)
1	1,000	80	80	1,000
2	1,000	80	80	1,000
3	1,000	80	80	1,000
4	1,000	80	80	1,000
5	1,000	80	80	1,000
6	1,000	80	80	1,000
7	1,000	80	80	1,000
8	1,000	80	80	1,000
9	1,000	80	80	1,000
10	1,000	80	80 + 1,000	–

However if, at the outset, the option *was* expected to be exercised, the effective interest rate of the *hybrid* would be 9.08% as this is the rate that discounts the expected cash flows of €80 per year for seven years, plus €1,100 at the end of seven years, to the initial carrying amount of €1,000. The table below provides information about the amortised cost, interest income and cash flows using this alternative assumption.

Year	(a) Amortised cost at start of year (€)	(b = a × 9.08%) Interest and similar income (€)	(c) Cash flows (€)	(d = a + b − c) Amortised cost at end of year (€)
1	1,000	91	80	1,011
2	1,011	92	80	1,023
3	1,023	93	80	1,036
4	1,036	94	80	1,050
5	1,050	95	80	1,065
6	1,065	97	80	1,082
7	1,082	98	80 + 1,100	–

On the face of it, therefore, comparing the amortised cost of the hybrid with the exercise price of the option at the date it could be exercised suggests the prepayment option might be considered closely related if it was likely to be exercised but not if exercise was unlikely.

However, even this is not the whole story. If the option (on inception) was not expected to be exercised, but at a later date exercise became likely, the amortised cost carrying amount would be revised so that it represented the expected future cash flows discounted at the original effective interest rate. For example, if at the end of Year 5, it became likely that the option would be exercised, the carrying amount would be revised so that it represented €80 discounted for one year at 8% plus €1,180 discounted for two years at 8% – in other words, €1,086 rather than €1,065. The difference of €21 would be recognised in profit or loss immediately and the amortised cost carrying amount would subsequently accrete so that it represented the final cash outflow (option exercise price of €1,100 plus coupon of €80) at the end of Year 7. So even in this situation there is an argument to suggest that the prepayment option should not be separated as the exercise price will always equal the amortised cost (at least to the extent that the option is expected to be exercised).

If the assessment was performed based on the amortised cost of the *host*, the initial fair value of the prepayment option is needed to determine the initial carrying amount of the host (see Chapter 47 at 3.4). From P's perspective it will have a positive fair value and for the purpose of this example this is assumed to be €50. Therefore, the initial value of the host will be €1,050 (€1,000 + €50). The effective interest rate of the host can be demonstrated to be 7.28% and the amortised cost each year would be as follows:

Year	(a) Amortised cost at start of year (€)	(b = a × 7.28%) Interest and similar income (€)	(c) Cash flows (€)	(d = a + b − c) Amortised cost at end of year (€)
1	1,050	76	80	1,046
2	1,046	76	80	1,042
3	1,042	76	80	1,038
4	1,038	76	80	1,034
5	1,034	75	80	1,029
6	1,029	75	80	1,024
7	1,024	75	80	1,019
8	1,019	74	80	1,013
9	1,013	74	80	1,007
10	1,007	73	80 + 1,000	–

In this case, the amortised cost at the date the option can be exercised is €1,019. Comparing this with the exercise price of €1,100 suggests the option may not be considered closely related in this case.

In fact if this analysis were applied to prepayment options for which there was no associated penalty (i.e. the instrument would always be redeemed at its principal amount), separating the embedded derivative in this way would artificially create a difference between the amortised cost of the *host* and the exercise price. However, we are entirely unconvinced it would be appropriate to separate an embedded derivative from such a simple instrument.

Unfortunately, the standard is silent on these issues and preparers of accounts will be required to exercise judgement as to the most appropriate method to use in their individual circumstances, although as noted in Chapter 43 at 5.1.3, one trade body has published guidance explaining that where early repayment fees are included in the calculation of effective interest, the prepayment option is likely to be closely related to the loan.[9]

3.3   Floating rate instruments

When estimating cash flows for a floating rate instrument, application of the basic requirements discussed at 3 above could produce some surprising results, as shown in the following example.

Example 48.11:   Effective interest method – variable rate loan

At the start of July 2016, Company G originates a floating rate debt instrument. Its fair value is equal to its principal amount of $1,000 and no transaction costs are incurred. The instrument pays, in arrears at the end of June, a variable rate coupon, determined by reference to 12 month LIBOR at the start of each previous July. It has a term of five years and is repayable at its principal amount at the end of June 2021.

On origination, 12 month LIBOR is 5% and this establishes the first payment, to be made in June 2017, at $50. Based on a market-derived yield curve, G estimates that the subsequent floating rate payments will be $60, $70, $80 and $90 (yield curve rises steeply). It can be demonstrated that the interest rate that exactly discounts these estimated coupon payments and the $1,000 principal at maturity to the current carrying amount of $1,000 is 6.87% (the definition does not acknowledge the possibility of more than one effective interest rate that would be reflective of a yield curve that is not flat).

In this situation, recognising interest at 6.87% in the first year would seem entirely counter-intuitive and is inconsistent with traditional notions of interest recognition for floating rate instruments. Nevertheless, there are some who believe, at least in principle, that such an approach is technically correct, even if it is not applied widely in practice.

The standard does contain additional guidance for applying the effective interest method to floating rate instruments. Normally, the effective interest rate remains constant over the life of an instrument. However, for floating rate instruments, it is stated that periodic re-estimation of cash flows to reflect movements in market interest rates *does* alter the effective interest rate. The standard goes on to explain that where such an instrument is initially recognised at an amount equal to the principal repayable on maturity, re-estimating the future interest payments normally has no significant effect on the carrying amount of the instrument. *[IAS 39.AG7].*

Typically this has been interpreted to mean that entities should simply account for periodic floating rate payments on an accruals basis in the period to which they relate. However, those that believe entities should forecast all future cash flows argue that this means that the calculated effective interest rate (6.87% in Example 48.11 above) is applied until estimated future cash flows are revised, at which point a new effective interest rate is calculated based on the revised cash flow expectations and the current carrying amount.

Whilst payments, receipts, discounts and premiums included in the effective interest method calculation are normally amortised over the expected life of the instrument, there may be situations when they are amortised over a shorter period (see 3 above). This will be the case when the variable to which they relate reprices to market rates before the instrument's expected maturity. In such cases, the appropriate amortisation period is to the next re-pricing date.

For example, if a premium or discount on a floating rate instrument reflects interest that has accrued since interest was last paid, or changes in market rates since the floating interest rate was reset to market rates, it will be amortised to the next date when the interest rate is reset to market rates. This is because the premium or discount relates to the period to the next interest reset date because, at that date, the variable to which the premium or discount relates (i.e. the interest rate) is reset to market rates. If, however, it results from a change in the credit spread over the floating rate specified in the instrument, or other variables that are not reset to market rates, it is amortised over the expected life of the instrument. *[IAS 39.AG6]*.

The following examples illustrate the requirements of applying a discount arising on acquisition of a debt instrument resulting from (a) a credit downgrade and (b) accrued interest.

Example 48.12: *Effective interest method –*
amortisation of discount arising from credit downgrade

A twenty year bond is issued at £100, has a principal amount of £100, and requires quarterly interest payments equal to current three month LIBOR plus 1% over the life of the instrument. The interest rate reflects the market-based required rate of return associated with the bond issue at issuance. Subsequent to issuance, the credit quality of the bond deteriorates resulting in a rating downgrade. It therefore trades at a discount, although there is no objective evidence of impairment. Company A purchases the bond for £95 and classifies it as held-to-maturity.

The discount of £5 is amortised to income over the period to the maturity of the bond and not to the next date interest rate payments are reset as it results from a change in credit spreads.[10]

Example 48.13: *Effective interest method –*
amortisation of discount arising from accrued interest

At the start of November 2016, Company P acquires the bond issued by Company G in Example 48.11 above – current interest rates have not changed since the end of July 2016 and G's credit risk has not changed since origination so P pays $1,017.

The premium of $17 paid by P relates to interest accrued since the last reset date and so is amortised to income over the period to the next re-pricing date, June 2017; further, the $50 cash flow received at the end of June 2017 is also 'amortised' over this period.

Consequently, for the eight months ended June 2017, P will record interest of $33 ($50 – $17), which is also the approximate equivalent of eight months interest at current rates (5%) earned on P's initial investment.

This treatment is consistent with the requirements of IAS 18 that apply when unpaid interest has accrued before the acquisition of an interest-bearing investment. In such cases, it is explained (in more traditional terms) that the subsequent receipt of interest should be allocated between pre-acquisition and post-acquisition periods and only the post-acquisition portion should be recognised as revenue. *[IAS 18.32]*. In fact for many floating rate instruments, it will often be appropriate to apply a simplistic method of accounting – for example, by amortising transaction costs on a straight line basis over the life of the instrument combined with a simple time apportionment approach to the floating rate coupons.

3.4   Perpetual debt instruments

The fact that an instrument is perpetual does not change how amortised cost is calculated. The present value of the perpetual stream of future cash payments is discounted at the effective interest rate, resulting in an amortised cost that equals the principal amount in each period. *[IAS 39.B.24]*.

However, in cases where interest is only paid over a limited amount of time, some or all of the interest payments are, from an economic perspective, repayments of the principal amount as illustrated in the following example. *[IAS 39.B.25]*.

Example 48.14:   Amortised cost –
*   perpetual debt with interest payments over a limited amount of time*

On 1 January 2016, Company A subscribes £1,000 for a debt instrument which yields 25% interest for the first five years and 0% in subsequent periods and is classified as a loan. It can be determined that the effective yield is 7.9% and the amortised cost is shown in the table below.[11]

Year	(a) Amortised cost at start of year (£)	(b = a × 7.9%) Interest income (£)	(c) Cash flows (£)	(d = a + b − c) Amortised cost at end of year (£)
2016	1,000	79	250	829
2017	829	66	250	645
2018	645	51	250	446
2019	446	36	250	232
2020	232	18	250	–
2021	–	–	–	–

3.5   Acquisition of credit impaired debt instruments

In some cases, financial assets are acquired at a deep discount that reflects incurred credit losses. IAS 39 requires such incurred (but not expected or future) credit losses to be included in the estimated cash flows when computing the effective interest rate. This is illustrated in the following example. *[IAS 39.AG5]*.

Example 48.15:   Purchase of impaired debt

On 1 January 2009, Company D issued a debt instrument that required it to pay an annual coupon of €800 in arrears and to repay the principal of €10,000 on 31 December 2019. By 2015, D was in financial difficulties and was unable to pay the coupon due on 31 December 2015. On 1 January 2016, Company V estimated that the holder could expect to receive a single payment of €4,000 at the end of 2017 and acquired the debt instrument at an arm's length price of €3,000.

It can be shown that using the contractual cash flows (including the €800 overdue) gives rise to an effective interest rate of 70.1% (the net present value of €800 now and annually thereafter until 2019 and €10,000 receivable at the end of 2019 is €3,000 when discounted at 70.1%). However, because the debt instrument is clearly credit impaired, V should calculate the effective interest rate using the estimated cash flows on the instrument. In this case, the effective interest rate is 15.5% (the net present value of €4,000 receivable in two years is €3,000 when discounted at 15.5%).

All things being equal, interest income of €464 (€3,000 × 15.5%) would be recognised on the instrument during 2016 and its carrying amount at the end of the year would be €3,464 (€3,000 + €464). However if at the end of the year the cash flow expected to be generated by the instrument had increased to €4,250 (still to be received at the end of 2017), an adjustment to the asset would be made as set out at 3.2.1 above. Accordingly, its carrying amount would be increased to €3,681 (€4,250 discounted over one year at 15.5%) and a further €217 income would be recognised in profit or loss. Of course, there would need to be a substantive and supportable basis for revising the cash flow estimates.

In the above example, let us say at the time of acquisition of the debt instrument, Company V forecasts that it has to incur collection costs of €200. These forecast collection costs would not normally be included in the estimated future cash flows when computing the effective interest rate of the acquired impaired debt instrument, since they should be treated as expenses when incurred rather than as a reduction in interest income. However, given that the standard requires incurred credit losses to be included in the estimated cash flows when computing the effective interest rate for financial assets acquired at a deep discount with incurred credit losses and paragraph AG84 requires the calculation of the present value of the estimated future cash flows of an impaired collateralised financial asset to reflect 'the cash flows that may result from foreclosure less costs for obtaining and selling the collateral', it would follow that costs associated with obtaining and selling collateral should normally be included in the estimated future cash flows when computing the effective interest rate for an acquired impaired debt instrument (see 4.2.2 below).

3.6 Inflation-linked debt

As noted in Chapter 43 at 5.1.5, the issuance of debt instruments whose cash flows are linked to changes in an inflation index is quite common and, typically, the embedded derivative representing the variability in cash flows is treated as closely related to the host instrument. Consequently, entities that hold or issue these instruments must apply the effective interest method to determine the amount of interest to be recognised in profit or loss each period (assuming the instrument is not classified at fair value through profit or loss).

In May 2008, the Interpretations Committee was asked to consider a request for guidance on this issue. Three ways of applying the effective interest method that were being used in practice were included in the request. These are summarised in the following example.[12]

Example 48.16: Application of the effective interest method to inflation-linked debt instruments[13]

On 1 January 2016, Company A issues a debt instrument for $100,000 that is linked to the local Consumer Prices Index ('CPI'). The terms of the instrument require it to be repaid in full after five years at an amount equal to $100,000 adjusted by the cumulative change in the CPI over those five years. Interest on the loan is paid at each year end at an amount equal to 5% of the principal ($100,000) adjusted by the cumulative change in the CPI from issuance of the instrument.

The following table sets out the expected annual inflation rates on issuance of the instrument and one year later:

	Expected annual inflation rates	
	At start of 2016	At start of 2017
2016	0.7%	
2017	2.6%	1.4%
2018	2.8%	1.9%
2019	2.8%	3.5%
2020	2.8%	3.5%

During 2016 actual inflation is 1.2%.

Method 1 – application of IAS 39.AG8 (the 'AG8 approach')

This approach follows the requirements set out at 3.2.1 above. Therefore, the effective interest rate is established on 1 January 2016 based on expected cash flows at that time:

Date: end of	Expected cash flow ($)	Calculation
2016	5,035	=5,000 × 1.007
2017	5,166	=5,000 × 1.007 × 1.026
2018	5,311	=5,000 × 1.007 × 1.026 × 1.028
2019	5,459	=5,000 × 1.007 × 1.026 × 1.028 × 1.028
2020	117,854	=105,000 × 1.007 × 1.026 × 1.028 × 1.028 × 1.028

It can be demonstrated that these expected cash flows produce an effective interest rate of 7.4075%, i.e. the net present value of these cash flows, discounted at 7.4075%, equals $100,000.

During 2016, A applies the effective interest rate to the financial liability to recognise a finance charge of $7,408 ($100,000 × 7.4075%), increasing the carrying amount of the financial liability to $107,408 ($100,000 + $7,408). At the end of the year A pays cash interest of $5,060 ($5,000 × 101.2%) reducing the liability to $102,348 ($107,408 – $5,060). In addition, A must adjust the carrying amount of the financial liability so that it equals the net present value of expected future cash flows discounted at the original expected interest rate.

The expected future cash flows are now as follows:

Date: end of	Cash flow ($)	Calculation
2017	5,131	=5,000 × 1.012 × 1.014
2018	5,228	=5,000 × 1.012 × 1.014 × 1.019
2019	5,411	=5,000 × 1.012 × 1.014 × 1.019 × 1.035
2020	117,615	=105,000 × 1.012 × 1.014 × 1.019 × 1.035 × 1.035

The net present value of these cash flows discounted at 7.4075% is $102,050. Therefore A reduces its finance charge by $298 ($102,050 – $102,348) so that the total finance charge for 2016 is $7,110 ($7,408 – $298).

Method 2 – application of IAS 39.AG7 using forecast future cash flows (the 'AG7 approach')

This approach is referred to at 3.3 above.

The initial effective interest rate is calculated and applied in the same way as Method 1. However, no adjustment is made to the carrying amount of the financial liability at the end of 2016 ($102,348) or to the finance charge for 2016 ($7,408) as a result of A, at the start of 2017, revising its expectations about inflation over the remaining term of the instrument.

Instead, a revised effective interest rate is calculated at the start of 2017 using the revised forecast cash flows (shown above under Method 1, i.e. $5,131 at the end of 2017, $5,228 at the end of 2018, $5,411 at the end of 2019 and $117,615 at the end of 2020) and the current carrying amount ($102,348). It can be demonstrated that this produces a revised effective interest rate of 7.3237%, i.e. the net present value of those cash flows, discounted at 7.3237% equals $102,348.

Applying this revised rate prospectively in 2017 (and assuming estimates of future inflation are not revised again until the start of 2018) there will be a finance charge for 2017 of $7,496 ($102,348 × 7.3237%).

Method 3 – application of IAS 39.AG6-AG7 without forecasting future cash flows

This method is based on the traditional method of accounting for floating rate debt instruments and is commonly used under other bodies of GAAP. Rather than taking account of expectations of future inflation it takes account of inflation only during the reporting period.

Therefore, in 2016, A would recognise a finance charge of $5,060 as a result of accruing the variable interest payment in respect of 2016. In addition, the actual inflation experienced during 2016 increases the amount of principal that will be paid from $100,000 to $101,200 ($100,000 × 1.012%). This increase, i.e. $1,200, is effectively a premium to be paid on the redemption of the financial liability. Paragraph AG6 of IAS 39 explains that a premium should normally be amortised over the expected life of an instrument. However, it goes on to explain that a shorter period should be used if this is the period to which the premium relates. *[IAS 39.AG6]*. In this case, the premium clearly relates to 2016 as it arises from inflation during that year and so it is appropriately amortised in that year.

Consequently, the total finance charge for 2016 using this method would be $6,260 ($5,060 + $1,200).

In analysing the submission, it initially appeared as if the Interpretations Committee staff completely rejected Method 3. The submission argued that Method 3 was justified by reference to IAS 29 – *Financial Reporting in Hyperinflationary Economies*. The staff concluded (quite correctly) that it was inappropriate to apply IAS 29 because that standard applies only to the financial statements of an entity whose functional currency is the currency of a hyperinflationary economy and instead the guidance in IAS 39 should be applied.[14]

However, the Interpretations Committee noted that paragraphs AG6 to AG8 of IAS 39 provide the relevant application guidance and that judgement is required to determine whether an instrument is floating rate and within the scope of paragraph AG7 or is within the scope of paragraph AG8.[15] Further, it was noted that IAS 39 is unclear as to whether future expectations about interest rates (and presumably, therefore, inflation) should be taken into account when applying paragraph AG7.[16] Consequently, in our view, all three methods noted in the example comply with the current requirements of IAS 39. This view is consistent with the opinion of one national standard-setter that operates in a jurisdiction where such instruments are extremely common.[17]

3.7 Other, more complex, instruments

The application of the effective interest method to instruments with unusual embedded derivatives that are deemed closely related to the host, or other embedded features that are not accounted for separately, is not always straightforward or intuitive. Specifically it is not always clear how to deal with changes in the estimated cash flows of the instrument and in any given situation one needs to assess which of the approaches set out at 3.2.1 above (changes in cash flows generally, or the 'AG8' approach) and 3.3 above (specific requirements for floating rate instruments, or the 'AG7' approach) is more appropriate.

Consider an entity that issues a debt instrument for its par value of €10m which is repayable in ten years' time and on which an annual coupon is payable comprising two elements: a fixed amount of 2.5% of the par value and a variable amount equating to 0.01% of the entity's annual revenues. The instrument is not designated at fair value through profit or loss and it is judged that the embedded feature is not a derivative as outlined in Example 43.4 in Chapter 43.

The AG7 approach and the AG8 approach could give rise to significantly different accounting treatments. In the latter case, the issuer would need to estimate the amount of payments to be made over the life of the bond (which will depend on its estimated revenues for the next ten years) in order to determine the effective interest rate to be applied. Any changes to these estimates would result in a catch-up adjustment to profit or loss and the carrying amount of the bond which, potentially, could give rise to significant volatility. In the former case the annual coupon would simply be accrued each year and changes in estimated revenues of future periods would have no impact on the accounting treatment until the applicable year.

In 2009, the Interpretations Committee was asked to consider the accounting treatment for an instrument with similar terms. However, it considered the issue without reconsidering the assumptions described in the request, namely that the financial liability (a) did not contain any embedded derivatives, (b) was measured at amortised cost using the effective interest method, and (c) did not meet the definition of a floating rate instrument.[18] In other words, whilst clearly indicating that the AG8 approach was acceptable, it did not explicitly preclude the use of the AG7 approach. In this situation we believe that it would often be appropriate to apply the AG8 approach, principally because the entity's revenue does not represent a floating rate that changes to reflect movements in market rates of interest, although as covered at 3.6 above, judgement is required to determine which approach is appropriate.[19]

For other instruments, the decision as to which approach to use is even less clear. For example, as set out at 3.6 above, it can be argued that simple inflation-linked bonds are similar enough to floating rate instruments to apply the AG7 approach. However, this approach would not extend to more exotic instruments, for example to an 'inverse floater' where coupons on an otherwise simple debt instrument are paid at a fixed rate minus LIBOR (subject to a floor of zero), even though re-estimation of cash flows will only reflect movements in market interest rates.

In other cases, it might be considered appropriate to apply a combination of both approaches if, for example, an instrument contains both fixed and floating rate features.

4   IMPAIRMENT

Although the impairment requirements of IAS 39 are less complex than those of IFRS 9 – *Financial Instruments*, they may appear somewhat over-engineered for what is a relatively simple subject for many entities, i.e. making appropriate provisions for bad and doubtful debts. The reason for this complexity is that IAS 39 is designed for use by all entities, including financial institutions for which impairment losses are often highly material. Accordingly, the IASB has tried to lay down clear guidelines as to when impairment losses should (and should not) be recognised in order to ensure that a consistent approach is taken both from period to period for individual entities and from entity to entity.

4.1 Impairment reviews

All financial assets, except for those measured at fair value through profit or loss, are subject to review for impairment. *[IAS 39.46]*. Assessments should be made at the end of each reporting period as to whether there is any objective evidence that a financial asset or group of assets is impaired. If such evidence exists, the requirements set out at 4.2, 4.3 or 4.4 below should be followed to determine the amount of any impairment loss. *[IAS 39.58]*.

A financial asset or a group of assets is impaired (and impairment losses are determined) if, and only if, there is objective evidence of impairment as a result of one or more events that occurred after initial recognition (a 'loss event') and that loss event (or events) has an impact on the estimated future cash flows of the financial asset or group of assets that can be reliably estimated. *[IAS 39.59]*.

Therefore, an entity should recognise an impairment loss on a group of loans even if the loss expectation since initial recognition of the loans has not changed, provided it could be estimated reliably, based on past history, that loss events have occurred after initial recognition, but before the reporting date.[20]

It may not be possible to identify a single, discrete event that caused the impairment; rather, the combined effect of several events may have caused the impairment. However, losses expected as a result of future events, no matter how likely, are not recognised. *[IAS 39.59]*. Therefore, an impairment loss is not permitted to be recognised at the time an asset is originated (i.e. before a loss event can have occurred) as illustrated in the following example. *[IAS 39.E.4.2]*.

Example 48.17: Immediate recognition of impairment

Bank B lends $1,000 to Customer M. Based on historical experience, B expects that 1% of the principal amount of loans given will not be collected, but an immediate impairment loss of $10 cannot be recognised. *[IAS 39.E.4.2]*.

4.1.1 Examples of loss events

Objective evidence that a financial asset or group of assets is impaired includes observable data that comes to the attention of the holder about the following loss events:

- significant financial difficulty of the issuer or obligor;
- breach of contract, such as a default or delinquency in interest or principal payments;
- the lender, for economic or legal reasons relating to the borrower's financial difficulty, granting to the borrower a concession that would not otherwise be considered;
- it becoming probable that the borrower will enter bankruptcy or other financial reorganisation;
- the disappearance of an active market for that asset because of financial difficulties (but not simply because the asset is no longer publicly traded *[IAS 39.60]*); or

- observable data indicating that there is a measurable decrease in the estimated future cash flows from a group of financial assets since initial recognition, although the decrease cannot yet be identified with the individual assets in the group, including:

  - adverse changes in the payment status of borrowers in the group (e.g. an increased number of delayed payments or an increased number of credit card borrowers who have reached their credit limit and are paying the minimum monthly amount); or

  - national or local economic conditions that correlate with defaults on the assets in the group (e.g. an increase in the unemployment rate in the geographical area of the borrowers, a decrease in property prices for mortgages in the relevant area, a decrease in oil prices for loan assets to oil producers, or adverse changes in industry conditions that affect the borrowers in the group). *[IAS 39.59].*

A downgrade of an entity's credit rating is not, of itself, evidence of impairment, although it may be when considered with other available information. *[IAS 39.60].* Other factors that would be considered in determining whether an impairment loss has been incurred include information about the debtors' or issuers' liquidity, solvency and business and financial risk exposures, levels of and trends in delinquencies for similar financial assets, national and local economic trends and conditions, and the fair value of collateral and guarantees. *[IAS 39.E.4.1].* A decline in the fair value of a financial asset below its cost or amortised cost is not necessarily evidence of impairment – for example, the fair value of a debt instrument may decline only from an increase in the risk-free interest rate. *[IAS 39.60, E.4.10].* Therefore, it is possible that an 'available-for-sale reserve' within equity can be negative.

4.1.2   Loss events related to investments in equity instruments

The standard explains that the following are objective evidence of impairment of an equity investment:

- information about significant changes with an adverse effect that have taken place in the technological, market, economic or legal environment in which the issuer operates, and indicates that the cost of the investment in the equity instrument may not be recovered; and

- a significant or prolonged decline in the fair value of an investment in such an instrument below its cost (see 4.1.3 below). *[IAS 39.61].*

These triggers apply in addition to those specified at 4.1.1 above, which focus on the assessment of impairment in debt instruments. *[IAS 39.BC107].*

4.1.3   Significant or prolonged declines in fair value

The meaning of the terms 'significant' and 'prolonged' is not defined or explained further. In March 2009, the Interpretations Committee received a request to provide guidance on the conceptual meaning of these terms as a result of considerable diversity in practice, sometimes driven by regulatory guidance issued in various jurisdictions.[21] The Interpretations Committee decided not to take the issue onto its agenda, but took the unusual step of outlining inappropriate applications of IAS 39 in recognising impairment on available-for-sale equity instruments,[22] including the following:[23]

- the standard cannot be read to require the decline in value to be both significant *and* prolonged. Thus, either a significant *or* a prolonged decline is sufficient to require the recognition of an impairment loss (although there is obviously some interaction between the notions of 'significant' and 'prolonged'[24]);

- because IAS 39 states that a significant or prolonged decline in the fair value of an investment in an equity instrument below its cost is objective evidence of impairment, when such a decline exists, recognition of an impairment loss is required. Therefore, it is not possible to consider such a decline only an indicator of possible impairment;[25]

- the fact that a decline in the value of an investment is in line with the overall level of decline in the relevant market does not mean that it can be concluded that the investment is not impaired;

- the existence of a significant or prolonged decline cannot be overcome by forecasts of an expected recovery of market values, regardless of their expected timing. Consequently, an anticipated market recovery is not relevant to the assessment of 'significant or prolonged'.

  To illustrate why such a recovery should not be anticipated, the Japanese Nikkei index reached its peak at 38,900 in December 1989, trended downwards to a low of 8,000 in March 2003, had a brief recovery to 17,900 in May 2007 and in May 2009 when it stood at 8,100, had not exceeded 20,000 since March 2000.[26]

  The Interpretations Committee was specifically asked to address whether an actual recovery in the fair value of an investment, after the end of the reporting period but before the financial statements were approved, could be taken into account. The Interpretations Committee staff noted that the impairment assessment was to be made at the end of the reporting period and noted that IAS 10 – *Events after the Reporting Period* – states that a decline in the fair value of an investment after the year end does not normally relate to the condition of the investment at the end of the reporting period. In the light of this they were clearly of the view that such a recovery was not relevant.[27] Ultimately, however, the Interpretations Committee did not state that it was inappropriate to take account of actual recoveries; and

- significant or prolonged declines must be assessed in the functional currency of the entity holding the instrument because that is how any impairment loss is determined – i.e. it is inappropriate to make the assessment in the foreign currency in which the equity investment is denominated.

  The Interpretations Committee was asked whether an impairment assessment made by a subsidiary in its functional currency should be reassessed when the financial statements of the subsidiary are translated to another currency (which could result in the reversal of an impairment recognised at the subsidiary level or *vice versa*). However, such a reassessment would not comply with the general requirements of IAS 21 – *The Effects of Changes in Foreign Exchange Rates*.[28]

The matters above are examples only and they are unlikely to be an exhaustive list of all the inconsistencies in the way the standard is applied that might exist in practice.

The determination of what constitutes a significant or prolonged decline is a matter of fact that requires the application of judgement. This is true even though an entity may develop internal guidance to assist it in applying that judgement consistently.[29] In fact more than one judgement may be necessary. For example, an entity may decide which criteria it uses to categorise investments by similar risk profiles, e.g. by geography, industry or price volatility. An entity may then decide which criteria are relevant for each category of investments to identify individual equity investments that require further analysis, e.g. any quantitative thresholds of percentage or duration of decline. These criteria should then be applied consistently in order to conclude whether or not the decline in fair value is significant or prolonged.[30]

Each equity investment is unique and should be evaluated individually. Accordingly the use only of 'bright line' tests is inappropriate. However, in our view, a decline of less than 10% would not normally be considered significant but, depending on the circumstances, it could be difficult to argue that a decline of more than 20% is not significant (although for a less liquid investment that has historically been particularly volatile, it may be possible to make a case for a larger decline, say 30%, not being significant). Similarly, whilst a decline that had persisted for less than six months would not normally be considered prolonged, we consider that a decline that had persisted for more than twelve months would typically be seen as prolonged.

When impairments of available-for-sale equity investments are material or potentially material it is appropriate to explain the judgements made in determining the existence of objective evidence and the amounts of impairment (see Chapter 3 at 5.1.1.B and Chapter 53 at 4.1).[31] Allianz provides the following disclosure indicating the quantitative thresholds it uses.

Extract 48.2: Allianz SE (2014)

Notes to the Consolidated Financial Statements [extract]
2.   Summary of significant accounting policies [extract]
Impairments of available-for-sale and held-to-maturity investments as well as loans and advances to banks and customers [extract]

An available-for-sale equity security is considered to be impaired if there is objective evidence that the cost may not be recovered. Objective evidence that the cost may not be recovered, in addition to qualitative impairment criteria, includes a significant or prolonged decline in the fair value below cost. The Allianz Group's policy considers a decline to be significant if the fair value is below the weighted average cost by more than 20%. A decline is considered to be prolonged if the fair value is below the weighted average cost for a period of more than nine months. If an available-for-sale equity security is impaired, any further declines in the fair value at subsequent reporting dates are recognized as impairments. Therefore, at each reporting period, for an equity security that was determined to be impaired, additional impairments are recognized for the difference between the fair value and the original cost basis, less any previously recognized impairment. Reversals of impairments of available-for-sale equity securities are not recorded through the income statement but recycled out of other comprehensive income when sold.

4.2 Financial assets carried at amortised cost

4.2.1 Individual and collective assessments

The standard requires that impairment assessments should be performed as follows:

- for assets that are individually significant, assessment should be made on an individual basis;
- other assets may also be assessed individually, although such an assessment is not necessarily required;
- assets that have been individually assessed, but for which there is no objective evidence of impairment, should be included within a group of assets with similar credit risk characteristics and collectively assessed for impairment;
- assets that are individually assessed for impairment and for which an impairment loss is (or continues to be) recognised cannot be subject to a collective impairment assessment; and
- any other assets, i.e. those that have not been individually assessed, should also be the subject of a collective assessment. *[IAS 39.64]*.

The above requirements might be read as allowing an asset that is not individually significant, but known to be impaired, to be included in a collective assessment thereby avoiding the recognition of a loss if, say, the fair value of other assets in the group exceed their amortised cost. However, the implementation guidance clearly states that if an entity knows that an individual financial asset carried at amortised cost is impaired, the impairment loss should be recognised. *[IAS 39.E.4.7]*.

The ability to include individual assets that have been reviewed for impairment in a collective assessment is a controversial one and two IASB members cited this as a reason for them voting against publication of the standard. *[IAS 39.DO2, DO4, DO7]*. The Basis for Conclusions contains an extensive discussion of the arguments for and against the proposal *[IAS 39.BC108, BC121]* but it is essentially a question of whether or not one believes a loan can actually be impaired even if a review has not identified it as such.

If, in performing an individual review, the lender had access to all relevant information about the loan and the borrower, it might seem quite reasonable to conclude that there is no need to perform an additional collective review. However, in practice, not all information is going to be readily available on a timely basis, and any individual assessment is likely to be incomplete. Therefore, in our view, it is entirely appropriate to require an additional collective review.

4.2.2 Measurement – general requirements

If there is objective evidence that an impairment loss has been incurred on loans and receivables or held-to-maturity investments, that loss should be measured as the difference between the asset's carrying amount and the present value of estimated future cash flows. Those cash flows, which should exclude future credit losses that have not been incurred, should be discounted at the original effective interest rate of the financial asset, i.e. the effective interest rate computed at initial recognition. *[IAS 39.63]*. The original effective interest rate is used because discounting at the

Chapter 48

current market interest rate would, in effect, impose fair-value measurement on assets that would otherwise be measured at amortised cost. *[IAS 39.AG84]*.

The standard allows the carrying amount of an impaired asset to be reduced, either directly or through use of an allowance account, but emphasises that the loss should always be recognised in profit or loss. *[IAS 39.63]*.

If the terms of an instrument are renegotiated or otherwise modified because of the borrower's financial difficulties and assuming this is not regarded as an event that leads to derecognition of the original asset (see Chapter 50 at 3.4), impairment should be measured using the original effective interest rate. For variable rate assets, the discount rate for measuring the impairment loss is the current effective interest rate(s) determined under the contract. As a practical expedient, impairment may be measured based on an instrument's fair value using an observable market price. *[IAS 39.AG84]*. In the original standard, this concession was allowed only for floating rate assets,[32] but it may now be used for fixed rate assets too. There is little conceptual merit in this, but it aligns IAS 39 more closely with US GAAP. *[IAS 39.BC221(f)]*. If an entity applies this practical expedient, then the IFRS 13 fair value measurement and disclosure requirements would apply.

The implementation guidance makes it clear that recognition of impairment losses in excess of those that are determined based on objective evidence (either at an individual asset or collective group level) is not permitted. *[IAS 39.E.4.6]*.

These basic principles are illustrated in the following example.

Example 48.18:   Impairment – changes in amount or timing of payments

A bank is concerned that, because of financial difficulties, five customers, Companies A to E, will not be able to make all principal and interest payments due on originated loans in a timely manner. It negotiates a restructuring of the loans and expects the customers will meet their restructured obligations. The restructured terms are as follows:

- A will pay the full principal amount of the original loan five years after the original due date, but none of the interest due under the original terms;

- B will pay the full principal amount of the original loan on the original due date, but none of the interest due under the original terms;

- C will pay the full principal amount of the original loan on the original due date but with interest at a lower interest rate than the interest rate inherent in the original loan;

- D will pay the full principal amount of the original loan five years after the original due date and all interest accrued during the original loan term, but no interest for the extended term; and

- E will pay the full principal amount of the original loan five years after the original due date and all interest, including interest on all outstanding amounts for both the original term of the loan and the extended term.

An impairment loss has been incurred if there is objective evidence of impairment – this is assumed to be the case here because of the customers' financial difficulties. The amount of the impairment loss for a loan measured at amortised cost is the difference between the loan's carrying amount and the present value of future principal and interest payments, discounted at the loan's original effective interest rate.

For A to D, the present value of the future principal and interest payments discounted at the loan's original effective interest rate will be lower than the carrying amount of the loan. Therefore an impairment loss is recognised in those cases. For E, even though the timing of payments has changed, the bank will receive interest on interest, so that the present value of the future principal and interest payments, discounted at the loan's original effective interest rate, will equal the carrying amount of the loan. Therefore, there is no impairment loss. However, this fact pattern is unlikely given Company E's financial difficulties. *[IAS 39.E.4.3]*.

Accounting for and disclosure of banks' forbearance practices has become a common area of scrutiny by financial reporting regulators in the wake of the financial crisis. Please refer to Chapter 53 at 5.2.2.C for more details.

Consistent with the initial measurement requirements, cash flows relating to short-term receivables are not discounted if the effect of discounting is immaterial. *[IAS 39.AG84]*. This does not mean that such instruments are not, as a matter of principle, discounted, as illustrated in the following example.

Example 48.19:   Impairment of short-term receivable

A construction company, K, agrees to build a new stadium for a professional football club, L. The project takes approximately six months and payment of €10 million is due six weeks after completion. On completion, K has recognised revenue and a corresponding receivable of €10 million because the effect of discounting at the current annualised rate of 5% is immaterial.

Shortly after completion, it becomes apparent that L is in financial difficulties and is unlikely to be able to settle the €10 million debt. In order to avoid formal insolvency proceedings, L attempts to restructure its financial obligations and offers to pay K €1 million per year for the next 10 years. Because it believes this arrangement appears to offer the best prospects for the recovery of its debt, K accepts.

On the face of it (and assuming no defaults on the rescheduled debt are expected), it might be argued that K need not recognise an impairment loss because it will receive all of the money owed and the debt's original effective interest rate was 0%. However, the original receivable was, in principle, discounted – it is just that the effects of discounting were not reflected in the financial statements as they were not material. Therefore, the effect of discounting the rescheduled payments at 5% per annum (approximately €2.28 million) should be recognised as an impairment loss.

It is common practice for commercial companies to determine bad debt provisions on accounts receivable using a provisioning matrix or similar formula based on the number of days a loan or debt is overdue, e.g. 0% if less than 90 days, 20% if 90 to 180 days, 50% if 180 to 365 days and 100% if more than 365 days overdue. This will be acceptable only if the formula can be demonstrated to produce an estimate sufficiently close to one determined under the methodology specified in IAS 39. *[IAS 39.E.4.5]*.

In measuring the impairment of a collateralised or secured loan, the cash flows used should reflect those that may result from foreclosure less costs for obtaining and selling the collateral, whether or not foreclosure is probable. *[IAS 39.AG84]*. The collateral itself should not be recognised as a separate asset unless it meets the recognition criteria for an asset in another standard. *[IAS 39.E.4.8]*.

To a lender, guarantees provided by a third (sometimes related) party such as a parent, other shareholder or fellow subsidiary, are little different to collateral – they provide a source of funds in the event that the debtor defaults. In the original implementation guidance it was made clear that guarantees should be taken into account in determining the amount of an impairment loss.[33]

Chapter 48

The guarantee is clearly a financial instrument (see Chapter 42 at 2.2.3). Based on the analysis in Chapter 43 at 8, it will normally be considered a separate financial instrument, even if it cannot be transferred independently from the loan. This is because there will almost certainly be a substantive business purpose for structuring the arrangement in this way, i.e. to reduce the lender's exposure to default. The guarantee is likely to satisfy the definition of an insurance contract in IFRS 4 – *Insurance Contracts* – but will be excluded from the scope of that standard because it is a direct insurance contract held by the insured (who is not a cedant). *[IFRS 4.4(f)].* (A cedant is an insurer that is the policyholder under a reinsurance contract.) If the guarantee satisfies the definition of an insurance contract in IFRS 4 it is outside the scope of IAS 39 *[IAS 39.2(e)]* irrespective of whether it is within the scope of IFRS 4 (see Chapter 42 at 3.3 and 3.4). Therefore it is hard to avoid the conclusion that the guarantee is a contingent asset within the scope of IAS 37 because it is not 'covered' by another standard *[IAS 37.1(c), 37.5(e)]* (see Chapter 27 at 2.2.1.B).

What this means is that the guarantee can only be recognised as an asset when it is 'virtually certain' that a recovery will be made. In conceptual terms this seems a more onerous test than that for recognising an impairment loss on the associated loan asset. Therefore, it might seem necessary to recognise an impairment loss on the asset (that would be fully recovered under the guarantee) but without being able to recognise an offsetting recovery from the guarantee.

There is more than one counter-argument to this analysis. For example, it might be considered that the guarantee and the loan should be accounted for as a single 'synthetic' instrument, irrespective of what is said in Chapter 43 at 8, especially where the two parties are related. A degree of support for this treatment can be found in the Basis for Conclusions on IAS 39 where it is stated that 'the fair value of liabilities ... guaranteed by third parties ... is generally unaffected by changes in the entity's creditworthiness'. *[IAS 39.BC92].* This suggests that the IASB considers a third party guarantee of a borrowing to be an integral part of the borrowing arrangement rather than a separate instrument. Further, where the guarantor is a member of the same group as the borrower, IAS 32 – *Financial Instruments: Presentation* – requires both elements of the transaction to be considered together when determining the appropriate classification of the instrument from the point of view of the group's consolidated financial statements (see Chapter 44 at 4.8).

Even if it is considered that IAS 37 should apply to the guarantee, some might argue that it is more appropriate to characterise it as a 'reimbursement' in respect of the impairment loss, rather than as a standalone contingent asset. As set out in Chapter 27 at 4.5, a reimbursement is recognised as an asset when it is virtually certain that the reimbursement will be received if the obligation for which a provision has been established is settled. By analogy, therefore, the guarantee would be recognised as an asset to the extent it is virtually certain a recovery could be made if the lender suffered the impairment loss on the loan.

Finally, IFRS 4 explains that the holder of a financial guarantee contract will normally need to develop its accounting policy in accordance with the 'hierarchy' in IAS 8 – *Accounting Policies, Changes in Accounting Estimates and Errors* (see

Chapter 42 at 3.4.3 and Chapter 3 at 4.3) *[IFRS 4.IG2, Example 1.11]* suggesting an entity does not automatically apply IAS 37.

4.2.3 Measurement – detailed requirements

The standard contains a significant amount of detailed application guidance on the processes to be used for the assessment and calculation of impairment losses within groups of financial assets carried at amortised cost. In practice, this will be of limited relevance to entities that are determining a bad debt provision in respect of a portfolio of short-term trade receivables. However, for banks and other financial institutions with significant portfolios of loans and receivables, these detailed requirements will be highly relevant and could have a major impact on the way that loan impairments are assessed. This guidance might also be more relevant for entities providing goods or services on deferred settlement terms, such as retailers operating their own store-cards.

The guidance explains that the process for estimating impairment should consider all credit exposures, not only those of low credit quality. For example, if an internal credit grading system is used, all credit grades should be considered, not only those reflecting severe credit deterioration. *[IAS 39.AG85]*. In other words, the possibility of impairment existing in a portfolio of high quality assets that contain a low risk of default should not be ignored.

Whatever process is used to estimate an impairment loss, it may produce either a single amount or a range of possible amounts. In the latter case, the best estimate within the range should be recognised as the impairment loss. This estimate should take into account all relevant information about known conditions that existed at the end of the reporting period. The standard cross-refers to IAS 37 for guidance on selecting the best estimate in a range of possible outcomes (see Chapter 27 at 4.1). *[IAS 39.AG86]*.

When performing a collective evaluation of impairment, assets should be grouped on the basis of similar credit risk characteristics that are indicative of the debtors' ability to settle according to the contractual terms of the instruments concerned. For example, this may be done on the basis of a credit risk evaluation or grading process that considers some or all of the following characteristics depending on their relevance: asset type, industry, geographical location, collateral type, past-due status as well as other factors. *[IAS 39.AG87]*.

It is stated that loss probabilities and other loss statistics differ at a group level between (a) assets that have been individually evaluated for impairment and found not to be impaired, and (b) assets that have not been individually evaluated for impairment, with the result that a different amount of impairment may be required. *[IAS 39.AG87]*. In practice, the extent of the difference in approach to these groups will depend on the quality of the individual assessments – i.e. the less detailed or accurate the individual assessment is, the less the loss probabilities for assets in (a) and in (b) should differ.

Further, it is explained that if an entity does not have a group of assets with similar risk characteristics, it should not make any additional assessment over and above that performed at an individual level. *[IAS 39.AG87]*. It is this situation that the two dissenting IASB members found hard to accept. If one entity owned 50% of a loan asset for which there was no evidence of impairment when assessed on an individual basis, but it owned no similar assets, then it would recognise no impairment loss. However, if another entity owned the other 50% of the loan asset and also owned a number of similar assets, that entity may end up recognising an impairment loss in respect of its identical asset. *[IAS 39.DO4].*

This anomaly may be rationalised in a number of ways. For example, if a company owned only one significant asset, rather than a group of similar assets, it is quite likely to assess impairment of that asset in a more detailed manner than a company with a group of similar assets. Also, this situation is not dissimilar to the treatment of warranty claims under IAS 37 (at least the current version of that standard). If there was a small probability, say 1%, of a warranty claim arising on each sale made, a company that had sold one unit would not normally recognise a provision. However, a company that had sold thousands of identical units would almost certainly recognise a provision.

It is explained that impairment losses recognised on a group basis represent an interim step pending the identification of impairment losses on individual assets in the group. Accordingly, as soon as information is available that specifically identifies losses on individually impaired assets, those assets should be removed from the group. *[IAS 39.AG88].*

Estimates of future cash flows for a group of financial assets should be based on historical loss experience for assets with credit risk characteristics similar to those in the group. Entities that have no, or insufficient, entity-specific loss experience, should use peer group experience for comparable groups of assets. Historical loss experience should be adjusted on the basis of current observable data to reflect the effects of current conditions that did not affect the period on which the historical loss experience is based, and to remove the effects of conditions in the historical period that do not exist currently. Estimates of changes in future cash flows should reflect, and be directionally consistent with, changes in related observable data from period to period (such as changes in unemployment rates, property prices, commodity prices, payment status or other factors that are indicative of incurred losses in the group and their magnitude). The methodology and assumptions used for estimating future cash flows should be reviewed regularly to reduce any differences between loss estimates and actual loss experience. *[IAS 39.AG89].*

As an example of this approach, historical experience may demonstrate that one of the main causes of default on credit card loans is the death of the borrower. Although the death rate may be unchanged since the previous year, some of the group of borrowers could have died in the year. This would indicate that an impairment loss has occurred, even if it was not possible to identify which specific borrowers had died at the year-end, and it would be appropriate for an impairment loss to be recognised for these 'incurred but not reported' losses. However, it would not be appropriate to recognise an impairment loss for deaths that are expected to occur in a future period. In that case the necessary loss event (the death of the borrower) has not yet occurred. *[IAS 39.AG90].*

When using historical loss rates in estimating future cash flows, it is important that information about historical loss rates is applied to groups that are defined in a manner consistent with the groups for which the historical loss rates were observed. Therefore, the method used should enable each group to be associated with information about past loss experience in groups of assets with similar credit risk characteristics and relevant observable data that reflect current conditions. *[IAS 39.AG91].*

Formula-based approaches or statistical methods may be used to determine impairment losses in a group of financial assets (e.g. for smaller balance loans) as long as they are consistent with the general requirements of the standard. Therefore any model used should incorporate the effect of the time value of money, consider the cash flows for all of the remaining life of an asset (not only the next year), consider the age of the loans within the portfolio and not give rise to an impairment loss on initial recognition. *[IAS 39.AG92].*

Sometimes, the observable data required to estimate an impairment loss may be limited or no longer fully relevant to current circumstances, for example when a borrower is in financial difficulties and there are few available historical data relating to similar borrowers. In such cases, judgement and experience should be used to estimate the amount of any impairment loss and to adjust observable data for a group of financial assets to reflect current circumstances. The fact that an impairment loss is difficult to measure is not a reason for not recognising a loss that has been incurred. The use of reasonable estimates is an essential part of the preparation of financial statements and does not undermine their reliability. *[IAS 39.62].*

4.2.4 Impairment of assets subject to hedges

When a loan asset with fixed interest rate payments is hedged against the exposure to interest rate risk by a receive-variable, pay-fixed interest rate swap, the carrying amount of the asset will include an adjustment for fair value changes attributable to movements in interest rates (see Chapter 51 at 4.1). As a result, in accounting for the asset, the original effective interest rate and amortised cost of the asset are adjusted to take into account these recognised fair value changes and the adjusted effective interest rate is calculated using the adjusted carrying amount of the asset. *[IAS 39.E.4.4].*

Any impairment loss on such a hedged asset should be calculated after taking account of the adjustments noted above. In other words, it will be the difference between the carrying amount of the asset *after* adjustment for fair value changes attributable to the risk being hedged and the expected future cash flows of the loan discounted at the *adjusted* effective interest rate. *[IAS 39.E.4.4].*

When a loan is included in a portfolio hedge of interest rate risk (see Chapter 51 at 6) the change in the fair value of the hedged portfolio should be allocated to the loans (or groups of similar loans) being assessed for impairment on a systematic and rational basis. *[IAS 39.E.4.4].*

4.2.5   Reversal of impairment losses

If, in a subsequent period, the amount of the impairment or bad debt loss decreases and the decrease can be objectively related to an event occurring after the write-down (such as an improvement in the debtor's credit rating), the previously recognised impairment loss should be reversed, either directly or by adjusting an allowance account. The reversal should not result in a carrying amount of the asset that exceeds what its amortised cost would have been at the date of reversal, had the impairment not been recognised. The amount of the reversal should be recognised in profit or loss. *[IAS 39.65].*

4.3   Available-for-sale assets measured at fair value

4.3.1   Recognition of impairment

When a decline in the fair value of an available-for-sale asset has been recognised in other comprehensive income and there is objective evidence that the asset is impaired (see 4.1 above), the cumulative loss within equity should be reclassified to profit or loss even though the asset has not been derecognised. *[IAS 39.67].*

The amount of the loss that should be reclassified is the difference between the acquisition cost of the asset (net of any principal repayment and amortisation for assets measured using the effective interest method) and current fair value, less any impairment loss on that asset previously recognised in profit or loss. *[IAS 39.68].*

For debt instruments, this requirement is not uncontroversial. Unlike an impairment loss on an equivalent asset measured at amortised cost, the amount recognised in profit or loss is measured by reference to the fair value of the asset. This will include the effects of changes in interest rates and credit or liquidity spreads, whereas the impairment loss for, say, a loan or receivable, will reflect only the present value of the expected cash loss.

For non-monetary assets, such as equity instruments, the cumulative net loss included within equity will include any portion attributable to foreign currency changes. It follows that this element of the loss should also be reclassified to profit or loss if the asset becomes impaired. *[IAS 39.E.4.9].*

4.3.2   Impairment of available-for-sale equity instruments subject to fair value hedges

In assessing the impairment of available-for-sale equity instruments, IAS 39 requires an entity to use the 'cost' of the instrument as the basis to determine whether there has been a significant or prolonged decline in fair value. *[IAS 39.61].* Similarly, in recognising the impairment loss, the entity would reclassify the amount of the loss within equity to profit or loss based on the difference between the 'acquisition cost' and current fair value, less any amount already recognised in profit or loss (see 4.3.1 above). *[IAS 39.68].*

However, for an equity instrument that was previously subject to a fair value hedge and the hedge was subsequently terminated, it would make sense for the entity to adjust the 'cost' basis when assessing whether there has been a significant or prolonged decline in fair value. For example, an equity investment that was bought at a price of £100 and hedged for fair value decline to £80 (where the hedge was subsequently terminated), then the assessment of whether there is an impairment loss and subsequent calculation of that loss should be based on £80 rather than the original cost of £100.

The adjustment to the cost basis for impairment purposes is consistent with the guidance on assessing impairment for inventories and fixed interest rate loans subject to fair value hedges (see 4.2.4 above). *[IAS 39.E.4.4, F.3.6]*.

4.3.3 Reversals of impairment

If, in a subsequent period, the fair value of an available-for-sale *debt* instrument increases, and the increase can be objectively related to an event occurring after the loss was recognised in profit or loss, the impairment loss should be reversed and recognised in profit or loss. *[IAS 39.70]*. Judgement is required to determine whether a recovery in the fair value of an available-for-sale debt security relates to an event that occurred after the loss was recognised. Questions arise as to what to do when the fair value partially recovers or when there is evidence of an improvement in the credit quality of the debt instrument but the entity cannot determine that there is no longer any objective evidence of impairment. In these circumstances, we believe policy choices need to be made. This is illustrated in the following example:

Example 48.20: Increase in the fair value of an impaired available-for-sale debt investment

An entity purchased a debt instrument, which it designated as available-for-sale with a cost of £100. In year two, the fair value of the instrument decreased to £70 and the entity concluded that the instrument was impaired and consequently recognised an impairment loss of £30. In year three, the fair value of the instrument increases to £95.

Scenario 1 – The entity can determine that there is no longer any objective evidence of impairment. That is, the credit event triggering the impairment reverses in its entirety.

Scenario 2 – The entity cannot determine that there is no longer any objective evidence of impairment (that is, the credit event triggering the impairment did not entirely reverse) however, it can determine that the credit quality of the instrument improved compared to the situation when the instrument was impaired.

In both scenarios, the entity might have reversed a small part of the impairment loss through the application of the higher effective interest rate determined at the time the instrument was impaired. This effect is ignored in the conclusion below.

An entity can only reverse through profit or loss an increase in the fair value of an available-for-sale debt instrument that occurs subsequent to impairment if there is an actual improvement in the credit quality of the instrument. If there is no improvement in the credit quality, the entity recognises the increase in fair value in other comprehensive income (OCI). Judgement is required to determine whether the credit event triggering the impairment reversed in its entirety (i.e. there is no longer any objective evidence of impairment) or whether there is only some improvement in credit quality.

Scenario 1 – If there is no longer objective evidence of impairment, such that the event reversed in its entirety, we believe the entity has an accounting policy choice, which it must apply consistently:

The entity can recognise in profit or loss a reversal of impairment of £30 and recognise a loss of £5 in OCI or it can recognise in profit or loss a reversal of impairment of £25.

Scenario 2 – If there is some evidence of improvement in credit quality, but the credit event did not reverse, the entity has an accounting policy choice, which it must apply consistently:

The entity can recognise in profit or loss a reversal of impairment of £25. Alternatively, the entity could choose not to recognise any reversal of impairment in profit or loss, until the event reverses in its entirety. Therefore, the entity recognises an increase in fair value in OCI (of £25).

However, in the case of *equity* instruments, impairments cannot be reversed through profit or loss. *[IAS 39.69]*.

The Basis for Conclusions includes an explanation for the difference in treatment. In particular, in the context of the reversal of impairments on available-for-sale debt securities, it is noted that:

- the reversal of impairment losses of non-financial assets (e.g. inventories, property, plant and equipment and intangible assets) is required if circumstances change;

- the treatment provides consistency with the requirement to reverse impairment losses on loans and receivables and on assets classified as held-to-maturity; and

- determining an increase in fair value attributable to an improvement in credit standing is more objectively determinable than for equity instruments. *[IAS 39.BC128].*

The IASB could not find an acceptable way to distinguish reversals of impairment losses from other increases in fair value of available-for-sale equity instruments. Therefore, it decided that precluding such reversals for equity instruments was the only appropriate solution, even though a number of other approaches were considered. *[IAS 39.BC130].* In the end, this approach probably seemed most expedient as it is comparable to US GAAP under which reversals of impairment losses on equity instruments are not permitted. *[IAS 39.BC221(g)].* One IASB member formally disagreed with the approach adopted, not because he considered it appropriate to reverse an impairment loss but because he would have preferred all losses below original cost on equity instruments to be recognised as impairments, *[IAS 39.DO13],* i.e. in profit or loss.

4.3.4   Further declines in the fair value of impaired equity instruments

The question has arisen as to what the accounting treatment should be if, following an impairment, the fair value of an available-for-sale equity instrument declines further. This is illustrated in the following example.

Example 48.21:   Decline in the fair value of an impaired available-for-sale equity investment

Company A acquired 100 shares in Company X on 1 January 2015, for their fair value of €10,000. On 31 December 2015, A's year end, the fair value of the shares in X had fallen to €6,000 and A concluded the shares were impaired. Accordingly, in its 2015 financial statements, A recognised an impairment loss of €4,000 in profit or loss.

On 31 December 2016, the fair value of the shares in X had fallen a little further to €5,900. In its 2016 financial statements, should A automatically regard the loss of €100 as a further impairment (to be recognised in profit or loss) or should it regard it as a normal revaluation to be recognised in other comprehensive income?

The implementation guidance to the standard suggests that any further declines in the fair value of an impaired available-for-sale equity instrument should be recognised in profit or loss, although only in the context of explaining the treatment of portions of fair value movements arising from foreign currency changes. *[IAS 39.E.4.9].*

However, perhaps because the accounting treatment is said to be comparable to US GAAP (see 4.3.3 above), some considered that, once impaired, the asset acquired a new 'cost base' equal to the fair value at the date of impairment. Consequently, the €100 decline in fair value would be assessed for impairment as if the asset had been acquired on 31 December 2015 for €6,000. This approach would not necessarily result in the €100 being characterised as an impairment loss.

The Interpretations Committee has addressed this issue and took the view that impairments do not establish a new cost basis. Therefore, for an equity instrument for which a prior impairment loss has been recognised, in applying the indicators discussed at 4.1 above, 'significant' should be evaluated against the original cost at initial recognition and 'prolonged' should be evaluated against the period in which the fair value of the investment has been below original cost at initial recognition.[34] Consequently, any further decline in fair value, whatever its cause, should be recognised in profit or loss. Extract 48.2 at 4.1.3 above (Allianz) contains an accounting policy that explicitly addresses this requirement.

4.3.5 Timing of impairment tests and interaction with interim reporting

The standard does not discuss how frequently an available-for-sale equity instrument should be assessed for impairment, only that it should be done 'at the end of each reporting period'. *[IAS 39.58].* It might seem sensible to perform such reviews at the end of both interim and annual periods. However, this could give rise to what some see as anomalous results.

Consider, for example, an entity that purchases an equity share for €100 at the start of its reporting period. If the fair value of the share had fallen to €60 at the end of the half-year, it is very likely to conclude that the share had become impaired. Consequently, a €40 loss would be recognised in profit or loss. However, if the share price had recovered to €100 by the end of the full financial year, should this loss be reversed? IAS 34 – *Interim Financial Reporting* – states that '… the frequency of an entity's reporting (annual, half-yearly, or quarterly) shall not affect the measurement of its annual results.' *[IAS 34.28].* This might suggest that the impairment loss recognised at the half-year could be reversed at the year-end.

On the other hand, the guidance that accompanies IAS 34 states that the same impairment testing, recognition, and reversal criteria that would be applied at the year-end should be applied at an interim date. *[IAS 34.B36].* Further, the accounting requirements of IAS 39 are generally applied on a continuous basis and it might be argued that ignoring losses between the end of reporting periods (whatever their frequency) fails to apply properly the requirements of the standard.

This is an issue that has reached the Interpretations Committee's agenda. Early on in their deliberations it was made clear that the Interpretations Committee did not support an approach that would require entities to review for impairment on a continuous basis, leaving the apparent conflicts within IAS 34 and between IAS 34 and IAS 39 to be dealt with.[35]

In July 2006, the Interpretations Committee published an interpretation, IFRIC 10 – *Interim Financial Reporting and Impairment* – setting out how to resolve the conflicts. The Interpretations Committee took the view that the more specific requirements in IAS 39 should take precedence and, therefore, that impairments of available-for-sale equity instruments recognised in an interim period should not be reversed. *[IFRIC 10.8, BC9].* IFRIC 10 also deals with a similar conflict in the treatment of goodwill impairments but it contains a prohibition on extending by analogy its consensus to other areas of potential conflict between IAS 34 and other standards. *[IFRIC 10.9].*

Chapter 48

4.4   Financial assets carried at cost in accordance with IAS 39

As set out at 2.1 and 2.4 above, unquoted equity instruments and derivative assets that are linked to and must be settled by delivery of such instruments whose fair value cannot be reliably measured, are measured at cost.

If there is objective evidence that an impairment loss has been incurred on such an asset, the amount of the impairment loss is measured as the difference between the carrying amount of the financial asset and the present value of estimated future cash flows, discounted at the current market rate of return for a similar financial asset. *[IAS 39.66].* This requirement applies equally to financial assets classified as at fair value through profit or loss and to available-for-sale financial assets.

Consistent with the treatment for available-for-sale equity securities measured at fair value, any such impairment losses may not be reversed. *[IAS 39.66].* The requirements of IFRIC 10 apply to these assets as well as to available-for-sale assets measured at fair value. *[IFRIC 10.6].*

4.5   Interest income after impairment recognition

Once a financial asset, or group of similar assets, has been written down as a result of an impairment loss, interest income is thereafter recognised based on the rate of interest that was used to discount the future cash flows for the purpose of measuring the impairment loss. *[IAS 39.AG93].*

It is not clear how this requirement should be applied to a fixed interest rate debt instrument that is measured at amortised cost and has been written down to its fair value (rather than its net present value using the original effective interest rate of the instrument – see 4.2.2 above). Using an appropriate long-term interest rate at the date of the impairment would seem consistent with the measurement basis adopted, although this is not strictly in accordance with the standard.

5   FOREIGN CURRENCIES

5.1   Foreign currency instruments

The provisions of IAS 21 apply to transactions involving financial instruments in just the same way as they do for other transactions, although the manner in which certain hedges are accounted for can over-ride its general requirements.

Consequently, the statement of financial position measurement of a foreign currency financial instrument is determined as follows:

- firstly, it is recorded and measured in the foreign currency in which it is denominated, whether it is carried at fair value, cost, or amortised cost;
- secondly, that amount is retranslated to the entity's functional currency using:
  - closing rate, for all monetary items (e.g. a debt security) and for non-monetary items (e.g. an equity share) carried at fair value; or
  - a historical rate, for non-monetary items carried at cost because their fair value cannot be reliably measured.

Therefore, for a foreign currency denominated monetary asset carried at amortised cost, amortised cost is calculated in the currency in which it is denominated. That foreign currency amount is then retranslated into the entity's functional currency at the closing rate.

As an exception, if the non-monetary financial instrument carried at cost (for example, unquoted equity instruments) is designated as a hedged item in a fair value hedge of foreign currency exposure, it is remeasured for changes in foreign currency rates even if it would otherwise have been recognised using a historical rate (see Chapter 51 at 4.1).

The reporting of changes in the carrying amount of a financial instrument in profit or loss or in other comprehensive income depends on a number of factors, including whether it is an exchange difference or other change in carrying amount, whether the instrument is a monetary or non-monetary item and whether it is designated as part of a foreign currency cash flow hedge or hedge of a net investment.

Profit and loss items associated with financial instruments, e.g. dividends receivable, interest payable or receivable and impairments, are recorded at the spot rate ruling when they arise (although average rates may be used when they represent an appropriate approximation to spot rates throughout the period). Exchange differences arising on retranslating monetary items are generally recognised in profit or loss, although they may be recognised in other comprehensive income for instruments designated as hedges of future foreign currency transactions or net investments in foreign entities (see Chapter 51 at 4.2 and 4.3). All other fair value changes (e.g. the change in value of a debt instrument as a result of interest rate movements) are recognised in profit or loss if the instrument is classified at fair value through profit or loss, or other comprehensive income if it is available-for-sale.

In cases where some portion of the change in carrying amount is recognised in profit or loss and some in other comprehensive income, e.g. if the fair value of a bond has increased in foreign currency and decreased in the functional currency, those two components cannot be offset for the purposes of determining gains or losses that should be recognised in profit or loss and other comprehensive income. [IAS 39.AG83, E.3.4].

These principles are illustrated in the following example.

Example 48.22: Available-for-sale foreign currency debt security

On 31 December 2015, Company A, whose functional currency is the euro, acquires a dollar bond for its fair value of $1,000. The bond is the same as the one in Example 48.6 at 3.1 above, i.e. it has five years to maturity and a $1,250 principal, carries fixed interest of 4.7% paid annually ($1,250 × 4.7% = $59 per year), and has an effective interest rate of 10%.

A classifies the bond as available-for-sale. The exchange rate is $1 to €1.50 and the carrying amount of the bond is €1,500 ($1,000 × 1.50).

	€	€
Bond	1,500	
Cash		1,500

On 31 December 2016, the dollar has appreciated and the exchange rate is $1 to €2.00. The fair value of the bond is $1,060 and therefore its carrying amount is €2,120 ($1,060 × 2.00). Its amortised

cost is $1,041 (or €2,082 = $1,041 × 2.00) and the cumulative gain or loss to be included in other comprehensive income is the difference between its fair value and amortised cost, i.e. a gain of €38 (€2,120 – €2,082; or, alternatively, [$1,060 – $1,041] × 2.00).

Interest received on the bond on 31 December 2016 is $59 (or €118 = $59 × 2.00). Interest income determined in accordance with the effective interest method is $100 ($1,000 × 10%) of which $41 ($100 – $59) is the accretion of the initial discount.

It is assumed that the average exchange rate during the year is $1 to €1.75 and that the use of an average exchange rate provides a reliable approximation of the spot rates applicable to the accrual of interest during the year. Therefore, reported interest income is €175 ($100 × 1.75) including accretion of the initial discount of €72 (€41 × 1.75).

The exchange difference recognised in profit or loss is €525, which comprises three elements: a €500 gain from the retranslation of the initial amortised cost ($1,000 × [2.00 – 1.50]); a €15 gain from the retranslation of interest income received ($59 × [2.00 – 1.75]) and a €10 gain on the retranslation of the interest income accreted ($41 × [2.00 – 1.75]).

	€	€
Bond	620	
Cash	118	
Interest income (P&L)		175
Exchange gain (P&L)		525
Fair value change (equity)		38

On 31 December 2017, the dollar has appreciated further and the exchange rate is $1 to €2.50. The fair value of the bond is $1,070 and therefore its carrying amount is €2,675 ($1,070 × 2.50). Its amortised cost is $1,086 (or €2,715 = $1,086 × 2.50) and the cumulative gain or loss to be included in other comprehensive income is the difference between its fair value and the amortised cost, i.e. a loss of €40 (€2,675 – €2,715; or, alternatively, [$1,070 – $1,086] × 2.50). Therefore, there is a debit to other comprehensive income equal to the change in the difference during 2017 of €78 (€40 + €38).

Interest received on the bond on 31 December 2017 is $59 (or €148 = $59 × 2.50). Interest income determined in accordance with the effective interest method is $104 ($1,041 × 10%), of which $45 ($104 – $59) is the accretion of the initial discount.

Using the same assumptions as in the previous year, interest income is €234 ($104 × 2.25) including accretion of the initial discount of €101 ($45 × 2.25).

The exchange difference recognised in profit or loss is €547, which again comprises three elements: a €521 gain from the retranslation of the opening amortised cost ($1,041 × [2.50 – 2.00]); a €15 gain from the retranslation of interest income received ($59 × [2.50 – 2.25]) and an €11 gain on the retranslation of the interest income accreted ($45 × [2.50 – 2.25]). [IAS 39.E.3.2].

	€	€
Bond	555	
Cash	148	
Fair value change (equity)	78	
Interest income (P&L)		234
Exchange gain (P&L)		547

It is worth repeating that the treatment would be different for available-for-sale equity instruments. Under IAS 21, these are not considered monetary items and exchange differences would form part of the change in the fair value of the instrument, which would be recognised in other comprehensive income.

5.2 Foreign entities

IAS 39 does not amend application of the net investment method of accounting for foreign entities set out in IAS 21 (see Chapter 15 at 6). Therefore, for the purpose of preparing its own accounts for inclusion in consolidated accounts, a foreign entity that is part of a group applies the principles at 5.1 above by reference to its own functional currency. Consequently, the treatment of gains and losses on, say, trading assets held by a foreign entity should follow the treatment in the example below.

Example 48.23: Interaction of IAS 21 and IAS 39 – foreign currency debt investment

Company A is domiciled in the US and its functional currency and presentation currency is the US dollar. A has a UK domiciled subsidiary, B, whose functional currency is sterling. B is the owner of a debt instrument which is held for trading and is therefore carried at fair value.

In B's financial statements for 2015, the fair value and carrying amount of the debt instrument is £100. In A's consolidated financial statements, the asset is translated into US dollars at the spot exchange rate applicable at the end of the reporting period, say 2.0, and the carrying amount is US$200 (£100 × 2.0).

At the end of 2016, the fair value of the debt instrument has increased to £110. B reports the trading asset at £110 in its statement of financial position and recognises a fair value gain of £10 in profit or loss. During the year, the spot exchange rate has increased from 2.0 to 3.0 resulting in an increase in the fair value of the instrument from US$200 to US$330 (£110 × 3.0). Therefore, A reports the trading asset at US$330 in its consolidated financial statements.

Since B is classified as a foreign entity, A translates B's statement of comprehensive income 'at the exchange rates at the dates of the transactions'. Since the fair value gain has accrued through the year, A uses the average rate of 2.5 (= [3.0 + 2.0] ÷ 2) as a practical approximation. Therefore, while the fair value of the trading asset has increased by US$130 (US$330 − US$200), A recognises only US$25 (£10 × 2.5) of this increase in profit or loss. The resulting exchange difference, i.e. the remaining increase in the fair value of the debt instrument of US$105 (US$130 − US$25), is recognised in other comprehensive income until the disposal of the net investment in the foreign entity. *[IAS 39.E.3.3]*.

References

1 *IAS 39.70 (2000)*.
2 *IGC Q&A 70-1*.
3 *IFRIC Update*, November 2006.
4 The implementation guidance says the entire combined contract should be treated as held for trading (not designated at fair value through profit or loss). This reflects an earlier version of IAS 39 as the implementation guidance was not updated to reflect a subsequent amendment.
5 *Exposure Draft, Proposed Amendments to IAS 39 and IFRS 4, Financial Guarantee Contracts and Credit Insurance*, IASB, July 2004, BC18(a).
6 *ASC 944-20-15-69, Financial Guarantee Insurance Contracts*, FASB.

7 *IGC Q&A 73-1*.
8 *IGC Q&A 10-19*.
9 *Implementation of International Accounting Standards*, British Bankers' Association, July 2004, 10.
10 *IGC Q&A 76-1*.
11 Based on the example in IAS 39.B.25.
12 *IFRIC Update*, July 2008.
13 Information for Observers (May 2008 IFRIC meeting), *Application of the Effective Interest Rate Method*, IASB, May 2008, Appendix.
14 Information for Observers, 6.
15 *IFRIC Update*, July 2008.

Chapter 48

16 Information for Observers (July 2008 IFRIC meeting), *Application of the Effective Interest Rate Method*, IASB, July 2008, 4.

17 Position Paper, *IAS 39 – Financial Instruments: Recognition and Measurement – assets and liabilities linked to an inflation index which are not measured at fair value (continuation to the paper published in February 2008)*, Israel Accounting Standards Board, August 2008.

18 *IFRIC Update*, May 2009.

19 *IFRIC Update*, July 2008.

20 *IFRIC Update*, October 2004.

21 Staff Paper (May 2009 IFRIC Meeting), *IAS 39 Financial Instruments: Recognition and Measurement – Meaning of 'significant or prolonged' (Agenda reference 10)*, IASB, May 2009, 2 and 5.

22 *IASB Update*, July 2009.

23 *IFRIC Update*, July 2009.

24 Staff Paper (May 2009 IFRIC Meeting), 33.

25 Staff Paper (May 2009 IFRIC Meeting), 24.

26 Staff Paper (May 2009 IFRIC Meeting), 25.

27 Staff Paper (July 2009 IFRIC Meeting), *IAS 39 Financial Instruments: Recognition and Measurement – Meaning of 'significant or prolonged' (Agenda reference 21)*, IASB, July 2009, 15 to 18.

28 Staff Paper (July 2009 IFRIC Meeting), 19 to 28.

29 *IFRIC Update*, July 2009.

30 Staff Paper (July 2009 IFRIC Meeting), 11 to 14.

31 *IFRIC Update*, July 2009.

32 *IGC Q&A 113-3*.

33 *IGC Q&A 113-1*.

34 *IFRIC Update*, June 2005.

35 *IFRIC Update*, August 2005.

Chapter 49   Financial instruments: Subsequent measurement (IFRS 9)

Chapter 49

Chapter 49

List of examples

Chapter 49

Chapter 49   Financial instruments: Subsequent measurement (IFRS 9)

1   INTRODUCTION

The introduction to Chapter 41 provides a general background to the development of accounting for financial instruments. Chapter 42 deals with what qualify as financial assets and financial liabilities and other contracts that are treated as if they were financial instruments, and Chapter 46 discusses the classification of financial instruments under IFRS 9 – *Financial Instruments*. Chapter 47 deals with the question of when financial instruments should be recognised in financial statements and their initial measurement, and the related question of when a previously recognised financial instrument should be derecognised from the financial statements is dealt with in Chapter 50. Hedge accounting under IFRS 9 is dealt with in Chapter 52 and the presentation and disclosure of financial instruments are covered in Chapter 53.

This chapter discusses the subsequent measurement of financial instruments under IFRS 9, when applied, including the requirements relating to amortised cost, the effective interest method, foreign currency revaluation, impairment, effective date and the transition requirements.

Most, but not all, of the detailed requirements of IFRS governing the measurement of fair values are dealt with in IFRS 13 – *Fair Value Measurement* – which is covered in Chapter 14. IFRS 9 also contains some requirements addressing fair value measurements of financial instruments and these are covered at 2.6 below.

2   SUBSEQUENT MEASUREMENT AND RECOGNITION OF GAINS AND LOSSES

As explained in Chapter 46 at 2, following the application of IFRS 9, financial assets are classified into one of the following measurement categories: *[IFRS 9.4.1.1]*

- Debt instruments at amortised cost;
- Debt instruments at fair value through other comprehensive income (with cumulative gains and losses reclassified to profit or loss upon derecognition);
- Debt instruments, derivatives and equity instruments at fair value through profit or loss;
- Equity instruments designated as measured at fair value through other comprehensive income (with gains and losses remaining in other comprehensive income, without recycling); or
- Financial liabilities at either fair value through profit or loss or at amortised cost.

Following the initial recognition of financial assets and financial liabilities, their subsequent accounting treatment depends principally on the classification of the instrument, although there are a small number of exceptions. These requirements are summarised in the following table and are considered in more detail in the remainder of this section.

Classification	Instrument type	Statement of financial position	Fair value gains and losses	Interest and dividends	Impairment	Foreign exchange
Fair value through profit or loss (including derivatives not designated in effective hedges)	Debt, Equity or Derivative	Fair value	Profit or loss*†	Profit or loss*	–	Profit or loss
Equity investments at fair value through other comprehensive income	Equity	Fair value	Other comprehensive income‡	Profit or loss: dividends receivable	–	Other comprehensive income‡
Debt financial assets at fair value through other comprehensive income	Debt	Fair value	Other comprehensive income and recycled to profit or loss when derecognised	Profit or loss: using an effective interest rate	Profit or loss	Profit or loss
Financial assets and liabilities at amortised cost	Debt	Amortised cost	–	Profit or loss: using an effective interest rate	Profit or loss (assets)	Profit or loss

* Little guidance is given on how gains and losses should be disaggregated – see Chapter 53 at 7.1.1.

† The gain or loss on a financial liability attributable to changes in its credit risk is sometimes recognised in other comprehensive income – see 2.1.1 and 6.2.3 below.

‡ These gains and losses are not reclassified from equity to profit or loss, even on disposal.

In addition, IFRS 9 sets out the accounting treatment for certain financial guarantee contracts (see Chapter 42 at 3.4) and commitments to provide a loan at a below market interest rate (see Chapter 42 at 3.5).

2.1 Financial assets and financial liabilities measured at fair value through profit or loss

After initial recognition, financial assets and financial liabilities that are classified as measured at fair value through profit or loss (including derivatives that are not designated in effective hedging relationships) are measured at fair value, with no deduction for sale or disposal costs (see Chapter 46 at 2, 5.4 and 7). [IFRS 9.5.2.1, 5.3.1, 5.7.1].

The standard helpfully points out that if the fair value of a financial asset falls below zero it becomes a financial liability (assuming it is measured at fair value). [IFRS 9.B5.2.1]. The only real alternative would be treatment as a negative asset which would not be sensible. The standard does not explain what happens if the fair value of a financial liability becomes positive, but it is safe to assume that it becomes a financial asset and not a negative liability.

Gains and losses arising from remeasuring a financial asset or financial liability at fair value should normally be recognised in profit or loss. [IFRS 9.5.7.1]. However, there is an exception for most non-derivative financial liabilities that are *designated* as measured at fair value through profit or loss. For these liabilities the element of the gain or loss attributable to changes in credit risk (see 2.1.1 and 6.2.3 below) should normally be recognised in other comprehensive income (with the remainder recognised in profit or loss). [IFRS 9.5.7.7, B5.7.8]. These amounts presented in other comprehensive income should not be subsequently transferred to profit or loss. However, the cumulative gain or loss may be transferred within equity. [IFRS 9.B5.7.9].

This exception does not apply to loan commitments or financial guarantee contracts, nor does it apply if it would create or enlarge an accounting mismatch in profit or loss (see 2.1.2 below). [IFRS 9.5.7.8, 5.7.9]. In these cases, all changes in the fair value of the liability (including the effects of changes in the credit risk) should be recognised in profit or loss. [IFRS 9.B5.7.8].

2.1.1 Liabilities at fair value through profit or loss: calculating the gain or loss attributable to changes in credit risk

IFRS 7 – *Financial Instruments: Disclosures* – defines credit risk as 'the risk that one party to a financial instrument will cause a financial loss for the other party by failing to discharge an obligation', which is also part of non-performance risk as defined in IFRS 13 (see Chapter 14 at 11.3). [IFRS 7 Appendix A]. The change in fair value of a financial liability that is attributable to credit risk relates to the risk that the issuer will fail to perform on that particular liability. It may not solely relate to the creditworthiness of the issuer but may be influenced by other factors, such as collateral.

Chapter 49

For example, if an entity issues a collateralised liability and a non-collateralised liability that are otherwise identical, the credit risk of those two liabilities will be different, even though they are issued by the same entity. The credit risk on the collateralised liability will be less than the credit risk of the non-collateralised liability. In fact, the credit risk for a collateralised liability may be close to zero. *[IFRS 9.B5.7.13]*. It is important to distinguish between what the standard refers to as credit risk and what the sections which address impairment refer to as the risk of default, since the latter does not include the benefit of collateral.

For these purposes, credit risk is different from asset-specific performance risk. Asset-specific performance risk is not related to the risk that an entity will fail to discharge a particular obligation but rather it is related to the risk that a single asset or a group of assets will perform poorly (or not at all). *[IFRS 9.B5.7.14]*. For example, consider: *[IFRS 9.B5.7.15]*

(a)   a liability with a unit-linking feature whereby the amount due to investors is contractually determined on the basis of the performance of specified assets. The effect of that unit-linking feature on the fair value of the liability is asset-specific performance risk, not credit risk;

(b)   a liability issued by a structured entity with the following characteristics:

- the structured entity is legally isolated so the assets in the structured entity are ring-fenced solely for the benefit of its investors, even in the event of bankruptcy;

- the structured entity enters into no other transactions and the assets in the SPE cannot be hypothecated; and

- amounts are due to the structured entity's investors only if the ring-fenced assets generate cash flows.

Thus, changes in the fair value of the liability primarily reflect changes in the fair value of the assets. The effect of the performance of the assets on the fair value of the liability is asset-specific performance risk, not credit risk.

Unless an alternative method more faithfully represents the change in fair value of a financial liability that is attributable to credit risk, this amount should be determined as the amount of change in the fair value of the liability that is not attributable to changes in market conditions that give rise to market risk. *[IFRS 9.B5.7.16]*. Changes in market conditions that give rise to market risk include changes in a benchmark interest rate, the price of another entity's financial instrument, a commodity price, foreign exchange rate or index of prices or rates. *[IFRS 9.B5.7.17]*.

If the only significant relevant changes in market conditions for a financial liability are changes in an observed (benchmark) interest rate, the amount to be recognised in other comprehensive income can be estimated as follows: *[IFRS 9.B5.7.18]*

(a)   first, the liability's internal rate of return at the start of the period is computed using the fair value and contractual cash flows at that time and from this is deducted the observed (benchmark) interest rate at the start of the period, to arrive at an instrument specific component of the internal rate of return;

(b)   next, the present value of the cash flows associated with the liability is calculated using the liability's contractual cash flows at the end of the period and a discount rate equal to the sum of the observed (benchmark) interest rate at the end of the period and the instrument-specific component of the internal rate of return at the start of the period as determined in (a); and

(c)   the difference between the fair value of the liability at the end of the period and the amount determined in (b) is the change in fair value that is not attributable to changes in the observed (benchmark) interest rate and this is the amount to be presented in other comprehensive income.

This method is illustrated in the following example. *[IFRS 9.IE1-IE5]*.

Example 49.1:   Estimating the change in fair value of an instrument attributable to its credit risk

On 1 January 2016, Company J issues a 10-year bond with a par value of €150,000 and an annual fixed coupon rate of 8%, which is consistent with market rates for bonds with similar characteristics. J uses LIBOR as its observable (benchmark) interest rate. At the date of inception of the bond, LIBOR is 5%. At the end of the first year:

• LIBOR has decreased to 4.75%; and

• the fair value of the bond is €153,811 which is consistent with an interest rate of 7.6% [i.e. the remaining cash flows on the bond, €12,000 per year for nine years and €150,000 at the end of nine years, discounted at 7.6% equals €153,811].

J assumes a flat yield curve, that all changes in interest rates result from a parallel shift in the yield curve, and that the changes in LIBOR are the only relevant changes in market conditions.

The amount of change in the fair value of the bond that is not attributable to changes in market conditions that give rise to market risk is estimated as follows:

Step (a)

The bond's internal rate of return at the start of the period is 8%. Because the observed (benchmark) interest rate (LIBOR) is 5%, the instrument-specific component of the internal rate of return is 3%.

Step (b)

The contractual cash flows of the instrument at the end of the period are:

• interest: €12,000 [€150,000 × 8%] per year for each of years 2016 to 2025.

• principal: €150,000 in 2025.

The discount rate to be used to calculate the present value of the bond is thus 7.75%, which is the 4.75% end of period LIBOR rate, plus the 3% instrument-specific component calculated as at the start of the period, which gives a notional present value of €152,367 [€12,000 × (1 − 1.0775^{-9}) / 0.0775) + €150,000 × 1.0775^{-9}], on the assumption that there has been no change in the instrument-specific component.

Step (c)

The market price of the liability at the end of the period (which will reflect the real instrument-specific component at the end of the period within the 7.6% yield) is €153,811, therefore J should disclose €1,444 [€153,811 − €152,367] as the increase in fair value of the bond that is not attributable to changes in market conditions that give rise to market risk.

Chapter 49

This method assumes that changes in fair value other than those arising from changes in the instrument's credit risk or from changes in observed (benchmark) interest rates are not significant. It would not be appropriate to use this method if changes in fair value arising from other factors are significant. In such cases, an alternative method should be used that more faithfully measures the effects of changes in the liability's credit risk. For example, if the instrument in the example contained an embedded derivative, the change in fair value of the embedded derivative should be excluded in determining the amount to be presented in other comprehensive income. [IFRS 9.B5.7.19, B5.7.16(b)].

The above method will produce an amount which includes any changes in the liquidity spread charged by market participants, since such changes are not considered to be attributable to changes in market conditions that give rise to market risk. This solution is applied in practice as the effect of a liquidity spread cannot normally be isolated from that of the credit spread.

As with all estimates of fair value, the measurement method used for determining the portion of the change in the liability's fair value that is attributable to changes in its credit risk should make maximum use of market inputs. [IFRS 9.B5.7.20].

2.1.2   Liabilities at fair value through profit or loss: assessing whether an accounting mismatch is created or enlarged

If a financial liability is designated as at fair value through profit or loss, it must be determined whether presenting in other comprehensive income the effects of changes in the liability's credit risk would create or enlarge an accounting mismatch in profit or loss. An accounting mismatch would be created or enlarged if this treatment would result in a greater mismatch in profit or loss than if those amounts were presented in profit or loss. [IFRS 9.B5.7.5].

In making that determination, an assessment should be made as to whether the effects of changes in the liability's credit risk are expected to be offset in profit or loss by a change in the fair value of another financial instrument measured at fair value through profit or loss. Such an expectation should be based on an economic relationship between the characteristics of the liability and the characteristics of the other financial instrument. [IFRS 9.B5.7.6].

The determination should be made at initial recognition and is not reassessed. For practical purposes, all of the assets and liabilities giving rise to an accounting mismatch need not be entered into at exactly the same time – a reasonable delay is permitted provided that any remaining transactions are expected to occur. An entity's methodology for making this determination should be applied consistently for similar types of transactions. IFRS 7 requires an entity to provide qualitative disclosures in the notes to the financial statements about its methodology for making that determination – see Chapter 53 at 4.4.2.B. [IFRS 9.B5.7.7].

The following example describes a situation in which an accounting mismatch would be created in profit or loss if the effects of changes in the credit risk of the liability were presented in other comprehensive income. [IFRS 9.B5.7.10].

Example 49.2:   Liabilities at fair value through profit or loss: accounting mismatch in profit or loss

A mortgage bank provides loans to customers and funds those loans by selling bonds with matching characteristics (e.g. amount outstanding, repayment profile, term and currency) in the market. The contractual terms of the loan permit the mortgage customer to prepay its loan (i.e. satisfy its obligation to the bank) by buying the corresponding bond at fair value in the market and delivering that bond to the mortgage bank.

As a result of that contractual prepayment right, if the credit quality of the bond worsens (and, thus, the fair value of the mortgage bank's liability decreases), the fair value of the mortgage bank's loan asset also decreases. The change in the fair value of the asset reflects the mortgage customer's contractual right to prepay the mortgage loan by buying the underlying bond at fair value (which, in this example, has decreased) and delivering the bond to the mortgage bank. Therefore, the effects of changes in the credit risk of the liability (the bond) will be offset in profit or loss by a corresponding change in the fair value of a financial asset (the loan).

If the effects of changes in the liability's credit risk were presented in other comprehensive income there would be an accounting mismatch in profit or loss. Therefore, the mortgage bank is required to present all changes in fair value of the liability (including the effects of changes in the liability's credit risk) in profit or loss.

In the example above, there is a contractual linkage between the effects of changes in the credit risk of the liability and changes in the fair value of the financial asset (i.e. as a result of the mortgage customer's contractual right to prepay the loan by buying the bond at fair value and delivering the bond to the mortgage bank). However, an accounting mismatch may also occur in the absence of a contractual linkage. *[IFRS 9.B5.7.11]*.

For these purposes, an accounting mismatch is not caused solely by the measurement method that an entity uses to determine the effects of changes in a liability's credit risk. An accounting mismatch in profit or loss would arise only when the effects of changes in the liability's credit risk (as defined in IFRS 7 – see 2.1.1 above) are expected to be offset by changes in the fair value of another financial instrument. A mismatch that arises solely as a result of the measurement method (i.e. because changes in a liability's credit risk are not isolated from some other changes in its fair value) does not affect the determination above. For example, changes in a liability's credit risk may not be isolated from changes in liquidity risk. If the combined effect of both factors is presented in other comprehensive income, a mismatch may occur because changes in liquidity risk may be included in the fair value measurement of the entity's financial assets and the entire fair value change of those assets is presented in profit or loss. However, such a mismatch is caused by measurement imprecision, not the offsetting relationship and, therefore, does not affect the determination above. *[IFRS 9.B5.7.12]*.

2.2   Investments in equity investments designated at fair value through other comprehensive income

After initial recognition, investments in equity instruments not held for trading that are designated as measured at fair value through other comprehensive income (see Chapter 46 at 2.2) should be measured at fair value, with no deduction for sale or disposal costs. With the exception of dividends received, the associated gains and losses (including any related foreign exchange component) should be recognised in other comprehensive income. Amounts presented in other comprehensive income should not be subsequently transferred to profit or loss, although the cumulative gain or loss may be transferred within equity. *[IFRS 9.5.2.1, 5.7.5, B5.7.1, B5.7.3]*.

Dividends from such investments should be recognised in profit or loss when the right to receive payment is probable and can be measured reliably unless the dividend clearly represents a recovery of part of the cost of the investment. *[IFRS 9.5.7.1A, 5.7.6, B5.7.1]*. Determining when a dividend does or does not clearly represent a recovery of cost could prove somewhat judgmental in practice, especially as the standard contains no further explanatory guidance.

2.3   Debt instruments measured at fair value through other comprehensive income

For financial assets that are debt instruments measured at fair value through other comprehensive income (see Chapter 46 at 2.1), the IASB decided that both amortised cost and fair value information are relevant because debt instruments held by entities in this measurement category are held for both the collection of contractual cash flows and the realisation of fair values. *[IFRS 9.4.1.2A, BC4.150]*.

After initial recognition, investments in debt instruments that are classified as measured at fair value through other comprehensive income are measured at fair value in the statement of financial position (with no deduction for sale or disposal costs) and amortised cost information is presented in profit or loss. *[IFRS 9.5.7.10, 5.7.11]*.

Subsequent measurement of debt instruments at fair value through other comprehensive income involves the following: *[IFRS 9.5.7.1(d), 5.7.10, B5.7.1A]*

(a)   impairment gains and losses (see 5 below) are derived using the same methodology that is applied to financial assets measured at amortised cost and are recognised in profit or loss; *[IFRS 9.5.2.2, 5.5.2]*

(b)   foreign exchange gains and losses (see 4 below) are calculated based on the amortised cost of the debt instruments and are recognised in profit or loss; *[IFRS 9.B5.7.2, B5.7.2A]*

(c)   interest revenue is calculated using the effective interest method (see 3 below) and is recognised in profit or loss; *[IFRS 9.5.4.1]*

(d)   other fair value gains and losses are recognised in other comprehensive income; *[IFRS 9.5.7.10, B5.7.1A]*

(e)   when debt instruments are modified (see 5.7 below), the modification gains or losses are recognised in profit or loss;[1] *[IFRS 9.5.7.10, 5.7.11, 5.4.3]* and

(f)   when the debt instruments are derecognised, the cumulative gains or losses previously recognised in other comprehensive income are reclassified (i.e. recycled) from equity to profit or loss as a reclassification adjustment. *[IFRS 9. 5.7.10, B5.7.1A]*

It follows that the amount recognised in other comprehensive income is the difference between the total change in fair value and the amounts recognised in profit or loss (excluding any amounts received in cash, e.g. the coupon on a bond).

2.4 Financial assets measured at amortised cost

Financial assets that are measured at amortised cost require the use of the effective interest method and are subject to the IFRS 9 impairment rules. *[IFRS 9.5.2.1, 5.2.2]*. Gains and losses are recognised in profit or loss when the instrument is derecognised or impaired, as well as through the amortisation process. *[IFRS 9.5.7.2]*. The effective interest method of accounting is dealt with at 3 below, foreign currency retranslation is discussed at 4 below and impairment is addressed in 5 below.

2.5 Financial liabilities measured at amortised cost

Liabilities that are measured at amortised cost require the use of the effective interest method with gains and losses recognised in profit or loss when the instrument is derecognised as well as through the amortisation process. *[IFRS 9.5.3.1, 5.7.2]*. The effective interest method of accounting is dealt with at 3 below and foreign currency retranslation is discussed at 4 below.

2.6 Unquoted equity instruments and related derivatives

In contrast to the position in IAS 39 – *Financial Instruments: Recognition and Measurement*, IFRS 9 requires all investments in equity instruments and contracts on those instruments to be measured at fair value (see Chapter 14). However, it is recognised that in limited circumstances, cost may be an appropriate estimate of fair value. That may be the case if insufficient more recent information is available to determine fair value, or if there is a wide range of possible fair value measurements and cost represents the best estimate of fair value within that range. *[IFRS 9.B5.2.3]*.

Such guidance was provided to alleviate some of the concerns expressed by constituents and also, to replace the IAS 39 cost exception that was not brought forward to IFRS 9. IAS 39 contained an exception from fair value measurement for investments in equity instruments (and some derivatives linked to those investments) that do not have a quoted price in an active market and whose fair value cannot be reliably measured. Those equity investments were required to be measured at cost less impairment, if any. *[IFRS 9.BC5.13, BC5.16, BC5.18]*.

Indicators that cost might not be representative of fair value include: *[IFRS 9.B5.2.4]*

(a) a significant change in the performance of the investee compared with budgets, plans or milestones;

(b) changes in expectation that the investee's technical product milestones will be achieved;

(c) a significant change in the market for the investee's equity or its products or potential products;

(d) a significant change in the global economy or the economic environment in which the investee operates;

(e) a significant change in the performance of comparable entities, or in the valuations implied by the overall market;

(f) internal matters of the investee such as fraud, commercial disputes, litigation, changes in management or strategy; and

(g)   evidence from external transactions in the investee's equity, either by the investee (such as a fresh issue of equity), or by transfers of equity instruments between third parties.

This list is not intended to be exhaustive. All information about the performance and operations of the investee that becomes available after the date of initial recognition should be used and to the extent that any such relevant factors exist, they may indicate that cost might not be representative of fair value. In such cases, fair value should be estimated. *[IFRS 9.B5.4.16]*.

For the avoidance of doubt, IFRS 9 emphasises that cost is never the best estimate of fair value for investments in quoted equity instruments (or contracts on quoted equity instruments). *[IFRS 9.B5.4.17]*.

2.7   Reclassifications of financial assets

In certain situations financial assets classified as measured at fair value through profit or loss should be reclassified as measured at amortised cost and *vice versa*. The situations in which a reclassification might arise are considered in more detail in Chapter 46 at 9.

The reclassification should be applied prospectively from the reclassification date which is defined as 'the first day of the first reporting period following the change in business model that results in an entity reclassifying financial assets'. *[IFRS 9.5.6.1, Appendix A]*.

Accordingly, any previously recognised gains, losses (including impairment gains and losses) or interest should not be restated. *[IFRS 9.5.6.1]*. For example, when a financial asset is reclassified so that it is measured at fair value, its fair value is determined at the reclassification date. Any gain or loss arising from a difference between the previous carrying amount and fair value should be recognised in profit or loss of the current period without restating prior periods. *[IFRS 9.5.6.2]*. Accordingly, when a financial asset is reclassified so that it is measured at amortised cost, its fair value at the reclassification date becomes its new gross carrying amount. *[IFRS 9.5.6.3]*.

2.8   Financial guarantees and commitments to provide a loan at a below-market interest rate

Financial guarantees issued and commitments made to provide a loan at a below-market interest rate should be measured on initial recognition at their (negative) fair value and subsequently at the higher of:

- the amount of the loss allowance determined in accordance with the impairment requirements of IFRS 9 (see 5 below); and

- the amount initially recognised less, where appropriate, cumulative amortisation recognised in accordance with IAS 18 – *Revenue* (or when adopted the principles of IFRS 15 – *Revenue from Contracts with Customers*) (see Chapters 28 and 29).

This assumes that the instrument is not classified at fair value through profit or loss (in which case the requirements considered at 2.1 above apply) and, in the case of a financial guarantee contract, does not arise from a failed derecognition transaction (see 2.9.3 below). *[IFRS 9.4.2.1(a), 9.4.2.1(c), 4.2.1(d)]*.

2.9 Exceptions to the general principles

2.9.1 Hedging relationships

Financial assets and financial liabilities that are designated as hedged items are subject to measurement under the hedge accounting requirements of IFRS 9, or IAS 39 if the entity chooses as its accounting policy to continue to apply the hedge accounting requirements of IAS 39. *[IFRS 9.5.2.3, 5.3.2, 5.7.3, 7.2.21]*.

Also, derivatives and non-derivative debt financial instruments may be designated as hedging instruments which can affect whether fair value or foreign exchange gains and losses are recognised in profit or loss or in other comprehensive income. *[IFRS 9.B5.7.2]*. Hedge accounting is covered in Chapters 51 and 52.

2.9.2 Regular way transactions

IFRS 9 requires an entity to recognise a financial asset in its statement of financial position when, and only when, the entity becomes party to the contractual provisions of the instrument and to derecognise a financial asset when, and only when, the contractual rights to the cash flows from the financial asset expire (see Chapter 47 at 2.1). *[IFRS 9.3.1.1, 3.2.3]*. In other words, IFRS 9 requires a financial asset to be recognised or derecognised on a trade date basis, i.e. the date that an entity commits itself to purchase or sell an asset. *[IFRS 9.B3.1.5]*. However, the standard permits financial assets subject to so called 'regular way transactions' to be recognised, or derecognised, either as at the trade date or as at the settlement date (see Chapter 47 at 2.2), *[IFRS 9.3.1.2, B3.1.3, B3.1.5, B3.1.6]*. Whichever method is used, it is applied consistently and symmetrically (i.e. to acquisitions and disposals) to each of the main categories of financial asset identified by IFRS 9, i.e. *mandatorily* measured at amortised cost, at fair value through other comprehensive income or at fair value through profit or loss or *designated* as measured at fair value through profit or loss or at fair value through other comprehensive income (equity investments only) (see Chapter 47 at 2.2). *[IFRS 9.B3.1.3]*.

Where settlement date accounting is used for regular way transactions, any change in the fair value of the asset to be received arising between trade date and settlement date is not recognised for those assets that will be measured at amortised cost. For assets that will be recorded at fair value, such changes in value are recognised: *[IFRS 9.5.7.4, B3.1.6]*

- in profit or loss for assets to be classified as measured at fair value through profit or loss; and

- in other comprehensive income for investments in equity instruments to be designated as measured at fair value through other comprehensive income.

For financial assets measured at amortised cost or at fair value through other comprehensive income, IFRS 9 requires entities to use the trade date as the date of initial recognition for the purposes of applying the impairment requirements. *[IFRS 9.5.7.4]*. This means that entities that use settlement date accounting may have to recognise a loss allowance for financial assets which they have purchased but not yet recognised and, correspondingly, no loss allowance for assets that they have sold but not yet derecognised (see 5.6.2 below).

On disposal, changes in value of such assets between trade date and settlement date are not recognised because the right to changes in fair value ceases on the trade date. *[IFRS 9.D.2.2]*. This is illustrated in Chapter 47 at 2.2.3.

2.9.3   *Liabilities arising from failed derecognition transactions*

There are special requirements for financial liabilities (including financial guarantee contracts) that arise when transfers of financial assets do not qualify for derecognition, or are accounted for using the continuing involvement approach. *[IFRS 9.4.2.1(b)]*. These are dealt with in Chapter 50 at 5.3.

3   AMORTISED COST AND THE EFFECTIVE INTEREST METHOD

The amortised cost measurement requirements, including the calculation of effective interest rates under IFRS 9, are the same as under IAS 39, although the terminology has changed. IFRS 9 contains three key definitions relating to this method of accounting, which are set out below: *[IFRS 9 Appendix A]*

- The *amortised cost* is the amount at which the financial asset or financial liability is measured at initial recognition minus any principal repayments, plus or minus the cumulative amortisation using the effective interest method of any difference between that initial amount and the maturity amount and, for financial assets, adjusted for any loss allowance.

- The *gross carrying amount* is the amortised cost of a financial asset before adjusting for any loss allowance.

- The *effective interest method* is the method that is used in the calculation of the amortised cost of a financial asset or a financial liability and in the allocation and recognition of the interest revenue or interest expense in profit or loss over the relevant period. *[IFRS 9 Appendix A]*.

The *effective interest rate* is the rate that exactly discounts estimated future cash payments or receipts through the expected life of the financial asset or financial liability to the *gross carrying amount* of a financial asset or to the amortised cost of a financial liability. *[IFRS 9.5.4.1, IFRS 9 Appendix A]*. When calculating the effective interest rate, an entity should estimate the expected cash flows by considering all the contractual terms of the financial instrument (e.g. prepayment, extension, call and similar options). The calculation includes all fees and points paid or received between parties to the contract that are an integral part of the effective interest rate, transaction costs, and all other premiums or discounts. *[IFRS 9 Appendix A]*.

Guidance related to what elements should and should not be considered integral is also included in IFRS 9. Fees that are an integral part of the effective interest rate of a financial instrument are treated as an adjustment to the effective interest rate, unless the financial instrument is measured at fair value, with the change in fair value being recognised in profit or loss. In those cases, the fees are recognised as revenue or expense when the instrument is initially recognised. *[IFRS 9.B5.4.1]*.

Fees that are an integral part of the effective interest rate of a financial instrument include:

- origination fees received on the creation or acquisition of a financial asset. Such fees may include compensation for activities such as evaluating the borrower's financial condition, evaluating and recording guarantees, collateral and other security arrangements, negotiating the terms of the instrument, preparing and processing documents and closing the transaction. These fees are an integral part of generating an involvement with the resulting financial instrument;

- commitment fees received to originate a loan when the loan commitment is not measured at fair value through profit or loss and it is probable that the entity will enter into a specific lending arrangement. These fees are regarded as compensation for an ongoing involvement with the acquisition of a financial instrument. If the commitment expires without the entity making the loan, the fee is recognised as revenue on expiry; and

- origination fees paid on issuing financial liabilities measured at amortised cost. These fees are an integral part of generating an involvement with a financial liability. An entity distinguishes fees and costs that are an integral part of the effective interest rate for the financial liability from origination fees and transaction costs relating to the right to provide services, such as investment management services. *[IFRS 9.B5.4.2]*.

Fees that are not an integral part of the effective interest rate of a financial instrument and are accounted for in accordance with IFRS 15 include:

- fees charged for servicing a loan;

- commitment fees to originate a loan when the loan commitment is not measured at fair value through profit or loss and it is unlikely that a specific lending arrangement will be entered into; and

- loan syndication fees received to arrange a loan and the entity does not retain part of the loan package for itself (or retains a part at the same effective interest rate for comparable risk as other participants). *[IFRS 9. B5.4.3]*.

Except for purchased or originated financial assets that are credit-impaired on initial recognition, expected credit losses are not considered in the calculation of the effective interest rate. This is (because the recognition of expected credit losses is decoupled from the recognition of interest revenue (see 5.3.1 below). *[IFRS 9 Appendix A, BCZ5.67]*.

For a purchased or originated credit-impaired financial asset (see 5.3.3 below), the *credit-adjusted effective interest rate* is applied when calculating the interest revenue and it is the rate that exactly discounts the estimated future cash payments or receipts through the expected life of the financial asset to the amortised cost of a financial asset. An entity is required to include the initial expected credit losses in the estimated cash flows when calculating the credit-adjusted effective interest rate for such assets. *[IFRS 9.5.4.1, B5.4.7, Appendix A]*.

However, this does not mean that a credit-adjusted effective interest rate should be applied solely because the financial asset has high credit risk at initial recognition. The application guidance explains that a financial asset is only considered

Chapter 49

credit-impaired at initial recognition because the credit risk is very high or, in the case of a purchase, it is acquired at a deep discount. *[IFRS 9.B5.4.7]*.

It is important to note that the effective interest rate is normally based on estimated, not contractual, cash flows and there is a presumption that the cash flows and the expected life of a group of similar financial instruments can be estimated reliably. However, in those rare cases when it is not possible to estimate reliably the cash flows or the expected life of a financial instrument (or group of instruments), the contractual cash flows over the full contractual term of the financial instrument (or group of instruments) should be used. *[IFRS 9 Appendix A]*. During the development of IAS 39, the IASB considered whether the effective interest rate for all financial instruments should be calculated on the basis of *estimated* cash flows, or whether *contractual* cash flows should be used for individual financial instruments with the use of estimated cash flows being restricted to groups of financial instruments. The position adopted was chosen because the IASB believes it achieves consistent application of the effective interest method throughout the standard. *[IFRS 9.BCZ5.65]*.

When applying the effective interest method, an entity generally amortises any fees, points paid or received, transaction costs and other premiums or discounts that are included in the calculation of the effective interest rate over the expected life of the financial instrument. However, a shorter period is used if this is the period to which the fees, points paid or received, transaction costs, premiums or discounts relate. This will be the case when the related variable (e.g. interest rates) to which the fees, points paid or received, transaction costs, premiums or discounts relate is repriced to market rates before the expected maturity of the instrument. In such a case, the appropriate amortisation period is the period to the next such repricing date. *[IFRS 9.B5.4.4, BCZ5.70]*. For example, if a premium or discount on a floating-rate financial instrument reflects the interest that has accrued on that financial instrument since the interest was last paid, or changes in the market rates since the floating interest rate was reset to the market rates, it will be amortised to the next date when the floating interest is reset to market rates. This is because the premium or discount relates to the period to the next interest reset date because, at that date, the variable to which the premium or discount relates (i.e. interest rates) is reset to the market rates. If, however, the premium or discount results from a change in the credit spread over the floating rate specified in the financial instrument, or other variables that are not reset to the market rates, it is amortised over the expected life of the financial instrument. *IFRS 9.B5.4.4]*.

For floating-rate financial assets and floating-rate financial liabilities, periodic re-estimation of cash flows to reflect the movements in the market rates of interest alters the effective interest rate. If a floating-rate financial asset or a floating-rate financial liability is recognised initially at an amount equal to the principal receivable or payable on maturity, re-estimating the future interest payments normally has no significant effect on the carrying amount of the asset or the liability. *IFRS 9.B5.4.5]*. The application of the effective interest method to floating rate instruments and inflation-linked debt is considered in more detail at 3.3 and 3.5 below.

As set out in Chapter 44 at 6, an issued compound financial instrument such as a convertible bond is accounted for as a financial liability component and an equity component. In accounting for the financial liability at amortised cost, the expected cash flows should be those of the liability component only and the estimate should not take account of the bond being converted.

3.1 Fixed interest, fixed term instruments

The effective interest method is most easily applied to instruments that have fixed payments and a fixed term. The following examples, adapted from the Implementation Guidance to the standard, illustrate this. *IFRS 9.IG.B.26, IG.B.27].*

Example 49.3: **Effective interest method –**
amortisation of premium or discount on acquisition

At the start of 2016, a company purchases a debt instrument with five years remaining to maturity for its fair value of US$1,000 (including transaction costs). The instrument has a principal amount of US$1,250 and carries fixed interest of 4.7% payable annually (US$1,250 × 4.7% = US$59 per year). In order to allocate interest receipts and the initial discount over the term of the instrument at a constant rate on the carrying amount, it can be shown that interest needs to be accrued at the rate of 10% annually. The table below provides information about the gross carrying amount, interest income, and cash flows of the debt instrument in each reporting period.[2] *[IFRS 9.B.26].*

Year	(a) Gross carrying amount at the start of the year (US$)	(b = a × 10%) Interest income (US$)	(c) Cash flows (US$)	(d = a + b – c) Gross carrying amount at the end of the year (US$)
2016	1,000	100	59	1,041
2017	1,041	104	59	1,086
2018	1,086	109	59	1,136
2019	1,136	113	59	1,190
2020	1,190	119	1,250 + 59	–

Example 49.4: **Effective interest method – stepped interest rates**

On 1 January 2016, Company A acquires a debt instrument for its fair value of £1,250 (including transaction costs). The principal amount is £1,250 which is repayable on 31 December 2020. The rate of interest is specified in the debt agreement as a percentage of the principal amount as follows: 6% in 2016 (£75), 8% in 2017 (£100), 10% in 2018 (£125), 12% in 2019 (£150) and 16.4% in 2020 (£205). It can be shown that the interest rate that exactly discounts the stream of future cash payments to maturity is 10%. In each period, the amortised cost at the beginning of the period is multiplied by the effective interest rate of 10% and added to the gross carrying amount. Any cash payments in the period are deducted from the resulting balance. Accordingly, the gross carrying amount, interest income and cash flows of the debt instrument in each period are as follows:

Year	(a) Gross carrying amount at the start of the year (£)	(b = a × 10%) Interest income (£)	(c) Cash flows (£)	(d = a + b – c) Gross carrying amount at the end of the year (£)
2016	1,250	125	75	1,300
2017	1,300	130	100	1,330
2018	1,330	133	125	1,338
2019	1,338	134	150	1,322
2020	1,322	133	1,250 + 205	–

It can be seen that, although the instrument is issued for £1,250 and has a maturity amount of £1,250, its gross carrying amount does not equal £1,250 at each reporting date. *[IFRS 9.IG.B.27].*

Chapter 49

Methods for determining the effective interest rate for a given set of cash flows (as in the examples above) include simple trial and error techniques as well as more methodical iterative algorithms. Alternatively, many spreadsheet applications contain goal-seek or similar functions that can also be used to derive effective interest rates.

3.2   Prepayment, call and similar options

When calculating the effective interest rate, all contractual terms of the financial instrument, for example prepayment, call and similar options, should be considered. *[IFRS 9 Appendix A]*. The following simple example illustrates how this principle is applied.

Example 49.5:   Effective interest rate – embedded prepayment options

Bank ABC originates 1,000 ten year loans of £10,000 with 10% stated interest, prepayable at par. Prepayments are probable and it is possible to reasonably estimate their timing and amount. ABC determines that the effective interest rate including loan origination fees received by ABC is 10.2% based on the *contractual* payment terms of the loans as the fees received reduce the initial carrying amount.

However, if the *expected* prepayments were considered, the effective interest rate would be 10.4% since the difference between the initial amount and maturity amount is amortised over a shorter period.

The effective interest rate that should be used by ABC for this portfolio is 10.4%.[3]

3.2.1   Revisions to estimated cash flows

The standard contains an explanation of how changes to estimates of payments or receipts (e.g. because of a reassessment of the extent to which prepayments will occur) should be dealt with.

When there is a change in estimates of payments or receipts, excluding changes in estimates of expected credit losses, the gross carrying amount of the financial asset or amortised cost of a financial liability (or group of instruments) should be adjusted to reflect actual and revised estimated cash flows. More precisely, the gross carrying amount of the financial asset or amortised cost of the financial liability should be re-calculated by computing the present value of estimated future contractual cash flows that are discounted at the financial instrument's original effective interest rate (or if the instrument has been designated as the hedged item in a fair value hedge, the revised effective interest rate). Any consequent adjustment should be recognised immediately in profit or loss. *[IFRS 9.B5.4.6]*. This is equivalent to the IAS 39 approach set out in paragraph AG8 (see Chapter 48 at 3.6).

The revision of estimates is illustrated in the following example adapted from the Implementation Guidance to the standard. *[IFRS 9.IG.B.26]*.

Example 49.6:   Effective interest method – revision of estimates

At the start of 2016, a company purchases in a quoted market a debt instrument with the same terms as the instrument in Example 49.3 at 3.1 above, except that the contract also specifies that the borrower has an option to prepay the instrument and that no penalty will be charged for prepayment (i.e. any prepayment will be made at the principal amount of US$1,250 or a proportion thereof).

At inception, there is an expectation that the borrower will not prepay and so the information about the instrument's effective interest rate, gross carrying amount, interest income and cash flows in each reporting period would be the same as that in Example 49.3.

On the first day of 2018, the investor revises its estimate of cash flows. It now expects that 50% of the principal will be prepaid at the end of 2018 and the remaining 50% at the end of 2020. Therefore, the opening balance of the debt instrument in 2018 is adjusted to an amount calculated by discounting the amounts expected to be received in 2018 and subsequent years using the original effective interest rate (10%). This results in a revised balance of US$1,138. The adjustment of US$52 (US$1,138 – US$1,086) is recorded in profit or loss in 2018.

The table below provides information about the gross carrying amount, interest income and cash flows as they would be adjusted taking into account this change in estimate.

Year	(a) Gross carrying amount at start of year (US$)	(b = a × 10%) Interest and similar income* (US$)	(c) Cash flows (US$)	(d = a + b − c) Gross carrying amount at end of year (US$)
2016	1,000	100	59	1,041
2017	1,041	104	59	1,086
2018	1,086 + 52	114	625 + 59	568
2019	568	57	30	595
2020	595	60	625 + 30	–

*the standard and related guidance do not state whether the catch-up adjustment (US$52 in 2018 in this case) should be classified as interest income or as some other income or expense, simply that it should be recognised in profit or loss.

This above calculation would be applicable whether the instruments were classified as measured at amortised cost or FVOCI under IFRS 9.

In this example it is not clear why the prepayment option has not precluded amortised cost measurement under IFRS 9. The exercise price is US$1,250 and the option may be exercised at any time, yet the amortised cost is initially only US$1,000. We find it hard to believe that the IASB considers two numbers, one of which is 25% larger than the other, to be approximately equal and the instrument would probably fail the contractual cash flow characteristics test under IFRS 9 (see Chapter 46 at 6.3). More likely, the example rolled-forward from IAS 39 was not updated to reflect the contractual cash flow characteristics test under IFRS 9.

3.2.2   Interaction with the requirements for embedded derivatives

If a hybrid contract contains a host that is a liability within the scope of IFRS 9, any embedded derivative (e.g. a prepayment option) that is required to be separated from the host must be accounted for as a derivative (see Chapter 43 at 4 and 5). [IFRS 9.4.3.3]. Although not explained in the standard, the embedded derivative should not be taken into account in applying the effective interest method of the host.

This actually raises other questions with regards to the issue of whether prepayment and similar options should be regarded as closely related to the host instrument. In assessing whether the exercise price is approximately equal to the amortised cost at each exercise date, should one consider the amortised cost of the hybrid on the assumption the option is regarded as closely related, or the amortised cost of the host on the assumption that it is not? This conundrum is illustrated in the following

Chapter 49

simple example (which also provides further illustrations of the application of the effective interest method to instruments containing prepayment options).

Example 49.7:   Embedded prepayment option

Company P borrows €1,000 on terms that require it to pay annual fixed rate coupons of €80 and €1,000 principal at the end of ten years. The terms of the instrument also allow P to redeem the debt after seven years by paying the principal of €1,000 and a penalty of €100.

The debt instrument can be considered to comprise the following two components:

- a host debt instrument requiring ten annual payments of €80 followed by a €1,000 payment of principal; and

- an embedded prepayment option, exercisable only at the end of seven years with an exercise price of €1,100.

If, at inception, the prepayment option was expected *not* to be exercised, the effective interest rate of the *hybrid* would be 8%. This is the rate that would discount the expected cash flows of €80 per year for ten years plus €1,000 at the end of ten years to the initial carrying amount of €1,000. The table below provides information about the amortised cost, interest income and cash flows using this assumption.

Year	(a) Gross carrying amount at the start of the year (€)	(b = a × 8%) Interest and similar income (€)	(c) Cash flows (€)	(d = a + b − c) Gross carrying amount at the end of the year (€)
1	1,000	80	80	1,000
2	1,000	80	80	1,000
3	1,000	80	80	1,000
4	1,000	80	80	1,000
5	1,000	80	80	1,000
6	1,000	80	80	1,000
7	1,000	80	80	1,000
8	1,000	80	80	1,000
9	1,000	80	80	1,000
10	1,000	80	80 + 1,000	–

However if, at the outset, the option *was* expected to be exercised, the effective interest rate of the *hybrid* would be 9.08% as this is the rate that discounts the expected cash flows of €80 per year for seven years, plus €1,100 at the end of seven years, to the initial carrying amount of €1,000. The table below provides information about the amortised cost, interest income and cash flows using this alternative assumption.

Year	(a) Gross carrying amount at the start of the year (€)	(b = a × 9.08%) Interest and similar income (€)	(c) Cash flows (€)	(d = a + b − c) Gross carrying amount at the end of the year (€)
1	1,000	91	80	1,011
2	1,011	92	80	1,023
3	1,023	93	80	1,036
4	1,036	94	80	1,050
5	1,050	95	80	1,065
6	1,065	97	80	1,082
7	1,082	98	80 + 1,100	–

On the face of it, therefore, comparing the amortised cost of the hybrid with the exercise price of the option at the date it could be exercised suggests the prepayment option might be considered closely related if it was likely to be exercised but not if exercise was unlikely.

However, even this is not the whole story. If the option (on inception) was not expected to be exercised, but at a later date exercise became likely, the amortised cost carrying amount would be revised so that it represented the expected future cash flows discounted at the original effective interest rate. For example, if at the end of Year 5, it became likely that the option would be exercised, the carrying amount would be revised so that it represented €80 discounted for one year at 8% plus €1,180 discounted for two years at 8% – in other words, €1,086 rather than €1,065. The difference of €21 would be recognised in profit or loss immediately and the amortised cost carrying amount would subsequently accrete so that it represented the final cash outflow (option exercise price of €1,100 plus coupon of €80) at the end of Year 7. So even in this situation there is an argument to suggest that the prepayment option should not be separated as the exercise price will always equal the amortised cost (at least to the extent that the option is expected to be exercised).

If the assessment was performed based on the amortised cost of the *host*, the initial fair value of the prepayment option is needed to determine the initial carrying amount of the host (see Chapter 47 at 3.4). From P's perspective it will have a positive fair value and for the purpose of this example this is assumed to be €50. Therefore, the initial value of the host will be €1,050 (€1,000 + €50). The effective interest rate of the host can be demonstrated to be 7.28% and the amortised cost each year would be as follows:

Year	(a) Amortised cost at start of year (€)	(b = a × 7.28%) Interest and similar income (€)	(c) Cash flows (€)	(d = a + b − c) Amortised cost at end of year (€)
1	1,050	76	80	1,046
2	1,046	76	80	1,042
3	1,042	76	80	1,038
4	1,038	76	80	1,034
5	1,034	75	80	1,029
6	1,029	75	80	1,024
7	1,024	75	80	1,019
8	1,019	74	80	1,013
9	1,013	74	80	1,007
10	1,007	73	80 + 1,000	–

In this case, the amortised cost at the date the option can be exercised is €1,019. Comparing this with the exercise price of €1,100 suggests the option may not be considered closely related in this case.

In fact if this analysis were applied to prepayment options for which there was no associated penalty (i.e. the instrument would always be redeemed at its principal amount), separating the embedded derivative in this way would artificially create a difference between the amortised cost of the *host* and the exercise price. However, we are entirely unconvinced it would be appropriate to separate an embedded derivative from such a simple instrument.

Unfortunately, the standard is silent on these issues and preparers of accounts will be required to exercise judgement as to the most appropriate method to use in their individual circumstances, although as noted in Chapter 43 at 5.1.3, one trade body has published guidance explaining that where early repayment fees are included in the calculation of effective interest, the prepayment option is likely to be closely related to the loan.[4]

3.3   Floating rate instruments

When estimating cash flows for a floating rate instrument, application of the basic requirements discussed at 3 above could produce some surprising results, as shown in the following example. It is assumed that the instrument meets the criteria for measurement at amortised cost under IFRS 9.

Example 49.8:   Effective interest method – variable rate loan

At the start of July 2015, Company G originates a floating rate debt instrument. Its fair value is equal to its principal amount of $1,000 and no transaction costs are incurred. The instrument pays, in arrears at the end of June, a variable rate coupon, determined by reference to 12 month LIBOR at the start of each previous July. It has a term of five years and is repayable at its principal amount at the end of June 2020.

On origination, 12 month LIBOR is 5% and this establishes the first payment, to be made in June 2016, at $50. Based on a market-derived yield curve, G estimates that the subsequent floating rate payments will be $60, $70, $80 and $90 (the yield curve rises steeply). It can be demonstrated that the interest rate that exactly discounts these estimated coupon payments and the $1,000 principal at maturity to the current carrying amount of $1,000 is 6.87% (the definition does not acknowledge the possibility of more than one effective interest rate that would be reflective of a yield curve that is not flat).

In this situation, recognising interest at 6.87% in the first year would seem entirely counter-intuitive and is inconsistent with traditional notions of interest recognition for floating rate instruments. Nevertheless, there are some who believe, at least in principle, that such an approach is technically correct, even if it is not applied widely in practice.

The standard does contain additional guidance for applying the effective interest method to floating rate instruments. Normally, the effective interest rate remains constant over the life of an instrument. However, for floating rate instruments, it is stated that periodic re-estimation of cash flows to reflect the movements in the market interest rates *does* alter the effective interest rate. The standard goes on to explain that where a floating-rate financial asset or a floating-rate financial liability is initially recognised at an amount equal to the principal receivable or repayable on maturity, re-estimating the future interest payments normally has no significant effect on the carrying amount of the asset or the liability. *[IFRS 9.B5.4.5].* This is equivalent to the IAS 39 approach set out in paragraph AG7 (see Chapter 48 at 3.3).

Typically, this has been interpreted to mean that entities should simply account for periodic floating rate payments on an accrual basis in the period they relate to. However, those that believe entities should forecast all future cash flows argue that this means that the calculated effective interest rate (6.87% in the example above) is applied until estimated future cash flows are revised, at which point a new effective interest rate is calculated based on the revised cash flow expectations and the current carrying amount.

Whilst payments, receipts, discounts and premiums included in the effective interest method calculation are normally amortised over the expected life of the instrument, there may be situations when they are amortised over a shorter period (see 3 above). This will be the case when the variable to which they relate reprices to market rates before the instrument's expected maturity. In such cases, the appropriate amortisation period is to the next repricing date.

For example, if a premium or discount on a floating rate instrument reflects interest that has accrued since interest was last paid, or changes in market rates since the floating interest rate was reset to market rates, it will be amortised to the next date when the interest rate is reset to market rates. This is because the premium or discount relates to the period to the next interest reset date because, at that date, the variable to which the premium or discount relates (i.e. the interest rate) is reset to market rates. If, however, the premium or discount results from a change in the credit spread over the floating rate specified in the financial instrument, or other variables that are not reset to market rates, it is amortised over the expected life of the instrument. *[IFRS 9.B5.4.4]*.

The following examples illustrate the requirements of applying a discount arising on acquisition of a debt instrument resulting from (a) a credit downgrade and (b) accrued interest.

Example 49.9:   Effective interest method –
amortisation of discount arising from credit downgrade

A twenty year bond is issued at £100, has a principal amount of £100, and requires quarterly interest payments equal to current three month LIBOR plus 1% over the life of the instrument. The interest rate reflects the market-based required rate of return associated with the bond issue at issuance. Subsequent to issuance, the credit quality of the bond deteriorates resulting in a rating downgrade. It therefore trades at a discount, although it is assessed not to be credit-impaired (see 5.3.1 below). Company A purchases the bond for £95 and classifies it as measured at amortised cost.

The discount of £5 is amortised to income over the period to the maturity of the bond and not to the next date interest rate payments are reset as it results from a change in credit spreads.[5]

Example 49.10:   Effective interest method –
amortisation of discount arising from accrued interest

At the start of November 2015, Company P acquires the bond issued by Company G in Example 49.7 above – current interest rates have not changed since the end of July 2015 and G's credit risk has not changed since origination so P pays $1,017.

The premium of $17 paid by P relates to interest accrued since the last reset date and so is amortised to income over the period to the next repricing date, June 2016; further, the $50 cash flow received at the end of June 2016 is also amortised over this period.

Consequently, for the eight months ended June 2016, P will record interest of $33 ($50 – $17), which is also the approximate equivalent of eight months interest at current rates (5%) earned on P's initial investment.

This treatment is consistent with the requirements of IAS 18 that apply when unpaid interest has accrued before the acquisition of an interest-bearing investment. In such cases, it is explained (in more traditional terms) that the subsequent receipt of interest should be allocated between pre-acquisition and post-acquisition periods and only the post-acquisition portion should be recognised as revenue. *[IAS 18.32]*. In fact for many floating rate instruments, it will often be appropriate to apply a simplistic method of accounting – for example, by amortising transaction costs on a straight line basis over the life of the instrument combined with a simple time apportionment approach to the floating rate coupons. This guidance was not included in IFRS 15 or a consequential amendment to IFRS 9 as a result of the issuance of IFRS 15. We believe this was an oversight on part of the IASB and assume that this practice should not change.

3.4   Perpetual debt instruments

The fact that an instrument is perpetual does not change how the gross carrying amount is calculated. The present value of the perpetual stream of future cash payments, discounted at the effective interest rate, equals the gross carrying amount in each period. *[IFRS 9.IG.B.24].*

However, in cases where interest is only paid over a limited amount of time, some or all of the interest payments are, from an economic perspective, repayments of the gross carrying amount, as illustrated in the following example. *[IFRS 9.B.25].*

Example 49.11:   Amortised cost –
          perpetual debt with interest payments over a limited amount of time

On 1 January 2016, Company A subscribes £1,000 for a debt instrument which yields 25% interest for the first five years and 0% in subsequent periods. The instrument is classified as measured at amortised cost. It can be determined that the effective yield is 7.9% and the gross carrying amount is shown in the table below.[6]

Year	(a) Gross carrying amount at the start of the year (£)	(b = a × 7.9%) Interest income (£)	(c) Cash flows (£)	(d = a + b − c) Gross carrying amount at the end of the year (£)
2016	1,000	79	250	829
2017	829	66	250	645
2018	645	51	250	446
2019	446	36	250	232
2020	232	18	250	–
2021	–	–	–	–

3.5   Inflation-linked debt

As noted in Chapter 43 at 5.1.5, the issuance of debt instruments whose cash flows are linked to changes in an inflation index is quite common and typically, such an instrument would also often meet the contractual cash flow characteristics test as shown in Example 46.11 in Chapter 46. Consequently, entities that hold or issue these instruments must apply the effective interest method to determine the amount of interest to be recognised in profit or loss each period (assuming the instrument is not classified at fair value through profit or loss).

In May 2008, the Interpretations Committee was asked to consider a request for guidance on this issue. Three ways of applying the effective interest method that were being used in practice were included in the request. These are summarised in the following example that has been revised to reflect the requirements in IFRS 9 instead of IAS 39.[7]

Example 49.12:   Application of the effective interest method to inflation-linked debt
          instruments[8]

On 1 January 2016, Company A issues a debt instrument for $100,000 that is linked to the local Consumer Prices Index (CPI). The terms of the instrument require it to be repaid in full after five years at an amount equal to $100,000 adjusted by the cumulative change in the CPI over those five years. Interest on the loan is paid at each year end at an amount equal to 5% of the principal ($100,000) adjusted by the cumulative change in the CPI from issuance of the instrument. For IFRS 9 purposes, it is assumed that the inflation index is not leveraged and the principal is protected and thereby, the instrument meets the criteria for measurement at amortised cost.

The following table sets out the expected annual inflation rates on issuance of the instrument and one year later:

	Expected annual inflation rates	
	At start of 2016	At start of 2017
2016	0.7%	
2017	2.6%	1.4%
2018	2.8%	1.9%
2019	2.8%	3.5%
2020	2.8%	3.5%

During 2016 actual inflation is 1.2%.

Method 1 – application of IFRS 9.B5.4.6 (or the IAS 39 AG8 approach)

This approach follows the requirements set out at 3.2.1 above. Therefore, the effective interest rate is established on 1 January 2016 based on expected cash flows at that time:

Date: end of	Expected cash flow ($)	Calculation
2016	5,035	=5,000 × 1.007
2017	5,166	=5,000 × 1.007 × 1.026
2018	5,311	=5,000 × 1.007 × 1.026 × 1.028
2019	5,459	=5,000 × 1.007 × 1.026 × 1.028 × 1.028
2020	117,854	=105,000 × 1.007 × 1.026 × 1.028 × 1.028 × 1.028

It can be demonstrated that these expected cash flows produce an effective interest rate of 7.4075%, i.e. the net present value of these cash flows, discounted at 7.4075%, equals $100,000.

During 2016, A applies the effective interest rate to the financial liability to recognise a finance charge of $7,408 ($100,000 × 7.4075%), increasing the carrying amount of the financial liability to $107,408 ($100,000 + $7,408). At the end of the year A pays cash interest of $5,060 ($5,000 × 101.2%) reducing the liability to $102,348 ($107,408 – $5,060). In addition, A must adjust the carrying amount of the financial liability so that it equals the net present value of expected future cash flows discounted at the original expected interest rate.

The expected future cash flows are now as follows:

Date: end of	Cash flow ($)	Calculation
2017	5,131	=5,000 × 1.012 × 1.014
2018	5,228	=5,000 × 1.012 × 1.014 × 1.019
2019	5,411	=5,000 × 1.012 × 1.014 × 1.019 × 1.035
2020	117,615	=105,000 × 1.012 × 1.014 × 1.019 × 1.035 × 1.035

The net present value of these cash flows discounted at 7.4075% is $102,050. Therefore A reduces its finance charge by $298 ($102,050 – $102,348) so that the total finance charge for 2016 is $7,110 ($7,408 – $298).

Method 2 – application of IFRS 9.B5.4.5 using forecast future cash flows (or the IAS 39 AG7 approach)

This approach is referred to at 3.3 above.

The initial effective interest rate is calculated and applied in the same way as Method 1. However, no adjustment is made to the carrying amount of the financial liability at the end of 2016 ($102,348) or to the finance charge for 2015 ($7,408) as a result of A, at the start of 2017, revising its expectations about inflation over the remaining term of the instrument.

Instead, a revised effective interest rate is calculated at the start of 2017 using the revised forecast cash flows (shown above under Method 1, i.e. $5,131 at the end of 2017, $5,228 at the end of 2018, $5,411 at the end of 2019 and $117,615 at the end of 2020) and the current carrying amount ($102,348). It can be demonstrated that this produces a revised effective interest rate of 7.3237%, i.e. the net present value of those cash flows, discounted at 7.3237% equals $102,348.

Applying this revised rate prospectively in 2017 (and assuming estimates of future inflation are not revised again until the start of 2018) there will be a finance charge for 2017 of $7,496 ($102,348 × 7.3237%).

Method 3 – application of IFRS 9 B5.4.4-5 without forecasting future cash flows

This method is based on the traditional method of accounting for floating rate debt instruments and is commonly used under other bodies of GAAP. Rather than taking account of expectations of future inflation it takes account of inflation only during the reporting period.

Therefore, in 2016, A would recognise a finance charge of $5,060 as a result of accruing the variable interest payment in respect of 2016. In addition, the actual inflation experienced during 2016 increases the amount of principal that will be paid from $100,000 to $101,200 ($100,000 × 1.012%). This increase, i.e. $1,200, is effectively a premium to be paid on the redemption of the financial liability. Paragraph B5.4.4 of IFRS 9 explains that a premium should normally be amortised over the expected life of an instrument. However, it goes on to explain that a shorter period should be used if this is the period to which the premium relates. *[IFRS 9.B5.4.4]*. In this case, the premium clearly relates to 2016 as it arises from inflation during that year and so it is appropriately amortised in that year.

Consequently, the total finance charge for 2016 using this method would be $6,260 ($5,060 + $1,200).

In analysing the submission, it initially appeared as if the Interpretations Committee staff completely rejected Method 3. The submission argued that Method 3 was justified by reference to IAS 29 – *Financial Reporting in Hyperinflationary Economies.* The staff concluded (quite correctly) that it was inappropriate to apply IAS 29 because that standard applies only to the financial statements of an entity whose functional currency is the currency of a hyperinflationary economy and instead the guidance in IAS 39 should be applied.[9]

However, the Interpretations Committee noted that paragraphs AG6 to AG8 of IAS 39 provide the relevant application guidance and that judgement is required to determine whether an instrument is floating rate and within the scope of paragraph AG7 or is within the scope of paragraph AG8.[10] Further, it was noted that IAS 39 is unclear as to whether future expectations about interest rates (and presumably, therefore, inflation) should be taken into account when applying paragraph AG7.[11] Consequently, in our view, all three methods noted in the example comply with the current requirements of IAS 39 and therefore, since the requirements are unchanged, of IFRS 9. This view is consistent with the opinion of one national standard-setter that operates in a jurisdiction where such instruments are extremely common.[12]

3.6   More complex financial liabilities

The application of the effective interest method to instruments with unusual embedded derivatives that are deemed closely related to the host, or other embedded features that are not accounted for separately, is not always straightforward or intuitive. Specifically it is not always clear how to deal with changes in the estimated cash flows of the instrument and in any given situation one needs to assess which of the approaches set out above is more appropriate:

- the general requirements for changes in cash flows set out in paragraph B5.4.6 of IFRS 9, equivalent to the IAS 39 AG8 approach (see 3.2.1 above); and

- specific requirements for floating rate instruments under paragraph B5.4.5 of IFRS 9, equivalent to the IAS 39 AG7 approach (see 3.3 above).

Consider an entity that issues a debt instrument for its par value of €10m which is repayable in ten years' time on which an annual coupon is payable comprising two elements: a fixed amount of 2.5% of the par value and a variable amount equating to 0.01% of the entity's annual revenues. The instrument is not designated at fair value through profit or loss and it is judged that the embedded feature is not a derivative as outlined in Example 43.3 in Chapter 43.

The requirements under paragraph B5.4.5 and B5.4.6 of IFRS 9 could give rise to significantly different accounting treatments. In the latter case, the issuer would need to estimate the amount of payments to be made over the life of the bond (which will depend on its estimated revenues for the next ten years) in order to determine the effective interest rate to be applied. Any changes to these estimates would result in a catch-up adjustment to profit or loss and the carrying amount of the bond which, potentially, could give rise to significant volatility. In the former case the annual coupon would simply be accrued each year and changes in estimated revenues of future periods would have no impact on the accounting treatment until the applicable year.

In 2009, the Interpretations Committee was asked to consider the accounting treatment for an instrument with similar terms. However, the IFRIC considered the issue without reconsidering the assumptions described in the request, namely that the financial liability (a) did not contain any embedded derivatives, (b) was measured at amortised cost using the effective interest method, and (c) did not meet the definition of a floating rate instrument.[13] In other words, whilst clearly indicating that the B5.4.6 approach was acceptable, it did not explicitly preclude the use of the B5.4.5 approach. In this situation, we believe that it would often be appropriate to apply the requirements under paragraph B5.4.6 of IFRS 9 principally because the entity's revenue does not represent a floating rate that changes to reflect movements in market rates of interest, although as covered at 3.5 above, judgement is required to determine which approach is appropriate.[14]

For other instruments, the decision as to which approach to use is even less clear. For example, as set out at 3.5 above, it can be argued that simple inflation-linked bonds are similar enough to floating rate instruments to apply the requirements under paragraph B5.4.5 of IFRS 9. However, this approach would not extend to more exotic instruments, for example to an inverse floater where coupons on an otherwise simple debt instrument are paid at a fixed rate minus LIBOR (subject to a floor of zero), even though re-estimation of cash flows will only reflect movements in market interest rates.

Chapter 49

In other cases, it might be considered appropriate to apply a combination of both approaches if, for example, an instrument contains both fixed and floating rate features.

4   FOREIGN CURRENCIES

4.1   Foreign currency instruments

The provisions of IAS 21 – *The Effects of Changes in Foreign Exchange Rates* – apply to transactions involving financial instruments in just the same way as they do for other transactions, although the manner in which certain hedges are accounted for can over-ride its general requirements.

Consequently, the statement of financial position measurement of a foreign currency financial instrument is determined as follows:

- firstly, it is recorded and measured in the foreign currency in which it is denominated, whether it is carried at fair value, cost, or amortised cost;

- secondly, that amount is retranslated to the entity's functional currency using:

  - closing rate, for all monetary items (e.g. a debt security) and for non-monetary items (e.g. an equity share) carried at fair value; or

  - a historical rate, for non-monetary items carried at cost because their fair value cannot be reliably measured.

Therefore, for a foreign currency denominated monetary asset carried at amortised cost under IFRS 9, amortised cost is calculated in the currency in which it is denominated. That foreign currency amount is then retranslated into the entity's functional currency at the closing rate.

As an exception, if the financial instrument is designated as a hedged item in a fair value hedge of foreign currency exposure, it is remeasured for changes in foreign currency rates even if it would otherwise have been recognised using a historical rate (see Chapter 52 at 8).

The reporting of changes in the carrying amount of a financial instrument in profit or loss or in other comprehensive income depends on a number of factors, including whether it is an exchange difference or other change in carrying amount, whether the instrument is a monetary or non-monetary item and whether it is designated as part of a foreign currency cash flow hedge or hedge of a net investment.

Profit and loss items associated with financial instruments, e.g. dividends receivable, interest payable or receivable and impairments, are recorded at the spot rate ruling when they arise (although average rates may be used when they represent an appropriate approximation to spot rates throughout the period). Foreign exchange differences arising on retranslating monetary items, including debt instruments measured at fair value through other comprehensive income, are generally recognised in profit or loss. However, those exchange differences may be recognised in other comprehensive income for instruments designated as a hedging instrument in a cash flow hedge, a hedge of a net investment in a foreign operation (see Chapter 52 at 5) or a fair value hedge of an equity instrument for which an entity has elected to present changes in fair value in other comprehensive income (see 2.2 above).

[IFRS 9.B5.7.2, B5.7.2A]. All other fair value changes (e.g. the change in value of a debt instrument as a result of interest rate movements) are recognised in profit or loss if the instrument is classified at fair value through profit or loss, or other comprehensive income.

In cases where some portion of the change in carrying amount is recognised in profit or loss and some in other comprehensive income, e.g. if the amortised cost of a foreign currency bond measured at fair value through other comprehensive income has increased in foreign currency (resulting in a gain in profit or loss) but its fair value has increased in foreign currency, those two components cannot be offset for the purposes of determining gains or losses that should be recognised in profit or loss or in other comprehensive income. *[IFRS 9.B5.7.2, 5.7.2A, E.3.4]*.

4.2 Foreign entities

IFRS 9 does not amend application of the net investment method of accounting for foreign entities set out in IAS 21 (see Chapter 15 at 6). Therefore, for the purpose of preparing its own accounts for inclusion in consolidated accounts, a foreign entity that is part of a group applies the principles at 4.1 above by reference to its own functional currency.

5 IMPAIRMENT

5.1 Introduction

The IASB has sought to address a key concern that arose as a result of the financial crisis, that the incurred loss model in IAS 39 contributed to the delayed recognition of credit losses. To do so, it has introduced a forward-looking expected credit loss model in IFRS 9. The expected credit loss requirements and application guidance in the standard are accompanied by 14 Illustrative Examples.

This section discusses the new expected credit loss model as set out in IFRS 9. This section also briefly describes the new credit risk disclosures in relation to the expected credit loss model as set out in IFRS 7 (see 5.13 below). A more detailed discussion of the disclosure requirements can be found in Chapter 53 at 5.2.3.

5.1.1 Brief history and background of the impairment project

During the financial crisis, the delayed recognition of credit losses that are associated with loans and other financial instruments was identified as a weakness in existing accounting standards. This is primarily due to the fact that the current impairment requirements under IAS 39 are based on an incurred loss model, i.e. credit losses are not recognised until a credit loss event occurs. Since losses are rarely incurred evenly over the lives of loans, there is a mismatch in the timing of the recognition of the credit spread inherent in the interest charged on the loans over their lives and any impairment losses that only get recognised at a later date. A further identified weakness was the complexity of different entities using different approaches to calculate impairment.

As part of the joint approach by the IASB and the FASB to deal with the financial reporting issues arising from the financial crisis, the boards set up the Financial Crisis Advisory Group (FCAG) in October 2008 to consider how improvements in financial reporting could help to enhance investor confidence in financial markets. Not long after, the leaders of the Group of 20 (also known as the G20) published a report *Declaration on Strengthening the Financial System* in April 2009 that called on the accounting standard setters to reduce the complexity of accounting standards for financial instruments and to strengthen accounting recognition of loan-loss provisions by incorporating a broader range of credit information.[15]

In July 2009, the FCAG presented its report to the IASB and the FASB about the standard-setting implications of the global financial crisis. Consistent with the G20's recommendations, the FCAG also recommended both the IASB and the FASB to explore alternatives to the incurred loss model for loan loss provisioning that used more forward-looking information.[16]

In June 2009, the IASB published a request for information – *Impairment of Financial Assets: Expected Cash Flow Approach* – on the feasibility of an expected loss model for the impairment of financial assets. Following this, the IASB issued an Exposure Draft – *Financial Instruments: Amortised Cost and Impairment* – in November 2009, that proposed an impairment model based on expected losses rather than on incurred losses, for all financial assets recorded at amortised cost. In this approach, the initial expected credit losses were to be recognised over the life of a financial asset, by including them in the computation of the effective interest rate when the asset was first recognised. This would build an allowance for credit losses over the life of a financial asset and so match the recognition of credit losses with that of the credit spread implicit in the interest charged. Subsequent changes in credit loss expectations would be reflected in catch-up adjustments to profit or loss based on the original effective interest rate. Because the proposals were much more closely linked to credit risk management concepts, the IASB acknowledged that this would represent a fundamental change from how entities currently operate (i.e. typically, entities operate their accounting and credit risk management systems separately). Consequently, the IASB established a panel of credit risk experts, the Expert Advisory Panel (EAP), to provide input to the project. [IFRS 9.BC5.87].

Comments received on the 2009 Exposure Draft and during the IASB's outreach activities indicated that constituents were generally supportive of a model that distinguished between the effect of initial estimates of expected credit losses and subsequent changes in those estimates. However, they were also concerned about the operational difficulties in implementing the model proposed. These included: [IFRS 9.BC5.89]

- estimating the full expected cash flows for all financial instruments;
- applying a credit-adjusted effective interest rate to those cash flow estimates; and
- maintaining information about the initial estimate of expected credit losses.

Also, the proposals would not have been easy to apply to portfolios of loans managed on a collective basis, in particular, open portfolios to which new financial instruments are added over time, and concerns were expressed about the volatility of reported profit or loss arising from the catch up adjustments.

To address these operational challenges and as suggested by the EAP, the IASB decided to decouple the measurement and allocation of initial expected credit losses from the determination of the effective interest rate (except for purchased or originated credit-impaired financial assets). Therefore, the financial asset and the loss allowance would be measured separately, using an original effective interest rate that is not adjusted for initial expected credit losses. Such an approach would help address the operational challenges raised and allow entities to leverage their existing accounting and credit risk management systems and so reduce the extent of the necessary integration between these systems. *[IFRS 9.BC5.92]*.

By decoupling expected credit losses from the effective interest rate, an entity must measure the present value of expected credit losses using the original effective interest rate. This presents a dilemma, because measuring expected credit losses using such a rate double-counts the expected credit losses that were priced into the financial asset at initial recognition. In other words, because the fair value of the loan at original recognition already reflects the expected credit losses, to provide for the expected credit losses as an additional allowance would be to double count these losses. Hence, the IASB concluded that it was not appropriate to recognise lifetime expected credit losses on initial recognition. In order to address the operational challenges while trying to reduce the effect of double-counting as well as to replicate (approximately) the outcome of the 2009 Exposure Draft, the IASB decided to pursue a dual-measurement model that would require an entity to recognise: *[IFRS 9.BC5.93]*

- a portion of the lifetime expected credit losses from initial recognition as a proxy for recognising the initial expected credit losses over the life of the financial asset; and

- the lifetime expected credit losses when credit risk had increased since initial recognition (i.e. when the recognition of only a portion of the lifetime expected credit losses would no longer be appropriate because the entity has suffered a significant economic loss).

It is worth noting that any approach that seeks to approximate the outcomes of the model in the 2009 Exposure Draft without the associated operational challenges of a credit-adjusted effective interest rate will include a recognition threshold for lifetime expected credit losses. This will give rise to what has been referred to as a cliff effect i.e. the significant increase in allowance that represents the difference between the portion that was recognised previously and the lifetime expected credit losses. *[IFRS 9.BC5.95]*.

Subsequently, the IASB and FASB spent a considerable amount of time and effort developing a converged impairment model. In January 2011, the IASB issued with the FASB a Supplementary Document – *Financial Instruments:*

Chapter 49

Impairment – reflecting a joint approach that proposed a two-tier loss allowance: *[IFRS 9.BC5.96]*

- for the good book, an entity would recognise the higher of a time-proportionate allowance (i.e. the lifetime expected credit losses over the weighted average life of the portfolio of assets) or expected credit losses for the 'foreseeable future'; and

- for the bad book, an entity would recognise lifetime expected credit losses on those financial assets when the collectability of contractual cash flows had become so uncertain that the entity's credit risk management objective had changed from receiving the regular payments to recovery of all, or a portion of, the asset.

However, this approach received only limited support, because respondents were concerned about the operational difficulties in performing the dual calculation for the good book, that it also lacked conceptual merit and, potentially, would provide confusing information to users of financial statements. Moreover, concerns were also raised as to how foreseeable future should be interpreted and applied.

Many constituents emphasised the importance of achieving convergence and this encouraged the IASB and FASB to attempt to develop another joint alternative approach. In May 2011, the boards decided to develop jointly an expected credit loss model that would reflect the general pattern of increases in the credit risk of financial instruments, the so-called three-bucket model. *[IFRS 9.BC5.111]*.

However, due to concerns raised by the FASB's constituents about the model's complexity, the FASB decided to develop an alternative expected credit loss model. In December 2012, the FASB issued a proposed accounting standard update, *Financial Instruments Credit Losses (Subtopic 825-15)*, that would require an entity to recognise a loss allowance for expected credit losses from initial recognition at an amount equal to lifetime expected credit losses (see 5.1.4 below). *[IFRS 9.BC5.112]*.

In March 2013, the IASB published a new Exposure Draft – *Financial Instruments: Expected Credit Losses*, based on proposals that grew out of the joint project with the FASB. The 2013 Exposure Draft proposed that entities should recognise a loss allowance or provision at an amount equal to 12-month credit losses for those financial instruments that had not yet seen a significant increase in credit risk since initial recognition, and lifetime expected credit losses once there had been a significant increase in credit risk. This new model was designed to:

- ensure a more timely recognition of expected credit losses than the existing incurred loss model;

- distinguish between financial instruments that have significantly deteriorated in credit quality and those that have not; and

- better approximate the economic expected credit losses.[17]

This two-step model was designed to approximate the build-up of allowance as proposed in the 2009 Exposure Draft, but involving less operational complexity. Figure 49.1 below illustrates the stepped profile of the new model, shown by the solid line, compared to the steady increase shown by the black dotted line proposed in the 2009 Exposure Draft (based on the original expected credit loss assumptions and assuming no subsequent revisions of this estimate). It shows that the two step model first overstates the allowance (compared to the method set out in the 2009 Exposure Draft), then understates it as the credit quality deteriorates, and then overstates it once again, as soon as the deterioration is significant.

Figure 49.1 Accounting for expected credit losses – 2009 ED versus IFRS 9[18]

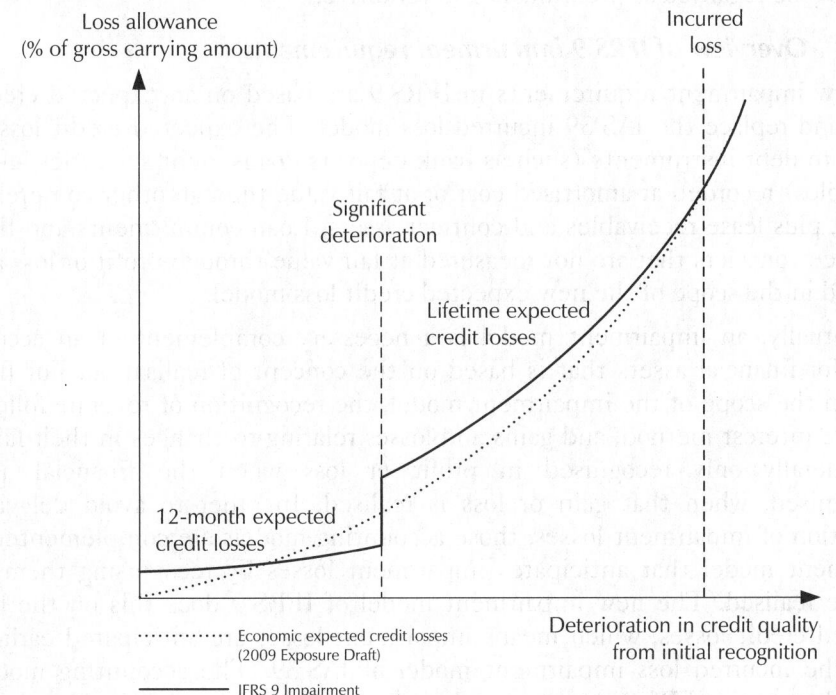

Feedback received on the IASB's 2013 Exposure Draft and the FASB's 2012 Proposed Update was considered at the joint board meetings. In general, non-US constituents preferred the IASB's proposals whilst the US constituents preferred the FASB's proposals. These differences in views arose in large part because of differences in the starting point of how preparers apply US GAAP for loss allowances from that for most IFRS preparers, while the interaction between the role of prudential regulators and calculation of loss allowances is historically stronger in the US. *[IFRS 9.BC5.116].*

Many respondents urged the IASB to finalise the proposals in the 2013 Exposure Draft as soon as possible, even if convergence could not be achieved, in order to improve the accounting for the impairment of financial assets in IFRSs. *[IFRS 9.BC5.114].* The IASB re-deliberated particular aspects of the 2013 Exposure Draft proposals, with the aim of providing further clarifications and additional guidance to help entities implement the proposed requirements. The IASB finalised the impairment requirements and issued them in July 2014, as part of the final IFRS 9.

Chapter 49

Also, the IASB has set up an IFRS Transition Resource Group for Impairment of Financial Instruments (ITG) (see 5.1.5 below) and the Basel Committee is expected to provide guidance to banks on the implementation of the IFRS 9 impairment model (see 5.1.6 and 5.6.1 below).

Given these initiatives and the development of consensus on the part of preparers, auditors and other stakeholders, any views that we express in this chapter must inevitably be regarded as preliminary and tentative.

5.1.2 Overview of IFRS 9 impairment requirements

The new impairment requirements in IFRS 9 are based on an expected credit loss model and replace the IAS 39 incurred loss model. The expected credit loss model applies to debt instruments (such as bank deposits, loans, debt securities and trade receivables) recorded at amortised cost or at fair value through other comprehensive income, plus lease receivables and contract assets. Loan commitments and financial guarantee contracts that are not measured at fair value through profit or loss are also included in the scope of the new expected credit loss model.

Conceptually, an impairment model is a necessary complement of an accounting model for financial assets that is based on the concept of realisation. For financial assets in the scope of the impairment model, the recognition of revenue follows the effective interest method, and gains and losses relating to changes in their fair value are generally only recognised in profit or loss when the financial asset is derecognised, when that gain or loss is realised. In order to avoid delaying the recognition of impairment losses, those accounting models are complemented by an impairment model that anticipates impairment losses by recognising them before they are realised. The new impairment model of IFRS 9 does this on the basis of expected credit losses, which means impairment losses are anticipated earlier than under the incurred loss impairment model of IAS 39. The accounting models for financial assets in IFRS 9 that are not based on the concept of realisation, i.e. those measured at fair value through profit or loss or at fair value through other comprehensive income without recycling (under the presentation choice for fair value changes of some investments in equity instruments, see Chapter 46 at 8 and 2.2 above) do not involve any separate impairment accounting. Those measurement categories implicitly include impairment losses in the fair value changes that are recognised immediately (and without any later reclassification entries between other comprehensive income and profit or loss when they are realised).

The guiding principle of the expected credit loss model is to reflect the general pattern of deterioration or improvement in the credit quality of financial instruments. The expected credit loss approach has been commonly referred to as the three-bucket approach, although IFRS 9 does not use this term. Figure 49.2 below summarises the general approach in recognising either 12-month or lifetime expected credit losses.

Figure 49.2 General approach

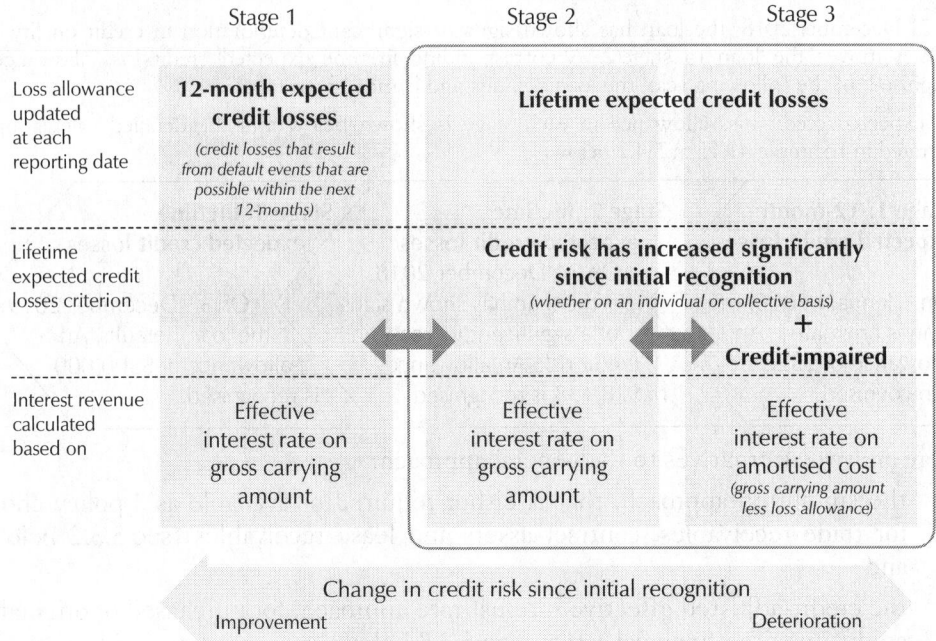

The amount of expected credit losses recognised as a loss allowance or provision depends on the extent of credit deterioration since initial recognition. Under the general approach (see 5.3.1 below), there are two measurement bases:

- 12-month expected credit losses (stage 1), which apply to all items as long as there is no significant deterioration in credit risk; and

- lifetime expected credit losses (stages 2 and 3), which apply when a significant increase in credit risk has occurred on an individual or collective basis.

When assessing significant increases in credit risk, there are a number of operational simplifications available, such as the low credit risk simplification (see 5.5.4 below).

Stages 2 and 3 differ in how interest revenue is recognised. Under stage 2 (as under stage 1), there is a full decoupling between interest recognition and impairment, and interest revenue is calculated on the gross carrying amount. Under stage 3 (where a credit event has occurred, defined similarly to an incurred credit loss under IAS 39), interest revenue is calculated on the amortised cost (i.e. the gross carrying amount adjusted for the impairment allowance).

The following example illustrates how the expected credit loss allowance changes when a loan moves from stage 1 to stage 3.

Example 49.13: Expected credit loss allowance in stages 1, 2 and 3 under the general approach

On 1 January 2016, Bank A originates a 10 year loan with a gross carrying amount of $1,000,000. There are no transaction costs and the loan contracts include no options (for example, prepayment or call options), premiums or discounts, points paid, or other fees.

At origination, the loan is in stage 1 and a corresponding 12-month expected credit loss allowance is recognised in the year ending 31 December 2016.

On 31 December 2018, the loan has shown signs of significant deterioration in credit quality and Bank A moves the loan to stage 2. A corresponding lifetime expected credit loss allowance is recognised. In the following year, the loan defaults and is moved to stage 3.

The expected credit loss allowance in each stage is shown below and the detailed calculation is illustrated in Example 49.15 at 5.4.2 below.

Stage 1: 12-month expected credit losses	Stage 2: lifetime expected credit losses	Stage 3: lifetime expected credit losses
On 1 January 2016, the loan is originated. An allowance of $320 is recognised.	On 31 December 2018, the loan has shown signs of a significant increase in credit risk. An allowance of $28,438 is recognised.	On 31 December 2019, the loan defaults. An allowance of $300,000 is recognised.

There are two alternatives to the general approach:

- the simplified approach, that is either required or available as a policy choice for trade receivables, contract assets and lease receivables (see 5.3.2 below); and

- the credit-adjusted effective interest rate approach, for purchased or originated credit-impaired financial assets (see 5.3.3 below).

Expected credit losses are an estimate of credit losses over the life of a financial instrument and when measuring expected credit losses (see 5.4 below), an entity needs to take into account:

- the probability-weighted outcome (see 5.4.4 below), as expected credit losses should not be simply either a best or a worst-case scenario, but should instead reflect the possibility that a credit loss occurs and the possibility that no credit loss occurs;

- the time value of money (see 5.4.5 below); and

- reasonable and supportable information that is available without undue cost or effort (see 5.4.8 below).

The expected credit loss requirements must be adopted with the other IFRS 9 requirements from 1 January 2018, with early application permitted if the other IFRS 9 requirements are adopted at the same time.

5.1.3   Key changes from the IAS 39 impairment requirements and the main implications of these changes

The new IFRS 9 impairment requirements eliminate the IAS 39 threshold for the recognition of credit losses, i.e. it is no longer necessary for a credit event to have occurred before credit losses are recognised. Instead, an entity always accounts for expected credit losses, and updates the loss allowance for changes in these expected credit losses at each reporting date to reflect changes in credit risk since initial recognition. Consequently, the holder of the financial asset needs to take into account more timely and forward-looking information in order to provide users of financial statements with useful information about the expected credit losses on financial instruments that are in the scope of these impairment requirements.

The main implications for both financial and non-financial entities are as follows:

- The scope of the impairment requirements is now much broader. Previously, under IAS 39, there were different impairment models for financial assets measured at amortised cost and available-for-sale financial assets. Under IFRS 9, there is a single impairment model for all debt instruments measured at amortised cost and at fair value through other comprehensive income. Furthermore, loan commitments and financial guarantee contracts that were previously in the scope of IAS 37 – *Provisions, Contingent Liabilities and Contingent Assets* – are now in the scope of the IFRS 9 impairment requirements (see 5.2 below).

- Previously, under IAS 39, loss allowances were only recorded for impaired exposures. The new impairment requirements result in earlier recognition of credit losses, by necessitating a 12-month expected credit loss allowance for all credit exposures not measured at fair value through profit or loss. In addition, there will be a larger allowance for all credit exposures that have significantly deteriorated (as compared to the recognition of individual incurred losses under IAS 39 today). While credit exposures in stage 3, as illustrated in Figure 49.2 above, are similar to those deemed by IAS 39 to have suffered individual incurred losses, credit exposure in stages 1 and 2 will essentially replace those exposures measured under IAS 39's collective approach.

- The expected credit loss model is more forward-looking than the IAS 39 impairment model. This is because holders of financial assets are not only required to consider historical information that is adjusted to reflect the effects of current conditions and information that provides objective evidence that financial assets are impaired in relation to incurred losses, but they are now required to consider reasonable and supportable information that includes forecasts of future economic conditions when calculating expected credit losses, on an individual and collective basis.

- The application of the new IFRS 9 impairment requirements is expected to increase the credit loss allowances (with a corresponding reduction in equity on first-time adoption) of many entities, particularly banks and similar financial institutions. However, the increase in the loss allowance will vary by entity, depending on its portfolio and current practices. Entities with shorter term and higher quality financial instruments are likely to be less significantly affected. Similarly, financial institutions with unsecured retail loans are more likely to be affected to a greater extent than those with collateralised loans such as mortgages.

- Moreover, the focus on expected losses will possibly result in higher volatility in the expected credit loss amounts charged to profit or loss, especially for financial institutions. The level of loss allowances will increase as economic conditions are forecast to deteriorate and will decrease as economic conditions are forecast to become more favourable. This may be compounded by the significant increase in the loss allowance when financial instruments move between 12-month and lifetime expected credit losses and *vice versa*.

- The need to incorporate forward-looking information means that the application of the standard will require considerable judgement as to how changes in macroeconomic factors will affect expected credit losses. Also, the increased level of judgement required in making the expected credit loss calculation may mean that it will be difficult to compare the reported results of different entities. However, the more detailed disclosures (compared with those required to complement IAS 39) that require entities to explain their inputs, assumptions and techniques used in estimating expected credit losses requirements, should provide greater transparency over entities' credit risk and provisioning processes. The Enhanced Disclosures Task Force, established in 2012 by the Financial Stability Board to recommend best practice market risk disclosures, is in the process of developing guidance to promote greater transparency and comparability about the application of the expected credit loss model (see Chapter 53 at 9.2).

- In financial institutions, finance and credit risk management systems and processes will have to be better connected than today because of the necessary alignment between risk and accounting in the new model. Risk models and data will have to be more extensively used to make the assessments and calculations required for accounting purposes, which are both a major difference from IAS 39 and a key challenge.

- In addition, financial institutions will need to fully understand the complex interactions between the IFRS 9 and regulatory capital requirements in relation to credit losses. At the time of writing, these have yet to be determined by the Basel Committee. In many cases, it is expected that the new IFRS 9 expected credit loss requirements will result in a reduction in the regulatory capital of financial institutions.

- For corporates, the expected credit loss model will most likely not cause a major increase in allowances for short-term trade receivables because of their short term nature. Moreover, the standard includes practical expedients, in particular the use of a provision matrix, which should help in measuring the loss allowance for short-term trade receivables. *[IFRS 9.B5.5.35]*. However, the model may give rise to challenges for the measurement of long-term trade receivables, bank deposits and debt securities which are measured at amortised cost or at fair value through other comprehensive income. For example, a corporate that has a large portfolio of debt securities that are currently held as available-for-sale under IAS 39, is likely to classify its holdings as measured at fair value through other comprehensive income if the contractual cash flow characteristics and business model test are met (see Chapter 46 at 5 and 6). For these securities, the corporate would be required to recognise a loss allowance based on 12-month expected credit losses even for debt securities that are highly rated (e.g. AAA- or AA-rated bonds).

5.1.4 Key differences from the FASB's proposals

In December 2012, the FASB issued a proposed accounting standard update, *Financial Instruments Credit Losses (Subtopic 825-15)*, that aimed to address the same fundamental issue that the IASB's expected credit loss model addresses, namely the delayed recognition of credit losses resulting from the incurred credit loss model. The FASB substantially completed its re-deliberations in April 2015 and its staff are drafting a final standard as of the time of writing this publication. The most significant differences between the FASB's Exposure Draft (as updated for decisions made in re-deliberations) and the IASB's expected credit loss model in IFRS 9 are, as follows:

• The FASB's proposed expected credit loss model would not be applied to debt securities measured at fair value through other comprehensive income (i.e. so-called available for sale securities under US GAAP). Rather, for these securities, the FASB's existing other-than-temporary impairment model would be modified to require an allowance for credit impairment rather than a direct write-down, among other things.

• The FASB proposed that expected credit losses would be calculated based on the current estimate of the contractual cash flows that an entity does not expect to collect. This is similar to the lifetime expected credit loss objective under IFRS 9. The FASB's proposed model would not include a 12-month expected credit loss to be recognised for any assets. As a result, the FASB's proposed model does not require an entity to assess whether there has been a significant deterioration in credit quality, in contrast to the assessment required by IFRS 9.

• For purchased credit-impaired assets, the FASB's proposed model would require an entity to increase the purchase price by the allowance for expected credit losses upon acquisition. In doing so, the FASB model would effectively gross-up the asset's carrying amount by the expected credit losses existing upon acquisition, but also recognise a corresponding credit loss allowance, thereby resulting in a net carrying amount equal to the purchase price (see 5.3.3 below for the accounting treatment of credit-impaired assets under IFRS 9).

• The FASB's proposed model would continue to allow the use of non-accrual accounting practice (i.e. ceasing recognition of interest income in certain circumstances) in lieu of specifically requiring a net interest income recognition approach for debt instruments where there is evidence of incurred credit losses.

The FASB is expected to publish its impairment requirements before the end of 2015.

5.1.5   The IFRS Transition Resource Group for Impairment of Financial Instruments (ITG)

The IASB has set up the ITG that aims to:[19]

- provide a public discussion forum to support stakeholders on implementation issues arising from the new impairment requirements that could create diversity in practice; and

- inform the IASB about the implementation issues, which will help the IASB determine what action, if any, will be needed to address them.

However, the ITG will not issue any guidance.

Members of the ITG include financial statement preparers and auditors from various geographical locations with expertise, skills or practical knowledge on credit risk management and accounting for impairment. Board members and observers from the Basel Committee on Banking Supervision and the International Organisation of Securities Commissions also attend the meetings.

The ITG agenda papers are prepared by the IASB staff and are made public before the meetings. The staff also provides ITG meeting summaries which are not authoritative. Both the staff papers and the meeting summaries represent educational reading on the issues submitted.[20]

Following its inaugural meeting in December 2014 to discuss its operating procedures, the ITG met on 22 April 2015 to discuss eight implementation issues raised by stakeholders. These included:

- when applying the impairment requirements at the reporting date, whether and how to incorporate events and forecasts, that occur after economic forecasts have been made but before the reporting date and between the reporting period end and the date of signing the financial statements (see 5.4.8.C below);

- whether the impairment requirements in IFRS 9 must also be applied to other commitments to extend credit, in particular, a commitment (on inception of a finance lease) to commence a finance lease at a date in the future and a commitment by a retailer through the issue of a store account to provide a customer with credit when the customer buys goods or services from the retailer in the future (see 5.10 below);

- whether there is a requirement to measure expected credit losses at dates other than the reporting date, namely the date of derecognition and the date of initial recognition (see 5.6.2 below);

- whether an entity should consider the ability to recover cash flows through an integral financial guarantee contract when assessing whether there has been a significant increase in the credit risk of the guaranteed debt instrument since initial recognition (see 5.5.1 below);

- the maximum period to consider when measuring expected credit losses on a portfolio of mortgage loans that have a stated maturity of 6 months, but contain a contractual feature whereby the term is automatically extended every 6 months subject to the lender's non-objection (see 5.4.3 below);

- the maximum period to consider when measuring expected credit losses for revolving credit facilities and the determination of the date of initial recognition of the revolving facilities for the purposes of assessing them for significant increases in credit risk (see 5.11 below);

- whether the measurement of expected credit losses for financial guarantee contracts issued should consider future premium receipts due from the holder and, if so, how (see 5.10 below); and

- the measurement of expected credit losses in respect of a modified financial asset, the calculation of the modification gain or loss and subsequent requirement to measure expected credit losses on the modified financial asset as well as the appropriate presentation and disclosure (see 5.7 below).

On 16 September 2015, the ITG held its third meeting to discuss six implementation issues raised by stakeholders. These included:

- how to identify a significant increase in credit risk for a portfolio of retail loans when identical pricing and contractual terms are applied to customers across broad credit quality bands (see 5.5.2);

- the possibility of using behavioural indicators of credit risk for the purpose of the assessment of significant increases in credit risk since initial recognition (see 5.5.2 below);

- when assessing for significant increases in credit risk, whether an entity would be required to perform an annual review to determine whether circumstances still support the use of the 12-month probability of default (PD) as an approximation of changes in the lifetime PD (see 5.5.4.C below);

- when measuring expected credit losses for revolving credit facilities, how an entity should estimate future drawdowns on undrawn lines of credit when an entity has a history of allowing customers to exceed their contractually set credit limits on overdrafts and other revolving credit facilities (see 5.11 below);

- at what level should forward-looking information be incorporated – at the level of the entity or on a portfolio-by-portfolio basis (see 5.4.8.C); and

- how to determine what is reasonable and supportable forward-looking information and how to treat shock events with material, but uncertain, economic consequences (see 5.4.8.C below).

The final meeting for 2015 is scheduled for 11 December 2015. The IASB is prepared to reconvene the ITG in 2016, if needed, although no meetings are currently scheduled.

It is expected that the FASB (see 5.1.4 above) will set up its own transition resource group and its discussions may prove relevant to the application of IFRS 9 in areas where the two expected credit loss models are similar.

Chapter 49

5.1.6   Basel Committee on Banking Supervision

On 2 February 2015, the Basel Committee on Banking Supervision issued a *Consultative Document: Guidance on accounting for expected credit losses* – that set out draft supervisory expectations regarding sound credit risk practices associated with implementing and applying an expected credit loss accounting framework. The draft guidance largely retained the Basel Committee's current principles on sound credit risk assessment and valuation of loans (SCRAVL) that were issued in 2006, but was revised to reflect the move from an incurred loss to an expected credit loss accounting model. The guidance, which is due to be published in its final form in the fourth quarter of 2015, is further discussed at 5.6.1 below.

5.2   Scope

IFRS 9 requires an entity to recognise a loss allowance for expected credit losses on: *[IFRS 9.5.5.1]*

- financial assets that are debt instruments such as loans, debt securities, bank balances and deposits and trade receivables (see 5.9 below) that are measured at amortised cost; *[IFRS 9.4.1.2]*

- financial assets that are debt instruments measured at fair value through other comprehensive income (see 5.8 below); *[IFRS 9.4.1.2A]*

- lease receivables under IAS 17 – *Leases* (see 5.9 below and Chapter 24);

- contract assets under IFRS 15 (see 5.9 below and Chapter 29). IFRS 15 defines a contract asset as an entity's right to consideration in exchange for goods or services that the entity has transferred to a customer when that right is conditioned on something other than the passage of time (for example, the entity's future performance); *[IFRS 15 Appendix A, IFRS 9 Appendix A]*

- loan commitments that are not measured at fair value through profit or loss under IFRS 9 (see 5.10 and 5.11 below). The scope excludes loan commitments designated as financial liabilities at fair value through profit and loss and loan commitments that can be settled net in cash or by delivering or issuing another financial instrument; and *[IFRS 9.2.1(g), 2.3, 4.2.1(a), 4.2.1(d)]*

- financial guarantee contracts that are not measured at fair value through profit or loss under IFRS 9 (see 5.10 below).

5.3   Approaches

In applying the IFRS 9 impairment requirements, an entity needs to follow one of the approaches below:

- the general approach (see 5.3.1 below);

- the simplified approach (see 5.3.2 below); or

- the purchased or originated credit-impaired approach (see 5.3.3 below).

Figure 49.3 below, based on a diagram from the standard, summarises the process steps in recognising and measuring expected credit losses.

Figure 49.3 Application of the impairment requirements at a reporting date

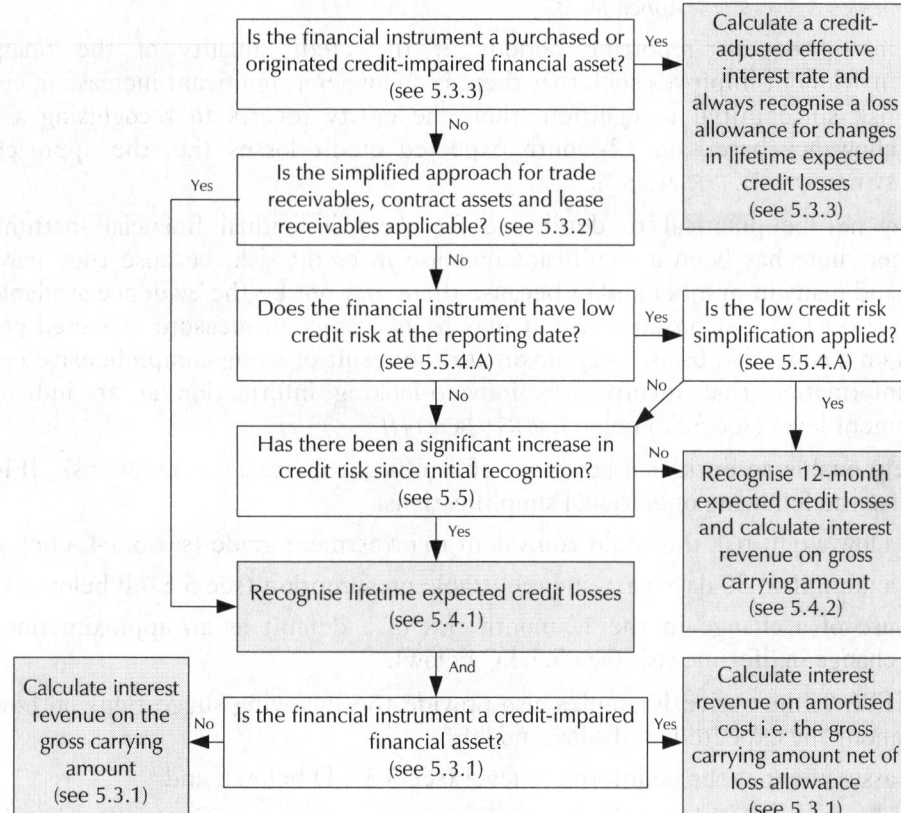

5.3.1 General approach

Under the general approach, at each reporting date, an entity recognises a loss allowance based on either 12-month expected credit losses or lifetime expected credit losses, depending on whether there has been a significant increase in credit risk on the financial instrument since initial recognition. *[IFRS 9.5.5.3, 5.5.5].* The changes in the loss allowance balance are recognised in profit or loss as an impairment gain or loss. *[IFRS 9.5.5.8, Appendix A].*

Essentially, an entity must make the following assessment at each reporting date:

* for credit exposures where there have not been significant increases in credit risk since initial recognition, an entity is required to provide for 12-month expected credit losses, i.e. the portion of lifetime expected credit losses that represent the expected credit losses that result from default events that are possible within the 12-months after the reporting date (stage 1 in Figure 49.2 at 5.1.2 above). *[IFRS 9.5.5.3, Appendix A].*

* for credit exposures where there have been significant increases in credit risk since initial recognition on an individual or collective basis, a loss allowance is required for lifetime expected credit losses, i.e. expected credit losses that result from all possible default events over the expected

life of a financial instrument (stages 2 and 3 in Figure 49.2 at 5.1.2 above). *[IFRS 9.5.5.4, 5.5.5, Appendix A]*.

- in subsequent reporting periods, if the credit quality of the financial instrument improves such that there is no longer a significant increase in credit risk since initial recognition, then the entity reverts to recognising a loss allowance based on 12-month expected credit losses (i.e. the approach is symmetrical). *[IFRS 9.5.5.7]*.

It may not be practical to determine for every individual financial instrument whether there has been a significant increase in credit risk, because they may be small and many in number and/or because there may not be the evidence available to do so. *[IFRS 9.B5.5.1]*. Consequently, it may be necessary to measure expected credit losses on a collective basis, to approximate the result of using comprehensive credit risk information that incorporates forward-looking information at an individual instrument level (see 5.5.5 below). *[IFRS 9.BC5.141]*.

To help enable an entity's assessment of significant increases in credit risk, IFRS 9 provides the following operational simplifications:

- a low credit risk threshold equivalent to investment grade (see 5.5.4.A below);
- a more than 30 days past due rebuttable presumption (see 5.5.4.B below); and
- use of a change in the 12-month risk of a default as an approximation for change in lifetime risk (see 5.5.4.C below).

The IFRS 9 Illustrative Examples also provide the following suggestions on how to implement the expected credit loss model:

- assessment at the counterparty level (see 5.5.4.D below); and
- a set transfer threshold by determining maximum initial credit risk for a portfolio (see 5.5.4.E below).

In stages 1 and 2, there is a complete decoupling between interest recognition and impairment. Therefore, interest revenue is calculated on the gross carrying amount (without deducting the loss allowance). If a financial asset subsequently becomes credit-impaired (stage 3 in Figure 49.2 at 5.1.2 above), an entity is required to calculate the interest revenue by applying the effective interest rate in subsequent reporting periods to the amortised cost of the financial asset (i.e. the gross carrying amount net of loss allowance) rather than the gross carrying amount (see 3 above for further details on amortised cost and the effective interest method). *[IFRS 9.5.4.1, Appendix A]*. Financial assets are assessed as credit-impaired using substantially the same criteria as for the impairment assessment of an individual asset under IAS 39. *[IAS 39.59, IFRS 9 Appendix A]*.

A financial asset is credit-impaired when one or more events that have a detrimental impact on the estimated future cash flows of that financial asset have occurred. Evidence that a financial asset is impaired includes observable data about such events. IFRS 9 provides a list of events that are substantially the same as the IAS 39 loss events for an individual asset assessment: *[IFRS 9 Appendix A]*

- significant financial difficulty of the issuer or the borrower;
- a breach of contract, such as a default or past due event;

- the lender(s) of the borrower, for economic or contractual reasons relating to the borrower's financial difficulty, having granted to the borrower a concession(s) that the lender(s) would not otherwise consider;

- it is becoming probable that the borrower will enter bankruptcy or other financial reorganisation;

- the disappearance of an active market for that financial asset because of financial difficulties; or

- the purchase or origination of a financial asset at a deep discount that reflects the incurred credit losses.

It may not be possible for an entity to identify a single discrete event. Instead, the combined effect of several events may have caused the financial asset to become credit-impaired. *[IFRS 9 Appendix A].*

In subsequent reporting periods, if the credit quality of the financial asset improves so that the financial asset is no longer credit-impaired and the improvement can be related objectively to the occurrence of an event (such as an improvement in the borrower's credit rating), then the entity should once again calculate the interest revenue by applying the effective interest rate to the gross carrying amount of the financial asset. *[IFRS 9.5.4.2].*

When the entity has no reasonable expectations of recovering the financial asset, then the gross carrying amount of the financial asset should be directly reduced in its entirety. A write-off constitutes a derecognition event (see 5.12.1.A below).

5.3.2 Simplified approach

The simplified approach does not require an entity to track the changes in credit risk, but instead requires the entity to recognise a loss allowance based on lifetime expected credit losses at each reporting date. *[IFRS 9.5.5.15].*

An entity is required to apply the simplified approach for trade receivables or contract assets that result from transactions within the scope of IFRS 15 and that do not contain a significant financing component, or when the entity applies the practical expedient for contracts that have a maturity of one year or less, in accordance with IFRS 15 (see Chapter 29). *[IFRS 9.5.5.15(a)(i)].* Paragraphs 60-65 of IFRS 15 provide the requirements for determining the existence of a significant financing component in the contract, including the use of the practical expedient for contracts that are one year or less.

A contract asset is defined as an entity's right to consideration in exchange for goods or services that the entity has transferred to a customer when that right is conditioned on something other than the passage of time (for example, the entity's future performance). *[IFRS 15 Appendix A].* IFRS 15 describes contracts with a significant financing component as those for which the agreed timing of payment provides the customer or the entity with a significant benefit of financing on the transfer of goods or services to the customer and hence, in determining the transaction price, an entity is required to adjust the promised amount of consideration for the effects of the time value of money. *[IFRS 15.60].* However, if the entity expects at contract inception that the period between when the entity transfers a promised good or service to a customer and when the customer pays for that good or service will be one year or less, as a practical expedient, an entity need not adjust the promised amount of consideration for the effects of a significant financing component. *[IFRS 15.63].*

Application of the simplified approach to trade receivables and contract assets that do not contain a significant financing component intuitively makes sense. In particular, for trade receivables and contract assets that are due in 12-months or less, the 12-month expected credit losses are the same as the lifetime expected credit losses.

However, an entity has a policy choice to apply either the simplified approach or the general approach for the following: *[IFRS 9.5.5.16]:*

- all trade receivables or contract assets that result from transactions within the scope of IFRS 15, and that contain a significant financing component in accordance with IFRS 15. The policy choice may be applied separately to trade receivables and contract assets (see 5.9.1 below and Chapter 29); *[IFRS 9.5.5.15(a)(ii)]* and

- all lease receivables that result from transactions that are within the scope of IAS 17. The policy choice may be applied separately to finance and operating lease receivables (see 5.9.2 below and Chapter 24). *[IFRS 9.5.5.15(b)].*

The IASB noted that offering this policy choice would reduce comparability. However, the IASB believes it would alleviate some of the practical concerns of tracking changes in credit risk for entities that do not have sophisticated credit risk management systems. *[IFRS 9. BC5.225].*

5.3.3   Purchased or originated credit-impaired financial assets

On initial recognition of a financial asset, an entity is required to determine whether the asset is credit-impaired. The criteria are set out at 5.3.1 above. *[IFRS 9.5.5.3, 5.5.5, 5.5.13].*

A financial asset may be purchased credit-impaired because it has already met the criteria. Such an asset is likely to be acquired at a deep discount. However, this does not mean that an entity is required to apply the credit-adjusted effective interest rate to a financial asset solely because the financial asset has a high credit risk at initial recognition, if it has not yet met those criteria. *[IFRS 9.B5.4.7].*

In some unusual circumstances, it may be possible that an entity originates a credit-impaired financial asset, for example following a substantial modification of a distressed financial asset that resulted in the derecognition of the original financial asset (see 5.7 below). *[IFRS 9.B5.5.26].*

Consider an example of a bank originating a loan of €100,000 with interest of 30% per annum charged over the term of the loan, payable in monthly amortising instalments. The bank's customer has a high credit risk on origination and the bank expects a large portion of this type of customer to pay late or fail to pay some or all of their instalment payments. Although the loan is of high credit risk (which is supported by the high interest rate), none of the loss events listed above *have occurred* and the loan was not the result of a substantial modification and derecognition of a distressed debt, hence, the bank should assess the loan not to be credit-impaired on origination.

For financial assets that are considered to be credit-impaired on purchase or origination, the effective interest rate (see 3 above) is calculated taking into account the initial lifetime expected credit losses in the estimated cash flows. *[IFRS 9.B5.4.7, Appendix A, BC5.214, BC5.217].*

This accounting treatment is the same as that under IAS 39. *[IAS 39.AG5].* It is also consistent with the original method for measuring impairment proposed in the 2009 Exposure Draft.

Consequently, no allowance is recorded for 12-month expected credit losses for financial assets that are credit-impaired on initial recognition. The rationale for not recording a 12-month expected credit loss allowance for these assets is that the losses are already reflected in the fair values at which they are initially recognised. The same logic could be applied to all the other financial assets which are not credit-impaired, arguing that they, too, are initially recognised at a fair value that reflects expectations of future losses. The distinction is made because the double-counting of 12-month expected credit losses on initial recognition would be too large for assets with such a high credit risk, and the exclusion of initial expected credit losses from the computation of the effective interest rate would lead to a distortion that would be too significant to be acceptable.

For financial assets that were credit-impaired on purchase or origination, the credit-adjusted effective interest rate is also used subsequently to discount the expected credit losses. In subsequent reporting periods an entity is required to recognise:

- in the statement of financial position, the cumulative changes in lifetime expected credit losses since initial recognition, discounted at the credit-impaired effective interest rate (see 5.4.5 below), as a loss allowance; *[IFRS 9.5.5.13, B5.5.45]* and

- in profit or loss, the amount of any change in lifetime expected credit losses as an impairment gain or loss. An impairment gain is recognised if favourable changes result in the lifetime expected credit losses estimate becoming lower than the original estimate that was incorporated in the estimated cash flows on initial recognition when calculating the credit-adjusted effective interest rate. *[IFRS 9.5.5.14].*

For favourable changes that result in a lower lifetime expected credit losses than the original estimate on initial recognition, IFRS 9 does not provide guidance on where in the statement of financial position the debit entry should be booked. In our view, the impairment gain should be recognised as a direct adjustment to the gross carrying amount. This is supported by paragraph B5.4.6 as, for purchased or originated credit-impaired financial assets, the expected credit losses are included in the estimated cash flows when calculating the credit-adjusted effective interest rate and hence, the changes in estimates of expected credit losses should adjust the gross carrying amount of the financial asset. An alternative treatment would be to recognise a negative loss allowance which would reflect the favourable changes in lifetime expected credit losses.

Chapter 49

Along with the other credit risk disclosures requirements (see 5.13 below and Chapter 53 at 5.2.3), the holder is required to explain how it has determined that assets are credit-impaired (including the inputs, assumptions and estimation techniques used). It is also required to disclose the total amount of undiscounted expected credit losses at initial recognition for financial assets initially recognised during the reporting period that were purchased or originated credit-impaired. *[IFRS 7.35H(c)].*

The accounting treatment for a purchased credit-impaired financial asset is illustrated in the following example.

Example 49.14:   Calculation of the credit-adjusted effective interest rate and recognition of a loss allowance for a purchased credit-impaired financial asset

On 1 January 2010, Company D issued a bond that required it to pay an annual coupon of €800 in arrears and to repay the principal of €10,000 on 31 December 2019. By 2015, Company D was in significant financial difficulties and was unable to pay the coupon due on 31 December 2015. On 1 January 2016, Company V estimates that the holder could expect to receive a single payment of €4,000 at the end of 2017. It acquires the bond at an arm's length price of €3,000. Company V determines that the debt instrument is credit-impaired on initial recognition, because of evidence of significant financial difficulty of Company D and because the debt instrument was purchased at a deep discount.

It can be shown that using the contractual cash flows (including the €800 overdue) gives rise to an effective interest rate of 70.1% (the net present value of €800 now and annually thereafter until 2019 and €10,000 receivable at the end of 2019 equals €3,000 when discounted at 70.1%). However, because the bond is credit-impaired, V should calculate the effective interest rate using the estimated cash flows of the instrument. In this case, the effective interest rate is 15.5% (the net present value of €4,000 receivable in two years equals €3,000 when discounted at 15.5%).

All things being equal, interest income of €464 (€3,000 × 15.5%) would be recognised on the instrument during 2016 and its carrying amount at the end of the year would be €3,464 (€3,000 + €464). However if at the end of the year, based on reasonable and supportable evidence, the cash flow expected to be received on the instrument had increased to, say, €4,250 (still to be received at the end of 2017), an adjustment would be made to the asset's amortised cost. Accordingly, its carrying amount would be increased to €3,681 (€4,250 discounted over one year at 15.5%) and an impairment gain of €217 would be recognised in profit or loss.

5.4   Measurement of expected credit losses

The standard defines credit loss as the difference between all contractual cash flows that are due to an entity in accordance with the contract and all the cash flows that the entity expects to receive (i.e. all cash shortfalls), discounted at the original effective interest rate (or credit-adjusted effective interest rate for purchased or originated credit-impaired financial assets). When estimating the cash flows, an entity is required to consider: *[IFRS 9 Appendix A]*

- all contractual terms of the financial instrument (including prepayment, extension, call and similar options) over the expected life (see 5.4.3 below) of the financial instrument. The maximum period to consider when measuring expected credit losses is the maximum contractual period (including extension options) over which the entity is exposed to credit risk (with an exception for revolving facilities).

- cash flows from the sale of collateral held (see 5.4.7 below) or other credit enhancements that are integral to the contractual terms.

Also, the standard goes on to define expected credit losses as 'the weighted average of credit losses with the respective risks of a default occurring as the weights'. *[IFRS 9 Appendix A].*

The standard does not prescribe specific approaches to estimate expected credit losses, but stresses that that the approach used must reflect the following: *[IFRS 9.5.5.17]*

- an unbiased and probability-weighted amount that is determined by evaluating a range of possible outcomes (see 5.4.4 below);

- the time value of money (see 5.4.5 below); and

- reasonable and supportable information that is available without undue cost or effort at the reporting date about past events, current conditions and forecasts of future economic conditions (see 5.4.8 below).

5.4.1 *Lifetime expected credit losses*

IFRS 9 defines lifetime expected credit losses as the expected credit losses that result from all possible default events over the expected life of a financial instrument (i.e. an entity needs to estimate the risk of a default occurring on the financial instrument during its expected life). *[IFRS 9 Appendix A, B5.5.43].* The expected life considered for the measurement of lifetime expected credit losses cannot be longer than the maximum contractual period (including extension options) over which the entity is exposed to credit risk. However, there is an exception for revolving facilities (see 5.11 below).

Expected credit losses should be estimated based on the present value of all cash shortfalls over the remaining expected life of the financial asset, i.e. the difference between: *[IFRS 9.B5.5.29]*

- the contractual cash flows that are due to an entity under the contract; and

- the cash flows that the holder expects to receive.

As expected credit losses take into account both the amount and the timing of payments, a credit loss arises even if the holder expects to receive all the contractual payments due, but at a later date. *[IFRS 9.B5.5.28].*

When estimating lifetime expected credit losses for undrawn loan commitments (see 5.10 below), the provider of the commitment needs to:

- estimate the expected portion of the loan commitment that will be drawn down over the expected life of the loan commitment (capped at the maximum contractual period, including extension options, over which the entity is exposed to credit risk (with the exception for revolving facilities)) (see 5.4.2 below for 12-month expected credit losses); *[IFRS 9.B5.5.31]* and

- calculate the present value of cash shortfalls between the contractual cash flows that are due to the entity if the holder of the loan commitment draws down that expected portion of the loan and the cash flows that the entity expects to receive if that expected portion of the loan is drawn down. *[IFRS 9.B5.5.30].*

Chapter 49

For a financial guarantee contract (see 5.10 below), the guarantor is required to make payments only in the event of a default by the debtor in accordance with the terms of the instrument that is guaranteed. Accordingly, the estimate of lifetime expected credit losses would be based on the present value of the expected payments to reimburse the holder for a credit loss that it incurs less any amounts that the guarantor expects to receive from the holder, the debtor or any other party. If the asset is fully guaranteed, the expected credit loss estimate for the financial guarantee contract would be the same as the estimated cash shortfall estimate for the asset subject to the guarantee. *[IFRS 9.B5.5.32]*.

5.4.2   12-month expected credit losses

The 12-month expected credit losses is defined as a portion of the lifetime expected credit losses that represent the expected credit losses that result from default events on a financial instrument that are possible within the 12 months after the reporting date. *[IFRS 9 Appendix A]*. The standard explains further that the 12-month expected credit losses are a portion of the lifetime expected credit losses that will result if a default occurs in the 12 months after the reporting date (or a shorter period if the expected life of a financial instrument is less than 12 months), weighted by the probability of that default occurring. *[IFRS 9.B5.5.43]*.

Because the calculation is based on the probability of default (PD), the standard emphasises that the 12-month expected credit loss is not the lifetime expected credit loss that an entity will incur on financial instruments that it *predicts* will default in the next 12 months (i.e. for which the PD over the next 12 months is greater than 50%). For instance, the PD might be only 25%, in which case this should be used to calculate 12-month expected credit losses, even though it is not probable that the asset will default. Also, the 12-month expected credit losses are not the cash shortfalls that are predicted over only the next 12 months. For an asset defaulting in the next 12 months, the lifetime expected credit losses that need to be included in the calculation will normally be significantly greater than just the cash flows that were contractually due in the next 12 months.

For undrawn loan commitments (see 5.10 below), an entity's estimate of 12-month expected credit losses should be based on its expectations of the portion of the loan commitment that will be drawn down within 12 months of the reporting date . *[IFRS 9.B5.5.31]*.

As already mentioned at 5.1.2 above, the IASB believes that the 12-month expected credit losses serve as a proxy for the recognition of initial expected credit losses over time, as proposed in the 2009 Exposure Draft, and they mitigate the systematic overstatement of interest revenue that is recognised under IAS 39. *[IFRS 9.BC5.135]*. This practical approximation was necessary as a result of the decision to decouple the measurement and allocation of initial expected credit losses from the determination of the effective interest rate following the re-deliberations of the 2009 Exposure Draft. *IFRS 9.BC5.199]*.

The stage 1, 12-month allowance overstates the necessary allowance for each financial instrument after initial recognition. However, this is offset by the fact that the allowance is not further increased (except for changes in the 12-month expected credit losses) until the instrument's credit risk has significantly increased and it is transferred to stage 2. For a portfolio of instruments, with various origination dates, the overall provision may (very approximately) be a similar size as might be achieved using a more conceptually robust approach. Although there is no conceptual justification for an allowance based on 12-month expected credit losses, it is a pragmatic solution to achieve an appropriate balance between faithfully representing the underlying economics of a transaction and the cost of implementation.

How accurate a proxy the 12-month and lifetime expected credit loss model is for a more conceptually pure approach will depend on the nature of the portfolio. Also, the effect of recording a 12-month expected credit loss in the first reporting period that a financial instrument is recognised will not have a significant effect on reported income if the portfolio is stable in size from one period to the next. The 12-month expected credit loss allowance will, however, reduce the reported income for entities which are expanding the size of their portfolio.

Although the choice of 12 months is arbitrary, it is the same time horizon as used for the more advanced bank regulatory capital calculation under the Basel framework.[21] The definition of 12-month expected credit losses is similar to the Basel Committee's definition of expected credit loss, although the modelling requirements differ significantly.[22] However, it should be stressed that the 12-month requirement under IFRS 9 will always differ from that computed for regulatory capital purposes, as the IFRS 9 measure is a point-in-time estimate, reflecting currently forecast economic conditions (see 5.4.8.C below), while the Basel regulatory figure is based on through-the-cycle assumptions of default and conservative estimates of losses given default. However, banks that use an advanced approach to calculate their capital requirements should be able to use their existing systems and methodologies as a starting point and make the necessary adjustments to flex the calculation to comply with IFRS 9.

Following from Example 49.13 at 5.1.2 above, calculations of the 12-month and lifetime expected credit losses are illustrated below.

Example 49.15: 12-month and lifetime expected credit loss measurement based on a PD approach

On 1 January 2016, Bank A originates a 10 year loan with a gross carrying amount of $1,000,000 (which is the exposure at default (EAD)). There are no transaction costs and the loan contracts include no options (for example, prepayment or call options), premiums or discounts, points paid, or other fees.

At origination, the loan is in stage 1 and a corresponding 12-month expected credit loss allowance is recognised in the year ending 31 December 2016. Taking into consideration the expectations for instruments of similar credit quality (using the most relevant information available, such as holder-specific data or industry data), the credit quality of the borrower, and the economic outlook for the next 12 months, Bank A estimates that the instrument has a 0.13% PD in the next 12 months. After valuing its collateral (and discounting the cash flows that would be received from the sale of the collateral, based on the time expected to be taken to realise it), Bank A assumes that 25 per cent of the gross carrying amount will be lost if the loan defaults (i.e. the loss given default or LGD). Bank A recognises a loss allowance at an amount equal to 12-month expected credit losses using the 0.13% 12-month PD that is discounted over 6 months (i.e. 0.5 years) as it is assumed that 6-months is the average point of default. The loss allowance for the 12-month expected credit losses is $320 (see detailed calculation below).

On 31 December 2018, Bank A considers forward-looking information, and updates its historical information for current economic conditions as well as reasonable and supportable forecasts of future economic conditions. The loan has shown signs of significant deterioration in credit quality and Bank A moves the loan to stage 2. Bank A uses the 'marginal expected credit loss approach' to derive the lifetime expected credit losses. Based on a cumulative PD for the remaining 7 years of 11.8% and, an LGD of 27% following the revaluation of the collateral, and discounting the losses from the mid-point of each year, Bank A recognises a loss allowance of $28,438 (see detailed calculation below).

In the following year, the loan defaults and is moved to stage 3. The lifetime PD is 100% and Bank A revises the LGD to 30% following the revaluation of the collateral. The loss allowance for the lifetime expected credit losses is $300,000 (see detailed calculation below).

Stage 1: 12-month expected credit losses of $320

At origination, the loan is in Stage 1 and a corresponding 12-month expected credit loss allowance is recognised in the year ending 31 December 2016.

Stage	Stage 1
12-month PD	0.13%
Lifetime PD (9 years)	2.7%
LGD	25%
EAD	$1,000,000
Effective interest rate (EIR)	3%
Years to maturity	9 years

For stage 1, the 12-month expected credit loss allowance is calculated as:

$$12\text{-month expected credit losses} = \frac{12\text{-month PD} \times \text{LGD} \times \text{EAD}}{(1 + \text{EIR})^{0.5}}$$

$$= \frac{0.13\% \times 25\% \times \$1,000,000}{(1 + 3\%)^{0.5}}$$

$$= \$320$$

Stage 2: lifetime expected credit losses of $28,438

On 31 December 2018, the loan has shown signs of significant increases in credit risk.

Stage	Stage 2
12-month PD	1%
Lifetime PD (2 years)	2.2%
Lifetime PD (3 years)	3.72%
Lifetime PD (4 years)	5.77%
Lifetime PD (5 years)	8.02%
Lifetime PD (6 years)	10.06%
Lifetime PD (7 years)	11.8%
LGD	27%
EAD	$1,000,000
Effective interest rate (EIR). Losses are discounted from the mid-point of each year.	3%
Years to maturity	7 years

For stage 2, the marginal expected credit loss approach is applied to derive the lifetime expected credit loss allowance. The calculation is as follows:

$$\text{Lifetime expected credit losses} = \frac{\text{change in lifetime PD} \times \text{LGD} \times \text{EAD}}{(1 + \text{EIR})^{(2t-1)/2}}$$

$$= \frac{1\% \times 27\% \times \$1{,}000{,}000}{(1 + 3\%)^{0.5}} + \dots + \frac{(11.81\% - 10.06\%) \times}{(1 + 3\%)^{6.5}}$$

$$= \$28{,}438$$

Time	Cumulative PD	Delta PD	LGD	EAD	Marginal expected credit losses	Cumulative expected credit losses
					(d) = (a) × (b) × (c) ÷ $(1+\text{EIR})^{(2t-1)/2}$	
		(a)	(b)	(c)		
1 year	1.00%	1.00%	27%	1,000,000	$2,660	$2,660
2 years	2.20%	1.20%	27%	1,000,000	$3,099	$5,760
3 years	3.72%	1.52%	27%	1,000,000	$3,812	$9,572
4 years	5.77%	2.04%	27%	1,000,000	$4,967	$14,539
5 years	8.02%	2.25%	27%	1,000,000	$5,318	$19,857
6 years	10.06%	2.04%	27%	1,000,000	$4,682	$24,539
7 years	11.81%	1.75%	27%	1,000,000	$3,899	$28,438

Stage 3: lifetime expected credit losses of $300,000

On 31 December 2019, the loan defaults and is moved to stage 3.

Stage	Stage 3
12-month PD	100%
Lifetime PD (6 years)	100%
LGD	30%
EAD	$1,000,000
Effective interest rate (EIR)	3%
Years to maturity	6 years

For stage 3, the lifetime expected credit loss allowance is calculated as:

$$\text{Lifetime expected credit losses} = \text{Lifetime PD} \times \text{LGD} \times \text{EAD}$$

$$= 100\% \times 30\% \times \$1{,}000{,}000$$

$$= \$300{,}000$$

Our observation of emerging practices reveals that most sophisticated banks are intending to develop their IFRS 9 solutions by adjusting and extending their existing Basel models. This is true for all types of component models, PD, loss given default (LGD) and exposure at default (EAD), particularly for LGD and EAD. This is perhaps unsurprising given the historical investment large banks have made in their Basel models, and the fact that IFRS 9 shares fundamental similarities in expected loss modelling. But, for many banks, creating lifetime estimates and altering models to satisfy the complex and detailed IFRS 9 requirements will still require significant work.

Chapter 49

5.4.2.A   Definition of default

Default is not defined for the purposes of determining the risk of a default occurring in the next 12 months. Because it is defined differently by different institutions (for instance, 30, 90 or 180 days past due), the IASB was concerned that defining default could result in a definition that is inconsistent with that applied internally for credit risk management. In particular, since default is the anchor point used to measure probabilities of default and losses given default in Basel modelling, requiring a different definition would require building a whole different set of models for accounting purposes. Therefore, the standard requires an entity to apply a definition of default that is consistent with how it is defined for its normal credit risk management practices, consistently from one period to another. It follows that an entity might have to use different default definitions for different types of financial instruments. However, the standard stresses that an entity needs to consider qualitative indicators of default when appropriate in addition to days past due, such as breaches of covenant. [IFRS 9.B5.5.37].

Expected credit loss calculations were not originally expected by the IASB to change as a result of differences in the definition of default, because of the counterbalancing interaction between the way an entity defines default and the credit losses that arise as a result of that definition of default. (For instance, if an entity uses a shorter delinquency period of 30 days past due instead of 60 days past due, the associated lifetime expected credit losses will be correspondingly smaller as it is to be expected that more debtors that are 30 days past due will in due course recover). [IFRS 9.BC5.248]. However, the notion of default is fundamental to the application of the model, particularly because it affects the subset of the population that is subject to the 12-month expected credit losses measure. [IFRS 9.BC5.249].

The standard restricts diversity resulting from this effect by establishing a rebuttable presumption that default does not occur later than when a financial asset is 90 days past due. This presumption may be rebutted only if an entity has reasonable and supportable information to support an alternative default criterion. [IFRS 9.B5.5.37, BC5.252].

A 90 day default definition would also be consistent with that used by banks for the advanced Basel II regulatory capital calculations (with a few exceptions). We observe that most banks intend to align their regulatory and accounting definitions of default. This generally means aligning the number of days past due trigger to 90 days under IFRS 9, with some exceptions for certain portfolios such as mortgages for which the regulatory definition may allow longer delinquency periods. (For these portfolios, not all banks who use the longer periods have yet decided whether to rebut the 90 DPD presumption or not). Most banks also intend to align the accounting definition of credit impaired for transfer to stage 3 with the definition of default.

5.4.2.B   *Measurement of 12-month expected credit losses based on a loss rate approach*

Not every entity calculates a separate risk of a default occurring and an LGD, but instead uses a loss rate approach. Using this approach, the entity develops loss-rate statistics on the basis of the amount written off over the life of the financial assets. It must then adjust these historical credit loss trends for current conditions and expectations about the future. The following Illustrative Example 9 from IFRS 9 is designed to illustrate how an entity measures 12-month expected credit losses using a loss rate approach. *[IFRS 9 IG Example 9, IE53-IE57].*

Example 49.16:   12-month expected credit loss measurement based on a loss rate approach

Bank A originates 2,000 bullet loans with a total gross carrying amount of $500,000. Bank A segments its portfolio into borrower groups (Groups X and Y) on the basis of shared credit risk characteristics at initial recognition. Group X comprises 1,000 loans with a gross carrying amount per client of $200, for a total gross carrying amount of $200,000. Group Y comprises 1,000 loans with a gross carrying amount per client of $300, for a total gross carrying amount of $300,000. There are no transaction costs and the loan contracts include no options (for example, prepayment or call options), premiums or discounts, points paid, or other fees.

Bank A measures expected credit losses on the basis of a loss rate approach for Groups X and Y. In order to develop its loss rates, Bank A considers samples of its own historical default and loss experience for those types of loans. In addition, Bank A considers forward-looking information, and updates its historical information for current economic conditions as well as reasonable and supportable forecasts of future economic conditions. Historically, for a population of 1,000 loans in each group, Group X's loss rates are 0.3 per cent, based on four defaults, and historical loss rates for Group Y are 0.15 per cent, based on two defaults.

	Number of clients in sample	Estimated per client gross carrying amount at default	Total estimated gross carrying amount at default	Historic per annum average defaults	Estimated total gross carrying amount at default	Present value of observed loss (a)	Loss rate
	A	B	C = A × B	D	E = B × D	F	G = F ÷ C
Group							
X	1,000	$200	$200,000	4	$800	$600	0.3%
Y	1,000	$300	$300,000	2	$600	$450	0.15%

(a) Expected credit losses should be discounted using the effective interest rate. However, for purposes of this example, the present value of the observed loss is assumed. *[IFRS 9.5.5.17(b)].*

At the reporting date, Bank A expects an increase in defaults over the next 12 months compared to the historical rate. As a result, Bank A estimates five defaults in the next 12 months for loans in Group X and three for loans in Group Y. It estimates that the present value of the observed credit loss per client will remain consistent with the historical loss per client.

On the basis of the expected life of the loans, Bank A determines that the expected increase in defaults does not represent a significant increase in credit risk since initial recognition for the portfolios. On the basis of its forecasts, Bank A measures the loss allowance at an amount equal to 12-month expected credit losses on the 1,000 loans in each group amounting to $750 and $675 respectively. This equates to a loss rate in the first year of 0.375 per cent for Group X and 0.225 per cent for Group Y.

Chapter 49

	Number of clients in sample	Estimated per client gross carrying amount at default	Total estimated gross carrying amount at default	Expected defaults	Estimated total gross carrying amount at default	Present value of observed loss	Loss rate
Group	A	B	C = A × B	D	E = B × D	F	G = F ÷ C
X	1,000	$200	$200,000	5	$1,000	$750	0.375%
Y	1,000	$300	$300,000	3	$900	$675	0.225%

Bank A uses the loss rates of 0.375 per cent and 0.225 per cent respectively to estimate 12-month expected credit losses on new loans in Group X and Group Y originated during the year and for which credit risk has not increased significantly since initial recognition.

The example above illustrates that under the loss rate approach, an entity would compute its loss rates by segmenting its portfolio into appropriate groupings (or sub-portfolios) based on shared credit risk characteristics and then updating its historical loss information with more forward-looking information. The loss rate was derived simply by computing the ratio between the present value of observed losses (the numerator) and the gross carrying amount of the loans (the denominator). Note that, although it does not require an explicit risk of a default occurring, there has to be an estimate of the number of defaults in order to determine whether there has been a significant increase in credit risk (see 5.5 below). Hence application will require any entities that intend to use this approach to track the incidence of default.

Expected credit losses should be discounted at the effective interest rate. However, in this example, the present value of the observed loss is just assumed.

5.4.3   *Expected life versus contractual period*

Lifetime expected credit losses are defined as the expected credit losses that result from all possible default events over the *expected life* of a financial instrument. *[IFRS 9 Appendix A]*. This is consistent with the requirement that an entity should assess whether the credit risk on a financial instrument has increased significantly since initial recognition by using the change in the risk of a default occurring over the *expected life* of the financial instrument. *[IFRS 9.5.5.9]*.

An entity must therefore estimate cash flows and the instrument's life by considering all contractual terms of the financial instrument (for example, prepayment, extension, call and similar options). There is a presumption that the expected life of a financial instrument can be estimated reliably. In those rare cases when it is not possible to reliably estimate the expected life of a financial instrument, the entity shall use the remaining contractual term of the financial instrument. *[IFRS 9 Appendix A, B5.5.51]*.

However, the maximum period to consider when measuring expected credit losses should be the maximum contractual period (including extension options) over which the entity is exposed to credit risk and not a longer period, even if that longer period is consistent with business practice. *[IFRS 9.5.5.19]*. Although an exception to this principle has been added for revolving facilities (see 5.11 below), the IASB remains of the view that the contractual period over which an entity is committed to provide credit (or a shorter period considering prepayments) is the correct conceptual outcome. The IASB noted that most loan commitments will expire at a specified date, and if an entity decides to renew or extend its commitment to extend credit, it will be a new instrument for which the entity has the opportunity to revise the terms and conditions. *[IFRS 9.BC5.260].*

This means that prepayment and extension options should only be reflected in the measurement of expected credit losses as long as this does not extend the horizon beyond the maximum contractual period over which the entity is exposed to credit risk.

Extension options at the discretion of the lender should therefore be excluded from the measurement of expected credit losses. Similarly, a lender's ability to require prepayment limits the horizon over which it is exposed to credit risk. The first prepayment date at the discretion of the lender should therefore represent the maximum period to be reflected in the expected loss calculation.

When assessing the impact of extension options at the discretion of the borrower, an entity should estimate both the probability of exercise of the extension option as well as the portion of the loan that will be extended (if the extension option can be exercised for a portion of the loan only). This is consistent with how lifetime expected losses must be assessed for loan commitments where an entity's estimate of expected credit losses must be consistent with its expectations of drawdowns on that loan commitment. *[IFRS 9.B.5.5.31].*

Expected prepayments at the discretion of borrowers should also be reflected in the measurement of expected credit losses. As with extension options, an entity should estimate both the probability of exercise of the prepayment option as well as the portion of the loan that will be prepaid (if the prepayment option can be exercised for a portion of the loan only). The standard does not specify whether prepayment patterns should be reflected through an amortising EAD (assessed at portfolio level) over the maximum contractual period of the financial instruments or, rather, by shortening the horizon over which to measure expected credit losses to the average life of the financial instruments. In our view, the former would seem the right conceptual answer, as shortening the horizon over which to measure expected losses would not reflect losses expected to occur beyond this average life.

Another degree of complexity in assessing expected prepayments and extensions arises if one considers that the behaviour of borrowers is affected by their creditworthiness. This means that prepayment and extension patterns should probably be estimated separately for stage 1 and stage 2 assets. This may represent a significant challenge, as making such estimates would require distinct historical observations for each of the stage 1 and 2 populations, which are unlikely to be available given that these populations were never identified in the past. Prepayment assumptions for stage 2 assets would need to factor in the probabilities that some may subsequently default and some may cure. A further complication is that expected prepayment and extension behaviour may vary with changes in the macro-economic outlook.

Chapter 49

The standard is clear that, for loan commitments and financial guarantee contracts, the time horizon to measure expected credit losses is the maximum contractual period over which an entity has a present contractual obligation to extend credit. *[IFRS 9.B5.5.38]*. However, for revolving credit facilities (e.g. credit cards and overdrafts) that do not have a fixed term or repayment structure and usually have a short contractual cancellation period (for example, one day), this period is extended beyond the maximum contractual period and includes the period over which the entity is exposed to credit risk and expected credit losses would not be mitigated by credit risk management actions (see 5.11). *[IFRS 9.5.5.20, B5.5.39, B5.5.40]*.

At its April 2015 meeting, the ITG (see 5.1.5 above) discussed, how to determine the maximum period for measuring expected credit losses, by reference to the flowing example.[23]

Example 49.17:   Determining the maximum contractual period when measuring expected credit losses

Bank A manages a portfolio of variable rate mortgages on a collective basis. The mortgage loans are issued to retail customers in Country X with the following terms:

- the stated maturity is 6 months with an automatic extension feature whereby, unless the borrower or lender take action to terminate the loan at the stated maturity date, the loan automatically extends for the following 6 months;

- the interest rate is fixed for each 6-month period at the beginning of the period. The interest rate is reset to the current market interest rate on the extension date; and

- the lender's right to refuse an extension is unrestricted.

It is assumed that the mortgage loans meet the criteria for amortised cost measurement under paragraph 4.1.2 of IFRS 9.

In practice, borrowers are generally expected not to elect to terminate their loans on the stated maturity date, because moving the mortgage to another bank, or applying for a new product, generally involves an administrative burden and has little or no economic benefit for the borrower.

Furthermore, Bank A does not complete regular credit file reviews for individual loans and as a result does not usually cancel the loans unless it receives information about an adverse credit event in respect of a particular borrower. On the basis of historical evidence, such loans extend many times and can last for up to 30 years.

The ITG noted that:

- IFRS 9 is clear that the maximum period to consider when measuring expected credit losses in this example would be restricted to 6 months, because this is the maximum contractual period over which the lender is exposed to credit risk, i.e. the period until the lender can next object to an extension. *[IFRS 9.B5.5.19]*.

- The standard requires that extension options must be considered when determining the maximum contractual period, but does not specify whether these are lender or borrower extension options. However, if the extension option is within the control of the lender, the lender cannot be forced to continue extending credit and therefore such an option cannot be considered as lengthening the maximum period of exposure to credit risk. Conversely, if a borrower holds an extension option that could force the lender to continue extending credit, this would have the effect of lengthening that maximum contractual period of credit exposure.

- The maximum contractual period over which the entity is exposed to credit risk should be determined in accordance with the substantive contractual terms of the financial instrument. To further illustrate this point, a situation in which a lender is legally prevented from exercising a contractual right should be seen as distinct from a situation in which a lender chooses not to exercise a contractual right for practical or operational reasons.

- In the example presented, the facility is not of a revolving nature and the borrower does not have any such flexibility regarding drawdowns. Consequently, it would not be appropriate to analogise the 6-month mortgage loan to a revolving credit facility that has been fully drawn at the reporting date. Hence, the example falls outside the narrow scope exception for revolving credit facilities (e.g. credit cards and overdraft facilities) in which the maximum period to consider when measuring expected credit losses is over the period that the entity is exposed to credit risk and expected credit losses would not be mitigated by credit risk management actions, even if that period extends beyond the maximum contractual period (see 5.11 below). *[IFRS 9.B5.5.20].*

- Consequently, it was acknowledged that there may be a disconnect between the accounting and credit risk management view in some situations (e.g. an entity may choose to continue extending credit to a long-standing customer despite being in a position to reduce or remove the exposure).

5.4.4   *Probability-weighted outcome*

Expected credit losses must reflect an unbiased and probability-weighted estimate of credit losses over the expected life of the financial instrument (i.e. the weighted average of credit losses with the respective risks of a default occurring as the weights). *[IFRS 9.5.5.17(a), Appendix A, B5.5.28].*

When measuring expected credit losses, in order to derive an unbiased and probability-weighted amount, an entity needs to evaluate a range of possible outcomes. *IFRS 9.5.5.17(a)].* This involves identifying possible scenarios that specify:

a)   the amount and timing of the cash flows for particular outcomes; and

b)   the estimated probability of these outcomes.

Although an entity does not need to identify every possible scenario, it will need to take into account the possibility that a credit loss occurs, no matter how low that probability is. *[IFRS 9.5.5.18].* This is not the same as a single estimate of the worst-case or best-case scenario or the most likely outcome (i.e. when there is a low risk or probability of a default with high loss outcomes, the most likely outcome could be no credit loss even though an allowance would be required based on probability-weighted cash flows). *[IFRS 9.B5.5.41].*

In practice, calculating a probability-weighted amount may not require a complex analysis or a detailed simulation of a large number of scenarios and the standard suggests that relatively simple modelling may be sufficient. For instance, the average credit losses of a large group of financial instruments with shared risk characteristics may be a reasonable estimate of the probability-weighted amount. *[IFRS 9.B5.5.42].*

See also the April and September 2015 ITG discussions at 5.4.8.C below.

Chapter 49

5.4.5   *Time value of money*

An entity needs to consider the time value of money when measuring expected credit losses, by discounting this amount to the reporting date using a rate that approximates the effective interest rate of the asset (see 3 above). *[IFRS 9.5.5.17, B5.5.44]*. This has two components:

- discounting recoveries to the date of default, hence 'a credit loss arises even if the entity expects to be paid in full but later than when contractually due'. *[IFRS 9.B5.5.28]*.

- discounting losses from the date of default to the reporting date. This is needed because the gross amortised cost of the asset is based on the contractual cash flows discounted at the effective interest rate, and so not to discount cash flows that are now not expected to be received would overstate the loss.

Of these two components, the first is typically included by banks in their calculation of the LGD, but the second will also need to be calculated to comply with the standard.

The discount rate is calculated as follows:

- for a fixed-rate financial asset, entities are required to determine or approximate the effective interest rate on the initial recognition of the financial asset, while for a floating-rate financial asset, entities are required to use the current effective interest rate; *[IFRS 9.B5.5.44]*

- for a purchased or originated credit-impaired financial asset (see 5.3.3 above), entities are required to discount expected credit losses using the credit-adjusted effective interest rate determined on the initial recognition of the financial asset; *[IFRS 9.B5.5.45]*

- for a loan commitment (see 5.10 below), entities are required to use the effective interest rate of the asset that will result once the commitment is drawn down. This would give rise to a consistent rate for a credit facility that includes both a loan (i.e. a financial asset) and an undrawn commitment (i.e. a loan commitment). If the effective interest rate of the resulting asset is not determinable, then entities are required to use the current risk-free rate (i.e. the discount rate that reflects the current market assessment of the time value of money). This should be adjusted for risks specific to the cash flows, but only if the cash flows have not already been adjusted for these risks, in order to avoid double counting; *[IFRS 9.B5.5.47, B5.5.48]*

- for financial guarantee contracts (see 5.10 below) entities are required to use the current risk-free rate adjusted for risks specific to the cash flow; *[IFRS 9.B5.5.48]* and

- for lease receivables (see 5.9.2 below), entities are required to discount the expected credit losses using the same discount rate used in the measurement of the lease receivables in accordance with IAS 17. *[IFRS 9.B5.5.46, IAS 17.4]*.

It is rare that customers just fail to pay amounts when due. In most cases, default also involves payments being paid late, while default can lead to the acceleration of payment of amounts that are not contractually due until a later date. Therefore, modelling losses involves modelling the timing of payments when default occurs and different patterns of timing of recoverable cash flows, such as the time it takes to foreclose on and sell collateral and complete bankruptcy proceedings, before the expected credit losses can be discounted back to the reporting date.

The standard and its Illustrative Examples are silent on how the calculation should be made. In Illustrative Example 9 the present value of the observed loss is assumed and in Illustrative Example 8, a footnote states that, 'Because the LGD represents a percentage of the present value of the gross carrying amount, this example does not illustrate the time value of money'. One approach would be to model various scenarios as to how cash is collected once the loan has defaulted, and probability-weight the discounted cash flows of these various scenarios.

LGD data available from Basel models should include a discounting factor, but this would only cover the period between default and subsequent recoveries. Therefore, entities will have to find ways to adjust their LGDs to reflect the discounting effect required by the standard (i.e. based on a rate that approximates the effective interest rate and over the entire period from recoveries back to the reporting date). Given the requirement to use an approximation to the effective interest rate, entities will need to work out how to determine a rate that is sufficiently accurate. One of the challenges is to interpret how much flexibility is afforded by the term 'approximation'.

5.4.6 Interaction between expected credit losses calculations and fair value hedge accounting

Another operational difficulty arises from the interplay between the new impairment model and fair value hedge accounting. For financial assets designated in a hedge, because the fair value hedge adjustment is a part of the carrying value of the financial asset that is hedged, the measurement of the loss allowance must take that adjustment into account. In other words, the fair value hedge adjustment changes the carrying amount that is assessed for impairment, which is achieved by adjusting the effective interest rate used to measure the impairment allowance.

This requirement was already illustrated by the implementation guidance of IAS 39. This pointed out that a portfolio hedge of interest rate risk creates the need to allocate the change in the fair value of the hedged portfolio to the loans (or groups of loans) being assessed for impairment on a systematic and rational basis. This was equally true for micro hedges. Consequently, the fair value hedge adjustment must be included in the carrying amount that is subject to the impairment requirements. Otherwise, for an asset in the scope of the impairment requirements, a part of its carrying amount would not have a loss allowance or the loss allowance would be overstated (in case of a negative fair value hedge adjustment). *[IAS 39.IG E.4.4].*

Chapter 49

However, the interaction between fair value hedge accounting and impairment will be more complex under the new impairment model of IFRS 9 because:

- Under IAS 39 an entity can often avoid the difficulty of measuring impairment losses on the financial assets it includes in the designation of a fair value hedge by designating only higher quality assets, which do not have any associated incurred losses under IAS 39.

- In contrast, under the new impairment model of IFRS 9, all financial assets in the scope of the impairment requirements, whether recorded at amortised cost or at fair value through other comprehensive income, require the measurement of a loss allowance, even if they are high quality assets and have not deteriorated. Many of these assets will have been designated as the hedged items in fair value hedge relationships.

- IFRS 9 allows expected losses to be discounted by a rate that approximates the effective interest rate. This approximation will need to take account of the effect of fair value hedge accounting.

- For portfolio hedging strategies it may not be possible to allocate fair value hedge adjustments to individual assets, so it will be necessary for entities to determine a basis of allocation of such hedges to those assets subject to a 12-month loss allowance and those for which lifetime expected credit losses are provided for. This is likely to be feasible only for groups of assets with similar credit characteristics, including maturities and effective interest rates. Even for micro hedges of individual assets, it may be difficult to link the hedge accounting and impairment processes, to calculate the consequences of hedge accounting for impairment.

The complexity of combining the expected credit loss impairment model and fair value hedge accounting is illustrated by Example 49.30 at 5.8.

5.4.7   Credit enhancements: collateral and financial guarantees

Although credit enhancements such as collateral and guarantees play only a limited role in assessing whether there has been a significant increase in credit risk (see 5.5.1 below), they do affect the measurement of expected credit losses. For example, for a mortgage loan, even if an entity determines that there has been a significant increase in credit risk on the loan since initial recognition because the borrower became unemployed and is expected to be unable to repay further monthly interest and capital repayments, if the expected proceeds from the collateral (i.e. the mortgaged property) exceeds the amount loaned, then the entity may have expected credit losses, and hence an allowance, of zero.

In measuring the expected credit losses and, hence, the expected cash shortfalls for a collateralised financial instrument, an entity should include the cash flows from the realisation of the collateral and other credit enhancements that are: *[IFRS 9.B5.5.55]*

• part of the contractual terms; and

• not recognised separately by the entity.

As is the case in IAS 39, the standard specifies that the estimate of cash flows from collateral should include the effect of a foreclosure, regardless of whether foreclosure is probable, and the resulting cash flows from foreclosure on the collateral less the costs of obtaining and selling the collateral, taking into account the amount and timing of these cash flows. *[IFRS 9.B5.5.55]*. The wording does not mean that the entity is required to assume that recovery will be through foreclosure only, but rather that the entity should calculate the cash flows arising from the various ways that the asset may be recovered, only some of which may involve foreclosure, and to probability-weight these different scenarios.

Although the standard does not refer to fair value when determining the valuation of the collateral, in practice, an entity is likely to estimate the cash flows from the realisation of the collateral, based on the fair value of the collateral. In the case of illiquid collateral, such as real estate, adjustments will probably need to be made for expected changes in the fair value, depending on the economic conditions at the estimated date of selling the collateral.

Also as in IAS 39, any collateral obtained as a result of foreclosure is not recognised as an asset that is separate from the collateralised financial instrument unless it meets the relevant recognition criteria for an asset in IFRS 9 or other standards. *[IFRS 9.B5.5.55]*.

If a loan is guaranteed by a third party as part of its contractual terms, it should carry an allowance for expected credit losses based on the combined credit risk of the guarantor and the guaranteed party, by reflecting the effect of the guarantee in the measurement of losses expected on default.

A challenge is interpreting what constitutes part of the contractual terms. In particular:

• if a loan is guaranteed but that guarantee would not pass to the new holder if the loan is transferred, can that guarantee be included in determining the PD and in estimating expected credit losses, or is it a separate financial instrument that needs to be accounted for on a standalone basis?

• the question gets more complicated when laws and regulations governing the contract means that guarantees may not be part of the contractual terms but implied (for instance, guarantees provided by the government).

Chapter 49

Currently, because there is no equivalent guidance in IAS 39 similar to paragraph B5.5.55 in IFRS 9, there is some diversity in practice as to how collateral is taken into account in loan loss impairment calculations. In practice, most banks incorporate the guarantees as part of their LGD measure in line with the guidance in IAS 39.IG.E.4.1.

As written, IFRS 9 appears to be quite restrictive and would not include, for instance, any recoveries from credit insurance or guarantees that are purchased separately from the original instrument. This raises the question as to how such collateral and credit enhancements should be separately measured by the holder. On this question, we note the following:

- A guarantee is likely to satisfy the definition of an insurance contract in IFRS 4 – *Insurance Contracts* – but will be excluded from the scope of IFRS 4 because it is a direct insurance contract held by the insured who is not a cedant (i.e. an insurer that is the policyholder under a reinsurance contract). *[IFRS 4.4(f)]*. If the guarantee satisfies the definition of an insurance contract in IFRS 4 it is outside the scope of IAS 39 irrespective of whether it is within the scope of IFRS 4. *[IAS 39.2(e)]*. IFRS 4 points to paragraphs 10 to 12 of IAS 8 – *Accounting Policies, Changes in Accounting Estimates and Errors* – which applies to situations where no IFRS specifically applies to a transaction, i.e. the holder of a financial guarantee contract will normally need to develop its accounting policy in accordance with the hierarchy in IAS 8. *[IFRS 4 IG Example 1.11]*.

- One possibility would be to apply IAS 37 to treat the guarantee as a contingent asset. This would mean that the guarantee would only be recognised as an asset when it is virtually certain that a recovery will be made. This is likely to result in a timing mismatch, since impairment losses will be recorded on an expected loss basis, long before they are virtually certain to occur.

- Another possibility might be to characterise the guarantee as a reimbursement in respect of the impairment loss, rather than as a standalone contingent asset. IAS 37 permits a reimbursement of a liability to be recognised as an asset when it is virtually certain that the reimbursement will be received if the obligation for which a provision has been established is settled. *[IAS 37.53]*. By analogy, it might be possible to argue that the guarantee would be recognised as an asset to the extent it is virtually certain a recovery could be made if the lender were to suffer the impairment loss on the loan. *[IAS 37.54]*.

This issue will be relevant for many retail banking mortgage portfolios where default insurance is acquired, either as a legal requirement or as part of the credit risk management strategy. The same issue will also be relevant when a bank receives a guarantee of a commercial lending arrangement from a parent or a sister company of the borrower. There may be also inconsistencies between the treatment in IFRS 9 and traditionally by credit risk managers, where any form of credit enhancement or guarantee is included in regulatory LGD calculations.

The above issues would usefully be brought to the ITG (see 5.1.5 above).

5.4.8 Reasonable and supportable information

IFRS 9 requires an entity to consider reasonable and supportable information that is available without undue cost or effort at the reporting date about past events, current conditions and forecasts of future economic conditions and that is relevant to the estimate of expected credit losses, including the effect of expected prepayments. *[IFRS 9.5.5.17(c), B5.5.51].*

5.4.8.A Undue cost or effort

The term undue cost or effort is not defined in the standard, although it is clear from the guidance that information available for financial reporting purposes is considered to be available without undue cost or effort. *[IFRS 9.B5.5.49].*

Beyond that, although the standard tells us that entities are not required to undertake an exhaustive search for information, it does include, as examples of relevant information, data from risk management systems, as described in the next section.

What is available without undue cost or effort would be an area subject to management judgement in assessing the costs and associated benefits. This is consistent with the Q&A (non-mandatory guidance) provided by the SME (small and medium-sized entities) Implementation Group in relation to the application of undue cost or effort when implementing IFRSs for SMEs.[24] The Q&A explains that application of a requirement would result in undue cost or effort if the cost or effort is excessive in comparison to the benefits that the users of the financial statements would receive from having the information. If the reporting entity is a bank, there would presumably be a higher hurdle to determine what credit risk information would require undue cost or effort, compared to a reporter that is not a bank, given that the benefit to users of its financial statements would be also expected to be higher. It is an issue on which we expect bank regulators to have a view (see 5.6.2 below).

5.4.8.B Sources of information

The standard states that the information used should include factors that are specific to the borrower, general economic conditions and an assessment of both the current as well as the forecast direction of conditions at the reporting date. Entities may use various sources of data, both internal (entity-specific) data and external data that includes internal historical credit loss experience, internal ratings, credit loss experience of other entities for comparable financial instruments, and external ratings, reports and statistics. Entities that have no, or insufficient, sources of entity-specific data may use peer group experience for the comparable financial instrument (or groups of financial instruments). *[IFRS 9.B5.5.51].*

Although the expected credit losses reflect an entity's own expectations of credit losses, an entity should also consider observable market information about the credit risk of particular financial instruments. *[IFRS 9.B5.5.54].* Therefore, although entities with in-house economic teams will inevitably want to use their internal economic forecasts, while loss estimation models will be built based on historical data, they should not ignore external market data.

5.4.8.C   *Information about past events, current conditions and forecasts of future economic conditions*

One of the significant changes from the IAS 39 impairment requirements is that entities are not only required to use historical information (e.g. their credit loss experience) that is adjusted to reflect the effects of current conditions, but they are also required to consider how forecasts of future conditions would affect their historical data.

The degree of judgement that is required to estimate expected credit losses depends on the availability of detailed information. An entity is not required to incorporate detailed forecasts of future conditions over the entire expected life of a financial instrument. The standard notes that as the forecast horizon increases, the availability of detailed information decreases and the degree of judgement required to estimate expected credit losses increases. Therefore, an entity is not required to perform a detailed estimate for periods that are far in the future and may extrapolate projections from available, more detailed information. *[IFRS 9.B5.5.50]*.

The wording suggests that entities may often be able to assume that economic conditions revert to their long-term average, beyond a horizon for which they can be reliably forecast. There are at least two versions of how this might be done: either by reverting to the average immediately beyond the forecast horizon, or by adjusting the forecast data to the long-term average over a few years. The latter would, perhaps, more effectively make use of all reasonable and supportable information.

Historical information should be used as a starting point from which adjustments are made to estimate expected credit losses on the basis of reasonable and supportable information that incorporates both current and forward-looking information: *[IFRS 9.B5.5.52]*

- in most cases, adjustments would be needed to incorporate these effects that were not present in the past or to remove these effects that are not relevant for the future; and

- in some cases, unadjusted historical information may be the best estimate, depending on the nature of the historical information and when it was calculated, compared to circumstances at the reporting date and the characteristics of the financial instrument being considered. But it should not be assumed to be appropriate in all circumstances. *[IFRS 9.BC5.281]*.

Additionally, when considering how, and to what extent, historical credit losses should be adjusted, an entity will need to consider various items, including:

- whether the historical data captures expected credit losses that are through-the-cycle (i.e. estimates based on historical credit loss events and experience over the entire economic cycle) or point-in-time (i.e. estimates based on information, circumstances and events at the reporting date); and

- the period of time over which its historical data has been captured and the corresponding economic conditions represented in that history. The historical data period may reflect unusually benign or harsh conditions unless it is long enough, while products, customers and lending behaviours all change over time; and when using historical credit loss experience, it is important that information about historical credit losses is applied to groups that are defined in a manner that is consistent with the groups for which the historical credit losses were observed.

The estimates of changes in expected credit losses should be directionally consistent with changes in related observable data from period to period (i.e. consistent with trends observed on payment status and macroeconomic data such as changes in unemployment rates, property prices, and commodity prices). Also, in order to reduce the differences between an entity's estimates and actual credit loss experience, the estimates of expected credit losses should be back-tested and re-calibrated, i.e. an entity should regularly review its inputs, assumptions, methodology and estimation techniques used as well as its groupings of sub-portfolios with shared credit risk characteristics (see 5.5.5 below).

Back testing will be considerably more challenging for forecasts over several years than may be the case for just the 12-month risk of default, because detailed information may not be available over the forecast horizon and the degree of judgement increases as the forecast horizon increases. *[IFRS 9.B5.5.52. B5.5.53]*. Also, economic forecasts are usually wrong, as reality is much more complex than can ever be effectively modelled. Therefore it is probably not a useful exercise to back test macroeconomic assumptions against what actually transpires, but it is useful to back test whether, for a given macroeconomic scenario, credit losses increase or decrease as expected.

In estimating expected credit losses, entities must consider how to bridge the gap between historical loss experience and current expectations. Estimating future economic conditions is only the first step of the exercise; having decided what will happen to macroeconomic factors such as interest rates, house prices, unemployment and GDP growth, entities then need to decide how they translate into expected credit losses. This will need to reflect how such changes in factors affected defaults in the past. However, it is possible that the forecast combination of factors may have never been seen historically together.

In practice, adjusting historical information to reflect current conditions and forecasts of future economic conditions may involve:

- using an econometric model or other statistical techniques in which current expectations and expectations about the future are used as a direct input into a forecasting model that relies on historical relationships between loss and macroeconomic factors such as unemployment and gross domestic product (GDP) growth; or

- using a base-case model that is based on historical information and, subsequently, adding a management estimate overlay (including a quantitative overlay outside of the primary model and qualitative adjustments based on management's evaluation of macro-level and portfolio-level factors) to adjust the historical data to reflect current expectations; and

- considering the data used for budgeting, forecasting and capital planning, and determining how this information will affect the expected credit loss estimates. This may include macroeconomic assumptions and forecasts and other more detailed data that is currently used by an entity for budgeting and forecasting purposes (including consensus forecasts by third-party providers) and other forward-looking information on emerging issues and uncertain future events that are not usually included in the entity's current budgeting and forecasting processes. However, it may be most appropriate to include such forward-looking information on emerging themes by way of overlays in order to reflect this information on a collective level to affected portfolios (see 5.5.5 below); and

- making use of publically available forecasts in order to challenge and validate economic forecasts made by the entity.

We observe that banks are also trying to align IFRS 9 to their existing risk management practices. Many banks intend to leverage and align their regulatory capital calculation and stress testing frameworks for their IFRS 9 calculations. This manifests itself in many of the individual decisions that banks are making as part of their development of IFRS 9 methodologies (e.g. definitions of default and alignment to stress testing). It is likely that regulators and standard-setters will concur with this approach. Basel PDs are used as a starting point and there is a need for a different calibration for IFRS 9, in order to transform a Basel PD into an unbiased point in time metric and include forward looking expectations. Stress testing resources, previously working almost exclusively with capital issues, will likely play a major role in calculating lifetime expected credit losses, although the scenarios modelled for IFRS 9 will not be stressed. However, estimating losses may still be challenging for many entities.

The ITG has discussed several aspects of the forecast of expected credit losses (see 5.1.5 above). In April 2015, the ITG debated whether and how to incorporate events and new information about forecasts of future economic conditions that occur after the expected credit losses have been estimated. Due to operational practicality, entities may perform their expected credit loss calculations before the reporting period end in order to publish their financial statements in a timely manner (e.g. forecasts of future economic conditions developed in November may be used as the basis for determining the expected credit losses at the reporting date as at 31 December). Further information may then become available after the period end. The ITG noted that:

- If new information becomes available before the reporting date, subject to materiality considerations in accordance with IAS 8, an entity is required to take into consideration this information in the assessment of significant increases in credit risk and the measurement of expected credit losses at the reporting date.

- IFRS 9 does not specifically require new information that becomes available after the reporting date to be reflected in the measurement of expected credit losses at the reporting date. If new information becomes available between the reporting date and the date the financial statements are authorised for issue, an entity needs to apply judgement, based on the specific facts and circumstances, to determine whether it is an adjusting or non-adjusting event in accordance with IAS 10 – *Events after the Reporting Period* (see Chapter 35 at 3). Similarly, materiality considerations apply in accordance with IAS 8.

- Expected credit losses are similar in nature to the measurement of fair value at the reporting date, in that movements in fair value after the reporting date are generally not reflected in the measurement of fair value at the reporting date. [IAS 10.11]. For example, a change in interest rates or the outcome of a public vote after the reporting date would not normally be regarded as adjusting events for the expected credit loss calculation.

- However, expected credit losses are a probability-weighted estimate of credit losses at the reporting date (see 5.4.4 above). Accordingly, the determination of expected credit losses should take into consideration relevant possible future scenarios based on a range of expectations at the reporting date, using the information available at that date. Hence, the probabilities attached to future expected movements in interest rates and expected outcomes of a future public vote based on information available at the reporting date would be reflected in the determination of expected credit losses at that date. Entities need robust processes and appropriate governance procedures for incorporating information, including forecasts of future economic conditions, to ensure transparent and consistent application of the impairment requirements in IFRS 9. This includes processes for updating expected credit losses for new information that becomes available after the initial modelling has taken place up until the reporting date.

At its meeting on 16 September 2015, the ITG (see 5.1.5 above) examined two further questions about the use of forward-looking information:[25]

- the level at which forward-looking information should be incorporated – whether at the level of the entity or on a portfolio-by-portfolio basis; and *[IFRS 9 B5.5.16]*

- how to determine what is reasonable and supportable forward-looking information and how to treat shock events with material, but uncertain, economic consequences. *[IFRS 9 B5.5.49 - B5.5.54].*

ITG members agreed that forward-looking information should be assessed at the level that matters and is relevant given the granularity of the information under consideration; this should be as granular as is necessary but will require entities to understand the significant drivers of losses.

On the second question, ITG members seemed to largely agree that a balance needs to be struck between:

- inappropriately excluding information that is relevant (and perhaps presenting opportunities for abuse or delays in recognition); and

- considering all views on future possibilities, including those of a speculative nature that have little or no basis (and may be considered unsupportable).

Some ITG members agreed that shock events for which the expected loss consequences cannot be reliably estimated should be rare. For most events, it should be possible to estimate and incorporate their consequences in the measurement of expected credit losses. If it is concluded that it is not possible to determine the loss consequences then, at the very least, that conclusion and the event should both be disclosed. Entities should make their best efforts, on a good faith basis, to establish the expected losses associated with shock events. In the first instance, this will inevitably be an approximation, but should be at least directionally consistent with the change in the risk. The measurement of this estimate will need to be refined as more information about the event and its consequences becomes available.

It was also noted that, in calculating the effect of shock events, it is important not to double count what may have already been built into longer-term macroeconomic

Chapter 49

forecasts, if they already anticipate more generic shocks and unknown events. However, larger shocks may ultimately require separate consideration.

ITG members also generally agreed that a structured approach should be consistently applied to shock events and that the judgements should be adequately documented, including how conclusions about whether items did or did not require separate consideration were determined. Good governance and control is required to manage this process.

5.5   General approach: determining significant increases in credit risk

One of the major challenges in implementing the general approach in the IFRS 9 expected credit loss model is to track and determine whether there have been significant increases in the credit risk of an entity's credit exposures since initial recognition. However, a number of operational simplifications and presumptions are available to help entities make this assessment (as described further below).

The assessment of significant deterioration is key in establishing the point of switching between the requirement to measure an allowance based on 12-month expected credit losses and one that is based on lifetime expected credit losses. The standard is prescriptive that an entity cannot align the timing of significant increases in credit risk and the recognition of lifetime expected credit losses with when a financial asset is regarded as credit-impaired or to an entity's internal definition of default. *[IFRS 9.B5.5.21]*. Financial assets should normally be assessed as having increased significantly in credit risk earlier than when they become credit-impaired (see 5.3.1 above) or default. *[IFRS 9.B5.5.7]*.

As this area involves significant management judgement, entities are required to provide both qualitative and quantitative disclosures under IFRS 7 to explain the inputs, assumptions and estimation used to determine significant increases in credit risk of financial instruments and any changes in those assumptions and estimates (see 5.13 below and Chapter 53 at 5.2.3). *[IFRS 7.35F(a), 35G(a)(ii), 35G(c)]*.

Similar to measuring expected credit losses, an entity may use different approaches for different financial instruments when assessing significant increases in credit risk. An approach that does not include PD as an explicit input can be consistent with the impairment requirements as long as the entity is able to separate the changes in the risk of a default occurring from changes in other drivers of expected credit losses (e.g. collateral) and considers the following when making the assessment: *[IFRS 9.B5.5.12]*

- the change in the risk of a default occurring since initial recognition;
- the expected life of the financial instrument; and
- reasonable and supportable information that is available without undue cost or effort that may affect credit risk.

In addition, because of the relationship between the expected life and the risk of default occurring, the change in credit risk cannot be assessed simply by comparing the change in the absolute risk of default over time, because the risk of default usually decreases as time passes if the credit risk is unchanged. *[IFRS 9.B5.5.11]*.

Entities that do not use probability of loss as an explicit input will have to use other criteria to identify a change in the risk of default occurring. These might include deterioration in a behavioural score or other indicators of a heightened risk of default. A collective approach may also be an appropriate substitute for an assessment at the individual instrument level (see 5.5.5 below).

5.5.1 Change in the risk of a default occurring

In order to make the assessment of whether there has been significant credit deterioration, an entity should consider reasonable and supportable information that is available without undue cost or effort and compare: *[IFRS 9.5.5.9]*

- the risk of a default occurring on the financial instrument as at the reporting date; and

- the risk of a default occurring on the financial instrument as at the date of initial recognition.

For loan commitments, an entity should consider changes in the risk of a default occurring on the potential loan to which a loan commitment relates. For financial guarantee contracts, an entity should consider the changes in the risk that the specified debtor will default. *[IFRS 9.B5.5.8]*.

At each reporting date, an entity is required to assess significant increases in credit risk based on the change in the risk of a default occurring over the expected life of the financial instrument rather than the change in the amount of expected credit losses. *[IFRS 9.5.5.9]*. In a departure from the Basel regulatory wording and to avoid suggesting that statistical models are necessarily required (including the probability of a default approach), the IASB changed the terminology from 'probability of a default occurring' to 'risk of a default occurring'. *[IFRS 9.BC5.157]*.

In order to make the IFRS 9 impairment model operational, the IASB considered a number of alternative methods for determining significant increases in credit risk, but these were rejected for the following reasons:

- Absolute level of credit risk: The IASB considered whether an entity should be required to recognise lifetime expected credit losses on all financial instruments at, or above, a particular credit risk at the reporting date. Although this approach is operationally simpler to apply (because an entity is not required to track changes in credit risk) such an approach may not provide useful information (including the economic effect of initial and subsequent changes in credit loss expectations) and may result in overstatement or understatement of expected credit losses, depending on the threshold set for recognising lifetime expected credit losses. *[IFRS 9.BC5.160]*. However, the IASB noted that an absolute approach could be used for portfolios of financial instruments with similar credit risk at initial recognition, by determining the maximum initial credit risk accepted and then comparing the maximum initial credit risk to the credit risk at the reporting date (see 5.5.4.E below). *[IFRS 9.BC5.161]*.

- Change in the credit risk management objective: The IASB also considered whether the assessment of significant deterioration should be based on whether an entity's credit risk management objective changes (e.g. monitoring of financial assets on an individual basis, or a change from collecting past due amounts to the recovery of these amounts). This approach is operationally relatively easy to apply. However, it is likely to have a similar effect to the IAS 39 incurred loss model and, hence, may result in the delayed recognition of expected credit losses. [IFRS 9.BC5.162].

- Credit underwriting policies: The IASB further considered whether the change in the entity's credit underwriting limit for a particular class of financial instrument at the reporting date (i.e. an entity would not originate new loans on the same terms) should form the basis of assessing significant increase in credit risk. The IASB noted that this approach is similar to the absolute approach above. Moreover, the change in an entity's credit underwriting limits may be driven by other factors that are not related to a change in the credit risk of its borrowers (e.g. the entity may incorporate favourable terms to maintain a good business relationship or to increase lending), or are dependent on circumstances existing at the reporting date that are not relevant to the particular vintages of financial instruments. [IFRS 9.BC5.163, BC5.164, BC5.165].

As already stressed, the assessment is based on the change in the lifetime risk of default, not the amount of expected credit losses. Hence the allowance for a fully collateralised asset may need to be based on lifetime expected credit losses (because there has been a significant increase in the risk of default) even though no loss is expected to arise. [IFRS 9.5.5.9]. In such instances, the fact that the asset is being measured using lifetime expected credit losses may have more significance for disclosure than for measurement (see 5.13 below).

The interaction between collateral, assessment of significant increases in credit risk and measurement of expected credit losses is illustrated in the following example from the standard. [IFRS 9 IG Example3, IE18-IE23].

Example 49.18:   Highly collateralised financial asset

Company H owns real estate assets which are financed by a five-year loan from Bank Z with a loan-to-value (LTV) ratio of 50 per cent. The loan is secured by a first-ranking security over the real estate assets. At initial recognition of the loan, Bank Z does not consider the loan to be credit-impaired as defined in Appendix A of IFRS 9.

Subsequent to initial recognition, the revenues and operating profits of Company H have decreased because of an economic recession. Furthermore, expected increases in regulations have the potential to further negatively affect revenue and operating profit. These negative effects on Company H's operations could be significant and ongoing.

As a result of these recent events and expected adverse economic conditions, Company H's free cash flow is expected to be reduced to the point that the coverage of scheduled loan payments could become tight. Bank Z estimates that a further deterioration in cash flows may result in Company H missing a contractual payment on the loan and becoming past due.

Recent third party appraisals have indicated a decrease in the value of the real estate properties, resulting in a current LTV ratio of 70 per cent.

At the reporting date, the loan to Company H is not considered to have low credit risk in accordance with paragraph 5.5.10 of IFRS 9. Bank Z therefore needs to assess whether there has been a significant increase in credit risk since initial recognition in accordance with paragraph 5.5.3 of IFRS 9, irrespective of the value of the collateral it holds. It notes that the loan is subject to considerable credit risk at the reporting date because even a slight deterioration in cash flows could result in Company H missing a contractual payment on the loan. As a result, Bank Z determines that the credit risk (i.e. the risk of a default occurring) has increased significantly since initial recognition. Consequently, Bank Z recognises lifetime expected credit losses on the loan to Company H.

Although lifetime expected credit losses should be recognised, the measurement of the expected credit losses will reflect the recovery expected from the collateral (adjusting for the costs of obtaining and selling the collateral) on the property as required by paragraph B5.5.55 of IFRS 9 and may result in the expected credit losses on the loan being very small.

The ITG (see 5.1.5 above) discussed in April 2015 whether an entity should consider the ability to recover cash flows through a financial guarantee contract that is integral to the contract when assessing whether there has been a significant increase in the credit risk of the guaranteed debt instrument since initial recognition. IFRS 9 requires that measurement of the expected credit losses of the guaranteed debt instrument includes cash flows from the integral financial guarantee contract (see 5.4.7 above). *[IFRS 9.B5.5.55]*. However, some ITG members commented that IFRS 9 is clear that recoveries from integral financial guarantee contracts should be excluded from the assessment of significant increases in credit risk of the guaranteed debt instrument. *[IFRS 9.5.5.9]*. This is because the focus of the standard is about the risk of the borrower defaulting when making such an assessment, as highlighted in the examples in B5.5.17. These examples clarify that information about a guarantee (or other credit enhancement) may be relevant to assessing changes in credit risk, but only to the extent that it affects the likelihood of the borrower defaulting on the instrument. *[IFRS 9.B5.5.17]*. Furthermore, excluding recoveries from the financial guarantee contract, when assessing significant increases in credit risk, would be consistent with the treatment of other forms of collateral.

While the value of collateral does not normally affect the assessment of significant increases in credit risk, if significant changes in the value of the collateral supporting the obligation are expected to reduce the borrower's economic incentive to make scheduled contractual payments, then this would have an effect on the risk of a default occurring. The standard provided an example that if the value of collateral declines because house prices decline, borrowers in some jurisdictions have a greater incentive to default on their mortgages. *[IFRS 9.B5.5.17(j)]*.

The other examples provided by the standard of situations where the value of a credit enhancement could have an impact on the ability or economic incentive of the borrower to repay relate to guarantees or financial support provided by a shareholder, parent entity or other affiliate and to interests issued in securitisations. These are included in the examples listed in the next section of this chapter (see 5.5.2 below), where subordinated interests are expected to be capable of absorbing expected credit losses:

- a significant change in the quality of the guarantee provided by a shareholder (or an individual's parents) if the shareholder (or parents) have an incentive and financial ability to prevent default by capital or cash infusion; and *[IFRS 9.B5.5.17(k)]*
- significant changes, such as reductions in financial support from a parent entity or other affiliate or an actual or expected significant change in the quality of credit enhancement, that are expected to reduce the borrower's ability to make scheduled contractual payments. Credit quality enhancements or support include the consideration of the financial condition of the guarantor

Chapter 49

and/or, for interests issued in securitisations, whether subordinated interests are expected to be capable of absorbing expected credit losses (for example, on the loans underlying the security). *[IFRS 9.B5.5.17(l)]*.

Under the loss rate approach, introduced at 5.4.2.B above, an entity develops loss-rate statistics on the basis of the amount written off over the life of the financial assets rather than using separate PD and LGD statistics. Entities then must adjust these historical credit loss trends for current conditions and expectations about the future.

The standard is clear that although a loss rate approach may be applied, an entity needs to be able to separate the changes in the risk of a default occurring from changes in other drivers of expected credit losses. *[IFRS 9.B5.5.12]*. Under the loss rate approach, the entity does not distinguish between a risk of a default occurring and the loss incurred following a default. This is not so much of an issue for measuring 12-month or lifetime expected credit losses. However, under the loss rate approach, an entity would not be able to implement the assessment of significant increases in credit risk that is based on the change in the risk of a default. Therefore, entities using the loss rate approach would need an overlay of measuring and forecasting the level of defaults, as illustrated in the extract of Example 9 from the Implementation Guidance (see Example 49.16 above). For entities that currently use only expected loss rates it may be easier to develop a PD approach than to use the method described in the Example.

5.5.2   *Factors or indicators of changes in credit risk*

Similar to measuring expected credit losses (see 5.4 above), when assessing significant increases in credit risk, an entity should consider all reasonable and supportable information that is available without undue cost or effort (see 5.4.8 above) and that is relevant for an individual financial instrument, a portfolio, portions of a portfolio, and groups of portfolios. *[IFRS 9.B5.5.15, B5.5.16]*.

The IASB notes that it did not intend to prescribe a specific or mechanistic approach to assess changes in credit risk and that the appropriate approach will vary for different levels of sophistication of entities, the financial instrument and the availability of data. *[IFRS 9.BC5.157]*. It is important to stress that the assessment of significant increases in credit risk often involves a multifactor and holistic analysis. The importance and relevance of each specific factor will depend on the type of product, characteristics of the financial instruments and the borrower as well as the geographical region. *[IFRS 9.B5.5.16]*. The guidance in the standard is clear that in certain circumstances, qualitative and non-statistical quantitative information may be sufficient to determine that a financial instrument has met the criterion for the recognition of lifetime expected credit losses. That is, the information does not need to flow through a statistical model or credit ratings process in order to determine whether there has been a significant increase in the credit risk of the financial instrument. In other cases, the assessment may be based on quantitative information or a mixture of quantitative and qualitative information. *[IFRS 9.B5.5.18]*.

The standard provides a non-exhaustive list of factors or indicators which an entity should consider when determining whether the recognition of lifetime expected credit losses is required. This list of factors or indicators is as follows: *[IFRS 9.B5.5.17]*

- significant changes in internal price indicators of credit risk as a result of a change in credit risk since inception, including, but not limited to, the credit spread that would result if a particular financial instrument, or similar financial instrument with the same terms and the same counterparty were newly originated or issued at the reporting date;

- other changes in the rates or terms of an existing financial instrument that would be significantly different if the instrument was newly originated or issued at the reporting date (such as more stringent covenants, increased amounts of collateral or guarantees, or higher income coverage) because of changes in the credit risk of the financial instrument since initial recognition;

- significant changes in external market indicators of credit risk for a particular financial instrument or similar financial instruments with the same expected life. Changes in market indicators of credit risk include, but are not limited to: the credit spread; the credit default swap prices for the borrower; the length of time or the extent to which the fair value of a financial asset has been less than its amortised cost; and other market information related to the borrower (such as changes in the price of a borrower's debt and equity instruments). The IASB noted that market prices are an important source of information that should be considered in assessing whether credit risk has changed, although market prices themselves cannot solely determine whether significant deterioration has occurred because market prices are also affected by non-credit risk related factors such as changes in interest rates or liquidity risks; *[IFRS 9.BC5.123]*

- an actual or expected significant change in the financial instrument's external credit rating;

- an actual or expected internal credit rating downgrade for the borrower or decrease in behavioural scoring used to assess credit risk internally. Internal credit ratings and internal behavioural scoring are more reliable when they are mapped to external ratings or supported by default studies;

- existing or forecast adverse changes in business, financial or economic conditions that are expected to cause a significant change in the borrower's ability to meet its debt obligations, such as an actual or expected increase in interest rates or an actual or expected significant increase in unemployment rates;

- an actual or expected significant change in the operating results of the borrower. Examples include actual or expected declining revenues or margins, increasing operating risks, working capital deficiencies, decreasing asset quality, increased balance sheet leverage, liquidity, management problems or changes in the scope of business or organisational structure (such as the discontinuance of a segment of the business) that result in a significant change in the borrower's ability to meet its debt obligations;

- significant increases in credit risk on other financial instruments of the same borrower;

- an actual or expected significant adverse change in the regulatory, economic, or technological environment of the borrower that results in a significant change in the borrower's ability to meet its debt obligations, such as a decline in the demand for the borrower's sales product because of a shift in technology;

- significant changes in the value of the collateral supporting the obligation or in the quality of third-party guarantees or credit enhancements, which are expected to reduce the borrower's economic incentive to make scheduled contractual payments or to otherwise have an effect on the probability of a default occurring. For example, if the value of collateral declines because house prices decline, borrowers in some jurisdictions have a greater incentive to default on their mortgages;

- a significant change in the quality of the guarantee provided by a shareholder (or an individual's parents) if the shareholder (or parents) have an incentive and financial ability to prevent default by capital or cash infusion;

- significant changes, such as reductions, in financial support from a parent entity or other affiliate or an actual or expected significant change in the quality of credit enhancement, that are expected to reduce the borrower's economic incentive to make scheduled contractual payments. For example, such a situation could occur if a parent decides to no longer provide financial support to a subsidiary, which as a result would face bankruptcy or receivership. This could in turn result in that subsidiary prioritising payments for its operational needs (such as payroll and crucial suppliers) and assigning a lower priority to payments on its financial debt, resulting in an increase in the risk of default on those liabilities. Credit quality enhancements or support include the consideration of the financial condition of the guarantor and/or, for interests issued in securitisations, whether subordinated interests are expected to be capable of absorbing expected credit losses (for example, on the loans underlying the security);

- expected changes in the loan documentation (i.e. changes in contract terms) including an expected breach of contract that may lead to covenant waivers or amendments, interest payment holidays, interest rate step-ups, requiring additional collateral or guarantees, or other changes to the contractual framework of the instrument;

- significant changes in the expected performance and behaviour of the borrower, including changes in the payment status of borrowers in the group (for example, an increase in the expected number or extent of delayed contractual payments or significant increases in the expected number of credit card borrowers who are expected to approach or exceed their credit limit or who are expected to be paying the minimum monthly amount);

- changes in the entity's credit management approach in relation to the financial instrument, i.e. based on emerging indicators of changes in the credit risk of the financial instrument, the entity's credit risk management practice is expected to become more active or to be focused on managing the instrument, including the instrument becoming more closely monitored or controlled, or the entity specifically intervening with the borrower; and

- past due information, including the more than 30 days past due rebuttable presumption (see 5.5.4.B below).

This list raises the question as to whether an entity will be required to look at each of these factors or indicators as soon as the information is readily available, even though they may not be fully integrated in the entity's credit risk management systems and processes. This relates to our earlier discussion about which information is available without undue cost or effort (see 5.4.8.A above).

We also make the following observations:

- Many financial institutions should have readily available information about the pricing and terms of various types of loans issued to a specific customer (e.g. overdraft, credit cards and mortgage loans) in their credit risk management systems and processes. However, in practice, it would often be difficult to use such information because changes in pricing and terms on the origination of a similar financial instrument at the reporting date may not be so obviously related to a change in credit risk as other, more commercial, factors come into play (e.g. different risk appetites, change in management approach and underwriting standards). It may be challenging to link the two sets of information (i.e. pricing processes on the one hand and credit risk management on the other).

- Some of the factors or indicators are only relevant for the assessment of significant deterioration on an individual basis and not on a portfolio basis. For example, change in external market indicators of credit risk, including the credit spread, the credit default swap prices of the borrower and the extent of decline in fair value. However, it is worth noting that external market information that is available for a quoted instrument may be useful to help assess another instrument that is not quoted but which is issued by the same debtor or one who operates in the same sector.

- It is important to stress that the approach required by the standard is more holistic and qualitative than is necessarily captured by external credit ratings, which are adjusted for discrete events and do not reflect gradual degradations in credit quality. External credit ratings should not, therefore, be used on their own but only in conjunction with other qualitative information. Furthermore, although ratings are forward-looking, it is sometimes suggested that changes in credit ratings may not be reflected in a timely matter. Therefore, entities may have to take account of expected change in ratings in assessing whether exposures are low risk. The same point can of course be made about the use of internal credit ratings, especially if they are only reassessed on an annual basis.

- Also, some of the factors or indicators are very forward-looking, such as forecasts of adverse changes in business, financial or economic conditions that are expected to result in significant future financial difficulty of the borrower in repaying its debt. In practice it will be challenging to link such forecasts to whether they lead to significant increases in credit risk for particular exposures.

With IFRS 9 not being prescriptive, we observe some differences in how banks intend to implement the assessment of significant increase in credit risk. These differences reflect various schools of thought along with differences in credit processes, business model, sophistication, use of advanced models for regulatory capital purposes, availability of data (e.g. historic data at origination) and consistency of definitions across businesses or multiple systems. It is likely that these factors will lead to a number of approaches being adopted within one bank.

The consideration of various factors or indicators when assessing significant increases in credit risk since initial recognition is illustrated in the following Examples 49.19 and 49.20, based on Examples 1 and 2 in the Implementation Guidance for the standard. *[IFRS 9 IG Example 1, IG Example 2, IE7-IE17].*

Example 49.19:   Significant increase in credit risk

Company Y has a funding structure that includes a senior secured loan facility with different tranches. The security on the loan affects the loss that would be realised if a default occurs, but does not affect the risk of a default occurring, so it is not considered when determining whether there has been a significant increase in credit risk since initial recognition as required by paragraph 5.5.3 of IFRS 9. Bank X provides a tranche of that loan facility to Company Y. At the time of origination of the loan by Bank X, although Company Y's leverage was relatively high compared with other issuers with similar credit risk, it was expected that Company Y would be able to meet the covenants for the life of the instrument. In addition, the generation of revenue and cash flow was expected to be stable in Company Y's industry over the term of the senior facility. However, there was some business risk related to the ability to grow gross margins within its existing businesses.

At initial recognition, because of the considerations outlined above, Bank X considers that despite the level of credit risk at initial recognition, the loan is not an originated credit-impaired loan because it does not meet the definition of a credit-impaired financial asset in Appendix A of IFRS 9.

Subsequent to initial recognition, macroeconomic changes have had a negative effect on total sales volume and Company Y has underperformed on its business plan for revenue generation and net cash flow generation. Although spending on inventory has increased, anticipated sales have not materialised. To increase liquidity, Company Y has drawn down more on a separate revolving credit facility, thereby increasing its leverage ratio. Consequently, Company Y is now close to breaching its covenants on the senior secured loan facility with Bank X.

Bank X makes an overall assessment of the credit risk on the loan to Company Y at the reporting date, by taking into consideration all reasonable and supportable information that is available without undue cost or effort and that is relevant for assessing the extent of the increase in credit risk since initial recognition. This may include factors such as:

(a) Bank X's expectation that the deterioration in the macroeconomic environment may continue in the near future, which is expected to have a further negative impact on Company Y's ability to generate cash flows and to deleverage.

(b) Company Y is closer to breaching its covenants, which may result in a need to restructure the loan or reset the covenants.

(c) Bank X's assessment that the trading prices for Company Y's bonds have decreased and that the credit margin on newly originated loans have increased reflecting the increase in credit risk, and that these changes are not explained by changes in the market environment (for example, benchmark interest rates have remained unchanged). A further comparison with the pricing of Company Y's peers shows that reductions in the price of Company Y's bonds and increases in credit margin on its loans have probably been caused by company-specific factors.

(d) Bank X has reassessed its internal risk grading of the loan on the basis of the information that it has available to reflect the increase in credit risk.

Bank X determines that there has been a significant increase in credit risk since initial recognition of the loan in accordance with paragraph 5.5.3 of IFRS 9. Consequently, Bank X recognises lifetime expected credit losses on its senior secured loan to Company Y. Even if Bank X has not yet changed the internal risk grading of the loan it could still reach this conclusion – the absence or presence of a change in risk grading in itself is not determinative of whether credit risk has increased significantly since initial recognition.

Example 49.20: No significant increase in credit risk

Company C is the holding company of a group that operates in a cyclical production industry. Bank B provided a loan to Company C. At that time, the prospects for the industry were positive, because of expectations of further increases in global demand. However, input prices were volatile and given the point in the cycle, a potential decrease in sales was anticipated.

In addition, in the past Company C has been focused on external growth, acquiring majority stakes in companies in related sectors. As a result, the group structure is complex and has been subject to change, making it difficult for investors to analyse the expected performance of the group and to forecast the cash that will be available at the holding company level. Even though leverage is at a level that is considered acceptable by Company C's creditors at the time that Bank B originates the loan, its creditors are concerned about Company C's ability to refinance its debt because of the short remaining life until the maturity of the current financing. There is also concern about Company C's ability to continue to service interest using the dividends it receives from its operating subsidiaries.

At the time of the origination of the loan by Bank B, Company C's leverage was in line with that of other customers with similar credit risk and based on projections over the expected life of the loan, the available capacity (i.e. headroom) on its coverage ratios before triggering a default event, was high. Bank B applies its own internal rating methods to determine credit risk and allocates a specific internal rating score to its loans. Bank B's internal rating categories are based on historical, current and forward-looking information and reflect the credit risk for the tenor of the loans. On initial recognition, Bank B determines that the loan is subject to considerable credit risk, has speculative elements and that the uncertainties affecting Company C, including the group's uncertain prospects for cash generation, could lead to default. However, Bank B does not consider the loan to be originated credit-impaired.

Subsequent to initial recognition, Company C has announced that three of its five key subsidiaries had a significant reduction in sales volume because of deteriorated market conditions but sales volumes are expected to improve in line with the anticipated cycle for the industry in the following months. The sales of the other two subsidiaries were stable. Company C has also announced a corporate restructure to streamline its operating subsidiaries. This restructuring will increase the flexibility to refinance existing debt and the ability of the operating subsidiaries to pay dividends to Company C.

Despite the expected continuing deterioration in market conditions, Bank B determines, in accordance with paragraph 5.5.3 of IFRS 9, that there has not been a significant increase in the credit risk on the loan to Company C since initial recognition. This is demonstrated by factors that include:

(a) Although current sale volumes have fallen, this was as anticipated by Bank B at initial recognition. Furthermore, sales volumes are expected to improve, in the following months.

(b) Given the increased flexibility to refinance the existing debt at the operating subsidiary level and the increased availability of dividends to Company C, Bank B views the corporate restructure as being credit enhancing. This is despite some continued concern about the ability to refinance the existing debt at the holding company level.

(c) Bank B's credit risk department, which monitors Company C, has determined that the latest developments are not significant enough to justify a change in its internal credit risk rating.

As a consequence, Bank B does not recognise a loss allowance at an amount equal to lifetime expected credit losses on the loan. However, it updates its measurement of the 12-month expected credit losses for the increased risk of a default occurring in the next 12 months and for current expectations of the credit losses that would arise if a default were to occur.

At its meeting on 16 September 2015, the ITG (see 5.1.5 above) discussed two issues concerning how an entity should determine whether there has been a significant increase in credit risk:

- How to identify a significant increase in credit risk for a portfolio of retail loans when identical pricing and contractual terms are applied to customers across broad credit quality bands.

- The possibility of using behavioural indicators of credit risk for the purpose of the assessment of significant increases in credit risk since initial recognition.[26]

The first question was influenced by one of the operational simplifications introduced by the IASB, discussed at 5.5.4.E, which allows an entity to assess if there has been a significant increase in credit risk by determining the maximum initial credit risk accepted for portfolios with similar credit risks on original recognition, and by reviewing which exposures now exceed this limit. The question was whether, if the loan pricing is the same for loans with various credit qualities, it is possible to assert that there has been no significant increase in credit risk as long as the pricing of a loan has not changed.

ITG members generally agreed that pricing alone is likely not a determinative factor in assessing a significant increase in credit risk. *[IFRS 9.5.5.4].* If, within the same portfolio, there are customers with significantly different credit risks at origination, an entity cannot disregard this fact. ITG members suggested two possible ways of assessing whether significant increases in credit risk have occurred. First, an entity could achieve greater granularity by segmenting portfolios by groups of loans with shared credit risk characteristics. *[IFRS 9.B5.5.5].* Second, an entity could design more sophisticated indicators that take into account different initial credit qualities within the same collectively assessed portfolio.

The second question was whether the following behavioural indicators could be used, on their own, to determine if there has been a significant increase in credit risk:

- where a customer has made only the minimum monthly repayment for a specified number of months;

- where a customer has failed to make a payment on a loan with a different lender; or

- where a customer has failed to make a specified number of minimum monthly repayments.

The ITG members generally agreed that behavioural indicators can only be used on their own to assess a significant increase in credit risk if a correlation can be established between the behavioural indicators and the risk of a default occurring (in accordance with paragraphs 5.5.4 and 5.5.9 of IFRS 9). ITG members also noted that behavioural indicators are usually backward looking and an entity will also need to consider forward-looking information, possibly through a collective approach (see 5.5.5 below). Whatever the approach, it should aim to ensure that exposures move to stage 2 before they become delinquent. *[IFRS 9.B5.5.2].* Also, the majority of ITG members were in general agreement that behavioural information should not rely solely on an entity's own experience, but should make use of other readily available credit information, such as credit bureau data, if available.

Other behavioural indicators, beyond those mentioned in the IASB Staff Paper, including items such as the level of cash advances, changes in expected payment patterns (e.g. moving from full payment to something less than full payment), and higher-than-expected utilisation of the facility, were raised at the meeting. Individually, these kinds of behaviours may not be determinative of a significant increase in credit risk but, when observed together, they may prove to be more indicative. By combining these indicators, an entity has the potential to transfer assets between stage 1 and stage 2 more meaningfully.

We also note that that one of the challenges with using behavioural information is that it depends on the starting point. That is, if the obligor's risk of default initially is consistent with a super-prime rating, the kind of deteriorating behaviour noted above would likely signal a significant shift. However, if the obligor originally had a sub-prime rating, then such behaviour might not indicate a significant increase in risk. Also, while indicators that are more lagging may show a greater correlation with subsequent default, they are also likely to be less forward-looking and so make it more necessary to apply an additional collective approach.

5.5.3 What is significant?

The assessment of whether credit risk has significantly increased depends, critically, on an interpretation of the word 'significant'. Some constituents who commented on the 2013 Exposure Draft requested the IASB to quantify the term significant, however, the IASB decided not to do so, for the following reasons: *[IFRS 9.BC5.171, BC5.172]*

- specifying a fixed percentage change in the risk of default would require all entities to use the risk of default approach. As not all entities (apart from regulated financial institutions) use PDs as an explicit input, this would have increased the costs and effort for those entities that do not use such an approach; and

- defining the amount of change in the risk of a default occurring would be arbitrary and this would depend on the type of products, maturities and initial credit risk.

The standard emphasises that the determination of the significance of the change in the risk of a default occurring depends on:

- the original credit risk at initial recognition: the same absolute change in PD for a financial instrument with a lower initial credit risk will be more significant than those with a higher initial credit risk (see 5.5.4.E below and Example 49.24). *[IFRS 9.B5.5.9]*.

- the expected life or term structure: the risk of a default occurring for financial instruments with similar credit risk increases the longer the expected life of the financial instruments. Due to the relationship between the expected life and the risk of a default occurring, an entity cannot simply compare the absolute risk of a default occurring over time. For example, if the risk of a default occurring for a financial instrument with an expected life of 10 years at initial recognition is the same after five years, then this indicates that the credit risk has increased. The standard also states that, for financial instruments that have significant payment obligations close to the maturity of the financial instrument (e.g. those where the principal is only repaid at maturity), the risk of a default occurring may not necessarily decrease as time passes. In such cases, an entity needs to consider other qualitative factors. We note, however, that while the risk of default may decrease less quickly for an instrument with payment obligations throughout its contractual life, normally, the risk of default will still decrease as maturity approaches. *[IFRS 9.B5.5.10, B5.5.11].*

Examining the historical levels of default associated with the credit ratings of agencies, such as Standard & Poor's, it is apparent that the PDs increase at a geometrical, rather than an arithmetic, rate as the credit ratings decline. Hence, the absolute increase in the PD between two relatively low risk credit ratings is considerably less than between two relatively higher risk ratings. The relative increase in PD between each of these ratings might be considered significant, since most involve a doubling or trebling of the PD. In contrast, because credit rating is an art rather than a science, the smaller changes in credit risk associated with the plus or minus notches in the grading system are less likely to be viewed as significant. In addition, as the time horizon increases, the PDs also increase across all credit ratings (i.e. the PD increases with a longer maturity).

The majority of credit exposures that are assessed for significant credit deterioration will not have been rated by a credit rating agency. However, the same logic will apply when entities have developed their own PD models and are able to classify their exposure by PD levels. It is important to stress that the approach required by the standard is more holistic and qualitative than is necessarily captured by external credit ratings, which are adjusted for discrete events and do not reflect gradual degradations in credit quality. External credit ratings should not, therefore, be used on their own but only in conjunction with other qualitative information. The same point can of course be made about the use of internal credit ratings, especially if they are only reassessed on an annual basis.

The determination of what is significant will, for the larger banks, be influenced by the guidance issued by banking regulators (see 5.6.1 below).

5.5.4   Operational simplifications

When assessing significant increases in credit risk, there are a number of operational simplifications available. These are discussed below.

5.5.4.A   Low credit risk operational simplification

The standard contains an important simplification, that if a financial instrument has a low credit risk, then an entity is allowed to assume at the reporting date that no significant increases in credit risk have occurred. The low credit risk concept was intended, by the IASB, to provide relief for entities from tracking changes in the credit risk of high quality financial instruments. This simplification is only optional and the low credit risk simplification can be elected on an instrument-by-instrument basis. *[IFRS 9.BC5.184].*

This is a change from the 2013 Exposure Draft, in which a low risk exposure was deemed not to have suffered significant deterioration in credit risk. *[IFRS 9.BC5.181, BC5.182, BC5.183].*

The amendment to make the simplification optional was made in response to requests from constituents, including regulators. The consultative Basel Committee guidance (see 5.6.1 below) considers the use of the low credit risk simplification a low-quality implementation of the expected credit loss model and expects it to be used in rare and appropriate circumstances, except for holdings in securities.

For low risk instruments for which the simplification is used, the entity would recognise an allowance based on 12-month expected credit losses. *[IFRS 9.5.5.10]*. However, if a financial instrument is not or no longer considered to have low credit risk at the reporting date, it does not follow that the entity is required to recognise lifetime expected credit losses. In such instances, the entity has to assess whether there has been a significant increase in credit risk since initial recognition which requires the recognition of lifetime expected credit losses. *[IFRS 9.5.5.24]*.

The standard states that a financial instrument is considered to have low credit risk if: *[IFRS 9.5.5.22]*

- the financial instrument has a low risk of default;
- the borrower has a strong capacity to meet its contractual cash flow obligations in the near term; and
- adverse changes in economic and business conditions in the longer term may, but will not necessarily, reduce the ability of the borrower to fulfil its contractual cash flow obligations.

A financial instrument is not considered to have low credit risk simply because it has a low risk of loss (e.g. for a collateralised loan, if the value of the collateral is more than the amount lent (see 5.4.7 above)) or it has lower risk of default compared to the entity's other financial instruments or relative to the credit risk of the jurisdiction within which the entity operates. *[IFRS 9.B5.5.22]*.

The description of low credit risk is equivalent to investment grade quality assets, equivalent to a Standard and Poor's rating of BBB– or better, Moody's rating of Baa3 or better and Fitch's rating of BBB– or better. When applying the low credit risk simplification, financial instruments are not required to be externally rated. However, the IASB's intention was to use a globally comparable notion of low credit risk instead of a level of risk determined, for example, by an entity or jurisdiction's view of risk based on entity-specific or jurisdictional factors. *[IFRS 9.BC5.188]*. Therefore, an entity may use its internal credit ratings to assess what is low credit risk as long as this is consistent with the globally understood definition of low credit risk (i.e. investment grade) or the market's expectations of what is deemed to be low credit risk, taking into consideration the terms and conditions of the financial instruments being assessed. *[IFRS 9.B5.5.23]*.

The Consultative guidance of the Basel Committee guidance (see 5.6.1 below) states that the investment grade category used by ratings agencies is not considered homogeneous enough to be automatically considered low credit risk, and internationally active and sophisticated banks are expected to rely primarily on their own credit assessments.

Chapter 49

In practice, entities with internal credit ratings will attempt to map their internal rating to the external credit ratings and definitions, such as Standard & Poor's, Moody's and Fitch. The description of the credit quality ratings by these major rating agencies are illustrated below.[27]

Figure 49.4 External credit ratings and definitions from the 3 major rating agencies

Standard & Poor's	Moody's	Fitch
Investment grade would usually refer to categories AAA to BBB (with BBB– being lowest investment grade considered by market participants).	Investment grade would usually refer to categories Aaa to Baa (with Baa3 being lowest investment grade considered by market participants).	Investment grade would usually refer to categories AAA to BBB (with BBB– being lowest investment grade considered by market participants).
BBB **Adequate capacity** to meet financial commitments, but more subject to **adverse economic conditions**.	**Baa** Obligations rated Baa are judged to be medium-grade and subject to moderate credit risk and as such may possess certain speculative characteristics.	**BBB: Good credit quality** Indicates that expectations of **default risk are currently low**. The capacity for payment of financial commitments is considered adequate but adverse business or economic conditions are more likely to impair this capacity.
The dividing line between investment grade and speculative grade		
BB Less vulnerable in the near-term but faces major on-going uncertainties to adverse business, financial and economic conditions.	**Ba** Obligations rated Ba are judged to be speculative and are subject to substantial credit risk.	**BB: Speculative** Indicates an elevated vulnerability to default risk, particularly in the event of adverse changes in business or economic conditions over time; however, business or financial flexibility exists which supports the servicing of financial commitments.

Examining the historical levels of default associated with the credit ratings of agencies such as Standard & Poor's, the PD of a BBB-rated loan is approximately treble that of one that is rated A. Hence, many entities would consider the increase in credit risk to be significant, if the low risk simplification is not used.

The low credit risk simplification will not be relevant if an entity originates or purchases a financial instrument with a credit risk which is already non-investment grade. Similarly, this simplification will also have limited use when the financial instrument is originated or purchased with a credit quality that is marginally better than a non-investment grade (i.e. at the bottom of the investment grade rating), because any credit deterioration into the non-investment grade rating would require the entity to assess whether the increase in credit risk has been significant.

Partly because of the Basel Committee guidance, most sophisticated banks intend to apply the low risk simplification only to securities. It is yet to be seen whether less sophisticated banks will use this operational simplification widely for their loan portfolios. Investors that hold externally rated debt instruments are more likely to rely on external rating agencies data and use the low credit risk simplification. However, some sophisticated banks are intending not to use it at all, preferring to use the same criteria as for other exposures. It is also important to emphasise that:

- The default rates provided by external rating agencies are historical information. Entities need to understand the sources of these historical default rates and update the data for current and forward-looking information (see 5.4.8 above) when measuring expected credit losses or assessing credit deterioration, as illustrated by Example 49.22 below.

- Although ratings are forward-looking, it is sometimes suggested that changes in credit ratings may not be reflected in a timely matter. Therefore, entities may have to take account of expected change in ratings in assessing whether exposures are low risk.

The following example from the standard illustrates the application of the low credit risk simplification. *[IFRS 9 IG Example 4, IE24-IE28].*

Example 49.21: Public investment-grade bond

Company A is a large listed national logistics company. The only debt in the capital structure is a five-year public bond with a restriction on further borrowing as the only bond covenant. Company A reports quarterly to its shareholders. Entity B is one of many investors in the bond. Entity B considers the bond to have low credit risk at initial recognition in accordance with paragraph 5.5.10 of IFRS 9. This is because the bond has a low risk of default and Company A is considered to have a strong capacity to meet its obligations in the near term. Entity B's expectations for the longer term are that adverse changes in economic and business conditions may, but will not necessarily, reduce Company A's ability to fulfil its obligations on the bond. In addition, at initial recognition the bond had an internal credit rating that is correlated to a global external credit rating of investment grade.

At the reporting date, Entity B's main credit risk concern is the continuing pressure on the total volume of sales that has caused Company A's operating cash flows to decrease.

Because Entity B relies only on quarterly public information and does not have access to private credit risk information (because it is a bond investor), its assessment of changes in credit risk is tied to public announcements and information, including updates on credit perspectives in press releases from rating agencies.

Entity B applies the low credit risk simplification in paragraph 5.5.10 of IFRS 9. Accordingly, at the reporting date, Entity B evaluates whether the bond is considered to have low credit risk using all reasonable and supportable information that is available without undue cost or effort. In making that evaluation, Entity B reassesses the internal credit rating of the bond and concludes that the bond is no longer equivalent to an investment grade rating because:

(a) The latest quarterly report of Company A revealed a quarter-on-quarter decline in revenues of 20 per cent and in operating profit by 12 per cent.

(b) Rating agencies have reacted negatively to a profit warning by Company A and put the credit rating under review for possible downgrade from investment grade to non-investment grade. However, at the reporting date the external credit risk rating was unchanged.

(c) The bond price has also declined significantly, which has resulted in a higher yield to maturity. Entity B assesses that the bond prices have been declining as a result of increases in Company A's credit risk. This is because the market environment has not changed (for example, benchmark interest rates, liquidity, etc. are unchanged) and comparison with the bond prices of peers shows that the reductions are probably company specific (instead of being, for example, changes in benchmark interest rates that are not indicative of company-specific credit risk).

While Company A currently has the capacity to meet its commitments, the large uncertainties arising from its exposure to adverse business and economic conditions have increased the risk of a default occurring on the bond. As a result of the factors described above, Entity B determines that the bond does not have low credit risk at the reporting date. As a result, Entity B needs to determine whether the increase in credit risk since initial recognition has been significant. On the basis of its assessment, Company B determines that the credit risk has increased significantly since initial recognition and that a loss allowance at an amount equal to lifetime expected credit losses should be recognised in accordance with paragraph 5.5.3 of IFRS 9.

Some of the challenges in assessing whether there has been a significant increase in credit risk (including the use of the low credit risk simplification) and estimating the expected credit losses, are illustrated in the following example. It illustrates different ways of identifying a significant change in credit quality and different input parameters for calculating expected credit losses for a European government bond, which result in very different outcomes and volatility of the IFRS 9 expected credit loss allowance.

Example 49.22:   Use of credit ratings and/or CDS spreads to determine whether there have been significant increases in credit risk and to estimate expected credit losses

Introduction

A significant challenge in applying the IFRS 9 impairment requirements to quoted bonds is that the credit ratings assigned by agencies such as Standard & Poor's (S&P), and the historical experience of losses by rating grade, can differ significantly with the view of the market, as reflected in, for instance, credit default swap (CDS) spreads and bond spreads.

To illustrate the challenges of applying IFRS 9 to debt securities, we have examined how the expected credit loss could be determined for a real bond issued by a European government on 16 September 2008 and due to mature in 2024. For three dates, we applied the IFRS 9 calculations to this bond, which is assumed to have been acquired at inception. In January 2009, the Standard & Poor's credit rating of the government was AA+, as at origination, but by January 2012, its rating was downgraded to A. The bond was further downgraded to BBB– in March 2014 before recovery to BBB in May 2014.

Three approaches

Shown below are three approaches:

- Approach 1: Use of S&P credit ratings both to determine whether the bond has significantly increased in credit risk and to estimate expected credit losses.

- Approach 2: Use of S&P credit ratings to determine whether the bond has significantly increased in credit risk and CDS spreads to estimate expected credit losses.

- Approach 3: Use of CDS spreads both to determine whether the bond has significantly increased in credit risk and to estimate expected credit losses.

Based on the historical corporate PDs from each assessed S&P credit rating (approach 1) and based on the CDS spreads (approaches 2 and 3), the loan loss percentages were calculated below. For the calculations, an often used LGD of 60% was applied.

The percentage loss allowances were, as follows:

	Credit ratings	12-month PD	Lifetime PD	Approach 1	Approach 2	Approach 3
1 January 2009	AA+	0.44%	16.69%	–	–	–
31 January 2009	AA+	1.84%	18.29%	0.01	1.10	18.29
31 January 2012	A	4.96%	30.89%	0.04	2.98	30.89
31 March 2014	BBB–	0.57%	13.81%	0.18	0.34	13.81

Approach 1

According to the credit ratings, the bond was investment grade throughout this period. Hence, using the low risk simplification, the loss allowance would have been based on 12-month expected credit losses. Using the corporate historical default rates implied by the credit ratings and an assumption of 60% LGD to calculate the expected credit losses, the 12-month allowance would have increased from 0.01% on 31 January 2009 to 0.04% three years later, increasing to 0.18% by 31 March 2014. It should be stressed that the historical default rates implied by credit ratings are historical rates for corporate debt and so they would not, without adjustment, satisfy the requirements of the standard. IFRS 9 requires the calculation of expected credit losses, based on current conditions and forecasts of future conditions, to be based on reasonable and supportable information. This is likely to include market indicators such as CDS and bond spreads, as illustrated by Approach 2.

Approach 2

In contrast to Approach 1, using credit default swap spreads to calculate the expected credit losses and the same assumption of 60% LGD to calculate the expected credit losses, the 12-month allowance would have increased from 1.1% on 31 January 2009 to 2.98% three years later, declining to 0.34% by 31 March 2014. The default rates implied by the CDSs are significantly higher than would have been expected given the ratings of these bonds. The loss allowances are, correspondingly, very much higher and very volatile. It might be argued that CDS spreads are too responsive to short term market sentiment to calculate long term expected credit losses, but it may appear difficult to find other reasonable and supportable information to adjust these rates so as to dampen the effects of market volatility.

Approach 3

Credit ratings are often viewed by the market as lagging indicators. For these bonds, the ratings are difficult to reconcile with the default probabilities as assessed by the markets. It might be argued that it is not sufficient to focus only on credit ratings when assessing whether assets are low risk since, according to CDS spreads, the bond was not low risk at any time in the period covered in this example, as it showed a significant increase in 1 year PD after inception (based on CDS spreads). The 1 year PDs increased from 0.44% on issue to 1.84% by 31 January 2009. Assessing the bond as requiring a lifetime expected credit loss at all three dates, based on CDS spreads, would have given much higher loss allowances of 18.29%, 30.89% and 13.81%.

The counter-view might be that CDS spreads are too volatile to provide a sound basis for determining significant deterioration. Perhaps the best way to make the assessment of whether a bond has increased significantly in credit risk is to use more than one source of data and to take account of the qualitative indicators as described in the standard.

Conclusion

The calculated expected credit loss figures differ significantly depending on the approach taken as to how to determine a significant change in credit quality and the parameters used for the calculation. Those based on CDS spreads are both large and very volatile, reflecting the investor uncertainty during the period, when the possibility of default depended more on the political will of the European Union to maintain the integrity of the Eurozone than the economic forecasts for the particular country. As a result, the disparity between the effect of the use of credit grades and CDSs is probably more marked than for most other security investments. Nevertheless, the same challenges will be found with other securities, albeit on a smaller scale.

5.5.4.B   *Past due status and more than 30 days past due rebuttable presumption*

The IASB is concerned that past due information is a lagging indicator. Typically, credit risk increases significantly before a financial instrument becomes past due or other lagging borrower-specific factors (for example, a modification or restructuring) are observed. Consequently, when reasonable and supportable information that is more forward-looking than past due information is available without undue cost or

Chapter 49

effort, it must be used to assess changes in credit risk and an entity cannot rely solely on past due information. *[IFRS 9.5.5.11, B5.5.2].* However, the IASB acknowledged that many entities manage credit risk on the basis of information about past due status and have a limited ability to assess credit risk on an instrument-by-instrument basis in more detail on a timely basis. *[IFRS 9 BC5.192].* Therefore, if more forward-looking information (either on an individual or collective basis) is not available without undue cost or effort, an entity may use past due information to assess changes in credit risks. *[IFRS 9.5.5.11].*

This simplification goes with the rebuttable presumption that the credit risk on a financial asset has increased significantly since initial recognition when contractual payments are more than 30 days past due. *[IFRS 9.5.5.11].* The IASB decided that this rebuttable presumption was required to ensure that its application does not result in an entity reverting to an incurred loss model. *[IFRS 9.BC5.190].*

The more than 30 days past due rebuttable presumption is intended to serve as a backstop even when forward-looking information is used (e.g. macroeconomic factors on a portfolio level). *[IFRS 9.B5.5.19].* This presumption would therefore not apply if significant increases in credit risk have already occurred before contractual payments are more than 30 days past due.

Moreover, as already stressed earlier, the standard is clear that an entity cannot align the definition and criteria used to identify significant increases in credit risk (and the resulting recognition of lifetime expected credit losses) to when a financial asset is regarded as credit-impaired or to an entity's internal definition of default. *[IFRS 9.B5.5.21].* An entity should normally identify significant increases in credit risk and recognise lifetime expected credit losses before default occurs or the financial asset becomes credit-impaired, either on an individual or collective basis (see 5.5.5 below).

An entity can rebut the presumption if it has reasonable and supportable information that is available without undue cost or effort, that demonstrates that credit risk has not increased significantly even though contractual payments are more than 30 days past due. *[IFRS 9.5.5.11].* Such evidence may include knowledge that a missed non-payment is because of administrative oversight rather than financial difficulty of the borrower, or historical information suggests significant increases in credit risks only occur when payments are more than 60 days past due. *[IFRS 9.B5.5.20].*

Similar to the low credit risk simplification discussed above (see 5.5.4.A above), the Basel Committee guidance (see 5.6.1 below) has proposed that sophisticated banks should only use the 30 days past due simplification rarely for their loan portfolios.

Given the wording in the standard, it will be interesting to see whether any less sophisticated banks will argue that they do not have, or are unable to use, more forward-looking indicators (either at an individual or a collective level) to supplement past due status.

Our observations of emerging practice amongst the more sophisticated banks include:

- delinquency is generally considered as a lagging indicator and, for wholesale loans, 30 days past due is likely to be used only as a backstop, as opposed to a primary driver of significant increase in credit risk. Also, most do not intend to rebut the 30 days past due presumption.

- delinquency is likely to more widely used for retail loans, although in combination with other criteria or, again, as a backstop. Those sophisticated banks who intend to use delinquency as a primary individual indicator generally intend to supplement this with a collective approach to reflect more forward looking criteria (see 5.5.5 below). Most do not intend to rebut the 30 days presumption and those who do are more likely to do so only for credit card facilities.

5.5.4.C   12-month risk as an approximation for change in lifetime risk

In determining whether there has been a significant increase in credit risk, an entity must assess the change in the risk of default occurring over the expected life of the financial instrument. Despite this, the standard says that: '...changes in the risk of a default occurring over the next 12 months may be a reasonable approximation...unless circumstances indicate that a lifetime assessment is necessary'. *[IFRS 9.B5.5.13]*.

The IASB observed in its Basis for Conclusions that changes in the risk of a default occurring within the next 12 months generally should be a reasonable approximation of changes in the risk of a default occurring over the remaining life of a financial instrument and thus would not be inconsistent with the requirements. Also, some entities use a 12-month PD measure for prudential regulatory requirements and these entities can continue to use their existing systems and methodologies as a starting point for determining significant increases in credit risk, thus reducing the costs of implementation. *[IFRS 9.BC5.178]*.

However, for some financial instruments, or in some circumstances, the use of changes in the risk of default occurring over the next 12 months may not be appropriate to determine whether lifetime expected credit losses should be recognised. For a financial instrument with a maturity longer than 12 months, the standard gives the following examples: *[IFRS 9.B5.5.14]*

- the financial instrument only has significant payment obligations beyond the next 12 months;
- changes in relevant macroeconomic or other credit-related factors occur that are not adequately reflected in the risk of a default occurring in the next 12 months; or
- changes in credit-related factors only have an impact on the credit risk of the financial instrument (or have a more pronounced effect) beyond 12 months.

At its meeting on 16 September 2015, the ITG (see 5.1.5 above) discussed whether an entity would be required to perform an annual review to determine whether circumstances still support the use of the 12-month risk of default as an approximation of changes in the lifetime risk of default.

The ITG members agreed that there has to be some method of periodic reassessment of whether a 12-month risk of default is a reasonable approximation of the lifetime risk. There was no consensus on how to perform the subsequent reassessments, other than they do not need to be solely quantitative exercises.

Chapter 49

It should, however, be stressed that while ITG members agreed that a 12-month risk of default could possibly be used for *assessing* significant increases in credit risk, it is not suitable as a proxy for lifetime PD when *measuring* lifetime credit losses. Entities will still need to calculate a lifetime PD when assets are in stage 2 or stage 3 (see 5.3.1 above).

The majority of the more sophisticated banks currently intend to use the 12-month risk of default for assessing if there has been a significant increase in credit risk. Movements in a 12-month risk of default are, for most products and conditions, strongly correlated with movements in the lifetime risk. However, these banks appreciate that 12-month PDs may need to be adjusted or calibrated to reflect the longer term macroeconomic outlook. Also, there are products such as interest-only mortgages and those with an introductory period in which no repayments are required, where additional procedures may need to be implemented in order to ensure that they are transferred to stage 2 appropriately.

5.5.4.D   Assessment at the counterparty level

As indicated by Example 7 in the Implementation Guidance of IFRS 9, assessment of significant deterioration in credit risk can be made at the level of the counterparty rather than the individual financial instrument. Such assessment at the counterparty level is only allowed if the outcome would not be different to the outcome if the financial instruments had been individually assessed. *[IFRS 9.BC5.168].* In certain circumstances, assessment at the counterparty level would not be consistent with the impairment requirements. Both these situations are illustrated in the example below, based on Example 7 in the Implementation Guidance for the standard. *[IFRS 9 IG Example 7, IE43-IE47].*

Example 49.23:   Counterparty assessment of credit risk

Scenario 1

In 2009 Bank A granted a loan of $10,000 with a contractual term of 15 years to Company Q when the company had an internal credit risk rating of 4 on a scale of 1 (lowest credit risk) to 10 (highest credit risk). The risk of a default occurring increases exponentially as the credit risk rating deteriorates so, for example, the difference between credit risk rating grades 1 and 2 is smaller than the difference between credit risk rating grades 2 and 3. In 2014, when Company Q had an internal credit risk rating of 6, Bank A issued another loan to Company Q for $5,000 with a contractual term of 10 years. In 2016 Company Q fails to retain its contract with a major customer and correspondingly experiences a large decline in its revenue. Bank A considers that as a result of losing the contract, Company Q will have a significantly reduced ability to meet its loan obligations and changes its internal credit risk rating to 8.

Bank A assesses credit risk on a counterparty level for credit risk management purposes and determines that the increase in Company Q's credit risk is significant. Although Bank A did not perform an individual assessment of changes in the credit risk on each loan since its initial recognition, assessing the credit risk on a counterparty level and recognising lifetime expected credit losses on all loans granted to Company Q, meets the objective of the impairment requirements as stated in paragraph 5.5.4 of IFRS 9. This is because, even since the most recent loan was originated, its credit risk has increased significantly. The counterparty assessment would therefore achieve the same result as assessing the change in credit risk for each loan individually.

Scenario 2

Bank A granted a loan of $150,000 with a contractual term of 20 years to Company X in 2009 when the company had an internal credit risk rating of 4. During 2014 economic conditions deteriorate and demand for Company X's products has declined significantly. As a result of the reduced cash flows from lower sales, Company X could not make full payment of its loan instalment to Bank A. Bank A re-assesses Company X's internal credit risk rating, and determines it to be 7 at the reporting date. Bank A considered the change in credit risk on the loan, including considering the change in the internal credit risk rating, and determines that there has been a significant increase in credit risk and recognises lifetime expected credit losses on the loan of $150,000.

Despite the recent downgrade of the internal credit risk rating, Bank A grants another loan of $50,000 to Company X in 2015 with a contractual term of 5 years, taking into consideration the higher credit risk at that date.

The fact that Company X's credit risk (assessed on a counterparty basis) has previously been assessed to have increased significantly, does not result in lifetime expected credit losses being recognised on the new loan. This is because the credit risk on the new loan has not increased significantly since the loan was initially recognised. If Bank A only assessed credit risk on a counterparty level, without considering whether the conclusion about changes in credit risk applies to all individual financial instruments provided to the same customer, the objective in paragraph 5.5.4 of IFRS 9 would not be met.

Most banks manage their credit exposures on a counterparty basis. Therefore, the standard's requirement to assess if there has been an increase in credit risk at a counterparty level, only if it would make no difference from doing it at an individual instrument level, is challenging. This is particularly the case for those banks who are seeking to use their existing processes, such as the use of watch lists, to make the assessment. It may be necessary for them to add procedures to track increase in the risk of default at the instrument level in order to comply with the standard.

5.5.4.E   Determining maximum initial credit risk for a portfolio

The IFRS 9 credit risk assessment that determines whether a financial instrument should attract a lifetime expected credit loss allowance, or only a 12-month expected credit loss allowance, is based on whether there has been a *relative* increase in credit risk. One of the challenges identified by some constituents in responding to the 2013 Exposure Draft is that many credit risk systems monitor *absolute* levels of risk, without tracking the history of individual loans (see 5.5.1 above). To help address this concern the standard contains an approach that turns a relative system into an absolute one, by segmenting the portfolio sufficiently by loan quality at origination.

As indicated by Illustrative Example 6 in the Implementation Guidance of IFRS 9 on which Example 49.24 below is based, an entity can determine the maximum initial credit risk accepted for portfolios with similar credit risks on initial recognition. *IFRS 9 IG Example 6, IE40-IE42].* Thereby, an entity may be able to establish an absolute threshold for recognising lifetime expected credit losses.

Example 49.24:   Comparison to maximum initial credit risk

Bank A has two portfolios of automobile loans with similar terms and conditions in Region W. Bank A's policy on financing decisions for each loan is based on an internal credit rating system that considers a customer's credit history, payment behaviour on other products with Bank A and other factors, and assigns an internal credit risk rating from 1 (lowest credit risk) to 10 (highest credit risk) to each loan on origination. The risk of a default occurring increases exponentially as the credit risk rating deteriorates so, for example, the difference between credit risk rating grades 1 and 2 is smaller than the difference between credit risk rating grades 2 and 3. Loans in Portfolio 1 were only offered to existing customers with a similar internal credit risk rating and at initial recognition all loans were rated 3 or 4 on the internal rating scale. Bank A determines that the maximum initial credit risk rating at initial recognition it would accept for Portfolio 1 is an internal rating of 4. Loans in Portfolio 2 were offered to customers that responded to an advertisement for automobile loans and the internal credit risk ratings of these customers range between 4 and 7 on the internal rating scale. Bank A never originates an automobile loan with an internal credit risk rating worse than 7 (i.e. with an internal rating of 8-10).

For the purposes of assessing whether there have been significant increases in credit risk, Bank A determines that all loans in Portfolio 1 had a similar initial credit risk. It determines that given the risk of default reflected in its internal risk rating grades, a change in internal rating from 3 to 4 would not represent a significant increase in credit risk but that there has been a significant increase in credit risk on any loan in this portfolio that has an internal rating worse than 5. This means that Bank A does not have to know the initial credit rating of each loan in the portfolio to assess the change in credit risk since initial recognition. It only has to determine whether the credit risk is worse than 5 at the reporting date to determine whether lifetime expected credit losses should be recognised in accordance with paragraph 5.5.3 of IFRS 9..

However, determining the maximum initial credit risk accepted at initial recognition for Portfolio 2 at an internal credit risk rating of 7, would not meet the objective of the requirements as stated in paragraph 5.5.4 of IFRS 9. This is because Bank A determines that significant increases in credit risk arise not only when credit risk increases above the level at which an entity would originate new financial assets (i.e. when the internal rating is worse than 7). Although Bank A never originates an automobile loan with an internal credit rating worse than 7, the initial credit risk on loans in Portfolio 2 is not of sufficiently similar credit risk at initial recognition to apply the approach used for Portfolio 1. This means that Bank A cannot simply compare the credit risk at the reporting date with the lowest credit quality at initial recognition (for example, by comparing the internal credit risk rating of loans in Portfolio 2 with an internal credit risk rating of 7) to determine whether credit risk has increased significantly because the initial credit quality of loans in the portfolio is too diverse. For example, if a loan initially had a credit risk rating of 4 the credit risk on the loan may have increased significantly if its internal credit risk rating changes to 6.

At its September meeting, the ITG discussed identification of a significant increase of credit risk for a portfolio of retail loans with identical pricing and contractual terms (see 5.5.2). However, in the fact pattern, the same terms were applied to customers across a broad credit quality band. The ITG members generally agreed that it is not appropriate to assume that just because loans are priced the same that they share similar risk characteristics.

5.5.5   Collective assessment

Banks have hundreds of thousands, or even millions, of small exposures to retail customers and small businesses. Much of the information available to monitor them is based on whether payments are past due and behavioural information that is mostly historical rather than forward-looking. As a result such exposures tend to be managed on an aggregated basis, combining past due and behavioural data with historical statistical experience and sometimes macroeconomic indicators, such as interest rates and unemployment levels, that tend to correlate with future defaults. Also, even when exposures are managed on an individual basis, as is the case for most commercial loans, the information used to manage them may not be sufficiently forward-looking to comply with the standard.

To address these concerns, the standard introduces the idea of making a collective assessment for financial assets, to determine if there has been a significant increase in credit risk, if an entity cannot make the assessment adequately on an individual instrument level. It is, however, worth noting that the language on when this is required is not consistent within the standard. Paragraph B5.5.1 states that 'it *may be* necessary to perform the assessment' on a collective basis, which is consistent with the requirement in paragraph 5.5.11, that 'an entity cannot rely on solely on past due information if reasonable and supportable forward-looking information is available without undue cost or effort'. However, paragraph B5.5.4 says that if 'an entity does not have reasonable and supportable information that is available without undue cost or effort to measure lifetime expected credit losses on an individual instrument basis...lifetime credit losses *shall be* recognised on a collective basis' (emphasis added for each quotation). Banking regulators will probably ensure that this 'shall be' wording will be applied, at least for more sophisticated banks (see 5.1.6 above and 5.6.1 below).

But then that raises a second concern: once significant deterioration has been identified for a portfolio, whether the entire portfolio would have to be measured using lifetime expected credit losses. This outcome would result in sudden, massive increases in provisions as soon as conditions begin to decline. Consequently the Board, in finalising the standard, also had to devise a method by which only a segment or portion of the portfolio would be changed to lifetime expected credit losses.

Illustrative Example 5 in the Implementation Guidance for the standard illustrates how an entity may assess whether its individual assessment should be complemented with a collective one whenever the information at individual level is not sufficiently comprehensive and updated. The following examples have been adapted from that Guidance.

As a benchmark, Scenario 1 (an individual assessment) illustrates a situation where a bank has sufficient information at individual exposure level to identify a significant deterioration of credit quality.

Example 49.25: Individual assessment in relation to responsiveness to changes in credit risk

The bank assesses each of its mortgage loans on a monthly basis by means of an automated behavioural scoring process based on current and historical past due statuses, levels of customer indebtedness, loan-to-value (LTV) measures, customer behaviour on other financial instruments with the bank, the loan size and the time since the origination of the loan. It is said that historical data indicates a strong correlation between the value of residential property and the default rates for mortgages.

The bank updates the LTV measures on a regular basis through an automated process that re-estimates property values using recent sales in each post code area and reasonable and supportable forward-looking information that is available without undue cost or effort. Therefore, an increased risk of a default occurring due to an expected decline in residential property value adjusts the behavioural scores and the Bank is therefore able to identify significant increases in credit risk on individual customers before a mortgage becomes past due if there has been a deterioration in the behavioural score.

The example concludes that if the bank is unable to update behavioural scores to reflect the expected declines in property prices, it would use reasonable and supportable information that is available without undue cost or effort to undertake a collective assessment to determine the loans on which there has been a significant increase in credit risk since initial recognition and recognize lifetime expected credit losses for those loans.

Chapter 49

It should be noted that, in this example, the main source of forward-looking information is expected future property prices. No account would appear to be taken of other economic data such as future levels of employment or interest rates. We assume that the Board took this approach to make the example simple, but it implies that future property prices are considered to provide a sufficiently good guide to future defaults that it is not necessary to take account of other data as well.

If an entity does not have reasonable and supportable information that is available without undue cost or effort to measure lifetime expected credit losses on an individual instrument basis, the standard first specifies that it must assess lifetime losses on a collective basis. This exercise must consider comprehensive information that incorporates not only past due data but other relevant credit information, such as forward-looking macro-economic information. The objective is to approximate the result of using comprehensive credit information that incorporates forward-looking information at an individual instrument level. *[IFRS 9.B5.5.4]*.

Hence, even if a financial asset is normally managed on an individual basis, it should also be assessed collectively (i.e. based on macro-economic indicators), if the entity does not have sufficient forward-looking information at the individual level to make the determination. The way that this might work is not very different from the IAS 39 requirement to assess an asset collectively for impairment if it has already been assessed individually and found not to be impaired.

Next, the standard sets out how financial instruments may be grouped together in order to determine whether there has been a significant increase in credit risk. Any instruments assessed collectively must possess shared credit risk characteristics. It is not permitted to aggregate exposures that have different risks and, in so doing, obscure significant increases in risk that may arise on a sub-set of the portfolio. Examples of shared credit risk characteristics given in the standard include, but are not limited to: *[IFRS 9.B5.5.5]*

- instrument type;
- credit risk ratings;
- collateral type;
- date of initial recognition;
- remaining term to maturity;
- industry;
- geographical location of the borrower; and
- the value of collateral relative to the asset (the loan-to-value or LTV ratio), if this would have an impact on the probability of a default occurring.

The standard also states that the basis of aggregation of financial instruments to assess whether there have been changes in credit risk on a collective basis may have to change over time, as new information on groups of, or individual, financial instruments becomes available. *[IFRS 9.B5.5.6]*.

We make the following observations:

- As has been stressed earlier, the assessment of significant deterioration is intended to reflect the risk of default, not the risk of loss, hence collateral should normally be ignored for the assessment. The standard nonetheless explains that the value of collateral relative to the financial asset would be relevant to the collective assessment if it has an impact on the risk of a default occurring. It cites, as an example, non-recourse loans in certain jurisdictions. The question of when such an arrangement would always meet the IFRS 9 classification and measurement characteristics of the asset test is beyond the scope of this chapter. However, the standard also gives, as an example, LTV ratios, without explaining why these are likely to have an impact on the risk of a default occurring. *[IFRS 9.B5.5.5]*. LTV or a house price index may be a useful indicator of significant collective deterioration in a wider range of circumstances than just where the loans are non-recourse. First, house prices are themselves a useful barometer of the economy and so higher LTVs and lower indices correlate with declining economic conditions. Second, loans that were originally advanced at higher LTVs may reflect more aggressive lending practices, with the consequence that such loans may exhibit a higher PD if economic conditions decline.

- By date of original recognition, we assume that the Board did not intend that loans should be assessed in separate groups for each year of origination, but that vintages may be aggregated into groups that share similar credit risk characteristics. Loan products and lending practices, including the extent of due diligence, and key ratios, such as the LTV and loan to income, change over time, often reflecting the economic conditions at the time of origination. The consequence is that loans from particular years are inherently more risky than others. For some banks, this might mean isolating those loans advanced just prior to the financial crisis from those originated earlier or in the subsequent, more careful lending environment. Also, there is a phenomenon termed seasoning, which describes how loans that been serviced adequately for a number of years, over a business cycle, are statistically less likely to default in future, suggesting that older loans should be assessed separately

- Although the examples in the standard refer to regions, as the geographical location of borrowers, the groupings could be much larger, such as by country, or much smaller, if there are particular issues associated with particular towns. Hence the choice of geographical groupings will depend very much on the environment in which a bank operates.

- Other ways that loans might be grouped according to shared credit risk characteristics could include by credit score, by payment history, whether previously restructured or subject to forbearance but subsequently restored to a 12-month expected credit loss allowance, and manner of employment (as featured in Illustrative Example 5 in the Implementation Guidance for the standard under the bottom up assessment discussed in Example 49.26 below).

- The requirement that financial instruments that are assessed together must share similar credit risk characteristics means that a bank may have a substantial number of portfolios. Even a relatively small bank might have six

Chapter 49

different products (taking into account terms to maturity and types of collateral), three regions and three different vintage groups which, multiplied out, would give fifty four different assessment groups. A larger, global bank might need to monitor many more different portfolios. However, a balance will need to be struck between ensuring that portfolios are small enough to have sufficient homogeneity and yet not so small that there is too little historical data for losses to be reliably estimated.

- Also, the requirement that groupings may have to be amended over time means that there must be put in place processes to reassess whether loans continue to share similar credit risk characteristics. Yet, in practice, there will need to be a sufficient level of stability in the construction of portfolios to allow enough historical data to be gathered for reliable estimation of losses.

- Finally, paragraph B5.5.6 in IFRS 9 adds that, 'if an entity is not able to group financial instruments for which the credit risk is considered to have increased significantly since original recognition based on shared credit risk characteristics, the entity should recognise lifetime expected credit losses on a portion of the financial assets for which credit risk is deemed to have increased significantly'. This is designed to deal with situations in which the lender cannot distinguish between the different exposures, and so is unable to determine significant deterioration identified at portfolio level based on macroeconomic indicators. A bank would, but for this guidance, need to measure lifetime expected credit losses for the whole portfolio.

The main standard does not amplify how a collective assessment would be made but Illustrative Example 5 in the Implementation Guidance of IFRS 9 provides two scenarios that explore the approach. *[IFRS 9 IG Example 5, IE29-IE39].*

Example 49.26:   Collective assessment in relation to responsiveness to changes in credit risk ('bottom up' approach)

Region Two of Illustrative Example 5 in the Implementation Guidance for the standard introduces the so-called bottom up method. It deals with a mining community within a region that faces unemployment risk due to a decline in coal exports and, consequently, anticipated future mine closures. Although most of the loans are not yet 30 days past due and, further, the borrowers are not yet unemployed, the bank re-segments its mortgage portfolio so as to separate loans to customers employed in the mining industry (based on information in the original mortgage application form).

For these loans (plus any others that are more than 30 days past due), Bank ABC recognises lifetime expected credit losses, while it continues to recognise 12-month expected credit losses for the other mortgage loans in the region. Any new loans to borrowers who rely on the coal industry would also attract only a 12-month allowance, until they also demonstrate a significant increase in credit risk.

The bottom up method is described as an example of how to assess credit deterioration by using information that is more forward-looking than past due status. But this example also illustrates that collectively assessed groups may need to change over time, to ensure that they share similar credit risk characteristics. Once the coal mining industry begins to decline, those loans connected with it would no longer share the same risk characteristics as other loans to borrowers in the region, and so would need to be assessed separately. We also note that this example assumes that macroeconomic factors can be linked to the expected credit losses of a very specific portfolio. Further, in practice, most banks may not have the data to achieve this level of segmentation.

As already described above (possible criteria for grouping of financial assets with similar credit risk characteristics), the bottom up approach could be applied to sub-portfolios differentiated by type of instrument, risk rating, type of collateral, date of initial recognition, remaining term to maturity, industry, geographical location of the borrower, or the LTV ratio. A good example of this approach might be for exposures to borrowers that are expected to suffer major economic difficulties due to war or political upheaval. In addition, as underwriting standards may vary or change, the portfolio might be sub-divided so as to reflect this. Note that the coal mines closures are, as yet, only anticipated, hence this example helps show how the standard is intended to look much further forward than the consequent unemployment that would probably trigger an IAS 39 impairment provision. The need to look forward is also illustrated in the next example.

Example 49.27:   Collective assessment in relation to responsiveness to changes in credit risk ('top down' approach)

For Region Three of Illustrative Example 5 in the Implementation Guidance for the standard, Bank ABC anticipates an increase in defaults following an expected rise in interest rates. We are told that, historically, an increase in interest rates has been a lead indicator of future defaults on floating rate mortgages in the region. The bank regards the portfolio of variable rate mortgage loans in that region to be homogenous and it is incapable of identifying particular sub portfolios on the basis of shared credit risk characteristics. Hence, it uses what is described as a top down method.

Based on historical data, the bank estimates that a 200 basis points rise in interest rates will cause a significant increase in credit risk on 20 per cent of the mortgages. As a result, presumably because the bank expects a 200 basis points rise in rates, it recognises lifetime expected credit losses on 20 per cent of the portfolio (along with those loans that are more than 30 days past due) and 12-month expected credit losses on the remainder of mortgages in the region.

The challenge posed by the top down method is how to calculate the percentage of loans that have significantly deteriorated. That a rise in interest rates will likely lead to a significant deterioration in credit risk for some floating rate borrowers, is not controversial. But working out whether they make up 5 per cent, 20 per cent or 35 per cent of the portfolio would appear to be more of an art than science, and no two banks are likely to arrive at the same figure. The example in the standard bases the percentage on historical experience, but it is more than 20 years since most developed countries last saw a 200 basis points rise in interest rates, and products and lending practices were then very different, as was the level of interest rates before they began to rise and the extent of the increase. Hence, the past may not be a reliable guide to the future.

A further issue with the top down approach is the question of what the lender should do if it subsequently finds that differences in risk characteristics emerge within the portfolio, such that certain assets need to be measured using lifetime expected credit losses using the bottom up approach. A similar question arises if individual assets subsequently need to be measured using lifetime expected credit losses, for instance, because they become 30 days past due. Presumably, in each case the lender will need to reallocate part of the portion of the portfolio already measured using lifetime losses based on the top down approach, but just how much? For example, if

20% of the portfolio had been assessed using the top down approach and now a further 15% must be measured using lifetime losses due to the bottom up approach, should the lender assume that the entire 15% were already covered by the top down lifetime loss allowance, or would this apply to only 20% of the 15%?

Presumably a portion of the loans that are measured using lifetime expected credit losses can be measured once again using 12-month expected credit losses if economic conditions are expected to improve. However, the standard seem to make it clear that it is not possible to rebut the 30 days past due presumption just because of a favourable economic outlook. [IFRS 9.B5.5.19].

Furthermore, the use of a top down approach becomes yet more complex if some of the financial assets in the collective assessment are designated in a fair value hedge relationship, as it may be necessary to measure a portion of the hedge adjustment using lifetime expected credit losses.

Because of these and similar difficulties, we are not currently aware of any banks who intend to use the top down approach in the manner set out in the Illustrative Example. Banks prefer to know which loans are measured using lifetime expected credit losses, rather than a notional percentage of the population. In practice, the methods that are being explored by banks are closer to a mixture of the bottom up and top down approaches, as described in the Examples. Macroeconomic indicators are assessed, as in the top down approach, but the effect is determined by assessing the effect on particular exposures. One possible method is to determine the expected migration of loans through a bank's risk classification system, by recalibrating the probabilities of default based on forward-looking data. This could be used to forecast how many additional loans will get downgraded as well as the associated expected credit losses. Another is to focus on more vulnerable categories of lending, such as interest only mortgages, secured loans with high loan-to-value ratios, or property development loans, and assess how these might respond to the economic outlook, The more information about customers that a lender possesses, the more this might look like the illustrated bottom up approach. It is likely that banks will use different approaches for different portfolios, depending on how they are managed and what data is available.

All the examples in the Illustrative Examples simplify the fact pattern to focus on just one driver of credit losses, whereas in reality there will be many, and it may not be possible to find a historical precedent for the combination of economic indicators that may now be present. Further, to delve into the past to predict the future requires a level of data that banks may lack. In practice, banks will need to determine the main macroeconomic variables that correlate with credit losses and focus on modelling these key drivers of loss. The banks can make use of work that has already been carried out for stress testing.

The example of an anticipated increase in interest rates is very topical, given that rates in many countries are expected to rise in future from the all-time low levels that have been experienced since the financial crisis. This gives rise to an observation that is relevant to any expected credit loss model: banks and (hopefully) borrowers have presumably known that new variable loans made since the crisis would likely increase in rate as the economy improves. If the increase was anticipated at the time of origination, expectation of a rise in interest rate should not be viewed as a significant deterioration in credit risk. Yet, there is a concern that rising rates will bring difficulty for many borrowers who have over stretched themselves, implying that the inevitable rise was not fully factored into lending decisions. With any forward-looking approach it is necessary to understand what risks were already taken into account when loans are first made, to assess whether there has been a significant increase in risk.

Some kind of collective adjustment or overlay will be needed for many retail lending portfolios, given that most customer-specific information will not be forward looking. For commercial loans, the lender will typically have access to much more information and a forward-looking approach may already have been built into loan grading systems. Nevertheless, we are aware of some banks who consider that they might need to introduce an additional overlay for commercial loans so as to be more responsive to emerging macroeconomic and other risk developments. Other banks intend to achieve this by using their existing watch list approaches, to supplement using their credit grading system to assess significant increases in credit risk, because watch list systems tend to be more reactive to changing circumstances than formal credit gradings. Any one bank is likely to employ a variety of methods, depending on its products, systems and data.

5.6   Other matters and issues in relation to the IFRS 9 impairment requirements

In addition to the challenges in assessing significant increases in credit risk (see 5.5 above), this section discusses other matters and issues when applying the IFRS 9 impairment requirements.

5.6.1   Basel Committee guidance on accounting for expected credit losses

At the time of writing this publication the Basel Committee is revising its guidance in the light of constituents' comments, and the final guidance is expected to be issued in late 2015 (see 5.1.6 above). The brief summary that follows is based on the Consultative Document. The Basel Committee's guidance will apply to internationally active banks and more sophisticated banks in the business of lending. For less complex banks, supervisors may determine a proportionate approach in implementing the guidance that is commensurate with the size, nature and complexity of their lending exposures (excluding securities).

The main section of the Basel Committee's guidance is intended to be applicable in all jurisdictions (i.e. in the US as well as for banks reporting under IFRS) and will contain 11 supervisory principles on sound credit risk practices. The main requirements of this section that relate to accounting include:

1.   Forward-looking information and related credit quality factors used in regulatory expected credit loss estimates should be consistent with input to other relevant estimates in the financial statements, budgets, strategic and capital plans and other regulatory reporting.

2.   Banks should seek consistency in credit ratings assigned to lending exposures for regulatory capital calculations and financial reporting. In addition, the grouping of lending exposures into portfolios with shared credit risk characteristics must be re-evaluated regularly (including re-segmentation in light of relevant new information). Groupings must be granular enough to assess changes in credit risk and changes in a part of the portfolio must not be masked by the performance of the portfolio as a whole. Moreover, the draft guidance suggests that the entire portfolio should migrate to a higher credit risk rating if the level of credit risk is assessed to have increased on a group basis.

3.   When forward-looking information and macroeconomic factors cannot be applied at the individual exposure level, these exposures should be placed in a group with shared credit risk characteristics and assessed collectively (see 5.5.5 above). Also, robust methodologies to estimate expected credit losses should consider the full spectrum of reasonable information and different potential scenarios and not rely purely on subjective, biased or overly optimistic considerations.

4.   Incorporating forward-looking information and macroeconomic factors into the estimate of expected credit losses is challenging, costly and requires significant judgement. However, the consideration of forward-looking information and macroeconomic factors is critical to a robust implementation of an expected credit loss model. As such, banks are required to incorporate all reasonably available forward-looking information and macroeconomic factors when estimating expected credit losses. The associated costs should not be avoided on the basis that they are excessive or unnecessary. Also, the Basel Committee recognises that it may not always be possible to demonstrate a strong link in formal statistical terms between the set of information and credit risk of some exposures and that a bank's experienced credit judgement will be crucial in establishing the appropriate level for the individual or collective allowance.

5.   The Basel Committee encourages banks to improve their disclosures in order to fairly depict their exposures to credit risk and underwriting practices.

The guidance is supplemented by an appendix that outlines additional supervisory requirements specific to jurisdictions applying the IFRS 9 expected credit loss model. The key areas are outlined below:

1.   A bank's definition of default adopted for accounting purposes should be guided by the definition used for regulatory purposes, which includes both a qualitative unlikeliness to pay criterion and a quantitative 90-days-past-due criterion, described by the Committee as a 'backstop'. The regulatory definition should be supplemented by other elements such as a collective assessment and adjustments to reflect current conditions, forward-looking information and macroeconomic factors, to ensure the 12-month expected credit loss is sufficiently sensitive to all relevant sources of credit risk. Exposures originated with a high credit risk are expected to be monitored closely and move quickly to lifetime expected credit loss measurement.

2.   Banks should look widely and holistically for information, including forward-looking information and macroeconomic factors, that are relevant to the assessment of whether increases in credit risk are significant It is critical that banks have processes in place to ensure that financial instruments, whether assessed individually or collectively, are moved from the 12-month to the lifetime expected credit loss measurement as soon as credit risk has increased significantly. It is important that banks' analysis considers that credit losses very often begin to deteriorate a considerable period of time before an actual delinquency occurs.

Chapter 49

3.   In assessing whether there has been a significant increase in credit risk, banks should not rely solely on quantitative analysis. The guidance emphasises that certain conditions would suggest a significant increase in credit risk (e.g. an increased credit spread for a particular loan, a downgrade by a credit rating agency, expectation of forbearance). Also, the guidance stresses that the sensitivity of the risk of a default occurring to rating downgrades increases strongly as rating quality declines. For example, although a downgrade from AAA to AA may not be indicative of a significant increase in credit risk, it is possible that a significant increase in credit risk could occur even before a one-notch downgrade. Particular care should be taken when some, but not all, of a bank's exposures to a counterparty are deemed to have significantly deteriorated.

4.   IFRS 9 includes a number of practical expedients (see 5.5.4 above). However, as banks are in the business of lending and it is unlikely that obtaining relevant information will involve undue cost or effort, the Basel Committee emphasises that many of these practical expedients are inappropriate for use by internationally active banks and those banks more sophisticated in the business of lending. For instance:

   a.   The long-term benefit of a high-quality implementation of an expected credit loss model that takes into account all reasonable and supportable information far outweighs the associated costs.

   b.   The use of the low credit risk simplification is considered a low-quality implementation of the expected credit loss model and is expected to be used in rare and appropriate circumstances, except for holdings in securities. Also, the investment grade category used by ratings agencies is not considered homogeneous enough to be automatically considered low credit risk. Banks are expected to rely primarily on their own credit assessments.

   c.   Significant reliance on past-due information would be considered a very low-quality implementation of the expected credit loss model. Banks are not expected to fall back on the more than 30 days past due rebuttable presumption, unless they have demonstrated that no forward-looking factors have any substantive correlation with the level of credit losses.

   d.   The Committee notes that the simplification in IFRS 9 allowing banks to set a maximum credit risk for a portfolio on initial recognition is only relevant if segmentation of the portfolio is sufficiently granular to enable the analysis to be consistent with IFRS 9.

During the ITG meeting on 16 September 2015 (see 5.1.5 above), the Basel Committee observer provided an update on the Basel Committee's revisions to their guidance on credit risk and IFRS 9 implementation. The observer confirmed that the Basel Committee guidance will only apply to internationally active banks and will continue to prohibit the use of certain of the practical expedients offered in IFRS 9. The observer also confirmed that no disclosure requirements will be included in the Basel Committee guidance. The Basel Committee will leave further guidance on disclosures to regulators and the Enhanced Disclosure Task Force (EDTF). The Basel Committee has sought to ensure that the guidance does not conflict with US GAAP and IFRS and will forward it to the FASB and IASB before publication for a final fatal flaw review. The final guidance is expected to be published in October or November 2015.

5.6.2 Measurement dates of expected credit losses

5.6.2.A Derecognition and initial recognition for foreign currency exposures

Impairment must be assessed and measured at the reporting date. IFRS 9 also requires a derecognition gain or loss to be measured relative to the carrying amount at the date of derecognition (see Chapter 53 at 4.2.1 and 7.1.1). This necessitates an assessment and measurement of expected credit loses for that particular asset as at the date of derecognition, as was confirmed by the discussions at the April 2015 ITG meeting.

At that meeting, the ITG also discussed a more difficult question, whether impairment must be measured as at the date of initial recognition, for foreign currency monetary assets. The significance of this is whether subsequent gains and losses arising from foreign currency retranslation in the first accounting period should be calculated based on the initial gross amortised cost or a net amount, after deducting an impairment allowance. This would affect the allocation of subsequent gains and losses of the asset in this period to impairment or to foreign currency retranslation, so that it would be reported in different lines of the profit or loss account.

Differing views were expressed at the April 2015 ITG meeting:

- A few ITG members supported the view that while IFRS 9 does not expressly require expected credit losses to be measured at the date of initial recognition, the requirements of other IFRSs, e.g. IAS 21 may result in an entity measuring expected credit losses at the date of initial recognition. Also, Illustrative Example 14 in IFRS 9 implies the need to include expected credit losses on initial recognition in the measurement of foreign exchange gains and losses in respect of a foreign currency-denominated asset (see Example 49.30 at 5.8 below). However, these members questioned the frequency with which an entity needed to perform that calculation and pointed out that considerations of materiality would be a key factor in making this decision.

- Some other ITG members were of the view that an entity is required to measure a financial asset at its fair value upon initial recognition and that consequently measuring expected credit losses at initial recognition would be inconsistent with that requirement. *[IFRS 9.5.1.1]*. IFRS 9 includes impairment as part of the subsequent measurement of a financial asset and, consequently, only requires an entity to begin measuring expected credit losses at the first reporting date after initial recognition (or on derecognition if that occurs earlier). *[IFRS 9.3.2.12, 5.5.3, 5.5.5, 5.5.13]*. While the requirements of other IFRSs should be applied to the loss allowance at that point, the application of those requirements should not result in an entity having to measure expected credit losses at a date earlier than that specifically required by IFRS 9.

Also, the ITG noted that the illustrative examples are non-authoritative and illustrate only one way of applying the requirements of IFRS 9. Measuring a 12 month expected loss using point in time, forward-looking information, every time that a foreign

Chapter 49

currency exposure is first recognised would not be feasible. Given that there was no consensus on this issue, we expect that there may be diversity in practice.

A similar issue is whether impairment needs to be measured at the date that an asset is modified (see 5.7 below).

5.6.2.B   Trade date and settlement date accounting

For financial assets measured at amortised cost or at fair value through other comprehensive income, IFRS 9 requires entities to use the trade date as the date of initial recognition for the purposes of applying the impairment requirements. *[IFRS 9.5.7.4]*. This means that entities that use settlement date accounting may have to recognise a loss allowance for financial assets which they have purchased but not yet recognised and, correspondingly, no loss allowance for assets that they have sold but not yet derecognised. (See Chapter 47 at 2.2 for further details on trade date accounting and settlement date accounting).

Irrespective of the accounting policy choice for trade date accounting versus settlement date accounting, the recognition of the loss allowance on the trade date ensures that entities recognise the loss allowance at the same time; otherwise entities could choose settlement date accounting to delay recognising the loss allowance until the settlement date. The effect of this is similar to accounting for fair value changes on financial assets measured at fair value through other comprehensive income and those measured at fair value through profit or loss when settlement date accounting is applied (i.e. a measurement change needs to be recognised in profit or loss and the statement of financial position even if the related assets that are being measured are only recognised slightly later).

For settlement date accounting, the recognition of a loss allowance for an asset that has not yet been recognised raises the question of how that loss allowance should be presented in the statement of financial position. The time between the trade date and the settlement date is somewhat similar to a loan commitment in that the accounting is off balance sheet, which suggests presentation of the loss allowance as a provision.

In practice, some entities tend to opt for settlement date accounting for financial assets recorded at amortised cost, because they do not need the additional systems capabilities to account for the financial assets on trade date (i.e. they do not need to account for financial assets that will be measured at amortised cost until settlement date). The change from the IAS 39 incurred loss model to the IFRS 9 expected credit loss model means that the settlement date accounting simplification for financial assets measured at amortised cost would lose much of its benefit from an operational perspective.

5.6.3   Interaction between the initial measurement of debt instruments acquired in a business combination and the impairment model of IFRS 9

Consistent with IFRS 9 and IFRS 13, IFRS 3 – *Business Combinations* – requires financial assets acquired in a business combination to be measured by the acquirer on initial recognition at their fair value (see Chapter 47 at 3.2.4 and Chapter 9 at 5.5.5). *[IFRS 3.18, IFRS 3.36]*. IFRS 3 contains application guidance explaining that an acquirer should not recognise a separate valuation allowance (i.e. loss allowance for expected credit losses) in respect of loans and receivables acquired in a business combination for contractual cash flows that are deemed to be uncollectible at the acquisition date. This is because the effects of uncertainty about future cash flows are included in the fair value measure. *[IFRS 3.B41].*

Consequently, the accounting for impairment of debt instruments measured at amortised cost or fair value through other comprehensive income under IFRS 9 does not affect the accounting for the business combination. At the acquisition date, the acquired debt instruments are measured at their acquisition-date fair value in accordance with IFRS 3. No loss allowance is recognised as part of the accounting for the business combination (i.e. no loss allowance is recognised as part of the initial measurement of debt instruments that are acquired in a business combination).

Subsequent accounting for debt instruments acquired in a business combination after their initial recognition is in the scope of IFRS 9. The impairment requirements in IFRS 9 are part of the subsequent measurement of those debt instruments. *[IFRS 9.5.5, 5.2.1, 5.2.2].* At the first reporting date after the business combination, following the guidance in IFRS 9, a loss allowance is recognised. *[IFRS 9.5.5.3, 5.5.5].* This will result in an impairment loss that is recognised in profit or loss (rather than an adjustment to goodwill), just as would be the case if the entity were to originate those assets or acquire them as a portfolio, rather than acquire them through a business combination. *[IFRS 9.5.5.8].*

Despite the colloquial reference to a 'day one' loss that results from the expected credit loss impairment model in IFRS 9, it is important to understand that the recognition of a loss allowance for newly acquired (whether purchased or originated) debt instruments that are in the scope of the impairment requirements of IFRS 9 is a matter of subsequent measurement of those financial instruments. This means that the acquirer recognises the loss allowance for all debt instruments acquired in a business combination (that are subject to impairment accounting) in the reporting period that includes the business combination but not as part of that business combination, and with a corresponding impairment loss in profit or loss.

The only exception to this is the specific accounting for purchased or originated credit-impaired financial assets which applies to the extent that the portfolio includes financial assets which are credit-impaired at the acquisition date (i.e. the effective interest rate is determined using a cash flow estimate that includes all expected credit losses and no allowance is made for expected credit losses). A financial asset is credit-impaired when one or more events that have a detrimental impact on the estimated future cash flows of that financial asset have occurred (see 5.3.1 above).

5.7 Modified financial assets

If the contractual cash flows on a financial asset are renegotiated or modified, the holder needs to assess whether the financial asset should be derecognised (see Chapter 50 at 3.4 and 6.2 for further details on modification and derecognition). While IAS 39 contains guidance on when financial liabilities that have been renegotiated or modified should be derecognised, it does not do so for financial assets. Similarly, as the derecognition literature in IAS 39 has been carried forward to IFRS 9, the IASB has still not established criteria for analysing when a modification of a financial asset constitutes a derecognition event. However, an entity may refer to the decision made by the IFRS Interpretations Committee in May 2012. The Interpretations Committee was asked to consider the accounting treatment of Greek government bonds (GGBs). The principal issue raised was whether the portion of the old GGBs to be exchanged for new bonds with different maturities and interest rates should result in derecognition of the whole asset, or only part of it, in accordance with IAS 39 or, conversely, be accounted for as a modification that would not require derecognition. The Interpretations Committee concluded that this assessment can be made, either on the basis of:

- the extinguishment of the contractual rights to the cash flows from the assets as per paragraph 17(a) of IAS 39 (now under paragraph 3.2.3 of IFRS 9); or

- by analogising to the notion of a substantial change of the terms of financial liabilities to these assets as per paragraph 40 of IAS 39 (now under paragraph 3.3.2 of IFRS 9).[28]

IFRS 9 acknowledges that in some circumstances, the renegotiation or modification of the contractual cash flows of a financial asset can lead to the derecognition of the existing financial asset and subsequently, the recognition of a new financial asset. *[IFRS 9.B5.5.25]*. This means that the entity is starting afresh and the date of the modification will also be the date of initial recognition of the new financial asset. Typically, the entity will recognise a loss allowance based on 12-month expected credit losses at each reporting date until the requirements for the recognition of lifetime expected credit losses are met. However, in some unusual circumstances following a modification that results in derecognition of the original financial asset, there may be evidence that the new financial asset is credit-impaired on initial recognition (see 5.3.3 above), and thus, the financial asset should be recognised as an originated credit-impaired financial asset. *[IFRS 9.B5.5.26]*.

In other circumstances, the renegotiation or modification of the contractual cash flows of a financial asset does not lead to the derecognition of the existing financial asset as per IFRS 9. In such situations, the entity will:

- continue with its current accounting treatment for the existing asset that has been modified;

- recognise a modification gain or loss in profit or loss by recalculating the gross carrying amount of the financial asset as the present value of the renegotiated or modified contractual cash flows, discounted at the financial asset's original effective interest rate (or the credit-adjusted effective interest rate for purchased or originated credit-impaired financial assets). Any costs or fees incurred adjust the carrying amount of the modified financial asset and are amortised over the remaining term of the modified financial asset (see 3 above); *[IFRS 9.5.4.3, Appendix A]*

- assess whether there has been a significant increase in the credit risk of the financial instrument, by comparing the risk of a default occurring at the reporting date (based on the modified contractual terms) and the risk of a default occurring at initial recognition (based on the original, unmodified contractual terms). A financial asset that has been renegotiated or modified is not automatically considered to have lower credit risk. The assessment should consider the credit risk over the expected life of the asset based on historical and forward-looking information, including information about the circumstances that led to the modification. Evidence that the criteria for the recognition of lifetime expected credit losses are subsequently no longer met may include a history of up-to-date and timely payment in subsequent periods. This means a minimum period of observation will often be necessary before a financial asset may qualify to return to stage 1; *[IFRS 9.5.5.12, B5.5.27]* and

- make the appropriate quantitative and qualitative disclosures required for renegotiated or modified assets to enable users of financial statements to understand the nature and effect of such modifications (including the effect on the measurement of expected credit losses) and how the entity monitors its assets that have been modified (see 5.13 below and Chapter 53 at 5.2.3). *[IFRS 7.35F(f), B8B, 35J]*.

The following example has been adapted from Example 11 of the Implementation Guidance in the standard to illustrate the accounting treatment of a loan that is modified. *[IFRS 9 IG Example 11, IE66-IE73]*.

Example 49.28: Modification of contractual cash flows

Bank A originates a five-year loan that requires the repayment of the outstanding contractual amount in full at maturity. Its contractual par amount is €1,000 with an interest rate of 5 per cent, payable annually. The effective interest rate is 5 per cent. At the end of the first reporting period in Year 1, Bank A recognises a loss allowance at an amount equal to 12-month expected credit losses because there has not been a significant increase in credit risk since initial recognition. A loss allowance balance of €20 is recognised. In Year 2, Bank A determines that the credit risk on the loan has increased significantly since initial recognition. As a result, Bank A recognises lifetime expected credit losses on the loan. The loss allowance balance is €150.

At the end of Year 3, following significant financial difficulty of the borrower, Bank A modifies the contractual cash flows on the loan. It forgoes interest payments and extends the contractual term of the loan by one year so that the remaining term at the date of the modification is three years. The modification does not result in the derecognition of the loan by Bank A.

As a result of that modification, Bank A recalculates the gross carrying amount of the financial asset as the present value of the modified contractual cash flows discounted at the loan's original effective interest rate of 5 per cent. The difference between this recalculated gross carrying amount and the gross carrying amount before the modification is recognised as a modification gain or loss. Bank A recognises the modification loss (calculated as €136) against the gross carrying amount of the loan, reducing it to €864, and a modification loss of €136 in profit or loss.

Bank A also remeasures the loss allowance, taking into account the modified contractual cash flows and evaluates whether the loss allowance for the loan should continue to be measured at an amount equal to lifetime expected credit losses. Bank A compares the current credit risk (taking into consideration the modified cash flows) to the credit risk (on the original unmodified cash flows) at initial recognition. Bank A determines that the loan is not credit-impaired at the reporting date but that credit risk has still significantly increased compared to the credit risk at initial recognition. It

Chapter 49

continues to measure the loss allowance at an amount equal to lifetime expected credit losses, which are €110 at the reporting date.

At each subsequent reporting date, Bank A continues to evaluate whether there has been a significant increase in credit risk by comparing the loan's credit risk at initial recognition (based on the original, unmodified cash flows) with the credit risk at the reporting date (based on the modified cash flows).

Two reporting periods after the loan modification (Year 5), the borrower has outperformed its business plan significantly compared to the expectations at the modification date. In addition, the outlook for the business is more positive than previously envisaged. An assessment of all reasonable and supportable information that is available without undue cost or effort indicates that the overall credit risk on the loan has decreased and that the risk of a default occurring over the expected life of the loan has decreased, so Bank A adjusts the borrower's internal credit rating at the end of the reporting period.

Given the positive overall development, Bank A re-assesses the situation and concludes that the credit risk of the loan has decreased and there is no longer a significant increase in credit risk since initial recognition. As a result, Bank A once again measures the loss allowance at an amount equal to 12-month expected credit losses.

Year	Beginning gross carrying amount	Impairment (loss)/gain	Modification (loss)/gain	Interest revenue	Cash flows	Ending gross carrying amount	Loss allowance	Ending amortised cost amount
	A	B	C	D Gross: A × 5%	E	F = A + C + D − E	G	H = F − G
1	€1,000	(€20)		€50	€50	€1,000	€20	€980
2	€1,000	(€130)		€50	€50	€1,000	€150	€850
3	€1,000	€40	(€136)	€50	€50	€864	€110	€754
4	€864	€24		€43		€907	€86	€821
5	€907	€72		€45		€952	€14	€938
6	€952	€14		€48	€1,000	€0	€0	€0

The ITG (see 5.1.5 above) discussed the measurement of expected credit losses in respect of a modified financial asset where the modification does not result in derecognition, but the cash flows have been renegotiated to be consistent with those previously expected to be paid.[29]

The ITG noted that IFRS 9 is clear that an entity is required to calculate a new gross carrying amount and the gain or loss on modification taken to profit or loss should be based on the renegotiated or modified contractual cash flows and excludes expected credit losses unless it is a purchased or originated credit-impaired financial asset. *[IFRS 9.5.4.3, Appendix A]*. Consequently, an entity must calculate the gain or loss on modification as a first step before going on to consider the revised expected credit loss allowance required on the modified financial asset. Thereafter, the entity is required to continue to apply the impairment requirements to the modified financial asset in the same way as it would for other unmodified financial instruments, taking into account the revised contractual terms. *[IFRS 9.5.5.12]*. The revised expected credit loss cannot be assumed to be nil as, in accordance with paragraph 5.5.18 of IFRS 9, an entity is required to consider the possibility that a credit loss occurs, even if the likelihood of that credit loss occurring is very low. *[IFRS 9.5.18]*.

The ITG also discussed the appropriate presentation and disclosure requirements pertaining to modifications. These are discussed further in Chapter 53 at 7.1.1.

We note that if an entity has no reasonable expectations of recovering a portion of the financial asset, which is subsequently forgiven, then this amount should arguably be written off, as a partial derecognition. The gross carrying amount would be reduced directly before a modification gain or loss is calculated. *[IFRS 9.5.4.4, B5.4.9].* This will mean that the loss will be recorded as an impairment loss, rather than as a loss on modification, and presented differently in the profit or loss account. Whether it is possible to treat as forgiveness of a portion of a loan as a write off event rather than as a modification might usefully be addressed by the ITG.

5.8 Financial assets measured at fair value through other comprehensive income

Based on the accounting treatment of financial assets measured at fair value through other comprehensive income (described at 2.3 above), the expected credit losses do not reduce the carrying amount of the financial assets in the statement of financial position, which remains at fair value. Instead, an amount equal to the allowance that would arise if the asset was measured at amortised cost is recognised in other comprehensive income as the 'accumulated impairment amount'. *[IFRS 9.4.1.2A, 5.5.2, Appendix A].*

The accounting treatment and journal entries for debt instruments measured at fair value through other comprehensive income are illustrated in the following example, based on Illustrative Example 13 in the Implementation Guidance for the standard. *[IFRS 9 IG Example 13, IE78-IE81].*

Example 49.29: Debt instrument measured at fair value through other comprehensive income

An entity purchases a debt instrument with a fair value of £1,000 on 15 December 2016 and measures the debt instrument at fair value through other comprehensive income (FVOCI). The instrument has an interest rate of 5 per cent over the contractual term of 10 years, and has a 5 per cent effective interest rate. At initial recognition the entity determines that the asset is not purchased or originated credit-impaired.

	Debit	Credit
Financial asset – FVOCI	£1,000	
Cash		£1,000

(To recognise the debt instrument measured at its fair value)

On 31 December 2016 (the reporting date), the fair value of the debt instrument has decreased to £950 as a result of changes in market interest rates. The entity determines that there has not been a significant increase in credit risk since initial recognition and that expected credit losses should be measured at an amount equal to 12-month expected credit losses, which amounts to £30. For simplicity, journal entries for the receipt of interest revenue are not provided.

	Debit	Credit
Impairment loss (profit or loss)	£30	
Other comprehensive income[a]	£20	
Financial asset – FVOCI		£50

(To recognise 12-month expected credit losses and other fair value changes on the debt instrument)

(a) The cumulative loss in other comprehensive income at the reporting date was £20. That amount consists of the total fair value change of £50 (i.e. £1,000 – £950) offset by the change in the accumulated impairment amount representing 12-month expected credit losses that was recognised (£30).

Disclosure would be provided about the accumulated impairment amount of £30.

Chapter 49

On 1 January 2017, the entity decides to sell the debt instrument for £950, which is its fair value at that date.

	Debit	Credit
Cash	£950	
Financial asset – FVOCI		£950
Loss (profit or loss)	£20	
Other comprehensive income		£20

(To derecognise the fair value through other comprehensive income asset and recycle amounts accumulated in other comprehensive income to profit or loss, i.e. £20).

This means that in contrast to financial assets measured at amortised cost, there is no separate allowance but, instead, impairment gains or losses are accounted for as an adjustment of the revaluation reserve accumulated in other comprehensive income, with a corresponding charge to profit or loss (which is then reflected in retained earnings).

Practically, for financial assets measured at fair value through other comprehensive income, the manner of accounting for impairment gains or losses required by the standard means that it becomes a matter of a disaggregation of accumulated other comprehensive income into impairment-related and other amounts. *[IFRS 9.4.1.2A, Appendix A, IFRS 7.35H].*

The above example is relatively straightforward. A more complicated one, based on a foreign currency denominated financial asset which is also the subject of an interest rate hedge, is provided below. It also illustrates the complexity that arises from the interaction between fair value (FV) hedge accounting and the new impairment model (see 5.4.6 above). It is based on Illustrative Example 14 in the Implementation Guidance for the standard but extended so as to illustrate the complexities that could arise in practice. *[IFRS 9.IE82-IE102].*

Example 49.30:   Interaction between the fair value through other comprehensive income measurement category and foreign currency denomination, fair value hedge accounting and impairment

The example assumes the following fact pattern and that, on initial recognition, expected credit losses are included when measuring foreign exchange gains and losses (see 5.6.2 above):

- An entity purchases a bond denominated in a foreign currency (FC) for its fair value of FC100,000 on 1 January 2016.
- The bond is held within a business model whose objective is achieved by both collecting contractual cash flows and selling financial assets and has contractual cash flows which are solely payments of principal and interest on the principal amount outstanding. Therefore, the entity classifies the bond as measured at fair value through other comprehensive income.
- The bond has five years remaining to maturity and a fixed coupon of 5 per cent over its contractual life on the contractual par amount of FC100,000.
- The entity hedges the bond for its interest rate related fair value risk. The fair value of the corresponding interest rate swap at the date of initial recognition is nil.
- On initial recognition, the bond has a 5 per cent effective interest rate which results in a gross carrying amount that equals the fair value at initial recognition.
- The entity's functional currency is its local currency (LC).
- As at 1 January 2016, the exchange rate is FC1 to LC1.
- At initial recognition, the entity determines that the bond is not purchased credit-impaired. The entity applies a 12-month PD for its impairment calculation and assumes that payment default

occurs at the end of the reporting period (i.e. after 12 months). In particular, the entity estimates the PD over the next 12 months at 2 per cent and the LGD at FC60,000, resulting in an (undiscounted) expected cash shortfall of FC1,200 (the discounted expected cash shortfall is FC1,143 at 5 per cent effective interest rate).

• For simplicity, amounts for interest revenue are not provided. It is assumed that interest accrued is received in the period. Differences of 1 in the calculations and reconciliations are due to rounding.

The entity hedges its risk exposures using the following risk management strategy:

(a) for fixed interest rate risk (in FC) the entity decides to link its interest receipts in FC to current variable interest rates in FC. Consequently, the entity uses interest rate swaps denominated in FC under which it pays fixed interest and receives variable interest in FC; and

(b) for foreign exchange (FX) risk, the entity decides not to hedge against any variability in LC arising from changes in foreign exchange rates.

The entity designates the following hedging relationship: a fair value hedge of the bond in FC as the hedged item with changes in benchmark interest rate risk in FC as the hedged risk. The entity enters into a swap that pays fixed and receives variable interest in FC on the same day and designates the swap as the hedging instrument. The tenor of the swap matches that of the hedged item (i.e. five years). This example assumes that all qualifying criteria for hedge accounting are met (see paragraph 6.4.1 of IFRS 9). The description of the designation is solely for the purpose of understanding this example (i.e. it is not an example of the complete formal documentation required in accordance with paragraph 6.4.1 of IFRS 9).

This example assumes that no hedge ineffectiveness arises in the hedging relationship. This assumption is made in order to better focus on illustrating the accounting mechanics in a situation that entails measurement at fair value through other comprehensive income of a foreign currency financial instrument that is designated in a fair value hedge relationship, and also to focus on the recognition of impairment gains or losses on such an instrument.

Situation as per 1 January 2016

The table below illustrates the amounts recognised in the financial statements as per 1 January 2016, as well as the shadow amortised cost calculation for the bond, based on the fact pattern described above (debits are shown as positive numbers and credits as negative numbers):

	Financial Statements			Shadow Calculation	
	FC	LC		FC	LC
	Statement of financial position				
Bond (FV)	100,000	100,000	Gross carrying amount	100,000	100,000
Swap (FV)	–	–	Loss allowance	(1,143)	(1,143)
			Amortised cost	98,857	98,857
	Statement of profit or loss				
Impairment	1,143	1,143	FV hedge adjustment	–	–
FV hedge (bond)	–	–	Adjusted gross carrying amt.	100,000	100,000
FX gain/loss (bond)	–	–	Adjusted amortised cost	98,857	98,857
FV hedge (swap)	–	–			
FX gain/loss (swap)	–	–			
	Statement of OCI				
FV changes	–	–			
Impairment offset	(1,143)	(1,143)			
FV hedge recycling	–	–			

As per 1 January 2016, the entity recognises the bond and the swap at their initial fair values of LC100,000 and nil, respectively. The loss allowance of FC1,143 is recognised in profit or loss. The amount is calculated as the difference between all contractual cash flows that are due to the entity in accordance with the contract and all the cash flows that the entity expects to receive (i.e. all cash shortfalls), discounted at the original effective interest of 5 per cent, and weighted by the probability of the scenario occurring. To keep the example simple, it is assumed that default on the bond occurs one year after the date of the initial recognition, at which point the recoverable amount of the bond is received. This means that in the case of a default the entity expects cash flows of FC45,000 (which is the principal of FC100,000 plus one year of interest of FC5,000 less the LGD of FC60,000). The latter loss is discounted by the 5 per cent EIR and weighted by the 2 per cent PD to arrive at the loss allowance. The table below shows the calculation:

1 January 2016		Year 1	Year 2	Year 3	Year 4	Year 5
Contractual cash flows		5,000	5,000	5,000	5,000	105,000
Gross carrying amount	100,000					
EIR	5%					
Expected cash flows		45,000				
Amortised cost (NPV[1] at 5%)	42,857					
Expected cash shortfalls		40,000	(5,000)	(5,000)	(5,000)	(105,000)
NPV at 5%	(57,143)					
PD	2%					
Net present value (probability weighted) – this is the expected credit loss	(1,143)					

1   Stands for net present value

2   Stands for present value

The table above shows how the expected credit loss is calculated as the net present value of the cash shortfalls, i.e. the difference between contractual and expected cash flows on each relevant date. An alternative is to calculate the probability-weighted present value for the two scenarios (FC100,000 × 98% plus FC42,857 × 2% = FC98,857) and determine the difference to the gross carrying amount (FC98,857 – FC100,000 = (FC1,143)).

In accordance with paragraph 16A of IFRS 7, the loss allowance for financial assets measured at fair value through other comprehensive income is not presented separately as a reduction of the carrying amount of the financial asset. As a consequence, the offsetting entry to the impairment loss of LC1,143 is recorded in other comprehensive income in the same period.

Situation as at 31 December 2016

As of 31 December 2016 (the reporting date), the entity observes the following facts:

- The fair value of the bond has decreased from FC100,000 to FC96,370, mainly because of an increase in market interest rates.

- The fair value of the swap has increased to FC1,837.

- In addition, as at 31 December 2016, the entity determines that there has been no change to the credit risk on the bond since initial recognition. The entity still estimates the PD over the next 12 months at 2 per cent and the LGD at FC60,000, resulting in an (undiscounted) expected shortfall of FC1,200.

- As at 31 December 2016, the exchange rate is FC1 to LC1.4.

The table below illustrates the amounts recognised in the financial statements between 1 January 2016 (after the entries for the impairment loss of FC1,143 at 1 January, shown above) and 31 December 2016, as well as the shadow amortised cost calculation for the bond (debits are shown as positive numbers and credits as negative numbers):

	Financial Statements			Shadow Calculation	
	Statement of financial position				
Bond (FV)	96,370	134,918	Gross carrying amount	100,000	140,000
Swap (FV)	1,837	2,572	Loss allowance	(1,110)	(1,555)
			Amortised cost	98,890	138,445
	Statement of profit or loss				
Impairment	(32)	(45)	FV hedge adjustment	(1,837)	(2,572)
FV hedge (bond)	1,837	2,572	Adjusted gross carrying amount	98,163	137,428
FX gain/loss (bond)		(39,543)	Adjusted amortised cost	97,053	135,874
FV hedge (swap)	(1,837)	(2,572)			
FX gain/loss (swap)	–	–			
	Statement of OCI				
FV changes	3,630	4,625			
Impairment offset	32	45			
FV hedge recycling	(1,837)	(2,572)			

At this point, the example reveals the operational complexity of the fact pattern. As highlighted in the introduction to this example, it is important to understand that the hedging relationship adjusts the gross carrying amount and the amortised cost of the bond which leads to an adjusted effective interest rate. This follows from the definition of the effective interest rate as 'the rate that exactly discounts the estimated future cash payments or receipts through the expected life of the financial asset or the financial liability to the gross carrying amount of a financial asset or to the amortised cost of a financial liability.' and the effect of a fair value hedge, that is, the hedging gain/loss adjusts the carrying amount of the hedged item. [IFRS 9 Appendix A].

The table below outlines the calculation:

31 December 2016		Year 2	Year 3	Year 4	Year 5
Contractual cash flows		5,000	5,000	5,000	105,000
Adjusted gross carrying amount[1]	98,163				
Updated EIR[2]	5.5%				
Expected cash flows		45,000			
Adjusted amortised cost (NPV at 5.5%)	42,644				
Expected cash shortfalls		40,000	(5,000)	(5,000)	(105,000)
NPV at 5.5%	(55,519)				
PD	2%				
Net present value (probability weighted) – this is the expected credit loss	(1,110)				

1   The adjusted gross carrying amount equals the gross carrying amount adjusted for the fair value hedge adjustment and forms the new basis of the EIR calculation

2   The updated EIR is the interest rate that exactly discounts the contractual cash flows to the adjusted gross carrying amount

Again, the table above shows how the expected credit loss is calculated as the net present value of the cash shortfalls, i.e. the difference between contractual and expected cash flows on each relevant date. The alternative calculation based on the probability-weighted present value for the two scenarios (FC98,163 × 98% plus FC42,644 × 2% = FC97,053) and then determining the difference to the gross carrying amount (including the fair value hedge adjustment) gives the same result (FC97,053 − FC98,163 = (FC1,110)).

This calculation means that there is an impairment gain recognised in profit or loss of FC32 (or LC45, respectively). This is because, to show more clearly how the accounting works, we have maintained the same expected cash flows as a year earlier, even though interest rates have now increased by 0.5 per cent. With a higher EIR, the expected credit losses are discounted at a higher rate. There are three effects that influence the impairment loss: the unwinding of the discount, the adjustment of the EIR and the change in the estimate of the timing of the payment default, which has moved 12 months into the future (i.e. from 31 December 2016 to 31 December 2017). The table below provides a reconciliation of those amounts:

31 December 2016 (values in FC)		
Loss allowance at the end of 1 January 2016	(1,143)	
Previous loss allowance rolled forward to reporting date (at 5% EIR)	(1,200)	
Unwinding of discount		**(57)**
Effect of adjusting the EIR		**32**
Effect of changes in estimate		**57**
Total change in loss allowance		**32**

Because we have maintained the expected cash shortfall pattern and its probability of occurring, the change in estimate is just the effect of deferral by a year of the expected date of default, which exactly offsets the unwinding of the discount.

In accordance with paragraph 16A of IFRS 7, the loss allowance for financial assets measured at fair value through other comprehensive income is not presented separately as a reduction of the carrying amount of the financial asset. As a consequence, the offsetting entry of the impairment gain FC32 (LC45) is recorded as a debit to other comprehensive income in the same period.

The bond is a monetary asset. Consequently, the entity recognises the changes arising from movements in foreign exchange rates in profit or loss in accordance with paragraphs 23(a) and 28 of IAS 21 and recognises other changes in accordance with IFRS 9. For the purposes of applying paragraph 28 of IAS 21, the asset is treated as an asset measured at amortised cost in the foreign currency.

The change in the fair value of the bond since 1 January 2015 amounts to LC34,918 and is recognised as a fair value adjustment to the carrying amount of the bond on the entity's statement of financial position.

The gain of LC39,543 due to the changes in foreign exchange rates is recognised in profit or loss. It consists of the impact of the change in the exchange rates during 2016:

- on the original gross carrying amount of the bond, amounting to LC40,000;
- offset by the loss allowance of the bond, amounting to LC457 (i.e. the difference of FC1,143 translated at the exchange rate as at 1 January 2016 of FC1 to LC1 and FC1,143 translated at the exchange rate as at 31 December 2016 of FC1 to LC1.4).

The difference between the change in fair value (LC34,918) and the gain recognised in profit or loss that is due to the changes in foreign exchange rates (LC39,543) is recognised in OCI. That difference amounts to LC4,625.

A gain of LC2,572 (FC1,837) on the swap is recognised in profit or loss and, because it is assumed that there is no hedge ineffectiveness, this amount coincides with the loss on the hedged item (as an absolute amount). Because this is a fair value hedge of a debt instrument at fair value through other comprehensive income this loss is recycled from other comprehensive income in the same period.

Situation as at 31 December 2017

As of 31 December 2017 (the reporting date), the entity observes the following facts:

- The fair value of the bond has further decreased from FC96,370 to FC87,114.
- The fair value of the swap has increased to FC2,092.
- Based on adverse macroeconomic developments in the industry in which the bond issuer operates, the entity assumes a significant increase in credit risk since initial recognition, and recognises the lifetime expected credit loss for the bond.

- The entity updates its impairment estimate and now estimates the lifetime PD at 20 per cent and the LGD at FC48,500, resulting in (undiscounted) expected cash shortfalls of FC9,700. (For simplicity, this example assumes that payment default will happen on maturity when the entire face value becomes due).

- As at 31 December 2017, the exchange rate is FC1 to LC1.25.

The table below illustrates the amounts recognised in the financial statements between 31 December 2016 and 31 December 2017, as well as the shadow amortised cost calculation for the bond (debits are shown as positive numbers and credits as negative numbers):

Financial Statements			Shadow Calculation	
Statement of financial position				
Bond (FV)	87,114	108,893	Gross carrying amount	100,000	125,000
Swap (FV)	2,092	2,615	Loss allowance	(8,195)	(10,244)
			Amortised cost	91,805	114,756
Statement of profit or loss				
Impairment	7,085	8,856	FV hedge adjustment	(2,092)	(2,615)
FV hedge (bond)	255	319	Adj. gross carrying amt.	97,908	122,385
FX gain/loss (bond)		14,558	Adj. amortised cost	89,713	112,141
FV hedge (swap)	(255)	(319)			
FX gain/loss (swap)		276			
Statement of OCI				
FV changes	9,256	11,468			
Impairment offset	(7,085)	(8,856)			
FV hedge recycling	(255)	(319)			

Similar to the situation as at 31 December 2016, the fair value hedge adjustment leads to an adjusted EIR. The table below illustrates the calculation:

31 December 2017 (values in FC)		Year 3	Year 4	Year 5
Contractual cash flows		5,000	5,000	105,000
Adjusted gross carrying amount[1]	97,908			
Updated EIR[2]	5.8%			
Expected cash flows		5,000	5,000	56,500
Adjusted amortised cost (NPV at 5.8%)	56,931			
Expected cash shortfalls		–	–	(48,500)
NPV at 5.8%	(40,977)			
PD	20%			
Net present value (probability weighted) – this is the expected credit loss	(8,195)			

1 The adjusted gross carrying amount equals the gross carrying amount adjusted for the fair value hedge adjustment and forms the new basis of the EIR calculation

2 The updated EIR is the interest rate that exactly discounts the contractual cash flows to the adjusted gross carrying amount

Again, the table above shows how the expected credit loss is calculated as the net present value of the cash shortfalls, i.e. the difference between contractual and expected cash flows on each relevant date. The alternative calculation based on the probability-weighted present value for the two scenarios (FC97,908 × 80% plus FC56,931 × 20% = FC89,713) and then determining the difference to the gross carrying amount (including the fair value hedge adjustment) gives the same result (FC FC89,713 – FC97,908 = (FC8,195)).

As at 31 December 2017, there are three effects that influence the impairment loss of FC8,398 (LC10,498) recognised in profit or loss: the unwinding of the discount, the adjustment of the EIR and the increase in credit risk (change in estimate). The table below provides a reconciliation of those amounts:

31 December 2017 (values in FC)	
Loss allowance at the beginning of the period	(1,110)
Previous loss allowance rolled forward to reporting date (at 5.5% EIR)	(1,172)
Unwinding of discount	**(61)**
Effect of adjusting the EIR	**60**
Effect of changes in estimate	**(7,083)**
Total change in loss allowance	**(7,085)**

The offsetting entry of the impairment loss FC7,085 (LC8,856) is recorded in other comprehensive income in the same period.

The change in the fair value of the bond since 31 December 2016 amounts to a decrease of LC26,026 and is recognised as a fair value adjustment to the carrying amount of the bond on the entity's statement of financial position.

The loss of LC14,558 due to the changes in foreign exchange rates is recognised in profit or loss. It consists of the impact of the change in the exchange rates during 2017:

- on the original gross carrying amount of the bond, amounting to a loss of LC15,000;
- on the loss allowance of the bond, amounting to a gain of LC167;
- on the fair value hedge adjustment, amounting to a gain of LC276.

The difference between the change in fair value (decrease of LC26,026) and the loss recognised in profit or loss that is due to the changes in foreign exchange rates (–LC14,558) is recognised in OCI. That difference amounts to LC11,468.

A gain of LC319 (FC255) on the swap is recognised in profit or loss and, because it is assumed that there is no hedge ineffectiveness, this amount coincides with the loss on the hedged item (as an absolute amount). Because this is a fair value hedge of a debt instrument at fair value through other comprehensive income this loss is recycled from other comprehensive income in the same period.

Situation as at 1 January 2018

On 1 January 2018, the entity decides to sell the bond for FC87,114, which is its fair value at that date and also closes out the swap at its fair value. For simplicity, all amounts, including the foreign exchange rate, are assumed to be the same as at 31 December 2017.

Upon derecognition, the entity reclassifies the cumulative amount recognised in OCI of (LC3,248) ((FC2,599)) to profit or loss. This amount is equal to the difference between the fair value and the adjusted amortised cost amount of the bond at the time of its derecognition. The table below presents a reconciliation of those amounts.

Reconciliation of loss on derecognition (values in LC) to cumulative OCI				
Fair value per 1 January 2018	87,114			
Adjusted amortised cost per 1 January 2018	89,713			
Loss	**(2,599)**			
	Cum. OCI	1 January 2016	31 December 2016	31 December 2017
FV changes	12,886	–	3,630	9,256
Impairment	(8,195)	(1,143)	32	(7,085)
FV hedge recycling	(2,092)	–	(1,837)	(255)
Total OCI to be reclassified	**2,599**			

This table presents the amount that has not yet been recycled and, therefore, must be reclassified to profit or loss on derecognition.

5.9   Trade receivables, contract assets and lease receivables

The standard provides some operational simplifications to trade receivables, contract assets and lease receivables. This includes the requirement or policy choice to apply the simplified approach that does not require entities to track changes in credit risk (see 5.3.2 above) and the practical expedient to calculate expected credit losses on trade receivables using a provision matrix (see 5.9.1 below).

5.9.1   Trade receivables and contract assets

It is a requirement for entities to apply the simplified approach for trade receivables or contract assets that do not contain a significant financing component. However, entities have a policy choice to apply either the general approach (see 5.3.1 above) or the simplified approach separately to trade receivables and contract assets that do contain a significant financing component (see 5.3.2 above). *[IFRS 9.5.5.15(a)]*.

Also, entities are allowed to use practical expedients when measuring expected credit losses, as long as the approach reflects a probability-weighted outcome, the time value of money and reasonable and supportable information that is available without undue cost or effort at the reporting date about past events, current conditions and forecasts of future economic conditions. *[IFRS 9.5.5.17, B5.5.35]*.

One of the approaches suggested in the standard is the use of a provision matrix as a practical expedient for measuring expected credit losses on trade receivables. For instance, the provision rates might be based on days past due (e.g. 1 per cent if not past due, 2 per cent if less than 30 days past due, etc.) for groupings of various customer segments that have similar loss patterns. The grouping may be based on geographical region, product type, customer rating, the type of collateral or whether covered by trade credit insurance, and the type of customer (such as wholesale or retail). To calibrate the matrix, the entity would adjust its historical credit loss experience with forward-looking information. *[IFRS 9.B5.5.35]*.

In practice, many corporates use a provision matrix to calculate their current impairment allowances. However, in order to comply with the IFRS 9 requirements, corporates would need to consider how current and forward-looking information might affect their customers' historical default rates and, consequently, how the information would affect their current expectations and estimates of expected credit losses. The use of the provision matrix is illustrated in the following example. *[IFRS 9 IG Example 12, IE74-IE77]*.

Example 49.31:   Provision matrix

Company M, a manufacturer, has a portfolio of trade receivables of €30 million in 2015 and operates only in one geographical region. The customer base consists of a large number of small clients and the trade receivables are categorised by common risk characteristics that are representative of the customers' abilities to pay all amounts due in accordance with the contractual terms. The trade receivables do not have a significant financing component in accordance with IFRS 15. In accordance with paragraph 5.5.15 of IFRS 9, the loss allowance for such trade receivables is always measured at an amount equal to lifetime time expected credit losses.

To determine the expected credit losses for the portfolio, Company M uses a provision matrix. The provision matrix is based on its historical observed default rates over the expected life of the trade receivables and is adjusted for forward-looking estimates. At every reporting date, the historical observed default rates are updated and changes in the forward-looking estimates are analysed. In this case it is forecast that economic conditions will deteriorate over the next year.

On that basis, Company M estimates the following provision matrix:

	Current	1-30 days past due	31-60 days past due	61-90 days past due	More than 90 days past due
Default rate	0.3%	1.6%	3.6%	6.6%	10.6%

The trade receivables from the large number of small customers amount to €30 million and are measured using the provision matrix.

	Gross carrying amount	Lifetime expected credit loss allowance (Gross carrying amount × lifetime expected credit loss rate)
Current	€15,000,000	€45,000
1-30 days past due	€7,500,000	€120,000
31-60 days past due	€4,000,000	€144,000
61-90 days past due	€2,500,000	€165,000
More than 90 days past due	€1,000,000	€106,000
	€30,000,000	**€580,000**

It should be noted that this example, like many in the standard, ignores the need to consider explicitly the time value of money, presumably in this case because the effect is considered immaterial.

5.9.2   Lease receivables

For lease receivables, entities have a policy choice to apply either the general approach (see 5.3.1 above) or the simplified approach (see 5.3.2 above) separately to finance and operating lease receivables (see Chapter 24). *[IFRS 9.5.5.15(b)]*.

In addition, when measuring expected credit losses for lease receivables, an entity should:

- use the cash flows that are used in measuring the lease receivables in accordance with IAS 17; *[IFRS 9.B5.5.34, IAS 17.36-38]* and

- discount the expected credit losses using the same discount rate used in the measurement of the lease receivables in accordance with IAS 17. *[IFRS 9.B5.5.46, IAS 17.4]*.

5.10   Loan commitments and financial guarantee contracts

The description of 'loan commitment' and the definition of 'financial guarantee contract' remain unchanged from IAS 39. Loan commitments (see Chapter 42 at 3.5) are described in IFRS 9 as 'firm commitments to provide credit under pre-specified terms and conditions', while a financial guarantee contract (see Chapter 42 at 3.4) is defined as 'a contract that requires the issuer to make specified payments to reimburse the holder for a loss it incurs because a specified debtor fails to make payment when due in accordance with the original or modified terms of a debt instrument'. *[IFRS 9.BCZ2.2, Appendix A, IAS 39.9, BC15].*

The IFRS 9 impairment requirements apply to loan commitments and financial guarantee contracts that are not measured at fair value through profit or loss under IFRS 9, with some exceptions (see 5.2 above).

The ITG (see 5.1.5 above) discussed in April 2015 whether the impairment requirements in IFRS 9 must also be applied to other commitments to extend credit such as:

- a commitment at the inception of a finance lease that has not yet commenced (i.e. a commitment to transfer the right to use an asset at the lease commencement date in return for a payment or series of payments in the future); and

- a commitment by a retailer through the issue of a store account to provide a customer with credit when the customer buys goods or services from the retailer in the future.

The ITG appeared to agree with the IASB's staff analysis that the impairment requirements of IFRS 9 apply to an agreement that contains a commitment to extend credit by virtue of paragraph 2.1(g) if:

- the agreement meets the description of a loan commitment; *[IFRS 9.BCZ2.2]*

- the agreement meets the definition of a financial instrument; *[IAS 32.11]* and

- none of the specific exemptions from the requirements of IFRS 9 apply. *[IFRS 9.2.1].*

The IASB staff paper stated that some contracts, such as irrevocable finance lease agreements, might clearly contain a firm commitment at inception to provide credit under pre-specified terms and conditions. However, other cases might not be so clear cut, depending upon the specific terms of the agreement and other facts and circumstances (e.g. if the issuer of a store account has the discretion to refuse to sell products or services to a customer with a store card and hence can avoid extending credit).[30]

In the examples discussed above, the finance lease and store account do not meet the definition of a financial instrument until the contractual right to receive cash is established, that is likely to be at the commencement of the lease term or when goods or services are sold. *[IAS 32.11 and AG20].* Only lease receivables are scoped into the IFRS 9 impairment requirements (see 5.9.2 above). *[IFRS 9.2.1(b)].*

The application of the model to financial guarantees and loan commitments warrants some further specification regarding some of the key elements, such as the determination of the credit quality on initial recognition, cash shortfalls and the effective interest rate to be used in the expected credit losses calculations. These specifications are summarised in the table below, which also highlights the differences in recognising and measuring expected credit losses for financial assets measured at amortised cost or at fair value through other comprehensive income, loan commitments and financial guarantee contracts.

Chapter 49

	Financial assets measured at amortised cost or at fair value through other comprehensive income	Loan commitments	Financial guarantee contracts
Date of initial recognition in applying the impairment requirements (see 5.6.2 above and 6.2.1 below)	Trade date. *[IFRS 9.5.7.4]*.	Date that an entity becomes a party to the irrevocable commitment. *[IFRS 9.5.5.6]*.	Date that an entity becomes a party to the irrevocable commitment. *[IFRS 9.5.5.6]*.
Period over which to estimate expected credit losses (see 5.4.3 above)	The expected life up to the maximum contractual period (including extension options) over which the entity is exposed to credit risk and not a longer period. *[IFRS 9.5.5.19]*.	The expected life up to the maximum contractual period over which an entity has a present contractual obligation to extend credit. *[IFRS 9.B5.5.38]*. However, for revolving credit facilities (see 5.11 below), this period extends beyond the contractual period over which the entity is exposed to credit risk and the expected credit losses would not be mitigated by credit risk management actions. *[IFRS 9.5.5.20, B5.5.39, B5.5.40]*.	The expected life up to the maximum contractual period over which an entity has a present contractual obligation to extend credit. *[IFRS 9.B5.5.38]*.
Cash shortfalls in measuring expected credit losses (see 5.4.1 above)	Cash shortfalls between the cash flows that are due to an entity in accordance with the contract and the cash flows that the entity expects to receive. *[IFRS 9.B5.5.28]*.	Cash shortfalls between the contractual cash flows that are due to the entity if the holder of the loan commitment draws down the loan and the cash flows that the entity expects to receive if the loan is drawn down. *[IFRS 9.B5.5.30]*.	Cash shortfalls are the expected payments to reimburse the holder for a credit loss that it incurs less any amounts that the entity (issuer) expects to receive from the holder, the debtor or any other party. *[IFRS 9.B5.5.32]*.
Effective interest rate used in discounting expected credit losses (see 5.4.5 above)	The effective interest rate is determined or approximated at initial recognition of the financial instrument. *[IFRS 9.B5.5.44]*.	The effective interest rate of the resulting asset will be applied and if this is not determinable, then the current rate representing the risk of the cash flows is used. *[IFRS 9.B5.5.47, B5.5.48]*.	The current rate representing the risk of the cash flows is used. *[IFRS 9.B5.5.48]*.
Assessment of significant increases in credit risk (see 5.5 above)	An entity considers changes in the risk of a default occurring on the financial asset. *[IFRS 9.5.5.9]*.	An entity considers changes in the risk of a default occurring on the loan to which a loan commitment relates. *[IFRS 9.B5.5.8]*.	An entity considers the changes in the risk that the specified debtor will default on the contract. *[IFRS 9.B5.5.8]*.

At its meeting in April 2015, the ITG (see 5.1.5 above) also discussed the measurement of expected credit losses for an issued financial guarantee contract that requires the holder to pay further premiums in the future. Some members of the ITG agreed with the staff's analysis that the issuer of a financial guarantee contract should exclude future premium receipts due from the holder when measuring expected credit losses in respect of the expected cash outflows payable under the guarantee.[31] When estimating the cash shortfalls, the amounts that the entity expects to receive from the holder should relate only to recoveries or reimbursements of claims for losses and would not include receipts of premiums. *[IFRS 9.B5.5.32]*. Moreover, the expected cash outflows under the guarantee depend upon the risk of default of the guaranteed asset, while the expected future premiums receipts are subject to the risk of default by the holder of the guarantee. Hence, these risks of default should be considered separately. We note that this conclusion implies that, on 'day one', the issuer of the financial guarantee contract records a gross liability and an asset for the future premiums receivable.

In addition, an ITG member noted that the terms of a financial guarantee contract may affect the period of exposure to credit risk on the guarantee, for example if the guarantee were contingent or cancellable. This should be taken into consideration when measuring the expected credit losses of the guarantee.

5.11 Revolving credit facilities

The 2013 Exposure Draft specified that the maximum period over which expected credit losses are to be calculated should be limited to the contractual period over which the entity is exposed to credit risk.[32] This would mean that the allowance for commitments that can be withdrawn at short notice by a lender, such as overdrafts and credit card facilities, would be limited to the expected credit losses that would arise over the notice period, which might be only one day. However, banks will not normally exercise their right to cancel the commitment until there is already evidence of significant deterioration, which exposes them to risk over a considerably longer period. The IASB responded to the concerns of respondents by setting out further guidance and an example, addressing such arrangements.

The guidance relates to financial instruments that 'include both a loan and an undrawn commitment component and for which the entity's contractual ability to demand repayment and cancel the commitment does not limit the entity's exposure to credit losses to the contractual notice period'. *[IFRS 9.5.5.20]*. Despite the use of the word 'both', the ITG agreed, in April 2015, that this guidance applies even if the facility has yet to be drawn down. It also applies if the facility has been completely drawn down, as it is the nature of revolving facilities that the drawn down component is periodically paid off before further amounts will be drawn down again in future.

The standard goes on to describe three characteristics generally associated with such instruments: *[IFRS 9.B5.5.39]*

- they usually have no fixed term or repayment structure and usually have a short contractual cancellation period;
- the contractual ability to cancel the contract is not enforced in day-to-day management, but only when the lender is aware of an increase in credit risk at the facility level; and
- they are managed on a collective basis.

According to the standard, 'for such financial instruments, and only those financial instruments, the entity shall measure expected credit losses over the period that the entity is exposed to credit risk and expected credit losses would not be mitigated by credit risk management actions, even if that period extends beyond the maximum contractual period'. *[IFRS 9.5.5.20]*. In order to calculate the period for which expected credit losses are assessed, 'an entity should consider factors such as historical information and experience about:

(a) the period over which the entity was exposed to credit risk on similar financial instruments;

(b) the length of time for related defaults to occur on similar financial instruments following a significant increase in credit risk; and

(c) the credit risk management actions that an entity expects to take once the credit risk on the financial instrument has increased, such as the reduction or removal of undrawn limits.' *[IFRS 9.B5.5.40]*.

This wording in the standard is not very easy to interpret or apply.

The ITG (see 5.1.5 above), in April 2015, discussed how to determine the appropriate period when measuring expected credit losses for a portfolio of revolving credit card exposures in stages 1, 2 and 3 and commented that:

- An entity's ability to segment and stratify the portfolio into different sections of exposures in accordance with how those exposures are being managed will be relevant. For example, an entity may be able to identify exposures with specific attributes that are considered more likely to default and consequently would have shorter average lives than those that are expected to continue performing (see 5.5.5 above).

- While IFRS 9 requires a period in excess of the maximum contractual period to be used when measuring expected credit losses, the fundamental aim was still to determine the period over which the entity is exposed to credit risk and an entity must consider all three factors set out in paragraph B5.5.40. Consequently, expected defaults or potential credit risk management actions such as reduction or removal of undrawn limits could result in a shorter period of exposure than that indicated by the historical behavioural life of the facility. That is, the time horizon is not the period over which the lender expects the facility to be used, but the period over which the lender is, in practice, exposed to credit risk.

The ITG discussion left it unclear as to how long the period should be. Most banks believe that an argument can be made for the period being more than a year, in which case the actual period becomes irrelevant for stage 1 facilities, whose loss allowances are calculated based on a 12-month period. Hence the question for them is how long to use when calculating facilities in stage 2, whose credit risk may have increased significantly since origination, but are still deemed low enough risk that the facility has not been withdrawn. For some stage 2 facilities, the period over which an entity is exposed to credit risk is likely to be lower than for stage 1 facilities, as they are being more closely monitored, but other facilities in stage 2 can be expected to cure and for them the period may be as long as for facilities in stage 1. There are other banks who believe that their credit procedures are sufficiently active that the exposure period is less than a year.

As there were many diverse views and questions raised, many of the ITG members indicated that they would benefit from more examples on revolving credit facilities. These examples should seek to explain how assumptions and credit risk management actions are linked to the determination of the appropriate period when measuring expected credit losses and how the assessment differs for assets measured at 12-month and lifetime expected credit losses, and credit-impaired assets. It is expected that this issue will be brought back to the ITG meeting in December 2015.

At its April 2015 meeting, the ITG also discussed the date of initial recognition when assessing significant increases in credit risk for a portfolio of revolving credit facilities. There will typically be a diverse customer base, ranging from long-standing customers who have been with the bank for many years, to new customers who have only recently opened an account. One view is that the date of initial recognition is the date the facility was issued and this should only be changed if there had been a derecognition of the original facility. The challenge would be how to determine when changes are sufficiently significant to result in a derecognition of the original facility and recognition of a new facility. Judgement would be required in making this assessment, which would depend on the specific facts and circumstances. For example:

- in some circumstances, issuing a new card may be indicative that the original facility has been derecognised (e.g. replacement of a student credit card with a new credit card upon graduation), but in other cases, this may be a purely operational process and thus would not indicate that a new facility has been issued; and

- credit reviews or revision to credit limits in themselves may not indicate that a new facility has been issued.

Against the view that it is necessary to look back to an original recognition date, others would argue that this is inappropriate for a revolving facility, since the credit decisions are periodically refreshed and those made on origination are no longer relevant. Particularly, if there is a periodic formal reassessment, as thorough as that as on original recognition, the date of this reassessment may be a more appropriate reference date. This is consistent with paragraph BC5.260, 'if an entity decides to renew or extend its commitment to extend credit, it will be a new instrument for which the entity has the opportunity to revise the terms and conditions'.

This following example illustrates the calculation of impairment for revolving credit facilities, based on Illustrative Example 10 in the Implementation Guidance for the standard. *[IFRS 9 IG Example 10, IE58-IE65]*. For the sake of clarity, the assumptions and calculations have been adapted from the IASB example as it is not explicit on the source of the parameters and how they are computed. The example has also been expanded to show the calculation of the loss allowances. However, to simplify the example, we have ignored the need to discount expected credit losses.

Example 49.32:   *Revolving credit facilities*

Bank A provides credit cards with a one day cancellation right and manages the drawn and undrawn commitment on each card together, as a facility. Bank A sub-divides the credit card portfolio by segregating those amounts for which a significant increase in credit risk was identified at the individual facility level from the remainder of the portfolio. The remainder of this example only illustrates the calculation of expected credit losses for the sub-portfolio for which a significant increase in credit risk was not identified at the individual facility level. At the reporting date, the outstanding balance on the sub-portfolio is £6,000,000 and the undrawn facility is £4,000,000. The Bank determines the sub-portfolio's expected life as 30 months (using the guidance set out above) and that the credit risk on 25 per cent of the sub-portfolio has increased significantly since initial origination, making up £1,500,000 of the outstanding balance and £1,000,000 of the undrawn commitment (see the calculation of the exposure in the table below).

To calculate its EAD, Bank A uses an approach whereby it adds the amounts that are drawn at the reporting date and additional draw-downs that are expected in the case that a customer defaults. For those expected additional draw-downs, Bank A uses a credit conversion factor that represents the estimate of what percentage of that part of committed credit facilities that is unused at the reporting date would be drawn by a customer before he defaults. Using its credit models, the bank determines this credit conversion factor as 95 per cent. The EAD on the portion of facilities measured on a lifetime expected credit loss basis is therefore £2,450,000, made up of the drawn balance of £1,500,000 and £950,000 of expected further draw-downs before the customers default. For the remainder of the facilities, the EAD that is measured on a 12-month expected credit loss basis is £7,350,000, being the remaining drawn balance of £4,500,000 plus additional expected draw-downs for customers defaulting over the next 12 months of £2,850,000 (see the calculation for the EAD in the table below).

Bank A has estimated that the PD for the next 12 months is 5 per cent, and 30 per cent for the next 30 months. The estimate for the LGD on the credit cards in the sub-portfolio is 90 per cent. That results in lifetime expected credit losses of £661,500 and 12-month expected credit losses of £330,750 (see calculation for expected credit losses in the table below).

For the presentation in the statement of financial position, the expected credit losses against the drawn amount of £607,500 would be recognised as an allowance against the credit card receivables and the remainder of the expected credit losses that relates to the undrawn facilities of £384,750 would be recognised as a liability (see table below).

Determination made at facility level		Drawn	Undrawn	Total
Facility		£6,000,000	£4,000,000	£10,000,000
Exposure				
Subject to lifetime expected credit losses (25% of the facility has been determined to have significantly increased in credit risk)	25%	£1,500,000	£1,000,000	£2,500,000
Subject to 12-month expected credit losses (the remaining 75% of the facility)	75%	£4,500,000	£3,000,000	£7,500,000
Credit conversion factor (CCF)	95%			
A uniform CCF is used irrespective of deterioration, which reflects that the CCF is contingent on default which is the same reference point for a 12-month and lifetime expected credit loss calculation				
EAD				
EAD for undrawn balances is calculated as exposure × CCF				
Subject to lifetime expected credit losses		£1,500,000	£950,000	£2,450,000
Subject to 12-month expected credit losses		£4,500,000	£2,850,000	£7,350,000
PD				
Exposures subject to lifetime expected credit losses	30%			
Exposures subject to 12-month expected credit losses	5%			
LGD	90%			
Expected credit losses (EAD × PD × LGD)				
Exposures subject to lifetime expected credit losses		£405,000	£256,500	£661,500
Exposures subject to 12-month expected credit losses		£202,500	£128,250	£330,750
		£607,500 *presented as loss allowance against assets*	£384,750 *presented as provision*	£992,250

We make the following observations:

- In Example 10 of the standard (on which our Example 49.32 above is based), we have assumed that the 25 per cent has been calculated using the top down method described at 5.5.5 above, which also sets out various challenges in its application. This means that the bank does not know which of the facilities are

Chapter 49

deemed to have significantly deteriorated. It might, alternatively, be calculated using a bottom up approach.

• Example 10 in the standard does not show how the 30-month period was calculated. The calculation of the period is likely to be challenging and require the use of judgement.

• We use the same credit conversion factor, of 95%, for calculating the EAD, irrespective of whether it is an input for 12-month or lifetime expected credit losses. This is based on an assumption that the extent of future draw-downs in the event that the customer defaults do not differ depending on whether at the reporting date there had been a significant increase in credit risk. This reflects that, in practice, for many credit cards the exposure in case of a default reaches close to the limit of the total facility (credit limit). In this context it is important to be aware that the use of a conventional credit conversion factor model for estimating the EAD creates some problems. For instance, in practice, the credit limit is often exceeded when the customer reaches the state of default, in which case the credit conversion factor would be greater than 100%.

At its meeting on 16 September 2015, the ITG (see 5.1.5 above) discussed how an entity should estimate future drawdowns on undrawn lines of credit when an entity has a history of allowing customers to exceed their contractually set credit limits on overdrafts and other revolving credit facilities.

Some ITG participants thought that the ultimate economic risk of loss should be reflected, regardless of what is contractually agreed. However, there appears to be no support in the standard for including amounts in excess of the limits.

Some ITG members noted that a limit is not always explicitly stipulated in the contract. There was no consensus on how to deal with these circumstances, although one member suggested looking at the bank's internally established limit in its systems or credit policies. This issue has been flagged to the IASB for further consideration.

5.12   Presentation of expected credit losses in the statement of financial position

IFRS 9 uses the term 'loss allowance' throughout the standard as an umbrella term for expected credit losses that are recognised in the statement of financial position. However, that umbrella term leaves open the question of how those expected credit losses should be presented in that statement. Their presentation differs by the type of the credit risk exposures that are in scope of the impairment requirements. *[IFRS 9 Appendix A]*. This section explains how presentation applies in the different situations.

Any adjustment to the loss allowance balance due to an increase or decrease of the amount of expected credit losses recognised in accordance with IFRS 9, is reflected in profit or loss in a separate line as an impairment gain or loss. *[IAS 1.82(ba), IFRS 9.5.5.8, Appendix A]*.

5.12.1 Allowance for financial assets measured at amortised cost, contract assets and lease receivables

Expected credit losses on financial assets measured at amortised cost, lease receivables (see Chapter 24) and contract assets (see Chapter 29) are presented as an allowance, i.e. as an integral part of the measurement of those assets in the statement of financial position. Unlike the requirement to show impairment losses as a separate line item in the statement of profit or loss, there is no similar consequential amendment to IAS 1 – *Presentation of Financial Statements* – to present the loss allowance as a separate line item in the statement of financial position. *[IAS 1.82(ba)]*. It is clear from the standard that the definition of *amortised cost* of a financial asset is after adjusting for any loss allowance and hence, the loss allowance would reduce the *gross carrying amount* in the statement of financial position (which is why an allowance is sometimes referred to as a contra asset account). *[IFRS 9 Appendix A]*. Accordingly, financial assets measured at amortised cost, contract assets and lease receivables should be presented net of the loss allowance at their amortised cost in the statement of financial position.

IFRS 9 provides guidance on when the allowance should be used, i.e. when it should be applied against the gross carrying amount of a financial asset. This occurs when there is a write-off on a financial asset (see 5.12.1.A below). This represents a change from IAS 39, where no similar guidance is provided and its derecognition guidance does not refer to write-offs.

5.12.1.A Write-off

An entity is required to reduce the gross carrying amount of a financial asset when the entity has no reasonable expectations of recovering the contractual cash flows on a financial asset in its entirety or a portion thereof. A write-off is considered a derecognition event. *[IFRS 9.5.4.4, B3.2.16(r)]*.

For example, a lender plans to enforce the collateral on a loan and expects to recover no more than 30 per cent of the value of the loan from selling the collateral. If the lender has no reasonable prospects of recovering any further cash flows from the loan, it should write off the remaining 70 per cent. *[IFRS 9.B5.4.9]*. The example given in the standard demonstrates that write-offs can be for only a partial amount instead of the entire gross carrying amount.

If the amount of loss on write-off is greater than the accumulated loss allowance, the difference will be an additional impairment loss. In situations where a further impairment loss occurs, the question has arisen as to how it should be presented: simply as a loss in profit or loss with a credit directly to the gross carrying amount or, first, as an addition to the allowance that is then applied against the gross carrying amount. The difference between those alternatives is whether the additional impairment loss flows through the allowance, showing up in a reconciliation of the allowance as an addition and a use (i.e. a write-off), or whether such additional impairment amounts bypass the allowance. The IASB's original 2009 Exposure Draft (see 5.1.1 above) explicitly mandated that all write-offs could only be debited against the allowance, meaning that any direct write-offs against profit or loss without flowing through the allowance were prohibited.[33]

Chapter 49

IFRS 9 does not include any similar explicit guidance on this issue, which may not be material for most entities.

In addition, IFRS 7 requires an entity to disclose its policies in relation to write-offs and also, the amounts written off during the period that are still subject to enforcement activity (see 5.13 below and Chapter 53 at 5.2.3). *[IFRS 7.35F(e), 35L]*. It should be noted that there is a tension between this requirement and the criteria in an IFRS 9 for write-off, since it may be difficult to argue that there is no reasonable expectation of recovering the contractual cash flows if the loan is still subject to enforcement activity.

5.12.1.B   Presentation of the gross carrying amount and expected credit loss allowance for credit-impaired assets

For financial assets that are credit-impaired in stage 3, the application of the effective interest rate to the amortised cost of the financial asset applies only to the calculation and presentation of interest revenue, but does not seem to affect the measurement of the gross carrying amount and the loss allowance. *[IFRS 9.BC5.75]*. If the asset was not credit-impaired on initial recognition, the effective interest rate is based on the contractual cash flows, excluding expected credit losses and this does not change when the asset becomes credit-impaired. *[IFRS 9.B5.4.4, Appendix A]*. Consequently, the calculation of the gross carrying amount and the expected credit loss allowance are not affected by the recognition of interest revenue moving from a gross to a net basis.

A calculation of the interest income and the gross amortised cost and loss allowance is shown in the following example.

Example 49.33:   Calculation of the gross carrying amount and expected credit loss allowance for credit-impaired assets in stage 3

On 1 January 2016, a zero coupon loan is repayable at £5,000 in 2 years' time and has an effective interest rate of 10%. The loan was assessed to be credit-impaired in accordance with the criteria outlined in Appendix A of IFRS 9 at this date and the expected cash flows at maturity are expected to be only £1,000.

If the calculation of the gross carrying amount and expected credit loss allowance are not affected by the recognition of interest revenue moving from a gross to a net basis, the following computation would apply:

All figures are in £	1 January 2016	Net interest revenue (profit or loss)	Gross-up of carrying amount and allowance	Total effective interest rate (EIR) accrual	31 December 2016	
Gross carrying amount	4,132	83	330	413	4,545	£5,000 discounted for two years and then one year at 10%
Expected credit loss allowance	(3,305)		(330)		(3,635)	Difference between gross carrying amount and amortised cost.
Amortised cost	827	83	0	413	910	£1,000 discounted for two years and then one year at 10%

Note:
- Interest revenue of £83 is calculated based on the 10% effective interest rate on the amortised cost balance of £827.
- Gross interest accrual of £413 is based on the 10% effective interest rate on the gross amortised cost of £4,132.

Although this is how we think the standard was intended to be read, others may argue that it is possible to interpret the standard not to require the 'gross up' entries to the gross carrying amount and to impairment, so that just the net £83 is added to the gross carrying amount. Given that this only affects the disclosure of the components of the amortised cost, the difference between the two approaches will often not be material.

5.12.2   Provisions for loan commitments and financial guarantee contracts

In contrast to the presentation of impairment of assets, expected credit losses on loan commitments and financial guarantee contracts are presented as a provision in the statement of financial position, i.e. as a liability. *[IFRS 9 Appendix A]*.

For financial institutions that offer credit facilities, commitments may often be partially drawn down, i.e. an entity may have a facility that includes both a loan (a financial asset) and an undrawn commitment (a loan commitment). If the entity cannot separately identify the expected credit losses attributable to the drawn and the undrawn commitment, IFRS 7 requires an entity to present the provision for expected credit losses on the loan commitment together with the allowance for the financial asset. IFRS 7 states, further, that if the combined expected credit losses exceed the gross carrying amount of the financial asset, then the expected credit losses should be recognised as a provision. *[IFRS 7.B8E]*.

Chapter 49

5.12.3   Accumulated impairment amount for debt instruments measured at fair value through other comprehensive income

Rather than presenting expected credit losses on financial assets measured at fair value through other comprehensive income as an allowance, this amount is presented as the 'accumulated impairment amount' in other comprehensive income. This is because financial assets measured at fair value through other comprehensive income are measured at fair value in the statement of financial position and the accumulated impairment amount cannot reduce the carrying amount of these assets (see 5.8 above for further details). *[IFRS 9.4.1.2A, 5.5.2, Appendix A]*.

5.13   Disclosures

The credit risk disclosure requirements are less onerous than were proposed in the 2013 Exposure Draft. Nevertheless, they have been expanded significantly when compared to those currently in IFRS 7 and are supplemented by some detailed implementation guidance. The disclosure requirements in relation to the IFRS 9 expected credit loss model are dealt with in more detail in Chapter 53 at 5.2.3, and this section provides only a high level summary.

The new credit risk disclosure requirements will enable users of financial statements to understand better an entity's credit risk management practices, its credit risk exposures, expected credit losses estimates and changes in credit risks. *[IFRS 7.35B]*. In order to meet this objective, an entity will need to disclose both quantitative and qualitative information that includes the following:

- inputs, assumptions and estimation used (and any changes) to determine significant increases in credit risk of financial instruments, including the application of the low credit risk and more than 30 days past due operational simplifications (see 5.5 above); *[IFRS 7.35F(a), 35G(a)(ii), 35G(c)]*

- inputs, assumptions and techniques used (and any changes) in measuring 12-month and lifetime expected credit losses, including the definition of default and the incorporation of forward-looking information (see 5.4 above); *[IFRS 7.35F(b), 35G(a)(i), 35G(b), 35G(c), B8A]*

- how the financial instruments were grouped if the measurement of expected credit losses was performed on a collective basis (see 5.5.5 above); *[IFRS 7.35F(c)]*

- how collateral and other credit enhancements affect the estimate of expected credit losses, including a description of the nature and quality of collateral held and quantitative information about the collateral for financial assets that are credit-impaired (see 5.4.7 above); *[IFRS 7.35K, B8F, B8G]*

- a reconciliation of the opening and closing balance of the loss allowance and explanations of the changes. This disclosure is required to be shown separately for:

  - financial instruments that are measured using 12-month expected credit losses;

  - those that are measured using lifetime expected credit losses; financial assets that are credit-impaired on initial recognition;

  - those that are subsequently credit-impaired; and

- trade receivables, contract assets and lease receivables measured under the simplified approach; *[IFRS 7.35H]*
- explanation of how significant changes in the gross carrying amount of financial instruments during the period contributed to changes in the loss allowance; *[IFRS 7.35I]*
- inputs, assumptions and techniques used (and any changes) to determine whether a financial asset is credit-impaired (see 5.3.1 and 5.3.3 above); *[IFRS 7.35F(d), 35G(a)(iii), 35G(c)]*
- for modified financial assets (see 5.7 above):
  - the credit risk management practices (how an entity determines that a financial asset that is modified when its loss allowance was measured based on lifetime expected credit losses has improved to the extent that its allowance can now be reduced to 12-month expected credit losses, and how an entity monitors the extent to which such a loss allowance should subsequently be brought back to lifetime expected credit losses);
  - the amortised cost before the modification and the net modification gain or loss recognised during the period for modified financial assets with a loss allowance measured at lifetime expected credit losses;
  - the gross carrying amount of those modified financial assets for which the loss allowance has changed from lifetime to 12-month expected credit losses during the period; and
  - quantitative information that will assist users to understand any subsequent increase in credit risk, including information about modified financial assets for which the loss allowance has reverted from 12-month expected credit losses to lifetime expected credit losses; *[IFRS 7.35F(f), B8B, 35J]*
- the entity's credit risk exposure and significant credit risk concentrations, including the gross carrying amount of financial assets and the exposure to credit risk on loan commitments and financial guarantee contracts, by credit risk rating grades or past due status. This disclosure is required to be shown separately for:
  - those instruments that are measured using 12-month expected credit losses;
  - those that are measured using lifetime expected credit losses;
  - financial assets that are credit-impaired on initial recognition;
  - those that are subsequently credit-impaired; and
  - trade receivables, contract assets and lease receivables measured under the simplified approach; *[IFRS 7.35M, B8H, B8I]* and
- the write-off policy and amounts written off during the period that are still subject to enforcement activity (see 5.12.1.A above). *[IFRS 7.35F(e), 35L]*.

It is critical for entities to align their credit risk management and financial reporting systems and processes, not only to estimate the loss allowance for expected credit losses, but also to produce a sufficient level of detailed information to meet the disclosure requirements in IFRS 7.

In addition, the EDTF will also be developing common expected credit loss disclosure practices (see Chapter 53 at 9.2).

6   EFFECTIVE DATE AND TRANSITION

This section provides a high level summary of the transition issues specific to subsequent measurement. This summary covers only the requirements that are applicable when an entity applies the final version of IFRS 9 (issued in July 2014) and had not applied the earlier versions of IFRS 9. The requirements that are applicable for the earlier versions are not covered in this edition, but are described in earlier editions of this publication.

6.1   Effective date

IFRS 9 is effective for annual periods beginning on or after 1 January 2018. Entities are permitted to apply the standard earlier, although if they do, this fact should be disclosed and all of the requirements (including the classification and measurement, impairment and hedge accounting requirements) in the standard must be applied at the same time. *[IFRS 9.7.1.1]*. However, early application may be subject to approval or endorsement by the local jurisdiction.

Previously, the IASB moved the mandatory effective date of IFRS 9 from annual periods beginning on or after 1 January 2013 to 1 January 2015. Its later decision to defer the mandatory effective date to annual periods beginning on or after 1 January 2018, was intended to allow sufficient time for entities to develop systems and processes and to gather historical data in order to make the calculations.

It is likely that systems and processes will be based on those used for credit risk management and regulatory capital calculations. However, most banks will need, at least in part, to build new systems and processes in order to comply with the standard, while there will need to be a much closer alignment of credit risk management and financial reporting functions than may currently be the case.

Many banks are seeking to run the new processes in parallel with the old during 2017, which means that at the time of this publication they have only another year to complete the design, building and testing of the new systems and processes. An advantage of a 2017 parallel run is that such banks would have a robust basis to be able to communicate the effect of transition to stakeholders, such as shareholders and regulators, in advance of the effective date.

6.2   Transition

IFRS 9 contains a general requirement that it should be applied retrospectively, including the impairment requirements. However, the standard does specify a number of exceptions and reliefs. *[IFRS 9.7.2.1, 7.2.15, 7.2.17]*. These are covered below.

6.2.1   Date of initial application

A number of the transition provisions refer to the 'date of initial application'. This is the beginning of the first reporting period in which the entity adopts IFRS 9, and not the beginning of the first restated comparative period presented. It must be the beginning of a reporting period after the issue of the standard. [IFRS 9.7.2.2].

6.2.2   Restatement of comparatives

Notwithstanding the general requirement to apply the standard retrospectively, perhaps the most important transitional relief is that IFRS 9 does not require restatement of prior periods. Indeed, an entity is permitted to restate prior periods only if it is able to do so without the use of hindsight. [IFRS 9.7.2.15]. The IASB noted that as entities were not required to recognise or disclose expected credit losses for accounting purposes in the past, there was a risk that hindsight would be needed to recognise and measure the amount of expected credit losses in prior periods. [IFRS 9.BC7.75(b)]. This applies to situations where it is impracticable to calculate the period-specific effect or the cumulative effect of the change and hence, it is impossible for entities to objectively distinguish the historical information that is relevant for estimating expected credit losses from the information that would not have been available at that earlier date. [IFRS 9.BC7.74, IAS 8.50-53].

It should be stressed that other IFRS transition requirements, such as the requirement that the business model should be assessed as at the date of initial application and that the application is not retrospective for assets derecognised prior to that date, may mean that comparative information may not, in any case, be very meaningful. To the extent financial assets were held during any prior periods but were sold before the date of initial application, their impairment will be measured under IAS 39 if comparative information is restated.

We are aware that some banks are considering providing pro forma comparative impairment information in their annual report in the year of initial application as if IFRS 9 were applied to all financial assets throughout the comparative period. Such entities will need to make it clear that these do not represent comparative numbers according to IFRS 9.

If an entity is required to provide comparative information for two prior periods (e.g. US Foreign Private Issuers as required by the US Securities Exchange Commission), we believe that the requirement in paragraph 7.2.15 of IFRS 9 does not represent an all-or-nothing option, i.e. if the entity can only restate the latest comparative period without the use of hindsight but would need to use hindsight to restate the earlier comparative period, this does not preclude a restatement only of the latest comparative period. Therefore, the entity could choose to restate the latest comparative period for which the financial information does not involve the use of hindsight, while it would not restate the earlier comparative period for which the use of hindsight would be involved. Such circumstances may arise if the entity has chosen to do a parallel run for impairment only a year before the mandatory application date of IFRS 9, in which case they would be able to restate the latest comparative period without the use of hindsight but may not be able to do so for the earlier period. The same applies to any other information about prior periods, such as historical summaries of financial data. This treatment is consistent with the requirements in IAS 8 where for retrospective application of a new accounting policy, an entity need to only go back to the beginning of the earliest period for which retrospective applicable is practicable. *[IAS 8.24, 25, 26, IFRS 9.BC7.13]*.

When prior periods are not restated, any difference between the previously reported carrying amounts and the new carrying amounts of financial instruments at the beginning of the annual reporting period that includes the date of initial application must be recognised in the opening retained earnings (or other component of equity, as appropriate) of the annual reporting period that includes the date of initial application. However, if an entity restates prior periods, the restated financial statements must reflect all of the requirements in the standard. *[IFRS 9.7.2.15]*. For impairment purposes, the cumulative impairment loss allowance is recognised in the opening retained earnings for all credit exposures.

Where interim financial reports are prepared in accordance with IAS 34 – *Interim Financial Reporting*, the requirements in IFRS 9 need not be applied to interim periods prior to the date of initial application if it is impracticable (as defined in IAS 8). *[IFRS 9.7.2.16]*.

6.2.3   Own credit requirements

The 2013 version of IFRS 9 made the own credit requirements for non-derivative financial liabilities available for early application before the completed version of the standard was issued. These provisions require an entity to present in other comprehensive income the fair value gains and losses attributable to changes in the entity's own credit risk for non-derivative financial liabilities designated as measured at fair value through profit or loss (see 2.1 above). This would mean that, before the mandatory effective date of IFRS 9, entities may elect to change only their accounting policy for own credit risk while continuing to account for their financial instruments in accordance with IAS 39. If an entity elects to apply early only those provisions, it shall disclose that fact and provide on an ongoing basis the related disclosures. *[IFRS 9.7.1.2]*.

6.2.4   Hybrid financial assets measured at fair value through profit or loss

A hybrid financial asset that is measured at fair value through profit or loss in accordance with IFRS 9, may previously have been accounted for as a host financial asset and a separate embedded derivative in accordance with IAS 39. In these circumstances, at the end of each comparative reporting period, the fair value of the hybrid contract is deemed to be the sum of the fair values of the components (i.e. the non-derivative host and the embedded derivative) where the fair value of the hybrid contract had not been determined in those comparative reporting periods. *[IFRS 9.7.2.6]*.

At the date of initial application, any difference between the fair value of the entire hybrid contract at the date of initial application and the sum of the fair values of the components of the hybrid contract at the date of initial application should be recognised in the opening retained earnings (or other component of equity, as appropriate) of the reporting period that includes the date of initial application. *[IFRS 9.7.2.7]*.

6.2.5   Effective interest rate

It may be impracticable to apply retrospectively the effective interest method to a financial asset or financial liability that is measured at amortised cost in accordance with IFRS 9, e.g. if it was previously classified at fair value through profit or loss. In those circumstances, the fair value of the financial asset or financial liability at the end of each comparative period should be treated as the gross carrying amount or the amortised cost amount, respectively. Also, the fair value of the financial asset or financial liability at the date of initial application should be treated as its new gross carrying amount or amortised cost amount, respectively, at that date. *[IFRS 9.7.2.11]*.

6.2.6   Unquoted equity investments

An investment in an unquoted equity instrument (or a derivative that is linked to and must be settled by delivery of such an unquoted equity instrument) might previously have been measured at cost in accordance with IAS 39. In those circumstances the instrument should be measured at fair value at the date of initial application of IFRS 9. Any difference between the previous carrying amount and fair value should be recognised in the opening retained earnings of the reporting period that includes the date of initial application. *[IFRS 9.7.2.12-13]*. This means that that previous periods cannot be restated. The Board explains that this is because as an entity would not have previously determined the fair value of an investment in an unquoted equity instrument and it will not now have the necessary information to determine fair value retrospectively without using hindsight. *[IFRS 9.BC7.15]*.

6.2.7   Initial credit risk and significant increases in credit risk on transition

At the date of initial application, in order to determine the loss allowance that would be recognised under the IFRS 9 impairment requirements, an entity is required to determine whether there has been a significant increase in credit risk since initial recognition, by comparing: *[IFRS 9.7.2.18, B8E]*

- the credit risk at the date that a financial instrument was initially recognised (or for loan commitments and financial guarantee contracts, at the date that the entity became a party to the irrevocable commitment); and

- the credit risk at the date of initial application of IFRS 9.

On transition, the standard allows an entity to *approximate* the credit risk on initial recognition of the financial instrument (or for loan commitments and financial guarantee contracts the date that the entity became a party to the irrevocable commitment), by considering all reasonable and supportable information that is available without undue cost or effort (see 5.4.8.A above). *[IFRS 9.7.2.18, B7.2.2, B8E]*. An entity may consider internal and external information, including information used for collective assessment (see 5.5.5 above) and information about similar products or peer group experience for comparable financial instruments. *[IFRS 9.B7.2.3, B7.2.4]*. When determining whether there have been significant increases in credit risk since initial recognition, an entity is not required to undertake an exhaustive search for information. *[IFRS 9.B7.2.2]*.

Chapter 49

In addition, when determining whether there has been a significant increase in credit risk since initial recognition, an entity may use the low credit risk operational simplification (see 5.5.4.A above) or the more than 30 days past due rebuttable presumption if significant deterioration is assessed solely based on delinquency (see 5.5.4.B above). *[IFRS 9.7.2.19]*. The IASB also noted that an entity can assess the change in the credit risk of a financial instrument on a portfolio basis if the initial credit risk is not determinable for an individual financial instrument (see 5.5.5 above). *[IFRS 9.BC7.81]*.

As with the approximation of effective interest rates (see 5.4.5 above), entities will be faced with the challenge in interpreting how much flexibility is afforded by the term 'to approximate'. Also, it is unclear to what extent entities would need to search for information that is available without undue cost or effort.

If an entity is unable to determine whether there have been significant increases in credit risk since initial recognition without undue cost or effort, then the entity must recognise a loss allowance based on lifetime expected credit losses at each reporting date until the financial instrument is derecognised. However, if at subsequent reporting dates, the entity is able to determine that the financial instrument has low credit risk at the reporting date, then it would recognise a loss allowance based only on 12-month expected credit losses. *[IFRS 9.B7.2.2, 7.2.20]*.

The requirement to recognise lifetime expected credit losses may encourage entities to look for and use information about the initial credit risk and hence, will enhance comparability and the quality of the information provided. On the other hand, some entities may be discouraged to use such information if they are able to absorb lifetime expected credit losses on transition. While such an approach may result in inconsistency between entities, the IASB believes that the transition requirements and reliefs are the best way to balance the provision of useful and relevant information with the associated cost of providing it. *[IFRS 9.BC7.79]*.

References

1 Whilst paragraph 5.7.10 of IFRS 9 could be read as saying that the modification gains or losses should not be recognised in profit or loss, we understand that it was the IASB's intention that they should be recognised in profit or loss. This is clear from reading paragraph 5.7.11 of IFRS 9 in conjunction with paragraph 5.4.3 of IFRS 9, and therefore we view this as drafting error in paragraph 5.7.10 of IFRS 9.

2 *IGC Q&A 73-1.*

3 *IGC Q&A 10-19.*

4 *Implementation of International Accounting Standards,* British Bankers' Association, July 2004, 10.

5 *IGC Q&A 76-1.*

6 Based on the example in IAS 39.B.25.

7 *IFRIC Update,* July 2008.

8 Information for Observers (May 2008 IFRIC meeting), *Application of the Effective Interest Rate Method,* IASB, May 2008, Appendix.

9 Information for Observers, 6.

10 *IFRIC Update*, July 2008.

11 Information for Observers (July 2008 IFRIC meeting), *Application of the Effective Interest Rate Method*, IASB, July 2008, 4.

12 Position Paper, *IAS 39 – Financial Instruments: Recognition and Measurement – assets and liabilities linked to an inflation index which are not measured at fair value (continuation to the paper published in February 2008)*, Israel Accounting Standards Board, August 2008.

13 *IFRIC Update*, May 2009.

14 *IFRIC Update*, July 2008.

15 G20 Declaration on Strengthening the Financial System, April 2009.

16 Report of the Financial Crisis Advisory Group, July 2009.

17 IASB Snapshot: Financial Instruments: Expected Credit Losses Exposure Draft, March 2013.

18 Based on illustration provided by the IASB in *Snapshot: Financial Instruments: Expected Credit Losses Exposure Draft*, p.9, March 2013.

19 IASB Website Announcement. IASB to establish transition resource group for impairment of financial instruments, 23 June 2014 and Transition Resource Group for Impairment of Financial Instruments – Meeting Summary, 22 April 2015.

20 IASB Transition Resource Group for Impairment of Financial Instruments, Meeting Summary, 22 April 2015.

21 Basel Committee on Banking Supervision, *International Convergence of Capital Measurement and Capital Standards*, June 2006 and *Basel III:A global regulatory framework for more resilient banks and banking systems*, June 2011.

22 Regulation (EU) No 575/2013 of the European Parliament and of the Council of 26 June 2013 on prudential requirements for credit institutions and investment firms and amending Regulation (EU) No 648/2012.

23 Transition Resource Group for Impairment of Financial Instruments, Agenda ref 1, *The maximum period to consider when measuring expected credit losses,* 22 April 2015.

24 Q&A 2012/01 IFRS for SMEs General topics: Application of 'undue cost or effort', April 2012, para. 2.

25 Transition Resource Group for Impairment of Financial Instruments, Agenda ref 4, *Forward-looking information*, 16 September 2015.

26 Transition Resource Group for Impairment of Financial Instruments, Agenda ref 1, *Significant increases in credit risk,* 16 September 2015.

27 IASB Agenda paper 5B, Financial Instruments: Impairment, Operational simplifications – 30dpd and low credit risk, 28 October – 1 November 2013.

28 *IFRIC update*, May 2012.

29 Transition Resource Group for Impairment of Financial Instruments, Agenda ref 8, *Measurement of expected credit losses in respect of a modified financial asset*, 22 April 2015.

30 Transition Resource Group for Impairment of Financial Instruments, Agenda ref 3, *Loan Commitments – Scope*, 22 April 2015.

31 Transition Resource Group for Impairment of Financial Instruments, Agenda ref 6, *Measurement of expected credit losses for an issued financial guarantee contract,* 22 April 2015.

32 *Exposure Draft – Financial Instruments: Expected Credit Losses*, March 2013, para. 17.

33 *Exposure Draft – Financial Instruments: Amortised Cost and Impairment*, November 2009, para. B23.

Chapter 49

Chapter 50   Financial instruments: Derecognition

Chapter 50

List of examples

Chapter 50

Chapter 50   Financial instruments: Derecognition

1   INTRODUCTION

This Chapter deals with the question of when financial instruments should be removed ('derecognised') from financial statements. At what point should an item already recognised in financial statements cease to be included? If an entity sells a quoted share in the financial markets, it may cease to be entitled to all the benefits, and exposed to all the risks, inherent in owning that share somewhat earlier than the date on which it ceases to be registered as the legal owner. However, the question of derecognition goes much further than this, as it encroaches on what is commonly referred to as 'off-balance sheet' finance.

1.1   Off-balance sheet finance

In order to understand the rationale for the requirements of IFRS for the derecognition of financial assets and financial liabilities, it is necessary to appreciate the fact that those requirements, and those in equivalent national standards, have their origins in the response by financial regulators to the growing use of off-balance sheet finance from the early 1980s onwards.

'Off-balance sheet' transactions can be difficult to define, and this poses the first problem in discussing the subject. The term implies that certain things belong on the statement of financial position and that those which escape the net are deviations from this norm. The practical effect of off-balance sheet transactions is that the financial statements do not fully present the underlying activities of the reporting entity. This is generally for one of two reasons. The items in question may be included in the statement of financial position but presented 'net' rather than 'gross' – for example, by netting off loans received against the assets they finance. Alternatively, the items might be excluded from the statement of financial position altogether on the basis that they do not represent present assets and liabilities. Examples include operating lease commitments and certain contingent liabilities.

The result in all cases will be that the statement of financial position may suggest less exposure to assets and liabilities than really exists, with a consequential flattering effect on certain ratios, such as the debt/equity ratio and return on assets employed. There is usually an income statement dimension to be considered as well, perhaps because assets taken off-balance sheet purport to have been sold (with a possible profit effect), and also more generally because the presentation of off-balance sheet activity influences the timing or disclosure of associated revenue items. In particular, the presence or absence of items in the statement of financial position usually affects whether the finance cost implicit in a transaction is reported as such or included within another item of income or expense.

Depending on their roles, different people react differently to the term 'off-balance sheet finance'. To some accounting standard setters, or other financial regulators, the expression carries the connotation of devious accounting, intended to mislead the reader of financial statements. Off-balance sheet transactions are those which are designed to allow an entity to avoid reflecting certain aspects of its activities in its financial statements. The term is therefore pejorative and carries the slightly self-righteous inference that those who indulge in such transactions are up to no good and need to be stopped. However, there is also room for a more honourable use of the term 'off-balance sheet finance'. Entities may wish, for sound commercial reasons, to engage in transactions which share with other parties the risks and benefits associated with certain assets and liabilities.

In theory, it should be possible to determine what items belong in the statement of financial position by reference to general principles such as those in the IASB's *Conceptual Framework for Financial Reporting* and similar concepts statements. In practice, however, such principles on their own have not proved adequate to deal with off-balance sheet finance, including routine transactions such as debt factoring and mortgage securitisation.

Accordingly, standard-setters throughout the world, including the IASB, have developed increasingly detailed rules to deal with the issue. This 'anti-avoidance' aspect of the derecognition rules helps to explain why, rather unusually, IFRS considers not only the economic position of the entity at the reporting date, but also prior transactions which gave rise to that position and the reporting entity's motives in undertaking them.

For example, an entity that enters into a forward contract to purchase a specified non-derivative asset for a fixed price will normally recognise that arrangement as a derivative. However, an entity which previously owned the specified non-derivative asset and entered into an identical forward contract at the same time as selling the asset would normally recognise the entire arrangement as a financing transaction. It would leave the (sold) asset on its statement of financial position and recognise a non-derivative liability for the purchase price specified in the forward contract.

The IASB has recently proposed changes to its conceptual framework, including the addition of new guidance addressing derecognition. These proposals are covered in more detail at 7 below.

2   DEVELOPMENT OF IFRS

Under IFRS, many definitions relating to financial instruments are in IAS 32 – *Financial Instruments: Presentation* – while derecognition of financial assets and financial liabilities is currently addressed in IAS 39 – *Financial Instruments: Recognition and Measurement* – or IFRS 9 – *Financial Instruments*.

The provisions of IFRS 10 – *Consolidated Financial Statements* – are also very relevant to certain aspects of the derecognition of financial assets and financial liabilities. IFRS 10 is discussed in Chapter 6, but it is also referred to at various points below.

Whilst IFRS 9 introduces major changes to the way in which financial instruments are reflected in financial statements, its requirements relating to derecognition are substantially the same as those in IAS 39. Disclosure requirements in respect of transfers of financial assets are included in IFRS 7 – *Financial Instruments: Disclosures* – and these are discussed in Chapter 53 at 6.

2.1   Definitions

The following definitions in IAS 32, IAS 39, IFRS 9 and IFRS 13 – *Fair Value Measurement* – are generally relevant to the discussion in this Chapter.

A *financial instrument* is any contract that gives rise to a financial asset of one entity and a financial liability or equity instrument of another entity. *[IAS 32.11].*

A *financial asset* is any asset that is:

(a)   cash;

(b)   an equity instrument of another entity;

(c)   a contractual right:

    (i)   to receive cash or another financial asset from another entity; or

    (ii)   to exchange financial assets or financial liabilities with another entity under conditions that are potentially favourable to the entity; or

(d)   a contract that will or may be settled in the entity's own equity instruments and is:

    (i)   a non-derivative for which the entity is or may be obliged to receive a variable number of the entity's own equity instruments; or

    (ii)   a derivative that will or may be settled other than by the exchange of a fixed amount of cash or another financial asset for a fixed number of the entity's own equity instruments. For this purpose the entity's own equity instruments do not include puttable financial instruments classified as equity ..., instruments that impose on the entity an obligation to deliver to another party a *pro rata* share of the net assets of the entity only on liquidation and are classified as equity ..., or instruments that are themselves contracts for the future receipt or delivery of the entity's own equity instruments. *[IAS 32.11].*

A *financial liability* is any liability that is:

(a)   a contractual obligation:

    (i)   to deliver cash or another financial asset to another entity; or

    (ii)   to exchange financial assets or financial liabilities with another entity under conditions that are potentially unfavourable to the entity; or

(b)   a contract that will or may be settled in the entity's own equity instruments and is:

    (i)   a non-derivative for which the entity is or may be obliged to deliver a variable number of the entity's own equity instruments; or

    (ii)   a derivative that will or may be settled other than by the exchange of a fixed amount of cash or another financial asset for a fixed number of the entity's own equity instruments. For this purpose the entity's own equity instruments do not include puttable financial instruments classified as equity ..., instruments that impose on the entity an obligation to deliver to another party a *pro rata* share of the net assets of the entity only on liquidation and are classified as equity ..., or instruments that are themselves contracts for the future receipt or delivery of the entity's own equity instruments. *[IAS 32.11].*

An *equity instrument* is any contract that evidences a residual interest in the assets of an entity after deducting all of its liabilities. *[IAS 32.11].*

A *derivative* is a financial instrument or other contract within the scope of IAS 39 or IFRS 9 (see Chapter 43 at 2) with all three of the following characteristics:

- its value changes in response to the change in a specified interest rate, financial instrument price, commodity price, foreign exchange rate, index of prices or rates, credit rating or credit index, or other variable, provided in the case of a non-financial variable that the variable is not specific to a party to the contract (sometimes called the 'underlying');

- it requires no initial net investment or an initial net investment that is smaller than would be required for other types of contracts that would be expected to have a similar response to changes in market factors; and

- it is settled at a future date. *[IAS 39.9, IFRS 9 Appendix A].*

Fair value is the price that would be received to sell an asset or paid to transfer a liability in an orderly transaction between market participants at the measurement date. *[IFRS 13.9, Appendix A].*

3 DERECOGNITION – FINANCIAL ASSETS

3.1 Background

The requirements of IAS 39 and IFRS 9 for derecognition of financial assets are primarily designed to deal with the accounting challenges posed by various types of off-balance sheet finance. As a result, the real focus of many of the rules for derecognition of assets is in fact the recognition of liabilities. The starting point for most of the transactions discussed below is that the reporting entity receives cash or other consideration in return for a transfer or 'sale' of all or part of a financial asset. This raises the question of whether such consideration should be treated as sales proceeds or as a liability. IAS 39 and IFRS 9 effectively answer that question by determining whether the financial asset to which the consideration relates should be derecognised (the consideration is treated as sales proceeds and there is a gain or loss on disposal) or should continue to be recognised while the consideration is treated as a liability.

This underlying objective of the derecognition criteria helps to explain why IAS 39 and IFRS 9 consider not only the economic position of the entity at the reporting date, but also prior transactions which gave rise to that position and the reporting entity's motives in undertaking them. For example, if, at a reporting date, an entity has two identical forward contracts for the purchase of a financial asset, the accounting treatment of the contracts may vary significantly if one contract relates to the purchase of an asset previously owned by the entity and the other does not.

This is because the derecognition rules of IAS 39 and IFRS 9 are based on the premise that, if a transfer of an asset leaves the transferor's economic exposure to the transferred asset much as if the transfer had never taken place, the financial statements should represent that the transferor still holds the asset. Thus, if an entity sells (say) a listed bond subject to a forward contract to repurchase the bond from the buyer at a fixed price, IAS 39 and IFRS 9 argue that the entity is exposed to the risks and rewards of that bond as if it had never sold it, but has simply borrowed an amount equivalent to the original sales proceeds secured on the bond. IAS 39 and IFRS 9 therefore conclude that the bond should not be removed from the statement of financial position and the sale proceeds should be accounted for as a liability (in effect the obligation to repurchase the bond under the forward contract – see 4 below).

By contrast, if the entity were to enter into a second identical forward contract over another bond (i.e. one not previously owned by the entity), IAS 39 and IFRS 9 would simply require it to be accounted for as a derivative at fair value (see Chapter 43). This might seem a rather counter-intuitive outcome of a framework that purports to report economically equivalent transactions in a consistent and objective manner. However, the IASB would argue that the two transactions are not economically equivalent: they are distinguished by the fact that, on entering into the forward contract over the originally owned asset, the entity received a separate cash inflow (i.e. the 'sale' proceeds from the counterparty), whereas, on entering into the second contract, it did not. This reinforces the point that the real focus of IAS 39 and IFRS 9 is to determine the appropriate accounting treatment for that cash inflow and not that of the previously owned bond *per se*.

3.2   Decision tree

The provisions of IAS 39 and IFRS 9 concerning the derecognition of financial assets are complex, but are summarised in the flowchart below. *[IAS 39.AG36, IFRS 9.B3.2.1]*. It may be helpful to refer to this while reading the discussion that follows.

It will be seen that the process presupposes that the reporting entity has correctly consolidated all its subsidiaries in accordance with IFRS 10, including any entities identified as consolidated structured entities, often called special purpose entities (SPEs) (see Chapter 6).

Under IFRS, a vehicle (or a structured entity) that, though not meeting a traditional definition of a subsidiary based on ownership of equity, is still controlled by the entity is often referred to as a (consolidated) special purpose entity or SPE. IFRS 10 requires a reporting entity to consolidate another entity, including an SPE, when the reporting entity is exposed, or has rights, to variable returns from its involvement with the investee entity and has the ability to affect those returns through its power over the investee entity (see 3.6 below).

It is clearly highly significant from an accounting perspective that an entity to which a financial asset or liability is transferred is a subsidiary or a consolidated SPE of the transferor. A financial asset (or financial liability) transferred from an entity to its subsidiary or consolidated SPE (on whatever terms) will continue to be recognised in the entity's consolidated financial statements through the normal consolidation procedures set out in IFRS 10. Thus, the requirements discussed at 3.3 to 3.9 below are irrelevant to the treatment, in an entity's consolidated financial statements, of any transfer of a financial asset by the entity to a subsidiary or consolidated SPE. Requiring consolidation of subsidiaries and certain SPEs means that the same derecognition analysis applies whether the entity transfers the financial assets directly to a third party investor or to a subsidiary or consolidated SPE that carries out the transfer.

However, the criteria may be relevant to any onward transfer by the subsidiary or consolidated SPE, and to the transferor's separate financial statements, if prepared (see Chapter 8). Moreover, the criteria may well be relevant to determining whether the transferee is an SPE that should be consolidated. A transfer that leaves the entity, through its links with the transferee, exposed to risks and rewards similar to those arising from its former direct ownership of the transferred asset, may in itself indicate that the transferee is an SPE that should be consolidated.

Figure 50.1: *Derecognition flowchart* *[IAS 39.AG36, IFRS 9.B3.2.1]*

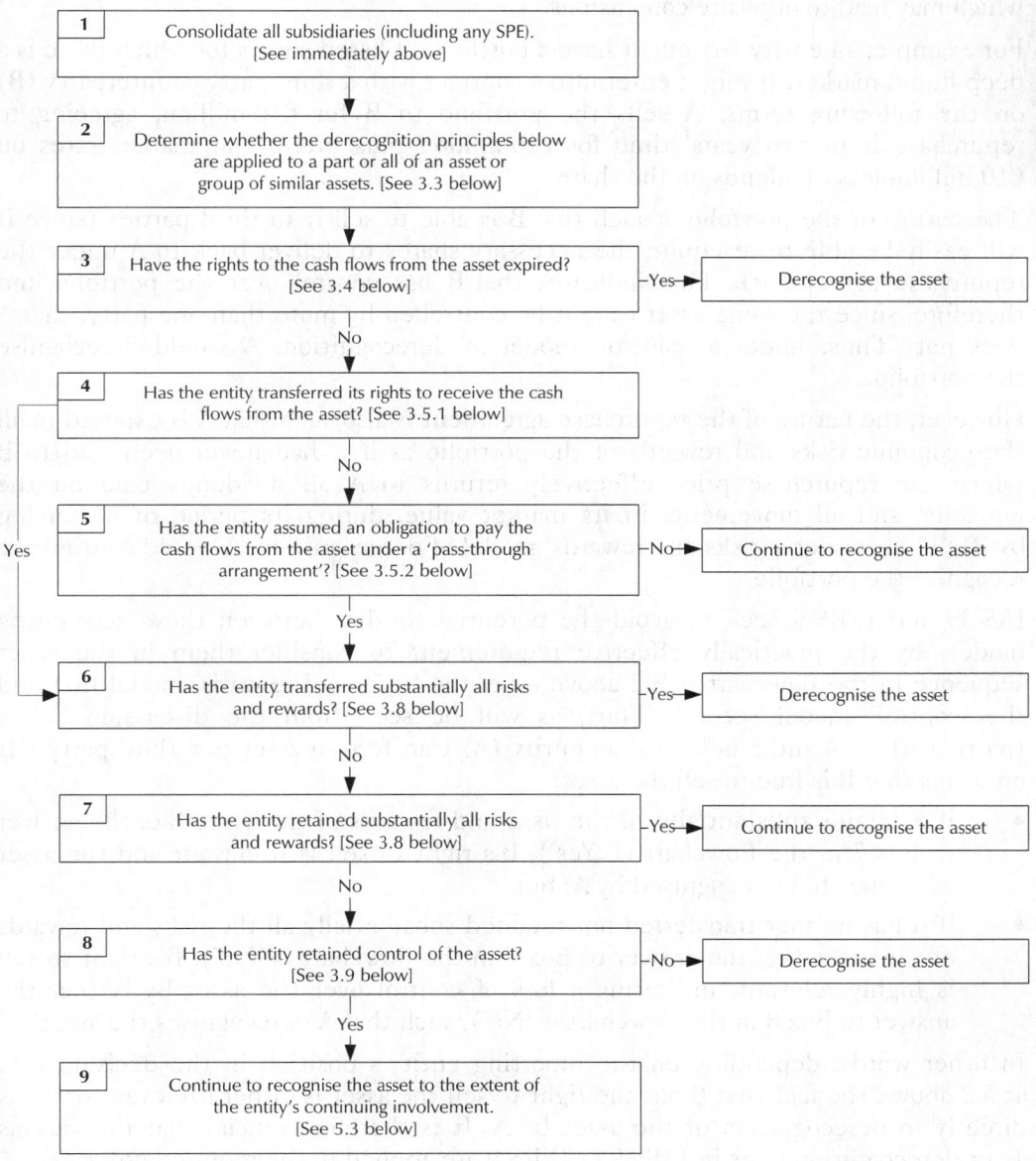

The subsequent steps towards determining whether derecognition is appropriate are discussed below. Some examples of how these criteria might be applied to some common transactions in financial assets are given in 4 below. The accounting consequences of the derecognition of a financial asset are discussed at 5 below.

3.2.1 *Importance of applying tests in sequence*

The derecognition rules in IAS 39 and IFRS 9 are based on several different accounting concepts, in particular a 'risks and rewards' model and a 'control' model, which may lead to opposite conclusions.

For example, an entity (A) might have a portfolio of listed shares for which there is a deep liquid market. It might enter into a contract with a third party counterparty (B) on the following terms. A sells the portfolio to B for €10 million, agreeing to repurchase it in two years' time for €10 million plus interest at market rates on €10 million less dividends on the shares.

The nature of the portfolio is such that B is able to sell it to third parties (since it will easily be able to reacquire the necessary shares to deliver back to A under the repurchase agreement). This indicates that B has control over the portfolio and therefore, since the same asset cannot be controlled by more than one party, that A does not. Thus, under a 'control' model of derecognition, A would derecognise the portfolio.

However, the nature of the repurchase agreement is also such that A is exposed to all the economic risks and rewards of the portfolio as if it had never been sold to B (since the repurchase price effectively returns to A all dividends paid on the portfolio, and all movements in its market value, during its period of ownership by B). Thus, under a 'risks and rewards' model of derecognition, A would continue to recognise the portfolio.

IAS 39 and IFRS 9 seek to avoid the potential conflict between those accounting models by the practically effective requirement to consider them in the strict sequence in the flowchart in 3.2 above – i.e. the 'risks and rewards' model first and the 'control' model second. Thus, as will be seen from the discussion below (particularly at 4 and 5 below) if an entity (A) transfers an asset to a third party (B) on terms that B is free to sell the asset:

- if A retains substantially all the risks and rewards of the asset (i.e. the answer to Box 7 in the flowchart is 'Yes'), B's right to sell is irrelevant and the asset continues to be recognised by A; but

- if A has neither transferred nor retained substantially all the risks and rewards of the asset (i.e. the answer to Box 7 in the flowchart is 'No'), B's right to sell is highly relevant, indicating a loss of control over the asset by A (i.e. the answer to Box 8 in the flowchart is 'No'), such that A derecognises the asset.

In other words, depending on the reporting entity's position in the decision tree at 3.2 above, the fact that B has the right to sell the asset is either irrelevant or leads directly to derecognition of the asset by A. It is therefore crucial that the various asset derecognition tests in IAS 39 or IFRS 9 are applied in the required order.

3.3 Derecognition principles, parts of assets and groups of assets

The discussion in this section relates to Box 2 in the flowchart at 3.2 above.

IAS 39 and IFRS 9 require an entity, before evaluating whether, and to what extent, derecognition is appropriate, to determine whether the provisions discussed at 3.4

and following below should be applied to the whole, or a part only, of a financial asset (or the whole or, a part only, of a group of similar financial assets).

It is important to remember throughout the discussion below that these are criteria for determining at what level the derecognition rules should be applied, not for determining whether the conditions in those rules have been satisfied.

The derecognition provisions must be applied to a part of a financial asset (or a part of a group of similar financial assets) if, and only if, the part being considered for derecognition meets one of the three conditions set out in (a) to (c) below.

(a)   The part comprises only specifically identified cash flows from a financial asset (or a group of similar financial assets).

   For example, if an entity enters into an interest rate strip whereby the counterparty obtains the right to the interest cash flows, but not the principal cash flows, from a debt instrument, the derecognition provisions are applied to the interest cash flows.

(b)   The part comprises only a fully proportionate (*pro rata*) share of the cash flows from a financial asset (or a group of similar financial assets).

   For example, if an entity enters into an arrangement in which the counterparty obtains the rights to 90% of all cash flows of a debt instrument, the derecognition provisions are applied to 90% of those cash flows. The test in this case is whether the reporting entity has retained a 10% proportionate share of the *total* cash flows. If there is more than one counterparty, it is not necessary for each of them to have a proportionate share of the cash flows.

(c)   The part comprises only a fully proportionate (*pro rata*) share of specifically identified cash flows from a financial asset (or a group of similar financial assets).

   For example, if an entity enters into an arrangement whereby the counterparty obtains the rights to a 90% share of interest cash flows from a financial asset, the derecognition provisions are applied to 90% of those interest cash flows. The test is whether the reporting entity has (in this case) retained a 10% proportionate share of the *interest* cash flows. As in (b), if there is more than one counterparty, it is not necessary for each of them to have a proportionate share of the specifically identified cash.

If none of the criteria in (a) to (c) above is met, the derecognition provisions are applied to the financial asset in its entirety (or to the group of similar financial assets in their entirety). For example, if an entity transfers the rights to the first or the last 90% of cash collections from a financial asset (or a group of financial assets), or the rights to 90% of the cash flows from a group of receivables, but provides a guarantee to compensate the buyer for any credit losses up to 8% of the principal amount of the receivables, the derecognition provisions are applied to the financial asset (or a group of similar financial assets) in its entirety. *[IAS 39.16, IFRS 9.3.2.2].*

The various examples above illustrate that the tests in (a) to (c) are to be applied very strictly. It is essential that the entity transfers 100%, or a lower fixed proportion, of a definable cash flow. In the arrangement in the previous paragraph, the transferor provides a guarantee the effect of which is that the transferor may have to return some part of the consideration it has already received. This has the effect that the derecognition provisions must be applied to the asset in its entirety and not just to the proportion of cash flows transferred. If the guarantee had not been given, the arrangement would have satisfied condition (b) above, and the derecognition provisions would have been applied only to the 90% of cash flows transferred.

The criteria above must be applied to the whole, or a part only, of a financial asset or the whole, or a part only, of a group of similar financial assets. This raises the question of what comprises a 'group of similar financial assets' – an issue that has been discussed by the Interpretations Committee and the IASB but without them being able to reach any satisfactory conclusions (see 3.3.2 below).

3.3.1   Credit enhancement through transferor's waiver of right to future cash flows

IAS 39 and IFRS 9 give an illustrative example, the substance of which is reproduced as Example 50.15 at 5.4.4 below, of the accounting treatment of a transaction in which 90% of the cash flows of a portfolio of loans are sold. All cash collections are allocated 90:10 to the transferee and transferor respectively, but subject to any losses on the loans being fully allocated to the transferor until its 10% retained interest in the portfolio is reduced to zero, and only then allocated to the transferee. IAS 39 and IFRS 9 indicate that in this case it is appropriate to apply the derecognition criteria to the 90% sold, rather than the portfolio as whole.

At first sight, this seems inconsistent with the position in the scenario in the penultimate paragraph of 3.3 above, where application of the derecognition criteria to the 90% transferred is precluded by the transferor's having given a guarantee to the transferee. Is not the arrangement in Example 50.15 below (whereby the transferor may have to cede some of its right to receive future cash flows to the transferee) a guarantee in all but name?

Whilst IAS 39 and IFRS 9 do not expand on this explicitly, a possible explanation could be that the two transactions can be distinguished as follows:

(a)   the transaction in Example 50.15 may result in the transferor losing the right to receive a future cash inflow, whereas a guarantee arrangement may give rise to an obligation to return a past cash inflow;

(b)   the transaction in Example 50.15 gives the transferee a greater chance of recovering its full 90% share, but does not guarantee that it will do so. For example, if only 85% of the portfolio is recovered, the transferor is under no obligation to make up the shortfall.

It must be remembered that, at this stage, we are addressing the issue of whether or not the derecognition criteria should be applied to all or part of an asset, not whether derecognition is actually achieved.

In many cases an asset transferred subject to a guarantee by the transferor would not satisfy the derecognition criteria, since the guarantee would mean that the transferor had not transferred substantially all the risks of the asset. For derecognition to be possible, the scope of the guarantee would need to be restricted so that some significant risks are passed to the transferee. However, if the guarantee has been acquired from a third party, there are additional issues to consider that may affect the derecognition of the asset and/or the guarantee (see 3.3.2 below).

3.3.2 Derecognition of groups of financial assets

As described above, the derecognition provisions of IAS 39 and IFRS 9 apply to the whole, or a part only, of a financial asset or a group, or a part of a group, of *similar* financial assets (our emphasis). However, transfers of financial assets, such as debt factoring or securitisations (see 3.6 below), typically involve the transfer of a group of assets (and possibly liabilities) comprising:

- the non-derivative financial assets (i.e. the trade receivables or securitised assets) that are the main focus of the transaction;

- financial instruments taken out by the transferor in order to mitigate the risk of those financial assets. These arrangements may either have already been in place for some time, or they may have been entered into to facilitate the transfer; and

- non-derivative financial guarantee contracts that are transferred with the assets. These are not always recognised separately as financial assets, e.g. mortgage indemnity guarantees which compensate the lending bank if the borrower defaults and there is a deficit when the secured property is sold. Such guarantees may be transferred together with the mortgage assets to which they relate.

Financial instruments transferred with the 'main' assets typically include derivatives such as interest rate and currency swaps. The entity may have entered into such arrangements in order to swap floating rate mortgages to fixed rate, or to change the currency of cash flows receivable from financial assets to match the currency of the borrowings, e.g. sterling into euros.

Both the Interpretations Committee and the IASB have considered whether the reference to transfers of 'similar' assets in IAS 39 (and hence in IFRS 9) is intended to require:

- a single derecognition test for the whole 'package' of transferred non-derivative assets, and any associated financial instruments, as a whole; or

- individual derecognition tests for each type of instrument (e.g. debtor, interest rate swap, guarantee or credit insurance) transferred.

The IASB and Interpretations Committee did not succeed in clarifying the meaning of 'similar assets'. The Interpretations Committee came to a tentative decision but passed the matter to the IASB, together with some related derecognition issues, in particular, the types of transaction that are required to be treated as 'pass through' and the effect of conditions attached to the assets that have been transferred (discussed at 3.5 below). In November 2006 the Interpretations Committee issued a tentative decision not to provide formal guidance, based on the views publicly expressed by the IASB in the *IASB Update* for September 2006. The Interpretations Committee's decision not to proceed was withdrawn in January 2007 on the basis of comment letters received by the Interpretations Committee that demonstrated that the IASB's 'clarification' was, in fact, unworkable and further guidance was required after all. The Interpretations Committee announced this as follows:

> 'In November 2006, the IFRIC published a tentative agenda decision not to provide guidance on a number of issues relating to the derecognition of financial assets. After considering the comment letters received on the tentative agenda decision, the IFRIC concluded that additional guidance is required in this area. The IFRIC therefore decided to withdraw the tentative agenda decision [not to provide further guidance] and add a project on derecognition to its agenda. The IFRIC noted that any Interpretation in this area must have a tightly defined and limited scope, and directed the staff to carry out additional research to establish the questions that such an Interpretation should address.'[1]

The next section describes the Interpretations Committee's and IASB's attempts to establish the meaning of 'similar', which demonstrated the absence of a clear principle. There is bound to be diversity in practice in the light of the failure to provide an interpretation, so it is most important that entities establish an accounting policy that they apply consistently to the derecognition of groups of financial assets.

3.3.2.A   The IASB's view and the Interpretations Committee's tentative conclusions

Although the Interpretations Committee initially tended to the view that the IASB intended a single test to be undertaken,[2] the IASB itself indicated that derivatives transferred together with non-derivative financial assets were not 'similar' to non-derivative financial assets for the purposes of paragraph 16 of IAS 39 (paragraph 3.2.2 of IFRS 9). Therefore, an entity would apply the derecognition tests in IAS 39 or IFRS 9 to non-derivative financial assets (or groups of similar non-derivative financial assets) and derivative financial assets (or groups of similar derivative financial assets) separately, even if they were transferred at the same time.[3] The IASB also indicated that, in order to qualify for derecognition, transferred derivatives that could be assets or liabilities (such as interest rate swaps) would have to meet both the financial asset and the financial liability derecognition tests[4] – see the further discussion of this issue at 6.4 below. Whilst the IASB's published decision referred only to derivatives transferred with the main non-derivative assets, observers of the relevant meeting reported that the IASB also took the view that the derecognition tests must also be applied separately to other financial assets, such as guarantees and credit insurance, transferred with the main assets.

This could have had practical effects on many securitisations as currently structured (see 3.6 below). The interpretation could have made it easier to derecognise certain items (particularly non-derivative assets) than at present. Many derivatives themselves might not meet the appropriate derecognition criteria at all and would continue to be recognised. By contrast, a transaction might achieve a transfer of substantially all the risks and rewards (see Box 6 in Figure 50.1 at 3.2 above, and 3.8 below) of a transferred asset considered separately from any associated derivatives or guarantees, but not if the asset and the associated derivatives or guarantees are considered as a whole. However, the interpretation could well have resulted in far more arrangements falling into the category of 'continuing involvement', where the entity has neither retained nor disposed of substantially all of the risks and rewards of ownership.

Suppose that an entity transfers a fixed rate loan subject to prepayment risk and a credit guarantee, but retains prepayment risk through an amortising interest rate swap, linked to the principal amount of the transferred loan, with the transferee. On the view that the loan and guarantee should be considered for derecognition as a whole, there was no real credit risk prior to the transfer because of the guarantee. The entity was exposed to prepayment risk and the risk of failure by the counterparty to the guarantee. On the assumption that the latter risk could be considered negligible, the only real risk was prepayment risk. Thus, on the view that the loan and guarantee should be considered for derecognition as a whole, they would probably not be derecognised because the entity would retain the only substantial risk (prepayment risk) to which it was exposed before the transfer – i.e. the transaction would fail the test of transferring substantially all risks and rewards in Box 6 in Figure 50.1.

Following the IASB's decision, the implication is that the derecognition criteria would be applied separately to the loan and the guarantee. Considered individually, the loan gives rise to prepayment risk and credit risk. On this analysis, the transfer would leave the entity with only one of the two substantial risks (i.e. prepayment risk, but not credit risk) that it bore previously. This could lead to the conclusion that the entity had neither transferred nor retained substantially all the risks of the loan, and that the loan would therefore be recognised only to the extent of the entity's continuing involvement (in this example, the interest rate swap) – see Box 9 in Figure 50.1 at 3.2 above, and 5.3 below.

This could well lead to more transactions being accounted for as a continuing involvement than previously. This is unfortunate since, as discussed further at 5.3 below, IAS 39 and IFRS 9 give no clear general principles to be applied in accounting for continuing involvements.

3.3.2.B   What are 'similar assets'?

There are a number of different derivative and derivative-like instruments that can be transferred together with a non-derivative, including:

*   hedging instruments that are always assets, e.g. interest rate caps;
*   hedging instruments that are always liabilities, e.g. written options;
*   hedging instruments that may be an asset or liability at any point in time, e.g. interest rate swaps;
*   purchased financial guarantee contracts and credit insurance; and
*   guarantees that are not financial guarantee contracts but are commonly accounted for as derivatives, e.g. mortgage indemnity guarantee contracts.

The IASB's interpretation, repeated in its Exposure Draft – *Derecognition* – referred to at 2 above, would require each of the first three to meet different derecognition treatments. Derivatives that could be financial assets or financial liabilities depending on movements in market value (e.g. interest rate and credit default swaps) would need to meet both the financial asset and financial liability derecognition requirements of IAS 39 or IFRS 9 (even though at any one time they would be either an asset or a liability). The derecognition of liabilities requires *inter alia* legal release by the counterparty (see 6 below). In many securitisations there is no cancellation, novation or discharge of swaps 'transferred' to a structured entity, in which case the transferor would not be able to derecognise the instrument. This would raise issues regarding the treatment of the retained swap, as it does not actually expose the entity to risks and rewards. This is discussed further at 3.6.5 below.

The interpretation raises the difficulty of allocating the single cash flow received from the transferee to the various financial instruments transferred. This is discussed further at 3.5.1 below.

Given the withdrawal of the Interpretations Committee 'non-interpretation', there is no underlying principle that would prevent any of the instruments described above being considered 'similar' to the main non-derivative. Therefore, an entity must establish an accounting policy that it applies consistently to all transactions involving the derecognition of assets, not only to those associated with securitisation arrangements. It must bear in mind that a narrow concept of 'similar', in which instruments are treated as separate assets, may make it easier to derecognise some of them but more likely to have to engage with the problems of continuing involvement and more difficult to achieve pass through (see 3.5.2 below). Regardless of the accounting policy followed, a derivative that involves two-way payments between parties (i.e. the payments are, or could be, from or to either of the parties) should be derecognised only when both the derecognition criteria for a financial asset and the derecognition criteria for a financial liability are met (see 6.4 below).

Once an entity has determined what is 'similar', it must consider the derecognition tests (pass through and transfer of risk and rewards) by reference to the same group of 'similar' assets (see 3.5 below).

3.3.3   *Transfer of asset (or part of asset) for only part of its life*

The examples given in IAS 39 and IFRS 9 implicitly appear to have in mind the transfer of a tranche of cash flows from the date of transfer for the remainder of the life of an instrument. This raises the question of the appropriate accounting treatment where (for example) an entity with a loan receivable repayable in 10 years' time enters into a transaction whereby all the interest flows for the next 5 years only (or those for years 6 to 10) are transferred to a third party. There is no reason why such a transaction could not be considered for partial derecognition.

3.3.4   *'Financial asset' includes whole or part of a financial asset*

In the derecognition provisions in IAS 39 and IFRS 9, as well as the discussion in sections 3 to 5 of this Chapter, the term 'financial asset' is used to refer to either the whole, or a part, of a financial asset (or the whole or a part of a group of similar financial assets). *[IAS 39.16, IFRS 9.3.2.2]*. It is therefore important to remember throughout the following discussion that a reference to an asset being derecognised 'in its entirety' does not necessarily mean that 100% of the asset is derecognised. It may mean, for example, that there has been full derecognition of, say, 80% of the asset to which the derecognition rules have applied separately (in accordance with the criteria above).

3.4   Have the contractual rights to cash flows from the asset expired?

The discussion in this section refers to Box 3 in the flowchart at 3.2 above.

The first step in determining whether derecognition of a financial asset is appropriate is to establish whether the contractual rights to the cash flows from that asset have expired. If they have, the asset is derecognised. Examples might be:

* a loan receivable is repaid;
* the holder of a perpetual debt, whose terms provide for ten annual 'interest' payments that, in effect, provide both interest and a return of capital, receives the final payment of interest; or
* a purchased option expires unexercised.

If the cash flows from the financial asset have not expired, it is derecognised when, and only when, the entity 'transfers' the asset within the specified meaning of the term in IAS 39 and IFRS 9 (see 3.5 below), and the transfer has the effect that the entity has either:

* transferred substantially all the risks and rewards of the asset (see 3.8 below); or
* neither transferred nor retained substantially all the risks and rewards of the asset (see 3.8 below), and has not retained control of the asset (see 3.9 below). *[IAS 39.17, IFRS 9.3.2.3].*

3.4.1   *Renegotiation of the terms of an asset*

It is common for an entity, particularly but not necessarily when in financial difficulties, to approach its major creditors for a restructuring of its debt commitments. The restructuring may involve a modification to the terms of a loan or an exchange of one debt instrument issued by the borrower for another. In these circumstances, IAS 39 contains accounting requirements for the borrower to apply which address whether the restructured debt should be regarded as:

* the continuation of the original liability, with no gain or loss recognised as a consequence of the restructuring; or
* a new financial liability which replaces the original liability that is hence derecognised. In this case the borrower would recognise a gain or loss based on the difference between the fair value of the restructured debt and the carrying amount of the original liability (see 6.2 below).

However, IAS 39 contains no equivalent requirements for the lender.

In practice, different entities have developed their own accounting policies for such arrangements, often based broadly on the guidance for financial liabilities. Nevertheless, IAS 39 is clear that a loss should be recognised on a renegotiated or modified asset that is impaired (see Chapter 48 at 4.2.2). Therefore, it would be inappropriate to maintain the carrying amount of an impaired financial asset (as one might do for a financial liability) to avoid recognising such a loss.[5]

This could be an important accounting policy for banks and other financial institutions if they frequently renegotiate the terms of their loans and receivables and, accordingly, IFRS 7 suggests such policies should be disclosed (see Chapter 53 at 4.1). HSBC includes the following in its financial statements:

Extract 50.1: HSBC Holdings plc (2014)

Notes on the Financial Statements [extract]
1 – Basis of preparation and significant accounting policies [extract]
(k) Impairment of loans and advances and available-for-sale financial assets [extract]
Renegotiated loans [extract]

[...] A loan that is renegotiated is derecognised if the existing agreement is cancelled and a new agreement made on substantially different terms or if the terms of an existing agreement are modified such that the renegotiated loan is substantially a different financial instrument. [...]

The requirements in IFRS 9 for determining when to derecognise financial assets are unchanged from those in IAS 39, but the basis for conclusions does contain some new references to this topic. In particular, it is noted that some modifications of contractual cash flows result in the derecognition of a financial instrument and the recognition of a new instrument, but frequently they do not. *[IFRS 9.BC5.216, BC5.227]*. Those observations are consistent with the discussions above and in the next section. The measurement consequences for financial assets that are classified at amortised cost or debt instrument measured at fair value through other comprehensive income in accordance with IFRS 9 and which are modified but not derecognised are considered in Chapter 49 at 5.7.

3.4.2   Interpretations Committee discussions on asset restructuring in the context of Greek government debt

In February 2012, the Greek government announced the terms of a restructuring of certain of its issued bonds. One aspect involved the exchange of 31.5% of the principal amount of the bonds for twenty new bonds with different maturities and interest rates. The remaining portions of the bonds were either forgiven or exchanged for other securities issued by the European Financial Stability Facility, a special purpose entity established by eurozone states. In addition, for each new bond, the holder received another security issued by the Greek government, payments on which are linked to Greece's gross domestic product.

Soon afterwards, the Interpretations Committee was asked to address the appropriate accounting treatment for certain aspects of the restructuring, which they did initially in May 2012. One question the Committee considered was whether the exchange of 31.5% of the principal amount of the original bonds for new bonds could be regarded as a continuation of that portion of the original asset or whether that portion should also be derecognised (it being widely accepted that the remaining portions of the bonds should be derecognised).

In addressing this question, the Committee made an assumption that it was appropriate to analyse this aspect of the restructuring in isolation even though many individual members expressed the view during their discussions that the restructuring should be analysed as a whole. (The IFRIC was clear that if the analysis considered the restructuring as a whole, the bonds should be derecognised in their entirety.)

The committee first addressed whether the exchange should be regarded as a transfer. They noted that the bonds were transferred back to the issuer rather than to a third party and, as a consequence, concluded this particular restructuring should not be regarded as a transfer (see 3.5.1 below). Instead, it should be evaluated to determine whether it amounted to an actual or in-substance expiry or extinguishment of the original cash flows.

The staff analysis was clear that a modification of terms *can* result in expiry of the asset's original rights to cash flows, although it would not always do so. This is because it is implicit within the requirements for measuring impairment losses that a modification would sometimes be regarded as a continuation of the original, albeit impaired, asset. Therefore an entity would assess the modifications made against the notion of 'expiry' of the rights to the cash flows.[6]

The staff analysis indicated that the 'hierarchy' in IAS 8 – *Accounting Policies, Changes in Accounting Estimates and Errors* – would be applied in developing an appropriate accounting policy. Whilst this requires the application of judgement, it is not an absolute discretion. Consequently, it would be appropriate to analogise, at least to some extent, to those requirements in IAS 39 applying to modifications and exchanges of financial liabilities, particularly the notion of 'substantial modification' and the fact that modifications and exchanges between an existing lender and borrower are seen as equivalent. However, applying the '10% test' to determine whether a modification is substantial would not always be appropriate because of potential inconsistencies with the requirements in IAS 39 for impaired financial assets.[7] For example, IAS 39 envisages some modifications of cash flows that are accounted for as impairment of the original financial asset (for instance, a deferral of the due dates of the original cash flows), *[IAS 39.IG.E.4.3]*, that could well produce a difference in discounted cash flows of greater than 10% (see Chapter 48 at 4.2.2).

The committee did not explicitly conclude on this part of the staff analysis, particularly the question of when it would be appropriate to regard a modification or exchange as the expiry or in-substance extinguishment of the original asset. Instead they simply noted that, in their view, derecognition of the original Greek government bonds would be the appropriate accounting treatment however this particular transaction was assessed, i.e. whether it was viewed as (a) an actual expiry of the rights of the original asset or (b) as a substantial modification that should be accounted for as an extinguishment of the original asset (because of the extensive changes in the assets' terms). An agenda decision setting out the committee's conclusions was published in September 2012.[8]

Whilst that discussion resolved most of the issues associated with the restructuring of Greek government bonds, the wider topic continues to require the application of judgement and, as a result, potentially leads to inconsistent approaches being applied by different entities. In responding to the committee's tentative agenda decision published in May 2012, some important regulators, particularly in Europe, called for the topic to be addressed more comprehensively.[9]

3.4.3   *Novation of contracts to intermediary counterparties*

A change in the terms of a contract may take the legal form of a 'novation'. In this context novation means that the parties to a contract agree to change that contract so that an original counterparty is replaced by a new counterparty.

For example, a derivative between a reporting entity and a bank may be novated to a central counterparty (CCP) as a result of the introduction of new laws or regulations. In these circumstances, the IASB explains that through novation to a CCP the contractual rights to cash flows from the original derivative have expired and as a consequence the novation meets the derecognition criteria for a financial asset. *[IAS 39.BC220A-220F].*

Whilst the IASB reached the above conclusion in relation to novations of over-the-counter derivatives, it is our view that the principle is applicable to all novations of contracts underlying a financial instrument. Accordingly, when a counterparty changes as a result of a novation, the financial instrument should be derecognised and a new financial instrument should be recognised. Although such a change may not be expected to give rise to a significant gain or loss when the financial instrument derecognised and the new financial instrument recognised are both measured at fair value through profit or loss, the bid/ask spread and the effect of change in counterparty on credit risk may cause some value differences. Furthermore, a novation may result in discontinuation of hedge accounting if the original financial instrument was a derivative designated in a hedging relationship (see Chapter 51 at 4.2.3.A and Chapter 52 at 11.3 for further details).

3.4.4   *Write-offs*

When an entity applies IFRS 9, it is required to directly reduce the gross carrying amount of a financial asset when it has no reasonable expectations of recovery. Such a write-off is regarded as the asset being derecognised – effectively it is seen as an in-substance expiry of the associated rights. Write-offs can also relate to a portion of an asset. For example, consider an entity that plans to enforce the collateral on a financial asset and expects to recover no more than 30% of the financial asset from the collateral. If the entity has no reasonable prospects of recovering any further cash flows from the financial asset, it should write off the remaining 70%. *[IFRS 9.5.4.4, B3.2.16(r) and B5.4.9].*

3.5 Has the entity 'transferred' the asset?

An entity is regarded by IAS 39 and IFRS 9 as 'transferring' a financial asset if, and only if, it either:

(a) transfers the contractual rights to receive the cash flows of the financial asset (see 3.5.1 below); or

(b) retains the contractual rights to receive the cash flows of the financial asset, but assumes a contractual obligation to pay the cash flows on to one or more recipients in an arrangement that meets the conditions in 3.5.2 below *[IAS 39.18, IFRS 9.3.2.4]* (a so-called 'pass-through arrangement').

This might be the case where the entity is a special purpose entity or trust, and issues to investors beneficial interests in financial assets that it owns and provides servicing of those assets. *[IAS 39.AG37, IFRS 9.B3.2.2].*

These conditions are highly significant for securitisations and similar transactions that fall within (b) because the entity retains the contractual right to receive cash.

3.5.1 Transfers of contractual rights to receive cash flows

The discussion in this section refers to Box 4 in the flowchart at 3.2 above.

IAS 39 and IFRS 9 do not define what they mean by the phrase 'transfers the contractual rights to receive the cash flows of the financial asset' in (a) in 3.5 above, possibly on the assumption that this is self-evident. However, this is far from the case, since the phrase raises a number of questions of interpretation.

There are two key uncertainties about the meaning of 'transferring the contractual rights' (which in turn determines whether a transaction falls within (a) or (b) in 3.5 above):

- whether it is restricted to transfers of legal title only or also encompasses transfers of equitable title or an equitable interest (see 3.5.1.A below); and

- the effect of conditions attached to the transfers (see 3.5.1.B below).

While both of these are of great significance to securitisations (see 3.6 below), they also have implications for other transactions. These issues were discussed in 2006 by both the Interpretations Committee and the IASB. However, as described at 3.3.2 above, the Interpretations Committee's tentative decision not to issue further guidance and the interpretation of the issues that had so far been published were both withdrawn in January 2007. There is no clear evidence that practice has changed as a result of the views that had been expressed by the IASB and the Interpretations Committee but, as this has demonstrated a lack of clear underlying principles, it would be no surprise to find that entities have different interpretations of the requirements.

In the context of the restructuring of Greek government bonds (see 3.4.2 above), the Interpretations Committee considered whether an exchange of debt instruments between a borrower and a lender should be regarded as a transfer. It was noted that the bonds were transferred back to the issuer rather than to a third party and, as a consequence, it was agreed that this particular restructuring should not be regarded as a transfer.[10] However, it was noted during the committee's discussion and in the comment process that applying such a conclusion more widely might not always be appropriate, e.g. in the case of a short-term sale and repurchase agreement over a bond with the bond issuer or the simple repurchase of a bond by the issuer for cash.

3.5.1.A   Meaning of 'transfers the contractual rights to receive the cash flows'

In many jurisdictions, the law recognises two types of title to property: (a) legal title; and (b) 'equitable', or beneficial title. In general, legal title defines who owns an asset at law and equitable title defines who is recognised as entitled to the benefit of the asset. Transfers of legal title give the transferee the ability to bring an action against a debtor to recover the debt in its own name. In equitable transfers, however, the transferee joins the transferor in an action to sue the debtor for recovery of debt. As noted above, the issue here is whether 'transfers of contractual rights' are limited to transfers of legal title.

We have commented in previous editions of this book that the requirement to transfer 'the *contractual* rights to receive cash flows' suggests that transfer must have the effect that the transferee has a direct legal claim on those cash flows. Under this interpretation, if a corporate entity securitises the future cash flows from a portfolio of trade receivables it has arguably 'transferred' them for the purposes of IAS 39 or IFRS 9 if, and only if, the finance provider could, directly and in its own name, sue the debtor for default (see 3.6 below). In many jurisdictions, this would simply not be possible without either:

- a tri-partite agreement between the corporate entity, the finance provider and the debtor; or

- a clause in the standard terms of trade allowing such a transfer at the sole discretion of the corporate entity without the express consent of the debtor, so that transfer can be effected by a subsequent bi-partite agreement between the corporate entity and the finance provider.

The consent of the debtor is not normally obtained, or indeed practically obtainable, in many securitisations and similar transactions. In these arrangements, all cash flows that are collected are contractually payable to a new eventual recipient – i.e. the debtor continues to pay the transferor, while the transferor loses the right to retain any cash collected from the debtor without actually transferring the contract itself.

In March 2006 the Interpretations Committee began to consider whether there can be a transfer of the contractual right to receive cash flows in an equitable transfer.[11] The Interpretations Committee had already concluded, in November 2005, that retaining servicing rights (i.e. continuing to administer collections and distributions of cash as agent for the transferee) does not in itself preclude derecognition.[12] However, the Interpretations Committee then considered whether retention by the transferor of the contractual right to receive the cash from debtors for distribution on to other parties (as must inevitably happen if debtors are not notified) means that such a transaction does not meet test (a) in 3.5 above, and thus must meet test (b) (pass-through) in order to achieve derecognition. The Interpretations Committee referred this issue to the IASB, which indicated in September 2006 that:

> 'a transaction in which an entity transfers all the contractual rights to receive the cash flows (without necessarily transferring legal ownership of the financial asset), would not be treated as a pass-through. An example might be a situation in which an entity transfers all the legal rights to specifically identified cash flows of a financial asset (for example, a transfer of the interest or principal of a debt instrument). Conversely, the pass-through test would be applicable when the entity does not transfer all the contractual rights to cash flows of the financial asset, such as disproportionate transfers.'[13] (Disproportionate transfers are discussed at 3.3 above).

The statement that such a transaction 'would not be treated as a pass-through' means (in terms of the flowchart in Figure 50.1 at 3.2 above) that the answer to Box 4 is 'Yes', such that the pass-through test in Box 5 (see 3.5.2 below) is by-passed.

The IASB's conclusion appears to concede that the reference in IAS 39 (and hence in IFRS 9) to a transfer of the 'contractual' right to cash flows was intended to include an *equitable* transfer of those rights, a conclusion that the IASB repeated in its April 2009 Exposure Draft – *Derecognition.*

The IASB commented that 'the pass-through test would be applicable when the entity does not transfer all the contractual rights to cash flows of the financial asset, such as disproportionate transfers'.

For example, if an entity transfers the rights to 90% of the cash flows from a group of receivables but provides a guarantee to compensate the buyer for any credit losses up to 8% of the principal amount of the receivables, the derecognition provisions are applied to the group of financial assets in its entirety. *[IAS 39.16(b), IFRS 9.3.2.2(b)].* This means that the answer to Box 4 in the flowchart will be 'No' (since some, not all, of the cash flows of the entire group of assets have been transferred), thus requiring the pass-through test in Box 5 to be applied. In contrast, the pass-through test would not need to be applied where the entity transfers the contractual right to receive 100% of the cash flows even if it guarantees losses up to a certain percentage of the principal.

It is hard to see the circumstances in which the pass-through test would ever be successfully applied to a disproportionate transfer. Accordingly, this view from the IASB would, in effect, disqualify virtually all disproportionate transfers from derecognition.

The IASB's interpretation gives no answer to an even more critical question. If the derecognition rules need to be applied separately to loans and derivatives or guarantees, how does this affect:

- the definition of a 'transfer' (if all the cash flows are transferred); or

- the application of the pass-through test (if the transfer is of a disproportionate share of the cash flow)?

Before this re-examination by the IASB of the meaning of 'transfer', it was common in some jurisdictions to apply the legal title test to transfers of financial assets to a

SPE in securitisation arrangements, rather than relying on an equitable transfer. After the withdrawal of the 'non-interpretation' (see 3.3.2 above), it is likely that those entities have continued to apply their previous practice. However the discussions have, yet again, highlighted the uncertainty at the heart of the derecognition rules in IAS 39 and IFRS 9 which means that there must be different treatments in practice. Until there is a conclusive interpretation, entities must establish an accounting policy that they apply consistently to all such transactions, whether they are transfers or pass-throughs.

The implications of the IASB's discussion on securitisation transactions are discussed further at 3.6.5 below.

3.5.1.B   Transfers subject to conditions

An entity may transfer contractual rights to cash flows but subject to conditions. The Interpretations Committee identified the following main types of condition:

- *Conditions relating to the existence and legal status of the asset at the time of the transfer*

  These include normal warranties as to the condition of the asset at the date of transfer and other guarantees affecting the existence and accuracy of the amount of the receivable that may not be known until after the date of transfer.

- *Conditions relating to the performance of the asset after the time of transfer*

  These include guarantees covering future default, late payment or changes in credit risk, guarantees relating to changes in tax, legal or regulatory requirements, where the buyer may be able to require additional payments if it is disadvantaged or – in some cases – demand reversal of the transaction, or guarantees covering future performance by the seller that might affect the recoverable amount of the debtor.

- *Offset arrangements*

  The original debtor may have the right to offset amounts against balances owed to the transferor for which the transferor will compensate the transferee. There may also be tripartite offset arrangements where a party other than the original debtor (e.g. a subcontractor) has such offset rights.[14]

All securitisations (and indeed, most derecognitions, whether of financial or non-financial assets) include express or implied warranties regarding the condition of the asset at the date of transfer. In the case of a securitisation of credit card receivables, these might include a representation that, for example, all the debtors transferred are resident in a particular jurisdiction, or have never been in arrears for more than one month in the previous two years. In our view, such warranties should not affect whether or not the transaction achieves derecognition.

It is a different matter when it comes to guarantees of post-transfer performance. In particular, one of the issues identified by the Interpretations Committee – guarantees covering future default, late payment or changes in credit risk – links to the related debate regarding the transfer of groups of financial assets where the guarantees may have been provided by a third party (see 3.3.2 above).

In July 2006 the Interpretations Committee decided to refer this issue to the IASB, which considered it at its September 2006 meeting. The IASB broadly confirmed our view as set out above. In its view neither conditions relating to the existence and value of transferred cash flows at the date of transfer nor conditions relating to the future performance of the asset would affect whether the entity has transferred the contractual rights to receive cash flows[15] (i.e. Box 4 in Figure 50.1 at 3.2 above). In other words, a transaction with such conditions that otherwise met the criteria in Box 4 would not be subject to the pass-through test in Box 5.

However, the existence of conditions relating to the future performance of the asset might affect the conclusion related to the transfer of risks and rewards (i.e. Box 6 in Figure 50.1 at 3.2 above) as well as the extent of any continuing involvement by the transferor in the transferred asset (i.e. Box 9 in Figure 50.1 at 3.2. above).[16]

These interpretations were also withdrawn by the Interpretations Committee in January 2007 together with the views that had been expressed regarding 'similar' assets and transfers of assets (see 3.3.2 above). Although the IASB repeated them in the April 2009 Exposure Draft – *Derecognition* – an entity must take a view that is consistent with its policies on these matters and, as in these other cases, hold this view consistently when considering the derecognition of any financial asset.

An example of a two-party offset arrangement is when the original debtor (e.g. a borrower or customer) has the right to offset amounts it is owed by the transferor (e.g. balances in a deposit account or arising from a credit note issued by the transferor) against the transferred asset. If such a right is exercised after the asset is transferred the transferor would be required to compensate the transferee. This would not, in our view, normally affect whether the entity has transferred the contractual rights to receive the cash flows of the original financial asset. Payments made by the transferor to the transferee as a result of the right of offset being exercised simply transfer to the transferee the value the transferor obtained when its liability to the original debtor was settled.

3.5.2 Retention of rights to receive cash flows subject to obligation to pay over to others (pass-through arrangement)

The discussion in this section refers to Box 5 in the flowchart at 3.2 above.

It is common in certain securitisation and debt sub-participation transactions (see 3.6 below) for an entity to enter into an arrangement whereby it continues to collect cash receipts from a financial asset (or more typically a pool of financial assets), but is obliged to pass on those receipts to a third party that has provided finance in connection with the financial asset. Whilst the term 'pass-through' for these arrangements does not actually appear in IAS 39 or IFRS 9 it has become part of the language of the financial markets.

Under IAS 39 and IFRS 9, an arrangement whereby the reporting entity retains the contractual rights to receive the cash flows of a financial asset (the 'original asset'), but assumes a contractual obligation to pay the cash flows to one or more recipients (the 'eventual recipients') is regarded as a transfer of the original asset if, and only if, all of the following three conditions are met:

(a)   the entity has no obligation to pay amounts to the eventual recipients unless it collects equivalent amounts from the original asset. Short-term advances by the entity with the right of full recovery of the amount lent plus accrued interest at market rates do not violate this condition (see 3.6.1 and 3.6.2 below);

(b)   the entity is prohibited by the terms of the transfer contract from selling or pledging the original asset other than as security to the eventual recipients for the obligation to pay them cash flows; and

(c)   the entity has an obligation to remit any cash flows it collects on behalf of the eventual recipients without material delay. In addition, the entity is not entitled to reinvest such cash flows, except in cash or cash equivalents as defined in IAS 7 – *Statement of Cash Flows* (see Chapter 37 at 3) during the short settlement period from the collection date to the date of required remittance to the eventual recipients, with any interest earned on such investments being passed to the eventual recipients. *[IAS 39.19, IFRS 9.3.2.5].*

These conditions are discussed further at 3.6.4 below.

IAS 39 and IFRS 9 note that an entity that is required to consider the impact of these conditions on a transaction is likely to be either:

•   the originator of the financial asset in a securitisation transaction (see 3.6 below); or

•   a group that includes a consolidated special purpose entity that has acquired the financial asset and passes on cash flows to unrelated third party investors. *[IAS 39.AG38, IFRS 9.B3.2.3].*

3.6   Securitisations

Securitisation is a process whereby finance can be raised from external investors by enabling them to invest in parcels of specific financial assets. The first main type of assets to be securitised was domestic mortgage loans, but the technique is regularly extended to other assets, such as credit card receivables, other consumer loans, or lease receivables. Securitisations are a complex area of financial reporting beyond the scope of a general text such as this to discuss in detail. However, it may assist understanding of the IASB's thinking to consider a 'generic' example of such a transaction.

A typical securitisation transaction involving a portfolio of mortgage loans would operate as follows. The entity which has initially advanced the loans in question (the 'originator') will sell them to another entity set up for the purpose (the 'issuer'). The issuer will typically be a subsidiary or consolidated SPE of the originator (and therefore consolidated – see 3.2 above) and its equity share capital, which will be small, will often be owned by a trustee on behalf of a charitable trust. The issuer will finance its purchase of these loans by issuing loan notes on interest terms which will be related to the rate of interest receivable on the mortgages and to achieve this it may need to enter into derivative instruments such as interest rate swaps. The swap counterparty may be the originator or a third party. The originator will continue to administer the loans as before, for which it will receive a service fee from the issuer.

The structure might therefore be as shown in this diagram:

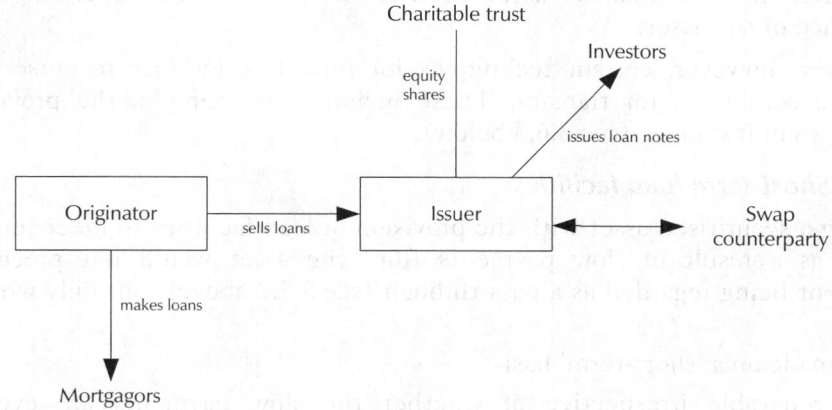

Potential investors in the mortgage-backed loan notes will want to be assured that their investment is relatively risk-free and the issue will normally be supported by obtaining a high rating from a credit rating agency. This may be achieved by using a range of credit enhancement techniques which will add to the security already inherent in the quality of the mortgage portfolio. Such techniques can include the following:

- limited recourse to the originator in the event that the income from the mortgages falls short of the interest payable to the investors under the loan notes and other expenses. This may be made available in a number of ways; for example, by the provision of subordinated loan finance from the originator to the issuer; by the deferral of part of the consideration for the sale of the mortgages; or by the provision of a guarantee (see 3.6.1 below);

- the provision of loan facilities to meet temporary shortfalls as a result of slow payments of mortgage interest (see 3.6.2 below); or

- insurance against default on the mortgages (see 3.6.3 below).

The overall effect of the arrangement is that outside investors have been brought in to finance a particular portion of the originator's activities. These investors have first call on the income from the mortgages which back their investment. The originator is left with only the residual interest in the differential between the rates paid on the notes and earned on the mortgages, net of expenses; generally, this profit element is extracted by adjustments to the service fee or through the mechanism of interest rate swaps. It has thus limited its upside interest in the mortgages, while its remaining downside risk on the whole arrangement will depend on the extent to which it has assumed obligations under the credit enhancement measures.

3.6.1   *Recourse to originator*

The conditions in 3.5.2 above clearly have the effect that an arrangement that does not transfer the contractual rights to receive the cash flows but provides for direct recourse to the originator does not meet the definition of a 'transfer' for the purposes of pass-through and therefore does not qualify to be considered for derecognition. Direct recourse would include an arrangement whereby part of the consideration for the financial asset transferred was deferred depending on the performance of the asset.

In our view, however, certain techniques for providing indirect recourse do not breach the conditions for transfer. These include, for example, the provision of certain types of insurance (see 3.6.3 below).

3.6.2   Short-term loan facilities

Enhancing a securitised asset with the provision of loan facilities to meet temporary shortfalls as a result of slow payments from the asset would not preclude an arrangement being regarded as a pass-through (see 3.5.2 above), but only where the loans:

*   are made on a 'short-term' basis;
*   are repayable irrespective of whether the slow payments are eventually received; and
*   bear interest at market rates.

The purpose of these restrictions is to ensure that IAS 39 and IFRS 9 allow derecognition of assets subject to such facilities only where the facilities are providing a short-term cash flow benefit to the investor, and not when they effectively transfer slow payment risk back to the originator (as would be the case if the originator made significant interest-free loans to the investor). Clearly, therefore, the circumstances in which such funds can be advanced must be very tightly defined if pass-through is to be achieved.

3.6.3   Insurance protection

The conditions for 'transfer' are not, in our view, breached by the originator purchasing an insurance contract for the benefit of investors in the event of a shortfall in cash collections from the securitised assets, provided that the investors' only recourse is to the insurance policy. In other words, the originator cannot give a guarantee to investors to make good any shortfalls should the insurer become insolvent, nor can the originator provide any support to the insurer through a guarantee arrangement or a reinsurance contract.

The implications of the derecognition and pass-through requirements of IAS 39 (and hence of IFRS 9) for transfers of groups of financial assets including insurance contracts have been reconsidered by the Interpretations Committee and the IASB but their tentative conclusions were withdrawn. For a discussion of the issues and the alternative interpretations of 'similar' assets, see 3.3.2 above.

3.6.4   Treatment of collection proceeds

Securitisation contracts rarely require any amount received on the securitised assets to be immediately transferred to investors. This is for the obvious practical reason that it would be administratively inefficient, in the case of a securitisation of credit card receivables for example, to transfer the relevant portion of each individual, and relatively small, cash flow received from the hundreds, if not thousands, of cards in the portfolio. Instead, it is usual for transfers to be made in bulk on a periodic basis (e.g. weekly or monthly). This raises the question of what happens to the cash in the period between receipt by the issuer and onward transfer to the investors.

IAS 39 and IFRS 9 require cash flows from transferred financial assets for which derecognition is sought to be:

- passed to the eventual recipients 'without material delay'; and
- invested only in cash or cash equivalents as defined in IAS 7 entirely for the benefit of the investors (see condition (c) in 3.5.2 above).

These requirements mean that many securitisation arrangements may well fail to satisfy the pass-through test in 3.5.2 above, as explained below.

Suppose that a credit card issuer wishes to raise five year finance secured on its portfolio of credit card receivables. The assets concerned are essentially short term (being in most cases settled in full within four to eight weeks), whereas the term of the borrowings secured on them is longer. In practice, what generally happens is that, at the start of the securitisation, a 'pool' of balances is transferred to the issuer. The cash receipts from that 'pool' are used to pay interest on the borrowings, and to fund new advances on cards in the 'pool' or to purchase other balances. Such an arrangement, commonly referred to as a 'revolving' structure, appears to breach the requirement of the pass-through tests to:

- pass on cash receipts without material delay (since only the amount of cash receipts necessary to pay the interest on the borrowings is passed on, with the balance being reinvested until the principal of the borrowings falls due); and
- only invest in cash or cash equivalents as defined in IAS 7 in the period prior to passing them onto the investor. This is because the cash not required to pay interest on the borrowings is invested in further credit card receivables, which are not cash or cash equivalents as defined in IAS 7.

The Interpretations Committee confirmed in November 2005 that 'revolving' structures do not meet the requirements of the pass-through test for funds to be passed on without material delay and to be invested only in cash and cash equivalents.[17]

In practice, we have observed the pass-through tests are applied very strictly such that any arrangement that provides for even a small tranche of the interest from such short-term deposits to be retained by or for the benefit of the originator will not satisfy the criteria for transfer under IAS 39 or IFRS 9. Moreover, IAS 39 and IFRS 9 require that the reporting entity 'is not entitled' to invest the cash other than in cash or cash equivalents as described above. Thus, it appears that the criteria for transfer are not satisfied merely where the entity does not in fact invest the cash in any other way – it must be contractually prohibited from doing so. In practice, this is often achieved by having the funds paid into a trustee bank account that can be used only for the benefit of the providers of finance.

The IASB does not expand further on the term 'without material delay'. It is not, in our view, intended to require settlement to noteholders on an unrealistically frequent basis such as daily, although we would normally expect payments to be made by the next quarterly coupon payment date to meet this condition.

The strict requirements of IAS 39 and IFRS 9 in respect of cash received from assets subject to a pass-through arrangement raise the related, but broader, issue of the appropriate treatment of client money which is discussed at 3.7 below.

3.6.5   Transfers of non-optional derivatives along with a group of financial assets

As discussed at 3.3.2. above, interest rate swaps that are transferred along with a group of non-derivative financial assets may be derecognised only when any associated obligation is discharged, cancelled or expires (see 6 below). This, however, does not occur in most securitisations.

In a securitisation transaction involving the equitable transfer of an interest rate swap to an SPE, the swap would continue to be recognised by the transferor. The ongoing accounting consequences of this are less clear. The swap must clearly continue to be measured at fair value through profit or loss in accordance with the general requirement of IAS 39 or IFRS 9 for the measurement of derivatives not in a hedging relationship (see Chapter 43). However, this would have the effect that the reporting entity reflected gains and losses in the income statement for a derivative in which it no longer has a beneficial interest. In such a case, the entity should presumably recognise the notional back-to-back swap which it has effectively entered into with the transferee, so as to offset the income statement effect of the original swap.

3.6.6   'Empty' subsidiaries or SPEs

If an entity enters into a transaction whereby:

- the entity transfers an asset to a subsidiary or SPE; and
- the subsidiary or SPE transfers the asset to noteholders on terms that satisfy the pass-through derecognition criteria in IAS 39 or IFRS 9 discussed at 3.5.2 and 3.6 above,

the overall effect will be that the individual financial statements of the subsidiary or SPE will include neither the transferred asset nor the finance raised from noteholders. This may well mean that the financial statements show nothing apart from the relatively small amount of equity of the entity and any related assets. This analysis is likely to be applicable only for relatively simple transfers, and not, for example, when derivatives are transferred along with the non-derivative assets.

3.7   Client money

A number of financial institutions and other entities hold money on behalf of clients. The terms on which such money is held can vary widely. In the case of normal deposits with a bank, the bank is free to use the client's money for its own purposes, with the client being protected by the capital requirements imposed by the regulatory authorities. By contrast there are cases (e.g. in the case of certain monies held by legal advisers on behalf of their clients in some jurisdictions) where funds held on behalf of clients must be kept in a bank account completely separate from that of the depositary entity itself, with all interest earned on the account being for the benefit of clients. There are also intermediate situations where, for example:

- funds are required to be segregated in separate bank accounts but the depositary entity is allowed to retain some or all of the interest on the client accounts; or

- client funds are allowed to be commingled with those of the depositary entity, but some or all income on the funds must be passed on to clients.

This raises the question of how client monies should be accounted for in the financial statements under IFRS. In particular, whether the assets should be recognised in the first place, and if so whether, in the absence of specific guidance, the rules for the treatment of funds received under a pass-through arrangement (see 3.6.4 above) should be applied.

The types of arrangement to deal with client money are so varied that it is impossible to generalise as to the appropriate treatment. Key considerations include:

- which party is at risk from the failure of assets, such as bank accounts, in which the client money is held;

- the status of the funds in the event of the insolvency of either the reporting entity or its client;

- whether the reporting entity can use the cash for its own purposes as opposed to administering the cash on behalf of the client in its capacity as an agent; and

- which party has the benefit of income from the assets.

The analysis for the two extreme cases seems relatively straightforward. In the case of a bank deposit (or any arrangement where the entity may freely use client cash for its own benefit), the general recognition criteria of IAS 39 and IFRS 9 indicate that an asset and a liability should be recognised. Conversely, where the entity is required to hold funds held on behalf of clients in a bank account completely separate from that of the entity itself, with all interest earned on the account being for the benefit of clients, it is hard to see how such funds meet the general definition of an asset under the *Conceptual Framework for Financial Reporting*. Whilst the entity administers such funds in its capacity as an agent on behalf of the client, it can derive no economic benefits from them. The intermediate cases may be harder to deal with.

Sometimes the appropriate analysis will be that the depositary entity enjoys sufficient use of the client money that it should be recognised as an asset with a corresponding liability due to the client. This will be the case, for example, if the client money is commingled with the reporting entity's cash for a short period of time. During this period the reporting entity is exposed to the credit risk associated with the cash and is entitled to all income accruing. Hence, the reporting entity would recognise the cash as an asset and a corresponding liability. If the cash is later moved to a segregated client trust account, an analysis should be performed to determine whether or not the cash and the corresponding liability should be removed from the reporting entity's statement of financial position.

3.8   Has the entity transferred or retained substantially all the risks and rewards of ownership?

The discussion in this section refers to Boxes 6 and 7 in the flowchart at 3.2 above.

Once an entity has established that it has transferred a financial asset (see 3.5 above), IAS 39 and IFRS 9 then require it to evaluate the extent to which it retains the risks and rewards of ownership of the financial asset. *[IAS 39.20, IFRS 9.3.2.6]*.

If the entity transfers substantially all the risks and rewards of ownership of the financial asset, the entity must derecognise the financial asset and recognise separately as assets or liabilities any rights and obligations created or retained in the transfer. *[IAS 39.20(a), IFRS 9.3.2.6(a)]*. Examples of such transactions are given at 3.8.1 and 4.1. If an entity determines that, as a result of the transfer, it has transferred substantially all the risks and rewards of ownership of the transferred asset, it does not recognise the transferred asset again in a future period, unless it reacquires the transferred asset in a new transaction. *[IAS 39.AG41, IFRS 9.B3.2.6]*.

If the entity retains substantially all the risks and rewards of ownership of the financial asset, the entity continues to recognise the financial asset. *[IAS 39.20(b), IFRS 9.3.2.6(b)]*. Examples of such transactions are given at 3.8.2, 4.1 and 4.3 below.

If the entity neither transfers nor retains substantially all the risks and rewards of ownership of the financial asset (see 3.8.3 below), the entity determines whether it has retained control of the financial asset *[IAS 39.20(c), IFRS 9.3.2.6(c)]* (see 3.9 below).

IAS 39 and IFRS 9 clarify that the transfer of risks and rewards should be evaluated by comparing the entity's exposure, before and after the transfer, to the variability in the amounts and timing of the net cash flows of the transferred asset. *[IAS 39.21, IFRS 9.3.2.7]*. Often it will be obvious whether the entity has transferred or retained substantially all risks and rewards of ownership. In other cases, it will be necessary to determine this by computing and comparing the entity's exposure to the variability in the present value (discounted at an appropriate current market interest rate) of the future net cash flows before and after the transfer. All reasonably possible variability in net cash flows is considered, with greater weight being given to those outcomes that are more likely to occur. *[IAS 39.22, IFRS 9.3.2.8]*.

3.8.1   *Transfers resulting in transfer of substantially all risks and rewards*

An entity has transferred substantially all the risks and rewards of ownership of a financial asset if its exposure to the variability in the amounts and timing of the net cash flows of the transferred asset is no longer significant in relation to the total such variability. IAS 39 and IFRS 9 give the following examples of transactions that transfer substantially all the risks and rewards of ownership:

- an unconditional sale of a financial asset;

- a sale of a financial asset together with an option to repurchase the financial asset at its fair value at the time of repurchase (since this does not expose the entity to any risk of loss or give any opportunity for profit);

- a sale of a financial asset together with a put or call option that is deeply out of the money (i.e. an option that is so far out of the money it is highly unlikely to go into the money before expiry); or

- the sale of a fully proportionate share of the cash flows from a larger financial asset in an arrangement, such as a loan sub-participation, that satisfies the criteria for a 'transfer' in 3.5.2 above. *[IAS 39.21, AG39, IFRS 9.3.2.7, B3.2.4].*

Such transactions are discussed in more detail at 4 below.

It is important to note that, in order for derecognition to be achieved, it is necessary that the entity's exposure to the variability in the amounts and timing of the net cash flows of the transferred asset is considered not in isolation, but 'in relation to the total such variability' (see above). Thus derecognition is not achieved simply because the entity's remaining exposure to the risks or rewards of an asset is small in absolute terms. It has also become clear, from the Interpretations Committee and IASB's discussions described at 3.3.2 above, that derecognition also depends on the interpretation of 'asset' and of groups of similar assets that is applied by the entity.

3.8.2 *Transfers resulting in retention of substantially all risks and rewards*

An entity has retained substantially all the risks and rewards of ownership of a financial asset if its exposure to the variability in the present value of the future net cash flows from the financial asset does not change significantly as a result of the transfer. IAS 39 and IFRS 9 give the following examples of transactions in which an entity has retained substantially all the risks and rewards of ownership:

- a sale and repurchase transaction where the repurchase price is a fixed price or the sale price plus a lender's return;

- a securities lending agreement;

- a sale of a financial asset together with a total return swap that transfers the market risk exposure back to the entity;

- a sale of a financial asset together with a deeply in the money put or call option (i.e. an option that is so far in the money that it is highly unlikely to go out of the money before expiry). It will be in the holder's interest to exercise such an option, so that the asset will almost certainly revert to the transferor; and

- a sale of short-term receivables in which the entity guarantees to compensate the transferee for credit losses that are likely to occur. *[IAS 39.21, AG40, IFRS 9.3.2.7, B3.2.5].*

Such transactions are discussed in more detail at 4.1 below.

3.8.3   Transfers resulting in neither transfer nor retention of substantially all risks and rewards

IAS 39 and IFRS 9 give the following examples of transactions in which an entity has neither transferred nor retained substantially all the risks and rewards of ownership:

- a sale of a financial asset together with a put or call option that is neither deeply in the money nor deeply out of the money. *[IAS 39.AG51(g)-(h), IFRS 9.B3.2.16(g)-(h)].* The effect of such an option is that the transferor will have either (in the case of purchased call option) capped its exposure to a loss in value of the asset but have potentially unlimited access to increases in value or (in the case of a written put option) capped its potential access to increases in value in the asset but assumed potential exposure to a total loss in value of the asset; and

- a sale of 90% of a loan portfolio with significant transfer of prepayment risk, but retention of a 10% interest, with losses allocated first to that 10% retained interest. *[IAS 39.AG52, IFRS 9.B3.2.17].*

Such transactions are discussed in more detail at 4 below.

3.8.4   Evaluating the extent to which risks and rewards are transferred – practical example

The following example illustrates one approach to evaluating the extent to which risks and rewards associated with a portfolio of assets have been transferred.

Example 50.1:   Risks and rewards analysis – variability in the amounts and timing of net cash flows

Entity X sells a portfolio of trade receivables with a face value of £1 million and an average due date of 45 days from the issuance of the invoice to Entity Y, an unrelated third party. After the sale, X does not retain any residual beneficial interests in the receivables. However, X guarantees losses on the transferred portfolio up to a percentage of the total face value. Default losses, including late payments, as a percentage of face value ranged historically from 3% to 5%.

Assume the following two hypothetical situations:

- Fact pattern 1 – Entity X guarantees first losses on the portfolio up to 3.5% of the total face value.
- Fact pattern 2 – Entity X guarantees first losses on the portfolio up to 4% of the total face value.

The following calculations illustrate one possible approach for calculating the exposure to the variability in the amounts and timing of net cash flows.

Under this approach the reporting entity (Entity X) determines a number of reasonably possible scenarios that reflect the expected variability in the amounts and timing of net cash flows; these scenarios are then assigned a probability, with greater weighting being given to those outcomes that are more likely to occur. Next, Entity X calculates the expected future net cash flows for each scenario, discounted using an appropriate current market rate. The expected variability is then calculated using an appropriate statistical technique. The above steps are duplicated for net cash flows that the transferor, Entity X, remains exposed to after the transfer. Finally, the exposure to expected variability of net cash flows post transfer is compared to the corresponding expected variability before the transfer.

In this example, the expected variability is calculated by adding up the individual (negative or positive) deviations of the expected discounted future net cash flows for each scenario from the total expected value of the net cash flows for all possible scenarios. As the receivables are relatively short-term, the calculations below focus primarily on credit risk, including delinquency risk. For simplicity, the calculations below ignore the effect of discounting.

Fact pattern 1: Entity X guarantees first losses on the portfolio up to 3.5% of total face value.

Based on historical experience and supportable expectations Entity X has defined five scenarios of possible variability, each of which has been assigned a probability based on historical experience and current market information. These scenarios and probabilities are set out below.

Before Transfer

Face value = £1,000,000 = A

Possible credit loss B	Discounted expected cash flows C= A – [A×B] £	Probability D	Probability weighted discounted cash flows E=C×D £	Variability F=C–Σ(E) £	Probability weighted negative variability G= F×D if F<0 £	Probability weighted positive variability H=F×D if F>0 £
3.0%	970,000	3.5%	33,950	11,550	–	404.25
3.5%	965,000	20.0%	193,000	6,550	–	1,310.00
4.0%	960,000	30.0%	288,000	1,550	–	465.00
4.5%	955,000	35.0%	334,250	(3,450)	(1,207.50)	–
5.0%	950,000	11.5%	109,250	(8,450)	(971.75)	–
		100.0%	958,450		(2,179.25)	2,179.25
					K	K
		I	£41,550	=A – Σ(E)		

After Transfer

Face value = £1,000,000 = A

Possible credit loss B	Discounted expected cash flows C=[A×(B)], max 35,000 £	Probability D	Probability weighted discounted cash flows E=C×D £	Variability F=C–Σ(E) £	Probability weighted negative variability G=F×D if F<0 £	Probability weighted positive variability H=F×D if F>0 £
3.0%	30,000	3.5%	1,050	(4,825)	(168.88)	–
3.5%	35,000	20.0%	7,000	175	–	35.00
4.0%	35,000	30.0%	10,500	175	–	52.50
4.5%	35,000	35.0%	12,250	175	–	61.25
5.0%	35,000	11.5%	4,025	175	–	20.13
		100.0%	34,825		(168.88)	168.88
			M		L	L

Percentage of variability retained by Entity X   L÷K   (7.75)%   7.75%

To avoid a mechanical determination and to leave room for judgement, IAS 39 does not establish any bright-lines on what constitutes 'substantially all' risks and rewards of ownership. Therefore, judgement is needed to assess what is 'substantially all' in each particular situation considering, for example, the sensitivity of the calculation to certain changes in assumptions.

Assuming that Entity X determined that 'substantially all' represents 90% of total expected variability in the amounts and timing of net cash flows, it will conclude that it has transferred substantially all risks and rewards of ownership.

This conclusion may seem counterintuitive given that Entity X has retained 83.81% of the total expected losses (M÷I=34,825÷41,550). However, IAS 39 is clear that the transfer of risks and rewards should be evaluated by comparing the transferor's exposure, before and after the transfer, to the variability in the amounts and timing of net cash flows of the transferred asset. In practice, even when factoring with limited recourse, the transferor very often retains exposure to losses in excess of those reasonably expected to arise such that substantially all the variability is retained by the transferor.

Fact pattern 2: Entity X guarantees first losses on the portfolio up to 4% of the total face value.

Face value = £1,000,000 = A

Before Transfer

Possible credit loss B	Discounted expected cash flows C= A − [A×B] £	Probability D	Probability weighted discounted cash flows E=C×D £	Variability F=C−Σ(E) £	Probability weighted negative variability G= F×D if F<0 £	Probability weighted positive variability H=F×D if F>0 £
3.0%	970,000	3.5%	33,950	11,550	–	404.25
3.5%	965,000	20.0%	193,000	6,550	–	1,310.00
4.0%	960,000	30.0%	288,000	1,550	–	465.00
4.5%	955,000	35.0%	334,250	(3,450)	(1,207.50)	–
5.0%	950,000	11.5%	109,250	(8,450)	(971.75)	–
		100.0%	958,450		**(2,179.25)**	**2,179.25**
					K	K
		I	£41,550	A − Σ(E)		

After Transfer

Possible credit loss B	Discounted expected cash flows C=[A×(B), max 40,000] £	Probability D	Probability weighted discounted cash flows E=C×D £	Variability F=C−Σ(E) £	Probability weighted negative variability G=F×D if F<0 £	Probability weighted positive variability H=F×D if F>0 £
3.0%	30,000	3.5%	1,050	(8,650)	(302.75)	–
3.5%	35,000	20.0%	7,000	(3,650)	(730.00)	–
4.0%	40,000	30.0%	12,000	1,350	–	405.00
4.5%	40,000	35.0%	14,000	1,350	–	472.50
5.0%	40,000	11.5%	4,600	1,350	–	155.25
		100.0%	38,650		**(1,032.75)**	**1,032.75**
			M		L	L
Percentage of variability retained by Entity X				L÷K	**(47.39)%**	**47.39%**

Now that Entity X stands ready to cover first losses up to 4% which is in the middle of the range of expected losses (3% to 5%), it is not a surprise that its exposure to variability has increased to 47.39%. This means that Entity X has neither transferred nor retained substantially all risks and rewards of ownership in this case. Again, the fact that the seller now covers, after the sale, 93.02% (M÷I=38,650÷41,550) of the total expected losses is not relevant to the analysis.

In this case, derecognition will depend on whether the transferee (Entity Y) has the practical ability to sell the trade receivables unilaterally and without imposing additional restrictions on the transfer. The conclusion needs to take into account many factors. For example: (i) whether the transferee has legal title to the transferred receivables (ii) whether there is a market for the transferred receivables or not; (iii) whether or not the seller has a call option or has written a put option over the transferred receivables; (iv) whether or not the guarantee of Entity X is transferable with the receivables; (v) whether the receivables are 'ring-fenced' in a SPE as a pledge for securities collateralised by the transferred assets, etc. This aspect of the analysis is covered in 3.9 below.

3.9   Has the entity retained control of the asset?

The discussion in this section relates to Boxes 8 and 9 of the flowchart at 3.2 above.

If the transferring entity has neither transferred nor retained substantially all the risks and rewards of a transferred financial asset, IAS 39 and IFRS 9 require the entity to determine whether or not it has retained control of the financial asset. If the entity has not retained control, it must derecognise the financial asset and recognise separately as assets or liabilities any rights and obligations created or retained in the transfer. If the entity has retained control, it must continue to recognise the financial asset to the extent of its continuing involvement in the financial asset (see 5.3 below). *[IAS 39.20(c), IFRS 9.3.2.6(c)].*

IAS 39 and IFRS 9 require the question of whether the entity has retained control of the transferred asset to be determined by the transferee's ability to sell the asset. If the transferee:

- has the practical ability to sell the asset in its entirety to an unrelated third party; and
- is able to exercise that ability unilaterally and without needing to impose additional restrictions on the transfer,

the entity has not retained control (see below).

In all other cases, the entity has retained control. *[IAS 39.23, IFRS 9.3.2.9].*

3.9.1   *Transferee's 'practical ability' to sell the asset*

IAS 39 and IFRS 9 clarify that the transferee will have the practical ability to sell a transferred asset if the asset is traded in an active market, on the basis that the transferee will have the ability to repurchase the transferred asset in the market if it needs to return the asset to the entity.

If a transferred asset is sold subject to an option that allows the entity to repurchase it, the transferee may (subject to the further considerations discussed below) have the practical ability to sell the asset if it can readily obtain the transferred asset in the market if the option is exercised. *[IAS 39.AG42, IFRS 9.B3.2.7].*

The transferee has the practical ability to sell the transferred asset only if the transferee can sell the transferred asset in its entirety to an unrelated third party and is able to exercise that ability unilaterally and without imposing additional restrictions on the transfer. IAS 39 and IFRS 9 require that to be determined by considering what the transferee is able to do in practice, rather than solely by reference to any contractual rights or prohibitions. The standard notes that a contractual right to dispose of the transferred asset has little practical effect if there is no market for the transferred asset. *[IAS 39.AG43, IFRS 9.B3.2.8].*

An ability to dispose of the transferred asset also has little practical effect if it cannot be exercised freely. Accordingly, the transferee's ability to dispose of the transferred asset must be a unilateral ability independent of the actions of others. In other words, the transferee must be able to dispose of the transferred asset without needing to attach conditions to the transfer (e.g. conditions about how a loan asset is serviced, or an option giving the transferee the right to repurchase the asset). *[IAS 39.AG43, IFRS 9.B3.2.8]*.

For example, the entity might sell a financial asset to a transferee but the transferee has an option to put the asset back to the entity or has a performance guarantee from the entity. IAS 39 and IFRS 9 argue that such an option or guarantee might be so valuable to the transferee that it would not, in practice, sell the transferred asset to a third party without attaching a similar option or other restrictive conditions. Instead, the transferee would hold the transferred asset so as to obtain payments under the guarantee or put option. Under these circumstances IAS 39 and IFRS 9 regard the transferor as having retained control of the transferred asset. *[IAS 39.AG44, IFRS 9.B3.2.9]*.

However, the fact that the transferee is simply unlikely to sell the transferred asset does not, of itself, mean that the transferor has retained control of the transferred asset. *[IAS 39.AG44, IFRS 9.B3.2.9]*.

4　PRACTICAL APPLICATION OF THE DERECOGNITION CRITERIA

IAS 39 and IFRS 9 give a number of practical examples of the application of the derecognition criteria, which are discussed below. In some cases, it has to be said that the guidance in IAS 39 and IFRS 9 is less than satisfactory, amounting to little more than repetition of the standard.

In order to provide a link with Figure 50.1 at 3.2 above we have used the following convention:

'Box 6, Yes'	The transaction would result in the answer 'Yes' at Box 6 in the flowchart.
'Box 7, No'	The transaction would result in the answer 'No' at Box 7 in the flowchart.

4.1　Repurchase agreements ('repos') and securities lending

4.1.1　Agreements to return the same asset

If a financial asset is:

- sold under an agreement to repurchase it at a fixed price or at the sale price plus a lender's return; or
- loaned under an agreement to return it to the transferor,

the asset is not derecognised, because the transferor retains substantially all the risks and rewards of ownership *[IAS 39.AG51(a), IFRS 9.B3.2.16(a)]* (Figure 50.1, Box 7, Yes). The accounting treatment of such transactions is discussed at 5.2 below.

4.1.1.A   Transferee's right to pledge

If the transferee obtains the right to sell or pledge an asset that is the subject of such a transaction, the transferor reclassifies the asset on its statement of financial position as, for example, a loaned asset or repurchase receivable. *[IAS 39.AG51(a), IFRS 9.B3.2.16(a)]*.

It appears that this accounting treatment is required merely where the transferee has the 'right' to sell or pledge the asset. This contrasts with the requirements for determining whether an asset subject to a transaction in which the entity neither transfers nor retains substantially all the risks and rewards associated with the asset (Figure 50.1, Box 7, No) nevertheless qualifies for derecognition because the transferee has control (Figure 50.1, Box 8). In order for the transferee to be regarded as having control for the purposes of Box 8, any rights of the transferee to sell an asset must have economic substance – see 3.9 above.

The accounting treatment of such transactions is discussed at 5.2 below.

4.1.2   Agreements with right to return the same or substantially the same asset

If a financial asset is:

- sold under an agreement to repurchase the same or substantially the same asset at a fixed price or at the sale price plus a lender's return; or
- loaned under an agreement to return the same or substantially the same asset to the transferor,

the asset is not derecognised because the transferor retains substantially all the risks and rewards of ownership *[IAS 39.AG51(b), IFRS 9.B3.2.16(b)]* (Figure 50.1, Box 7, Yes). The accounting treatment of such transactions is discussed at 5.2 below.

4.1.3   Agreements with right of substitution

If a financial asset is the subject of:

- a repurchase agreement at a fixed repurchase price or a price equal to the sale price plus a lender's return; or
- a similar securities lending transaction,

that provides the transferee with a right to substitute assets that are similar and of equal fair value to the transferred asset at the repurchase date, the asset sold or lent is not derecognised because the transferor retains substantially all the risks and rewards of ownership *[IAS 39.AG51(c), IFRS 9.B3.2.16(c)]* (Figure 50.1, Box 7, Yes). The accounting treatment of such transactions is discussed at 5.2 below.

4.1.4   Net cash-settled forward repurchase

IAS 39 and IFRS 9 give some guidance on the treatment of net cash-settled options over transferred assets (see 4.2.5 below), which in passing refers to net cash-settled forward contracts. This guidance indicates that the key factor for determining whether derecognition is appropriate remains whether or not the entity has transferred substantially all the risks and rewards of the transferred asset. *[IAS 39.AG51(k), IFRS 9.B3.2.16(k)]*. This suggests that an asset sold subject to a fixed price net-settled forward contract to reacquire it should not be derecognised (see 4.1.1 to 4.1.3 above) until the forward contract is settled (Figure 50.1, Box 7, Yes).

The accounting treatment of such transactions is discussed at 5.2 below.

4.1.5   Agreement to repurchase at fair value

A transfer of a financial asset subject only to a forward repurchase agreement with a repurchase price equal to the fair value of the financial asset at the time of repurchase results in derecognition because of the transfer of substantially all the risks and rewards of ownership *[IAS 39.AG51(j), IFRS 9.B3.2.16(j)]* (Figure 50.1, Box 6, Yes). The accounting treatment of such transactions is discussed at 5.1 below.

4.1.6   Right of first refusal to repurchase at fair value

If an entity sells a financial asset and retains only a right of first refusal to repurchase the transferred asset at fair value if the transferee subsequently sells it, the entity derecognises the asset because it has transferred substantially all the risks and rewards of ownership *[IAS 39.AG51(d), IFRS 9.B3.2.16(d)]* (Figure 50.1, Box 6, Yes).

IAS 39 and IFRS 9 do not address the treatment of a financial asset sold with a right of first refusal to repurchase the transferred asset at a predetermined value that might well be lower or higher than fair value (e.g. an amount estimated, at the time at which the original transaction was entered into, as the future market value of the asset). One analysis might be that, since the transferee is under no obligation to put the asset up for sale, derecognition is still appropriate. Another analysis might be that, if the asset can ultimately only be realised by onward sale, the arrangement is nearer in substance to a transferor's call option (see 4.2 below).

4.1.7   Wash sale

A 'wash sale' is the repurchase of a financial asset shortly after it has been sold. Such a repurchase does not preclude derecognition provided that the original transaction met the derecognition requirements. However, if an agreement to sell a financial asset is entered into concurrently with an agreement to repurchase the same asset at a fixed price or the sale price plus a lender's return, then the asset is not derecognised. *[IAS 39.AG51(e), IFRS 9.B3.2.16(e)]*. Such a transaction would be equivalent to those in 4.1.1 to 4.1.4 above.

4.2   Transfers subject to put and call options

An option contract is a contract which gives one party to the contract the right, but not the obligation, to buy from, or sell to, the other party to the contract the asset that is the subject of the contract for a given price (often, but not always, a price that is fixed) at a future date (or during a longer period ending on a future date). An option giving the right to buy an asset is referred to as a 'call' option and one giving the right to sell as a 'put' option. An option is referred to as a 'bought' or 'purchased' option from the perspective of the party with the right to buy or sell (the 'holder') and as a 'written' option from the perspective of the party with the potential obligation to buy or sell. An option is referred to as 'in the money' when it would be in the holder's interest to exercise it and as 'out of the money' when it would not be in the holder's interest to exercise it.

Under IAS 39 and IFRS 9 an option is:

- 'deeply in the money' when it is so far in the money that it is highly unlikely to go out of the money before expiry; *[IAS 39.AG40(d), IFRS 9.B3.2.5(d)]* and

- 'deeply out of the money' when it is so far out of the money that it is highly unlikely to become in the money before expiry. *[IAS 39.AG39(c), IFRS 9.B3.2.4(c)].*

IAS 39 and IFRS 9 do not elaborate on what it means by 'highly unlikely' in this context, although the Implementation Guidance clarifies that 'highly probable' (in the context of a 'highly probable forecast transaction' subject to a hedge) indicates a much greater likelihood of happening than the term 'more likely than not'. *[IAS 39.F.3.7].*

Option contracts that are within the scope of IAS 39 or IFRS 9 (see Chapter 43 at 2) are recognised as assets or liabilities when the holder or writer becomes a party to the contract. *[IAS 39.AG35(d), IFRS 9.B3.1.2(d)].*

4.2.1 Deeply in the money put and call options

If a transferred financial asset can be called back by the transferor, and the call option is deeply in the money, the transfer does not qualify for derecognition because the transferor has retained substantially all the risks and rewards of ownership (Figure 50.1, Box 7, Yes).

Similarly, if the financial asset can be put back by the transferee, and the put option is deeply in the money, the transfer does not qualify for derecognition because the transferor has retained substantially all the risks and rewards of ownership *[IAS 39.AG51(f), IFRS 9.B3.2.16(f)]* (Figure 50.1, Box 7, Yes).

The accounting treatment for such transactions would be similar to that for 'repos' as set out in Example 50.9 at 5.2 below.

If a transferred asset continues to be recognised because of a transferor's call option or transferee's put option, but the option subsequently lapses unexercised, the asset and any associated liability would then be derecognised.

4.2.2 Deeply out of the money put and call options

A financial asset that is transferred subject only to a transferee's deeply out of the money put option, or a transferor's deeply out of the money call option, is derecognised. This is because the transferor has transferred substantially all the risks and rewards of ownership *[IAS 39.AG51(g), IFRS 9.B3.2.16(g)]* (Figure 50.1, Box 6, Yes).

4.2.3 Options that are neither deeply out of the money nor deeply in the money

Where a financial asset is transferred subject to an option (whether a transferor's call option or a transferee's put option) that is neither deeply in the money nor deeply out of the money, the result is that the entity neither transfers nor retains substantially all the risks and rewards associated with the asset *[IAS 39.AG51, IFRS 9.B3.2.16]* (Figure 50.1, Box 7, No). It is therefore necessary to determine whether or not the transferor has retained control of the asset under the criteria summarised in 3.9 above.

If a transferred asset continues to be recognised because of a transferor's call option or transferee's put option, but the option subsequently lapses unexercised, the asset and any associated liability would then be derecognised.

4.2.3.A   Assets readily obtainable in the market

If the transferor has a call option over a transferred financial asset that is readily obtainable in the market, IAS 39 and IFRS 9 consider that control of the asset has passed to the transferee (Figure 50.1, Box 8, No – see 3.9 above). *[IAS 39.AG51(h), IFRS 9.B3.2.16(h)].* This would presumably also be the conclusion where the transferee has a put option over a transferred financial asset that is readily obtainable in the market, although IAS 39 and IFRS 9 do not specifically address this.

4.2.3.B   Assets not readily obtainable in the market

If the transferor has a call option over a transferred financial asset that is not readily obtainable in the market, IAS 39 and IFRS 9 consider that control of the asset remains with the transferor (Figure 50.1, Box 8, Yes – see 3.9 above). Accordingly, derecognition is precluded to the extent of the amount of the asset that is subject to the call option. *[IAS 39.AG51(h), IFRS 9.B3.2.16(h)].*

If the transferee has a put option over a transferred financial asset that is not readily obtainable in the market, IAS 39 and IFRS 9 require the transferee's likely economic behaviour to be assessed – in effect to determine whether the option gives the transferee the practical ability to sell the transferred asset (see 3.9.1 above).

If the put option is sufficiently valuable to prevent the transferee from selling the asset, the transferor is considered to retain control of the asset and should account for the asset to the extent of its continuing involvement *[IAS 39.AG51(i), IFRS 9.B3.2.16(h)]* (Figure 50.1, Box 9). The accounting treatment required is discussed at 5.3 below.

If the put option is not sufficiently valuable to prevent the transferee from selling the asset, the transferor is considered to have ceded control of the asset, and should derecognise it *[IAS 39.AG51(i), IFRS 9.B3.2.16(i)]* (Figure 50.1, Box 8, No).

The requirements above beg two questions. First the question of whether or not a put option is sufficiently valuable to prevent the transferee from selling the asset is not a matter of objective fact, but rather a function of the transferee's appetite for risk, its need for liquidity and so forth. It is not clear how the transferor can readily assess these factors.

Second, IAS 39 and IFRS 9 are not explicit as to the accounting consequences (if any) of an option that was considered at the time of the original transfer to be deeply out of the money subsequently becoming neither deeply in the money nor deeply out of the money, or even deeply in the money, (or any other of the possible permutations). This is discussed further at 4.2.9 below.

4.2.4   Option to put or call at fair value

A transfer of a financial asset subject only to a put or call option with an exercise price equal to the fair value of the financial asset at the time of repurchase results in derecognition because of the transfer of substantially all the risks and rewards of ownership *[IAS 39.AG51(j), IFRS 9.B3.2.16(j)]* (Figure 50.1, Box 6, Yes).

4.2.5 Net cash-settled options

Where a transfer of a financial asset is subject to a put or call option that will be settled net in cash, IAS 39 and IFRS 9 require the entity to evaluate the transfer so as to determine whether it has retained or transferred substantially all the risks and rewards of ownership. *[IAS 39.AG51(k), IFRS 9.B3.2.16(k)].* IAS 39 and IFRS 9 comment that 'if the entity has not retained substantially all the risks and rewards of ownership of the transferred asset, it determines whether it has retained control of the transferred asset' – a repetition of the basic principles of the standard adding no clarification specific to this type of transaction.

4.2.6 Removal of accounts provision

A 'removal of accounts provision' is an unconditional repurchase (i.e. call) option that gives an entity the right to reclaim transferred assets subject to some restrictions. Provided that such an option results in the entity neither retaining nor transferring substantially all the risks and rewards of ownership, IAS 39 and IFRS 9 allow derecognition, except to the extent of the amount subject to repurchase (assuming that the transferee cannot sell the assets).

For example, if an entity transfers loan receivables with a carrying amount of €100,000 for proceeds of €100,000, subject only to the right to call back any individual loan(s) up to a maximum of €10,000, €90,000 of the loans would qualify for derecognition. *[IAS 39.AG51(l), IFRS 9.B3.2.16(l)].*

4.2.7 Clean-up call options

A 'clean-up call' option is an option held by an entity that services transferred assets (and may be the transferor of those assets) to purchase remaining transferred assets when the cost of servicing the assets exceeds the entity's participation in their benefits. If such a clean-up call results in the entity neither retaining nor transferring substantially all the risks and rewards of ownership, and the transferee cannot sell the assets, IAS 39 and IFRS 9 preclude derecognition only to the extent of the amount of assets subject to the call option. *[IAS 39.AG51(m), IFRS 9.B3.2.16(m)].*

4.2.8 Same (or nearly the same) price put and call options

IAS 39 and IFRS 9 do not specifically address the transfer of an asset subject to both a transferee's option to put, and a transferor's option to call, the asset at a fixed price rather than at fair value (as discussed in 4.2.4 above). Assuming that:

- both options can be exercised simultaneously; and
- both the transferor and transferee behave rationally,

it will clearly be in the interest of either the transferor or the transferee to exercise its option, so that the asset will be reacquired by the transferor. This indicates that the transferor has retained substantially all the risks and rewards of ownership.

However, if the two options were exercisable on different dates or at different prices the effects of each option would need to be considered carefully.

4.2.9   Changes in probability of exercise of options after initial transfer of asset

As noted at 4.2.3 above, IAS 39 and IFRS 9 are not explicit as to the accounting consequences (if any) of an option that was considered at the time of the original transfer to be deeply out of the money subsequently becoming neither deeply in the money nor deeply out of the money, or even deeply in the money, (or any other of the possible permutations). This is explored further in Examples 50.2 to 50.4 below.

Example 50.2:   Financial asset transferred subject only to deeply out of the money call option

On 1 January 2013 an entity transferred a financial asset to a counterparty, subject only to a call option to repurchase the asset at any time up to 31 December 2017. At 1 January 2013 the option was considered deeply out of the money and the asset was accordingly derecognised (see 4.2.2 above).

At 31 December 2016 market conditions have changed considerably and the option is now deeply in the money. What is the accounting consequence of this change?

There are no accounting consequences since, as noted at 3.8 above, IAS 39 paragraph AG41 (IFRS 9 paragraph B3.2.6) specifies that an asset previously derecognised because substantially all the risks and rewards associated with the asset have been transferred (as would be the analysis for an asset transferred subject only to a deeply out of the money call – see 4.2.2 above) is not re-recognised in a future period unless it is reacquired. Instead the increase in the fair value of the option would be captured in the financial statements as a gain under the normal requirement of IAS 39 or IFRS 9 to account for derivatives at fair value with changes in value reflected in profit or loss (see Chapter 43).

However, if the market changes were not demonstrably beyond any reasonable expectation as at 1 January 2015, there might be an argument (given the definition of a deeply out of the money option as an option that is 'highly unlikely' to become in the money before expiry – see 4.2.3 above) that the fact that the option is now not merely in the money, but deeply in the money, indicates that the original assessment that that option was deeply out of the money was in fact an accounting error requiring correction under IAS 8 (see Chapter 3 at 4.6).

Example 50.3:   Financial asset transferred subject only to deeply in the money call option

On 1 January 2013 an entity transferred a financial asset to a counterparty, subject only to a call option to repurchase the asset at any time up to 31 December 2017. At 1 January 2013 the option was considered deeply in the money and the asset was accordingly not derecognised (see 4.2.1 above).

At 31 December 2016 market conditions have changed considerably and the option is now deeply out of the money. What is the accounting consequence of this change?

This is the mirror image of the fact pattern in Example 50.2. However, whereas IAS 39 and IFRS 9 make it clear that an asset previously derecognised is not re-recognised, there is no comparable provision that an asset that previously did not qualify for derecognition on the origination of a particular transaction may not later be derecognised as a result of a subsequent change in the assessed likely impact of the transaction. Because the standard does not explain the consequences, it is not clear when the asset is derecognised or whether there is any basis for derecognising the asset before the expiry of the option.

In our view, however, the original assessment as to whether or not the asset should be derecognised should not be subsequently revisited, unless (in exceptional circumstances) the original assessment was an accounting error within the scope of IAS 8. Thus, in Example 50.3 above the asset would not be derecognised. However, the fall in the value of the option indicates an impairment of the asset which is likely to be required to be reflected in the financial statements under the normal requirements of IAS 39 (see Chapter 48 at 4). This would in turn appear to require a corresponding adjustment to the liability recognised for the sale proceeds, so as to avoid recognising a net loss in the income statement that has not actually been suffered.

Example 50.4: *Financial asset transferred subject to call option neither deeply in the money nor deeply out of the money*

On 1 January 2013 an entity transferred a financial asset (an equity share) to a counterparty, subject only to a call option to repurchase the asset at any time up to 31 December 2017. At 1 January 2013 the option was considered to be neither deeply in the money nor deeply out of the money. However, the asset was readily marketable and freely transferable by the transferor and was accordingly derecognised because the entity, while neither transferring nor retaining substantially all the risks and rewards of the asset, no longer controls it (see 4.2.3 above).

At 31 December 2016 the financial asset that was the subject of the transfer ceases to be listed and is therefore not readily marketable. Had this been the case at the time of the original transfer, the entity would have been regarded as retaining control of the asset, which would not have been derecognised (see 4.2.3.B above). What is the accounting consequence of this change?

Again, matters are not entirely clear. The rule in paragraph AG41 of IAS 39 (paragraph B3.2.6 of IFRS 9) that a previously derecognised asset should not be re-recognised (other than on reacquisition of the asset) applies, as drafted, only where derecognition results from a transfer of substantially all the risks and rewards associated with the asset. In this case, derecognition has resulted from a loss of control over, not a transfer of substantially all the risks and rewards associated with, the asset. There is therefore some ambiguity as to whether AG41 is to be read:

- *generally* as prohibiting any re-recognition of a derecognised asset; or

- *specifically* as referring only to circumstances where derecognition results from transfer of substantially all the risks and rewards (i.e. it applies only to 'Box 6, Yes' transactions, and not to 'Box 8, No' transactions).

Again, however, we take the view that the original decision to derecognise the asset should not be revisited, unless (in exceptional circumstances) the original assessment was an accounting error within the scope of IAS 8. The fact that the asset was transferred on terms that the transferee could freely dispose of it means that the transferor did indeed lose control.

4.3 Subordinated retained interests and credit guarantees

Where a financial asset is transferred, an entity may provide the transferee with credit enhancement by subordinating some or all of its interest retained in the transferred asset. Alternatively, an entity may provide the transferee with credit enhancement in the form of a credit guarantee that could be unlimited or limited to a specified amount. *[IAS 39.AG51(n), IFRS 9.B3.2.16(n)]*. Such techniques are commonly used in securitisation transactions (see 3.6 above).

IAS 39 and IFRS 9 note that, if the entity retains substantially all the risks and rewards of ownership of the transferred asset, the asset continues to be recognised in its entirety. If the entity retains some, but not substantially all, of the risks and rewards of ownership and has retained control, derecognition is precluded to the extent of the amount of cash or other assets that the entity could be required to pay. *[IAS 39.AG51(n), IFRS 9.B3.2.16(n)]*. This 'guidance' is really no more than a repetition of the basic principles of the standard, adding no real clarification specific to this type of transaction.

4.4   Transfers by way of swaps

4.4.1   Total return swaps

An entity may sell a financial asset to a transferee and enter into a total return swap with the transferee, whereby the transferor pays an amount equivalent to fixed or floating rate interest on the consideration for the transfer and receives an amount equivalent to the cash flows from, together with any increases or decreases in the fair value of, the underlying asset. In such a case, derecognition of all of the asset is prohibited, *[IAS 39.AG51(o), IFRS 9.B3.2.16(o)]*, since the transaction has the effect that substantially all the risks and rewards associated with the asset are retained by the transferor (Figure 50.1, Box 7, Yes).

4.4.2   Interest rate swaps

An entity may transfer a fixed rate financial asset and enter into an interest rate swap with the transferee to receive a fixed interest rate and pay a variable interest rate based on a notional amount equal to the principal amount of the transferred financial asset. IAS 39 and IFRS 9 state that the interest rate swap does not preclude derecognition of the transferred asset, provided that the payments on the swap are not conditional on payments being made on the transferred asset. *[IAS 39.AG51(p), IFRS 9.B3.2.16(p)]*. It is interesting that this is included as guidance as it does not follow from the principles. There are situations in which the entity retains substantially all of the risks by retaining interest rate risk.

If, however, the transferor were to transfer an asset subject to prepayment risk (e.g. a domestic mortgage), and the transferor and transferee were to enter into an amortising interest rate swap (i.e. one whose notional amount amortises so that it equals the principal amount of the transferred financial asset outstanding at any point in time), the transferor would generally retain substantial prepayment risk through the swap. In this case, the transferor would (depending on the other facts of the transaction, such as the transfer or retention of credit risk) continue to recognise the transferred asset either in its entirety (Figure 50.1, Box 7, Yes) or to the extent of the transferor's continuing involvement (Figure 50.1, Box 9). *[IAS 39.AG51(q), IFRS 9.B3.2.16(q)]*.

Conversely, if the transferor and the transferee were to enter into an amortising interest rate swap, the amortisation of the notional amount of which is not linked to the principal amount outstanding on the transferred asset, the transferor would no longer retain prepayment risk. Therefore such a swap would not preclude derecognition of the transferred asset, provided the payments on the swap were not conditional on interest payments being made on the transferred asset and the swap did not result in the entity retaining any other significant risks and rewards of ownership on the transferred asset. *[IAS 39.AG51(q), IFRS 9.B3.2.16(q)].*

4.5 Factoring of trade receivables

IAS 39 and IFRS 9 do not specifically address one of the more common forms of 'off-balance sheet finance' – the factoring of trade receivables. The common aim of all factoring structures is to provide cash flow from trade receivables quicker than would arise from normal cash collections, which is generally achieved by a 'sale' of all, or certain selected, receivables to a financial institution. However, the conditions of such 'sales' are extremely varied (which may well explain the lack of any generic guidance in the standard), ranging from true outright sales and pass-through arrangements (resulting in full derecognition), to transactions with continuing involvement through guarantee or subordination arrangements. It will therefore be necessary for an entity to consider the terms of its particular debt-factoring arrangement(s) carefully in order to determine the appropriate application of the derecognition provisions of IAS 39 or IFRS 9. Operational matters, for example how cash receipts from a debtor are allocated to particular invoices outstanding, could also be relevant to the analysis.

Depending on circumstances, Examples 50.5 (see 5.1 below), 50.6 (see 5.1.1 below), 50.10 (see 5.4.1 below) and 50.15 (see 5.4.4 below) may also be of particular relevance.

5 ACCOUNTING TREATMENT

This part of the Chapter deals with the accounting consequences of the derecognition criteria for financial assets – in other words how the principles discussed above translate into accounting entries.

In order to provide a link with Figure 50.1 at 3.2 above we have used the following convention:

'Box 6, Yes'   The transaction would result in the answer 'Yes' at Box 6 in the flowchart.

'Box 7, No'   The transaction would result in the answer 'No' at Box 7 in the flowchart.

5.1 Transfers that qualify for derecognition

It is important to remember throughout this section that references to an asset being derecognised in its entirety include situations where a part of an asset to which the derecognition criteria are applied separately is derecognised in its entirety (see 3.3 above). In this context, IAS 39 and IFRS 9 use the phrase 'in its entirety' in contrast to the accounting treatment applied to assets where there is continuing involvement (see 5.3 below) where some, but not all, of a financial asset, or part of an asset, is derecognised.

If, as a result of a transfer, a financial asset is derecognised in its entirety but the transfer results in the transferor obtaining a new financial asset or servicing asset or assuming a new financial liability, or a servicing liability (see 5.1.2 below), IAS 39 and IFRS 9 require the entity to recognise the new financial asset, servicing asset, financial liability or servicing liability at fair value. *[IAS 39.24-25, IFRS 9.3.2.10-11].*

On derecognition of a financial asset in its entirety, IAS 39 and IFRS 9 require the difference between:

(a)   the carrying amount of the asset; and

(b)   the consideration received (including any new asset obtained less any new liability assumed)

to be recognised in profit or loss. *[IAS 39.26, IFRS 9.3.2.12].* In addition, any cumulative gain or loss in respect of that asset which was previously recognised in other comprehensive income should be reclassified from equity to profit or loss if the asset is:

- classified as available-for-sale in accordance with IAS 39; *[IAS 39.26, 55(b)]* or
- a debt instrument accounted for at fair value through other comprehensive income under IFRS 9. *[IFRS 9.3.2.10].*

Example 50.5 illustrates these requirements.

Example 50.5:   Derecognition of whole of financial asset in its entirety

At 1 October 2016 an entity has an available-for-sale financial asset carried at €1,400 in respect of which a cumulative gain of €200 has been recognised in equity. At that date, the asset is unconditionally sold to a third party in exchange for cash of €2,500 and a loan note issued to the third party. The loan note bears a fixed rate interest below current market rates and is repayable at €1,150 but is considered to have a fair value of €1,100. The following accounting entries are made by the entity to record the disposal:

	€	€
Cash	2,500	
Equity ('recycling' of cumulative gain on asset)	200	
Gain on disposal		200
Asset		1,400
Loan note		1,100

Thereafter the loan note will be accreted up to its repayable amount of €1,150 over its expected life using the effective interest method (see Chapter 48 at 3).

If the asset had been of a type eligible for accounting using the amortised cost method, and had been so accounted for, and had a carrying amount of (say) €1,300 at the date of the transfer, the accounting entry would have been:

	€	€
Cash	2,500	
Profit on disposal		100
Asset		1,300
Loan note		1,100

5.1.1   Transferred asset part of larger asset

If the transferred asset is part of a larger financial asset, for example when an entity transfers interest cash flows that are part of a debt instrument (see 3.3 above), and the part transferred qualifies for derecognition in its entirety, IAS 39 and IFRS 9 require the previous carrying amount of the larger financial asset to be allocated between the part that continues to be recognised and the part that is derecognised. The allocation is based on the relative fair values of those parts on the date of the transfer. For this purpose, a retained servicing asset (see 5.1.2 below) is to be treated as a part that continues to be recognised.

IAS 39 and IFRS 9 require the difference between:

(a)   the carrying amount allocated to the part derecognised; and

(b)   the sum of:

   (i)   the consideration received for the part derecognised (including any new asset obtained less any new liability assumed); and

   (ii)   any cumulative gain or loss allocated to it previously recognised directly in equity

to be recognised in profit or loss. Any cumulative gain or loss that had been recognised in equity is allocated between the part that continues to be recognised and the part that is derecognised, based on the relative fair values of those parts. *[IAS 39.27, IFRS 9.3.2.13].*

The requirement in (b)(ii) above for 'recycling' of any cumulative gain or loss previously recognised directly in equity applies to assets accounted for as available-for-sale in accordance with IAS 39 and the same logic would apply to debt instruments accounted for at fair value through other comprehensive income under IFRS 9.

IAS 39 and IFRS 9 note that the accounting treatment prescribed for the derecognition of a part (or parts) of a financial asset requires an entity to determine the fair value of the part(s) that continue to be recognised. Where the entity has a history of selling parts similar to the part that continues to be recognised, or other market transactions exist for such parts, IAS 39 and IFRS 9 require recent prices of actual transactions to be used to provide the best estimate of its fair value. When there are no price quotations or recent market transactions to support the fair value of the part that continues to be recognised, the best estimate of the fair value is the difference between:

• the fair value of the larger financial asset as a whole; and

• the consideration received from the transferee for the part that is derecognised. *[IAS 39.28, IFRS 9.3.2.14].*

The requirements of IFRS 13 that deal with the determination of fair value should also be used *[IAS 39.AG46, IFRS 9.B3.2.11]* – see Chapter 14.

Example 50.6 illustrates the requirements for full derecognition of a part of an asset.

Example 50.6:   Derecognition of part of financial asset in its entirety

On 1 January 2011 an entity invested €1 million in a loan with a par value of €1 million. The loan pays interest of €75,000 on 31 December annually in arrears and is to be redeemed at par on 31 December 2020. The entity accounts for the loan at amortised cost.

On 1 January 2016 it unconditionally sells the right to receive the remaining five interest payments to a bank. The derecognition provisions of IAS 39 or IFRS 9 are applied to the interest payments as an identifiable part of the asset, leading to the conclusion that they are required to be derecognised.

The consideration received for, and the fair value of, the future interest payments (based on the net present value, as at 1 January 2016, of the payments at the current market interest rate that would be available to the borrower of 5%)^{18} is €324,711 (€75,000 × [1/1.05 + 1/1.05² ... + 1/1.05⁵]). By the same methodology the fair value of the principal repayment can be calculated as €783,526 (€1,000,000 × 1/1.05⁵), giving a total fair value for the loan of €1,108,237.

In order to calculate the gain or loss on disposal, the total carrying value of the loan of €1,000,000 is allocated between the part disposed of and the part retained, based on the fair values of those parts. This allocates €292,998 (€1,000,000 × 324,711 ÷ 1,108,237) to the interest payments disposed of and €707,002 (€1,000,000 × 783,526 ÷ 1,108,237) to the retained right to the repayment of principal. This generates the accounting entry:

	€	€
Cash	324,711	
Loan (portion of carrying amount allocated to interest payments)		292,998
Gain on disposal		31,713

If the loan had instead been a quoted bond accounted for as available-for-sale, it would have already have been carried at €1,108,237, so that the basic disposal journal would simply be:

	€	€
Cash	324,711	
Bond (portion of carrying amount allocated to interest payments)		324,711

However, as the bond was accounted for as available-for-sale, it would also be necessary to recycle that portion of the cumulative revaluation gain of €108,237 that relates to the interest 'component' of the total carrying value from equity to the income statement. IAS 39 requires a pro-rata allocation of the cumulative gain or loss in equity based on the total fair value of the interest and principal – this would deem €31,713 (€108,237 × €324,711 ÷ 1,108,237) of the cumulative revaluation gain to relate to interest. This would give rise to the further journal, resulting in the same gain on disposal as above:

	€	€
Equity	31,713	
Gain on disposal (income statement)		31,713

5.1.2   Servicing assets and liabilities

It is common for an entity to transfer a financial asset (or part of a financial asset) in its entirety, but to retain the right or obligation to service the asset, i.e. to collect payments as they fall due and undertake other administrative tasks, in return for a fee.

When an entity transfers a financial asset in a transfer that qualifies for derecognition in its entirety and retains the right to service the financial asset for a fee, IAS 39 and IFRS 9 require the entity to recognise either a servicing asset or a servicing liability for that servicing contract, as follows:

- If the fee to be received is not expected to compensate the entity adequately for performing the servicing, the entity should recognise a servicing liability for the servicing obligation at its fair value.

- If the fee to be received is expected to be more than adequate compensation for the servicing, the entity should recognise a servicing asset for the servicing right. This should be recognised at an amount determined on the basis of an allocation of the carrying amount of the larger financial asset (as described in 5.1.1 above). *[IAS 39.24, IFRS 9.3.2.10].*

It is not immediately clear what is meant by this requirement. The application guidance expands on the point, as follows.

An entity may retain the right to a part of the interest payments on transferred assets as compensation for servicing those assets. The part of the interest payments that the entity would give up upon termination or transfer of the servicing contract is allocated to the servicing asset or servicing liability. The part of the interest payments that the entity would not give up is an interest-only strip receivable.

For example, if the entity would not give up any interest upon termination or transfer of the servicing contract, the entire interest spread is an interest-only strip receivable. Presumably, as the entity will still have a liability to service the portfolio, it will have to account for this if it allocates none of the interest spread to a servicing asset. For the purposes of applying the requirements for disposals of part of an asset discussed in 5.1.1 above, the fair values of the servicing asset and interest-only strip receivable are used to allocate the carrying amount of the receivable between the part of the asset that is derecognised and the part that continues to be recognised. If there is no servicing fee specified, or the fee to be received is not expected to compensate the entity adequately for performing the servicing, a liability for the servicing obligation is recognised at fair value. *[IAS 39.AG45, IFRS 9.B3.2.10].*

Unfortunately, IAS 39 and IFRS 9 do not provide examples of what exactly is meant here, but we believe that something along the lines of Example 50.7 below was intended.

Example 50.7:   Servicing assets and liabilities

An entity has a portfolio of originated domestic mortgages which are accounted for at amortised cost and have a carrying amount of £10 million. The mortgages bear interest at a fixed rate of 7.5%. The average life of the mortgages in the portfolio (taking account of prepayment risk) is 12 years and the fair value of the portfolio is £11 million, representing £4.5 million in respect of future interest payments and £6.5 million in respect of the principal amounts. The entity assesses the amount that would compensate it for servicing the assets to be £0.5 million.

The entity sells the entire portfolio to a bank (on terms such that it qualifies for derecognition under IAS 39 or IFRS 9) but continues to service the portfolio. If the entity does not retain any part of the interest payments, the selling price would be the fair value of the assets of £11 million (or very close to it). It would then assume a servicing liability of £0.5 million, giving rise to the accounting entry:

	£m	£m
Cash	11.0	
Mortgage portfolio		10.0
Servicing liability		0.5
Profit on disposal		0.5

Alternatively, it retains interest payments of 1% and the right to service the portfolio. The entity estimates that the fair value of the right to receive interest payments of 1% is £0.6 million. In this case, the bank would be expected to pay fair value of £10.4 million (or very close to it).

The standard states – see above – that, if (as is the case here) the entity would not give up any interest on termination or transfer of the contract, then the whole of the interest spread is an interest-only strip receivable. In order to calculate the amount of the portfolio to be derecognised, the carrying value of £10 million is pro-rated (as in Example 50.6 above) as to £9.45 million disposed of (£10m × 10.4/11) and the part retained of £0.55 million (£10m × 0.6/11). However, as it has allocated the full amount of the interest spread to an interest-only strip receivable, it would need to recognise a servicing liability of £0.5 million in respect of its obligations under the contract. This gives rise to the following accounting entry:

	£m	£m
Cash	10.40	
Interest-only strip receivable	0.55	
Mortgage portfolio (£9.45m disposed of plus £0.55m reclassified as interest-only strip receivable)		10.00
Servicing liability		0.50
Profit on disposal		0.45

If the entity were to retain only £0.1 million of the interest spread on termination or transfer of the servicing contract, then IAS 39 and IFRS 9 require – see above:

- the part of the interest payments that the entity would not give up, i.e. the part which is not contingent on fulfilment of the servicing obligation (£0.1 million) to be treated as an interest-only strip receivable; and

- the part of the interest payments that the entity would give up (i.e. £0.45 million – £0.55 million as above less £0.1 million in previous bullet) upon termination or transfer of the servicing contract to be allocated to the servicing asset or servicing liability.

This suggests that the following accounting entry would be made:

	£m	£m
Cash	10.40	
Interest-only strip receivable	0.10	
Mortgage portfolio (£9.45m disposed of plus £0.1m reclassified as interest-only strip receivable and £0.45m allocated to servicing liability)		10.00
Servicing liability (£0.5m gross cost less interest payments that would be lost on termination or transfer – £0.45m)		0.05
Profit on disposal		0.45

A servicing asset is a non-financial asset representing a right to receive a higher than normal amount for performing future services. Accordingly it would normally be accounted for in accordance with IAS 38 – *Intangible Assets*. Similarly, a servicing liability represents consideration received in advance for services to be performed in the future and would normally be accounted for as deferred revenue in accordance with IAS 18 – *Revenue* – or IFRS 15 – *Revenue from Contracts with Customers*.

5.2 Transfers that do not qualify for derecognition through retention of risks and rewards

If a transfer does not result in derecognition because the entity has retained substantially all the risks and rewards of ownership of the transferred asset (see 3.8 above), IAS 39 and IFRS 9 require the entity to continue to recognise the transferred asset in its entirety and recognise a financial liability for any consideration received. In subsequent periods, the entity recognises any income on the transferred asset and any expense incurred on the financial liability. *[IAS 39.29, IFRS 9.3.2.15]*. This treatment is illustrated by Examples 50.8 and 50.9 below.

It should be noted that these provisions apply only where derecognition does not occur as a result of retention by the transferor of substantially all the risks and rewards of ownership of the transferred asset (Figure 50.1, Box 7, Yes). They do not apply where derecognition does not occur as a result of continuing involvement in an asset of which substantially all the risks and rewards of ownership are neither retained nor transferred (Figure 50.1, Box 8, Yes). Such transactions are dealt with by the separate provisions discussed in 5.3 and 5.4 below.

Example 50.8: Asset not qualifying for derecognition (risks and rewards retained)

An entity holds a loan of £1,000 made on 1 January 2012, paying interest of £65 annually in arrears and redeemable at par on 31 December 2016, which it accounts for at amortised cost (see Chapter 48 at 3).

On 1 January 2016 it enters into a transaction whereby the loan is sold to a bank for its then fair value of €985, but with full recourse to the entity for any default on the loan. The guarantee provided by the entity has the effect that it retains substantially all the risks and rewards of the loan, which is therefore not derecognised (Figure 50.1, Box 7, Yes – see 3.8.2 above). *[IAS 39.AG47, IFRS 9.B3.2.12]*.

The entity therefore continues to recognise the loan, and interest on it, as if it still held the loan. It accounts for the £985 proceeds as a liability which must be accreted up using the effective interest method (see Chapter 48 at 3) so that it will be equal to the carrying amount of the asset on the date on which it is expected that the asset will be derecognised.

In this case, the asset will be derecognised at maturity on 31 December 2016, when a payment of £1,065 (the final instalment of interest of £65 and return of principal of £1,000) is due. Accordingly, the liability must be accreted from £985 to £1,065 during the year ended 31 December 2016. The following accounting entries are made by the entity:

	£	£
1 January 2016		
Cash	985	
Liability		985
Consideration received from bank		
1 January-31 December 2016		
Loan (£1,065 at 31.12.16 – £1,000 at 1.1.16)	65	
Interest on loan (income statement)		65
Interest on liability (income statement)	80	
Liability (£1,065 at 31.12.16 – £985 at 1.1.16)		80
Accretion of interest income loan and liability		
31 December 2016		
Liability	1,065	
Loan receivable		1,065
'Redemption' of loan and 'discharge' of liability		

This accounting treatment recognises an overall loss of £15 in 2016, which would be expected, as representing the difference between the carrying value of the asset at the date of transfer (£1,000) and the consideration received (£985). However, IAS 39 and IFRS 9 require the various elements of the transaction to be shown separately – it would not have been acceptable for the income statement simply to show a net loss of £15.

If the transferred asset had been accounted for at fair value through profit or loss, it would already have been carried at £985 at the date of transfer – i.e. the loss of £15 would already have been reflected in the financial statements. The accounting entries at 1 January and 31 December 2016 would be the same as above. However, the following accounting entries would then have been made during the year ended 31 December:

	£	£
1 January-31 December 2016		
Interest on liability (income statement)	80	
Liability (£1,065 at 31.12.16 – £985 at 1.1.16)		80
Loan (£1,065 at 31.12.16 – £985 at 1.1.16)	80	
Interest on loan (income statement)		65
Change in fair value of loan (income statement)		15

Recognition of interest on, and change in fair value of, loan and accretion of interest on liability

Whilst the total amounts recorded in the income statement net to nil, they are arrived at by different methodologies – the £80 increase in the carrying value of the loan receivable is recognised as it occurs whereas the £80 interest on the liability is accrued at a constant effective rate. This means that, if the entity were to prepare financial statements at an interim date, it might well show a net gain or loss on the transaction at that date, notwithstanding that ultimately no gain or loss will be reflected.

It would presumably be possible for the entity to avoid this result by designating the liability as at fair value through profit or loss (see Chapter 45 at 2.2 and Chapter 46 at 7), such that changes in the fair value of the liability would be matched in line with those in the fair value of the asset.

Example 50.9: Asset not qualifying for derecognition ('repo' transaction)

An entity holds a government bond of £2,000 issued on 1 January 2012, paying interest of £50 semi-annually in arrears and redeemable at par on 31 December 2017, which it accounts for as a held-to-maturity investment at amortised cost (see Chapter 48 at 3).

A   Gross-settled transaction

On 1 January 2016 the entity enters into a transaction whereby the bond is sold to a bank for its then fair value of £1,800, and the entity agrees to repurchase it on 1 January 2017 for £1,844. As the legal owner of the loan at 30 June 2016 and 31 December 2016, the bank will receive the £100 interest payable on the bond for the calendar year 2016. This £100, together with the £44 difference between the sale and repurchase price gives the bank £144, representing a lender's return of 8% on the £1,800 sale proceeds. Accordingly, the effect of the transaction is that the entity has retained substantially all the risks and rewards of ownership of the bond (Figure 50.1, Box 7, Yes – see 4.1 above).

The entity therefore continues to recognise the bond, and interest on it, as if it still held the bond. It accounts for the £1,800 proceeds as a liability which must be accreted up to £1,844 (the repurchase price due on 31 December 2016) over the period to 31 December 2016 using the effective interest method (see Chapter 48 at 3). The following accounting entries are made by the entity:

	£	£
1 January 2016		
Cash	1,800	
Liability		1,800

Consideration received from bank

	£	£
1 January-31 December 2016		
Interest on liability (income statement)	144	
Liability (£1,944 at 31.12.16 – £1,800 at 1.1.16)		144
Bond (£2,100 at 31.12.16 – £2,000 at 1.1.16)	100	
Interest on bond (income statement)		100

Accretion of income on bond and finance cost of liability

1 January-31 December 2016

Liability	100	
Bond		100

Notional receipt of interest on bond at 30 June and 31 December and notional transfer thereof to bank

1 January 2017

Liability	1,844	
Cash		1,844

Execution of repurchase contract

The above is arguably the strict translation into accounting entries of the accounting analysis of IAS 39 or IFRS 9 that the entity still retains ownership of the bond throughout 2016. As a matter of practicality, however, the same overall result could have been obtained by the following 'short-cut' approach, which avoids recording the notional receipt and transfer to the bank of bond interest received on 30 June and 31 December:

	£	£
1 January 2016		
Cash	1,800	
Liability		1,800

Consideration received from bank

	£	£
1 January-31 December 2016		
Interest on liability (income statement)	144	
Interest on bond (income statement)		100
Liability (statement of financial position)		44

Accretion of income on bond and finance cost of liability

1 January 2017		
Liability	1,844	
Cash		1,844

Execution of repurchase contract

If (as would be likely, given the nature of the transferred asset) the bank has the right to sell or pledge the bond during the period of its legal ownership, it would be necessary to reclassify the bond as a repurchase receivable during the period of the bank's ownership (see 4.1.1.A above). In other words, the following additional accounting entries would be required.

	£	£
1 January 2016		
Repurchase receivable	2,000	
Bond		2,000
1 January 2017		
Bond	2,000	
Repurchase receivable		2,000

B   *Net-settled transaction*

The entity might enter into the transaction above, but on terms that the repurchase contract was to be net-settled. In other words, on 1 January 2017, a payment would be made to or by the bank for the difference between £1,844 (the notional repurchase price) and the fair value of the bond at that date. Assuming that the fair value of the bond at 1 January 2017 is £1,860, the bank would be required to pay the entity £16 (£1,860 – £1,844).

In this case, matters are further complicated by the fact that the economic effect of the net-settled forward is the same as if the entity sold the bond on 1 January 2017. As this is before the maturity date of the bond, it is questionable whether the entity can any longer classify it as held-to-maturity. In such a case, IAS 39 requires it to be reclassified as available-for-sale (see Chapter 45 at 3.3). The following accounting entries would be made:

	£	£
1 January 2016		
Cash	1,800	
Liability		1,800
Consideration received from bank		
Equity	200	
Bond (£2,000 carrying amount less £1,800 fair value)		200
Restatement of bond to fair value		
Repurchase receivable	1,800	
Bond		1,800
Reclassification of bond as receivable (see 4.1.1.A above)		
1 January-31 December 2016		
Interest on liability (income statement)	144	
Interest on bond (income statement)		100
Liability (statement of financial position)		44
Repurchase receivable	60	
Equity		60
Accretion of income on bond and finance cost of liability and restatement of repurchase receivable (represented by fair value of underlying bond accounted for as available-for-sale – £1,860)		
1 January 2017		
Cash	16	
Liability	1,844	
Repurchase receivable		1,860
Loss on disposal	140	
Equity		140
Net settlement of repurchase contract and 'recycling' of cumulative losses in equity		

The loss on disposal at 1 January 2017 of £140 arises because the net-settled contract is equivalent to the entity disposing of the bond for its then fair value of £1,860, which is £140 lower than its amortised cost, at the date of reclassification from held-to-maturity to available-for-sale, of £2,000.

This illustrates the point that, where the terms of net-settled forward contract over a transferred asset are such that the original asset cannot be derecognised, the result will be that the entity's statement of financial position shows a gross position – i.e. the original asset and a liability for the consideration for the transfer. This may seem a strange accounting reflection of a contract that is required to be settled net. However, the IASB was to some extent forced into this approach as an anti-avoidance measure. It is clear from the analysis in 4.1.1 to 4.1.4 above that an asset sold subject to the obligation to repurchase the same or similar asset at a fixed price should not be derecognised. If the accounting treatment were to vary merely because the contract was net-settled, it would be possible to avoid the requirements of IAS 39 or IFRS 9 for continued recognition of assets subject to certain forward repurchase agreements simply by altering the terms of the agreement to allow net settlement.

5.3   Transfers with continuing involvement – summary

If an entity neither transfers nor retains substantially all the risks and rewards of ownership of a transferred asset, but retains control of the transferred asset (see 3.9 above), IAS 39 and IFRS 9 require the entity to continue to recognise the transferred asset to the extent of its 'continuing involvement' – i.e. the extent to which it is exposed to changes in the value of the transferred asset. *[IAS 39.30, IFRS 9.3.2.16]*. Such transactions fall within Box 9 of the flowchart at 3.2 above.

The concept of 'continuing involvement' was first introduced in the exposure draft of proposed amendments to IAS 32 and IAS 39 published in June 2002. The IASB's intention at that time was to move towards an accounting model for derecognition based entirely on continuing involvement. However, this approach (or at least the methodology for implementing it proposed in the exposure draft) received little support in the exposure period and the IASB decided to abandon it and revert largely to an accounting model for derecognition based on the transfer of risks and rewards. *[IAS 39.BC44-BC52,   IFRS 9.BCZ3.4-BCZ3.12]*. However, the continuing involvement approach remains relevant for certain transactions – mainly transfers of assets which result in the sharing, rather than the substantial transfer, of the risks and rewards.

The accounting requirements in respect of assets in which the entity has continuing involvement are particularly complex, and are summarised at 5.3.1 to 5.3.5 below, with worked examples at 5.4 below. In particular, and in contrast to the treatment for transactions that do not qualify for derecognition through retention of risks and rewards (see 5.2 above), the associated liability is often calculated as a balancing figure that will not necessarily represent the proceeds received as the result of the transfer (see 5.3.3 below).

We have a general concern regarding the required accounting treatment for a continuing involvement, namely that IAS 39 and IFRS 9 provide examples of how to deal with certain specific transactions rather than clear underlying principles. It can be difficult to determine the appropriate treatment for a continuing involvement that does not correspond fairly exactly to one of the examples in IAS 39 or IFRS 9.

5.3.1   Guarantees

When the entity's continuing involvement takes the form of guaranteeing the transferred asset, the extent of the entity's continuing involvement is the lower of:

- the carrying amount of the asset; and
- the maximum amount of the consideration received that the entity could be required to repay ('the guarantee amount'). *[IAS 39.30(a), IFRS 9.3.2.16(a)]*.

An example of this treatment is given at 5.4.1 below.

It follows that if the transferor guarantees the entire amount of the transferred asset, no derecognition would be achieved, even though it may have passed other significant risks to the transferee.

5.3.2   Options

When the entity's continuing involvement takes the form of a written and/or purchased option (including a cash-settled option or similar provision) on the transferred asset, the extent of the entity's continuing involvement is the amount of the transferred asset that the entity may repurchase. However, in case of a written put option (including a cash-settled option or similar provision) on an asset measured at fair value, the extent of the entity's continuing involvement is limited to the lower of the fair value of the transferred asset and the option exercise price. *[IAS 39.30(b)-(c), IFRS 9.3.2.16(b)-(c)].*

Examples of this treatment are given at 5.4.2 and 5.4.3 below.

5.3.3   Associated liability

When an entity continues to recognise an asset to the extent of its continuing involvement, IAS 39 and IFRS 9 require the entity to recognise an associated liability. *[IAS 39.31, IFRS 9.3.2.17].* IAS 39 and IFRS 9 provide that 'despite the other measurement requirements in this Standard', the transferred asset and the associated liability are to be measured on a basis that reflects the rights and obligations that the entity has retained. The associated liability is measured in such a way that the net carrying amount of the transferred asset and the associated liability is equal to:

*   if the transferred asset is measured at amortised cost, the amortised cost of the rights and obligations retained by the entity; or

*   if the transferred asset is measured at fair value, the fair value of the rights and obligations retained by the entity when measured on a stand-alone basis. *[IAS 39.31, IFRS 9.3.2.17].*

This has the effect that the 'liability' is often calculated as a balancing figure that will not necessarily represent the proceeds received as the result of the transfer (see Examples 50.10 to 50.13 at 5.4 below). This does not fit very comfortably with the normal rules in IAS 39 and IFRS 9 for the initial measurement of financial liabilities (see Chapter 47 at 3) – hence the comment that this treatment applies 'despite the other measurement requirements in this Standard'.

5.3.4   Subsequent measurement of assets and liabilities

IAS 39 and IFRS 9 require an entity to continue to recognise any income arising on the transferred asset to the extent of its continuing involvement and to recognise any expense incurred on the associated liability. *[IAS 39.32, IFRS 9.3.2.18].* This is comparable to the requirements in respect of assets not derecognised through retention of substantially all risks and rewards (see 5.2 above).

When the transferred asset and associated liability are subsequently measured, IAS 39 and IFRS 9 require recognised changes in the fair value of the transferred asset and the associated liability to be accounted for consistently with each other in accordance with the general provisions of IAS 39 and IFRS 9 for measuring gains and losses (see Chapter 48 at 2 and Chapter 49 at 2) and not offset. *[IAS 39.33, IFRS 9.3.2.19].* Moreover, if the transferred asset is measured at amortised cost, the option in IAS 39 and IFRS 9 to designate a financial liability as at fair value through profit or loss (see Chapter 45 at 2.2 and Chapter 46 at 7) is not applicable to the associated liability. *[IAS 39.35, IFRS 9.3.2.21].*

5.3.5   *Continuing involvement in part only of a larger asset*

An entity may have continuing involvement in a part only of a financial asset, for example where the entity retains an option to repurchase part of a transferred asset, or retains a residual interest in part of an asset, such that the entity does not retain substantially all the risks and rewards of ownership, but does retain control.

In such a case, IAS 39 and IFRS 9 require the entity to allocate the previous carrying amount of the financial asset between the part that it continues to recognise under continuing involvement, and the part that it no longer recognises on the basis of the relative fair values of those parts on the date of the transfer. The allocation is to be made on the same basis as applies on derecognition of part only of a larger financial asset – see 5.1.1 and 5.1.2 above.

The difference between:

(a)   the carrying amount allocated to the part that is no longer recognised; and

(b)   the sum of:

   (i)   the consideration received for the part no longer recognised; and

   (ii)   any cumulative gain or loss allocated to it that had been recognised directly in equity

is recognised in profit or loss. A cumulative gain or loss that had been recognised in equity is allocated between the part that continues to be recognised and the part that is no longer recognised on the basis of the relative fair values of those parts. [IAS 39.27, IFRS 9.3.2.13].

The requirement in (b)(ii) above for 'recycling' of any cumulative gain or loss previously recognised directly in equity applies to assets accounted for as available-for-sale in accordance with IAS 39 and the same logic would apply to debt instruments accounted for at fair value through other comprehensive income under IFRS 9.

This topic is discussed further at 5.4.4 below.

5.4   Transfers with continuing involvement – accounting examples

The provisions summarised at 5.3 above, even judged by the standards of IAS 39 and IFRS 9, are unusually impenetrable. However, the application guidance provides a number of clarifications and examples, the substance of which is reproduced below.

5.4.1   *Transfers with guarantees*

If a guarantee provided by an entity to pay for default losses on a transferred asset prevents the transferred asset from being derecognised to the extent of the continuing involvement, IAS 39 and IFRS 9 require:

(a)   the transferred asset at the date of the transfer to be measured at the lower of:

   (i)   the carrying amount of the asset; and

   (ii)   the maximum amount of the consideration received in the transfer that the entity could be required to repay ('the guarantee amount'); and

(b)   the associated liability to be initially measured at the guarantee amount plus the fair value of the guarantee (which is normally the consideration received for the guarantee).

Subsequently, the initial fair value of the guarantee is recognised in profit or loss on a time proportion basis in accordance with IAS 18 or IFRS 15 and the carrying value of the asset is reduced by any impairment losses. *[IAS 39.AG48(a), IFRS 9.B3.2.13(a)].*

This is illustrated in Example 50.10 below (which is based on the circumstances in Example 50.15 below).

Example 50.10:   Continuing involvement through guarantee

An entity has a loan portfolio carried at €10 million with a fair value of €10.5 million. It sells the rights to 100% of the cash flows to a third party for a payment of €10.55 million, which includes a payment of €50,000 in return for the entity agreeing to absorb the first €1 million of default losses on the portfolio. The loans are fixed rate loans with significant prepayment risk.

The guarantee has the effect that the entity has transferred substantially all the rewards, but not substantially all the risks, of the portfolio (Figure 50.1, Box 6, No). The prepayment risk and interest rate risk have been transferred to the transferee, so that the entity does not retain all significant risks of the loans (Figure 50.1, Box 7, No). The portfolio is not a readily marketable asset, so that the entity retains control of the asset (Figure 50.1, Box 8, Yes – see also 3.9 above), and the continuing involvement provisions of IAS 39 and IFRS 9 apply (Figure 50.1, Box 9).

The entity turns to the requirements above. The continuing involvement in the transferred asset must be measured at the lower of:

(i)   the amount of the asset transferred – i.e. €10 million; and

(ii)   the maximum amount of the consideration received in the transfer that the entity could be required to repay – i.e. €1 million (the amount guaranteed).

Therefore, the entity will set up an asset that represents its continuing involvement in the transferred asset of €1 million.

The entity then considers the carrying amount of the liability. This is required to be measured at the guarantee amount (i.e. €1 million) plus the fair value of the guarantee (i.e. the €50,000 guarantee payment), a total of €1.05 million. Therefore, the entity's continuing involvement in the transaction will be reflected as follows:

	€m	€m
Cash	10.55	
Loan portfolio transferred		10.00
Continuing involvement in the transferred asset	1.00	
Liability		1.05
Profit on disposal*		0.50

> *   Cash received (€10.55m) less guarantee payment (€50,000) = consideration
>   for portfolio (€10.5m) less carrying amount of portfolio (€10m).

Over the remaining life of the transaction, the €50,000 of the liability that represents the consideration received for the guarantee is amortised to the income statement on a time proportion basis. This has the effect that the income earned by the entity for entering into the guarantee arrangement is reported as revenue on a time proportion basis. This is exactly the same result as would have been obtained by simply recognising the €50,000 as a liability and amortising it (as would have been required by IAS 18 or IFRS 15).

If in a subsequent period credit losses of €0.2 million are suffered, requiring a payment under the guarantee, IAS 39 and IFRS 9 require the following accounting entries to be made: *[IAS 39.AG52, IFRS 9.B3.2.17]*

	€m	€m
Profit or loss (loss under guarantee)	0.20	
Cash (paid to transferee)		0.20
Liability	0.20	
Continuing involvement in the transferred asset		0.20

5.4.2 Transfers of assets measured at amortised cost

If a put or call option prevents derecognition (see 3.8.3 and 4 above) of a transferred asset measured at amortised cost, IAS 39 and IFRS 9 require the associated liability to be measured at cost (i.e. the consideration received) and subsequently adjusted for the amortisation of any difference between that cost and the amortised cost of the transferred asset at the expiration date of the option, as illustrated by Example 50.11 below. *[IAS 39.AG48(b), IFRS 9.B3.2.13(b)].*

Example 50.11: Asset measured at amortised cost

An entity has a financial asset, accounted for at amortised cost, carried at £98. It transfers the asset to a third party in return for consideration of £95. The asset is subject to a call option whereby the entity can compel the transferee to sell the asset back to the entity for £102. The amortised cost of the asset on the option exercise date will be £100. The option is considered to be neither deeply in the money nor deeply out of the money. IAS 39 and IFRS 9 therefore require the entity to continue to recognise the asset to the extent of its continuing involvement (Figure 50.1, Box 9 – see also 4.2.3 above).

The initial carrying amount of the associated liability is £95. This is then accreted to £100 (i.e. the amortised cost of the asset on exercise date – *not* the £102 exercise price) through profit or loss using the effective interest method. Because the transferred asset is measured at amortised cost, the associated liability must also be accounted for at amortised cost, and not at fair value through profit or loss (see 5.3.4 above). This will give rise to the accounting entries:

	£	£
Date of transfer		
Cash	95	
Liability		95
After date of transfer		
Interest on liability	5	
Liability (£100 – £95)		5
Asset (£100 – £98)	2	
Income on asset		2

If the option is exercised, any difference between the carrying amount of the associated liability and the exercise price is recognised in profit or loss. This last requirement has the possibly counter-intuitive effect that the question of whether the entity records a profit or loss on exercise of the option is essentially a function of the difference between the liability (representing the amortised cost of the transferred asset) and the cash paid, not of whether it has in fact (i.e. in economic terms) made a gain or loss.

Thus, if the entity were to exercise its option at £102 it would apparently record the accounting entry:

	£	£
Liability	100	
Loss	2	
Cash		102

However, the entity would not have exercised the option unless the asset had been worth at least £102 (i.e. £2 more than its carrying amount), suggesting that the more appropriate treatment would be to add the £2 to the cost of the asset.

Likewise, if instead of the entity having a call option, the transferee had a put option at £98 which it exercised, the entity would apparently record the accounting entry:

	£	£
Liability	100	
Profit		2
Cash		98

However, the transferee would not have exercised its option unless the asset had been worth less than £98 (i.e. £2 less than its carrying amount). In this case, however, the IASB's thinking may have been that the exercise of the transferee's put option suggests an impairment of the asset which is required to be recognised in the financial statements (see Chapter 48 at 4). This would not necessarily be the case (e.g. where a fixed-interest asset has a fair value below cost because of movements in interest rates but is not intrinsically impaired).

If the option were to lapse unexercised, the entity would simply derecognise the transferred asset and the associated liability, i.e.:

	£	£
Liability	100	
Asset		100

5.4.3 *Transfers of assets measured at fair value*

IAS 39 and IFRS 9 discuss the application of continuing involvement accounting to transferred assets measured at fair value in terms of transferred assets subject to:

- a transferor's call option (see 5.4.3.A below);
- a transferee's put option (see 5.4.3.B below); and
- a 'collar' – i.e. a transferor's call option combined with a transferee's put option (see 5.4.3.C below).

The way in which the rules are articulated in IAS 39 and IFRS 9 is somewhat confusing, but in general the effect is that the transferred asset is recognised at:

- in the case of an asset subject to a transferor call option, its fair value (on the basis that the call option gives the transferor access to any increase in the fair value of the asset); and

- in the case of an asset subject to a transferee put option, the lower of fair value and the option exercise price (on the basis that the put option denies the transferor access to any increase in the fair value of the asset above the option price).

This methodology summarised below is applied both on the date on which the option is written and subsequently.

5.4.3.A *Transferor's call option*

If a transferor's call option prevents derecognition (see 3.8.3 and 4 above) of a transferred asset measured at fair value, the asset continues to be measured at its fair value. The associated liability is measured:

- if the option is in or at the money, at the option exercise price less the time value of the option; or

- if the option is out of the money, at the fair value of the transferred asset less the time value of the option.

The adjustment to the measurement of the associated liability ensures that the net carrying amount of the asset and the associated liability is the fair value of the call option right, as illustrated by Example 50.12 below. *[IAS 39.AG48(c), IFRS 9.B3.2.13(c)].*

Example 50.12:   Asset measured at fair value subject to transferor's call option

An entity has a financial asset, accounted for at fair value through profit or loss, carried at €80. It transfers the asset to a third party, subject to a call option whereby the entity can compel the transferee to sell the asset back to the entity for €95. At the date of transfer, the call option has a time value of €5.

The option is considered to be neither deeply in the money nor deeply out of the money. IAS 39 and IFRS 9 therefore require the entity to continue to recognise the asset to the extent of its continuing involvement (Figure 50.1, Box 9 – see also 4.2.3 above), and to continue recording it at fair value. At the date of transfer, the call option is out of the money. IAS 39 and IFRS 9 therefore require the liability to be measured at the fair value of the transferred asset less the time value of the option, i.e. €80 – €5 = €75. This has the result that the net of the carrying value of the asset (€80) and the carrying value of the liability (€75) equals the time value of the option (€5), i.e.

	€	€
Date of transfer		
Cash	75	
Liability		75

A   *Transferred asset increases in value*

Suppose that one year later the fair value of the asset is €100 and the time value of the option is now €3. The option is now in the money, so that the liability is measured at the option exercise price less the time value of the option, i.e. €95 – €3 = €92. This has the result that the net of the carrying value of the asset (€100) and the carrying value of the liability (€92) equals the fair value of the option (€8, representing €3 time value and €5 intrinsic value). The liability could have been more straightforwardly calculated as the fair value of the asset (€100) less the fair value of the option (€8) = €92. This gives rise to the following accounting entries:

	€	€
During year 1		
Asset (€100 – €80)	20	
Liability (€92 – €75)		17
Gain (profit or loss)		3

The €3 gain recorded in profit or loss effectively represents the increase in the fair value of the option from €5 to €8 over the period. If the entity were able to exercise the option at this point, and did so, it would record the entry:

	€	€
Liability	92	
Loss (profit or loss)	3	
Cash		95

The particular transaction results in no overall gain or loss being reflected in profit or loss (i.e. €3 gain during the year less €3 loss on exercise of option). This represents the net of the €20 gain in the fair value of the asset (€100 at the end of period less €80 at the start) and the net cash outflow of €20 (€75 in on initial transfer, €95 out on exercise of option).

B   *Asset decreases in value*

Suppose instead that during the first year the fair value of the asset fell to €65 and the time value of the option at the end of the year was only €1. The liability would be measured at the fair value of the transferred asset less the time value of the option, i.e. €65 – €1 = €64. This would generate the accounting entries:

	€	€
During year 1		
Liability (€64 – €75)	11	
Loss (profit or loss)	4	
Asset (€65 – €80)		15

Again the overall loss shown in profit or loss represents the movement in the fair value of the option over the period from €5 to €1. Suppose that one year later there was no change in the fair value of the asset, and the option expired unexercised. The entity would then record the accounting entry:

	€	€
At end of year 2		
Liability	64	
Loss (profit or loss)	1	
Asset (statement of financial position)		65

This results in an overall loss for the transaction as a whole of €5 (€4 in year 1 and €1 in year 2), which represents the difference between the carrying value of the asset at the date of original transfer (€80) and the proceeds received (€75).

The amount of any consideration received is in principle not relevant to the measurement of the liability. If, for example, the entity originally received consideration of €72, it would still record a liability of €75 and a 'day one' loss of €3. If it received consideration of €80, it would still record a liability of €75 and a 'day one' profit of €5. The IASB no doubt presumed that such transactions are likely to be undertaken only by sophisticated market participants such that the consideration received will always be equivalent to the fair value of the asset less the fair value of the option. However, there may well be instances where this is not the case, such as in transactions between members of the same group or other related parties.

5.4.3.B   Transferee's put option

If a transferee's put option prevents derecognition (see 3.8.3 and 4 above) of a transferred asset measured at fair value, IAS 39 and IFRS 9 require the asset to be measured at the lower of fair value and the option exercise price. The basis for this treatment is that the entity has no right to increases in the fair value of the transferred asset above the exercise price of the option. The associated liability is measured at the option exercise price plus the time value of the option. This ensures that the net carrying amount of the asset and the associated liability is the fair value of the put option obligation, as illustrated by Example 50.13 below. *[IAS 39.AG48(d), IFRS 9.B3.2.13(d)].*

Example 50.13:   Asset measured at fair value subject to transferee's put option

An entity has a financial asset, accounted for at fair value. On 1 January 2016 it transfers the asset, then carried at €98, to a third party, subject to a put option whereby the transferee can compel the entity to reacquire the asset for €100. The option is considered to be neither deeply in the money nor deeply out of the money. IAS 39 and IFRS 9 therefore require the entity to continue to recognise the asset to the extent of its continuing involvement (Figure 50.1, Box 9 – see also 4.2.3 above), and to continue recording it at the lower of (a) fair value and (b) €100 (the exercise price of the option). Assuming that the transferee pays €106 for the asset, representing €98 fair value of the asset plus €8 time value of the option, the entity would record the accounting entry:

	€	€
1 January 2016		
Cash	106	
Liability		106

A   *Transferred asset increases in value*

Suppose that at 31 December 2016, the option has a time value of €5 and the fair value of the asset is €120. IAS 39 and IFRS 9 require the carrying value of the asset to be restricted to €100 (the exercise price of the option). The liability is measured at the exercise price plus the time value of the option,[19] i.e. €100 + €5 = €105. This has the result that the net of the carrying value of the asset (€100) and the carrying value of the liability (€105) equals the fair value of the option to the transferor (–€5).

This gives the accounting entry:

	€	€
31 December 2016		
Asset (€100 – €98)	2	
Liability (€105 – €106)	1	
Gain (profit or loss)		3

The gain of €3 effectively represents the decrease in the time value of the option (a *gain* from the transferor's perspective) from €8 to €5.

If the option were then to lapse unexercised, with no further change in the fair value of the asset, the entity would record the accounting entry:

	€	€
On lapse of option		
Liability	105	
Asset		100
Gain (profit or loss)		5

The total gain on the transaction of €8 (€3 in Year 1 and €5 on lapse) represents the option premium of €8 (i.e. the difference between the total consideration of €106 and the carrying value of the asset of €98) received at the outset.

B   *Transferred asset decreases in value*

Suppose instead that at 31 December 2016, the option has a time value of €5 but the fair value of the asset is €90. IAS 39 and IFRS 9 require the carrying value of the asset to be measured at its fair value of €90. The liability is measured at the exercise price plus the time value of the option (i.e. to the transferee), i.e. €100 + €5 = €105.

This gives the accounting entry:

	€	€
31 December 2016		
Liability (€105 – €106)	1	
Loss (profit or loss)	7	
Asset (€90 – €98)		8

This has the result that the net of the carrying value of the asset (€90) and the liability (€105), i.e. €(–15) represents the fair value of the option to the transferor (i.e. intrinsic value €(–10) [€100 exercise price versus €90 value of asset] + time value €(−5)). The €7 loss represents the increase in the fair value of the option (a loss to the transferor) from €8 at the outset to €15 at 31 December 2016.

If the transferee were able to, and did, exercise its option at that point, the entity would record the accounting entry:

	€	€
On exercise of option		
Liability	105	
Cash		100
Gain (profit or loss)		5

The overall €2 loss (i.e. €5 gain above and €7 loss during Year 1) represents the net cash of €8 received from the transferee (€108 in at inception less €100 out on exercise) less the €10 fall in fair value of the transferred asset (€100 at inception less €90 at exercise).

5.4.3.C   'Collar' put and call options

Assets may be transferred in a way designed to ensure that the transferee is shielded from excessive losses on the transferred asset but has to pass significant gains on the asset back to the transferor. Such an arrangement is known as a 'collar', on the basis that it allocates a range of potential value movements in the asset to the transferee, with movements outside that range accruing to the transferor. A simple example would be the transfer of an asset subject to a purchased call option (allowing the transferor to reacquire the asset if it increases in value beyond a certain level) and a written put option (allowing the transferee to compel the transferor to reacquire the asset if it falls in value beyond a certain level).

If a collar, in the form of a purchased call and written put option, prevents derecognition (see 3.8.3 and 4 above) of a transferred asset measured at fair value, IAS 39 and IFRS 9 require the entity to continue to measure the asset at fair value. The associated liability is measured at:

• if the call option is in or at the money, the sum of the call exercise price and the fair value of the put option less the time value of the call option; or

• if the call option is out of the money, the sum of the fair value of the asset and the fair value of the put option less the time value of the call option.

The adjustment to the associated liability ensures that the net carrying amount of the asset and the associated liability is the fair value of the options held and written by the entity, as illustrated by Example 50.14 below. *[IAS 39.AG48(e), IFRS 9.B3.2.13(e)].*

Example 50.14:   Asset measured at fair value subject to collar put and call options

An entity has a financial asset, accounted for at fair value, carried at €100. On 1 January 2016 it transfers the asset to a third party, subject to:

• a call option whereby the entity can compel the transferee to sell the asset back to the entity for €120; and

• a put option whereby the transferee can compel the entity to reacquire the asset for €80.

The options are considered to be neither deeply in the money nor deeply out of the money. IAS 39 and IFRS 9 therefore require the entity to continue to recognise the asset to the extent of its continuing involvement (Figure 50.1, Box 9 − see also 4.2.3 above), and to continue recording it at fair value.

At the date of transfer, the time value of the put and call are €1 and €5 respectively. At the date of transfer, the call option is out of the money, so that the associated liability is calculated as the sum of the fair value of the asset and the fair value of the put option less the time value of the call option, i.e. (€100+€1) – €5 = €96. The net of this and the fair value of the asset (€100) is €4 which is the net fair value of the two options (call €5 less put €1). Assuming that the transaction is undertaken at arm's length, the transferee would pay €96 for the asset and the entity would record the accounting entry:

	€	€
Cash	96	
Liability		96

A   Transferred asset increases in value

Suppose that, at 31 December 2016, the fair value of the asset is €140, and the time value of the put and call are €0.5 and €2 respectively. The call option is now in the money, so that IAS 39 and IFRS 9 require the entity to recognise a liability equal to the sum of the call exercise price and fair value of the put option less the time value of the call option, i.e. (€120 + €0.5) – €2 = €118.5. The net of this and the carrying value of the asset (€140) is €21.5 which is the net fair value of the two options (call €22 [time value €2 plus intrinsic value €20] less put €0.5 = €21.5). This gives the accounting entry:

	€	€
31 December 2016		
Asset (€140 – €100)	40.0	
Gain (profit or loss)		17.5
Liability (€118.5 – €96)		22.5

The gain represents the increase in fair value of the call option of €17 (€5 at outset and €22 at 31 December 2016) plus the €0.5 decrease (a gain from the transferor's perspective) in the fair value of the put option (€1 at outset and €0.5 at 31 December 2016).

If the entity were able to, and did, exercise its call option, it would record the entry:

	€	€
Exercise of call option		
Liability	118.5	
Loss (profit or loss)	1.5	
Cash		120.0

The overall gain of €16 on the transaction (€1.5 loss above and €17.5 profit recorded in 2016) represents the increase in fair value of the asset of €40 (€100 at outset, €140 at 31 December 2016) less the net €24 paid to the transferee (€120 paid on exercise of call less €96 received on initial transfer).

B   Transferred asset decreases in value

Suppose instead that, at 31 December 2016, the fair value of the asset is €78, and the time value of the put and call are €0.5 and €2 respectively. The call option is now out of the money, so that IAS 39 and IFRS 9 require the entity to recognise a liability equal to the sum of the fair value of the asset and the fair value of the put option (i.e. €2.5 – time value €0.5 plus intrinsic value €2 [€80 exercise price versus €78 fair value of asset]) less the time value of the call option, i.e. (€78 + €2.5) – €2 = €78.5.

The net of this and the carrying value of the asset (€78) is €(–0.5) which is the net fair value of the two options (call €2 less put €2.5 = €(–0.5)). This gives the accounting entry:

	€	€
31 December 2016		
Liability (€78.5 – €96)	17.5	
Loss (profit or loss)	4.5	
Asset (€78 – €100)		22.0

The loss represents the decrease in the fair value of the call option of €3 (€5 at outset and €2 at 31 December 2016) plus the €1.5 increase (a decrease from the transferor's perspective) in the fair value of the put option (€1 at outset and €2.5 at 31 December 2016).

If the transferee were able to, and did, exercise its put option, the entity would record the entry:

	€	€
Exercise of put option		
Liability	78.5	
Loss (profit or loss)	1.5	
Cash		80.0

The overall loss of €6 on the transaction (€1.5 loss above and €4.5 loss recorded in 2016) represents the decrease in fair value of the asset of €22 (€100 at outset, €78 at 31 December 2016) offset by the net €16 received from the transferee (€96 received on initial transfer less €80 paid on exercise of put).

5.4.4   *Continuing involvement in part only of a financial asset*

IAS 39 and IFRS 9 give the following example of the application of the continuing involvement approach to continuing involvement in part only of a financial asset. *[IAS 39.AG52, IFRS 9.B3.2.17].*

Example 50.15:   Continuing involvement in part only of a financial asset

An entity has a portfolio of prepayable loans whose coupon and effective interest rate is 10% and whose principal amount and amortised cost is €10 million. It enters into a transaction in which, in return for a payment of €9.115 million, the transferee obtains the right to €9 million of any collections of principal plus 9.5% interest.

The entity retains rights to €1 million of any collections of principal plus interest at 10%, plus the remaining 0.5% ('excess spread') on the remaining €9 million of principal. Collections from prepayments are allocated between the entity and the transferee proportionately in the ratio of 1:9, but any defaults are deducted from the entity's interest of €1 million until that interest is exhausted.

The fair value of the loans at the date of the transaction is €10.1 million and the estimated fair value of the excess spread of 0.5 per cent is €40,000.

The entity determines that it has transferred some significant risks and rewards of ownership (for example, significant prepayment risk) but has also retained some significant risks and rewards of ownership because of its subordinated retained interest (Figure 50.1, Box 7, No) and has retained control (Figure 50.1, Box 8, Yes). It therefore applies the continuing involvement approach (Figure 50.1, Box 9).

The entity analyses the transaction as:

- a retention of a fully proportionate retained interest of €1 million, plus
- the subordination of that retained interest to provide credit enhancement to the transferee for credit losses.

The entity calculates that €9.09 million (90% of €10.1 million) of the consideration received of €9.115 million represents the consideration for a fully proportionate 90% share. The remainder of the consideration (€25,000) received represents consideration received by the entity for subordinating its retained interest to provide credit enhancement to the transferee for credit losses. In addition, the excess spread of 0.5% represents consideration received for the credit enhancement. Accordingly, the total consideration received for the credit enhancement is €65,000 (€25,000 received from transferee plus €40,000 fair value of excess spread).

The entity first calculates the gain or loss on the sale of the 90% share of cash flows. Assuming that separate fair values of the 10% part transferred and the 90% part retained are not available at the date of the transfer, the entity allocates the carrying amount of the asset pro-rata to the fair values of those parts (see 5.1.1 and 5.1.2 and 5.3.5 above). The total fair value of the portfolio is considered to be €10.1 million (see above), and the fair value of the consideration for the part disposed of €9.09 million. The carrying amount of the whole portfolio is €10 million. This implies a carrying amount for the part disposed of €10m × 9.09/10.1 = €9 million, and for the part retained €1 million. The gain on the sale of the 90% is therefore €90,000 (€9.09 million – €9 million).

In addition, IAS 39 and IFRS 9 require the entity to recognise the continuing involvement that results from the subordination of its retained interest for credit losses. Accordingly, it recognises an asset of €1 million (the maximum amount of the cash flows it would forfeit under the subordination), and an associated liability of €1.065 million (the maximum amount of the cash flows it would forfeit under the subordination, i.e. €1 million, plus the consideration for the subordination of €65,000). It also recognises an asset for the fair value of the excess spread which forms part of the consideration for the subordination.

This gives rise to the accounting entry:

	€000	€000
Cash	9,115	
Asset for the subordination of the residual interest	1,000	
Excess spread received for subordination	40	
Loan portfolio		9,000
Liability for subordination		1,065
Gain on disposal		90

It is crucial to an understanding of this example that, as a result of the transaction, the original asset (the portfolio of prepayable loans) is being accounted for as two separate assets. Because the cash flows from the portfolio are split in fully proportionate (pro-rata) shares (see 3.3 above), each of these assets must be considered separately.

The first of these assets, the right to cash flows of €9 million, continues to be recognised only to the extent of the entity's continuing involvement, which in this case is via the credit enhancement. The approach is very similar to continuing involvement through guarantee (see Example 50.10 at 5.4.1 above), except that the liability for subordination includes the maximum cash flow that the entity might not receive from its retained share (i.e. €1 million) rather than, as in Example 50.10, a potential cash outflow (the guarantee amount, which is the maximum amount that the entity could be required to repay). This is aggregated with the fair value of the amount received in respect of the credit enhancement, in order to calculate the full liability for subordination. This is similar to the way in which the fair value of the guarantee is added to the guarantee amount in order to calculate the associated liability. [IAS 39.AG48(a), IFRS 9.B3.2.13(a)].

The second asset is the entity's proportionate retained share of €1 million. It is, seemingly, irrelevant to the accounting analysis in IAS 39 and IFRS 9 that this has already been taken into account in calculating the entity's continuing involvement in the remaining €9 million of the portfolio.

The effect is to gross up the statement of financial position with a subordination asset and liability. As IAS 39 and IFRS 9 note, immediately following the transaction, the carrying amount of the asset is €2.04 million (i.e. €1 million part retained plus €1 million subordination asset plus €40,000 excess spread) – in respect of an asset whose fair value is only €1.01 million!

We have some reservations concerning the example above. First, we challenge whether, as a point of principle, it is appropriate to apply the derecognition criteria to part of an asset where the part that is retained provides credit enhancement for the transferee. As discussed more fully at 3.3.1 above, it is possible that IAS 39 and IFRS 9 are implicitly drawing a distinction between:

- a guarantee that could result in an outflow of the total resources of the transferor, or a return of consideration for the transfer already received (which would not allow partial derecognition); and

- a guarantee that could result in the transferor losing the right to receive a specific future cash inflow, but not being obliged to make any other payment should that specific future cash inflow not materialise.

Moreover, even in the context of the analysis presented by IAS 39 and IFRS 9, we do not understand the basis of the treatment of the excess spread. The example simply asserts that this forms part of the consideration for providing the subordination, although it is not clear that it forms any more or any less of the consideration for the subordination than the interest and principal on the 10% of the portfolio retained.

In our view, a more logical analysis would have been that:

- the entity has disposed of not 90% of the whole portfolio, but 90% of the principal balances and 9.5% interest on that 90%; and

- the consideration for the subordination is still €65,000, on the basis that if:

  - the fair value of the consideration for a fully proportionate share of 90% (i.e. including 10% interest) is €9,090,000; and

  - the fair value of the excess spread of 0.5% interest is €40,000, then

  the fair value of consideration for a fully proportionate share less the excess spread is €9,050,000 (i.e. €9,090,000 less €40,000). This in turn means that the balance of the total consideration of €9,115,000 (i.e. €65,000) relates to the subordination.

In addition, of course, Example 50.15 ignores the possibility that the excess spread is retained by the transferor because it continues to service the portfolio, although this may be an attempt to avoid overcomplicating matters even further.

A further issue is that, if the excess spread is regarded as part of the asset retained, rather than the consideration received, it would seem more appropriate to recognise it on a basis consistent with the accounting treatment of the original transferred asset (typically, amortised cost) rather than at fair value.

5.5 Miscellaneous provisions

IAS 39 and IFRS 9 contain a number of accounting provisions generally applicable to transfers of assets, as discussed below.

5.5.1 *Offset*

IAS 39 and IFRS 9 provide that, if a transferred asset continues to be recognised, the entity must not offset:

- the asset with the associated liability; or

- any income arising from the transferred asset with any expense incurred on the associated liability. *[IAS 39.36, IFRS 9.3.2.22]*.

Whilst IAS 39 and IFRS 9 do not say so specifically, this is clearly intended to apply both to assets that continue to be recognised in full and to those that continue to be recognised to the extent of their continuing involvement.

This requirement apparently over-rides the offset criteria in IAS 32 *[IAS 32.42]*, as illustrated, for example, by the various situations highlighted in the discussion at 4 and 5.1 to 5.4 above where a transaction required to be net-settled (which would normally be required to be accounted for as such under IAS 32) is accounted for as if it were to be gross-settled.

5.5.2 Collateral

If a transferor provides non-cash collateral (such as debt or equity instruments) to the transferee, the accounting treatment for the collateral by both the transferor and the transferee depends on:

- whether the transferee has the right to sell or repledge the collateral; and
- whether the transferor has defaulted.

If the transferee has the right by contract or custom to sell or repledge a collateral asset, the transferor should reclassify that asset in its statement of financial position (e.g. as a loaned asset, pledged equity instruments or repurchase receivable) separately from other assets.

If the transferee sells collateral pledged to it, it recognises the proceeds from the sale and a liability measured at fair value for its obligation to return the collateral.

If the transferor defaults under the terms of the contract and is no longer entitled to redeem the collateral, it derecognises the collateral, and the transferee either:

- recognises the collateral as its asset initially measured at fair value; or
- if it has already sold the collateral, derecognises its obligation to return the collateral.

In no other circumstances should the transferor derecognise, or the transferee recognise, the collateral as an asset. *[IAS 39.37, IFRS 9. 3.2.23].*

5.5.3 Rights or obligations over transferred assets that continue to be recognised

Where a transfer of a financial asset does not qualify for derecognition, the transferor may well have contractual rights or obligations related to the transfer, such as options or forward repurchase contracts that are derivatives of a type that would normally be required to be recognised under IAS 39 and IFRS 9.

IAS 39 and IFRS 9 prohibit separate recognition of such derivatives, if recognition of the derivative together with either the transferred asset or the liability arising from the transfer would result in recognising the same rights or obligations twice.

For example, IAS 39 and IFRS 9 note that a call option retained by the transferor may prevent a transfer of financial assets from being accounted for as a sale (see 4 above). In that case, the call option must not be separately recognised as a derivative asset. *[IAS 39.AG49, IFRS 9.B3.2.14].*

5.6   Reassessing derecognition

IAS 39 and IFRS 9 state that if an entity determines that, as a result of the transfer, it has transferred substantially all the risks and rewards of ownership of the transferred asset, it does not recognise the transferred asset again in a future period, unless it reacquires the transferred asset in a new transaction. *[IAS 39.AG41, IFRS 9.B3.2.6]*. We have noted earlier that there is some ambiguity as to whether this rule in AG41 is to be read generally as prohibiting any re-recognition of a derecognised asset or specifically as referring only to circumstances where derecognition results from transfer of substantially all the risks and rewards (i.e. it applies only to 'Box 6, Yes' transactions, and not to 'Box 8, No' transactions). Our view, as expressed at 4.2 above, is that the broader interpretation should be applied and the requirement still applies if derecognition occurs for another reason, e.g. loss of control.

The risks and rewards of ownership retained by the entity may change as a result of market changes in such a way that, had the revised conditions existed at inception, they would have prevented derecognition of the asset. However, the original decision to derecognise the asset should not be revisited, unless (in exceptional circumstances) the original assessment was an accounting error within the scope of IAS 8.

5.6.1   Reassessment of consolidation of subsidiaries and SPEs

The effect of IFRS 10, combined with the derecognition provisions of IAS 39 or IFRS 9 is that a transaction (commonly, but not exclusively, in a securitisation) may result in derecognition of the financial asset concerned in the seller's own financial statements, but the 'buyer' may be a consolidated SPE, so that the asset is immediately re-recognised in the consolidated financial statements in which the seller is included. However, an entity may derecognise assets if they are transferred to an SPE that is not consolidated because, having considered all of the facts and circumstances, the entity concludes that it does not control the SPE. The assessment as to whether a particular SPE is controlled by the reporting entity is discussed in Chapter 6.

IFRS 10 requires an investor to reassess whether it controls an investee if facts and circumstances indicate that there are changes to any elements of control, including the investor's exposure, or rights, to variable returns from its involvement with the investee (see Chapter 6). *[IFRS 10.8]*.

6   DERECOGNITION – FINANCIAL LIABILITIES

The provisions of IAS 39 and IFRS 9 with respect to the derecognition of financial liabilities are generally more straightforward and less subjective than those for the derecognition of financial assets. However, they are also very different from the asset derecognition rules which focus primarily on the economic substance of the transaction. By contrast, the rules for derecognition of liabilities, like the provisions of IAS 32 for the identification of instruments as financial liabilities (see Chapter 44), focus more on legal obligations than on economic substance – or, as the

IASB would doubtless argue, they are based on the view that the economic substance of whether an entity has a liability to a third party is ultimately dictated by the legal rights and obligations that exist between them.

IAS 39 and IFRS 9 contain provisions relating to:

- the extinguishment of debt (see 6.1 below);
- the substitution or modification of debt by the original lender (see 6.2 below); and
- the calculation of any profit or loss arising on the derecognition of debt (see 6.3 below).

6.1 Extinguishment of debt

IAS 39 and IFRS 9 require an entity to derecognise (i.e. remove from its statement of financial position) a financial liability (or a part of a financial liability – see 6.1.1 below) when, and only when, it is 'extinguished', that is, when the obligation specified in the contract is discharged, cancelled, or expires. *[IAS 39.39, IFRS 9.3.3.1]*. This will be achieved when the debtor either:

- discharges the liability (or part of it) by paying the creditor, normally with cash, other financial assets, goods or services; or
- is legally released from primary responsibility for the liability (or part of it) either by process of law or by the creditor. *[IAS 39.AG57, IFRS 9.B3.3.1]*. Extinguishment of liabilities by legal release is discussed further at 6.1.2 below.

If the issuer of a debt instrument repurchases the instrument, the debt is extinguished even if the issuer is a market maker in that instrument, or otherwise intends to resell or reissue it in the near term. *[IAS 39.AG58, IFRS 9.B3.3.2]*. IAS 39 and IFRS 9 focus only on whether the entity has a legal obligation to reissue the debt, not on whether there is a commercial imperative for it to do so.

6.1.1 What constitutes 'part' of a liability?

The requirements of IAS 39 and IFRS 9 for the derecognition of liabilities apply to all or 'part' of a financial liability. It is not entirely clear what is meant by 'part' of a liability in this context. The rules, and the examples, in IAS 39 and IFRS 9 seem to be drafted in the context of transactions that settle all remaining cash flows (i.e. interest and principal) of a proportion of a liability, such as the repayment of £25 million of a £100 million loan, together with any related interest payments.

However, these provisions are presumably also intended to apply in situations where an entity prepays the interest only (or a proportion of future interest payments) or the principal only (or a proportion of future principal payments) on a loan.

6.1.2 Legal release by creditor

A liability can be derecognised by a debtor if the creditor legally releases the debtor from the liability. It is clear that IAS 39 and IFRS 9 regard legal release as crucial, with the effect that very similar (if not identical) situations may lead to different results purely because of the legal form.

For example, IAS 39 and IFRS 9 provide that:

- where a debtor is legally released from a liability, derecognition is not precluded by the fact that the debtor has given a guarantee in respect of the liability; *[IAS 39.AG57(b), IFRS 9.B3.3.1(b)]* but

- if a debtor pays a third party to assume an obligation and notifies its creditor that the third party has assumed the debt obligation, the debtor derecognises the debt obligation if, and only if, the creditor legally releases the debtor from its obligations. *[IAS 39.AG60, IFRS 9.B3.3.4].*

The effect of these requirements is shown by Example 50.16.

Example 50.16:   Transfer of debt obligations with and without legal release

Scenario 1

Entity A issues bonds that have a carrying amount and fair value of $1,000,000. A pays $1,000,000 to Entity B for B to assume responsibility for paying interest and principal on the bonds to the bondholders. The bondholders are informed that B has assumed responsibility for the debt. However, A is not legally released from the obligation to pay interest and principal by the bondholders. Accordingly, if B does not make payments when due, the bondholders may seek payment from A.

Scenario 2

Entity A issues bonds that have a carrying amount and fair value of $1,000,000. A pays $1,000,000 to Entity B for B to assume responsibility for paying interest and principal on the bonds to the bondholders. The bondholders are informed that B has assumed responsibility for the debt and legally release A from any further obligation under the debt. However, A enters into a guarantee arrangement whereby, if B does not make payments when due, the bondholders may seek payment from A.

It is clear, in our view, that in either scenario above the bondholders are in the same economic and legal position – they will receive payments from B and, if B defaults, they will have recourse to A.

However, IAS 39 and IFRS 9 give rise to the, in our view, anomalous result that:

- Scenario 1 is accounted for by the continuing recognition of the debt because no legal release has been obtained; but

- Scenario 2 is accounted for by derecognition of the debt, and recognition of the guarantee, notwithstanding that the effect of the guarantee is to put A back in the same position as if it had not been released from its obligations under the original bond.

IAS 39 and IFRS 9 also clarify that, if a debtor:

- transfers its obligations under a debt to a third party and obtains legal release from its obligations by the creditor; but

- undertakes to make payments to the third party so as to enable it to meet its obligations to the creditor,

it should derecognise the original debt, but recognise a new debt obligation to the third party. *[IAS 39.AG60, IFRS 9.B3.3.4].*

Legal release may also be achieved through the novation of a contract to an intermediary counterparty. For example, a derivative between a reporting entity and a bank may be novated to a central counterparty (CCP). In these circumstances, the IASB explains that the novation to the CCP releases the bank from the responsibility to make payments to the reporting entity. Consequently, the original derivative meets the derecognition criteria for a financial liability and a new derivative with the CCP is recognised. *[IAS 39.BC220D]*. However, for hedge accounting purposes only, it is sometimes possible in these circumstances to treat the new derivative as a continuation of the original (see Chapter 51 at 4.2.3.A and Chapter 52 at 11.3).

6.1.3   'In-substance defeasance' arrangements

Entities sometimes enter into so-called 'in-substance defeasance' arrangements in respect of financial liabilities. These typically involve a lump sum payment to a third party (other than the creditor) such as a trust, which then invests the funds in (typically) very low-risk assets to which the entity has no, or very limited, rights of access. These assets are then applied to discharge all the remaining interest and principal payments on the financial liabilities that are purported to have been defeased. It is sometimes argued that the risk-free nature of the assets, and the entity's lack of access to them, means that the entity is in substance in no different position than if it had actually repaid the original financial liability.

IAS 39 and IFRS 9 regard such arrangements as not giving rise to derecognition of the original liability in the absence of legal release by the creditor. *[IAS 39.AG59, IFRS 9.B3.3.3]*.

6.1.4   Extinguishment in exchange for transfer of assets not meeting the derecognition criteria

IAS 39 and IFRS 9 note that in some cases legal release may be achieved by transferring assets to the creditor which do not meet the criteria for derecognition (see 3 above). In such a case, the debtor will derecognise the liability from which it has been released, but recognise a new liability relating to the transferred assets that may be equal to the derecognised liability. *[IAS 39.AG61, IFRS 9.B3.3.5]*. It is not entirely clear what is envisaged here, but it may be some such scenario as the following.

Example 50.17:   Extinguishment of debt in exchange for transfer of assets not meeting derecognition criteria

An entity has a bank loan of €1 million. The bank agrees to accept in full payment of the loan the transfer to it by the entity of a portfolio of corporate bonds with a market value of €1 million. The entity and the bank then enter into a put and call option over the bonds, the effect of which will be that the entity will repurchase the bonds in three years' time at a price that gives the bank a lender's return on €1 million. As discussed further at 4.2.8 above, this would have the effect that the entity is unable to derecognise the bonds.

Under the provisions of IAS 39 and IFRS 9, the entity would be able to derecognise the original bank loan, as it has been legally released from it. The provisions under discussion here have the overall result that a loan effectively continues to be recognised. Strictly, however, the analysis is that the original loan has been derecognised and a new one recognised. In effect the accounting is representing that the entity has repaid the original loan and replaced it with a new one secured on a bond portfolio.

However, as the new loan is required to be initially recognised at fair value whereas the old loan may well have been recognised at amortised cost (see Chapter 48 at 3), there may well be a gain or loss to record as the result of the different measurement bases being used – see 6.2 and 6.3 below.

6.2   Exchange or modification of debt by original lender

It is common for an entity, particularly but not necessarily when in financial difficulties, to approach its major creditors for a restructuring of its debt commitments – for example, an agreement to postpone the repayment of principal in exchange for higher interest payments in the meantime, or to roll up interest into a single 'bullet' payment of interest and principal at the end of the term. Such changes to the terms of debt can be effected in a number of ways, in particular:

- a notional repayment of the original loan followed by an immediate re-lending of all or part of the proceeds of the notional repayment as a new loan ('exchange'); or

- legal amendment of the original loan agreement ('modification').

The accounting issue raised by such transactions is essentially whether there is, in fact, anything to account for. For example, if an entity owes £100 million at floating rate interest and negotiates with its bankers to change the interest to a fixed coupon of 7%, should the accounting treatment reflect that fact that:

(a)   the entity still owes £100 million to the same lender, and so is in the same position as before; or

(b)   the modification of the interest profile has altered the net present value of the total obligations under the loan?

IAS 39 and IFRS 9 require an exchange between an existing borrower and lender of debt instruments with 'substantially different' terms to be accounted for as an extinguishment of the original financial liability and the recognition of a new financial liability. Similarly, a substantial modification of the terms of an existing financial liability, or a part of it, (whether or not due to the financial difficulty of the debtor) should be accounted for as an extinguishment of the original financial liability and the recognition of a new financial liability. *[IAS 39.40, IFRS 9.3.3.2]*.

The accounting consequences for an exchange or a modification that results in extinguishment and one that does not lead to extinguishment are discussed in further detail at 6.2.1 to 6.2.3 below.

IAS 39 and IFRS 9 regard the terms of exchanged or modified debt as 'substantially different' if the net present value of the cash flows under the new terms (including any fees paid net of any fees received) discounted at the original effective interest rate is at least 10% different from the discounted present value of the remaining cash flows of the original debt instrument. *[IAS 39.AG62, IFRS 9.B3.3.6]*. This comparison is commonly referred to as 'the 10% test'.

Whilst IAS 39 and IFRS 9 do not say so explicitly, it seems clear that the discounted present value of the remaining cash flows of the original debt instrument used in the 10% test must also be determined using the original effective interest rate, so that there is a 'like for like' comparison. This amount should also represent the amortised cost of the liability prior to modification.

Also, it is not clear from the standards whether the cash flows under the new terms should include only fees payable to the lender or whether they should also include other fees and costs that would be considered transaction costs, such as amounts payable to the entity's legal advisers. Read literally the standards suggest only fees should be included, but as the accounting treatment for fees and costs incurred on a modification are identical, some would argue that both should be included in the test. In our view, either approach is an acceptable interpretation.

IAS 39 and IFRS 9 do not explicitly prohibit an entity from accounting for an exchange or modification of a liability where the net present value of the cash flows under the new terms is less than 10% different from the discounted present value of the remaining cash flows of the original debt instrument. Indeed, there may be situations where the modification of the debt is so fundamental that immediate derecognition is appropriate whether or not the 10% test is satisfied. The following are examples of situations where derecognition of the original instrument could be required:

• An entity has issued a 'plain vanilla' debt instrument and restructures the debt to include an embedded equity instrument.

• An entity has issued a 5% euro-denominated debt instrument and restructures the instrument to an 18% Turkish lire-denominated debt instrument.

The present value of the cash flows of the restructured debts, discounted at the original effective interest rate, may not be significantly different from the discounted present value of the remaining cash flows of the original financial liability. However, even if the 10% test is not satisfied, the introduction of the equity-linked feature or a change in currency could significantly alter the future economic risk exposure of the instrument. In these circumstances the modification of terms should, in our view, be regarded as representing a substantial change which would lead to derecognition of the original liability.

6.2.1 Costs and fees

An entity will almost always be required to pay fees to the lender and incur costs (such as legal expenses) on an exchange or modification of a financial liability.

If an exchange of debt instruments or modification of terms is accounted for as an extinguishment of the original debt, IAS 39 and IFRS 9 require any costs or fees incurred to be recognised as part of the gain or loss on the extinguishment (see 6.3 below). *[IAS 39.AG62, IFRS 9.B3.3.6]*.

Where the exchange or modification is not accounted for as an extinguishment, any costs or fees incurred adjust the carrying amount of the liability and are amortised over the remaining term of the modified liability. *[IAS 39.AG62, IFRS 9.B3.3.6]*. Neither IAS 39 nor IFRS 9 specify a particular method for amortising such costs and fees. In our view, applying the effective interest method or another approach that approximates this such as a straight-line method would be appropriate. This is illustrated in the following example.

Example 50.18:   Fees and costs incurred on modification of debt not treated as extinguishment

On 1 January 2014 an entity borrowed $100 million on, at that time, arm's length market terms, so that interest of 6% was to be paid annually in arrears and the loan repaid in full on 31 December 2018. Transaction costs of $4 million were incurred. Assuming that the loan had run to term, the entity would have recorded the following amounts using the effective interest method.

The loan is originally recorded at the issue proceeds of $100 million less transaction costs of $4 million, and the effective interest rate of 6.975% is derived by a computer program or trial and error. For a more detailed discussion of the effective interest method, see Chapter 48 at 3 and Chapter 49 at 3.

Year	Liability b/f $m	Interest at 6.975% $m	Cash paid $m	Liability c/f $m
1.1.2014	96.00			96.00
2014	96.00	6.70	(6.00)	96.70
2015	96.70	6.74	(6.00)	97.44
2016	97.44	6.80	(6.00)	98.24
2017	98.24	6.85	(6.00)	99.09
2018	99.09	6.91	(106.00)	–

During the latter part of 2015 the entity considers expanding its business in a way that would crystallise the lender's right to demand immediate repayment of the loan because such an action is not permitted under the detailed terms of the loan. Therefore the entity approaches the lender with a view to amending those terms to permit the planned expansion, but without changing the cash flows on the loan. On 1 January 2016, the lender agrees to amend the terms in return for which it charges the entity a fee of $450,000. The entity also incurs directly attributable legal costs of $50,000, bringing the total fees and costs incurred to $500,000.

It can be shown that the net present value of the cash flows under the new terms, including the $0.45 million of fees paid, discounted at the original effective interest rate is $97.89 million. This compares to the carrying amount of $97.44 million and because the remaining cash flows have not changed, the difference between the two simply represents the fees paid. This difference is just 0.46% of the original carrying amount, significantly less than 10%. If the legal costs were also included in the 10% test, the difference would be $0.50 million or 0.51% of the original carrying amount. The entity does not consider the changes to the detailed terms of the loan to be substantial and therefore concludes the modification should not result in the extinguishment of the liability.

Accordingly the carrying amount of the liability is adjusted by the $500,000 fees and costs incurred so that the revised carrying amount is $96.94 million ($97.44 million less $0.50 million). In order to amortise this adjustment over the remaining term of the loan, the entity could reset the effective interest rate of the loan, in this case to 7.169%, so that it is amortised in accordance with the effective interest method as follows.

Year	Liability b/f $m	Interest at 7.169% $m	Cash paid $m	Liability c/f $m
1.1.2016	96.94			96.94
2016	96.94	6.95	(6.00)	97.89
2017	97.89	7.02	(6.00)	98.91
2018	98.91	7.09	(106.00)	–

Another way would be to view the liability as comprising two components: the unadjusted carrying amount of $97.44 million, to which the effective interest method would be applied using the original effective interest rate of 6.975%; and the adjustment of $500,000 which would be amortised on some other basis, such as straight line. This would give rise to substantially the same interest expense in each period, detailed calculations showing a slight change in 2016 and 2018 to $6.96 million and $7.08 million respectively.

6.2.2 Modification gains and losses

In Example 50.18 above, the remaining cash flows on the loan remained the same after the modification, but in practice they will often change. For example, in the situation set out in Example 50.18, the lender might have agreed to charge additional interest of, say, $170,000 per year for the remaining three year term of the loan instead of the $450,000 fee at the time of the modification. Detailed calculations show an almost identical outcome when applying the 10% test to these revised facts, with the net present value of the cash flows under revised terms being $97.89 million excluding the $50,000 of costs, a difference of $0.45 million or 0.46% ($97.94 million including costs, a difference of $0.50 million or 0.51%). Again it would be concluded that the modification does not result in derecognition of the liability.

As noted at 6.2.1 above, the standards are clear that the costs and fees incurred should be amortised over the remaining term of the liability, but how should the entity account for changes to the future contractual cash flows? Neither IAS 39 nor IFRS 9 provide a conclusive answer to this question. Guidance to the original version of IAS 39[20] made it clear that the difference between the present values under the old and new terms was to be amortised over the remaining term of the liability. This treatment applied irrespective of the extent to which the difference arose from fees or costs incurred at the time of the modification or from changes to the remaining cash flows. Given the related requirements of the original version of IAS 39 were carried forward into the current version (and now into IFRS 9) without major change, it could be argued that this approach remains appropriate.

However, other parts of IAS 39 and IFRS 9 might suggest a different treatment. In particular, both IAS 39 and IFRS 9 are clear that if an entity's estimates of the contractual cash flows on a debt instrument change, the amortised cost of the instrument should be adjusted to the net present value of the revised cash flows discounted at the original effective interest rate, with the difference recognised in profit or loss (see Chapter 48 at 3.2.1 and Chapter 49 at 3.2.1). Although this requirement is intended to apply to changes in estimated cash flows under the terms of an unmodified contract, some would argue it is appropriate to apply a similar approach when the contractual terms change. Further, IFRS 9 is clear that modifications to the contractual cash flows of a financial asset measured at amortised cost that do not result in derecognition of that asset give rise to a modification gain or loss (see Chapter 49 at 5.7).

In our view, in the absence of more definitive guidance, both approaches are acceptable. In our experience, the approach commonly applied is that based on the guidance to the original version of IAS 39. When IFRS 9 is applied, the more explicit requirements for modifications of financial assets should lead entities to review, and possibly change, their accounting policies for modifications to financial liabilities, although that remains to be seen.

Applying the second approach to the situation discussed above would result in the entity recognising a modification loss of $0.45 million, being the net present value of the additional interest payable of $170,000 per annum, discounted at the original effective interest rate of 6.975%. This might seem counter-intuitive to some when compared to the original facts in Example 50.18. The only difference between the two scenarios is that in the first the borrower makes an immediate cash payment to the lender of $0.45 million in the form of a fee, whereas in the second it makes payments to the lender over the next three years (in the form of additional interest) which have a net present value of $0.45 million. Therefore, one might ask, why would the timing of the associated expense depend on the form and timing of the cash flows? Nevertheless, this treatment is clearly required by IFRS 9 for financial assets.

6.2.3 Illustrative examples

Examples 50.19 and 50.20 below illustrate some more complex modifications of debt.

Example 50.19: Modification of debt not treated as extinguishment

On 1 January 2011 an entity borrowed £100 million on, at that time, arm's length market terms, so that interest of 7% was to be paid annually in arrears and the loan repaid in full on 31 December 2020. Transaction costs of £5 million were incurred. Assuming that the loan had run to term, the entity would have recorded the following amounts using the effective interest method. The loan is originally recorded at the issue proceeds of £100 million less transaction costs of £5 million, and the effective interest rate is 7.736%.

Year	Liability b/f £m	Interest at 7.736% £m	Cash paid £m	Liability c/f £m
1.1.2011	95.00			95.00
2011	95.00	7.35	(7.00)	95.35
2012	95.35	7.38	(7.00)	95.73
2013	95.73	7.40	(7.00)	96.13
2014	96.13	7.44	(7.00)	96.57
2015	96.57	7.47	(7.00)	97.04
2016	97.04	7.51	(7.00)	97.55
2017	97.55	7.55	(7.00)	98.10
2018	98.10	7.59	(7.00)	98.69
2019	98.69	7.63	(7.00)	99.32
2020	99.32	7.68	(107.00)	–

During 2015 the entity is in financial difficulties and approaches the lender for a modification of the terms of the loan. These are agreed on 1 January 2016, as follows. No cash interest will be paid in 2016 or 2017, although a fee of £2 million must be paid to the lender immediately. From 2018 onwards interest of 9% will be paid annually in arrears and the term of the loan will be extended for two years until 31 December 2022. Legal fees and other costs incurred are not material.

The entity is required to compute the present value of the new arrangement using the original effective interest rate of 7.736%. This gives a net present value for the modified debt of £92.53 million, calculated as follows:

Year	Cash flow	£m	Discount factor	£m
1.1.2016	Fee	2.00	1	2.00
2018	Interest	9.00	$1/1.07736^3$	7.20
2019	Interest	9.00	$1/1.07736^4$	6.68
2020	Interest	9.00	$1/1.07736^5$	6.20
2021	Interest	9.00	$1/1.07736^6$	5.75
2022	Interest and principal	109.00	$1/1.07736^7$	64.70
			Total	92.53

This represents 95.4% of the current carrying value of the debt as at the end of 2015 of £97.04 million, so that the net present value of the modified loan (discounted at the effective interest rate of the original loan) is 4.6% different from that of the original loan. This is less than 10%, so that the modification is not automatically required to be treated as an extinguishment under IAS 39 or IFRS 9.

If the entity selects an accounting policy to recognise modification gains or losses over the remaining term of the liability, the current carrying value of £97.04 million must stand and a new effective interest rate is derived.

Under this approach the carrying value of the loan at the end of 2015 of £97.04 million, net of the £2 million fees, is treated as a new borrowing of £95.04 million, accounted for as follows, using a newly derived effective interest rate of 6.905%.

Year	Liability b/f £m	Interest at 6.905% £m	Cash paid £m	Liability c/f £m
2016	95.04	6.56		101.60
2017	101.60	7.01		108.61
2018	108.61	7.50	(9.00)	107.11
2019	107.11	7.40	(9.00)	105.51
2020	105.51	7.28	(9.00)	103.79
2021	103.79	7.17	(9.00)	101.96
2022	101.96	7.04	(109.00)	–

However, the entity may have selected an accounting policy under which it recognises an immediate gain or loss when the cash flows on a loan are modified and the liability is not derecognised. The application of such an approach in this situation would result in the recognition of a gain of £6.51 million (£97.04 million current carrying value less £90.53 million recalculated net present value, excluding the fees, which as set out at 6.2.1 above adjust the carrying amount of the liability and are amortised over its remaining term). Allocating the fee based upon the effective interest method would result in an increase in the effective interest rate to 8.1213%.

The adjusted carrying amount of the liability £88.53 million (£90.53 million net present value of cash flows on the borrowing less £2 million fee) would be accreted using the effective interest method as follows:

Year	Liability b/f £m	Interest at 8.1213% £m	Cash paid £m	Liability c/f £m
2016	88.53	7.19	–	95.72
2017	95.72	7.77	–	103.49
2018	103.49	8.41	(9.00)	102.90
2019	102.90	8.36	(9.00)	102.26
2020	102.26	8.30	(9.00)	101.56
2021	101.56	8.25	(9.00)	100.81
2022	100.81	8.19	(109.00)	–

Example 50.20: Modification of debt treated as extinguishment

Assume the same facts as in Example 50.19 above, except that on 1 January 2016 the entity comes to an arrangement with the lender to modify the terms of the loan as follows.

No cash interest will be paid in 2016 or 2017, although a fee of £2 million must be paid to the lender immediately. From 2018 onwards interest of 12.5% will be paid annually in arrears, and the term of the loan will be extended for three years until 31 December 2023. Legal fees and other costs incurred are not material.

As in Example 50.19 above, the entity is required to compute the net present value of the new arrangement using the original effective interest rate of 7.736%. This gives a net present value for the modified debt of £107.3 million calculated as follows.

Year	Cash flow	£m	Discount factor	£m
1.1.2016	Fee	2.00	1	2.00
2018	Interest	12.50	$1/1.07736^3$	10.00
2019	Interest	12.50	$1/1.07736^4$	9.28
2020	Interest	12.50	$1/1.07736^5$	8.61
2021	Interest	12.50	$1/1.07736^6$	7.99
2022	Interest	12.50	$1/1.07736^7$	7.42
2023	Interest and principal	112.50	$1/1.07736^8$	61.98
			Total	107.28

This represents 110.6% of the current carrying value of the debt as at the end of 2015 of £97.04 million, so that the net present value of the modified loan (discounted at the effective interest rate of the original loan) is 10.6% different from that of the original loan. This is greater than 10%, so that the modification is required to be treated as an extinguishment under IAS 39 and IFRS 9.

This will involve derecognising the existing liability and recognising a new liability. The issue is then at what amount the new liability should be recognised. It is not the £107.28 million above, since this includes the fee of £2 million, which is required to be treated as integral to the cash flows of the modified loan for the purposes of comparing it with the original loan, but is then required to be expensed immediately if the test identifies an extinguishment.

Moreover, as the accounting treatment is intended to represent the derecognition of an existing liability and the recognition of a new one, the modified loan must – in accordance with the initial measurement provisions of IAS 39 and IFRS 9 (see Chapter 47) – be recognised at fair value and amortised using its own effective interest rate, not that applicable to the original loan.

The difficulty is obviously in determining the fair value of the modified loan. If the loan was in the form of a quoted bond, a market value might be available. Another possible approach might be to discount the cash flows of the modified loan at the interest rate at which the entity could have issued a new loan on similar terms to the modified loan. However, where (as may well be the case) the modification is being undertaken because the entity is in serious financial difficulty, it might be that no lender would be prepared to advance new finance, so that there is no readily available 'notional' borrowing rate. Nevertheless, IAS 39 and IFRS 9 contain no exemption from making an estimate of the fair value of the modified loan.

If the view were taken that the fair value of the modified loan was £98 million, the accounting treatment for the modification would be (see also 6.3 below):

	£m	£m
Original loan	97.04	
Loss on extinguishment of debt (income statement)	2.96	
Modified loan		98.00
Cash (fee)		2.00

In this particular case, this has the result that the actual gain or loss recognised is actually somewhat smaller than the difference calculated between the net present value of the original and modified loan that led to the requirement to recognise the gain or loss in the first place. This differential will obviously be reflected in higher interest costs as the transaction matures. If the borrower was in financial difficulties, it is possible for the fair value of the modified loan to be significantly below its principal amount, which could give rise to a large profit on modification followed by very high interest charges over the remaining term.

6.2.4   Settlement of financial liability with issue of new equity instrument

A related area is the accounting treatment to be adopted where an entity issues non-convertible debt, but subsequently enters into an agreement with the debt-holder to discharge the liability under the debt in full or in part for an issue of equity instruments. This most often occurs when the entity is in financial difficulties. This topic is now dealt with in IFRIC 19 – *Extinguishing Financial Liabilities with Equity Instruments* – which is discussed in Chapter 44 at 7.

6.3   Gains and losses on extinguishment of debt

When a financial liability (or part of a liability) is extinguished or transferred to another party, IAS 39 and IFRS 9 require the difference between the carrying amount of the transferred financial liability (or part of a liability) and the consideration paid, including any non-cash assets transferred or liabilities assumed, to be recognised in profit or loss. *[IAS 39.41, IFRS 9.3.3.3].*

If an entity repurchases only a part of a financial liability, it calculates the carrying value of the part disposed of (and hence the gain or loss on disposal) by allocating the previous carrying amount of the financial liability between the part that continues to be recognised and the part that is derecognised based on the relative fair values of those parts on the date of the repurchase. *[IAS 39.42, IFRS 9.3.3.4].* In other words, the carrying amount of the liability is not simply reduced by consideration received.

This is illustrated in Example 50.21 below.

Example 50.21:   Partial derecognition of debt

On 1 January 2013 an entity issues 500 million €1 10-year bonds which are traded in the capital markets. Issue costs of €15 million were incurred and the carrying value of the bonds at 31 December 2016 is €490 million. On 31 December 2016 the entity makes a market purchase of 120 million bonds at their then current market price of €0.97. The entity records the following accounting entry:

	€m	€m
Bonds (120/500 × €490m)	117.6	
Cash (120m × €0.97)		116.4
Gain on repurchase of debt		1.2

In some cases, as discussed in 6.2 above, a creditor may release a debtor from its present obligation to make payments, but the debtor assumes an obligation to pay if the party assuming primary responsibility defaults. In such a case, IAS 39 and IFRS 9 require the debtor to recognise:

(a)   a new liability based on the fair value for the obligation for the guarantee; and

(b)   a gain or loss based on the difference between

   (i)   any proceeds; and

   (ii)   the carrying amount of the original liability (including any related unamortised costs) less the fair value of the new liability. *[IAS 39.AG63, IFRS 9.B3.3.7].*

6.4   Derivatives that can be financial assets or financial liabilities

Historically, IAS 39 did not address the required treatment for the transfer of a non-optional derivative, such as a swap or forward contract, that by its nature can be either a financial asset or a financial liability at various times during its life. However, in finalising the amendments made to IAS 39 and IFRS 9 that addressed hedge accounting when a hedging instrument is novated to a central counterparty (see 3.4.3 above, Chapter 51 at 4.2.3.A and Chapter 52 at 11.3), the IASB noted that 'a derivative should be derecognised only when it meets both the derecognition criteria for a financial asset and the derecognition criteria for a financial liability in circumstances in which the derivative involves two-way payments between parties, i.e. the payments are or could be from and to each of the parties'. *[IAS 39.BC220B, IFRS 9.BC6.333]*. In practice, any transfer of such derivatives is likely to require the consent of the counterparty to the entity's legal release from its obligations under the contract, and the possible payment of a fee to compensate the counterparty for the difference between the creditworthiness of the entity and that of the transferee. Such procedures are much closer to those envisaged in the derecognition rules for financial liabilities than those implicit in the derecognition rules for financial assets.

On many occasions, the IASB has made it clear that a non-optional derivative that could be either an asset or liability can be derecognised only if the derecognition criteria for both assets and liabilities are satisfied (see 3.3.2 above).

6.5   Supply-chain finance

An increasingly common type of arrangement involves the provision of finance linked to the supply of goods or services. These arrangements, which can vary significantly in both form and substance, are often referred to as 'supply-chain finance', but other terms are also used including 'supplier finance', 'reverse factoring' and 'structured payable transactions'. Whilst the terms of such arrangements can vary widely, they typically contain a number of the following features:

- they involve a purchaser of goods and/or services, a group of its suppliers and a financial intermediary;

- the purchaser is often a large, creditworthy entity that uses a number of suppliers, many of which will have a higher credit risk than the purchaser;

- the arrangement is nearly always initiated by the purchaser rather than the supplier;

- the arrangements operate continuously for all future purchases until the arrangement is cancelled;

- they are often put in place in connection with the purchaser attempting to secure extended payment terms from its suppliers;

- the intermediary/service provider is often a financial institution who will normally make available IT systems to facilitate the arrangement;

- the intermediary makes available to suppliers an optional invoice discounting or factoring facility for invoices accepted or agreed by the purchaser, often on terms that enable the supplier to derecognise the receivable;

- the purchaser will commit to pay the invoice on the due date, sometimes by using a payment facility operated by the intermediary;
- interest terms will be included in the supply agreement to protect the intermediary in the event of the purchaser defaulting or missing the payment date;
- those interest terms will be similar to ones included in most supply agreements, although they are rarely enforced by suppliers;
- the credit risk the intermediary is taking on is that of the purchaser, but it may be able to charge a higher financing cost to the supplier (in the form of the discount) than it would if lending to the supplier directly; and
- it can be difficult to determine the overall financing costs of the arrangement, and who bears those costs, especially if the supply involves items for which the pricing is subjective/unobservable.

The primary accounting concern with these types of arrangement is whether the purchaser should present the resulting financial liability as debt or as a trade or similar payable. This determination could have a significant impact on the purchaser's financial position, particularly its leverage or gearing ratios. However, whilst IFRS does not address the issue directly, a number of standards could be regarded as relevant.

IAS 1 – *Presentation of Financial Statements* – addresses the presentation of the statement of financial position and can certainly be relevant to this determination. IAS 1 requires that entities include line items that present (a) trade and other payables and (b) other financial liabilities. *[IAS 1.54]*. These are considered sufficiently different in nature or function to warrant separate presentation, *[IAS 1.57]* but additional line items should be presented when relevant to an understanding of the entity's financial position, for example depending on the size, nature or function of the item. This may be achieved by disaggregating the two line items noted above. *[IAS 1.55, 57]*. In addition, it may be appropriate to amend the descriptions used and the ordering of items or aggregation of similar items according to the nature of the entity and its transactions. *[IAS 1.57]*.

These requirements provide a framework for determining the structure of an entity's statement of financial position. Liabilities that are clearly financing in nature, for example those arising from bonds, bank borrowings and other loans, are normally presented together and described as debt or another similar term. Conversely, liabilities that are more clearly in the nature of working capital are normally presented within trade and other payables, with further analysis of the component balances within the notes. In this context, IAS 7 might also be considered relevant given an entity is required to classify its cash flows according to whether they arise from operating, financing or investing activities and one would expect broad consistency between the statement of cash flows and the statement of financial position. Therefore the definitions of operating activities and financing activities (see Chapter 37 at 4) might assist an entity in determining the appropriate presentation of liabilities.

The requirements in IAS 39 and IFRS 9 dealing with derecognition of financial liabilities can be relevant in determining the appropriate presentation of liabilities arising from supply-chain financing arrangements. If the arrangement results in derecognition of the original liability (e.g. if the purchaser is legally released from its original obligation to the supplier), an entity will need to determine the appropriate classification of the new liability which may well represent an amount due to the intermediary rather than the supplier. As the intermediary is typically a financial institution, presentation as debt could be more appropriate than as a trade or other payable. Derecognition can also occur and presentation as debt can also be appropriate if the purchaser is not legally released from the original obligation but the terms of the obligation are amended in a way that is considered a substantial modification. Where those revised terms are more consistent with a financing transaction than a trade or other payable, classification of that new liability as debt will be appropriate.

However, even when the arrangement results in derecognition of the original trade payable, there is a view that if there are no significant changes to the payment terms, the new liability is not necessarily in the nature of debt and so presentation as trade or other payables might be appropriate. Conversely, even if the original liability is not derecognised, other factors may indicate that the substance and nature of the arrangements mean that the liability should no longer be presented as a trade payable. Instead the liability would be reclassified and presented as debt (in a similar way to transferred assets that are not derecognised, which IAS 39 and IFRS 9 require to be reclassified within the statement of financial position – see 4.1.1.A above). Circumstances which could result in reclassification include the payment of referral fees or commissions by the intermediary to the purchaser.

In practice, the appropriate presentation of any such arrangement is likely to involve a high degree of judgement in the light of specific facts and circumstances. Whatever the presentation adopted, we believe additional disclosures will often be necessary to explain the nature of the arrangements and the financial reporting judgements made. In fact, the need for clear disclosure of complex supplier arrangements under IFRS is something that has been emphasised by at least one European regulator[21] and the SEC has, in the past, highlighted the presentation of these arrangements under US GAAP as an area of focus. Therefore, it is quite possible this topic will become the focus of wider regulatory scrutiny in the future, and perhaps also be subject to consideration by the IFRS Interpretations Committee.

7   FUTURE DEVELOPMENTS

The IASB's *Conceptual Framework for Financial Reporting* is discussed in Chapter 2. The current version does not address derecognition in any meaningful way. However, in May 2015, the IASB issued an exposure draft proposing a revised version which would contain a new chapter addressing both recognition and derecognition of assets and liabilities. The exposure draft proposes that accounting requirements for derecognition should aim to represent faithfully both:[22]

(a)   the assets and liabilities retained after the transaction or other event that led to the derecognition (including any asset or liability acquired, incurred or created as part of the transaction or other event); and

(b)   the change in the entity's assets and liabilities as a result of that transaction or other event:

and goes on to explain that those aims are normally achieved by:[23]

- derecognising any assets or liabilities that have been transferred, consumed, collected or fulfilled, or have expired and recognising any resulting income or expense; and
- continuing to recognise the assets or liabilities retained, if any (the retained component), which become a separate unit of account. Accordingly, no income or expenses are recognised on the retained component as a result of the derecognition of the transferred component.

The exposure draft explains that if an entity transfers a previously recognised asset (or liability) to another party that is acting as its agent the asset is still controlled by the transferor (the liability is still an obligation of the transferor) and derecognition would not faithfully represent the transferor's assets, liabilities, income and expenses.[24] Further, if an entity retains exposure to positive or negative variations in the amount of economic benefits produced by an economic resource, this may indicate that the entity retains control of that economic resource, in which case derecognition is not appropriate.[25] However, the IASB has not advocated a 'control' approach in all circumstances, nor does it advocate a 'risks and rewards' approach. Instead, it notes that the aim set out in (a) above is more consistent with a control approach and the aim set out in (b) more consistent with a risks and rewards approach.[26]

The IASB acknowledges it will sometimes be difficult to achieve both of the aims set out above. This might be the case if, for example, the transferor of an asset retains a disproportionate exposure to variations in the asset's economic benefits or if it must or may repurchase the asset. In these circumstances, derecognition may not faithfully represent the extent of changes in the entity's assets and liabilities and might in fact misrepresent the entity's financial position.[27] In some such situations derecognition might meet the aims set out above if supported by separate presentation or explanatory disclosure in the notes to the financial statements, but in others there may be a need to continue recognising the transferred component as well as the retained component, perhaps separately presented or with explanatory disclosure.[28]

The exposure draft also addresses the modification of contracts, which will include those giving rise to financial assets and financial liabilities. The proposals note that modifications normally do one or both of the following:[29]

- reduce or eliminate existing rights and obligations (for which the discussions above are relevant in deciding whether to derecognise those rights or obligations); and
- add new rights or new obligations.

For rights and obligations created by a modification that are distinct from those created by the original terms of the contract, it may be appropriate to treat the additions as new assets or liabilities.[30] However, if they are not distinct it may be appropriate to treat the new rights and obligations as part of the same unit of account as the existing rights and obligations.[31] Furthermore, some modifications both reduce or eliminate existing rights and obligations and add new rights and obligations. The combined effects of such changes would be considered in order to provide the most relevant information in the way that most faithfully represents their effect.[32]

The proposed recognition and derecognition chapter does not address whether partial derecognition (where the transferred component is derecognised and the retained component continues to be recognised) or full derecognition (where the entire asset or liability is derecognised and any retained component is recognised as a new asset or liability) should be used. This question is seen as more closely linked to how the 'unit of account' is determined and how the measurement basis for the retained component is selected, topics addressed elsewhere in the exposure draft.[33]

At the time of writing the IASB has not committed itself to finalising these proposals in a particular timescale, noting only that it expects to decide the direction of the project at some point after January 2016. Even if the proposals are finalised in their current form, it seems unlikely the IASB would make any changes to the related requirements in IAS 39 or IFRS 9 in the short- or medium-term. However, the proposals could potentially influence the way in which entities develop their accounting policies when dealing with situations for which the requirements in the standards are not clear.

References

1 *IFRIC Update*, January 2007.
2 *IFRIC Update*, May 2006.
3 *IASB Update*, September 2006.
4 *IASB Update*, September 2006.
5 Staff Paper (May 2012 Interpretations Committee Meeting), *IAS 39 Financial Instruments: Recognition and Measurement – Derecognition of financial assets (Agenda reference 10-B)*, IASB, May 2012, paras. 8 to 10.
6 Staff Paper (May 2012 Interpretations Committee Meeting), *IAS 39 Financial Instruments: Recognition and Measurement – Derecognition of financial assets (Agenda reference 10-A)*, IASB, May 2012, paras. 32 to 36.
7 Staff Paper (May 2012 Interpretations Committee Meeting), *IAS 39 Financial Instruments: Recognition and Measurement – Derecognition of financial assets (Agenda reference 10-A)*, IASB, May 2012, paras. 37 to 42.
8 *IFRIC Update*, September 2012.

9 For example, *The IFRS Interpretations Committee's tentative agenda decision on IAS 39 Financial Instruments: Recognition and Measurement – Accounting for different aspects of restructuring Greek government bonds*, ESMA, July 2012 and *Final Comment Letter on the IFRS Interpretations Committee tentative rejection notice in relation to the restructuring of Greek government bonds*, EFRAG, August 2012.
10 *IFRIC Update*, September 2012.
11 *Information for Observers*, IFRIC, March 2006.
12 *IFRIC Update*, November 2005.
13 *IASB Update*, September 2006.
14 *Information for Observers*, IFRIC, March 2006.
15 *IASB Update*, September 2006.
16 *IASB Update*, September 2006.
17 *IFRIC Update*, November 2005.
18 In practice, other factors might be relevant to the valuation.

19 The fair value of an in the money option is positive for the buyer and negative for the writer.

20 IGC Q&A 62-1

21 Press Release 74/14, *FRC urges clarity in the reporting of complex supplier arrangements by retailers and other businesses,* FRC, December 2014.

22 Exposure Draft ED/2015/3, *Conceptual Framework for Financial Reporting,* IASB, May 2015, para. 5.26.

23 Exposure Draft ED/2015/3, *Conceptual Framework for Financial Reporting,* IASB, May 2015, para. 5.27.

24 Exposure Draft ED/2015/3, *Conceptual Framework for Financial Reporting,* IASB, May 2015, para. 5.28.

25 Exposure Draft ED/2015/3, *Conceptual Framework for Financial Reporting,* IASB, May 2015, para. 5.29.

26 Exposure Draft ED/2015/3, *Conceptual Framework for Financial Reporting,* IASB, May 2015, para. BC5.57.

27 Exposure Draft ED/2015/3, *Conceptual Framework for Financial Reporting,* IASB, May 2015, para. 5.30.

28 Exposure Draft ED/2015/3, *Conceptual Framework for Financial Reporting,* IASB, May 2015, paras. 5.31 and 5.32.

29 Exposure Draft ED/2015/3, *Conceptual Framework for Financial Reporting,* IASB, May 2015, para. 5.33.

30 Exposure Draft ED/2015/3, *Conceptual Framework for Financial Reporting,* IASB, May 2015, para. 5.34.

31 Exposure Draft ED/2015/3, *Conceptual Framework for Financial Reporting,* IASB, May 2015, para. 5.35.

32 Exposure Draft ED/2015/3, *Conceptual Framework for Financial Reporting,* IASB, May 2015, para. 5.36.

33 Exposure Draft ED/2015/3, *Conceptual Framework for Financial Reporting,* IASB, May 2015, para. BC5.58.

Chapter 50

Chapter 51   Financial instruments: Hedge accounting (IAS 39)

Chapter 51

Chapter 51

Chapter 51   Financial instruments: Hedge accounting (IAS 39)

1   INTRODUCTION

1.1   Background

Chapter 41 provides a general background to the development of accounting for financial instruments and notes the fundamental changes that have been experienced in international financial markets. The markets for derivatives, especially, have seen remarkable and continued growth over the past two to three decades. This reflects the increasing use of such instruments by businesses, commonly to 'hedge' their financial risks. Accordingly, the accounting treatment for derivatives and hedging activities has taken on a high degree of importance. Historically, however, the accounting guidance has struggled to keep up with business practices and, at best, issues were dealt with very much on a piecemeal basis. Therefore, until the development of standards such as IAS 39 – *Financial Instruments: Recognition and Measurement*, entities were left largely to their own devices in developing accounting policies for hedges so that their financial statements reflected the objectives for entering into such transactions.

'Hedging' itself is a much wider topic than hedge accounting and is *not* the primary subject of this chapter. It is an imprecise term although standard setters frequently describe hedging in terms of designating a hedging instrument that has a value that is expected, wholly or partly, to offset changes in the value or cash flows of a 'hedged position'.[1] In this context, hedged positions normally include those arising from recognised assets and liabilities, contractual commitments and expected, but uncontracted, future transactions. Whilst this may be an appropriate description for many hedges, it does not necessarily capture the essence of all risk management activities involving financial instruments. Nevertheless, it forms the basis for the hedge accounting requirements under IFRS.

1.2 What is hedge accounting?

Hedge accounting is often seen as 'correcting' deficiencies in the accounting requirements that would otherwise apply to each leg of the hedge relationship. These deficiencies are an inevitable consequence of using a mixed-measurement model of accounting. Typically, hedge accounting involves recognising gains and losses on a hedging instrument in the same period(s) and/or in the same place in the financial statements as gains or losses on the hedged position. It may be used in a number of situations, for example to adjust (or correct) for:

- *Measurement differences*

  These might arise where the hedge is of a recognised asset or liability that is measured on a different basis to the hedging instrument. An example might be inventory that is recorded in the financial statements at cost, but whose value is hedged by a forward contract that enables inventory of the same nature to be sold at a predetermined price. In this case, both the hedging instrument and the hedged position exist and are recognised in the financial statements, but they are likely to be measured on different bases.

  Avoiding the measurement difference could in this situation theoretically be achieved in a number of ways. One alternative would be not to recognise unrealised gains or losses on the forward contract, and realised gains or losses could be deferred (e.g. separately as assets or liabilities or by including them within the carrying amount of the inventory) until the inventory is sold. On the other hand, if unrealised gains or losses on the forward contract were recognised in profit or loss, the measurement basis of the inventory could be changed to reflect changes in its fair value in profit or loss;

- *Performance reporting differences*

  Even if the measurement bases of the hedging instrument and hedged item are the same, performance reporting differences might arise if gains and losses are reported in a different place in the financial statements. An example might be where an investment in shares is classified as available-for-sale (see Chapter 45 at 5) and whose value is hedged by a put option. The investment and the put option are both measured at fair value. However, gains or losses on the investment are recognised in other comprehensive income whilst those on the put option are recognised in profit or loss, therefore resulting in a mismatch in the income statement (or statement of comprehensive income). Similarly, gains or losses on retranslating the net assets of a foreign operation are recorded in other comprehensive income whilst retranslation gains or losses on a borrowing used to hedge that net investment are, absent any form of hedge accounting, recorded in profit or loss.

  In the case of the inventory and the forward contract, hedge accounting might involve reporting gains and losses on the inventory in profit or loss, or gains and losses on the forward contract in other comprehensive income. For the foreign operation, hedge accounting normally involves reporting the retranslation gains and losses on both the borrowing and the foreign operation in other comprehensive income;

- *Recognition differences*

  These might arise where the hedge is of contractual rights or obligations that are not recognised in the financial statements. An example is a foreign currency denominated operating lease where the unrecognised contractual commitment to pay lease rentals in another currency is hedged by a series of forward currency contracts (i.e. each payment is effectively 'fixed' in functional currency terms).

  In this case, one solution might be to treat the lease as a 'synthetic' functional currency denominated lease. A similar outcome would be obtained if unrealised gains and losses on each forward contract remained unrecognised until the accrual of the lease payment it was hedging;

- *Existence differences*

  These might arise where the hedge is of cash flows arising from an uncontracted future transaction, i.e. a transaction that does not yet exist. An example is a foreign currency denominated sale expected next year that is hedged by a forward currency contract.

  Again, a solution to this issue might involve treating the future sale as a 'synthetic' functional currency sale or it might involve deferring the gain or loss on the forward contract until the sale is recognised in profit or loss.

1.3 Development of hedge accounting standards

The first comprehensive hedge accounting requirements issued by the IASB were contained in IAS 39. This standard was published in 1999 (see Chapter 41 at 1.2), and since then has been subject to numerous amendments.

In November 2013, as part of its project to replace IAS 39, the IASB published amendments to IFRS 9 – *Financial Instruments* – including revised requirements for hedge accounting. IFRS 9 is effective for periods beginning on or after 1 January 2018 and will replace substantially all of IAS 39, including the hedge accounting requirements. However, IFRS 9 allows entities an accounting policy choice to continue applying the hedge accounting requirements of IAS 39 instead of those in IFRS 9. *[IFRS 9.7.2.21]*. The hedge accounting requirements of IFRS 9 are discussed in Chapter 52.

IFRS 9 does not provide any particular solutions specifically tailored to so-called 'macro hedge' accounting, the term used to describe the more complex risk management practices used by entities such as banks. In May 2012 the Board decided to decouple accounting for macro hedging from IFRS 9, and a separate project was set up to develop an accounting solution for dynamic risk management. In consideration of this fact, for a fair value hedge of the interest rate exposure of a portfolio of financial assets or financial liabilities (and only for such a hedge), an entity may apply the hedge accounting requirements in IAS 39 instead of those in IFRS 9. This choice relates only to a fair value portfolio hedge as described in IAS 39 81A, 89A and AG114-AG132 of IAS 39. A decision to continue to apply this IAS 39 guidance is not part of the accounting policy choice to defer IAS 39 mention above.

In April 2014, the IASB issued the Discussion Paper – *Accounting for Dynamic Risk Management: a Portfolio Revaluation Approach to Macro Hedging.* The six-month comment period ended in October 2014. Most respondents supported the need for the project, but there was no consensus on a solution (see 6 below).

2   HEDGING INSTRUMENTS AND HEDGED ITEMS

In the terminology of IAS 39, the two main ingredients of a hedge are the hedging instrument and the hedged item. The definition of these and related terms are as follows:

- *Hedging instrument:* a designated derivative or (for a hedge of the risk of changes in foreign currency exchange rates only) a designated non-derivative financial asset or non-derivative financial liability whose fair value or cash flows are expected to offset changes in the fair value or cash flows of a designated hedged item.

- *Hedged item:* an asset, liability, firm commitment, highly probable forecast transaction or net investment in a foreign operation that (a) exposes the entity to risk of changes in fair value or future cash flows and (b) is designated as being hedged.

- *Firm commitment:* a binding agreement for the exchange of a specified quantity of resources at a specified price on a specified future date or dates.

  In addition to simple agreements to purchase a given quantity of units on a given date for a given amount of money, other arrangements may also be firm commitments, for example construction contracts under which payments are made periodically based on documented progress or achievement of milestones.

- *Forecast transaction:* an uncommitted but anticipated future transaction. *[IAS 39.9].*

2.1   Hedging instruments

There are a number of restrictions on what type of item may be used as the hedging instrument in a 'valid' hedge, i.e. one that can qualify for hedge accounting, and these operate on many levels as set out below. One of these restrictions stems from the definition of a hedging instrument and requires an entity to have an expectation that its fair value or cash flows will offset changes in the fair value or cash flows of the hedged item attributable to the hedged risk. This requirement principally manifests itself in the provisions on hedge effectiveness, which are dealt with at 5.3 below. Hedging instruments must also involve a party that is external to the reporting group. *[IAS 39.73].* More detail is provided on this point at 2.3 below.

2.1.1   Derivative financial instruments

The distinction between derivative and non-derivative financial instruments is covered in Chapter 43. With the exception of certain written options (see 2.1.1.A below), the circumstances in which a derivative may be designated as a hedging instrument are not restricted, provided the conditions for hedge accounting set out at 5 below are met. *[IAS 39.72]*. Those conditions mean that a derivative that is not carried at fair value, because it is linked to and must be settled by delivery of an unquoted equity instrument whose fair value cannot be reliably measured (see Chapter 48 at 2.6), cannot be designated as a hedging instrument. *[IAS 39.AG96]*.

In order to be able to qualify as a hedging instrument, the derivative must be accounted for as such under IAS 39. Therefore, an embedded derivative that is accounted for separately from its host contract (see Chapter 43 at 4) can be used as a hedging instrument. However, a contract that is considered a normal sale or purchase, and is therefore accounted for as an executory contract, cannot (see Chapter 42 at 4). *[IAS 39.F.1.2]*.

Example 51.1:   Hedging with a sales commitment

Company J has the Japanese yen as its functional currency. J has issued a fixed-rate debt instrument with semi-annual interest payments that matures in two years with principal due at maturity of US$5 million. It has also entered into a fixed price sales commitment for US$5 million that matures in two years and is not accounted for as a derivative because it qualifies for the normal sales exemption.

Because the sales commitment is accounted for as a firm commitment rather than a derivative instrument it cannot be a hedging instrument in a hedge of the foreign currency risk associated with the debt instrument. However, if the foreign currency component of the sales commitment was required to be separated as an embedded derivative (essentially a forward contract to buy US dollars for yen) that component could be designated as the hedging instrument in such a hedge. *[IAS 39.F.1.2]*.

Similarly, a forecast transaction or planned future transaction cannot be the hedging instrument as it is not a recognised financial instrument, *[IAS 39.AG35(e), F.1.6]*, and is therefore not a derivative.

2.1.1.A   Options and collars

It is explained in IAS 39 that an option an entity writes is not effective in reducing the profit or loss exposure of a hedged item. In other words, the potential loss on a written option could be significantly greater than the potential gain in value of a related hedged item. Therefore, a written option is prohibited from qualifying as a hedging instrument unless it is designated as an offset to a purchased option, including one that is embedded in another financial instrument. An example of this might be a written call option that is used to hedge a callable liability. In contrast, a purchased option has potential gains equal to or greater than losses and therefore has the potential to reduce profit or loss exposure from changes in fair values or cash flows. Accordingly, a purchased option can qualify as a hedging instrument. *[IAS 39.AG94]*.

It follows that a derivative such as an interest rate collar that includes a written option cannot be designated as a hedging instrument if it is a net written option. *[IAS 39.77]*. However, a derivative instrument that includes a written option may be designated as a hedging instrument if it is a net purchased option or zero cost collar. *[IAS 39.F.1.3(a)]*.

The following factors, taken together, indicate that an instrument is not a net written option:

- no net premium is received, either at inception or over the life of the instrument – the distinguishing feature of a written option is the receipt of a premium to compensate for the risk incurred;

- except for the strike prices, the critical terms and conditions of the written and purchased option components are the same, including underlying variable(s), currency denomination and maturity date; and

- the notional amount of the written option component is not greater than that of the purchased option component. *[IAS 39.F.1.3(b)]*.

The application of these requirements is illustrated in the following two examples.

Example 51.2:   Foreign currency collar (or 'cylinder option')

Company E, which has sterling as its functional currency, has forecast that it is highly probable it will receive €1,000 in six months' time in respect of an expected sale to a customer in France.

E is concerned that sterling might have appreciated by the time the payment is received and wishes to protect the profit margin on the sale without paying the premium that would be required with an ordinary currency option. E also wishes to benefit from some of the upside in the event that sterling depreciates, so would prefer not to use a forward contract.

Accordingly, E enters into an instrument under which it effectively:

- purchases an option that allows it to buy sterling for €1,000 from the counterparty at €1.53:£1.00; and

- sells an option that allows the counterparty to sell sterling to E for €1,000 at €1.47:£1.00.

In the foreign currency markets, such an instrument is often called a 'cylinder option' rather than a 'collar' and it operates as follows. If, in six months' time, the spot exchange rate exceeds €1.53:£1.00, E will exercise its option to sell €1,000 at €1.53:£1.00, effectively fixing its minimum proceeds on the sale (in sterling terms) at £654. Similarly, if the rate is below €1.47:£1.00, the counterparty will exercise its option to buy €1,000 at €1.47:£1.00, effectively capping E's maximum proceeds on the sale at £680. If the rate is between €1.47:£1.00 and €1.53:£1.00, both options will lapse unexercised and E will be able to sell its €1,000 for sterling at the spot rate, generating between £654 and £680.

The premium that E would pay to acquire the purchased option equals the premium it would receive to sell the written option and therefore no premium is paid or received on inception. The critical terms and conditions, including the notional amounts, of the written and purchased option components are the same except for the strike price. Therefore, E concludes that the instrument is not a net written option and, consequently, it may be used as the hedging instrument in a hedge of the foreign currency risk associated with the future sale.

It is possible that the counterparty might, instead, have offered E a variation on the instrument described above. If the notional amount on E's purchased option component had been reduced, say to €500, the counterparty could have offered a better rate on that component, say €1.51. However, in this case, the notional amount on the written option component is twice that of the purchased option component and the instrument would be seen as a net written option. Accordingly, even if E had very good business reasons for using such an instrument to manage its foreign exchange risk, it could not qualify as a hedging instrument under IAS 39. Therefore, hedge accounting would be precluded.

Example 51.3: 'Knock-out' swap

Company Y has a significant amount of long-dated floating rate borrowings. In order to hedge the cash flow interest rate risk arising from these borrowings, Y has entered into a number of matching pay-fixed, receive-floating interest rate swaps that effectively convert the interest rates on the borrowings to fixed-rate.

Under the terms of one of these swaps, on each fifth anniversary of its inception until maturity the swap counterparty may choose to simply terminate the swap at no cost. This is often referred to as a knock-out feature. In return for agreeing to this, Y benefits by paying a lower interest rate on the fixed leg of the swap than it would on a conventional swap. In other words, Y receives a premium for taking on the risk of the counterparty cancelling the swap.

This instrument contains a net written option, i.e. the knock-out feature, and therefore cannot be used as a hedging instrument unless it is used in a hedge of an equivalent purchased option. (In practice, it is unlikely that the hedged borrowings will contain such an option feature.)

2.1.1.B   Credit break clauses

It is not uncommon for certain derivatives (e.g. long-term interest rate swaps) to contain terms that allow the counterparties to settle the instrument at a so-called 'fair value' in certain circumstances. The 'fair value' is usually not a true fair value as it excludes changes in credit risk. Such terms, often called 'credit break clauses', enable the counterparties to manage their credit risk in markets where collateral or margin accounts and master netting agreements are not used. They are particularly common where a long-duration derivative is transacted between a financial and non-financial institution. For example, the terms of a twenty-year interest rate swap may allow either party to settle the instrument at fair value on the fifth, tenth and fifteenth anniversary of its inception.

These terms can be seen as options on counterparty credit risk. However, provided the two parties have equivalent rights to settle the instrument at 'fair value', the credit break clause will generally not prevent the derivative from qualifying as a hedging instrument. Particularly, in assessing whether a premium is received for agreeing to the incorporation of such terms into an instrument, care needs to be exercised. For example, marginally better underlying terms offered by one potential counterparty (as a result of market imperfections) should not be mistaken for a very small option premium.

2.1.2   Cash instruments

In contrast to the position for derivatives, there are significant restrictions over the use as hedging instruments of non-derivative financial assets and liabilities, or 'cash instruments' as the IASB sometimes refer to them. *[IAS 39.BC144]*. Essentially, a cash instrument may be designated as a hedging instrument only for a hedge of foreign currency risk. *[IAS 39.72]*.

This would allow, say, a held-to-maturity investment carried at amortised cost to be designated as a hedging instrument in a hedge of foreign currency risk, *[IAS 39.AG95]*, as well as other instruments such as loans and receivables, available for sale debt instruments and borrowings. However, an investment in an unquoted equity instrument that is not carried at fair value because its fair value cannot be reliably measured (see Chapter 48 at 2.6), cannot be designated as a hedging instrument. *[IAS 39.AG96]*.

The following two examples illustrate the types of permitted hedge relationships where the hedging instrument is a non-derivative.

Example 51.4:   Hedging with a non-derivative liability

In Example 51.1 above, Company J had issued a fixed rate debt instrument with principal due at maturity in two years of US$5 million. J had also entered into a fixed price sales commitment, accounted for as an executory contract, for US$5 million that matured in two years as well.

J could not designate the debt instrument as a hedge of the exposure to *all* fair value changes of the fixed price sales commitment because the hedging instrument is a non-derivative (and it would not be a good economic hedge anyway). However, J could designate the fixed rate debt instrument as a hedge of the foreign currency exposure associated with the future receipt of US dollars on the fixed price sales commitment. *[IAS 39.F.1.2].*

Example 51.5:   Hedge of foreign currency bond

Company J has also issued US$5 million five year fixed rate debt and owns a US$5 million five year fixed rate bond, which is classified as available for sale.

J's bond has exposure to changes in both foreign currency and interest rates, as does the liability. However, the liability can only be designated as a hedge of the bond's foreign currency, not interest rate, risk because it is a non-derivative instrument.

In Example 51.5 above, hedge accounting is unnecessary because the amortised cost of the hedging instrument and the hedged item are both remeasured using closing rates with differences recognised in profit or loss as required by IAS 21 – *The Effects of Changes in Foreign Exchange Rates. [IAS 39.F.1.1].*

In principle, there is no reason why a non-derivative financial instrument cannot be a hedging instrument in one hedge (of foreign currency risk) and a hedged item in another hedge (for example in a hedge of interest rate risk).

In developing the hedge accounting requirements for inclusion in IFRS 9 the IASB has decided that a non-derivative financial asset or financial liability measured at fair value through profit or loss may qualify as a hedging instrument, including for risks other than foreign currency risk, provided it is not a financial liability designated as at fair value through profit or loss with changes in its credit risk recognised in other comprehensive income (see Chapter 52 at 4.2). *[IFRS 9.6.2.2].*

2.1.3   Combinations of instruments

Two or more derivatives, or proportions of them (see 2.1.4 below) may be viewed in combination and jointly designated as a hedging instrument. This is the case even when the risk(s) arising from some derivatives offset(s) those arising from others. However, two or more instruments (or proportions of them) may be designated as a hedging instrument only if *none of them* is a written option or a net written option. *[IAS 39.77].* Although this restriction on individual net written options does not appear in IFRS 9 (see Chapter 52 at 4.1), there is still a requirement that any combination can only be designated as a hedged item if the combination is not a net written option.

In practice, many zero cost collars are transacted as legally separate written and purchased options. On the face of it, therefore, such transactions cannot be treated as a combined hedging instrument, even if the combination is not a net written option. However, we are not at all convinced the IASB intended such a prohibition to take effect in practice. This is especially the case if the reason the collar takes the legal form of two options is for the seller's administrative ease, which would in many cases be irrelevant to the entity purchasing the collar. In fact, if it can be demonstrated that the only substantive business purpose for entering into such an arrangement is to purchase a zero cost collar to hedge an underlying exposure, the logic in some of the implementation guidance would *require* these contracts to be treated as a single instrument for this purpose (see 2.3.3 below and Chapter 43 at 3.2). We therefore believe that a combination of two or more derivatives, having the same critical terms, but including a derivative that on its own is a written (or net written) option, may be treated as one hedging instrument, provided the written and purchased options:

- were transacted at the same time;
- with the same counterparty;
- in anticipation of one another; and
- the combined instrument does not meet the definition of a net written option. (see 2.1.1.A above)

In the case of a hedge of foreign currency risk, the standard also allows two or more non-derivatives, or proportions of them, to be viewed in combination and designated as a hedging instrument. Further, a combination of derivatives and non-derivatives, or proportions of them, may be similarly combined. [IAS 39.77].

Unlike for combinations of derivatives, the standard does not clarify whether it is acceptable for these combinations to contain offsetting terms although in the absence of an indication to the contrary we believe it is.

For example, an entity with the euro as its functional currency may have issued a yen denominated floating rate borrowing and entered into a matching receive-yen floating (plus principal at maturity), pay-US dollar floating (plus principal at maturity) cross-currency interest rate swap. These instruments, which effectively synthesise a US dollar floating rate borrowing, contain offsetting terms, i.e. the whole of the borrowing and the yen leg of the swap. The entity could designate the combination of these two instruments in a hedge of the entity's foreign currency risk arising from, say, an asset with an identifiable exposure to US dollar exchange rates.

2.1.4   Portions and proportions of hedging instruments

In contrast to the position for hedged financial items (see 2.2.1 below), there are significant restrictions on what components of an individual financial instrument can be carved out and designated as a hedging instrument. It is explained that there is normally a single fair value measure for a hedging instrument in its entirety and the factors that cause changes in its fair value are co-dependent. Normally, therefore, a financial instrument (or proportion thereof – see 2.1.4.C below) can only be designated as a hedging instrument in its entirety. [IAS 39.74].

Example 51.6:   Combination of written and purchased options

Company Y transacts a combination of a written option and purchased option (such as an interest rate collar) as a single instrument with one counterparty. Y cannot split the derivative instrument into its written and purchased option components and designate just the purchased option component as a hedging instrument. [IAS 39.F.1.8].

Similarly, the 'knock-out swap' in Example 51.3 above could not be split into a conventional interest rate swap, to be used as a hedging instrument, and the knock-out feature (a written swaption, i.e. an option for the counterparty to enter into an offsetting interest rate swap with the same terms as the conventional swap).

However, there are a number of exceptions to this general rule:

- the time value of options may be separated (see 2.1.4.A below);
- interest elements of forwards may be separated (see 2.1.4.B below);
- a proportion only of a hedging instrument may be designated in a hedging relationship (see 2.1.4.C below);
- the spot rate retranslation risk of a foreign currency cash instrument may be separated (see 2.1.4.D below); and
- a derivative may be separated into notional component parts when each part is designated as a hedge and qualifies for hedge accounting (see 2.1.4.E below).

2.1.4.A   Time value of options

IAS 39 permits an entity to separate the intrinsic value and time value of an option contract and designate as the hedging instrument only the change in intrinsic value of the option and exclude changes in its time value. This is permitted because, as the standard explains, the intrinsic value of the option can generally be measured separately. *[IAS 39.74]*. However, this explanation is slightly hollow as the same would apply to the type of instrument discussed in Example 51.6 above.

An entity may choose to designate the variability of future cash flow outcomes resulting from a price increase (but not a decrease) of a forecast commodity purchase. In such a situation, only cash flow losses that result from an increase in the price above the specified level are designated. However, only the intrinsic value of a purchased option, not its time value, reflects this one-sided risk in the hedged item (assuming that it has the same principal terms as the designated risk). The hedged risk of, say, a forecast transaction does not have features similar to the time value of a purchased option because that is not a component of the forecast transaction that affects profit or loss (see 5.3.10 below). *[IAS 39.AG99BA]*.

Excluding the time value may make it administratively easier to process the hedges and it can certainly improve a hedge's effectiveness from an accounting perspective. However, even though separated from the hedging relationship, the changes in the fair value of time value over the term of the hedge still affect profit or loss.

The use of this exception is not mandatory. For example, a dynamic hedging strategy that assesses both the intrinsic value and time value of an option contract can qualify for hedge accounting (see 5.1.2 below), *[IAS 39.74]*, although the time value is likely to result in some ineffectiveness.

2.1.4.B   Interest elements of forwards

IAS 39 also permits (but does not require) an entity to separate the interest element and spot price of a forward contract because the premium on the forward can generally (like the time value of an option) be measured separately. *[IAS 39.74]*.

Excluding this portion may be consistent with the entity's overall hedging strategy, such as where the interest element of forward contracts are managed with the rest of the entity's interest rate exposures rather than in conjunction with the associated spot rate exposures. Similar to the treatment of the time value of an option, if the interest element of a forward contract is excluded from the hedge relationship, changes in the fair value of that element will continue to impact profit or loss. (see 5.3.3 below)

2.1.4.C   *Proportions of instruments*

In addition to the above exceptions, a proportion of the entire hedging instrument, such as 50% of the notional amount, may also be designated in a hedging relationship. However, a hedging relationship may not be designated for only a portion of the time period in which the hedging instrument is outstanding. *[IAS 39.75].*

A literal reading of the second sentence in paragraph 75 might suggest that a hedge relationship may not be designated for a shorter period of time than the period for which the hedging instrument can remain outstanding. For example, if an interest rate swap has a remaining maturity of five years, then it might be concluded this could not be a hedging instrument in a hedge relationship that would only last four years. However, we do not believe that this is the intended meaning of the guidance. We believe that there is no restriction on the period of the hedge relationship itself, but only a restriction on what can be used as the hedging instrument. For example, in the case of the interest rate swap above, the payments and receipts over the next four years (i.e. ignoring those in year five) could not be designated as the hedging instrument. Instead, the whole derivative (i.e. including payments and receipts in year five) must be designated as the hedging instrument, although the hedging relationship may itself last for only four years. However, hedge accounting can only be applied if the hedge is determined to be effective, which may be difficult where there are significant mismatches in maturity between the hedged item and the hedging instrument.

2.1.4.D   *Cash instruments*

There is one further situation where a portion of an instrument may be designated as a hedging instrument (in fact, is required to be). In the case of a cash instrument used as a hedge of foreign currency risk, it is essentially only the spot rate retranslation risk of, say, a borrowing that is used as the hedging instrument and not the other components, such as its changes in fair value arising from interest rate risk.

2.1.4.E   *Notional decomposition*

We also believe it is acceptable in certain circumstances to split a derivative (or allowable portion thereof – see 2.1.4.A to 2.1.4.C above) into component parts provided all of those components are designated and qualify for hedge accounting. For example a 'functional currency leg' could be introduced into a derivative that is denominated in two currencies (such as a forward contract or cross-currency interest rate swap) and the components designated separately in more than one hedging relation. In fact, the implementation guidance effectively contains examples of just such an approach (see Examples 51.7 and 51.8 and 2.1.6 below for further details) and the IFRS Interpretations Committee has confirmed that it considers such an approach to be acceptable.[2]

2.1.4.F   Restructuring of derivatives

An entity may exchange a derivative that does not qualify as a hedging instrument (say, the knock-out swap in Example 51.3 above) for two separate derivatives that, together, have the same fair value as the original instrument (say, a conventional interest rate swap and a written swaption). Such an exchange is likely to be motivated by a desire to obtain hedge accounting for one of these new instruments.

In order to determine whether the new arrangement can be treated as two separate derivatives, rather than a continuation of the original derivative, we believe it is necessary to determine whether the exchange transaction has any substance, which is clearly a matter of judgement. If the exchange has no substance then hedge accounting would still be precluded as the two 'separate' derivatives would in substance be a continuation of the original derivative (see Chapter 43 at 3.2).

In the case of the knock-out swap, if the two new contracts had the same counterparty and, in aggregate, the same terms as the original contract this would not necessarily lead to the conclusion that the exchange lacked substance. However if, in addition, the swaption would be settled by delivery of the conventional interest rate swap in the event that it was exercised, this is a strong indicator that the exchange does lack substance.

2.1.5   Reduction of risk

The implementation guidance explains that risk exposures should be assessed on a transaction basis and, therefore, a hedging instrument need not reduce risk at an entity-wide level. For example, if an entity has a fixed rate asset and a fixed rate liability, each with the same principal terms, it may enter into a pay-fixed, receive-variable interest rate swap to hedge the fair value of the asset even though the effect of the swap is to create an interest rate exposure for the entity that previously did not exist. *[IAS 39.F.2.6].* However, such a hedge designation would of course only make sense when the hedge is offsetting an economic risk. For example, in the situation described above, the hedge designation might only be a proxy for a hedge of a cash flow risk that does not qualify for hedge accounting.

The IASB discussed the concept of proxy hedging as part of the deliberations on the IFRS 9 hedge accounting guidance and decided that proxy hedging is permitted, provided the designation is directionally consistent with the actual risk management activities (see Chapter 52 at 5.5).

A derivative which does not reduce risk at the transaction level cannot be a hedging instrument. Consider a 'basis swap' that effectively converts one variable interest rate index (say a central bank base rate) on a liability to another (say LIBOR). A relationship of this nature would not normally qualify for hedge accounting because the hedging instrument does not reduce or eliminate risk in any meaningful way – it simply converts one risk to another similar risk. For this reason, such an economic strategy would not qualify as either a fair value or cash flow hedge relationship (see 3.1 and 3.2 below).

A basis swap or similar instrument may qualify as a hedging instrument when considered in combination with another instrument (see 2.1.3 above). For example, the basis swap described above and a pay-fixed, receive-LIBOR interest rate swap may qualify as a hedging instrument in a cash flow hedge of a borrowing that pays interest based on a central bank rate. It may also be used on its own in a hedge of offsetting asset and liability positions (see 2.1.6 below).

2.1.6 Hedging different risks with one instrument

A single hedging instrument may be designated as a hedge of more than one type of risk, provided that:

- the risks hedged can be identified clearly;
- the effectiveness of the hedge can be demonstrated ; and
- it is possible to ensure that there is specific designation of the hedging instrument and different risk positions. *[IAS 39.76]*.

The implementation guidance provides the following example to illustrate this point.

Example 51.7:   Foreign currency forward hedging positions in two foreign currencies

Company J, which has Japanese yen as its functional currency, issues five year floating rate US dollar debt and acquires a ten year fixed rate sterling bond. The principal amounts of the asset and liability, when converted into Japanese yen, are the same. J enters into a single foreign currency forward contract to hedge its foreign currency exposure on both instruments under which it receives US dollars and pays sterling at the end of five years.

Designating a single hedging instrument as a hedge of multiple types of risk is permitted if three conditions are met:

- the hedged risks can be clearly identified.

  In this case the risks are exposures to changes in the US dollar/yen and yen/sterling exchange rates respectively;

- the effectiveness of the hedge can be demonstrated.

  For the sterling bond, effectiveness can be measured as the degree of offset between the fair value of the principal repayment in sterling and the fair value of the sterling payment on the forward exchange contract.

  For the US dollar liability, effectiveness can be measured as the degree of offset between the fair value of the principal repayment in US dollars and the US dollar receipt on the forward exchange contract.

  Even though the bond has a ten year life and the forward only protects it for the first five years, hedge accounting is permitted for only a portion of the exposure (see 2.2.1.B below); and

- it is possible to ensure that there is a specific designation of the hedging instrument and the different risk positions.

  The hedged exposures are identified as the principal amounts of the liability and the bond in their respective currency of denomination.

The hedging instrument satisfies all of these conditions and J can designate the forward as a hedging instrument in a cash flow hedge against the foreign currency exposure on the principal repayments of both instruments and qualify for hedge accounting. *[IAS 39.F.1.13]*.

In this example, the hedging instrument is effectively decomposed and viewed as two forward contracts, each with an offsetting position in yen, i.e. J's functional currency. Each of the decomposed forward contracts is then designated in an eligible hedge accounting relationship.

The implementation guidance also explains that a single hedging instrument may be designated in both a cash flow hedge and a fair value hedge, provided the above conditions are met (section 3 covers the three different types of hedge recognised by IAS 39). For example, entities may use a cross currency interest rate swap to convert a variable rate position in a foreign currency to a fixed rate position in the functional currency. Such a swap could be designated separately as a fair value hedge of the currency risk and a cash flow hedge of the interest rate risk. *[IAS 39.F.1.12]*. However it could also be designated as a single cash flow hedge of foreign exchange and interest rate risk with the interest rate and currency swap in combination as the hedging instrument.

The IASB's implementation guidance takes the concept of hedging different risks a little further, as set out in the following example.

Example 51.8:   Cross-currency interest rate swap hedging two foreign currency exchange rate exposures and fair value interest rate exposure

Company J issues five-year floating rate US dollar debt and acquires a ten-year fixed rate sterling bond and wishes to hedge the foreign currency exposure on both the bond and the debt as well as the fair value interest rate exposure on the bond. To do this it enters into a matching cross-currency interest rate swap to receive floating rate US dollars, pay fixed rate sterling and exchange the US dollars for sterling at the end of five years.

Hedge accounting is permitted for components of risk, provided effectiveness can be measured. A single hedging instrument may be designated as a hedge of more than one type of risk if the risks can be identified clearly, effectiveness can be demonstrated, and specific designation of the hedging instrument and the risk positions can be ensured.

Therefore, the swap may be designated as a hedging instrument in a fair value hedge of the sterling bond against exposure to changes in its fair value associated with the interest rate payments on the bond until year five and the change in value of the principal payment due at maturity to the extent affected by changes in the yield curve relating to the five years of the swap (see Example 51.11 at 2.2.1.B below) as well as the exchange rate between sterling and US dollars.

In summary, the swap would be measured at fair value with changes in fair value recognised in profit or loss. The carrying amount of the receivable would be adjusted for changes in its fair value caused by changes in UK interest rates for the first five-year portion of the yield curve. Both the receivable and payable are remeasured using spot exchange rates under IAS 21 and the changes to their carrying amounts recognised in profit or loss. *[IAS 39.F.2.18]*.

Taken literally, the designation set out above takes no account of the existence of the US dollar liability and thereby suggests that the exchange rate between sterling and US dollars (the hedged risk) is seen as a component of the risk associated with the sterling bond (the hedged item). Mathematically this is clearly true from the point of view of a yen functional entity – together, the sterling/US dollar rate and the US dollar/yen rate give the sterling/yen exchange rate, i.e. the true foreign currency risk arising on the sterling bond. However, without considering the US dollar liability (which does not appear to be part of the designated hedge relationship) the hedge provides no real offset against the currency risk of the sterling liability. Instead it simply converts one foreign currency risk (exposure to sterling) to another (exposure to US dollars) and this would not normally be considered an acceptable hedging relationship. The IASB obviously sees the existence of the US dollar liability as important (otherwise it would not have been introduced into the example) but the point it is trying to articulate is not perfectly clear. In all likelihood, their failure to refer to the US dollar liability in the description of the hedge designation was simply an oversight. We believe that a hedge relationship to reflect the hedge of the foreign exchange risk on the US dollar liability would also need to be designated.

By analogy with Examples 51.7 and 51.8 above, we believe it would be acceptable to use a basis swap as a hedge of relevant asset and liability positions. For example, an entity may have made a $1m loan that earns LIBOR based interest and incurred a $1m liability that pays interest based on the central bank rate. In this case it may use as a hedging instrument an interest rate swap under which it pays LIBOR based interest and receives interest based on the central bank rate on a notional amount of $1m. In this case, the basis swap could be decomposed into two interest rate swaps, both with an offsetting $1m fixed rate leg, to facilitate hedge designations for each of the LIBOR loan and central bank deposit within separate cash flow hedges.

Decomposition of a derivative hedging instrument by imputing a notional leg is an acceptable means of splitting the fair value of a derivative hedging instrument into multiple components in order to achieve hedge accounting, as long as the split does not result in the recognition of cash flows that do not exist in the contractual terms of the derivative instrument.

The guidance above discussed combinations of (a) different cash flow hedges, (b) different fair value hedges and (c) a cash flow hedge and a fair value hedge. However, there appears to be no reason why a single instrument could not, in theory, be designated in other combinations of hedges, for example a cash flow hedge and a hedge of a net investment.

When a single hedging instrument is designated as a hedge of more than one type of risk, the IFRS Interpretations Committee has confirmed that the method of effectiveness testing is not prescribed. The method of assessing effectiveness should be captured in the hedge documentation on designation. Accordingly, the effectiveness assessment may be carried out for the total hedged position, i.e. incorporating all risks identified if these risks are inextricably linked, or for the decomposed parts separately, i.e. individually each for hedge relationship that includes a decomposed part of the derivative.[3] However, if the assessment is undertaken separately we believe that the assessment needs to be passed for each hedge relationship that includes a decomposed part, otherwise the assessment fails overall. This restriction is necessary as a financial instrument can only be designated as hedging instrument in its entirety (see 2.1.4 above). *[IAS 39.74]*.

2.1.7 Own equity instruments

An entity's own equity instruments are not financial assets or liabilities of the entity and, therefore, cannot be hedging instruments. *[IAS 39.AG97]*. This prohibition would also apply to instruments that give rise to non-controlling interests in consolidated financial statements – under IFRS it is clear that non-controlling interests are part of a reporting entity's equity.

2.2   Hedged items

The basic requirement for a hedged item is for it to be one of the following:

- a recognised asset or liability;
- an unrecognised firm commitment;
- a highly probable forecast transaction; or
- a net investment in a foreign operation,

and it should expose the entity to the risk of changes in fair value or future cash flows. *[IAS 39.78]*.

Recognised assets and liabilities can include financial items and non-financial items such as inventory. They can also include recognised firm commitments that are not routinely recognised as assets or liabilities absent the effects of hedge accounting for such items. Most internally-generated intangibles (e.g. for a bank, a core deposit intangible – see 2.2.10 below) are not recognised assets and therefore cannot be hedged items. *[IAS 39.F.2.3]*.

In general, for hedge accounting purposes, only exposures that involve a party external to the entity can be designated as hedged items. However, there are some exceptions which are covered at 2.3.4 below. *[IAS 39.80]*.

Financial assets and liabilities need not be within the scope of IAS 39 to qualify as hedged items. For example, although rights and obligations under lease agreements are for most purposes scoped out of IAS 39, finance lease payables or receivables still meet the definition of a financial instrument and could therefore be hedged items in a hedge of interest rate or foreign currency risk.

In the case of a financial asset or liability containing an embedded derivative (see Chapter 43 at 4), if the embedded derivative is accounted for separately from the host instrument, the hedged item would be the host instrument or cash flows from the host (or portion thereof – see 2.2.1 below); otherwise it would be based on the hybrid instrument (i.e. the instrument including the embedded derivative) or cash flows from the hybrid.

As well as designating all changes in the cash flows or fair value of a hedged item in a hedging relationship, an entity can also designate only changes in the cash flows or fair value of a hedged item above or below a specified price or other variable (a one-sided risk). For example, an entity can designate the variability of future cash flow outcomes resulting from a price increase of a forecast commodity purchase, without including the risk of a price decrease within the hedge relationship. Such a situation may arise if the entity wanted to retain the opportunity to benefit from lower commodities prices, but protect itself against an increase. In such a situation, only cash flow losses that result from an increase in the price above the specified level are designated. *[IAS 39.AG99BA]*. Although this already seemed to be clear, the July 2008 amendments to IAS 39 dealing with eligible hedged items added implementation guidance to clarify this.

2.2.1   *Financial items: portions and proportions*

If the hedged item is a financial asset or liability, the standard contains a general principle that it may be a hedged item with respect to the risks associated with only a portion of its cash flows or fair value, such as one or more selected contractual cash flows or portions of them or a percentage of the fair value (i.e. a proportion of the asset or liability) provided that effectiveness can be measured. *[IAS 39.81]*. The ability to designate a proportion or a percentage of an exposure as a hedged item is similar to the guidance for hedging instruments. However the ability to identify a portion of an exposure as the hedged item is very different to the restrictions imposed on hedging instruments discussed in 2.1.4 above. For example:

(a)   all of the cash flows of a financial instrument may be designated for cash flow or fair value changes attributable to some (but not all) risks; or

(b)   some (but not all) of the cash flows of a financial instrument may be designated for cash flow or fair value changes attributable to all or only some risks (i.e. a 'portion' of the cash flows of the financial instrument may be designated for changes attributable to all or only some risks). *[IAS 39.AG99E]*.

Only the portion of cash flows or fair value of a financial instrument that are designated as the hedged item are subject to the hedge accounting requirements. The accounting for other portions that are not designated as the hedged item remains unchanged.

The guidance also adds that to be eligible for hedge accounting, the designated risks and portions must be separately identifiable components of the financial instrument, and changes in the cash flows or fair value of the entire financial instrument arising from the designated risks and portions must be reliably measurable. *[IAS 39.AG99F]*. This is considered further below.

2.2.1.A   *Benchmark portions of interest rate risk*

As an example of the general principle above, an identifiable and separately measurable portion of the interest rate exposure of an interest-bearing asset or liability may be designated as the hedged risk. Such a portion might be a risk-free interest rate or other benchmark interest rate component of the total interest rate exposure of a hedged financial instrument. This is always subject to the proviso that effectiveness can be measured (see 5.3 below). *[IAS 39.81]*.

For a fixed-rate financial instrument hedged for changes in fair value attributable to changes in a risk-free or other benchmark interest rate, the implementation guidance explains that the risk-free or other benchmark rate is normally regarded as both a separately identifiable component of the financial instrument and reliably measurable. *[IAS 39.AG99F(a)]*.

For example, consider an entity that issues five year debt with a fixed coupon of 5%, for which the pricing was based on a prevailing benchmark curve of 2% for five years, plus 3% credit risk spread. The entity then transacts an interest rate swap at the prevailing five year benchmark rate (i.e. pay benchmark, receive 2%). It would be possible for the entity to designate the portion of the debt's cash flow represented by the debt principal and a 2% benchmark component of the coupon as the hedged item. In general, if a portion of the cash flows of a financial asset or liability is designated as the hedged item, that designated portion must be less than its total cash flows. For example, in the case of a liability whose effective interest rate is below LIBOR, designating the following components is not permitted:

- a portion of the liability equal to the principal amount plus interest at LIBOR; and
- a negative residual portion.

This restriction gives risk to what is often referred to as the sub-LIBOR issue. In these cases, all of the cash flows of the entire financial asset or liability may be designated as the hedged item in a hedge of only one particular risk (e.g. only for changes that are attributable to changes in LIBOR). Consider a financial liability whose effective interest rate is 100 basis points (1%) below LIBOR (i.e. the cash flows represent repayment of the principal plus interest at LIBOR minus 100 basis points). It is not possible to designate cash flows representing a LIBOR component of that liability, but the entire liability can be designated as the hedged item in a hedge of changes in the fair value or cash flows attributable to changes in LIBOR. This means that the full cash flows from the liability are designated within the hedge relationship, but for changes in LIBOR. Nevertheless, the standard explains that some ineffectiveness will occur and, in order to improve the effectiveness of the hedge, a hedge ratio of other than one-to-one may be chosen. *[IAS 39.AG99C]*. This is relevant for hedged items in both cash flow hedges (e.g. a floating rate debt security which refixes to 3 month LIBOR less a 0.5% spread every 3 months) and fair value hedges (e.g. a fixed rate loan with an effective interest rate which is 1% less than the prevailing benchmark rate for that term). See Chapter 52 at 3.4.5 for further information on this topic.

The guidance goes on to explain that, if a fixed rate financial instrument is hedged some time after its origination, and interest rates have changed in the meantime, a portion equal to a benchmark rate that is actually higher than the contractual rate paid on the item *can* be designated as the hedged item in some circumstances. This is provided that the benchmark rate is less than the effective interest rate calculated on the assumption that the instrument had been purchased on the day it was first designated as the hedged item. *[IAS 39.AG99D]*. This is illustrated below.

Example 51.9:   Hedge of a portion of an existing fixed rate financial asset following a rise in interest rates

Company B originates a fixed rate financial asset of €100 that has an effective interest rate of 6% at a time when LIBOR is 4%. B begins to hedge that asset some time later when LIBOR has increased to 8% and the fair value of the asset has decreased to €90.

B calculates that if it had purchased the asset on the date it first designated it as the hedged item for its then fair value of €90, the effective yield would have been 9.5%. Because LIBOR is less than this effective yield, the entity can designate a LIBOR portion of 8% that consists partly of the contractual interest cash flows and partly of the difference between the current fair value (€90) and the amount repayable on maturity (€100). *[IAS 39.AG99D]*.

The guidance illustrated in Example 51.9 above will assist entities in designating hedges in a way that significantly reduces ineffectiveness. In fact, as noted at 5.3.8

below, the ability to designate a portion of a financial instrument as the hedged item can enable many hedges to be designated in a way that minimises or even eliminates ineffectiveness in some cases.

The negative interest rate environment in some countries, mainly Switzerland and certain countries in the Eurozone, has further implications on the designation of risk components in connection with the sub-LIBOR issue. The following example illustrates this.

Example 51.10: Negative interest rates and fair value hedges

Assume the following scenarios

a)   Bank A enters into a €1 million loan to a corporate at a fixed coupon of 3.5%. The coupon has been determined considering the negative EONIA rate (the benchmark) of –0.15% plus a credit spread of 3.65%.

b)   Bank B acquires a government debt security in the secondary market with the same terms as the loan in scenario a). In this fact pattern the debt was issued some years ago when benchmark interest rates were much higher. The purchase price of the debt was €1.185 million which resulted in an effective interest rate of –0.18%, consisting of the negative EONIA rate (the benchmark) when the debt was acquired of –0.15% and a credit spread of –0.03%.

Both, Bank A and Bank B want to hedge the fixed rate benchmark component and enter into an interest rate swap paying fixed –0.15% and receiving EONIA. The banks wish to designate the benchmark component in a fair value hedge for changes in EONIA.

In scenario a) it seems acceptable for the bank to designate the benchmark risk component because:

- it is included in the pricing of the hedged item and therefore separately identifiable and reliably measureable;

- the benchmark can be positive or negative, therefore the cash flows representing that benchmark rate can also be positive or negative, even if they are part of overall positive cash flows (which is similar to a benchmark component of 4% hedging the benchmark risk in a coupon of 5%, except that the benchmark is negative in this case); and

- the benchmark cash flows are less than the cash flows in the hedged items (i.e. minus 0.15% which is less than 3.5%).

We would find it difficult to reach the same conclusion for scenario b) as the benchmark rate is higher than the effective interest rate (i.e. minus 0.15% which is greater than minus 0.18%). *[IAS 39.AG99D]*. This is consistent with the fact that if a debt instrument were to be issued at par bearing a coupon of –0.18%, which included credit spread of –0.03%, when the benchmark rate was –0.15% it would not be possible to identify a benchmark component for hedge accounting purposes. *[IAS 39 AG99C]*.

In both scenarios, the banks would not be permitted to designate a payment of 0.15% of the principal as an eligible component of a receipt of a 3.5% coupon, as it is difficult to argue that a payment of 0.15% of the principal is a portion of a receipt of 3.5% of that principal. However, this is not that relevant in scenario a) as it would be possible to designate a separately identifiable benchmark component in the total cash flows, as noted above. *[IAS 39.AG99E(b)]*.

Notwithstanding the above, in both cases, the banks can designate all the cashflows in the financial asset for changes in the benchmark rate, although this is likely to result in some ineffectiveness. *[IAS 39.AG99E(a)]*.

2.2.1.B   Partial term hedging

The example below illustrates a different portion of interest rate risk that is eligible for designation. It is the ability to designate a hedged item for the portion of risk that represents only part of the term that a hedged item remains outstanding.

Example 51.11:   Partial term hedging

Company A acquires a 10% fixed-rate government bond with a remaining term to maturity of ten years and classifies it as available-for-sale. To hedge against the fair value exposure on the bond associated with the first five years' interest payments, it acquires a five year pay-fixed receive-floating swap.

The swap may be designated as hedging the fair value exposure of the interest rate payments on the government bond until year five and the change in value of the principal payment due at maturity to the extent affected by changes in the yield curve relating to the five years of the swap. *[IAS 39.F.2.17].*

2.2.1.C   Foreign currency risk associated with publicly quoted shares

The implementation guidance explains that the foreign currency risk associated with a holding of publicly traded shares may be hedged if they give rise to a clear and identifiable exposure to changes in foreign exchange rates. It is asserted that this will be the case if:

- the shares are not traded on an exchange, or other established market, in which trades are denominated in the same currency as the holder's functional currency; and

- dividends on the shares are not denominated in that currency.

Consequently, if the share trades in multiple currencies, one of which is the holder's functional currency, hedge accounting would not be permitted. *[IAS 39.F.2.19].* However, this restriction does not stand up to close scrutiny, as illustrated in the following example.

Example 51.12:   Foreign currency risk associated with equity shareholding

ABC plc, a UK company whose functional currency is sterling, acquires a small shareholding in IJK Limited. IJK is a South African company whose operations are based solely in that country and whose income, expenditure and dividends are all denominated in South African rand. IJK's shares are listed on the Johannesburg Stock Exchange where trades are denominated in rand.

The implementation guidance suggests that, potentially, ABC could hedge the foreign currency risk arising from the sterling/rand exchange rate on its IJK holding, which appears quite sensible. If, on day 1, the shares trade at R50 and the exchange rate is R10 to £1, the shares would have a sterling value of £5.00 (= R50 ÷ 10). If, on day 2, the exchange rate moves to R8 to £1, all other things being equal, the rand value of IJK should not change, but its sterling value would be £6.25 (= R50 ÷ 8), exactly mirroring the exchange rate movement.

If IJK subsequently obtained a secondary listing on the London Stock Exchange where trades were denominated in sterling, but its business fundamentals were unchanged, in the scenario outlined above ABC's foreign exchange exposure would be exactly the same. In fact, the operation of the markets should ensure that the share price in London on the equivalent of days 1 and 2 is £5.00 and £6.25 respectively. However, the guidance suggests that because of the secondary listing, ABC no longer has a clear and identifiable exposure to changes in foreign exchange rates on the IJK shares and therefore hedge accounting would not be permitted.

2.2.1.D   Inflation risk

Although there has been significant debate by many interested parties over the years, the implementation guidance in IAS 39 states that inflation is not separately identifiable and reliably measurable and cannot be designated as a risk portion of a financial instrument. There is one exception: the contractually specified inflation portion of the cash flows of a recognised inflation-linked bond (assuming there is no requirement to account for an embedded derivative separately) is considered to be separately identifiable and reliably measurable as long as other cash flows of the instrument are not affected by the inflation portion. Therefore inflation risk would not be eligible as a designated risk or portion of a fixed interest rate borrowing that does not also reference inflation. *[IAS 39.AG99F(b)-(c), BC11D, BC172C].*

However, this prohibition will be softened on application of IFRS 9 which introduces a rebuttable presumption that, unless contractually specified, inflation is not separately identifiable and reliably measurable (see Chapter 52 at 3.4.4).

2.2.1.E   Other portions

While IAS 39 permits hedging of some portions of risk for financial assets or liabilities, there are intended to be some restrictions, i.e. a portion cannot be simply anything. It also noted that IAS 39 requires a hedged portion to have an effect on the price of the hedged item or transaction that is separately measurable from the hedged item or transaction itself. Consequently, a portion cannot be a residual; i.e. an entity is not permitted to designate as a portion the residual fair value or cash flows of a hedged item or transaction if that residual does not have a separately measurable effect on the hedged item or transaction. It is for this reason that it is not considered possible to determine that credit risk is an eligible risk component of a debt instrument.

This position was reaffirmed by the IASB in IFRS 9. *[IAS 39.BC6.470].* However, IFRS 9 does introduce an alternative accounting solution for entities undertaking economic credit risk hedging activity (see Chapter 52 at 10.1).

2.2.2   Non-financial items: portions

It is explained that changes in the price of an ingredient or component of a non-financial asset or liability generally do not have a predictable, separately measurable effect on the price of the item that is comparable to the effect of, say, a change in market interest rates on the price of a bond. Therefore, because of the difficulty of isolating and measuring the appropriate portion of cash flows or fair value changes attributable to specific risks (other than foreign currency risks) a non-financial asset or liability can be designated as a hedged item only:

- in its entirety for all risks; or
- for foreign exchange risks. *[IAS 39.82, AG100].*

A number of commentators disagree with this assertion, at least in certain situations, and some urged the IASB in revising IAS 39 to reconsider this restriction. For example, Swiss International Air Lines, in responding to the June 2002 exposure draft, wrote the following:

> 'Like any airline SWISS is short of jet fuel. The Company is exposed to the daily price fluctuations of crude oil and the prices of inter product spreads (cracks, differentials) that convert crude oil into gas oil and finally into jet fuel.
>
> There is more liquidity in crude oil for positions beyond two years. Therefore, it is part of SWISS' fuel risk management strategy to do long-term hedges with

crude oil. These positions are then rolled into gas oil and jet fuel as they move closer to the settlement dates.

Paragraphs 129-130 [of the Exposure Draft] state that non-financial assets and liabilities can only be hedged in their entirety or separately with respect to foreign exchange risk.

Crude oil hedges therefore must be designated as hedging the risk of price movements of jet fuel in its entirety. The critical terms of the hedging instrument and the hedged item therefore do not perfectly match – frequently a certain ineffectiveness will result. Even if the hedge can be expected to be highly effective due to a high historical correlation of the price movements of crude and jet fuel, actual effectiveness might fall outside the 80-125% range in some periods and the hedge will have to be dedesignated.

We believe that due to the special properties of jet fuel prices, it should be allowed to designate the price changes of a jet fuel component such as crude oil as the hedged risk.

The reason given in paragraphs 129 and 130 is that risk components of non-financial instruments generally do not have a predictable, separately measurable effect on the price of the entire item. This is a generalization that does not account for the special properties of jet fuel pricing.

Jet fuel is a derivative of crude oil. Crude oil is then converted into gas oil. The difference of the crude and the gas oil price is called gas oil crack. Gas oil is finally converted into jet fuel, the price difference being called jet differential.

It is not difficult to isolate and measure the portion of the changes of jet fuel prices attributable to the price risk of these components. Crude, gas oil crack, and jet differential are separately traded and market prices are available through market information systems such as Platt's as for jet fuel itself. The price of jet fuel actually is calculated from the prices of its components.

Changes in the price of the components of jet fuel do have a predictable, separately measurable effect on the price of jet fuel. This effect can be compared to the effect of a change in the market interest rates on the price of a bond.'[4]

However, in spite of protestations such as this, the IASB noted that, in many cases, changes in the cash flows or fair value of a portion of a non-financial hedged item *are* difficult to isolate and measure and therefore the restriction was retained largely unchanged. [IAS 39.BC137, BC138]. This was much to the disappointment of various airlines and entities with similar fuel requirements who would have preferred the standard to adopt a different approach, e.g. to establish a 'rebuttable presumption' that components could not be identified and separately hedged. In fact, it appears that this message had not been fully appreciated because it was again put to the IFRS Interpretations Committee and discussed in October 2004, where it was again reiterated that it was not possible to designate a risk component of a non-financial item other than foreign exchange risk.[5]

Interestingly, with the aim of bringing hedge accounting closer to risk management practices, the IASB has revisited risk components of non-financial items when developing the revised hedge accounting requirements for inclusion in IFRS 9. The hedge accounting requirements of IFRS 9 pick up the above jet fuel hedging example and permit risk components of non-financial items to be eligible hedged items, provided the risk component is separately identifiable and reliably measurable (see Chapter 52 at 3.4.3).

However, it is possible for an amount of highly probable forecast non-financial hedged items to be designated in a hedge relationship that is less than the full amount expected to occur. Such a designation is only possible if the forecast transaction can be identified and documented with sufficient specificity so that when the transaction occurs, it is clear whether the transaction is or is not the hedged transaction (see 5.2 below).

Furthermore, the guidance in IAS 39 does not prevent an entity hedging a specified range of absolute values of a non-financial item, i.e. a one sided risk (see 2.2 above). For example, an entity may hedge the risk that its gold inventory will fall in value by purchasing a cash-settled at-the-money put option that allows (but does not require) the entity to sell a fixed amount of gold for a price that is fixed at its market value at inception of the contract – in this case the hedged risk is the risk that the value of the gold inventory will fall below a specified price.

The IASB also considered whether the interest rate risk portion of loan servicing rights could be designated as the hedged item on the grounds that this portion can be separately identified and measured, and that changes in market interest rates have a predictable and separately measurable effect on the value of such rights. In fact the possibility of treating loan servicing rights as financial assets rather than non-financial assets, perhaps on an elective basis, was also considered. However, it was concluded that no exceptions should be permitted for this matter either. *[IAS 39.BC140-BC143].*

It seems reasonably clear from the logic of the above restriction that an entity may also hedge a non-financial exposure for all risks *except* foreign currency risk (even if it is not clear from the standard itself), as illustrated in the following example.

Example 51.13:   Hedge of foreign currency denominated commodity risk

Company P has the FC as its functional currency. It has forecast, with a high probability, the need to purchase a fixed quantity of crude oil for US Dollars in twelve months' time. To hedge part of its exposure to the price risk inherent in this purchase P enters into an exchange traded twelve-month cash-settled crude oil forward contract. The strike price of the forward is denominated in US dollars (there is no active market in FC denominated crude oil futures) and P therefore fixes the US dollar price of the oil to be purchased. P chooses not to hedge the risk associated with FC to US dollar exchange rates. This might be because of illiquidity in the foreign currency markets for FCs or, perhaps, because P has forecast US dollar inflows that provide a natural hedge of the foreign exchange risk.

P may designate the forward contract as the hedging instrument in a hedge of the exposure to the US dollar denominated price risk associated with its forecast purchase of crude oil.

In many cases it will be difficult to identify a separately measurable effect on non-financial assets, even for foreign currency risk, as illustrated in the following example from the implementation guidance.

Example 51.14:   Foreign currency borrowings hedging fixed assets

A Danish shipping company, D, has a US subsidiary that has the same functional currency as the parent, the Danish krone. Accordingly in D's consolidated financial statements, ships owned by the subsidiary, which are carried at depreciated historical cost, are reported in Danish krone using historical exchange rates. To hedge the potential currency risk on the disposal of the ships in US dollars, purchases of ships are normally financed with loans denominated in US dollars.

US dollar borrowings cannot be classified as fair value hedges of a ship because ships do not contain any separately measurable foreign currency risk even if their purchase was, and sale is likely to be, denominated in US dollars.

The proceeds from the anticipated sale of the ship may, however, be designated in a cash flow hedge, provided all the hedging criteria are met. Those conditions require that the sale is highly probable, which is only likely if the sale is expected to occur in the immediate future. *[IAS 39.F.6.5]*.

Unfortunately, the statement that a ship does not contain any separately measurable foreign currency risk is not explained any further, which makes it difficult to apply this guidance in other situations. For example, it is hard to argue that a commodity such as crude oil, which is traded throughout the world in US dollars, does not contain a measurable exposure to US dollars. If another commodity is regularly traded and quoted both in US dollars and in euro (the implementation guidance suggests this might be the case for natural gas – see Chapter 43 at 5.2.1.B) it might seem sensible to treat that commodity as containing both US dollar and euro exposures. However, by analogy with the guidance on quoted shares (see 2.2.1.C above), *[IAS 39 F.2.19]*, a commodity that is traded and quoted in more than one currency would probably be deemed to create no measurable currency exposure for an entity whose functional currency is one of those currencies.

Inevitably, for many hedges of non-financial items there will be a difference between the terms of the hedging instrument and the hedged item. As well as the restriction on hedging portions of the non-financial item, there may simply be no perfectly matching hedging instruments. For example, a forward contract to purchase Colombian coffee might be used as a hedge of the forecast purchase of Brazilian coffee on otherwise similar terms. Such a hedge may, nonetheless, qualify for hedge accounting, provided all the hedging criteria are met. *[IAS 39.AG100]*.

To meet these criteria, it must be expected that the hedge will be highly effective. For this purpose, the amount of the hedging instrument may be greater or less than that of the hedged item if this improves the effectiveness of the hedging relationship (see 5.3 below for more on assessing the hedge effectiveness). For example, a regression analysis could be performed to establish a statistical relationship between the hedged item (e.g. a transaction in Brazilian coffee) and the hedging instrument (e.g. a transaction in Columbian coffee). If there is a valid statistical relationship between the two variables (i.e. between the unit prices of Brazilian coffee and Columbian coffee), the slope of the regression line can be used to establish the designated hedge ratio that will maximise expected effectiveness. For example, if the slope of the regression line is 1.02, a hedge ratio based on 0.98 quantities of hedged items to 1.00 quantities of the hedging instrument maximises expected effectiveness. However, the hedging relationship may result in ineffectiveness that is recognised in profit or loss during the term of the hedging relationship. *[IAS 39.AG100]*. The continued existence of a valid statistical relationship is required to be proven as part of the ongoing hedge effectiveness assessment in order to continue with hedge accounting prospectively (see 5.3 below). This idea is a recurring theme in the standard and is referred to a number of times.

As discussed in Chapter 42 at 2.2.1, current tax receivable (payable) is a non-financial asset (liability) because it arises from statutory requirements imposed by governments rather than a contract. Therefore it is not possible to designate a portion of current tax as a hedged item except for foreign exchange risk. This is the case even where the portion arises indirectly from foreign exchange risk. For example, an entity may be taxed at, say, 30% on exchange gains or losses arising on a specified monetary item but the portion of its tax charge which is payable or receivable in respect of those foreign currency gains and losses may not be a hedged item. Consequently, gains and losses on the hedging instrument (which in some cases will offset the corresponding portion of the tax charge or credit in the right period without the need for hedge accounting) could not be offset against the tax charge in profit or loss (see Chapter 53 at 7.1.3).

2.2.3 Groups of items as hedged items

The standard explains that a hedged item can be a single item or a group of such items with similar risk characteristics. *[IAS 39.78]*. To aggregate and hedge similar assets or liabilities as a group, the individual items need to share the risk exposure for which they are hedged. Further, the standard requires that fair value changes attributable to the hedged risk for each individual item should be approximately proportional to the equivalent fair value change of the entire group. *[IAS 39.83]*.

For example, a group of mortgage loans may be considered a hedged item with respect to interest rate risk as long as the changes in fair value attributable to changes in the hedged risk for each loan are expected to be approximately proportional to the overall change in fair value of the entire group of loans due to the hedged risk. Factors to consider might include the interest rate applied to the individual mortgage loans in the group (fixed or floating) the actual coupon rate for fixed rate mortgages, the denominated currency and the maturity of the loans. However, the risk characteristics of the individual shares in a portfolio designed to replicate a share index will be different from each other and from the portfolio as a whole. For example the fair value of an individual share may go up whereas the fair value of the portfolio as a whole goes down. Therefore, the portfolio could not be hedged with respect to movements in the index *[IAS 39.F.2.20]* even though, in economic terms, the portfolio of shares may well be perfectly (or near perfectly) hedged. In situations like this, an entity may be able to designate the assets within the portfolio at fair value through profit or loss so that gains and losses from the hedging instrument and hedged items should offset within profit or loss (but of course designation could only take place on initial recognition and all fair value movements would be recognised, not just those with respect to the hedged risk – see Chapter 45 at 2.2).

The IFRS 9 guidance on hedge accounting for groups of items no longer requires that fair value changes attributable to the hedged risk for each individual item should be approximately proportional to the equivalent fair value change of the entire group (see Chapter 52 at 3.6.1).

IAS 39 states that, in general, hedge effectiveness is assessed by comparing the change in value or cash flow of hedging instruments and of hedged items. Therefore an overall net position, e.g. the net of all fixed rate assets and fixed rate liabilities with similar maturities, cannot be a hedged item. *[IAS 39.84]*. Similarly, the net cash flows arising from a portfolio of floating rate assets and liabilities cannot be designated as the hedged item. *[IAS 39.F.2.21]*. Accordingly, many financial institutions apply the special portfolio hedge accounting solutions (see 6 below).

However, approximately the same effect on profit or loss can be achieved by designating a gross part of the underlying items as the hedged position. For example, a European company with firm commitments to make purchases and sales of US$100 and US$90 respectively could hedge the net exposure by acquiring a derivative and designating it as a hedging instrument associated with gross purchases of US$10. Similarly, a bank with €100 of assets and €90 of liabilities with risks and terms of a similar nature could hedge the net exposure by designating €10 of those assets as the hedged item. *[IAS 39.AG101]*.

2.2.4   Hedges of general business risk

To qualify for hedge accounting, the hedge must relate to a specific identified and designated risk, and not merely to the entity's general business risks; also, it must ultimately affect profit or loss (see the definitions of the types of hedging relationships in IAS 39 at 3 below). A hedge of the risk of obsolescence of a physical asset or the risk of expropriation of property by a government is not eligible for hedge accounting (effectiveness cannot be measured because those risks are not measurable reliably). *[IAS 39.AG110]*. Similarly, the risk that a transaction will not occur is an overall business risk that is not eligible as a hedged item. *[IAS 39.F.2.8]*.

2.2.5   Hedges of a firm commitment to acquire a business

A firm commitment to acquire a business in a business combination cannot be a hedged item, except for foreign exchange risk (see further discussion at 4.4 below), because the other risks being hedged cannot be specifically identified and measured. These other risks are also said to be general business risks. *[IAS 39.AG98]*. However, transactions of the business to be acquired (for example floating rate interest payments on its borrowings) may potentially qualify as hedged items. For this to be the case, it would need to be demonstrated that, from the perspective of the acquirer, those hedged transactions are highly probable which may not be straightforward as this requirement applies to both the business combination and the hedged transactions themselves.

2.2.6   Held-to-maturity investments

Unlike loans and receivables, a held-to-maturity investment (whether it pays fixed or floating interest rates) cannot be a hedged item with respect to interest rate risk or prepayment risk. This is because designating an investment as held-to-maturity requires an intention to hold the investment until maturity without regard to changes in the fair value or cash flows of such an instrument attributable to changes in interest rates (see Chapter 45 at 3). *[IAS 39.79, F.2.9]*.

However, a held-to-maturity investment (or related cash flows) can be a hedged item in the following circumstances:

- the investment may be a hedged item with respect to risks from changes in foreign currency exchange rates and credit risk; *[IAS 39.79]*

- the forecast purchase of such an investment may be a hedged item, say to lock in current interest rates – this is because an investment is not given an IAS 39 classification until it is actually recognised; *[IAS 39.F.2.10]* and

- the forecast reinvestment of fixed or variable interest receipts can be hedged items with respect to the risk of interest rate changes, as these hedged interest flows relate to forecast debt instruments that have not yet been classified for accounting purposes. *[IAS 39.F.2.11]*.

  It should be noted that this hedge relationship is significantly different from a hedge of the interest rate risk on the held-to-maturity investment itself. The hedge of interest flows from forecast reinvestment is most commonly used as a building block in the cash flow macro-hedging model (see 6 below).

2.2.7 Derivatives

A derivative cannot be a hedged item, the implementation guidance explains that this is because such instruments are always deemed held for trading and measured at fair value with gains and losses recognised in profit or loss unless they are designated and effective hedging instruments. *[IAS 39.F.2.1]*.

This has the effect that cash flows from a forecast derivative transaction cannot be hedged items. For example, a company with the euro as its functional currency that expects to issue floating rate debt in three months' time may wish to enter into a forward starting euro denominated pay-fixed receive-floating interest rate swap to fix the cash flows on that debt before it is issued, and those cash flows could qualify as hedged items. However, that entity may instead expect to issue US dollar denominated debt and, immediately after issuance, swap it into floating rate euro debt by way of a cross currency interest rate swap. In this case, the forecast floating rate euro interest payments are not valid hedged items as they partly arise from a forecast derivative contract.

Consider a further example where a commodity trading entity (which produces part of the commodities that it trades) accounts for all of its sales contracts at fair value through profit or loss (see Chapter 42 at 4). The costs of production are incurred in euros, which is also the entity's functional currency. Commodities are traded in US dollars and the entity has US dollar debt that was used to finance the production assets. In this example, the entity cannot hedge the foreign exchange risk arising from its expected gross sales in US dollars (i.e. the forecast transaction) with its US dollar debt as the expected gross sales arise from forecast derivatives.

Similarly, a 'synthetic hedged item' created by combining a derivative with a non-derivative financial instrument cannot be a hedged item. For example, if an entity issued foreign currency denominated fixed rate debt and converted it into functional currency floating rate debt using a cross-currency interest rate swap, it would not be possible to designate the synthetic functional currency floating rate debt as a hedged item, as it is made up of combination of debt and a derivative.[6]

In what is a significant change, the IASB decided to allow aggregated exposures (i.e. a combination of a derivative and a risk exposure) to qualify as a hedged item under the IFRS 9 hedge accounting requirements. This allows hedge accounting to be applied to many common risk management strategies, such as where an entity initially only hedges the price risk of a highly probable forecast purchase of a raw material denominated in a foreign currency, then later hedges the foreign exchange risk too (see Chapter 52 at 3.3).

2.2.8   *Forecast acquisition or issuance of foreign currency monetary items*

Changes in foreign exchange rates prior to acquisition or issuance of a monetary item denominated in a foreign currency do not impact profit or loss. Therefore an entity cannot hedge the foreign currency risk associated with the forecast acquisition or issuance of a monetary item denominated in a foreign currency, such as the expected issuance for cash of borrowings denominated in a currency other than the entity's functional currency. This is because there is a need for the hedged risk to have the potential to impact profit or loss in order to achieve hedge accounting. *[IAS 39.86(b)]*.

2.2.9   *Own equity instruments*

Transactions in an entity's own equity instruments (including distributions to holders of such instruments) are generally recognised directly in equity by the issuer (see Chapter 44) and do not affect profit or loss. Therefore, such instruments cannot be designated as a hedged item. Similarly, a forecast transaction in an entity's own equity instruments (e.g. a forecast dividend payment) cannot qualify as a hedged item. However, a declared dividend that qualifies for recognition as a financial liability, e.g. because the entity has become legally obliged to make the payment, may qualify as a hedged item. For example, a recognised liability to pay a dividend in a foreign currency would give rise to foreign exchange risk. *[IAS 39.F.2.7]*.

2.2.10   *Core deposits*

Financial institutions often receive a significant proportion of their funding from demand deposits, such as current account balances, savings accounts and other accounts that behave in a similar manner. Even though the total balance from all such customer deposits may vary, a financial institution typically determines a level of core deposits that it believes will be maintained for a particular time frame, and hence will behave for that time frame like a fixed interest rate exposure from an interest rate risk perspective.

These customer deposits or accounts usually pay a zero or low, stable interest rate which is generally insensitive to changes in market interest rates. Hence both existing and new deposits are generally considered fungible for interest rate risk management purposes as new deposits will usually be on the same terms as any withdrawn deposits that they replace. Financial institutions cannot determine which customer deposits will make up the core deposits. While these deposits can be withdrawn at little or short notice, typically they are left as a deposit for a long and generally predictable time despite the low interest paid.

Risk management of the 'deemed' fixed rate interest rate risk exposure that financial institutions attribute to core deposits will often result in the need to transact interest rate derivatives, although achieving hedge accounting for these derivatives can be difficult.[7]

In order for items to be eligible hedged items in a fair value hedge, the fair value of the hedged items must vary with the hedged risk. However, IFRS 13 – *Fair Value Measurement* – states that the fair value of a financial liability with a demand feature (e.g. a demand deposit) is not less than the amount payable on demand, discounted from the first date that the amount could be required to be paid. *[IFRS 13.47]*. Therefore the fair value of demand deposits will not vary with the hedged risk, and fair value hedge accounting is precluded.

An alternative consideration is whether it is possible to designate a core deposit intangible (representing the value of this source of funding to the financial institution) as an eligible hedged item. The term 'core deposit intangible' could be used to represent the difference between:

(a)   the fair value of a portfolio of core deposits; and

(b)   the aggregate of the individual fair values of the liabilities within the portfolio, normally calculated in accordance with the requirements of IAS 39.

Generally, an internally-generated core deposit intangible cannot be a hedged item because it is not a recognised asset. If a core deposit intangible is acquired together with a related portfolio of deposits, it is required to be recognised separately as an intangible asset (or as part of the related acquired portfolio of deposits) if it meets the recognition criteria in IAS 38 – *Intangible Assets* – *[IAS 39.F.2.3]* which it normally will (see Chapter 9 at 5.5.2).

Theoretically, therefore, a recognised core deposit intangible asset could be designated as a hedged item. However this will only be the case if it meets the conditions for hedge accounting, including the requirement that the effectiveness of the hedge can be measured reliably. The implementation guidance explains that, because it is often difficult to measure reliably the fair value of a core deposit intangible asset other than on initial recognition, it is unlikely that this requirement will be met. *[IAS 39.F.2.3]*. In fact, this probably understates the difficulty.

For the reasons set out above, financial institutions are not able to designate core deposits with the associated hedging instruments in hedge accounting relationships, despite the economic validity of these risk management activities. Accordingly, many financial institutions apply the special portfolio hedge accounting guidance (see 6 below).

2.2.11   Pension scheme assets

An entity may wish to enter into transactions to hedge the risk associated with assets held by a pension scheme or other long-term employee benefit fund. We consider that, for many reasons, plan assets are unlikely to qualify as hedged items under IAS 39. For example, a pension scheme is, in many respects, a non-financial asset or liability and, therefore, the portion of the risk associated with only the assets could not be a hedged item (see 2.2.2 above).

2.3   Internal hedges and other group accounting issues

One of the most pervasive impacts that IAS 39 can have on groups, especially those operating centralised treasury functions, is the need to reassess hedging strategies that involve intra-group transactions. To a layman this might come as something of a surprise because the standard does little more than reinforce the general principle that transactions between different entities within a group should be eliminated in the consolidated financial statements of that group. Nevertheless, a significant amount of the standard and related implementation guidance is devoted to this subject.

2.3.1   *Internal hedging instruments*

The starting point for this guidance is the principle of preparing consolidated financial statements in IFRS 10 – *Consolidated Financial Statements* – that requires 'intragroup assets and liabilities, equity, income, expenses and cash flows to be eliminated in full'. *[IFRS 10.B86, IAS 39.F.1.4].*

Although individual entities within a consolidated group (or divisions within a single legal entity) may enter into hedging transactions with other entities within the group (or divisions within the entity), such as internal derivative contracts to transfer risk exposures between different companies (or divisions), any such intragroup (or intra-entity) transactions are eliminated on consolidation. Therefore, such hedging transactions do not qualify for hedge accounting in the consolidated financial statements of the group, *[IAS 39.73, F.1.4]*, (or in the individual or separate financial statements of an entity for hedging transactions between divisions of the entity). Effectively, this is because they do not exist in an accounting sense.

As a consequence, IAS 39 makes it very clear that for hedge accounting purposes only instruments that involve a party external to the reporting entity (i.e. external to the group or individual entity that is being reported on) can be designated as hedging instruments. *[IAS 39.73].*

The implementation guidance explains that IAS 39 does not specify how an entity should *manage* its risk. Accordingly, where an internal contract is offset with an external party, the external contract may be regarded as the hedging instrument. In such cases, the hedging relationship (which is between the external transaction and the item that is the subject of the internal hedge) may qualify for hedge accounting. *[IAS 39.F.1.4].* The following example illustrates this.

Example 51.15:   Internal derivatives

The banking division of Bank A enters into an internal interest rate swap with A's trading division. The purpose is to hedge the interest rate risk exposure of a loan (or group of similar loans) in the banking division's loan portfolio. Under the swap, the banking division pays fixed interest payments to the trading division and receives variable interest rate payments in return.

Assuming a hedging instrument is not acquired from an external party, hedge accounting treatment for the hedging transaction undertaken by the banking and trading divisions is not allowed, because only derivatives that involve a party external to the entity can be designated as hedging instruments. Further, any gains or losses on intragroup or intra-entity transactions should be eliminated on consolidation.

Therefore, transactions between different divisions within A cannot qualify for hedge accounting treatment in Bank A's financial statements. Similarly, transactions between different entities within a group cannot qualify for hedge accounting treatment in A's consolidated financial statements.

However, if, in addition to the internal swap in the above example, the trading division entered into an interest rate swap or other contract with an external party that offset the exposure hedged in the internal swap, hedge accounting would be permitted. For the purposes of IAS 39, the hedged item is the loan (or group of similar loans) in the banking division and the hedging instrument is the external interest rate swap or other contract.

The trading division may aggregate several internal swaps or portions of them that are not offsetting each other (see 2.3.2 below) and enter into a single third party derivative contract that offsets the aggregate exposure. Such external hedging transactions may qualify for hedge accounting treatment provided that the hedged items in the banking division are identified and the other conditions for hedge accounting are met. *[IAS 39.F.1.4]*.

It follows that internal hedges may qualify for hedge accounting in the individual or separate financial statements of individual entities within the group, provided they are external to the individual entity that is being reported on. *[IAS 39.73]*.

The implementation guidance contains the following summary of the application of IAS 39 to internal hedging transactions:

- IAS 39 does not preclude an entity from using internal derivative contracts for risk management purposes and it does not preclude internal derivatives from being accumulated at the treasury level or some other central location so that risk can be managed on an entity-wide basis or at some higher level than the separate legal entity or division;

- Internal derivative contracts between two separate entities within a consolidated group can qualify for hedge accounting by those entities in their individual or separate financial statements, even though the internal contracts are not offset by derivative contracts with a party external to the consolidated group;

- Internal derivative contracts between two separate divisions within the same legal entity can qualify for hedge accounting in the individual or separate financial statements of that legal entity only if those contracts are offset by derivative contracts with a party external to the legal entity;

- Internal derivative contracts between separate divisions within the same legal entity and between separate entities within the consolidated group can qualify for hedge accounting in the consolidated financial statements only if the internal contracts are offset by derivative contracts with a party external to the consolidated group;

- If the internal derivative contracts are not offset by derivative contracts with external parties, the use of hedge accounting by group entities and divisions using internal contracts must be reversed on consolidation. *[IAS 39.F.1.4]*.

The premise on which the restriction on internal hedging instruments is based is not completely true. In fact, foreign currency intragroup balances may well give rise to gains and losses in profit or loss under IAS 21 that are not fully eliminated on consolidation. Such intra-group monetary items, as well as forecast intragroup transactions, may qualify as a hedged item in the consolidated financial statements if the other conditions for hedge accounting are met (see 2.3.4 below). However, this does not change the fact that internal transactions, even those that affect consolidated profit or loss, cannot be used as hedging instruments in consolidated financial statements. This is somewhat surprising as one might consider the same arguments that led to the exception permitting intragroup monetary items and forecast intragroup transactions to be hedged items to support allowing intragroup monetary items to be hedging instruments. However, during its deliberations of the hedge accounting model under IFRS 9 the IASB decided to retain this restriction. *[IFRS 9.BC6.142-147]*.

IFRS 8 – *Operating Segments* – requires disclosure of segment information that is reported to the chief operating decision maker even if this is on a non-GAAP basis (see Chapter 33 at 3.1). Consequently, for a hedge to qualify for hedge accounting in segment reporting, it is not always necessary for the hedging instrument to involve a party external to the segment.

2.3.2   Offsetting internal hedging instruments

As noted at 2.3.1 above, if an internal contract used in a hedging relationship is offset with an external party, the external contract may be regarded as a hedging instrument and the hedge may qualify for hedge accounting. *[IAS 39.F.1.4]*. The implementation guidance elaborates on this further in the context of both interest rate and foreign currency risk management, particularly in the situation where the exposure from internal derivatives are offset before being laid off with a third party.

2.3.2.A   Interest rate risk

Sometimes, central treasury functions enter into internal derivative contracts with subsidiaries and, perhaps, divisions within the consolidated group to manage interest rate risk on a centralised basis. If, before laying off the risk, the internal contracts are first netted against each other and only the net exposure is offset in the marketplace with external derivative contracts, the internal contracts cannot qualify for hedge accounting in the consolidated financial statements. *[IAS 39.F.1.5]*.

An internal contract designated at the subsidiary level, or by a division, as a hedge results in the recognition of changes in the fair value of the item being hedged in profit or loss (for a fair value hedge – see 4.1.1 below) or in the recognition of the changes in the fair value of the internal derivative in other comprehensive income (for a cash flow hedge – see 4.2.1 below). On consolidation, there is no basis for changing the measurement attribute of the item being hedged in a fair value hedge unless the exposure is offset with an external derivative. Similarly, on consolidation, there is no basis for including the gain or loss on the internal derivative in other comprehensive income for one entity and recognising it in profit or loss by the other entity unless it is offset with an external derivative. *[IAS 39.F.1.5]*.

Where two or more internal derivatives used to manage interest rate risk on assets or liabilities at the subsidiary or division level are offset at the treasury level, the effect of designating the internal derivatives as hedging instruments is that the hedged non-derivative exposures at the subsidiary or division levels would be used to offset each other on consolidation. Accordingly, since IAS 39 does not permit designating non-derivatives as hedging instruments (except for foreign currency exposures) – see 2.1.2 above, the results of hedge accounting from the use of internal derivatives at the subsidiary or division level that are not laid off with external parties must be reversed on consolidation. *[IAS 39.F.1.5]*.

It should be noted, however, that if the hedges were perfectly effective at the subsidiary level, there will be no effect on profit or loss and equity of reversing the effect of hedge accounting on consolidation for internal derivatives that offset each other at the consolidation level if they are used in the same type of hedging relationship at the subsidiary or division level and, in the case of cash flow hedges, where the hedged items affect profit or loss in the same period. Just as the internal derivatives offset at the treasury level, their use as fair value hedges by two separate entities or divisions within the consolidated group will also result in the offset of the fair value amounts recognised in profit or loss. Similarly, their use as cash flow hedges by two separate entities or divisions within the consolidated group will also result in the fair value amounts being offset against each other in other comprehensive income. *[IAS 39.F.1.5]*.

However, there may be an effect on individual line items in both the consolidated income statement (or statement of comprehensive income) and the consolidated statement of financial position, for example when internal derivatives that hedge assets (or liabilities) in a fair value hedge are offset by internal derivatives that are used as a fair value hedge of other assets (or liabilities) that are recognised in a different statement of financial position or income statement (or statement of comprehensive income) line item. In addition, to the extent that one of the internal contracts is used as a cash flow hedge and the other is used in a fair value hedge, the effect on profit or loss and equity would not offset since the gain (or loss) on the internal derivative used as a fair value hedge would be recognised in profit or loss and the corresponding loss (or gain) on the internal derivative used as a cash flow hedge would be recognised in other comprehensive income. *[IAS 39.F.1.5]*. However, the reversal of the fair value hedge adjustment would also be recognised in profit or loss when reversing hedge accounting on consolidation for internal derivatives.

Notwithstanding this, under the principles set out at 2.2.3 above, it may be possible to designate the external derivative as a hedge of *some* of the underlying exposures as illustrated in the following example.

Example 51.16: Single external derivative offsets internal contracts on a net basis

Company A uses what it describes as internal derivative contracts to document the transfer of responsibility for interest rate risk exposures from individual divisions to a central treasury function. The central treasury function aggregates the internal derivative contracts and enters into a single external derivative contract that offsets the internal derivative contracts on a net basis.

On one particular day the central treasury function enters into three internal receive-fixed, pay-variable interest rate swaps that lay off the exposure to variable interest cash flows on variable rate liabilities in other divisions and one internal receive-variable, pay-fixed interest rate swap that lays off the exposure to variable interest cash flows on variable rate assets in another division. It enters into an interest rate swap with an external counterparty that exactly offsets the four internal swaps.

A hedge of an overall net position does not qualify for hedge accounting. However, designating a part of the underlying items as the hedged position on a gross basis is permitted. *[IAS 39.84, AG101]*. Therefore, even though the purpose of entering into the external derivative was to offset internal derivative contracts on a net basis, hedge accounting is permitted if the hedging relationship is defined and documented as a hedge of a part of the underlying cash inflows or cash outflows on a gross basis and assuming that the hedge accounting criteria are met. *[IAS 39.F.2.15]*.

2.3.2.B   Foreign exchange risk

Although much of the discussion at 2.3.2.A above applies equally to hedges of foreign currency risk, there is one important distinction between the two situations. IAS 39 allows non-derivative financial instruments to be used as the hedging instrument in the hedge of foreign currency risk. Therefore, in this case, internal derivatives may be used as a basis for *identifying* non-derivative external transactions that could qualify as hedging instruments or hedged items, provided that the internal derivatives represent the transfer of foreign currency risk on underlying non-derivative financial assets or liabilities (see Case 3 in Example 51.16 below). However, for consolidated financial statements, it is necessary to *designate* the hedging relationship so that it involves only external transactions. *[IAS 39.F.1.6]*.

Forecast transactions and unrecognised firm commitments cannot qualify as hedging instruments under IAS 39. Accordingly, to the extent that two or more offsetting internal derivatives represent the transfer of foreign currency risk on such items, hedge accounting cannot be applied. As a result, if any cumulative net gain or loss on an internal derivative has been included in the initial carrying amount of an asset or liability (a 'basis adjustment') or recognised in other comprehensive income (see 4.2.1 and 4.2.2 below), it would have to be reversed on consolidation if it cannot be demonstrated that the offsetting internal derivative represented the transfer of a foreign currency risk on a financial asset or liability to an external hedging instrument. *[IAS 39.F.1.6]*.

The following example illustrates this principle – it also illustrates the mechanics of accounting for fair value hedges and cash flow hedges, which are discussed in more detail at 4.1 and 4.2 below.

Example 51.17:   Using internal derivatives to hedge foreign currency risk [IAS 39.F.1.7]

In each of the following cases, 'FC' represents a foreign currency, 'LC' represents the local currency (which is the entity's functional currency) and 'TC' the group's treasury centre.

Case 1: Offset of fair value hedges

Subsidiary A has trade receivables of FC100, due in 60 days, which it hedges using a forward contract with TC. Subsidiary B has payables of FC50, also due in 60 days, which it hedges using a forward contact with TC.

TC nets the two internal derivatives and enters into a net external forward contract to pay FC50 and receive LC in 60 days.

At the end of month 1, FC weakens against LC. A incurs a foreign exchange loss of LC10 on its receivables, offset by a gain of LC10 on its forward contract with TC. B makes a foreign exchange gain of LC5 on its payables, offset by a loss of LC5 on its forward contract with TC. TC makes a loss of LC10 on its internal forward contract with A, a gain of LC5 on its internal forward contract with B and a gain of LC5 on its external forward contract.

Accordingly, the following entries are made in the individual or separate financial statements of A, B and TC at the end of month 1 (assuming that forward foreign exchange and spot exchange rates are exactly the same, which is unlikely in reality). Entries reflecting intra-group transactions or events are shown in italics.

A's entries

	LC	LC
Foreign exchange loss	10	
Receivables		10
Internal contract (TC)	*10*	
Internal gain (TC)		*10*

B's entries

	LC	LC
Payables	5	
Foreign exchange gain		5
Internal loss (TC)	*5*	
Internal contract (TC)		*5*

TC's entries

	LC	LC
Internal loss (A)	*10*	
Internal contract (A)		*10*
Internal contract (B)	*5*	
Internal gain (B)		*5*
External forward contract	5	
Foreign exchange gain		5

Both A and B could apply hedge accounting in their individual financial statements provided all necessary conditions were met. However, because gains and losses on the internal derivatives and the offsetting losses and gains on the hedged receivables and payables are recognised immediately in profit or loss without hedge accounting, hedge accounting is unnecessary (see 3.3 for further information on hedges of foreign currency denominated monetary items).

In the consolidated financial statements, the internal derivative transactions are eliminated. In economic terms, B's payable hedges FC50 of A's receivables. The external forward in TC hedges the remaining FC50 of A's receivable. In the consolidated financial statements, hedge accounting is again unnecessary because monetary items are measured at spot foreign exchange rates under IAS 21 irrespective of whether hedge accounting is applied.

The net balances, before and after elimination of the accounting entries relating to the internal derivatives, are the same, as set out below. Accordingly, there is no need to make any further accounting entries to meet the requirements of IAS 39.

	LC	LC
Receivables	–	10
Payables	5	–
External forward contract	5	–
Gains and losses	–	–
Internal contracts	–	–

Case 2: Offset of cash flow hedges

To extend the example, A also has highly probable future revenues of FC200 on which it expects to receive cash in 90 days. B has highly probable future expenses of FC500 (advertising cost), also to be paid for in 90 days. A and B enter into separate forward contracts with TC to hedge these exposures and TC enters into an external forward contract to receive FC300 in 90 days.

As before, FC weakens at the end of month 1. A incurs a 'loss' of LC20 on its anticipated revenues because the LC value of these revenues decreases and this is offset by a gain of LC20 on its forward contract with TC. Similarly, B incurs a 'gain' of LC50 on its anticipated advertising cost because the LC value of the expense decreases and this is offset by a loss of LC50 on its transaction with TC.

TC incurs a gain of LC50 on its internal transaction with B, a loss of LC20 on its internal transaction with A and a loss of LC30 on its external forward contract.

Both A and B complete the necessary documentation, the hedges are effective and both A and B qualify for hedge accounting in their individual financial statements. A recognises the gain of LC20 on its internal derivative transaction in other comprehensive income and B does the same with its loss of LC50. TC does not claim hedge accounting, but measures both its internal and external derivative positions at fair value, which net to zero.

Accordingly, the following entries are made in the individual or separate financial statements of A, B and TC at the end of month 1. Entries reflecting intra-group transactions or events are shown in italics.

A's entries

	LC	LC
Internal contract (TC)	*20*	
Other comprehensive income		*20*

B's entries

	LC	LC
Other comprehensive income	*50*	
Internal contract (TC)		*50*

TC's entries

	LC	LC
Internal loss (A)	*20*	
Internal contract (A)		*20*
Internal contract (B)	*50*	
Internal gain (B)		*50*
Foreign exchange loss	30	
External forward contract		30

IAS 39 requires that, in the consolidated financial statements, the accounting effects of the internal derivative transactions must be eliminated.

If there were no hedge designation for the consolidated financial statements, the gains and losses recognised in other comprehensive income and profit or loss on the internal derivatives would be reversed. Consequently, a loss of LC30 would be recognised in profit or loss in respect of the external forward contract held by TC.

However, for the consolidated financial statements, TC's external forward contract on FC300 *is* designated, at the beginning of month 1, as a hedging instrument of the first FC300 of B's highly probable future expenses. Therefore, LC30 of the gain recognised in other comprehensive income by B may remain in other comprehensive income on consolidation, because it involves an external derivative. Accordingly, the net balances, before and after elimination of the accounting entries relating to the internal derivatives, are as set out below and there is no need to make any further accounting entries in order for the requirements of IAS 39 to be met.

	LC	LC
External forward contract	–	30
Other comprehensive income	30	–
Gains and losses	–	–
Internal contracts	–	–

Case 3: Offset of fair value and cash flow hedges

The example is extended further and it is assumed that the exposures and the internal derivative transactions are the same as in Cases 1 and 2. In other words, Subsidiary A has trade receivables of FC100, due in 60 days, and highly probable future revenues of FC200 on which it expects to receive cash in 90 days. Subsidiary B has payables of FC50, due in 60 days, and highly probable future expenses of FC500 to be paid for in 90 days. Each of these exposures is hedged using forward contacts with TC. However, in this case, instead of entering into two external derivatives to hedge separately the fair value and cash flow exposures, TC enters into a single net external derivative to receive FC250 in exchange for LC in 90 days.

Consequently, TC has four internal derivatives, two maturing in 60 days and two maturing in 90 days. These are offset by a net external derivative maturing in 90 days. The interest rate differential between FC and LC is minimal, and therefore the ineffectiveness resulting from the mismatch in maturities is expected to have a minimal effect on profit or loss in TC.

As in Cases 1 and 2, A and B apply hedge accounting for their cash flow hedges and TC measures its derivatives at fair value. A recognises a gain of LC20 on its internal derivative transaction in other comprehensive income and B does the same with its loss of LC50.

Accordingly, the following entries are made in the individual or separate financial statements of A, B and TC at the end of month 1. Entries reflecting intra-group transactions or events are shown in italics.

A's entries

	LC	LC
Foreign exchange loss	10	
Receivables		10
Internal contract (TC)	*10*	
Internal gain (TC)		*10*
Internal contract (TC)	*20*	
Other comprehensive income		*20*

B's entries

	LC	LC
Payables	5	
Foreign exchange gain		5
Internal loss (TC)	*5*	
Internal contract (TC)		*5*
Other comprehensive income	*50*	
Internal contract (TC)		*50*

TC's entries

	LC	LC
Internal loss (A)	*10*	
Internal contract (A)		*10*
Internal loss (A)	*20*	
Internal contract (A)		*20*
Internal contract (B)	*5*	
Internal gain (B)		*5*
Internal contract (B)	*50*	
Internal gain (B)		*50*
Foreign exchange loss	25	
External forward contract		25

The gains and losses recognised on the internal contracts in A and B can be summarised as follows:

	A LC	B LC	Total LC
Profit or loss (fair value hedges)	10	(5)	5
Other comprehensive income (cash flow hedges)	20	(50)	(30)
Total	30	(55)	(25)

In the consolidated financial statements, IAS 39 requires the accounting effects of the internal derivative transactions to be eliminated.

If there were no hedge designation for the consolidated financial statements, the gains and losses recognised in other comprehensive income and profit or loss on the internal derivatives would be reversed. Consequently, a loss of LC30 would be recognised in profit or loss in respect of the external receivable and payable held by A (loss LC10) and B (gain LC5) respectively and the external forward contract held by TC (loss LC25).

However, for the consolidated financial statements, the following designations are made at the beginning of month 1:

- the payable of FC50 in B is designated as a hedge of the first FC50 of the highly probable future revenues in A.

  Therefore, at the end of month 1, the following entries are made in the consolidated financial statements: Dr Payable LC5; Cr Other comprehensive income LC5;

- the receivable of FC100 in A is designated as a hedge of the first FC100 of the highly probable future expenses in B.

  Therefore, at the end of month 1, the following entries are made in the consolidated financial statements: Dr Other comprehensive income LC10, Cr Receivable LC10; and

- the external forward contract on FC250 in TC is designated as a hedge of the next FC250 of highly probable future expenses in B.

  Therefore, at the end of month 1, the following entries are made in the consolidated financial statements: Dr Other comprehensive income LC25; Cr External forward contract LC25.

Combining these entries produces the total net balances as follows:

	LC	LC
Receivables	–	10
Payables	5	–
External forward contract	–	25
Other comprehensive income	30	–
Gains and losses	–	–
Internal contracts	–	–

Case 4: Offset of fair value and cash flow hedges with adjustment to carrying amount of inventory

Similar transactions to those in Case 3 are assumed except that the anticipated cash outflow of FC500 in B relates to the purchase of inventory that is delivered after 60 days. It is also assumed that the entity has a policy of basis-adjusting hedged forecast non-financial items (see 4.2.2 below).

To recap, Subsidiary A has trade receivables of FC100, due in 60 days, and highly probable future revenues of FC200 on which it expects to receive cash in 90 days. Subsidiary B has payables of FC50, due in 60 days, and a highly probable future purchase of inventory for FC500, to be delivered in 60 days and paid for in 90 days. Each of these exposures is hedged using forward contracts with TC, and TC enters into a single net external derivative to receive FC250 in exchange for LC in 90 days.

At the end of month 2, there are no further changes in exchange rates or fair values. At that date, the inventory is delivered and the loss of LC50 on B's internal derivative, recognised in other comprehensive income in month 1, is removed from equity and adjusts the carrying amount of inventory in B. The gain of LC20 on A's internal derivative is recognised in other comprehensive income as before.

In the consolidated financial statements, there is now a mismatch compared with the result that would have been achieved by unwinding and redesignating the hedges. The external derivative (FC250) and the proportion of receivable (FC50) in A offset FC300 of the anticipated inventory purchase in B. Offset will occur between the FC50 payable in B and a FC50 proportion of the receivable in A. There is a natural hedge between the remaining FC200 of anticipated cash outflow in B (inventory) and the anticipated cash inflow of FC200 in A (revenue). This last relationship does not qualify for hedge accounting under IAS 39 as no valid hedging instrument exists, hence this time there is only a partial offset between gains and losses on the internal derivatives that hedge these amounts.

Accordingly, the following entries are made in the individual or separate financial statements of A, B and TC at the end of month 1. Entries reflecting intra-group transactions or events are shown in italics.

A's entries (all at the end of month 1)

	LC	LC
Foreign exchange loss	10	
Receivables		10
Internal contract (TC)	*10*	
Internal gain (TC)		*10*
Internal contract (TC)	*20*	
Other comprehensive income		*20*

B's entries (at the end of month 1)

	LC	LC
Payables	5	
Foreign exchange gain		5
Internal loss (TC)	*5*	
Internal contract (TC)		*5*
Other comprehensive income	50	
Internal contract (TC)		*50*

B's entries (at the end of month 2)

	LC	LC
Inventory	50	
Other comprehensive income		50

TC's entries (all at the end of month 1)

	LC	LC
Internal loss (A)	*10*	
Internal contract (A)		*10*
Internal loss (A)	*20*	
Internal contract (A)		*20*
Internal contract (B)	*5*	
Internal gain (B)		*5*
Internal contract (B)	*50*	
Internal gain (B)		*50*
Foreign exchange loss	25	
External forward contract		25

Chapter 51

The gains and losses recognised on the internal contracts in A and B can be summarised as follows:

	A LC	B LC	Total LC
Profit or loss (fair value hedges)	10	(5)	5
Other comprehensive income (cash flow hedges)	20	–	20
Basis adjustment (inventory)	–	(50)	(50)
Total	30	(55)	(25)

Combining these amounts with the external transactions (i.e. those not marked in italics above) produces the total net balances before elimination of the internal derivatives as follows:

	LC	LC
Receivables	–	10
Payables	5	–
External forward contract	–	25
Other comprehensive income	–	20
Basis adjustment (inventory)	50	–
Gains and losses	–	–
Internal contracts	–	–

For the consolidated financial statements, the following designations are made at the beginning of month 1:

- The payable of FC50 in B is designated as a hedge of the first FC50 of the highly probable future revenues in A.

  Therefore, at the end of month 1, the following entry is made in the consolidated financial statements: Dr Payables LC5; Cr Other comprehensive income LC5.

- The receivable of FC100 in A is designated as a hedge of the first FC100 of the highly probable future inventory purchase in B.

  Therefore, at the end of month 1, the following entries are made in the consolidated financial statements: Dr Other comprehensive income LC10; Cr Receivable LC10; and at the end of month 2, Dr Inventory LC10; Cr Other comprehensive income LC10.

- The external forward contract on FC250 in TC is designated as a hedge of the next FC250 of highly probable future inventory purchase in B.

  Therefore, at the end of month 1, the following entry is made in the consolidated financial statements: Dr Other comprehensive income LC25; Cr External forward contract LC25; and at the end of month 2, Dr Inventory LC25; Cr Other comprehensive income LC25.

This leaves FC150 of the future revenue in A and FC150 of future inventory purchase in B not designated in a hedge accounting relationship in the consolidated financial statements.

The total net balances after elimination of the accounting entries relating to the internal derivatives are as follows:

	LC	LC
Receivables	–	10
Payables	5	–
External forward contract	–	25
Other comprehensive income	–	5
Basis adjustment (inventory)	35	–
Gains and losses	–	–
Internal contracts	–	–

These total net balances are different from those that would be recognised if the internal derivatives were not eliminated, and it is these net balances that IAS 39 requires to be included in the consolidated financial statements. The accounting entries required to adjust the total net balances before elimination of the internal derivatives are as follows:

- to reclassify LC15 of the loss on B's internal derivative that is included in inventory to reflect that FC150 of the forecast purchase of inventory is not hedged by an external instrument (neither the external forward contract of FC250 in TC nor the external payable of FC100 in A); and

- to reclassify the gain of LC15 on A's internal derivative to reflect that the forecast revenues of FC150 to which it relates is not hedged by an external instrument.

The net effect of these two adjustments is as follows:

	LC	LC
Other comprehensive income	15	
Inventory		15

It is apparent that extending the principles set out in this relatively simple example to the more complex and higher volume situations that are likely to be encountered in practice is not going to be straightforward.

2.3.3   Offsetting external hedging instruments

The implementation guidance explains that where two offsetting derivatives are transacted at the same time, it is generally not permitted to designate one of them as a hedging instrument in a hedge when the derivatives are viewed as one unit. The two derivatives would not be accounted for as one unit if:

- the second derivative was not entered into in contemplation of the first; or

- there is a 'substantive business purpose' for structuring the transactions separately.

This issue is also discussed in Chapter 43 at 8. It is emphasised that judgement should be applied in determining what is a substantive business purpose. For example, a centralised treasury entity may enter into third party derivative contracts on behalf of other subsidiaries to hedge their interest rate exposures and, to track those exposures within the group, enter into internal derivative transactions with those subsidiaries. It may also enter into a derivative contract with the same counterparty during the same business day with substantially the same terms as a contract entered into as a hedging instrument on behalf of another subsidiary as part of its trading operations, or because it wishes to rebalance its overall portfolio risk. In this case, there is a valid business purpose for entering into each contract. However, a desire to achieve fair value accounting for the hedged item is deemed not to be a substantive business purpose. *[IAS 39.F.1.14]*.

The following example, based on the implementation guidance, explores this issue a little further.

Example 51.18:   External derivative contracts settled net

A company uses internal derivative contracts to transfer interest rate risk exposures from individual divisions to a central treasury function. For each internal derivative contract, the central treasury function enters into a derivative contract with a single external counterparty that offsets the internal derivative contract. For example, if the central treasury function has entered into a receive-5% fixed, pay-LIBOR interest rate swap with another division that has entered into the internal contract with central treasury to hedge the exposure to variability in interest cash flows on a pay-LIBOR borrowing, central treasury would enter into a pay-5% fixed, receive-LIBOR interest rate swap on the same principal terms with the external counterparty.

Although each external derivative contract is formally documented as a separate contract, only the net of the payments on all of the external derivative contracts is settled since there is a netting agreement with the external counterparty.

Even though the external derivatives are settled on a net basis, the individual external derivative contracts, such as the pay-5% fixed, receive-LIBOR interest rate swap above, can generally be designated as hedging instruments of underlying gross exposures, such as the exposure to changes in variable interest payments on the pay-LIBOR borrowing above, assuming that all the other hedge accounting criteria are met.

External derivative contracts that are legally separate contracts and serve a valid business purpose, such as laying off risk exposures on a gross basis, qualify as hedging instruments even if those external contracts are settled on a net basis with the same external counterparty, provided the hedge accounting criteria in IAS 39 are met. *[IAS 39.F.2.16]*.

In the context of interest rate instruments, the facts in this example appear a little unlikely. This is because most master netting agreements have a practical effect only in the event of default by, or insolvency of, one of the counterparties – otherwise payments tend to be made gross. However, the above situation has become more relevant as many jurisdictions recently introduced (or plan to introduce) requirements to settle over-the-counter derivatives through a central clearing house (discussed at 4.2.3.A below).

For foreign currency instruments, a number of financial institutions provide services that are broadly analogous to the one described in Example 51.18 above. Under these arrangements a treasury function will transact, say, legally separate forward exchange contracts with the financial institution to offset each internal derivative it has entered into with a subsidiary or division. These contracts will be administered under a centralised facility with settlements being made on a net basis. Further, the financial institution will often price these contracts to reflect the reduced credit risk and administrative burden associated with the arrangements so that the cost of transacting individual contracts is significantly reduced.

Some may express surprise that the guidance explains that arrangements such as those illustrated in Example 51.18 above may qualify for hedge accounting. In substance, they are little different from the entity offsetting its internal contracts before entering into an offsetting external transaction, which as explained at 2.3.2 above, would not permit hedge accounting to be applied for each item hedged using an internal contract. However, this is nothing compared to what follows. The implementation guidance considers an extension to the arrangement set out above:

> 'Treasury observes that by entering into the external offsetting contracts and including them in the centralised portfolio, it is no longer able to evaluate the exposures on a net basis. Treasury wishes to manage the portfolio of offsetting external derivatives separately from other exposures of the entity. Therefore, it enters into an additional, single derivative to offset the risk of the portfolio.' *[IAS 39.F.2.16]*.

The guidance explains that the purpose of structuring the external derivatives like this is consistent with the entity's risk management policies and strategies and, generally, hedge accounting may still be used. Even if this final external derivative is effected with the same counterparty under the same netting arrangement, and notwithstanding the fact that all exposures with that counterparty will, as a result, net to zero, it is implied that this constitutes a substantive business purpose as described at the start of this sub-section. *[IAS 39.F.2.16].*

In essence, the guidance appears to suggest that the use of internal derivatives for hedge accounting is allowed, provided that an agreement is reached with a third party to give the appearance of laying off the exposure even though the risk is immediately taken back again. This seems a long way from what the standard requires and, in fact, begs the question of why an entity should even go to the trouble of creating such an artificial external agreement that appears to lack any commercial substance. We have serious reservations over this part of the guidance, particularly we question whether it really would be possible to demonstrate the existence of a valid business purpose for such an arrangement.

2.3.4 *Internal hedged items*

Only assets, liabilities, firm commitments or highly probable forecast transactions that involve a party external to the entity can be designated as hedged items. It follows that hedge accounting can be applied to transactions between entities in the same group only in the individual or separate financial statements of those entities and not in the consolidated financial statements of the group. However, there are two exceptions – intragroup monetary items and forecast intragroup transactions, discussed at 2.3.4.A and 2.3.4.B below. *[IAS 39.80].*

2.3.4.A *Intragroup monetary items*

IAS 39 allows the foreign currency risk of an intra-group monetary item (e.g. a payable or receivable between two subsidiaries) to qualify as a hedged item in the consolidated financial statements if it results in an exposure to foreign exchange rate gains or losses under IAS 21 that are not fully eliminated on consolidation. Foreign exchange gains and losses on such items are not fully eliminated on consolidation when they are transacted between two group entities that have different functional currencies (see Chapter 15 at 6.3), *[IAS 39.80]*, as illustrated in the following example.

Example 51.19: Intragroup monetary items that will affect consolidated profit or loss

Company A has two subsidiaries, Company B and Company C. A and B have the euro as their functional currencies, while C has the US dollar as its functional currency. On 31 March, C purchases goods from B for US$110, payable on 30 June.

In this case, the intragroup monetary item of US$110 may be designated as a hedged item in a hedge of foreign currency risk both by B in its separate financial statements and by A in its consolidated financial statements.

While B's foreign currency receivable is eliminated against C's foreign currency payable on consolidation, the exchange differences that arise for B cannot be eliminated since C has no corresponding exchange differences.

Thus, the intragroup monetary item results in an exposure to variability in the foreign currency amount of the intra-group monetary item that will affect profit or loss in the consolidated financial statements. Therefore, the intragroup monetary item may be designated as a hedged item in a foreign currency hedge.[8]

2.3.4.B   Forecast intragroup transactions

IAS 39 also contains a second exception allowing the foreign currency risk of a highly probable forecast intragroup transaction to qualify as a hedged item in a cash flow hedge in consolidated financial statements in certain circumstances. The transaction must be denominated in a currency other than the functional currency of the entity entering into that transaction (e.g. parent, subsidiary, associate, joint venture or branch) and the foreign currency risk must affect consolidated profit or loss (otherwise it cannot qualify as a hedged item). *[IAS 39.80, AG99A]*.

Normally, royalty payments, interest payments and management charges between members of the same group will not affect consolidated profit or loss unless there is a related external transaction. However, by way of example, a forecast sale or purchase of inventory between members of the same group will affect profit or loss if there is an onward sale of the inventory to a party external to the group. Similarly, a forecast intragroup sale of plant and equipment from the group entity that manufactured it to a group entity that will use it in its operations may affect consolidated profit or loss. This could occur, for example, because the plant and equipment will be depreciated by the purchasing entity and the amount initially recognised for the plant and equipment may change if the forecast intragroup transaction is denominated in a currency other than the functional currency of the purchasing entity. *[IAS 39.AG99A]*.

Although the standard refers exclusively to forecast intragroup transactions, we believe there is no reason why these provisions should not also apply to intragroup firm commitments.

2.3.5   Hedged item and hedging instrument held by different group entities

The implementation guidance explains that, in a group, it is not necessary for the hedging instrument to be held by the same entity as the one that has the exposure being hedged in order to qualify for hedge accounting in the consolidated financial statements. *[IAS 39.F.2.14]*. This is illustrated in the following example.

Example 51.20:   Subsidiary's foreign exchange exposure hedged by parent

Company S is based in Switzerland and prepares consolidated financial statements in Swiss francs. It has an Australian subsidiary, Company A, whose functional currency is the Australian dollar and is included in the consolidated financial statements of S. A has forecast purchases in Japanese yen that are highly probable and S enters into a forward contract to hedge the change in yen relative to the Australian dollar.

Because A did not hedge the foreign currency exchange risk associated with the forecast purchases in yen, the effects of exchange rate changes between the Australian dollar and the yen will affect A's profit or loss and, therefore, would also affect consolidated profit or loss. Therefore that hedge may qualify for hedge accounting in S's consolidated financial statements provided the other hedge accounting criteria in IAS 39 are met. *[IAS 39.F.2.14]*.

3   TYPES OF HEDGING RELATIONSHIPS

There are three types of hedging relationship defined in IAS 39: *[IAS 39.86]*

- *fair value hedge:* a hedge of the exposure to changes in the fair value of a recognised asset or liability or an unrecognised firm commitment, or an identified portion of such an asset, liability or firm commitment, that is attributable to a particular risk and could affect profit or loss;

- *cash flow hedge:* a hedge of the exposure to variability in cash flows that:

    (i)   is attributable to a particular risk associated with a recognised asset or liability (such as all or some future interest payments on variable rate debt) or a highly probable forecast transaction; and

    (ii)   could affect profit or loss; and

- *hedge of a net investment in a foreign operation:* as defined in IAS 21 (see Chapter 15 at 2.3).

These definitions are considered further in the remainder of this section.

3.1   Fair value hedges

An example of a fair value hedge is a hedge of the exposure to changes in the fair value of a fixed rate debt instrument (not measured at fair value through profit or loss) as a result of changes in interest rates – if interest rates increase, the fair value of the debt decreases and *vice versa*. Such a hedge could be entered into either by the issuer or by the holder, *[IAS 39.AG102]*, (provided, in the case of the holder, it was not classified as held-to-maturity – see 2.2.6 above).

On the face of it, if a fixed rate loan that is classified within loans and receivables is held until it matures (as is the case for many such loans), changes in the fair value of the loan would not affect profit or loss. However, the implementation guidance explains that such assets may be hedged items in a fair value hedge because the loan *could* be sold, in which case fair value changes *would* affect profit or loss. *[IAS 39.F.2.13]*. The same would be true of a fixed rate borrowing for which settlement before maturity is very unlikely.

A variable rate debt may be the hedged item in a fair value hedge in certain circumstances. For example, the fair value of such an instrument will change if the issuer's credit risk changes. Accordingly variable rate debt could be designated in a hedge of all changes in its fair value. There may also be changes in its fair value relating to movements in the market rate in the periods between which the variable rate is reset. For example, if a debt instrument provides for annual interest payments reset to the market rate each year, a portion of the debt instrument has an exposure to changes in fair value during the year. *[IAS 39.F.3.5]*.

The exposure to changes in the price of inventories that are carried at the lower of cost and net realisable value may also be the subject of a fair value hedge because their fair value will affect profit or loss when they are sold or written down. For example, a copper forward may be used as the hedging instrument in a hedge of the copper price associated with copper inventory. *[IAS 39.F.3.6].*

An equity method investment cannot be a hedged item in a fair value hedge because the equity method recognises in profit or loss the investor's share of the associate's profit or loss, rather than changes in the investment's fair value. For a similar reason, an investment in a consolidated subsidiary cannot be a hedged item in a fair value hedge because consolidation recognises in profit or loss the subsidiary's profit or loss, rather than changes in the investment's fair value. *[IAS 39.AG99].*

The ongoing accounting for fair value hedges is described at 4.1 below.

3.1.1   Hedges of firm commitments

A hedge of a firm commitment (e.g. a hedge of the change in fuel price relating to an unrecognised contractual commitment by an electricity utility to purchase fuel at a fixed price) is considered a hedge of an exposure to a change in fair value. Accordingly, such a hedge is a fair value hedge. However, a hedge of the foreign currency risk of a firm commitment may be accounted for as a fair value hedge or a cash flow hedge (this is discussed further at 3.2.2 below). *[IAS 39.87, AG104].*

3.1.2   Hedges of foreign currency monetary items

A foreign currency monetary asset or liability that is hedged using a forward exchange contract may be treated as a fair value hedge because its fair value will change as foreign exchange rates change. Alternatively, it may be treated as a cash flow hedge because changes in exchange rates will affect the amount of cash required to settle the item (as measured by reference to the entity's functional currency) (see 4.2.2 below). *[IAS 39.F3.3-F3.4].*

3.2   Cash flow hedges

An example of a cash flow hedge is the use of an interest rate swap to change floating rate debt to fixed rate debt, i.e. a hedge of a future transaction where the future cash flows being hedged are the future interest payments. *[IAS 39.AG103].*

As noted at 3.1 above, a hedge of the exposure to changes in the fair value of a fixed rate debt instrument as a result of changes in interest rates could be treated as a fair value hedge. This could not be a cash flow hedge because changes in interest rates will not affect the cash flows on the hedged item, only its fair value. *[IAS 39.F.3.1].*

It was also noted at 3.1 above that a copper forward, say, may be used in a fair value hedge of copper inventory. Alternatively, the same hedging instrument may qualify as a cash flow hedge of the future sale of the inventory. *[IAS 39.F.3.6].*

The following example from the implementation guidance explains how a company might lock in current interest rates by way of a cash flow hedge of the anticipated issuance of fixed rate debt.

Example 51.21: Hedge of anticipated issuance of fixed rate debt

Company R periodically issues new bonds to refinance maturing bonds, provide working capital, and for various other purposes. When R decides it will be issuing bonds, it sometimes hedges the risk of changes in long-term interest rates to the date the bonds are issued. If long-term interest rates go up (down), the bond will be issued either at a higher (lower) rate, with a higher (smaller) discount or with a smaller (higher) premium than was originally expected. The higher (lower) rate being paid or decrease (increase) in proceeds is normally offset by the gain (loss) on the hedge.

In August 2016 R decides it will issue £2m seven-year bonds in January 2017. Historical correlation studies suggest that a seven-year treasury bond adequately correlates to the bonds R expects to issue, assuming a hedge ratio of 0.93 future contracts to one debt unit. Therefore, it hedges the anticipated issuance of the bonds by selling ('shorting') £1.86m worth of futures on seven-year treasury bonds.

From August 2016 to January 2017 interest rates increase and the short futures positions are closed on the date the bonds are issued. This results in a £120,000 gain, which offsets the increased interest payments on the bonds and, therefore, will affect profit or loss over the life of the bonds. The hedge may qualify as a cash flow hedge of the interest rate risk on the forecast debt issuance (assuming all other conditions for hedge accounting are met). *[IAS 39.F.2.2].*

Similarly, the forecast reinvestment of interest cash flows from a fixed rate asset can be the subject of a cash flow hedge using, say, a forward rate agreement to lock in the interest rate that will be received on that reinvestment. *[IAS 39.F.3.2].*

The ongoing accounting for cash flow hedges is described at 4.2 below.

3.2.1 All-in-one hedges

There are situations where an instrument that is accounted for as a derivative under IAS 39 is expected to be settled gross by delivery of the underlying asset in exchange for the payment of a fixed price. The implementation guidance states that such an instrument can be designated as the hedging instrument in a cash flow hedge of the variability of the consideration to be paid or received in the future transaction that will occur on gross settlement of the derivative contract itself. It is explained that this is acceptable because there *would* be an exposure to variability in the purchase or sale price without the derivative. It is important to note that, in order to qualify for a hedge of a highly probable forecast transaction, the hedging entity must have the intention (and the ability) to gross settle the derivative. For example, consider an entity that enters into a fixed price contract to sell a commodity and that contract is accounted for as a derivative under IAS 39 (see Chapter 42 at 4). This might be because the entity has a practice of settling such contracts net in cash or of taking delivery of the underlying and selling it within a short period after delivery for the purpose of generating a profit from short-term fluctuations in price or dealer's margin. In this case, the fixed price contract may be designated as a cash flow hedge of the variability of the consideration to be received on the sale of the asset (a future transaction) even though the fixed price contract is the contract under which the asset will be sold. *[IAS 39.F.2.5].*

Similarly, an entity may enter into a forward contract to purchase a debt instrument (which will not be classified at fair value through profit or loss) that will be settled by delivery, but the forward contract is a derivative. This will be the case if its term exceeds the regular way delivery period in the marketplace (see Chapter 47 at 2.2). In this case the forward may be designated as a cash flow hedge of the variability of the consideration to be paid to acquire the debt instrument (a future transaction), even though the derivative is the contract under which the debt instrument will be acquired. *[IAS 39.F.2.5]*. If the debt instrument was to be classified at fair value through profit or loss, the all-in-one hedge strategy could not be applied (see 2.2.7 above).

It might come as a surprise to many entities that such contracts are, in fact, derivatives as defined. *[IAS 39.9]*. Therefore, the use of an 'all-in-one hedge' strategy for such instruments could prove useful in keeping fair value gains and losses, on what might be considered little more than purchase or sale orders, from being recognised immediately in profit or loss.

However, it seems best to accept the all-in-one hedge for what it is, i.e. a pragmatic concession, rather than trying to determine how it is derived from the principles of the standard. For example, the hedged item in each of the above two paragraphs, i.e. the spot price payment on the future purchase or sale of the asset, appears to be a cash flow that will never happen because the asset will be purchased or sold for the fixed price specified in the contract. Further, the hedged item (i.e. the contracted sale or purchase) also appears to be accounted for as a derivative, which is generally prohibited (see 2.2.7 above).

3.2.2   Hedges of firm commitments

A hedge of the foreign currency risk of a firm commitment may be accounted for as a cash flow hedge or a fair value hedge (see 3.1.1 above). *[IAS 39.87, AG104]*. This is because foreign currency risk affects both the cash flows and the fair value of the hedged item. Accordingly, a foreign currency cash flow hedge of a forecast transaction need not be redesignated as a fair value hedge when the forecast transaction becomes a firm commitment. *[IAS 39.BC154]*.

3.2.3   Hedges of foreign currency monetary items

A foreign currency monetary asset or liability that is hedged using a forward exchange contract may be treated as a fair value hedge because its fair value will change as foreign exchange rates change. Alternatively, it may be treated as a cash flow hedge because changes in exchange rates will affect the amount of cash required to settle the item (as measured by reference to the entity's functional currency) (see 4.2.2 below). *[IAS 39.F3.3-F3.4]*.

3.3   Hedges of net investments in foreign operations

Many reporting entities have investments in foreign operations which may be subsidiaries, associates, joint ventures or branches. As set out in Chapter 15 at 4, IAS 21 requires an entity to determine the functional currency of each of its foreign operations as the currency of the primary economic environment of that operation. When translating the results and financial position of its foreign operation into a presentation currency, it should recognise foreign exchange differences in other comprehensive income until disposal of the foreign operation. *[IFRIC 16.1]*.

From the perspective of an investor (e.g. a parent) it is clear that an investment in a foreign operation is likely to give rise to a degree of foreign currency exchange rate risk and an entity with many foreign operations may be exposed to a number of foreign currency risks. *[IFRIC 16.4]*. Whilst equity method investments and investments in consolidated subsidiaries cannot be hedged items in a fair value hedge because changes in the investments' fair value are not recognised in profit or loss, they may be designated in a net investment hedge relationship. A hedge of a net investment in a foreign operation is said to be different because it is a hedge of the foreign currency exposure, not a fair value hedge of the change in the value of the investment. *[IAS 39.AG99]*.

Conceptually, net investment hedging is somewhat unsatisfactory, as it mixes foreign currency translation risk (largely an accounting exposure) with transactional risk (much more an economic exposure). IFRIC 16 – *Hedges of a Net Investment in a Foreign Operation* – addresses the question of what does and does not constitute a valid hedging relationship, a topic on which IAS 39 provided very little guidance.

IFRIC 16 applies to any entity that hedges the foreign currency risk arising from its net investments in foreign operations and wishes to qualify for hedge accounting in accordance with IAS 39. *[IFRIC 16.7]*. It only applies to those hedges and should not be applied by analogy to other types of hedge accounting. *[IFRIC 16.8]*. For the avoidance of doubt, IFRIC 16 explains that such a hedge can be applied only when the net assets of that foreign operation are included in the financial statements. This will be the case for consolidated financial statements, financial statements in which investments such as associates or joint ventures are accounted for using the equity method or those that include a branch or a joint operation (as defined in IFRS 11 – *Joint Arrangements*). *[IFRIC 16.2]*. For convenience, IFRIC 16 refers to such an entity as a parent entity and to the financial statements in which the net assets of foreign operations are included as consolidated financial statements and this section follows this convention.

Investments in foreign operations may be held directly by a parent entity or indirectly by its subsidiary or subsidiaries.

The requirements of IFRIC 16 are discussed in more detail at 3.3.1 to 3.3.4 below and, in the case of assessing and measuring the effectiveness of such a hedge, at 5.3.12 below.

3.3.1 Nature of the hedged risk

Perhaps the most important decision made by the IFRS Interpretations Committee was that hedge accounting may be applied only to the foreign exchange differences arising between the functional currency of the foreign operation and the parent entity's functional currency. *[IFRIC 16.10]*. Furthermore, the hedged risk may be designated as the foreign currency exposure arising between the functional currency of the foreign operation and the functional currency of any parent entity (the immediate, intermediate or ultimate parent entity) of that foreign operation. The fact that the net investment may be held through an intermediate parent does not affect the nature of the economic risk arising from the foreign currency exposure to the ultimate parent entity. *[IFRIC 16.12]*. This principle is illustrated in the following example.

Example 51.22:   Nature of the hedged risk in a net investment hedge

Company P is the ultimate parent entity of a group and presents its consolidated financial statements in its functional currency of euro. It has two direct wholly owned subsidiaries, Company A whose functional currency is Japanese yen and Company B whose functional currency is sterling. B has a wholly owned subsidiary, Company C, whose functional currency is US dollars. P's net investment in A is ¥400,000 million which includes A's external borrowings of US$300 million. P's net investment in B is £500 million including the equivalent of £159 million representing B's net investment in C of US$300 million. This corporate structure is illustrated as follows:

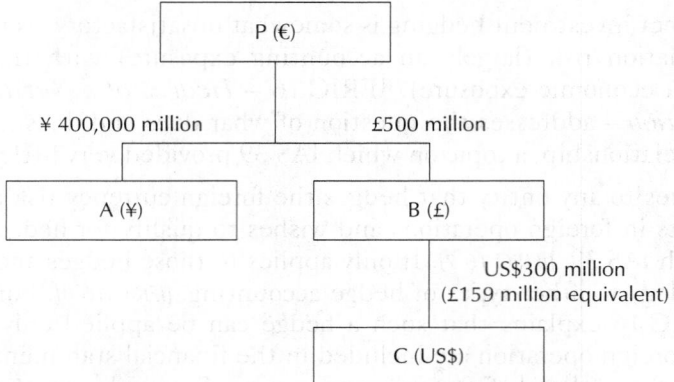

P, in its consolidated financial statements, could hedge its net investment in each of A, B and C for the foreign exchange risk between their functional currencies (Japanese yen, sterling and US dollars respectively) and euro. P could also hedge the foreign exchange risk between the functional currencies of B (sterling) and C (US dollars).

In its consolidated financial statements, B could hedge its net investment in C for the foreign exchange risk between C's functional currency (US dollars) and its own (pounds sterling). *[IFRIC 16.AG1-AG3]*.

Where a non-derivative instrument is used as the hedging instrument, the designated risk should be the spot foreign exchange risk; if the hedging instruments were forward contracts, the forward foreign exchange risk could be designated as the hedged risk. *[IFRIC 16.AG2]*.

3.3.2   Amount of the hedged item for which a hedging relationship may be designated

The hedged item can be an amount of net assets equal to or less than the carrying amount of the net assets of the foreign operation in the consolidated financial statements of the parent entity. *[IFRIC 16.11]*.

Example 51.23:   Amount of hedged item in a net investment hedge

The facts are as in Example 51.22 above. If P wished to hedge the foreign exchange risk from its net investment in C, the hedged item could be an amount of net assets equal to or less than the US$300 million carrying amount of C in P's consolidated financial statements. *[IFRIC 16.AG4]*.

The carrying amount of the net investment takes account of monetary items receivable from or payable to a foreign operation for which settlement is neither planned nor likely to occur in the future. Under IAS 21 these balances are considered to be, in substance, part of the reporting entity's net investment in the foreign operation. In the case of a loan made to the foreign operation this will increase the amount that can be hedged; if a loan is made by the foreign operation, the amount that can be hedged will be reduced. *[IFRIC 16.AG14].*

In many cases the full economic value of a net investment will not be recognised in the financial statements. The most common reason will be the existence of, say, goodwill or intangible assets that are either not recognised or measured at an amount below their current value. In these situations, if an investor hedges the entire economic value of its net investment it will not be able to obtain hedge accounting for the proportion of the hedging instrument that exceeds the recognised net assets.

A single hedging instrument can hedge the same designated risk only once. Consequently, in Examples 51.22 and 51.23 above, P could not in its consolidated financial statements designate A's external borrowing in a hedge of both the €/US$ spot foreign exchange risk and the £/US$ spot foreign exchange risk in respect of its net investment in C. *[IFRIC 16.AG6].*

The carrying amount of the net assets of a foreign operation that may be designated as the hedged item in the consolidated financial statements of a parent depends on whether any lower level parent of the foreign operation has applied hedge accounting for all or part of the net assets of that foreign operation and whether that accounting has been maintained in the parent's consolidated financial statements. *[IFRIC 16.11].* An exposure to foreign currency risk arising from a net investment in a foreign operation may qualify for hedge accounting only once in the consolidated financial statements. Therefore, if the same net assets of a foreign operation are hedged by more than one parent entity within the group (for example, both a direct and an indirect parent entity) for the same risk, only one hedging relationship will qualify for hedge accounting in the consolidated financial statements of the ultimate parent. *[IFRIC 16.13].* This is illustrated in the following example.

Example 51.24: Amount of hedged item in a net investment hedge (different hedged risks)

The facts are the same as in Examples 51.22 and 51.23 above except that P's net assets include £500 million and US$300 million of external borrowings. If P wished to hedge the foreign exchange risk in relation to its net investments in B and C, the designations it could make in its consolidated financial statements include the following: *[IFRIC 16.AG10]*

- US$300 million of the US dollar borrowings designated as a hedge of the net investment in C with the risk being the spot foreign exchange exposure (€/US$) between P and C and up to £341 million of the sterling borrowings designated as a hedge of the net investment in B with the risk being the spot foreign exchange exposure (€/£) between P and B; or

- US$300 million of the US dollar borrowings as a hedge of the net investment in C with the risk being the spot foreign exchange exposure (£/US$) between B and C and up to £500 million of the sterling borrowings designated as a hedge of the net investment in B with the risk being the spot foreign exchange exposure (€/£) between P and B.

The €/US$ risk from P's net investment in C is a different risk from the €/£ risk from P's net investment in B. However, in the first case described above, P would have already fully hedged the €/US$ risk from its net investment in C and if P also designated its £500 million of borrowings as a hedge of its net investment in B, £159 million of that net investment, representing the sterling equivalent of its US dollar net investment in C, would be hedged twice for £/€ risk in P's consolidated financial statements. *[IFRIC 16.AG11]*. In the second case described above, because the designation of the US$/£ risk between B and C does not include the £/€ risk, P is also able to designate up to £500 million of its net investment in B with the risk being the spot foreign exchange exposure (£/€) between P and B. *[IFRIC 16.AG12]*.

A hedging relationship designated by one parent entity in its consolidated financial statements need not be maintained by another higher level parent entity. However, if it is not maintained by the higher level parent entity, the hedge accounting applied by the lower level parent must be reversed before the higher level parent's hedge accounting is recognised. *[IFRIC 16.13]*. This is illustrated in the following example.

Example 51.25:   Hedge accounting applied by intermediate parent

The facts are the same as in Examples 51.22 and 51.23 above, except that P's net assets include £500 million of external borrowings and B's net assets of £341 million include US$300 million of external borrowings which it designates as a hedge of the £/US$ risk of its net investment in C in its own consolidated financial statements.

P could maintain B's designation of that hedging instrument as a hedge of its net investment in C for the £/US$ risk and P could designate its £500 million external borrowings as a hedge of its entire net investment in B. The first hedge, designated by B, would be assessed by reference to B's functional currency (sterling) and the second hedge, designated by P, would be assessed by reference to P's functional currency (euro). In this case, only the £/US$ risk from P's net investment in C has been hedged in its consolidated financial statements by B's US dollar borrowings, not the entire €/US$ risk. Therefore, the entire €/£ risk from P's net investment in B may be hedged in P's consolidated financial statements. *[IFRIC 16.AG13]*.

Alternatively, P could reverse the hedging relationship designated by B. In this case, it could designate B's US$300 million external borrowing as a hedge of its net investment in C for the €/US$ risk and designate £341 million of its borrowings as a hedge of part of the net investment in B. In this case the effectiveness of both hedges would be computed by reference to P's functional currency (euro). Consequently, both the US$/£ and £/€ changes in value of B's US$300 million borrowing would be included in P's foreign currency translation reserve. Because P has already fully hedged the €/US$ risk from its net investment in C, it could hedge only up to £341 million for the €/GBP risk of its net investment in B. *[IFRIC 16.AG15]*.

3.3.3   *Where the hedging instrument can be held*

The hedging instrument(s) may be held by any entity or entities within the group, including the foreign operation being hedged, provided the designation, documentation and effectiveness requirements of IAS 39 are satisfied. The hedging strategy of the group should be clearly documented because of the possibility of different designations at different levels of the group (see 3.3.2 above). *[IFRIC 16.14]*.

Where the entity holding the hedging instrument has a functional currency that is not the same as the parent by which the hedged risk is defined, this could result in the recognition of ineffectiveness in profit or loss – this is discussed further at 5.3.11 below.

Clearly the reporting entity (which, in the case of consolidated financial statements, includes any subsidiary consolidated by the parent) must be a party to the hedging instrument. In Examples 51.22 and 51.23 above, therefore, B could not apply hedge accounting in its consolidated financial statements in respect of a hedge involving the US$300 million borrowing issued by A because the hedging instrument is held outside of the group headed by B. *[IFRIC 16.AG6]*.

3.3.4   Disposal of a hedged foreign operation

When a foreign operation that was hedged is disposed of, the amount reclassified from the foreign currency translation reserve to profit or loss in respect of the hedging instrument is the amount that IAS 39 requires to be identified, being the cumulative gain or loss on the hedging instrument that was determined to be an effective hedge (see 5.3.11 below). *[IFRIC 16.16]*. If the step-by-step method of consolidation is used, this amount could be different to the equivalent amount of gains or losses accumulated within equity arising on the retranslation of that entity (see Chapter 15 at 6.1.5 and at 6.6). *[IFRIC 16.17]*.

Example 51.26:   Disposal of foreign operation

The facts are the same as in Examples 51.22 and 51.23 above. If C were disposed of, the amounts reclassified to profit or loss in P's consolidated financial statements from its foreign currency translation reserve would be: *[IFRIC 16.17, AG8]*

- in respect of A's borrowing, the amount that IAS 39 requires to be identified, i.e. the total change in value in respect of foreign exchange risk that was recognised in other comprehensive income as the effective portion of the hedge; and

- in respect of the net investment in C, the amount determined by the entity's consolidation method. If P uses the direct method, its foreign currency translation reserve ('FCTR') in respect of C will be determined directly by the EUR/USD foreign exchange rate. If P uses the step-by-step method, its FCTR in respect of C will be determined by the FCTR recognised by B reflecting the GBP/USD foreign exchange rate, translated to P's functional currency using the EUR/GBP foreign exchange rate. P's use of the step-by-step method for consolidation in prior periods does not require it to or preclude it from determining the amount of FCTR to be reclassified when it disposes of C to be the amount that it would have recognised if it had always used the direct method, however, it is an accounting policy choice which should be followed consistently for all net investments.

4   ACCOUNTING FOR EFFECTIVE HEDGES

If there is a designated hedging relationship between a hedging instrument and a hedged item as described at 3 above and it meets the conditions set out at 5 below, the accounting for the gain or loss on the hedging instrument and the hedged item will be as set out in the remainder of this section. *[IAS 39.71]*. This is referred to as 'hedge accounting' and is said to recognise the offsetting effects on profit or loss of changes in the fair values of the hedging instrument and the hedged item. *[IAS 39.85]*.

4.1   Fair value hedges

4.1.1   Ongoing fair value hedge accounting

If a fair value hedge (see 3.1 above) meets the qualifying conditions set out at 5 below during the period, it should be accounted for as follows:

- the gain or loss from remeasuring the hedging instrument at fair value (for a derivative hedging instrument) or the foreign currency component of its carrying amount measured in accordance with IAS 21 (for a non-derivative hedging instrument) is recognised in profit or loss; and

- the carrying amount of the hedged item is adjusted for the change in its value attributable to the hedged risk and the gain or loss is recognised in profit or loss. This applies if the hedged item is an available-for-sale financial asset (and that gain or loss would otherwise be recognised in other comprehensive income) or if it is otherwise measured at cost. *[IAS 39.89].*

It will be rare for the change in fair value of the hedging instrument (or, for non-derivative hedging instruments, foreign exchange gains or losses) to be exactly the same as the change in fair value of the hedged item attributable to the hedged risk, even for highly effective hedges. To the extent these amounts differ, a net amount will be recognised in profit or loss. The recognition of this difference is commonly referred to as the measurement of hedge ineffectiveness. Although not clearly evident from the standard, we believe the gain or loss from remeasuring the hedging instrument and the gain or loss from adjusting the hedged item should be recognised in the same line item in profit or loss to reflect the offsetting effect of hedge accounting (see Chapter 53 at 7.1.3).

The following simple example illustrates how the treatment above might apply to a hedge of fair value interest rate risk on an investment in fixed rate debt.

Example 51.27:   Fair value hedge

At the beginning of Year 1 an investor purchases a fixed rate debt security for £100 and classifies it as available-for-sale. At the end of Year 1, the fair value of the asset is £110. To protect this value, the investor enters into a hedge by acquiring a derivative with a nil fair value. By the end of Year 2, the derivative has a fair value of £5 and the debt security has a corresponding decline in fair value (its fair value does not change as a result of any factors other than interest rates).

The investor would record the following accounting entries:

Year 1

Beginning of year	£	£
Debt security	100	
Cash		100

To reflect the acquisition of the security.

End of year	£	£
Debt security	10	
Other comprehensive income		10

To record the increase in the security's fair value in other comprehensive income.

Year 2

Beginning of year	£	£
Derivative	–	
Cash		–

To record the acquisition of the derivative at its fair value of nil.

End of year	£	£
Derivative	5	
Profit or loss		5

To recognise the increase in the derivative's fair value in profit or loss.

	£	£
Profit or loss	5	
Debt security		5

To recognise the decrease in the security's fair value in profit or loss.

The example is taken from the original version of the standard and was not carried forward into the December 2003 version of the standard, although it is not entirely clear why not. Even if it was considered too simplistic to be a useful practical example (it does not deal, for example, with net cash settlements on the derivative, coupon payments on the debt or the subsequent impact on the recognition of interest under the effective interest method), it does illustrate the basic mechanics of fair value hedge accounting quite well.

The standard explains that if only particular risks attributable to a hedged financial instrument are hedged, the recognised changes in the fair value of the hedged item that are unrelated to the hedged risk should be recognised as set out in Chapter 48 at 2. *[IAS 39.90]*. Therefore, for instruments measured at amortised cost, these other gains and losses would generally not be recognised; for available-for-sale assets those gains and losses would generally be recognised in other comprehensive income. Exceptions to this would include foreign currency retranslation gains or losses on monetary items and impairment losses, which would be recognised in profit or loss in any event. The following example illustrates this.

Example 51.28: Hedging foreign currency risk of publicly traded shares

Company C, whose functional currency is sterling, acquires 100,000 shares in a listed US corporation for US$1m, which it classifies as available-for-sale. It is assumed the shares gives rise to a clear and identifiable exposure to changes in the US dollar/sterling exchange rate and to protect itself from changes in this exchange rate, C enters into a forward contract to sell US$0.75m which it intends to roll over for as long as the shares are held.

A portion of an exposure may be designated as a hedged item, and so the forward contract may be designated as a hedge of part of the shareholding. It could be a fair value hedge of the foreign exchange exposure of US$0.75m associated with the shares (alternatively it could be a cash flow hedge of a forecast sale of the shares but only if the timing of the sale is identified with sufficient certainty). Any variability in the fair value of the shares in US dollars would not affect the assessment of hedge effectiveness unless their fair value fell below US$0.75m. *[IAS 39.F.2.19]*.

Gains and losses on the forward contract would be recognised in profit or loss. Gains and losses arising from remeasuring the dollar value of the hedged portion of the shares to sterling would also be recognised in profit or loss and the remainder would be recognised in other comprehensive income (as would all of the foreign currency amount were it not for the hedge relationship).

The basic hedge accounting treatment above applies equally to fair value hedges of unrecognised firm commitments. Therefore, where an unrecognised firm commitment is designated as a hedged item in a fair value hedge, the subsequent cumulative change in its fair value attributable to the hedged risk should be recognised as an asset or liability with a corresponding gain or loss recognised in profit or loss. Thereafter, the firm commitment would be a *recognised* asset or liability (albeit that its carrying amount will not represent either its cost or, necessarily, its fair value). The changes in the fair value of the hedging instrument would also be recognised in profit or loss. *[IAS 39.93]*.

It can be seen that applying fair value hedge accounting adjustments does not change the accounting for the hedging instrument. This is true whether the hedging instrument is a derivative or non-derivative instrument (in a hedge of foreign currency risk). For example, if a foreign currency cash instrument was designated as the hedging instrument in a fair value hedge (see 2.1.2 above), the foreign currency component of its carrying amount would continue to be measured in accordance with IAS 21. *[IAS 39.89(a)]*.

4.1.2   *Dealing with adjustments to the hedged item*

In general, adjustments to the hedged asset or liability arising from the application of hedge accounting as described at 4.1.1 above are dealt with in accordance with the normal accounting treatment for that item. For example, copper inventory might be the hedged item in a fair value hedge of the exposure to changes in the copper price. In this case, the adjusted carrying amount of the copper inventory becomes the cost basis for the purpose of applying the lower of cost and net realisable value test under IAS 2 – *Inventories* (see Chapter 22 at 3). *[IAS 39.F.3.6].*

Where the hedged item is a financial instrument for which the effective interest method of accounting is used, the adjustment should be amortised to profit or loss. Amortisation may begin as soon as the adjustment exists and should begin no later than when the hedged item ceases to be adjusted for changes in its fair value attributable to the hedged risk. The adjustment should be based on a recalculated effective interest rate at the date amortisation begins and should be fully amortised by maturity. *[IAS 39.92].*

When an entity enters into a firm commitment to acquire an asset or assume a liability that is a hedged item in a fair value hedge, the initial carrying amount of the asset or liability that results from the entity meeting the firm commitment is adjusted to include the cumulative change in the fair value of the firm commitment attributable to the hedged risk that was recognised in the statement of financial position. *[IAS 39.94].*

Example 51.29:   Hedge of a firm commitment to acquire equipment

Company X has the euro as its functional currency. It has chosen to treat all hedges of foreign currency risk associated with firm commitments as fair value hedges. In January 2016 it contracts with a US supplier (with the US dollar as its functional currency) to purchase an item of machinery it intends to use in its business. The machine will be delivered at the start of July 2016 and the contracted price, payable on delivery, is US$1,000.

X has no appetite to take on foreign currency exchange risk in relation to euro/US dollar exchange rates and so contracts with a bank to purchase US$1,000 at the start of July in exchange for €900 (six month forward exchange rate is US$1:€0.90). In other words, X has effectively fixed the price it will pay for the machine (in euro terms) at €900.

If the fair value of the forward contract at the end of March 2016 (X's year end) is €30 positive to X, on delivery is €50 positive to X (spot exchange rate is US$1:€0.95) and assuming the hedge is perfectly effective (this might be the case if the hedged risk is identified as the forward exchange rate rather than the spot rate – see 5.3.3 below) and meets all the requirements for hedge accounting, the journal entries to record this hedging relationship would be as follows:

January 2016

No entries are required as the firm commitment is unrecognised, the forward contract is recognised but has a zero fair value and no cash is paid or received.

March 2016

	€	€
Forward contract	30	
Profit or loss		30

To recognise the change in fair value of the forward contract in profit or loss.

	€	€
Profit or loss	30	
Firm commitment		30

To recognise the change in fair value of the (previously) unrecognised firm commitment in respect of changes in forward exchange rates in profit or loss.

July 2016

	€	€
Forward contract	20	
Profit or loss		20

To recognise the change in fair value of the forward contract in profit or loss.

	€	€
Profit or loss	20	
Firm commitment		20

To recognise the change in fair value of the (now recognised) firm commitment in respect of changes in forward exchange rates in profit or loss.

	€	€
Cash	50	
Forward contract		50

To record the settlement of the forward contract at its fair value.

	€	€
Machine	950	
Cash		950

To record the settlement of the firm commitment at the contracted price of US$1,000 at the spot rate of US$1:€0.95.

	€	€
Firm commitment	50	
Machine		50

To remove the carrying amount of the firm commitment from the statement of financial position and adjust the initial carrying amount of the machine that results from the firm commitment.

In summary, the result of these accounting entries is as follows:

	€	€
Machine	900	
Cash		900

which is somewhat reassuring given the starting presumption, i.e. that X had effectively fixed the purchase price of its machine at €900.

4.1.3   Discontinuing fair value hedge accounting

The ongoing fair value hedge accounting set out at 4.1.1 above should be discontinued prospectively if any one of the following occurs:

- the hedging instrument expires or is sold, terminated, or exercised.

    For this purpose, the replacement or a rollover of a hedging instrument into another is not an expiration or termination if that is part of the documented hedging strategy.

    Further, an expiration or termination of the hedging instrument is not considered to have occurred for this purpose if:

    - as a consequence of laws or regulations or the introduction of laws or regulations, the parties to the hedging instrument agree that one or more clearing counterparties replace their original counterparty to become the new counterparty to each of the parties. For this purpose, a clearing counterparty is a central counterparty (sometimes called a 'clearing organisation' or 'clearing agency') or an entity or entities, for example, a clearing member of a clearing organisation or a client of a clearing member of a clearing organisation, that are acting as counterparty in order to effect clearing by a central counterparty. However, when the parties to the hedging instrument replace their original counterparties with different counterparties this paragraph shall apply only if each of those parties effects clearing with the same central counterparty; and

    - other changes, if any, to the hedging instrument are limited to those that are necessary to effect such a replacement of the counterparty. Such changes are limited to those that are consistent with the terms that would be expected if the hedging instrument were originally cleared with the clearing counterparty. These changes include changes in the collateral requirements, rights to offset receivables and payables balances, and charges levied;

- the hedge no longer meets the hedge effectiveness criteria for hedge accounting; or

- the designation is revoked. *[IAS 39.91]*.

If the reason the hedge no longer meets the criteria for qualification for hedge accounting is that it does not meet the hedge effectiveness criteria, hedge accounting should be discontinued from the last date on which compliance with hedge effectiveness was demonstrated. However, if the event or change in circumstances that caused the hedging relationship to fail the effectiveness criteria can be identified, and it can be demonstrated that the hedge was effective before the event or change in circumstances occurred, the hedge accounting should be discontinued from the date of the event or change in circumstances. *[IAS 39.AG113]*.

Example 51.30: Hedge of foreign exchange risk from currency pegged to the US dollar

Company Z has the euro as its functional currency and prepares annual financial statements for the year ended 31 December. It also prepares interim financial statements for the six months ended 30 June and, in general, assesses the effectiveness of hedges at these dates.

In January 2016, Z acquires an equity instrument issued by a company whose functional currency is the FC. It is assumed the investment has a clear and identifiable exposure to changes in the FC/euro exchange rate and is classified as available-for-sale. For many years the value of the FC has been pegged to the US dollar and historical studies show that during this time the FC/US dollar exchange rate has never moved outside of a corridor representing 2.5% of the mean rate. Furthermore, there is no evidence to suggest that the peg will not continue for the foreseeable future.

Accordingly, in January 2016, Z is able to designate a US dollar denominated borrowing as a highly effective hedge of the foreign currency risk associated with part of the equity instrument.

At the end of June 2016, Z performs an effectiveness assessment and determines that the hedge has been highly effective and, therefore, changes in the value of the equity instrument attributable to changes in the FC/euro exchange rate are recognised in profit or loss rather than other comprehensive income, together with the exchange differences on the US dollar borrowing.

At the beginning of October 2016, there is an unexpected financial crisis, the peg ceases and the FC is devalued by 25% relative to the US dollar.

When Z assesses the effectiveness of the hedge in December 2016 it concludes that, because of the cessation of the peg and consequent devaluation, the hedge can no longer be regarded as highly effective and that hedge accounting should cease.

However, Z is able to determine that the failure of the hedge arose because of the cessation of the FC/US dollar peg and subsequent devaluation at the beginning of October 2016. Therefore, it is able to apply hedge accounting for the first three months of its second interim period. Thus, changes in the value of the equity instrument attributable to changes in the FC/euro exchange rate for that period will be recognised in profit or loss, but thereafter will be recognised in other comprehensive income when accounting for the available-for-sale asset at fair value.

In other cases, hedge accounting should be discontinued from the date the hedging instrument expires or is sold, terminated or exercised, or the hedge designation is revoked. For example, if the forward contract in Example 51.29 above were settled (or the hedge designation was revoked) at the end of March 2016, no further adjustments to the carrying value of the firm commitment (€30) would be made after that date.

4.2 Cash flow hedges

4.2.1 Ongoing cash flow hedge accounting

If a cash flow hedge (see 3.2 above) meets the qualifying conditions set out in 5 below, it should be accounted for as follows:

- the portion of the gain or loss on the hedging instrument that is determined to be an effective hedge should be recognised in other comprehensive income; and

- the ineffective portion should be recognised immediately in profit or loss. *[IAS 39.95, F.4.5].*

More specifically, the accounting should be as follows:

- the separate component of equity associated with the hedged item is adjusted to the lesser of the following (in absolute amounts):
  - (i) the cumulative gain or loss on the hedging instrument from inception of the hedge; and
  - (ii) the cumulative change in fair value (present value) of the expected future cash flows on the hedged item from inception of the hedge;
- any remaining gain or loss on the hedging instrument or designated component of it (that is not an effective hedge) is recognised in profit or loss; and
- if the documented risk management strategy for a particular hedging relationship excludes from the assessment of hedge effectiveness a specific component of the gain or loss or related cash flows on the hedging instrument, that excluded component of gain or loss is recognised as set out in Chapter 48 at 2 (effectively in profit or loss for a derivative hedging instrument).

  Those excluded components can include the time value of an option, the interest element of a forward contract or a proportion of an instrument (see 2.1.4 above). *[IAS 39.96].*

The requirements set out in the first two bullets are often referred to as the 'lower of' requirements. This accounting treatment is illustrated in the following examples.

Example 51.31: Cash flow hedge of anticipated commodity sale

On 30 September 2016, Company A hedges the anticipated sale of 24 tonnes of pulp on 1 March 2017 by entering into a short forward contract. The contract requires net settlement in cash, determined as the difference between the future spot price of 24 tonnes of pulp on a specified commodity exchange and £1m. A expects to sell the pulp in a different, local market.

A determines that the forward contract is an effective hedge of the anticipated sale and that the other conditions for hedge accounting are met. It assesses hedge effectiveness by comparing the entire change in the fair value of the forward contract with the change in the fair value of the expected cash inflows. On 31 December 2016, the spot price of pulp has increased both in the local market and on the exchange, although the increase in the local market exceeds the increase on the exchange. As a result, the present value of the expected cash inflow from the sale on the local market is £1.1m and the fair value of the forward is £85,000 negative. The hedge is determined to be still highly effective.

The cumulative change in the fair value of the forward contract is £85,000, while the fair value of the cumulative change in expected future cash flows on the hedged item is £100,000. Ineffectiveness is not recognised in the financial statements because the cumulative change in the fair value of the hedged cash flows exceeds the cumulative change in the value of the hedging instrument. The whole of the fair value change in the forward contract would be recognised in other comprehensive income.

December 2016

	£'000	£'000
Other comprehensive income	85	
Forward contract		85

However, if A concluded that the hedge was no longer highly effective, it would discontinue hedge accounting prospectively as from the date the hedge ceased to be highly effective (see 4.2.3 below). *[IAS 39.F.5.3].*

Example 51.32:   Cash flow hedge of a floating rate liability

Company A has a floating rate liability of £1m with five years remaining to maturity. It enters into a five year pay-fixed, receive-floating interest rate swap with the same principal terms to hedge the exposure to variable cash flow payments on the floating rate liability attributable to interest rate risk.

At inception, the swap's fair value is £nil. Subsequently, there is an increase of £49,000 which consists of a change of £50,000 resulting from an increase in market interest rates and a change of minus £1,000 resulting from an increase in the credit risk of the swap counterparty. There is no change in the fair value of the floating rate liability, but the fair value (present value) of the future cash flows needed to offset the exposure to variable interest cash flows on the liability increases by £50,000.

Even if A determines that the hedge of interest rate risk is 'highly effective' (simplistically, the offset ratio is 49,000 ÷ 50,000 or 98%, so this is quite likely), it is not fully effective if part of the change in the fair value of the derivative is due to the counterparty's credit risk (see 5.3.4 below). However, because the hedge relationship is still 'highly effective', A credits the effective portion of the swap's fair value change, £49,000, to other comprehensive income. There is no debit to profit or loss for the change in fair value of the swap attributable to the deterioration in the credit quality of the swap counterparty because the cumulative change in the present value of the future cash flows needed to offset the exposure to variable interest cash flows on the hedged item, £50,000, exceeds the cumulative change in value of the hedging instrument, £49,000. If A concluded that the hedge was no longer highly effective, it would discontinue hedge accounting prospectively as from the date the hedge ceased to be highly effective (see 4.2.3 below).

Alternatively, if the fair value of the swap increased to £51,000 of which £50,000 results from the increase in market interest rates and £1,000 from a decrease in the swap counterparty's credit risk, there would be a credit to profit or loss of £1,000 for the change in the swap's fair value attributable to the improvement in the counterparty's credit quality. This is because the cumulative change in the value of the hedging instrument, £51,000, exceeds the cumulative change in the present value of the future cash flows needed to offset the exposure to variable interest cash flows on the hedged item, £50,000. The difference of £1,000 represents the excess ineffectiveness attributable to the swap, and is recognised in profit or loss. *[IAS 39.F.5.2]*.

It can be seen that the measurement of hedge ineffectiveness differs for a cash flow hedge when compared to a fair value hedge. In a cash flow hedge, if the fair value of the derivative increases by €10 and the present value of the hedged expected cash flows change by only €8, the €2 difference is recognised in profit or loss (as would be the case for a fair value hedge). However, if the present value of the hedged expected cash flows changes by €10, but the fair value of the derivative changes by only €8, this €2 of hedge ineffectiveness is *not* recognised in profit or loss (which would not be the case for a fair value hedge).

Because of this, an entity might consider deliberately under-hedging an exposure in a cash flow hedge. It might do this by targeting an offset of, say, 85% to 90%, which would keep it within the prescribed 80% to 125% range (see 5.3.1 below) but avoid the need to recognise ineffectiveness in profit or loss. However, such an approach is not permitted by IAS 39. *[IAS 39.AG107A, BC136A]*.

4.2.2   *Reclassification of gains and losses recognised in other comprehensive income from equity to profit or loss*

If a hedged forecast transaction subsequently results in the recognition of a *financial* asset or liability, the associated gains or losses that were recognised in other comprehensive income should be reclassified from equity to profit or loss in the same period(s) during which the hedged forecast cash flows (or asset acquired or liability assumed) affect profit or loss, e.g. in the periods that interest income or interest expense is recognised. This reclassification is often referred to as 'recycling'. However, if it is expected that all or a portion of a loss recognised in other comprehensive income will not be recovered in one or more future periods, the amount that is not expected to be recovered should be reclassified from equity to profit or loss immediately. *[IAS 39.97]*.

If a hedged forecast transaction subsequently results in the recognition of a *non-financial* asset or liability (or a forecast transaction for a *non-financial* asset or liability becomes a firm commitment for which fair value hedge accounting is applied) then a choice of accounting policies is available. In these circumstances, an entity should either:

- reclassify the associated gains and losses that were recognised in other comprehensive income from equity to profit or loss in the same period(s) during which the asset acquired or liability assumed affects profit or loss, e.g. in the periods that depreciation expense or cost of sales is recognised. However, if it is expected that all or a portion of a loss recognised in other comprehensive income will not be recovered in one or more future periods, the amount that is not expected to be recovered should be reclassified from equity to profit or loss. Essentially this is the same treatment as for hedges of financial items; or

- remove the associated gains and losses that were recognised in other comprehensive income and include them in the initial cost or other carrying amount of the asset or liability *[IAS 39.98]* as a 'basis adjustment'.

An entity should adopt one of these as its accounting policy and apply it consistently to all relevant hedges. *[IAS 39.99]*. These treatments are illustrated in the following example.

Example 51.33:   Hedge of a firm commitment to acquire equipment

Consider a variation of the situation in Example 51.29 at 4.1.2 above whereby Company X has chosen to treat all hedges of foreign currency risk associated with firm commitments as cash flow hedges, rather than as fair value hedges, as permitted by the standard (see 3.2.2 above). In the first case, X's accounting policy is to apply a basis adjustment to cash flow hedges that result in the recognition of non-financial assets or liabilities; in the second case it does not. Otherwise, the underlying facts and assumptions are the same. The accounting entries made at the end of March 2016 have not been shown separately (as they were in Example 51.29) because they are not relevant to the issue being illustrated.

Case 1: Basis adjustment

The journal entries to record this hedging relationship would be as follows:

January 2016

No entries are required as the firm commitment is unrecognised, the forward contract is recognised but has a zero fair value and no cash is paid or received.

July 2016

	€	€
Forward contract	50	
Other comprehensive income		50

To recognise the change in fair value of the forward contract and, because no ineffectiveness arises, the whole of this change is recognised in other comprehensive income.

	€	€
Cash	50	
Forward contract		50

To record the settlement of the forward contract at its fair value.

	€	€
Machine	950	
Cash		950

To record the settlement of the firm commitment at the contracted price of US$1,000 at the spot rate of US$1:€0.95.

	€	€
Other comprehensive income	50	
Machine		50

To remove the gain recognised in other comprehensive income and adjust the carrying amount of the machine that results from the hedged transaction by this amount.

In summary, the result of these accounting entries is as follows:

	€	€
Machine	900	
Cash		900

which again reflects the starting presumption, i.e. that X had effectively fixed the purchase price of its machine at €900.

Case 2: No basis adjustment

The journal entries to record this hedging relationship would be as follows:

January 2016

No entries are required as the firm commitment is unrecognised, the forward contract is recognised but has a zero fair value and no cash is paid or received.

July 2016

	€	€
Forward contract	50	
Other comprehensive income		50

To recognise the change in fair value of the forward contract and, because no ineffectiveness arises, the whole of this change is recognised in other comprehensive income.

	€	€
Cash	50	
Forward contract		50

To record the settlement of the forward contract at its fair value.

	€	€
Machine	950	
Cash		950

To record the settlement of the firm commitment at the contracted price of US$1,000 at the spot rate of US$1:€0.95.

In summary, the result of these accounting entries is as follows:

	€	€
Machine	950	
Cash		900
Other comprehensive income		50

The gain recognised in other comprehensive income would be reclassified from equity to profit or loss as the machine affects profit or loss, e.g. as it is depreciated, impaired or derecognised. If the machine has a very long useful economic life, this might involve tracking this adjustment for many years. The result might be considered less intuitive than the outcome on case 1.

The hedge accounting requirements of IFRS 9 eliminate the accounting policy choice and require a basis adjustment (see Chapter 52 at 8.1).

For all other cash flow hedges (i.e. those that do not result in the recognition of an asset or a liability), amounts that had been recognised in other comprehensive income should be reclassified from equity to profit or loss in the same period or periods during which the hedged forecast cash flows (or transaction) affects profit or loss, e.g. when a forecast sale occurs, *[IAS 39.100]*, or when variable rate interest income or expense is recognised. Although not clearly evident from the standard, we believe the reclassification from accumulated other comprehensive income to profit or loss should be recognised in the same line item in profit or loss as the hedged transaction to reflect the offsetting effect of hedge accounting (see Chapter 53 at 7.1.3).

When instruments such as conventional interest rate swaps are used as a hedging instrument in a cash flow hedge, it is common for entities to recognise net interest income or expense on the hedging instrument directly in profit or loss on an accruals basis. Other changes in fair value of the hedging instrument (i.e. the 'clean value' – excluding accrued interest) are recognised in other comprehensive income, subject to the 'lower of' requirements (see 4.2.1 above). Such an approach avoids the need to reclassify from equity to profit or loss the net interest as the hedged item impacts profit or loss. However, care must be taken to ensure the portion of the gain or loss on the hedging instrument that is recognised in other comprehensive income appropriately excludes ineffectiveness, which should be recognised in profit or loss. The hedging derivative would still be recognised in the statement of financial position at the full fair value.

If a hedge of a forecast intragroup transaction qualifies for hedge accounting (see 2.3.4.B above), any gain or loss that is recognised in other comprehensive income should be reclassified from equity to profit or loss in the same period(s) during which the foreign currency risk of the hedged transaction affects consolidated profit or loss. *[IAS 39.AG99B]*.

It was stated at 3.2.3 above that using a forward exchange contract to hedge a foreign currency payable or receivable could be treated either as a fair value hedge, or a cash flow hedge, under IAS 39. In a fair value hedge, the gain or loss on remeasurement of the forward contract and the hedged item are recognised immediately in profit or loss. However, in a cash flow hedge, the gain or loss on remeasuring the forward contract is recognised in other comprehensive income and reclassified from equity to profit or loss when the payable or receivable affects profit or loss. Because the payable or receivable is remeasured continuously in respect of changes in foreign exchange rates, the gain or loss on the forward contract will be reclassified from equity to profit or loss as the payable or receivable is remeasured, not when the payment occurs. *[IAS 39.F.3.3-F.3.4].* Where cash flow hedge accounting is applied, the effective portion of the gain or loss on the forward contract should be recognised in other comprehensive income and then reclassified from equity to profit or loss in the same period or periods during which the hedged item(s) impact profit or loss.

The interest element of the fair value of a forward may be excluded from the designated hedge relationship (designation of the spot exchange risk only – see 2.1.4.B above) although in this case changes in the fair value of the interest element would be recognised immediately in profit or loss, outside the hedge accounting. *[IAS 39.F.6.4].* Designating the forward exchange rate or the spot exchange rate as the hedged risk could result in different results as illustrated in Example 51.37 at 5.3.3 below.

4.2.3 Discontinuing cash flow hedge accounting

Cash flow hedge accounting should be discontinued prospectively in any of the following circumstances:

(a) the hedging instrument expires or is sold, terminated, or exercised.

In this case the cumulative gain or loss that has been recognised in other comprehensive income in the period when the hedge was effective should remain in equity until the forecast transaction occurs. That is, the cumulative gain or loss on the hedging instrument that has been recognised in other comprehensive income should be reclassified from equity to profit or loss in the same period(s) during which the hedged forecast cash flows (or asset acquired or liability assumed) affect profit or loss. The standard does not entertain the possibility that, subsequently, the hedged forecast transaction might not occur. However, it would only make sense to deal with this situation in the same way as for hedges where the hedged instrument has not been terminated, i.e. as in (c) below;

The replacement or rollover of a hedging instrument into another hedging instrument is not an expiration or termination if such replacement or rollover is part of the entity's documented hedging strategy.

As a result of amendments made to IAS 39 in July 2013, for this purpose an expiration or termination of the hedging instrument is not considered to have occurred if:

- as a consequence of laws or regulations or the introduction of laws or regulations, the parties to the hedging instrument agree that one or more clearing counterparties replace their original counterparty to become the new counterparty to each of the parties. For this purpose, a clearing counterparty is a central counterparty (sometimes called a 'clearing organisation' or 'clearing agency') or an entity or entities, for example, a clearing member of a clearing organisation or a client of a clearing member of a clearing organisation, that are acting as counterparty in order to effect clearing by a central counterparty. However, when the parties to the hedging instrument replace their original counterparties with different counterparties this paragraph shall apply only if each of those parties effects clearing with the same central counterparty;

- other changes, if any, to the hedging instrument are limited to those that are necessary to effect such a replacement of the counterparty. Such changes are limited to those that are consistent with the terms that would be expected if the hedging instrument were originally cleared with the clearing counterparty. These changes include changes in the collateral requirements, rights to offset receivables and payables balances, and charges levied.

(b)   the hedge no longer meets the criteria for hedge accounting.

In this case, the cumulative gain or loss that has been recognised in other comprehensive income is dealt with in same way as in (a) above;

(c)   the forecast transaction is no longer expected to occur.

In this case, the cumulative gain or loss on the hedging instrument that has been recognised in other comprehensive income should be reclassified from equity to profit or loss. However, a forecast transaction that is no longer highly probable (and therefore the hedge no longer meets the criteria for hedge accounting) may still be expected to occur, in which case (b) above will apply, not (c);

(d)   the designation as a hedge is revoked.

In this case, the cumulative gain or loss that has been recognised in other comprehensive income is dealt with in same way as in (a) above. However, if the transaction is no longer expected to occur, (c) applies. *[IAS 39.101]*.

As for fair value hedges, if the reason the hedge no longer meets the criteria for qualification for hedge accounting is that it does not meet the hedge effectiveness criteria, hedge accounting should normally be discontinued from the last date on which compliance with hedge effectiveness was demonstrated. However, if the event or change in circumstances that caused the hedging relationship to fail the effectiveness criteria can be identified, and it can be demonstrated that the hedge was effective before the event or change in circumstances occurred, the hedge accounting should be discontinued from the date of the event or change in circumstances. *[IAS 39.AG113]*.

4.2.3.A   Impact of central clearing regulations on cash flow hedges

The collapse of some financial institutions during the financial crisis highlighted the potential impact of credit risk on the global derivatives markets. In response to this, several jurisdictions have introduced, or are in the process of introducing, legal or regulatory requirements that require over-the-counter (OTC) derivatives to be novated to a central clearing party (CCP) or incentivise financial institutions to do so. The CCP would usually require the derivatives to be collateralised, thereby reducing (potentially significantly) the counterparty credit risk. Examples of such legislation include the Dodd-Frank Wall Street Reform and Consumer Protection

Act (Dodd-Frank Act) in the United States and the European Market Infrastructure Regulation (EMIR) in the European Union.

Following an urgent request, the IFRS Interpretation Committee concluded in January 2013 that an entity is required to discontinue hedge accounting where an OTC derivative that is designated as hedging instrument in a hedging relationship is novated to a CCP (unless, very unusually, the novation represented a replacement or rollover of the hedging instrument as part of a documented hedging strategy). This is because the novated derivative is derecognised and the new derivative contract, with the CCP as a counterparty, is recognised at the time of the novation. However, if the new derivative was designated in a cash flow hedge relationship accounting ineffectiveness would likely arise if the derivative had a fair value other than zero (see 5.3.5 below). Consequently, the Interpretations Committee decided to recommend that the IASB make a narrow-scope amendment to IAS 39 to permit continuation of hedge accounting in such narrow circumstances.[9] In July 2013 the IASB amended IAS 39 after the publication of an exposure draft in February 2013.

The exception applies to some, but not all, voluntary novations to a CCP. In order for hedge accounting to continue, a voluntary novation should at least be associated with laws or regulations that are relevant to central clearing of derivatives. For example, a voluntary novation could be in anticipation of regulatory changes. However, the mere possibility of laws or regulations being introduced is not, in the view of the IASB, a sufficient basis for continuation of hedge accounting. *[IAS 39.BC220O-BC220Q].*

Further, the exception applies to so-called 'indirect clearing' arrangements where a clearing member of a CCP provides an indirect clearing service to its client or where a group entity is clearing on behalf of another entity within the same group since they are consistent with the objective of the amendments. *[IAS 39.BC220R, BC220S].*

For this purpose, a clearing counterparty is a central counterparty (sometimes called a 'clearing organisation' or 'clearing agency') or an entity or entities, for example, a clearing member of a clearing organisation or a client of a clearing member of a clearing organisation, that are acting as counterparty in order to effect clearing by a central counterparty. However, when the parties to the hedging instrument replace their original counterparties with different counterparties this paragraph shall apply only if each of those parties effects clearing with the same central counterparty. *[IAS 39.101(a)(i)].*

Finally, in order to qualify for the exception, any changes (if any) to the hedging instrument, as a result of a novation, should be limited to those that are necessary to effect the novation. Such changes are limited to those that are consistent with the terms that would be expected if the hedging instrument were originally cleared with the clearing counterparty. These changes include changes in the collateral requirements, rights to offset receivables and payables balances, and charges levied. *[IAS 39.101(a)(ii)].*

The other criteria for achieving hedge accounting will still need to be met in order to continue hedge accounting, including the effectiveness assessment (see at 5.3.4.A below).

Chapter 51

4.2.4   *Acquisitions and disposals*

Where a reporting entity acquires a subsidiary that is applying cash flow hedge accounting, additional considerations arise. In applying the purchase method of accounting in its consolidated financial statements, the reporting entity does not inherit the subsidiary's existing cash flow hedge reserve, since this clearly represents cumulative pre-acquisition gains and losses.[10] This has implications for the assessment of hedge effectiveness and the measurement of ineffectiveness because, so far as the group is concerned, it has effectively started a new hedge relationship with a hedging instrument that is likely to have a non-zero fair value (see 5.1.1 and 5.3.5 below).

The standard does not address the situation when the hedge relationship ceases because there is a change in the relationship between the reporting entity and the entity that is holding the hedging instrument and/or is exposed to the hedged transaction, for example when a subsidiary is disposed of. This issue is covered in more detail in Chapter 7 at 3.2.

4.3   Accounting for hedges of a net investment in a foreign operation

Hedges of a net investment in a foreign operation (see 3.3 above), including a hedge of a monetary item that is accounted for as part of the net investment (see Chapter 15 at 6.3.1), should be accounted for in a similar way to cash flow hedges: *[IAS 39.102]*

- the portion of the gain or loss on the hedging instrument that is determined to be an effective hedge should be recognised in other comprehensive income and (as clarified by IFRIC 16) included with the foreign exchange differences arising on translation of the results and financial position of the foreign operation; *[IFRIC 16.3]* and

- the ineffective portion should be recognised in profit or loss.

The gain or loss on the hedging instrument relating to the effective portion of the hedge that has been recognised in other comprehensive income should be reclassified from equity to profit or loss on disposal or, in certain circumstances, partial disposal of the foreign operation in accordance with IAS 21 (see Chapter 15 at 6.6). *[IAS 39.102]*.

The meaning of 'in a similar way to cash flow hedges' is not immediately clear. It is readily understood that the portion of the gain or loss on the hedging derivative that is determined to be an effective hedge should be recognised in other comprehensive income (as it would for a cash flow hedge). However, the wording in the standard also seems to indicate that ineffectiveness should be measured in the same way as for cash flow hedges, i.e. no ineffectiveness is recognised in profit or loss if the gain or loss on the hedging instrument is less, in absolute terms, than the gain or loss on the hedged item, (see 4.2.1 above). This is despite the fact that there appears to be no good reason why ineffectiveness should not also be recognised in profit or loss if the gain or loss on the hedging instrument is less, in absolute terms, than the gain or loss on the hedged item. This is different to the accounting for net investment hedges under US GAAP,[11] for which it is clear that ineffectiveness should be recognised in profit or loss for under-hedges as well as over-hedges.

4.4   Hedges of a firm commitment to acquire a business

A firm commitment to acquire a business in a business combination cannot be a hedged item, except for foreign exchange risk (see 2.2.5 above).

Consider the situation where an entity with euro as its functional currency enters into a binding agreement to purchase a subsidiary in six months. The subsidiary's functional currency is the US dollar. The consideration is denominated in US dollars and is payable in cash. The entity decides to enter into a forward contract to buy US dollars for euros to hedge its foreign currency risk on the firm commitment. The following options exist and the entity may choose the most appropriate accounting treatment:

- Because the hedge is a *purchase* of US dollars, it is, arguably, not a fair value hedge of the acquisition, since the acquisition is itself naturally hedged for changes in the fair value in the US dollar – that is, the entity is committed to buy a group of US dollar denominated assets and liabilities for a price denominated in US dollars. Nevertheless, the entity may still designate the transaction as the hedged item in a fair value hedge relationship, *[IAS 39.87]*, although this may not make intuitive sense.

- The entity could instead designate the forward contract as a hedge of the cash flows associated with the committed purchase, which is a cash flow hedge. *[IAS 39.87]*.

- If the anticipated business combination in this example is only a highly probable forecast transaction and not a firm commitment, then the entity can only apply cash flow hedging.

If the transaction is a fair value hedge, then the carrying amount of the hedged item is adjusted for the gain or loss attributable to the hedged risk. Since separately identifiable assets acquired and liabilities assumed must be recognised on initial consolidation at fair value in the consolidated financial statements of the acquirer, it follows that the gain or loss attributable to the hedged risk must be included in the consideration paid. In other words, the impact of the hedge affects the calculation of goodwill, that is otherwise determined by the application of IFRS 3 – *Business Combinations* – see Chapter 9 at 6.[12]

During the hedging period, the effective portion of the gain or loss on a hedging instrument in a cash flow hedge is recognised in other comprehensive income. Upon initial recognition of the acquisition, gains or losses recognised in other comprehensive income may be:

- deferred in other comprehensive income until the goodwill acquired affects profit or loss; or

- included in the consideration paid for the business combination that is designated as the hedged item. *[IAS 39.98]*.

The adjusted carrying amount of goodwill, including the gain or loss from hedge accounting, will then be subject to the normal requirements to test for annual impairment (see Chapter 20 at 5).

Once the purchase price is paid and the transaction is completed, the entity is 'long' US dollars as a result of recognising the US dollar net assets of the acquired entity. Those net assets would then be eligible for net investment hedging which would require selling US dollars to create an eligible hedging instrument, for example by entering into a foreign currency forward (see 3.3 and 4.3 above).

5   QUALIFYING CONDITIONS FOR HEDGE ACCOUNTING

A hedging relationship qualifies for hedge accounting as set out at 4 above if, and only if, all of the following conditions are met:

- at the inception of the hedge there is formal designation and documentation both of the hedging relationship and the entity's risk management objective and strategy for undertaking the hedge;

- the hedge is expected to be highly effective in achieving offsetting changes in fair value or cash flows attributable to the hedged risk, consistently with the originally documented risk management strategy for that particular hedging relationship;

- a forecast transaction that is the subject of a cash flow hedge must be highly probable and must present an exposure to variations in cash flows that could ultimately affect net profit or loss;

- the effectiveness of the hedge can be reliably measured, i.e. the fair value or cash flows of the hedged item that are attributable to the hedged risk and the fair value of the hedging instrument can be reliably measured (see Chapter 14 for guidance on determining fair value and Chapter 48 at 2.6 for a discussion of when fair values may not be reliably measurable); and

- the hedge is assessed on an ongoing basis and determined actually to have been highly effective throughout the financial reporting periods for which the hedge was designated. *[IAS 39.88]*.

These conditions are considered in further detail in the remainder of this section.

5.1   Documentation and designation

The documentation supporting the hedge should include the identification of:

- the hedging instrument;
- the hedged item or transaction;
- the nature of the risk being hedged; and
- how the entity will assess the hedging instrument's effectiveness in offsetting the exposure to changes in the hedged item's fair value or cash flows attributable to the hedged risk. *[IAS 39.88(a)]*.

Designation of a hedge relationship takes effect prospectively from the date all of the criteria at 5 above are met. In particular, hedge accounting can be applied only from the date all of the necessary documentation is completed. Therefore, hedge relationships cannot be designated retrospectively. *[IAS 39.F.3.8]*.

Where an ongoing hedge relationship fails the retrospective effectiveness test (see 5.3.1 below), an entity is not precluded from redesignating the hedging instrument in a hedge of the same financial asset or liability. Therefore, hedge accounting may be obtained for a subsequent period in which the hedge is effective provided the hedge meets the requirements set out at 5 above.[13] This would require documentation as a new hedge relationship. Similarly, an instrument that has been dedesignated as a hedging instrument may be redesignated in a new hedge relationship for which the hedged item is the same or a different exposure provided all other conditions for hedge accounting are met.

Hedge designation need not take place at the time a hedging instrument is entered into. For example, a derivative contract may be designated and formally documented as a hedging instrument any time after entering into the derivative contract. Hedge accounting will apply prospectively from designation, provided all other conditions are met. *[IAS 39.F.3.9]*. However, there is often a hidden danger when designating a derivative as a hedging instrument subsequent to its inception. For non-option derivatives, such as forwards or interest rate swaps, any fair value is likely to create 'noise' in a hedge effectiveness assessment that may not be fully offset by changes in the hedged item, especially in the case of a cash flow hedge. Consequently, there is likely to be more ineffectiveness recognised and, in extremis, could cause the hedge not be regarded as highly effective (see 5.3.5 below). Only by coincidence will a derivative still have a fair value that is zero, or close to zero, which would minimise this problem.

5.1.1   *Business combinations*

In a business combination accounted for using the purchase method of accounting where the acquiree has designated hedging relationships, the question arises of whether the acquirer should:

*   be permitted to continue to apply the hedge accounting model to hedge relationships designated previously by the acquiree, assuming it is consistent with the acquirer's strategies and policies; or

*   be required to re-designate hedge relationships at the acquisition date.[14]

IFRS 3 provides guidance that in order to obtain hedge accounting in their consolidated financial statements, acquirers are required to redesignate the acquiree's hedges. *[IFRS 3.15, 16(b)]*. Further, the acquirer should not recognise in its consolidated financial statements any amounts in equity in respect of any cash flow hedges of the acquiree relating to the period prior to acquisition. Redesignating the hedge relationships at the acquisition date means that if the hedging instrument has a fair value other than zero, it is likely that ineffectiveness will be introduced in a hedge that may have been nearly 100% effective prior to the acquisition. In fact, it is possible that a hedge relationship that would continue to be effective for the acquiree had the business combination not occurred will fail to qualify for hedge accounting in the acquirer's consolidated financial statements if the hedging instrument has a significant fair value at the acquisition date, particularly for cash flow hedges. To mitigate this, the acquirer may, subsequent to the combination, choose to settle the hedging instruments and replace them with more effective ones.

5.1.2   Dynamic hedging strategies

The standard explains that a dynamic hedging strategy that assesses both the intrinsic value and time value of an option contract can qualify for hedge accounting. *[IAS 39.74]*. The implementation guidance explains that this allows the use of a delta-neutral hedging strategy as well as other dynamic hedging strategies under which the quantity of the hedging instrument is constantly adjusted in order to maintain a desired hedge ratio (e.g. to achieve a delta-neutral position, insensitive to changes in the fair value of the hedged item), to qualify for hedge accounting. For example, a portfolio insurance strategy that seeks to ensure that the fair value of the hedged item does not drop below a certain level, while allowing the fair value to increase, may qualify for hedge accounting. *[IAS 39.F.1.9]*.

For a dynamic hedging strategy to qualify for hedge accounting, the documentation must specify how the hedge will be monitored and updated and how effectiveness will be measured. In addition, the entity must be able to track properly all terminations and redesignations of the hedging instrument, in addition to demonstrating that all other criteria for hedge accounting are met. Also, the entity must demonstrate that the hedge is expected to be highly effective for a specified short period of time during which adjustment of the hedge is not expected. *[IAS 39.F.1.9]*. However, this does not mean that no ineffectiveness will arise.

This guidance is applicable when the quantity of the hedging instrument is constantly adjusted in order to maintain a desired hedge ratio for the existing hedged item(s), often referred to as a closed portfolio. Accounting for dynamic risk management of open portfolios, to which new exposures are frequently added, existing exposures mature, where frequent changes also occur to the hedged item(s), and the associated risk is managed directly was the subject of a Discussion Paper DP/2014/1 – *Accounting for Dynamic Risk management: A Portfolio Revaluation Approach to Macro Hedging* (see at 6 below).

5.2   Forecast transactions

In the case of a hedge of a forecast transaction, the documentation should identify the date on, or time period in which, the forecast transaction is expected to occur. This is because, in order to qualify for hedge accounting:

- the hedge must relate to a specific identified and designated risk;
- it must be possible to measure its effectiveness reliably; and
- the hedged forecast transaction must be highly probable.

To meet these criteria, entities are not required to predict and document the exact date a forecast transaction is expected to occur. However, the time period in which the forecast transaction is expected to occur should be identified and documented within a reasonably specific and generally narrow range of time from a most probable date, as a basis for assessing hedge effectiveness. To determine that the hedge will be highly effective, it is necessary to ensure that changes in the fair value of the expected cash flows are offset by changes in the fair value of the hedging instrument. The implementation guidance suggests in one example that this test may be met only if the timing of the cash flows occur within close proximity to each other. *[IAS 39.F.3.11]*. However, the approach adopted elsewhere in the implementation guidance (see paragraph below) focuses more on the need to pass the effectiveness assessment, which would reflect differences in timing of the hedged and hedging cash flows.

If a forecast transaction such as a commodity sale is properly designated in a cash flow hedge relationship and, subsequently, its expected timing changes to an earlier (or later) period, this does not affect the validity of the original designation. If the entity can conclude that this transaction is the same as the one designated as being hedged, then hedge accounting may be able to continue. However, this is subject to passing the effectiveness assessment, which may well be affected by the change in timing, as the assessment would be based on the up to date expectation of the timing of the hedged forecast transaction (see 5.3.3 below). For example, if the forecast transaction was now expected earlier than originally thought, the hedging instrument will be designated for the remaining period of its existence, which will exceed the period to the forecast sale. *[IAS 39.F.5.4]*.

Further, hedged forecast transactions must be identified and documented with sufficient specificity so that when the transaction occurs, it is clear whether the transaction is, or is not, the hedged transaction. Therefore, a forecast transaction may be identified as the sale of the first 15,000 units of a specific product during a specified three-month period, but it could not be identified as the last 15,000 units of that product sold because they cannot be identified when they occur. For the same reason, a forecast transaction cannot be specified solely as a percentage of sales or purchases during a period. *[IAS 39.F.3.10]*.

Finally, the standard requires a forecast transaction that is the subject of a cash flow hedge to be 'highly probable'. The implementation guidance explains that this term indicates a *much* greater likelihood of happening than the term 'more likely than not' (a term used throughout the IASB's work to describe, or define, 'probable'). The guidance states that probability should be supported by observable facts and attendant circumstance and should not be based solely on management intent, because intentions are not verifiable. In making this assessment, consideration should be given to the following circumstances:

- the frequency of similar past transactions;
- the financial and operational ability to carry out the transaction;
- substantial commitments of resources to a particular activity, e.g. a manufacturing facility that can be used in the short run only to process a particular type of commodity;
- the extent of loss or disruption of operations that could result if the transaction does not occur;
- the likelihood that transactions with substantially different characteristics might be used to achieve the same business purpose, e.g. there are several ways of raising cash ranging from a short-term bank loan to a public share offering; and
- the entity's business plan.

The length of time until a forecast transaction is projected to occur is also a consideration in determining probability. Other factors being equal, the more distant a forecast transaction is, the less likely it is to be considered highly probable and the stronger the evidence that would be needed to support an assertion that it is highly probable. For example, a transaction forecast to occur in five years may be less likely to occur than a transaction forecast to occur in one year. However, forecast interest payments for the next 20 years on variable-rate debt would typically be highly probable if supported by an existing contractual obligation.

In addition, other factors being equal, the greater the physical quantity or future value of a forecast transaction in proportion to transactions of the same nature, the less likely it is that the transaction would be considered highly probable and the stronger the evidence that would be required to support such an assertion. For example, less evidence would generally be needed to support forecast sales of 100,000 units in the next month than 950,000 units when recent sales have averaged 950,000 units for each of the past three months. *[IAS 39.F.3.7]*.

The implementation guidance uses the following example to elaborate on this:

Example 51.34:   Hedge of foreign currency revenues

An airline operator uses sophisticated models based on past experience and economic data to project its revenues in various currencies. If it can demonstrate that forecast revenues for a period of time into the future in a particular currency are 'highly probable', it may designate the future revenue stream in a cash flow hedge.

However, it is unlikely that 100% of revenues for a future year could be reliably predicted. On the other hand, it is possible that a portion of predicted revenues, normally those expected in the short-term, will meet the 'highly probable' criterion. *[IAS 39.F.2.4]*.

It is also explained that cash flows arising after the prepayment date on an instrument that is prepayable at the issuer's option may be highly probable for a group or pool of similar assets for which prepayments can be estimated with a high degree of accuracy, e.g. mortgage loans, or if the prepayment option is significantly out of the money. In addition, the cash flows after the prepayment date may be designated as the hedged item if a comparable option exists in the hedging instrument. *[IAS 39.F.2.12]*.

The implementation guidance states that a history of having designated hedges of forecast transactions and then determining that the forecast transactions are no longer expected to occur, calls into question both the ability to accurately predict forecast transactions and the propriety of using hedge accounting in the future for similar forecast transactions. *[IAS 39.F.3.7]*. This is clearly common sense, however the standard contains no prescriptive 'tainting' provisions in this area akin to those applied to held-to-maturity investments (see Chapter 45 at 3.3). Therefore, entities are not automatically prohibited from using cash flow hedge accounting if a forecast transaction fails to occur. Instead, whenever such a situation arises the particular facts, circumstances and evidence should be assessed to determine whether doubt has, in fact, been cast on an entity's ongoing hedging strategies.

5.3   Assessing hedge effectiveness

One of the fundamental requirements of IAS 39 is that to use hedge accounting, the hedge must be an effective one. To this end, hedge effectiveness is defined as:

> 'the degree to which changes in the fair value or cash flows of the hedged item that are attributable to a hedged risk are offset by changes in the fair value or cash flows of the hedging instrument.' *[IAS 39.9]*.

There is little doubt that demonstrating the effectiveness of a hedge can be one of the most challenging aspects of IAS 39. The assessment of a hedge's effectiveness has the potential to be an extremely difficult exercise, involving the use of complex statistical techniques and valuation models of which many accountants have, at best, only limited experience. All of this is not helped by the fact that the IASB has provided very limited practical guidance on how to go about testing effectiveness and the IFRS Interpretations Committee has shied away from developing application guidance in this area.[15]

5.3.1 Basic requirements

Three of the qualifying conditions for hedge accounting involve hedge effectiveness as follows:

- the entity should expect the hedge to be highly effective in achieving offsetting changes in fair value or cash flows attributable to the hedged risk, consistently with the originally documented risk management strategy for that particular hedging relationship;

- the effectiveness of the hedge can be reliably measured, i.e. the fair value or cash flows of the hedged item that are attributable to the hedged risk and the fair value of the hedging instrument can be reliably measured; and

- the hedge should be assessed on an ongoing basis and determined actually to have been highly effective throughout the financial reporting periods for which the hedge was designated. [IAS 39.88].

Qualification for hedge accounting is based on an expectation of future (prospective) effectiveness, the objective of which is to ensure there is firm evidence to support an expectation of high effectiveness, and an evaluation of actual (retrospective) effectiveness. [IAS 39.BC136, BC136B]. The application guidance explains that a hedge is regarded as highly effective only if both of the following conditions are met:

(a)   at the inception of the hedge, and in subsequent periods, the hedge is expected to be highly effective in achieving offsetting changes in fair value or cash flows attributable to the hedged risk during the period for which the hedge is designated.

Such an expectation can be demonstrated in various ways, including a comparison of past changes in the fair value or cash flows of the hedged item that are attributable to the hedged risk with past changes in the fair value or cash flows of the hedging instrument, or by demonstrating a high statistical correlation between the fair value or cash flows of the hedged item and those of the hedging instrument. A hedge ratio of other than one to one may be chosen in order to improve the effectiveness of the hedge (see 2.2.2 above); and

(b)   the actual results of the hedge are within a range of 80% to 125%.

For example, if actual results are such that the loss on the hedging instrument is €120 and the gain on the cash instrument is €100, offset can be measured by $120 \div 100$, which is 120%, or by $100 \div 120$, which is 83%. In this example, assuming the hedge meets the condition in (a), it would be concluded that the hedge has been highly effective. [IAS 39.AG105].

Chapter 51

Effectiveness should be assessed, at a minimum, at the time annual or interim financial reports are prepared. *[IAS 39.AG106]*. However, there is nothing to prevent effectiveness assessments being performed more frequently. In fact this might be desirable if there is a risk of the hedge ceasing to be considered highly effective (although the prospective test should ensure such a risk is actually very low). The sooner an ineffective hedge is identified, the sooner the accounting volatility that results from a failure to obtain hedge accounting can be managed. For example, following a failure, it might be possible to redesignate the hedge (perhaps with some adjustment to the hedging instrument) but hedge accounting for that new hedge relationship will be available only prospectively.

No single method for assessing hedge effectiveness is specified by IAS 39 – the method used will depend on the entity's risk management strategy adopted. For example, if the risk management strategy is to adjust the amount of the hedging instrument periodically to reflect changes in the hedged position, it needs to be demonstrated that the hedge is expected to be highly effective only for the period until the amount of the hedging instrument is next adjusted. *[IAS 39.AG107]*.

Hedge effectiveness may also be assessed on a pre-tax or after-tax basis. If effectiveness is to be assessed on an after-tax basis, this should be designated at inception as part of the formal documentation of the hedging strategy. *[IAS 39.F.4.1]*.

In some cases, an entity will adopt different methods for different types of hedges. The documentation of its hedging strategy should include its procedures for assessing effectiveness and those procedures should state whether the assessment will include all of the gain or loss on a hedging instrument or whether the time value of the instrument is excluded (see 2.1.4 above). *[IAS 39.AG107]*.

The appropriateness of a given method will depend on the nature of the risk being hedged and the type of hedging instrument used. The method must be reasonable and consistent with other similar hedges unless different methods are explicitly justified. An entity is required to document, at the inception of the hedge, how effectiveness will be assessed and then to apply that effectiveness test on a consistent basis for the duration of the hedge. Several mathematical techniques can be used including ratio analysis, i.e. a comparison of hedging gains and losses to the corresponding gains and losses on the hedged item at a point in time, and statistical measurement techniques such as regression analysis (see 5.3.6 below). If regression analysis is used, the entity's documented policies for assessing hedge effectiveness must specify how the results of the regression will be assessed. *[IAS 39.F.4.4]*.

Expected hedge effectiveness may be assessed on a cumulative basis if that is how the hedge is designated and that condition is reflected in the hedging documentation. Therefore, even if a hedge is not expected to be highly effective in a particular period, hedge accounting is not precluded if effectiveness is expected to remain sufficiently high over the life of the hedging relationship. *[IAS 39.F.4.2]*. Whether hedge effectiveness is to be assessed on a cumulative or period to period basis should form part of the hedge documentation.

Example 51.35: Cumulative hedge effectiveness

A company designates an interest rate swap linked to LIBOR as a hedge of a borrowing whose interest is a UK base rate plus a margin. The UK base rate changes, perhaps, once each quarter or less, in increments of 25 to 50 basis points, while LIBOR changes daily. Over a one to two year period, the hedge is expected to be highly effective. However, there will be quarters when the UK base rate does not change at all while LIBOR has changed significantly. This would not necessarily preclude hedge accounting. *[IAS 39.F.4.2]*.

The time value of money will generally need to be considered in assessing the effectiveness of a hedge. The fair value of an interest rate swap derives from its net settlements and the fixed and variable rates on a swap can be changed without affecting the net settlement if both are changed by the same amount. In other words, a pay-7% fixed, receive-LIBOR swap should have the same fair value as a pay-6% fixed, receive-LIBOR minus 1% swap with otherwise identical terms. Consequently, the fixed rate on a hedged item need not exactly match the fixed rate on a swap designated as a fair value hedge. Nor does the variable rate on an interest-bearing asset or liability need to be the same as the variable rate on a swap designated as a cash flow hedge. *[IAS 39.AG112]*.

In the case of interest rate risk, it is suggested that hedge effectiveness may be assessed by preparing a maturity schedule for financial assets and liabilities that shows the net interest rate exposure for each time period, provided that the net exposure is associated with a specific asset or liability (or a specific group of assets or liabilities or a specific portion of them) giving rise to the net exposure, and hedge effectiveness is assessed against that asset or liability. *[IAS 39.AG111]*. The macro-hedging models (see 6 below) have their origins in just such an approach.

An important point to note is that the method used in the *assessment* of hedge *effectiveness* need not be the same as that used in the *measurement* (i.e. recognition in profit or loss) of hedge *ineffectiveness*. Therefore, even if the calculations used to measure ineffectiveness would not support a retrospective hedge effectiveness test performed using the 'dollar-offset' method (see 5.3.2 below), hedge accounting would not necessarily be precluded, provided the hedge passed the originally documented retrospective hedge effectiveness test, for example regression analysis (see 5.3.6 below).[16]

5.3.2 The 'dollar-offset' method

One method that may be used to assess hedge effectiveness is a comparison of hedging gains and losses to the corresponding gains and losses on the hedged item at a point in time. *[IAS 39.F.4.4]*.

This method essentially uses the mechanics of *measuring* hedge ineffectiveness set out at 4.1.1 and 4.2.1 above as a basis for *assessing* effectiveness. In other words, it compares the monetary amounts of the change in fair value of the hedging instrument with the monetary amount of the change in fair value or cash flows of the hedged item or transactions attributable to the hedged risk over the assessment period. To the extent that dividing these monetary amounts results in a fraction between 0.80 and 1.25, the hedge will be seen as highly effective on a retrospective basis. Largely because of the terminology used under US GAAP, this has become known as the 'dollar-offset' method.

The dollar-offset method is commonly used as a basis for assessing hedge effectiveness on an ongoing basis because it uses the calculations that have to be performed for determining the hedge accounting bookkeeping entries (i.e. measurement of hedge ineffectiveness), therefore it requires limited additional effort and is relatively easily understood.

Example 51.36 below contains a very comprehensive illustration of the dollar-offset method for a cash flow hedge that is based on the implementation guidance to IAS 39. Although it is somewhat esoteric, and many accountants will find the calculations difficult to follow, it is an important example. Particularly, it establishes two relatively practical methods of measuring ineffectiveness, and assessing effectiveness, for cash flow hedges. They are normally referred to as the 'hypothetical derivative method' and the 'change in fair value method' (which is what they are called under US GAAP).

As its name suggests, the hypothetical derivative method involves establishing a notional derivative that would be the ideal hedging instrument for the hedged exposure (normally an interest rate swap or forward contract with no unusual terms and a zero fair value at inception of the hedge relationship). The fair value of the hypothetical derivative is then used as a proxy for the net present value of the hedged future cash flows against which changes in value of the actual hedging instrument are compared to assess effectiveness and measure ineffectiveness.

Example 51.36:   Measuring effectiveness for a hedge of a forecast transaction in a debt instrument

A forecast investment in an interest-earning asset or forecast issue of an interest-bearing liability creates a cash flow exposure to interest rate changes because the related interest payments will be based on the market rate that exists when the forecast transaction occurs. The objective of a cash flow hedge of the exposure to interest rate changes is to offset the effects of future changes in interest rates so as to obtain a single fixed rate, usually the rate that existed at the inception of the hedge that corresponds with the term and timing of the forecast transaction. However, during the period of the hedge, it is not possible to determine what the market interest rate for the forecast transaction will be at the time the hedge is terminated or when the forecast transaction occurs.

During this period, effectiveness can be measured on the basis of changes in interest rates between the designation date and the interim effectiveness measurement date. The interest rates used to make this measurement are the interest rates that correspond with the term and occurrence of the forecast transaction that existed at the inception of the hedge and that exist at the measurement date as evidenced by the term structure of interest rates.

Generally it will not be sufficient simply to compare cash flows of the hedged item with cash flows generated by the derivative hedging instrument as they are paid or received, since such an approach ignores the entity's expectations of whether the cash flows will offset in subsequent periods and whether there will be any resulting ineffectiveness.

It is assumed that Company X expects to issue a €100,000 one-year debt instrument in three months. The instrument will pay interest quarterly with principal due at maturity. X is exposed to interest rate increases and establishes a hedge of the interest cash flows of the debt by entering into a forward starting interest rate swap. The swap has a term of one year and will start in three months to correspond with the terms of the forecast debt issue. X will pay a fixed rate and receive a variable rate, and it designates the risk being hedged as the LIBOR-based interest component in the forecast issue of the debt.

Yield curve

The yield curve provides the foundation for computing future cash flows and the fair value of such cash flows both at the inception of, and during, the hedging relationship. It is based on current market yields on applicable reference bonds that are traded in the marketplace. Market yields are converted to spot interest rates ('spot rates' or 'zero coupon rates') by eliminating the effect of coupon payments on the market yield. Spot rates are used to discount future cash flows, such as principal and interest rate payments, to arrive at their fair value. Spot rates also are used to compute forward interest rates that are used to compute the estimated variable future cash flows. The relationship between spot rates and one-period forward rates is shown by the following formula:

Spot-forward relationship

$$F = \frac{(1 + SR_t)^t}{(1 + SR_{t-1})^{t-1}} - 1$$

where   F = forward rate (%)

SR = spot rate (%)

t = period in time (e.g. 1, 2, 3, 4, 5)

It is assumed that the following quarterly-period term structure of interest rates using quarterly compounding exists at the inception of the hedge.

Yield curve at inception (beginning of period 1)

Forward periods	1	2	3	4	5
Spot rates	3.75%	4.50%	5.50%	6.00%	6.25%
Forward rates	3.75%	5.25%	7.51%	7.50%	7.25%

The one-period forward rates are computed on the basis of spot rates for the applicable maturities. For example, the current forward rate for Period 2 calculated using the formula above is equal to $[1.0450^2 \div 1.0375] - 1 = 5.25\%$. The current one-period forward rate for Period 2 is different from the current spot rate for Period 2, since the spot rate is an interest rate from the beginning of Period 1 (spot) to the end of Period 2, while the forward rate is an interest rate from the beginning of Period 2 to the end of Period 2.

Hedged item

In this example, X expects to issue a €100,000 one-year debt instrument in three months with quarterly interest payments. X is exposed to interest rate increases and would like to eliminate the effect on cash flows of interest rate changes that may happen before the forecast transaction takes place. If that risk is eliminated, X would obtain an interest rate on its debt issue that is equal to the one-year forward coupon rate currently available in the marketplace in three months. That forward coupon rate, which is different from the forward (spot) rate, is 6.86%, computed from the term structure of interest rates shown above. It is the market rate of interest that exists at the inception of the hedge, given the terms of the forecast debt instrument. It results in the fair value of the debt being equal to par at its issue.

At the inception of the hedging relationship, the expected cash flows of the debt instrument can be calculated on the basis of the existing term structure of interest rates. For this purpose, it is assumed that interest rates do not change and that the debt would be issued at 6.86% at the beginning of Period 2. In this case, the cash flows and fair value of the debt instrument would be as follows at the beginning of Period 2.

Issue of fixed rate debt (beginning of period 2) – no rate changes (spot based on forward rates)

	Total	1	2	3	4	5
Original forward periods		1	2	3	4	5
Remaining periods			1	2	3	4
Spot rates			5.25%	6.38%	6.75%	6.88%
Forward rates			5.25%	7.51%	7.50%	7.25%
	€		€	€	€	€
Cash flows:						
Fixed interest at 6.86%			1,716	1,716	1,716	1,716
Principal						100,000
Fair value:						
Interest*	6,592		1,694	1,663	1,632	1,603
Principal*	93,408					93,408
	100,000					

* cash flow discounted at the spot rate for the relevant period, e.g. fair value of principal is calculated as €100,000 ÷ (1 + [0.0688 ÷ 4])^4 = €93,408

Since it is assumed that interest rates do not change, the fair value of the interest and principal amounts equals the par amount of the forecast transaction. The fair value amounts are computed on the basis of the spot rates that exist at the inception of the hedge for the applicable periods in which the cash flows would occur had the debt been issued at the date of the forecast transaction. They reflect the effect of discounting those cash flows on the basis of the periods that will remain after the debt instrument is issued. For example, the spot rate of 6.38% is used to discount the interest cash flow that is expected to be paid in Period 3, but it is discounted for only two periods because it will occur two periods after the forecast transaction.

The forward interest rates are the same as shown previously, since it is assumed that interest rates do not change. The spot rates are different but they have not actually changed. They represent the spot rates one period forward and are based on the applicable forward rates.

Hedging instrument

The objective of the hedge is to obtain an overall interest rate on the forecast transaction and the hedging instrument that is equal to 6.86%, which is the market rate at the inception of the hedge for the period from Period 2 to Period 5. This objective is accomplished by entering into a forward starting interest rate swap that has a fixed rate of 6.86%. Based on the term structure of interest rates that exist at the inception of the hedge, the interest rate swap will have such a rate. At the inception of the hedge, the fair value of the fixed rate payments on the interest rate swap will equal the fair value of the variable rate payments, resulting in the interest rate swap having a fair value of zero. The expected cash flows of the interest rate swap and the related fair value amounts are shown as follows:

Interest rate swap

	Total	1	2	3	4	5
Original forward periods		1	2	3	4	5
Remaining periods			1	2	3	4
	€		€	€	€	€
Cash flows:						
Fixed interest at 6.86%			1,716	1,716	1,716	1,716
Forecast variable interest*			1,313	1,877	1,876	1,813
Forecast based on forward rate			5.25%	7.51%	7.50%	7.25%
Net interest			(403)	161	160	97

Fair value

Discount rate (spot)			5.25%	6.38%	6.75%	6.88%
Fixed interest	6,592		1,694	1,663	1,632	1,603
Forecast variable interest	6,592		1,296	1,819	1,784	1,693
Fair value of interest rate swap	0		(398)	156	152	90

* forecast variable rate cash flow based on forward rate, e.g. €1,313 = €100,000 × (0.0525 ÷ 4)

At the inception of the hedge, the fixed rate on the forward swap is equal to the fixed rate X would receive if it could issue the debt in three months under terms that exist today.

Measuring hedge effectiveness

If interest rates change during the period the hedge is outstanding, the effectiveness of the hedge can be measured in various ways.

Assume that interest rates change as follows immediately before the debt is issued at the beginning of Period 2 (this effectively uses the yield curve existing at Period 1 with a 200 basis point (2%) shift).

Yield curve assumption

Forward periods	*1*	*2*	*3*	*4*	*5*
Remaining periods		*1*	*2*	*3*	*4*
Spot rates		5.75%	6.50%	7.50%	8.00%
Forward rates		5.75%	7.25%	9.51%	9.50%

Under the new interest rate environment, the fair value of the pay-fixed at 6.86%, receive-variable interest rate swap that was designated as the hedging instrument would be as follows.

Fair value of interest rate swap

	Total					
Original forward periods		*1*	*2*	*3*	*4*	*5*
Remaining periods			*1*	*2*	*3*	*4*
	€		€	€	€	€
Cash flows:						
Fixed interest at 6.86%			1,716	1,716	1,716	1,716
Forecast variable interest			1,438	1,813	2,377	2,376
Forecast based on new forward rate			*5.75%*	*7.25%*	*9.51%*	*9.50%*
Net interest			(279)	97	661	660

	Total					
Original forward periods		*1*	*2*	*3*	*4*	*5*
Remaining periods			*1*	*2*	*3*	*4*
	€		€	€	€	€
Fair value						
New discount rate (spot)			5.75%	6.50%	7.50%	8.00%
Fixed interest	6,562		1,692	1,662	1,623	1,585
Forecast variable interest	7,615		1,417	1,755	2,248	2,195
Fair value of interest rate swap	1,053		(275)	93	625	610

In order to compute the effectiveness of the hedge, it is necessary to measure the change in the present value of the cash flows or the value of the hedged forecast transaction. There are at least two methods of accomplishing this measurement.

Method A – Compute change in fair value of debt

	Total		1	2	3	4	5
Original forward periods			1	2	3	4	5
Remaining periods				1	2	3	4
		€		€	€	€	€
Cash flows:							
Fixed interest at 6.86%				1,716	1,716	1,716	1,716
Principal							100,000
Fair value:							
New discount rate (spot)				5.75%	6.50%	7.50%	8.00%
Interest	6,562			1,692	1,662	1,623	1,585
Principal	92,385						*92,385
Total	98,947						
Fair value at inception	100,000						
Difference	(1,053)						

$* \text{€}100{,}000 \div (1 + [0.08 \div 4])^{4}$

Under Method A, a computation is made of the fair value in the new interest rate environment of debt that carries interest that is equal to the coupon interest rate that existed at the inception of the hedging relationship (6.86%). This fair value is compared with the expected fair value as of the beginning of Period 2 that was calculated on the basis of the term structure of interest rates that existed at the inception of the hedging relationship, as illustrated above, to determine the change in the fair value. Note that the difference between the change in the fair value of the swap and the change in the expected fair value of the debt (€1,053) exactly offset in this example, since the terms of the swap and the forecast transaction match each other.

Method B – Compute change in fair value of cash flows

	Total		1	2	3	4	5
Original forward periods			1	2	3	4	5
Remaining periods				1	2	3	4
Market rate at inception				6.86%	6.86%	6.86%	6.86%
Current forward rate				5.75%	7.25%	9.51%	9.50%
Rate difference				1.11%	(0.39%)	(2.64%)	(2.64%)
Cash flow difference (principal × rate)				€279	(€97)	(€661)	(€660)
Discount rate (spot)				5.75%	6.50%	7.50%	8.00%
Fair value of difference	(€1,053)			€275	(€93)	(€625)	(€610)

Under Method B, the present value of the change in cash flows is computed on the basis of the difference between the forward interest rates for the applicable periods at the effectiveness measurement date and the interest rate that would have been obtained if the debt had been issued at the market rate that existed at the inception of the hedge. The market rate that existed at the inception of the hedge is the one-year forward coupon rate in three months. The present value of the change in cash flows is computed on the basis of the current spot rates that exist at the effectiveness measurement date for the applicable periods in which the cash flows are expected to occur. This method also could be referred to as the 'theoretical swap' method (or 'hypothetical derivative' method) because the comparison is between the hedged fixed rate on the debt and the current variable rate, which is the same as comparing cash flows on the fixed and variable rate legs of an interest rate swap.

As before, the difference between the change in the fair value of the swap and the change in the present value of the cash flows exactly offset in this example.

Other considerations

There is an additional computation that should be performed to compute ineffectiveness before the expected date of the forecast transaction that has not been considered for the purpose of this illustration. The fair value difference has been determined in each of the illustrations as of the expected date of the forecast transaction immediately before the forecast transaction, i.e. at the beginning of Period 2. If the assessment of hedge effectiveness is performed before the forecast transaction occurs, the difference should be discounted to the current date to arrive at the actual amount of ineffectiveness. For example, if the measurement date were one month after the hedging relationship was established and the forecast transaction is now expected to occur in two months, the amount would have to be discounted for the remaining two months before the forecast transaction is expected to occur to arrive at the actual fair value. This step would not be necessary in the examples provided above because there was no ineffectiveness. Therefore, additional discounting of the amounts, which net to zero, would not have changed the result.

Under Method B, ineffectiveness is computed on the basis of the difference between the forward coupon interest rates for the applicable periods at the effectiveness measurement date and the interest rate that would have been obtained if the debt had been issued at the market rate that existed at the inception of the hedge. Computing the change in cash flows based on the difference between the forward interest rates that existed at the inception of the hedge and the forward rates that exist at the effectiveness measurement date is inappropriate if the objective of the hedge is to establish a single fixed rate for a series of forecast interest payments. This objective is met by hedging the exposures with an interest rate swap as illustrated in the above example. The fixed interest rate on the swap is a blended interest rate composed of the forward rates over the life of the swap. Unless the yield curve is flat, the comparison between the forward interest rate exposures over the life of the swap and the fixed rate on the swap will produce different cash flows whose fair values are equal only at the inception of the hedging relationship. This difference is shown in the table below.

	Total	1	2	3	4	5
Original forward periods		1	2	3	4	5
Remaining periods			1	2	3	4
Forward rate at inception			5.25%	7.51%	7.50%	7.25%
Current forward rate			5.75%	7.25%	9.51%	9.50%
Rate difference			(0.50%)	0.26%	(2.00%)	(2.25%)
Cash flow difference (principal × rate)			(€125)	€64	(€501)	(€563)
Discount rate (spot)			*5.75%*	*6.50%*	*7.50%*	*8.00%*
Fair value of difference	€1,055		(€123)	€62	(€474)	(€520)
Fair value of interest rate swap	€1,053					
Ineffectiveness	(€2)					

If the objective of the hedge is to obtain the forward rates that existed at the inception of the hedge, the interest rate swap is ineffective because the swap has a single blended fixed coupon rate that does not offset a series of different forward interest rates. However, if the objective of the hedge is to obtain the forward coupon rate that existed at the inception of the hedge, the swap is effective, and the comparison based on differences in forward interest rates suggests ineffectiveness when none may exist. Computing ineffectiveness based on the difference between the forward interest rates that existed at the inception of the hedge and the forward rates that exist at the effectiveness measurement date would be an appropriate measurement of ineffectiveness if the hedging objective is to lock in those forward interest rates. In that case, the appropriate hedging instrument would be a series of forward contracts each of which matures on a repricing date that corresponds with the date of the forecast transactions.

It also should be noted that it would be inappropriate to compare only the variable cash flows on the interest rate swap with the interest cash flows in the debt that would be generated by the forward interest rates. That methodology has the effect of measuring ineffectiveness only on a portion of the derivative, and IAS 39 does not permit the bifurcation of a derivative for the purposes of assessing effectiveness in this situation[17] – see 2.1.4 above. It is recognised, however, that if the fixed interest rate on the interest rate swap is equal to the fixed rate that would have been obtained on the debt at inception, there will be no ineffectiveness assuming that there are no differences in terms and no change in credit risk or it is not designated in the hedging relationship. *[IAS 39.F.5.5]*.

Although the calculations are set out in longhand, the above example is still simplified. The 'hypothetical derivative' method should not be seen as a method in its own right that results in zero ineffectiveness for a hedge with matching terms. There are likely to be elements that are relevant for determining the fair value of the hedging instrument, such as credit risk, that are either not present in the hedged item or that differ between the hedged item and the hedging instrument (see also 5.3.4 below and Chapter 52 at 5.3 and 6.4.2).

5.3.2.A   Law of small numbers

The dollar-offset method of assessing effectiveness is commonly used because it requires limited additional effort over and above that required to determine the amount of ineffectiveness to be recognised in profit or loss. However, there can be significant problems in achieving high correlation, particularly when the actual movements in fair value or cash flows of the hedging instrument and hedged item are both small.

Consider a fair value hedge of a fixed interest rate bond where interest rates barely change in the period. The change in fair value of the hedging instrument for the period might be €1,000 and the corresponding change in fair value of the hedged item €2,000, being an increase from €1,000,000 to €1,002,000. This would indicate that the hedging relationship was only 50% effective and would therefore not qualify for hedge accounting. However, the changes in fair value are very small in relation to the fair value of the contract being hedged. In fact, it might be possible to demonstrate that had interest rates moved by a more noticeable amount, the change in value of the hedged item and the hedging instrument would have been, say, €50,000 and €49,000 respectively, i.e. the strategy would actually have been highly effective. This scenario is often described as 'the law of small numbers' problem. Although well documented, the standard does not address this phenomenon and certainly offers no insight as to how an entity might deal with it.

A common approach, for the purposes of *assessing* hedge effectiveness, is simply to ignore changes in fair value that are below a given fixed limit (strictly, for the purpose of *measuring* ineffectiveness, these amounts should be recognised but they will not be material). This limit should be established at the inception of the hedge and should be included in the hedge documentation. Care should be taken in setting this limit – too high and the entity could be accused of not establishing an appropriate method of assessing effectiveness; too low and the risk of failing the assessment is increased.

5.3.3   Dollar-offset: comparison of spot rate and forward rate methods

It was explained at 2.1.4.B above that the spot and interest elements of a forward contract could be treated separately for the purposes of hedge designation. The next example, based on the implementation guidance, contrasts two variations of the dollar-offset method. Case 1 can be used when the whole of a forward contract is treated as the hedging instrument and the hedged risk is identified by reference to changes attributable to the forward rate (forward rate method). Case 2 can be used when the interest component is excluded and the hedged risk is identified by reference to changes attributable to the spot rate (spot rate method).

To demonstrate these methods, the implementation guidance uses a type of hedge that is very common in practice, the hedging of foreign currency risk associated with future purchases using a forward exchange contract. The example also illustrates the difference in the accounting for such hedges depending on whether the spot and interest elements of a forward contract are treated separately for the purposes of hedge designation.

Example 51.37: Cash flow hedge of firm commitment to purchase inventory in a foreign currency

Company A has the Local Currency (LC) as its functional and presentation currency. A's accounting policy is to apply basis adjustments to non-financial assets that result from hedged forecast transactions and it chooses to treat hedges of the foreign currency risk of a firm commitment as cash flow hedges.

On 30 June 2016, A enters into a forward exchange contract to receive Foreign Currency (FC) 100,000 and deliver LC109,600 on 30 June 2017 at an initial cost and fair value of zero. On inception, it designates the forward exchange contract as a hedging instrument in a cash flow hedge of a firm commitment to purchase a certain quantity of paper for FC100,000 on 31 March 2017 and, thereafter, as a fair value hedge of the resulting payable of FC100,000, which is to be paid on 30 June 2017. It is assumed that all hedge accounting conditions in IAS 39 are met.

The relevant foreign exchange rates and associated fair values for the forward exchange contract are provided in the following table:

Date	Spot rate	Forward rate to 30 June 2017	Fair value of forward contract
30 June 2016	1.072	1.096	–
31 December 2016	1.080	1.092	(388)
31 March 2017	1.074	1.076	(1,971)
30 June 2017	1.072	–	(2,400)

The applicable yield curve in the local currency is flat at 6% per annum throughout the period. The fair value of the forward exchange contract is negative LC388 on 31 December 2016 ($\{[1.092 \times 100,000] - 109,600\} \div 1.06^{(6/12)}$), negative LC1,971 on 31 March 2017 ($\{[1.076 \times 100,000] - 109,600\} \div 1.06^{(3/12)}$), and negative LC2,400 on 30 June 2017 ($1.072 \times 100,000 - 109,600$).

Case 1: Changes in the fair value of the forward contract are designated in the hedge

Ignoring ineffectiveness that may arise from other elements that have an impact on the fair value of the hedging instrument, the hedge is expected to be fully effective because the critical terms of the forward exchange contract and the purchase contract are otherwise the same. The assessments of hedge effectiveness are based on the forward price.

The accounting entries are as follows.

30 June 2016

	LC	LC
Forward	–	
Cash		–

To record the forward exchange contract at its initial fair value, i.e. zero.

31 December 2016

	LC	LC
Other comprehensive income	388	
Forward – liability		388

To recognise the change in the fair value of the forward contract between 30 June 2016 and 31 December 2016, i.e. $388 - 0 = LC388$, in other comprehensive income. The hedge is fully effective because the loss on the forward exchange contract, LC388, exactly offsets the change in cash flows associated with the purchase contract based on the forward price $\{([1.092 \times 100,000] - 109,600) \div 1.06^{(6/12)}\} - \{([1.096 \times 100,000] - 109,600) \div 1.06\} = -LC388$. The negative figure denotes a reduction in the net present value of cash outflows and, therefore, effectively represents a 'gain' to offset the loss on the forward in other comprehensive income.

31 March 2017

	LC	LC
Other comprehensive income	1,583	
Forward – liability		1,583

To recognise the change in the fair value of the forward contract between 1 January 2017 and 31 March 2017, i.e. $1,971 - 388 = LC1,583$, in other comprehensive income. The hedge is fully effective because the loss on the forward exchange contract, LC1,583, exactly offsets the change in cash flows associated with the purchase contract based on the forward price $\{([1.076 \times 100,000] - 109,600) \div 1.06^{(3/12)}\} - \{([1.092 \times 100,000] - 109,600) \div 1.06^{(6/12)}\} = -LC1,583$. The negative figure denotes a reduction in the net present value of cash outflows and, therefore, effectively represents a 'gain' to offset the loss on the forward in other comprehensive income.

	LC	LC
Paper (purchase price)	107,400	
Paper (hedging loss)	1,971	
Other comprehensive income		1,971
Payable		107,400

To record the purchase of the paper at the spot rate ($1.074 \times 100,000 = LC\,107,400$) and remove the cumulative loss on the forward recognised in other comprehensive income from equity, LC1,971, and include it in the initial measurement of the purchased paper. Accordingly, the initial measurement of the purchased paper is LC 109,371 consisting of a purchase consideration of LC 107,400 and a hedging loss of LC 1,971. The payable is recorded as a foreign currency monetary item of FC100,000, equivalent to LC107,400 ($100,000 \times 1.074$) on initial recognition.

30 June 2017

	LC	LC
Payable	107,400	
Cash		107,200
Profit or loss		200

To record the settlement of the payable at the spot rate ($100,000 \times 1.072 = LC107,200$) and recognise the associated exchange gain of $LC200 = 107,400 - 107,200$ in profit or loss.

	LC	LC
Profit or loss	429	
Forward – liability		429

To recognise the loss on the forward exchange contract between 1 April 2017 and 30 June 2017, i.e. $2,400 - 1,971 = LC429$) in profit or loss. The hedge is considered to be fully effective because the loss on the forward exchange contract, LC429, exactly offsets the change in the fair value of the payable based on the forward price [1.072 × 100,000] − 109,600 − {([1.076 × 100,000] − 109,600) ÷ 1.06$^{(3/12)}$} = −LC429. The negative figure denotes a reduction in the net present value of the payable and, therefore represents a gain to offset the loss on the forward contract.

	LC	LC
Forward – liability	2,400	
Cash		2,400

To record the net settlement of the forward exchange contract.

Although this arrangement has been set up to be a 'perfect hedge', the loss on the forward in the last three months is significantly different from the exchange gain recognised on retranslating the hedged payable. The principal reason for this is that the change in the fair value of the forward contract includes changes in its interest element, as well as its currency element, whereas the payable is translated at the spot foreign exchange rate. [IAS 21.23(a)].

Case 2: Changes in the spot element of the forward contract only are designated in the hedge

Ignoring ineffectiveness that may arise from other elements that have an impact on the fair value of the hedging instrument, the hedge is expected to be fully effective because the critical terms of the forward exchange contract and the purchase contract are the same and the change in the premium or discount on the forward contract is excluded from the assessment of effectiveness.

30 June 2016

	LC	LC
Forward	–	
Cash		–

To record the forward exchange contract at its initial fair value, i.e. zero.

31 December 2016

	LC	LC
Profit or loss (interest element of forward)	1,165	
Other comprehensive income (spot element)		777
Forward – liability		388

To recognise the change in the fair value of the forward contract between 30 June 2016 and 31 December 2016, i.e. 388 − 0 = LC388. The change in the present value of spot settlement of the forward exchange contract is a gain of LC777 = {([1.080 × 100,000] − 107,200) ÷ 1.06$^{(6/12)}$} − {([1.072 × 100,000] − 107,200) ÷ 1.06}), which is recognised in other comprehensive income. The change in the interest element of the forward exchange contract (the residual change in fair value) is a loss of LC1,165 = 388 + 777, which is recognised in profit or loss. The hedge is fully effective because the gain in the spot element of the forward contract, LC777, exactly offsets the change in the purchase price at spot rates {([1.080 × 100,000] − 107,200) ÷ 1.06$^{(6/12)}$} − {([1.072 × 100,000] − 107,200) ÷ 1.06} = LC777. The positive figure denotes an increase in the net present value of cash outflows and, therefore, effectively represents a 'loss' to offset the gain on the forward in other comprehensive income.

31 March 2017

	LC	LC
Other comprehensive income (spot element)	580	
Profit or loss (interest element)	1,003	
Forward – liability		1,583

To recognise the change in the fair value of the forward contract between 1 January 2017 and 31 March 2017, i.e. 1,971 − 388 = LC1,583. The change in the present value of spot settlement of the forward exchange contract is a loss of LC580 = {([1.074 × 100,000] − 107,200) ÷ 1.06$^{(3/12)}$} − {([1.080 × 100,000] − 107,200) ÷ 1.06$^{(6/12)}$}, which is recognised in other comprehensive income. The change in the interest element of the forward contract (the residual change in fair value) is a loss of LC1,003 = 1,583 − 580), which is recognised in profit or loss. The hedge is fully effective because the loss in the spot element of the forward contract, LC580, exactly offsets the change in the purchase price at spot rates {([1.074 × 100,000] − 107,200) ÷ 1.06$^{(3/12)}$} − {([1.080 × 100,000] − 107,200) ÷ 1.06$^{(6/12)}$} = −LC580. The negative figure denotes a reduction in the net present value of cash outflows and, therefore, effectively represents a 'gain' to offset the loss on the forward in other comprehensive income.

	LC	LC
Paper (purchase price)	107,400	
Other comprehensive income	197	
Paper (hedging gain)		197
Payable		107,400

To recognise the purchase of the paper at the spot rate (1.074 × 100,000 = LC 107,400) and remove the cumulative gain on the spot element of the forward contract that has been recognised in other comprehensive income (777 − 580 = LC197) and include it in the initial measurement of the purchased paper. Accordingly, the initial measurement of the purchased paper is LC107,203 consisting of a purchase consideration of LC107,400 and a hedging gain of LC197.

30 June 2017

	LC	LC
Payable	107,400	
Cash		107,200
Profit or loss		200

To record the settlement of the payable at the spot rate (100,000 × 1.072 = LC107,200) and recognise the associated exchange gain of LC200 (= − [1.072 − 1.074] × 100,000) in profit or loss.

	LC	LC
Profit or loss (spot element)	197	
Profit or loss (interest element)	232	
Forward – liability		429

To recognise the change in the fair value of the forward between 1 April 2017 and 30 June 2017, i.e. 2,400 − 1,971 = LC429). The change in the present value of spot settlement of the forward exchange contract is a loss of LC197 = {[1.072 × 100,000] − 107,200 − {([1.074 × 100,000] − 107,200) ÷ 1.06$^{(3/12)}$}, which is recognised in profit or loss. The change in the interest element of the forward contract (the residual change in fair value) is a loss of LC232 = 429 − 197, which is recognised in profit or loss. The hedge is fully effective because the loss in the spot element of the forward contract, LC197, exactly offsets the gain on the payable reported using spot rates = {[1.072 × 100,000] − 107,200 − {([1.074 × 100,000] − 107,200) ÷ 1.06$^{(3/12)}$} = −LC197. The negative figure denotes a reduction in the net present value of the payable and, therefore represents a gain to offset the loss on the forward contract.

	LC	LC
Forward – liability	2,400	
Cash		2,400

To record the net settlement of the forward exchange contract.

The following table provides an overview of the components of the change in fair value of the hedging instrument over the term of the hedging relationship. It illustrates that the way in which a hedging relationship is designated affects the subsequent accounting for that hedging relationship, including the assessment of hedge effectiveness and the recognition of gains and losses. *[IAS 39.F.5.6].*

Period ending	Change in spot settlement LC	Fair value of change in spot settlement LC	Change in forward settlement LC	Fair value of change in forward settlement LC	Fair value of change in interest element LC
30 June 2016	–	–	–	–	–
31 December 2016	800	777	(400)	(388)	(1,165)
31 March 2017	(600)	(580)	(1,600)	(1,583)	(1,003)
30 June 2017	(200)	(197)	(400)	(429)	(232)
Total	–	–	(2,400)	(2,400)	(2,400)

Ignoring ineffectiveness that may arise from elements that affect the fair value of the hedging instrument only or that may be different from the hedged item to the hedging instrument, both designations result in effective hedges as a result of the way effectiveness is measured. However, there is a significant difference in profit or loss. In part (a) all gains and losses on the forward are recognised in other comprehensive income when designated as a cash flow hedge whereas in part (b) changes in the fair value of the interest element of the forward are immediately recognised in profit or loss. The example also sets out how a single hedge can initially be a cash flow hedge of the future sale and then become a fair value hedge of the associated payable, provided it is documented as such.

The example also indicates that the time value of money is relevant for the assessment of effectiveness even when the spot element is designated in a hedge relationship. However, diversity in practice exists with respect to discounting of the spot element for hedge effectiveness purposes. This is perhaps because in many circumstances the effect of discounting the revaluation of the spot element is not be material.

5.3.4 The impact of the hedging instrument's credit quality

The application guidance to IAS 39 states that a hedge of interest rate risk using a derivative would not be fully effective if part of the change in the fair value of the derivative is attributable to the counterparty's credit risk. *[IAS 39.AG109].* The implementation guidance explains that when assessing effectiveness, both at inception and thereafter, the risk of counterparty default should be considered. For a fair value hedge, the implications of this guidance are clear. If there is a change in the derivative counterparty's creditworthiness, the hedging instrument's fair value will change but there is unlikely to be an offsetting change in fair value for the hedged item. This will affect its effectiveness as measured and should also be taken into account in the assessment of whether it continues to qualify for hedge accounting. *[IAS 39.F.4.3].*

For a cash flow hedge, the implications of the guidance are slightly less clear. The application guidance noted above is included within a section of the standard titled 'Assessing hedge effectiveness'. This strongly suggests that it is applicable to the assessment of cash flow hedges as well as to their measurement (for which the credit risk of the counterparty is certainly something to be taken into account – see Example 51.32 above).

Some might argue that, to qualify for hedge accounting, the test is that the hedging instrument will be highly effective in achieving offsetting changes in fair value *or cash flows* attributable to the hedged risk. *[IAS 39.88(b), 88(d), AG105(a)]*. Further, in the context of a cash flow hedge, the implementation guidance explains that, if default becomes probable, the hedging relationship is unlikely to achieve offsetting cash flows and hedge accounting will be discontinued. *[IAS 39.F.4.3]*. Together, these might suggest that the assessment of a cash flow hedge's effectiveness should be affected only by significant changes in the counterparty's credit risk, i.e. where default became probable. This is the approach US GAAP adopts. Under US GAAP, if a hedged cash flow is probable of occurring, hedge accounting is permitted and changes in the risk of non-performance (e.g. credit spreads) within certain ranges, all of which still reflect the cash flow remaining probable of occurring, are not relevant to the measurement of hedge ineffectiveness because they will not *change* the amount of the ultimate cash flow or represent a source of variability. In other words, as long as the cash flows remain probable overall, changes in degrees of probability, as long as overall probability can still be asserted, are not measured under any of the three permitted methods for measuring ineffectiveness in cash flow hedges.[18] Each method contains accommodations for cash flow hedges that are intended to eliminate the generation of hedge ineffectiveness attributable to the use of different yield curves for measuring cash flows related to the hedged item and the derivative. These accommodations involve utilizing the *same* credit adjusted discount curve for both the derivative and the hedged item in all three methods. However, there is no equivalent guidance in IAS 39. Also, some would view ignoring changes in the credit risk component of a hedging instrument's fair value as inappropriately excluding a portion of the hedging instrument from the hedge relationship (see 2.1.4 above).

We note that the application guidance of IFRS 9 states in the context of the 'hypothetical derivative' method that one cannot include features in the value of the hedged item that only exist in the hedging instrument, but not in the hedged item. Arguably, both the hedged item and the hedging instrument include credit risk. However, the credit risk in the hedged item is likely to be different from the credit risk in the hedging instrument. Consequently, at least when applying IFRS 9, credit risk also needs to be considered when assessing the effectiveness of cash flow hedges (see Chapter 52 at 5.3). *[IFRS 9.B6.5.5]*.

In addition to changes in the counterparty's credit risk, changes in the reporting entity's own credit risk may also affect the fair value of the hedging instrument in ways that are not replicated in the hedged item (see Chapter 52 at 5.3 and Chapter 14 at 11.3). The impact will be more pronounced where the hedging derivative is longer term, has a significant negative fair value and there exist no other credit enhancements such as collateral agreements or credit break clauses. Consequently, changes in the hedging instrument's fair value arising from the reporting entity's own credit risk will need to be considered when measuring hedge effectiveness and assessing the effectiveness of fair value hedges. The extent to which they need to be considered when assessing the effectiveness of a cash flow hedge is subject to the same uncertainties as noted further above.

During the financial crisis the IASB's Expert Advisory Panel acknowledged that, in practice, this is an area that had received limited attention by many entities, possibly because such changes in value have been considered insignificant or immaterial. However the financial crisis, which started in the second half of 2007, brought the related issues into focus as the fair values of some instruments were impacted to a greater extent by credit risk than they had historically and IFRS 13 is clear that credit risk should be taken into account when measuring the fair value of derivatives (see Chapter 14 at 11.3).

Nowadays, most over-the-counter derivative contracts between financial institutions are cash collateralised. Furthermore, current initiatives in several jurisdictions, such as, the European Market Infrastructure Regulation (EMIR) in the European Union or the Dodd-Frank Act in the United States, will result in more derivative contracts being collateralised by cash. Cash collateralisation significantly reduces the credit risk for both parties involved.

5.3.4.A   Discount rates for calculating the fair value of derivatives

Historically, the fair values of derivatives have been calculated using LIBOR-based swap curve as the discount factor, since it reflected the cost of funding for banks. However, the use of LIBOR as the standard discount rate ignores the fact that a number of derivative transactions are collateralised. For cash collateralised trades, a more relevant discount rate is an overnight rate rather than LIBOR.

While there has always been a difference between LIBOR and the overnight index swap (OIS) rates, the difference had historically been equal to a few basis points. However, the basis differential widened significantly during the 2008 financial crisis and is not expected to revert in the foreseeable future. Therefore, market participants generally consider an instrument's real cash flows including collateral, and OIS rate curves are generally being used to discount those derivatives that are fully cash collateralised. In other words, LIBOR (forward) rates are only used to project the future floating cash flows but the cash flows are then discounted using OIS rates.

The use of two different yield curves (often referred to as the 'multi curve issue') has an effect on the fair value of the derivative and therefore also can have an effect on hedge accounting if the derivative is used in a hedge accounting relationship:

- For fair value hedges, it is likely that there will be ineffectiveness. This is because different curves are used for the calculation of future floating cash flows and discounting the cash flows from the derivative, while only one curve is used for discounting the hedged item's fixed cash flows.

- In the case of cash flow hedges, the situation is less clear and comes back to the discussion about the use of the 'hypothetical derivative' method set out above at 5.3.4 above.

- A derivative that is novated to a central clearing party may as a result become cash collateralised (see 4.2.3.A above). The application guidance clarifies that the change in the fair value of the hedging instrument that results from the changes to the contract in connection with the novation (e.g. a change in the collateral arrangements) must be included in measurement of hedge ineffectiveness. This would also affect the hedge effectiveness assessment. *[IAS 39.AG113A].*

5.3.4.B   Currency basis risk in cross-currency interest rate swaps

Another phenomenon of the financial crisis is the increase in currency basis spreads. The currency basis is the charge above the risk-free rate in a foreign country to compensate for country and liquidity risk. Consequently, currency basis is sensitive to changes in the relative sovereign ratings of the two currencies involved. Historically, basis spreads had been low, but increased significantly after the financial crisis and the following sovereign crisis. Volatility in currency basis can create hedge ineffectiveness when using a cross currency interest rate swap (CCIRS) to hedge the foreign exchange and interest rate risk of a debt instrument issued in a foreign currency.

When designating the CCIRS in a fair value hedge, the gain or loss on the hedged item attributable to changes in the hedged interest rate risk is determined based on the foreign currency interest rate curve, therefore excluding currency basis. IAS 21 then requires such a monetary item in a foreign currency to be translated to the functional currency using the spot exchange rate. *[IAS 21.23].* Contrary, the fair value of the CCIRS incorporates the currency basis spread which results in ineffectiveness.

By contrast, IFRS 9 identifies cross currency basis spread as a 'cost of hedging' for which a new accounting approach was developed. Guidance in IFRS 9 permits an appropriate portion of the change in the fair value of cross currency basis spreads to be taken to OCI rather than immediately recognised in the profit, see Chapter 52 at 7.2.2.

5.3.5   Hedging using instruments with a non-zero fair value

The application guidance to IAS 39 states that a hedge of a highly probable forecast purchase of a commodity with a forward contract is likely to be highly effective if, among other things, the fair value of the forward contract at inception is zero *[IAS 39.AG108].* (see 5.3.8 below). A non-optional derivative, such as a forward or swap contract, that has a non-zero fair value is unlikely to be a perfectly effective hedging instrument, especially in a cash flow hedge. This is because the derivative contains a 'financing' element (the initial fair value), gains and losses on which will not be replicated in the hedged item and therefore the hedge contains an inherent source of ineffectiveness. In extreme cases it may not be possible to determine that the hedge will be highly effective. This situation can arise when a derivative is designated or redesignated in a hedging relationship subsequent to its initial recognition or in a business combination (see 5.1.1 above).[19]

5.3.6   Regression analysis and other statistical methods

The use of regression analysis is referred to in the standard in the context of optimising the ratio of hedging instrument quantities to hedged item quantities in order to improve the effectiveness of a hedge. *[IAS 39.AG100].* The implementation guidance also explains that statistical measurement techniques such as regression analysis may also be used for assessing hedge effectiveness. *[IAS 39.F.4.4].* This section sets out the basic concepts underlying linear regression analysis, together with guidelines and considerations that we believe are appropriate when determining whether a hedge relationship can be considered highly effective when using this approach to test effectiveness.

5.3.6.A   Basic concepts of regression

Linear regression is a method of identifying and describing the relationship between variables, for example y and x; linear refers to the assumption of a straight-line relationship between the variables. Regression analysis identifies a line of 'best fit' through a swarm of data using least squares analysis to minimise the total squared distances of the plotted points from the line. Some regression analyses will indicate a wider scatter of data points around the regression line than others; these wider scatters indicate a relationship between the variables that is less strong than a regression with a narrow scatter.

The regression is represented by the algebraic formula:

$$y = \alpha + \beta x + \varepsilon$$

In this equation, y is the dependent variable, x is the independent variable, α is the intercept, β is the slope of the regression line, and ε is the residual, or error term. In the context of hedge effectiveness, it is convenient to define y as the change in the fair value of the hedged item, and x as the change in fair value of the hedging instrument.

The following example of a regression describes the formula's terms in more detail:

Figure 51.1:   *The line of best fit, drawn through a series of correlated observations of changes in the x and y variables (such a line is likely to incorporate a non-zero intercept, if only due to random error)*

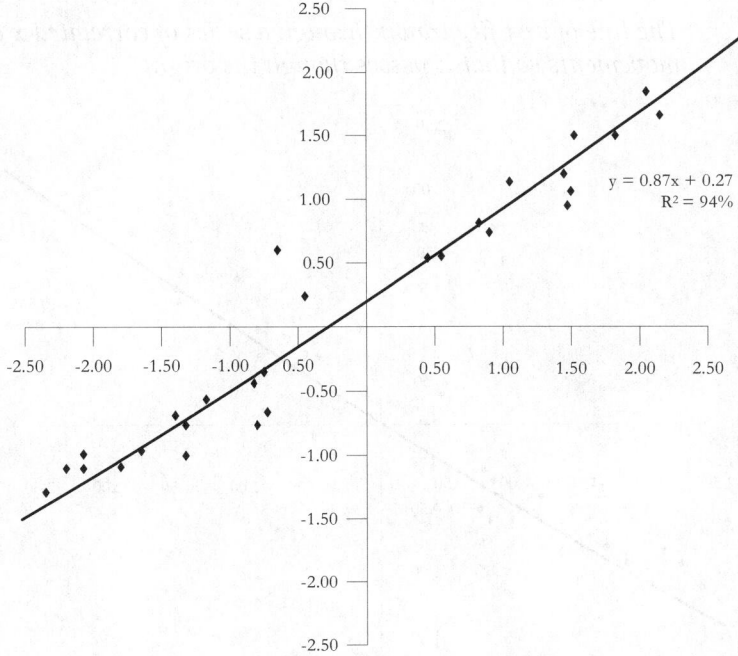

The coefficient of determination, R^2, is the percentage of the variance in y that is 'explained' by x, and is a measure of the tightness of the distribution around the regression line. In the example above, an R^2 value of 94% indicates that 94% of the variance in y can be explained by x. When assessing hedge effectiveness, the closer the line is to the actual results, the less ineffectiveness there will be. Higher R^2 values indicate a stronger relationship. The square root of this value, R, is often referred to as the coefficient of correlation. We consider that the value of R^2 should be at least 80% in order to indicate an effective hedge relationship.

The slope of the regression line is known as β or beta. In Figure 51.1 above, the slope of 0.87 indicates that, given an increase in x of 1, we would expect an increase in y of 0.87.

As noted at 2.2.2 above, IAS 39 describes a situation in which expected hedge effectiveness is maximised if the ratio between the hedging instrument and the hedged item is set at a level other than 1.00. In such circumstances it may be easier to demonstrate hedge effectiveness by multiplying the y observations by the hedge ratio so as to bring the slope closer to 1.

The intercept is the point at which the regression line crosses the y-axis – the expected value of y when x is 0. In Figure 51.1 above, the intercept is 0.27. The presence of a non-zero intercept increases the likelihood of hedge ineffectiveness, as it implies that y will change even when there is no change in x. While a small y intercept will not necessarily invalidate a hedging relationship, it is easier to demonstrate that a hedge is effective by forcing the line of regression to have a y intercept of zero, although this will reduce the value of R^2, and may also alter the slope. The chart below illustrates the impact of forcing the regression line through the origin. The effect is a reduction of the R^2 to 88% but (as described further below) an increase in the 'confidence' of the estimate.

Figure 51.2:   The line of best fit, drawn through a series of correlated x and y movements so that it passes though the origin

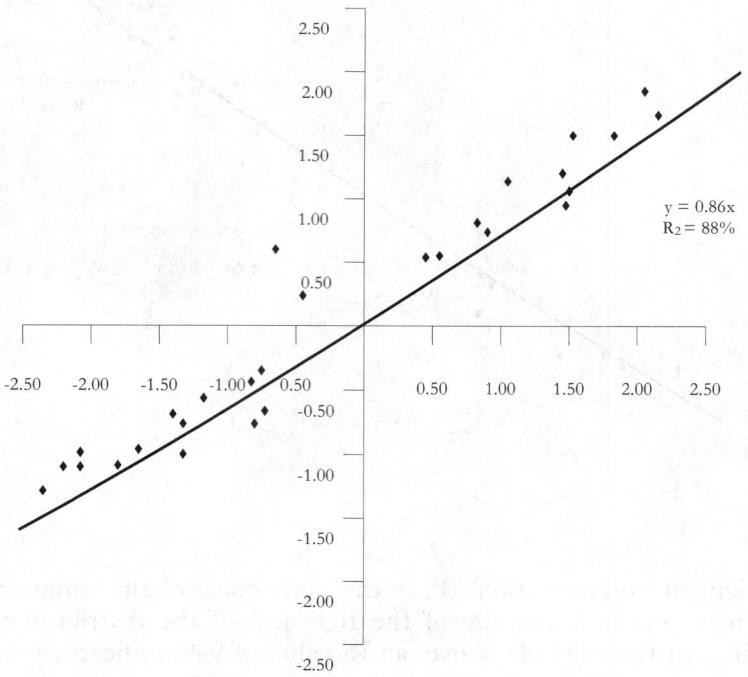

When performing regression analysis, an important notion is the concept of the sample as opposed to the population. The sample represents observations, whereas the population is the relationship between the variables that we are attempting to find. Estimates of the parameters of the population are based on the parameters of the sample. Statistical techniques can be used to express the confidence in the estimate.

For this reason, it is important to consider the statistical significance of the sample regression parameters: the degree to which the sample will provide an indication of the true (population) regression parameters. This will largely be driven by the number of data points sampled and the consistency between these points. Without some consideration of the confidence in the regression analysis, it is possible that a high R^2 could be calculated and an appropriate slope based on the sample (implying that a hedge will be highly effective), even though the sample is not a fair reflection of the population as a whole. If this were the case, it would not be appropriate to conclude that the hedge relationship will be highly effective, and there is a higher possibility of the hedge relationship failing to satisfy a retrospective test of effectiveness in future periods. In practice, when an entity enters into a new hedge relationship, it may not have the number of data points necessary to generate a reasonable population for regression analysis. In such situations, entities often generate additional data points by looking to periods prior to the inception of the hedge relationship. Effectively, the historic data points are used to help simulate how the hedge relationship would have performed under historically observed conditions, but this only makes sense provided such data is representative of those subsequent to inception. This issue is particularly relevant for relationships that include hedged items with an embedded floor within economies presently experiencing a negative interest rate environment but for which historically it was more common for positive interest rates to be applied, for example in some European countries – see Chapter 52 at 5.2.

There are a number of methods that can be used to assess the significance of the regression, including the sample size, T tests, F tests and P statistics. While these tests, when performed appropriately, are largely consistent, we recommend incorporating all tests into a single methodology to ensure sufficient statistical significance e.g. a 95% confidence that the actual population slope (as compared to the sample slope) is within the 80% to 125% range.

The following graph illustrates this concept. Regression theory explains that the slope follows a t-distribution, where the shape is largely determined by the number of data points available. Using this distribution, the likelihood of the true slope being within the 80% to 125% range can be determined. For example, Figure 51.3 illustrates a sample in which there is a 96.4% probability that the slope is within the desired range.

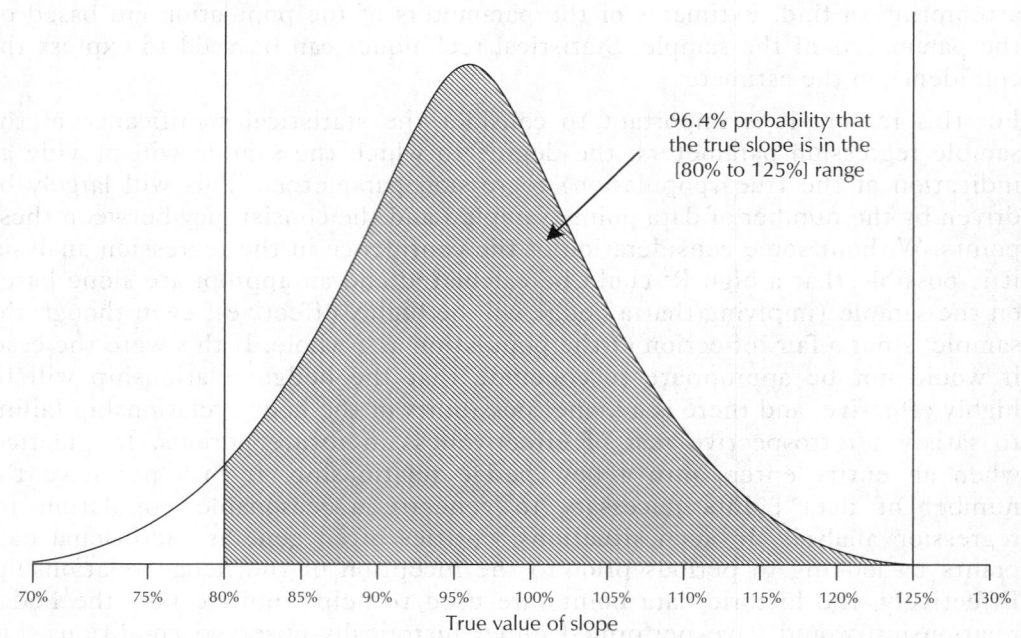

Figure 51.3:   The probability distribution of the true slope, for the given sample, follows a t-distribution, with a 96.4% probability that the slope is within the 80% to 125% range

The error term ε represents the unpredicted or unexplained variation in the hedged item. In a perfectly valid regression, the error terms should be normally distributed, with constant variance, and should be independent of each other (i.e. should have no 'autocorrelation'[20]). This is an impossible expectation for real market data as financial markets almost always incorporate autocorrelation of some sort. However the imperfections most likely to invalidate regression conclusions, such as significant trends, are less likely to occur in financial price data due to the existence of arbitrage activities that take advantage of such inefficiencies.

Finally, when considering whether to use regression analysis, we believe that there must be a logical, a priori, expectation of a relationship between the relevant variables (sometimes referred to as causality). It would be inappropriate to establish a hedge relationship based solely on statistics, as there is a greater possibility of the hedge relationship being coincidental or temporary, and so breaking down in the future if it has no ongoing economic or intuitive rationale. In fact, the hedge accounting requirements under IFRS 9 explicitly require an economic relationship between the hedged item and the hedging instrument to qualify for hedge accounting (see Chapter 52 at 5.2).

5.3.6.B   Summary

In order to assess a hedge relationship as highly effective (either on a prospective or retrospective basis) using regression analysis, we believe that all of the following criteria should normally be met:

- the line of best fit passes through the origin;
- the value of R^2 is at least 80%;
- there is at least 95% confidence that the true population slope of the line is within the 80% to 125% range; and
- there is an intuitive economic rationale for the hedge relationship.

Whilst a regression analysis that does not comply with these guidelines is not necessarily invalid, in such circumstances, consideration should be given so that inappropriate reliance on the regression analysis is avoided.

Finally, the IFRS Interpretations Committee concluded that if regression analysis, as the originally documented method for assessing the hedge's retrospective hedge effectiveness, demonstrated that a hedge had been effective but a 'dollar-offset' test would have fallen outside of the 80-125% range, hedge accounting would not necessarily be precluded.[21] However, in such instances, care should be taken to ensure that the regression analysis remains valid, especially if the dollar-offset comparison regularly falls outside of the range.

5.3.7   'Short-cut method'

Under US GAAP, an entity is allowed to assume that there will be no ineffectiveness in a hedge of interest rate risk using an interest rate swap as the hedging instrument, provided specified criteria are met. This is known as the 'short-cut method' for assessing hedge effectiveness. [IAS 39.BC132]. The original version of IAS 39 precluded such an approach and during the improvements project many commentators urged the IASB to permit the use of the short-cut method under IAS 39. [IAS 39.BC133]. However, one of the general principles of IAS 39 is that ineffectiveness in a hedging relationship is measured and recognised in profit or loss and the IASB did not want to make an exception to this principle. Therefore, IAS 39 was not amended to permit the short-cut method. [IAS 39.BC134].

5.3.8   'Critical terms match' approach

The application guidance explains that if the principal terms of the hedging instrument and of the hedged asset, liability, firm commitment or highly probable forecast transaction are the same, the changes in fair value and cash flows attributable to the risk being hedged may be likely to offset each other fully, both when the hedge is entered into and afterwards. For example, a hedge of a highly probable forecast purchase of a commodity with a forward contract is likely to be highly effective if:

- the forward contract is for the purchase of the same quantity of the same commodity at the same time and location as the hedged forecast purchase;
- the fair value of the forward contract at inception is zero; and
- either the change in the discount or premium on the forward contract is excluded from the assessment of effectiveness and included directly in profit or loss or the change in expected cash flows on the forecast transaction is based on the forward price for the commodity (see 5.3.3 above). [IAS 39.AG108].

Similarly, an interest rate swap is likely to be an effective hedge if the notional and principal amounts, term, repricing dates, dates of interest and principal receipts and payments, and basis for measuring interest rates are the same for the hedging instrument and the hedged item. *[IAS 39.AG108]*. However, an entity would of course have to consider other potential elements of ineffectiveness, such as the ones described at 5.3.4 above.

Sometimes the hedging instrument offsets only part of the hedged risk. For example, if the hedging instrument and hedged item are denominated in different currencies that do not move in tandem, the hedge would not be fully effective. *[IAS 39.AG109]*.

In deciding not to permit the short-cut method, the IASB noted that IAS 39 permits the hedging of portions of financial assets and liabilities in cases where US GAAP does not. Therefore, an entity may hedge a portion of a financial instrument (e.g. interest rate risk – see 2.2.1 above) and if the critical terms of the hedging instrument and the hedged item are the same, the entity will, in many cases, recognise no ineffectiveness. *[IAS 39.BC135]*. The implementation guidance continues with this theme and explains that, to improve hedge effectiveness, an entity may designate only certain risks in an overall exposure as being hedged. For example, if an interest rate swap issued by a counterparty with a AA credit rating is used to hedge the fair value of a fixed interest rate debt instrument, designating only the exposure in the debt related to AA rated interest rate movements will reduce the impact on effectiveness of market changes in the debt counterparty credit spreads. *[IAS 39.F.4.7]*.

Therefore it can be seen, at least for hedges of financial items, that the designation of the hedge can be tailored to reduce the ineffectiveness that can feasibly occur, sometimes significantly. However, because ineffectiveness may still arise as a result of other attributes (e.g. liquidity of the hedging instrument or its credit risk – see 5.3.4 above), hedge effectiveness cannot be assumed throughout the life of the hedge even if the principal terms of the hedging instrument and hedged item are the same. *[IAS 39.F.4.7]*.

It is clear from the guidance discussed above that IAS 39 acknowledges a method of assessing *prospective* hedge effectiveness that involves comparing the critical terms of the hedging instrument and the hedged item, supplemented by a qualitative review of counterparty credit risk and other factors such as liquidity and credit risk of the hedging instrument (a 'critical terms match' approach). US GAAP also allows a 'critical terms match' approach to be used for retrospectively assessing the effectiveness of cash flow hedges,[22] but the lack of any equivalent guidance in IAS 39 has led some to say that a quantitative assessment is always necessary.

In fact the extent of testing that is required to qualify for hedge accounting is not an accounting question, but more a regulatory issue. We have seen increasing evidence of financial reporting (and auditing) regulators setting their own benchmarks as to what they consider to be appropriate methods to use in practice, with many being reluctant to accept retrospective assessments based on the matching of critical terms and other qualitative factors. Recent years have seen new challenges to the use of seemingly simple methods for assessing hedge effectiveness, including:

- the emergence of the multi-curve issue in determining the fair value of derivatives (see 5.3.4.A above);

- a widening of basis risk spreads within cross-currency interest rate swaps (see 5.3.4.B above) and the IASB's identification of basis risk as a source of hedge ineffectiveness in the hedge accounting requirements of IFRS 9 (see Chapter 52 at 7.2.2); and

- the increased impact of credit risk on the fair value of derivatives, including an explicit requirement in IFRS 13 to take account of credit risk, including the reporting entity's own credit risk, when estimating fair values (see Chapter 14 at 11.3).

These make it increasingly difficult to justify the use of such methods and whilst they have sometimes been accepted by regulators in the past, we would advise strong caution against their continued use. In general, a quantitative method will give rise to a much lower risk of challenge than a qualitative method. The risk is heightened because, if it is determined that the selected method of assessing effectiveness is inappropriate, then hedge accounting should arguably never have been applied even if the hedge was demonstrably effective by other means such as a simple dollar-offset calculation (an approach the SEC appears to follow rigorously).[23]

5.3.9   Interest accruals and 'clean' versus 'dirty' values

Another problem that entities can face when assessing the effectiveness of hedging instruments such as interest rate swaps, is the fair value 'noise' that is generated between interest rate reset dates. The payments on an interest rate swap are typically established at the beginning of a reset period and paid at the end of that period. Between these two dates the swap is no longer a pure pay-fixed receive-variable (or *vice versa*) instrument because both the next payment and the next receipt are fixed. Accordingly, the corresponding changes in the fair value of the hedged item (e.g. fixed rate debt) will not strictly mirror that of the swap. This problem becomes more acute the less frequently variable interest rates are reset to market rates.

The IASB does not seem to see this as a potential source of ineffectiveness. For example, it is stated in IAS 39 that 'an interest rate swap is likely to be an effective hedge if the notional and principal amounts, term, repricing dates, dates of interest and principal receipts and payments, and basis for measuring interest rates are the same for the hedging instrument and the hedged item.' *[IAS 39.AG108]*. Further, given the IASB's statements (see 5.3.7 above) regarding the decision not to permit the short-cut method, which is only available for hedge relationships involving interest rate swaps, it seems safe to assume that they do not normally expect ineffectiveness from interest rate repricings to arise on such relationships where the hedge is 'perfect'. In fact, it is interesting to note that the one comprehensive example showing the measurement of effectiveness of an interest rate swap (see Example 51.36 at 5.3.2 above) completely avoids this issue.

Entities are therefore left with little practical guidance in dealing with the ineffectiveness that results from hedges that seem highly effective. In deliberating the accounting for macro hedging (see 6 below) the IASB staff concluded that 'hedge ineffectiveness can arise from movements in the fair value of hedging instruments owing to changes in ... floating legs within hedging derivatives'.[24]

A common approach to avoid much of this noise is to use 'clean' fair values (which effectively ignore the effects of the next net settlement or interest payment) rather than 'dirty' fair values (which includes them) for assessment of effectiveness. The mathematics of an effectiveness assessment using this approach should mean there is a much lower likelihood of the hedge failing the test. This approach is likely to prove acceptable in many situations, especially where the interval between repricings is frequent enough, e.g. quarterly rather than yearly, so as to minimise the changes in fair value from the fixed net settlement or next interest payment.

However, ineffectiveness should always be measured and recognised in profit or loss. This ineffectiveness is likely to be more significant when interest are more volatile, as experienced by a number of entities during the 'credit crunch' starting in the second half of 2007.

5.3.10   Effectiveness of options

It was explained at 2.1.4.A above that the time value of an option may be excluded from the hedge relationship and, in many cases, this may make it easier to demonstrate the effectiveness of a hedge. In such cases, if the documented hedged risk is appropriately customised there will, in many cases, be no ineffectiveness to recognise, as set out in the following example.

Example 51.38:   Out of the money put option used to hedge an equity share

Company A has an investment in one hundred shares of Company Z. The share is classified as available-for-sale, therefore associated fair value gains and losses are recognised in other comprehensive income. The shares have a quoted price of £100 each and to partially protect itself against decreases in the share price, A acquires a put option, which gives it the right to sell one hundred shares in Z for £90 each.

A is permitted to designate changes in the option's intrinsic value as the hedging instrument. The changes in the intrinsic value of the option provide protection against the risk of variability in Z's share price below or equal to the strike price of the put of £90. For prices above £90, the option is out of the money and has no intrinsic value. Accordingly, gains and losses on the shares in Z for prices above £90 are not attributable to the hedged risk for the purposes of assessing hedge effectiveness and recognising gains and losses on the hedged item.

Therefore, changes in the fair value of the shares in Z are recognised in other comprehensive income if associated with variations in share price above £90. Changes in the fair value of the shares in Z associated with price declines below £90 form part of the designated fair value hedge and are recognised in profit or loss. Assuming the hedge is effective, those changes are offset by changes in the intrinsic value of the put, which are also recognised in profit or loss (see 4.1.1 above).

Changes in the time value of the put are excluded from the designated hedging relationship and recognised in profit or loss as they arise. *[IAS 39.F.1.10]*.

Under US GAAP, implementation guidance sets out a method of assessing effectiveness and measuring ineffectiveness of an entire option (i.e. including its time value) in certain cash flow hedges, which normally resulted in the measurement of no ineffectiveness.[25] This allows entities to recognise all changes in the fair value of an option (including the time value) in other comprehensive income until the hedged transaction affects profit or loss.

This guidance appears to be an exception to, rather than an interpretation of, the general principles of hedge accounting under US GAAP. Consequently, the use of this method was seen by many as incompatible with IAS 39. The topic was brought to the attention of the IFRS Interpretations Committee and in September 2007 the committee decided not to take the issue onto its agenda as the IASB's project on 'portions' would make it clear that such an approach is not allowed by IAS 39.[26]

The IASB's project resulted in amendments to IAS 39 being issued in July 2008 which added implementation guidance to the standard. The guidance reiterates that if the principal terms of a forecast transaction and an option are the same, excluding the time value of the option from the hedging instrument may result in a hedging relationship that is perfectly effective in achieving offsetting changes in cash flows attributable to the hedged one-sided risk. *[IAS 39.AG110A].*

Conversely, if a purchased option is designated in its entirety as the hedging instrument of a one-sided risk arising from a forecast transaction, the hedging relationship will not be perfectly effective. This is because the premium paid for the option includes time value and, as discussed at 2.1.4.A above, a designated one-sided risk does not include the time value of an option. Therefore, in this situation, there will be no offset between the cash flows relating to the time value of the option premium paid and the designated hedged risk. *[IAS 39.AG110B].*

5.3.11 Net investment hedges: identifying the effective portion

As set out at 3.3.1 above, IFRIC 16 explains that the hedged risk in a net investment hedge is defined by reference to the functional currency of a parent of the foreign operation that is the subject of the hedge. For the purpose of assessing effectiveness, the change in value of the hedging instrument in respect of foreign exchange risk should be computed by reference to the functional currency of this parent entity. *[IFRIC 16.15].* This change in value is also the amount that should be reclassified from equity to profit or loss if the hedged foreign operation is disposed of. *[IFRIC 16.16].*

Depending on where the hedging instrument is held, in the absence of hedge accounting the total change in its value might be recognised in profit or loss, in other comprehensive income, or both. *[IFRIC 16.15].* For example, consider the situation outlined in Example 51.22 above (see 3.3.1 above). In the absence of hedge accounting, the total US\$/€ foreign exchange difference on A's US\$300 million external borrowing would be recognised in P's consolidated financial statements as follows: *[IFRIC 16.AG5]*

- US\$/¥ spot foreign exchange rate change, translated to euro, in profit or loss, and

- ¥/€ spot foreign exchange rate change in other comprehensive income.

The interpretation states that the assessment of effectiveness should not be affected by where the change in value of the hedging instrument would be recognised. In applying hedge accounting, the total effective portion of the change should be included in other comprehensive income. *[IFRIC 16.15].* Nevertheless, the application guidance indicates that in certain situations there may be ineffectiveness recognised in profit or loss.

Consider the situation set out in Example 51.22 above. If A's borrowings were designated in a hedge of the €/US$ spot risk associated with P's net investment in C, the application guidance states that all of the €/US$ foreign exchange difference would, after the application of hedge accounting, be recognised in other comprehensive income and be included in the foreign currency translation reserve relating to C. The guidance says this is because the change in value of both the hedging instrument and the hedged item are computed by reference to the functional currency of P (euro) against the functional currency of C (US dollars). *[IFRIC 16.AG4, AG7].*

However, if the borrowing was designated as a hedge of the £/US$ spot foreign exchange risk between C and B, the guidance states that the total US$/€ foreign exchange difference on A's borrowing would instead be recognised in P's consolidated financial statements as follows: *[IFRIC 16.AG5]*

- the £/US$ spot foreign exchange rate change (the effective portion of the hedging instrument) in the foreign currency translation reserve relating to C;
- £/¥ spot foreign exchange rate change, translated to euro, in profit or loss; and
- ¥/€ spot foreign exchange rate change in other comprehensive income.

Finally, it states that if P held the US$ denominated borrowings and designated them in a hedge of the spot foreign exchange exposure (£/US$) between B and C, only the £/US$ part of the change in the value of the borrowings (the effective portion of the hedging instrument) would be included in P's foreign currency translation reserve relating to C. The remainder of the change (equivalent to the £/€ change on £159 million) would be included in P's consolidated profit or loss. *[IFRIC 16.AG12].*

The assessment of effectiveness is not affected by whether the hedging instrument is a derivative or a non-derivative instrument or by the method of consolidation. *[IFRIC 16.15, AG7].*

5.3.12   Net investment hedges: other practical issues

There can be a number of other issues surrounding what constitutes a valid net investment hedge and the remainder of this section deals with some of the other practical aspects of such hedges on the assumption that the hedge relationship is considered valid.

5.3.12.A   Non-derivative liabilities used as the hedging instrument

A foreign currency denominated non-derivative financial liability, such as a borrowing, can be used as the hedging instrument in a hedge of a net investment in a foreign operation. This can be seen as a pure 'accounting' hedge, i.e. the retranslation gain or loss on the borrowing (an accounting entry representing a part of its change in fair value that is accounted for on a continuous basis) can offset the retranslation gain or loss on the net investment (another accounting entry). In fact, if the liability is:

- denominated in the same currency as the functional currency of the hedged net investment;
- held by an entity with the same functional currency as the parent by which the hedged risk is defined;
- has an amortised cost that is lower than the net investment in the foreign operation; and
- is designated appropriately,

the hedge is likely to be perfectly effective in terms of the offsetting retranslation gains and losses on the liability and the hedged proportion of the net investment.

If a borrowing or similar liability is denominated in a different currency to the functional currency of the net investment, it may still be possible to designate it as the hedging instrument. However, it will need to be demonstrated that the two currencies are sufficiently correlated so that the hedging instrument is expected to result in offsetting gains and losses over the period that the hedge is designated. This might be the case if the two currencies are formally pegged or otherwise linked to one another or if the relevant exchange rates move in tandem because of, say, similarities in the underlying economies.

Even if such a hedge is highly effective, it is likely to result in some ineffectiveness. Under US GAAP it is suggested that the retranslation gains and losses on the actual instrument should be compared to those on a hypothetical non-derivative (e.g. a borrowing in the correct currency) with any difference recognised in profit or loss.[27] This approach should normally be acceptable under IAS 39, if applied in conjunction with the accounting requirements for net investment hedges (see 4.3 above).

5.3.12.B   Derivatives used as the hedging instrument

It is harder to determine what types of derivative may be used in a hedge of a net investment. The same definition of effectiveness applies to such hedges as to others, but what are the changes in the fair value or cash flows of the hedged item that are attributable to the hedged risk that are to be offset by changes in the fair value or cash flows of the hedging instrument? In many respects it is only an accounting entry that is being hedged but, unlike in 5.3.12.A above, the hedging instrument will be accounted for at fair value. Even for the simplest derivative that fair value is likely to reflect factors other than changes in the spot exchange rate.

Chapter 51

Under US GAAP a number of interpretations to ASC 815 have been issued setting out what types of derivative may be designated in a net investment hedge and how changes in the value of those derivatives should be accounted for. This guidance is summarised in the following table:[28]

Type of derivative	Method of assessing effectiveness under USGAAP*	
	Spot rate method	Forward rate method
Forward contract	Changes in value attributable to spot rate changes recognised in other comprehensive income Changes in value of interest element recognised in profit or loss	All changes in value (including interest element) recognised in other comprehensive income
Purchased option	Changes in intrinsic value recognised in other comprehensive income Changes in time value recognised in profit or loss	All changes in value (including time value) recognised in other comprehensive income
Cross-currency interest rate swap: both legs floating rate	Interest settlements accrued in profit or loss All other changes in value recognised in other comprehensive income	All changes in value (including interest settlements) recognised in other comprehensive income
Cross-currency interest rate swap: both legs fixed rate	Changes in value from retranslating notional at spot exchange rates recognised in other comprehensive income Interest settlements accrued in profit or loss Other changes in value (e.g. from changes in interest rates) recognised in profit or loss	All changes in value (including interest settlements) recognised in other comprehensive income
Cross-currency interest rate swap: one floating rate leg, one fixed	Hedge accounting not available	Hedge accounting not available

* one method to be applied consistently for all derivatives designated as hedges of a net investment.

This table assumes the contracts are denominated in the same currency as the functional currency of the hedged net investment and that there are no other sources of ineffectiveness. The applicability of this guidance to IAS 39 is considered below.

I   Forward currency contracts

It is very common for forward currency contracts to be used as the hedging instrument in a hedge of a net investment – in fact, this is the one example that is acknowledged in the implementation guidance. Therefore, applying the US GAAP guidance under IAS 39 seems relatively uncontroversial and has effectively been endorsed in IFRIC 16. *[IFRIC 16.15, AG2]*. However, implementation guidance in IAS 39 makes it clear that where the spot rate method is used (i.e. the interest element of the forward is excluded from the hedge relationship) the premium or discount cannot be amortised to profit or loss. *[IAS 39.F.6.4]*. Inevitably, therefore, some volatility will arise in profit or loss and the longer the term of the forward, the greater is the potential volatility.

Some may wonder why entities might choose the spot rate method over the forward rate method. Prior to the development of standards such as IAS 39, the interest element of a forward contract (and similar instruments) was commonly recognised as interest on an accruals basis. Depending on the relative interest rates of the two currencies in the forward, accounting for the interest element in this way could potentially result in a credit to profit or loss, which is clearly desirable from the perspective of preparers of the financial statements. Where an entity is prepared to accept the volatility associated with this method, a similar effect on profit or loss (over time) may be achieved by using the spot rate method.

If the forward contract is denominated in a different currency to the functional currency of the net investment it is likely that, at best, some ineffectiveness will arise (unless the link between the two currencies is perfect). Under US GAAP, a comparison of the forward contract with a hypothetical derivative (a forward contract in the right currency) would be made to measure the amount of ineffectiveness[29] and this approach would normally be acceptable under IAS 39.

II   Purchased options

The spot rate method involves designating the intrinsic value of a purchased option as the hedging instrument (i.e. its time value is excluded from the hedge relationship). This is clearly acceptable under IAS 39 (see 2.1.4.A and 5.3.10 above), although this will cause some volatility in profit or loss, which over time will always result in an expense being recognised in profit or loss as the time value decays.

Under the forward rate method applied under US GAAP, the whole option would be designated as the hedging instrument. However, as discussed at 5.3.10 above, designating the entire purchased option as the hedging instrument under IAS 39 is likely to result in high levels of ineffectiveness which could result in hedge failure. This is because no offset will arise for changes in the time value of the purchased option, as the time value is not a component of the hedged net investment. *[IAS 39.AG110B].*

III   Cross-currency interest rate swaps

Like forward contracts, these instruments are commonly used as hedging instruments in net investment hedges. At a conceptual level, it is easy to see that the changes in value of a cross-currency swap with two floating-rate legs are likely to offset the retranslation gains and losses of a net investment, provided the floating rate resets sufficiently frequently. It is also reasonably easy to see that a swap with one floating-rate leg and one fixed-rate leg is unlikely to provide the necessary offset because the fixed rate leg will give rise to changes in the swap's value that are unrelated to changes in exchange rates.

It is less easy to see that the change in value of a swap with two fixed-rate legs will provide a good hedge against the retranslation gains and losses (again the fixed-rate legs will give rise to changes in the swap's value that are unrelated to changes in exchange rates). However, such an instrument may be viewed as a combination of forward contracts, albeit ones that, individually, are likely to have non-zero fair values, which could be designated in a hedge of a net investment based on the forward rate method (see I above). Designating a fixed-for-fixed currency swap in a cash flow hedge based on the forward rate implies that the amount of hedged item would be equal to the sum of the undiscounted foreign currency interest and principal payments which would be higher than the notional amount of the swap. However, since the conceptual basis of a net investment hedge is not that clear, we do not think such designation by analogy to a cash flow hedge would be required.

The 'spot rate' treatment under US GAAP which permits changes in value other than the retranslation of the notional at spot exchange rates to be included in other comprehensive income, however, is generally considered to have limited technical merit. We believe that application of the US GAAP spot rate method as described for forward contracts is more appropriate.

5.3.12.C   Combinations of derivative and non-derivative instruments used as the hedging instrument

It is not uncommon for entities to hedge their net investments using synthetic foreign currency debt instruments. For example, consider a parent with the euro as its functional currency that has a net investment in a Japanese subsidiary with yen as its functional currency. The parent might borrow in US dollars and enter into a pay-Japanese yen, receive-US dollar cross-currency interest rate swap. In this way the two instruments might be considered a synthetic Japanese yen borrowing, although they are required to be accounted for separately (see Chapter 43 at 8).

As noted at 2.1.3 above, a combination of derivatives and non-derivatives may be viewed in combination and jointly designated as a hedging instrument under IAS 39. *[IAS 39.77].* However, all the hedging instruments must be clearly identified in the hedge documentation. *[IAS 39.88(a)].*

The Japanese parent in the above fact pattern may wish to designate the spot rate only when hedging a net investment with a combination of derivatives and non-derivatives (see 5.3.12.B III above). Designation of the combination as hedging a forward rate is more problematic given the issues noted in see 5.3.12.B III above and the fact that the hedging instrument includes a foreign currency monetary item for which the accounting for foreign exchange is at the spot rate. *[IAS 21.23(a)].*

Another alternative may be to notionally decompose the cross currency swap by introducing an interest bearing functional currency denominated leg and designating one part as a hedge of the borrowing and the other as a hedge of the net investment (see 2.1.4.E).

5.3.12.D   Individual or separate financial statements

It is common for an entity with an investment in a subsidiary, associate or joint venture to be party to a financial instrument (a borrowing, say) that in the entity's consolidated financial statements is designated as the hedging instrument in a hedge of its net investment in the subsidiary, associate or joint venture. However, in the entity's individual or separate financial statements, the investment will generally be accounted for as an asset measured at cost or as a financial asset in accordance with IAS 39. *[IAS 27.10].* In other words, it will not be accounted for by way of consolidation or the equity method.

Accordingly, from the perspective of the individual or separate financial statements, the reporting entity will not have a net investment in a foreign operation. Therefore, the borrowing could not be designated as the hedging instrument in a net investment hedge for the purposes of the separate financial statements. However, if hedge accounting is desirable, it may be possible to designate the borrowing as the hedging instrument in another type of hedge. Typically, this would be a fair value hedge of the foreign currency risk arising from the investment. This will be an independent hedge relationship, separate from the net investment hedge in the consolidated financial statements. Therefore, all of the other hedge accounting criteria (including the documentation requirements) will need to be met for this hedge too. Of course, the effects of this hedge accounting will need to be reversed when preparing the group's consolidated financial statements (otherwise those financial statements will reflect as an asset or liability certain changes in the fair value of a parent's investment in its subsidiary which would be contrary to the general principles of IFRS 10).

6 PORTFOLIO (OR MACRO) HEDGING

At a detailed level, the topic of portfolio (or macro) hedging for banks and similar financial institutions is beyond the scope of a general financial reporting publication such as this. However, no discussion of hedge accounting would be complete without an overview of the high level issues involved and an explanation of how the standard setters have tried to accommodate these entities.

The underlying philosophy of IAS 39's approach to hedge accounting is that individual hedging instruments are designated as hedging individual assets, liabilities or other risk exposures. However, banks and similar financial institutions typically manage their interest rate risk exposures dynamically on a portfolio (or macro) level. New exposures are frequently added to the portfolio and existing exposures mature. So as the net risk of the portfolio changes, risk managers will react accordingly to meet the risk management objective. Given that the focus is on the net risk position and natural offsets frequently arise as the exposures in the portfolio change, the distinction between hedged item and hedging instrument becomes less relevant. Accordingly, there is a fundamental difference between the risk management activities of the financial institution and the main hedge accounting requirements of the standard.

IAS 39 includes some specific guidance that was developed with a view to assist financial institutions in achieving hedge accounting for their portfolio interest rate risk management activities. This guidance is as follows:

- Fair value hedge of the interest rate exposure of a portfolio of financial assets or financial liabilities; *[IAS 39.78, 81A, 89A, 92, AG114-AG132, BC173-220, IE1-IE31, DO1-DO2]*

- Management of interest rate risk in financial institutions (colloquially known as the macro cash flow approach). *[IAS 39.F.6.1-F.6.3].*

Unfortunately, even with these two approaches, it is often difficult to accommodate the risk management activities of financial institutions within the IAS 39 hedge accounting requirements. In particular, there are significant restrictions on the way the fair value of financial liabilities with a demand feature are measured (see Chapter 14 at 11.5) and this effectively prevents banks from applying fair value hedge accounting to the majority of their current and deposit accounts (see 2.2.10 above). In fact, the EC endorsed version of IAS 39 has certain parts of the hedge accounting requirements carved out in a direct response to the cited difficulties of financial institutions achieving hedge accounting under IAS 39,[30] thereby allowing the use of hedge accounting in situations that the full version of IAS 39 would not.

In view of these factors, a project was set up by the IASB to develop a new accounting approach for dynamic risk management that would be based on an entity's risk management activities. This project was originally part of the IASB's project to replace IAS 39 with IFRS 9. However, the IASB realised that developing the new accounting model would take time and probably be a different concept from hedge accounting. In May 2012, the Board therefore decided to decouple the part of the project that related to accounting for dynamic risk management from IFRS 9, allowing more time to develop an accounting model without affecting the timeline for the completion of the other elements of IFRS 9.[31]

Although mainly focused on financial institutions, the accounting model for dynamic risk management might also be beneficial for some corporate entities applying macro-type hedging strategies.

In April 2014, the IASB issued the Discussion Paper – *Accounting for Dynamic Risk Management: a Portfolio Revaluation Approach to Macro Hedging*. The six-month comment period ended in October 2014. Most respondents supported the need for the project, but there was no consensus on a solution. Given the diversity in views, in July 2015 the IASB concluded that the insights that it had received from the comment letters and feedback so far did not enable it to develop proposals for an exposure draft. Accordingly, the IASB decided that the project should remain in the research programme, with the aim of publishing a second discussion paper. The next step for the project will be to focus on identifying the information needed to provide more decision useful information on dynamic risk management.

References

1 For example, see IAS 39 (2000), *Financial Instruments: Recognition and Measurement*, IASC, December 1998 to October 2000, para. 10.
2 *IFRIC Update*, July 2007.
3 *IFRIC Update*, July 2007.

4 *Comments of Swiss International Air Lines Ltd. on Paragraphs 129 and 130 of the 'Exposure Draft of Proposed Amendments to IAS 39 Financial Instruments: Recognition and Measurement'*, Swiss International Air Lines Ltd, October 2002.

5 *IFRIC Update*, October 2004.

6 *IFRIC Update*, July 2009.

7 *DP/2014/1* 1.14 -1.15 and 3.9.1-3.9.16.

8 IGC Q&A 137-13.

9 *IFRIC Update*, January 2013.

10 Information for Observers (February 2007 IASB meeting), *Business Combinations II: Reassessments (Agenda Paper 2B)*, IASB, February 2007, para. 28 and Information for Observers (April 2007 IASB meeting), *Classification and Designation of Assets, Liabilities and Equity Instruments Acquired or Assumed in a Business Combination (Agenda Paper 2B)*, IASB, April 2007, item #5, table following para. 14.

11 ASC 815-35-35-1 through 35-26 (formerly, Statement 133 Implementation Issue H8, *Foreign Currency Hedges: Measuring the Amount of Ineffectiveness in a Net Investment Hedge*).

12 *IFRIC Update*, January 2011.

13 *IFRIC Update*, June 2005.

14 Information for Observers (February 2007 IASB meeting), *Business Combinations II: Reassessments (Agenda Paper 2B)*, IASB, February 2007, para. 25.

15 *IFRIC Update*, September 2006.

16 *IFRIC Update*, November 2006.

17 *IFRIC Update*, March 2007.

18 ASC 815-30-35-10 through 35-32 (formerly, Statement 133 Implementation Issue G7, *Cash Flow Hedges: Measuring the Ineffectiveness of a Cash Flow Hedge under Paragraph 30(b) When the Shortcut Method is not Applied*) and ASC 815-20-35-14 through 35-18 (formerly, Statement 133 Implementation Issue G10, *Cash Flow Hedges: Need to Consider Possibility of Default by the Counterparty to the Hedging Derivative*).

19 IAS 39.AG108, *IFRIC Update*, March 2007, Information for Observers (January 2007 IFRIC meeting), *IAS 39 Financial Instruments: Recognition and Measurement – Assessing Hedge Effectiveness of an Interest Rate Swap in a Cash Flow Hedge (Agenda Paper 14(v))*, IASB, January 2007, Information for Observers (February 2007 IASB meeting), *Business Combinations II: Reassessments (Agenda Paper 2B)*, IASB, February 2007, para. 29 and Information for Observers (April 2007 IASB meeting), *Classification and Designation of Assets, Liabilities and Equity Instruments Acquired or Assumed in a Business Combination (Agenda Paper 2B)*, IASB, April 2007, item #5, table following para. 14.

20 Autocorrelation is the correlation of a variable with itself (i.e. the risk of repeating patterns in the error term).

21 *IFRIC Update*, November 2006.

22 ASC 815-20-25-84 (formerly, SFAS 133.65).

23 Speech by SEC Staff, *Remarks Before the 2006 AICPA National Conference on Current SEC and PCAOB Developments by Timothy S. Kviz*, U.S. Securities and Exchange Commission, December 2006.

24 Staff paper 4A, paragraph 14, October 2012 IASB Meeting.

25 ASC 815-20-25-126 to 25-129, 55-209 through 55-211, 815-30-35-33 to 35-37 and 55-127 (formerly, Statement 133 Implementation Issue G20, *Cash Flow Hedges: Assessing and Measuring the Effectiveness of a Purchased Option Used in a Cash Flow Hedge*).

26 *IFRIC Update*, September 2007.

27 ASC 815-35-35-1 to 35-26 (formerly, Statement 133 Implementation Issue H8, *Foreign Currency Hedges: Measuring the Amount of Ineffectiveness in a Net Investment Hedge*).

28 ASC 815-35-35-1 to 35-26 (formerly, Statement 133 Implementation Issue H8, Question 1) and ASC 815-20-25-67 to 25-68A; 25-71 (formerly, Statement 133 Implementation Issue H9, *Foreign Currency Hedges: Hedging a Net Investment with a Compound Derivative That Incorporates Exposure to Multiple Risks*).

29 ASC 815-35-35-1 to 35-26 (formerly, Statement 133 Implementation Issue H8, Question 2).

30 IAS 39, *Financial Instruments: Recognition and Measurement, Regulation* No. 2086/2004, European Commission, 19 November 2004, paras. 35, AG107A, AG124(a) and AG130 and parts of paras. 81A, AG31, AG99C, AG99D, AG114(c) and (g), AG118, AG119(d), (e) and (f), AG121, AG122, AG124(d), AG126, AG127 and AG129.

31 *IASB Update*, May 2012.

Chapter 51

Chapter 52   Financial instruments: Hedge accounting (IFRS 9)

List of examples

Chapter 52

Chapter 52

Chapter 52   Financial instruments: Hedge accounting (IFRS 9)

1   INTRODUCTION

1.1   Background

The majority of the IASB's current work on financial instruments began in conjunction with the FASB as part of their Memorandum of Understanding,[1] when both Boards agreed to work jointly on a research project to reduce the complexity of the accounting for financial instruments. As part of this project, the Boards had a joint objective to simplify or eliminate the need for hedge accounting.[2] In March 2008 the IASB issued a discussion paper – *Reducing Complexity in Reporting Financial Instruments* – which contained many proposals, including a number related to hedge accounting.[3] Although this was not a joint IASB-FASB document, the FASB also published it so as to obtain input for its own efforts at simplifying the accounting for financial instruments.[4]

Meanwhile, the financial crisis resulted in a significant amount of political pressure being brought to bear on standard setters in general and the IASB specifically. Responding to this pressure, in April 2009 the IASB announced a detailed six-month timetable for publishing a proposal to replace IAS 39 – *Financial Instruments: Recognition and Measurement.*[5] In order to expedite the replacement of IAS 39, the IASB divided the project into three phases: classification and measurement; amortised cost and impairment of financial assets; and hedge accounting.

In December 2010, the IASB issued the Exposure Draft ('ED' or the exposure draft) *Hedge Accounting*, being the proposals for the third part of IFRS 9 – *Financial Instruments*. After redeliberating the proposals in 2011, in September 2012 the Board published a draft of *Chapter 6 – Hedge Accounting –* of IFRS 9, together with consequential changes to other parts of IFRS 9 and other IFRSs (the draft standard).

The idea of the draft standard was to enable constituents to familiarise themselves with the new requirements.[6]

Although the IASB did not ask for comments, a number of constituents asked the IASB to clarify certain elements of the draft standard. As a result, the IASB redeliberated some elements of the IFRS 9 hedge accounting requirements in its January 2013 and April 2013 meetings.

This resulted in the third version of IFRS 9, issued in November 2013, which included the new hedge accounting requirements. Finally, in July 2014 the IASB issued the all-encompassing final version of IFRS 9 that includes the new impairment requirements (see Chapter 49 at 5) and some amendments to the classification and measurement requirements (see Chapter 46). This also involved some minor consequential amendments to the hedge accounting requirements in IFRS 9, mainly because of the introduction of a new category for debt instruments measured at fair value through other comprehensive income with subsequent reclassification adjustments.

The standard does not provide any particular solutions specifically tailored to so-called 'macro hedge' accounting, the term used to describe the more complex risk management practices used by entities such as banks. In May 2012 the Board decided to decouple accounting for macro hedging from IFRS 9.[7] An accounting model specifically for macro hedging is being developed in a separate project and the discussion paper – *Accounting for Dynamic Risk Management: a Portfolio Revaluation Approach to Macro Hedging* – was published in April 2014 (see 3.6.5 below).

1.2   The main changes in the IFRS 9 hedge accounting requirements

Hedge accounting under IAS 39 is often criticised as being complex and rules-based, and thus, ultimately not reflecting an entity's risk management activities. This is unhelpful for preparers and users of the financial statements alike. The IASB took this concern as the starting point of its project for a new hedge accounting model. Consequently, the objective of IFRS 9 is to reflect the effect of an entity's risk management activities in the financial statements. *[IFRS 9.6.1.1]*.

This means that the new model specifically aims to provide a better linkage between an entity's risk management strategy and objective in and the impact of hedging on the financial statements. Because of this aim, it is important for an entity to understand the difference between the risk management strategy and risk management objective. The latter determines whether or not an entity can designate a hedging relationship or whether or not it needs to discontinue an existing hedging relationship. Risk management strategy and risk management objective are covered at 2 below, the general eligibility criteria are described at 5.1 below and the criteria for discontinuation at 6.3 below.

In addition, IFRS 9 widens the range of eligible hedged items. This is particularly helpful for non-financial institutions as it opens up the possibility for more hedging activities to meet the criteria for hedge accounting. It includes, for example, the possibility to designate an aggregated exposure which includes a derivative as the hedged item in a second hedging relationship (see 3.3 below). It also includes the possibility to designate non-financial risk components as the hedged risk. This was so far only possible for financial items (see 3.4 below). The standard also introduces further guidance related to hedging of layer components (see 3.4 below) and the hedging of groups of items including net positions (see 3.5 below).

Qualifying hedging instruments are covered at 4 below. Probably the most significant change related to hedging instruments is that under IFRS 9, entities are permitted to designate, as hedging instruments, non-derivative financial assets or non-derivative financial liabilities that are accounted for at fair value through profit or loss (see 4.2 below).

Perhaps the most significant change compared to IAS 39 is the replacement of rules as to whether a hedge relationship is eligible with more principle-based requirements. This includes deleting some of the arbitrary rules, such as the 80%-125% effectiveness requirement. The new effectiveness requirements are based only on whether there is an economic relationship and the effect of credit risk on that relationship. The effectiveness test is now only prospective and will normally be qualitative. The qualifying criteria are described at 5 and the subsequent assessment of the hedge effectiveness at 6.1 below.

It should be emphasised, however, that while the standard relaxes the criteria for hedge accounting, so that many more hedge relationships will qualify for hedge accounting and far fewer will 'fail', any actual ineffectiveness must continue to be measured and recognised in profit or loss.

In order to align hedge accounting further with actual risk management, the standard allows an entity to rebalance a hedging relationship should the hedged item and hedging instrument no longer offset each other to the extent originally expected, due to basis risk. In such cases, an entity can (or is even required to) adjust the quantity of the hedged item or hedging instrument on a prospective basis, such that the respective changes in the fair value are expected to offset in future periods. Rebalancing is covered in more detail at 6.2 below.

Further, IFRS 9 introduces the possibility that the time value of an option, the forward element of a forward contract and any foreign currency basis spread can be excluded from the designation of a financial instrument as the hedging instrument, and need to be (for the time value of option) or can be (for the forward points or the foreign currency basis spread) accounted for as 'costs of hedging'. This means that, instead of the fair value changes of these elements affecting profit or loss like a trading instrument, these amounts get allocated to profit or loss in a similar manner to transaction costs, while fair value changes are temporarily recognised in other comprehensive income. Cost of hedging is further covered at 7 below.

Chapter 52

Most of the basics of hedge accounting do not change as a result of IFRS 9. There are still three types of hedging relationships:

- fair value hedges;
- cash flow hedges; and
- hedges of net investments in foreign operations. *[IFRS 9.6.5.2]*.

Hedges of net investments in foreign operations must still be accounted for similarly to cash flow hedges. *[IFRS 9.6.5.13]*. There are only some consequential amendments to IFRIC 16 – *Hedges of a Net Investment in a Foreign Operation*.

While IFRS 9 does not significantly change how the different types of hedges are presented (see 8 below), it extends the range of disclosures an entity is required to provide. Consistent with the objective of the standard, the disclosures should allow the reader of the financial statements to understand the risk management of the entity, the amount, timing and uncertainty of future cashflows as well as the effect of hedge accounting on the financial position and performance of the entity. More information related to disclosures is provided at 9 below.

Hedge accounting remains optional and can only be applied to hedging relationships that meet the qualifying criteria (discussed at 5 below). *[IFRS 9.6.5.1]*. This means that an entity does not have to designate hedging relationships to the same extent or in exactly the same manner as it hedges for risk management purposes. The standard also introduces alternatives to hedge accounting such as the fair value option for credit risk exposures and a fair value option for own use contracts. Both alternatives are described at 10 below.

Rather than providing a comprehensive summary of hedge accounting, this chapter focuses on the differences between hedge accounting under IAS 39 and the hedge accounting requirements in IFRS 9. Therefore, much of what is discussed in Chapter 51 also applies to this chapter.

2   RISK MANAGEMENT

2.1   Objective of hedge accounting

Every entity is exposed to business risks from its daily operations. Many of those risks have an impact on the cash flows or the value of assets and liabilities, and therefore, ultimately affect profit or loss. In order to manage these risk exposures, companies often enter into derivative contracts (or, less commonly, other financial instruments) to hedge them. Hedging can therefore be seen as a risk management activity in order to change an entity's risk profile.

Applying the IFRS accounting requirements to those risk management activities can result in accounting mismatches, when the gains or losses on a hedging instrument are not recognised in the same period(s) and/or in the same place in the financial statements as gains or losses on the hedged exposure. Many believe that the resulting accounting mismatches are not a good representation of those risk management activities (see Chapter 51 at 1.2). The objective of the IFRS 9 hedge accounting requirements is to 'represent, in the financial statements, the effect of an entity's risk management activities'. The aim of the objective is 'to convey the context of hedging instruments for which hedge accounting is applied in order to allow insight into their purpose and effect'. *[IFRS 9.6.1.1]*. Similar to IAS 39, this is achieved by reducing the accounting mismatch by changing either the measurement or (in the case of certain firm commitments) recognition of the hedged exposure, or the accounting for the hedging instrument, but with some important improvements.

This is a rather broad objective that focuses on an entity's risk management activities and reflects what the Board wanted to achieve with the new accounting requirements. However, this broad objective does not override any of the hedge accounting requirements, which is why the Board noted that hedge accounting is only permitted if all the new qualifying criteria are met (see 5 below). *[IFRS 9.BC6.82]*.

2.2 Risk management strategy versus risk management objective

Linking hedge accounting with an entity's risk management activities requires an understanding of what those risk management activities are. IFRS 9 distinguishes between the *risk management strategy* and the *risk management objective*.

The *risk management strategy* is established at the highest level of an entity and identifies the risks to which the entity is exposed, and whether and how the risk management activities should address those risks. For example, a risk management strategy could identify changes in interest rates of loans as a risk and define a specific target range for the fixed to floating rate ratio for those loans. The strategy is typically maintained for a relatively long period of time. However, it may include some flexibility to react to changes in circumstances. *[IFRS 9.B6.5.24]*.

IFRS 9 refers to the risk management strategy as normally being set out in 'a general document that is cascaded down through an entity through policies containing more specific guidelines.' *[IFRS 9.B6.5.24]*. However, in our view, this does not need to be a formal written document in all circumstances. Small and medium-sized entities with limited risk management activities that use financial instruments may not have a formal written document outlining their overall risk management strategy that they have in place. In some instances, there might be an informal risk management strategy empowering an individual within the entity to decide on what is done for risk management purposes. In such situations entities do not have the benefit of being able to incorporate the risk management strategy in their hedge documentation by reference to a formal policy document, but instead have to include a description of their risk management strategy directly in their hedge documentation. Also, there are disclosure requirements for the risk management strategy that apply irrespective of whether an entity uses a formal written policy document as part of its risk management activities. Consequently, a more informal risk management strategy should be both reflected in the disclosures and 'compensated' by a more detailed documentation of the hedging relationships.

Chapter 52

The risk management strategy is an important cornerstone of the hedge accounting requirements in IFRS 9. Consequently, the Board added specific disclosure requirements to IFRS 7 – *Financial Instruments: Disclosures* – that should allow users of the financial statements to understand the risk management activities of an entity and how they affect the financial statements (see 9 below).

The *risk management objective,* on the contrary, is set at the level of an individual hedging relationship and defines how a particular hedging instrument is designated to hedge a particular hedged item. For example, this would define how a specific interest rate swap is used to 'convert' a specific fixed rate liability into a floating rate liability. Hence, a risk management strategy would usually be supported by many risk management objectives. *[IFRS 9.B6.5.24].*

Example 52.1:   Risk management strategies with related risk management objectives
The table below shows two examples of a risk management strategy with a related risk management objective.

Risk management strategy	Risk management objective
Maintain 40% of financial debt at floating interest rate	Designate an interest rate swap as a fair value hedge of a GBP 100m fixed rate liability
Hedge foreign currency risk of up to 70% of forecast sales in USD up to 12 months	Designate a foreign exchange forward contract to hedge the foreign exchange risk of the first USD 100 sales in March 2016

It is essential to understand the difference between the risk management strategy and the risk management objective, as a change in a risk management objective, or a specific action without a corresponding change in the risk management objective, may affect the ability to continue applying hedge accounting. Furthermore, voluntary discontinuation of a hedging relationship without a respective change in the risk management objective is not allowed. This is described at 6.3 below.

3   HEDGED ITEMS

3.1   General requirements

The general requirements of what qualifies as an eligible hedged item are unchanged compared to IAS 39. A hedged item can be:

- a recognised asset or liability;
- an unrecognised firm commitment;
- a highly probable forecast transaction; or
- a net investment in a foreign operation.

All of above can either be a single item or a group of items, provided the specific requirements for group of items are met (see 3.6 below). *[IFRS 9.6.3.1].*

Only assets, liabilities, firm commitments and forecast transactions with an external party qualify for hedge accounting. *[IFRS 9.6.3.5]*. As an exception, a hedge of the foreign currency risk of an intragroup monetary item qualifies for hedge accounting if that foreign currency risk affects consolidated profit or loss. In addition, the foreign currency risk of a highly probable forecast intragroup transaction would also qualify as a hedged item if that transaction affects consolidated profit or loss. *[IFRS 9.6.3.6]*. These requirements are unchanged from IAS 39 (for further details see Chapter 51 at 2.3.4).

As with IAS 39, the item being hedged must still be reliably measurable. *[IFRS 9.6.3.2]*. Also unchanged from IAS 39, a forecast transaction must be highly probable. *[IFRS 9.6.3.3]*.

However, what has changed in IFRS 9, compared to IAS 39, is how hedged items are designated in a hedging relationship. In particular, the designation of risk components and nominal components, and the designation of aggregated exposures and groups of items have changed. These changes, which should ultimately lead to more risk management activities qualifying for hedge accounting, all stem from the broader goal of the hedge accounting project, to better align an entity's risk management approach with the accounting outcome.

In the remainder of this section, we focus on changes in the designation of hedged items compared to IAS 39.

3.2   Hedges of exposures affecting other comprehensive income

Only hedges of exposures that could affect profit or loss qualify for hedge accounting. The sole exception to this rule is when an entity is hedging an investment in equity instruments for which it has elected to present changes in fair value in other comprehensive income (OCI), as permitted by IFRS 9. Using that election, gains or losses on the equity investments will never be recognised in profit or loss (see Chapter 49 at 2.2). *[IFRS 9.6.5.3]*.

For such a hedge, the fair value change of the hedging instrument is recognised in OCI. *[IFRS 9.6.5.8]*. Ineffectiveness is also recognised in OCI. *[IFRS 9.6.5.3]*. On sale of the investment, gains or losses accumulated in OCI are not reclassified to profit or loss (see Chapter 50 at 5). Consequently, the same also applies for any accumulated fair value changes on the hedging instrument, including any ineffectiveness.

3.3   Aggregated exposures

Entities often purchase or sell items (in particular commodities) that expose them to more than one type of risk. When hedging those risk exposures, entities do not always hedge each risk for the same time period. This is best explained with an example:

Example 52.2:   Aggregated exposure – copper purchase in a foreign currency

An entity manufacturing electrical wires is expecting to purchase copper in 12 months. The functional currency of the entity is euro (EUR). The copper price is fluctuating and is denominated in US dollars (USD), which is a foreign currency for the entity. The entity is exposed to two main risks, the copper price risk and the foreign exchange risk.

The entity first decides to hedge the copper price fluctuation risk, using a copper futures contract. By doing so, the entity now has a fixed-price copper purchase denominated in a foreign currency and is therefore still exposed to foreign exchange risk. (In this example we assume there is no 'basis risk' between the copper price exposures in the expected purchase and the futures contract, such as the effect of quality and the location of delivery).

Three months later, the entity decides to hedge the foreign exchange risk by entering into a foreign exchange forward contract to buy a fixed amount of USD in nine months. By doing so, the entity is hedging the aggregated exposure, which is the combination of the original exposure to variability of the copper price and the copper futures contract. The diagram below illustrates the two hedging relationships.

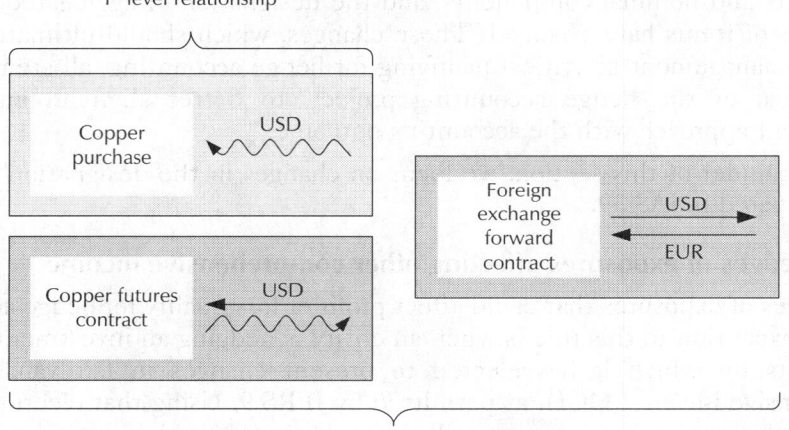

IAS 39 precludes derivatives from being designated as part of a hedged item for accounting purposes (see Chapter 51 at 2.2.7). Applying IAS 39 to the scenario in Example 52.2 above, an entity would have two choices:

- Discontinue the first hedging relationship (i.e. the copper price risk hedge) and re-designate a new relationship with joint designation of the copper futures contract and the foreign exchange forward contract as the hedging instrument. This is likely to lead to some 'accounting' hedge ineffectiveness as the copper futures contract will now have a non-zero fair value on designation of the new relationship (see Chapter 51 at 5.3.5).

- Maintain the copper price risk hedge and designate the foreign exchange forward contract in a second relationship as a hedge of the variable USD copper price. Even if the other IAS 39 requirements could be met, this means that the volume of hedged item is constantly changing as the variable copper price is hedged for foreign exchange risk, which will likely have an impact on the effectiveness of the hedging relationship.

IFRS 9 expands the range of eligible hedged items by including aggregated exposures that are a combination of an exposure that could qualify as a hedged item and a derivative. *[IFRS 9.6.3.4]*.

Consequently, in the scenario described in Example 52.2 above, the entity could designate the foreign exchange forward contract in a cash flow hedge of the combination of the original exposure and the copper futures contract (i.e. the aggregated exposure) without affecting the first hedging relationship. In other words, it would no longer be necessary to discontinue and re-designate the first hedging relationship.

It is important to keep in mind that the individual items in the aggregated exposure are accounted for separately, applying the normal requirements of hedge accounting (i.e. there is no change in the unit of account; the aggregated exposure is not treated as a 'synthetic' single item). For example, when hedging a combination of a variable rate loan and a pay fixed/receive variable interest rate swap (IRS), the loan would still be accounted for at amortised cost with the IRS presented separately in the statement of financial position. An entity would not be allowed to present the IRS and the loan (i.e. the aggregated exposure) together in one line item (i.e. as if it was one single fixed rate loan). *[IFRS 9.B6.3.4]*.

However, when assessing the effectiveness and measuring the ineffectiveness of a hedge of an aggregated exposure, the combined effect of the items in the aggregated exposure has to be taken into consideration. *[IFRS 9.B6.3.4]*. This is of particular relevance if the terms of the hedged item and the hedging instrument in the first hedging relationship do not perfectly match, e.g. if there is basis risk. Any ineffectiveness in the first level relationship would automatically also lead to some ineffectiveness in the second level relationship. However, this does not mean that the same ineffectiveness is recognised twice.

Basis risk, in the context of hedge accounting, refers to any difference in price sensitivity of the underlyings of the hedging instrument and the hedged item. Basis risk usually results in a degree of hedge ineffectiveness. For example, hedging a cotton purchase in India with NYMEX cotton futures contracts is likely to result in some ineffectiveness, as the hedged item and the hedging instrument do not share exactly the same underlying price.

The following two examples, partly derived from illustrative examples in the implementation guidance of IFRS 9, help explain the concept of a hedge of an aggregated exposure:

Example 52.3:   Fixed rate loan in a foreign currency – cash flow hedge of an aggregated exposure

An entity has a fixed rate borrowing denominated in a foreign currency (FC) and is therefore exposed to foreign exchange risk and fair value risk due to changes in interest rates. The entity decides to swap the borrowing into a functional currency (LC) floating rate borrowing using a cross currency interest rate swap (CCIRS). The CCIRS is designated as the hedging instrument in a fair value hedge (first-level relationship). By doing so, the entity has eliminated both the foreign exchange risk and the fair value risk due to changes in interest rates. However, it is now exposed to variable functional currency interest payments.

Later, the entity decides to fix the amount of functional currency interest payments by entering into an interest rate swap (IRS) to pay fixed and receive floating interest in its functional currency. By doing so, the entity is hedging the aggregated exposure, which is the combination of the original exposure and the CCIRS. The IRS is designated as the hedging instrument in a cash flow hedge (second-level relationship). *[IFRS 9.IE128]*. The diagram below illustrates the two hedging relationships.

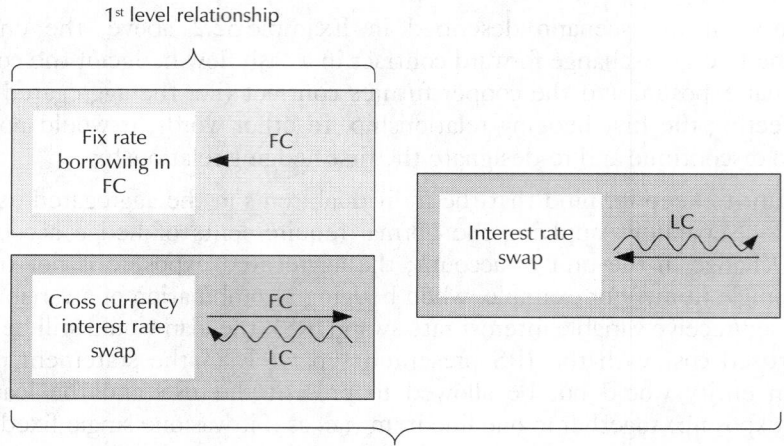

The complexity of this example lies in the calculation of the present value (PV) of the variability of cash flows of the aggregated exposure, which is the basis for the ineffectiveness calculation in the second level relationship. As explained in the illustrative examples in the implementation guidance, this can be done by creating a 'synthetic' aggregated exposure for calculation purposes. This aggregated exposure has a variable leg, based on the aggregate future cash flows on the liability in foreign currency and the local and foreign currency CCIRS cash flows, as well as a fixed leg in local currency based on a blended nominal rate.

The blended rate on the fixed leg of the 'synthetic' aggregated exposure must be calibrated at the date of designation of the second level relationship such that the synthetic aggregated exposure has a present value of nil. This involves calculating the present value in local currency of all gross future cash flows on the liability in foreign currency as well as the local and foreign currency cash flows on the CCIRS, to give the present value of the variable leg. The blended rate on the fixed leg can then be determined as the rate that results in an equal and opposite present value to the variable leg of the 'synthetic' aggregated exposure.

The illustrative examples indicate that valuation techniques used to calculate the present value for each cash flow making up the variable leg must be appropriate for the instrument from which the cash flows arise. For example, the local currency present value of the foreign currency cash flows on the liability and the CCIRS may not offset completely, due to valuation differences such as cross currency basis spreads or the credit risk of the CCIRS. Accordingly gross cash flows must be considered, without any aggregation of cash flows from separate instruments. *[IFRS 9.IE134(a)]*. However, the illustrative examples do not indicate whether the same the same considerations about valuation techniques have to be made for the 'synthetic' fixed rate leg of the aggregated exposures.

The diagram below illustrates the methodology described above. The grey field indicates the unknown in this equation (i.e. the fixed rate of the synthetic aggregated exposure).

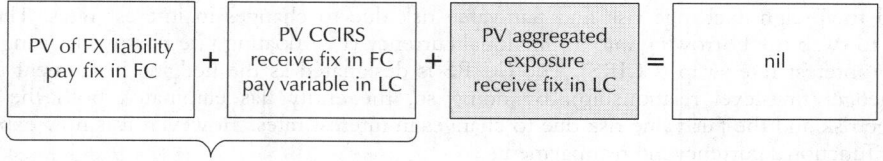

While, as stated above, the implementation guidance indicates that that valuation techniques used to calculate the present value for each cash flow making up the variable leg must be appropriate for the instrument from which the cash flows arise, it is not entirely clear which valuation basis should be used when determining the synthetic fixed rate leg such that the synthetic aggregated exposure has a zero present value on designation.

In each subsequent period, the present values are updated for the changes in the variable cash flows and discount rates while holding the previously calibrated blended fixed rate on the aggregated exposure constant, similar to a hypothetical derivative (see 6.4.2 below). The sum of the resulting present values of cash flows (which previously was calibrated to be nil as per designation) then equals the present value of the cash flow variability of the aggregated exposure. *[IFRS 9.IE134]*.

This is illustrated in the diagram below. The unknown in this equation is now the present value of the cash flow variability of the aggregated exposure.

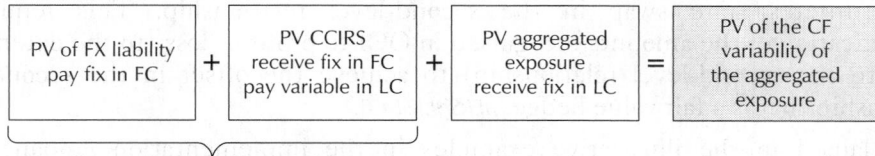

Ineffectiveness is then determined using the calculated present value of the cash flow variability of the aggregated exposure and the fair value of the hedging instrument, (i.e. the local currency IRS).

Example 52.4: Floating rate loan in a foreign currency – fair value hedge of an aggregated exposure

An entity has a floating rate borrowing denominated in a foreign currency (FC) and is therefore exposed to foreign exchange risk and cash flow risk due to changes in interest rates. The entity decides to swap the borrowing into a functional currency (LC) fixed rate borrowing using a cross currency interest rate swap (CCIRS). The CCIRS is designated as the hedging instrument in a cash flow hedge (first-level relationship). By doing so, the entity has eliminated both the foreign exchange risk and the cash flow risk due to changes in interest rates. However, it is now exposed to a fair value risk resulting from changes in the functional currency interest rate curve.

Later, the entity decides to hedge this fair value risk and enters into an interest rate swap (IRS) that receives fixed rate and pays floating rate interest in its functional currency. By doing so, the entity is hedging the aggregated exposure, which is the combination of the original exposure and the CCIRS. The IRS is designated as the hedging instrument in a fair value hedge (second-level relationship). *[IFRS 9.IE138]*. The diagram below illustrates the two hedging relationships.

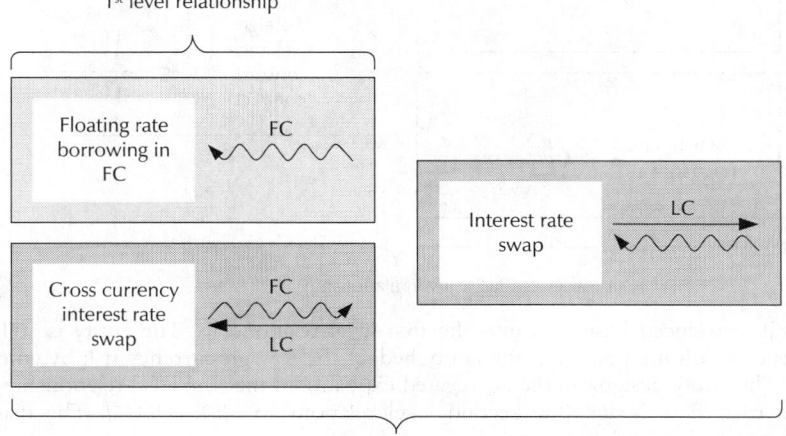

The concept of hedging aggregated exposures as such is straightforward. However, the accounting for such relationships includes some (necessary) complexity. The accounting mechanics are explained in detail in the illustrative examples in the implementation guidance of IFRS 9. In Example 52.4 above, where an entity has a cash flow hedge in the first-level relationship that is then designated as the hedged item in a fair value hedge, the cross-currency interest rate swap is both a hedging instrument and part of a hedged item at the same time but in different hedging relationships. Its fair value changes are recognised in other comprehensive income (OCI), but at the same time, should also offset the fair value changes in profit or loss of the interest rate swap in the second-level relationship. This requires a reclassification of the amounts recognised in OCI to profit or loss (to the extent they relate to the second-level relationship) to achieve the offset in the second-level relationship that is a fair value hedge. *[IFRS 9.IE143].*

As explained in the illustrative examples in the implementation guidance, the application of hedge accounting to an aggregated exposure gets even more complicated when basis risk is involved in one of the hedging relationships, in particular if basis risk is present in the first-level relationship. This is shown in Example 52.5 below.

Example 52.5:   Hedge of a commodity price risk as an aggregated exposure in a cash flow hedge of foreign currency risk

Entity A with functional currency LC enters into a coffee benchmark price forward contract to hedge its highly probably coffee purchases in foreign currency (FC) in five years. It designates the benchmark forward contract and the highly probably forecast transaction as a cash flow hedge (the first level relationship). The entity designates the entire price risk and not only the benchmark risk as it was not able to separately identify a benchmark component in the hedged item (see 3.4.3 below).

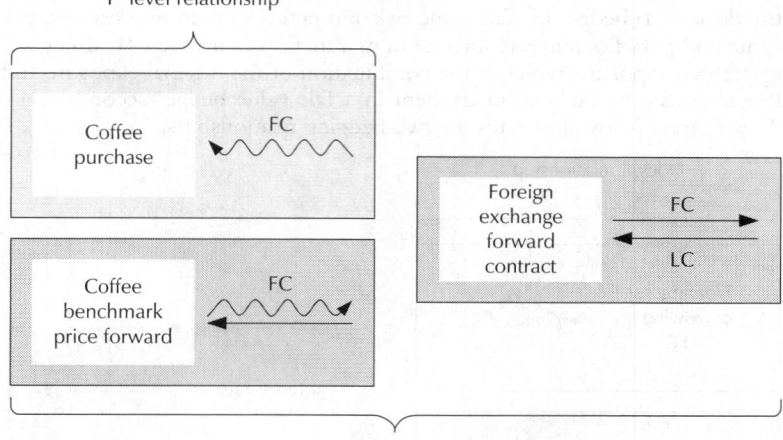

By doing so it introduced basis risk into the first level relationship. The entity is still exposed to foreign currency risk. One year later, the entity hedges the foreign currency risk by entering into an FX forward. The entity designates the aggregated exposure in the first level relationship and the FX forward as a cash flow hedge (the second level relationship). *[IFRS 9.IE117].* The diagram below illustrates the two hedging relationships.

Illustrative example 16 in the implementation guidance of IFRS 9 demonstrates why the accounting effort for this can be more than trivial. First, the entity calculates the fair value of the hedged item and hedging instrument in the first level relationship in foreign currency and translates them into local currency, using spot rates. On this basis, the entity calculates the ineffectiveness in the first level hedging relationship in the usual way. Second, the entity calculates the fair value of the aggregated exposure and the second-level hedging instrument in local currency. This results in the second level ineffectiveness.

The aggregated exposure is a combination of the foreign currency cash flows expected from the highly probable coffee purchases and the gain or loss on the commodity hedging contract. Accordingly changes in the commodity basis risk that exists in the aggregated exposure (and the first level hedging relationship) will impact the amount of expected foreign currency cash flows making up the aggregate exposure. As the hedging instrument in the second level relationship is just an FX forward contract, fair value change in the hedging instrument are insensitive to commodity basis risk, and so additional ineffectiveness may arise. *[IFRS 9.IE117]*.

There are several complications in the example in the implementation guidance. To reduce the basis risk the entity choses a hedge ratio other than 1:1 for the first level relationship. Furthermore, the entity designates the second level relationship based on the implied forward price, which assumed the entity's original long term expectations of the basis spread. This expectation is neither the basis spread at the time of designation nor does it necessarily correspond with future actual basis spreads.

An additional complication is that the aggregated exposure is a combination of the foreign currency cash flows expected from the highly probable coffee purchases and the gain or loss on the commodity hedging contract. If the first level relationship was a 'perfect hedge', the resultant foreign currency cash flow to be hedged in the second level relationship would be known. However, as commodity basis risk exists in the second level relationship, the hedged amount of foreign currency in the second level relationship will vary as the basis between the price of the forecast coffee purchases and the underlying coffee price in the hedging contract varies. Accordingly, changes in the commodity basis that exists in the aggregated exposure (and the first level hedging relationship) will impact the amount of expected foreign currency cash flows making up the aggregated exposure. As the hedging instrument in the second level relationship is just an FX forward contract, fair value change in the hedging instrument are insensitive to commodity basis risk, and so additional ineffectiveness may arise.

For example, at inception of the second level relationship, an entity might have expected a hedged cash flow of FC 990 based on the price achieved in the commodity hedging contract and the level of basis that then existed. However, at the date when the entity calculates the ineffectiveness, the expected cash flow might be FC 1000 due to changes in the commodity basis in the first level relationship. If that is the case, an entity would need to measure effectiveness as if it always expected cash flows of FC 1000.

Another layer of complexity would be added if the entity subsequently needed to rebalance the hedge relationship because of changes in the expected basis. The example, however, does not include this.

Chapter 52

The definition of an aggregated exposure includes a forecast transaction of an aggregated exposure. *[IFRS 9.6.3.4]*. An example, where this might be helpful, is when pre-hedging the interest rate risk in a forecast foreign currency debt issue:

Example 52.6:   Aggregated exposure – interest rate pre-hedge of forecast foreign currency debt issue

Assume it is highly probable that an entity will issue fixed rate foreign currency debt in six months' time. It is also highly probable that on issue the entity will transact a CCIRS, converting the debt to functional currency variable rate. The combination of the forecast *foreign currency* fixed rate debt issuance and the forecast transaction of the CCIRS is economically a forecast *functional currency* variable rate debt issuance.

The entity wishes to hedge itself against increases in the variable functional currency interest rate between today and the issue of the debt in six months as well as the term of the debt. Therefore, the entity enters into a forward starting pay fixed/receive variable functional currency IRS. The entity designates the IRS as a hedging instrument in a cash flow hedge of the forecast aggregated exposure.

As an aggregated exposure is a combination of an exposure and a derivative, the aggregated exposure is often a hedging relationship itself (the first-level relationship). In order for the aggregated exposure to qualify for hedge accounting, IFRS 9 only requires that the first-level relationship *could* qualify for hedge accounting and not that hedge accounting is actually applied. However, applying hedge accounting to the aggregated exposure gets even more complex when hedge accounting is not applied to the first-level relationship, and the entity is also unlikely to achieve its desired accounting result. *[IFRS 9.BC6.167]*. Therefore, in many cases we expect entities to apply hedge accounting to the first-level relationship, even if not required.

However, just because an entity enters into an additional derivative transaction that relates to an existing hedging relationship does not mean that this relationship qualifies as an aggregated exposure. This is demonstrated by the following example.

Example 52.7:   Cash flow hedging of an exposure that includes a net investment in a foreign operation

Parent A with functional currency Australian dollars (AUD) has a US dollar (USD) net investment exposure. It transacts a pay floating USD receive floating AUD cross currency interest rate swap (CCIRS) and designates it in hedge of a net investment in a foreign operation. By doing so, the group is exposed to cash flow variability due to the floating rate exposure in AUD. The parent A enters into a pay floating/receive fixed AUD interest rate swap (IRS) and wishes to designate this derivative as the hedged item in a cash flow hedge for the aggregated exposure including the net investment in a foreign operation.

While there is an economic relationship between the net investment exposure and the CCIRS for foreign exchange risk, there is no economic relationship between the aggregated exposure and the IRS for interest rate risk. This is because the USD floating interest rate cash flows on the CCIRS are not offset by the USD net investment, as it does not have cash flow variability that is closely linked to interest rates. Furthermore, aggregated exposures can only be designated if they are managed as one exposure for a particular risk, which is unlikely to be the case in this fact pattern given the lack of interest risk associated with the net investment. *[IFRS 9.B6.3.3]*.

3.4 Risk components

3.4.1 General requirements

Instead of hedging the total changes in fair values or cash flows, risk managers often enter into derivatives to hedge only specific risk components. Managing a specific risk component reflects that hedging all risks is often not economical and hence not desirable, or not possible (because of a lack of suitable hedging instruments).

However, under IAS 39, a non-financial item can only be designated as the hedged item for its foreign currency risk or all its risks in their entirety (see Chapter 51 at 2.2.2). There is no such restriction for financial items, therefore creating an inconsistency in hedge accounting for risks of financial and non-financial items. This results in many risk management activities, in particular those of non-financial services entities, not qualifying for hedge accounting under IAS 39, or else hedge ineffectiveness being artificially overstated.

In what many believe to be the single most important change from IAS 39, the hedge accounting requirements in IFRS 9 now permit an entity to designate a risk component of a non-financial item as the hedged item in a hedging relationship, provided the risk is separately identifiable and reliably measurable. This is likely to enable many more common risk management strategies to qualify for hedge accounting and will result in less ineffectiveness in profit or loss.

A risk component may be contractually specified or it may be implicit in the fair value or the cash flows of the item to which the component belongs. *[IFRS 9.B6.3.10]*. However, the mere fact that a physical component is part of the make-up of the whole item does not mean that the component necessarily qualifies as risk component for hedge accounting purposes. A physical component is neither required nor by itself sufficient to meet the criteria for risk components that are eligible as a hedged item. However, depending on the market structure, a physical component can help meet those criteria (see 3.4.3 below). For example, just because rubber is a physical component of car tyres that does not mean that an entity can automatically designate rubber as a risk component in a hedge of forecast tyre purchases or sales, since the price of tyres may be related only indirectly to the price of rubber. Further analysis of the pricing structure of the whole car tyre would be required.

3.4.2 Contractually specified risk components

Purchase or sales agreements sometimes contain clauses that link the contract price via a specified formula to a benchmark price of a commodity. Examples of contractually specified risk components include:

- the price of natural gas contractually linked in part to a gas oil benchmark price and in part to a fuel oil benchmark price;
- the price of electricity contractually linked in part to a coal benchmark price and in part to transmission charges that include an inflation indexation;
- the price of wires contractually linked in part to a copper benchmark price and in part to a variable tolling charge reflecting energy costs; and
- the price of coffee contractually linked in part to a benchmark price of Arabica coffee and in part to transportation charges that include a diesel price indexation.

Chapter 52

In each case, it is assumed that the pricing component would not require separation as an embedded derivative (see Chapter 43 at 4 and 5). When contractually specified, a risk component would usually be considered *separately identifiable*. Further, the risk component element of a price formula would usually be referenced to observable data, such as a published price index. Therefore, the risk component would usually also be considered *reliably measurable*. However, entities would still have to consider what has become termed the 'sub-LIBOR issue' (discussed at 3.4.5 below).

Example 52.8:   Hedge of a contractually specified risk component – coal supply contract linked to the coal benchmark price and the Baltic Dry Index

An entity purchases coal from its coal supplier under a contract that sets out a variable price for coal linked to the coal benchmark price, represented by futures contracts for coal loaded at the Newcastle Coal Terminal in Australia, plus a logistics charge that is indexed to the Baltic Dry Index, reflecting that the delivery is at an overseas location. The contract sets out minimum purchase quantities for each month covered by its term.

The entity wishes to hedge itself against price changes related to the benchmark coal price but does not want to hedge the price variability resulting from the logistics costs represented by the indexation of the coal price to the Baltic Dry Index. Therefore, the entity enters into Newcastle coal futures contracts whereby it purchases coal for the relevant delivery months. For each relevant delivery month the entity designates the futures contracts as a hedging instrument in a cash flow hedge of the benchmark coal price risk component of the future coal purchases under its supply contract.

In this case the risk component is contractually specified by the pricing formula in the supply contract. This means it is separately identifiable, because the entity knows exactly which part of the change in the future purchase price of coal under its particular supply contract results from changes in the benchmark price for coal and what part of the price change results from changes in the Baltic Dry Index. The risk component can also be reliably measured using the price in the futures market for the relevant delivery months as inputs for calculating the present value of the cumulative change in the hedged cash flows. An entity could also decide to only hedge its exposure to variability in the coal price that is related to transportation costs. For example, the entity could enter into forward freight agreements and designate them as hedging instruments, with the hedged item being only the variability in the coal price under its supply contract that results from the indexation to the Baltic Dry Index.

3.4.3   Non-contractually specified risk components

Not all contracts define the various pricing elements and, therefore, specify risk components. In fact, we expect most risk components of financial and non-financial items not to be contractually specified. While it is certainly easier to determine that a risk component is separately identifiable and reliably measurable if it is specified in the contract, IFRS 9 is clear that there is no need for a component to be contractually specified in order to be eligible for hedge accounting. The assessment of whether a risk component qualifies for hedge accounting (i.e. whether it is separately identifiable and reliably measurable) has to be made 'within the context of the particular market structure to which the risk or risks relate and in which the hedging activity takes place'. *[IFRS 9.B6.3.9]*. We understand the relevance of the market structure to be that the risk component must have a distinguishable effect on changes in the value or the cash flows that an entity is exposed to. Depending on the situation, the market structure can reflect a 'market convention' that establishes, for example, a benchmark interest rate that has a pervasive effect on the value and cash flows for debt instruments. In other situations the market structure reflects the particular purchasing or selling market of an entity. For example, this is the case when an entity buys goods from its particular supplier based on a benchmark price plus other charges, as in the examples listed at 3.4.2 above. Even if the pricing under such a supply arrangement is not a wider 'market convention' its pricing formula represents the exposure of the particular entity to variability in cash flows from its purchases. The assessment is normally straightforward for contractually specified risk components. The existence of contractually specified risk components in similar transactions can be a relevant factor in the assessment of the market structure and so help identify non-contractually specified risk components such as risk components of forecast transactions that have not been contractually specified. The following example from the application guidance of IFRS 9 illustrates the 'separately identifiable and reliably measurable' assessment. *[IFRS 9.B6.3.10(b)].*

Example 52.9:   Hedge of a non-contractually specified risk component – coffee purchases with a benchmark price risk component

An entity purchases a particular quality of coffee of a particular origin from its supplier under a contract that sets out a variable price linked to the benchmark price for coffee. The price is represented by the coffee futures price plus a fixed spread, reflecting the different quality of the coffee purchased compared to the benchmark plus a variable logistics services charge reflecting that the delivery is at a specific manufacturing site of the entity. The fixed spread is set for the current harvest period. For the deliveries that fall into the next harvest period this type of supply contract is not yet available.

The entity analyses the market structure for its coffee supplies, taking into account how the eventual deliveries of coffee that it receives are priced. The entity can enter into similar supply contracts for each harvest period once the crop relevant for its particular purchases is known and the spread can be set. In that sense, the knowledge about the pricing under the supply contracts also informs the entity's analysis of the market structure more widely, including forecast purchases which are not yet contractually specified. This allows the entity to conclude that its exposure to variability of cash flows resulting from changes in the benchmark coffee price is a risk component that is separately identifiable and reliably measurable for coffee purchases under the variable price supply contract for the current harvest period as well as for forecast purchases that fall into the next harvest period.

In this case the entity can enter into coffee futures contracts to hedge its exposure to the variability in cash flows from the benchmark coffee price and designate that risk component as the hedged item. This means that changes in the coffee price from the variable logistics services charge as well as future changes in the spread reflecting the different coffee qualities would be excluded from the hedging relationship.

The assessment of whether a risk component qualifies for hedge accounting is mainly driven by an analysis of whether there are different pricing factors that have a distinguishable effect on the item as a whole (in terms of its value or its cash flows). This evaluation would always have to be based on relevant facts and circumstances.

The standard uses the refinement of crude oil to jet fuel as an example to demonstrate how the assessment of the market structure could be made to conclude that crude oil in a particular situation is an eligible risk component of jet fuel. *[IFRS 9.B6.3.10(c)]*. Crude oil is a physical input of the most common production process for jet fuel and there is a well-established price relationship between the two.

Extending this example, crude oil is also a major input in the production process for plastic. However, the manufacturing process is complex and involves a number of steps. The process starts with crude oil being distilled into its separate 'fractions', of which only one (naphtha) is used for making plastic. Naphtha then undergoes a number of further processes before the various types of plastic are finally produced.

Generally, the further 'downstream' in the production process an item is, the more difficult it is to find a distinguishable effect of any single pricing factor. The mere fact that a commodity is a major physical input in a production process does not automatically translate into a separately identifiable effect on the price of the item as a whole. For example, crude oil price changes are unlikely to have a distinguishable effect on the retail price of plastic toys even though, in the longer term, changes in the crude oil price might influence the price of such toys to some degree. Similarly, the price for pasta at food retailers in the medium to long term also responds to changes in the price for wheat, but there is no distinguishable direct effect of wheat prices changes on the retail price for pasta, which remains unchanged for longer periods even though the wheat price changes. If retail prices are periodically adjusted in a way that also directionally reflects the effect of wheat price changes, that is not sufficient to constitute a separately identifiable risk component.

Allowing non-contractually specified risk components as eligible hedged items opens up a new area for judgement. The assessment of the market structure will normally require the involvement of staff with a good understanding of the drivers of market prices (e.g. members of the sales or procurement departments responsible for the underlying transactions).

3.4.4   Inflation as a risk component

Under IAS 39, inflation cannot be designated as a hedged risk component for financial instruments, unless the inflation risk component is contractually specified (see Chapter 51 at 2.2.1.D. For non-financial instruments, inflation risk cannot be designated under IAS 39 as a risk component at all.

In contrast, for financial instruments IFRS 9 introduces a rebuttable presumption that, unless contractually specified, inflation is not separately identifiable and reliably measureable. This means that there are limited cases under which it is possible to identify a risk component for inflation and designate that inflation component in a hedging relationship. Similar to other non-contractually specified risk components, the analysis would have to be based on the particular circumstances in the respective market, which is, in this case, the debt market. *[IFRS 9.B6.3.13]*.

The example below, derived from the application guidance of IFRS 9, explains a situation in which the presumption that inflation does not qualify as a risk component of a financial instrument can be rebutted.

Example 52.10: Inflation risk as an eligible risk component of a debt instrument

An entity wishes to hedge the inflation risk component of a debt instrument. The debt instrument is issued in a currency and country in which inflation-linked bonds are actively traded in a significant volume. The volume, liquidity and term structure of these inflation-linked bonds allow the computation of a real interest yield curve. This situation supports that inflation is a factor that is separately considered in the debt market in a way that it is a separately identifiable and reliably measureable risk component. *[IFRS 9.B6.3.14].*

There are not many currencies with a liquid market for inflation-linked debt instruments, therefore limiting the availability of designating non-contractually specified inflation risk components of financial instruments.

IFRS 9 does not specify whether the analysis of inflation as an eligible risk component has to be made by currency or by country, or both. This is particularly relevant for countries forming a monetary union together with other countries, but having different inflation rates (e.g. within the Eurozone). The relevant 'market structure' for inflation will usually be given by the currency.

While IFRS 9 defines in what circumstances inflation can be a risk component for a financial instrument, inflation can under IFRS 9 be treated as a risk component for non-financial items in the same manner as any other risk component (as described at 3.4.2 and 3.4.3 above, i.e. the rebuttable presumption described in this section applies only to financial instruments). For example, a contractually specified inflation risk component would normally qualify as a hedged item (e.g. a sales contract with a price formula linked to the consumer price index) under IFRS 9, whereas it would not under IAS 39.

3.4.5 The 'sub-LIBOR issue'

Some financial institutions are able to raise funding at interest rates that are below a benchmark interest rate (e.g. LIBOR minus 15 basis points (bps)). In such a scenario, the entity may wish to remove the variability in future cash flows caused by movements in LIBOR benchmark interest rates. However, like IAS 39 (see Chapter 51 at 2.2.1.A), IFRS 9 does not allow the designation of a 'full' LIBOR risk component (i.e. LIBOR flat), as a component cannot be more than the total cash flows of the entire item. This is sometimes referred to as the 'sub-LIBOR issue'. *[IFRS 9.B6.3.22].*

The reason for this restriction is that a contractual interest cannot normally be less than zero. Hence, for a borrowing at, say, LIBOR minus 15bps, if benchmark interest rates decrease below 15bps, any further reduction in the benchmark would not cause any cash flow variability for the hedged item. Consequently, any designated component has to be less than or equal to the cash flows of the entire item. *[IFRS 9.B6.3.21].*

In the above scenario, where the interest rate is at LIBOR minus 15bps, the entity could instead designate, as the hedged item, the variability in cash flows of the entire liability (or a proportion of it) that is attributable to LIBOR changes. *[IFRS 9.B6.3.24].* This would result in some ineffectiveness for financial instruments that have an interest rate 'floor' of zero in situations in which the forward curve for a part of the remaining hedged term is below 15bps because the hedged item will have less variability in cash flows as a result of interest rate changes than a swap without such a floor.

While the example in the standard uses LIBOR as the benchmark component, it is clear that the requirement relates not just to financial items in general, or the LIBOR benchmark component in particular, but is a general prohibition on the cash flows of hedged risk components being larger than the cash flows of the entire hedged item. This means that the sub-LIBOR issue is also applicable to non-financial items where the contract price is linked to a benchmark price minus a differential. This is best demonstrated using an example derived from the application guidance of IFRS 9.

Example 52.11:   Sub-LIBOR issue – Selling crude oil at below benchmark price

Assume an entity has a long-term sales contract to sell crude oil of a specific quality to a specified location. The contract includes a clause that sets the price per barrel at West Texas Intermediate (WTI) minus USD 10 with a minimum price of USD 30. The entity wishes to hedge the WTI benchmark price risk by entering into a WTI future. As outlined above, the entity cannot designate a 'full' WTI component, i.e. a WTI component that ignores the price differential and the minimum price.

However, the entity could designate the WTI future as a hedge of the entire cash flow variability under the sales contract that is attributable to the change in the benchmark price. When doing so, the hedged item would have the same cash flow variability as a sale of crude oil at the WTI price (or above), as long as the forward price for the remaining hedged term does not fall below USD 40. *[IFRS 9.B6.3.25]*.

In some cases the contract price may not be defined as a benchmark price minus a fixed differential but as a benchmark price plus a pricing differential that is sometimes positive and sometimes negative (the 'basis spread'). The market structure may reveal that items are priced that way and there may even be derivatives available for the basis spread (i.e. basis swaps, for example the benchmark gas oil crack spread derivative which is a derivative for the price differential between crude oil and gas oil – a refining margin *[IFRS 9.B6.3.10(c)(i)]*). Similar to Example 52.11 above, an entity could not designate the benchmark price component as the hedged item given that the cash flows of the benchmark component could be more than the total cash flows of the entire item. Unfortunately, the standard does not provide any guidance as to how an entity has to assess whether the basis spread could be negative or not. For example, it is not clear whether an entity is only required to look at the forward benchmark prices or whether it has to consider all reasonably possible scenarios. The use of 'reasonably possible scenarios' in other places in IFRS 9 might indicate that the latter is the case.

A related question is whether the entity could designate the entire cash flow variability that is attributable to changes in only the benchmark risk (as the entity alternatively does in Example 52.11 above) if that risk is a non-contractually specified risk component. This assessment is likely to be similar to whether a non-contractually specified risk component is separately identifiable and reliably measureable (as outlined at 3.4.3 above) which would be required in order to determine the variability of the entire cash flows with respect to changes in the benchmark.

However, the presence of a spread that is sometimes negative could make this assessment more difficult. An entity needs to prove that the benchmark cash flows plus or minus the spread make up the total cash flows. This might be the case, for example, if it can be proven that there are quality differences, such that the benchmark is sometimes of better quality and sometimes worse than the hedged exposure. On the other hand, if the basis spread switches between positive and negative because of individual supply and demand drivers in the benchmark price and the price of the hedged exposure, this may indicate that the benchmark is not implicit in the fair value or cash flows of the hedged exposure. To illustrate this with an example, take WTI and Brent crude oil prices. While both prices might be highly correlated, WTI could not be identified as a benchmark component in Brent because both prices have their own supply and demand drivers. Furthermore, it would not be possible to determine whether either WTI is a risk component of Brent or *vice versa*, which demonstrates that there is no risk component.

The negative interest rate environment in some countries, mainly countries in the Eurozone and Switzerland has further implications on the designation of risk components in connection with the sub-LIBOR issue. However, this not only relates to hedge accounting under IFRS 9 but also under IAS 39 and is therefore covered in Chapter 51 at 2.2.1.A.

3.5   Components of a nominal amount

3.5.1   Definition

A component of a nominal amount is a specified part of the amount of an item. *[IFRS 9.6.3.7]*. This could be a proportion of an entire item (such as, 60% of a fixed rate loan of EUR 100 million) or a layer component (for example, the 'bottom layer' of EUR 60 million of a EUR 100 million fixed rate loan that can be prepaid at fair value. 'Bottom layer' here refers to the portion of the loan that will be prepaid last). *[IFRS 9.B6.3.16]*.

Nominal components are frequently used in risk management activities in practice. Examples include:

- Part of a monetary transaction volume.
  For example, the first USD 1 million cash flows from sales to customers in a given period.
- Part of a physical volume.
  For example, the 50 tonnes bottom layer of coal inventory in a particular location.
- A part of a physical or other transaction volume.
  For example, the sale of the first 15,000 units of widgets during January 2015.
- A layer from the nominal amount of the hedged item.
  For example, the top layer of a CHF 100 million fixed rate liability that can be prepaid at fair value. 'Top layer' refers to the portion of the liability that will be prepaid first. *[IFRS 9.B6.3.18]*.

3.5.2   Hedge accounting requirements in IAS 39

IAS 39 allows the designation of nominal components for a group of forecast cash flows, such as the sale of the first 15,000 units of widgets used as an example above.

Chapter 52

Such a designation accommodates the fact that there may be a level of uncertainty as to the quantity of the hedged item and that this uncertainty does not form part of the hedging relationship (see also Chapter 51 at 5.2).

However, IAS 39 does not allow the designation of layer components for fair value hedges. Consequently, an entity that wishes to hedge part of a group of items within a fair value hedge must identify specific items within the group (and designate those items only) or designate a percentage of the total as the hedged item. The premise of the IAS 39 model is to replicate, on a portfolio basis, the hedge accounting result that would arise on an individual hedged item basis.

Financial institutions often apply economic layer hedging strategies. However, as illustrated in the example below, they cannot be directly reflected in the financial statements by using hedge accounting in accordance with IAS 39.

Example 52.12:   Hedging a bottom layer of a loan portfolio (IAS 39)

A bank holds a portfolio of fixed rate loans with a total nominal amount of CU 100m. The borrowers can, at any time during the tenor, prepay 20% of their (original) loan amount at par.

For risk management purposes, the loans are considered together with variable rate borrowings of CU100m. As a result, the bank is exposed to an interest margin risk resulting from the fix-to-floating rate mismatch. The bank expects CU 20m of loans to be prepaid.

As part of the risk management strategy, the bank decides to hedge the interest margin by entering into a pay fixed/receive variable interest rate swap (IRS). The objective is to hedge the amount of loans that is not prepayable using an IRS with a notional amount of CU 80m. The IRS is designated as a fair value hedge of 80% of the CU 100m loan portfolio.

After two years loans of CU 10m are prepaid, which is less than 20% and therefore does not affect the economic hedge in place. However, because of the proportionate designation, this is considered a reduction in the hedged amount for hedge accounting purposes. As a result, the entity now has an IRS of CU 80m designated as a hedge of loans of CU 72m ([CU 100m – CU 10m] × 80%), which will inevitably lead to some ineffectiveness.

3.5.3   Hedge accounting requirements in IFRS 9

In what is seen by many as an important change, IFRS 9 now allows, for fair value hedges, the designation of layer components from a defined nominal amount or a defined, but open, population. *[IFRS 9.B6.3.18]*. This designation should be consistent with an entity's risk management objective. *[IFRS 9.B6.3.16]*. IFRS 9 still includes some restrictions, in particular that a layer component that includes a prepayment option does not qualify as a hedged item in a fair value hedge if the fair value of the prepayment option is affected by changes in the hedged risk (unless the changes in fair value of the prepayment option as a result of changes in the hedged risk are included when measuring the change in fair value of the hedged item – see Example 52.13 below). *[IFRS 9.B6.3.20]*.

If an entity has an option to prepay a loan at fair value, the fair value of the option is not affected by changes in the hedged risk. Consequently, an entity would be able to designate a hedge as described in Example 52.15 below:

Example 52.13:   Hedging a top layer of a loan

An entity borrows money by issuing a CU 10m five-year fixed rate loan. The entity has a prepayment option to pay back CU 5m at fair value. The entity wants to be able to make use of the prepayment option without the amount repayable on early redemption being affected by interest rate changes.

Consequently, the entity would like to hedge the fair value interest rate risk of the prepayable part of the loan. To achieve this, the entity enters into a five-year receive fixed/pay variable interest rate swap (IRS) with a notional amount of CU 5m. The entity designates the IRS in a fair value hedge of the interest rate risk of the CU 5m top layer of the loan attributable to the benchmark interest rate. As a result, the top layer is adjusted for changes in the fair value attributable to changes in the hedged risk. The bottom layer, which cannot be prepaid, remains at amortised cost.

The gain or loss on the IRS will offset the change in fair value on the top layer attributable to the hedged risk. On prepayment, the fair value hedge adjustment of the top layer is part of the gain or loss from derecognition of a part of the loan as the result of the early repayment.

The situation illustrated by Example 52.13 of a hedge of a top layer of a loan would not often be found in practice, as most prepayment options in loan agreements allow, in our experience, for prepayment at the nominal amount (instead of at fair value). Moreover, if a financial asset included an option that allowed prepayment at fair value, that would affect the assessment of the characteristics of the contractual cash flows. That assessment is a part of the classification of financial assets and such a prepayment option would not be consistent with payments that are solely principal and interest (see Chapter 46 at 6.4.5).

If prepayment is at the nominal amount, the fair value of the prepayment option would be affected by changes in the hedged interest rate risk. Therefore, a top or bottom layer would not normally qualify for hedge accounting unless the effect of the related prepayment option is included when measuring the fair value change of the hedged item. *[IFRS 9.B6.3.20]*. As it is usual for the entity to consider that the likelihood of prepayment in a bottom layer is insufficient to justify using a hedging instrument that can also be cancelled, the changes in the fair values of the hedging instrument and the hedged item will not normally be the same. The consequence is that there is likely to be a level of ineffectiveness in the accounting hedge relationship, to be measured and recognised. 'Bottom layer' hedging strategies that avoid this source of ineffectiveness can only be applied if the hedged layer is not affected by the prepayment risk. This is best demonstrated based on the scenario already used in Example 52.12 above, but this time making use of the new IFRS 9 designation for nominal components.

Example 52.14: Hedging a bottom layer of a loan portfolio (IFRS 9)

A bank holds a portfolio of fixed rate loans with a total nominal amount of CU 100m. The borrowers can, at any time during the tenor, prepay 20% of their (original) loan amount at par.

For risk management purposes, the loans are considered together with variable rate borrowings of CU 100m. As a result, the bank is exposed to an interest margin risk resulting from the fix-to-floating rate mismatch. The bank expects CU 20m of loans to be prepaid.

As part of the risk management strategy, the bank decides to hedge a part of the interest margin by entering into a pay fixed/receive variable interest rate swap (IRS). The objective is to hedge 95% of the amount of loans that is not prepayable using an IRS with a notional amount of CU 76m (95% of CU 80m). The hedged layer does not include a prepayment option. Therefore, the IRS is designated in a fair value hedge of the interest rate risk of the CU 76m bottom layer of the CU 100m loan portfolio.

As a result, the bottom layer is adjusted for changes in the fair value attributable to changes in the hedged risk (i.e. benchmark interest rate risk). The extent to which the borrowers exercise their prepayment option does not affect the hedging relationship. Also, if the bank were to derecognise any of the loans for any other reason, the first CU 4m of non-prepayable amount of derecognised loans would not be part of the hedged item (i.e. the CU 76m bottom layer).

As already mentioned above, IFRS 9 does not preclude hedge accounting for layers including a prepayment option. However, in order to achieve hedge accounting for

Chapter 52

such a designation, changes in fair value of the prepayment option as a result of changes in the hedged risk have to be included when measuring the change in fair value of the hedged item. Example 52.15 illustrates what this means in practice:

Example 52.15:   Hedging a bottom layer including prepayment risk

A bank originates a CU 10m five-year fixed rate loan with a prepayment option to pay back CU 5m at any time at par.

For risk management purposes, the loan is considered together with variable rate borrowings of CU 10m. As a result, the bank is exposed to an interest margin risk resulting from the fix-to-floating rate mismatch. The bank expects the borrower to prepay CU 2m and, therefore, wishes to hedge CU 8m only. The bank enters into a five-year pay fixed/receive variable interest rate swap (IRS) with a notional amount of CU 8m and designates CU 5m of the IRS in a fair value hedge of the benchmark interest rate risk of the CU 5m layer of the non-prepayable loan amount. In addition, the bank enters into a swaption with a notional amount of CU 3m that is jointly designated with CU 3m of the IRS to hedge the benchmark interest rate risk of the last remaining CU 3m of the CU 5m prepayable amount of the loan (a bottom layer).

As a result, the non-prepayable loan amount is adjusted for changes in the fair value attributable to changes in the hedged risk (the fixed rate benchmark interest rate risk of a fixed term instrument). However, the CU 3m bottom layer of the prepayable amount also needs to be adjusted for the effect of the prepayment option on the changes in the fair value attributable to the interest rate risk. The CU 2m top layer remains at amortised cost.

Therefore, the first CU 2m of prepayments would have a gain or loss on derecognition determined as the difference between the amortised cost of the prepaid amount and par. For any further prepayments exceeding CU 2m, the gain or loss on derecognition would be determined as the difference between the amortised cost including the fair value hedge adjustment and par.

While IFRS 9 provides an effective solution for portfolios that feature a bottom layer that is not prepayable, as explained in Examples 52.14 and 52.15 above, it does not provide an answer for portfolios that are fully prepayable. The IASB decided to address hedging of such portfolios in its separate macro hedging project, as described at 3.6.5 below. Until that project is finalised, entities are allowed to apply the portfolio hedging guidance in IAS 39 as described at 3.6.6 below and in Chapter 51 at 6).

3.6   Groups of items

Hedge accounting under IAS 39 was primarily designed from a single instrument view point. A hedging relationship would typically include a single hedging instrument (e.g. an interest rate swap) hedging a single item (e.g. a loan). However, for operational reasons entities often economically hedge several items together on a group basis. IAS 39 allows several items to be hedged together as a group, but there are restrictions such that there are relatively few types of groups that are eligible as hedged items (see Chapter 51 at 2.2.3).

Under IAS 39, a group of items is eligible as a designated hedged item for accounting purposes only if:

*   the individual items within the group share the same designated risk exposure; and

*   the change in the fair value attributable to the hedged risk for each individual item in the group is 'approximately proportional' to the overall change in the fair value attributable to the hedged risk of the group. *[IAS 39.83].*

Many hedges will fail to fulfil the second criterion. For example, when hedging a portfolio of shares that replicates a market index, the individual shares would usually not move in tandem with the entire portfolio.

3.6.1   General requirements

In an effort to address the issues raised by these restrictions, the IASB has broadened the eligibility criteria for groups of items in IFRS 9. Under IFRS 9, hedge accounting may be applied to a group of items if:

- the group consists of items or components of items that would individually qualify for hedge accounting; and

- for risk management purposes, the items in the group are managed together on a group basis. *[IFRS 9.6.6.1].*

Example 52.16:   Hedging a portfolio of shares

An entity holds a portfolio of shares of Swiss companies that replicates the Swiss Market Index (SMI). The entity elected to account for the shares at fair value through other comprehensive income without subsequent reclassification to profit or loss, as allowed by IFRS 9. The entity decides to lock in the current value of the portfolio by entering into corresponding SMI futures contracts.

The individual shares would be eligible hedged items if hedged individually. As the objective of the portfolio is to replicate the SMI, the entity can also demonstrate that the shares are managed together on a group basis. The entity also assesses the effectiveness criteria for hedge accounting (see 5 below). Consequently, the entity designates the SMI futures contracts as the hedging instrument in a hedge of the fair value of the portfolio. As a result, the gains or losses on the SMI futures are accounted for in OCI (without subsequent reclassification to profit or loss) as well, thus eliminating the accounting mismatch.

Whether the items in the group are managed together on a group basis is a matter of fact, i.e. it depends on an entity's behaviour and cannot be achieved by mere documentation.

3.6.2   Hedging a component of a group

A group designation can also consist of a component of a group of items, such as a layer component of a group. *[IFRS 9.6.6.3].* A component could also be a proportion of a group of items, such as 50% of a fixed rate bond series with a total volume of CU 100 million. Whether an entity designates a layer component or a proportionate component depends on the entity's risk management objective. *[IFRS 9.6.6.2, 6.6.3].*

The benefits of identifying a layer component, as discussed at 3.5.3 above, are relevant when applied to a group of items. The bottom layer hedging strategy discussed in Example 52.15 above is, in fact, a designation of a component of a group.

Another example is a bond issue of CU 50million that is made up of 50,000 fixed rate bonds with a face value of CU 1,000 each. If the issuer expects that it might repurchase up to CU 10million of the issue volume before maturity, it could hedge the benchmark component of the fair value interest rate risk with a receive fixed/pay variable interest rate swap that has a notional amount of CU 10million. From an economic perspective, that hedge would allow repurchases of up to CU 10million total face value for which the gain or loss from changes in the benchmark interest rate would be compensated by the gain or loss on the swap. However, this can only be reflected in the accounting if the entity can designate a CU 10million top layer (i.e. for the first CU 10million of face value that are repurchased, the entity would include a fair value hedge gain or loss on the full face value when determining the gain or loss on derecognition of the bonds). If it was not permitted to designate a layer of a group of items, entities would in such cases either have to identify individual items within the group and designate them on a standalone basis or prorate the fair value hedge gain or loss to the entire bond issue volume. The IASB believes this would result in arbitrary accounting results and decided to allow a layer component designation for a group of items. *[IFRS 9.BC6.438, BC6.439]*.

A layer component of a group of items only qualifies for hedge accounting if:

- the layer is separately identifiable and reliably measurable;
- the risk management objective is to hedge a layer component;
- the items in the group from which the layer is identified all share the same risk;
- for a hedge of existing items, the items in the group can be identified and tracked; and
- any items in the group containing prepayment options meet the requirements for components of a nominal amount (see 3.5.3 above). *[IFRS 9.6.6.3]*.

3.6.3   Cash flow hedge of a net position

Many entities are exposed to foreign exchange risk arising from purchases and sales of goods or services denominated in foreign currencies. Cash inflows and outflows occurring on forecast transactions in the same foreign currency are often economically hedged on a net basis. For example, consider an entity that has forecast foreign currency sales of FC 100 and purchases of FC 80, both in 6 months. It hedges the net exposure using a single foreign exchange forward contract to sell FC 20 in 6 months.

Hedging of such a net position does not qualify for hedge accounting under IAS 39 as hedge accounting for net positions is prohibited. However, hedge accounting could still be achieved by designating the foreign exchange forward contract as hedging FC 20 of the FC 100 forecast sales. By doing so, hedge accounting would result in FC 20 of the total forecast sales of FC 100 being recorded at the hedged rate, while the remaining sales and the purchases will be measured at the then prevailing spot rate (see Chapter 51 at 2.2.3).

When managing the foreign exchange risk on forecast transactions, treasury departments typically determine the net positions by adding the expected cash inflows and cash outflows for a given date or time period (e.g. week or month). The resulting net exposure is then hedged using a financial instrument. Under IAS 39, if the individual cash flows forming the net position affect profit or loss in different reporting periods they will not offset each other in the income statement, i.e. there will be no 'natural hedge' for accounting purposes.

Example 52.17:   Accounting mismatch for a 'natural hedge' of foreign currency cash flows (IAS 39)

An entity anticipates foreign currency denominated sales of FC 100 in 12 months and also intends to purchase fixed assets of FC 80 in 12 months (both denominated in the same foreign currency). The cash inflows of the forecast sales are hedged on a net basis together with the cash outflows for the forecast purchase of the fixed assets. The forecast sales will have an immediate effect upon profit or loss when they occur, while the forecast asset purchases will only affect profit or loss as the assets are depreciated over their useful lives.

In the Exposure Draft, the IASB proposed to permit a group of items that result in a net position to be an eligible hedged item. *[IFRS 9.BC6.432]*. However, the Board also decided to limit the application for cash flow hedges to groups where the offsetting risk positions affect profit or loss in the same period. *[IFRS 9.BC6.447]*. This was considered by many constituents to conflict with the broader goal of the hedge accounting project, to reflect risk management activities in the financial statements. *[IFRS 9.BC6.449]*.

When redeliberating the proposals, the Board has not only confirmed its earlier decision to allow net positions as eligible hedged items, but has also extended the eligibility for designation as a hedged item in a cash flow hedge to net positions that affect profit or loss in different periods. This is, however, limited to hedges of foreign exchange risk. *[IFRS 9.6.6.1(c)]*.

The standard mechanics of cash flow hedge accounting cannot be applied to a hedged net position whose cash flows affect profit or loss in different periods. Applying standard cash flow hedge accounting to Example 52.17 above, the gain or loss accumulated in other comprehensive income (OCI) on the FC 20 of hedging instrument would be reclassified to profit or loss when the revenue transaction occurs. However, this will only set off the gain or loss on FC 20 of the FC 100 hedged revenue while the remaining revenue of FC 80 and the fixed asset purchase of FC 80 (i.e. the economic hedge) would still be measured at the spot rate. This would result in the bottom line profit for the period(s) not reflecting the economic hedge.

IFRS 9 changes the cash flow hedge accounting for such a net position in that the foreign exchange gain or loss on the FC 80 revenue cash flows that affect profit or loss in the earlier period must be carried forward to offset the foreign exchange gain or loss on the fixed asset purchase cash flows that will affect profit or loss in later periods. This is achieved by deferring the gain or loss on the natural hedge in OCI, with a reclassification to profit or loss once the offsetting cash flows affect profit or loss (see Example 52.18 below).

However, the transactions that make up the net position would each need to be recognised when they arise and be measured at the spot foreign currency rate ruling at that time. Hence, they are not adjusted to reflect the result of the hedge. The whole impact of hedge accounting has to be presented in a separate line item in profit or loss. *[IFRS 9.6.6.4]*.

This separate line item includes:

- The reclassification adjustment of gains or losses on the hedge of the net position.
- The gain or loss on the natural hedge, with the counter-entry being recognised in OCI.
- The later reclassification adjustment of the gain or loss on the natural hedge from OCI to profit or loss.

The rather complicated accounting described above is best illustrated using an example:

Example 52.18: Cash flow hedge of a foreign currency net position

An entity having the CAD as functional currency anticipates sales of GBP 100m in 12 months and also plans a major capital expenditure (fixed assets) of GBP 80m in 12 months. The anticipated sales and capital expenditure (i.e. the group of forecast transactions) are designated as the hedged item and the resulting net position is hedged with a forward contract to sell GBP 20m in 12 months. The fixed assets will be depreciated on a straight-line basis over eight years. For simplicity, assume the spot rate equals the forward rate.

GBP/CAD spot rate	
At inception of the hedge (beginning of year 1)	1.50
After 12 months (end of year 1)	1.60

The entity would record the following journal entries (amounts in millions):

Year 1

	CAD	CAD
Other comprehensive income	2	
Hedging derivative		2

To account for the fair value change in the hedging instrument (GBP 20 × [1.50 – 1.60]).

Cash	160	
Revenue from sales		160

To account for the sales volume of GBP 100 at the current spot rate of 1.60 (GBP 100 × 1.60).

Property, plant and equipment	128	
Cash		128

To account for the purchase of GBP 80 fixed assets at the current spot rate of 1.60 (GBP 80 × 1.60).

Hedging derivative	2	
Cash		2

To account for the settlement of the forward contract.

Net position hedging gains/losses	2	
Other comprehensive income		2

To reclassify the cash flow hedge reserve from OCI to profit or loss.

Net position hedging gains/losses	8	
Other comprehensive income		8

To defer the natural hedge gain from profit or loss to OCI (GBP 80 × [1.60 – 1.50]).

The net profit for the period is CAD 150, which represents the sale of GBP 100 at the hedged rate of 1.50 (albeit presented in two different line items).

Years 2 to 9

Depreciation	16	
Property, plant and equipment		16

To account for the straight line depreciation of the fixed assets (CAD 128 × 12.5%).

Other comprehensive income	1	
Net position hedging gains/losses		1

To reclassify part of the deferred gain from OCI to profit or loss (CAD 8 × 12.5%).

The net loss for each period is 15, which represents depreciation (at 12.5%) of a fixed asset of GBP 80 purchased at the hedged rate of 1.50.

Overview

Income statement (CAD)	Y1	Y2	Y3	Y4	Y5	Y6	Y7	Y8	Y9	Total
Revenue from sale of goods	160									160
Depreciation		(16)	(16)	(16)	(16)	(16)	(16)	(16)	(16)	(128)
Net position hedging gains/losses	(10)	1	1	1	1	1	1	1	1	(2)
Profit for the period	150	(15)	(15)	(15)	(15)	(15)	(15)	(15)	(15)	30

Statement of financial position (CAD)	Y1	Y2	Y3	Y4	Y5	Y6	Y7	Y8	Y9
Cash	30								
Property, plant and equipment	128	112	96	80	64	48	32	16	0
Hedging reserve (OCI)	(8)	(7)	(6)	(5)	(4)	(3)	(2)	(1)	0

The transactions within a net position still have to be measured at their spot rates, while the effect of the hedge is presented in a separate line item. *[IFRS 9.B6.6.15]*. In other words, as although an entity may be economically hedged from a bottom line (or net) perspective, volatility will still arise in the amounts reported for the individual hedged transactions (on a gross basis), and it is only the bottom line of profit or loss that will reflect the benefits of the hedge.

For a net position to qualify for cash flow hedge accounting the hedge documentation has to include, for each type of item within the net position, its amount and nature as well as the reporting period in which it is expected to affect profit or loss. *[IFRS 9.6.6.1, B6.6.7-B6.6.8]*.

3.6.4   Nil net positions

As part of its introduction of the concept of net positions as hedged items, IFRS 9 also addresses hedges of nil net positions. Sometimes entities hedge a group of items where the hedged items themselves fully offset the risk that is managed. An example would be similar to the scenario illustrated by example 52.18 above but where the entity anticipates sales of GBP 100m in 12 months and also plans a major capital expenditure of GBP 100m in 12 months. An entity is allowed to designate such a nil net position in a hedging relationship, provided that:

- the hedge is part of a rolling net risk hedging strategy;

- hedging instruments are used to hedge the net risk when the hedged net position changes in size over the life of the rolling hedging strategy and is not a nil net position;

- the entity would normally apply hedge accounting to such net positions when the net position is not nil; and

- not applying hedge accounting to the nil net position would result in inconsistent accounting outcomes over time (because in a period in which the net position is nil, hedge accounting would not be available for what is otherwise the same type of exposure). [IFRS 9.6.6.6].

3.6.5   Macro hedging

Financial institutions, especially retail banks, have as a core business the collection of funds by depositors that are subsequently invested as loans to customers. This typically includes instruments such as current and savings accounts, deposits and borrowings, loans and mortgages that are usually accounted for at amortised cost. The difference between interest received and interest paid on these instruments (i.e. the net interest margin) is a main source of profitability.

A bank's net interest margin is exposed to changes in interest rates, a risk most banks (economically) hedge by entering into derivatives (mainly interest rate swaps). Applying the hedge accounting requirements (as set out in IAS 39 or IFRS 9) to such hedging strategies on an individual item-by-item basis can be difficult as a result of the characteristics of the underlying financial assets and liabilities:

- Prepayment options are common features of many fixed rate loans to customers. Customers exercise these options for many reasons, such as when they move house, and so not necessarily in response to interest rate movements. Their behaviour can be predicted better on a portfolio basis rather than an item-by-item basis.

- As a result of the sheer number of financial instruments involved, banks typically apply their hedging strategies on a macro (or portfolio) basis, with the number of individual instruments in the hedged portfolio constantly churning.

Although IAS 39 can be applied to macro hedging situations, and guidance exists for portfolio fair value and cash flow hedge accounting for interest rate risk, entities do not always use hedge accounting in those situations. This is because not all sources of interest rate risk qualify for hedge accounting, use of IAS 39 can be operationally complex and cash flow hedge solutions result in volatility of other comprehensive income. Some European banks have, instead, made use of the European Union's carve out of certain sections of the IAS 39 hedge accounting rules.

Instead of developing particular hedge accounting requirements in IFRS 9 that are specifically tailored to macro hedging strategies, the IASB is seeking to create a separate accounting model for macro hedging situations that would be based on an entity's risk management activities. The accounting for macro hedging was originally part of the IASB's project to replace IAS 39 with IFRS 9. However, the IASB realised that developing the new accounting model would take time and probably be a different concept from hedge accounting. In May 2012, the Board therefore decided to decouple the part of the project that is related to accounting for macro hedging from IFRS 9, allowing more time to develop an accounting model without affecting the timeline for the completion of the other elements of IFRS 9.[8]

Although mainly focused on financial institutions, the accounting model for macro hedging might also be beneficial for some corporate entities applying macro-type hedging strategies.

In April 2014, the IASB issued the Discussion Paper – *Accounting for Dynamic Risk Management: a Portfolio Revaluation Approach to Macro Hedging*. The six-month comment period ended in October 2014. Most respondents supported the need for the project, but there was no consensus on a solution. Given the diversity in views, in July 2015 the IASB concluded that the insights that it had received from the comment letters and feedback so far did not enable it to develop proposals for an Exposure Draft. Accordingly, the IASB decided that the project should remain in the Research Programme, with the aim of publishing a second Discussion Paper.[9] The next step for the project will be to focus on identifying the information needed to provide more decision useful information on Dynamic Risk Management.

3.6.6   *Applying hedge accounting for macro hedging strategies under IFRS 9*

Because of its pending project on an accounting model specifically tailored to macro hedging situations (see 3.6.5 above), the IASB created a scope exception from the IFRS 9 hedging accounting requirements that allows entities to use the specific fair value hedge accounting for portfolio hedges of interest rate risk, and only for such hedges, as defined and set out in IAS 39, until the project is finalised and becomes effective. The specific guidance that defines what is meant by the fair value hedge accounting for portfolios of interest rate risk is set out in IAS 39.81A, 89A, AG114-AG132 (see Chapter 51 at 6).

However, the implementation guidance accompanying IAS 39 also contains specific illustrations of the implementation of cash flow hedge accounting when financial institutions manage interest rate risk on a net basis. *[IAS 39.IG F.6.2, F.6.3]*. The IASB decided not to carry forward any implementation guidance on hedge accounting to IFRS 9.

As a result, many financial institutions were concerned that they would not be able to continue with their existing macro cash flow hedging strategies under IFRS 9.

In its January 2013 meeting, the IASB confirmed its earlier decision and clarified that not carrying forward the implementation guidance was without prejudice (i.e. it did not mean that the IASB had rejected that guidance and so had not intended to imply that entities cannot apply macro cash flow hedge accounting under IFRS 9).[10]

This was, however, not the end of the story. Several constituents continued to lobby EFRAG and the IASB to allow entities to either apply the hedge accounting requirements in IAS 39 or IFRS 9 until the project on accounting for macro hedging is finalised.[11]

Eventually, the IASB decided to give entities the following choices until the project on accounting for macro hedging is completed:

- to apply the new hedge accounting requirements as set out in IFRS 9, in full;

- to apply the new hedge accounting requirements as set out in IFRS 9 to all hedges except fair value hedges of the interest rate exposure of a portfolio of financial assets or financial liabilities; in that case an entity must also apply the paragraphs that were added to IAS 39 when that particular type of hedge was introduced (IAS 39.81A, 89A and AG114-AG132) – i.e. an entity must apply *all* the hedge accounting requirements of IAS 39 (e.g. the 80%-125% bright line effectiveness test) *including* the paragraphs that specifically address fair value hedges of the interest rate exposure of a portfolio of financial assets or financial liabilities); the choice to apply IAS 39 in these situations is the result of the scope of the hedge accounting requirements of IFRS 9 and available on a case-by-case basis (i.e. it is not an accounting policy choice); *[IFRS 9.6.1.3]*, or

- to continue applying hedge accounting as set out in IAS 39 until the project on accounting for macro hedging is completed, to all hedges; this is an accounting policy choice, *[IFRS 9.7.2.21]*. Because it is an accounting policy choice, an entity may later on change its policy and start applying the hedge accounting requirements of IFRS 9 (subject to the transition requirements of IFRS 9 for hedge accounting). However, even if an entity chooses to continue to apply the hedge accounting requirements of IAS 39, the entity still has to provide the new hedge accounting disclosures that were developed during the IFRS 9 project because those disclosure requirements have become a part of IFRS 7 for which no similar accounting policy choice to continue to apply the previous requirements was provided. *[IFRS 9.BC6.104]*. Once an entity changes its accounting policy and starts to apply the hedge accounting requirements of IFRS 9, it cannot go back to IAS 39.

3.6.7   *Hedged items held at fair value through profit or loss*

In general, it does not appear to be useful to designate a hedged item that is measured at fair value through profit or loss in a hedge relationship because such an item is either held for trading, measured on a fair value basis or designated as measured at fair value through profit or loss using the fair value option. This means that an entity either seeks to be exposed to fair value changes (in which case it makes no sense to hedge the exposure) or the fair value changes of the exposure and the derivative are, anyway, offset.

However, the classification model under IFRS 9 may require an entity to measure certain variable rate instruments at fair value through profit or loss because they fail the contractual cash flow characteristics test (see Chapter 46 at 6). An example would be a variable interest rate loan that contains a feature by which the lender gets a certain amount of shares free of charge if the borrower successfully lists its shares. Although such an instrument would be measured at fair value through profit or loss, an entity may still seek to hedge variability of cash flows by entering into an interest rate swap. Because of their variable nature, such instruments may not be significantly exposed to changes in fair value caused by movements in interest rates, whereas the swap will be. IFRS 9 does not seem to prevent an entity from being able to designate such an instrument in a cash flow hedge.

Notwithstanding the above, we do not believe that it is possible to apply cash flow hedge accounting for a forecast transaction that results in recognising an instrument at fair value though profit or loss, because such a transaction does not result in an exposure to variations in cash flows that could ultimately affect net profit or loss.

4 HEDGING INSTRUMENTS

IAS 39 places several restrictions on the types of instruments that can qualify as hedging instruments for hedge accounting purposes. This is to reflect that hedge accounting was mainly intended to address accounting mismatches that resulted from requiring derivatives to be accounted for at fair value through profit or loss (see Chapter 51 at 2.1). IFRS 9 takes a different approach that focuses on what instruments are used for hedging and expands the list of what can be permitted as a hedging instrument.

4.1 General requirements

Unchanged from IAS 39, derivatives measured at fair value through profit or loss qualify as hedging instruments. *[IFRS 9.6.2.1]*. The sole exception to this rule continues to be written options, unless the written option is designated to offset a purchased option. Purchased options include those that are embedded in another financial instrument. *[IFRS 9.B6.2.4]*.

Two or more financial instruments can be jointly designated as hedging instruments. *[IFRS 9.6.2.5]*. This was already permitted under IAS 39. Also unchanged is the requirement that a single instrument combining a written option and a purchased option, such as an interest rate collar, cannot be a hedging instrument if it is a net written option at the date of the designation. *[IFRS 9.6.2.6]*.

If options are transacted as legally separate contracts. IFRS 9 specifically permits them to be jointly designated as hedging instruments if the combined instrument is not a net written option at the date of designation. *[IFRS 9.6.2.6]*. This is consistent with how we interpreted IAS 39 (see Chapter 51 at 2.1.3).

Chapter 52

Example 52.19:   Hedging foreign exchange risk of a forecast transaction using a combined option instrument

An entity is exposed to foreign exchange risk resulting from a highly probably forecast transaction in a foreign currency. In order to hedge that exposure, the entity enters into a collar by combining a long call and a short put option. The premium paid on the long call option equals the premium received on the short put option (i.e. it is what is termed a 'zero cost collar').

The entity designates the combination of the two instruments in a cash flow hedge of its highly probable forecast transaction.

The requirement that the hedging instrument has to be a contract with a party external to the reporting entity remains. *[IFRS 9.6.2.3].*

4.2   Non-derivative financial instruments

Under IFRS 9, entities are permitted to designate, as hedging instruments, non-derivative financial assets or non-derivative financial liabilities that are accounted for at fair value through profit or loss. *[IFRS 9.6.2.2].* This is meant in a strict sense. Consequently:

- A liability designated as at fair value through profit or loss (for which the amount of its change in fair value that is attributable to changes in the credit risk of that liability is presented in other comprehensive income (OCI)) does not qualify as a hedging instrument. *[IFRS 9.6.2.2].* This is because the entire fair value change is not recognised in profit or loss, which would in effect allow the entity to ignore its own credit risk when assessing and measuring hedge ineffectiveness and thus conflict with the concepts of hedge accounting.

- An equity instrument for which an entity has elected to present changes in fair value in OCI does not qualify as a hedging instrument in a hedge of foreign currency risk. *[IFRS 9.6.2.2].* Again, this reflects that fair value changes are not recognised in profit or loss, which is incompatible with the mechanics of fair value hedges and cash flow hedges.

Example 52.20:   Hedge of a forecast commodity purchase with an investment in a commodity fund or an exchange traded commodity

An entity is exposed to variability in cash flows from highly probable forecast purchases of crude oil that is indexed to Brent crude oil. The entity wants to hedge its cash flow risk from changes in the price of Brent crude oil. Instead of using derivative contracts, the entity purchases exchange traded investments that replicate the performance of Brent futures contracts such as commodity funds or exchange traded commodities (ETCs). ETCs have the legal form of debentures that are coupled to the price development of a commodity (either directly at the spot price or with a commodity futures contract). They can be traded like exchange traded funds but, because they are legally debt securities, they involve credit risk of the issuer (which is usually mitigated by collateralisation through physically deposited commodities or other suitable collateral).

These investments are financial instruments that (under IFRS 9) would be accounted for at fair value through profit or loss. Consequently, they could qualify as hedging instruments if all other qualifying criteria for hedge accounting are met. In particular, the effectiveness assessment would have to consider that the fair value change of the investments will differ from the present value of the cumulative change in the cash flows for the forecast purchases of crude oil. This is because of aspects such as 'tracking errors' (i.e. that investment does not perfectly replicate the performance of futures contracts) and that the investments are fully funded cash-instruments whereas the cash flows on the forecast transactions will only occur in the future.

The ability to designate non-derivative hedging instruments can be helpful if an entity does not have access to derivatives markets (e.g. because of local regulations that prohibit the entity from holding such instruments), or if an entity does not want to be subject to margining requirements nor enter into uncollateralised over-the-counter derivatives. Purchasing and selling financial investments in such cases can be operationally easier for entities than transacting derivatives.

4.3 Hedges of a portion of a time period

IAS 39 contains a restriction that a hedging relationship cannot be designated for only a portion of the time period during which a hedging instrument remains outstanding (see Chapter 51 at 2.1.4.C). In essence, this restriction remains; however, it is now formulated more precisely, in that a hedging instrument may not be designated for a part of its change in fair value that results from only a portion of the time period during which the hedging instrument remains outstanding. This clarifies that an entity cannot designate a 'partial-term' component of a financial instrument as the hedging instrument, but only the entire instrument for its remaining life (notwithstanding that an entity may exclude from designation the time value of an option, the forward element of a forward contract or the foreign currency basis spread, see 7.1 and 7.2 below). *[IFRS 9.6.2.4].*

4.4 Hedges of foreign currency risk

For hedges of foreign currency risk, the foreign currency risk component of a non-derivative financial instrument is determined in accordance with IAS 21 – *The Effects of Changes in Foreign Exchange Rates. [IFRS 9.B6.2.3].* This means that an entity could, for example, hedge the spot risk of highly probable forecast sales in 12 months' time that are denominated in a foreign currency with a 7-year financial liability in the same foreign currency. However, when measuring ineffectiveness, IFRS 9 is now explicit that the revaluation of the forecast sales for foreign currency risk would have to be on a discounted basis (i.e. a present value calculation of the spot revaluation, reflecting the time between the reporting date and the future cash flow date), whereas the hedging instrument (i.e. the IAS 21-based foreign currency component of the financial liability) would not. This would result in some ineffectiveness (see 6.4.1 below). *[IFRS 9.B6.5.4].*

4.5 Time value of money, forward element and currency basis spread

Consistent with IAS 39, an entity can exclude from the designation as the hedging instrument the changes in fair value attributable to the time value of an option or the forward element of a forward contract (see 7.1 and 7.2 below). IFRS 9 expands this by also allowing the separation and exclusion of the foreign currency basis spread when designating a financial instrument as the hedging instrument (see 7.2.2 below).

In practice, there has been some debate how exactly a financial instrument should be split into parts that are included and excluded from the designation as the hedging instrument. In this context it is useful to think about the effect of the requirements for measuring ineffectiveness. These require taking into account the time value of money, which means the hedged item must be measured on a present value basis (see 6.4.1 below). *[IFRS 9.B6.5.4].*

5   QUALIFYING CRITERIA

5.1   General requirements

Unchanged from IAS 39, in order to qualify for hedge accounting, a hedging relationship has to consist of eligible hedging instruments and eligible hedged items (see 3 and 4 above). Also, at inception of the hedging relationship, there still has to be a formal designation and documentation. This would include the entity's risk management strategy and the objective underlying the hedging relationship. The documentation has to include an identification of the hedging instrument, the hedged item, the nature of the risk being hedged and how the entity will assess whether the hedging relationship meets the hedge effectiveness requirements. *[IFRS 9.6.4.1].*

However, compared to IAS 39, the entity's risk management strategy and objective are more important under IFRS 9 because of the effect on discontinuation of hedge accounting and the hedge accounting related disclosures. IFRS 9 also requires documentation of the hedge ratio and potential sources of ineffectiveness (that may have to be updated as part of a continuing hedging relationship). *[IFRS 9.B6.5.26, IFRS 7.22A].*

Entities can still only designate one of three types of hedging relationships: a fair value hedge, a cash flow hedge or a hedge of a net investment in a foreign operation. For hedges of the foreign currency risk of a firm commitment, an entity may still designate either a fair value hedge or a cash flow hedge. *[IFRS 9.6.5.2, 6.5.4].*

The requirements for assessing effectiveness are another major change compared to IAS 39. The effectiveness assessment under IFRS 9 is only prospective, does not involve any 'bright lines' and, depending on the circumstances, may often be qualitative. The method for assessing effectiveness may need to be changed in response to changes in circumstances. In such cases, the hedge documentation is updated but without resulting in discontinuation of the hedging relationship. *[IFRS 9.B6.4.17, B6.4.19].*

Under IFRS 9 a hedging relationship qualifies for hedge accounting if it meets *all* of the following effectiveness requirements:

- there is 'an economic relationship' between the hedged item and the hedging instrument;
- the effect of credit risk does not 'dominate the value changes' that result from that economic relationship; and
- 'the hedge ratio of the hedging relationship is the same as that resulting from the quantity of hedged item that the entity actually hedges and the quantity of the hedging instrument that the entity actually uses to hedge that quantity of hedged item. However, that designation shall not reflect an imbalance between the weightings of the hedged item and the hedging instrument that would create hedge ineffectiveness (irrespective of whether recognised or not) that could result in an accounting outcome that would be inconsistent with the purpose of hedge accounting'. *[IFRS 9.6.4.1(c)].* The second part of this requirement is an anti-abuse clause that is explained in more detail in at 5.4 below.

The required steps for designating a hedging relationship can be summarised in a flow chart as follows:

Figure 52.1:   How to achieve hedge accounting

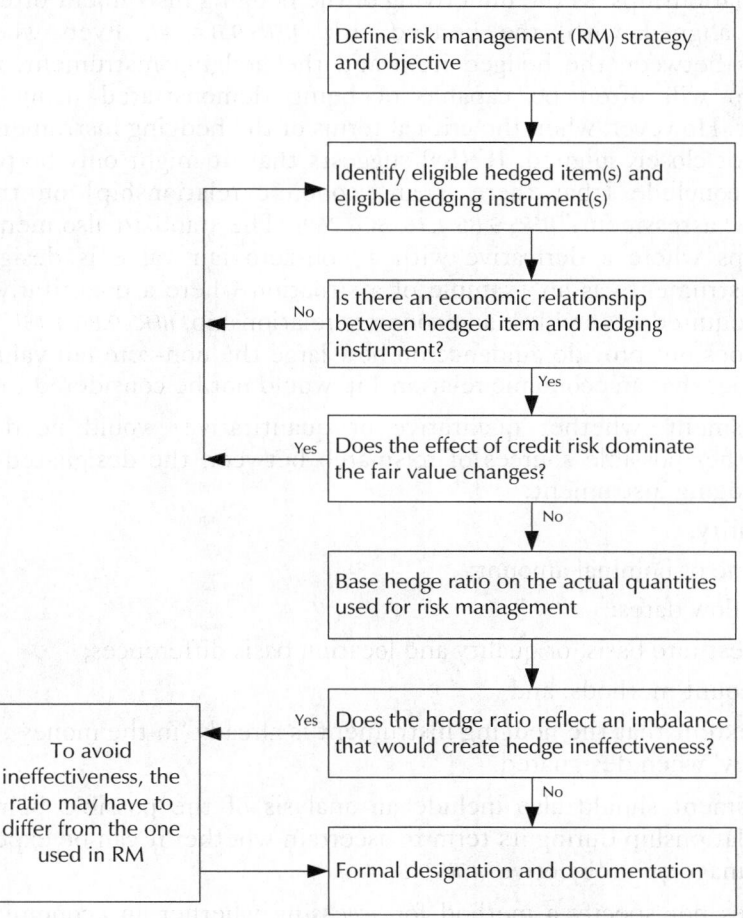

The individual steps in the new effectiveness assessment are discussed in more detail below.

5.2   Economic relationship

The first effectiveness requirement means that the hedging instrument and the hedged item must generally be expected to move in opposite directions as a result of a change in the hedged risk. *[IFRS 9.B6.4.4, B6.4.5, BC6.238]*. This should be based on an economic rationale rather than just by chance, as could be the case if the relationship is based only on a statistical correlation. That is, causality cannot be assumed purely from correlation or, to quote the IASB, 'the mere existence of a statistical correlation between two variables does not, by itself, support a valid conclusion that an economic relationship exists.'. *[IFRS 9.B6.4.6]*. However, a statistical correlation may provide corroboration of an economic rationale. It follows from the above, that a quantitative assessment alone is not enough to establish an economic relationship.

The requirement of an economic relationship will automatically be fulfilled for many hedging relationships, as the underlying of the hedging instrument often matches, or is closely aligned with, the hedged risk. *[IFRS 9.B.4.14]*. Even when there are differences between the hedged item and the hedging instrument, the economic relationship will often be capable of being demonstrated using a qualitative assessment. However, when the critical terms of the hedging instrument and hedged item are not closely aligned, IFRS 9 suggests that 'it might only be possible for an entity to conclude [that there is an economic relationship] on the basis of a quantitative assessment.' *[IFRS 9.B6.4.16, BC6.269]*. The standard also mentions hedging relationships where a derivative with a non-zero fair value is designated as the hedging instruments as an example of a situation where a quantitative assessment might be required to establish an economic relationship. *[IFRS 9.B6.4.15]*. However, the standard does not provide guidance on how large the non-zero fair value would have to be in order that an economic relationship would not be considered to exist.

The assessment, whether qualitative or quantitative, would need to consider, amongst other possible sources of mismatch between the designated hedged item and the hedging instrument:

- maturity;
- volume or nominal amount;
- cash flow dates;
- interest rate basis, or quality and location basis differences;
- day count methods; and
- the extent that the hedging instrument is already 'in the money', or 'out of the money' when designated.

The assessment should also include an analysis of the possible behaviour of the hedging relationship during its term to ascertain whether it can be expected to meet the risk management objective. *[IFRS 9.B6.4.6]*.

IFRS 9 does not specify a method for assessing whether an economic relationship exists. An entity should use a method capturing all the relevant characteristics of the hedging relationship. *[IFRS 9.B6.4.13]*. Which methods, including statistical methods such as regression or sensitivity analysis, as well as the thresholds attached to them, is certainly an area where we expect that best practice will emerge over time. However, it follows from the objective of the hedge accounting requirements to represent the effect of an entity's risk management activities, that the main source of information to perform the assessment would be an entity's risk management activities. *[IFRS 9.6.1.1, B6.4.18]*. In practice, an entity will have normally assessed the economic relationship for risk management purposes and, in most cases, assuming sound risk management, we would expect that this assessment to be appropriate for accounting purposes as well. However, in some cases, existing risk management techniques might not capture all sources of ineffectiveness, such that additional quantitative analysis may be required.

The standard also mentions that a quantitative method, (e.g. regression analysis), might help demonstrate a suitable hedge ratio (see 5.4 below). *[IFRS 9.B6.4.16].*

The following example illustrates an approach that uses a qualitative assessment.

Example 52.21: Economic relationship between HKD and USD

An entity has foreign currency exposures in both Hong Kong dollars (HKD) and US dollars (USD). The entity aggregates its exposures in the two currencies and only uses USD linked hedges to hedge those currency exposures.

Because the HKD is pegged to the USD in a way that allows fluctuations only within a very narrow band (between HKD 7.75 – HKD 7.85 per USD) the entity concludes that an economic relationship exists between its USD linked hedges (with the USD as the underlying) and its HKD denominated foreign currency exposures.

The entity monitors the currency peg for changes and treats the movements of the HKD within the narrow band as a source of some ineffectiveness for all hedges in which the hedged item relates to amounts denominated in HKD.

When using a statistical method such as regression analysis, either to corroborate an economic relationship or to determine a suitable hedging ratio, an entity is required to consider its expectations of future developments. A prominent recent example is negative interest rates in some European countries. Many variable debt instruments such as mortgages include an explicit or implicit floor while the interest rates swaps used to hedge the variability of cash flows of those exposures usually do not. Although the interest cash flows of the hedged item and the variable leg of the hedging instrument may well have been highly correlated in the past, in an environment where interest rates are expected to be negative in the foreseeable future, this may no longer be expected because of the floor in the hedged item. This means that an entity needs to incorporate changes in expectations and re-calibrate its regression analysis accordingly (see Chapter 51 at 5.3.6.A).

5.3 Impact of credit risk

IFRS 9 requires that, to achieve hedge accounting, the impact of credit risk should not be of a magnitude such that it dominates the value changes, even if there is an economic relationship between the hedged item and hedging instrument. Credit risk can arise on both the hedging instrument and the hedged item in the form of counterparty credit risk or the entity's own credit risk.

Judgement has to be used in determining when the impact of credit risk is 'dominating' the value changes. But clearly, to 'dominate' would mean that there would have to be a very significant effect on the fair value of the hedged item or the hedging instrument. The standard provides guidance that small effects should be ignored even when, in a particular period, they affect the fair values more than changes in the hedged risk. *[IFRS 9.B6.4.7].* An example of credit risk dominating a hedging relationship would be when an entity hedges an exposure to commodity price risk with an uncollateralised derivative and the credit standing of the counterparty to that derivative deteriorates severely, such that the effect of the changes in the counterparty's credit standing might outweigh the effect of changes in the commodity price on the fair value of the hedging instrument. *[IFRS 9.B6.4.8].*

Chapter 52

5.3.1   *Credit risk on the hedging instrument*

IFRS 13 – *Fair Value Measurement* – is clear that the effect of credit risk, both the counterparty's credit risk and the entity's own credit risk, has to be reflected in the measurement of fair value (see Chapter 14 at 11.3.2). The effect of credit risk on the measurement of the hedging instrument would obviously result in some hedge ineffectiveness. The expected effect of that ineffectiveness should not be of a magnitude that it frustrates the offsetting impact of a change in the values of the hedging instrument and the hedged item that results from the economic relationship (as explained at 5.2 above).

We expect the assessment of the effect of credit risk to be a qualitative assessment in most cases. For example, entities typically have counterparty risk limits defined as part of their risk management policy. The credit standing of the counterparties is monitored on a regular basis. However, a quantitative assessment of the impact of credit risk on the value changes of the hedging relationship might be required in some instances, if the customer's credit standing deteriorates.

Nowadays, most over-the-counter derivative contracts between financial institutions are cash collateralised. Furthermore, current initiatives in several jurisdictions, such as, the European Market Infrastructure Regulation (EMIR) in the European Union or the Dodd-Frank Act in the United States, will result in more derivative contracts being collateralised by cash. Cash collateralisation significantly reduces the credit risk for both parties involved, meaning that credit risk is unlikely to dominate the change in fair value of such hedging instruments.

5.3.2   *Credit risk on the hedged item*

The analysis of the hedged item is somewhat different, as credit risk does not apply to all types of hedged items. For example, inventory and forecast transactions would not have credit risk. Loan assets typically have counterparty credit risk, while financial liabilities bear the issuing entity's own credit risk.

Credit risk cannot dominate the value change in a hedge of a forecast transaction as the transaction is, by definition, only anticipated but not committed. *[IFRS 9 Appendix A]*. Credit risk is defined as 'risk that one party to a financial instrument will cause a financial loss for the other party by failing to discharge an obligation'. *[IFRS 7 Appendix A]*. For the same reason, inventory also does not involve credit risk. Consequently, credit risk can only apply if the entity enters into a contract (e.g. if the hedged item is a firm commitment or a financial instrument). This should be contrasted with the assessment of whether a forecast transaction is highly probable. Even though such a transaction does not involve credit risk, depending on the possible counterparties for the anticipated transaction, the credit risk that affects them can indirectly affect the assessment of whether the forecast transaction is highly probable. For example, assume an entity sells a product to only one particular customer abroad for which the sales are denominated in a foreign currency and the entity does not have alternative customers to sell the product to in that currency (or other sales in that currency). In that case, the credit risk of that particular customer would indirectly affect the likelihood of the entity's forecast sales in that currency occurring. Conversely, if the entity has a wider customer base for sales of its product that are denominated in the foreign currency then the potential loss of a particular customer would not significantly (or even not at all) affect the likelihood of the entity's forecast sales in that currency occurring.

For regulatory and accounting purposes, banks usually have systems in place to determine the credit risk on their loan portfolios. Therefore, banks should be able to identify loans for which credit risk is so high that it would require an assessment of whether credit risk is dominating the value changes in the hedging relationship. The new impairment model of IFRS 9 (see Chapter 49 at 5) raises the question of what the interaction is between:

- the different stages of the impairment model, i.e. the concept of a significant increase in credit risk (i.e. the move from 'stage one' to 'stage two') and the subsequent transfer of a credit-impaired financial assets to 'stage three'; and

- the concept of when the effect of credit risk dominates the value changes of the hedged item that represent the hedged risk.

There is no direct link between the stages of the impairment model and credit risk eligibility criterion of the hedge accounting model. However in practice, an entity may consider the indicators cited in the definition of a credit-impaired financial asset (see Chapter 49 at 5.3.3). This is because those indicators characterise situations with a magnitude of credit risk that normally suggests that its effect would dominate the value changes of the hedged item that represent the hedged risk. This suggests that normally the hedge effectiveness criteria would cease to be met no later than when a financial asset is classified as credit-impaired (i.e. in stage three). How much earlier the hedge effectiveness criteria might be failed is a matter of judgement, which also includes whether quantitative assessment might be needed in some situations. But also, in the context of stage three of the impairment model, it should be remembered that the effect of credit risk on the fair value of an item involves not only the probability of default but also the loss given default, whereas the indicators cited in the definition of a credit-impaired financial asset relate only to the probability of default. That difference is relevant when assessing whether credit risk is dominant in the case of items that are highly collateralised.

In practice, we expect that entities with a sound risk management would be unlikely to struggle with the assessment of when the effect of credit risk dominates the value changes of the hedged item that represent the hedged risk. This is because such entities would have developed suitable criteria for when risk exposures can no longer be hedged because credit risk creates too much uncertainty as to whether that exposure will eventually crystallise as per the terms in the contract from which it arises. Entities normally evaluate this for risk management purposes because they want to avoid being 'over-hedged' as a result of the offset from the hedged item for the gains or losses on the hedging instrument being eroded by credit risk. In other words, this is predominantly an economic question rather than an accounting consideration (similar to the discussion at 5.3.1 above regarding the credit risk of hedging instruments and entities' criteria for selecting counterparties for those instruments).

There is also interaction between the hedge accounting model and the impairment model regarding the effect that a fair value hedge has on the measurement of the expected credit loss for an item whose carrying amount is adjusted for fair value hedge gains and losses. Because the fair value hedge adjustment is a part of the carrying value of the financial asset that is hedged, the measurement of the loss allowance must take that adjustment into account. This is achieved by adjusting the effective interest rate used to measure the expected credit loss allowance. A similar requirement was already illustrated by the implementation guidance of IAS 39. *[IAS 39.IG E.4.4]*. The main difference compared to IAS 39 in terms of operational complexity is, of course, that under IFRS 9 every debt instrument recorded at amortised cost or at fair value through other comprehensive income has an associated loss allowance. This means, for every fair value hedge in relation to such financial assets, the measurement of the loss allowance requires taking into account the effect of the fair value hedge accounting. This is illustrated in Chapter 49 at 5.4.6.

The assessment of the effect of credit risk on value changes for hedge effectiveness purposes, which often may be made on a qualitative basis, should not be confused with the requirement to measure and recognise the impact of credit risk on the hedging instrument and, where appropriate, the designated hedged item, which will normally give rise to hedge ineffectiveness recognised in profit or loss (see Chapter 51 at 5.3.4).

The systems used to assess the credit risk of loans would also usually permit banks to determine the appropriate economic hedge when hedging the interest rate risk of such loans, as illustrated by Example 52.22 below:

Example 52.22:   Designating interest rate hedges of loan assets when credit risk is expected

Assume a bank wishes to hedge the interest rate risk of a portfolio of loans that have similar credit risk characteristics. Economically, the bank should hedge only the cash flows it expects to collect. When expecting to collect 95% of all cash flows in a loan portfolio, the bank should designate the first 95% of cash flows only. A designation of more than 95% would result in an economic over-hedge and would also increase the risk of credit risk dominating the value changes of the hedging relationship.

As a significant change compared to IAS 39, the designation of such a nominal component (often referred to as a bottom layer) is now possible under IFRS 9 (as discussed at 3.5.3 above). This type of designation would require that all items included in the layer are exposed to the same hedged risk so that the measurement of the hedged layer is not significantly affected by items that make up the 95% layer from the overall 100% of the portfolio. *[IFRS 9.6.6.3(c)]*. Therefore, the entity has to designate the same kind of benchmark interest rate risk component of each loan to make up the bottom layer. If there is a deterioration in the credit risk of a particular loan that results in credit risk dominating the economic relationship with the benchmark interest rate, such that its benchmark interest rate risk component will no longer qualify to be designated as a hedged item, it would not be considered to be part of the bottom layer unless and until those loans for which credit risk dominates the economic relationship would exceed 5% of the portfolio.

The example should not be taken to imply that for an individual loan with an expected loss of, say, 5% an entity may not hedge the interest rate risk using an interest rate swap that has a notional amount equal to the loan's face value. However, if the loan deteriorated in its credit quality to an extent where the credit risk-related changes in fair value start to dominate the interest rate risk-related changes, the hedging relationship would have to be discontinued.

5.4 Setting the hedge ratio

The hedge ratio is the ratio between the amount of hedged item and the amount of hedging instrument. For many hedging relationships, the hedge ratio would be 1:1 as the underlying of the hedging instrument perfectly matches the designated hedged risk.

Some hedging relationships may include basis risk such that the fair value changes of the hedged item and the hedging instrument do not have a simple 1:1 relationship. In such cases, risk managers will generally set the hedge ratio so as to be other than 1:1, in order to improve the effectiveness of the hedge. Consequently, the third effectiveness requirement is that the hedge ratio used for accounting should be the same as that used for risk management purposes. *[IFRS 9.6.4.1(c)(iii)].*

Example 52.23: Setting the hedge ratio

An entity purchases a raw material whose price is at a discount to the commodity benchmark price, reflecting that the raw material is not yet processed to the same extent as the benchmark commodity, as well as quality differences. The entity runs a rolling 12-month regression analysis at each month end to ascertain that the price of the commodity in the futures market and the price of the raw material remain highly correlated. The slopes of the regression analyses (commodity benchmark price to raw material price) over recent months varied between 1.237 and 1.276.

The entity considers that the pattern of its regression analyses is consistent with its longer term view that the raw material trades at an approximately 20% discount to the commodity benchmark price and does not indicate a change in trend but fluctuations around that discount. Therefore, the entity uses a notional amount of 1 tonne of a forward contract for the benchmark commodity to hedge highly probable forecast purchases of 1.25 tonnes of the raw material. Note that this is not exactly the same as the particular slope of the most recent monthly regression, which is not required because the standard requires only that the entity uses the hedge ratio that it actually uses for risk management purposes, and not that it is required to minimise ineffectiveness. The example also illustrates what the standard acknowledges: there is no 'right' answer, as different entities would run different regression analyses (e.g. in terms of frequency and data inputs used, which means there is no one hedge ratio that could be required). The fluctuation of the actual discount around the particular hedge ratio chosen for designating the hedging relationship will give rise to some ineffectiveness.

However, the standard requires the hedge ratio for accounting purposes to be different from the hedge ratio used for risk management if the latter hedge ratio reflects an imbalance that would create hedge ineffectiveness 'that could result in an accounting outcome that would be inconsistent with the purpose of hedge accounting.' *[IFRS 9.6.4.1(c)(iii), B6.4.10].* This complex language was introduced because the Board is specifically concerned with deliberate 'under-hedging', either to minimise recognition of ineffectiveness in cash flow hedges or the creation of additional fair value adjustments to the hedged item in fair value hedges. *[IFRS 9.B6.4.11].*

Example 52.24: Deliberate under-hedging in a cash flow hedge to avoid recognition of ineffectiveness

Consistent with the equivalent requirements of IAS 39 (see Chapter 51 at 4.2.1), IFRS 9 requires the cash flow hedge reserve to be adjusted for the lower of (a) the cumulative gain or loss on the hedging instrument or (b) the cumulative change in fair value of the hedged item. *[IFRS 9.6.5.11(a)].* If (a) exceeds (b), the difference is recognised in profit or loss as ineffectiveness. On the other hand, no ineffectiveness is recognised if (b) exceeds (a). An entity has highly probable forecast purchases of a raw material used in its manufacturing process. The average volume of raw material purchases is expected to be Russian Rouble (RUB) 200m per month. The entity wishes to hedge the commodity price risk on those forecast purchases. The only derivative available does not have an underlying risk exactly matching the one from the actual raw material hedged. The slope of a linear regression analysis is 0.93, indicating the ideal hedge ratio.

To seek to avoid recognition of accounting ineffectiveness, the entity ensures (b) will exceed (a), applying the accounting requirement discussed above. It enters into derivatives with a notional amount of only RUB 150m per month and designates the RUB 150m of forward contracts as hedging instruments in cash flow hedges of highly probable forecast purchases of RUB 200m (thereby setting the hedge ratio at 0.75:1).

In this scenario, the hedge ratio would be considered unbalanced and only entered into to avoid recognition of accounting ineffectiveness. For hedge accounting purposes, the hedge ratio would have to be based on the expected sensitivity between the hedged item and the hedging instrument (in this example possibly around the 0.93:1 based on the linear regression analysis, which would be a hedged volume of RUB 186m). As a result, if the relative change in the fair value of the hedging instrument is greater than that on the hedged item because the relationship between the underlyings changes, some ineffectiveness will have to be recognised.

Example 52.25:   Deliberate under-hedging in a fair value hedge to create fair value accounting

An entity acquires a CU 50million portfolio of debt instruments. The debt instruments fail the 'cash flow characteristics test' of IFRS 9 (i.e. the contractual cash flows do not solely represent payments of principal and interest on the principal amount outstanding) and are therefore accounted for at fair value through profit or loss (see Chapter 46 at 6). *[IFRS 9.4.1.2(b), 4.1.2A(b)].*

The treasurer dislikes the profit or loss volatility resulting from the fair value accounting. He realises that one of the entity's fixed rate bank borrowings has a similar term structure and that fair value changes on the liability would more or less offset the fair value changes on the asset portfolio. However, at the time of entering into the bank borrowing, the entity did not apply the fair value option to this liability (see Chapter 46 at 3).

The treasurer enters into a CU 1m receive fixed/pay variable interest rate swap (IRS) and designates the IRS in a fair value hedge of CU 50m of fixed rate liability (thereby setting the hedge ratio at 0.02:1). As a result, the entire CU 50m of liability would be adjusted for changes in the hedged interest rate risk.

In this scenario, the hedge ratio is unbalanced as the real purpose of the hedging relationship is to achieve fair value accounting (related to changes in interest rate risk) for CU 49m of the liability. The hedge ratio used for hedge accounting purposes would have to be different (likely close to 1:1).

The above examples are of course extreme scenarios and instances of unbalanced hedge designations are likely to be rare; IFRS 9 does not require an entity to designate a 'perfect hedge'. For instance, if the hedging instrument is only available in multiples of 25 metric tonnes as the standard contract size, an imbalance due to using, say, 400 metric tonnes nominal value of hedging instrument to hedge 409 metric tonnes of forecast purchases, would not be regarded as resulting in an outcome 'that would be inconsistent with the purpose of hedge accounting' and so would meet the qualifying criteria. *[IFRS 9.B6.4.11(b)].*

5.5   Designating 'proxy hedges'

The objective of the standard is 'to represent, in the financial statements, the effect of an entity's risk management activities'. *[IFRS 9.6.1.1].* However, this does not mean that an entity can only designate hedging relationships that exactly mirror its risk management activities. In some cases entities will designate so called 'proxy hedges' (i.e. designations that do not exactly represent the actual risk management). In redeliberating the September 2012 draft standard, the Board decided that proxy hedging is permitted, provided the designation is directionally consistent with the actual risk management activities.[12] *[IFRS 9.BC6.97-BC6.101].* The examples below are common proxy hedging designations:

Example 52.26:   Common proxy hedging designations

Net position cash flow hedging

An entity holds Australian Dollar (AUD) 2m of variable rate loan assets and AUD 10m of variable rate borrowings. The treasurer is hedging the cash flow risk exposure on the net position of AUD 8m, by entering into a pay fixed/receive variable interest rate swap (IRS) with a nominal amount of AUD 8m. Rather than designate the net AUD 8m as the hedged item, the entity designates the IRS in a hedge of variable rate interest payments on a portion of AUD 8m of its AUD 10m borrowing.

Macro hedging strategies

Permitting proxy hedging is of particular relevance for banks wishing to apply macro cash flow hedging strategies (see Chapter 51 at 6). Typically, banks manage the interest margin risk resulting from fixed-floating mismatches of financial assets and financial liabilities held at amortised cost on their banking books. Assume the assets are floating rate and the liabilities are fixed rate. The fixed-floating mismatches are offset by entering into receive fixed/pay variable interest rate swaps. There is no hedge accounting model that perfectly accommodates such hedges of the interest margin. Consequently, banks are forced to use either fair value hedge accounting for the liabilities or cash flow hedge accounting for the assets, although the actual risk management activity is neither to hedge fair values nor cash flows, but to hedge the interest margin. Both cash flow hedge accounting and fair value hedge accounting would be directionally consistent with the risk management activity and so acceptable as proxy hedging designations.

IFRS 9 limits the designation of net positions in cash flow hedges to hedges of foreign exchange risk (see 3.6.3 above). *[IFRS 9.6.6.1(c)].* However, in practice, entities often hedge other types of risk on a net cash flow basis. Such entities could still designate the net position as a gross designation.

6   SUBSEQUENT ASSESSMENT OF EFFECTIVENESS, REBALANCING AND DISCONTINUATION

6.1   Assessment of effectiveness

Under IFRS 9 there is no retrospective effectiveness assessment, and the IAS 39 quantitative assessment using the 80%-125% 'bright lines' has been removed. It is important, however, to stress that, unchanged from IAS 39, an entity still has to measure and recognise any ineffectiveness that has actually occurred, as described in Chapter 51 at 4.1.1 and 4.2.1. Also, the elimination of a retrospective effectiveness assessment does not mean that hedge accounting continues irrespective of how effective the hedge turns out to be. A prospective effectiveness assessment is still required on an ongoing basis, in a similar manner as at the inception of the hedging relationship (see 5.1 above) and, as a minimum, at each reporting date. *[IFRS 9.B6.4.12].*

Figure 52.2:   Effectiveness assessment and rebalancing

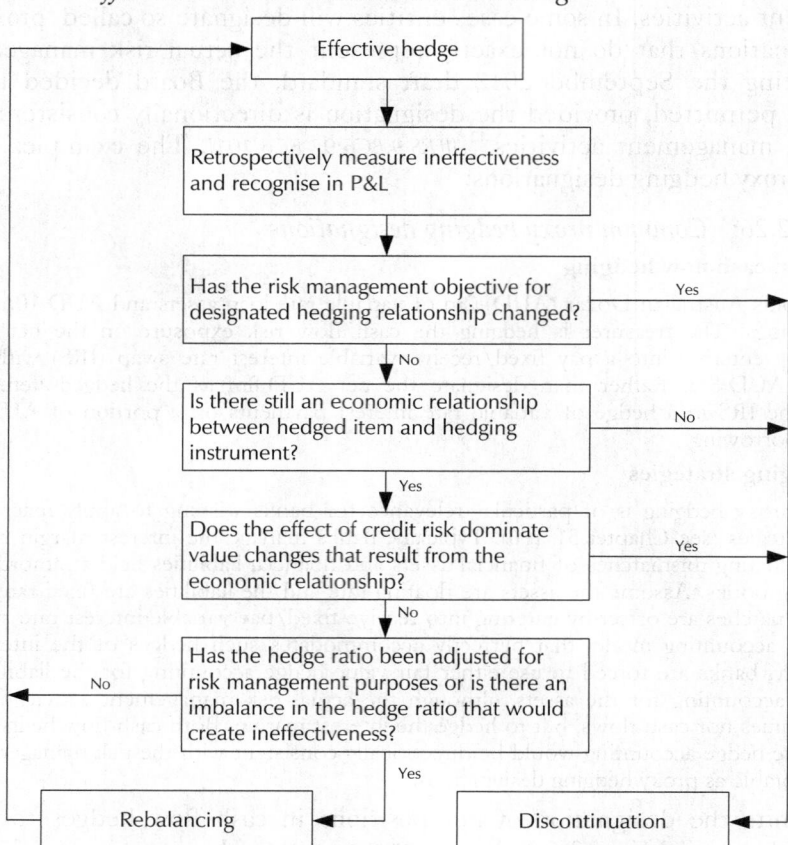

Each accounting period an entity first has to assess whether the risk management objective for the hedging relationship has changed. A change in risk management objective is a matter of fact that triggers discontinuation. Discontinuation of hedging relationships is discussed at 6.3 below.

An entity would also have to discontinue hedge accounting if it turns out that there is no longer an economic relationship. This makes sense as whether there is an economic relationship is a matter of fact that cannot be altered by adjusting the hedge ratio. The same is true for the impact of credit risk; if credit risk is now dominating the hedging relationship, then the entity has to discontinue hedge accounting. *[IFRS 9.6.5.6]*.

But the hedge ratio may need to be adjusted if it turns out that the hedged item and hedging instrument do not move in relation to each other as expected. The entity has to assess whether it expects this to continue to be the case going forward. If so, the entity is required to rebalance the hedge ratio to reflect the change in the relationship between the underlyings.

Currently, under IAS 39, when a hedge ratio is revised, entities have to discontinue the hedging relationship in its entirety and restart a new hedging relationship. For a cash flow hedge this is likely to lead to a degree of recognised ineffectiveness, as the hedging instrument will likely now have a non-zero fair value (colloquially known as the 'late hedge' issue, described in Chapter 51 at 5.3.5).

Rebalancing under IFRS 9 allows entities to refine their hedge ratio without discontinuation and so reducing this source of recorded ineffectiveness.

6.2 Rebalancing

6.2.1 Definition

The newly introduced concept of rebalancing only comprises prospective changes to the hedge ratio to reflect expected changes in the relationship between the hedged item and the hedging instrument. *[IFRS 9.B6.5.7]*. Any other changes made to the quantities of the hedged item or hedging instrument for instance, a reduction in the quantity of the hedged item because some cash flows are no longer highly probable, would not be rebalancing. Such other changes to the designated quantities would need to be treated as a partial discontinuation if the entity reduces the extent to which it hedges, and a new designation of a hedging relationship if the entity increases it. *[IFRS 9.B6.5.9]*. Changes that risk managers may make to improve hedge effectiveness but that do not alter the quantities of the hedged item or the hedging instrument are not rebalancing either. An example of such a change is the transaction of derivatives related to a risk that was not considered in the original hedge relationship.

Therefore, rebalancing is only relevant if there is basis risk between the hedged item and the hedging instrument. It only affects the expected relative sensitivity between the hedged item and the hedging instrument going forward, as ineffectiveness from past changes in the sensitivity will have already been recognised in profit or loss. The following example provides some indications as to how to distinguish rebalancing from other changes to a hedge relationship:

Example 52.27: Rebalancing

Fact pattern 1

An entity is exposed to price changes in commodity A which is not widely traded as a derivative. The entity has proven that there is an economic relationship between commodity A and B and commodity B is widely traded as a derivative. In that case, the entity may use commodity B derivatives to hedge the price risk in commodity A. An initial hedge ratio of 1:1.1 is based on the expected relationship between the prices of commodity A and commodity B. The relationship subsequently changes such that a ratio of 1:1.15 is expected to be more effective.

The entity can account for the changes in the hedging relationship as rebalancing because the difference between the prices is caused by basis risk.

Fact pattern 2

An entity swaps a base rate floating rate loan into a fixed interest rate using a pay LIBOR receive fixed swap. At inception, the entity is able to prove that there is an economic relationship between the base rate and LIBOR and designates the swap and the loan in a cash flow hedge, although it expects some level of ineffectiveness. Similar to fact pattern 1, the entity may use rebalancing to account for changes in the basis spread between the base rate and LIBOR.

Chapter 52

However, the entity subsequently transacts a LIBOR versus base rate swap in order to eliminate the basis risk. The accounting consequences would depend on the reason for doing so and here we consider two scenarios:

a)   The entity can no longer prove that there is an economic relationship between the base rate and LIBOR

b)   The entity can still prove that there is an economic relationship between the base rate and LIBOR, but no longer wishes to suffer the resultant ineffectiveness arising from the basis risk.

In scenario a), the hedging relationship no longer meets the eligibility criteria and needs to be discontinued, as there is no longer an economic relationship between the hedged item and the hedging instrument. The entity cannot use rebalancing to avoid discontinuation because the hedge no longer meets the qualifying criteria.

In scenario b), the entity tries to avoid ineffectiveness by contracting another hedging instrument. Arguably, the entity could continue with the original designation and account for the LIBOR versus base rate swap as a derivative measured at fair value through profit or loss. However, given that the entity seeks to avoid ineffectiveness, it might want to apply hedge accounting to the base rate swap as well. If the entity wants to include the LIBOR versus base rate swap in the original hedging relationship, it would represent a change in the documented risk management objective which requires discontinuation of the existing and re-designation of a new hedging relationship.

Fact pattern 3

An entity with functional currency of US dollars designated a fix rate loan denominated in EUR and a USD dollars /Euro forward exchange contract in a cash flow hedge. Subsequently, the borrower suffers significant financial difficulties and the entity only expects to receive 90% of the contractual cash flows on the loan.

The entity cannot apply rebalancing because the changes in the cash flows of the hedged item are not caused by basis risk but by credit risk. Instead, the entity is required to assess whether credit risk dominates the fair value changes of the hedged item in which case the hedging relationship needs to be discontinued (see 5.3 above). The entity might, however, still adjust the amount of the hedging instrument and treat this as a partial dedesignation.

Fact pattern 4

An airline with functional currency of Swiss francs enters into a firm commitment to purchase ten new airplanes in two years' time. The contract to purchase those airplanes is denominated in US dollars and the airline enters into a forward exchange contract to hedge the foreign currency exposure. The airline designates the firm commitment and the derivative in a fair value hedge. Six months into the contract, the aircraft manufacturer informs the airline that it has suffered significant delays in production and that the aircrafts will not be delivered in two years as originally planned but in three years. Payment is due when the airplanes are delivered.

The delay in payment may result in ineffectiveness as the forward exchange rates for two years and three years are likely to be different. However, the airline could not avoid this ineffectiveness by rebalancing, because the ineffectiveness is caused by the timing difference and not basis risk that was present in the original designation.

6.2.2   Requirement to rebalance

Whether an entity has to rebalance a hedging relationship is first and foremost a matter of fact, which is, whether the hedge ratio has changed for risk management purposes. An entity has to rebalance a hedging relationship if that relationship has an unchanged risk management objective but no longer meets the hedge effectiveness requirements regarding the hedge ratio. This will, in effect, be the case if the hedge ratio is no longer the one that is actually used for risk management (see 5.4 above). *[IFRS 9.6.5.5].*

However, as on initial designation, the hedge ratio for hedge accounting purposes would have to differ from the hedge ratio used for risk management if the latter would result in ineffectiveness that could result in an accounting outcome that would be inconsistent with the purpose of hedge accounting. *[IFRS 9.B6.5.14]*.

IFRS 9 clarifies that 'not every change in the extent of offset between the hedging instrument and the hedged item constitutes a change in the relationship' that requires rebalancing. For example, hedge ineffectiveness arising from a fluctuation around an otherwise valid hedge ratio cannot be reduced by adjusting the hedge ratio. *[IFRS 9.B6.5.11, B6.5.12]*. A trend in the amount of ineffectiveness on the other hand might suggest that retaining the hedge ratio would result in increased ineffectiveness going forward. This guidance in IFRS 9 further clarifies that an accounting outcome that would be inconsistent with the purpose of hedge accounting as the result of failing to adjust the hedge ratio for risk management purposes, would not meet the qualifying criteria for hedge accounting. This simply means that the qualifying criteria treat inappropriate hedge ratios in the same way, irrespective of whether they were achieved by acting (inappropriate designation) or failure to act (by not adjusting a designation that has become inappropriate). *[IFRS 9.B6.5.13]*.

6.2.3   Mechanics of rebalancing

Rebalancing can be achieved by:

- increasing the volume of the hedged item;
- increasing the volume of the hedging instrument;
- decreasing the volume of the hedged item; or
- decreasing the volume of the hedging instrument. *[IFRS 9.B6.5.16]*.

Decreasing the volume of the hedging instrument or hedged item does not mean that the respective transactions or items no longer exist or are no longer expected to occur. As demonstrated in Example 52.28 below, rebalancing only changes what is designated in the particular hedging relationship:

Example 52.28:   Rebalancing the hedge ratio by decreasing the volume of the hedging instrument

1 January

An entity expects to purchase 1m barrels of West Texas Intermediate (WTI) crude oil in 12 months. The entity designates a futures contract of 1.05m barrels of Brent crude oil in a cash flow hedge to hedge the highly probable forecast purchase of 1m barrels of WTI crude oil (hedge ratio of 1.05:1).

30 June

At 30 June, the cumulative change in the value of the hedged item is CU 200, while the cumulative change in the fair value of the hedging instrument is CU 229.

The entity would account for the hedging relationship as follows:

	CU	CU
Hedging gain/loss – other comprehensive income	200	
Hedge ineffectiveness	29	
Derivatives – hedging instruments		229

The treasurer of the entity is very sensitive to ineffectiveness and therefore considers rebalancing the hedging relationship.

The analysis of the treasurer shows that the sensitivity of Brent crude oil to WTI crude oil prices was not as expected. Going forward, the treasurer expects a different relationship between the two benchmark prices and decides to reset the hedge ratio to 0.98:1.

Rebalancing on 30 June

The treasurer can either designate more WTI exposure or de-designate part of the hedging instrument. The entity decides to do the latter, that is, discontinue hedge accounting for 0.07m barrels of Brent crude oil derivatives.

Of the total of 1.05m barrels of Brent derivative, 0.07m are no longer part of the hedging relationship. Therefore, the entity needs to reclassify 7/105 (or 6.7%) of the hedging instrument in the statement of financial position to a held for trading derivative, measured at fair value through profit or loss. The hedge documentation is updated accordingly.

The entity accounts for the rebalancing as follows:

	CU	CU
Derivatives – hedging instruments	15	
Derivatives – trading		15

To reflect that a part of the derivative is no longer part of a hedging relationship.

In Example 52.28 above, the entity no longer needs to hold this portion of the derivative any longer for hedging purposes and could, therefore, close it out. As mentioned, the entity could have also rebalanced by designating more WTI exposure (assuming that the higher level of exposure is highly probable of occurring). In that case, there would not be any immediate accounting entries; the entity would simply designate more WTI exposure. The same would be true when rebalancing by increasing the volume of hedging instrument, in which case the entity would simply designate additional volume of hedging instrument (provided, of course, it is available).

Example 52.29:   Rebalancing the hedge ratio by decreasing the volume of hedged item

1 April

An entity has highly probable forecast purchases of diesel over the next 12 months. The entity expects to get monthly deliveries of 10,000 metric tonnes at the local market price. The entity designates a futures contract referenced to the Platts Diesel D2 price with a nominal amount of 9,500 metric tonnes in a cash flow hedge, to hedge 10,000 metric tonnes of highly probable diesel purchases in September (giving a hedge ratio of 1:0.95).

30 June

At 30 June, the cumulative change in the value of hedged item is CU 820, while the cumulative change in the fair value of hedging instrument is CU 650.

The entity would account for the hedging relationship as follows:

	CU	CU
Hedging reserve – other comprehensive income	650	
Derivatives – hedging instruments		650

To account for the fair value change of the hedging instrument.

Despite the hedge only being 79% effective, no hedging ineffectiveness is recorded as a result of the 'lower of test' in the standard. *[IFRS 9.6.5.11(a)]*. As per that paragraph, the amount accumulated in other comprehensive income has to be the lower of:

i)   the cumulative gain or loss on the hedging instrument; and

ii)   the cumulative change in fair value of the hedged item, with any remaining gain or loss on the hedging instrument being recorded in profit or loss.

Based on an analysis, the entity now believes that the appropriate hedge ratio going forward is 1:1.05. Consequently, the entity can either increase the volume of hedging instrument or decrease the volume of hedged item. Based on a cost-benefit analysis the entity decides to reduce the volume of hedged item by 952 metric tonnes.

Rebalancing on 30 June

Rebalancing a hedge ratio by decreasing the volume of hedged item is considered a partial discontinuation of the hedging relationship. *[IFRS 9.B6.5.27]*. The entity is discontinuing 952 $(10,000 − (9,500/1.05) = 952)$ metric tonnes of diesel purchases while 9,048 metric tonnes of forecast purchases remain in the hedging relationship. The hedge documentation is updated accordingly. No accounting entry is required (however, the entity would have to retain the information that 952 metric tonnes of diesel were the hedged item for some part of the total life of the hedging relationship and which amount in the cash flow hedge reserve relates to this quantity of diesel).

Even though the standard allows adjusting either the quantity of hedging instrument or the quantity of the hedged item, when rebalancing, entities should consider that adjusting the hedged item will be operationally more complex than adjusting the hedging instrument because of the need to track the history of different quantities that were designated during the term of the hedging relationship. For example, if a quantity of 10 tonnes of a hedged item were added to increase the quantity of hedged item and later deducted to decrease it, those 10 tonnes would have been part of the hedged item for only a part of the life of the hedging relationship. However, any cash flow hedge adjustment would still, in part, relate to that quantity. This can get more complex in situations in which the hedging relationship needs frequent rebalancing, if not all hedged transactions occur at the same time, or in conjunction with the cost formulas used for the measurement of the cost of inventory. In addition, adjusting the hedged item might appear more as if the entity uses an accounting driven approach to hedge accounting, because risk management would normally adjust the quantity of the designated hedging instruments when rebalancing since the hedged exposure is the 'given' and drives what hedges are needed.

6.3   Discontinuation

As already discussed above, an entity would have to discontinue hedge accounting if the qualification criteria are no longer met. *[IFRS 9.6.5.6]*. As also mentioned at 6.1 above, this includes if the risk management objective for the hedging relationship has changed.

In an important change to IAS 39, IFRS 9 now introduces partial discontinuation of hedge accounting, which means that hedge accounting continues for the remaining part of the hedging relationship. *[IFRS 9.6.5.6]*.

The table below summarises the main scenarios resulting in either full or partial discontinuation:

Scenario	Discontinuation
The risk management objective has changed	Full or partial
There is no longer an economic relationship between the hedged item and the hedging instrument	Full
The effect of credit risk dominates the value changes of the hedging relationship	Full
As part of rebalancing, the volume of the hedged item or the hedging instrument is reduced	Partial
The hedging instrument expires	Full
The hedging instrument is (in full or in part) sold, terminated or exercised	Full or partial
The hedged item (or part of it) no longer exists or is no longer expected to occur	Full or partial

The application guidance in IFRS 9 contains three examples elaborating what constitutes a change in risk management objective. *[IFRS 9.B6.5.24].* We believe that a change in risk management objective has to be a matter of fact that can be observed in the entity's actual risk management. The examples below, the first of which is derived from the application guidance to IFRS 9, demonstrate how this could be assessed in practice.

Example 52.30:   Partial discontinuation as a result of a change in risk management objective

ABC Ltd is currently fully financed with variable rate borrowings (the tables in this example show nominal amounts in millions of Euro (EUR)):

Non-current financial liabilities as of 1 January 20x1	Variable rate	Fixed rate
Variable rate borrowings	100	
Fixed rate borrowings		0
Total	100	0
	100%	0%

Risk management strategy

To maintain between 20% and 40% of long term debt at a fixed rate.

Risk management activity

Consequently, the treasurer of ABC enters into a pay fixed/receive variable interest rate swap (IRS) and designates the IRS in a hedging relationship.

Risk management objective

Use a pay fixed/receive floating interest rate swap with a notional amount of EUR 30m in a cash flow hedge to hedge the interest payments on EUR 30m of the variable rate borrowings in order to maintain 30% of the long term borrowings at fixed rate.

Non-current financial liabilities as of 1 January 20x1	Variable rate	Fixed rate
Variable rate borrowings	100	
Fixed rate borrowings		0
Pay fixed/receive variable interest rate swap	(30)	30
Total	70	30
	70%	30%

On 31 March 20x2, the entity needs further funding and takes advantage of lower interest rates by issuing a EUR 50m fixed rate bond. At the same time, the entity decides to set its fixed rate exposure at 40% of total borrowings, still being within the risk management strategy.

Non-current financial liabilities as of 31 March 20x2	Variable rate	Fixed rate
Variable rate borrowings	100	
Fixed rate borrowings		50
Pay fixed/receive variable interest rate swap	(30)	30
Total	70	80
	47%	53%

It becomes evident that ABC is no longer within the target range of its risk management strategy. In order to execute the risk management strategy, ABC no longer needs part of its interest rate swap. In other words, the risk management objective for the hedging relationship has changed. Consequently, ABC discontinues EUR 20m of the hedging relationship (a partial discontinuation) and would most likely close out the risk from EUR 20m of the IRS.

Going forward, ABC's debt financing and risk profile will be as follows: *[IFRS 9.B6.5.24]*

Non-current financial liabilities as of 31 March 20x2	Variable rate	Fixed rate
Variable rate borrowings	100	
Fixed rate borrowings		50
Pay fixed/receive floating interest rate swap	(10)	10
Total	90	60
	60%	40%

The above example only illustrates the outcome of one particular course of action. The entity could also have adjusted its interest rate exposure in a different way in order to remain in the target range for its fixed rate funding, for instance by swapping EUR 20m of the new fixed rate bond into variable rate funding. In that case, instead of discontinuing a part of the already existing cash flow hedge the entity would have designated a new fair value hedge. The example in the application guidance of the standard is obviously a simplified one. In practice, entities tend to have staggered maturities for different parts of their financing. In such situations it would often be obvious from the maturity of the new interest rate swaps if they are a fair value hedge of the debt or a reduction of the already existing cash flow hedge volume. For example, if the new EUR 50m fixed rate bond is for a longer period than the existing debt and the new interest rate swap is for the same longer period, it would suggest that it is a fair value hedge of the new fixed rate bond instead of a reduction of the cash flow hedge for the already existing debt. Conversely, a reduction of the cash flow hedge volume would be consistent with entering into a new interest rate swap that has the same remaining maturity as the existing interest rate swap and offsets its fair value changes on a part of the notional amount.

Chapter 52

Example 52.31:   Partial discontinuation of an interest margin hedge

XYZ Bank is holding a combination of fixed and variable rate assets and liabilities on its banking book. For risk management purposes, the bank allocates all the assets and liabilities to time bands based on their contractual maturity. As of 1 January 20x1 the bank holds the following instruments in the 5-year time bucket (the tables in this example show nominal amounts in millions of Euro (EUR)):

Summary of instruments with a 5-year maturity	Assets: fixed rate	Liabilities: fixed rate	Assets: variable rate	Liabilities: variable rate
Bonds held			20	
Mortgages	30		10	
Retail loans	30		10	
Client term deposits				(60)
Bonds issued		(30)		(10)
Total	60	(30)	40	(70)
Fixed-variable interest mismatch		30		(30)

The fixed-variable mismatch results in interest margin risk due to changes in interest rates.

Risk management strategy

To eliminate the interest margin risk resulting from fixed-variable interest mismatches.

Risk management activity

In order to achieve the risk management strategy, XYZ Bank enters into a pay fixed/receive variable interest rate swap (IRS) with a notional amount of EUR 30m. For accounting purposes, the bank could either designate the IRS in a cash flow hedge of EUR 30m of specific variable rate liabilities or in a fair value hedge of EUR 30m of specific fixed rate assets. Under the local regulatory requirements, fair value hedges are more favourable for the bank's regulatory capital.

Risk management objective

Using a EUR 30m pay fixed/receive variable IRS in a fair value hedge of EUR 30m of fixed rate retail loans to hedge a fixed-variable interest mismatch on fixed and variable rate assets and liabilities in the 5-year time bucket of XYZ Bank's banking book.

At the beginning of year 20x3, XYZ Bank attracts EUR 10m of client term deposits as a result of a successful marketing campaign. The new term deposits all have a fixed interest rate for a maturity of three years, therefore, matching the (remaining) maturity of the instruments in the above time bucket. The XYZ Bank uses the proceeds from the new term deposits to buy back EUR 10m of variable rate bonds that it has issued. The new situation in the (now) 3-year time bucket is:

Summary of instruments with a 3-year maturity	Assets: fixed rate	Liabilities: fixed rate	Assets: variable rate	Liabilities: variable rate
Bonds held			20	
Mortgages	30		10	
Retail loans	30		10	
Client term deposits		(10)		(60)
Bonds issued		(30)		(0)
Total	60	(40)	40	(60)
Fixed-variable interest mismatch		20		(20)
Pay fixed/receive variable interest rate swap		(30)		30

As a result of the change in funding, the risk management objective of the hedging relationship has changed. XYZ Bank is over-hedged and needs to discontinue EUR10m of its hedging relationship.

A logical consequence of linking the discontinuation to the risk management objective is that voluntary discontinuations are no longer permitted just for accounting purposes. This change, gave rise to concern among some constituents who argued that, given hedge accounting is optional, voluntary discontinuation should be retained. *[IFRS 9.BC6.324]*.

In our view, entities have often voluntarily discontinued hedge accounting to adjust, for instance, the hedge ratio for a change in the expected relationship between the hedged item and the hedging instrument. Other reasons were because the entity wanted to hedge a secondary risk (i.e. an entity first hedged the commodity price risk in a commodity purchase contract in foreign currency but later decided to hedge the foreign currency risk as well), because the chosen effectiveness method no longer was appropriate, or because some of the hedged cash flows were no longer expected to occur.

This is addressed in IFRS 9 by introducing a new effectiveness assessment, rebalancing, the ability to achieve hedge accounting for aggregated exposures and partial discontinuation. Hence, voluntary discontinuation is no longer needed in such situations.

In its redeliberations, the IASB noted that hedge accounting is an exception to the general accounting principles in IFRS to (better) present in the financial statements a particular risk management objective of a risk management activity. If that risk management objective is unchanged and the qualifying criteria for hedge accounting are still met, a voluntary discontinuation would jeopardise the original (valid) reason for applying hedge accounting. The Board believes that hedge accounting, including its discontinuation, should have a meaning and should not be a mere accounting exercise. *[IFRS 9.BC6.327]*. Based on this, the IASB decided not to allow voluntary discontinuation for hedges with unchanged risk management objectives. *[IFRS 9.BC6.331]*.

It is important to note that the risk management objective of an individual hedging relationship can change although the risk management strategy of the entity remains unchanged. *[IFRS 9.BC6.331]*. In fact, in most cases where an entity might wish to voluntarily dedesignate a hedging relationship, this is usually driven by a change in the risk management objective in which case the entity would actually be required to amend its hedge accounting under IFRS 9. The standard only prohibits voluntary dedesignations when they are only made for accounting purposes.

6.4 Measuring ineffectiveness

IFRS 9 only adds two paragraphs in the application guidance on how to measure ineffectiveness, dealing with the time value of money and hypothetical derivatives. Although intended as a clarification, these two paragraphs might have wider implications for some practices currently used by entities. Except for the matters mentioned in this section, the guidance on measurement of ineffectiveness are the same as under IAS 39 and are covered in Chapter 51 at 4.1.1 and 4.2.1.

6.4.1   *The effect of the time value of money*

Entities have to consider the time value of money when measuring hedge ineffectiveness. This means that an entity has to determine the value of the hedged item on a present value basis (thereby including the effect of the time value of money). *[IFRS 9.B6.5.4]*.

The guidance in IFRS 9 does not clarify more than what was (theoretically) already clear under IAS 39 (see Chapter 51 at 5.3.1). In valuation practice, the effect of the time value of money is also included when measuring the fair value of financial instruments. Consequently, it is more than logical to apply the same principle to the hedged item as well.

Example 52.32:   Impact of time value of money when measuring ineffectiveness

A manufacturing company in India, having the Indian Rupee as its functional currency, is expecting forecast sales in USD. The company assesses sales of USD 1m per month for the next twelve months to be highly probable and wishes to hedge the related foreign currency exposure. The company also holds a borrowing of USD 20m. Instead of entering into foreign currency forward contracts, the company designates the US dollar borrowing as a hedging instrument in hedges of the spot risk of the monthly highly probable US dollar sales.

This hedge is a pure accounting hedge as the cash flows of the sales and the borrowing do not match. When measuring hedge ineffectiveness, the revaluation of the forecast sales for foreign currency risk would have to be on a discounted basis (i.e. a present value calculation reflecting the time between the reporting date and the future cash flow date), whereas the revaluation of the hedging instrument would not (as this follows the requirements of IAS 21).

It is suggested by some that use of a spot designation would override the general principle of IFRS 9 that measurement of ineffectiveness needs to be made on a discounted basis. *[IFRS 9.B6.5.4]*. The Guidance in Implementing IAS 39 contains an example where an entity designated changes in the spot element only. The example indicates that the time value of money is relevant for the assessment of effectiveness even when the spot element is designated in a hedge relationship, but this example has not been carried forward to IFRS 9. *[IAS 39.IG.F.5.6]*.

However, the requirement to calculate ineffectiveness on a present value basis intuitively makes sense in cases where the cash flows of the hedged item and hedging instrument are not aligned. It would seem inappropriate to have no ineffectiveness under a spot designation, for example in the situation described at 4.4 above where a 7-year financial liability denominated in a foreign currency is used as the hedging instrument of a 12 month forecast sale in that foreign currency.

However, currently under IAS 39 diversity in practice exists with respect to the discounting of the spot element for hedge effectiveness measurement purposes. This is perhaps because in many circumstances the effect of discounting the revaluation of the spot element is unlikely to be material. Although the requirement to measure effectiveness on a present value basis appears to be clearer in IFRS 9, the standard does not explicitly say that it applies to a spot designation. Hence, we expect this diversity to continue.

6.4.2 *Hypothetical derivatives for measuring ineffectiveness*

Although not specifically addressed in IAS 39, a method commonly used in practice to measure (and assess) ineffectiveness of cash flow hedges is the use of a so-called 'hypothetical derivative'. Although IFRS 9 brings more clarity in this regard, the basic method has not changed compared to IAS 39. The method involves establishing a notional derivative that has terms that match the critical terms of the hedged exposure (normally an interest rate swap or forward contract with no unusual terms and a zero fair value at inception of the hedging relationship). The fair value of the hypothetical derivative is then used to measure the change in the value of the hedged item against which changes in value of the actual hedging instrument are compared, to assess effectiveness and measure ineffectiveness (see Chapter 51 at 5.3.2).

IFRS 9 clarifies that use of a hypothetical derivative is one possible way of determining the change in the value of the hedged item when measuring ineffectiveness. However, IFRS 9 also clarifies that a hypothetical derivative has to be a replication of the hedged item and that any different method for determining the change in the value of the hedged item would have to have the same outcome. Consequently, an entity cannot include features in the hypothetical derivative that only exist in the hedging instrument, but not in the hedged item. *[IFRS 9.B6.5.5]*.

What appears to be a logical requirement may have wider implications for cash flow hedges than many would have expected. IFRS 9 is clear that the hypothetical derivative is supposed to represent the hedged item and not the 'perfect hedge'. In other words, an entity cannot simply assume no ineffectiveness for a cash flow hedge with matching terms (e.g. where the principle terms of the hedging instrument exactly match the principle terms of a hedged forecast transaction), since other features of the hedging instrument or the hedged item could differ.

For example, IFRS 13 requires an entity to reflect both the counterparty's credit risk and the entity's own credit risk in the measurement of a derivative. The counterparty credit risk of a derivative designated in a hedging relationship is likely to be different from the counterparty credit risk in the hedged item (if there is any). The difference in credit risk would result in some ineffectiveness (see 5.3 above and Chapter 51 at 5.3.2 and 5.3.4). Paragraph B6.5.5 of IFRS 9 is clear that, when using a hypothetical derivative for measuring ineffectiveness in a cash flow hedge, the counterparty credit risk on the hedging instrument could not be deemed to equally be a feature also present in the hedged item. *[IFRS 9.B6.5.5]*. For example, if the hedged item is a highly probable forecast transaction it would not involve any credit risk, so that there is no offset for any credit risk affecting the fair value of the hedging instrument, which would give rise to some ineffectiveness. Also, if the hedged item involves credit risk, the effect of that has to be established independently of the hedging instrument.

As a consequence of the above, a (maybe unexpected) source of ineffectiveness is the discount rate used for measuring the fair value of cash collateralised interest rate swaps (IRS). Historically, the fair values of interest rate swaps have been calculated using LIBOR-based discount rates. As per its definition, LIBOR is the average rate at which the reference banks can fund *unsecured* cash in the interbank market for a given currency and maturity.[13] However, the use of LIBOR as the standard discount rate ignores the fact that many derivative transactions are now collateralised and have therefore a lower credit risk than LIBOR would suggest. For cash-collateralised trades, a more relevant discount rate is an overnight rate rather than LIBOR. Overnight index swaps (OIS) are interest rate swaps where the floating leg is linked to an interest rate for overnight unsecured lending to a bank. OIS rates much better reflect the credit risk of cash collateralised IRS.

When measuring the fair value of cash-collateralised LIBOR indexed interest rate swap, an entity would have to use a LIBOR-based forward curve to determine the future floating cash flows, but these are then discounted using an OIS swap curve. This would result in a different fair value compared to a non-collateralised IRS for which both the forward rates and the discount rates are derived from the LIBOR swap curve. When, for example, a collateralised IRS is used as the designated hedging instrument in a fair value hedge of a fixed rate bond, this will likely lead to ineffectiveness because the calculation of the fair value of the bond is based on a discount rate that includes credit risk (such as LIBOR). The resulting ineffectiveness is sometimes referred to as the 'multi curve issue' (see also Chapter 51 at 5.3.4.A). For cash flow hedges, the situation is less clear under IAS 39. For example, a collateralised IRS is used to hedge the variability of cash flows of a variable rate bond due to changes in LIBOR. Consequentially, the IRS is designated as the hedging instrument in a cash flow hedge of the variable rate bond. The question arises which credit risk should be considered when the 'hypothetical derivative' is set up. However, by saying that 'the hypothetical derivative replicates the hedged item' IFRS 9 seems to clearly suggest that the 'hypothetical derivative' should be valued using a discount rate that represents the credit risk associated with the hedged risk. In this case, the appropriate discount rate would be LIBOR. *[IFRS 9.B6.5.5]*.

Historically, the difference between LIBOR and OIS rates has been equal to a few basis points only. However, the basis differential widened significantly during the financial crisis and is not expected to revert in the foreseeable future.

For cash-collateralised derivatives, both parties to the contract would have equal collateral requirements, significantly reducing the credit risk of both parties to the contract. This would improve the economic effectiveness of a hedging relationship while at the same time, may also result in more accounting ineffectiveness.

Another example of when the features of the hedging instrument and the hedging item could differ is when an entity hedges a debt instrument denominated in a foreign currency in a cash flow hedge (irrespective of whether it is fixed-rate or variable-rate debt). When using a hypothetical derivative to calculate ineffectiveness, the hypothetical derivative cannot simply impute a charge for exchanging different currencies (i.e. the foreign currency basis spread) even though actual derivatives (for example, cross-currency interest rate swaps) under which different currencies are exchanged might include such a charge. *[IFRS 9.B6.5.5]*. To address this, the IASB introduced the possibility to account for the foreign currency basis spread as a cost of hedging (see 7.2.2 below).

7 ACCOUNTING FOR THE COSTS OF HEDGING

Currently under IAS 39, entities can designate the intrinsic value of an option or the spot element of a forward contract. When doing so, the changes in fair value of the time value of the option or the forward points are accounted for in profit or loss, therefore resulting in volatility. This was criticised by many constituents as they see the time value or forward points as an unavoidable cost of hedging that should be accounted for accordingly. In response to these concerns, the IFRS 9 hedging model contains a new accounting requirement when only the intrinsic value or the spot element is designated in the hedge relationship. All the fluctuation in the fair value of the time value or forward points over time is recorded in other comprehensive income instead of profit or loss. This new treatment also applies to foreign currency basis spreads.

7.1 Time value of options

The fair value of an option consists of the intrinsic value and the time value. When using an option for hedging activities, only the intrinsic value is used for offsetting the fair value changes attributable to the hedged risk (unless the hedged item is also an option, see 4 above, or a delta-neutral hedging strategy is applied, see Chapter 51 at 5.1.2). Unchanged from IAS 39, an entity can either designate an option as a hedging instrument in its entirety, or it can separate the intrinsic value and the time value and designate only the intrinsic value. *[IFRS 9.6.2.4]*.

Under IAS 39, when designating the option in its entirety as a hedge of a non-option item, changes in the portion of the fair value attributable to the time value result in ineffectiveness. Depending on the level of ineffectiveness, an entity might even not pass the prospective effectiveness assessment or be forced to discontinue hedge accounting as a result of changes in the time value. Alternatively, when designating the intrinsic value of the option only, the time value has to be accounted for at fair value through profit or loss, thus, also resulting in potentially significant profit or loss volatility, albeit without the risk of failing the effectiveness assessment. In either case, the change in the time value will be recognised in profit or loss (see also Chapter 51 at 2.1.4.A).

From a risk management perspective, entities typically consider the premium paid on an option (which, on inception, is often only time value) as a cost of hedging rather than a trading position. Economically, the time value could be considered as a premium for protection against risk (i.e. an 'insurance premium'). *[IFRS 9.BC6.387]*. IFRS 9 does not change how an option is designated in a hedging relationship (i.e. whether in its entirety or the intrinsic value only). However, the IASB has acknowledged these concerns and introduced a new accounting treatment for changes in the fair value of the time value if only the intrinsic value is designated in the hedging relationship.

Changes in the fair value of the time value of options to the extent that they relate to the hedged item, are first recognised in other comprehensive income (OCI). The subsequent treatment depends on the nature of the hedged transaction. The standard differentiates between transaction related hedged items and time-period related hedged items: *[IFRS 9.6.5.15, B6.5.29]*

- Transaction related hedged item: the time value of an option used to hedge such an item has the character of part of the cost of the transaction. An example would be a hedge of a forecast commodity purchase.

  The amount that is accumulated in OCI is removed similarly to amounts accumulated in the cash flow hedge reserve (see 8.1 below), i.e. if the hedged transaction subsequently results in the recognition of a non-financial item, the amount becomes a 'basis adjustment', otherwise the amount is reclassified to profit or loss in the same period or periods during which the hedged cash flows affect profit or loss.

- Time-period related hedged item: the time value of an option used to hedge such an item has the character of the cost of protection against a risk over a particular period of time. An example would be a hedge of commodity inventory over a six month period.

  The amount that is accumulated in OCI is amortised on a systematic and rational basis to profit or loss as a reclassification adjustment. The amortisation period is the period during which the hedge adjustment for the option's intrinsic value could affect profit or loss (or other comprehensive income if the option is designated as a hedge of an equity instrument accounted for at fair value through other comprehensive income).

The distinction between transaction related hedged items and time-period related hedged items reflects that the accounting for the time value of the option should follow general IFRS principles for how to account for payments that are akin to insurance premiums (the 'insurance premium view' mentioned above). So, in making the distinction, an entity needs to consider how the accounting for the hedged item will eventually affect profit or loss.

If the hedged item later results in a transaction for which the transactions costs are accounted for as part of a one-off event (like a purchase or a sale of an item), the option's time value relates to a transaction related hedged item. Examples are hedges of forecast purchases of inventory or property, plant and equipment, and forecast sales, as well as purchases or sales resulting from firm commitments.

If the hedged item later results in protection against risk for a particular period that does not involve a transaction for which the transactions costs are accounted for as part of a one-off event, the option's time value relates to a time-period related hedged item. Examples are hedges of interest expense or income in particular periods, already existing inventory hedged for fair value changes or a hedge of a net investment in a foreign operation. In the case of a forward starting interest rate option, the time value would be amortised over the interest periods that the option covers (i.e. the amortisation period would exclude the initial part of the option's life).

It is important to note that because this accounting for 'costs of hedging' only applies if the time value of the option is excluded from the designation of the hedging relationship, the amounts deferred in accumulated other comprehensive income are not part of the cash flow hedge reserve but instead a different component of equity. The cash flow hedge reserve only includes amounts that are gains or losses on hedging instruments that are determined to be an effective hedge (i.e. amounts that are included in the designation of a hedging relationship). By default, the time value will be zero at expiry of an option contract. For a transaction related hedged item, recognising the fair value changes of the time value in OCI means that on expiry, the time value that existed at designation will have accumulated in OCI. Once the hedged transaction happens, the accounting for the accumulated time value follows the accounting for any changes in fair value of the intrinsic value of the option (that were also accumulated in OCI). *[IFRS 9.6.5.15].*

Example 52.33:   Hedging the purchase of equipment (transaction related)

In the first quarter of a year, a manufacturing entity plans to purchase a new machine for its manufacturing process. Delivery of the machine is expected in the third quarter and the purchase price will be Swedish Krona (SEK) 5m. The entity has the Norwegian Krone (NOK) as its functional currency and, therefore, is exposed to foreign currency risk on this forecast transaction. The entity buys a call option to purchase SEK 5m, as it wishes to hedge the downside risk only. The terms of the option match the terms of the forecast transaction. The entity designates only the intrinsic value of the call option in a cash flow hedge of the highly probable forecast purchase of the machine.

At inception, the time value of the option amounts to NOK 30,000. After inception, the time value of the option amounts to NOK 16,000 at the end of the first quarter, NOK 7,000 at the end of the second quarter and zero at maturity.

Applying the IFRS 9 accounting requirements to the time value of the option results in the following movement within other comprehensive income (OCI) and the reserve within equity for accumulating amounts in relation to the time value of options associated with transaction related hedged items:

(All amounts in NOK thousands)	Q1	Q2	Q3
Reserve at beginning of quarter	–	(14)	(23)
Change in time value of option	(14)	(9)	(7)
Basis adjustment to machine			30
Reserve at end of quarter	(14)	(23)	–
Effect on OCI for the period	(14)	(9)	(7)

For time-period related hedged items, the standard does not prescribe what 'on a systematic and rational basis' means in the context of amortising the time value from OCI to profit or loss. We believe a straight-line amortisation to be appropriate in most cases.

Example 52.34:   Hedging interest rate risk of a bond (time period related) (1)

An entity issues a seven-year floating rate bond and wishes to protect itself against increases in the interest expense for the first two years. Therefore, the entity purchases an interest rate cap with a maturity of two years. Only the intrinsic value of the cap is designated as a hedging instrument in a cash flow hedge.

The time value on designation is CU 20, which is amortised to profit or loss on a straight-line basis over the protection period (i.e. the first two years). After inception, the time value of the option amounts to CU 13 at the end of the first year.

Applying the IFRS 9 accounting requirements to the time value of the option results in the following movement within other comprehensive income (OCI) and the reserve within equity for accumulating amounts in relation to the time value of options associated with time-period related hedged items:

	Year 1	Year 2
Reserve at beginning of year	–	3
Change in time value of option	(7)	(13)
Amortisation of time value at inception	10	10
Reserve at end of year	3	–
Effect on OCI for the year	3	(3)
Effect on profit or loss for the year	(10)	(10)

The accounting for the time value of options would also apply to combinations of options, for example, when hedging a highly probable forecast transaction with a zero-cost collar. When designating the intrinsic value only, the volatility resulting from changes in the time values of the two options would be recognised in other comprehensive income. However, the amortisation (in the case of time-period related hedged items) or the transaction costs deferred at the end of the life of the hedging relationship (for transaction related hedged items) would be nil when using a zero-cost collar. *[IFRS 9.B6.5.31].*

Examples 52.30 and 52.31 above both assume that the critical terms of the option match the hedged item. However, in practice, this is not always the case. The accounting treatment described above applies only to the extent the time value relates to the hedged item. An additional assessment has to be made if the critical terms of the option do not match the hedged item. For that purpose, the actual time value has to be compared with that of a hypothetical option that perfectly matches the critical terms of the hedged item (in IFRS 9 referred to as the 'aligned time value'). *[IFRS 9.B6.5.32].*

When the terms of the option are not aligned with the hedged item, the accounting for the time value in situations in which the aligned time value exceeds the actual time value is different to situations in which the actual time value exceeds the aligned time value. *[IFRS 9.B6.5.33].*

If, at inception, the actual time value exceeds the aligned time value:

- the aligned time value at inception is amortised on a rational basis from OCI to profit or loss over the period the hedged item affects profit or loss (for a time-period related hedged item);
- the change in the fair value of the aligned time value is recognised in OCI; and
- the remaining difference in change in fair value between the actual time value and the aligned time value is recognised in profit or loss. *[IFRS 9.B6.5.33].*

If, at inception, the aligned time value exceeds the actual time value:

- the actual time value at inception is amortised on a rational basis from OCI to profit or loss over the period the hedged item affects profit or loss (for a time-period related hedged item);
- the lower of the cumulative change in the fair value of the actual time value and the aligned time value is recognised in OCI; and

- the remaining difference in change in fair value between the actual time value and the aligned time value, if any, is recognised in profit or loss. *[IFRS 9.B6.5.33].*

For the hedging strategy introduced in Example 52.35 above, this would change the accounting as follows:

Example 52.35: Hedging interest rate risk of a bond (time period related) (2)

Scenario 1: Actual time value exceeds aligned time value

The actual time value at inception is CU 20. The aligned time value at inception is CU 15.

	Year 1	Year 2
Change in actual time value of option	(7)	(13)
Change in aligned time value of option	(6)	(9)
Reserve in equity at beginning of year	–	1.5
Change in time value of option (based on aligned time value)	(6)	(9)
Amortisation of time value at inception (based on aligned time value)	7.5	7.5
Reserve in equity at end of year	1.5	–
Effect on OCI for the year	1.5	(1.5)
Remaining change in (actual) time value recognised in profit or loss (difference between the change in aligned time value and the actual time value of the option)	(1)	(4)
Effect on profit or loss for the year	(8.5)	(11.5)

The above accounting treats the difference between the actual and the aligned time value, consistent with its default classification, as a derivative at fair value through profit or loss.

Scenario 2: Actual time value is lower than aligned time value

The actual time value at inception is CU 20. The aligned time value at inception is CU 24.

	Year 1	Year 2
Change in actual time value of option	(7)	(13)
Change in aligned time value of option	(14)	(10)
Reserve in equity at beginning of year	–	2
Change in time value of option (based on the lower of the cumulative change in aligned time value and actual time value)	(7)	(13)
Amortisation of time value at inception (based on actual time value)	10	10
Reserve in equity at end of year	3	–
Effect on OCI for the year	3	(3)
Remaining change in (actual) time value recognised in profit or loss (zero, because the aligned time value of the option exceeds the actual time value of the option at inception)	–	–
Effect on profit or loss for the year	(10)	(10)

The above 'lower of test' for the accounting of the time value ensures that the entity does not recognise more expense in profit or loss than the entity actually incurred (based on the time value at inception).

IFRS 9 does not define the 'aligned time value' in much detail but it is clear that it is part of the concept of 'costs of hedging'. Therefore, regular pricing features, such as dealer margins, are part of the aligned time value of an option, reflecting that they are part of the fair value of the financial instrument whose intrinsic value is designated as the hedging instrument. This is different from using a hypothetical

Chapter 52

derivative, which has the purpose of measuring the hedged item. For that purpose, features that are only in the hedging instrument but not the hedged item cannot be taken into account, whereas the same rationale does not apply for the purpose of accounting for the costs of hedging. This becomes clearer from the example of the foreign currency basis spread (see 7.2.2 below); it cannot be included as part of a hypothetical derivative to measure the hedged item but it is a cost of hedging.

7.2 Forward element of forward contracts and foreign currency basis spread of financial instruments

7.2.1 General requirements

Under IAS 39, entities using foreign currency forward contracts in hedging relationships can designate the instrument in its entirety or designate the spot element. Designating the spot element results in the forward points (often also called the 'forward element') to be accounted for at fair value through profit or loss (see Chapter 51 at 2.1.4.B).

When designating the entire instrument, IAS 39 allows the hedged item alternatively to be measured at the forward rate instead of the spot rate. For example, when hedging a highly probable forecast transaction, the hedged item, once transacted, would be measured at the forward rate at designation. This is often referred to as the 'forward rate method' (see Chapter 51 at 5.3.3). However, IAS 21 requires monetary financial assets and liabilities denominated in a foreign currency to be measured at the spot rate. As a result, the forward rate method does not provide a similar solution for hedges of such monetary items because of how IAS 21 works. [IFRS 9.BC6.422].

The Exposure Draft did not propose changes to the accounting for forward points. However, many constituents, in particular financial institutions that are hedging the foreign exchange risk of loans and borrowings denominated in foreign currencies, have asked for an accounting treatment similar to the one for the time value of options. [IFRS 9.BC6.417]. As a change to the ED, IFRS 9 introduces an optional treatment similar to the accounting for time value of options when only the spot element is designated. This is, however, not an accounting policy choice, but an election for each designation.

When designating the spot element, the change in fair value of the forward element is recognised in other comprehensive income (OCI) and accumulated in a separate component of equity. The accounting for the forward element that exists at inception also follows the distinction between transaction related hedged items and time-period related hedged items that is made when accounting for the time value of an option (see at 7.1 above). This means, in the case of a transaction related hedged item, that the change in the fair value of the forward element is deferred in OCI and included, like transaction costs, in the measurement of the hedged item (or it is reclassified to profit or loss when a hedged sale occurs). In case of a time-period related hedged item, the forward element that exists at inception is amortised from the separate component of equity to profit or loss on a rational basis. [IFRS 9.6.5.16, B6.5.34].

As a result of the above accounting, fluctuations in the fair value of the forward element over time will affect other comprehensive income, and the amount accumulated in OCI will be recognised in profit or loss when the hedged item affects profit or loss (in case of a transaction related hedged item), or be amortised to profit or loss (in case of a time-period related hedged item).

Example 52.36:   Funding swaps – designating the spot risk only

A bank, having the Singapore Dollar (SGD) as its functional currency, borrows money by entering into a two-year fixed rate loan denominated in Japanese Yen (JPY). The bank transfers the JPY funds into its functional currency and lends the money as a SGD denominated two-year fixed rate loan. To hedge the SGD/JPY exchange risk, the bank enters into a foreign exchange forward contract to buy JPY against SGD in two years' time and designates it as a hedge of the JPY foreign exchange risk. The fair value of the forward element at inception is SGD 20,000 and it is SGD 13,000 at the end of the first year.

From an economic standpoint, the bank has now hedged the foreign exchange risk and locked in the interest margin for the entire two-year period.

In economic theory, the forward points represent the difference in interest rates between the two currencies involved. Hence, the forward element that exists at inception is seen as one element of the interest margin (however, see also 7.2.2 below).

Applying the IFRS 9 accounting for cost of hedging to the forward element of the forward contract results in the following movement within other comprehensive income (OCI):

(All amounts in SGD thousands)	Year 1	Year 2
Reserve in equity at beginning of year	–	3
Change in fair value of forward element	(7)	(13)
Amortisation of forward element at inception	10	10
Reserve in equity at end of year	3	–
Effect on OCI for the year	3	(3)
Effect on profit or loss for the year	(10)	(10)

The bank would present the amortisation of the forward element in the income statement within the interest margin, together with the interest income from the loan and the interest expense from the borrowing, showing the economically fixed interest margin in SGD of the transaction.

Just like for the accounting for the time value of an option, the accounting for the forward element as a cost of hedging applies only to the extent of the so-called 'aligned' forward element (i.e. only to the extent that the forward element relates to the hedged item – see 7.1 above).

7.2.2   Foreign currency basis spreads

IFRS 9 also introduces a new accounting treatment for currency basis spreads. The currency basis spread, a phenomenon that became very significant during the financial crisis, is a charge embedded in financial instruments that compensates for aspects such as country and liquidity risk as well as demand and supply factors. This charge only applies to transactions involving the exchange of foreign currencies at a future point in time (as, for example, in currency forward contracts or cross currency interest rate swaps (CCIRS)).

Historically, the difference between the spot and forward prices of currency forward contracts and CCIRS represented the differential between the interest rates of the two currencies involved. However, basis spreads increased significantly during the financial crisis and with the following sovereign debt crisis, and have become a significant and volatile component of the pricing of longer term forward contracts and CCIRS.

The standard cites currency basis spread as an example of an element that is only present in the hedging instrument, but not in a hedged item that is a single currency instrument. Consequently, this would result in some ineffectiveness even when using a hypothetical derivative for measuring ineffectiveness (see 6.4.2 above). *[IFRS 9.B6.5.5]*.

When using a foreign currency forward contract or a CCIRS in a hedge, the currency basis spread is an unavoidable 'cost' of the hedging instrument. In its redeliberations after the publication of the draft standard, the Board decided that currency basis spreads are a 'cost of hedging'. The cost of a hedging activity should be recognised in profit or loss at the same time as the hedged transaction. Consequently, the Board decided to expand the requirements regarding the accounting for costs of hedging to also include currency basis spreads in a way similar to the forward element of forward contracts.[14] This means that, when designating a hedging instrument, an entity may exclude the currency basis spread and account for it separately in the same way as the accounting for the forward element of the forward rate, as described in 7.2.1 above. *[IFRS 9.6.5.16]*. However, if an entity designates the entire hedging instrument, fair value changes due to changes in the currency basis spread would result in some ineffectiveness.

8   PRESENTATION

8.1   Cash flow hedges

The general mechanics of how ongoing cash flow hedges are presented does not change compared with IAS 39. Entities would continue to accumulate in what the standard now calls the 'cash flow hedge reserve' (i.e. in other comprehensive income in equity), the lower of the cumulative gain or loss on the hedging instrument and the cumulative change in fair value of the hedged item. *[IFRS 9.6.5.11(a)]*. This is often referred to as the 'lower-of-test' and basically ensures that, in line with the IASB's *Conceptual Framework*, an entity is not recognising an asset or liability that does not exist.

IFRS 9 is less flexible than IAS 39 as to how the amount accumulated in the hedging reserve is subsequently accounted for. IAS 39 provides an accounting policy choice to entities that hedge a forecast transaction resulting in the recognition of a non-financial item, to account for the amount accumulated in equity either as a basis adjustment or as a reclassification adjustment (see Chapter 51 at 4.2.2).

IFRS 9 also mentions 'periods that interest income or interest expense is recognised' as an example of a period over which the amount accumulated in the hedging reserve would have to be reclassified to profit or loss. *[IFRS 9.6.5.11(d)(ii)]*. This clarifies that entities cannot simply account for the net interest payment on an interest rate swap straight into profit or loss but would have to present this as a reclassification adjustment between OCI and profit or loss.

Apart from the above, IFRS 9 did not introduce further changes and the amount accumulated in the hedging reserve is subsequently accounted for depending on the nature of the underlying hedged transaction:

- If the hedged transaction subsequently results in the recognition of a non-financial item, the amount accumulated in equity is removed from the separate component of equity and included in the initial cost or other carrying amount of the hedged asset or liability. This accounting entry, sometimes referred to as 'basis adjustment', does not affect OCI of the period.

- The above accounting treatment would equally apply to situations where the hedged forecast transaction of a non-financial asset or non-financial liability subsequently becomes a firm commitment for which fair value hedge accounting is applied.

- For any other cash flow hedges, the amount accumulated in equity is reclassified to profit or loss as a reclassification adjustment in the same period or periods during which the hedged cash flows affect profit or loss. This accounting entry *does* affect OCI of the period. *[IFRS 9.6.5.11(d)]*.

If cash flow hedge accounting is discontinued, the amount that has been accumulated in OCI shall:

- remain in accumulated OCI if the hedged future cash flows are still expected to occur;

- be immediately reclassified to profit or loss as a reclassification adjustment if the hedged future cash flows are no longer expected to occur. *[IFRS 9.6.5.12]*.

After discontinuation, once the previously still expected hedged cash flow occurs, any amount remaining in accumulated OCI shall be accounted for depending on the nature of the underlying transaction (as described above). *[IFRS 9.6.5.12]*.

8.2 Fair value hedges

IFRS 9 does not change how fair value hedges are presented. Entities would continue to recognise the gain or loss on the hedging instrument in profit or loss and adjust the carrying amount of the hedged item for the hedging gain or loss with the adjustment being recognised in profit or loss. However, for hedged items that are debt instruments classified as at amortised cost, the interaction with the new impairment model in IFRS 9 means that fair value hedge accounting makes the overall accounting more complex. This is because it continuously changes the relevant effective interest rate that is needed to calculate the loss allowance (see Chapter 49 at 5.6.3). In contrast to IAS 39, the impairment model of IFRS 9 requires a loss allowance to be recognised for every debt instrument classified as at amortised cost throughout its entire life (see Chapter 49 at 5.3.1) so the issue affects every debt instrument classified at amortised cost, not just those with an incurred loss.

For hedged items that are debt instruments measured at fair value through OCI in accordance with paragraph 4.1.2A of IFRS 9, the gain or loss on the hedged item results in reclassification of that amount from accumulated OCI to profit or loss. This means fair value hedge accounting changes the timing of reclassification from the revaluation reserve of the debt instrument whereas the measurement of the debt

Chapter 52

instrument at fair value remains unaffected. Also, for these instruments, fair value hedge accounting makes the overall accounting more complex. Because the amounts recognised in profit or loss must be the same as if the instrument was measured at amortised cost, an entity needs to run a 'shadow' amortised cost calculation for such instruments. *[IFRS 9.5.7.11]*. This means the same complexity regarding the interaction with the new impairment model in IFRS 9 arises as described above for debt instruments classified as at amortised cost. But the complexity of the accounting is further compounded by the need for reclassification adjustments; this is illustrated in Chapter 49 at 2.3 for a debt instrument that is denominated in a foreign currency and for which fair value hedge accounting is used for a hedge of interest rate risk.

For hedged items that are equity instruments for which an entity has elected to present fair value changes in OCI without subsequent reclassification to profit or loss, the accounting for a fair value hedge is different because it does not affect profit or loss but instead only OCI (see 3.2 above). *[IFRS 9.6.5.8]*.

8.3 Hedges of groups of items

8.3.1 Cash flow hedges

When designating a group of items in a cash flow hedge, the presentation of the related hedging gains or losses in the statement of profit or loss depends on the nature of the group position. *[IFRS 9.B6.6.13-B6.6.15]*.

Nature of position	Line items affected in profit or loss	Presentation in the income statement
Gross position	One line item	The amount reclassified from equity to profit or loss has to be presented in the same line item as the underlying hedged transaction.
	Multiple line items	The amount reclassified from equity to profit or loss has to be allocated to the line items affected by the hedged items on a systematic and rational basis.
Net position	Multiple line items	The amount reclassified from equity to profit or loss has to be presented in a separate line item.

Note that the designation of a net position cash flow hedge is only permitted when hedging foreign currency risk (see 3.6.3 above).

The above requirement for net position cash flow hedges might not seem very attractive, as the presentation of the hedged transactions would not reflect the effect of the hedge. However, the Board was concerned that grossing-up the hedging gain or loss would result in non-existing gains or losses being recognised in the statement of profit or loss, which would be in conflict with general accounting principles. *[IFRS 9.BC6.457]*.

8.3.2 Fair value hedges

For fair value hedges of groups of items with offsetting risk positions (i.e. hedges of a net position), entities would have to present the hedging gains or losses in a separate line item in the income statement in order to avoid grossing up the hedging gain or loss on a single instrument into multiple line items. *[IFRS 9.6.6.4, B6.6.16]*.

However, the treatment in the statement of financial position is different, in that the individual items in the group are separately adjusted for the change in fair value due to changes in the hedged risk. *[IFRS 9.6.6.5].*

9 DISCLOSURES

For a comprehensive overview of the financial instruments related disclosure requirements of IFRS 7 see Chapter 53. This section on disclosures only addresses some of the hedge accounting related disclosures and aims primarily at illustrating them.

9.1 Background and general requirements

The disclosure requirements for entities applying hedge accounting are set out in IFRS 7. Those disclosure requirements were amended as a consequence of the new hedge accounting requirements.

Many constituents, users in particular, have asked for improved disclosures that link more clearly an entity's risk management activities and how it applies hedge accounting. *[IFRS 7.BC35C].* Linking the two requires an understanding of an entity's risk management strategy, which is why the IASB has introduced a requirement for a much more detailed qualitative description of the risk management strategy of the entity. *[IFRS 7.BC35P].* These disclosures of risk management strategies will, however, only be required where hedge accounting is applied. *[IFRS 7.21A].*

The objective of the new hedge accounting disclosures is that entities shall disclose information about:

- the risk management strategy and how it is applied to manage risks;

- how the risk management activities may affect the amount, timing and uncertainty of future cash flows; and

- the effect that hedge accounting has had on the statement of financial position, the statement of comprehensive income and the statement of changes in equity. *[IFRS 7.21A].*

In applying this objective an entity has to consider the necessary level of detail, the balance between different disclosure requirements, the appropriate level of disaggregation and whether additional explanations are necessary to meet the objective. *[IFRS 7.21D].*

The hedge accounting disclosures should be presented in a single note or a separate section of the financial statements. An entity may include information by cross-referencing to information presented elsewhere, such as a risk report, provided that information is available to users of the financial statements on the same terms as the financial statements and at the same time. *[IFRS 7.21B].*

The IASB made it clear that it would require entities to give clear disclosures about their risk management activities. *[IFRS 7.BC35D].* These should be specific to the entity rather than generic or 'boiler plate'.

9.2   Risk management strategy

The risk management strategy has to be described, by type of risk, and this description has to include how each risk arises and how, and to what extent, the risk is managed. This description must also include whether the entity hedges only a part of the risk exposure, such as a nominal component or selected contractual cash flows. *[IFRS 7.22A]*. To satisfy this requirement, an entity must disclose:

- the hedging instruments and how they are used to hedge the risk exposure;
- why the entity believes there is an economic relationship between the hedged item and the hedging instrument;
- how the hedge ratio is determined;
- the expected sources of ineffectiveness. *[IFRS 7.22B]*.

When only a risk component of an exposure is hedged, an entity must also disclose how it determined the component and how the component relates to the item in its entirety. *[IFRS 7.22C]*. In our view this would include a description of whether the risk component is contractually specified, and if not, how the entity determined that the non-contractually specified risk component is separately identifiable and reliably measurable.

Example 52.37:   Illustrative disclosure of risk management strategy for commodity price risk

Coffee price risk

Fluctuations in the coffee price are the main source of market risk for the Alpha Beta Coffee Group (the Group). The Group purchases Arabica coffee from various suppliers in South America. For this purpose, the Group enters into long-term contracts (for between one and three years) with its suppliers, in which the future coffee price is indexed to the USD Arabica benchmark coffee price, adjusted for transport cost that are indexed to diesel prices plus a quality coefficient that is reset annually for a crop period. In order to secure the volume of coffee needed, supply contracts are always entered into (or renewed) at least one year prior to harvest.

The Group forecasts the monthly volume of expected coffee purchases for a period of 18 months and manages the coffee price risk exposure on a 12-month rolling basis. For this purpose, the Group enters into futures contracts on the Arabica benchmark price and designates the futures contracts in cash flow hedges of the USD Arabica benchmark price risk component of its future coffee purchases. Some of those purchases are committed minimum volumes under the contracts and some purchases are highly probable forecast transactions (i.e. quantities in excess of the minimum purchases volumes and sometime for periods for which no contract has yet been entered into). The underlying risk of the coffee futures contracts is identical to the hedged risk component (i.e. the USD Arabica benchmark price). Therefore, the Group has established a hedge ratio of 1:1 for all its hedging relationships. The USD Arabica benchmark price risk component is contractually specified in its purchase contracts, therefore, the Group considers the risk component to be separately identifiable and reliably measurable based on the price of coffee futures.

The Group does not hedge its exposure to the variability in the purchase price of coffee that results from the annual reset of the quality coefficient, because hedging that risk would require highly bespoke financial instruments that in the Group's view are not economical.

The Group's exposure to the variability in the purchase price of coffee that results from the diesel price indexation of the transport costs is integrated into its general risk management of logistics costs that aggregates exposures resulting from various logistics processes of the Group (see Section XYZ below).

The Group determined the USD Arabica benchmark coffee price risk component that it designates as the hedged item on the basis of the pricing formula in the Group's coffee supply contracts (see the above description). That benchmark component is the largest pricing element. The quality coefficient depends on the particular crop in the region from which the Group sources its coffee, depending mainly on weather conditions that affect size and quality of the crop. Sometimes pest and plant diseases can have similar effects. Over the last 10 crop periods the quality coefficient ranged between US cents 2-27 per pound (lb). For the effect of the diesel price indexation, refer to the section 'Logistics costs management' in the Risk Management Report that is included in this Annual Report.

More information about how the Group manages its risk, including the extent to which the Group hedges, the hedging instruments used and sources of ineffectiveness, is provided in the Risk Management Report (see section 'Commodity Price Risk Management').

The risk management strategy disclosures are an important cornerstone of the new hedge accounting model, as they provide the link between an entity's risk management activities and how they affect the financial statements. The notes should also disclose the key judgements the entity has used in applying the new hedge accounting model (including those used to determine whether an economic relationship exists between the hedged item and the hedging instrument, how the hedge ratio was set and how risk components were identified, just to mention a few).

Disclosures have to be made by type of risk, rather than the type of hedging relationship (e.g. cash flow hedge or fair value hedge). *[IFRS 7.21C].* This should enable users to follow the various disclosures by type of risk, resulting in a much better understanding of the hedging activities and their impact on the financial statements.

9.3 The amount, timing and uncertainty of future cash flows

Further to the strategy, entities have to disclose the 'terms and conditions of hedging instruments and how they affect the amount, timing and uncertainty of future cash flows'. *[IFRS 7.23A].* More precisely, an entity has to disclose, by category of risk:

- a profile of the timing of the nominal amount of the hedging instrument; and

- if applicable, the average price or rate of the hedging instrument. This could be a strike price or a forward rate. *[IFRS 7.23B].*

In the Exposure Draft, the IASB proposed also to require the disclosure of the total volume of risk the entity managed, irrespective of whether the entity actually hedges the full exposure. *[IFRS 7.BC35U].* Many constituents disagreed with this proposal as they believed this to result in disclosure of commercially sensitive information. *[IFRS 7.BC35W].* The Board acknowledged this concern and decided not to carry this requirement forward to the final standard. *[IFRS 7.BC35X].*

Entities also have to disclose a description of the sources of hedge ineffectiveness that are expected to affect the hedging relationship during its term. *[IFRS 7.23D].* This would include an update of new sources of ineffectiveness that emerge in a hedging relationship over the term. *[IFRS 7.23E].*

Finally, if an entity has previously designated forecast transactions as hedged items in a cash flow hedging relationship and these are no longer expected to occur, this fact and a description of the forecast transaction have to be disclosed. *[IFRS 7.23F]*.

Example 52.38:   Illustrative disclosure of timing, nominal amount and average price of coffee futures contracts

As of 31 December 20x0, Alpha Beta Coffee Group is holding the following coffee futures contracts to hedge the exposure on its coffee purchases over the next twelve months:

	Jan	Feb	Mar	Apr	May	...	Dec	Total
Notional amount of coffee futures contracts (in lb thousands) by month of their maturity	1,275	1,425	1,350	1,312.5	1,350	...	1,200	**16,275**
Average hedged rate (in US cents per lb)	122	125	128	133	135	...	139	**133**

Disclosure of the profile of nominal amounts of hedging instruments and their average prices, as required by paragraph 23B of IFRS 7, would not be very meaningful when an entity applies a dynamic hedging process in which both the amount of hedged item and hedging instrument change frequently. *[IFRS 7.23B, BC35Z]*. Consequently, an entity using a dynamic hedging process is exempt from providing these disclosures. Instead, such an entity must disclose:

• a description of what the ultimate risk management strategy is in relation to those dynamic hedging relationships;

• a description of how it reflects this risk management strategy by using hedge accounting and designating those particular hedging relationships; and

• an indication of how frequently the hedging relationships are discontinued and restarted as part of the entity's process in relation to those hedging relationships. *[IFRS 7.23C]*.

If, at the reporting date, the volume of hedging relationships (which is part of the disclosures discussed at 9.4 below) to which the above exemption applies is not representative of the normal volumes hedged during the period, an entity has to disclose this fact and the reason it believes the volumes are not representative. *[IFRS 7.24D]*.

9.4   The effects of hedge accounting on the financial position and performance

IFRS 7 sets out a specific requirement to disclose the effect hedge accounting has on the entity's financial position and the performance. All disclosures are required to be provided in a tabular format and by type of risk. *[IFRS 7.24A-24C]*.

Instead of reproducing the specific requirements of IFRS 7 (see Chapter 53 at 4.3.2) we provide examples below of how those disclosures might look.

Example 52.39:   Illustrative disclosure of the effects of hedge accounting on the financial position and performance

The impact of hedging instruments designated in hedging relationships as of 31 December 20x0 on the statement of financial position of Alpha Beta Coffee Group (the Group) is as follows:

Cash flow hedges	Notional amount	Carrying amount	Line item in the statement of financial position	Change in fair value used for measuring ineffectiveness for the period
Coffee price risk			Short-term	
Arabica coffee	16,275lbs		derivative financial	
futures	(thousands)	(4.5)	liabilities	(1.0)
Interest rate risk				
Pay fixed/receive			Long-term	
variable interest rate			derivative financial	
swap	EUR 50m	4.0	assets	1.0

Fair value hedges	Notional amount	Carrying amount	Line item in the statement of financial position	Change in fair value used for measuring ineffectiveness for the period
Interest rate risk				
Receive fixed/pay			Long-term	
variable interest rate			derivative financial	
swap	EUR 200m	(10.0)	liabilities	(2.0)

The impact of hedged items designated in hedging relationships as of 31 December 20x0 on the statement of financial position of the Group is as follows:

Cash flow hedges	Change in value used for measuring ineffectiveness	Cash flow hedge reserve
Coffee price risk		
Coffee purchases	1.0	4.5
Interest rate risk		
Forecast interest		
payments	(0.9)	(3.9)

Fair value hedges	Carrying amount	Thereof accumulated fair value adjustments	Line item in the statement of financial position	Change in fair value used for measuring ineffectiveness for the period
Interest rate risk				
Fixed rate borrowings	211.0	11.0	Long-term borrowings	2.1

The above hedging relationships affected profit or loss and other comprehensive income as follows:

Cash flow hedges	Hedging gain or loss recognised in OCI	Ineffectiveness recognised in profit or loss	Line item in the statement of profit or loss	Amount reclassified from OCI to profit or loss	Line item in the statement of profit or loss
Coffee price risk Hedges of forecast coffee purchases	(1.0)				
Interest rate risk Forecast interest payments	0.9	0.1	Other financial income	0.5	Interest expense

Fair value hedges	Ineffectiveness recognised in profit or loss	Line item in the statement of profit or loss
Interest rate risk Hedge of fixed rate borrowings	(0.1)	Other financial expenses

Note that the cash flow hedges of the coffee price risk result in an adjustment to the purchase price of the coffee purchases (a basis adjustment), which means that the amounts that are removed from the cash flow hedge reserve are not reclassification adjustments and hence do not affect OCI or profit or loss (see 8.1 above).

IFRS 7 further requires a reconciliation of the components of equity that arise in connection with hedge accounting (such as the hedging reserve) and an analysis of OCI. That information needs to be disaggregated by risk category, which can be given in the notes to the financial statements. *[IFRS 7.24E, 24F].*

10   ALTERNATIVES TO HEDGE ACCOUNTING

10.1   Credit risk exposures

Many financial institutions hedge the credit risk arising from loans or loan commitments using credit default swaps (CDS). This would often result in an accounting mismatch, as loans and loan commitments are typically not accounted for at fair value through profit or loss. The most natural approach to hedge accounting would be to designate the credit risk as a risk component in a hedging relationship. However, the IASB noted that due to the difficulty in isolating the credit risk as a separate risk it does not meet the eligibility criteria for risk components. As a result, the accounting mismatch creates profit or loss volatility. *[IFRS 9.BC6.470].* The Exposure Draft leading up to IFRS 9 did not propose any changes in this area, however, the IASB asked its constituents to comment on three alternative approaches, none of which were that credit risk could be deemed an eligible risk component for hedge accounting. The feedback from constituents showed that accounting for credit risk hedging strategies is a major concern for many financial institutions. *[IFRS 9.BC6.491].*

In its redeliberations the Board reconfirmed its view that credit risk does not qualify as a separate risk component. *[IFRS 9.BC6.504].* However, the IASB decided that an entity undertaking economic credit risk hedging may, at any time, elect to account for a debt instrument (such as a loan or a bond), a loan commitment or a financial guarantee contract, to the extent that any of these instruments is managed for changes in its credit risk, at fair value through profit or loss. This was one of the alternative approaches set out in the Exposure Draft. This election can only be made if the asset referenced by the credit derivative has the same issuer and subordination as the hedged exposure (i.e. both the issuer's name and seniority of the exposure match). The accounting for the credit derivative would not change, i.e. it would continue to be accounted at fair value through profit or loss. *[IFRS 9.6.7.1]*.

If the election is made, the difference at that time between the carrying value (if any) and the fair value of the financial instrument designated as at fair value through profit or loss is immediately recognised in profit or loss; in case of a debt instrument accounted for as at fair value through other comprehensive income the carrying amount (i.e. fair value) does not change but instead the gain or loss that has been accumulated in the revaluation reserve has to be reclassified to profit or loss. *[IFRS 9.6.7.2]*. This gain or loss would not only reflect any change in credit risk, but also any change in other risks such as interest rate risk. Also different to a fair value hedge, once elected, the financial instruments hedged for credit risk are measured at their full fair value instead of just being adjusted for changes in the risk actually hedged. As a result, by hedging the credit risk exposure, the entity also has to revalue the financial instrument for the general effect of interest rate risk, which will result in profit or loss volatility.

An entity has to discontinue the specific accounting for credit risk hedges in line with its actual risk management. This would be the case when the credit risk either no longer exists or if the credit risk is no longer managed using credit derivatives (irrespective of whether the credit derivative still exists or is sold, terminated or settled). *[IFRS 9.6.7.3]*.

On discontinuation, the accounting for the financial instrument reverts to the same measurement category that had applied before the designation as at fair value through profit or loss. However, the fair value of the financial instrument on the date of discontinuing the accounting at fair value through profit or loss becomes the new carrying amount on that date. *[IFRS 9.6.7.4]*. For example, the fair value of a loan at the time of discontinuation becomes its new deemed amortised cost which is the basis to determine its new effective interest rate. This applies also to a debt instrument that reverts to accounting at fair value through other comprehensive income because it is required to affect profit or loss in the same way as a financial instrument at amortised cost. *[IFRS 9.5.7.11]*. This means the revaluation reserve only includes the gains and losses that arise after the date on which the accounting at fair value through profit or loss ceased. For a loan commitment or a financial guarantee contract the fair value at the date on which the accounting at fair value through profit or loss ceased is amortised over the remaining life of the instrument in accordance with the principles of IFRS 15 – *Revenue from Contracts with Customers* – unless the impairment requirements of IFRS 9 would require a higher amount than the remaining unamortised balance.

Chapter 52

In contrast to the fair value option under IFRS 9, the possibility to elect to measure at fair value through profit or loss those financial instruments whose credit risk is managed using credit derivatives, has the following advantages:

- the election can be made after initial recognition of the financial instrument;
- the election is available for a proportion of the instrument (instead of only the whole instrument); and
- the fair value through profit or loss accounting can be discontinued.

Consequently, even though it is not an equivalent to fair value hedge accounting, this accounting does address several concerns of entities that use CDSs for hedging credit exposures.

10.2   Own use contracts

Contracts accounted for in accordance with IFRS 9 include those contracts to buy or sell non-financial items that can be settled net in cash, as if they were financial instruments (i.e. they are in substance similar to financial derivatives). Many commodity purchase and sale contracts meet the criteria for net settlement in cash because the commodities are readily convertible to cash. However, such contracts are excluded from the scope of IFRS 9 if they were entered into and continue to be held for the purpose of the receipt or delivery of a non-financial item in accordance with the entity's expected purchase, sale or usage requirements. This is commonly referred to as the 'own use' scope exception. Own use contracts are further discussed in Chapter 42 at 4 (the scope exception was carried over to IFRS 9).

Own use contracts are accounted for as normal sales or purchase contracts (i.e. executory contracts), with the idea that any fair value change of the contract is not relevant given the contract is used for the entity's own use. However, some entities in certain industries enter into contracts for own use and similar financial derivatives for risk management purposes and manage all these contracts together. In such a situation, own use accounting leads to an accounting mismatch as the fair value change of the derivative positions used for risk management purposes cannot be offset against fair value changes of the own use contracts.

To eliminate the accounting mismatch, an entity could apply hedge accounting by designating an own use contract as the hedged item in a fair value hedging relationship. However, hedge accounting in these circumstances is administratively burdensome. Furthermore, entities enter into large volumes of commodity contracts and, within the large volume of contracts, some positions may offset each other. An entity would therefore typically hedge on a net basis.

Example 52.40:   Processing and brokerage of soybeans and sunflowers

An entity is in the business of procuring, transporting, storing, processing and merchandising soybeans and sunflower seeds. The inputs and the outputs are agricultural commodities which are traded in liquid markets. The entity has both a broker business and a processing business, which are operationally distinct. However, the entity analyses and monitors its net commodity risk position, comprising inventories, physically settled forward purchase and sales contracts and exchange traded futures and options. The target is to keep the net fair value risk position close to nil.

Under IAS 39, the physically settled forward contracts from the processing business have to be accounted for as own use contracts, whereas all other contracts are accounted for at fair value through profit or loss. The resulting accounting mismatch does not reflect how the entity is managing the overall fair value risk of those contracts.

As part of its project to replace IAS 39, the IASB introduced a fair value option for own use contracts. At inception of a contract, an entity may make an irrevocable designation to measure an own use contract at fair value through profit or loss (the 'fair value option'). However, such designation is only allowed if it eliminates or significantly reduces an accounting mismatch. *[IFRS 9.2.5]*.

When the IASB introduced this fair value option for own use contracts as part of the third phase of its project to replace IAS 39 (i.e. hedge accounting), it considered the need for specific transition requirements. As a result, the IASB allowed that on transition to the version of IFRS 9 issued in November 2013, entities can apply the fair value option on an 'all-or-nothing' basis for similar types of (already existing) own use contracts. This particular transition requirement was set out in IAS 39 as a consequential amendment by IFRS 9 issued in November 2013. *[IFRS 9.7.2.14A, BCZ2.36-38]*. At that time this was a consequential amendment of IAS 39 because the requirements for own use contracts are part of the scope of the financial instruments standard and IFRS 9 issued in November 2013 (incorporated the scope by reference to IAS 39). When finalising IFRS 9 in July 2014, the IASB relocated the scope section of IAS 39 to IFRS 9, including the fair value option for own use contracts.[15]

Some entities, especially in the power and utilities sector, enter into long-term own use contracts, sometimes for as long as 15 years. The business model of those entities would often be to manage those contracts together with other contracts on a fair value basis. However, there are often no derivatives available with such long maturities, while fair values for longer dated contracts may be difficult to determine. Hence, a fair value based management approach might only be used for the time horizon in which derivatives are available. The fair value option is, however, only available on inception of the own use contract. Consequently the fair value option will mainly be useful for entities that apply a fair value based risk management strategy for entire contracts, which is more likely to be the case for shorter-term own use contracts.

11   EFFECTIVE DATE AND TRANSITION

11.1   Effective date

The version of IFRS 9 issued in July 2014 has a mandatory effective date of annual periods beginning on or after 1 January 2018. Early application is permitted. *[IFRS 9.7.1.1]*. Early application can only start from the beginning of a reporting period, which is the date of initial application and must be after the date IFRS 9 was issued, i.e. after 24 July 2014. *[IFRS 9.7.2.2]*. Although not explicit in the standard, we believe that reporting period can be an annual reporting period or an interim reporting period.

This version of IFRS 9 supersedes the three earlier versions of IFRS 9 (issued in 2009, 2010 and 2013). However, the IASB provided a 'grace period' that allows an entity to adopt those earlier versions of IFRS 9 but only if it does so by choosing a date of initial application before 1 February 2015. *[IFRS 9.7.3.2]*.

Taken together, this means an entity that has early applied one of the earlier versions of IFRS 9 (when that option was still available) can continue to apply that version until the version issued in July 2014 becomes mandatorily effective in 2018. Furthermore, an entity that wants to apply the new hedge accounting requirements of IFRS 9 but does not want to early apply the new impairment model would have to apply the version of IFRS 9 issued in November 2013, choosing a date of initial application that is the beginning of an annual or interim reporting period beginning before 1 February 2015. Such an entity would have to apply the new impairment model (as well as the changes to classification and measurement that are included in IFRS 9 issued in July 2014) only from 2018.

As stated at 3.6.6 above, an entity has the accounting policy choice to continue applying hedge accounting as set out in IAS 39 to all hedges until the project on accounting for macro hedging is completed. *[IFRS 9.7.2.21].*

11.2   Prospective application in general

A hedging relationship can only be designated on a prospective basis, in order to avoid the use of hindsight. The same concern about using hindsight would also apply if the new hedge accounting requirements were to be applied retrospectively. Consequently, the IASB decided that hedge accounting in accordance with IFRS 9 has to be applied prospectively, with some limited exceptions. *[IFRS 9.7.2.22].* Because the date of initial application can only be the beginning of a reporting period, an entity can only start applying the new hedge accounting requirements of IFRS 9 prospectively from the beginning of a reporting period, and only if all qualifying criteria – including the hedge accounting documentation that conforms to IFRS 9 – are met on that date. *[IFRS 9.7.2.23, 7.2.2].*

Many preparers will already be applying hedge accounting under IAS 39 before transitioning to IFRS 9. For such entities, the standard clarifies that hedging relationships under IAS 39 which also qualify for hedge accounting under IFRS 9, are treated as continuing hedging relationships. *[IFRS 9.7.2.24].* Hedge accounting under IAS 39 ceases in the very same second as hedge accounting under IFRS 9 starts, therefore resulting in no accounting entries on transition. However, entities might have to rebalance their hedges on transition to fulfil the new effectiveness requirements under IFRS 9 in which case any resulting gain or loss must be recognised in profit or loss. *[IFRS 9.7.2.25].*

11.3   Limited retrospective application

The exceptions from prospective application of the new standard are for the new accounting treatment for the time value of options, when only the intrinsic value is designated; and, at the option of the entity, for the forward element of forward contracts, when only the spot element is designated, and the foreign currency basis spread of financial instruments (see 7 above).

The transition requirements for hedge accounting in IFRS 9 also replicate the retrospective application for the amendments that were made to IAS 39 by *Novation of Derivatives and Continuation of Hedge Accounting. [IFRS 9.7.2.26(c), IAS 39.108D].*

11.3.1 Accounting for the time value of options

Entities have to apply the new accounting treatment for the time value of options retrospectively, however, only to hedging relationships that existed at the beginning of the earliest comparative period and hedging relationships designated thereafter. *[IFRS 9.7.2.26(a)]*. This means that, for example, foreign entities registered and reporting with the United States Securities and Exchange Commission and required to present two comparative years of income statements, would have a longer period to cover for the retrospective application of the new requirements.

Applying the new accounting requirement retrospectively might have a much wider impact than anticipated. Depending on the type of hedging relationship, many line items in the primary statements and many disclosures in the notes might be affected.

Example 52.41: Retrospective application of accounting for time value of option

An entity applies the IFRS hedge accounting requirements as of 1 January 2015 and 1 January 2014 is the beginning of its earliest comparative period presented.

As of 1 January 2014, the entity had a hedging relationship in place in which the intrinsic value of an option was designated as the hedging instrument of a highly probable forecast purchase of a machine as of 31 March 2014. When preparing the 2015 financial statements, the entity would have to:

- determine the time value of that option as of 1 January 2014 and restate accumulated other comprehensive income (OCI) against retained earnings as of that date;

- determine the time value of that option as of 31 March 2014 and restate accumulated OCI against retained earnings as of that date;

- restate the initial carrying amount of the machine as of 31 March 2014 (the basis adjustment of amount accumulated in OCI);

- determine the new depreciation amount for 2014 and restate the carrying amount of the machine as of 31 December 2014 against retained earnings as of that date;

- reflect the restatement in the statement of profit or loss and other comprehensive income, the statement of changes in equity and the statement of financial position; and

- reflect the restatement in the notes disclosures.

11.3.2 Accounting for the forward element of forward contracts and foreign currency basis spread

Different to the accounting for the time value of options, entities will have an option to apply retrospectively the new accounting for the forward element of forward contracts. However, the option applies on an all or nothing basis (i.e. if an entity elects to apply the accounting retrospectively, it has to be applied to all hedging relationships that qualify for the election). The retrospective application would also only apply to those hedging relationships that existed at the beginning of the earliest comparative period or that were designated thereafter. *[IFRS 9.7.2.26(b)]*. Consequently, assets and liabilities cannot be adjusted to reflect hedges that had already finished at the start of the comparative period. A similar transition requirement applies for the accounting for foreign currency basis spreads (see at 7.2.2 above).

However, in contrast to the transition requirements for the forward element of forward contracts, the decision to apply retrospectively the cost of hedging guidance on foreign currency basis spreads can be made on a hedge by hedge basis, without a requirement that cross currency basis had been excluded from the designation under

IAS 39. This is owing to the differences in circumstances: IAS 39 did not have an exception for excluding a foreign currency basis spread from the designation of a financial instrument as a hedging instrument. *[IFRS 9.7.2.26(b), BC7.49]*.

11.3.3   *Re-designation of hedge relationships for non-financial risk components*

IFRS 9 permits the designation of eligible risk components in non-financial hedged items (see 3.4 above). Such a designation was not possible under IAS 39. This means, even if entities were economically hedging a risk component, they were obliged to designate the change in the entire hedged item as the hedged risk in order to achieve hedge accounting. Such a designation was likely to result in the recognition of ineffectiveness in profit or loss and in some cases failure of the effectiveness requirements.

On transition to IFRS 9, entities may wish to amend hedge accounting relationships such that the hedged risk is an eligible risk component for non-financial hedged items. The question is whether that change in the documented hedged risk must result in the discontinuation of the original hedge relationship and the start of a new hedge relationship, or whether it can be treated as an amendment to the original designation such that the original hedge relationship continues. This question is particularly relevant for cash flow hedges, as on re-designation the non-zero fair value of the hedging instrument can result in subsequent ineffectiveness recorded in profit or loss.

We believe that such a change in the documented hedged risk should be treated as a discontinuation of the original hedge relationship and the re-designation of a new hedge relationship because it can be seen as either a change in the hedged item or a change in the documented risk management objective which both require discontinuation of a hedging relationship. *[IFRS 9.B6.5.26(a)]*.

The IASB was very nervous of permitting any retrospective application of the IFRS 9 hedge accounting requirements, as such an application could involve the use of hindsight, for example as to whether it is beneficial or not to change the hedged risk to be an eligible risk component. The specific scenarios where retrospective application is permitted are those that either do not involve the use of hindsight as IFRS 9 application relied on particular choices that had already been made under IAS 39 (e.g. the designation of the intrinsic value of an option or the spot element of a forward) or where retrospective application was already permitted in IAS 39 (novation of a derivative through a central counterparty). *[IFRS 9.BC7.44-50]*. Due to the absence of a specific respective transition relief, it follows that such a hedge relationship cannot continue. A dual-designation at the inception of the hedge is not possible either because of the same arguments.

The logical follow-on question is whether an entity can continue with the original designation although it does not exactly represent the entity's risk management objective. We note that although the objective of hedge accounting under IFRS 9 is to represent an entity's risk management activities, *[IFRS 9.6.1.1]*, it does not require that it is an exact match. The Basis for Conclusions notes that, in some circumstances, the designation for hedge accounting purposes is inevitably not the same as an entity's risk management view of its hedging, but that the designation reflects risk management in that it relates to the same type of risk that is being managed and the instruments used for this purpose. The IASB refer to this situation as 'proxy hedging', which is an eligible way of designating the hedged item under IFRS 9 as long as that still reflects risk management. One example of proxy hedging mentioned is those instances where the risk management objective is to hedge a risk component but the accounting hedge designation is for the full price risk. Where there is a choice of accounting hedge designation, there is no requirement for an entity to select the designation that most closely matches the risk management view of hedging as long as the chosen approach still reflects risk management. *[IFRS 9.BC6.97,98,100(b)]*. Consequently, we believe that it is permitted, on transition, to continue with an accounting designation of the full price risk even if the management objective was always to hedge a component of risk.

Both questions above have been debated by the IFRS Interpretations Committee in September 2015. The tentative agenda decision reached by the IFRS Interpretations Committee is consistent with the analysis presented above.[16]

Chapter 52

References

1 *A Roadmap for Convergence between IFRSs and US GAAP* – 2006-2008, issued in February 2006, updated in 2008 and reaffirmed in November 2009.

2 *IASB Update*, October 2005 and April 2006 and Project Update, *Financial Instruments*, IASB, 18 January 2006.

3 Discussion Paper, *Reducing Complexity in Reporting Financial Instruments*, IASB, March 2008.

4 Invitation to Comment, *Reducing Complexity in Reporting Financial Instruments* (including IASB Discussion Paper, *Reducing Complexity in Reporting Financial Instruments*), FASB, March 2008.

5 Press Release, *IASB sets out timetable for IAS 39 replacement and its conclusions on FASB FSPs*, IASB, April 2009.

6 Press Release, *Draft of forthcoming IFRS on general hedge accounting*, September 2012.

7 *IASB Update*, May 2012.

8 *IASB Update*, May 2012.

9 *IASB Update*, July 2015.

10 *IASB Update*, January 2013.

11 For example: *Request to allow hedge accounting to comply with either IAS 39 or IFRS 9 while the macro hedging project is developed*, letter from EFRAG to the IASB, 22 March 2013.

12 *IASB Update*, January 2013.

13 www.bbalibor.com/explained/definitions (24 July 2013).

14 *IASB Update*, January 2013.

15 See consequential amendments made by IFRS 9 (issued July 2014), paragraph C40.

16 *IFRIC Update*, September 2015.

...an acquirer's risk management view of ... hedging, but that the designation reflects its alignment in that it relates to the same type of risk that is being managed and the instruments used for this purpose. The IASB refer to the situation as one in which ... an eligible way of designating ... hedged from those... IFRS 9 requires that entities risk management. This example at ... reflecting... mentioned to note instances where models ... ... observable... undertake a risk-management but the accounting hedge designation ... the full may differ. Where there is a mixture of designated and undesignated, there is no requirement for an entity to select the designation that most closely approaches the economic concept of hedging, as long as the chosen approach still reflects risk management... it is reasonable to be otherwise equitable. We believe that it is appropriate ... important to continue with an undertaking designation of the full under risk exposure... different management approach ... always manage a component of the ...

Both foundations above have been discussed by the IFRS Interpretations Committee in September 2018. The tentative agenda decision reached by the IFRS Interpretations Committee is consistent with the analysis presented above.

References

1 ... from the Interpretations Committee (AG) ... May 2017, IAS 2016 Basis based at Publication ... undated in 2016 and ... maximum ... September 2008.

2 Ibid, paras...

3 Issue ... in addition to ... management ... and financial ... hedging management ... IAS, September 2006.

4 Discussion Paper, Measuring Corporate ... Reporting Financial Risk exposures, 1338.

5 IAS 32 ... amounts, Aggregating Economic ...

6 IFRS 9, Para 6.1 para in the content ...

7 IS 4560 para inm, 5.10

8 ... in ... New 2017

9 IS 4560 para inm, 5.10

10 (IAS 9 para ... Para...) para...

11 ... para ...

... Assessment ... hedging items

... in black case more to Business Paper ...

... effective, that IFRSB ... to provide SL. ... mth 2016

... policy January 2018

... worldeconomics.com/climate-bulletins 2, July 2020.

... July paras January 60

... recommitment amendments. This ... Ibid, remitted July 2016, manipulates ...

16 Ibid. para ... Appendix 2019

4 Discussion ... amounts, Aggregating Economic ...
in ... in Disposal ... Paper Economic Exposures

5 Accounting ... 1338 ... amounts, Aggregating Economic ...

6 Initial Business ... IFRS 9 ... paras ...
... IAS, Supplement an ... items in ...
... IFRS 9, IAS 32 ... 5.5.6

Chapter 53   Financial instruments: Presentation and disclosure

Chapter 53

List of examples

Chapter 53

Chapter 53   Financial instruments: Presentation and disclosure

1   INTRODUCTION

Disclosure of financial instruments is largely dealt with in IFRS 7 – *Financial Instruments: Disclosures* – the development of which is outlined below.

1.1   IAS 32

The original version of IAS 32 – *Financial Instruments: Disclosure and Presentation* – was published in March 1995 and, as its title suggested, contained requirements about the disclosures entities should make about financial instruments. These requirements were superseded by IFRS 7 (see 1.2 below) which also changed the name of the standard to IAS 32 – *Financial Instruments: Presentation*.

One of the topics IAS 32 addresses is when entities should offset financial assets and financial liabilities, the associated requirements for which are discussed at 7.4.1 below. It also addresses the classification of financial instruments as equity, financial liabilities or financial assets, a topic covered in Chapter 44. IAS 32 has been amended a number of times since publication, including in December 2011 when the IASB addressed certain practical problems it had identified in its offsetting requirements.

1.2   IFRS 7

IFRS 7 emerged from a project principally focused on revising IAS 30 – *Disclosures in the Financial Statements of Banks and Similar Financial Institutions* – a standard which, at the time, set out additional disclosure requirements for banks and similar entities. It was published in August 2005 and superseded IAS 30.

The objective of IFRS 7 is to require entities to provide disclosures in their financial statements that enable users to evaluate: *[IFRS 7.1]*

- the significance of financial instruments for the entity's financial position and performance; and

- the nature and extent of risks arising from financial instruments to which the entity is exposed during the period and at the reporting date, and how the entity manages those risks.

These objectives manifest themselves in two disclosure principles (see 4 and 5 below) which are designed to complement those for recognising, measuring and presenting financial assets and financial liabilities in IAS 32, IAS 39 – *Financial Instruments: Recognition and Measurement* – and IFRS 9 – *Financial Instruments* (see Chapters 41 to 52). *[IFRS 7.2]*.

IFRS 7 has been subject to significant amendment since its original publication, in particular to address concerns raised during the financial crisis. These amendments aimed to improve the disclosures entities provide in a number of areas including liquidity risk, transfers of financial assets, offsetting and fair values (most of the disclosures for which are now included in IFRS 13 – *Fair Value Measurement* – see Chapter 14).

In July 2014, the IASB published the final version of IFRS 9, its replacement for IAS 39. The new standard changes the framework for classifying and measuring financial assets and financial liabilities; introduces an expected loss approach for determining impairment losses on financial assets and amends the requirements for applying hedge accounting. It also makes a number of consequential amendments to IFRS 7, introducing extensive new disclosures in respect of impairment (see 5.2.3 below) and hedge accounting (see 4.3.2 below) as well as making other changes which are noted throughout this chapter. The final version of IFRS 9 and its consequential amendments to IFRS 7 are effective for periods beginning on or after 1 January 2018.

2   SCOPE OF IFRS 7

2.1   Entities required to comply with IFRS 7

Although IFRS 7 evolved from a project to update IAS 30 (which applied only to banks and similar financial institutions) it applies to all entities preparing their financial statements in accordance with IFRS that have financial instruments. *[IFRS 7.BC6]*. The IASB considered exempting certain entities, including insurers, subsidiaries and those that are small or medium-sized (SMEs), but decided that IFRS 7 should apply to all entities whilst keeping the decision in respect of SMEs under review in its related project. *[IFRS 7.BC9, BC10, BC11]*. The IASB has now issued an IFRS for SMEs that requires reduced disclosures about financial instruments.

2.2   Financial instruments within the scope of IFRS 7

Sections 3 and 4 of Chapter 42 contain a detailed explanation of the scope of IFRS 7. It is important to recognise that the scope of IFRS 7 is generally somewhat wider than that of IAS 39 and IFRS 9. Therefore IFRS 7 can apply to instruments that are not subject to the recognition and measurement provisions of IAS 39 or IFRS 9, for example finance leases and certain loan commitments. *[IFRS 7.4]*. Conversely, some financial instruments within the scope of IAS 39 or IFRS 9, particularly those held in disposal groups or as part of discontinued operations, are not subject to all of the requirements in IFRS 7.

2.3 Interim reports

IAS 34 – *Interim Financial Reporting* – sets out the minimum content of an interim financial report. When an event or transaction is significant to an understanding of the changes in an entity's financial position or performance since the last annual financial period, IAS 34 requires the report to provide an explanation of, and update to, the information included in the last annual financial statements. *[IAS 34.15]*. The standard emphasises that relatively insignificant updates need not be provided. *[IAS 34.15A]*. The following disclosures which relate to financial instruments are required if significant: *[IAS 34.15B]*

- losses recognised from the impairment of financial assets;

- changes in the business or economic circumstances that affect the fair value of the entity's financial assets and financial liabilities, whether recognised at fair value or amortised cost;

- any loan default or breach of a loan agreement that has not been remedied on or before the end of the reporting period;

- transfers between levels of the fair value hierarchy used in the measurement of the fair value of financial instruments; and

- changes in the classification of financial assets as a result of a change in the purpose or use of those assets.

In considering the extent of disclosures necessary to meet the requirements above, IAS 34 refers to the guidance included in other IFRSs, *[IAS 34.15C]* which would include IFRS 7, but does not ordinarily require compliance with all the requirements in those standards.

IAS 34 also specifies additional disclosures to be given (normally on a financial year-to-date basis) about the fair value of financial instruments, including those discussed at 4.5 below and a number required by IFRS 13. *[IAS 34.16A(j)]*. This requirement is not subject to the qualifications noted above and so, as discussed in further detail in Chapter 38 at 4.5, these disclosures should always be given unless the information is not material.

The extent to which disclosures about offsetting of financial assets and financial assets (see 7.4.2 below) should be given in condensed interim financial statements was originally unclear. However, in September 2014 the IASB issued amendments to IFRS 7 clarifying that these disclosures need not be provided unless required by the more general requirements of IAS 34.

Chapter 53

3   STRUCTURING THE DISCLOSURES

The main text of IFRS 7 is supplemented by application guidance, which is an integral part of the standard,[1] and by implementation guidance, which accompanies, but is not part of, the standard.[2] The implementation guidance suggests possible ways of applying some of the requirements of the standard but, it is emphasised, does not create additional requirements. *[IFRS 7.IG1].*

Although the implementation guidance discusses each disclosure requirement in IFRS 7 separately, disclosures would normally be presented as an integrated package and individual disclosures might satisfy more than one requirement. For example, information about concentrations of risk might also convey information about exposure to credit or other risk. *[IFRS 7.IG2].* This chapter follows a similar approach whereby each topic is considered individually in the context of the requirements of the standard as well as related application and implementation guidance.

3.1   Level of detail

Entities need to decide, in the light of their circumstances, how much detail to provide to satisfy the requirements of IFRS 7, how much emphasis to place on different aspects of the requirements and how information is aggregated to display the overall picture without combining information with different characteristics. It is necessary to strike a balance between overburdening financial statements with excessive detail that may not assist users of financial statements and obscuring important information as a result of too much aggregation. For example, important information should not be obscured by including it among a large amount of insignificant detail. Similarly, information should not be aggregated so that it obscures important differences between individual transactions or associated risks. *[IFRS 7.B3].*

This means that not all of the information suggested, say, in the implementation guidance is necessarily required. *[IFRS 7.IG5].* On the other hand, there is a reminder that IAS 1 – *Presentation of Financial Statements* – requires additional disclosures when compliance with the specific requirements in IFRSs is insufficient to enable users to understand the impact of particular transactions, other events and conditions on the entity's financial position and financial performance (see Chapter 3 at 4.1.1.A). *[IFRS 7.IG6].*

3.2   Materiality

The implementation guidance to the original version of IFRS 7 drew attention to the definition of materiality in IAS 1 (see Chapter 3 at 4.1.5.A): *[IFRS 7(2010).IG3]*

> 'Omissions or misstatements of items are material if they could, individually or collectively, influence the economic decisions that users make on the basis of the financial statements. Materiality depends on the size and nature of the omission or misstatement judged in the surrounding circumstances. The size or nature of the item, or a combination of both, could be the determining factor.' *[IAS 1.7].*

It then noted that a specific disclosure requirement need not be satisfied if the information is not material *[IFRS 7(2010).IG3]* and drew attention to the following explanation in IAS 1: *[IFRS 7(2010).IG4]*

> 'Assessing whether an omission or misstatement could influence economic decisions of users, and so be material, requires consideration of the characteristics of those users. The *Framework for the Preparation and Presentation of Financial Statements* states ... that "users are assumed to have a reasonable knowledge of business and economic activities and accounting and a willingness to study the information with reasonable diligence."[3] Therefore, the assessment needs to take into account how users with such attributes could reasonably be expected to be influenced in making economic decisions.' *[IAS 1.7]*.

The inclusion of such guidance could have been seen as curious given that it is no more or less applicable to IFRS 7 than any other standard. What it amounted to was a degree of reassurance that entities with few financial instruments and few risks (for example a manufacturer whose only financial instruments are accounts receivable and accounts payable) will give few disclosures, something that was borne out in other references within the standard and accompanying material. *[IFRS 7.IN4, BC10]*.

However, in May 2010, the IASB removed all references to materiality from IFRS 7 because they thought that some of these references could imply that other disclosures in IFRS 7 are required even if those disclosures are not material, which was not the intention. *[IFRS 7.BC47A]*. Accordingly the above guidance continues to be relevant even though it has been removed from the standard.

3.3 Classes of financial instrument

Certain disclosures required by IFRS 7 should be provided by class of financial instrument (see 4.2.4, 4.4.7, 4.5.1, 4.5.2, 5.2.2, 5.2.3 and 6 below). For these, entities should group financial instruments into classes that are appropriate to the nature of the information disclosed and take into account the characteristics of those instruments. *[IFRS 7.6]*.

It is emphasised that these classes should be determined by the entity and are, thus, distinct from the categories of financial instruments specified in IAS 39 or IFRS 9 which determine how financial instruments are measured and where changes in fair value are recognised. *[IFRS 7.B1]*. However, in determining classes of financial instrument an entity should, as a minimum, distinguish instruments measured at amortised cost from those measured at fair value and treat as a separate class or classes those financial instruments outside the scope of IFRS 7. *[IFRS 7.B2]*.

For disclosures given by class of instrument, sufficient information should be provided to permit the information to be reconciled to the line items presented in the statement of financial position. *[IFRS 7.6]*.

Chapter 53

4   SIGNIFICANCE OF FINANCIAL INSTRUMENTS FOR AN ENTITY'S FINANCIAL POSITION AND PERFORMANCE

The IASB decided that the disclosure requirements in this area should result from the following disclosure principle:

> 'An entity shall disclose information that enables users of its financial statements to evaluate the significance of financial instruments for its financial position and performance.'

Further, they concluded that this principle could not be satisfied unless other specified disclosures (which are dealt with at 4.1 to 4.5 below) are also provided. *[IFRS 7.7, BC13]*.

4.1   Accounting policies

The main body of IFRS 7 contains a reminder of IAS 1's requirement for an entity to disclose its significant accounting policies, comprising the measurement basis (or bases) used in preparing the financial statements and the other accounting policies used that are relevant to an understanding of the financial statements. *[IFRS 7.21]*.

For financial assets or financial liabilities designated at fair value through profit or loss in accordance with IAS 39 (see Chapter 45 at 2.2), such disclosure may include: *[IFRS 7.B5(a)]*

- the nature of the financial assets or financial liabilities designated at fair value through profit or loss;
- the criteria for so designating such financial assets or financial liabilities on initial recognition; and
- how the conditions in IAS 39 for such designation have been satisfied.

  For instruments designated to eliminate or significantly reduce a measurement or recognition inconsistency, this should include a narrative description of the circumstances underlying the inconsistency that would otherwise arise.

  For groups of instruments that are managed and the performance evaluated on a fair value basis, this should include a narrative description of how designation at fair value through profit or loss is consistent with the entity's documented risk management or investment strategy.

For financial assets and financial liabilities designated as measured at fair value through profit or loss in accordance with IFRS 9 (see Chapter 46 at 7), such disclosure may include: *[IFRS 7.B5(a), B5(aa)]*

- the nature of the financial assets or financial liabilities designated as measured at fair value through profit or loss;
- the criteria for designating financial liabilities on initial recognition; and
- how the conditions or criteria in IFRS 9 for such designation have been satisfied.

Other policies that might be appropriate include: *[IFRS 7.B5(b), (c), (e), (f), (g)]*

- the criteria for designating financial assets as available for sale in accordance with IAS 39;
- whether regular way purchases and sales of financial assets are accounted for at trade date or at settlement date (see Chapter 47 at 2.2); and

- how net gains or net losses on each category of financial instrument are determined (see 4.2.1 below), for example whether the net gains or net losses on items measured at fair value through profit or loss include interest or dividend income.

  In our view, interest income and interest expense (including, for example, that arising on short positions) should be treated consistently, i.e. both included or both excluded from the net gains and losses disclosed;

- the criteria an entity applying IAS 39 uses to determine that there is objective evidence that an impairment loss has occurred; and

- for entities applying IAS 39, when the terms of financial assets that would otherwise be past due (see 5.2.2.C below) or impaired have been renegotiated, the accounting policy for financial assets that are the subject of renegotiated terms.

  In contrast to its specific requirements for the derecognition of financial liabilities, IAS 39 does not explicitly address whether or in what circumstances a financial asset whose terms are subject to renegotiation should be derecognised by the holder or whether it should be regarded as a continuation of the existing asset (see Chapter 50 at 3.4.1 and 3.4.2). Therefore, this could be an important accounting policy for banks and other financial institutions if they frequently renegotiate the terms of their loans and receivables.

  Such an accounting policy may also be relevant to entities applying IFRS 9, although when adopted, IFRS 7 is amended to specify additional disclosures about financial instruments that have been renegotiated and not derecognised (see 5.2.3 below).

For entities applying IAS 39, when an allowance account (such as a bad debt provision) is used to reduce the carrying amount of financial assets impaired by credit losses, the accounting policies may need to indicate: *[IFRS 7.B5(d)]*

- the criteria for determining when the carrying amount of impaired financial assets is reduced directly (or, in the case of a reversal of a write-down, increased directly) and when the allowance account is used; and

- the criteria for writing off amounts charged to the allowance account against the carrying amount of impaired financial assets (as set out at 4.4.7 below, a reconciliation of changes in the allowance account should be given).

When IFRS 9 is adopted, the guidance immediately above is deleted and replaced by extensive new disclosure requirements about impairments which are covered primarily at 5.2.3 below.

The application guidance also contains a reminder that IAS 1 requires entities to disclose the judgements, apart from those involving estimations, that management has made in the process of applying the entity's accounting policies and that have the most significant effect on the amounts recognised in the financial statements (see Chapter 3 at 5.1.1.B). *[IFRS 7.B5]*.

4.2 Income, expenses, gains and losses

Under IFRS 7, entities are required to disclose various items of income, expense, gains and losses. The disclosures below may be provided either on the face of the financial statements or in the notes. *[IFRS 7.20]*.

4.2.1 Gains and losses by measurement category

The IASB concluded that disclosure of net gains or net losses arising on the following categories of instrument is necessary to understand the financial performance of an entity's financial instruments given the different measurement bases in IAS 39: *[IFRS 7.20(a), BC33]*

- financial assets or financial liabilities at fair value through profit or loss, showing separately those on financial instruments designated as such upon initial recognition, and those on financial instruments classified as held for trading.

  The implementation guidance to IAS 39 explains that IFRS 7 neither requires nor prohibits the further analysis of gains and losses according to internal classifications used in an entity's business. For example, the change in fair value of those derivatives that IAS 39 classifies as held for trading but the entity classifies as part of risk management activities outside of the trading portfolio may be disclosed separately. *[IAS 39.G.1].*

  In our view, these amounts should not be shown net of funding costs if the associated financial liabilities are not classified at fair value through profit or loss;

- available-for-sale financial assets, showing separately the amount of gain or loss recognised directly in other comprehensive income during the period and the amount reclassified from equity to profit or loss for the period;

- held-to-maturity investments;

- loans and receivables; and

- financial liabilities measured at amortised cost.

These disclosures are designed to complement the statement of financial position disclosure requirement described at 4.4.1 below. *[IFRS 7.BC33].*

Some entities include interest and dividend income in gains and losses on financial assets and financial liabilities held for trading and others do not. To assist users in comparing income arising from financial instruments across different entities, entities are required to disclose how the income statement amounts are determined. For example, an entity should disclose whether net gains and losses on financial assets or financial liabilities held for trading include interest and dividend income (see 4.1 above). *[IFRS 7.BC34].*

On application of IFRS 9, the disclosure requirements above are amended to align them with that standard. Consequently, disclosure should be given of net gains or net losses arising on the following categories of instrument: *[IFRS 7.20]*

- financial assets or financial liabilities measured at fair value through profit or loss, showing separately those on financial assets or liabilities:

  - designated as such upon initial recognition (or subsequently when the credit risk of a financial asset is managed using a credit derivative); and

  - mandatorily measured at fair value in accordance with IFRS 9, e.g. liabilities held for trading.

  For financial liabilities designated at fair value through profit or loss, the amount of gain or loss recognised in other comprehensive income, i.e. relating to changes in fair value attributable to changes in credit risk (see Chapter 49 at 2.1), should be shown separately;

- financial assets measured at amortised cost.

IFRS 7 requires disclosure of an analysis of the gain or loss arising from derecognition of such assets showing separately gains and losses. The reasons for derecognition should also be given. *[IFRS 7.20A]*. These gains and losses should also be shown separately on the face of the income statement or statement of comprehensive income (see 7.1.1 below); *[IAS 1.82(aa)]*

- financial liabilities measured at amortised cost;

- investments in equity instruments designated at fair value through other comprehensive income; and

- debt instruments measured at fair value through other comprehensive income, showing separately:

  - the amount of gain or loss recognised in other comprehensive income during the period; and

  - the amount reclassified upon derecognition from accumulated other comprehensive income to profit or loss for the period.

4.2.2 Interest income and expense

For financial assets or financial liabilities that are not measured at fair value through profit or loss, total interest income and total interest expense (calculated using the effective interest method) should be disclosed. Interest income on impaired financial assets (accrued as described in Chapter 48 at 4.5) should be disclosed by entities applying IAS 39. Where IFRS 9 is applied, interest revenue for financial assets measured at amortised cost should be shown separately from interest revenue on debt instruments measured at fair value through other comprehensive income. *[IFRS 7.20(b), (d)]*.

Financial instruments containing discretionary participation features fall within the scope of IFRS 4 – *Insurance Contracts* – rather than IAS 39 or IFRS 9 (see Chapter 42 at 3.3.2 and Chapter 54 at 6). However, IFRS 7 does apply to such instruments and IFRS 4 acknowledges that the interest expense disclosed need not be calculated using the effective interest method. *[IFRS 4.35(d)]*.

Similarly, finance lease payables and receivables are within the scope of IFRS 7 (see Chapter 42 at 3.2) but are not accounted for using the effective interest method. However, there is no equivalent acknowledgement either in IAS 17 – *Leases* –IAS 39, or IFRS 9 that the disclosure of interest income and interest expense should be made on the basis of the finance cost and finance revenue recognised under IAS 17. Nevertheless, this seems little more than an oversight and we consider it appropriate to include in the disclosure the amounts actually recognised rather than amounts calculated in accordance with the effective interest method.

Chapter 53

4.2.3   Fee income and expense

Entities should disclose fee income and expense (excluding amounts included in the effective interest rate calculation) arising from: *[IFRS 7.20(c)]*

- financial assets or financial liabilities that are not measured at fair value through profit or loss; and

- trust and other fiduciary activities that result in the holding or investing of assets on behalf of individuals, trusts, retirement benefit plans, and other institutions.

This information is said to indicate the level of such activities and help users to estimate possible future income of the entity. *[IFRS 7.BC35].*

4.2.4   Impairment losses

For entities applying IAS 39, the amount of any impairment loss should be disclosed for each class of financial asset. *[IFRS 7.20(e)].* Significant additional disclosures are required for entities applying IFRS 9 which are covered at 5.2.3 below.

4.3   Hedge accounting

4.3.1   Hedge accounting disclosures for entities applying IAS 39

When hedge accounting is applied (see Chapter 51), entities applying IAS 39 are required to disclose the following, separately for each type of hedge (i.e. fair value hedges, cash flow hedges, and hedges of net investments in foreign operations): *[IFRS 7.22]*

- a description of each type of hedge;

- a description of the financial instruments designated as hedging instruments and their fair values at the reporting date; and

- the nature of the risks being hedged.

A single hedging instrument may be simultaneously designated in a cash flow hedge and a fair value hedge. The situations in which this might occur are considered further in Chapter 51 at 2.1.6. Such an instrument would need to be included separately in the disclosures above both for cash flow hedges and fair value hedges. *[IAS 39.F.1.12].*

For cash flow hedges, entities are also required to disclose: *[IFRS 7.23]*

- the periods when the cash flows are expected to occur and when they are expected to affect profit or loss;

- a description of any forecast transaction for which hedge accounting has previously been used, but which is no longer expected to occur;

- the amount that was recognised in other comprehensive income during the period;

- the amount that was reclassified from equity to profit or loss for the period, showing the amount included in each line item in the income statement; and

- the amount that was removed from equity during the period and included in the initial cost or other carrying amount of a non-financial asset or non-financial liability whose acquisition or incurrence was a hedged highly probable forecast transaction.

Finally, the following information is also required: *[IFRS 7.24]*

- for fair value hedges, gains or losses:
  - on the hedging instrument; and
  - on the hedged item attributable to the hedged risk;
- the ineffectiveness recognised in profit or loss that arises from cash flow hedges; and
- the ineffectiveness recognised in profit or loss that arises from hedges of net investments in foreign operations.

The financial statements of Deutsche Telekom include the following disclosure about hedges.

Extract 53.1: Deutsche Telekom AG (2014)

Notes to the consolidated financial statements [extract]

37. Financial instruments and risk management [extract]

Hedge accounting

Fair value hedges.

To hedge the fair value risk of fixed-interest liabilities, Deutsche Telekom primarily used interest rate swaps and forward interest rate swaps (pay variable, receive fixed) denominated in EUR, GBP, NOK and USD. Fixed-income bonds/MTNs denominated in EUR, GBP, NOK and USD were designated as hedged items. The changes in the fair values of the hedged items resulting from changes in the Euribor, GBP Libor, NOK OIBOR or USD Libor swap rate are offset against the changes in the value of the interest rate swaps. In addition, a cross-currency swap totalling AUD 125 million has been designated as fair value hedge, which converts a fixed-interest MTN into a variable interest-bearing security. The aim of this hedging is to transform the fixed-income bonds into variable-interest debt, thus hedging the fair value of the financial liabilities. Credit risks are not part of the hedging.

The effectiveness of the hedging relationship is tested prospectively and retrospectively at each reporting date using statistical methods in the form of a regression analysis. All hedging relationships were sufficiently effective as of the reporting date.

In the reporting period, new fair value hedges with a total nominal volume of EUR 3.5 billion were designated for reducing the fair value risk.

As the list of the fair values of derivatives shows (see TABLE 171, PAGE 257), Deutsche Telekom had interest rate derivatives with a net fair value of EUR 0.2 billion (December 31, 2013: EUR –0.2 billion) designated as fair value hedges at December 31, 2014. The remeasurement of the hedged items results in losses of EUR 0.4 billion being recorded in other financial income/expense in the 2014 financial year (2013: gains of EUR 0.4 billion); the changes in the fair values of the hedging transactions result in gains of EUR 0.4 billion (2013: losses of EUR 0.4 billion) being recorded in other financial income/expense.

Cash flow hedges – interest rate risks.

Deutsche Telekom entered into payer interest rate swaps and forward payer interest rate swaps (pay fixed, receive variable) to hedge the cash flow risk of variable-interest debt. The interest payments to be made in the hedging period are the hedged items and are recognized in profit or loss in the same period. The changes in the cash flows of the hedged items resulting from changes in the Euribor and Libor rates are offset against the changes in the cash flows of the interest rate swaps. The aim of this hedging is to transform the variable-interest bonds into fixed-income debt, thus hedging the cash flows of the financial liabilities. The terms of the hedging relationships will end in the years 2015 through 2018. Credit risks are not part of the hedging.

The effectiveness of the hedging relationship is tested prospectively and retrospectively using statistical methods in the form of a regression analysis.

Ineffectiveness of EUR 19 million (income) was recognized in profit or loss under other financial income/expense in the reporting year (2013:expense of EUR 21 million).

All designated hedging relationships were sufficiently effective as of the reporting date.

As the list of fair values of derivatives shows (see TABLE 171), Deutsche Telekom had interest rate derivatives with a fair value of EUR −0.3 billion (December 31, 2013: EUR −0.3 billion) amounting to a nominal total of EUR 3.1 billion (December 31, 2013: EUR 5.0 billion) designated as hedging instruments for the hedging of interest rate risks as part of cash flow hedges at December 31, 2014.

The recognition directly in equity of the change in the fair value of the hedging instruments resulted in losses (before taxes) of EUR 97 million (2013: gains of EUR 36 million) in shareholders' equity in the 2014 financial year. Losses amounting to EUR 77 million (2013: losses of EUR 124 million) recognized directly in equity were reclassified to other financial income/expense in the income statement in the 2014 financial year.

Cash flow hedges – currency risks.

Deutsche Telekom entered into currency derivative and cross-currency swap agreements to hedge cash flows not denominated in a functional currency. The payments in foreign currency to be made in the hedging period are the hedged items and are recognized in profit or loss in the same period. The terms of the hedging relationships will end in the years 2015 through 2033. The effectiveness of the hedging relationship is tested prospectively and retrospectively using statistical methods in the form of a regression analysis. All designated hedging relationships were sufficiently effective as of the reporting date.

No new cash flow hedges of this kind were designated in the reporting period.

In the 2014 financial year, gains (before taxes) totaling EUR 362 million (2013: losses of EUR 199 million) resulting from the change in the fair values of currency derivatives were taken directly to equity (hedging reserve). These changes constitute the effective portion of the hedging relationship. In the 2014 financial year, gains totalling EUR 338 million recognized directly in equity were reclassified to other financial income/expense and gains totalling EUR 6 million on were reclassified to profit/loss from operations (2013: losses of EUR 70 million were reclassified to other financial income/expense and gains of EUR 16 million to profit/loss from operations). There was no material ineffectiveness of these hedges recorded as of the reporting date.

As the list of the fair values of derivatives shows (see TABLE 171), Deutsche Telekom had currency forwards of a net fair value of EUR −5 million (December 31, 2013: EUR +21 million), that are the result of foreign currency purchases totalling EUR 0.2 billion and foreign currency sales totalling EUR 0.4 billion (December 31, 2013: foreign currency purchases of EUR 0.3 billion and foreign currency sales of EUR 0.8 billion), as well as cross-currency swaps of a net fair value of EUR 0.1 billion (December 31, 2013: EUR −0.3 billion) and a total volume of EUR 4.8 billion (December 31, 2013: EUR 4.8 billion) designated as hedging instruments for cash flow hedges as of December 31, 2014.

Hedging of a net investment.

The hedge of the net investment in T-Mobile US against fluctuations in the U.S. dollar spot rate designated in 2012 did not generate any effects in 2014. The level of gains/losses recognized directly in equity (total other comprehensive income) remained unchanged at EUR −0.4 billion (before taxes).

Derivatives.

TABLE 171 shows the fair values of the various derivatives carried. A distinction is made depending on whether these are part of an effective hedging relationship as set out in IAS 39 (fair value hedge, cash flow hedge, net investment hedge) or not. Other derivatives can also be embedded, i.e. a component of a composite instrument that contains a non-derivative host contract.

T 171
millions of €

	Net carrying amounts Dec. 31, 2014	Net carrying amounts Dec. 31, 2013
Assets		
Interest rate swaps		
Held for trading	53	54
In connection with fair value hedges	222	62
In connection with cash flow hedges	–	–
Currency forwards/currency swaps		
Held for trading	67	26
In connection with cash flow hedges	4	24
Cross-currency swaps		
Held for trading	531	358
In connection with fair value hedges	–	–
In connection with cash flow hedges	282	89
Other derivatives in connection with cash flow hedges	–	–
Other derivatives without a hedging relationship	1	–
Embedded derivatives	183	158
Liabilities and shareholders' equity		
Interest rate swaps		
Held for trading	235	226
In connection with fair value hedges	–	264
In connection with cash flow hedges	252	336
Currency forwards/currency swaps		
Held for trading	229	39
In connection with cash flow hedges	9	3
In connection with net investment hedges	–	–
Cross-currency swaps		
Held for trading	185	316
In connection with fair value hedges	8	12
In connection with cash flow hedges	162	387
Other derivatives in connection with cash flow hedges	–	–
Other derivatives without a hedging relationship	15	–
Embedded derivatives	–	–

4.3.2   Hedge accounting disclosures for entities applying IFRS 9

For entities applying IFRS 9, the disclosure requirements in respect of hedge accounting are expanded significantly when compared to IAS 39. Those requirements are also supplemented by some detailed implementation guidance. The hedge accounting requirements of IFRS 9 are dealt with in Chapter 52 which includes some discussion of the disclosure requirements set out below.

When an entity applies IFRS 9 it may choose to continue applying certain, or all, of the hedge accounting requirements of IAS 39 rather than those in IFRS 9 (see Chapter 51 at 1.3 and Chapter 52 at 3.6.6). In these circumstances the disclosure requirements introduced by IFRS 9 and covered in this section should be followed, rather than those set out at 4.3.1 above, even for those hedges that continue to be accounted for in accordance with IAS 39. *[IFRS 9.BC6.104].*

The requirements set out at 4.3.2.A to 4.3.2.D below apply for those risk exposures that an entity hedges and for which it elects to apply hedge accounting. The objective of these disclosures is to provide information about: *[IFRS 7.21A]*

- the entity's risk management strategy and how it is applied to manage risk (see 4.3.2.A below);

- how the entity's hedging activities may affect the amount, timing and uncertainty of its future cash flows (see 4.3.2.B below); and

- the effect that hedge accounting has had on the entity's statement of financial position, statement of comprehensive income and statement of changes in equity (see 4.3.2.C and 4.3.2.D below).

In order to meet these objectives, an entity will need to determine how much detail to disclose, how much emphasis to place on different aspects of the disclosure requirements, the appropriate level of aggregation or disaggregation and whether additional explanations are needed to evaluate the quantitative information disclosed. The level of aggregation or disaggregation should be consistent with that used for meeting the disclosure requirements of related information elsewhere in IFRS 7 and in IFRS 13 (see Chapter 14 at 20.1.2). *[IFRS 7.21D]*.

Some of the disclosure requirements at 4.3.2.A to 4.3.2.C are required to be given by 'risk category'. This is not a defined term, but each risk category should be determined on the basis of the risk exposures an entity decides to hedge and for which hedge accounting is applied. These categories should be determined consistently for all hedge accounting disclosures. *[IFRS 7.21C]*.

These disclosures should be presented in a single note or separate section of the financial statements. To avoid duplication, IFRS 7 allows this information to be incorporated by cross-reference from the financial statements to some other statement that is available to users of the financial statements on the same terms and at the same time, such as a management commentary or risk report. Without the information incorporated by cross-reference, the financial statements are incomplete. *[IFRS 7.21B]*.

4.3.2.A   The risk management strategy

An entity should explain its risk management strategy for each risk category of risk exposures that it decides to hedge and for which hedge accounting is applied. This explanation should enable users of financial statements to evaluate, for example: *[IFRS 7.22A]*

- how each risk arises;

- how each risk is managed.

    This includes whether the entity hedges an item in its entirety for all risks or hedges a risk component (or components) of an item and why; and

- the extent of risk exposures that are managed.

To meet these requirements, the information should include, but is not limited to, a description of: *[IFRS 7.22B]*

- the hedging instruments that are used (and how they are used) to hedge risk exposures;

- how the economic relationship between the hedged item and the hedging instrument is determined for the purpose of assessing hedge effectiveness;

- how the hedge ratio is established; and

- the sources of hedge ineffectiveness.

When a specific risk component is designated as a hedged item, qualitative or quantitative information should be provided about: *[IFRS 7.22C]*

- how the risk component that is designated as the hedged item was determined, including a description of the nature of the relationship between the risk component and the item as a whole; and

- how the risk component relates to the item in its entirety. For example, the designated risk component may historically have covered on average 80% of the changes in fair value of the item as a whole.

4.3.2.B   *The amount, timing and uncertainty of future cash flows*

For most hedge relationships, quantitative information should be disclosed by risk category that allows the evaluation of the terms and conditions of the hedging instruments and how they affect the amount, timing and uncertainty of future cash flows. *[IFRS 7.23A]*. This should include a breakdown disclosing the profile of the timing of the hedging instrument's nominal amount and, if applicable, its average price or rate (e.g. strike or forward prices). *[IFRS 7.23B]*. However, different information should be given where a dynamic hedging process is used.

A dynamic process may be used in which both the exposure and the hedging instruments used to manage that exposure remain the same for only short periods of time because both the hedging instrument and the hedged item frequently change and the hedging relationship is frequently reset (or discontinued and restarted). This might occur, for example, when hedging the interest rate risk of an open portfolio of debt instruments. In these situations, the following should be disclosed: *[IFRS 7.23C]*

- information about what the ultimate risk management strategy is in relation to those hedging relationships;

- a description of how the risk management strategy is reflected by using hedge accounting and designating those particular hedging relationships; and

- an indication of how frequently the hedging relationships are discontinued and restarted as part of the process in relation to those hedging relationships.

When the volume of hedging relationships in a dynamic process is unrepresentative of normal volumes during the period (i.e. the volume at the reporting date does not reflect the volumes during the period) that fact should be disclosed along with the reason volumes are believed to be unrepresentative. *[IFRS 7.24D]*.

For all hedges, a description of the sources of hedge ineffectiveness that are expected to affect the hedging relationship during its term should be disclosed by risk category. *[IFRS 7.23D]*. If other sources of hedge ineffectiveness emerge in a hedging relationship, those sources should be disclosed by risk category along with an explanation of the resulting hedge ineffectiveness. *[IFRS 7.23E]*.

Chapter 53

For cash flow hedges, a description of any forecast transaction for which hedge accounting had been used in the previous period, but which is no longer expected to occur, should be disclosed. *[IFRS 7.23F]*.

4.3.2.C   *The effects of hedge accounting on financial position and performance*

The following amounts related to designated hedging instruments should be disclosed:

- the carrying amount of the hedging instruments, presenting financial assets separately from financial liabilities;

- the line item in the statement of financial position that includes the hedging instrument;

- the change in fair value of the hedging instrument used as the basis for recognising hedge ineffectiveness for the period; and

- the nominal amounts (including quantities such as tonnes or cubic metres) of the hedging instruments.

This information should be given in a tabular format, separately by risk category and for fair value hedges, cash flow hedges and hedges of a net investment in a foreign operation *[IFRS 7.24A]* and the implementation guidance suggests it might be given in the following format. *[IFRS 7.IG13C]*.

Example 53.1:   Amounts related to hedged instruments

	Nominal amount of the hedging instrument	Carrying amount of the hedging instrument		Line item in the statement of financial position where the hedging instrument is located	Changes in fair value used for calculating hedge ineffective-ness for 20X1
		Assets	Liabilities		
Cash flow hedges					
Commodity price risk					
– Forward sales contracts	xx	xx	xx	Line item XX	xx
Fair value hedges					
Interest rate risk					
– Interest rate swaps	xx	xx	xx	Line item XX	xx
Foreign exchange risk					
– Foreign currency loan	xx	xx	xx	Line item XX	xx

The following amounts related to hedged items should be disclosed:

- for fair value hedges:

    - the carrying amount of the hedged item recognised in the statement of financial position, presenting assets separately from liabilities;

    - the accumulated amount of adjustments to the hedged item included in its carrying amount, again presenting assets separately from liabilities;

    - the line item in the statement of financial position that includes the hedged item;

- the change in value of the hedged item used as the basis for recognising hedge ineffectiveness for the period; and
- the accumulated amount of adjustments to hedged financial instruments measured at amortised cost that have ceased to be adjusted for hedging gains and losses and which remain in the statement of financial position;
- for cash flow hedges and hedges of a net investment in a foreign operation:
  - the change in value of the hedged item used as the basis for recognising hedge ineffectiveness for the period;
  - the balances in the cash flow hedge reserve and the foreign currency translation reserve for continuing hedges; and
  - the balances remaining in the cash flow hedge reserve and the foreign currency translation reserve from any hedging relationships for which hedge accounting is no longer applied.

This information should be given in a tabular format, separately by risk category *[IFRS 7.24B]* and the implementation guidance suggests it might be given in the following format. *[IFRS 7.IG13D]*.

Example 53.2: Amounts related to hedging items

	Carrying amount of the hedged item		Accumulated amount of fair value hedge adjustments on the hedged item included in the carrying amount of the hedged item		Line item in the statement of financial position in which the hedged item is included	Change in value used for calculating hedge ineffective-ness for 20X1	Cash flow hedge reserve
	Assets	Liabilities	Assets	Liabilities			
Cash flow hedges							
Commodity price risk							
– Forecast sales	n/a	n/a	n/a	n/a	n/a	xx	xx
– Discontinued hedges (forecast sales)	n/a	n/a	n/a	n/a	n/a	n/a	xx
Fair value hedges							
Interest rate risk							
– Loan payable	–	xx	–	xx	Line item XX	xx	n/a
– Discontinued hedges (Loan payable)	–	xx	–	xx	Line item XX	n/a	n/a
Foreign exchange risk							
– Firm commitment	xx	xx	xx	xx	Line item XX	xx	n/a

The following amounts affecting the statement of comprehensive income should be disclosed:

- for fair value hedges:
    - hedge ineffectiveness, i.e. the difference between the hedging gains or losses of the hedging instrument and the hedged item, recognised in profit or loss (or other comprehensive income for hedges of an equity instrument for which changes in fair value are presented in other comprehensive income); and
    - the line item in the statement of comprehensive income that includes the recognised hedge ineffectiveness;
- for cash flow hedges and hedges of a net investment in a foreign operation:
    - hedging gains or losses that were recognised in other comprehensive income in the reporting period;
    - hedge ineffectiveness recognised in profit or loss;
    - the line item in the statement of comprehensive income that includes the recognised hedge ineffectiveness;
    - the amount reclassified from the cash flow hedge reserve or the foreign currency translation reserve into profit or loss as a reclassification adjustment, differentiating in the case of cash flow hedges between:
        - amounts for which hedge accounting had previously been used, but for which the hedged future cash flows are no longer expected to occur; and
        - amounts that have been transferred because the hedged item has affected profit or loss;
    - the line item in the statement of comprehensive income that includes the reclassification adjustment; and
    - for hedges of net positions, the hedging gains or losses recognised in a separate line item in the statement of comprehensive income.

This information should be given in a tabular format, separately by risk category [IFRS 7.24C] and the implementation guidance suggests it might be given in the following format. [IFRS 7.IG13E].

Example 53.3:   *Amounts affecting the statement of comprehensive income.*

Cash flow hedges (a)	Separate line item recognised in profit or loss as a result of a hedge of a net position(b)	Change in the value of the hedging instrument recognised in other comprehensive income	Hedge ineffective-ness recognised in profit or loss	Line item in profit or loss (that includes hedge ineffectiveness)	Amount reclassified from the cash flow hedge reserve to profit or loss	Line item affected in profit or loss because of the reclassification
Commodity price risk						
Commodity X	n/a	xx	xx	Line item XX	xx	Line item XX
– Discontinued hedge	n/a	n/a	n/a	n/a	xx	Line item XX

(a) The information disclosed in the statement of changes in equity (cash flow hedge reserve) should have the same level of detail as these disclosures.

(b) This disclosure only applies to cash flow hedges of foreign currency risk.

Fair value Hedges	Ineffectiveness recognised in profit or loss	Line item(s) in profit or loss (that include(s) hedge ineffectiveness)
Interest rate risk	xx	Line item XX
Foreign exchange risk	xx	Line item XX

IAS 1 requires the presentation of a reconciliation of each component of equity and an analysis of other comprehensive income (see 7.2 and 7.3 below). The level of information given in the reconciliation and analysis should: *[IFRS 7.24E]*

- differentiate between hedging gains or losses recognised in other comprehensive income and amounts reclassified to profit or loss, separately for:
  - cash flow hedges for which the hedged future cash flows are no longer expected to occur;
  - those hedges for which the hedged item has affected profit or loss; and
  - amounts related to hedged forecast transactions that subsequently result in the recognition of a non-financial asset or liability, or a hedged forecast transaction for a non-financial asset or liability becomes a firm commitment for which fair value hedge accounting is applied, that are included directly in the initial cost or other carrying amount of the asset or the liability;
- differentiate between amounts associated with the time value of options that hedge transaction related hedged items and those that hedge time-period related hedged items where the time value of the option is recognised initially in other comprehensive income; and
- differentiate between amounts associated with forward elements of forward contracts and the foreign currency basis spreads of financial instruments that hedge transaction related hedged items and those that hedge time-period related hedged items where those amounts are recognised initially in other comprehensive income.

The information in the bullets above should be disclosed separately by risk category, although this disaggregation may be provided in the notes to the financial statements. *[IFRS 7.24F]*.

Further examples of how these disclosures might be provided are set out in Chapter 52 at 9.

4.3.2.D   Option to designate a credit exposure as measured at fair value through profit or loss

If a financial instrument, or a proportion of it, has been designated as measured at fair value through profit or loss because a credit derivative is used to manage the credit risk of that financial instrument, the following should be disclosed: *[IFRS 7.24G]*

- a reconciliation of each of the nominal amount and the fair value of the credit derivative at the beginning and end of the period;
- the gain or loss recognised in profit or loss on initial designation; and
- on discontinuation of measuring a financial instrument, or a proportion of it, at fair value through profit or loss, the fair value of that financial instrument that becomes the new carrying amount and the related nominal or principal amount.

   Except for providing comparative information in accordance with IAS 1, this information need not be given in subsequent periods.

4.4   Statement of financial position

4.4.1   Categories of financial assets and financial liabilities

For entities applying IAS 39, the carrying amounts of each of the following categories of financial instrument should be disclosed, either on the face of the statement of financial position or in the notes: *[IFRS 7.8]*

- financial assets at fair value through profit or loss, showing separately:
  - those designated as such upon initial recognition; and
  - those classified as held for trading;
- held-to-maturity investments;
- loans and receivables;
- available-for-sale financial assets;
- financial liabilities at fair value through profit or loss, showing separately:
  - those designated as such upon initial recognition; and
  - those classified as held for trading; and
- financial liabilities measured at amortised cost.

Although accounted for identically, the carrying amounts of financial instruments that are classified as held for trading and those designated at fair value through profit or loss are shown separately because designation is at the discretion of the entity. *[IFRS 7.BC15]*.

The IASB concluded that such disclosure would assist users in understanding the extent to which accounting policies affect the amounts at which financial assets and financial liabilities are recognised. *[IFRS 7.BC14]*.

On application of IFRS 9, the disclosure requirements above are amended to align them with that standard. Consequently, disclosure should be made using the following categories: *[IFRS 7.8]*

- financial assets measured at fair value through profit or loss, showing separately:
  - those designated as such upon initial recognition; and
  - those mandatorily measured at fair value in accordance with IFRS 9;
- financial liabilities at fair value through profit or loss, showing separately:
  - those designated as such upon initial recognition; and
  - those that meet the definition of held for trading in IFRS 9;
- financial assets measured at amortised cost;
- financial liabilities measured at amortised cost; and
- financial assets measured at fair value through other comprehensive income, showing separately:
  - debt instruments held within a business model to both collect contractual cash flows from, and to sell, the assets; and
  - investments in equity instruments designated to be measured as such upon initial recognition.

A derivative that is designated as a hedging instrument in an effective hedge relationship does not fall within any of the above categories and, strictly, should not be included in these disclosures. Disclosure requirements for hedges are set out at 4.3 above.

4.4.2   Financial liabilities designated at fair value through profit or loss

4.4.2.A   Entities applying IAS 39

Where a (non-derivative) financial liability has been designated at fair value through profit or loss, i.e. it is not classified as trading, the amount of change during the period and cumulatively (i.e. since initial recognition) in its fair value that is attributable to changes in credit risk should be disclosed.

Unless an alternative method more faithfully represents this amount, it should be determined as the amount of change in the fair value of the liability that is not attributable to changes in market conditions that give rise to market risk. Changes in market conditions that give rise to market risk include changes in a benchmark interest rate, commodity price, foreign exchange rate or index of prices or rates. For contracts that include a unit-linking feature, changes in market conditions include changes in the performance of an internal or external investment fund. *[IFRS 7.10(a)]*. If the only relevant changes in market conditions for a financial liability are changes in an observed (benchmark) interest rate, the amount to be disclosed can be estimated as follows:

(a)   first, the liability's internal rate of return at the start of the period is computed using the observed market price and contractual cash flows at that time and from this is deducted the observed (benchmark) interest rate at the start of the period, to arrive at an instrument specific component of the internal rate of return;

(b)   next, the present value of the cash flows associated with the liability is calculated using the liability's contractual cash flows at the end of the period and a discount rate equal to the sum of the observed (benchmark) interest rate at the end of the period and the instrument-specific component of the internal rate of return at the start of the period as determined in (a); and

(c)   the difference between the observed market price of the liability at the end of the period and the amount determined in (b) is the change in fair value that is not attributable to changes in the observed (benchmark) interest rate and this is the amount to be disclosed.

This assumes that changes in fair value other than those arising from changes in the instrument's credit risk or from changes in interest rates are not significant. If the instrument contained an embedded derivative, the change in fair value of the embedded derivative would be excluded in determining the amount to be disclosed. *[IFRS 7.B4]*.

The default method will produce an amount which includes any changes in the liquidity spread charged by market participants because such changes are not considered to be 'attributable to changes in market conditions that give rise to market risk'. This seems appropriate when the effect of a liquidity spread cannot be isolated from that of the credit spread.

This method is illustrated in the following example. *[IFRS 7.IG7]*.

Example 53.4:   Estimating the change in fair value of an instrument attributable to its credit risk

On 1 January 2016, Company J issues a 10-year bond with a par value of €150,000 and an annual fixed coupon rate of 8%, which is consistent with market rates for bonds with similar characteristics. J uses LIBOR as its observable (benchmark) interest rate. At the date of inception of the bond, LIBOR is 5%. At the end of the first year:

•   LIBOR has decreased to 4.75%; and

•   the fair value of the bond is €153,811, consistent with an interest rate of 7.6% [the remaining cash flows on the bond, i.e. €12,000 per year for nine years and €150,000 at the end of nine years, discounted at 7.6% equals €153,811].

J assumes a flat yield curve, that all changes in interest rates result from a parallel shift in the yield curve, and that the changes in LIBOR are the only relevant changes in market conditions.

The amount of change in the fair value of the bond that is not attributable to changes in market conditions that give rise to market risk is estimated as follows:

Step (a)

The bond's internal rate of return at the start of the period is 8%. Because the observed (benchmark) interest rate (LIBOR) is 5%, the instrument-specific component of the internal rate of return is 3%.

Step (b)

The contractual cash flows of the instrument at the end of the period are:

- interest: €12,000 [€150,000 × 8%] per year for each of years 2017 to 2025; and
- principal: €150,000 in 2025

The discount rate to be used to calculate the present value of the bond is thus 7.75%, which is the 4.75% end of period LIBOR rate, plus the 3% instrument-specific component calculated as at the start of the period which gives a notional present value of €152,367 [€12,000 × $(1 - 1.0775^{-9})$ ÷ 0.0775) + €150,000 × 1.0775^{-9}], on the assumption that there has been no change in the instrument-specific component.

Step (c)

The market price of the liability at the end of the period (which will reflect the real instrument-specific component at the end of the period) is €153,811, therefore J should disclose €1,444 [€153,811 − €152,367] as the increase in fair value of the bond that is not attributable to changes in market conditions that give rise to market risk. *[IFRS 7.IG8, IG9, IG10, IG11].*

If another method more faithfully represents the amount of change in the fair value of the liability that is attributable to changes in credit risk, that method should be used. *[IFRS 7.10(a)(ii)].*

Whatever the chosen method(s), it (they) should be disclosed. Further, if the disclosure is not considered to represent faithfully the change in the fair value of the financial liability attributable to changes in credit risk, the reasons for reaching this conclusion and the factors believed to be relevant should also be disclosed. *[IFRS 7.11].* This second requirement is somewhat curious and, where provided, could be regarded as undermining the entity's compliance with the requirements above.

In addition, the IASB concluded that the difference between the carrying amount of such a liability and the amount the entity would be contractually required to pay at maturity to the holder of the obligation should also be disclosed. *[IFRS 7.10(b)].* The fair value may differ significantly from the settlement amount, particularly for liabilities with a long duration when the entity has experienced a significant deterioration in creditworthiness subsequent to issuance and the IASB concluded that knowledge of this difference would be useful. Also, the settlement amount is important to some financial statement users, particularly creditors. *[IFRS 7.BC22]*

4.4.2.B   Entities applying IFRS 9

For entities applying IFRS 9, very similar disclosure requirements to those set out at 4.4.2.A above apply, although they are supplemented by a number of additional requirements. Further, entities should follow the requirements of IFRS 9 for determining changes in the fair value of a financial liability attributable to credit risk (see Chapter 49 at 2.1.1) rather than those in IFRS 7, although they are very similar. *[IFRS 7.10, 10A, 11].*

Where changes in the fair value of a financial liability attributable to credit risk are recognised in other comprehensive income (see Chapter 49 at 2.1), any transfers of the cumulative gain or loss within equity should be disclosed, including the reason for such transfers. *[IFRS 7.10(c)]*. Also, if a financial liability is derecognised during the period, the amount (if any) presented in other comprehensive income that was realised at derecognition should be disclosed. *[IFRS 7.10(d)]*.

When disclosing the method used to calculate the change in fair value attributable to changes in credit risk, a detailed description of that method should be given, including an explanation of why the method is appropriate. *[IFRS 7.11(a)]*.

Entities should also provide a detailed description of the methodology or methodologies used to determine whether presenting changes in the fair value of a liability attributable to credit risk in other comprehensive income would create or enlarge an accounting mismatch in profit or loss (see Chapter 49 at 2.1.2). Where an entity is required to present such changes in profit or loss, this disclosure should include a detailed description of the economic relationship between the financial liability and other financial instrument(s) measured at fair value through profit or loss that are expected to offset those changes. *[IFRS 7.11(c)]*.

4.4.3   Financial assets designated as measured at fair value through profit or loss

Additional disclosure requirements apply to loans and receivables (or groups of such assets) that are designated at fair value through profit or loss in accordance with IAS 39. Where IFRS 9 has been applied, the disclosure requirements apply to debt instruments that would otherwise be measured at fair value through other comprehensive income or at amortised cost.

These requirements are: *[IFRS 7.9]*

- the maximum exposure to credit risk (see 5.2.2.A or 5.2.3.D below) at the reporting date of the loan or receivable (or group of loans or receivables);

- the amount by which any related credit derivatives or similar instruments mitigate that maximum exposure to credit risk;

- the amount of change during the period and cumulatively (i.e. since initial recognition) in the fair value of the loan or receivable (or group of loans or receivables) that is attributable to changes in credit risk (see below); and

- the amount of change in the fair value of any related credit derivative or similar instrument that has occurred during the period and cumulatively since the loan or receivable was designated.

Calculating the change in fair value attributable to changes in credit risk is approached in the same way as for financial liabilities (see 4.4.2 above). It may be determined either as the amount of change in fair value that is not attributable to changes in market conditions that give rise to market risk or by using an alternative method that more faithfully represents the amount of change in its fair value that is attributable to changes in credit risk. *[IFRS 7.9]*. The chosen method(s) should be disclosed and if the disclosure is not considered to represent faithfully the change in the fair value of the financial asset attributable to changes in credit risk, the reasons for reaching this conclusion and the factors believed to be relevant should be disclosed. *[IFRS 7.11]*.

Although this is not addressed explicitly within the standard, we believe that the disclosure requirements above apply to hybrid financial assets that would, absent the designation, be accounted for as a loan or receivable and a separate embedded derivative in accordance with IAS 39, not just those financial assets that meet the definition of loans and receivables in their entirety.

On application of IFRS 9, very similar disclosure requirements to those set out above apply for a financial asset (or group of financial assets) designated as measured at fair value through profit or loss that would otherwise be measured at amortised cost. *[IFRS 7.9]*. When disclosing the method used to calculate the change in fair value attributable to changes in credit risk, an entity applying IFRS 9 should also provide a detailed description of that method, including an explanation of why the method is appropriate. *[IFRS 7.11(a)]*.

4.4.4   *Investments in equity instruments designated at fair value through other comprehensive income (IFRS 9)*

Where IFRS 9 is applied and investments in equity instruments have been designated to be measured at fair value through other comprehensive income (see Chapter 46 at 2 and 8), the following should be disclosed: *[IFRS 7.11A]*

*   which investments in equity instruments have been designated to be measured at fair value through other comprehensive income;
*   the reasons for using this presentation alternative;
*   the fair value of each such investment at the end of the reporting period;
*   dividends recognised during the period, showing separately those related to investments derecognised during the reporting period and those related to investments held at the end of the reporting period; and
*   any transfers of the cumulative gain or loss within equity during the period, including the reason for such transfers.

Where such investments are derecognised during the reporting period, the following should also be disclosed: *[IFRS 7.11B]*

*   the reasons for disposing of the investments;
*   the fair value of the investments at the date of derecognition; and
*   the cumulative gain or loss on disposal.

4.4.5   *Reclassification*

The circumstances in which financial instruments should or may be reclassified from one category to another are discussed in Chapter 45 at 6 for those entities applying IAS 39 and, where IFRS 9 is applied, in Chapter 46 at 9.

Chapter 53

4.4.5.A   Reclassifications in accordance with the October 2008 'reclassification' amendments to IAS 39

If an entity has reclassified a financial asset out of the fair value through profit or loss category (see Chapter 45 at 6.1.1) or out of the available-for-sale category (see Chapter 45 at 6.2) in accordance with the October 2008 amendments to IAS 39, it should disclose: *[IFRS 7.12A]*

(a)   the amount reclassified into and out of each category;

(b)   for each reporting period until derecognition, the carrying amounts and fair values of all financial assets that have been reclassified in the current and previous reporting periods;

(c)   if a financial asset was reclassified as a result of 'rare circumstances' (see Chapter 45 at 6.1.1.B), the rare situation and the facts and circumstances indicating that the situation was rare;

(d)   for the reporting period when the financial asset was reclassified, the fair value gain or loss on the financial asset recognised in profit or loss or other comprehensive income in that reporting period and in the previous reporting period;

(e)   for each reporting period following the reclassification (including the reporting period in which the financial asset was reclassified) until derecognition of the financial asset, the fair value gain or loss that would have been recognised in profit or loss or other comprehensive income if the financial asset had not been reclassified, and the gain, loss, income and expense recognised in profit or loss; and

(f)   the effective interest rate and estimated amounts of cash flows the entity expects to recover, as at the date of reclassification of the financial asset.

The IASB regarded such information as useful because the reclassification of a financial asset can have a significant effect on the financial statements. *[IFRS 7.BC23A]*. A survey by CESR of one hundred European financial companies' financial statements clearly demonstrates this to have been true. It found that €550 billion of assets had been reclassified in 2008 and the amount reported in profit or loss and other comprehensive income was an aggregate €28 billion higher as a result. Unfortunately, CESR also found some significant deficiencies in the compliance by these companies with the requirements above, particularly (d) and (f).[4]

4.4.5.B   Other reclassifications under IAS 39

Under IAS 39, financial assets should be reclassified from held-to-maturity investments to available-for-sale assets and *vice versa* in certain circumstances, for example as a result of a change in intention or ability to hold a debt instrument to maturity (see Chapter 45 at 6.3). Where this occurs, the amount reclassified into and out of each category should be disclosed, together with the reason for that reclassification.

This disclosure should also be provided for those unquoted equity instruments and related derivative assets that cease to be measured at cost or at fair value because a reliable measure of fair value becomes available or ceases to be available (see Chapter 48 at 2.1, 2.4 and 2.6). *[IFRS 7.12]*. Strictly, this requirement does not appear to apply to similar derivative liabilities whose measurement basis changes from cost to fair value or *vice versa*, although it would seem sensible to make equivalent disclosures.

4.4.5.C   Reclassifications of financial assets in accordance with IFRS 9

Where IFRS 9 is applied, there are circumstances in which a financial asset will be reclassified in response to a change in an entity's business model (see Chapter 46 at 9). If, in the current or previous reporting periods, any such reclassifications have occurred, the following should be disclosed: *[IFRS 7.12B]*

*   the date of reclassification;
*   a detailed explanation of the change in business model and a qualitative description of its effect on the entity's financial statements; and
*   the amount reclassified into and out of each category.

For assets previously measured at fair value through profit or loss that are reclassified so that they are measured at amortised cost or at fair value through other comprehensive income, the following information should be disclosed in each reporting period following reclassification until derecognition: *[IFRS 7.12C]*

*   the effective interest rate determined on the date of reclassification; and
*   the interest income or expense recognised.

Where financial assets previously measured at fair value through other comprehensive income have been reclassified since the last annual reporting date so that they are measured at amortised cost, the following should be disclosed: *[IFRS 7.12D]*

*   the fair value of the financial assets at the end of the reporting period; and
*   the fair value gain or loss that would have been recognised in profit or loss during the reporting period if the financial assets had not been reclassified.

4.4.6   *Collateral*

Where an entity has pledged financial assets as collateral for liabilities or contingent liabilities it should disclose the carrying amount of those assets and the terms and conditions relating to its pledge. This also applies to transfers of non-cash collateral where the transferee has the right, by contract or custom, to sell or repledge the collateral (see Chapter 50 at 5.5.2). *[IFRS 7.14]*.

When an entity holds collateral (of financial or non-financial assets) and is permitted to sell or repledge the collateral in the absence of default by the owner of the collateral, it should disclose: *[IFRS 7.15]*

*   the fair value of the collateral held;
*   the fair value of any such collateral sold or repledged, and whether the entity has an obligation to return it; and
*   the terms and conditions associated with its use of the collateral.

Although some respondents to the exposure draft that preceded IFRS 7 (ED 7) argued for an exemption from this disclosure in cases where it is impracticable to obtain the fair value of the collateral held, the IASB concluded that it is reasonable to expect an entity to know the fair value of collateral that it holds and can sell even where there is no default. *[IFRS 7.BC25].* Entities have continued to question the usefulness of this requirement and requested that it be removed, but the IASB has shown no inclination do so.[5]

4.4.7   *Allowance account for credit losses*

For entities applying IAS 39, IFRS 7 requires disclosures to be made when impairments of financial assets are recorded in a separate account (for example, an allowance account used to record individual impairments or a similar account used to record a collective impairment of assets) rather than directly reducing the carrying amount of the asset. In such cases an entity should disclose a reconciliation of changes in that account during the period for each class of financial assets. *[IFRS 7.16].* The components of the reconciliation are not specified, thereby allowing entities flexibility in determining the most appropriate format for their needs. *[IFRS 7.BC26].*

Equivalent information is not required for entities that do not use an allowance account. However, the IASB believes that IAS 39's requirement to consider impairment on a group or collective basis (see Chapter 48 at 4) necessitates the use of an allowance or similar account for virtually all entities. The disclosures required by IFRS 7 in respect of accounting policies (see 4.1 above) also include information about the use of direct adjustments to carrying amounts of financial assets. *[IFRS 7.BC27].*

This requirement applies to all entities, not just financial institutions, and the following extracts from the financial statements of Deutsche Telekom and the Nationwide Building Society show how this requirement has been dealt with in practice.

Extract 53.2: Deutsche Telekom AG (2014)

Notes to the consolidated statement of financial position [extract]
2   Trade and other receivables [extract]

The allowances on trade receivables developed as follows:

millions of €	2014	2013
Allowances as of January 1	**1,344**	1,316
Currency translation adjustments	15	(15)
Additions (allowances recognized as expense)	641	642
Use	(410)	(479)
Reversal	(222)	(120)
Allowances as of December 31	**1,368**	1,344

Extract 53.3: Nationwide Building Society (2015)

Notes to the Accounts [extract]

10 Impairment provisions on loans and advances to customers [extract]

The following provisions have been deducted from the appropriate asset values in the balance sheet:

2015 Group	Prime residential	Specialist residential	Consumer banking	Commercial lending	Other lending	Total
	£m	£m	£m	£m	£m	£m
At 5 April 2014	18	84	173	1,001	12	1,288
Charge for the year	13	45	89	52	34	233
Amounts written off during the year	(10)	(41)	(56)	(276)	(6)	(389)
Amounts recovered during the year	1	1	15	15	–	32
Disposals	–	–	–	(428)	(36)	(464)
Unwind of discount	–	(1)	(5)	(42)	–	(48)
At 4 April 2015	22	88	216	322	4	652

2014 Group	Prime residential	Specialist residential	Consumer banking	Commercial lending	Other lending	Total
	£m	£m	£m	£m	£m	£m
At 5 April 2013	32	133	87	958	14	1,224
Charge for the year	–	–	60	309	11	380
Amounts written off during the year	(15)	(52)	(3)	(215)	(9)	(294)
Amounts recovered during the year	1	4	33	10	–	48
Disposals	–	–	–	–	(4)	(4)
Unwind of discount	–	(1)	(4)	(61)	–	(66)
At 4 April 2014	18	84	173	1,001	12	1,288

The Group impairment provision of £652 million at 4 April 2015 (2014: £1,288 million) comprises individual provisions of £341 million (2014: £959 million) and collective provisions of £311 million (2014: £329 million).

The charge for the year for prime and specialist residential loans primarily results from refinements to credit risk provision assumptions, which reflect a segmental review of actual loss experience and take account of the impacts of the prolonged low interest rate environment.

The increase in impairment provisions on consumer banking is driven by a change in the accounting treatment for charged off accounts in 2014. Previously these accounts had been written off in full with subsequent recoveries taken to profit when received. Balances on charged off accounts are now held on the balance sheet, together with relevant provisions, where at least partial recovery is still expected.

The £464 million for disposals relates to divestment activity undertaken during the year in relation to non-core commercial real estate lending and out of policy treasury assets.

Chapter 53

When IFRS 9 is applied, the requirement above is withdrawn and replaced by a requirement to disclose in the notes the loss allowance in respect of debt instruments measured at fair value through other comprehensive income. *[IFRS 7.16A]*. In addition, more extensive disclosures about credit risk and loss allowances on financial assets measured at amortised cost are required as set out at 5.2.3 below.

4.4.8   *Compound financial instruments with multiple embedded derivatives*

Where an instrument has been issued that contains both a liability and an equity component and the instrument has multiple embedded derivatives whose values are interdependent, such as a callable convertible debt instrument (see Chapter 44 at 6.4.2), the existence of these features should be disclosed. *[IFRS 7.17].* Accordingly, the impact on the amounts reported as liabilities and equity will be highlighted, something the IASB sees as important given the acknowledged arbitrary nature of the allocation under IAS 32 of the joint value attributable to this interdependence. *[IFRS 7.BC31].*

4.4.9   *Defaults and breaches of loans payable*

Loans payable are defined as 'financial liabilities other than short-term trade payables on normal credit terms.' *[IFRS 7 Appendix].* It is considered that disclosures about defaults and breaches of loans payable and other loan agreements provide relevant information about the entity's creditworthiness and its prospects of obtaining future loans. *[IFRS 7.BC32].*

Accordingly, for any loans payable recognised at the reporting date, an entity is required to disclose: *[IFRS 7.18]*

- details of any defaults during the period of principal, interest, sinking fund, or redemption terms;
- the carrying amount of the loans payable in default at the reporting date; and
- whether the default was remedied, or the terms of the loans payable were renegotiated, before the financial statements were authorised for issue.

If, during the period, there were breaches of loan agreement terms other than those described above, the same information should be disclosed if those breaches permitted the lender to demand accelerated repayment (unless the breaches were remedied, or the terms of the loan were renegotiated, on or before the reporting date). *[IFRS 7.19].*

It is noted that any defaults or breaches may affect the classification of the liability as current or non-current in accordance with IAS 1 (see Chapter 3 at 3.1.4). *[IFRS 7.IG12].*

4.4.10   *Interests in other entities accounted for in accordance with IAS 39 or IFRS 9*

IAS 28 – *Investments in Associates and Joint Ventures* – allows an interest in an associate or a joint venture held by a venture capital or similar organisation to be measured at fair value through profit or loss in accordance with IAS 39 or IFRS 9 (see Chapter 11 at 5.3). In these circumstances, IFRS 12 – *Disclosure of Interests in Other Entities* – contains additional disclosure requirements, over and above those in IFRS 7, which are dealt with in Chapter 13 at 2.2.3.D and 5.

4.5   Fair values

4.5.1   *General disclosure requirements*

The IASB sees the disclosure of information about the fair value of financial assets and liabilities as being an important requirement. It is explained in the following terms:

'Many entities use fair value information internally in determining their overall financial position and in making decisions about individual financial instruments. It is also relevant to many decisions made by users of financial statements because, in many circumstances, it reflects the judgement of the financial markets about the present value of expected future cash flows relating to an instrument. Fair value information permits comparisons of financial instruments having substantially the same economic characteristics, regardless of why they are held and when and by whom they were issued or acquired. Fair values provide a neutral basis for assessing management's stewardship by indicating the effects of its decisions to buy, sell or hold financial assets and to incur, maintain or discharge financial liabilities.'

Therefore, when financial assets or liabilities are not measured on a fair value basis, information on fair values should be given by way of supplementary disclosures to assist users in comparing entities on a consistent basis. *[IFRS 7.BC36]*.

More specifically, except as set out below, the fair value of each class of financial assets and liabilities should be disclosed in a way that permits comparison with the corresponding carrying amounts. *[IFRS 7.25]*. In providing this disclosure, instruments should be offset only to the extent that their related carrying amounts are also offset in the statement of financial position. *[IFRS 7.26]*. IFRS 13 contains guidance on determining fair values and includes more extensive disclosure requirements about the fair values disclosed. These are discussed in Chapter 14 at 20.

Pragmatically, disclosure of fair values is not required for instruments whose carrying amount reasonably approximates their fair value, for example short-term trade receivables and payables. *[IFRS 7.29(a)]*.

Fair values need not be given for investments in unquoted equity instruments, or derivatives linked to such instruments, that are measured at cost because their fair value cannot be measured reliably (see Chapter 48 at 2.6). When IFRS 9 is applied, this concession ceases to apply. *[IFRS 7.29(b)]*.

As set out in Chapter 42 at 3.3.2 some instruments (normally life insurance policies) contain a discretionary participation feature. If the fair value of that feature cannot be reliably measured, disclosures of fair value are not required. *[IFRS 7.29(c)]*.

However, additional disclosures should be given about instruments for which the fair value cannot be reliably measured. This is to assist users of the financial statements in making their own judgements about the extent of possible differences between the carrying amount of such contracts and their fair value. In particular, the following should be disclosed: *[IFRS 7.30]*

- the fact that fair value has not been disclosed because it cannot be reliably measured;

- a description of the instruments, their carrying amount, and an explanation of why fair value cannot be measured reliably;

- information about the market for the instruments;

- information about whether and how the entity intends to dispose of the instruments; and

- for instruments whose fair value previously could not be reliably measured that are derecognised:

  - that fact;

  - their carrying amount at the time of derecognition; and

  - the amount of gain or loss recognised.

For all other financial instruments, the IASB believes it is reasonable to expect that fair value can be determined with sufficient reliability within constraints of timeliness and cost. It therefore concluded that there should be no exception from the requirement to disclose fair value information for these instruments. *[IFRS 7.BC37]*.

4.5.2   Day 1 profits

In certain situations there will be a difference between the transaction price for a financial asset or financial liability and the fair value that would be determined at that date in accordance with IFRS 13 (commonly known as a day 1 profit). *[IFRS 7.28]*. As set out in Chapter 47 at 3.2, an entity should not recognise a day 1 profit on initial recognition of the financial instrument if the fair value is neither evidenced by a quoted price in an active market for an identical asset or liability (known as a Level 1 input) nor based on a valuation technique that uses only data from observable markets. Instead, the difference will be recognised in profit or loss in subsequent periods in accordance with IAS 39 or IFRS 9 and the entity's accounting policy. *[IFRS 7.IG14]*.

Where such a difference exists, IFRS 7 requires disclosure, by class of financial instrument of: *[IFRS 7.28]*

- the accounting policy for recognising that difference in profit or loss to reflect a change in factors (including time) that market participants would take into account when setting a price for the financial instrument;

- the aggregate difference yet to be recognised in profit or loss at the beginning and end of the period and a reconciliation of changes in the amount of this difference; and

- why it was concluded that the transaction price was not the best evidence of fair value, including a description of the evidence that supports the fair value.

In other words, disclosure is required of the profits an entity might think it has made but which it is prohibited from recognising, at least for the time being. This disclosure is illustrated in the following example based on the implementation guidance. It is rather curious in that it illustrates a day 1 *loss*.

Example 53.5:   Disclosure of deferred day 1 profits

On 1 January 2015 Company R purchases financial assets that are not traded in an active market for €15 million which represents their fair value at initial recognition. After initial recognition, R applies a valuation technique to measure the fair value of the financial assets. This valuation technique uses inputs other than data from observable markets. At initial recognition, the same valuation technique would have resulted in an amount of €14 million, which differs from fair value by €1 million. R has only one class of such financial assets with existing differences of €5 million at 1 January 2015. The disclosure in R's 2016 financial statements would include the following: *[IFRS 7.IG14]*

Accounting policies

R uses the following valuation technique to measure the fair value of financial instruments that are not traded in an active market: [insert description of technique, not included in this example] Differences may arise between the fair value at initial recognition (which, in accordance with IFRS 13 and IAS 39 or IFRS 9, is normally the transaction price) and the amount determined at initial recognition using the valuation technique. Any such differences are [description of R's accounting policy].

In the notes to the financial statements

As discussed in note X, [insert name of valuation technique] is used to measure the fair value of the following financial instruments that are not traded in an active market. However, in accordance with IFRS 13 and IAS 39 or IFRS 9, the fair value of an instrument at inception is normally the transaction price. If the transaction price differs from the amount determined at inception using the valuation technique, that difference is [description of R's accounting policy].

The differences yet to be recognised in profit or loss are as follows:

	2016 €m	2015 €m
Balance at beginning of year	5.3	5.0
New transactions	–	1.0
Recognised in profit or loss during the year	(0.7)	(0.8)
Other increases	(0.1)	(0.1)
Balance at end of year	4.5	5.3

UBS discloses the following information about recognition of day 1 profits.

Extract 53.4: UBS AG (2014)

Notes to the UBS AG consolidated financial statements [extract]
24   Fair value measurement [extract]
d)   Valuation adjustments [extract]
Day-1 reserves [extract]

For new transactions where the valuation technique used to measure fair value requires significant inputs that are not based on observable market data, the financial instrument is initially recognized at the transaction price. The transaction price may differ from the fair value obtained using a valuation technique, and any such difference is deferred and not recognized in the income statement. These day-1 profit or loss reserves are reflected, where appropriate, as valuation adjustments.

The table below provides the changes in deferred day-1 profit or loss reserves during the respective period. Amounts deferred are released and gains or losses are recorded in *Net trading income* when pricing of equivalent products or the underlying parameters become observable or when the transaction is closed out.

Deferred day-1 profit or loss	For the year ended		
CHF *million*	31.12.14	31.12.13	31.12.12
Balance at the beginning of the year	486	474	433
Profit/(loss) deferred on new transactions	344	694	424
(Profit)/loss recognized in the income statement	(384)	(653)	(367)
Foreign currency translation	35	(29)	(16)
Balance at the end of the year	480	486	474

4.6   Business combinations

IFRS 3 – *Business Combinations* – requires an acquirer to disclose additional information about financial instruments arising from business combinations that occur during the reporting period. These requirements are discussed below.

4.6.1   Acquired receivables

Some constituents were concerned that prohibiting the use of an allowance account when accounting for acquired receivables at fair value (see Chapter 47 at 3.2.4) could make it impossible to determine the contractual cash flows due on those assets and the amount of those cash flows not expected to be collected. They asked for additional disclosure to help in assessing considerations of credit quality used in estimating those fair values, including expectations about receivables that will be uncollectible. *[IFRS 3.BC258]*. Consequently, the IASB decided to require the following disclosures to be made about such assets acquired in a business combination:

- fair value of the receivables;
- gross contractual amounts receivable; and
- the best estimate at the acquisition date of the contractual cash flows not expected to be collected.

This information should be provided by major class of receivable, such as loans, direct finance leases and any other class of receivables. *[IFRS 3.B64(h)]*.

Although these requirements will produce some of the information users need to evaluate the credit quality of receivables acquired, the IASB acknowledged that it may not provide all such information. However, this is seen as an interim measure and the IASB will monitor a related FASB project with a view to improving the disclosure requirements in the future *[IFRS 3.BC260]*, although it is not clear when such a project might be completed.

4.6.2   *Contingent consideration and indemnification assets*

The following information about contingent consideration arrangements and indemnification assets (see Chapter 42 at 3.7.1 and 3.12 respectively) should be given: *[IFRS 3.B64(g)]*

- the amount recognised as at the acquisition date;
- a description of the arrangement and the basis for determining the amount of the payment; and
- an estimate of the range of outcomes (undiscounted) or, if a range cannot be estimated, that fact and the reasons why a range cannot be estimated.

   If the maximum amount of the payment is unlimited, that fact should be disclosed.

These are requirements of IFRS 3 and apply irrespective of whether such items meet the definition of a financial instrument (which they normally will).

5   NATURE AND EXTENT OF RISKS ARISING FROM FINANCIAL INSTRUMENTS

IFRS 7 establishes a second key principle, namely:

   'An entity shall disclose information that enables users of its financial statements to evaluate the nature and extent of risks arising from financial instruments to which the entity is exposed at the reporting date.' *[IFRS 7.31]*.

Again this is supported by related disclosure requirements which focus on qualitative and quantitative aspects of the risks arising from financial instruments and how those risks have been managed. *[IFRS 7.32]*.

Providing qualitative disclosures in the context of quantitative disclosures enables users to link related disclosures and hence form an overall picture of the nature and extent of risks arising from financial instruments. The interaction between qualitative and quantitative disclosures contributes to disclosure of information in a way that better enables users to evaluate an entity's exposure to risks. *[IFRS 7.32A]*.

These risks typically include, but are not limited to, credit risk, liquidity risk and market risk, which are defined as follows: *[IFRS 7 Appendix]*

(a) *Credit risk*, the risk that one party to a financial instrument will cause a financial loss for the other party by failing to discharge an obligation;

(b) *Liquidity risk*, the risk that an entity will encounter difficulty in meeting obligations associated with financial liabilities that are settled by delivering cash or another financial asset.

(c) *Market risk*, the risk that the fair value or future cash flows of a financial instrument will fluctuate because of changes in market prices. It comprises three separate types of risk:

(i) *Currency risk*, the risk that the fair value or future cash flows of a financial instrument will fluctuate because of changes in foreign exchange rates.

Currency risk (or foreign exchange risk) arises on financial instruments that are denominated in a foreign currency, i.e. in a currency other than the functional currency in which they are measured. For the purpose of IFRS 7, currency risk does not arise from financial instruments that are non-monetary items or from financial instruments denominated in an entity's functional currency. *[IFRS 7.B23]*. Therefore if a parent with the euro as its functional and presentation currency owns a subsidiary with the pound sterling as its functional currency, monetary items held by the subsidiary that are denominated in sterling do not give rise to any currency risk in the consolidated financial statements of the parent;

(ii) *Interest rate risk*, the risk that the fair value or future cash flows of a financial instrument will fluctuate because of changes in market interest rates.

It is explained that interest rate risk arises on interest-bearing financial instruments recognised in the statement of financial position (e.g. debt instruments acquired or issued) and on some financial instruments not recognised in the statement of financial position (e.g. some loan commitments); *[IFRS 7.B22]*

(iii) *Other price risk*, the risk that the fair value or future cash flows of a financial instrument will fluctuate because of changes in market prices (other than those arising from interest rate risk or currency risk), whether those changes are caused by factors specific to the individual financial instrument or its issuer, or factors affecting all similar financial instruments traded in the market.

Other price risk arises on financial instruments because of changes in, for example, commodity prices, equity prices, prepayment risk (i.e. the risk that one party to a financial asset will incur a financial loss because the other party repays earlier or later than expected), and residual value risk (e.g. a lessor of motor cars that writes residual value guarantees is exposed to residual value risk). *[IFRS 7.B25, IG32]*.

Two examples of financial instruments that give rise to equity price risk are a holding of equities in another entity, and an investment in a trust, which in turn holds investments in equity instruments. Other examples include forward contracts and options to buy or sell specified quantities of an equity instrument and swaps that are indexed to equity prices. The fair values of such financial instruments are affected by changes in the market price of the underlying equity instruments. *[IFRS 7.B26]*.

The specified disclosures can be provided either in the financial statements or may be incorporated by cross-reference from the financial statements to some other statement that is available to users of the financial statements on the same terms and at the same time, such as a management commentary or risk report (preparation of which might be required by a regulatory authority). Without the information incorporated by cross-reference, the financial statements are incomplete. *[IFRS 7.B6, BC46]*.

Consistent with the approach outlined at 3 above, it is emphasised that the extent of these disclosures will depend on the extent of an entity's exposure to risks arising from financial instruments. *[IFRS 7.BC41]*. Therefore, entities with many financial instruments and related risks should provide more disclosure and those with few financial instruments and related risks may provide less extensive disclosure. *[IFRS 7.BC40(b)]*.

The IASB recognised that entities view and manage risk in different ways and that some entities undertake limited management of risks. Therefore, disclosures based on how risk is managed are unlikely to be comparable between entities and, for some entities, would convey little or no information about the risks assumed. Accordingly, whilst at a high level the disclosures are approached from the perspective of information provided to management (see 5.2 below), certain minimum disclosures about risk exposures are specified to provide a common and relatively easy to implement benchmark across different entities. Obviously, those entities with more developed risk management systems would provide more detailed information. *[IFRS 7.BC42]*.

It is explained in the basis for conclusions that the implementation guidance, which illustrates how an entity might apply IFRS 7, is consistent with the disclosure requirements for banks developed by the Basel Committee (known as Pillar 3), so that banks can prepare, and users receive, a single co-ordinated set of disclosures about financial risk. *[IFRS 7.BC41]*. Since the standard was originally written before the financial crisis there have been a number of initiatives to improve the reporting of risk by financial institutions, both from a regulatory and a financial reporting perspective, for example as set out at 9 below and in Chapter 41.

In developing the standard, the IASB considered various arguments that risk disclosures should not be included within the financial statements (even by cross-reference). For example, concerns were expressed that the information would be difficult and costly to audit and that it did not meet the criteria of comparability, faithful representation and completeness because it is subjective, forward-looking and based on management's judgement. It was also suggested that the subjectivity involved in the sensitivity analyses could undermine the credibility of the fair values recognised in the financial statements. However, the IASB was not persuaded and these arguments were rejected. *[IFRS 7.BC43, BC44, BC45, BC46].*

5.1   Qualitative disclosures

For each type of risk arising from financial instruments, an entity is required to disclose: *[IFRS 7.33(a), (b)]*

(a)   the exposures to risk and how they arise; and

(b)   its objectives, policies and processes for managing the risk and the methods used to measure the risk.

Any changes in either (a) or (b) above compared to the previous period, together with the reasons for the change, should be disclosed. These changes may result from changes in exposure to risk or the way those exposures are managed. *[IFRS 7.33(c), IG17].*

The type of information that might be disclosed to meet these requirements includes, but is not limited to, a narrative description of: *[IFRS 7.IG15]*

- the entity's exposures to risk and how they arose, which might include details of exposures, both gross and net of risk transfer and other risk-mitigating transactions;
- the entity's policies and processes for accepting, measuring, monitoring and controlling risk, which might include:
  - the structure and organisation of the entity's risk management function(s), including a discussion of independence and accountability;
  - the scope and nature of the entity's risk reporting or measurement systems;
  - the entity's policies for hedging or mitigating risk, including its policies and procedures for taking collateral; and
  - the entity's processes for monitoring the continuing effectiveness of such hedges or mitigating devices; and
- the entity's policies and procedures for avoiding excessive concentrations of risk.

It is noted that information about the nature and extent of risks arising from financial instruments is more useful if it highlights any relationship between financial instruments that can affect the amount, timing or uncertainty of an entity's future cash flows. The extent to which a risk exposure is altered by such relationships might be apparent from other required disclosures, but in some cases further disclosures might be useful. *[IFRS 7.IG16].*

The following extract from the financial statements of Origin Energy shows the type of disclosure that can be seen in practice.

Extract 53.5: Origin Energy Limited (2014)

Notes to the Financial Statements [extract]

24.   Financial Instruments [extract]

(A)   Financial risk management

Financial risk factors

The consolidated entity's activities expose it to a variety of financial risks: market risk (including foreign exchange risk and price risk), credit risk, liquidity risk and interest rate risk.. The consolidated entity's overall risk management program focuses on the unpredictability of financial and commodity markets and seeks to manage potential adverse effects of these on the consolidated entity's financial performance. The consolidated entity uses a range of derivative financial instruments to hedge these exposures.

Risk management is carried out under policies approved by the Board of Directors. Financial risks are identified, evaluated and hedged in close co-operation with the consolidated entity's operating units. The consolidated entity has written policies covering specific areas, such as foreign exchange risk, interest rate risk, electricity price risk, oil price risk, credit risk, use of derivative financial instruments and non-derivative financial instruments, and the investment of excess liquidity.

(i)   Market risk

Foreign exchange risk

The consolidated entity operates internationally and is exposed to foreign exchange risk arising from various currency exposures, primarily with respect to the New Zealand dollar, US dollar and Euro. Foreign exchange risk arises from future commercial transactions (including interest payments and principal debt repayments on long-term borrowings, the sale of oil, the sale and purchase of LPG and the purchase of capital equipment), the recognition of assets and liabilities (including foreign receivables and borrowings) and net investments in foreign operations.

To manage the foreign exchange risk arising from future commercial transactions, the consolidated entity uses forward foreign exchange contracts. To manage the foreign exchange risk arising from the future principal and interest payments required on foreign currency denominated long-term borrowings, the consolidated entity uses cross currency interest rate swaps (both fixed to fixed and fixed to floating) which convert the foreign currency denominated future principal and interest payments into the functional currency for the relevant entity for the full term of the underlying borrowings. In certain circumstances borrowings are left in the foreign currencies, or hedged from one foreign currency to another to match payments of interest and principal against expected future business cash flows in that foreign currency.

External derivative contracts are designated at the consolidated entity level as hedges of foreign exchange risk on specific assets, liabilities or future transactions on a gross basis.

The consolidated entity has certain investments in foreign operations whose net assets are exposed to foreign currency translation risk. Currency exposure arising from the net assets of the consolidated entity's foreign operations is managed primarily through borrowings denominated in the relevant foreign currencies.

Price risk

The consolidated entity is exposed to price risk from the purchase and sale of electricity, oil, gas, environmental scheme certificates and related commodities. To manage its price risks, the consolidated entity utilises a range of financial and derivative instruments including fixed priced swaps, options, futures and fixed price forward purchase contracts.

The consolidated entity's risk management policy for commodity price risk is to hedge forecast future transactions. The consolidated entity has a risk management policy framework that manages the exposure arising from its commodity-based activities. The policy permits the active hedging of price and volume exposure arising from the retailing, generation and portfolio management activities, within prescribed risk capacity limits. The policy prescribes the maximum risk exposures permissible over prescribed periods for each commodity within the portfolio, under defined worse case scenarios. The full portfolio is subject to ongoing testing against these limits at prescribed intervals, and reported monthly.

(ii) Credit risk

The consolidated entity manages its exposure to credit risk via credit risk management policies which allocate credit limits based on the overall financial and competitive strength of the counterparty. Publicly available credit information from recognised providers is utilised for this purpose where available. Credit policies cover exposures generated from the sale of products and the use of derivative instruments. Derivative counterparties are limited to high-credit-quality financial institutions and other organisations in the relevant industry. The consolidated entity has Board approved policies that limit the amount of credit exposure to each financial institution and derivate counterparty. The consolidated entity also utilises International Swaps and Derivative Association (ISDA) agreements with all derivative counterparties in order to limit exposure to credit risk through the netting of amounts receivable from and amounts payable to individual counterparties.

The carrying amounts of financial assets recognised in the statement of financial position, and disclosed in more detail in notes 6, 7 and 19 best represents the consolidated entity's maximum exposure to credit risk at the reporting date. In respect of those financial assets and the credit risk embodied within them, the consolidated entity holds no significant collateral as security and there are no other significant credit enhancements in respect of these assets. The credit quality of all financial assets that are neither past due nor impaired is constantly monitored in order to identify any potential adverse changes in the credit quality. There are no significant financial assets that have had renegotiated terms that would otherwise, without that renegotiation, have been past due or impaired.

The consolidated entity has provided certain funding to Australia Pacific LNG by way of subscription up to an amount of $3.75 billion for mandatorily redeemable cumulative preference shares (MRCPS) issued by Australia Pacific LNG. Each holder of the ordinary shares of Australia Pacific LNG also holds MRCPS in an equivalent proportion to its share in the ordinary equity of the joint venture entity. The MRCPS attract a market-based fixed dividend, reflective of the assessed credit risk of Australia Pacific LNG, have a mandatory redemption date of 31 December 2022 and accordingly are recorded in "other non-current financial assets". The carrying value of the loan at 30 June 2014, as disclosed in note 7, reflects the consolidated entity's view that the shares will be fully redeemed for their full issue price prior to 31 December 2022 from the cash flows generated from Australia Pacific LNG's export operations. There are no conditions existing at the reporting date which indicate that Australia Pacific LNG will be unable to repay the full carrying value. Accordingly, the loan is valued at amortised cost, and reflects the cash provided to Australia Pacific LNG.

(iii) Liquidity risk

Prudent liquidity risk management implies maintaining sufficient cash and marketable securities, the availability of funding through an adequate amount of committed credit facilities and the ability to close out market positions. Due to the dynamic nature of the underlying businesses, the consolidated entity aims to maintain flexibility in funding by keeping committed credit lines available. Certain of the consolidated entity's interest-bearing liability obligations are subject to change in control provisions under the agreements with third-party lenders. As at 30 June 2014 those provisions were not triggered.

(iv) Interest rate risk (cash flow and fair value)

The consolidated entity's income and operating cash flows are substantially independent of changes in market interest rates. The consolidated entity's interest rate risk arises from long-term borrowings. Borrowings issued at variable rates expose the consolidated entity to cash flow interest rate risk. Borrowings issued at fixed rates expose the consolidated entity to fair value interest rate risk. The consolidated entity's risk management policy is to manage interest rate exposures using Profit at Risk and Value at Risk methodologies using 95 per cent statistical confidence levels. Exposure limits are set to ensure that the consolidated entity is not exposed to excess risk from interest rate volatility. The consolidated entity manages its cash flow interest rate risk by using floating-to-fixed interest rate swaps. Such interest rate swaps have the economic effect of converting borrowings from floating rates to fixed rates.

5.2   Quantitative disclosures

5.2.1   *General matters*

For each type of risk arising from financial instruments (see 5 above), entities are required to disclose summary quantitative data about their exposure to that risk at the reporting date. It should be based on the information provided internally to key management personnel of the entity as defined in IAS 24 – *Related Party Disclosures* (see Chapter 36 at 2.2.1.D), for example the board of directors or chief executive officer. *[IFRS 7.34(a)].*

This 'management view' approach was adopted by the IASB because it was considered to: *[IFRS 7.BC47]*

- provide a useful insight into how the entity views and manages risk;

- result in information that has more predictive value than information based on assumptions and methods that management does not use, for instance, in considering the entity's ability to react to adverse situations;

- be more effective in adapting to changes in risk measurement and management techniques and developments in the external environment;

- have practical advantages for preparers of financial statements, because it allows them to use the data they use in managing risk; and

- be consistent with the approach used in segment reporting (see Chapter 33).

When several methods are used to manage a risk exposure, the information disclosed should use the method(s) that provide the most relevant and reliable information. It is noted, in this context, that IAS 8 – *Accounting Policies, Changes in Accounting Estimates and Errors* – discusses relevance and reliability (see Chapter 3 at 4.3). *[IFRS 7.B7].*

Where the quantitative data disclosed as at the reporting date are unrepresentative of an entity's exposure to risk during the period, further information that is representative should be provided. *[IFRS 7.35].* For example, if an entity typically has a large exposure to a particular currency, but at year-end unwinds the position, the entity might disclose a graph that shows the exposure at various times during the period, or it might disclose the highest, lowest and average exposures. *[IFRS 7.IG20].*

In developing IFRS 7, the IASB considered whether quantitative information about average risk exposures should be given in all cases. However, this is more informative only if the risk exposure at the reporting date is not representative of the exposure during the period and would be onerous to prepare and, consequently, they decided that disclosure by exception was appropriate. *[IFRS 7.BC48].*

5.2.2   *Credit risk (entities applying IAS 39)*

Many of the credit risk disclosures are to be given by class and it is noted that financial instruments in the same class should reflect shared economic characteristics with respect to the risk being disclosed, credit risk in this case (see 3.3 above). Therefore, a lender might determine that residential mortgages, unsecured consumer loans, and commercial loans each have different economic characteristics. *[IFRS 7.IG21].*

Chapter 53

5.2.2.A   Maximum exposure to credit risk

For each class of financial instrument, entities should disclose the amount that best represents its maximum exposure to credit risk at the reporting date without taking account of any collateral held or other credit enhancements (e.g. netting agreements that do not qualify for offset in accordance with IAS 32). This disclosure is not required for financial instruments whose carrying amount best represents this amount. *[IFRS 7.36(a)].*

For a financial asset, the maximum exposure to credit risk is typically the gross carrying amount, net of any amounts offset in accordance with IAS 32 (see 7.4.1 below) and any impairment losses recognised in accordance with IAS 39 (see Chapter 48 at 4). *[IFRS 7.B9].* This disclosure is required even if there are no identified problems in, say, a loan portfolio. *[IFRS 7.BC49].*

Activities that give rise to credit risk and the associated maximum exposure to credit risk include, but are not limited to: *[IFRS 7.B10]*

- granting loans to customers and placing deposits with other entities. In these cases, the maximum exposure to credit risk is the carrying amount of the related financial assets;

- entering into derivative contracts, e.g. foreign exchange contracts, interest rate swaps and purchased credit derivatives. When a resulting asset is measured at fair value, the maximum exposure to credit risk at the reporting date will equal the carrying amount;

   It is recognised that this disclosure does not always reflect potential *future* exposure to credit risk (because fair value could increase), but the disclosure requirement is for the exposure *at the reporting date;* *[IFRS 7.BC50]*

- granting financial guarantees. In this case, the maximum exposure to credit risk is the maximum amount the entity could have to pay if the guarantee is called on, which may be significantly greater than the amount recognised as a liability; and

- making a loan commitment that is irrevocable over the life of the facility or is revocable only in response to a material adverse change. If the issuer cannot settle the loan commitment net in cash or another financial instrument, the maximum credit exposure is the full amount of the commitment. This is because it is uncertain whether the amount of any undrawn portion may be drawn upon in the future. This may be significantly greater than the amount recognised as a liability.

The following extracts from the financial statements of Deutsche Telekom and HSBC illustrate how these disclosures may be provided in practice – clearly credit risk is much more significant to an entity such as HSBC.

Extract 53.6: Deutsche Telekom AG (2014)

Notes to the consolidated financial statements [extract]

37.   Financial instruments and Risk management. [extract]

Credit risks. Deutsche Telekom is exposed to a credit risk from its operating activities and certain financing activities. As a rule, transactions with regard to financing activities are only concluded with counterparties that have at least a credit rating of BBB+/Baa1, in connection with an operational credit management system. At the level of operations, the outstanding debts are continuously monitored in each area, i.e. locally. Credit risks are taken into account through individual and collective allowances.

The solvency of the business with corporate customers, especially international carriers, is monitored separately. In terms of the overall risk exposure from the credit risk, however, the receivables from these counterparties are not so extensive as to justify extraordinary concentrations of risk.

Offsetting is applied in particular to receivables and liabilities and Deutsche Telekom AG and Telekom Deutschland GmbH for the routing of international calls via the fixed network and for roaming fees in the mobile network.

In line with the contractual provisions, in the event of insolvency all derivatives with a positive or negative fair value that exist with the respective counterparty are offset against each other, leaving a net receivable or liability. The net amounts are normally recalculated every bank working day and offset against each other. When the netting of the positive and negative fair values of all derivatives was positive from Deutsche Telekom's perspective, the counterparty provided Deutsche Telekom with cash pursuant to the collateral contracts mentioned in Note 1 "Cash and cash equivalents.". The credit risk was thus further reduced.

When the netting of the positive and negative fair values of all derivatives was negative from Deutsche Telekom's perspective, Deutsche Telekom provided cash collateral to counterparties pursuant to collateral agreements. The net amounts are normally recalculated every bank working day and offset against each other. The cash collateral paid (please also refer to Note 8 "Other financial assets", PAGE 214) is offset by corresponding negative net derivative positions of EUR 467 million at the reporting date, which is why it was not exposed to any credit risks in this amount as of the reporting date. The collateral paid is reported under originated loans and receivables within other financial assets. On account of its close connection to the corresponding derivatives, the collateral paid constitutes a separate class of financial assets. Likewise, the collateral received, which is reported as other interest-bearing liabilities under financial liabilities, constitutes a separate class of financial liabilities on account of its close connection to the corresponding derivatives.

In accordance with the terms of bonds issued by a Deutsche Telekom subsidiary, this subsidiary has the right to terminate the bonds prematurely under specific conditions. The rights of termination constitute embedded derivatives and are accounted for separately as derivative financial assets. The conversion rights maintained in Mandatory Convertible Preferred Stock issued by a subsidiary of Deutsche Telekom constitute an embedded derivative and are recognized separately as a derivative. Since these rights of termination and conversion rights are not exposed to a credit risk, they constitute a separate class of financial instruments.

No other significant agreements reducing the maximum exposure to the credit risks of financial assets existed. The maximum exposure to credit risk of the other financial assets thus corresponds to their carrying amounts.

In addition, Deutsche Telekom is exposed to a credit risk through the granting of financial guarantees. Guarantees amounting to a nominal total of EUR 50 million had been pledged as of the reporting date (December 31, 2013: EUR 70 million), which also represent the maximum exposure to credit risk.

There were no indications as of the reporting date that Deutsche Telekom will incur a loss from a financial guarantee.

Chapter 53

Extract 53.7: HSBC Holdings plc (2014)

Report of the Directors: Risk [extract]

Maximum exposure to credit risk *(Audited)* [extract]

The table presents our maximum exposure to credit risk from balance sheet and off-balance sheet financial instruments before taking account of any collateral held or other credit enhancements (unless such enhancements meet accounting offsetting requirements). For financial assets recognised on the balance sheet, the maximum exposure to credit risk equals their carrying amount; for financial guarantees and similar contracts granted, it is the maximum amount that we would have to pay if the guarantees were called upon. For loan commitments and other credit-related commitments, it is generally the full amount of the committed facilities.

The offset in the table relates to amounts where there is a legally enforceable right of offset in the event of counterparty default and where, as a result, there is a net exposure for credit risk purposes. However, as there is no intention to settle these balances on a net basis under normal circumstances, they do not qualify for net presentation for accounting purposes.

In the case of derivatives the offset column also includes collateral received in cash and other financial assets.

While not disclosed as an offset in the 'Maximum exposure to credit risk' table, other arrangements are in place which reduce our maximum exposure to credit risk. These include a charge over collateral over borrowers' specific assets such as residential properties. Other credit risk mitigants include short positions in securities and financial assets held as part of linked insurance/investment contracts where the risk is predominantly borne by the policyholder. In addition, we hold collateral in the form of financial instruments that are not recognised on the balance sheet.

Maximum exposure to credit risk (Audited)		2014	
	Maximum exposure	**Offset**	**Net**
	US$m	US$m	US$m
Cash and balances at central banks	129,957	–	129,957
Items in the course of collection from other banks	4,927	–	4,927
Hong Kong Government certificates of indebtedness	27,674	–	27,674
Trading assets	228,944	–	228,944
-Treasury and other eligible bills	16,170	–	16,170
-debt securities	141,532	–	141,532
-loan and advances to banks	27,581	–	27,581
-loans and advances to customers	43,661	–	43,661
Financial assets designated at fair value	9,031	–	9,031
-Treasury and other eligible bills	56	–	56
-debt securities	8,891	–	8,891
-loan and advances to banks	84	–	84
-loans and advances to customers	–	–	–
Derivatives	345,008	(313,300)	31,708

Loans and advances to customers held at amortised cost	974,660	(67,094)	907,556
-personal	388,954	(4,412)	384,542
-corporate and commercial	535,184	(59,197)	475,987
-financial (non-bank financial institutions)	50,522	(3,485)	47,037
Loans and advances to banks held at amortised cost	112,149	(258)	111,891
Reverse repurchase agreements – non trading	161,713	(5,750)	155,963
Financial investments	404,773	–	404,773
-Treasury and other similar bills	81,517	–	81,517
-debt securities	323,256	–	323,256
Other assets	35,264	–	35,264
-assets held for sale	1,375	–	1,375
-endorsements and acceptances	10,775	–	10,775
-other	23,114	–	23,114
Financial guarantees and similar contracts	47,078	–	47,078
Loan and other credit-related commitments	651,380	–	651,380
At 31 December	3,132,558	(386,402)	2,746,156

Entities should provide by class of financial instrument a description of collateral held as security and of other credit enhancements, and their financial effect (e.g. a quantification of the extent to which collateral and other credit enhancements mitigate credit risk) in respect of the amount that best represents the maximum exposure to credit risk (whether disclosed separately or represented by the carrying amount of a financial instrument). *[IFRS 7.36(b)].*

The requirement may be met by disclosing: *[IFRS 7.IG22]*

- the policies and processes for valuing and managing collateral and other credit enhancements obtained;

- a description of the main types of collateral and other credit enhancements (examples of the latter being guarantees and credit derivatives, as well as netting agreements that do not qualify for offset in accordance with IAS 32);

- the main types of counterparties to collateral and other credit enhancements and their creditworthiness; and

- information about risk concentrations within the collateral or other credit enhancements.

It is not entirely clear how detailed this additional information is intended to be. For example, whilst the standard suggests it should, or at least could, involve disclosure of quantitative information, the implementation guidance implies more discursive disclosures might suffice in some cases. In practice, entities will need to make a judgment based on their own specific circumstances and in the light of emerging practice.

Chapter 53

5.2.2.B   Credit quality of financial assets

Entities should also provide information about the credit quality of financial assets that are neither past due (see 5.2.2.C below) nor impaired. *[IFRS 7.36(c)]*. The IASB believes this gives a greater insight into the credit risk of assets and helps users assess whether such assets are more or less likely to become impaired in the future. Because this information will vary between entities, no particular method for giving this information is specified. Rather, each entity should devise a method that is appropriate to its circumstances. *[IFRS 7.BC54]*. This might include: *[IFRS 7.IG23]*

- an analysis of credit exposures using an external or internal credit grading system;

    When external ratings are considered when managing and monitoring credit quality, information might be disclosed about: *[IFRS 7.IG24]*

    - the amounts of credit exposures for each external credit grade;
    - the rating agencies used;
    - the amount of an entity's rated and unrated credit exposures; and
    - the relationship between internal and external ratings.

    When internal credit ratings are considered when managing and monitoring credit quality, information might be disclosed about: *[IFRS 7.IG25]*

    - the internal credit ratings process;
    - the amounts of credit exposures for each internal credit grade; and
    - the relationship between internal and external ratings.

- the nature of the counterparty;
- historical information about counterparty default rates; and
- any other information used to assess credit quality.

It should be noted that the above disclosures do not need to include the fair value of all collateral held (except where the lender is entitled to sell or repledge in the absence of default – see 4.4.6 above). The IASB recognised that such information would often be onerous to collect and may sometimes be misleading (for example if information about over- and under-collateralised assets is aggregated). Of more relevance will be the extent of under-collateralised loans. *[IFRS 7.BC51, BC52]*.

The following extracts from the financial statements of Volkswagen, Essentra, Aviva and the Coventry Building Society illustrate a variety of ways in which these disclosures have been dealt with in practice. Volkswagen discloses an analysis of receivables by internal credit ratings; Essentra analyses current trade receivables between new and established customers; Aviva shows an analysis of investments by external credit ratings and Coventry Building Society provides various information about its loan assets including the extent of collateral.

Extract 53.8: Volkswagen Aktengeselschaft (2014)

Notes to the Consolidated Financial Statements [extract]
34 **Financial risk management and financial instruments** [extract]
2. **Credit and Default Risk** [extract]

CREDIT RATING OF THE GROSS CARRYING AMOUNTS OF FINANCIAL ASSETS THAT ARE NEITHER PAST DUE NOR IMPAIRED

€ million	Risk class 1	Risk class 2	Dec. 31, 2014	Risk class 1	Risk class 2	Dec. 31, 2013
Measured at amortized cost						
Financial services receivables	**86,099**	**13,696**	**99,795**	71,592	14,996	86,588
Trade receivables	**8,546**	**137**	**8,682**	8,218	1	8,219
Other receivables	**10,765**	**35**	**10,800**	9,402	40	9,442
Measured at fair value	**13,593**	**–**	**13,593**	12,009	–	12,009
	119,003	**13,868**	**132,871**	101,221	15,037	116,258

The Volkswagen Group performs a credit assessment of borrowers in all loan and lease agreements, using scoring systems for the high-volume business and rating systems for corporate customers and receivables from dealer financing. Receivables rated as good are contained in risk class 1. Receivables from customers whose credit rating is not good but have not yet defaulted are contained in risk class 2.

Extract 53.9: Essentra plc (2014)

Notes [extract]
1. **Financial risk management** [extract]
i) ***Credit risk*** [extract]
Trade and other receivables

Essentra's exposure to credit risk is driven by the profile of its customers. This is influenced by the demographics of the customer base, including the industry and country in which customers operate. Trade and other receivables are generally due from customers who are unlikely to seek credit ratings as part of their normal course of business.

Essentra monitors significant customers' credit limits and there is an allowance for impairment that represents the estimate of potential losses in respect of trade and other receivables. The components of this allowance are a specific allowance for individual losses and a collective allowance for losses that have been incurred but not yet identified. The collective allowance takes account of historical experience and the profile of customers.

As at 31 December 2014, gross trade receivables were £151.8m (2013: £130.7m) of which £25.1m (2013: £19.4m) were past due but not impaired. The ageing analysis of trade receivables past due but not impaired is as follows:

	2014 £m	2013 £m
Up to 3 months	**25.1**	19.4

As at 31 December 2014, trade receivables of £6.3m (2013: £5.7m) were provided for as they were considered to be impaired. The ageing of the impaired receivables provided for is as follows:

	2014 £m	2013 £m
Up to 3 months	1.6	2.1
Over 3 months	4.7	3.6
	6.3	5.7

The movement in the provision for impaired receivables is as follows:

	2014 £m	2013 £m
Beginning of year	5.7	4.9
Impaired receivables acquired	0.5	1.5
Impairment loss recognised	2.8	0.6
Release in the year	(1.6)	(0.4)
Utilisation	(1.1)	(0.9)
End of year	6.3	5.7

Derivative assets

Credit risk with respect to derivatives is controlled by limiting transactions to major banking counterparties where internationally agreed standard form documentation exists. The credit ratings of these counterparties are monitored.

Cash and cash equivalents

Credit risk relating to cash and cash equivalents is monitored daily, on a counterparty by counterparty basis. The credit limits imposed specify the maximum amount of cash which can be invested in, or with, any single counterparty. These limits are determined by geographic presence, expertise and credit rating. Essentra monitors the credit ratings of counterparties.

The following credit risk table provides information regarding the credit risk exposure of Essentra by classifying derivative assets and cash and cash equivalents according to credit ratings of the counterparties. AAA is the highest possible rating and all of the assets are neither impaired nor past due.

							2014
	AAA £m	AA £m	A £m	BBB £m	BB £m	Not rated £m	Total £m
Derivative assets	–	0.1	0.3	3.5	–	–	3.9
Cash and cash equivalents	–	2.6	13.9	27.5	1.0	1.0	46.0
	–	2.7	14.2	31.0	1.0	1.0	49.9

							2013
	AAA £m	AA £m	A £m	BBB £m	BB £m	Not rated £m	Total £m
Derivative assets	–	–	0.2	–	–	–	0.2
Cash and cash equivalents	–	9.5	29.0	3.6	0.6	1.4	44.1
	–	9.5	29.2	3.6	0.6	1.4	44.3

Essentra's maximum credit risk exposure is £209.4m (2013: £180.3m) and no collateral is held against this amount (2013: £nil).

Extract 53.10: Aviva plc (2014)

Notes to the consolidated financial statements [extracts]
58   Risk management [extract]
(b)   Credit risk [extracts]
Financial exposures by credit ratings [extracts]

Financial assets are graded according to current external credit ratings issued. AAA is the highest possible rating. Investment grade financial assets are classified within the range of AAA to BBB ratings. Financial assets which fall outside this range are classified as sub-investment grade. The following table provides information regarding the aggregated credit risk exposure of the Group for financial assets with external credit ratings, excluding assets 'held for sale'. 'Not rated' assets capture assets not rated by external ratings agencies.

As at 31 December 2014	AAA	AA	A	BBB	Speculative grade	Not rated	Carrying value including held for sale	Less: Amounts classified as held for sale	Carrying value £m
Debt securities	13.6%	35.6%	21.3%	21.9%	2.1%	5.5%	131,661	–	131,661
Reinsurance assets	0.3%	71.3%	21.9%	0.1%	0.0%	6.4%	7,958	–	7,958
Other investments	0.0%	0.1%	1.3%	0.0%	0.2%	98.4%	35,358	–	35,358
Loans	1.3%	9.0%	2.1%	0.2%	0.0%	87.4%	25,260	–	25,260
Total							200,237	–	200,237

As at 31 December 2013	AAA	AA	A	BBB	Speculative grade	Not rated	Carrying value including held for sale	Less: Amounts classified as held for sale	Carrying value £m
Debt securities	13.0%	33.1%	20.8%	24.9%	2.8%	5.4%	126,805	(2,420)	124,385
Reinsurance assets	0.3%	53.6%	37.1%	1.1%	0.1%	7.8%	7,257	(37)	7,220
Other investments	0.0%	0.2%	0.7%	1.0%	0.1%	98.0%	32,517	(201)	32,316
Loans	3.8%	12.1%	1.2%	0.0%	0.3%	82.6%	23,879	–	23,879
Total							190,458	(2,658)	187,800

Chapter 53

Extract 53.11: *Coventry Building Society (2014)*
Risk Management Report [extracts]
Retail credit risk [extracts]

Retail credit risk profile

The nature of the Society's lending has remained focused on low risk residential mortgage business, including buy to let. Limited non-traditional lending in the form of near-prime mortgages and self-certification was discontinued in 2008 and 2009 respectively and these portfolios are reducing over time. Commercial loans in the Stroud & Swindon portfolio were added to the Society's assets upon merger of the two Societies in 2010. These balances also continue to reduce over time, with no new lending activity being undertaken in this portfolio. There has been no new unsecured lending since 2009.

Loans and advances to customers, gross of impairment provisions, are shown below:

Loans and advances to customers (Audited)	2014 £m	2014 %	2013 £m	2013 %
Residential mortgages: owner-occupier	16,835.2	62.4	15,161.1	62.8
Residential mortgages: buy to let	9,657.4	35.8	8,419.8	34.9
Total traditional residential mortgages	26,492.6	98.2	23,580.9	97.7
Residential near-prime mortgages	105.2	0.4	116.0	0.5
Residential self-certification mortgages	331.6	1.2	382.6	1.6
Commercial mortgages	6.3	–	8.3	–
Total non-traditional mortgages	443.1	1.6	506.9	2.1
Unsecured personal loans	50.0	0.2	56.7	0.2
Total gross balance	26,985.7	100.0	24,144.5	100.0

Geographical concentration (Audited)

The residential mortgage portfolio is well diversified and reflects the national coverage of the Society's distribution channels. The geographical split of residential mortgages by balance, gross of impairment provisions is shown below:

Region	2014 %	2013 %
East of England	12.6	12.4
London	14.8	14.2
Midlands	15.1	16.0
North East	9.0	9.1
North West	8.6	8.6
Scotland & Northern Ireland	4.6	4.6
South Central	12.9	12.6
South East	10.8	10.6
South West & Wales	11.6	11.9
Total	100.0	100.0

Loan to value

The Society's low risk approach to lending is reflected in the loan to value profile of the residential mortgage book. The estimated value of the residential mortgage portfolio is updated on a quarterly basis using the Nationwide regional House Price Index.

The residential mortgage book as at 31 December 2014 is analysed below, together with an analysis of gross new lending in the year. The following tables are by value unless stated otherwise:

Total mortgage book profile (by number of accounts) (Audited)	2014 %	2013 %
Indexed loan to value:		
<50%	48.1	45.0
50% to 65%	25.9	26.6
65% to 75%	13.0	13.7
75% to 85%	8.8	9.1
85% to 95%	3.7	4.1
> 95%	0.5	1.5
Total	100.0	100.0
Average indexed loan to value of stock (simple average)	48.6	50.0
Average indexed loan to value of stock (balance weighted)	55.6	57.7

New business profile (Gross lending) (Audited)	2014 %	2013 %
Owner-occupier purchase	38.8	36.7
Owner-occupier remortgages	23.8	24.0
Buy to let	37.4	39.3
Total	100.0	100.0
Average loan to value (simple average)	64.6	63.6
Average loan to value (balance weighted)	66.6	66.5

Chapter 53

Identifying impaired loans (Audited)

Loans are categorised by arrears status in line with industry practice and are identified as being either not past due and not impaired (if up to date at the balance sheet date), past due up to three months but not impaired, or impaired if more than three months in arrears or in possession.

In terms of impaired mortgages, the Society's performance is compared with figures published by the Council of Mortgage Lenders (CML). From these figures it can be seen that the performance of the Society has remained strong, with arrears reducing over the year, and favourable to the industry.

The Society's number of accounts in arrears as a percentage of loans and advances to customers compared with the CML data is shown below:

	2014		2013	
	Society	CML	Society	CML
(Audited)	%	%	%	%
Greater than three months	0.68	1.33	0.90	1.68
Greater than six months	0.26	0.70	0.41	0.91
Greater than one year	0.08	0.28	0.12	0.37
In possession	0.02	0.06	0.03	0.08

An analysis of past due and impaired loans by loan to value is shown below:

As at 31 December 2014

	Not impaired		Impaired				
(Audited)							
Indexed loan to value:	Not past due	Past due up to three months	Past due over three to six months	Past due over six months or in litigation	In possession	Impairment provision	Total
	£m	£m	£m	£m	£m	£m	£m
<50%	9,697.5	97.3	24.3	10.9	0.1	(3.7)	9,826.4
50% to 65%	8,324.8	92.7	28.3	16.6	0.2	(4.3)	8,458.3
65% to 75%	4,228.2	62.4	19.9	15.5	0.4	(2.7)	4,323.7
75% to 85%	2,871.0	50.7	14.9	13.3	0.2	(3.0)	2,947.1
85% to 95%	1,140.5	28.5	15.1	11.7	0.9	(2.8)	1,193.9
>95%	131.6	15.2	8.4	8.7	5.9	(5.2)	164.6
Unsecured	45.6	3.5	0.6	0.3	–	(4.4)	45.6
Total	26,439.2	350.3	111.5	77.0	7.7	(26.1)	26,959.6

The Society held properties valued at £6.4 million (2013: £9.1 million) pending their sale against balances of £5.8 million (net of provisions) (2013: £8.2 million). Shortfalls between expected sale proceeds (less anticipated costs) and the balance outstanding are fully provided.

The table below provides further information regarding the impaired status of mortgages and loans. Balances are shown gross of impairment provisions.

As at 31 December 2014 (Audited)	Not impaired		Impaired				
	Not past due £m	Past due up to three months £m	Past due over three to six months £m	Past due over six months or in litigation £m	In possession £m	Impairment provision £m	Total £m
Residential mortgages							
Owner-occupier	16,484.3	223.1	73.6	51.6	2.6	(9.0)	16,826.2
Buy to let	9,562.9	69.9	13.1	9.4	2.1	(9.5)	9,647.9
Non-traditional mortgages							
Residential near-prime	57.9	22.7	14.1	9.2	1.3	(1.1)	104.1
Residential self-certified	283.1	30.3	10.1	6.4	1.7	(1.3)	330.3
Commercial lending	5.5	0.8	–	–	–	(0.8)	5.5
Unsecured	45.5	3.5	0.6	0.4	–	(4.4)	45.6
Total	26,439.2	350.3	111.5	77.0	7.7	(26.1)	26,959.6

5.2.2.C   *Financial assets that are either past due or impaired*

A financial asset is defined as 'past due' when a counterparty has failed to make a payment when contractually due. *[IFRS 7 Appendix]*. For example, consider an entity that enters into a lending agreement that requires interest to be paid every month. On the first day of the next month, if interest has not been paid, the loan is past due. Past due does not mean that the counterparty will never pay, but it can trigger various actions such as renegotiation, enforcement of covenants, or legal proceedings. *[IFRS 7.IG26]*.

This definition may seem rigid when compared to internal management reporting, which may not classify an asset as overdue provided payment is made within a commercially accepted interval, e.g. 30 days after the contractual due date. However, the IASB is not inclined to change the definition and notes that entities are encouraged to disclose their methods used to measure credit risk which would allow them to explain any differences between internal reporting and the ageing analysis required by IFRS 7.[6]

When the terms and conditions of financial assets that have been classified as past due are renegotiated (a practice often referred to as forbearance), the terms and conditions of the new contractual arrangement should be applied to determine whether the financial asset remains past due. *[IFRS 7.IG27]*. Accounting for and disclosure of banks' forbearance practices has become a common area of scrutiny by financial reporting regulators in the wake of the financial crisis.

To provide information about financial assets with the greatest credit risk, entities are required to disclose the following for each class of financial asset (including trade receivables): *[IFRS 7.37, BC55]*

- an analysis of the age of financial assets that are past due as at the reporting date but not impaired (essentially to identify those financial assets that are more likely to become impaired and help users to estimate the level of future impairment losses *[IFRS 7.BC55(a)]*).

  Judgement should be used to determine an appropriate number of time bands. For example, the following time bands might be considered appropriate: *[IFRS 7.IG28]*

  - not more than three months;
  - more than three months and not more than six months;
  - more than six months and not more than one year; and
  - more than one year.

  In most cases it will be appropriate to analyse the assets by reference to the period of time the asset has been past due rather than, say, by reference to the amount of time since the financial asset was initially recognised. For example, if a borrower had missed only the most recent interest payment due 20 days before the lender's reporting date, the fact that the payment is 20 days past due seems far more relevant to assessing its credit risk than the date the asset was originated which could have been many years earlier.

  There is no exemption from this disclosure requirement for financial assets classified as at fair value through profit or loss or as available for sale. Consequently, an ageing analysis of such financial assets should be provided, even though their carrying amounts reflect their credit status;[7] and

- an analysis of financial assets that are individually determined to be impaired as at the reporting date, including the factors the entity considered in determining that they are impaired.

  This analysis might include: *[IFRS 7.IG29]*

  - the carrying amount, before deducting any impairment loss;
  - the amount of any related impairment loss; and
  - the nature and fair value of collateral available and other credit enhancements obtained.

  It might also include an analysis of such assets by factors other than age, such as the nature of the counterparty or a geographical analysis of the impaired assets. *[IFRS 7.BC55(b)]*.

Extracts 53.9 and 53.11 above (Essentra and Coventry Building Society) contain examples of how this disclosure requirement has been dealt with in practice.

5.2.2.D   *Collateral and other credit enhancements obtained*

When an entity obtains financial or non-financial assets during the period by taking possession of collateral it holds as security, or calling on other credit enhancements such as guarantees, and these assets meet the recognition criteria in other standards, it should disclose for such assets held at the reporting date: *[IFRS 7.38]*

- the nature and carrying amount of the assets; and

- when the assets are not readily convertible into cash, its policies for disposing of such assets or for using them in its operations.

This disclosure is intended to provide information about the frequency of such activities and the entity's ability to obtain and realise the value of the collateral. *[IFRS 7.BC56]*.

5.2.3 Credit risk (entities applying IFRS 9)

For entities applying IFRS 9, the disclosure requirements in respect of impairment are expanded significantly when compared to IAS 39. Those requirements are also supplemented by some detailed implementation guidance. The requirements of IFRS 9 relating to the measurement of impairments are dealt with in Chapter 49 at 5.

5.2.3.A Scope and objectives

The objective of these disclosures is to enable users to understand the effect of credit risk on the amount, timing and uncertainty of future cash flows. To achieve this objective, the disclosures should provide: *[IFRS 7.35B]*

- information about the entity's credit risk management practices and how they relate to the recognition and measurement of expected credit losses, including the methods, assumptions and information used to measure those losses (see 5.2.3.B below);

- quantitative and qualitative information that allows users of financial statements to evaluate the amounts in the financial statements arising from expected credit losses, including changes in the amount of those losses and the reasons for those changes (see 5.2.3.C below); and

- information about the entity's credit risk exposure, i.e. the credit risk inherent in its financial assets and commitments to extend credit, including significant credit risk concentrations (see 5.2.3.D below).

An entity will need to determine how much detail to disclose, how much emphasis to place on different aspects of the disclosure requirements, the appropriate level of aggregation or disaggregation and additional explanations or information necessary to evaluate the quantitative information disclosed and meet the objectives above. *[IFRS 7.35D, 35E]*.

To avoid duplication, IFRS 7 allows this information to be incorporated by cross-reference from the financial statements to some other statement that is available to users of the financial statements on the same terms and at the same time, such as a management commentary or risk report. Without the information incorporated by cross-reference, the financial statements are incomplete. *[IFRS 7.35C]*.

A number of the disclosures about credit risk are required to be given by class (see 3.3 above). In determining these classes, financial instruments in the same class should reflect shared economic characteristics with respect to credit risk. A lender, for example, might determine that residential mortgages, unsecured consumer loans and commercial loans each have different economic characteristics. *[IFRS 7.IG21]*.

Unless otherwise stated, the disclosure requirements set out at 5.2.3.B to 5.2.3.D below are applicable only to financial instruments to which the impairment requirements in IFRS 9 are applied. *[IFRS 7.35A]*.

5.2.3.B   *Credit risk management practices*

An entity should explain its credit risk management practices and how they relate to the recognition and measurement of expected credit losses. To meet this objective it should disclose information that enables users to understand and evaluate: *[IFRS 7.35F]*

- how it has determined whether the credit risk of financial instruments has increased significantly since initial recognition, including if and how:
  - financial instruments are considered to have low credit risk; and
  - the presumption that there have been significant increases in credit risk since initial recognition when financial assets are more than 30 days past due has been rebutted;
- its definitions of default, including the reasons for selecting those definitions. This may include: *[IFRS 7.B8A]*
  - the qualitative and quantitative factors considered in defining default;
  - whether different definitions have been applied to different types of financial instruments; and
  - assumptions about the cure rate, i.e. the number of financial assets that return to a performing status, after a default has occurred on the financial asset;
- how the instruments were grouped if expected credit losses were measured on a collective basis;
- how it has determined that financial assets are credit-impaired;
- its write-off policy, including the indicators that there is no reasonable expectation of recovery and information about the policy for financial assets that are written-off but are still subject to enforcement activity.

  An asset (or portion thereof) should be written off only if there is no reasonable expectation of recovery. *[IFRS 9.5.4.4]*. Consequently, it is not entirely clear in which circumstances such an asset might still be subject to enforcement activity; and
- how the requirements for the modification of contractual cash flows of financial instruments have been applied, including how the entity:
  - determines whether the credit risk on a financial asset that has been modified while the loss allowance was measured at an amount equal to lifetime expected credit losses has improved to the extent that the loss allowance reverts to being measured at an amount equal to 12-month expected credit losses; and
  - monitors the extent to which the loss allowance on financial assets meeting the criteria in the previous bullet is subsequently remeasured at an amount equal to lifetime expected credit losses.

> Quantitative information that will assist users in understanding the subsequent increase in credit risk of modified financial assets may include information about modified financial assets meeting the criteria above for which the loss allowance has reverted to being measured at an amount equal to lifetime expected credit losses, i.e. a deterioration rate. *[IFRS 7.B8B]*.

An entity should also explain the inputs, assumptions and estimation techniques used to apply the impairment requirements of IFRS 9. For this purpose it should disclose: *[IFRS 7.35G]*

- the basis of inputs and assumptions and the estimation techniques used to:
  - measure 12-month and lifetime expected credit losses;
  - determine whether the credit risk of financial instruments has increased significantly since initial recognition; and
  - determine whether a financial asset is credit-impaired.

  This may include information obtained from internal historical information or rating reports and assumptions about the expected life of financial instruments and the timing of the sale of collateral; *[IFRS 7.B8C]*
- how forward-looking information has been incorporated into the determination of expected credit losses, including the use of macroeconomic information; and
- changes in estimation techniques or significant assumptions made during the reporting period and the reasons for those changes.

5.2.3.C   Quantitative and qualitative information about amounts arising from expected credit losses

An entity should explain the changes in the loss allowance and reasons for those changes by presenting a reconciliation of the opening balance to the closing balance. This should be given in a table for each relevant class of financial instruments, showing separately the changes during the period for: *[IFRS 7.35H]*

- the loss allowance measured at an amount equal to 12-month expected credit losses;
- the loss allowance measured at an amount equal to lifetime expected credit losses for:
  - financial instruments for which credit risk has increased significantly since initial recognition but that are not credit-impaired financial assets;
  - financial assets that are credit-impaired at the reporting date (but were not credit-impaired when purchased or originated); and
  - trade receivables, contract assets or lease receivables for which the loss allowance is measured using a simplified approach based on lifetime expected credit losses; and
- financial assets that were credit-impaired when purchased or originated.

  The total amount of undiscounted expected credit losses on initial recognition of any such assets during the reporting period should also be disclosed.

In addition, it may be necessary to provide a narrative explanation of the changes in the loss allowance during the period. This narrative explanation may include an analysis of the reasons for changes in the loss allowance during the period, including: *[IFRS 7.B8D]*

- the portfolio composition;
- the volume of financial instruments purchased or originated; and
- the severity of the expected credit losses.

For loan commitments and financial guarantee contracts the loss allowance is recognised as a provision. Information about changes in the loss allowance for financial assets should be shown separately from those for loan commitments and financial guarantee contracts. However, if a financial instrument includes both a loan (i.e. financial asset) and an undrawn loan commitment (i.e. loan commitment) component and the expected credit losses on the loan commitment component cannot be separately identified from those on the financial asset component, the expected credit losses on the loan commitment should be recognised together with the loss allowance for the financial asset. To the extent that the combined expected credit losses exceed the gross carrying amount of the financial asset, the expected credit losses should be recognised as a provision. *[IFRS 7.B8E]*.

An explanation should also be provided of how significant changes in the gross carrying amount of financial instruments during the period contributed to changes in the loss allowance. This information should be provided separately for financial instruments that represent the loss allowance as listed in paragraph 35H of IFRS 7 (see above). Examples of changes in the gross carrying amount of financial instruments that contribute to changes in the loss allowance may include: *[IFRS 7.35I]*

- changes because of financial instruments originated or acquired during the reporting period;
- the modification of contractual cash flows on financial assets that do not result in a derecognition of those financial assets;
- changes because of financial instruments that were derecognised, including those that were written-off during the reporting period; and
- changes arising from the measurement of the loss allowance moving from 12-month expected credit losses to lifetime losses (or *vice versa*).

The information disclosed should provide an understanding of the nature and effect of modifications of contractual cash flows on financial assets that have not resulted in derecognition as well as the effect of such modifications on the measurement of expected credit losses. The following information should therefore be given: *[IFRS 7.35J]*

- the amortised cost before the modification and the net modification gain or loss recognised for financial assets for which the contractual cash flows have been modified during the reporting period while they had a loss allowance based on lifetime expected credit losses; and
- the gross carrying amount at the end of the reporting period of financial assets that have been modified since initial recognition at a time when the loss

allowance was based on lifetime expected credit losses and for which the loss allowance has changed during the reporting period to an amount equal to 12-month expected credit losses.

These requirements apply to all modifications whether they are as a result of credit related or other commercial reasons. However, if an entity has the ability to separately identify different types of modifications and considers that the separate disclosure of these items is relevant to achieving the overall objective of the disclosures in this section, the entity could provide this additional detail as part of the disclosure.[8]

The following example illustrates how this information might be presented. *[IFRS 7.IG20B]*.

Example 53.6: Information about changes in the loss allowance

Mortgage loans – loss allowance	12-month expected credit losses	Lifetime expected credit losses (collectively assessed)	Lifetime expected credit losses (individually assessed)	Credit-impaired financial assets (lifetime expected credit losses)
CU'000				
Loss allowance as at 1 January	X	X	X	X
Changes due to financial instruments recognised as at 1 January:				
– Transfer to lifetime expected credit losses	(X)	X	X	–
– Transfer to credit-impaired financial assets	(X)	–	(X)	X
– Transfer to 12-month expected credit losses	X	(X)	(X)	–
– Financial assets that have been derecognised during the period	(X)	(X)	(X)	(X)
New financial assets originated or purchased	X	–	–	–
Write-offs	–	–	(X)	(X)
Changes in models/risk parameters	X	X	X	X
Foreign exchange and other movements	X	X	X	X
Loss allowance as at 31 December	X	X	X	X

Significant changes in the gross carrying amount of mortgage loans that contributed to changes in the loss allowance were:

- The acquisition of the ABC prime mortgage portfolio increased the residential mortgage book by x per cent, with a corresponding increase in the loss allowance measured on a 12-month basis.

- The write off of the CUXX DEF portfolio following the collapse of the local market reduced the loss allowance for financial assets with objective evidence of impairment by CUX.

- The expected increase in unemployment in Region X caused a net increase in financial assets whose loss allowance is equal to lifetime expected credit losses and caused a net increase of CUX in the lifetime expected credit losses allowance.

Chapter 53

The significant changes in the gross carrying amount of mortgage loans are further explained below:

Mortgage loans – gross carrying amount	12-month expected credit losses	Lifetime expected credit losses (collectively assessed)	Lifetime expected credit losses (individually assessed)	Credit impaired financial assets (lifetime expected credit losses)
CU'000				
Gross carrying amount as at 1 January	X	X	X	X
Individual financial assets transferred to lifetime expected credit losses	(X)	–	X	–
Individual financial assets transferred to credit-impaired financial assets	(X)	–	(X)	X
Individual financial assets transferred from credit-impaired financial assets	X	–	X	(X)
Financial assets assessed on collective basis	(X)	X	–	–
New financial assets originated or purchased	X	–	–	–
Write-offs	–	–	(X)	(X)
Financial assets that have been derecognised	(X)	(X)	(X)	(X)
Changes due to modifications that did not result in derecognition	(X)	–	(X)	(X)
Other changes	X	X	X	X
Gross carrying amount as at 31 December	X	X	X	X

Where the loss allowance for trade receivables or lease receivables is measured using a simplified approach based on lifetime expected credit losses, the information about modifications need be given only if those financial assets are modified while more than 30 days past due. *[IFRS 7.35A(a)]*.

To provide an understanding of the effect of collateral and other credit enhancements on the amounts arising from expected credit losses, the following should be disclosed by class of financial instrument: *[IFRS 7.35K]*

- the amount that best represents the maximum exposure to credit risk at the end of the reporting period without taking account of any collateral held or other credit enhancements (e.g. netting agreements that do not qualify for offset in accordance with IAS 32);
- a narrative description of collateral held as security and other credit enhancements, including:
    - a description of the nature and quality of the collateral held;
    - an explanation of any significant changes in the quality of that collateral or credit enhancements as a result of deterioration or changes in the entity's collateral policies during the reporting period; and
    - information about financial instruments for which a loss allowance has not been recognised because of the collateral.

This might include information about: *[IFRS 7.B8G]*

- the main types of collateral held as security and other credit enhancements, examples of the latter being guarantees, credit derivatives and netting agreements that do not qualify for offset in accordance with IAS 32;
- the volume of collateral held and other credit enhancements and its significance in terms of the loss allowance;
- the policies and processes for valuing and managing collateral and other credit enhancements;
- the main types of counterparties to collateral and other credit enhancements and their creditworthiness; and
- information about risk concentrations within the collateral and other credit enhancements; and
- quantitative information about the collateral held as security and other credit enhancements, e.g. quantification of the extent to which collateral and other credit enhancements mitigate credit risk, on financial assets that are credit-impaired at the reporting date.

Disclosure of information about the fair value of collateral and other credit enhancements is not required, nor is a quantification of the exact value of the collateral included in the calculation of expected credit losses (i.e. the loss given default). *[IFRS 7.B8F]*. Further, these requirements do not apply to lease receivables. *[IFRS 7.35A(b)]*.

For a financial asset, the maximum exposure to credit risk is typically the gross carrying amount, net of any amounts offset in accordance with IAS 32 and any impairment losses recognised in accordance with IFRS 9. *[IFRS 7.B9]*. Activities that give rise to credit risk and the associated maximum exposure to credit risk include, but are not limited to: *[IFRS 7.B10]*

- granting loans to customers and placing deposits with other entities. In these cases, the maximum exposure to credit risk is the carrying amount of the related financial assets;
- entering into derivative contracts, e.g. foreign exchange contracts, interest rate swaps and purchased credit derivatives. When the resulting asset is measured at fair value, the maximum exposure to credit risk at the reporting date will equal the carrying amount;
- granting financial guarantees. In this case, the maximum exposure to credit risk is the maximum amount the entity could have to pay if the guarantee is called on, which may be significantly greater than the amount recognised as a liability; and
- making a loan commitment that is irrevocable over the life of the facility or is revocable only in response to a material adverse change. If the issuer cannot settle the loan commitment net in cash or another financial instrument, the maximum credit exposure is the full amount of the commitment. This is because it is uncertain whether the amount of any undrawn portion may be drawn upon in the future. This may be significantly greater than the amount recognised as a liability.

Chapter 53

The contractual amount outstanding on financial assets that were written off during the reporting period and which are still subject to enforcement activity should be disclosed. *[IFRS 7.35L].*

5.2.3.D   Credit risk exposure

Users should be able to assess an entity's credit risk exposure and understand its significant credit risk concentrations. Therefore, an entity should disclose, by 'credit risk rating grades' (see below), the gross carrying amount of financial assets and the exposure to credit risk on loan commitments and financial guarantee contracts. This information should be provided separately for financial instruments: *[IFRS 7.35M]*

- for which the loss allowance is measured at an amount equal to 12-month expected credit losses;
- for which the loss allowance is measured at an amount equal to lifetime expected credit losses and that are:
  - financial instruments for which credit risk has increased significantly since initial recognition but are not credit-impaired financial assets;
  - financial assets that are credit-impaired at the reporting date (but were not credit-impaired when purchased or originated); and
  - trade receivables, contract assets or lease receivables for which the loss allowances are measured using a simplified approach based on lifetime expected credit losses. Information for these assets may be based on a provision matrix; and *[IFRS 7.35N]*
- that are financial assets that were credit-impaired when purchased or originated.

The following examples illustrate how this information might be presented. *[IFRS 7.IG20C, 20D]*

Example 53.7:   Information about credit risk exposures and significant credit risk concentrations

Consumer loan credit risk exposure by internal rating grades

20XX CU'000	Consumer–credit card Gross carrying amount		Consumer–automotive Gross carrying amount	
	Lifetime	12-month	Lifetime	12-month
Internal Grade 1-2	X	X	X	X
Internal Grade 3-4	X	X	X	X
Internal Grade 5-6	X	X	X	X
Internal Grade 7	X	X	X	X
Total	X	X	X	X

Corporate loan credit risk profile by external rating grades

20XX	Corporate–equipment		Corporate–construction	
	Gross carrying amount		Gross carrying amount	
CU'000	Lifetime	12-month	Lifetime	12-month
AAA-AA	X	X	X	X
A	X	X	X	X
BBB-BB	X	X	X	X
B	X	X	X	X
CCC-CC	X	X	X	X
C	X	X	X	X
D	X	X	X	X
Total	X	X	X	X

Corporate loan risk profile by probability of default

20XX	Corporate–unsecured		Corporate–secured	
	Gross carrying amount		Gross carrying amount	
CU'000	Lifetime	12-month	Lifetime	12-month
0.00-0.10	X	X	X	X
0.11-0.40	X	X	X	X
0.41-1.00	X	X	X	X
1.01-3.00	X	X	X	X
3.01-6.00	X	X	X	X
6.01-11.00	X	X	X	X
11.01-17.00	X	X	X	X
17.01-25.00	X	X	X	X
25.01-50.00	X	X	X	X
50.00+	X	X	X	X
Total	X	X	X	X

Example 53.8:   Information about credit risk exposures using a provision matrix

The reporting entity manufactures cars and provides financing to both dealers and end customers. It discloses its dealer financing and customer financing as separate classes of financial instruments and applies the simplified approach to its trade receivables so that the loss allowance is always measured at an amount equal to lifetime expected credit losses. The following table illustrates the use of a provision matrix as a risk profile disclosure under the simplified approach:

20XX CU'000	Trade receivables days past due				
Dealer financing	**Current**	**More than 30 days**	**More than 60 days**	**More than 90 days**	**Total**
Expected credit loss rate	0.10%	2%	5%	13%	
Estimated total gross carrying amount at default	CU20,777	CU1,416	CU673	CU235	CU23,101
Lifetime expected credit losses – dealer financing	CU21	CU28	CU34	CU31	CU114
Customer financing					
Expected credit loss rate	0.20%	3%	8%	15%	
Estimated total gross carrying amount at default	CU19,222	CU2,010	CU301	CU154	CU21,687
Lifetime expected credit losses – customer financing	CU38	CU60	CU24	CU23	CU145

Credit risk rating grades are defined as ratings of credit risk based on the risk of a default occurring on the financial instrument. *[IFRS 7.A]*. The number of credit risk rating grades used to disclose the information above should be consistent with the number that the entity reports to key management personnel for credit risk management purposes. If past due information is the only borrower-specific information available and past due information is used to assess whether credit risk has increased significantly since initial recognition, an analysis by past due status should be provided for that class of financial assets. *[IFRS 7.B8I]*.

When expected credit losses are measured on a collective basis, it may not be possible to allocate the gross carrying amount of individual financial assets or the exposure to credit risk on loan commitments and financial guarantee contracts to the credit risk rating grades for which lifetime expected credit losses are recognised. In that case, the disclosure requirement above should be applied to those financial instruments that can be directly allocated to a credit risk rating grade and separate disclosure should be given of the gross carrying amount of financial instruments for which lifetime expected credit losses have been measured on a collective basis. *[IFRS 7.B8J]*.

A concentration of credit risk exists when a number of counterparties are located in a geographical region or are engaged in similar activities and have similar economic characteristics that would cause their ability to meet contractual obligations to be similarly affected by changes in economic or other conditions. Information should be provided to enable users to understand whether there are groups or portfolios of financial instruments with particular features that could affect a large portion of that group of financial instruments, such as concentration to particular risks. This could include, for example, loan-to-value groupings, geographical, industry or issuer-type concentrations. *[IFRS 7.B8H]*.

For financial instruments within the scope of IFRS 7 to which the impairment requirements in IFRS 9 are *not* applied, disclosure should be given by class of instrument of the amount that best represents the entity's maximum exposure to credit risk at the reporting date (see 5.2.2.A above). The amount disclosed should not take account of any collateral held or other credit enhancements (e.g. netting agreements that do not qualify for offset in accordance with IAS 32). This disclosure is not required for financial instruments whose carrying amount best represents this amount. *[IFRS 7.36(a)]*.

Entities should also provide, by class of financial instrument to which the impairment requirements in IFRS 9 are not applied, a description of collateral held as security and of other credit enhancements, and their financial effect (e.g. a quantification of the extent to which collateral and other credit enhancements mitigate credit risk) in respect of the amount that best represents the maximum exposure to credit risk. This applies irrespective of whether the maximum exposure to credit risk is disclosed separately or is represented by the carrying amount of a financial instrument. *[IFRS 7.36(b)]*. The requirement may be met by disclosing: *[IFRS 7.IG22]*

- the policies and processes for valuing and managing collateral and other credit enhancements obtained;
- a description of the main types of collateral and other credit enhancements (examples of the latter being guarantees and credit derivatives, as well as netting agreements that do not qualify for offset in accordance with IAS 32);
- the main types of counterparties to collateral and other credit enhancements and their creditworthiness; and
- information about risk concentrations within the collateral or other credit enhancements.

It is not entirely clear how detailed this additional information is intended to be. For example, whilst the standard suggests it should, or at least could, involve disclosure of quantitative information, the implementation guidance implies more discursive disclosures might suffice in some cases. In practice, entities will need to make a judgment based on their own specific circumstances and in the light of emerging practice.

5.2.3.E   Collateral and other credit enhancements obtained

When an entity obtains financial or non-financial assets during the period by taking possession of collateral it holds as security, or calling on other credit enhancements such as guarantees, and these assets meet the recognition criteria in other standards, it should disclose for such assets held at the reporting date: *[IFRS 7.38]*

- the nature and carrying amount of the assets; and

- when the assets are not readily convertible into cash, its policies for disposing of such assets or for using them in its operations.

This disclosure is intended to provide information about the frequency of such activities and the entity's ability to obtain and realise the value of the collateral. *[IFRS 7.BC56]*.

5.2.4   *Liquidity risk*

5.2.4.A   *Information provided to key management*

As set out at 5.2.1 above, an entity should disclose summary quantitative data about its exposure to risk on the basis of the information provided internally to key management personnel and IFRS 7 emphasises that this requirement applies to liquidity risk too. *[IFRS 7.B10A, BC58A(b)]*.

Entities should provide an explanation of how the data disclosed are determined. If the outflows of cash (or other financial assets) included in the data could occur significantly earlier than indicated, that fact should be stated and quantitative information should be provided to enable users of the financial statements to evaluate the extent of this risk, unless that information is included in the contractual maturity analyses (see 5.2.4.B below). Similar information should be given if the outflows of cash (or other financial assets) could be for significantly different amounts than those indicated in the data. This might be required, for example, if a derivative is included in the data on a net settlement basis, but the counterparty has the option of requiring gross settlement. *[IFRS 7.B10A]*.

5.2.4.B   *Maturity analyses*

To illustrate liquidity risk, the principal minimum numerical disclosures required are: *[IFRS 7.39(a), (b)]*

- a maturity analysis for non-derivative financial liabilities (including issued financial guarantee contracts) that shows their remaining contractual maturities; and

- a maturity analysis for derivative financial liabilities which includes the remaining contractual maturities for those derivative financial liabilities for which contractual maturities are essential for an understanding of the timing of the cash flows.

  The contractual maturities of the following would be essential for an understanding of the timing of the cash flows: *[IFRS 7.B11B]*

  - an interest rate swap with a remaining maturity of five years in a cash flow hedge of a variable rate financial asset or liability.

  - all loan commitments.

  Derivatives entered into for trading purposes that are typically settled before their contractual maturity (e.g. in response to fair value movements) are an example of the type of instrument that might not need to be included in the maturity analysis.[9]

These requirements are discussed further in the remainder of this sub-section.

Although these minimum disclosures address only financial liabilities, other aspects of IFRS 7 mean that most financial institutions will be required to disclose a maturity analysis of financial assets too (see 5.2.4.C below).

I   *Time bands*

The time bands to be used in the maturity analyses are not specified. Rather, entities should use their judgement to determine what is appropriate. For example, an entity might determine that the following are appropriate: *[IFRS 7.B11]*

• not later than one month;

• later than one month and not later than three months;

• later than three months and not later than one year; and

• later than one year and not later than five years.

In practice it is rare for entities outside of the financial services sector to present more than one time band covering amounts payable within one year. However, it is quite common for more than one time band to be given covering amounts payable later than one year and within five years as Unilever and Nestlé have done (Extracts 53.13 and 53.14 respectively at VII below). For banks and similar institutions an 'on demand' category could also be relevant.

When a counterparty has a choice of when an amount is paid, the liability should be included on the basis of the earliest date on which the entity can be required to pay. For example, financial liabilities such as demand deposits that an entity can be required to repay on demand should be included in the earliest time band. *[IFRS 7.B11C(a)]*. This means that the disclosure shows a worst case scenario, even if there is only a remote possibility that the entity could be required to pay its liabilities earlier than expected *[IFRS 7.BC57]* (although the disclosures at 5.2.4.C below may be relevant in these circumstances, i.e. those which are based on the information used by management to manage liquidity risk).

No guidance is given on how to deal with instruments where the issuer has a choice of when an amount is paid. For example, borrowings containing embedded issuer call or issuer prepayment options might be included in the analysis for non-derivative financial liabilities based on the earliest, latest or expected contractual payment dates. Where an entity has a material amount of such instruments it would be appropriate to explain the basis of the analyses presented.

When an entity is committed to make amounts available in instalments, each instalment should be allocated to the earliest period in which the entity can be required to pay. For example, an undrawn loan commitment would be included in the time band containing the earliest date it could be drawn down. *[IFRS 7.B11C(b)]*.

For issued financial guarantee contracts, amounts included in the maturity analysis should be allocated to the earliest period in which the guarantee could be called. *[IFRS 7.B11C(c)]*.

II   Cash flows: general requirements

The amounts that should be disclosed in the maturity analyses are the contractual undiscounted cash flows, for example:

* gross finance lease obligations (before deducting finance charges);
* prices specified in forward agreements to purchase financial assets for cash;
* net amounts for pay-floating/receive-fixed interest rate swaps for which net cash flows are exchanged;
* contractual amounts to be exchanged in a derivative financial instrument (e.g. a currency swap) for which gross cash flows are exchanged; and
* gross loan commitments.

These undiscounted cash flows will differ from the amount included in the statement of financial position because the latter amount is based on discounted cash flows. *[IFRS 7.B11D]*.

When the amount payable is not fixed, the amount disclosed should be determined by reference to the conditions existing at the reporting date. For example, if the amount payable varies with changes in an index, the amount disclosed may be based on the level of the index at the reporting date. *[IFRS 7.B11D]*. The standard does not explain whether the amount should be based on the spot or forward price of the index and, in practice, both approaches are used. Where a material difference between the two approaches could arise it would be appropriate to explain the basis on which the information is prepared as Berendsen plc does.

Extract 53.12: Berendsen plc (2014)

Notes to the consolidated financial statements [extract]
17.   Financial risk management [extract]
17.1   Financial risk factors [extract]
c)   Liquidity risk [extract]

The table below analyses the group's financial liabilities, excluding break clauses, which will be settled on a net basis into relative maturity groupings based on the remaining period at the balance sheet to the contract maturity date. The amounts disclosed in the table are contractual undiscounted cash flows using spot interest and foreign exchange rates at 31 December 2014. Balances due within 12 months equal their carrying balances as the impact of the discount is not significant.

The definition of liquidity risk includes only financial liabilities that will result in the outflow of cash or another financial asset (see 5 above) which means that financial liabilities that will be settled in the entity's own equity instruments and liabilities within the scope of IFRS 7 that are settled with non-financial assets will not be included in the maturity analysis. *[IFRS 7.BC58A(a)]*.

III   Cash flows: borrowings

It follows from the requirements at II above that the cash flows included in the analysis of non-derivative financial liabilities in respect of interest-bearing borrowings should reflect coupon as well as principal payments (although the standard does not say this explicitly). Quite how perpetual debt obligations should be dealt with in this analysis remains to be seen because the amount the standard requires in the latest maturity category is infinity!

A number of companies show coupon payments separately from payments of principal, for example Unilever (Extract 53.13 at VII below). However, separate disclosure is not required and coupon payments are commonly aggregated with principal payments as Nestlé and Volkswagen have (Extracts 53.14 and 53.15 respectively).

The following example illustrates the cash flows that should be included in the maturity analysis for non-derivative financial liabilities for a simple floating rate borrowing.

Example 53.9: Maturity analysis: floating rate borrowing

On 1 January 2016, Company P borrowed €100 million from a bank on the following terms: coupons are payable on the entire principal on 30 June and 31 December each year at the annual rate of LIBOR plus 1% as determined on the previous 1 January and 1 July; the principal is repayable on 31 December 2019.

At the end of 2016, P's reporting period, LIBOR is 5% and there is no difference between spot and forward interest rates (i.e. the yield curve is flat). Accordingly, P would include the following cash flows in its maturity analysis:

	€ million
30 June 2017	3
31 December 2017	3
30 June 2018	3
31 December 2018	3
30 June 2019	3
31 December 2019	103
Total	118

IV Cash flows: derivatives

In the case of derivatives that are settled by a gross exchange of cash flows, it is not entirely clear whether entities should disclose the related cash inflow as well as the cash outflow, although such information might be considered useful. Further, because the analysis is of financial liabilities, it seems clear that, strictly, cash outflows from a derivative *asset* that is settled by a gross exchange of cash should not be included. However, the contractual cash flows on these instruments would appear to be no less relevant than on those that have a negative fair value and should be disclosed where relevant.

A number of approaches to these issues were seen in practice as illustrated in Extracts 53.13 to 53.16 at VII below. Unilever and Nestlé both included cash inflows as well as outflows whereas Volkswagen showed only the cash outflows; Unilever included only derivative liabilities whereas Nestlé and Volkswagen included gross-settled derivative assets too. The size of the figures disclosed by entities with gross-settled derivatives can be staggering – Volkswagen, for example, disclosed gross cash outflows of nearly €30 billion from its derivatives.

The IASB staff has been clear that disclosure of only the outflow on derivatives that were in a liability position was explicitly required. However, IFRS 7 now emphasises the need to provide a maturity analysis of assets where such information is necessary to enable users of financial statements to evaluate the nature and extent of the entity's liquidity risk (see 5.2.4.C below). This change is likely to bring derivative assets within the scope of the maturity analyses[10] and, by analogy, related gross cash inflows. Similar issues can arise on commodity contracts that are accounted for under IAS 39 or IFRS 9 which will often be settled by exchanging the commodity for cash. An additional complication with these is that one leg of the contract may not involve a cash flow.

Further issues can arise in the case of a derivative liability settled by exchanging net cash flows in a number of future periods. For example, the relevant index for a long-term interest rate swap might predict that in some periods the entity could have cash inflows. Although this issue was identified by the IASB staff,[11] it has not been addressed and it remains unclear whether and how these inflows should be included within the analyses.

V   Cash flows: embedded derivatives

The application guidance to IFRS 7 explains that where an embedded derivative is separated from a hybrid (combined) financial instrument (see Chapter 43 at 4), the entire instrument should be dealt with in the maturity analysis for non-derivative instruments. *[IFRS 7.B11A]*.

No guidance is given for dealing with embedded derivatives separated from non-financial contracts. However, applying a similar approach to those separated from financial instruments would result in them being excluded from the maturity analyses altogether. This is because the hypothecated cash flows of the embedded derivative would be treated as cash flows of the non-financial contract and such contracts are not within the scope of IFRS 7. This is consistent with the IASB staff analysis when developing the above requirement: they planned to exclude from the maturity analysis all separated embedded derivatives except those for which the hybrid contract was a financial liability because including them was unhelpful in understanding the liquidity information provided.[12]

VI   Cash flows: financial guarantee contracts and written options

For issued financial guarantee contracts, IFRS 7 requires the maximum amount of the guarantee to be included in the maturity analysis, *[IFRS 7.B11C(c)]*, but credit default swaps and written options are not directly addressed. However, the IASB staff have noted that the question of what to include in the maturity analysis is the same for such instruments and, in our view, the maximum amount that could be payable should be included in the analysis.[13]

VII   Examples of disclosures in practice

The following extracts from the financial statements of Unilever, Nestlé, Volkswagen and Royal Bank of Scotland show a variety of ways that companies applied the requirements of IFRS 7 in practice.

Extract 53.13: Unilever PLC and Unilever N.V. (2014)

Notes to the Consolidated Financial Statements [extract]

16A.   Management of liquidity risk [extract]

The following table shows Unilever's contractually agreed undiscounted cash flows, including expected interest payments, which are payable under financial liabilities at the balance sheet date:

Undiscounted cash flows	€ million Due within 1 year	€ million Due between 1 and 2 years	€ million Due between 2 and 3 years	€ million Due between 3 and 4 years	€ million Due between 4 and 5 years	€ million Due after 5 years	€ million Total	€ million Net carrying amount as shown in balance sheet
2014								
Non-derivative financial liabilities:								
Preference shares	(4)	(4)	(4)	(4)	(4)	(72)	(92)	(68)
Bank loans and overdrafts	(601)	(257)	(272)	–	–	–	(1,130)	(1,114)
Bonds and other loans	(4,758)	(647)	(1,289)	(511)	(1,418)	(4,513)	(13,136)	(10,573)
Finance lease creditors	(25)	(48)	(23)	(19)	(18)	(172)	(305)	(199)
Other financial liabilities	(230)	–	–	–	–	(188)	(418)	(418)
Trade payables excluding social security and sundry taxes	(12,051)	(378)	–	–	–	–	(12,429)	(12,429)
Issued financial guarantees	(11)	–	–	–	–	–	(11)	–
	(17,680)	(1,334)	(1,588)	(534)	(1,440)	(4,945)	(27,521)	(24,801)
Derivative financial liabilities:								
Interest rate derivatives:								
Derivatives contracts – receipts	289	229	230	17	–	–	765	
Derivative contracts – payments	(429)	(255)	(277)	(19)	–	–	(980)	
Foreign exchange derivatives:								
Derivatives contracts – receipts	9,957	2	–	347	–	–	10,306	
Derivative contracts – payments	(10,284)	(2)	–	(304)	–	–	(10,590)	
Commodity derivatives:								
Derivatives contracts – receipts	405	–	–	–	–	–	405	
Derivative contracts – payments	(421)	–	–	–	–	–	(421)	
	(483)	(26)	(47)	41	–	–	(515)	(514)
Total	(18,163)	(1,360)	(1,635)	(493)	(1,440)	(4,945)	(28,036)	(25,315)

Chapter 53

Extract 53.14: Nestlé S.A. (2014)

Notes [extract]
13.   Financial instruments [extract]
13.2b   Liquidity risk [extract]
Contractual maturities of financial liabilities and derivatives (including interest)[extract]

In millions of CHF

	In the first year	In the second year	In the third to the fifth year	After the fifth year	Contractual amount	Carrying amount
Financial assets						**27,833**
Trade and other payables	**(17,437)**	**(357)**	**(60)**	**(1,474)**	**(19,328)**	**(19,279)**
Commercial paper (a)	(5,573)	–	–	–	(5,573)	(5,569)
Bonds (a)	(672)	(1,419)	(6,403)	(5,042)	(13,536)	(12,257)
Other financial debt	(2,963)	(203)	(326)	(115)	(3,607)	(3,380)
Total financial debt	**(9,208)**	**(1,622)**	**(6,729)**	**(5,157)**	**(22,716)**	**(21,206)**
Financial liabilities	**(26,645)**	**(1,979)**	**(6,789)**	**(6,631)**	**(42,044)**	**(40,485)**
Non-currency derivative assets	39	5	3	(6)	41	41
Non-currency derivative liabilities	(215)	(29)	(42)	(7)	(293)	(289)
Gross amount receivable from currency derivatives	11,589	458	2,204	495	14,746	14,553
Gross amount payable from currency derivatives	(11,370)	(489)	(2,435)	(550)	(14,844)	(14,662)
Net derivatives	**43**	**(55)**	**(270)**	**(68)**	**(350)**	**(357)**
Net financial position						**(13,009)**
Of which derivatives under cash flow hedges (b)	(105)	(29)	(42)	(7)	(183)	(180)

(a)   Commercial paper of CHF 3571 million and bonds of CHF 76 million have maturities of less than three months.

(b)   The periods when the cash flow hedges affect the income statement do not differ significantly from the maturities disclosed above.

Extract 53.15: Volkswagen Aktiengesellschaft (2014)

Notes to the Consolidated Financial Statements [extract]

34.   Financial risk management and financial instruments [extract]

3.   LIQUIDITY RISK [extract]

The solvency and liquidity of the Volkswagen Group are ensured at all times by rolling liquidity planning, a liquidity reserve in the form of cash, confirmed credit lines and globally available debt issuance programs.

Local cash funds in certain countries (e.g. Brazil, Argentina, Ukraine, Malaysia, India and Taiwan) are only available to the Group for cross-border transactions subject to exchange controls. There are no significant restrictions over and above these.

The following overview shows the contractual undiscounted cash flows from financial instruments.

MATURITY ANALYSIS OF UNDISCOUNTED CASH FLOWS FROM FINANCIAL INSTRUMENTS

€ million	under one year	Remaining contractual maturities within one to five years	over five years	2014
Put options and compensation rights granted to noncontrolling interest shareholders	3,185	–	–	3,185
Financial liabilities	67,634	63,926	12,011	142,941
Trade payables	19,526	4	–	19,530
Other financial liabilities	4,652	1,470	94	6,216
Derivatives	61,623	51,265	207	113,094
	156,619	116,034	12,312	284,965

When calculating cash outflows related to put options and compensation rights, it was assumed that shares would be tendered at the earliest possible repayment date.

Derivatives comprise both cash flows from derivative financial instruments with negative fair values and cash flows from derivatives with positive fair values for which gross settlement has been agreed. The cash outflows from derivatives for which gross settlement has been agreed are matched in part by cash inflows. These cash inflows are not reported in the maturity analysis. If these cash inflows were also recognized, the cash outflows presented would be substantially lower.

The cash outflows from irrevocable credit commitments are presented in note 38, classified by contractual maturities.

The maximum potential liability under financial guarantees amounted to €674 million as of December 31, 2014. Financial guarantees are assumed to be due immediately in all cases. They relate primarily to guarantees.

Chapter 53

Extract 53.16: The Royal Bank of Scotland Group plc (2014)

Notes on the consolidated accounts [extract]

12.   Financial instruments – maturity analysis [extracts]

Assets and liabilities by contractual cash flow maturity [extract]

The tables below show the contractual undiscounted cash flows receivable and payable, up to a period of 20 years, including future receipts and payments of interest of financial assets and liabilities by contractual maturity.

Financial liabilities are included at the earliest date on which the counterparty can require repayment, regardless of whether or not such early repayment results in a penalty. If the repayment of a financial instrument is triggered by, or is subject to, specific criteria such as market price hurdles being reached, the asset is included in the time band that contains the latest date on which it can be repaid, regardless of early repayment.

The liability is included in the time band that contains the earliest possible date on which the conditions could be fulfilled, without considering the probability of the conditions being met.

For example, if a structured note is automatically prepaid when an equity index exceeds a certain level, the cash outflow will be included in the less than three months period, whatever the level of the index at the year end. The settlement date of debt securities in issue, issued by certain securitisation vehicles consolidated by RBS, depends on when cash flows are received from the securitised assets. Where these assets are prepayable, the timing of the cash outflow relating to securities assumes that each asset will be prepaid at the earliest possible date. As the repayments of assets and liabilities are linked, the repayment of assets in securitisations is shown on the earliest date that the asset can be prepaid, as this is the basis used for liabilities.

The principal amounts of financial assets and liabilities that are repayable after 20 years or where the counterparty has no right to repayment of the principal are excluded from the table, as are interest payments after 20 years.

Held-for-trading assets of £498.2 billion (2013 - £452.1 billion; 2012 - £666.5 billion) and liabilities of £477.1 billion (2013 - £423.3 billion; 2012 - £628.2 billion) have been excluded from the following tables in view of their short term nature.

2014	0-3 months £m	3-12 months £m	1-3 years £m	3-5 years £m	5-10 years £m	10-20 years £m
Liabilities by contractual maturity						
Deposits by banks	8,287	754	793	8	575	140
Debt securities in issue	2,591	7,585	12,952	8,536	8,897	1,926
Subordinated liabilities	1,243	2,731	3,045	4,365	13,394	3,698
Settlement balances and other liabilities	6,295	5	4	–	–	–
Total maturing liabilities	18,416	11,075	16,794	12,909	22,866	5,764
Customer accounts	328,158	7,884	3,170	1,082	114	23
Derivatives held for hedging	140	348	789	543	949	1,010
	346,714	19,307	20,753	14,534	23,929	6,797
Maturity gap	82,122	(4,772)	(11,561)	(8,179)	(16,748)	(3,162)
Cumulative maturity gap	82,122	77,350	65,789	57,610	40,862	37,700
Guarantees and commitments – notional amounts						
Guarantees	16,721	–	–	–	–	–
Commitments	212,777	–	–	–	–	–
	229,498	–	–	–	–	–

5.2.4.C   Management of associated liquidity risk

In addition to the maturity analyses for financial liabilities, the entity should provide a description of how it manages the liquidity risk inherent in those analyses. *[IFRS 7.39(c)].*

These disclosures are, in effect, intended to 'reconcile' the maturity analyses which are prepared on a worst case scenario notion (see 5.2.4.B above) with how an entity actually manages liquidity risk (see 5.2.4.A above).[14]

It is emphasised that a maturity analysis of financial assets held for managing liquidity risk (e.g. financial assets that are readily saleable or expected to generate cash inflows to meet cash outflows on financial liabilities) is required if that information is necessary to enable users of financial statements to evaluate the nature and extent of the entity's liquidity risk. *[IFRS 7.B11E, BC58D]*. IFRS 7 does not specify the basis on which such an analysis should be provided and in practice they are often prepared on the basis of expected rather than contractual maturities as this is considered more relevant information.

Other factors that might be considered when making this disclosure include, but are not limited to, whether the entity: *[IFRS 7.B11F]*

- has committed borrowing facilities (e.g. commercial paper facilities) or other lines of credit (e.g. stand-by credit facilities) that it can access to meet liquidity needs;
- holds deposits at central banks to meet liquidity needs;
- has very diverse funding sources;
- has significant concentrations of liquidity risk in either its assets or its funding sources;
- has internal control processes and contingency plans for managing liquidity risk;
- has instruments that include accelerated repayment terms (e.g. on the downgrade of the entity's credit rating);
- has instruments that could require the posting of collateral (e.g. margin calls for derivatives);
- has instruments that allow the entity to choose whether it settles its financial liabilities by delivering cash (or another financial asset) or by delivering its own shares; or
- has instruments that are subject to master netting agreements.

5.2.4.D Puttable financial instruments classified as equity

Certain puttable financial instruments that meet the definition of financial liabilities are classified as equity instruments (see Chapter 44 at 4.6). In spite of this classification, the IASB recognises that these instruments give rise to liquidity risk and consequently requires the following disclosures about them: *[IAS 1.136A]*

- summary quantitative data about the amount classified as equity;
- the entity's objectives, policies and processes for managing its obligation to repurchase or redeem the instruments when required to do so by the instrument holders, including any changes from the previous period;
- the expected cash outflow on redemption or repurchase of that class of financial instruments; and
- information about how the expected cash outflow on redemption or repurchase was determined.

5.2.5   *Market risk*

IFRS 7 requires entities to provide disclosure of their sensitivity to market risk in one of two ways which are set out at 5.2.5.A and 5.2.5.B below. The sensitivity analyses should cover the whole of an entity's business, but different types of sensitivity analysis may be provided for different classes of financial instruments. *[IFRS 7.B21]*. This is considered by the IASB to be simpler and more suitable than the disclosure of terms and conditions of financial instruments previously required by IAS 32 and for which there is no direct equivalent within IFRS 7. *[IFRS 7.BC59]*.

No sensitivity analysis is required for financial instruments that an entity classifies as equity instruments. Such instruments are not remeasured so that neither profit or loss nor equity will be affected by the equity price risk of those instruments. *[IFRS 7.B28]*.

5.2.5.A   *'Basic' sensitivity analysis*

Except where the disclosures set out at 5.2.5.B below are provided, entities should disclose: *[IFRS 7.40]*

- a sensitivity analysis for each type of market risk to which the entity is exposed at the reporting date, showing how profit or loss and equity would have been affected by changes in the relevant risk variable that were reasonably possible at that date.

  The sensitivity of profit or loss (which arises, for example, from instruments measured at fair value through profit or loss and, where IFRS 9 is not applied, impairments of available-for-sale financial assets) should be disclosed separately from the sensitivity of equity (which arises, for example, from instruments classified as available for sale or, where IFRS 9 is applied, from investments in equity instruments whose changes in fair value are presented in other comprehensive income). *[IFRS 7.B27]*.

  The term 'profit or loss' is used in IAS 1 to mean profit after tax. Therefore, it might well be argued that the amounts disclosed should take account of any related tax effects, a view corroborated by the illustrative disclosures in the implementation guidance to IFRS 7 (see Example 53.10 below). However, as noted below, the application guidance suggests this requirement should (and the implementation guidance might suggest it could) be met by disclosing the impact on interest expense, a pre-tax measure of profit. Given this conflicting guidance, it is difficult to say that a pre-tax approach fails to comply with the standard and, in practice, both approaches are seen.

  Where a post-tax figure is disclosed, it will not always be straightforward to determine the related tax effects, especially for a multinational group, and it may be appropriate to use the guidance in Chapter 30 at 10 which deals with the allocation of income tax between profit or loss, other comprehensive income and equity.

  This requirement focuses exclusively on accounting sensitivity, and does not include market risk sensitivities that do not directly impact profit and loss or equity, e.g. interest rate risk arising on fixed rate financial assets held at amortised cost. In December 2008, the IASB considered encouraging entities to discuss the effect of changes in the relevant risk variable on economic value not manifest in profit and loss or equity, but decided not to;[15]

- the methods and assumptions used in preparing the sensitivity analysis; and
- changes from the previous period in the methods and assumptions used, and the reasons for such changes.

The standard contains a reminder of the general guidance at 3.1 above and explains that an entity should decide how it aggregates information to display the overall picture without combining information with different characteristics about exposures to risks from significantly different economic environments. For example, an entity that trades financial instruments might disclose this information separately for financial instruments held for trading and those not held for trading. Similarly, an entity would not aggregate its exposure to market risks from areas of hyperinflation with its exposure to the same market risks from areas of very low inflation. However, an entity that has exposure to only one type of market risk in only one economic environment, would not show disaggregated information. *[IFRS 7.B17]*.

Risk variables that are relevant to disclosing market risk include, but are not limited to: *[IFRS 7.IG32]*

- the yield curve of market interest rates.

    It may be necessary to consider both parallel and non-parallel shifts in the yield curve;

- foreign exchange rates.

    The standard requires a sensitivity analysis to be disclosed for each currency to which an entity has significant exposure; *[IFRS 7.B24]*

- prices of equity instruments; and
- market prices of commodities.

When disclosing how profit or loss and equity would have been affected by changes in the relevant risk variable, there is no requirement to determine what the profit or loss for the period would have been if the relevant risk variables had been different during the reporting period. The requirement is subtly different because the effect that is disclosed assumes that a reasonably possible change in the relevant risk variable had occurred *at the reporting date* and had been applied to the risk exposures in existence *at that date*. For example, if an entity has a floating rate liability at the reporting date, the entity would disclose the effect on profit or loss (i.e. interest expense) for the current year if interest rates had varied by reasonably possible amounts. Further, this disclosure is not required for each change within a range of reasonably possible changes, only at the limits of the reasonably possible range. *[IFRS 7.B18]*. The following example illustrates how this requirement might be applied – for simplicity, tax effects are ignored.

Example 53.10:   Illustration of how sensitivity disclosures can be determined

Company X, which has the euro as its functional currency, is party to the following instruments at 31 December 2016, X's reporting date:

- a €100m floating rate loan;
- a forward contract to sell US$10m in July 2017 that is designated in an effective hedge of a highly probable forecast sale that is denominated in US dollars;
- a short-term loan of £10m made to a related party;
- an interest rate swap that is not designated as a hedge;
- investments in fixed rate debt securities that are classified as held-to-maturity
- investments in similar securities that are classified as available-for-sale; and
- investments in a portfolio of US equities with a fair value of US$50m.

Floating rate loan

Changes in interest rates will result in this instrument impacting on X's profit or loss. If X concludes that a reasonably possible change in interest rates is 50 basis points (0.5%), €0.5m [€100m × 0.5%] would be included in the amount disclosed as the impact on profit or loss of this reasonably possible change.

Forward contract

Changes in exchange rates will have an impact on the fair value (and carrying value) of this instrument, but this would be recognised in other comprehensive income, not profit or loss (assuming ineffectiveness is insignificant). If a reasonably possibly change in exchange rates would change the value of the contract by €0.3m, this would be included in the amount disclosed as the impact on equity of this reasonably possible change.

Foreign currency loan

Changes in spot exchange rates will have an impact on the carrying amount of this asset with changes recognised in profit or loss as a result of the application of IAS 21 – *The Effects of Changes in Foreign Exchange Rates*. If a reasonably possible change in the exchange rate would alter the carrying value of the contract by €1.0m, this would be included in the amount disclosed as the impact on profit or loss of this reasonably possible change.

If the loan were made to a subsidiary of X that had sterling as its functional currency, the loan itself would eliminate on consolidation but the impact of retranslating it into euros in X's own financial statements would remain in consolidated profit or loss. Therefore, in these circumstances, the loan would still be included in the sensitivity analysis for X's consolidated financial statements.

Interest rate swap

Changes in interest rates will have an impact on the fair value (and carrying value) of this instrument and such changes would be recognised in profit or loss. If a reasonably possible change of 50 basis points in interest rates would change the value of the contract by €0.4m, this would be included in the amount disclosed as the impact on profit or loss of this reasonably possible change.

Fixed rate debt securities

Changes in interest rates will have an impact on the fair value of all these instruments. However, because those classified as held-to-maturity are measured at amortised cost, the carrying amount only of those that are classified as available-for-sale will change as interest rates move and such change will normally be recognised in other comprehensive income. Therefore, if a reasonably possible 50 basis point change in interest rates would change the fair value of each group of instruments by €0.5m, only the amount in respect of the available-for-sale securities would be included in the sensitivity disclosure as an impact on equity. Of course there would be nothing to preclude disclosure, as additional information (if considered relevant), of the sensitivity of the fair value of held-to-maturity investments to changes in interest rates.

US equity securities

The impact of a reasonably possible change in the market prices of these securities should be included in the amount disclosed as X's sensitivity to equity price risk. Changes in exchange rates might be considered to impact the fair value of these investments. However, as noted at (c)(i) at 5 above, financial instruments that are non-monetary items do not give rise to foreign currency risk for the purposes of IFRS 7 – essentially the foreign currency risk is seen as part of the market price risk associated with such instruments. Therefore, X should take no account of these investments when disclosing its sensitivity to changes in the euro/US dollar exchange rate. Nevertheless, this information may be provided as additional disclosure where it is considered relevant.

Relevant risk variables for the purpose of this disclosure might include: *[IFRS 7.IG33]*

- prevailing market interest rates, for interest-sensitive financial instruments such as a variable-rate loan; or
- currency rates and interest rates, for foreign currency financial instruments such as foreign currency bonds.

For interest rate risk, the sensitivity analysis might show separately the effect of a change in market interest rates on:

- interest income and expense;
- other line items of profit or loss (such as trading gains and losses); and
- when applicable, equity.

An entity might disclose a sensitivity analysis for interest rate risk for each currency in which the entity has material exposures to interest rate risk. *[IFRS 7.IG34]*.

In determining what a reasonably possible change in the relevant risk variable is, the economic environment(s) in which the entity operates and the time frame over which it is making the assessment should be considered. A reasonably possible change should not include remote or 'worst case' scenarios or 'stress tests'. Moreover, if the rate of change in the underlying risk variable is stable, the chosen reasonably possible change in the risk variable need not be altered.

For example, assume that interest rates are 5 percent and an entity determines that a fluctuation in interest rates of ±50 basis points is reasonably possible. It would disclose the effect on profit or loss and equity if interest rates were to change to 4.5 percent or 5.5 percent. In the next period, interest rates have increased to 5.5 percent. The entity continues to believe that interest rates may fluctuate by ±50 basis points (i.e. that the rate of change in interest rates is stable). The entity would disclose the effect on profit or loss and equity if interest rates were to change to 5 percent or 6 percent. The entity would not be required to revise its assessment that interest rates might reasonably fluctuate by ±50 basis points, unless there is evidence that interest rates have become significantly more volatile. *[IFRS 7.B19]*.

However, when market conditions change significantly, for example as occurred in many markets in the second half of 2008, an entity's assessment of what constitutes a reasonably possible change should be reassessed.[16]

The time frame over which a reasonably possible change should be assessed is defined by the period until these disclosures will next be presented. This will normally coincide with the next annual reporting period, *[IFRS 7.B19]*, although in some jurisdictions such information may be included in interim reports.

Because the factors affecting market risk will vary according to the specific circumstances of each entity, the appropriate range to be considered in providing a sensitivity analysis of market risk will also vary for each entity and for each type of market risk. *[IFRS 7.IG35].*

Where an entity has exposure to other price risk, it might disclose the effect of a decrease in a specified stock market index, commodity price, or other risk variable. For example, if residual value guarantees that are financial instruments are given, the disclosure could include an increase or decrease in the value of the assets to which the guarantee applies. *[IFRS 7.B25].*

The following example from the implementation guidance illustrates the type of disclosure that might be provided.

Example 53.11:   Illustrative disclosure of sensitivity analyses

Interest rate risk

At 31 December 2016, if interest rates at that date had been 10 basis points lower with all other variables held constant, post-tax profit for the year would have been €1.7 million (2015: €2.4 million) higher, arising mainly as a result of lower interest expense on variable borrowings, and other comprehensive income would have been €2.8 million (2015: €3.2 million) higher, arising mainly as a result of an increase in the fair value of fixed rate financial assets classified as available-for-sale.

If interest rates had been 10 basis points higher, with all other variables held constant, post-tax profit would have been €1.5 million (2015: €2.1 million) lower, arising mainly as a result of higher interest expense on variable borrowings, and other comprehensive income would have been €3.0 million (2015: €3.4 million) lower, arising mainly as a result of a decrease in the fair value of fixed rate financial assets classified as available-for-sale.

Profit is more sensitive to interest rate decreases than increases because of borrowings with capped interest rates. The sensitivity is lower in 2016 than in 2015 because of a reduction in outstanding borrowings that has occurred as the entity's debt has matured (see note X).

Foreign currency exchange rate risk

At 31 December 2016, if the euro had weakened 10 percent against the US dollar with all other variables held constant, post-tax profit for the year would have been €2.8 million (2015: €6.4 million) lower, and other comprehensive income would have been €1.2 million (2015: €1.1 million) higher.

Conversely, if the euro had strengthened 10 percent against the US dollar with all other variables held constant, post-tax profit would have been €2.8 million (2015: €6.4 million) higher, and other comprehensive income would have been €1.2 million (2015: €1.1 million) lower.

The lower foreign currency exchange rate sensitivity in profit in 2016 compared with 2015 is attributable to a reduction in foreign currency denominated debt. Equity is more sensitive in 2016 than in 2015 because of the increased use of hedges of foreign currency purchases, offset by the reduction in foreign currency debt. *[IFRS 7.IG36].*

The following extracts from the financial statements of Hunting illustrates how one company has addressed this disclosure requirement in respect of certain of its interest rate and foreign currency exposures. Extract 53.18 (BP) at 5.2.5.B below contains another example, this time for its exposure to embedded derivatives.

Extract 53.17: Hunting plc (2014)

Notes to the Financial Statements [extract]

31.   Financial Instruments: Sensitivity Analysis [extract]

The following sensitivity analysis is intended to illustrate the sensitivity to changes in market variables on the Group's and Company's financial instruments and show the impact on profit or loss and shareholders' equity. Financial instruments affected by market risk include cash and cash equivalents, borrowings, deposits and derivative financial instruments. The sensitivity analysis relates to the position as at 31 December 2014.

The analysis excludes the impact of movements in market variables on the carrying value of pension and other post-retirement obligations, provisions and on the non-financial assets and liabilities of foreign operations.

The following assumptions have been made in calculating the sensitivity analysis:

- Foreign exchange rate and interest rate sensitivities have an asymmetric impact on the Group's results, that is, an increase in rates does not result in the same amount of movement as a decrease in rates.

- For floating rate assets and liabilities, the amount of asset or liability outstanding at the balance sheet date is assumed to be outstanding for the whole year.

- Fixed rate financial instruments that are carried at amortised cost are not subject to interest rate risk for the purpose of this analysis.

- The carrying values of financial assets and liabilities carried at amortised cost do not change as interest rates change.

Positive figures represent an increase in profit or equity.

(i) Interest Rate Sensitivity

The sensitivity rate of 0.25% (2013 – 0.25%) for US interest rates represents management's assessment of a reasonably possible change, based on historical volatility and a review of analysts' research and banks' expectations of future interest rates.

Group

The post-tax impact on the income statement, with all other variables held constant, at 31 December, for an increase of 0.25% (2013 – 0.25%) in US interest rates, is to reduce profits by $0.2m (2013 – $0.5m). If US interest rates were to decrease by 0.25% (2013 – 0.25%), then the post-tax impact on the income statement would be to increase profits by $0.2m (2013 – $0.5m). The movements arise on US dollar denominated borrowings. There is no impact on other comprehensive income ("OCI") for a change in interest rates.

(ii) Foreign Exchange Rate Sensitivity

The sensitivity rate of 10% (2013 – 10%) for Sterling and Canadian dollar exchange rates represents management's assessment of a reasonably possible change, based on historical volatility and a review of analysts' research and banks' expectations of future foreign exchange rates.

The table below shows the post-tax impact for the year of a reasonable change in foreign exchange rates, with all other variables held constant, at 31 December.

	2014		2013	
	Income statement	OCI	Income statement	OCI
	$m	$m	$m	$m
Sterling exchange rates +10% (2013: +10%)	(0.5)	1.6	(12.6)	18.6
Sterling exchange rates −10% (2013: −10%)	0.9	(2.0)	2.1	(22.4)
Canadian dollar exchange rates +10% (2013: +10%)	(0.8)	(5.1)	(0.1)	(1.8)
Canadian dollar exchange rates −10% (2013: −10%)	0.9	5.5	0.1	2.2

The movements in the income statement arise from cash, bank overdrafts, intra-group balances and accrued expenses where the functional currency of the entity is different from the currency that the monetary items are denominated in.

The movements in OCI in 2014 arise from net Sterling and Canadian dollar borrowings designated in a hedge of net investments in foreign subsidiaries and from US and Canadian dollar denominated loans that have been recognised as part of the Group's net investment in foreign subsidiaries. The movements in OCI in 2013 arise from Sterling and Canadian dollar denominated loans that have been recognised as part of the Group's net investment in foreign subsidiaries.

5.2.5.B   *Value-at-risk and similar analyses*

Where an entity prepares a sensitivity analysis, such as value-at-risk, that reflects interdependencies between risk variables (e.g. interest rates and exchange rates) and uses it to manage financial risks, it may disclose that analysis in place of the information specified at 5.2.5.A above. *[IFRS 7.41]*. If this disclosure is given, the effects on profit or loss and equity at 5.2.5.A above need not be given. *[IFRS 7.BC61]*.

In these cases the following should also be disclosed: *[IFRS 7.41]*

• an explanation of the method used in preparing such a sensitivity analysis, and of the main parameters and assumptions underlying the data provided; and

• an explanation of the objective of the method used and of limitations that may result in the information not fully reflecting the fair value of the assets and liabilities involved.

This applies even if such a methodology measures only the potential for loss and does not measure the potential for gain. Such an entity might comply with the disclosure requirements above by detailing the type of value-at-risk model used (e.g. whether the model relies on Monte Carlo simulations), an explanation about how the model works and the main assumptions (e.g. the holding period and confidence level). Entities might also disclose the historical observation period and weightings applied to observations within that period, an explanation of how options are dealt with in the calculations, and which volatilities and correlations (or, alternatively, Monte Carlo probability distribution simulations) are used. *[IFRS 7.B20]*.

The basic sensitivity analysis considered at 5.2.5.A above incorporates only the effects of financial instruments and other contracts within the scope of IFRS 7. In contrast, value-at-risk and similar analyses can incorporate the effects of items outside the scope of IFRS 7, for example trading inventories, own use contracts and insurance contracts. This is because the standard requires entities to disclose the analysis actually used in the management of the business which will often include such items.

It has been suggested that disclosure of potential losses due to stress conditions would be of greater use than the disclosure requirements for value-at-risk and similar methodologies that do not contemplate extraordinary market movements. However, in December 2008, the IASB noted this would be inconsistent with the 'basic' sensitivity analysis (see A above) and decided not to add such a requirement to IFRS 7.[17]

BP provides the following market risk disclosures which includes the value-at-risk limit it uses to manage that risk.

Extract 53.18: BP p.l.c. (2014)

Notes on financial statements [extract]
27 Financial instruments and financial risk factors [extract]
(a) Market risk [extract]

Market risk is the risk or uncertainty arising from possible market price movements and their impact on the future performance of a business. The primary commodity price risks that the group is exposed to include oil, natural gas and power prices that could adversely affect the value of the group's financial assets, liabilities or expected future cash flows. The group enters into derivatives in a well-established entrepreneurial trading operation. In addition, the group has developed a control framework aimed at managing the volatility inherent in certain of its natural business exposures. In accordance with the control framework the group enters into various transactions using derivatives for risk management purposes.

The major components of market risk are commodity price risk, foreign currency exchange risk and interest rate risk, each of which is discussed below.
(i) Commodity price risk

The group's integrated supply and trading function uses conventional financial and commodity instruments and physical cargoes and pipeline positions available in the related commodity markets. Oil and natural gas swaps, options and futures are used to mitigate price risk. Power trading is undertaken using a combination of over-the-counter forward contracts and other derivative contracts, including options and futures. This activity is on both a standalone basis and in conjunction with gas derivatives in relation to gas-generated power margin. In addition, NGLs are traded around certain US inventory locations using over-the-counter forward contracts in conjunction with over-the-counter swaps, options and physical inventories.

The group measures market risk exposure arising from its trading positions in liquid periods using value-at-risk techniques. These techniques make a statistical assessment of the market risk arising from possible future changes in market prices over a one-day holding period. The value-at-risk measure is supplemented by stress testing. Trading activity occurring in liquid periods is subject to value-at-risk limits for each trading activity and for this trading activity in total. The board has delegated a limit of $100 million value at risk in support of this trading activity. Alternative measures are used to monitor exposures which are outside liquid periods and which cannot be actively risk managed.

5.2.5.C Other market risk disclosures

When the sensitivity analyses discussed at 5.2.5.A and 5.2.5.B above are unrepresentative of a risk inherent in a financial instrument, that fact should be disclosed together with the reason for believing the sensitivity analyses are unrepresentative. *[IFRS 7.42].*

This can occur when the year-end exposure does not reflect the exposure during the year *[IFRS 7.42]* or a financial instrument contains terms and conditions whose effects are not apparent from the sensitivity analysis, e.g. options that remain out of (or in) the money for the chosen change in the risk variable. *[IFRS 7.IG37(a)].* Additional disclosures in this second case might include:

- the terms and conditions of the financial instrument (e.g. the options);
- the effect on profit or loss if the term or condition were met (i.e. if the options were exercised); and
- a description of how the risk is hedged.

For example, an entity may acquire a zero-cost interest rate collar that includes an out-of-the-money leveraged written option (e.g. the entity pays ten times the amount of the difference between a specified interest rate floor and the current market interest rate if that current rate is below the floor). The entity may regard the collar as an inexpensive economic hedge against a reasonably possible increase in interest rates. However, an unexpectedly large decrease in interest rates might trigger payments under the written option that, because of the leverage, might be significantly larger than the benefit of lower interest rates. Neither the fair value of the collar nor a sensitivity analysis based on reasonably possible changes in market variables would indicate this exposure. In this case, the entity might provide the additional information described above. *[IFRS 7.IG38]*.

Where financial assets are illiquid, e.g. when there is a low volume of transactions in similar assets and it is difficult to find a counterparty, additional disclosures might be required, *[IFRS 7.IG37(b)]*, for example the reasons for the lack of liquidity and how the risk is hedged. *[IFRS 7.IG39]*.

A large holding of a financial asset that, if sold in its entirety, would be sold at a discount or premium to the quoted market price for a smaller holding could also require additional disclosure. *[IFRS 7.IG37(c)]*. This might include: *[IFRS 7.IG40]*

- the nature of the security (e.g. entity name);
- the extent of holding (e.g. 15 percent of the issued shares);
- the effect on profit or loss; and
- how the entity hedges the risk.

5.2.6   Concentrations of risk

Concentrations of risk should be disclosed if not otherwise apparent from the disclosures made to comply with the requirements set out at 5.2.1 to 5.2.5 above. *[IFRS 7.34(c)]*. This should include:

- a description of how management determines concentrations;
- a description of the shared characteristic that identifies each concentration (for example, counterparty, geographical area, currency or market).

  For example, the shared characteristic may refer to geographical distribution of counterparties by groups of countries, individual countries or regions within countries; *[IFRS 7.IG19]* and
- the amount of the risk exposure associated with all financial instruments sharing that characteristic.

Concentrations of risk arise from financial instruments that have similar characteristics and are affected similarly by changes in economic or other conditions. It is emphasised that the identification of concentrations of risk requires judgement taking into account the circumstances of the entity. *[IFRS 7.B8]*. For example, they may arise from:

- Industry sectors.

  If an entity's counterparties are concentrated in one or more industry sectors (such as retail or wholesale), it would disclose separately exposure to risks arising from each concentration of counterparties;

- Credit rating or other measure of credit quality.

  If an entity's counterparties are concentrated in one or more credit qualities (such as secured loans or unsecured loans) or in one or more credit ratings (such as investment grade or speculative grade), it would disclose separately exposure to risks arising from each concentration of counterparties;

- Geographical distribution.

  If an entity's counterparties are concentrated in one or more geographical markets (such as Asia or Europe), it would disclose separately exposure to risks arising from each concentration of counterparties; and

- A limited number of individual counterparties or groups of closely related counterparties.

Similar principles apply to identifying concentrations of other risks, including liquidity risk and market risk. For example, concentrations of liquidity risk may arise from the repayment terms of financial liabilities, sources of borrowing facilities or reliance on a particular market in which to realise liquid assets. Concentrations of foreign exchange risk may arise if an entity has a significant net open position in a single foreign currency, or aggregate net open positions in several currencies that tend to move together. *[IFRS 7.IG18]*.

5.2.7 *Operational risk*

In developing IFRS 7, the IASB considered whether disclosure of information about operational risk should be required by the standard. However, the definition and measurement of operational risk were considered to be in their infancy and were not necessarily related to financial instruments. Also, such disclosures were believed to be more appropriately located outside the financial statements. Consequently, this issue was deferred for consideration in the management commentary project (see Chapter 3 at 2.3). *[IFRS 7.BC65]*.

5.2.8 *Capital disclosures*

The IASB considers that the level of an entity's capital and how it is managed are important factors for users of financial statements to consider in assessing the risk profile of an entity and its ability to withstand unexpected adverse events. It might also affect an entity's ability to pay dividends. Consequently, ED 7 contained proposed disclosures about capital. *[IAS 1.BC86]*.

However, some commentators questioned the relevance of the capital disclosures in a standard dealing with disclosures relating to financial instruments and the IASB noted that an entity's capital does not relate solely to financial instruments and, thus, they have more general relevance. Accordingly, whilst these disclosures were retained, they were included in IAS 1, rather than IFRS 7. *[IAS 1.BC88]*. Those disclosures required by IAS 1 are dealt with in Chapter 3 at 5.4.

Chapter 53

6   TRANSFERS OF FINANCIAL ASSETS

The objective of these requirements, which were introduced into IFRS 7 in October 2010, is that entities should disclose information that enables users of its financial statements: *[IFRS 7.42B]*

(a)   to understand the relationship between transferred financial assets that are not derecognised in their entirety and the associated liabilities; and

(b)   to evaluate the nature of, and risks associated with, the entity's continuing involvement in derecognised financial assets.

The standard specifies detailed disclosure requirements to support objectives (a) and (b) which are discussed below at 6.2 and 6.3 below respectively. However, an entity should disclose any additional information, over and above that specified by IFRS 7, that it considers necessary to meet these objectives. *[IFRS 7.42H]*.

Rather unusually, the standard specifies that these disclosures should be presented in a single note to the financial statements. *[IFRS 7.42A]*. Presumably this is to prevent entities 'hiding' these disclosures by having the detailed information scattered across a number of notes.

These requirements supplement the other requirements of IFRS 7 and apply when an entity transfers financial assets. They apply for all transferred financial assets that are not derecognised, and for any continuing involvement in a transferred asset, that exist at the reporting date, irrespective of when the related transfer occurred. *[IFRS 7.42A]*.

6.1   The meaning of 'transfer'

For the purposes of applying the disclosure requirements in this section, an entity transfers all or a part of a financial asset (the transferred financial asset) if, and only if, it either: *[IFRS 7.42A]*

(a)   transfers the contractual rights to receive the cash flows of that financial asset; or

(b)   retains the contractual rights to receive the cash flows of that financial asset, but assumes a contractual obligation to pay the cash flows to one or more recipients in an arrangement.

The transactions encompassed by (a) should be the same ones that would be regarded as transfers under the derecognition requirements of IAS 39 or IFRS 9 (see Chapter 50 at 3.5.1).

However, the transactions falling within (b) represent a larger group than those which would be regarded as 'pass-through arrangements' for the purposes of those requirements (see Chapter 50 at 3.5.2).

6.2   Transferred financial assets that are not derecognised in their entirety

Financial assets may have been transferred in such a way that part or all of the financial assets do not qualify for derecognition. This might occur if:

- the contractual rights to the cash flows have been transferred but substantially all risks and rewards are retained, e.g. a sale and repurchase agreement, so that the assets are not derecognised;

- the rights to the cash flows have been transferred, the risks and rewards partially transferred and control of the assets has been retained so that the assets continue to be recognised to the extent of the entity's continuing involvement; or

- an obligation has been assumed to pay the cash flows from the asset to other parties but in a way that does not meet the 'pass-through' requirements (see Chapter 50 at 3.5.2).

  Where securitisations and similar arrangements do not meet the pass-through requirements, careful analysis will be required to determine whether they are within the scope of these disclosures. If such a transaction is not considered to be within the scope of these requirements, the disclosures about collateral discussed at 4.4.6 above are likely to be applicable.

The following disclosures should be given for each class of transferred financial assets that are not derecognised in their entirety: *[IFRS 7.42D]*

(a)   the nature of the transferred assets;

(b)   the nature of the risks and rewards of ownership to which the reporting entity is exposed;

(c)   a description of the nature of the relationship between the transferred assets and the associated liabilities, including restrictions arising from the transfer on the reporting entity's use of the transferred assets;

(d)   when the counterparty (counterparties) to the associated liabilities has (have) recourse only to the transferred assets, a schedule that sets out the fair value of the transferred assets, the fair value of the associated liabilities and the net position, i.e. the difference between the fair value of the transferred assets and the associated liabilities;

(e)   when the reporting entity continues to recognise all of the transferred assets, the carrying amounts of the transferred assets and the associated liabilities; and

(f)   when the reporting entity continues to recognise the assets to the extent of its continuing involvement, the total carrying amount of the original assets before the transfer, the carrying amount of the assets that the entity continues to recognise, and the carrying amount of the associated liabilities.

These disclosures should be given at each reporting date at which the entity continues to recognise the transferred financial assets, regardless of when the transfers occurred. *[IFRS 7.B32]*.

The above requirements clearly apply to transfers of entire financial assets where the transferred assets continue to be recognised in their entirety. They also apply to transfers of entire assets where the transferred assets are recognised to the extent of the transferor's continuing involvement.

However, the derecognition criteria in IAS 39 and IFRS 9 are sometimes applied to specified parts of a financial asset (or group of similar financial assets). For example, an entity might transfer a proportion of an entire financial asset, such as 50% of all cash flows on a bond. Similarly, it may transfer specified cash flows from a financial asset, such as all the coupon payments or only the principal payment on a bond, commonly known as an interest strip and principal strip respectively. Further, if the derecognition criteria are met, it is possible for the specified parts of the financial asset to be derecognised whilst the remainder of the asset remains on the statement of financial position (see Chapter 50, particularly at 3.3). Should the disclosure requirements in this section be applied to such transfers?

Whilst the financial asset has not been derecognised in its entirety, it will normally be the case that the asset has not been transferred in its entirety either. Therefore, it might seem more appropriate for the disclosure requirements to follow the way in which the derecognition requirements of IAS 39 or IFRS 9 have been applied, i.e. they should focus on the specified part of the asset that has been transferred, not necessarily the entire asset. Nevertheless, in the absence of specific guidance, we believe the alternative view could be supported too.

In our view these disclosure requirements do not apply where an entity provides non-cash financial assets as collateral to a third party and the transferee's right to control the asset (normally evidenced by its ability to resell or repledge those assets) is conditional on default of the transferor. Instead the disclosures about collateral set out at 4.4.6 above would apply.

The following example illustrates how an entity that has not adopted IFRS 9 might meet the quantitative disclosure requirements in (d) and (e) above. *[IFRS 7.IG40C].*

Example 53.12:   Quantitative disclosures for transferred assets not fully derecognised

	Financial assets at fair value through profit or loss		Loans and receivables		Available-for-sale financial assets
	CU million		CU million		CU million
	Trading securities	Derivatives	Mortgages	Consumer loans	Equity investments
Carrying amount of assets	X	X	X	X	X
Carrying amount of associated liabilities	(X)	(X)	(X)	(X)	(X)
For those liabilities that have recourse only to the transferred assets:					
Fair value of assets	X	X	X	X	X
Fair value of associated liabilities	(X)	(X)	(X)	(X)	(X)
Net position	X	X	X	X	X

Very similar disclosures could be given by an entity that has adopted IFRS 9, although the asset classifications would be different. *[IFRS 7.IG40B].*

6.3 Transferred financial assets that are derecognised in their entirety

An entity may have transferred financial assets in such a way that they are derecognised in their entirety but the entity has 'continuing involvement' in those assets. Where this is the case, the additional disclosures set out at 6.3.2 below should be given. In this context, the term continuing involvement has a different meaning to that used in the derecognition requirements of IAS 39 or IFRS 9 (see Chapter 50 at 3.2 and 5.3) which is discussed at 6.3.1 below.

In practice the application of these requirements is likely to be limited given that few transfers with any form of continuing involvement (as that term is used here) will qualify for full derecognition. One example is a transfer of a readily obtainable financial asset subject to a call option that is neither deeply in the money nor deeply out of the money (see Chapter 50 at 4.2.3.A).

An entity may have derecognised financial assets under its previous GAAP, or an early version of IAS 39, in a transaction that would not have qualified for derecognition under IAS 39. Further, IFRS 1 – *First-time Adoption of International Financial Reporting Standards* – or the transitional provisions of IAS 39 mean these financial assets may remain derecognised. In our view it is not clear whether the disclosures covered in this section should be given for any remaining continuing involvement in such assets and an entity should establish an accounting policy and apply that policy consistently to all similar transactions.

6.3.1 Meaning of continuing involvement

In this context, continuing involvement arises if, as part of the transfer, the entity retains any of the contractual rights or obligations inherent in the transferred financial asset or obtains any new contractual rights or obligations relating to it. *[IFRS 7.42C]*.

For example, a financial asset transferred subject only to either (a) a deeply out of the money put option granted to the transferee or (b) a deeply out of the money call option retained by the transferor would be derecognised. This is because substantially all the risks and rewards of ownership have been transferred. *[IAS 39.AG51(g), IFRS 9.B3.2.16(g)]*. However, the put or call option would constitute continuing involvement in the asset.

Similarly, a readily obtainable asset transferred subject to a call option that is neither deeply in the money nor deeply out of the money would also be derecognised. This is because the entity has neither transferred nor retained substantially all of the risks and rewards of ownership and has not retained control. *[IAS 39.AG51(h), IFRS 9.B3.2.16(h)]*. However, the call option would constitute continuing involvement in the asset.

The following do not constitute continuing involvement for these purposes: *[IFRS 7.42C]*

(a)   normal representations and warranties relating to fraudulent transfer and concepts of reasonableness, good faith and fair dealings that could invalidate a transfer as a result of legal action;

(b)   forward, option and other contracts to reacquire the transferred financial asset for which the contract price (or exercise price) is the fair value of the transferred financial asset; or

(c)   an arrangement whereby an entity retains the contractual rights to receive the cash flows of a financial asset but assumes a contractual obligation to pay the cash flows to one or more entities in a 'pass-through arrangement' (see Chapter 50 at 3.5.2).

An entity does not have a continuing involvement in a transferred financial asset if, as part of the transfer, it neither retains any of the contractual rights or obligations inherent in the transferred financial asset nor acquires any new contractual rights or obligations relating to the transferred financial asset. Also, an entity does not have continuing involvement in a transferred financial asset if it has neither an interest in the future performance of the transferred financial asset nor a responsibility under any circumstances to make payments in respect of the transferred financial asset in the future. The term 'payment' in this context does not include cash flows of the transferred financial asset that an entity collects and is required to remit to the transferee. *[IFRS 7.B30]*.

When an entity transfers a financial asset, it may retain the right to service that financial asset for a fee, e.g. by entering into a servicing contract. As originally published IFRS 7 was unclear whether servicing rights or obligations related to derecognised financial assets represented continuing involvement for the purpose of these disclosure requirements. However, in September 2014 the IASB added application guidance to clarify its intention. This guidance is effective for periods commencing on or after 1 January 2016 and earlier application is permitted, although an entity should disclose that it has done so. However, the guidance need not be applied for any period presented that begins before the annual period for which an entity first applies that guidance. *[IFRS 7.44AA]*. In other words, comparative periods need not be restated.

The new guidance requires a servicing contract to be assessed in accordance with the more general guidance above to determine whether it gives rise to continuing involvement for the purposes of these disclosures. For example, a servicer will have continuing involvement in the transferred financial asset if the servicing fee is dependent on the amount or timing of the cash flows collected from the transferred financial asset. Similarly, the right to a fixed fee that would not be paid in full as a result of non-performance of the transferred financial asset would also represent continuing involvement. This is because the servicer has an interest in the future performance of the transferred financial asset. Any such assessment is independent of whether the fee to be received is expected to compensate the entity adequately for performing the servicing. *[IFRS 7.B31]*.

An entity might transfer a fixed rate financial asset and at the same time enter into an interest rate swap with the transferee that has the same notional amount as the transferred asset. If payments on the swap are not conditional on payments being made on the transferred financial asset and the notional of the swap is not linked to the notional amount of the loan this would not, in our view, represent continuing involvement.

The assessment of continuing involvement in a transferred financial asset should be made at the level of the reporting entity. For example, a subsidiary may transfer to an unrelated third party a financial asset in which the parent of the subsidiary has continuing involvement. In the subsidiary's stand-alone financial statements the parent's involvement should not be included in the assessment of whether the reporting entity (the subsidiary) has continuing involvement in the transferred asset. However, in the parent's consolidated financial statements, its continuing involvement (or that of another member of the group) in a financial asset transferred by its subsidiary would be included in determining whether the group has continuing involvement in the transferred asset. *[IFRS 7.B29]*.

Continuing involvement in a transferred financial asset may result from contractual provisions in the transfer agreement or in a separate agreement with the transferee or a third party entered into in connection with the transfer. *[IFRS 7.B31]*. In our view it would not encompass arrangements entered into some time after the financial asset was transferred that were not contemplated at the time of the transfer.

6.3.2　Disclosure requirements

When an entity derecognises transferred financial assets in their entirety but has continuing involvement in those assets, it should disclose, as a minimum, the following for each type of continuing involvement at each reporting date: *[IFRS 7.42E]*

(a)　the carrying amount of the assets and liabilities that are recognised in the entity's statement of financial position and represent the entity's continuing involvement in the derecognised financial assets, and the line items in which the carrying amount of those assets and liabilities are recognised;

(b)　the fair value of the assets and liabilities that represent the entity's continuing involvement in the derecognised financial assets;

(c)　the amount that best represents the entity's maximum exposure to loss from its continuing involvement in the derecognised financial assets, and information showing how the maximum exposure to loss is determined;

(d)　the undiscounted cash outflows that would or may be required to repurchase derecognised financial assets (e.g. the strike price in an option agreement) or other amounts payable to the transferee in respect of the transferred assets.

　　If the cash outflow is variable then the amount disclosed should be based on the conditions that exist at each reporting date;

(e)　a maturity analysis of the undiscounted cash outflows that would or may be required to repurchase the derecognised financial assets or other amounts payable to the transferee in respect of the transferred assets, showing the remaining contractual maturities of the entity's continuing involvement.

Chapter 53

This analysis should distinguish between cash flows that are required to be paid (e.g. forward contracts), cash flows the entity may be required to pay (e.g. written put options) and cash flows the entity might choose to pay (e.g. purchased call options). *[IFRS 7.B34]*.

Entities should use judgement to determine an appropriate number of time bands in preparing the maturity analysis. For example, it might be determined that the following maturity time bands are appropriate: *[IFRS 7.B35]*

(i)   not later than one month;

(ii)   later than one month and not later than three months;

(iii)   later than three months and not later than six months;

(iv)   later than six months and not later than one year;

(v)   later than one year and not later than three years;

(vi)   later than three years and not later than five years; and

(vii)   more than five years.

If there is a range of possible maturities, the cash flows should be included on the basis of the earliest date on which the entity can be required or is permitted to pay; *[IFRS 7.B36]* and

(f)   qualitative information that explains and supports the quantitative disclosures set out in (a) to (e) above.

This should include a description of the derecognised financial assets and the nature and purpose of the continuing involvement retained after transferring those assets. It should also include a description of the risks to which an entity is exposed, including: *[IFRS 7.B37]*

(i)   a description of how the entity manages the risk inherent in its continuing involvement in the derecognised financial assets;

(ii)   whether the entity is required to bear losses before other parties, and the ranking and amounts of losses borne by parties whose interests rank lower than the entity's interest in the asset (i.e. its continuing involvement in the asset); and

(iii)   a description of any triggers associated with obligations to provide financial support or to repurchase a transferred financial asset.

The types of continuing involvement into which these disclosures and those referred to below are analysed should be representative of the entity's exposure to risks. For example, the analysis may be given by type of financial instrument (e.g. guarantees or call options) or by type of transfer (e.g. factoring of receivables, securitisations and securities lending). *[IFRS 7.B33]*.

If an entity has more than one type of continuing involvement in respect of a particular derecognised financial asset the information above may be aggregated and reported under one type of continuing involvement. *[IFRS 7.42F]*.

The following example illustrates how an entity that has not adopted IFRS 9 might meet the quantitative disclosure requirements in (a) to (e) above. *[IFRS 7.IG40C]*.

Example 53.13: Quantitative disclosures for transferred assets fully derecognised

Type of continuing involvement	Cash outflows to repurchase transferred (derecognised) assets CU million	Carrying amount of continuing involvement in statement of financial position CU million			Fair value of continuing involvement CU million		Maximum exposure to loss CU million
		Held for trading	Available-for-sale financial assets	Financial liabilities at fair value through profit or loss	Assets	Liabilities	
Written put options	(X)			(X)		(X)	X
Purchased call options	(X)	X			X		X
Securities lending	(X)		X	(X)	X	(X)	X
		X	X	(X)	X	(X)	X

Undiscounted cash flows to repurchase transferred assets
Maturity of continuing involvement
CU million

Type of continuing involvement	Total	less than 1 month	1-3 months	3-6 months	6 months-1 year	1-3 years	3-5 years	more than 5 years
Written put options	X			X	X	X	X	
Purchased call options	X				X	X	X		X
Securities lending	X	X	X					

Very similar disclosures could be given by an entity that has adopted IFRS 9, although the asset classifications would be different. *[IFRS 7.IG40B].*

In addition to the information above, the following should be disclosed for each type of continuing involvement: *[IFRS 7.42G]*

(a) the gain or loss recognised at the date of transfer of the assets.

Disclosure should also be given if a gain or loss on derecognition arose because the fair values of the components of the previously recognised asset (i.e. the interest in the asset derecognised and the interest retained by the entity) were different from the fair value of the previously recognised asset as a whole. In that situation, disclosure should be made of whether the fair value measurements included significant inputs that were not based on observable market data; *[IFRS 7.B38]*

(b) income and expenses recognised, both in the reporting period and cumulatively, from the entity's continuing involvement in the derecognised financial assets (e.g. fair value changes in derivative instruments); and

(c) if the total amount of proceeds from transfer activity (that qualifies for derecognition) in a reporting period is not evenly distributed throughout the reporting period (e.g. if a substantial proportion of the total amount of transfer activity takes place in the closing days of a reporting period):

(i)   when the greatest transfer activity took place within that reporting period (e.g. the last five days before the end of the reporting period);

(ii)   the amount (e.g. related gains or losses) recognised from transfer activity in that part of the reporting period; and

(iii) the total amount of proceeds from transfer activity in that part of the reporting period.

This information should be provided for each period for which a statement of comprehensive income is presented. *[IFRS 7.42G]*.

7   PRESENTATION ON THE FACE OF THE FINANCIAL STATEMENTS AND RELATED DISCLOSURES

Although it requires certain minimum disclosures, IFRS 7 provides little guidance as to where financial instruments and related gains and losses should be presented on the face of the financial statements nor how such items should be disaggregated. Further, the disclosures required need not always reflect how items are presented on the face of the statements. Therefore, for the time being at least, management must use its judgement in deciding how best to present much of the information relating to financial instruments, taking account of the minimum requirements of IFRS 7 and other related standards such as IAS 1.

7.1   Gains and losses recognised in profit or loss

7.1.1   *Presentation on the face of the statement of comprehensive income (or income statement)*

The effects of an entity's various activities, transactions and other events (including those relating to financial instruments) differ in frequency, potential for gain or loss and predictability. Accordingly, IAS 1 explains, disclosing the components of financial performance assists in providing an understanding of the financial performance achieved and in making projections of future results. *[IAS 1.86]*.

IAS 1 prescribes requirements for line items to be included on the face of the statement of comprehensive income (or income statement). Where IFRS 9 is applied, these requirements include:

*   gains and losses arising from the derecognition of financial assets measured at amortised cost. *[IAS 1.82(aa)]*. In order to determine the amount of this gain or loss, the carrying amount of the financial asset should, in principle, be updated to the date of derecognition. It should, therefore, include a revised estimate of expected credit losses determined as at the date of derecognition. However, considerations of materiality would also need to be taken into account;[18]

*   impairment losses (including reversals of impairment losses or impairment gains) determined in accordance with IFRS 9. *[IAS 1.82(ba)]*.

Some might argue this line item should also include modification gains or losses, particularly if the reason for the modification was credit-related. However, a summary of the April 2015 meeting of the Transition Resource Group for Impairment of Financial Instruments, published on the IASB's website, suggests this would not be appropriate. Instead, it says that if disclosing gains and losses from impairments and modifications on a net basis would provide relevant information (for example, if the reason for the modification was credit-related), this could be dealt with through additional disclosure in the notes.

The summary also says that modification gains and losses should be presented separately if considered appropriate.[19] Consequently, another way in which a net figure could be presented on the face of the income statement involves presenting modification gains and losses (or at least those arising from credit-related events) in a separate line item that is adjacent to the one showing impairment losses and gains, together with a subtotal that includes these two amounts;

- where a financial asset previously measured at amortised cost is reclassified so that it is measured at fair value through profit or loss, any gain or loss arising from a difference between the previous carrying amount and its fair value at the reclassification date; *[IAS 1.82(ca)]* and

- where a financial asset previously classified at fair value through other comprehensive income is reclassified as measured at fair value through profit or loss, any cumulative gain or loss previously recognised in other comprehensive income that is reclassified to profit or loss. *[IAS 1.82(cb)]*.

Otherwise, only one caption, 'finance costs', clearly relates to financial instruments. *[IAS 1.82(b)]*. The implementation guidance to IFRS 7 explains that this caption includes total interest expense (see 4.2.2 above) but may also include amounts associated with non-financial liabilities, for example the unwinding of the discount on long-term provisions (see Chapter 27 at 4.3.5). *[IFRS 7.IG13]*.

The Interpretations Committee concluded that it is not permissible to present a line item 'net finance costs' (or a similar term) on the face of the statement without showing the finance costs and finance revenue composing it. However, the presentation of finance revenue followed immediately by finance costs and a subtotal, e.g. 'net finance costs', is allowed.[20]

The demand for safe investments can sometimes result in a negative yield on very high quality financial assets (e.g. certain government bonds or reserve bank deposits). The IFRS Interpretations Committee has considered this phenomenon and in January 2015 noted that interest resulting from a negative effective interest rate on a financial asset does not meet the definition of interest revenue in IAS 18 – *Revenue* – because it reflects a gross outflow, not a gross inflow, of economic benefits. Consequently, such expenses should not be presented as interest revenue, but in an appropriate expense classification.[21] This might be a separate line item titled, for example, 'financial expenses on liquid short term assets' or 'other financial expenses' or using another appropriate description. Alternatively, it could be appropriate to include within another expense line, for example, 'other expenses'.

Chapter 53

Similarly, we believe negative interest on financial liabilities, which will represent a form of income, should not be offset against positive interest expense.

Additional line items, headings and subtotals should be presented on the face of the statement of comprehensive income (or income statement) when such presentation is relevant to an understanding of the elements of an entity's financial performance. Factors that should be considered include materiality and the nature and function of the components of income and expenses. For example, a financial institution may amend the descriptions to provide information that is relevant to the operations of a financial institution. *[IAS 1.85, 86]*. This may also be relevant where an entity recognises negative interest on financial assets or financial liabilities.[22]

Any additional subtotals presented should: *[IAS 1.85A]*

- comprise line items made up of amounts recognised and measured in accordance with IFRS;
- be presented and labelled in a manner that makes the line items that constitute the subtotal clear and understandable;
- be consistent from period to period, as required by IAS 1 (see Chapter 3 at 4.1.4); and
- not be displayed with more prominence than the subtotals and totals required in IFRS for the statement(s) presenting profit or loss and other comprehensive income.

The following items should also be disclosed on the face of the statement of comprehensive income (or income statement) as allocations of profit or loss for the period: *[IAS 1.81B(a)]*

- profit or loss attributable to non-controlling interests; and
- profit or loss attributable to owners of the parent.

7.1.2   *Further analysis of gains and losses recognised in profit or loss*

As noted at 4.2.2 above, entities are required to disclose total interest income and total interest expense, calculated using the effective interest method, for financial assets and financial liabilities that are not at fair value through profit or loss. Whilst finance leases are included within the scope of IFRS 7, strictly they are not accounted for using the effective interest method (although for most leases the method prescribed in IAS 17 results in a very similar treatment). Accordingly, where material, it appears that finance income (charges) arising on finance leases should be shown separately from the interest income (expense) shown above. Until IFRS 15 – *Revenue from Contracts with Customers* – is applied, IAS 18 also requires separate disclosure of interest income arising on assets that do not arise from leases. *[IAS 18.6(a), 35(b)(iii)]*. In fact, it will often be appropriate to include such items within the same caption on the face of the statement of comprehensive income (or income statement) and include a sub-analysis in the notes.

Dividends classified as an expense (for example those payable to holders of redeemable preference shares) may be presented either with interest on other liabilities or as a separate item. Such items are subject to the requirements of IAS 1.

In some circumstances, because of the differences between interest and dividends with respect to matters such as tax deductibility, it is desirable to disclose them separately in the statement of comprehensive income (or income statement). *[IAS 32.40]*.

The following gains and losses reported in profit or loss should also be disclosed:

- the amount of revenue arising from dividends. *[IAS 18.35(b)(iv)]*. Where IFRS 9 is applied and equity investments are designated at fair value through other comprehensive income, dividends recognised should be disclosed, showing separately the amounts arising on investments derecognised during the reporting period and those related to investments held at the end of the reporting period; *[IFRS 7.11A(d)]*

- changes in fair value that relate to instruments at fair value through profit or loss (see 4.2.1 above).

  Little guidance is given on disaggregating gains and losses from instruments classified as at fair value through profit or loss. For example, the components of the change in fair value of a debt instrument can include:

  - interest accruals;
  - foreign currency retranslation;
  - movements arising from changes in the issuer's credit risk; and
  - changes in market interest rates.

  An entity is neither required to disaggregate, nor prohibited from disaggregating, these components on the face of the statement of comprehensive income (or income statement) provided the minimum disclosure requirements are met (e.g. see 4.2 above). Accordingly, in our view the interest accrual component, say, may be included separately within an interest receivable caption or it may be included within the same caption as other components of the gain or loss such as dealing profit. As noted at 4.1 above, whatever the entity's approach, it should be explained in its accounting policies; and

- the amount of exchange differences recognised in profit or loss under IAS 21 except for those arising on financial instruments measured at fair value through profit or loss. *[IAS 21.52(a)]*.

When IFRS 9 is applied, dividends recognised during the period arising on equity investments designated at fair value through other comprehensive income should be disclosed. Those dividends arising on investments derecognised during the reporting period and those arising on investments held at the end of the reporting period should be shown separately. *[IFRS 7.11A(d)]*.

In IAS 1 it is explained that when items of income and expense are material, their nature and amount are required to be disclosed separately. *[IAS 1.97]*. Circumstances that can give rise to separate disclosure include the disposal of investments *[IAS 1.98]* (e.g. available-for-sale assets) and the early settlement of liabilities. However, gains and losses should not be reported as extraordinary items, either on the face of the statement of comprehensive income (or income statement) or in the notes. *[IAS 1.87]*.

Chapter 53

7.1.3   Offsetting and hedges

IAS 1 explains that income and expenses should not be offset unless required or permitted by another standard. This is because offsetting detracts from the ability of users to understand fully the transactions, other events and conditions that have occurred and to assess the entity's future cash flows (except where it reflects the substance of the transaction or other event). *[IAS 1.32, 33]*. It goes on to explain that gains and losses on the disposal of non-current investments (such as many available-for-sale assets) are reported by deducting the carrying amount of the asset and related selling expenses from the proceeds on disposal rather than showing gross proceeds as revenue *[IAS 1.34]* – in the case of available-for-sale assets the profit or loss on disposal will also include any gains and losses that are reclassified from equity. It also explains that gains and losses arising from groups of similar transactions should be reported on a net basis, for example gains and losses arising on financial instruments held for trading or foreign exchange differences. The individual transactions should, however, be reported separately if they are material. *[IAS 1.35]*.

Whilst IAS 32 prescribes when financial assets and liabilities should be offset in the statement of financial position (see 7.4.1 below) it contains no guidance on when related income and expenses should be offset. IAS 39 states that hedge accounting 'recognises the offsetting effects on profit or loss of changes in the fair values of the hedging instrument and the hedged item.' *[IAS 39.85]*. This is a little short of an explicit requirement or permission to show income or expenses net of related hedging gains and losses. However, it is entirely consistent with the objective of hedge accounting to include within a caption in profit or loss related hedging gains and losses even if that results in a degree of offset. Further support for this position was found within IAS 30, which explained that income and expense items 'shall not be offset except for those relating to hedges and to assets and liabilities that have been offset...',[23] although we believe it would also be acceptable to present gains and losses on hedging instruments in a separate line item.

Example 53.14:   Presenting the effects of a hedge of a forecast sale

Company K has the euro as its functional currency. On 1 January 2016 it forecasts the sale of certain goods in dollars in six months and, to hedge that exposure, enters into a forward foreign exchange contract maturing on 1 July 2016. The hedge is designated as a cash flow hedge and meets the conditions for hedge accounting throughout the term of the hedge.

On 1 July 2016 the forecast sale occurs and is recorded using the prevailing spot rate resulting in, say, €1,000 being recognised in revenue. The forward contract is settled on this date at which point a related loss of, say, €100 has been recognised in other comprehensive income.

The mechanics of cash flow hedge accounting require the €100 loss to be reclassified from equity to profit or loss on 1 July 2016. Using the analysis above, K presents the €100 loss as a deduction from revenue resulting in the hedged sale being recognised at a net amount of €900.

Although the €100 loss reclassified from equity is being offset in profit or loss it will, however, be disclosed in the statement of comprehensive income or statement of changes in equity (see 7.2 below) or notes thereto.

IFRS 9 is more prescriptive than IAS 39 about the presentation of gains or losses on hedging instruments, specifying the following:

*   if a group of hedged items in a cash flow hedge contains no offsetting risk positions and will affect different line items in profit or loss, the gains or losses on the hedging instrument should be apportioned to the line items affected by the hedged items when reclassified to profit or loss.

    This might be the case, for example, if a group of foreign currency expense transactions are hedged for foreign currency risk and those expenses will affect, say, both distribution costs and administrative expenses

    The basis of apportionment between line items should be systematic and rational and not result in the grossing up of net gains or losses arising from a single hedging instrument; *[IFRS 9.B6.6.13, B6.6.14]*

*   if a group of hedged items contains offsetting risk positions, i.e. a net position is hedged and the hedged risk affects different line items in profit or loss, the gains or losses on the hedging instrument should be presented in a line separate from those affected by the hedged items. Consequently, the line item relating to the hedged item will remain unaffected by the hedge accounting. *[IFRS 9.6.6.4, B6.6.13]*.

    This would apply, for example, to a cash flow hedge of a group of foreign currency denominated sales and expenses. The hedging gains or losses would be presented in a line item that is separate from both revenue and the relevant expense line item(s). *[IFRS 9.B6.6.15]*.

    Another example would be a fair value hedge of a net position involving a fixed-rate asset and a fixed-rate liability. Hedge accounting would normally involve recognising the net interest accrual on the interest rate swap in profit or loss. In this case the net interest accrual should be presented in a line item separate from gross interest revenue and gross interest expense.

    This is to avoid the grossing up of net gains or losses on a single instrument into offsetting gross amounts and recognising them in different line items. *[IFRS 9.B6.6.16]*.

These requirements imply that gains and losses from hedging instruments in other hedging relationships would be presented in the same line item that is affected by the hedged item (at least to the extent the hedge is effective) rather than being shown separately, although this is not explicitly stated in IFRS 9.

7.1.4   Embedded derivatives

IAS 39 and IFRS 9 explicitly state that they do not address whether embedded derivatives should be presented separately in the statement of financial position. However, both standards are silent about the presentation in profit or loss. *[IAS 39.11, IFRS 9.4.3.4]*. In practice, it will depend on the nature both of the hybrid and the host whether related gains and losses are included in the same or separate captions within profit or loss.

For example, an investment in a credit linked note that is accounted for as a debt instrument host and an embedded credit derivative might give rise to interest income and credit losses respectively that would normally be reported in separate captions within profit or loss. Alternatively, changes in the fair value of an embedded prepayment option in a host debt instrument that is accounted for separately may be included in the same caption within profit or loss as interest on the debt instrument if the value of the option varies largely as a result of change in interest rates.

7.1.5   Entities whose share capital is not equity

Gains and losses related to changes in the carrying amount of a financial liability are recognised as income or expense in profit or loss even when they relate to an instrument that includes a right to the residual interest in the assets of the entity in exchange for cash or another financial asset, such as shares in mutual funds and co-operatives (see Chapter 44 at 4.6). Any gain or loss arising from the remeasurement of such an instrument (including the impact of dividends paid, where appropriate) should be presented separately on the face of the statement of comprehensive income (or income statement) when it is relevant in explaining the entity's performance. [IAS 32.41].

The following example illustrates a format for a statement of comprehensive income (or income statement) that may be used by entities such as mutual funds that do not have equity as defined in IAS 32, although other formats may be acceptable.

Example 53.15:   Statement of comprehensive income (or income statement) format for a mutual fund

Statement of comprehensive income (income statement) for the year ended 31 December 2016 [IAS 32.IE32]

	2016 €	2015 €
Revenue	2,956	1,718
Expenses (classified by nature or function)	(644)	(614)
Profit from operating activities	2,312	1,104
Finance costs		
– other finance costs	(47)	(47)
– distributions to members	(50)	(50)
Change in net assets attributable to unit holders	2,215	1,007

Although it may not be immediately clear, the final line item in this format is an expense. Therefore the entity's 'profit or loss' (as that term is used in IAS 1) for 2016 is €2,312 – €47 – €50 – €2,215 = €nil.

The next example illustrates a format for a statement of comprehensive income (or income statement) that may be used by entities whose share capital is not equity as defined in IAS 32 because the entity has an obligation to repay the share capital on demand, for example co-operatives, but which do have some equity (such as other reserves). Again, other formats may be acceptable.

Example 53.16:   Statement of comprehensive income (income statement) format for a co-operative

Statement of comprehensive income (income statement) for the year ended 31 December 2016 *[IAS 32.IE33]*

	2016	2015
	€	€
Revenue	472	498
Expenses (classified by nature or function)	(367)	(396)
Profit from operating activities	105	102
Finance costs		
– other finance costs	(4)	(4)
– distributions to members	(50)	(50)
Change in net assets attributable to members	51	48

In this example, the line item 'Finance costs – distributions to members' is an expense and the final line item is equivalent to 'profit or loss'.

Corresponding statement of financial position formats for both of these examples are shown at 7.4.6 below.

7.2   Gains and losses recognised in other comprehensive income

IAS 1 requires income and expense not recognised within profit or loss to be included in a statement of comprehensive income. *[IAS 1.82A]*.

Material items of income and expense and gains and losses that result from financial assets and financial liabilities which are included in other comprehensive income are required to be disclosed separately and should include at least the following:

- changes in fair value of available-for-sale financial assets, *[IAS 39.G.1]*, including: *[IFRS 7.20(a)(ii)]*

  - the amount of any gain or loss recognised in other comprehensive income during the period; and

  - the amount that was reclassified from equity to profit or loss for the period; and

- for cash flow hedges: *[IFRS 7.23(c), (d), (e)]*

  - the amount of gains or losses on designated hedging instruments recognised in other comprehensive income for the period;

  - the amount reclassified from equity to profit or loss during the period; and

  - the amount removed from equity during the period and included in the initial measurement of the acquisition cost of hedged non-financial assets or liabilities.

The implementation guidance to IAS 39 states that disclosure should be provided of changes in the fair value of hedging instruments that are recognised in other comprehensive income. *[IAS 39.G.1]*. This will include, in aggregate, gains and losses on hedging instruments in both cash flow hedges and hedges of net investments. However, this may often be dealt with by presenting for hedges of net investments similar information to that noted above for cash flow hedges.

When IFRS 9 is applied, the available-for-sale financial assets category is eliminated, although gains and losses on other categories of instrument are recognised in other comprehensive income which should be disclosed as follows:

- the amount of gain or loss attributable to changes in a liability's credit risk for those financial liabilities designated as at fair value through profit or loss; *[IFRS 7.20(a)(i)]*

- the revaluation gain or loss arising on equity investments designated at fair value through other comprehensive income; *[IFRS 7.20(a)(vii)]* and

- revaluation gains or losses arising on debt instruments measured at fair value through other comprehensive income, showing separately: *[IFRS 7.20(a)(viii)]*

  - the amount of gain or loss recognised in other comprehensive income during the period; and

  - the amount reclassified upon derecognition from accumulated other comprehensive income to profit or loss for the period.

In finalising IFRS 9, the IASB reconsidered the journal entry that arises when an entity removes a gain or loss on a cash flow hedge that was recognised in other comprehensive income in order to include it in the initial cost or other carrying amount of a non-financial asset or liability. It decided this should not be regarded as a reclassification adjustment and hence should not affect, or be included within, other comprehensive income. *[IFRS 9.BC6.380]*.

The following items should also be disclosed on the face of the statement of comprehensive income as allocations of total comprehensive income for the period: *[IAS 1.81B(b)]*

- total comprehensive income attributable to non-controlling interests; and

- total comprehensive income attributable to owners of the parent.

7.3   Statement of changes in equity

The following information should be included in the statement of changes in equity: *[IAS 1.106]*

- total comprehensive income for the period, showing separately the total amounts attributable to owners of the parent and to non-controlling interests; and

- for each component of equity, a reconciliation between the carrying amount at the beginning and the end of the period, separately disclosing changes resulting from:

  - profit or loss;

  - other comprehensive income; and

  - transactions with owners acting in their capacity as owners, showing separately:

    - contributions by and distributions to owners; and

    - changes in ownership interests in subsidiaries that do not result in a loss of control.

An analysis of other comprehensive income by item should be presented for each component of equity, either in the statement or in the notes. *[IAS 1.106A]*.

Where hedge accounting is applied in accordance with IFRS 9, IFRS 7 specifies additional information that should be presented within the reconciliation and analysis noted above or the notes thereto. This is covered in more detail at 4.3.2.C above.

In finalising IFRS 9, the IASB also reconsidered the nature of the journal entry that arises when an entity removes a gain or loss on a cash flow hedge that was recognised in other comprehensive income in order to include it in the initial cost or other carrying amount of a non-financial asset or liability. It decided it should not be regarded as a reclassification adjustment and hence should not affect, or be included within, other comprehensive income. *[IFRS 9.BC6.380]*. Such an entry should be presented within the statement of changes of equity (because it affects an entity's net assets and hence its equity), albeit separately from other comprehensive income.

The amount of dividends recognised as distributions to owners during the period should be disclosed on the face of the statement of changes in equity or in the notes. *[IAS 1.107]*.

In addition, IAS 32 notes that IAS 1 requires the amount of transaction costs accounted for as a deduction from equity in the period to be disclosed separately. *[IAS 32.39]*.

If an entity reacquires its own equity instruments from related parties disclosure should be provided in accordance with IAS 24 (see Chapter 36). *[IAS 32.34]*.

If an entity such as a mutual fund or a co-operative has no issued equity instruments, it may still need to present a statement of changes in equity. For example, such an entity may have gains or losses arising on available-for-sale assets that are recognised in equity; also co-operatives, for example, may have a balance on equity.

7.4 Statement of financial position

7.4.1 Offsetting financial assets and financial liabilities

It is common for reporting entities to enter into offsetting arrangements with their counterparties. Offsetting arrangements allow market participants to manage counterparty credit risks, and manage liquidity risk. In particular, netting arrangements generally reduce the credit risk exposures of market participants to counterparties relative to their gross exposures. Such mechanisms also permit the management of existing market risk exposures by taking on offsetting contracts with the same counterparty rather than assuming additional counterparty risk by entering into an offsetting position with a new counterparty. Furthermore, for a regulated financial institution, position netting may also have regulatory capital implications.

IAS 1 sets out a general principle that assets and liabilities should not be offset except where such offset is permitted or required by an accounting standard or interpretation (see Chapter 3 at 4.1.5.B). *[IAS 1.32]*. This general prohibition on offset is due to the fact that net presentation of assets and liabilities generally does not provide a complete depiction of the assets and liabilities of an entity. In particular, offsetting obscures the existence of some assets and liabilities in the statement of financial position and it impacts key financial ratios such as gearing, and measures such as total assets or liabilities.

IAS 32 provides some exceptions to this general rule in the case of financial assets and liabilities. IAS 32 *requires* a financial asset and a financial liability to be offset and the net amount reported in the statement of financial position when, and only when, an entity:

(a)   currently has a legally enforceable right to set off the recognised amounts; and

(b)   intends either to settle on a net basis, or to realise the asset and settle the liability simultaneously.

These two conditions are often called the *IAS 32 Offsetting Criteria*. There is, however, one exception to the offsetting requirement. This exception arise when a transferred financial asset does not qualify for derecognition. In such a circumstance, the transferred asset and the associated liability must not be offset, *[IAS 32.42]*, even if they otherwise satisfy the offsetting criteria (see Chapter 50 at 5.5.1).

IAS 32 argues that offset is appropriate in the circumstances set out in (a) and (b) above, because the entity has, in effect, a right to, or an obligation for, only a single net future cash flow and, hence, a single net financial asset or financial liability. In other circumstances, financial assets and financial liabilities are presented separately from each other, consistently with their characteristics as resources or obligations of the entity. *[IAS 32.43]*. Furthermore, the amount resulting from offsetting must also reflect the reporting entity's expected future cash flows from settling two or more separate financial instruments. *[IAS 32.BC94]*.

Offset is not equivalent to derecognition, since offsetting does not result in the financial asset or the financial liability being removed from the statement of financial position, but in net presentation of a net financial asset or a net financial liability. Moreover, no gain or loss can ever arise on offset, but may arise on derecognition. *[IAS 32.44]*.

IAS 32 acknowledges that an enforceable right to set off a financial asset and a financial liability affects the rights and obligations associated with that asset and liability and may affect an entity's exposure to credit and liquidity risk. However, such a right is not, in itself, a sufficient basis for offsetting. The entity may still realise the asset and liability separately and, in the absence of an intention to exercise the right or to settle simultaneously, the amount and timing of an entity's future cash flows are not affected. Similarly, an intention by one or both parties to settle on a net basis without the legal right to do so is not sufficient to justify offsetting because the rights and obligations associated with the individual financial asset and financial liability remain unaltered. *[IAS 32.46, AG38E]*.

IAS 32 elaborates further on the detail of the offsetting criteria as set out in the following subsections.

7.4.1.A   Criterion (a): Legal right of set-off

IAS 32 describes a right of set-off as a debtor's legal right, by contract or otherwise (for example, it may arise as a result of a provision in law or a regulation), to settle or otherwise eliminate all or a portion of an amount due to a creditor by applying against that amount an amount due from the creditor. The enforceability of the right of set-off is thus essentially a legal matter, so that the specific conditions supporting the right may vary from one legal jurisdiction to another. *[IAS 32.45]*. Care must therefore be taken to establish which laws apply to the relationships between the parties.

In unusual circumstances, a debtor (A) may have a legal right to apply an amount due from a third party (B) against an amount due to a creditor (C), provided that there is an agreement among A, B and C that clearly establishes A's right to set off amounts due from B against those due to C. *[IAS 32.45]*. For example, a foreign branch of a US bank makes a loan to a foreign subsidiary of a US parent with the parent required to deposit an amount equal to the loan in the US bank for the same term. The terms of the transactions may give the bank a legal right to set off the amount due to the parent against the amount owed by the foreign subsidiary. Another example is bank accounts maintained for a group of companies where each member of the group agrees that its credit balance may be the subject of set-off in respect of debit balances of other members of the group. In our experience, not all jurisdictions recognise this type of contractual multilateral set-off arrangement, particularly in bankruptcy scenarios.

Prior to the December 2011 amendments to IAS 32, the standard contained only limited additional guidance about this criterion. However, as part of the joint project that attempted to align US GAAP and IFRS in this area, the IASB identified inconsistencies in the way this criterion and the related guidance was being interpreted and applied in practice. Therefore it decided to supplement the application guidance in IAS 32 to clarify its meaning. *[IAS 32.BC78, BC79]*. The remainder of this subsection considers this revised guidance.

A right of set-off may currently be available or it may be contingent on a future event (e.g. the right may be triggered or exercisable only on the occurrence of some future event, such as the default, insolvency or bankruptcy of one of the counterparties). Even if the right of set-off is not contingent on a future event, it may only be legally enforceable in the normal course of business, or in the event of default, or in the event of insolvency or bankruptcy, of one or all of the counterparties. *[IAS 32.AG38A]*.

The revised application guidance makes it clear that, in order for an entity to currently have a legally enforceable right of set-off, the right: *[IAS 32.AG38B]*

- must not be contingent on a future event; and
- must be legally enforceable in all of the following circumstances:
  - the normal course of business;
  - the event of default; and
  - the event of insolvency or bankruptcy of the entity and all of the counterparties.

The nature and extent of the right of set-off, including any conditions attached to its exercise and whether it would remain in the event of default or insolvency or bankruptcy, may vary from one legal jurisdiction to another. Consequently, it cannot be assumed that the right of set-off is automatically available outside of the normal course of business. For example, the bankruptcy or insolvency laws of a jurisdiction may prohibit, or restrict, the right of set-off in the event of bankruptcy or insolvency in some circumstances. *[IAS 32.AG38C]*. Therefore, contractual provisions, the laws governing the contract, or the default, insolvency or bankruptcy laws applicable to the parties need to be considered to ascertain whether the right of set-off is enforceable in the circumstances set out above. *[IAS 32.AG38D]*. In assessing whether an agreement meets these conditions, entities will need to make a legal determination, which may involve obtaining legal advice.

The basis for conclusions suggests that to meet the criteria for offsetting, these rights must exist for all counterparties. Thus, if one party, including the reporting entity, will not or cannot perform under the contract, the other counterparties will be able to enforce that right to set-off against the party that has defaulted or become insolvent or bankrupt. *[IAS 32.BC80]*. However, the revised application guidance above appears to focus only on whether the rights of the reporting entity are legally enforceable. It is also clear that the above reference to 'all of the counterparties' pertains to the legal enforceability in the circumstances listed (i.e. the normal course of business, the events of default, insolvency or bankruptcy), and not who holds the set-off right.

In our view, normally the standard and its application guidance would prevail over the basis for conclusions and we consider that the IASB's most likely intention, consistent with the wording in the body and application guidance of the standard, was to require only the reporting entity to have a legal right to set off in the circumstances noted above – including, in the event of the reporting entity's own default, insolvency or bankruptcy.

The requirement that a reporting entity must be able to legally enforce a right of set-off in the event of its own bankruptcy means that the counterparty (or counterparties) to a netting agreement must not have the ability to force gross settlement in the event of the reporting entity's default, insolvency or bankruptcy. It also means that the reporting entity may need to obtain legal advice as to whether its legal right to net settle will survive the bankruptcy laws of the jurisdiction in which it is located.

Many contracts give only the non-defaulting party the right to enforce the netting provisions in case of default, insolvency or bankruptcy of any of the parties to the agreement. Unless the insolvency laws in the relevant jurisdiction would force net settlement, such contracts would fail the IAS 32 criteria because the reporting entity cannot enforce such rights of set-off in the event of its own bankruptcy, regardless of the fact that in practice it is highly unlikely that the non-defaulting party would insist on gross settlement. In practice, most of these contracts would not achieve offsetting under IAS 32 anyway, because the legal right of set-off available under such contracts is usually not enforceable in the normal course of business. Generally speaking, these contracts are structured this way because entities do not intend to settle net other than in situations of default. In other circumstances, entities need to determine if the right to enforce net settlement would survive their own bankruptcy.

A right of set-off that can be exercised only upon the occurrence of a future event is often referred to as a 'conditional' right of set-off. For example, an entity may have a right of set-off that is exercisable on changes to particular legislation or change in control of the counterparties. Conditional rights of set-off such as these do not meet the offsetting criteria and, hence, the financial asset and financial liability subject to such rights of set-off would not qualify to be offset.

As the description of a right of set-off itself envisages an amount being due to each party either now or in the future, the passage of time and uncertainties relating to amounts to be paid do not preclude an entity from currently having a legally enforceable right of set-off. The fact that payments subject to a right of set-off will only arise at a future date is not in itself a condition or form of contingency that prevents offsetting. *[IAS 32.BC83]*.

However, if the right of set-off is not exercisable during a period when amounts are due and payable, then the entity does not meet the offsetting criterion as it has no right to set off those payments. Similarly, a right of set-off that could disappear or that would no longer be enforceable after a future event that could take place in the normal course of business or in the event of default, or in the event of insolvency or bankruptcy, such as a ratings downgrade, would not meet the currently (legally enforceable) criterion. *[IAS 32.BC84]*.

Some contracts include representation clauses under which the right to set-off is automatically invalidated if any undertakings or representations in the contract turns out to be incorrect in a material respect. In our view, such clauses would generally not render the right of set-off a conditional right of set-off.

In certain circumstances, an entity may, in order to exercise its right of set-off, need to unilaterally take a procedural action within its control. For example, an entity may be required to notify the counterparty, in the form of a letter in advance, in order to effect net settlement under the terms of the contract. In some cases, an entity may need to apply to a court to effect set-off when a counterparty becomes bankrupt (as a matter of process), although that right is assured and is upheld in the event of default of a counterparty in that jurisdiction. In our view, the mere fact that such actions are needed before an entity can exercise the right of set-off would not make the exercisability of that right contingent on a future event. However, in the latter example, the probability of favourable or unfavourable judgement from the court would have to be assessed separately as part of the 'legal enforceability' requirement to conclude whether the right of set-off meets the offsetting criteria in IAS 32.

Unlike US GAAP, IAS 32 does not specify a particular level of assurance required to meet the 'legally enforceable' criterion. Instead, it leaves such determination to judgement and consideration of the relevant facts and circumstances. In practice, entities are expected, in their day to day business, to obtain reasonable assurance on enforceability of contractual rights as part of prudent risk management regardless of the accounting requirements.

7.4.1.B   Master netting agreements

It is common practice for an entity that undertakes a number of financial instrument transactions with a single counterparty to enter into a 'master netting arrangement' with that counterparty. These arrangements are typically used by financial institutions to restrict their exposure to loss in the event of bankruptcy or other events that result in a counterparty being unable to meet its obligations. Such an agreement commonly creates a conditional right of set-off that becomes enforceable, and affects the realisation or settlement of individual financial assets and financial liabilities, only following a specified event of default or in other circumstances not expected to arise in the normal course of business. Entities who enter into such master netting agreements other than not meeting the legal right of setoff requirement also typically do not intend to settle net in the normal course of business.

Where an entity has entered into such an agreement, the agreement does not provide the basis for the offset of assets and liabilities unless both of the offsetting criteria are satisfied. *[IAS 32.50, AG38]*. For enforceable master netting arrangements that create a conditional right of set off, this will typically be the case only if the default (or other event specified in the contract) has actually occurred. When financial assets and financial liabilities subject to a master netting arrangement are not offset, the effect of the arrangement falls within the scope of the disclosure requirements of IFRS 7(see 7.4.2 below).

7.4.1.C   Criterion (b): Intention to settle net or realise the gross amount simultaneously ('the net settlement criterion')

An entity's intention to settle net or settle simultaneously may be demonstrated through its past experience of executing set-off or simultaneous settlement in similar situations, its usual operating practices or by reference to its documented risk policies. Thus, incidental net or simultaneous settlement of a financial asset or financial liability does not meet the criterion above.

The requirement for an intention to settle net or to settle simultaneously is, however, considered only from the reporting entity's perspective.

IAS 32 notes that an entity's intentions with respect to settlement of particular assets and liabilities may be influenced by its normal business practices, the requirements of the financial markets and other circumstances that may limit the ability to settle net or simultaneously. *[IAS 32.47]*.In practice, even though a reporting entity has the right to settle net, it may settle gross either because of lack of appropriate arrangements or systems to effect net settlement or to facilitate operations. In such circumstances, the entity presents such assets and liabilities on a net basis in the statement of financial position only when the entity intends to settle the asset and the liability simultaneously.

Simultaneous settlement of two financial instruments may occur through, for example, the operation of a clearing house in an organised financial market or a face-to-face exchange. *[IAS 32.48]*. The procedures of the clearing house or exchange may provide that the amount to be paid or received for different products be settled gross. However, such payments may be made simultaneously. Hence, even though the parties may make payment or receive payment separately for different product types, settlement occur at the same moment and there is exposure only to the net amount.

The standard states that the reference to 'simultaneous' settlement in the conditions for offset above is to be interpreted literally, as applying only to the realisation of a financial asset and settlement of a financial liability at the same moment. *[IAS 32.48]*. For example, the settlement of a financial asset and a financial liability at the same nominal time but in different time zones is not considered to be simultaneous.

Nevertheless, it became apparent to the IASB that there was diversity in practice related to the interpretation of 'simultaneous' settlement in IAS 32. In practice, due to processing constraints, settlement of gross amounts rarely occurs at exactly the same moment, even when using a clearing house or settlement system. Rather, actual settlement takes place over a period of time (e.g. clearing repos and reverse repos in batches during the day). Arguably, therefore, 'simultaneous' is not operational and ignores settlement systems that are established to achieve what is economically equivalent to net settlement. Consequently, IAS 32 has often been interpreted to mean that settlement through a clearing house does meet the simultaneous settlement criterion, even if not occurring at the same moment. The IASB agreed that some, but not all, settlement systems should be seen as equivalent to net settlement and, in order to reduce diversity of accounting treatment, introduced guidance into IAS 32 in December 2011 to clarify how criterion (b) should be assessed in these circumstances. *[IAS 32.BC94-BC100].*

The amendments explain that if an entity can settle amounts in a manner such that the outcome is, in effect, equivalent to net settlement, the entity will meet the net settlement criterion. This will occur if, and only if, the gross settlement mechanism has features that (i) eliminate or result in insignificant credit and liquidity risk, and that (ii) will process receivables and payables in a single settlement process or cycle. For example, a gross settlement system that has all of the following characteristics would meet the net settlement criterion: *[IAS 32.AG38F]*

- financial assets and financial liabilities eligible for set-off are submitted at the same point in time for processing;

- once the financial assets and financial liabilities are submitted for processing, the parties are committed to fulfil the settlement obligation;

- there is no potential for the cash flows arising from the assets and liabilities to change once they have been submitted for processing (unless the processing fails – see next item below);

- assets and liabilities that are collateralised with securities will be settled on a securities transfer or similar system (e.g. delivery versus payment), so that if the transfer of securities fails, the processing of the related receivable or payable for which the securities are collateral will also fail (and *vice versa*);

- any transactions that fail, as outlined in the previous item above, will be re-entered for processing until they are settled;

- settlement is carried out through the same settlement institution (e.g. a settlement bank, a central bank or a central securities depository); and

- an intraday credit facility is in place that will provide sufficient overdraft amounts to enable the processing of payments at the settlement date for each of the parties, and it is virtually certain that the intraday credit facility will be honoured if called upon.

The IASB deliberately chose the language above so that it was clear that settlement systems established by clearing houses or other central counterparties should not automatically be assumed to meet the net settlement criterion. Conversely, irrespective of the names used in a particular jurisdiction, other settlement systems

Chapter 53

may meet the net settlement criterion if that system eliminates or results in insignificant credit and liquidity risk and processes receivables and payables in the same settlement process or cycle. [IAS 32.BC101].

7.4.1.D   Situations where offset is not normally appropriate

An entity may enter into a number of different financial instruments designed to replicate, as a group, the features of a single financial instrument (such a replication is sometimes referred to as creating a 'synthetic instrument'). For example, if an entity issues floating rate debt and then enters into a 'pay fixed/receive floating' interest rate swap, the combined economic effect is that the entity has issued fixed rate debt.

IAS 32 argues that each of the individual financial instruments that together constitute a 'synthetic instrument':

- represents a contractual right or obligation with its own terms and conditions;
- may be transferred or settled separately; and
- is exposed to risks that may differ from those to which the other financial instruments in the 'synthetic instrument' are exposed.

Accordingly, when one financial instrument in a 'synthetic instrument' is an asset and another is a liability, they are not offset and presented on an entity's statement of financial position on a net basis unless they meet the offsetting criteria. [IAS 32.49(a), AG39].

Other circumstances where the offsetting criteria are generally not met, and therefore offsetting is usually inappropriate, include: [IAS 32.49(b), (c), (d), (e)]

(a)   financial assets and financial liabilities arise from financial instruments having the same primary risk exposure (e.g. assets and liabilities within a portfolio of forward contracts or other derivative instruments) but involving different counterparties;

(b)   financial or other assets are pledged as collateral for non-recourse financial liabilities (see 7.4.1.E below);

(c)   financial assets are set aside in trust by a debtor for the purpose of discharging an obligation without those assets having been accepted by the creditor in settlement of the obligation (e.g. a sinking fund arrangement); or

(d)   obligations incurred as a result of events giving rise to losses are expected to be recovered from a third party by virtue of a claim made under an insurance policy.

Derivative assets and liabilities that are not transacted through central clearing systems are very unlikely to qualify for offsetting. For example, it is rare that they will be settled net in the normal course of business and even where associated offsetting agreements exist they are usually conditional on the default of one of the counterparties.

7.4.1.E   Offsetting collateral amounts

Many central counterparty clearing houses require cash collateral in the form of variation margin to cover the fluctuations in the market value of 'over-the-counter' and exchange-traded derivatives. Historically IAS 32 has not addressed the offsetting of collateral although entities sometimes did offset the market values of the derivatives against the cash collateral, on the basis that all payments on the derivatives will be made net using the cash collateral already provided. In effect, the collateral is represented as an advance payment for settlement of the cash flows arising on the derivatives.

In the basis for conclusions to the 2011 amendment, the IASB clarified that the offsetting criteria do not give special consideration to items referred to as 'collateral'. Accordingly, a recognised financial instrument designated as collateral should be set off against the related financial asset or financial liability if, and only if, it meets the offsetting criteria in IAS 32. This might be the case, for instance, if variation margin is used to settle cash flows on derivative contracts. However, the IASB also noted that if an entity can be required to return or receive back collateral, the entity would not currently have a legally enforceable right of set-off in all relevant circumstances and therefore offsetting would not be appropriate. *[IAS 32.BC103]*.

In practice, to set off collateral against related financial assets and liabilities, a reporting entity would also need to assess, among other factors: (i) whether the amounts paid or received can be construed as partial settlement of the amounts due under the derivative contracts (see below); (ii) whether the right of offset is legally enforceable in the event of default, insolvency or bankruptcy of either party as well as in the normal course of business; (iii) whether the right to offset the collateral and the open position is conditional on a future event; (iv) whether the collateral will form part of the actual net settlement of the underlying contracts ; and (v) whether there is a single process for both the settlement of the underlying contracts and the transfer of the collateral.

The analysis of whether payments or receipts described as margin payments are in fact partial settlements of an open position, and hence result in partial derecognition of the derivative, requires the application of significant judgement, including an assessment of the legal relationship between the clearing member and the clearing house. When the strike price of a derivative contract is effectively reset each day following a margin payment based on the contract's change in fair value, this might indicate it is appropriate to regard the margin payment as a partial settlement of the derivative. This situation sometimes occurs with exchange traded futures for which gains and losses on the open position are realised over time as opposed to being accumulated until the final settlement date.

7.4.1.F   Unit of account

IAS 32 does not specify the 'unit of account' to which the offsetting requirements should be applied. For example, they could be applied to individual financial instruments, such as entire derivative assets or liabilities, or they could be applied to identifiable cash flows arising on those financial instruments. In practice, both approaches are seen with the former being more commonly applied by financial institutions and the latter by energy producers and traders. This diversity became apparent to the IASB during its project that amended IAS 32 in December 2011. Nevertheless, whilst the IASB considered imposing an approach based on individual cash flows (which, on a conceptual level, it favoured), it concluded that the different interpretations applied today do not result in inappropriate application of the offsetting criteria. The Board also concluded that the benefits of amending IAS 32 would not outweigh the costs for preparers. *[IAS 32.BC105-BC111]*. Accordingly, IAS 32 was not amended, thereby allowing this diversity to continue. Reporting entities should establish an accounting policy and apply that policy consistently.

7.4.2 *Offsetting financial assets and financial liabilities: disclosure*

This section discusses the requirements of IFRS 7 introduced by the IASB in December 2011. These requirements are similar to requirements introduced into US GAAP by the FASB at around the same time and are intended to assist users in identifying major differences between the effects of the IFRS and US GAAP offsetting requirements (without requiring a full reconciliation). *[IAS 32.BC77]*.

7.4.2.A Objective

The objective of these requirements is to disclose information to enable users of financial statements to evaluate the effect or potential effect of netting arrangements, including rights of set-off associated with recognised financial assets and liabilities, on the reporting entity's financial position. *[IFRS 7.13B]*.

To meet this objective, the minimum quantitative disclosure requirements considered at 7.4.2.C below may need to be supplemented with additional (qualitative) disclosures. Whether such disclosures are necessary will depend on the terms of an entity's enforceable master netting arrangements and related agreements, including the nature of the rights of set-off, and their effect or potential effect on the entity's financial position. *[IFRS 7.B53]*.

7.4.2.B Scope

The disclosure requirements considered at 7.4.2.C below are applicable not only to all recognised financial instruments that are set off in accordance with IAS 32 (see 7.4.1 above), but also to recognised financial instruments that are subject to an *enforceable* master netting arrangement or 'similar agreement' that covers similar financial instruments and transactions, irrespective of whether they are set off in accordance with IAS 32. *[IFRS 7.13A, B40]*.

In this context, enforceability has two elements: first, enforceability as a matter of law under the governing laws of the contract; and second, consistency with the bankruptcy laws of the jurisdictions where the reporting entity and counterparty are located. The latter is critical since, regardless of the jurisdiction selected to govern the contract, local insolvency laws in an insolvent counterparty's jurisdiction can override contractual terms in the event of insolvency. Determining whether an agreement is enforceable for the purposes of these disclosures may require judgement based on a legal analysis that is sometimes, but not necessarily, based on legal advice.

These 'similar agreements' include, but are not limited to, derivative clearing agreements, global master repurchase agreements, global master securities lending agreements, and any related rights to financial collateral. The 'similar financial instruments and transactions' include, but are not restricted to, derivatives, sale and repurchase agreements, reverse repurchase agreements, securities borrowing and securities lending agreements. However, loans and customer deposits with the same financial institution would not be within the scope of these disclosure requirements, unless they are set off in the statement of financial position; nor would financial instruments that are subject *only* to a collateral agreement. *[IFRS 7.B41].*

The breadth of scope of these disclosure requirements resulted in the US FASB restricting the application of the equivalent disclosures in US GAAP to the items identified in the implementation guidance, namely derivatives, repurchase and reverse repurchase agreements and securities lending and borrowing arrangements. In November 2012, the IASB staff debriefed the IASB on the FASB's decision and recommended that the IASB should not make a similar amendment. Whilst the IASB did not make any formal decisions, its 'non-objection' to the staff's recommendation confirms that the scope of the new disclosure requirements is broader than many had realised. As a result, reporting entities should carefully examine their contracts to determine whether they have netting arrangements or similar agreements in place. In particular, trade or other receivables and payables such as balances with brokers that are subject to an umbrella netting arrangement (normally where an entity's customer is also a supplier, and *vice versa*), are likely to fall within the scope of these disclosure requirements. Extract 53.19 (BP) illustrates one company providing these disclosures about receivables and payables in addition to derivatives.

7.4.2.C   Disclosure requirements

To meet the objective at 7.4.2.A above, the standard requires entities to disclose, at the end of the reporting period, in a tabular format unless another format is more appropriate, the following information separately for recognised financial assets and for recognised financial liabilities. *[IFRS 7.13C].* References to Amounts (a), (b), et seq. can be traced through to Example 53.17 at 7.4.2.D below.

- the gross amounts of those recognised financial assets and recognised financial liabilities within the scope of the disclosures (see 7.4.2.B above) [Amount (a)].

    This excludes any amounts recognised as a result of collateral agreements that do not meet the offsetting criteria in IAS 32. Instead these will be disclosed in Amount (d) (see below); *[IFRS 7.B43]*

- the amounts that are set off in accordance with the criteria in IAS 32 when determining the net amounts presented in the statement of financial position [Amount (b)].

    These amounts will be disclosed in both the financial asset and financial liability disclosures. However, the amounts disclosed (in, for example, a table) should be limited to the amounts subject to set-off. For example, an entity may have a recognised derivative asset and a recognised derivative liability that meet the offsetting criteria. If the gross amount of the asset is larger than the gross amount of the liability, the financial asset disclosure table will include the entire amount of the derivative asset in Amount (a) and the entire amount of the derivative liability in Amount (b). However, while the financial liability disclosure table will include the entire amount of the derivative liability in

Amount (a), it will only include the amount of the derivative asset that is equal to the amount of the derivative liability in Amount (b); *[IFRS 7.B44]*

- the net amounts presented in the statement of financial position [Amount (c) = Amount (a) – Amount (b)].

For instruments that are within the scope of these disclosure requirements but which do not meet the offsetting criteria in IAS 32, the amounts included in Amount (c) would equal the amounts included in Amount (a). *[IFRS 7.B45]*.

Amount (c) should be reconciled to the individual line item amounts presented in the statement of financial position. For example, if an entity determines that the aggregation or disaggregation of individual line item amounts provides more relevant information, it should reconcile the aggregated or disaggregated amounts included in Amount (c) back to the individual line item amounts presented in the statement of financial position; *[IFRS 7.B46]*

- the amounts subject to an enforceable master netting arrangement or similar agreement that are not included in the amounts subject to set-off above [Amount (d)], including:

  - amounts related to recognised financial instruments that do not meet some or all of the offsetting criteria in IAS 32 [Amount (d)(i)].

    This might include, for example, current rights of set-off where there is no intention to settle the open positions subject to these rights net or simultaneously, or conditional rights of set-off that are enforceable and exercisable only in the event of the default, insolvency or bankruptcy of any of the counterparties; *[IFRS 7.B47]* and

  - amounts related to *financial* collateral (including cash collateral) [Amount (d)(ii)].

    The fair value of those financial instruments that have been pledged or received as collateral should be disclosed. To ensure that the disclosures reflect the maximum net exposure to credit risk, the amendments require the amounts disclosed for financial collateral not offset to include *actual* collateral received, whether recognised or not as well as actual collateral pledged. The amounts disclosed should not relate to any payables or receivables recognised to return or receive back such collateral. *[IFRS 7.B48]*. The amounts disclosed for collateral would exclude non-financial collateral, for instance, land and buildings.

The total amount included in Amount (d) for any instrument is limited to the amount included in Amount (c) for that instrument. *[IFRS 7.13D]*. In other words, an entity takes into account the effects of over-collateralisation by financial instrument, so that, for example, an over-collateralisation on one asset does not make an under-collateralisation on another. To do so, it first deducts the amounts included in Amount (d)(i) from the amount included in Amount (c). It then limits the amounts included in Amount (d)(ii) to the remaining amount in Amount (c) for the related financial instrument. However, if rights to collateral are available to cover multiple contracts with the same counterparty, for example through a cross collateralisation agreement, such rights can be taken into account in arriving at Amount (d)(ii). *[IFRS 7.B49]*.

Entities should provide a description of the rights of set-off associated with the entity's financial instruments included in Amount (d), including the nature and type of those rights. For example, conditional rights would need to be described. For instruments subject to rights of set-off that are not contingent on a future event but that do not meet the remaining criteria in IAS 32, the description should include the reasons why the criteria are not met. For any financial collateral received or pledged, it would be appropriate to disclose the terms of the collateral (such as why the collateral is restricted); *[IFRS 7.13E, B50]* and

- the net amount after deducting Amount (d) from Amount (c) [Amount (e)].

The financial instruments disclosed in accordance with the requirements above may be subject to different measurement requirements, for example a payable related to a repurchase agreement may be measured at amortised cost, while a derivative will be measured at fair value. Instruments should be included at their recognised amounts and any resulting measurement differences should be described in the related disclosures. *[IFRS 7.B42]*.

The disclosures may be grouped by type of financial instrument or transaction (e.g. derivatives, repurchase and reverse repurchase agreements or securities borrowing and securities lending agreements). *[IFRS 7.B51]*.

Alternatively, disclosure of Amounts (a) to (c) may be grouped by type of financial instrument with disclosure of Amounts (c) to (e) by counterparty. Amounts that are individually significant in terms of total counterparty amounts should be separately disclosed with the remaining individually insignificant counterparty amounts aggregated into one line item. Names of the counterparties need not be given, although designation of counterparties (Counterparty P, Counterparty Q, Counterparty R, etc.) should remain consistent from year to year for the periods presented to maintain comparability. Qualitative disclosures should be considered so that further information can be given about the types of counterparties. *[IFRS 7.B52]*.

If the above quantitative and qualitative disclosures are included in more than one note to the financial statements, the amendments require the information in the individual notes to be cross-referenced to each other. This is intended to increase the transparency of the disclosures and enhance the value of information. *[IFRS 7.13F]*.

7.4.2.D   *Offsetting disclosures – illustrative examples*

The amendment that introduced the disclosures related to offsetting financial instruments provides the following example illustrating ways in which an entity might provide the required quantitative disclosures described above. However, these illustrations do not address all possible ways of applying the disclosure requirements. *[IFRS 7.IG40D]*.

Example 53.17:   Illustration of offsetting disclosures

Background

An entity has entered into transactions subject to an enforceable master netting arrangement or similar agreement with the following counterparties. The entity has the following recognised financial assets and financial liabilities resulting from those transactions that meet the scope of the disclosure requirements.

Counterparty A:

The entity has a derivative asset (fair value of CU100 million) and a derivative liability (fair value of CU80 million) with Counterparty A that meet the IAS 32 offsetting criteria. Consequently, the gross derivative liability is set off against the gross derivative asset, resulting in the presentation of a net derivative asset of CU20 million in the entity's statement of financial position. Cash collateral has also been received from Counterparty A for a portion of the net derivative asset (CU10 million). The cash collateral of CU10 million does not meet the IAS 32 offsetting criteria, but it can be set off against the net amount of the derivative asset and derivative liability in the case of default and insolvency or bankruptcy, in accordance with an associated collateral arrangement.

Counterparty B:

The entity has a derivative asset (fair value of CU100 million) and a derivative liability (fair value of CU80 million) with Counterparty B that do not meet the IAS 32 offsetting criteria, but which the entity has the right to set off in the case of default and insolvency or bankruptcy. Consequently, the gross amount of the derivative asset (CU100 million) and the gross amount of the derivative liability (CU80 million) are presented separately in the entity's statement of financial position. Cash collateral has also been received from Counterparty B for the net amount of the derivative asset and derivative liability (CU20 million). The cash collateral of CU20 million does not meet the IAS 32 offsetting criteria, but it can be set off against the net amount of the derivative asset and derivative liability in the case of default and insolvency or bankruptcy, in accordance with an associated collateral arrangement.

Counterparty C:

The entity has entered into a sale and repurchase agreement with Counterparty C that is accounted for as a collateralised borrowing. The carrying amount of the financial assets (bonds) used as collateral and posted by the entity for the transaction is CU79 million and their fair value is CU85 million. The carrying amount of the collateralised borrowing (repo payable) is CU80 million.

The entity has also entered into a reverse sale and repurchase agreement with Counterparty C that is accounted for as a collateralised lending. The fair value of the financial assets (bonds) received as collateral (and not recognised in the entity's statement of financial position) is CU105 million. The carrying amount of the collateralised lending (reverse repo receivable) is CU90 million.

The transactions are subject to a global master repurchase agreement with a right of set-off only in default and insolvency or bankruptcy and therefore do not meet the IAS 32 offsetting criteria. Consequently, the related repo payable and repo receivable are presented separately in the entity's statement of financial position.

Illustration of the disclosures by type of financial instrument

Financial assets subject to offsetting, enforceable master netting arrangements and similar agreements

CU million

As at 31 December 20XX	(a)	(b)	(c)=(a)−(b)	(d) Related amounts not set off in the statement of financial position		(e)=(c)−(d)
	Gross amounts of recognised financial assets	Gross amounts of recognised financial liabilities set off in the statement of financial position	Net amounts of financial assets presented in the statement of financial position	(d)(i), (d)(ii) Financial instruments	(d)(ii) Cash collateral received	Net amount
Description						
Derivatives	200	(80)	120	(80)	(30)	10
Reverse repurchase, securities borrowing and similar agreements	90	–	90	(90)	–	–
Other financial instruments	–	–	–	–	–	–
Total	290	(80)	210	(170)	(30)	10

Financial liabilities subject to offsetting, enforceable master netting arrangements and similar agreements

CU million

As at 31 December 20XX	(a)	(b)	(c)=(a)−(b)	(d) Related amounts not set off in the statement of financial position		(e)=(c)−(d)
	Gross amounts of recognised financial liabilities	Gross amounts of recognised financial assets set off in the statement of financial position	Net amounts of financial liabilities presented in the statement of financial position	(d)(i), (d)(ii) Financial instruments	(d)(ii) Cash collateral pledged	Net amount
Description						
Derivatives	160	(80)	80	(80)	–	–
Repurchase, securities lending and similar agreements	80	–	80	(80)	–	–
Other financial instruments	–	–	–	–	–	–
Total	240	(80)	160	(160)	–	–

Chapter 53

Illustration of amounts offset disclosed by type of financial instrument and amounts not offset by counterparty

Financial assets subject to offsetting, enforceable master netting arrangements and similar agreements

CU million

As at 31 December 20XX	(a) Gross amounts of recognised financial assets	(b) Gross amounts of recognised financial liabilities set off in the statement of financial position	(c)=(a)−(b) Net amounts of financial assets presented in the statement of financial position
Description			
Derivatives	200	(80)	120
Reverse repurchase, securities borrowing and similar agreements	90	–	90
Other financial instruments	–	–	–
Total	290	(80)	210

Net financial assets subject to enforceable master netting arrangements and similar agreements, by counterparty

CU million

As at 31 December 20XX	(c) Net amounts of financial assets presented in the statement of financial position	(d)(i), (d)(ii) Financial instruments	(d)(ii) Cash collateral received	(e)=(c)−(d) Net amount
		Related amounts not set off in the statement of financial position		
Counterparty A	20	–	(10)	10
Counterparty B	100	(80)	(20)	–
Counterparty C	90	(90)	–	–
Other	–	–	–	–
Total	210	(170)	(30)	10

Financial liabilities subject to offsetting, enforceable master netting arrangements and similar agreements

CU million

As at 31 December 20XX	(a) Gross amounts of recognised financial liabilities	(b) Gross amounts of recognised financial assets set off in the statement of financial position	(c)=(a)–(b) Net amounts of financial liabilities presented in the statement of financial position
Description			
Derivatives	160	(80)	80
Repurchase, securities lending and similar agreements	80	–	80
Other financial instruments	–	–	–
Total	240	(80)	160

Net financial liabilities subject to enforceable master netting arrangements and similar agreements, by counterparty

CU million

As at 31 December 20XX	(c) Net amounts of financial liabilities presented in the statement of financial position	(d)(i), (d)(ii) Financial instruments	(d)(ii) Cash collateral pledged	(e)=(c)–(d) Net amount
		Related amounts not set off in the statement of financial position		
Counterparty A	–	–	–	–
Counterparty B	80	(80)	–	–
Counterparty C	80	(80)	–	–
Other	–	–	–	–
Total	160	(160)	–	–

Chapter 53

BP provides the following disclosures about the extent of its offsetting.

Extract 53.19: BP p.l.c. (2014)

Notes on financial statements[extract]
27. Financial instruments and financial risk factors [extract]
(b) Credit risk [extract]

Financial instruments subject to offsetting, enforceable master netting arrangements and similar agreements

The following table shows the gross amounts of recognized financial assets and liabilities (i.e. before offsetting) and the amounts offset in the balance sheet.

Amounts which cannot be offset under IFRS, but which could be settled net under the terms of master netting agreements if certain conditions arise, and collateral received or pledged, are also shown in the table to show the total net exposure of the group.

$ million

| At 31 December 2014 | Gross amounts of recognized financial assets (liabilities) | Amounts set off | Net amounts presented on the balance sheet | Related amounts not set off in the balance sheet | | Net amount |
				Master netting arrange-ments	Cash collateral (received) pledged	
Derivative assets	11,515	(2,383)	9,132	(1,164)	(458)	7,510
Derivative liabilities	(8,971)	2,383	(6,588)	1,164	–	(5,424)
Trade receivables	10,502	(6,080)	4,422	(485)	(145)	3,792
Trade payables	(9,062)	6,080	(2,982)	485	–	(2,497)

7.4.3   Assets and liabilities

IAS 1 does not prescribe the order or format in which items are to be presented on the face of the statement of financial position, but states that the following items relating to financial instruments, are sufficiently different in nature or function to warrant separate presentation: *[IAS 1.54, 57]*

- trade and other receivables;
- cash and cash equivalents;
- other financial assets;
- trade and other payables;
- provisions; and
- other financial liabilities.

However, additional line items, headings and subtotals should be presented on the face of the statement of financial position when the size, nature or function of an item or aggregation of similar items is such that separate presentation is relevant to an understanding of the entity's financial position. Additional line items may also be presented by disaggregating the line items noted above. *[IAS 1.55, 57(a)]*.

Any additional subtotals presented should: *[IAS 1.55A]*

- comprise line items made up of amounts recognised and measured in accordance with IFRS;

- be presented and labelled in a manner that makes the line items that constitute the subtotal clear and understandable;

- be consistent from period to period, as required by IAS 1 (see Chapter 3 at 4.1.4); and

- not be displayed with more prominence than the subtotals and totals required in IFRS for the statement of financial position.

The judgement on whether additional items are presented separately should be based on an assessment of: *[IAS 1.58]*

- the nature and liquidity of assets;

- the function of assets within the entity; and

- the amounts, nature and timing of liabilities.

The descriptions used and the ordering of items or aggregation of similar items may be amended according to the nature of the entity and its transactions, to provide information that is relevant to an understanding of the entity's financial position. For example, a financial institution may amend the descriptions to provide information that is relevant to the operations of a financial institution. *[IAS 1.57(b)]*.

Although, for measurement purposes, IAS 39 classifies financial assets into four categories (see Chapter 45), other descriptors for these categories or other categorisations may be used when presenting information on the face of the financial statements. *[IAS 39.45]*. Whilst not explicitly stated in IFRS 9, entities should also be able to use categorisations that are different from the measurement categories in that standard (see Chapter 46) when it is applied.

However, the use of different measurement bases for different classes of assets suggests that their nature or function differs and, therefore, that they should be presented as separate line items. *[IAS 1.59]*. For example, loans and receivables measured at amortised cost would normally be presented separately from available-for-sale assets measured at fair value, particularly by a financial institution.

As noted at 7.1.4 above, IAS 39 and IFRS 9 explicitly state that they do not address whether embedded derivatives should be presented separately in the statement of financial position. *[IAS 39.11, IFRS 9.4.3.4]*. Although the guidance in the previous paragraph suggests that embedded derivatives will often be presented separately on the face of the statement of financial position, this will not always be the case, e.g. for the 'puttable instruments' shown in Example 53.18 below, which is based on IAS 32.

Further sub-classifications of the line items presented should be disclosed, either on the face of the statement of financial position or in the notes, classified in a manner appropriate to the entity's operations. *[IAS 1.77]*. The detail provided in sub-classifications will depend on the size, nature and function of the amounts involved and will vary for each item. For example, receivables should be disaggregated into amounts receivable from trade customers, receivables from related parties and other

Chapter 53

amounts. Assets included within receivables that are not financial instruments, such as many prepayments, should also be shown separately. *[IAS 1.78(b)]*.

The presentation in the statement of financial position of liabilities arising from supply-chain financing arrangements is an area where particular judgement is necessary. This issue is discussed in more detail in Chapter 50 at 6.5.

7.4.4   *The distinction between current and non-current assets and liabilities*

For entities presenting a statement of financial position that distinguishes between current and non-current assets and liabilities, the requirements of IAS 1 for determining whether items are classified as current or non-current are dealt with in Chapter 3 at 3.1.1 to 3.1.4. This section deals with five interpretive issues that have arisen in applying those requirements.

7.4.4.A   *Derivatives*

IAS 1 requires assets and liabilities held 'primarily for the purpose of trading' to be classified as current. *[IAS 1.66, 69]*. Where a derivative is not designated as a hedging instrument in an effective hedge, it is classified by IAS 39 or IFRS 9 as held for trading irrespective of the purpose for which it is held (see Chapter 45 at 2.1 and Chapter 46 at 4). *[IAS 39.9, IFRS 9.A]*. This does not mean that any derivative not designated as a hedging instrument in an effective hedge must always be classified as current because the IAS 39 or IFRS 9 classification is for measurement purposes only. Whilst a derivative held primarily for trading purposes should be presented as current regardless of its maturity date, other derivatives should be classified as current or non-current on the basis of their settlement date. Accordingly, derivatives that have maturities of less than 12 months from the end of the reporting period, or derivatives that have maturities of more than 12 months from the end of the reporting period but are expected to be settled within 12 months should be presented as a current asset or liability. Conversely, derivatives that have a maturity of more than twelve months and are expected to be held for more than twelve months after the reporting period should be presented as non-current assets or liabilities. *[IAS 1.BC38B, BC38C]*.

Although the Interpretations Committee and the IASB have considered how to split into current and non-current components the carrying amount of derivatives with staggered payment dates, both have decided not to address this issue. Consequently, entities will need to apply judgement in determining an appropriate split. For example, the current component of a five-year interest rate swap with interest payments exchanged quarterly could be determined as the present value of the net interest cash flows of the swap for the forthcoming twelve months after the reporting date.[24]

7.4.4.B   *Convertible loans*

Where an entity issues convertible bonds that are accounted for as an equity component (i.e. the holders' rights to convert the bonds into a fixed number of the issuer's equity instruments) and a liability component (i.e. the entity's obligation to deliver cash to holders at the maturity date), the issue arises whether the liability component should be classified as current or non-current if the conversion option may be exercised at any time before maturity. IAS 1 now explains that any terms of a liability which could, at the option of the counterparty, result in its settlement by the issue of equity instruments do not affect its classification. *[IAS 1.69(d)]*. In other words, provided the entity could not be required to settle the liability component directly within one year, it would be classified as non-current even if the holder could exercise the conversion (thereby requiring the liability component to be derecognised) within one year.

7.4.4.C   Long-term loans with repayment on demand terms

IAS 1 requires liabilities for which the entity does not have an unconditional right to defer settlement for at least twelve months after the reporting date to be classified as current. *[IAS 1.69(d)]*. Some long-term loan agreements, particularly in Hong Kong, contain clauses allowing the lender an absolute right to demand repayment at any time before maturity. Historically, borrowers often approached these clauses in the same way as more conventional covenants because the risk of exercise was considered very low (except in situations that might adversely affect the borrower's ability to repay). Consequently, the clause would result in classification of a loan as current only if such adverse matters relating to the borrower existed at the end of the reporting period.[25]

However, in 2010, the Interpretations Committee addressed this situation, noting that the requirements of IAS 1 are clear, i.e. such terms should always result in the loan being classified as current.[26]

7.4.4.D   Debt with refinancing or roll over agreements

IAS 1 states that if an entity expects, and has the discretion, to refinance or roll over an obligation for at least twelve months after the reporting period under an existing loan facility, the obligation should be classified as non-current even if it would otherwise be due within a shorter period. *[IAS 1.73]*. The Interpretations Committee has been considering the circumstances in which the guidance in paragraph 73 should apply for some time.

One particular area of concern has been the classification of liabilities arising from a short-term commercial paper programme that is backed by a long-term loan facility. In these arrangements the commercial paper is typically issued for a term of 90 or 180 days; the issuer will normally attempt to issue new instruments to replace those maturing; and a bank (often the sponsor or manager of the scheme) will have provided the entity with a longer-term loan facility that may be drawn down if any issue of commercial paper is under-subscribed. In this situation, *prima facie* the entity has in place an agreement (the loan facility) that can be used to refinance the short-term liability (from the commercial paper) on a long-term basis and might consider classifying the liability arising from commercial paper as non-current.

However, in January 2011 after analysing outreach requests, the IFRS Interpretations Committee noted that there is no charted diversity in practice where an agreement is reached to refinance an existing borrowing with a different lender – here paragraph 73 is not considered applicable, whatever the terms of the new facility, and the existing borrowing would be classified as current. Therefore the commercial paper liabilities should be classified as current.[27] In February 2015 the IASB proposed an amendment to IAS 1 that would remove the reference in paragraph 73 to 'refinance' and bring the wording of the standard into line with the committee's view on how it should be (and is being) applied.

Chapter 53

7.4.4.E   *Loan covenants*

If an entity does not have an unconditional right to defer settlement of the liability for at least twelve months after the reporting period the liability should be reported as current. *[IAS 1.69(a)]*. Further, when an entity breaches a provision of a long-term loan arrangement (commonly called a covenant) on or before the end of the reporting period with the effect that the liability becomes payable on demand, the liability should be classified as current because, at the end of the reporting period, it does not have an unconditional right to defer settlement for at least twelve months after that date. *[IAS 1.73]*. The application of these requirements, including in some commonly occurring situations, and proposals by the IASB to clarify these requirements are discussed in more detail in Chapter 3 at 3.1.4 and 6.3 respectively.

7.4.5   *Equity*

IAS 1 explains that the face of the statement of financial position should include line items that present the following amounts within equity: *[IAS 1.54(q), (r)]*

*   non-controlling interests, presented within equity; and
*   issued capital and reserves attributable to owners of the parent.

As for assets and liabilities, additional line items, headings and subtotals should be presented on the face of the statement of financial position when such presentation is relevant to an understanding of the entity's financial position and additional line items may also be presented by disaggregating the line items noted above. *[IAS 1.55]*. Further sub-classifications of the line items presented should be disclosed, either on the face of the statement of financial position or in the notes, classified in a manner appropriate to the entity's operations. *[IAS 1.77]*. The detail provided in the sub-classifications will depend on the size, nature and function of the amounts involved and will vary for each item. For example, equity capital and reserves should be disaggregated into various classes, such as paid-in capital, share premium and reserves. *[IAS 1.78(e)]*. A description of the nature and purpose of each reserve within equity should also be provided. *[IAS 1.79(b)]*.

For each class of share capital, the following information should be disclosed, either on the face of the statement of financial position or in the notes: *[IAS 1.79(a)]*

*   the number of shares authorised;
*   the number of shares issued and fully paid, and issued but not fully paid;
*   par value per share, or that the shares have no par value;
*   a reconciliation of the number of shares outstanding at the beginning and at the end of the period;
*   the rights, preferences and restrictions attaching to that class including restrictions on the distribution of dividends and the repayment of capital;
*   shares in the entity held by the entity or by its subsidiaries (treasury shares *[IAS 32.34]*) or associates; and
*   shares reserved for issue under options and contracts for the sale of shares, including the terms and amounts.

An entity without share capital, such as a partnership or trust, should disclose equivalent information, showing changes during the period in each category of equity interest, and the rights, preferences and restrictions attaching to each category of equity interest *[IAS 1.80]* (assuming of course it has actually issued instruments that meet the definition of equity).

Where puttable financial instruments and obligations arising on liquidation (see Chapter 44 at 4.6) are reclassified between financial liabilities and equity, entities are required to disclose the amount reclassified into and out of each category and the timing and reason for that reclassification. *[IAS 1.80A]*. This requirement was introduced by the amendments to IAS 32 and IAS 1 dealing with the classification of puttable financial instruments and obligations arising on liquidation.

7.4.6   Entities whose share capital is not equity

Continuing Examples 53.15 and 53.16 at 7.1.5 above, the following examples illustrate corresponding statement of financial position formats that may be used by entities such as mutual funds that do not have equity as defined in IAS 32, or entities such as co-operatives whose share capital is not equity as defined in IAS 32 because the entity has an obligation to repay the share capital on demand.

Example 53.18:   Statement of financial position format for a mutual fund

Statement of financial position at 31 December 2016 *[IAS 32.IE32]*

	2016		2015	
	€	€	€	€
ASSETS				
Non-current assets (classified in accordance with IAS 1)	91,374		78,484	
Total non-current assets		91,374		78,484
Current assets (classified in accordance with IAS 1)	1,422		1,769	
Total current assets		1,422		1,769
Total assets		92,796		80,253
LIABILITIES				
Current liabilities (classified in accordance with IAS 1)	647		66	
Total current liabilities		(647)		(66)
Non-current liabilities excluding net assets attributable to unit holders (classified in accordance with IAS 1)	280		136	
		(280)		(136)
Net assets attributable to unit holders		91,869		80,051

As for the equivalent income statement format, it may not be immediately clear what the final line item in this format represents. It is, in fact, a liability and therefore the entity's 'equity' (as that term is used in IAS 1) at the end of 2016 is €92,796 – €647 – €280 – €91,869 = €nil.

Example 53.19:   Statement of financial position format for a co-operative

Statement of financial position at
31 December 2016 *[IAS 32.IE33]*

	2016		2015	
	€	€	€	€
ASSETS				
Non-current assets (classified in accordance with IAS 1)	908		830	
Total non-current assets		908		830
Current assets (classified in accordance with IAS 1)	383		350	
Total current assets		383		350
Total assets		1,291		1,180
LIABILITIES				
Current liabilities (classified in accordance with IAS 1)	372		338	
Share capital repayable on demand	202		161	
Total current liabilities		(574)		(499)
Total assets less current liabilities		717		681
Non-current liabilities (classified in accordance with IAS 1)	187		196	
		187		196
RESERVES*				
Reserves, e.g. revaluation reserve, retained earnings	530		485	
		530		485
		717		681
MEMORANDUM NOTE **TOTAL MEMBERS' INTERESTS**				
Share capital repayable on demand		202		161
Reserves		530		485
		732		646

*In this example, the entity has no obligation to deliver a share of its reserves to its members.

The line item 'Share capital repayable on demand' is part of the entity's liabilities and the items within 'Reserves' represent its equity.

Although not required by IAS 1, an entity adopting this type of format for its statement of financial position may choose to present an analysis of movements in (or reconciliation of) total members' interests (often defined as equity plus share capital repayable on demand, perhaps adjusted for other balances with members) if this is considered to provide useful information; this would not remove the need to present a statement of changes in equity.

7.5   Statement of cash flows

The implementation guidance to IAS 39 and IFRS 9 acknowledges that the terminology in IAS 7 – *Statement of Cash Flows* – was not updated to reflect the publication of these standards, but does explain that the classification of cash flows arising from hedging instruments within the statement of cash flows should be consistent with the classification of these instruments as hedging instruments. In other words, such cash flows should be classified as operating, investing or financing activities, on the basis of the classification of the cash flows arising from the hedged item. *[IAS 39.G.2, IFRS 9.G.2].*

8   EFFECTIVE DATES AND TRANSITIONAL PROVISIONS

This section contains information that is relevant for annual periods beginning on or after 1 January 2015. For earlier periods, equivalent requirements are dealt with in *International GAAP 2014* and other predecessors to this publication.

8.1   Adoption of IFRS 9: effective date and transitional provisions

This section is prepared for entities applying the version of IFRS 9 published in July 2014 in its entirety. IFRS 9 and the consequential amendments to IFRS 7 and IAS 1, which are noted throughout this chapter, are effective for periods beginning on or after 1 January 2018. Entities are permitted to apply the standard earlier, however if they do, this fact should be disclosed. *[IFRS 9.7.1.1].* Comparative periods need not be restated when IFRS 9 is first applied. *[IFRS 9.7.2.15].*

8.2   Adoption of IFRS 9: disclosure requirements

When IFRS 9 is first applied, the following information should be disclosed, in a table unless another format is more appropriate, for each class of financial assets and financial liabilities at the date of initial application: *[IFRS 7.42I]*

- the original measurement category and carrying amount determined in accordance with IAS 39;

- the new measurement category and carrying amount determined in accordance with IFRS 9; and

- the amount of any financial assets and financial liabilities that were previously designated as measured at fair value through profit or loss but are no longer so designated, distinguishing between those that are required to be reclassified and those which an entity elects to reclassify.

In addition, qualitative information should be disclosed to provide an understanding of: *[IFRS 7.42J]*

- how the classification requirements in IFRS 9 were applied to those financial assets whose classification has changed as a result of applying IFRS 9; and

- the reasons for any designation or de-designation of financial assets or financial liabilities as measured at fair value through profit or loss.

Chapter 53

The following additional disclosures should also be provided on the application of IFRS 9: *[IFRS 7.44S, IFRS 9.7.2.13]*

- at the date of initial application of IFRS 9, changes in the classifications of financial assets and financial liabilities, showing separately: *[IFRS 7.42L]*

  - changes in the carrying amounts on the basis of their measurement categories in accordance with IAS 39 (i.e. not resulting from a change in measurement attribute on transition to IFRS 9); and

  - the changes in the carrying amounts arising from a change in measurement attribute on transition to IFRS 9; and

- in the reporting period in which IFRS 9 is initially applied, for financial assets and financial liabilities that have been reclassified so that they are measured at amortised cost and, in the case of financial assets, that have been reclassified out of fair value through profit or loss so that they are measured at fair value through other comprehensive income, as a result of the transition to IFRS 9: *[IFRS 7.42M]*

  - the fair value of the financial assets or financial liabilities at the end of the reporting period; and

  - the fair value gain or loss that would have been recognised in profit or loss or other comprehensive income during the reporting period if the financial assets or financial liabilities had not been reclassified;

- for financial assets and financial liabilities that have been reclassified out of fair value through profit or loss as a result of the transition to IFRS 9: *[IFRS 7.42N]*

  - the effective interest rate determined on the date of initial application; and

  - the interest income or expense recognised.

If an entity treats the fair value of a financial asset or a financial liability as its amortised cost at the date of initial application (see Chapter 46 at 10.2.7.B), these disclosures should be made for each reporting period following reclassification until derecognition. *[IFRS 7.42N]*.

These disclosures, together with other information in the financial statements, must permit reconciliation as at the date of initial application between: *[IFRS 7.42O]*

- the measurement categories presented in accordance with IAS 39 and IFRS 9; and

- the class of financial instrument.

Information should be disclosed that permits the reconciliation as at the date of initial application of the ending impairment allowances in accordance with IAS 39 and the provisions in accordance with IAS 37 – *Provisions, Contingent Liabilities and Contingent Assets* – to the opening loss allowances determined in accordance with IFRS 9. For financial assets, this disclosure should be provided by the related financial assets' measurement categories in accordance with IAS 39 and IFRS 9 and show separately the effect of the changes in the measurement category on the loss allowance at that date. *[IFRS 7.42P]*.

In the reporting period that includes the date of initial application of IFRS 9, an entity is not required to disclose the line item amounts that would have been reported in accordance with the classification and measurement requirements (including the requirements related to amortised cost measurement of financial assets and impairment) of IFRS 9 for prior periods or IAS 39 for the current period: *[IFRS 7.42Q]*

If, at the date of initial application of IFRS 9, it is impracticable (as defined in IAS 8) to assess:

- a modified time value of money element based on the facts and circumstances that existed at the initial recognition of a financial asset; or

- whether the fair value of a prepayment feature was insignificant based on the facts and circumstances that existed at the initial recognition of a financial asset,

the contractual cash flow characteristics of that asset should be based on the facts and circumstances that existed at that time without taking into account the requirements related to the modification of the time value of money or the exception for prepayment features as appropriate. The carrying amount of the financial assets whose contractual cash flow characteristics have been assessed in this way should be disclosed, separately for each of the two situations above, at each reporting date until those financial assets are derecognised. *[IFRS 7.42R, 42S]*.

These disclosures should be provided irrespective of whether comparatives are restated.

8.3   Other amendments to IFRS 7

The application guidance added to IFRS 7 that clarifies the meaning of 'continuing involvement' for the purposes of disclosures about transfers of financial assets (see 6.3.1 above) is effective for periods commencing on or after 1 January 2016 and earlier application is permitted, although an entity should disclose that it has done so. However, the guidance need not be applied for any period presented that begins before the annual period for which an entity first applies that guidance. *IFRS 7.44AA]*. In other words, comparative periods need not be restated.

The amendments clarifying that disclosures about offsetting are not normally required in interim reports (see 2.3 above) has the same effective date and same requirement to disclose if this is applied in earlier periods. *[IFRS 7.44AA]*.

9   FUTURE DEVELOPMENTS

9.1   General developments

Disclosure requirements are considered important by the IASB and those in respect of financial instruments have been expanded significantly as a result of changes made following the financial crisis. However, it seems unlikely that further major changes will be forthcoming in the near term.

The IASB's disclosure initiative (see Chapter 3 at 6.1) may influence the way entities present their disclosures about financial instruments. Initiatives by other bodies, such as reports and surveys of the Enhanced Disclosure Task Force of the Financial Stability Board (see 9.2 below) and the Basel Committee on Banking Supervision, may also influence the disclosures provided, particularly by financial institutions. In addition, we may see a gradual evolution of disclosure requirements in the light of practical experience.

In the longer term, any new accounting requirements arising from the IASB's project addressing macro hedge accounting (see Chapter 52 at 3.6.5) will likely be accompanied by extensive new disclosure requirements.

9.2   Enhanced Disclosure Task Force

The Enhanced Disclosure Task Force ('EDTF') is a private sector group comprising representatives from financial institutions, investors and analysts, credit rating agencies and external auditors. It was formed by the Financial Stability Forum in May 2012 and its objectives include the development of principles for enhanced disclosures about market conditions and risks, including ways to enhance the comparability of those disclosures and identifying those disclosures seen as leading practice.

In October 2012 the EDTF issued its first report. Seven fundamental principles for achieving enhanced risk disclosures were identified, namely that disclosures should:

- be clear, balanced and understandable;
- be comprehensive and include all of the bank's key activities and risks;
- present relevant information;
- reflect how the bank manages its risks;
- be consistent over time;
- be comparable among banks; and
- be provided on a timely basis.

The report also identified a number of detailed recommendations for enhancing risk disclosures, grouped under the following subjects (as well as addressing more general matters):

- risk governance and risk management strategies/business model;
- capital adequacy and risk-weighted assets;
- liquidity;
- funding;
- market risk;
- credit risk; and
- other risks.

These were accompanied by illustrative examples as well as observations on and extracts from recent reports issued by banks. The EDTF issued two further reports in August 2013 and September 2014 which charted the progress of a number of banks in applying the principles and recommendations set out in the first report.

High quality disclosure will be particularly important when introducing an expected credit loss impairment approach since it will differ from the calculation of expected losses for regulatory capital purposes and because model-based provisioning is inherently complex. At the time of writing, the EDTF is developing guidance for banks in this area. This will aim to enhance their disclosures, help the market understand the upcoming change in provisioning based on expected credit losses (whether under IFRS or US GAAP) and promote consistency and comparability of disclosures across internationally-active banks.

The guidance is expected to build on the existing fundamental principles and recommendations noted above and address the following key areas of focus:

- concepts, interpretations and policies developed to implement the new expected credit loss approaches, including the significant credit deterioration assessment required by IFRS 9;

- the specific methodologies and estimation techniques developed;

- the impact of moving from an incurred to an expected credit loss approach;

- understanding the dynamics of changes in impairment allowances and their sensitivity to significant assumptions;

- any changes made to the governance, processes and controls over financial reporting, and how they link with existing governance, processes and controls over other areas including credit risk management and regulatory reporting; and

- understanding the differences between the expected credit losses applied in and in determining regulatory capital.

We anticipate the EDTF will publish a report containing this guidance before the end of 2015 and, as a result, banks will be expected to start explaining the impacts of adopting IFRS 9 in their next annual reports.

Chapter 53

References

1 IFRS 7, Appendix B, Application guidance, para. after main heading.
2 IFRS 7, Guidance on implementing, para. after main heading.
3 In September 2010 the IASB replaced the *Framework* with the *Conceptual Framework for Financial Reporting*, Chapter 3 of which contains guidance on materiality. However, the guidance on materiality in IAS 1 has not been updated to reflect this.

4 CESR Statement, *Application of and disclosures related to the reclassification of financial instruments*, CESR, July 2009.
5 Information for Observers (December 2008 IASB Meeting), *IFRS 7 Financial Instruments: Disclosures – Minor Amendments (Agenda paper 14)*, IASB, December 2008, paras. 93 to 98 and *IASB Update*, December 2008.

6 Information for Observers (December 2008 IASB Meeting), *IFRS 7 Financial Instruments: Disclosures – Minor Amendments (Agenda paper 14)*, IASB, December 2008, paras. 30 to 40 and *IASB Update*, December 2008.

7 Information for Observers (December 2008 IASB Meeting), *IFRS 7 Financial Instruments: Disclosures – Minor Amendments (Agenda paper 14)*, IASB, December 2008, para. 32.

8 Transition Resource Group for Impairment of Financial Instruments, *Meeting Summary -22 April 2015*, IASB, April 2015, para. 57(b).

9 Information for Observers (January 2009 IASB Meeting), *Proposed amendments on liquidity risk disclosures (Agenda paper 14B)*, IASB, January 2009, para. 32.

10 Information for Observers (September 2008 IASB Meeting), *IFRS 7 Financial Instruments: Disclosures, Liquidity risk (Agenda paper 2A)*, IASB, September 2008, para. 34(b) and Information for Observers (January 2009 IASB Meeting), *Proposed amendments on liquidity risk disclosures (Agenda paper 14B)*, IASB, January 2009, para. 35(a).

11 Information for Observers (September 2008 IASB Meeting), *IFRS 7 Financial Instruments: Disclosures, Liquidity risk (Agenda paper 2A)*, IASB, September 2008, para. 34(c).

12 Information for Observers (September 2008 IASB Meeting), *IFRS 7 Financial Instruments: Disclosures, Liquidity risk (Agenda paper 2A)*, IASB, September 2008, paras. 40 and 41.

13 Information for Observers (September 2008 IASB Meeting), *IFRS 7 Financial Instruments: Disclosures, Liquidity risk (Agenda paper 2A)*, IASB, September 2008, paras. 34(d).

14 Information for Observers (September 2008 IASB Meeting), *IFRS 7 Financial Instruments: Disclosures, Liquidity risk (Agenda paper 2A)*, IASB, September 2008, para. 25.

15 Information for Observers (December 2008 IASB Meeting), *IFRS 7 Financial Instruments: Disclosures – Minor Amendments (Agenda paper 14)*, IASB, December 2008, paras. 71 to 79 and IASB Update, December 2008.

16 Information for Observers (December 2008 IASB Meeting), *IFRS 7 Financial Instruments: Disclosures – Minor Amendments (Agenda paper 14)*, IASB, December 2008, para. 86.

17 Information for Observers (December 2008 IASB Meeting), *IFRS 7 Financial Instruments: Disclosures – Minor Amendments (Agenda paper 14)*, IASB, December 2008, paras. 80 to 88 and IASB Update, December 2008.

18 Transition Resource Group for Impairment of Financial Instruments, *Meeting Summary -22 April 2015*, IASB, April 2015, paras. 24 and 25.

19 Transition Resource Group for Impairment of Financial Instruments, *Meeting Summary -22 April 2015*, IASB, April 2015, para. 57(a).

20 *IFRIC Update*, October 2004 and November 2006.

21 *IFRIC Update*, January 2015.

22 *IFRIC Update*, January 2015.

23 IAS 30, *Disclosures in the Financial Statements of Banks and Similar Financial Institutions*, IASB, August 1990 to December 2003, para. 13.

24 Information for Observers (March 2007 IFRIC meeting), *Current or non-current presentation of derivatives that are not designated as hedging instruments in effective hedges*, IASB, March 2007, paras. 14 and 17 and Information for Observers (11 March 2008 IASB meeting), *ED Annual improvements process – Comment analysis: IAS 1 Current/non-current classification of derivatives (Q6)*, IASB, March 2008, para. 12.

25 Staff Paper (September 2010 IFRS Interpretations Committee Meeting), *Current/non-current classification of callable term loan*, IASB, September 2010.

26 *IFRIC Update*, September 2010.

27 *IFRIC Update*, January 2011 and Staff Paper (January 2011 IFRS Interpretations Committee Meeting), *IAS 1 Presentation of Financial Statements – current/non-current classification of debt (rollover agreements) – outreach results*, IASB, January 2011.

Chapter 54   Insurance contracts

Chapter 54

List of examples

Chapter 54

Chapter 54   Insurance contracts

1   INTRODUCTION

1.1   The history of the IASB's insurance project

The IASB and its predecessor, the IASC, have been attempting to develop a comprehensive standard on insurance contracts since 1997 when a Steering Committee was established to carry out the initial project work. *[IFRS 4.BC3]*. It was decided to develop a standard on insurance contracts because:

(a) there was no standard on insurance contracts, and insurance contracts were excluded from the scope of existing standards that would otherwise have been relevant; and

(b) accounting practices for insurance contracts are diverse, and also often differ from practices in other sectors. *[IFRS 4.BC2]*.

Historically, the IASB and its predecessor have avoided dealing with specific accounting issues relating to insurance contracts by excluding them from the scope of their accounting standards. Currently, insurance contracts are excluded from the scope of the following standards:

- IAS 18 – *Revenue*;
- IAS 32 – *Financial Instruments: Presentation*;
- IAS 36 – *Impairment of Assets*;
- IAS 37 – *Provisions, Contingent Liabilities and Contingent Assets*;
- IAS 38 – *Intangible Assets*;
- IAS 39 – *Financial Instruments: Recognition and Measurement*;
- IFRS 7 – *Financial Instruments: Disclosures*;
- IFRS 9 – *Financial Instruments*; and
- IFRS 15 – *Revenue from Contracts with Customers*.

An alternative to developing a standard on insurance contracts would have been for the IASB to remove the insurance contract scope exemptions from these standards. Revenue would then have to be measured in accordance with IAS 18 (or IFRS 15) and most insurance contract liabilities would have to be recognised in accordance with either IAS 39 (or IFRS 9) or IAS 37 depending on their nature. However, the IASB and its predecessor were persuaded that an insurance contract is sufficiently unique to warrant its own accounting standard and have so far spent thirteen years attempting to decide what accounting that standard should require.

The Steering Committee established in 1997 published an Issues Paper – *Insurance* – in December 1999 which attracted 138 comment letters. Following a review of the comment letters, the committee developed a report to the IASB that was published in 2001 as a *Draft Statement of Principles – Insurance Contracts* (DSOP). The DSOP was never approved. *[IFRS 4.BC3].*

The IASB began discussing the DSOP in November 2001. However, at its May 2002 meeting the IASB concluded that it would not be realistic to expect the implementation of a full recognition and measurement standard for insurance contracts by 2005 (in time for the adoption of IFRS in the EU).[1]

Consequently, the insurance project was split into two phases: Phase I, which became IFRS 4 – *Insurance Contracts* – and Phase II, which encompasses the IASB's subsequent work to develop a full recognition and measurement standard for insurance contracts. Although the IASB did not approve the DSOP or invite formal comments on it a significant part of its wording has found its way into IFRS 4.

Phase II was later suspended in January 2003 due to other IASB priorities and subsequently restarted in September 2004. A Discussion Paper (DP) – *Preliminary Views on Insurance Contracts* – was issued in May 2007, an Exposure Draft (2010 ED), *ED 2010/8 – Insurance Contracts* – was published in July 2010 and a revised Exposure Draft (revised ED), ED/2013/7 – *Insurance Contracts* – was published in June 2013. The revised ED is discussed at 11 below.

1.2   The development of IFRS 4

IFRS 4 was the result of Phase I of the IASB's insurance contract project. It was finalised in a relatively short period by the IASB once it became clear that a standard was required in time for the EU adoption of IFRS in 2005. An exposure draft, ED 5 – *Insurance Contracts* – was issued in July 2003 with a comment period expiring on 31 October 2003. The IASB was extremely responsive to comment letters with most of the major concerns of the insurance industry being addressed in the final standard when it was issued in March 2004. IFRS 4 was first applicable for accounting periods beginning on or after 1 January 2005 with earlier adoption encouraged. *[IFRS 4.41].*

One significant concern that the IASB was unable to address was the mismatching of financial assets and insurance liabilities. Under IAS 39, many financial investments are held at fair value and, if those assets are classified as available-for-sale, unrealised fair value movements are recognised in other comprehensive income. By contrast all movements in insurance liabilities are normally recognised in profit or loss and most non-life insurance liabilities under most existing local GAAP models are undiscounted. A number of respondents to ED 5 suggested the creation of an investment category called 'investments held to back insurance contracts' (or words similar to that). Investments in this category would be held at amortised cost. However, the IASB concluded that changing the measurement requirements for financial assets in IAS 39, even temporarily, would diminish the relevance and reliability of an insurer's financial statements. In the view of the IASB this mismatch is caused by imperfections in the insurance liability measurement model rather than deficiencies in the financial investments measurement model and hence the suggestion went no further. *[IFRS 4.BC166-174]*.

Although IFRS 4 has now been in force for eleven years the standard was intended originally to be a temporary one that would last no more than a few years. As discussed at 11 below, a final standard is unlikely to be issued until 2016 and the effective date is unlikely to be before 2020.

1.3   Existing accounting practices for insurance contracts

Existing local accounting practices for insurance contracts are diverse. Typically such practices, including the definition of what constitutes an insurance contract, are driven by regulatory requirements. There may also be separate GAAP and regulatory rules for insurers. For example, in the European Union, there are separate financial statement presentation requirements for insurance entities which differ from those for non-insurance entities.

Many jurisdictions have also evolved different accounting rules for non-life (property/casualty) or short-term insurance and life or long-term insurance. However, the boundaries between what is considered non-life and life insurance can vary between jurisdictions and even within jurisdictions.

1.3.1   Non-life insurance

Non-life or short-term insurance transactions under local GAAP are typically accounted for on a deferral and matching basis. This means that premiums are normally recognised as revenue over the contract period, usually on a time apportionment basis. Claims are usually recognised on an incurred basis with no provision for claims that have not occurred at the reporting date. Within this basic model differences exist across local GAAPs on various points of detail which include:

- whether or not claims liabilities are discounted;
- the basis for measuring claims liabilities (e.g. best estimate or a required confidence level);
- whether and what acquisition costs are deferred;
- whether a liability adequacy test (see 7.2.2 below) is performed on the unearned revenue or premium balance and the methodology and level of aggregation applied in such a test; and
- whether reinsurance follows the same model as direct insurance and whether immediate gains on retroactive reinsurance contracts are permitted or not (see 7.2.6 below).

Chapter 54

1.3.2   *Life insurance*

Most local GAAP life insurance accounting models recognise premiums when receivable and insurance contract liabilities are typically measured under some form of discounted cash flow approach that calculates the cash flows expected over the lifetime of the contract. In many jurisdictions the key inputs to the calculation (e.g. discount rates, mortality rates) are set by regulators. Key assumptions may be current or 'locked-in' at the contract inception. Differences across jurisdictions also include:

- whether or not certain investment-type products are subject to 'deposit accounting' (i.e. only fees are recognised as revenue rather than all cash inflows from policyholders);

- if, and how (contracts with) discretionary participation features are accounted for (discussed at 6 below);

- whether and what acquisition costs are deferred;

- how to account for options and guarantees embedded within contracts; and

- the use of contingency reserves or provisions for adverse deviation.

1.3.3   *Embedded value*

The embedded value (EV) of a life insurance business is an estimate of its economic worth excluding any value which may be attributed to future new business. The EV is the sum of the value placed on the entity's equity and the value of the in-force business. Typically, an embedded value calculation would involve discounting the value of the stream of after tax profits. For insurance liabilities the income stream would normally be calculated by using the income stream from the backing invested assets as a proxy.

EV is used as an alternative (non-GAAP) performance measure by some life insurers to illustrate the performance and value of their business because local accounting is rarely seen as providing this information. This is because local accounting is often driven by what management consider are 'unrealistic' regulatory rules and assumptions. *[IFRS 4.BC140]*.

There is no standardised global measure of embedded value and embedded value practices are diverse. For example, in Europe, the CFO Forum, an organisation comprising the Chief Financial Officers of Europe's leading life and property and casualty insurers, has published both *European Embedded Values (EEV)* and *Market Consistent Embedded Value Principles (MCEV)*. Either of these embedded value models can be applied by Forum members.[2]

The potential use of embedded value under IFRS 4 is discussed at 8.2.4 below.

2 THE OBJECTIVES AND SCOPE OF IFRS 4

2.1 The objectives of IFRS 4

The stated objectives of IFRS 4 are:

(a) to make limited improvements to accounting by insurers for insurance contracts; and

(b) to require disclosures that identify and explain the amounts in an insurer's financial statements arising from insurance contracts and help users of those financial statements understand the amount, timing and uncertainty of future cash flows from insurance contracts. *[IFRS 4.1].*

It is not IFRS 4's stated objective to determine, in a comprehensive way, how insurance contracts are recognised, measured and presented. This will be addressed by the Phase II standard. Instead, issuers of insurance contracts are permitted, with certain limitations, to continue to apply their existing, normally local, GAAP. This is discussed further at 7 below.

2.2 The scope of IFRS 4

2.2.1 Definitions

The following definitions are relevant to the application of IFRS 4.

An *insurer* is the party that has an obligation under an insurance contract to compensate a policyholder if an insured event occurs.

An *insurance contract* is a contract under which one party (the insurer) accepts significant insurance risk from another party (the policyholder) by agreeing to compensate the policyholder if a specified uncertain future event (the insured event) adversely affects the policyholder.

A *reinsurer* is the party that has an obligation under a reinsurance contract to compensate a cedant if an insured event occurs.

A *reinsurance contract* is an insurance contract issued by one insurer (the reinsurer) to compensate another insurer (the cedant) for losses on one or more contracts issued by the cedant.

An *insured event* is an uncertain future event that is covered by an insurance contract and creates insurance risk.

An *insurance asset* is an insurer's net contractual rights under an insurance contract.

A *reinsurance asset* is a cedant's net contractual rights under a reinsurance contract.

An *insurance liability* is an insurer's net contractual obligations under an insurance contract.

A *cedant* is the policyholder under a reinsurance contract.

A *policyholder* is a party that has a right to compensation under an insurance contract if an insured event occurs.

Fair value is the price that would be received to sell an asset or paid to transfer a liability in an orderly transaction between market participants at the measurement date. This definition of fair value is the same as in IFRS 13 – *Fair Value Measurement*.

Guaranteed benefits are payments or other benefits to which a particular policyholder or investor has an unconditional right that is not subject to the contractual discretion of the issuer.

A *discretionary participation feature* (DPF) is a contractual right to receive, as a supplement to guaranteed benefits, additional benefits:

(a)   that are likely to be a significant portion of the total contractual benefits;

(b)   whose amount or timing is contractually at the discretion of the issuer; and

(c)   that are contractually based on:

   (i)   the performance of a specified pool of contracts or a specified type of contract;

   (ii)   realised and/or unrealised investment returns on a specified pool of assets held by the issuer; or

   (iii)   the profit or loss of the company, fund or other entity that issues the contract.

A *financial guarantee contract* is a contract that requires the issuer to make specified payments to reimburse the holder for a loss it incurs because a specified debtor fails to make payment when due in accordance with the original or modified terms of a debt instrument. *[IFRS 4 Appendix A].*

2.2.2   Transactions within the scope of IFRS 4

Unless specifically excluded from its scope (see 2.2.3 below) IFRS 4 must be applied to:

(a)   insurance contracts (including reinsurance contracts) issued by an entity and reinsurance contracts that it holds; and

(b)   financial instruments that an entity issues with a discretionary participation feature (see 6.2 below). *[IFRS 4.2].*

It can be seen from this that IFRS 4 applies to insurance contracts and not just to entities that specialise in issuing insurance contracts. Consistent with other IFRSs it is a transaction-based standard. Consequently, non-insurance entities will be within its scope if they issue contracts that meet the definition of an insurance contract.

IFRS 4 describes any entity that issues an insurance contract as an insurer whether or not the entity is regarded as an insurer for legal or supervisory purposes. *[IFRS 4.5].*

Often an insurance contract will meet the definition of a financial instrument but IAS 39 (and IFRS 9) contains a scope exemption for both insurance contracts and for contracts that would otherwise be within its scope but are within the scope of IFRS 4 because they contain a discretionary participation feature (see 6 below). *[IAS 39.2(e); IFRS 9.2.1(e)].*

Although the recognition and measurement of financial instruments (or investment contracts) with a discretionary participation feature is governed by IFRS 4, for disclosure purposes they are within the scope of IFRS 7. *[IFRS 4.2(b)].*

Contracts that fail to meet the definition of an insurance contract are within the scope of IAS 39 or IFRS 9 if they meet the definition of a financial instrument (unless they contain a DPF). This will be the case even if such contracts are regulated as insurance contracts under local legislation. These contracts are commonly referred to as 'investment contracts'.

Consequently, under IFRS, many insurers have different measurement and disclosure requirements applying to contracts that, under local GAAP or local regulatory rules, might, or might not, have been subject to the same measurement or disclosure requirements. The following table illustrates the standards applying to such contracts.

Type of contract	Recognition and Measurement	Disclosure
Insurance contract issued (both with and without a DPF)	IFRS 4	IFRS 4
Reinsurance contract held and issued	IFRS 4	IFRS 4
Investment contract with a DPF	IFRS 4	IFRS 7/IFRS 13
Investment contract without a DPF	IAS 39/IFRS 9	IFRS 7/IFRS 13

Many local GAAPs and local regulatory regimes prescribe different accounting requirements for life (long term) and non-life (short-term) insurance contracts (see 1.3 above). However, IFRS 4 does not distinguish between different types of insurance contracts.

IFRS 4 confirms that a reinsurance contract is a type of insurance contract and that all references to insurance contracts apply equally to reinsurance contracts. *[IFRS 4.6].*

Because all rights and obligations arising from insurance contracts and investment contracts with a DPF are also scoped out of IAS 39 (and IFRS 9), IFRS 4 applies to all the assets and liabilities arising from insurance contracts. *[IAS 39.2(e); IFRS 9.2.1(e)].* These include:

- insurance and reinsurance receivables owed by the policyholder direct to the insurer;
- insurance receivables owed by an intermediary to an insurer on behalf of the policyholder where the intermediary is acting in a fiduciary capacity;
- insurance claims agreed with the policyholder and payable;
- insurance contract policy liabilities;
- claims handling cost provisions;
- the present value of acquired in-force business (discussed at 9.1 below);
- deferred or unearned premium reserves;
- reinsurance assets (i.e. expected reinsurance recoveries in respect of claims incurred);
- deferred acquisition costs; and
- discretionary participation features (DPF).

However, payables and receivables arising out of investment contracts fall within the scope of IAS 39 (or IFRS 9) and the capitalisation and deferral of costs arising from such contracts currently fall within the scope of IAS 18, IAS 38 and IAS 39 (or IFRS 9).

Receivables due from intermediaries to insurers that have a financing character and balances due from intermediaries not acting in a fiduciary capacity, for example loans to intermediaries repayable from commissions earned, would also seem to be outside the scope of IFRS 4 as they do not arise from insurance contracts.

2.2.3   *Transactions not within the scope of IFRS 4*

With the exception of certain matters which are relevant when an entity first applies IFRS 4 (see 7 below) the standard does not address other aspects of accounting by insurers such as accounting for financial assets held and financial liabilities issued. The recognition and measurement requirements for these transactions are contained in IAS 39 (or IFRS 9) and the disclosure requirements are contained in IFRS 7. *[IFRS 4.3]*.

IFRS 4 describes transactions to which IFRS 4 is not applied. These primarily relate to transactions covered by other standards that could potentially meet the definition of an insurance contract. It was not the intention of the IASB in issuing IFRS 4 to reopen issues addressed by other standards unless the specific features of insurance contracts justified a different treatment. *[IFRS 4.BC10(c)]*. These transactions are discussed below.

2.2.3.A   *Product warranties*

Product warranties issued directly by a manufacturer, dealer or retailer are outside the scope of IFRS 4. These are accounted for under IAS 18 and IAS 37. *[IFRS 4.4(a)]*.

Without this exception many product warranties would have been covered by IFRS 4 as they would normally meet the definition of an insurance contract. The IASB has excluded them from the scope of IFRS 4 because they are closely related to the underlying sale of goods and because IAS 37 addresses product warranties while IAS 18 (or IFRS 15 – *Revenue from Contracts with Customers*) deals with the revenue received for such warranties. *[IFRS 4.BC71]*.

However, a product warranty is within the scope of IFRS 4 if an entity issues it on behalf of another party i.e. the contract is issued indirectly. *[IFRS 4.BC69]*.

Other types of warranty are not specifically excluded from the scope of IFRS 4. For example, a warranty given by a vendor to the purchaser of a business, such as in respect of contingent liabilities related to unagreed tax computations of the acquired entity, is an example of a transaction that may also fall within the scope of this standard. However, since IFRS 4 does not prescribe a specific accounting treatment, issuers of such warranties are likely to be able to apply their existing accounting policies.

2.2.3.B   *Assets and liabilities arising from employment benefit plans*

Employers' assets and liabilities under employee benefit plans and retirement benefit obligations reported by defined benefit retirement plans are excluded from the scope of IFRS 4. These are accounted for under IAS 19 – *Employee Benefits*, IFRS 2 – *Share-based Payment* – and IAS 26 – *Accounting and Reporting by Retirement Benefit Plans*. *[IFRS 4.4(b)]*.

Many defined benefit pension plans and similar post-employment benefits meet the definition of an insurance contract because the payments to pensioners are contingent on uncertain future events such as the continuing survival of current or retired employees. Without this exception they would have been within the scope of IFRS 4.

2.2.3.C   Contingent rights and obligations related to non-financial items

Contractual rights or contractual obligations that are contingent on the future use of, or right to use, a non-financial item (for example, some licence fees, royalties, contingent lease payments and similar items) are excluded from the scope of IFRS 4, as well as a lessee's residual value guarantee embedded in a finance lease which is accounted for under IAS 17 – *Leases*. *[IFRS 4.4(c)]*.

2.2.3.D   Financial guarantee contracts

Financial guarantee contracts are excluded from the scope of IFRS 4 unless the issuer has previously asserted explicitly that it regards such contracts as insurance contracts and has used accounting applicable to insurance contracts, in which case the issuer may elect to apply either IAS 32, IAS 39 (or IFRS 9) and IFRS 7 or IFRS 4 to them. The issuer may make that election contract by contract, but the election for each contract is irrevocable. *[IFRS 4.4(d)]*.

Where financial guarantees are not accounted for under IFRS 4 they should normally be measured on initial recognition at their (negative) fair value and subsequently at the higher of:

- the amount recognised under IAS 37; and
- the amount initially recognised less, where appropriate, cumulative amortisation recognised in accordance with IAS 18.

Where an insurer elects to use IFRS 4 to account for its financial guarantee contracts, its accounting policy defaults to its previous GAAP for such contracts (subject to any limitations discussed at 7.2 below) unless subsequently modified as permitted by IFRS 4 (see 8 below).

IFRS 4 does not elaborate on the phrase 'previously asserted explicitly'. However, the application guidance to IAS 39 and IFRS 9 states that assertions that an issuer regards contracts as insurance contracts are typically found throughout the issuer's communications with customers and regulators, contracts, business documentation and financial statements. Furthermore, insurance contracts are often subject to accounting requirements that are distinct from the requirements for other types of transaction, such as contracts issued by banks or commercial companies. In such cases, an issuer's financial statements typically include a statement that the issuer has used those accounting requirements. *[IAS 39.AG4A; IFRS 9.B2.6]*. Therefore, it is likely that insurers that have previously issued financial guarantee contracts and accounted for them under an insurance accounting and regulatory framework will meet these criteria. It is unlikely that an entity not subject to an insurance accounting and regulatory framework, or new insurers (start-up companies) and existing insurers that had not previously issued financial guarantee contracts would meet this criteria because they would not have previously made the necessary assertions.

The proposed treatment of financial guarantee contracts in the revised ED is the same as IFRS 4.

2.2.3.E   Contingent consideration payable or receivable in a business combination

Contingent consideration payable or receivable in a business combination is outside the scope of IFRS 4. *[IFRS 4.4(e)]*. Contingent consideration in a business combination is required to be recognised at fair value at the acquisition date with subsequent remeasurements of non equity consideration included in profit or loss. *[IFRS 3.58]*.

2.2.3.F   Direct insurance contracts in which the entity is the policyholder

Accounting by policyholders of direct insurance contracts (i.e. those that are not reinsurance contracts) is excluded from the scope of IFRS 4 because the IASB did not regard this as a high priority for Phase I. *[IFRS 4.4(f), BC73]*. However, holders of reinsurance contracts (cedants) are required to apply IFRS 4. *[IFRS 4.4(f)]*. The IASB originally intended to address accounting by policyholders of direct insurance contracts in the Phase II standard but changed its mind and excluded them from the revised ED on the grounds that there are 'no pressing reasons to address this topic'.[3]

A policyholder's rights and obligations under an insurance contract are also excluded from the scope of IAS 32, IAS 39 (or IFRS 9) and IFRS 7. However, the IAS 8 – *Accounting Policies, Changes in Accounting Estimates and Errors* – hierarchy does apply to policyholders when determining an accounting policy for direct insurance contracts. IAS 37 addresses accounting for reimbursements from insurers for expenditure required to settle a provision and IAS 16 – *Property, Plant and Equipment* – addresses some aspects of compensation from third parties for property, plant and equipment that is impaired, lost or given up. *[IFRS 4.BC73]*.

The principal outlined in IAS 37 is that reimbursements and contingent assets can only be recognised if an inflow of economic benefits is virtually certain. *[IAS 37.33, 56]*. IAS 16 requires that compensation from third parties for property, plant and equipment impaired, lost or given up is included in profit or loss when it 'becomes receivable'. *[IAS 16.66(c)]*. These are likely to be more onerous recognition tests than any applied under IFRS 4 for cedants with reinsurance assets which will be based on local insurance GAAP.

2.2.4   The product classification process

Because of the need to determine which transactions should be within the scope of IFRS 4, and which transactions are not within its scope, one of the main procedures required of insurers as part of their first-time adoption of IFRS 4 is to conduct a product classification review.

Many large groups developed a product classification process to determine the appropriate classification on a consistent basis. In order to ensure consistency, the product classification process is typically set out in the group accounting manual.

The assessment of the appropriate classification for a contract will include an assessment of whether the contract contains significant insurance risk (discussed at 3 below), and whether the contract contains embedded derivatives (discussed at 4 below), deposit components (discussed at 5 below) or discretionary participation features (discussed at 6 below).

The diagram below illustrates a product classification decision tree.

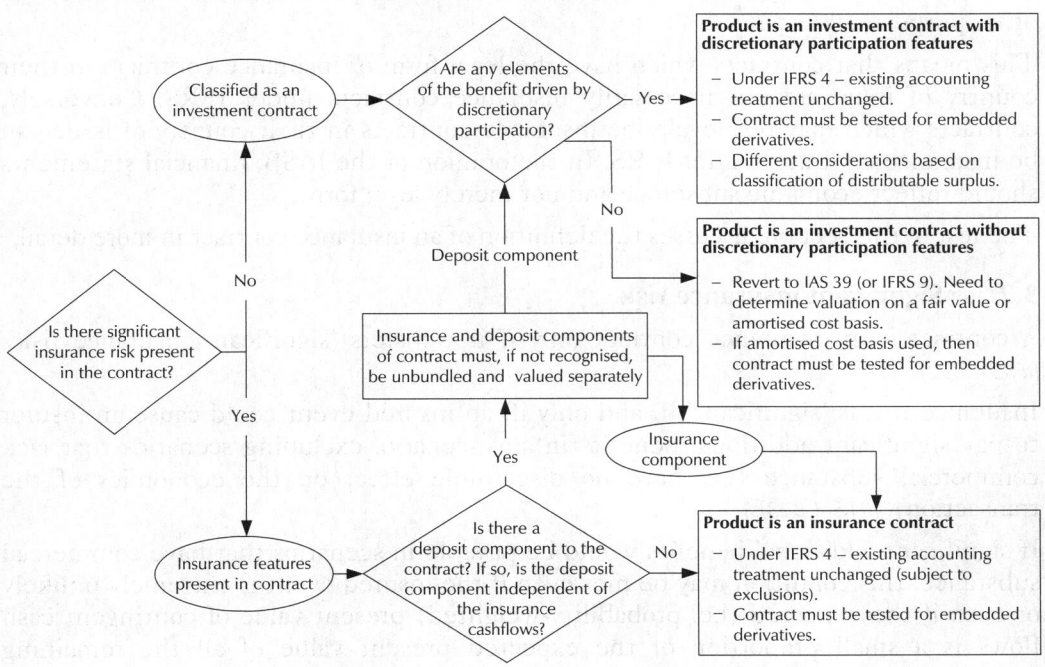

3 THE DEFINITION OF AN INSURANCE CONTRACT

3.1 The definition

The definition of an insurance contract in IFRS 4 is:

'A contract under which one party (the insurer) accepts significant insurance risk from another party (the policyholder) by agreeing to compensate the policyholder if a specified uncertain future event (the insured event) adversely affects the policyholder'. *[IFRS 4 Appendix A]*.

This definition determines which contracts are within the scope of IFRS 4 rather than other standards.

The IASB rejected using existing national definitions because they believed it unsatisfactory to base the definition used in IFRS on definitions that may vary from country to country and may not be the most relevant for deciding which IFRS ought to apply to a particular type of contract. *[IFRS 4.BC12]*.

In response to concerns that the definition in IFRS 4 could ultimately lead to changes in definitions used for other purposes, such as insurance law, insurance supervision or tax, the IASB made it clear that any definition within IFRS is solely for financial reporting and is not intended to change or pre-empt definitions used for other purposes. *[IFRS 4.BC13].*

This means that contracts which have the legal form of insurance contracts in their country of issue are not necessarily insurance contracts under IFRS. Conversely, contracts which may not legally be insurance contracts in their country of issue can be insurance contracts under IFRS. In the opinion of the IASB, financial statements should reflect economic substance and not merely legal form.

The rest of this section discusses the definition of an insurance contract in more detail.

3.2   Significant insurance risk

A contract is an insurance contract only if it transfers 'significant insurance risk'. *[IFRS 4.B22].*

Insurance risk is 'significant' if, and only if, an insured event could cause an insurer to pay significant additional benefits in any scenario, excluding scenarios that lack commercial substance (i.e. have no discernible effect on the economics of the transaction). *[IFRS 4.B23].*

If significant additional benefits would be payable in scenarios that have commercial substance, this condition may be met even if the insured event is extremely unlikely or even if the expected (i.e. probability-weighted) present value of contingent cash flows is a small proportion of the expected present value of all the remaining contractual cash flows. *[IFRS 4.B23].*

From this, we consider the IASB's intention was to make it easier, not harder, for contracts regarded as insurance contracts under most local GAAPs to be insurance contracts under IFRS 4.

Local GAAP in many jurisdictions prohibits insurance contract accounting if there are restrictions on the timing of payments or receipts. IFRS 4 has no such restrictions, provided there is significant insurance risk, although clearly the existence of restrictions on the timing of payments may mean that the policy does not transfer significant insurance risk.

3.2.1   The meaning of 'significant'

No quantitative guidance supports the determination of 'significant' in IFRS 4. This was a deliberate decision because the IASB considered that if quantitative guidance was provided it would create an arbitrary dividing line that would result in different accounting treatments for similar transactions that fall marginally on different sides of that line and would therefore create opportunities for accounting arbitrage. *[IFRS 4.BC33].*

The IASB also rejected defining the significance of insurance risk by reference to the definition of materiality within IFRS because, in their opinion, a single contract, or even a single book of similar contracts, could rarely generate a loss that would be material to the financial statements as a whole. *[IFRS 4.BC34].* The IASB also rejected the notion of defining significance of insurance risk by expressing the expected (probability weighted) average of the present values of the adverse outcomes as a proportion of the expected present value of all outcomes, or as a proportion of the premium. This idea would have required the constant monitoring of contracts over their life to see whether they continued to transfer insurance risk. As discussed at 3.3 below, an assessment of whether significant insurance risk has been transferred is normally only required at the inception of a contract. *[IFRS 4.BC35].*

The IASB believes that 'significant' means that the insured benefits certainly must be greater than 101% of the benefits payable if the insured event did not occur and it expressed this in the implementation guidance as illustrated below. It is, however, unclear how much greater than 101% the insured benefits must be to meet the definition of 'significant'.

Example 54.1: Significant insurance risk

Entity A issues a unit-linked contract that pays benefits linked to the fair value of a pool of assets. The benefit is 100% of the unit value on surrender or maturity and 101% of the unit value on death.

In this situation the implementation guidance states that if the insurance component (the additional death benefit of 1%) is not unbundled then the whole contract is an investment contract. The insurance component in this arrangement is insignificant in relation to the whole contract and so would not meet the definition of an insurance contract in IFRS 4. *[IFRS 4.IG2 E1.3].*

Some jurisdictions have their own guidance as to what constitutes significant insurance risk. However, as with IFRS 4, other jurisdictions offer no quantitative guidance. Some US GAAP practitioners apply a guideline that a reasonable possibility of a significant loss is a 10% probability of a 10% loss although this guideline does not appear in US GAAP itself. *[IFRS 4.BC32].* It is not disputed in the basis for conclusions that a 10% chance of a 10% loss results in a transfer of significant insurance risk and, indeed, the words 'extremely unlikely' and 'a small proportion' (see 3.2 above) suggests to us that the IASB envisages that significant insurance risk can exist at a different threshold than a 10% probability of a 10% loss.

This lack of a quantitative definition means that insurers must apply their own judgement as to what constitutes significant insurance risk. Although the IASB did not want to create an 'arbitrary dividing line', the practical impact of this lack of guidance is that insurers have to apply their own criteria to what constitutes significant insurance risk and there probably is inconsistency in practice as to what these dividing lines are, at least at the margins.

There is no requirement under IFRS 4 for insurers to disclose any thresholds used in determining whether a contract has transferred significant insurance risk. However, IAS 1 – *Presentation of Financial Statements* – requires an entity to disclose the judgements that management has made in the process of applying the

Chapter 54

entity's accounting policies that have the most significant effect on the amounts recognised in the financial statements (see Chapter 3 at 5.1.1.B). Liverpool Victoria made the following disclosures about significant insurance risk in its 2013 financial statements.

Extract 54.1: Liverpool Victoria Friendly Society Limited (2013)

Notes to the financial statements [extract]
Note 1.3   Accounting policies [extract]
b.   Contract classification [extract]

Insurance contracts are those contracts that transfer significant insurance risk. Such contracts may also transfer financial risk. As a general guideline, the Group defines as significant insurance risk the possibility of having to pay benefits on the occurrence of an insured event that are at least 10% more than the benefits payable if the insured event did not occur.

The revised ED contains application guidance which states that a contract does not transfer significant insurance risk if there is no scenario that has commercial substance in which the present value of the net cash flows paid by the issuer can exceed the present value of the premiums. However, if a reinsurance contract does not expose the issuer to the possibility of a significant loss, that contract would be deemed to transfer significant insurance risk if it transfers to the reinsurer substantially all of the insurance risk relating to the reinsured portions of the underlying insurance contracts. This would be a change from IFRS 4.[4] In subsequent discussions, the IASB has tentatively decided to clarify the guidance in the revised ED that significant insurance risk only occurs when there is a possibility that an issuer will incur a loss on a present value basis.[5]

3.2.2   The level at which significant insurance risk is assessed

Significant insurance risk must be assessed by individual contract, rather than by blocks of contracts or by reference to materiality to the financial statements. Thus, insurance risk may be significant even if there is a minimal probability of material losses for a whole book of contracts. *[IFRS 4.B25].*

The IASB's reasons for defining significant insurance risk in relation to a single contract were that:

(a)   although contracts are often managed and measured on a portfolio basis, the contractual rights and obligations arise from individual contracts; and

(b)   an assessment contract by contract is likely to increase the proportion of contracts that qualify as insurance contracts. The IASB intended to make it easier, not harder, for a contract previously regarded as an insurance contract under local GAAP to meet the IFRS 4 definition. *[IFRS 4.BC34].*

However, where a relatively homogeneous book of small contracts is known to consist of contracts that all transfer insurance risk, the standard does not require that an insurer examine each contract within that book to identify a few non-derivative contracts that transfer insignificant insurance risk. *[IFRS 4.B25].*

Multiple, mutually linked contracts entered into with a single counterparty (or contracts that are otherwise interdependent) should be considered a single contract for the purposes of assessing whether significant insurance risk is transferred. *[IFRS 4.B25fn].* This requirement is intended to prevent entities entering into contracts that individually transfer significant insurance risk but collectively do not and accounting for part(s) of what is effectively a single arrangement as (an) insurance contract(s).

If an insurance contract is unbundled (see 5 below) into a deposit component and an insurance component, the significance of insurance risk transferred is assessed by reference only to the insurance component. The significance of insurance risk transferred by an embedded derivative is assessed by reference only to the embedded derivative (see 4 below). *[IFRS 4.B28].*

3.2.2.A Self insurance

An insurer can accept significant insurance risk from a policyholder only if it issues an insurance contract to an entity separate from itself. Therefore, 'self insurance', such as a self-insured deductible where the insured cannot claim for losses below the excess limit of an insurance policy, is not insurance because there is no insurance contract. Accounting for self insurance and related provisions is covered by IAS 37 which requires that a provision is recognised only if there is a present obligation as a result of a past event, if it is probable that an outflow of resources will occur and a reliable estimate can be determined. *[IAS 37.14].*

3.2.2.B Insurance mutuals

A mutual insurer accepts risk from each policyholder and pools that risk. Although policyholders bear the pooled risk collectively in their capacity as owners, the mutual has still accepted the risk that is the essence of an insurance contract and therefore IFRS 4 applies to those contracts. *[IFRS 4.B17].*

3.2.2.C Intragroup insurance contracts

Where there are insurance contracts between entities in the same group these would be eliminated in the consolidated financial statements as required by IFRS 10 – *Consolidated Financial Statements*. If any intragroup insurance contract is reinsured with a third party that is not part of the group this third party reinsurance contract should be accounted for as a direct insurance contract in the consolidated financial statements of a non-insurer because the intragroup contract will be eliminated on consolidation. This residual direct insurance contract (i.e. the policy with the third party) is outside the scope of IFRS 4 from the viewpoint of the consolidated financial statements of a non-insurer because policyholder accounting is excluded from IFRS 4 as discussed at 2.2.3.F above.

3.2.3   Significant additional benefits

The 'significant additional benefits' described at 3.2 above refer to amounts that exceed those that would be payable if no insured event occurred. These additional amounts include claims handling and claims assessment costs, but exclude:

(a)   the loss of the ability to charge the policyholder for future services, for example where the ability to collect fees from a policyholder for performing future investment management services ceases if the policyholder of an investment-linked life insurance contract dies. This economic loss does not reflect insurance risk and the future investment management fees are not relevant in assessing how much insurance risk is transferred by a contract;

(b)   the waiver on death of charges that would be made on cancellation or surrender of the contract. Because the contract brought these charges into existence, the waiver of them does not compensate the policyholder for a pre-existing risk. Hence, they are not relevant in determining how much insurance risk is transferred by a contract;

(c)   a payment conditional on an event that does not cause a significant loss to the holder of the contract, for example where the issuer must pay one million currency units if an asset suffers physical damage causing an insignificant economic loss of one currency unit to the holder. The holder in this case has transferred to the insurer the insignificant insurance risk of losing one currency unit. However, at the same time the contract creates non-insurance risk that the issuer will need to pay 999,999 additional currency units if the specified event occurs;

(d)   possible reinsurance recoveries. The insurer will account for these separately; *[IFRS 4.B24]* and

(e)   the original policy premium (but not additional premiums payable in the event of claims experience – see Example 54.26 below).

The definition of insurance risk refers to risk that the insurer accepts from the policyholder. Consequently, insurance risk must be a pre-existing risk transferred from the policyholder to the insurer. A new risk, such as the inability to charge the policyholder for future services, is not insurance risk. *[IFRS 4.B12]*. The following example illustrates this.

Example 54.2:   Loan contract with prepayment fee

A loan contract contains a prepayment fee that is waived if the prepayment results from the borrower's death.

This is not an insurance contract since before entering into the contract the borrower faced no risk corresponding to the prepayment fee. Hence, although the loan contract exposes the lender to mortality risk, it does not transfer a pre-existing risk from the borrower. Thus, the risk associated with the possible waiver on death of the prepayment fee is not insurance risk. *[IFRS 4.IG2 E1.23]*.

It follows from this that if a contract pays a death benefit exceeding the amount payable on survival (excluding waivers under (b) above), the contract is an insurance contract unless the additional death benefit is insignificant (judged by reference to the contract rather than to an entire book of contracts). Similarly, an annuity contract that pays out regular sums for the rest of a policyholder's life is an insurance contract, unless the aggregate life-contingent payments are insignificant. In this case, the insurer could suffer a significant loss on an individual contract if the annuitant survives longer than expected. *[IFRS 4.B26]*.

Additional benefits could include a requirement to pay benefits earlier than expected if the insured event occurs earlier provided the payment is not adjusted for the time value of money. An example could be whole life insurance cover that provides a fixed death benefit whenever a policyholder dies. Whilst it is certain that the policyholder will die, the timing of death is uncertain and the insurer will suffer a loss on individual contracts when policyholders die early, even if there is no overall expected loss on the whole book of contracts. *[IFRS 4.B27]*.

3.3 Changes in the level of insurance risk

It is implicit within IFRS 4 that an assessment of whether a contract transfers significant insurance risk should be made at the inception of a contract. *[IFRS 4.B29]*. Further, a contract that qualifies as an insurance contract at inception remains an insurance contract until all rights and obligations are extinguished or expire. *[IFRS 4.B30]*. This applies even if circumstances have changed such that insurance contingent rights and obligations have expired. The IASB considered that requiring insurers to set up systems to continually assess whether contracts continue to transfer significant insurance risk imposed a cost that far outweighed the benefit that would be gained from going through the exercise. *[IFRS 4.BC38]*.

Conversely, contracts that do not transfer insurance risk at inception may become insurance contracts if they transfer insurance risk at a later time, as explained in the following example. This is because IFRS 4 imposes no limitations on when contracts can be assessed for significant insurance risk. The reclassification of contracts as insurance contracts occurs based on changing facts and circumstances, although there is no guidance on accounting for the reclassification.

Example 54.3:   Deferred annuity with policyholder election

Entity A issues a deferred annuity contract whereby the policyholder will receive, or can elect to receive, a life-contingent annuity at rates prevailing when the annuity begins.

This is not an insurance contract at inception if the insurer can reprice the mortality risk without constraints. However, it will become an insurance contract when the annuity rate is fixed (unless the contingent amount is insignificant in all scenarios that have commercial substance). *[IFRS 4.IG2 E1.7]*.

In practice, in the accumulation phase of an annuity, there are other guaranteed benefits such as premium refunds that might still make this an insurance contract prior to the date when the annuity rate is fixed.

Some respondents to ED 5 suggested that a contract should not be regarded as an insurance contract if the insurance-contingent rights and obligations expire after a very short time. The IASB considered that the requirement to ignore scenarios that lack commercial substance in assessing significant insurance risk and the fact that there is no significant transfer of pre-existing risk in some contracts that waive surrender penalties on death is sufficient to cover this issue. *[IFRS 4.BC39]*.

Chapter 54

IFRS 3 – *Business Combinations* – confirms that there should be no reassessment of the classification of contracts previously classified as insurance contracts under IFRS 4 which are acquired as a part of a business combination. *[IFRS 3.17(b)].*

3.4   Uncertain future events

Uncertainty (or risk) is the essence of an insurance contract. Accordingly, IFRS 4 requires at least one of the following to be uncertain at the inception of an insurance contract:

(a)   whether an insured event will occur;

(b)   when it will occur; or

(c)   how much the insurer will need to pay if it occurs. *[IFRS 4.B2].*

An insured event will be one of the following:

- the discovery of a loss during the term of the contract, even if the loss arises from an event that occurred before the inception of the contract;

- a loss that occurs during the term of the contract, even if the resulting loss is discovered after the end of the contract term; *[IFRS 4.B3]* or

- the discovery of the ultimate cost of a claim which has already occurred but whose financial effect is uncertain. *[IFRS 4.B4].*

This last type of insured event arises from 'retroactive' contracts, i.e. those providing insurance against events which have occurred prior to the policy inception date. An example is a reinsurance contract that covers a direct policyholder against adverse development of claims already reported by policyholders. In this case the insured event is the discovery of the ultimate cost of those claims.

Local GAAP in some jurisdictions, including the US, prohibits the recognition of gains on inception of retroactive reinsurance contracts. IFRS 4 contains no such prohibition. Therefore, such gains would be recognised if that was required by an insurer's existing accounting policies. However, as discussed at 10.1.3 below, the amount of any such gains recognised should be disclosed.

3.5   Payments in kind

Insurance contracts that require or permit payments to be made in kind are treated the same way as contracts where payment is made directly to the policyholder. For example, some insurers replace an article directly rather than compensating the policyholder. Others use their own employees, such as medical staff, to provide services covered by the contract. *[IFRS 4.B5].*

3.5.1   *Service contracts*

Some fixed-fee service contracts in which the level of service depends on an uncertain event may meet the definition of an insurance contract. However, in some jurisdictions these are not regulated as insurance contracts. For example, a service provider could enter into a maintenance contract in which it agrees to repair specified equipment after a malfunction. The fixed service fee is based on the expected number of malfunctions but it is uncertain whether a particular machine will break down. Similarly, a contract for car breakdown services in which the provider agrees, for a fixed annual fee, to provide roadside assistance or tow the car to a nearby garage could meet the definition of an insurance contract even if the provider does not agree to carry out repairs or replace parts. *[IFRS 4.B6].*

In respect of the type of service contracts described above, their inclusion within IFRS 4 seems an unintended consequence of the definition of an insurance contract. However, the IASB stresses that applying IFRS 4 to these contracts should be no more burdensome than applying other IFRSs since:

(a)   there are unlikely to be material liabilities for malfunctions and breakdowns that have already occurred;

(b)   if the service provider applied accounting policies consistent with IAS 18, this would be acceptable either as an existing accounting policy or, possibly, an improvement of existing policies (see 8 below);

(c)   whilst the service provider would be required to apply the liability adequacy test discussed at 7.2.2 below if the cost of meeting its contractual obligation to provide services exceeded the revenue received in advance, it would have been required to apply IAS 37 to determine whether its contracts were onerous if IFRS 4 did not apply; and

(d)   the disclosure requirements in IFRS 4 are unlikely to add significantly to the disclosures required by other IFRSs. *[IFRS 4.B7].*

The revised ED proposes to exclude from the scope of the standard fixed-fee service contracts that have, as their primary purpose, the provision of services and meet all of the following conditions:

•   the entity does not reflect an assessment of the risk that is associated with an individual customer in setting the price of the contract with that customer;

•   the contracts compensate customers by providing a service, rather than cash payment; and

•   the insurance risk that is transferred by the contract arises primarily from the customer's use of services.

These contracts will be accounted for under the new revenue recognition standard.[6]

However, in subsequent discussions the IASB tentatively decided that entities should be permitted an accounting policy choice whether to apply IFRS 15 to the fixed fee service contracts that meet the criteria above or whether to account for these contracts under the new insurance accounting standard.[7]

3.6   The distinction between insurance risk and financial risk

The definition of an insurance contract refers to 'insurance risk' which is defined as 'risk, other than financial risk, transferred from the holder of a contract to the issuer'. *[IFRS 4 Appendix A].*

A contract that exposes the reporting entity to financial risk without significant insurance risk is not an insurance contract. *[IFRS 4.B8].* 'Financial risk' is defined as 'the risk of a possible future change in one or more of a specified interest rate, financial instrument price, foreign exchange rate, index of prices or rates, credit rating or credit index or other variable, provided in the case of a non-financial variable that variable is not specific to a party to the contract'. *[IFRS 4 Appendix A]*.

An example of a non-financial variable that is not specific to a party to the contract is an index of earthquake losses in a particular region or an index of temperature in a particular city. An example of a non-financial variable that is specific to a party to the contract is the occurrence or non-occurrence of a fire that damages or destroys an asset of that party.

The risk of changes in the fair value of a non-financial asset is not a financial risk if the fair value reflects not only changes in the market prices for such assets (a financial variable) but also the condition of a specific non-financial asset held by a party to the contract (a non-financial variable). For example if a guarantee of the residual value of a specific car exposes the guarantor to the risk of changes in that car's condition, that risk is insurance risk. *[IFRS 4.B9]*.

Example 54.4:   Residual value insurance

Entity A issues a contract to Entity B that provides a guarantee of the fair value at the future date of an aircraft (a non-financial asset) held by B. A is not the lessee of the aircraft (residual value guarantees given by a lessee under a finance lease are within the scope of IAS 17).

This is an insurance contract (unless changes in the condition of the asset have an insignificant effect on its value). The risk of changes in the fair value of the aircraft is not a financial risk because the fair value reflects not only changes in market prices for similar aircraft but also the condition of the specific asset held.

However, if the contract compensated B only for changes in market prices and not for changes in the condition of B's asset, the contract would be a derivative and within the scope of IAS 39 or IFRS 9. *[IFRS 4.IG2 E1.15]*.

Contracts that expose the issuer to both financial risk and significant insurance risk can be insurance contracts. *[IFRS 4.B10]*.

Example 54.5:   Contract with insurance and financial risk

Entity A issues a catastrophe bond to Entity B under which principal, interest payments or both are reduced significantly if a specified triggering event occurs and the triggering event includes a condition that B has suffered a loss.

The contract is an insurance contract because the triggering event includes a condition that B has suffered a loss, and contains an insurance component (with the issuer as policyholder and the holder as the insurer) and a deposit component. A discussion of the separation of these two components is set out at 5 below. *[IFRS 4.IG2 E1.20]*.

Contracts where an insured event triggers the payment of an amount linked to a price index are insurance contracts provided the payment that is contingent on the insured event is significant.

An example would be a life contingent annuity linked to a cost of living index. Such a contract transfers insurance risk because payment is triggered by an uncertain future event, the survival of the annuitant. The link to the price index is an embedded derivative but it also transfers insurance risk. If the insurance risk transferred is significant the embedded derivative meets the definition of an insurance contract (see 4 below for a discussion of derivatives embedded within insurance contracts). *[IFRS 4.B11]*.

3.7 Adverse effect on the policyholder

For a contract to be an insurance contract the insured event must have an adverse effect on the policyholder. In other words, there must be an insurable interest.

Without the notion of insurable interest the definition of an insurance contract would have encompassed gambling. The IASB believed that without this notion the definition of an insurance contract might have captured any prepaid contract to provide services whose cost is uncertain and that would have extended the scope of the term 'insurance contract' too far beyond its traditional meaning. *[IFRS 4.BC26-28]*. In the IASB's opinion the retention of insurable interest gives a principle-based distinction, particularly between insurance contracts and other contracts that happen to be used for hedging and they preferred to base the distinction on a type of contract rather than the way an entity manages a contract or group of contracts. *[IFRS 4.BC29]*.

The adverse effect on the policyholder is not limited to an amount equal to the financial impact of the adverse event. So, the definition includes 'new for old' coverage that replaces a damaged or lost asset with a new asset. Similarly, the definition does not limit payment under a term life insurance contract to the financial loss suffered by a deceased's dependents nor does it preclude the payment of predetermined amounts to quantify the loss caused by a death or accident. *[IFRS 4.B13]*.

A contract that requires a payment if a specified uncertain event occurs which does not require an adverse effect on the policyholder as a precondition for payment is not an insurance contract. Such contracts are not insurance contracts even if the holder uses the contract to mitigate an underlying risk exposure. Conversely, the definition of an insurance contract refers to an uncertain event for which an adverse effect on the policyholder is a contractual precondition for payment. This contractual precondition does not require the insurer to investigate whether the uncertain event actually caused an adverse effect, but permits the insurer to deny payment if it is not satisfied that the event caused an adverse effect. *[IFRS 4.B14]*.

The following example illustrates the concept of insurable interest.

Example 54.6: Reinsurance contract with 'original loss warranty' clause

Entity A agrees to provide reinsurance cover to airline insurer B for $5m against losses suffered. The claims are subject to an original loss warranty of $50m meaning that only losses suffered by B up to $5m from events exceeding a cost of $50m in total can be recovered under the contract. This is an insurance contract as B can only recover its own losses arising from those events.

If the contract allowed B to claim up to $5m every time there was an event with a cost exceeding $50m regardless of whether B had suffered a loss from that event then this would not be an insurance contract because there would be no insurable interest in this arrangement.

3.7.1 Lapse, persistency and expense risk

Lapse or persistency risk (the risk that the policyholder will cancel the contract earlier or later than the issuer had expected in pricing the contract) is not insurance risk because, although this can have an adverse effect on the issuer, the cancellation is not contingent on an uncertain future event that adversely affects the policyholder. *[IFRS 4.B15]*.

Similarly, expense risk (the risk of unexpected increases in the administrative costs incurred by the issuer associated with the serving of a contract, rather than the costs associated with insured events) is not insurance risk because an unexpected increase in expenses does not adversely affect the policyholder. *[IFRS 4.B15]*.

Therefore, a contract that exposes the issuer to lapse risk, persistency risk or expense risk is not an insurance contract unless it also exposes the issuer to significant insurance risk.

3.7.2   *Insurance of non-insurance risks*

If the issuer of a contract which does not contain significant insurance risk mitigates the risk of that contract by using a second contract to transfer part of that first contract's risk to another party, this second contract exposes that other party to insurance risk because the policyholder of the second contract (the issuer of the first contract) is subject to an uncertain event that adversely affects it and thus it meets the definition of an insurance contract. *[IFRS 4.B16]*. This is illustrated by the following example.

Example 54.7:   Insurance of non-insurance risks

Entity A agrees to compensate Entity B for losses on a series of contracts issued by B that do not transfer significant insurance risk. These could be investment contracts or, for example, a contract to provide services.

The contract is an insurance contract if it transfers significant insurance risk from B to A, even if some or all of the underlying individual contracts do not transfer significant insurance risk to B. The contract is a reinsurance contract if any of the contracts issued by B are insurance contracts. Otherwise, the contract is a direct insurance contract. *[IFRS 4.IG2 E1.29]*.

3.8   Accounting differences between insurance and non insurance contracts

Making a distinction between insurance and non-insurance contracts is important because the accounting treatment will usually differ.

Insurance contracts under IFRS 4 will normally be accounted for under local GAAP (see 7 below). Typically, local GAAP (see 1.3 above) will recognise funds received or due from a policyholder as premiums (revenue) and amounts due to a policyholder as claims (an expense). However, if a contract does not transfer significant insurance risk and is therefore not an insurance contract under IFRS 4 it will probably be accounted for as an investment contract under IAS 39 (or IFRS 9). Under IAS 39 (or IFRS 9) the receipt of funds relating to financial assets or financial liabilities will result in the creation of a liability for the value of the remittance rather than a credit to profit or loss. This accounting treatment is sometimes called 'deposit accounting'. *[IFRS 4.B20]*.

A financial liability within the scope of IAS 39 (or IFRS 9) is measured at either amortised cost or fair value or possibly a mixture (e.g. if the instrument contains an embedded derivative). However, under IFRS 4, an insurance liability is measured under the entity's previous local GAAP accounting policies, unless these have been subsequently changed as discussed at 8 below. These may well result in the measurement of a liability that is different from that obtained by applying IAS 39 (or IFRS 9).

Additionally, the capitalisation of any acquisition costs related to the issuance of a contract is also likely to be different for insurance and investment contracts. IAS 18 (and IFRS 15) permits only incremental costs to be capitalised for the acquisition of investment management contracts. IAS 39 (or IFRS 9) requires transaction costs directly attributable to a financial asset or financial liability not at fair value through profit or loss to be included in its initial measurement. Transaction costs relating to financial assets and financial liabilities held at fair value through profit or loss are required to be expensed immediately. IFRS 4 does not provide any guidance as to what acquisition costs can be capitalised so reference to existing local accounting policies should apply (see 7.2.6.B below). In most cases, these will differ from the requirements outlined in IAS 18 (or IFRS 15) and IAS 39 (or IFRS 9).

If non-insurance contracts (see 3.9.2 below) do not create financial assets or financial liabilities then IAS 18 or IFRS 15 applies to the recognition of associated revenue. The principle outlined in IAS 18 is to recognise revenue associated with a transaction involving the rendering of services by reference to the stage of completion of the transaction if the revenue can be estimated reliably. The principle outlined in IFRS 15 is to recognise revenue associated with a transaction involving the rendering of services when (or as) an entity satisfies a performance obligation by transferring the promised service to a customer in an amount that reflects the consideration to which the entity expects to be entitled. *[IFRS 4.B21]*. This could differ from revenue recognition for insurance contracts measured under local GAAP.

3.9 Examples of insurance and non-insurance contracts

The section contains examples given in IFRS 4 of insurance and non-insurance contracts.

3.9.1 Examples of insurance contracts

The following are examples of contracts that are insurance contracts, if the transfer of insurance risk is significant:

(a) insurance against theft or damage to property;

(b) insurance against product liability, professional liability, civil liability or legal expenses;

(c) life insurance and prepaid funeral plans (although death is certain, it is uncertain when death will occur or, for some types of life insurance, whether death will occur within the period covered by the insurance);

(d) life-contingent annuities and pensions (contracts that provide compensation for the uncertain future event – the survival of the annuitant or pensioner – to assist the annuitant or pensioner in maintaining a given standard of living, which would otherwise be adversely affected by his or her survival);

(e) disability and medical cover;

(f) surety bonds, fidelity bonds, performance bonds and bid bonds (i.e. contracts that provide compensation if another party fails to perform a contractual obligation, for example an obligation to construct a building);

(g) credit insurance that provides for specified payments to be made to reimburse the holder for a loss it incurs because a specified debtor fails to make payment when due under the original or modified terms of a debt instrument. These contracts could have various legal forms, such as that of a guarantee, some types of letter of credit, a credit derivative default contract or an insurance contract. Although these contracts meet the definition of an

Chapter 54

insurance contract they also meet the definition of a financial guarantee contract and are within the scope of IAS 39 (or IFRS 9) and IFRS 7 and not IFRS 4 unless the issuer has previously asserted explicitly that it regards such contracts as insurance contracts and has used accounting applicable to such contracts (see 2.2.3.D above);

(h)   product warranties issued by another party for goods sold by a manufacturer, dealer or retailer are within the scope of IFRS 4. However, as discussed at 2.2.3.A above, product warranties issued directly by a manufacturer, dealer or retailer are outside the scope of IFRS 4;

(i)   title insurance (insurance against the discovery of defects in title to land that were not apparent when the contract was written). In this case, the insured event is the discovery of a defect in the title, not the title itself;

(j)   travel assistance (compensation in cash or in kind to policyholders for losses suffered while they are travelling);

(k)   catastrophe bonds that provide for reduced payments of principal, interest or both if a specified event adversely affects the issuer of the bond (unless the specified event does not create significant insurance risk, for example if the event is a change in an interest rate or a foreign exchange rate);

(l)   insurance swaps and other contracts that require a payment based on changes in climatic, geological and other physical variables that are specific to a party to the contract; and

(m)   reinsurance contracts. *[IFRS 4.B18].*

These examples are not intended to be an exhaustive list.

The following illustrative examples provide further guidance on situations where there is significant insurance risk:

Example 54.8:   *Deferred annuity with guaranteed rates*

Entity A issues a contract to a policyholder who will receive, or can elect to receive, a life-contingent annuity at rates guaranteed at inception.

This is an insurance contract unless the transfer of insurance risk is not significant. The contract transfers mortality risk to the insurer at inception, because the insurer might have to pay significant additional benefits for an individual contract if the annuitant elects to take the life-contingent annuity and survives longer than expected. *[IFRS 4.IG2 E1.6].*

This example contrasts with Example 54.3 above where the rates were not set at the inception of the policy and therefore that was not an insurance contract at inception.

Example 54.9:   *Guarantee fund established by contract*

A guarantee fund is established by contract. The contract requires all participants to pay contributions to the fund so that it can meet obligations incurred by participants (and, perhaps, others). Participants would typically be from a single industry, e.g. insurance, banking or travel.

The contract that establishes the guarantee fund is an insurance contract. *[IFRS 4.IG2 E1.13].*

This example contrasts with Example 54.15 below where a guarantee fund has been established by law and not by contract.

Example 54.10: *Insurance contract issued to employees related to a defined contribution pension plan*

An insurance contract is issued by an insurer to its employees as a result of a defined contribution pension plan. The contractual benefits for employee service in the current and prior periods are not contingent on future service. The insurer also issues similar contracts on the same terms to third parties.

This is an insurance contract. However, if the insurer pays part or all of its employee's premiums, the payment by an insurer is an employee benefit within the scope of IAS 19 and is not accounted for under IFRS 4 because the insurer is the employer and would be paying its own insurance premiums. *[IFRS 4.IG2 E1.22].*

Defined benefit pension liabilities are outside the scope of IFRS 4 as discussed at 2.2.3.B above.

Example 54.11: *No market value adjustment for maturity benefits*

A contract permits the issuer to deduct a market value adjustment (MVA), a charge which varies depending on a market index, from surrender values or death benefits to reflect current market prices for the underlying assets. It does not permit an MVA for maturity benefits.

The policyholder obtains an additional survival benefit because no MVA is applied at maturity. That benefit is a pure endowment because the insured person receives a payment on survival to a specified date but beneficiaries receive nothing if the insured person dies before then. If the risk transferred by that benefit is significant, the contract is an insurance contract. *[IFRS 4.IG2 E1.25].*

Example 54.12: *No market value adjustment for death benefits*

A contract permits the issuer to deduct a market value adjustment (MVA) from surrender values or maturity payments to reflect current market prices for the underlying assets. It does not permit an MVA for death benefits.

The policyholder obtains an additional death benefit because no MVA is applied on death. If the risk transferred by that benefit is significant, the contract is an insurance contract. *[IFRS 4.IG2 E1.26].*

3.9.2 Examples of transactions that are not insurance contracts

The following are examples of transactions that are not insurance contracts:

(a) investment contracts that have the legal form of an insurance contract but do not expose the insurer to significant insurance risk, for example life insurance contracts in which the insurer bears no significant mortality risk;

(b) contracts that have the legal form of insurance, but pass all significant risk back to the policyholder through non-cancellable and enforceable mechanisms that adjust future payments by the policyholder as a direct result of insured losses, for example some financial reinsurance contracts or some group contracts;

(c) self insurance, in other words retaining a risk that could have been covered by insurance. There is no insurance contract because there is no agreement with another party (see 3.2.2.A above);

(d) contracts (such as gambling contracts) that require a payment if an unspecified uncertain future event occurs, but do not require, as a contractual precondition for payment, that the event adversely affects the policyholder. However, this does not preclude the specification of a predetermined payout to quantify the loss caused by a specified event such as a death or an accident (see 3.7 above);

(e) derivatives that expose one party to financial risk but not insurance risk, because they require that party to make payment based solely on changes in

Chapter 54

one or more of a specified interest rate, financial instrument price, commodity price, foreign exchange rate, index of prices or rates, credit rating or credit index or other variable, provide in the case of a non-financial variable that the variable is not specific to a party to the contract;

(f) a credit-related guarantee (or letter of credit, credit derivative default contract or credit insurance contract) that requires payments even if the holder has not incurred a loss on the failure of a debtor to make payments when due;

(g) contracts that require a payment based on a climatic, geological or other physical variable that is not specific to a party to the contract. These are commonly described as weather derivatives and are accounted for under IAS 39 (or IFRS 9); and

(h) catastrophe bonds that provide for reduced payments of principal, interest or both, based on a climatic, geological or other physical variable that is not specific to a party to the contract. *[IFRS 4.B19]*.

The following examples illustrate further situations where IFRS 4 is not applicable.

Example 54.13:   Investment contract linked to asset pool

Entity A issues an investment contract in which payments are contractually linked (with no discretion) to returns on a pool of assets held by the issuer.

This contract is within the scope of IAS 39 (or IFRS 9) because the payments are based on asset returns and there is no significant insurance risk. *[IFRS 4.IG2 E1.10]*.

Example 54.14:   Credit-related guarantee

Entity A issues a credit-related guarantee that does not, as a precondition for payment, require that the holder is exposed to, and has incurred a loss on, the failure of the debtor to make payments on the guaranteed asset when due.

This is a derivative within the scope of IAS 39 (or IFRS 9) because there is no insurable interest. *[IFRS 4.IG2 E1.12]*.

Example 54.15:   Guarantee fund established by law

Guarantee funds established by law exist in many jurisdictions. Typically they require insurers to contribute funds into a pool in order to pay policyholder claims in the event of insurer insolvencies. They may be funded by periodic (usually annual) levies or by levies only when an insolvency arises. The basis of the funding requirement varies although typically most are based on an insurer's premium income.

The commitment of participants to contribute to the fund is not established by contract so there is no insurance contract. Obligations to guarantee funds are within the scope of IAS 37. *[IFRS 4.IG2 E1.14]*.

Example 54.16:   Right to recover future premiums

Entity A issues an insurance contract which gives it an enforceable and non-cancellable contractual right to recover all claims paid out of future premiums, with appropriate compensation for the time value of money.

Insurance risk is insignificant because all claims can be recovered from future premiums and consequently the insurer cannot suffer a significant loss. Therefore the contract is a financial instrument within the scope of IAS 39 (or IFRS 9). *[IFRS 4.IG2 E1.18]*.

Example 54.17: Catastrophe bond linked to index

Entity A issues a catastrophe bond in which principal, interest payments or both are reduced if a specified triggering event occurs and that triggering event does not include a condition that the issuer of the bond suffered a loss.

This is a financial instrument with an embedded derivative. Both the holder and the issuer should measure the embedded derivative at fair value through profit or loss under IAS 39 (or IFRS 9). *[IFRS 4.IG2 E1.19].*

Example 54.18: Insurance policy issued to defined benefit pension plan

Entity A issues an insurance contract to either (a) a defined benefit pension plan, covering the employees of A, and/or (b) the employees of another entity consolidated within the same group financial statements as A.

This contract will generally be eliminated on consolidation from the group financial statements which will include:

(a) the full amount of the pension obligation under IAS 19 with no deduction for the plan's right under the contract;

(b) no liability to policyholders under the contract; and

(c) the assets backing the contract. *[IFRS 4.IG2 E1.21].*

In January 2008, the Interpretations Committee considered a request for guidance on the accounting for investment or insurance policies that are issued by an entity to a pension plan covering its own employees (or the employees of an entity that is consolidated into the same group as the entity issuing the policy). The Interpretations Committee noted the definitions of plan assets, assets held by a long-term employee benefit plan and a qualifying insurance policy as defined by IAS 19 and considered that, if a policy was issued by a group company to the employee benefit fund then the treatment would depend on whether the policy was a 'non-transferable financial instrument issued by the reporting entity'. Since the policy was issued by a related party, the Interpretations Committee concluded that it could not meet the definition of a qualifying insurance policy as defined by IAS 19. Because of the narrow scope of this issue the Interpretations Committee declined to either issue an Interpretation or to add the issue to its agenda.[8]

Example 54.19: Market value adjustment without death or maturity benefits

A contract permits the issuer to deduct an MVA from surrender payments to reflect current market prices for the underlying assets. The contract does not permit a MVA for death and maturity benefits. The amount payable on death or maturity is the amount originally invested plus interest.

The policyholder obtains an additional benefit because no MVA is applied on death or maturity. However, that benefit does not transfer insurance risk from the policyholder because it is certain that the policyholder will live or die and the amount payable on death or maturity is adjusted for the time value of money. Therefore, the contract is an investment contract because there is no significant insurance risk. This contract combines the two features discussed in Examples 54.11 and 54.12 at 3.9.1 above. When considered separately, these two features transfer insurance risk. However, when combined, they do not transfer insurance risk. Therefore, it is not appropriate to separate this contract into two insurance components.

If the amount payable on death were not adjusted in full for the time value of money, or were adjusted in some other way, the contract might transfer insurance risk. *[IFRS 4.IG2 E1.27].*

Chapter 54

4   EMBEDDED DERIVATIVES

Insurance contracts may contain policyholder options or other clauses that meet the definition of an embedded derivative under IAS 39 (or IFRS 9). A derivative is a financial instrument within the scope of IAS 39 (or IFRS 9) with all three of the following characteristics:

- its value changes in response to a change in a specified interest rate, financial instrument price, commodity price, foreign exchange rate, index of prices or rates, credit rating or credit index, or other variable, provided in the case of a non-financial variable that the variable is not specific to the underlying of the contract;

- it requires no initial net investment or an initial net investment that would be smaller than would be required for other types of contracts that would be expected to have a similar response to changes in market factors; and

- it is settled at a future date. *[IAS 39.9, IFRS 9 Appendix A].*

An embedded derivative is a component of a hybrid (combined) instrument that also includes a non-derivative host contract. An embedded derivative causes some or all of the cash flows that would otherwise be required by the contract to be modified according to a specified interest rate, financial instrument price, commodity price, foreign exchange rate, index of prices or rates, credit rating or credit index, or other variable provided that in the case of a non-financial variable that the variable is not specific to the party to the contract. *[IAS 39.10, IFRS 9.4.3.1].*

The following are examples of embedded derivatives that may be found in insurance contracts:

- benefits, such as death benefits, linked to equity prices or an equity index;

- options to take life-contingent annuities at guaranteed rates;

- guarantees of minimum interest rates in determining surrender or maturity values;

- guarantees of minimum annuity payments where the annuity payments are linked to investment returns or asset prices;

- a put option for the policyholder to surrender a contract. These can be specified in a schedule, based on the fair value of a pool of interest-bearing securities or based on an equity or commodity price index;

- an option to receive a persistency bonus (an enhancement to policyholder benefits for policies that remain in-force for a certain period);

- an industry loss warranty where the loss trigger is an industry loss as opposed to an entity specific loss;

- a catastrophe trigger where a trigger is defined as a financial variable such as a drop in a designated stock market;

- an inflation index affecting policy deductibles;

- contracts where the currency of claims settlement differs from the currency of loss; and

- contracts with fixed foreign currency rates.

IAS 39 requires that an embedded derivative is separated from its host contract and measured at fair value with changes in fair value included in profit or loss if:

- its economic characteristics and risks are not closely related to the economic characteristics and risks of the host contract;
- it meets the definition of a derivative; and
- the combined instrument is not measured at fair value through profit or loss. *[IAS 39.11].*

IFRS 9 has identical requirements, although they do not apply to contracts that are financial assets. *[IFRS 9.4.3.3].*

The IASB considered and rejected arguments that insurers should be exempt from the requirement to separate embedded derivatives contained in a host insurance contract under IAS 39 (or IFRS 9) because, in the IASB's opinion, fair value is the only relevant measure for derivatives. *[IFRS 4.BC190].*

However, the IASB decided to exclude derivatives embedded in an insurance contract from the IAS 39 (or IFRS 9) measurement requirements if the embedded derivative is itself an insurance contract. *[IFRS 4.7].*

The IASB determined that it would be contradictory to require the measurement at fair value of an embedded derivative that met the definition of an insurance contract when such accounting is not required for a stand-alone insurance contract. Similarly, the IASB concluded that an embedded derivative is closely related to the host insurance contract if the embedded derivative and the host insurance contract are so interdependent that an entity cannot measure the embedded derivative separately. Without this conclusion IAS 39 (or IFRS 9) would have required an insurer to measure the entire insurance contract at fair value. *[IFRS 4.BC193].*

This means that derivatives embedded within insurance contracts do not have to be separated and accounted for under IAS 39 (or IFRS 9) if the policyholder benefits from the embedded derivative only when the insured event occurs.

IFRS 4 also states that an insurer need not (but may) separate, and measure at fair value, a policyholder's option to surrender an insurance contract for a fixed amount (or for an amount based on a fixed amount and an interest rate) even if the exercise price differs from the carrying amount of the host insurance liability. This appears to overrule the requirement in IAS 39 (or IFRS 9) that a call, put or prepayment option embedded in a host insurance contract must be separated from the host insurance contract unless the option's exercise price is approximately equal on each exercise date to the carrying amount of the host insurance contract. *[IAS 39.AG30(g), IFRS 9.B4.3.5(e)].* Because surrender values of insurance contracts often do not equal their amortised cost, without this concession in IFRS 4 fair value measurement of the surrender option would be required. *[IFRS 4.8].* This relief also applies to investment contracts with a discretionary participation feature. *[IFRS 4.9].*

The diagram below illustrates an embedded derivative decision tree.

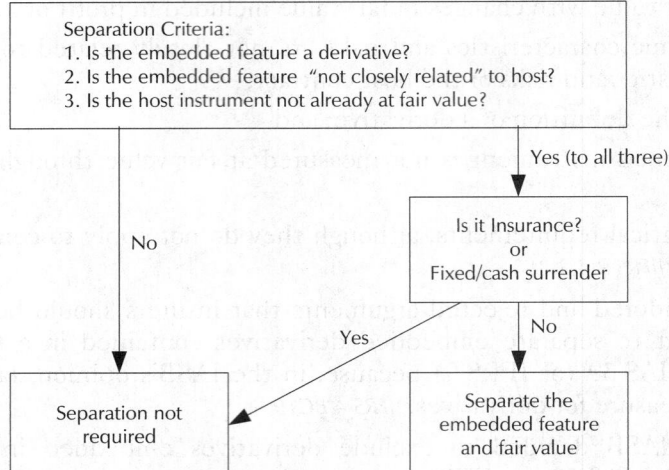

The example below illustrates an embedded derivative in an insurance contract that is not required to be separated and accounted for under IAS 39 (or IFRS 9).

Example 54.20:   Death or annuitisation benefit linked to equity prices or index

A contract has a death benefit linked to equity prices or an equity index and is payable only on death or when annuity payments begin and not on surrender or maturity.

The equity-index feature meets the definition of an insurance contract (unless the life-contingent payments are insignificant) because the policyholder benefits from it only when the insured event occurs. The embedded derivative is not required to be separated for accounting purposes. *[IFRS 4.IG4 E2.1]*.

The following two examples illustrate the application of the concession that IFRS 4 gives from the requirements in IAS 39 (or IFRS 9) to separate and measure at fair value surrender options for which the exercise price is not amortised cost as discussed above.

Example 54.21:   Life contingent annuity option

An insurance contract gives the policyholder the option to take a life-contingent annuity at a guaranteed rate i.e. a combined guarantee of interest rates and mortality changes.

The embedded option is an insurance contract (unless the life-contingent payments are insignificant) because the option is derived from mortality changes. Fair value measurement is not required but not prohibited even though the guaranteed rate may differ from the carrying amount of the insurance liability. *[IFRS 4.IG4 E2.3]*.

Example 54.22:   Policyholder option to surrender contract for cash surrender value

An insurance contract gives the policyholder the option to surrender the contract for a cash surrender value specified in a schedule i.e. not indexed and does not accumulate interest.

Fair value measurement is not required (but not prohibited) because the surrender option is for a fixed amount even though that fixed amount may differ from the carrying amount of the insurance liability. The surrender value may be viewed as a deposit component, but IFRS 4 does not require an insurer to unbundle a contract if it recognises all its obligations arising under the deposit component (see 5 below).

If this was an investment contract measured at amortised cost then fair value measurement of the option would be required if the surrender value was not approximately equal to the amortised cost at each exercise date. *[IFRS 4.IG4 E2.12]*.

The relief from applying IAS 39 (or IFRS 9) to certain surrender options discussed above does not apply to put options or cash surrender options embedded in an insurance contract if the surrender value varies in response to the change in a financial variable (such as an equity or commodity price or index) or a non-financial variable that is not specific to a party to the contract. Furthermore, the requirement to separate and fair value the embedded derivative also applies if the holder's ability to exercise the put option or cash surrender option is triggered by a change in such a variable, for example a put option that can be exercised if a stock market index reaches a specified level. *[IFRS 4.8]*. This is illustrated by the following example.

Example 54.23: *Policyholder option to surrender contract for value based on a market index*

An insurance contract gives the policyholder the option to surrender the contract for a surrender value based on an equity or commodity price or index.

The option is not closely related to the host insurance contract because the surrender value is derived from an index and is not specific to a party to the contract. Therefore, measurement of the option at its fair value is required. *[IFRS 4.IG4 E2.14]*.

Embedded derivatives in insurance contracts are also required to be separated where they do not relate to insurance risk and are not otherwise closely related to the host contract. An example of this is illustrated below.

Example 54.24: *Persistency bonus*

An insurance contract gives policyholders a persistency bonus paid at maturity in cash (or as a period-certain maturity).

The embedded derivative (the option to receive the persistency bonus) is not an insurance contract because, as discussed at 3.7 above, insurance risk does not include lapse or persistency risk. Therefore, measurement of the option at its fair value is required. *[IFRS 4.IG4 E2.17]*.

If the persistency bonus was paid at maturity as an enhanced life-contingent annuity then the embedded derivative would be an insurance contract and separate accounting would not be required. *[IFRS 4.IG4 E2.18]*.

Non-guaranteed participating dividends contained in an insurance contract are discretionary participation features rather than embedded derivatives and are discussed at 6 below.

Although the relief given by IFRS 4 from the requirements of IAS 39 (or IFRS 9) to separately account for embedded derivatives is therefore significant, some derivatives embedded in insurance contracts may still be required to be separated from the host instrument and accounted for at fair value under IAS 39 (or IFRS 9) as illustrated in Examples 54.23 and 54.24 above. In some circumstances this can be a challenging and time consuming task.

The revised ED contains similar requirements to IFRS 4. It proposes that an entity should separate an embedded derivative from the host contract and account for the embedded derivative under IAS 39 (or IFRS 9) if, and only if:

- the economic characteristics and risks of the embedded derivative are not closely related to the economic characteristics and risks of the host contract; and

- a separate financial instrument with the same terms as the embedded derivative would meet the definition of a derivative and would be within the scope of IAS 39 or IFRS 9 (for example, the derivative itself is not an insurance contract).[9]

Chapter 54

4.1   Unit-linked features

A unit-linked feature (i.e. a contractual term that requires payments denominated in units of an internal or external investment fund) embedded in a host insurance contract (or financial instrument) is considered to be closely related to the host contract if the unit-denominated payments are measured at current unit values that reflect the fair values of the assets of the fund. *[IAS 39.AG33(g), IFRS 9.B4.3.8(g)].*

IAS 39 (or IFRS 9) also considers that unit-linked investment liabilities should be normally regarded as puttable instruments that can be put back to the issuer at any time for cash equal to a proportionate share of the net asset value of an entity, i.e. they are not closely related. Nevertheless, the effect of separating an embedded derivative and accounting for each component is to measure the combined instrument at the redemption amount that is payable at the reporting date if the unit holders had exercised their right to put the instrument back to the issuer. *[IAS 39.AG32, IFRS 9.B4.3.7].* This seems somewhat to contradict the fact that the unit-linked feature is regarded as closely related (which means no separation of the feature is required) but the accounting treatment is substantially the same.

5   UNBUNDLING OF DEPOSIT COMPONENTS

The definition of an insurance contract distinguishes insurance contracts within the scope of IFRS 4 from investments and deposits within the scope of IAS 39 (or IFRS 9). However, most insurance contracts contain both an insurance component and a 'deposit component'. *[IFRS 4.10].* Indeed, virtually all insurance contracts have an implicit or explicit deposit component, because the policyholder is generally required to pay premiums before the period of the risk and therefore the time value of money is likely to be one factor that insurers consider in pricing contracts. *[IFRS 4.BC40].*

A deposit component is 'a contractual component that is not accounted for as a derivative under IAS 39 (or IFRS 9) and would be within the scope of IAS 39 (or IFRS 9) if it were a separate instrument'. *[IFRS 4 Appendix A].*

IFRS 4 requires an insurer to 'unbundle' those insurance and deposit components in certain circumstances, *[IFRS 4.10],* i.e. to account for the components of a contract as if they were separate contracts. *[IFRS 4 Appendix A].* In other circumstances unbundling is either allowed (but not required) or is prohibited.

Unbundling has the following accounting consequences:

(a)   the insurance component is measured as an insurance contract under IFRS 4;

(b)   the deposit component is measured under IAS 39 (or IFRS 9) at either amortised cost or fair value which may not be consistent with the measurement basis used for the insurance component;

(c)   premiums for the deposit component are not recognised as revenue, but rather as changes in the deposit liability. Premiums for the insurance component are typically recognised as revenue (see 3.8 above); and

(d)   a portion of the transaction costs incurred at inception is allocated to the deposit component if this allocation has a material effect. *[IFRS 4.12, BC41].*

The IASB's main reason for making unbundling mandatory only in limited circumstances was to give relief to insurers from having to make costly systems changes. These changes might be needed to identify and separate the various deposit components that might exist in certain contracts (e.g. surrender values in traditional life insurance contracts) which may then need to be reversed in Phase II (see 11 below). However, the IASB generally regards unbundling as appropriate for all large customised contracts, such as some financial reinsurance contracts, because a failure to unbundle them might lead to the complete omission of material contractual rights and obligations from the statement of financial position. *[IFRS 4.BC44-46].*

The revised ED proposes to require separation of any investment component of an insurance contract and account for it in accordance with IAS 39 or IFRS 9 if that investment component is distinct. An investment component is distinct if a contract with equivalent terms is sold, or could be sold, separately in the same market or same jurisdiction either by entities that issue insurance contracts or by other entities. However, if the investment component and insurance component are highly interrelated the entire contract would be accounted for as an insurance contract. This would be the case if:

- the entity is unable to measure the one without considering the other, e.g. the value of one component varies according to the value of the other; or

- the policyholder is unable to benefit from one component unless the other is also present, e.g. if the lapse or maturity of one component in a contract causes the lapse or maturity of the other.[10]

5.1 The unbundling requirements

Unbundling is required only if both the following conditions are met:

(a) the insurer can measure the deposit component (including any embedded surrender options) separately (i.e. without considering the insurance component); and

(b) the insurer's accounting policies do not otherwise require it to recognise all obligations and rights arising from the deposit component. *[IFRS 4.10(a)].*

Unbundling is permitted, but not required, if the insurer can measure the deposit component separately as in (a) but its accounting policies require it to recognise all obligations and rights arising from the deposit component. This is regardless of the basis used to measure those rights and obligations. *[IFRS 4.10(b)].*

Unbundling is prohibited when an insurer cannot measure the deposit component separately. *[IFRS 4.10(c)].*

Example 54.25: Unbundling

A cedant receives compensation for losses from a reinsurer but the contract obliges the cedant to repay the compensation in future years. That obligation arises from a deposit component.

If the cedant's accounting policies would otherwise permit it to recognise the compensation as income without recognising the resulting obligation, unbundling is required. *[IFRS 4.11].*

5.2   Unbundling illustration

The implementation guidance accompanying IFRS 4 provides an illustration of the unbundling of the deposit component of a reinsurance contract which is reproduced in full below.

Example 54.26:   Unbundling a deposit component of a reinsurance contract

Background

A reinsurance contract has the following features:

(a)   the cedant pays premiums of CU10 every year for five years;

(b)   an 'experience account' is established equal to 90% of the cumulative premiums (including the additional premiums discussed in (c) below) less 90% of the cumulative claims;

(c)   if the balance in the experience account is negative (i.e. cumulative claims exceed cumulative premiums), the cedant pays an additional premium equal to the experience account balance divided by the number of years left to run on the contract;

(d)   at the end of the contract, if the experience account balance is positive (i.e. cumulative premiums exceed cumulative claims), it is refunded to the cedant; if the balance is negative, the cedant pays the balance to the reinsurer as an additional premium;

(e)   neither party can cancel the contract before maturity; and

(f)   the maximum loss that the reinsurer is required to pay in any period is CU200.

The contract is an insurance contract because it transfers significant risk to the reinsurer. For example, in case 2 discussed below, the reinsurer is required to pay additional benefits with a present value, in year 1, of CU35, which is clearly significant in relation to the contract.

The following discussion addresses the accounting by the reinsurer. Similar principles apply to the accounting by the cedant.

Application of requirements: case 1 – no claims

If there are no claims, the cedant will receive CU45 in year 5 (90% of the cumulative premiums of CU50). In substance, the cedant has made a loan, which the reinsurer will repay in one instalment of CU45 in year 5.

If the reinsurer's accounting policies require it to recognise its contractual liability to repay the loan to the cedant, unbundling is permitted but not required. However, if the reinsurer's accounting policies would not require it to recognise the liability to repay the loan, the reinsurer is required to unbundle the contract.

If the reinsurer is required, or elects, to unbundle the contract, it does so as follows. Each payment by the cedant has two components: a loan advance (deposit component) and a payment for insurance cover (insurance component). Applying IAS 39 or IFRS 9 to the deposit component, the reinsurer is required to measure it initially at fair value. Fair value could be determined by discounting the future cash flows from the deposit component. Assume that an appropriate discount rate is 10% and that the insurance cover is equal in each year, so that the payment for insurance cover is the same in each year. Each payment of CU10 by the cedant is then made up of a loan advance of CU6.7 and an insurance premium of CU3.3.

The reinsurer accounts for the insurance component in the same way it accounts for a separate insurance contract with an annual premium of CU3.3.

The movements in the loan are shown below.

Year	Opening balance	Interest at 10%	Advance (repayment)	Closing balance
	CU	CU	CU	CU
0	0.00	0.00	6.70	6.70
1	6.70	0.67	6.70	14.07
2	14.07	1.41	6.70	22.18
3	22.18	2.21	6.70	31.09
4	31.09	3.11	6.70	40.90
5	40.90	4.10	(45.00)	0.00
Total		11.50	(11.50)	

Application of requirements: case 2 – claim of CU150 in year 1

Consider now what happens if the reinsurer pays a claim of CU150 in year 1. The changes in the experience account, and the resulting additional premiums, are as follows:

Year	Premium	Additional premium	Total premium	Cumulative premium	Claims	Cumulative claims	Cumulative premiums less claims	Experience account
	CU	CU	CU	CU	CU	CU	CU	CU
0	10	0	10	10	0	0	10	9
1	10	0	10	20	(150)	(150)	(130)	(117)
2	10	39	49	69	0	(150)	(81)	(73)
3	10	36	46	115	0	(150)	(35)	(31)
4	10	31	41	156	0	(150)	6	6
Total		106	156		(150)			

Incremental cash flows because of the claim in year 1

The claim in year 1 leads to the following incremental cash flows, compared with case 1:

Year	Additional premium	Claims	Refund in case 2	Refund in case 1	Net incremental cash flow	Present value at 10%
	CU	CU	CU	CU	CU	CU
0	0	0			0	0
1	0	(150)			(150)	(150)
2	39	0			39	35
3	36	0			36	30
4	31	0			31	23
5	0	0	(6)	(45)	38	27
Total	106	(150)	(6)	(45)	(5)	(35)

The incremental cash flows have a present value, in year 1, of CU35 (assuming a discount rate of 10% is appropriate). Applying paragraphs 10-12 of IFRS 4, the cedant unbundles the contract and applies IAS 39 or IFRS 9 to this deposit component (unless the cedant already recognises its contractual obligation to repay the deposit component to the reinsurer). If this were not done, the cedant might recognise the CU150 received in year 1 as income and the incremental payments in years 2-5 as expenses. However, in substance, the reinsurer has paid a claim of CU35 and made a loan of CU115 (CU150 less CU35) that will be repaid in instalments.

Chapter 54

The following table shows the changes in the loan balance. The table assumes that the original loan shown in case 1 and the new loan shown in case 2 meet the criteria for offsetting in IAS 32. Amounts shown in the table are rounded.

Year	Opening balance CU	Interest at 10% CU	Payments per original schedule CU	Additional payments in case 2 CU	Closing balance CU
0	–	–	6	–	6
1	6	1	7	(115)	(101)
2	(101)	(10)	7	39	(65)
3	(65)	(7)	7	36	(29)
4	(29)	(3)	6	31	5
5	5	1	(45)	39	0
Total		(18)	(12)	30	

Although the example refers to 'in year' the calculations indicate that most of the cash flows occur at the end of each year. The present value table showing the incremental cash flows resulting from the claim 'in year 1' appear to show the present values at the end of year 1. *[IFRS 4.IG5 E3]*.

5.3   Practical difficulties

In unbundling a contract the principal difficulty is identifying the initial fair value of any deposit component. In the IASB's illustration at 5.2 above a discount rate is provided but in practice contracts will not have a stated discount rate. The issuer and the cedant will therefore have to determine an appropriate discount rate in order to calculate the fair value of the deposit component. The IASB illustration is also unclear as to whether the discount rate is a risk adjusted rate. Fair value measurement would require an adjustment for credit risk.

However, the potential burden on insurers is reduced by the fact that the IASB has limited the requirement to unbundle to only those contracts where the rights and obligations arising from the deposit component are not recognised under insurance accounting. As noted above the IASB is principally concerned with ensuring that large reinsurance contracts with a significant financing element have all of their obligations properly recorded, although the requirements apply equally to direct insurance contracts. *[IFRS 4.IG5]*.

Some examples of clauses within insurance contracts that might indicate the need for unbundling are:

- 'funds withheld' clauses where part or all of the premium is never paid to the reinsurer or claims are never received;

- 'no claims bonus', 'profit commission' or 'claims experience' clauses which guarantee that the cedant will receive a refund of some of the premium;

- 'experience accounts' used to measure the profitability of the contract. These are often segregated from other funds and contain interest adjustments that may accrue to the benefit of the policyholder;

- 'finite' clauses that limit maximum losses or create a 'corridor' of losses not reinsured under a contract;

- contracts that link the eventual premium to the level of claims;

- commutation clauses whose terms guarantee that either party will receive a refund of amounts paid under the contract; and
- contracts of unusual size where the economic benefits to either party are not obviously apparent.

The unbundling requirements in IFRS 4 do not specifically address the issue of contracts artificially separated through the use of side letters, the separate components of which should be considered together. The IASB believes that it is a wider issue for a future project on linkage (accounting for separate transactions that are connected in some way). However, IFRS 4 does state that linked contracts entered into with a single counterparty (or contracts that are otherwise interdependent) form a single contract, for the purposes of assessing whether significant insurance risk is transferred, although the standard is silent on linked transactions with different counterparties (see 3.2.2 above). *[IFRS 4.BC54].*

6 DISCRETIONARY PARTICIPATION FEATURES

A discretionary participation feature (DPF) is a contractual right to receive, as a supplement to guaranteed benefits, additional benefits:

(a) that are likely to be a significant portion of the total contractual benefits;

(b) whose amount or timing is contractually at the discretion of the issuer; and

(c) that are contractually based on:

  (i) the performance of a specified pool of contracts or a specified type of contract;

  (ii) realised and/or unrealised investment returns on a specified pool of assets held by the issuer; or

  (iii) the profit or loss of the company, fund or other entity that issues the contract. *[IFRS 4 Appendix A].*

Guaranteed benefits are payments or other benefits to which the policyholder or investor has an unconditional right that is not subject to the contractual discretion of the issuer. Guaranteed benefits are always accounted for as liabilities.

Insurance companies in many countries have issued contracts with discretionary participation features. For example, in Germany, insurance companies must return to the policyholders at least 90% of the investment profits on certain contracts, but may give more. In France, Italy, the Netherlands and Spain, realised investment gains are distributed to the policyholder, but the insurance company has discretion over the timing of realising the gains. In the United Kingdom, bonuses are added to the policyholder account at the discretion of the insurer. These are normally based on the investment return generated by the underlying assets but sometimes include allowance for profits made on other contracts. The following are two examples of contracts with a DPF.

Chapter 54

Example 54.27:   Unitised with-profits policy

Premiums paid by the policyholder are used to purchase units in a 'with-profits' fund at the current unit price. The insurer guarantees that each unit added to the fund will have a minimum value which is the bid price of the unit. This is the guaranteed amount. In addition, the insurer may add two types of bonus to the with-profits units. These are a regular bonus, which may be added daily as a permanent increase to the guaranteed amount, and a final bonus that may be added on top of those guaranteed amounts when the with-profits units are cashed in. Levels of regular and final bonuses are adjusted twice per year. Both regular and final bonuses are discretionary amounts and are generally set based on expected future returns generated by the funds.

Example 54.28:   DPF policy with minimum interest rates

An insurance contract provides that the insurer must annually credit each policyholder's 'account' with a minimum interest rate (3%). This is the guaranteed amount. The insurer then has discretion with regard to whether and what amount of the remaining undistributed realised investment returns from the assets backing the participating policies are distributed to policyholders in addition to the minimum. The contract states that the insurer's shareholders are only entitled to share up to 10% in the underlying investment results associated with the participating policies. As that entitlement is up to 10%, the insurer can decide to credit the policyholders with more than the minimum sharing rate of 90%. Once any additional interest above the minimum interest rate of 3% is credited to the policyholder it becomes a guaranteed liability.

DPF can appear in both insurance contracts and investment contracts. However, to qualify as a DPF, the discretionary benefits must be likely to be a 'significant' portion of the total contractual benefits. The standard does not quantify what is meant by 'significant' but it could be interpreted in the same sense as in the definition of an insurance contract (see 3.2.1 above).

The definition of a DPF does not capture an unconstrained contractual discretion to set a 'crediting rate' that is used to credit interest or other returns to policyholders (as found in contracts described in some countries as 'universal life' contracts). For example, some contracts may not meet the criterion of (c) above if the discretion to set crediting rates is not contractually bound to the performance of a specified pool of assets or the profit or loss of the entity or fund that issues the contract. The IASB, however, acknowledges that some view these features as similar to a DPF because crediting rates are constrained by market forces and it proposed to revisit the treatment of these features in Phase II. *[IFRS 4.BC162].* However, the revised ED does not specifically revisit the treatment of these features. That is because the definition of DPF has been changed (see below).

With contracts that have discretionary features, the issuer has discretion over the amount and/or timing of distributions to policyholders although that discretion may be subject to some contractual constraints (including related legal and regulatory constraints) and competitive constraints. Distributions are typically made to policyholders whose contracts are still in force when the distribution is made. Thus, in many cases, a change in the timing of a distribution, apart from the change in the value over time, means that a different generation of policyholders might benefit. *[IFRS 4.BC154].*

Although the issuer has contractual discretion over distributions it is usually likely that current or future policyholders will ultimately receive some, if not most, of the accumulated surplus available at the reporting date. In Example 54.28 above policyholders are contractually entitled to a minimum of 90% of any discretionary distribution. Management can decide on any (total) amount. The main accounting question is whether that part of the discretionary surplus is a liability or a component of equity. *[IFRS 4.BC155]*.

The problem caused by discretionary features is that it is difficult to argue they meet the definition of a liability under IFRS. However, they can be integral to the economics of a contract and would clearly have to be considered in determining its fair value.

The definition of a liability in the IASB's *Conceptual Framework for Financial Reporting* ('*Framework*') requires there to be a present obligation. An obligation is a duty or responsibility to act or perform in a certain way. *[Framework 4.15]*. This can be contractual or constructive. However, a financial liability under IAS 32 must be a 'contractual obligation' *[IAS 32.11]* and discretionary obligations normally would not meet this requirement because of their discretionary nature.

IAS 37 requires provisions to be established once an 'obligating event' has occurred. Obligating events can be constructive but constructive obligations do require an entity to have indicated its responsibilities to other parties by an established pattern of past practice, published policies, or a sufficiently specific current statement, such that the entity has created a valid expectation on the part of those other parties that it will discharge those responsibilities. *[IAS 37.10]*. Say, for example, that an entity has previously paid discretionary bonuses to policyholders in the past five years of 5%, 15%, 0%, 10% and 5%. What 'valid expectation' has it created at the reporting date to policyholders in the absence of any public statement of management intent or, say, a published policy that discretionary bonuses will be linked to a particular profit figure?

If a DPF does not meet the definition of a liability then, under IAS 32, it would default to being equity, which is the residual interest in an entity's assets after deduction of its liabilities. This appears counter-intuitive and would result in discretionary distributions to policyholders being recorded as equity transactions outside of profit or loss or other comprehensive income. Taking this approach, a contract with a DPF would be bifurcated between liability and equity components like a bond convertible into equity shares.

The IASB's response to this difficult conceptual issue is to ignore it altogether in IFRS 4 and permit entities to have a choice as to whether to present contracts with a DPF within liabilities or equity. The difficult decisions have been deferred until Phase II. The IASB considers that the factor making it difficult to determine the appropriate accounting for these features is 'constrained discretion', being the combination of discretion and constraints on that discretion. If participation features lack discretion they are embedded derivatives and are within the scope of IAS 39. *[IFRS 4.BC161]*.

There may be timing differences between accumulated profits under IFRS and distributable surplus (i.e. the accumulated amount that is contractually eligible for distribution to holders of a DPF), for example, because distributable surplus excludes unrealised investment gains that are recognised under IAS 39 or IFRS 9. IFRS 4 does not address the classification of such timing differences. *[IFRS 4.BC160]*.

Chapter 54

In November 2005, the Interpretations Committee rejected a request for further interpretative guidance on the definition of a DPF. The Interpretations Committee had been informed of concerns that a narrow interpretation of a DPF would fail to ensure clear and comprehensive disclosure about contracts that included these features. In response, the Interpretations Committee noted that disclosure was particularly important in this area, drawing attention to the related implementation guidance, discussed at 10 below, but declined to add the topic to its agenda because it involved some of the most difficult questions that the IASB will need to resolve in Phase II.[11]

In January 2010, the Interpretations Committee also rejected a request to provide guidance on whether features contained in ownership units issued by certain Real Estate Investment Trusts (REITs) met the definition of a DPF. In some of the cases, the contractual terms of the ownership units require the REIT to distribute 90% of the Total Distributable Income (TDI) to investors. The remaining 10% may be distributed at the discretion of management. The request was to provide guidance on whether the discretion to distribute the remaining 10% of TDI met the definition of a DPF. If so, IFRS 4 would permit the ownership units to be classified as a liability in its entirety rather than a compound instrument with financial liability and equity components under IAS 32. The Interpretations Committee noted that the definition of a DPF in IFRS 4 requires, among other things, that the instrument provides the holder with guaranteed benefits and that the DPF benefits are in addition to these guaranteed benefits. Furthermore, it noted that such guaranteed benefits were typically found in insurance contracts. In other words, the Interpretations Committee was very sceptical about this presentation. However, it considered that providing guidance on this issue would be in the nature of application rather than interpretive guidance and therefore declined to add the issue to its agenda.[12]

The lack of interpretative guidance as to what constitutes a DPF has led to diversity in practice as to what is recognised as a DPF liability. For example, IFRS 4 is silent as to whether that part of an undistributed surplus on a participating contract which does not belong to policyholders should be treated as a liability or equity. This is illustrated by the following example.

Example 54.29:   DPF recognition

A minimum of 90% of an investment surplus on a participating contract may be distributed to policyholders although any distribution is entirely at the discretion of the insurer. However, IFRS 4 is silent as to whether the 10% of the surplus which does not belong to policyholders is part of the DPF if it has not been distributed and consequentially there is diversity in practice among insurers about whether the undistributed DPF liability includes the amount attributable to shareholders. Some insurers recognise the 90% as a liability and the 10% as a component of equity whereas others recognise the entire 100% as a liability until it is distributed.

The revised ED states that an investment contract with a DPF is within the scope of the proposed insurance contract standard provided that the reporting entity also issues insurance contracts, which is a change from IFRS 4. All insurance contracts, both with and without a DPF, are within the scope of the revised ED. Compared with the definition of a DPF in IFRS 4, the definition of an investment contract with a DPF in the revised ED requires that the additional returns must be contractually based on the returns from a specified pool of *insurance* contracts or a specified type of *insurance* contract rather just a contract or contracts *per se*.[13]

In subsequent discussions on accounting for participating contracts, the IASB has tentatively decided to create a class of participating contracts described as 'contracts with direct participation features' which will be eligible for a measurement model described as the 'variable fee' approach (discussed at 11.3 below). These are contracts for which:

- the contractual terms specify that the policyholder participates in a defined share of a clearly identified pool of underlying items;

- the entity expects to pay to the policyholder an amount equal to a substantial share of the returns from the underlying items; and

- a substantial proportion of the cash flows that the entity expects to pay to the policyholder should be expected to vary with the cash flows from the underlying items.[14]

The IASB has not yet discussed the measurement model for participating contracts that do not have 'direct participation features'.

6.1 Discretionary participation features in insurance contracts

Whilst IFRS 4 permits previous accounting practices for insurance contracts (see 7 below), the IASB considered there was a need to specify special accounting requirements for DPF features within these contracts. This might seem odd but the IASB's main concerns were:

- to prevent insurers classifying contracts with a DPF as an intermediate category that is neither liability nor equity as may have been permitted under some existing local accounting practices, such an intermediate category being incompatible with the *Framework*; *[IFRS 4.BC157]* and

- to ensure consistency with the treatment of DPF in investment contracts. *[IFRS 4.BC158]*.

IFRS 4 requires any guaranteed element (i.e. the obligation to pay guaranteed benefits included in a contract that contains a DPF) within an insurance contract to be recognised as a liability. However, insurers have an option as to whether to present a DPF either as a liability or as a component of equity. The following requirements apply:

(a) where the guaranteed element is not recognised separately from the DPF the whole contract must be classified as a liability;

(b) where the DPF is recognised separately from the guaranteed element the DPF can be classified as either a liability or as equity. IFRS 4 does not specify how an insurer determines whether the DPF is a liability or equity. The insurer may split the DPF into liability and equity components but must use a consistent accounting policy for such a split; and

(c) a DPF cannot be classified as an intermediate category that is neither liability nor equity. *[IFRS 4.34(a)-(b)]*.

An insurer may recognise all premiums received as revenue without separating any portion that relates to the equity component. *[IFRS 4.34(c)]*. The use of the word 'may' means that an insurer can classify some of the DPF as equity but continue to record all of the contract premiums as income. Conceptually, the IASB has admitted that if part or all of the DPF is classified as a component of equity, then the related portion of the premium should not be included in profit or loss. However, it concluded that requiring each incoming premium on a contract with a DPF to be split between liability and equity would requires systems changes beyond the scope of Phase I. Therefore, it decided that an issuer could recognise the entire premium as revenue without separating the portion that relates to the equity component. *[IFRS 4.BC164]*. This conclusion is inconsistent with those discussed at 4 and 5 above where IFRS 4 requires the separation of embedded derivatives and deposit elements of contracts in certain circumstances regardless of the 'systems changes' that may be required as a result.

Subsequent changes in the measurement of the guaranteed element and in the portion of the DPF classified as a liability must be recognised in profit or loss. If part or all of the DPF is classified in equity, that portion of profit or loss may be attributable to that feature (in the same way that a portion may be attributable to a non-controlling interest). The insurer must recognise the portion of profit or loss attributable to any equity component of a DPF as an allocation of profit or loss, not as expense or income. *[IFRS 4.34(c)]*.

IFRS 4 also requires an insurer to:

(a)   apply IAS 39 (or IFRS 9) to a derivative embedded within an insurance contract containing a DPF if it is within the scope of IAS 39 (or IFRS 9) (see 4 above); and

(b)   continue its existing accounting policies for such contracts, unless it changes those accounting policies in a way that complies with IFRS 4 (subject to the constraints noted above and those discussed at 8 below). *[IFRS 4.34(d)-(e)]*.

AMP provide the following detail as to how DPF contracts have been allocated in their income statement and statement of financial position.

Extract 54.2: AMP Limited (2008)

Notes to the financial statements [extract]

Note 1   **Summary of significant accounting policies** [extract]

Allocation of operating profit and unvested policyholder benefits

The operating profit arising from discretionary participating contracts is allocated between shareholders and participating policyholders by applying the MoS principles in accordance with the Life Insurance Act 1995 (Life Act).

Once profit is allocated to participating policyholders it can only be distributed to these policyholders. Any distribution of this profit to shareholders is only allowed for overseas business with specific approval of the regulators.

Profit allocated to participating policyholders is recognised in the Income statement as an increase in policy liabilities. Both the element of this profit that has not yet been allocated to specific policyholders (i.e. unvested) and that which has been allocated to specific policyholders by way of bonus distributions (i.e. vested) are included within life insurance contract liabilities.

Bonus distributions to participating policyholders are merely a change in the nature of the liability from unvested to vested and, as such, do not alter the amount of profit attributable to shareholders.

The principles of allocation of the profit arising from discretionary participating business determined under the Life Act and MoS are as follows:

(i) Investment income (net of tax and investment expenses) on retained earnings in respect of discretionary participating business is allocated between policyholders and shareholders in proportion to the balances of policyholders' and shareholders' retained earnings, being 80:20.

(ii) Other MoS profits arising from discretionary participating business (excluding the additional tax attributable to shareholders in respect of Australian superannuation business) are allocated 80% to policyholders and 20% to shareholders, with the following exceptions:

– The profit arising from New Zealand corporate superannuation business is apportioned such that shareholders are allocated 15% of the profit allocated to policyholders.

– The profit arising in respect of Preservation Superannuation Account business is allocated 92.5% to policyholders and 7.5% to shareholders.

(iii) Additional tax on taxable income to shareholders in respect of Australian superannuation business is allocated to shareholders only.

(iv) All profits arising from non-participating business, including net investment returns on shareholder capital and retained earnings in life statutory funds (excluding retained earnings dealt with in (i) above) are allocated to shareholders.

6.2 Discretionary participation features in financial instruments

As discussed at 2.2.2 above, a financial instrument containing a DPF is also within the scope of IFRS 4, not IAS 39 (or IFRS 9), and issuers of these contracts are permitted to continue applying their existing accounting policies to them rather than apply the rules in IAS 39 or IFRS 9.

The requirements discussed at 6.1 above apply equally to financial instruments that contain a DPF. However, in addition:

(a) if the issuer classifies the entire DPF as a liability, it must apply the liability adequacy test discussed at 7.2.2 below to the whole contract, i.e. to both the guaranteed element and the DPF. The issuer need not determine separately the amount that would result from applying IAS 39 (or IFRS 9) to the guaranteed element;

(b) if the issuer classifies part or all of the DPF of that instrument as a separate component of equity, the liability recognised for the whole contract shall not be less than the amount that would result from applying IAS 39 (or IFRS 9) to the guaranteed element. That amount shall include the intrinsic value of an option to surrender the contract, but need not include its time value if IFRS 4 exempts that option from fair value measurement (see 4 above). The issuer need not disclose the amount that would result from applying IAS 39 (or IFRS 9) to the guaranteed element, nor need it present the guaranteed amount separately. Furthermore, it need not determine the guaranteed amount if the total liability recognised for whole contract is clearly higher; and

(c) the issuer may continue to recognise all premiums (including the premiums from the guaranteed element) as revenue and recognise as an expense the resulting increase in the carrying amount of the liability even though these contracts are financial instruments.

Chapter 54

The IASB has admitted that, conceptually, the premium for the guaranteed element of these investment contracts is not revenue but believes that the treatment of the discretionary element could depend on matters that will not be resolved until Phase II. It has also decided to avoid requiring entities to make systems changes in order to split the premium between the guaranteed and discretionary elements which might later become redundant. Therefore, entities can continue to present premiums or deposits received from investment contracts with a DPF as revenue, with an expense representing the corresponding change in the liability. *[IFRS 4.BC163]*.

AXA's accounting policy for revenue recognition gives an example of an accounting policy that includes premiums from investment contracts with a DPF as revenue.

Extract 54.3: AXA Group (2008)

Notes to the Consolidated Financial Statements of AXA Group [extract]

1.18.   Revenue Recognition [extract]

1.18.1. Gross written premiums

Gross written premiums correspond to the amount of premiums written by insurance and reinsurance companies on business incepted in the year with respect to both insurance contracts and investment contracts with discretionary participating features, net of cancellations and gross of reinsurance ceded. For reinsurance, premiums are recorded on the basis of declarations made by the ceding company, and may include estimates of gross written premiums.

The disclosure requirements of IFRS 7 and IFRS 13 apply to financial instruments containing a DPF even though they are accounted for under IFRS 4. *[IFRS 4.2(b)]*. However, disclosure of the fair value of a contract containing a DPF (as described in IFRS 4) is not required if the fair value of that DPF cannot be measured reliably. *[IFRS 7.29(c)]*. Further, IFRS 4 allows the disclosed amount of interest expense for such contracts to be calculated on a basis other than the effective interest method. *[IFRS 4.35(d)]*. All of the other disclosure requirements of IFRS 7 and IFRS 13 apply to investment contracts with a DPF without modification, for example the contractual maturity analysis showing undiscounted cash flows and the fair value hierarchy categorisation if the contracts are measured at fair value.

As discussed at 6 above, an investment contract with a DPF is within the scope of the revised ED provided that the reporting entity also issues insurance contracts, which is a change from IFRS 4. In addition, the definition of an investment contract with a DPF is modified such that the additional returns must be contractually based on the returns from a specified pool of *insurance* contracts or a specified type of *insurance* contract rather just a contract or contracts.

6.3 Practical issues

6.3.1 Negative DPF

Cumulative unallocated realised and unrealised returns on investments backing insurance and investment contracts with a DPF may become negative and result in an unallocated amount that is negative (a cumulative unallocated loss).

Negative DPF is not addressed in IFRS 4 and does not appear to have been contemplated by the IASB at the time the standard was issued.

Assuming an insurer normally classifies contracts with a DPF as a liability, where such amounts become negative we believe that the insurer is prohibited from recognising an asset or debiting the contract liability related to the cumulative unallocated losses (realised or unrealised) on the investments backing contracts that include DPF features except to the extent that:

- the insurer is contractually entitled to pass those losses to the contract holders; or
- the insurer's previous local GAAP accounting for insurance or investment contracts with a DPF permitted the recognition of such an asset or the debiting of the contract liability when the unallocated investment results of the investments backing a DPF contract were negative.

An insurer is permitted to continue existing GAAP accounting for insurance contracts and investment contracts with a DPF as discussed at 7 below. If an existing GAAP accounting policy specifically allows the recognition of an asset or the reduction of contract liabilities related to cumulative unallocated DPF losses then in our view continuation of that policy is permitted because IFRS 4 specifically excludes accounting policies for insurance contracts from paragraphs 10-12 of IAS 8. If the existing GAAP accounting policy does not permit the recognition of an asset or the reduction of contract liabilities in such circumstances then the introduction of such a policy would need to satisfy the relevance and reliability criteria discussed at 8.1 below to be permissible.

Examples of situations in which an insurer is contractually entitled to (partially) recover losses can include contracts with a fixed surrender charge or a market value adjustment feature.

6.3.2 Contracts with switching features

Some contracts may contain options for the counterparty to switch between terms that would, *prima facie*, result in classification as an investment contract without DPF features (accounted for under IAS 39 (or IFRS 9)) and terms that would result in a classification as an investment contract with DPF features (accounted for under IFRS 4).

Chapter 54

We believe that the fact that this switch option makes these contracts investment contracts with a DPF means that the issuer should continuously be able to demonstrate that the DPF feature still exists and also be able to demonstrate actual switching to a DPF in order to classify these contracts as investment contracts with a DPF under IFRS 4.

7   SELECTION OF ACCOUNTING POLICIES

IFRS 4 provides very little guidance on accounting policies that should be used by an entity that issues insurance contracts or investment contracts with a DPF (hereafter for convenience, at 7 and 8 below, referred to as 'insurance contracts').

Instead of providing detailed guidance, the standard:

(a)   creates an exemption from applying the hierarchy in IAS 8 (the 'hierarchy exemption') that specifies the criteria an entity should use in developing an accounting policy if no IFRS applies specifically to an item (see 7.1 below);

(b)   limits the impact of the hierarchy exemption by imposing five specific requirements relating to catastrophe provisions, liability adequacy, derecognition, offsetting and impairment of reinsurance assets (see 7.2 below); and

(c)   permits some existing practices to continue but prohibits their introduction (see 8.2.1 below).

The importance of the hierarchy exemption is that without it certain existing accounting practices would be unlikely to be acceptable under IFRS as they would conflict with the *Framework* or other standards such as IAS 37, IAS 39 (or IFRS 9), IAS 18 or IFRS 15. For example, the deferral of acquisition costs that are not incremental or directly attributable to the issue of an insurance contract are unlikely to meet the *Framework's* definition of an asset. Similarly, a basis of liability measurement, such as the gross premium valuation, which includes explicit estimates of future periods' cash inflows in respect of policies which are cancellable at the policyholder's discretion would be unlikely to be acceptable.

The IASB considered that, without the hierarchy exemption, establishing acceptable accounting policies for insurance contracts could have been costly and that some insurers might have made major changes to their policies on adoption of IFRS followed by further significant changes in Phase II. *[IFRS 4.BC77].*

The practical result of the hierarchy exemption is that an insurer is permitted to continue applying the accounting policies that it was using when it first applied IFRS 4, subject to the exceptions noted at 7.2 below. *[IFRS 4.BC83].*

Usually, but not exclusively, these existing accounting policies will be the insurer's previous GAAP, but IFRS 4 does not specifically require an insurer to follow its local accounting pronouncements. This is mainly because of the problems in defining local GAAP. Also, some insurers, such as non-US insurers with a US listing, apply US GAAP to their insurance contracts rather than the GAAP of their own country which would have given rise to further definitional problems. *[IFRS 4.BC81].*

Additionally, the IASB wanted to give insurers the opportunity to improve their accounting policies even if there was no change to their local GAAP. *[IFRS 4.BC82].*

The practical result of this is a continuation of the diversity in accounting practices whose elimination was one of the primary objectives of the IASC's project on insurance contracts originally initiated in 1997.

To illustrate this point, below are extracts from the financial statements of Prudential and Münchener Rück (Munich Re), both of which apply IFRS. Prudential is a UK insurance group and applies UK GAAP to its insurance contracts whereas Munich Re is a German insurance group that applies US GAAP to its insurance contracts.

Extract 54.4: Prudential plc (2008)

Note on the Group financial statements [extract]
A3   Critical accounting policies, estimates and judgements[extract]

Insurance contract accounting

With the exception of certain contracts described in note D1, the Group's life assurance contracts are classified as insurance contracts and investment contracts with discretionary participating features. As permitted by IFRS 4, assets and liabilities of these contracts (see below) are accounted for under previously applied GAAP. Accordingly, except as described below, the modified statutory basis (MSB) of reporting as set out in the revised Statement of Recommended Practice (SORP) issued by the Association of British Insurers (ABI) in November 2003 has been applied.

Extract 54.5: Münchener Rückversicherungs – Gesellschaft Aktiengesellschaft (2008)

Note to the consolidated financial statements [extract]
Application of International Financial Reporting Standards [extract]

In accordance with the rules of IFRS 4, underwriting items are recognised and measured on the basis of US GAAP (United States Generally Accepted Accounting Principles). We have also observed the German accounting standards (DRSs) adopted by the German Standardisation Council (DSR) provided they do not contradict the applicable IFRSs.

7.1   The hierarchy exemption

Paragraphs 10-12 of IAS 8 provide guidance on the development and application of accounting policies in the absence of a standard or interpretation that specifically applies to a transaction. In particular, it explains the applicability and relative weighting to be given to other IFRS sources, the use of guidance issued by other standard-setting bodies and other accounting literature and accepted industry practices.

An insurer is not required to apply paragraphs 10-12 of IAS 8 for:

(a)   insurance contracts that it issues (including related acquisition costs and related intangible assets); and

(b)   reinsurance contracts that it holds. *[IFRS 4.13].*

What this means is that an insurer need not consider:

- whether its existing accounting policies are consistent with the *Framework*;
- whether those accounting policies regarding insurance contracts are consistent with other standards and interpretations dealing with similar and related issues; or
- whether they result in information that is 'relevant' or 'reliable'.

This exemption was controversial within the IASB and resulted in five members of the IASB dissenting from the issue of the standard. It was also opposed by some respondents to ED 5 on the grounds that it would permit too much diversity in practice and allow fundamental departures from the *Framework* that could prevent an insurer's financial statements from presenting information that is understandable, relevant, reliable and comparable. The IASB admitted that the exemption is 'unusual' but believed that it was necessary to minimise disruption in 2005 for both users and preparers. *[IFRS 4.BC79].*

7.2   Limits on the hierarchy exemption

In order to prevent insurers continuing with accounting policies that the IASB considered would either not be permitted in Phase II or which conflict too greatly with other standards, such as IAS 39 (or IFRS 9) or IAS 37, IFRS 4 imposes several limits on the hierarchy exception. These are in respect of:

- catastrophe and equalisation provisions;
- liability adequacy testing;
- derecognition of insurance liabilities;
- offsetting of reinsurance contracts against relating direct insurance contracts; and
- impairment of reinsurance assets. *[IFRS 4.14].*

These are discussed below.

7.2.1   *Catastrophe and equalisation provisions*

Catastrophe provisions are provisions that are generally built up over the years out of premiums received, perhaps following a prescribed regulatory formula, until an amount, possibly specified by the regulations, is reached. These provisions are usually intended to be released on the occurrence of a future catastrophic loss that is covered by current and future contracts. Equalisation provisions are usually intended to cover random fluctuations of claim expenses around the expected value of claims for some types of insurance contract (such as hail, credit guarantee and fidelity insurance) perhaps using a formula based on experience over a number of years. *[IFRS 4.BC87].* Consequently, these provisions tend to act as income smoothing mechanisms that reduce profits in reporting periods in which insurance claims are low and reduce losses in reporting periods in which insurance claims are high. As catastrophe and/or equalisation provisions are normally not available for distribution to shareholders, the solvency position of an insurer can be improved.

The recognition of a liability (such as catastrophe and equalisation provisions) for possible future claims, if these claims arise from insurance contracts that are not in existence at the end of the reporting period, is prohibited. *[IFRS 4.14(a)].*

The IASB considers there is no credible basis for arguing that equalisation or catastrophe provisions are recognisable liabilities under IFRS. Such provisions are not liabilities as defined in the *Framework* because the insurer has no present obligation for losses that will occur after the end of the contract period. Without the hierarchy exemption the recognition of these provisions as liabilities would have been allowed and therefore this requirement preserves that prohibition. Further, there is no realistic prospect that the IASB will permit them in Phase II. *[IFRS 4.BC89-90].*

The IASB views the objective of financial statements as not to enhance solvency but to provide information that is useful to a wide range of users for economic decisions. *[IFRS 4.BC89(d)].* Present imperfections in the measurement of insurance liabilities do not, in the IASB's opinion, justify the recognition of items that do not meet the definition of a liability. *[IFRS 4.BC92(a)].*

Although the recognition of catastrophe and equalisation provisions in respect of claims arising from insurance contracts that are not in force at the end of the reporting period are prohibited, such provisions are permitted to the extent that they were permitted under previous accounting policies and they are attributable to policies in force at the end of the reporting period.

Although IFRS 4 prohibits the recognition of these provisions as a liability, it does not prohibit their segregation as a component of equity. Consequently, insurers are free to designate a proportion of their equity as an equalisation or catastrophe provision. *[IFRS 4.BC93].*

Aviva Insurance Limited discloses that its equalisation provisions are included within retained earnings in equity.

Extract 54.6: Aviva Insurance Limited (2013)

Accounting policies [extract]
(AA)   **Equalisation provision**

Equalisation provisions are established in accordance with UK company law. These provisions are in addition to the provisions required to meet the anticipated ultimate cost of settlement of outstanding claims at the balance sheet date. Under IFRS, the provisions are not reported in the balance sheet as no liability exists but are included within the non-distributable element of retained earnings, net of attributable tax relief.

Where a catastrophe or equalisation provision has a tax base but is not recognised in the IFRS financial statements, then a taxable temporary difference will arise that should be accounted for under IAS 12 – *Income Taxes*.

7.2.2   Liability adequacy testing

Many existing insurance accounting models have mechanisms to ensure that insurance liabilities are not understated, and that related amounts recognised as assets, such as deferred acquisition costs, are not overstated. However, because there is no guarantee that such tests are in place in every jurisdiction and are effective, the IASB was concerned that the credibility of IFRS could suffer if an insurer claims to comply with IFRS but fails to recognise material and reasonably foreseeable losses arising from existing contractual obligations.

Therefore, a requirement for the application of a 'liability adequacy test' (an assessment of whether the carrying amount of an insurance liability needs to be increased, or the carrying amount of related deferred acquisition costs or related intangible assets decreased, based on a review of future cash flows) was introduced into IFRS 4. This assessment of liability adequacy is required at each reporting date. *[IFRS 4.BC94].*

If the assessment shows that the carrying amount of the recognised insurance liabilities (less related deferred acquisition costs and related intangible assets such as those acquired in a business combination or portfolio transfer discussed at 9 below) is inadequate in the light of the estimated future cash flows, the entire deficiency must be recognised immediately in profit or loss. *[IFRS 4.15].*

The purpose of this requirement is to prevent material liabilities being unrecorded.

7.2.2.A   Using a liability adequacy test under existing accounting policies

As many existing insurance accounting models have some form of liability adequacy test, the IASB was keen to ensure that insurers using such models, as far as possible, did not have to make systems changes. Therefore, if an insurer applies a liability adequacy test that meets specified minimum requirements, IFRS 4 imposes no further requirements. The minimum requirements are the following:

(a)   the test considers current estimates of all contractual cash flows, and of related cash flows such as claims handling costs, as well as cash flows resulting from embedded options and guarantees; and

(b)   if the test shows that the liability is inadequate, the entire deficiency is recognised in profit or loss. *[IFRS 4.16].*

If the insurer's liability adequacy test meets these requirements then the test should be applied at the level of aggregation specified in that test. *[IFRS 4.18].*

The standard does not specify:

* what criteria in the liability adequacy test determine when existing contracts end and future contracts start;

* at what level of aggregation the test should be performed;

* whether or how the cash flows are discounted to reflect the time value of money or adjusted for risk and uncertainty;

* whether the test considers both the time value and intrinsic value of embedded options and guarantees; or

* whether additional losses recognised because of the test are recognised by reducing the carrying amount of deferred acquisition costs or by increasing the carrying amount of the related insurance liabilities. *[IFRS 4.BC101].*

Additionally, the standard does not state whether this existing liability adequacy test can be performed net of expected related reinsurance recoveries. However, the liability adequacy test discussed at 7.2.2.B below explicitly excludes reinsurance.

The standard provides only minimum guidelines on what a liability adequacy test comprises. This avoids insurers having to make systems changes that may have to be reversed in Phase II but allows the continuation of a diversity of practice among insurers, for example in the use (or not) of discounting. However, some existing practices may not meet these minimum requirements, for example if they use cash flows locked-in at inception rather than current estimates.

An example of the details of a liability adequacy test can be found in the financial statements of Allianz.

Extract 54.7: Allianz SE (2008)

Notes to the consolidated financial statements [extract]

Note 2   Summary of significant accounting policies [extract]

Reserves for insurance and investment contracts and financial liabilities for unit-linked contracts [extract]

Liability adequacy tests are performed for each insurance portfolio on the basis of estimates of future claims, costs, premiums earned and proportionate investment income. For short duration contracts, a premium deficiency is recognised if the sum of expected claim costs and claim adjustment expenses, expected dividends to policyholders, unamortized acquisition costs, and maintenance expenses exceeds related unearned premiums while considering anticipated investment income. For long duration contracts, if actual experience regarding investment yields, mortality, morbidity, terminations or expense indicate that existing contract liabilities, along with the present value of future gross premiums, will not be sufficient to cover the present value of future benefits and to recover deferred policy acquisition costs, then a premium deficiency is recognised.

7.2.2.B   Using the liability adequacy test specified in IFRS 4

If an insurer's accounting policies do not require a liability adequacy test that meets the minimum criteria discussed, it should:

(a)   determine the carrying amount of the relevant insurance liabilities less the carrying amount of:

(i)   any related deferred acquisition costs; and

(ii)   any related intangible assets. However, related reinsurance assets are not considered because an insurer assesses impairment for them separately (see 7.2.5 below).

(b)   determine whether the amount described in (a) is less than the carrying amount that would be required if the relevant insurance liabilities were within the scope of IAS 37. If it is less, the entire difference should be recognised in profit or loss and the carrying amount of the related deferred acquisition costs or related intangible assets should be reduced or the carrying amount of the relevant insurance liabilities should be increased. *[IFRS 4.17].*

This test should be performed at the level of a portfolio of contracts that are subject to broadly similar risks and managed together as a single portfolio. *[IFRS 4.18].*

Investment margins should be reflected in the calculation if, and only if, the carrying amounts of the liabilities and any related deferred acquisition costs and intangible assets also reflect those margins. *[IFRS 4.19].*

IAS 37 was used as a basis for this liability adequacy test as it was an existing measurement basis that minimised the need for exceptions to existing IFRS principles. *[IFRS 4.BC95, 104].*

IAS 37 requires an amount to be recognised as a provision that is the best estimate of the expenditure required to settle the present obligation. This is the amount that an entity would rationally pay to settle the obligation at the reporting date or transfer it to a third party at that time. *[IAS 37.36-47].* Although IAS 37 refers to 'expenditure' there appears to be no specific prohibition from considering future premiums. This might be appropriate if it can be argued that the expenditures are a function of the future premiums.

The end result is that the IAS 37 requirements are potentially more prescriptive and onerous than those applying if an insurer has an existing liability adequacy test which meets the minimum IFRS 4 criteria discussed above.

7.2.2.C   Investment contracts with a discretionary participation feature

As discussed at 6.2 above the accounting requirements for investment contracts with a DPF depend on whether the entity has classified the DPF as a liability or as equity. Where the DPF is classified entirely as a liability then the liability adequacy test is applied to the whole contract, i.e. both the guaranteed element and the DPF. Where the DPF is classified in part or in total as a separate component of equity then IFRS 4 states that the amount recognised as a liability for the whole contract shall be not less than the amount that would result from applying IAS 39 (or IFRS 9) to the guaranteed element. IFRS 4 does not specify whether the IAS 39 (or IFRS 9) measurement basis should be amortised cost or fair value. It is also not clear if this requirement relates to the gross liability or to the net carrying amount, i.e. less any related deferred acquisition costs or related intangible assets. *[IFRS 4.35(b)].*

7.2.2.D   Interaction between the liability adequacy test and shadow accounting

IFRS 4 does not address the interaction between the liability adequacy test and shadow accounting (discussed at 8.3 below). The liability adequacy test requires all deficiencies to be recognised in profit or loss whereas shadow accounting permits certain unrealised losses to be recognised in other comprehensive income.

We believe that a company can apply shadow accounting to offset an increase in insurance liabilities to the extent that the increase is caused directly by market interest rate movements that lead to changes in the value of investments that are recognised directly in other comprehensive income. Although IFRS 4 does not specify the priority of shadow accounting over the LAT, because the LAT is to be applied as a final test to the amount recognised under the insurer's accounting policies, it follows that shadow accounting has to be applied first. This is illustrated in the example below.

Example 54.30:   Shadow loss recognition

An insurer has classified certain investments backing insurance liabilities as available-for-sale financial assets. It has issued a guaranteed single premium product backed by an investment in a government bond with the same effective interest rate, duration and currency.

The opening position in the statement of financial position, perfectly matched in currency, interest rates and duration is as follows:

	CU		CU
Bond @ 6% effective rate, initial value	100	Equity	10
Other assets	10	Contract @ 6% guarantee	100
Total assets	110	Total liabilities and equity	110

The position in the statement of financial position, one year after issuance, after a significant decline in market interest rates is as follows:

	CU		CU
Bond @ market value	116	Equity	20
Other assets	10	Contract @ 6% guarantee	106
Total assets	126	Total liabilities and equity	126

Given the market interest rate movement, the 'matched' situation no longer shows in the statement of financial position as the investment is valued at CU 116 and the liability at CU 106. The current market return on the assets funding the insurance contract at the time of performing the liability adequacy test (LAT) is no longer 6%. It is now 5.2% (CU 6 ÷ CU 116).

The increase in shareholders' equity could be used for, or considered available for, dividend payments. Part of the cash value of the investment is no longer allocated to the insurance liability, but to shareholders' equity. This is not correct because the entire investment, regardless of its carrying amount, is needed to provide the annual investment return (CU 6) to fund the growth of the liability (CU 6).

The bond's unrealised gain results in a decline in its market interest yield to below 6%. Therefore the liability needs to increase (in other words a higher amount of the investment needs to be allocated to it) to the level where the nominal CU 6 is earned.

IFRS 4 states that any increase in the liability needs to be charged to profit or loss. However, in this case the increase is caused by a market interest movement that has produced an unrealised gain on an investment. This unrealised gain has been credited to other comprehensive income rather than profit or loss. If the liability increase is charged to profit or loss there will be a mismatch between this and the related unrealised gain in other comprehensive income.

To the extent that the increase in the liability is related to other causes, the insurer should recognise a loss in the income statement.

This example assumes that the effect of the change in market interest rates on the fair value of investments is recorded in other comprehensive income and was exactly the same as the opposite change in the fair value of the liability. In reality these two effects may not match exactly, so there could be a difference between the change in the fair value of the available-for-sale (AFS) assets and the change required in the carrying amount of the liability before the LAT is performed. The impact of shadow accounting needs to be limited to the change in value that was directly recorded in other comprehensive income arising from changes in the fair value carrying amount of the AFS assets.

7.2.3   *Insurance liability derecognition*

An insurance liability, or a part of such a liability, can be removed from the statement of financial position (derecognised) when, and only when, it is extinguished i.e. when the obligation specified in the contract is discharged, cancelled or expires. *[IFRS 4.14(c)].*

This requirement is identical to that contained in IAS 39 (or IFRS 9) for the derecognition of financial liabilities. *[IAS 39.39, IFRS 9.3.3.1]*. The IASB said it could identify no reasons for the derecognition requirements for insurance liabilities to differ from those for financial liabilities. *[IFRS 4.BC105]*.

Accordingly, insurance liabilities should not normally be derecognised as a result of entering into a reinsurance contract because this does not usually discharge the insurer's liability to the policyholder. This applies even if the insurer has delegated all claims settlement authority to the reinsurer or if a claim has been fully reinsured.

Derecognition should be distinguished from remeasurement. The carrying amounts of many insurance liabilities are estimates and an insurer should re-estimate its claims liabilities, and hence change their carrying amounts, if that is required by its accounting policies. However, in certain situations the distinction between the two concepts can be blurred, for example where there is a dispute or other uncertainty over the contractual terms of an insurance policy.

IFRS 4 contains no guidance on when or whether a modification of an insurance contract might cause derecognition of that contract. The revised ED contains detailed guidance on when a modification of an insurance contract results in derecognition of that contract and recognition of a new contract. The revised ED states that if an insurance contract does not meet the criteria for derecognition due to modification, it is derecognised when, and only when, it is extinguished (i.e. when the obligation specified in the insurance contract is discharged, cancelled or expired).[15]

7.2.4   Offsetting of insurance and related reinsurance contracts

IFRS 4 prohibits offsetting of:

(a)   reinsurance assets against the related insurance liabilities; and

(b)   income or expense from reinsurance contracts against the expense or income from the related insurance contracts. *[IFRS 4.14(d)]*.

This prohibition broadly aligns the offsetting criteria for insurance assets and liabilities with those required for financial assets and financial liabilities under IAS 32, which requires that financial assets and financial liabilities can only be offset where an entity:

(a)   has a legally enforceable right to set-off the recognised amounts; and

(b)   intends to settle on a net basis, or to realise both the asset and settle the liability simultaneously. *[IAS 32.42]*.

Because a cedant normally has no legal right to offset amounts due from a reinsurer against amounts due to the related underlying policyholder the IASB considers a gross presentation gives a clearer picture of the cedant's rights and obligations. *[IFRS 4.BC106]*.

As a result, balances due from reinsurers should be shown as assets in the statement of financial position, whereas the related insurance liabilities should be shown as liabilities. Because of the relationship between the two, some insurers provide linked disclosures in the notes to their IFRS financial statements as discussed at 10.1.2.A below.

The IFRS 4 requirements, however, appear to be less flexible than those in IAS 32 in that they provide no circumstances in which offsetting can be acceptable. So, for example, 'pass through' contracts that provide for reinsurers to pay claims direct to the underlying policyholder would still have to be shown gross in the statement of financial position. IAS 32 also does not address offsetting in the income statement.

The revised ED requires separate presentation of portfolios of insurance and reinsurance contracts and also separate presentation of portfolios of insurance and reinsurance contracts that are assets from those that are liabilities. This means that balances on individual contracts within a portfolio that are assets are presented on a net basis together with balances on individual contracts that are liabilities.[16] In the statement of profit or loss and other comprehensive income, the revised ED requires that an entity should not offset income or expense from reinsurance contracts against the expense or income from insurance contracts and that income or expense from the underlying items is not offset against expense or income from the insurance contract.[17]

7.2.5   *Impairment of reinsurance assets*

If the IASB had required that the impairment model in IAS 36 be applied to reinsurance assets (as proposed in ED 5) many cedants would have been compelled to change their accounting model for reinsurance contracts in a way that was inconsistent with the accounting for the underlying direct insurance liability. This would have required the cedant to address matters such as discounting and risk, together with the attendant systems implications. Consequently, the IASB concluded that the impairment test should focus on credit risk (arising from the risk of default by the reinsurer and also from disputes over coverage) and not address matters arising from the measurement of the underlying direct insurance liability. It decided the most appropriate way to achieve this was to introduce an incurred loss model based on that contained in IAS 39. *[IFRS 4.BC107-108].*

Consequently, a reinsurance asset should be impaired if, and only if:

(a)   there is objective evidence, as a result of an event that occurred after initial recognition of the asset, that the cedant may not receive all amounts due to it under the terms of the contract; and

(b)   that event has a reliably measureable impact on the amounts that the cedant will receive from the reinsurer. *[IFRS 4.20].*

Where a reinsurance asset is impaired, its carrying amount should be reduced accordingly and the impairment loss recognised in profit or loss.

IAS 39 provides various indicators of impairment for financial assets, such as the significant financial difficulty of the obligor and a breach of contract, such as a default in interest or principal payments. IFRS 4 does not provide any specific indicators of impairment relating to reinsurance assets. In the absence of such indicators, it would seem appropriate for insurers to refer to those in IAS 39 as a guide to determining whether reinsurance assets are impaired.

Chapter 54

Zurich Financial Services discloses details of impairment indicators considered in determining whether reinsurance assets are impaired.

Extract 54.8: Zurich Financial Services Group (2008)

Notes to the consolidated financial statements [extract]

Note 3   Summary of significant accounting policies [extract]

b)   Insurance contracts and investment contracts with discretionary participating features
[extract]

Reinsurance [extract]

Reinsurance assets are assessed for impairment on a regular basis for any events that may trigger impairment. Triggering events may include legal disputes with third parties, changes in capital and surplus levels, change in credit ratings of a counterparty and historic experience regarding collectability from specific reinsurers.

The use of this impairment model means that provisions cannot be recognised in respect of credit losses expected to arise from future events.

IAS 39 permits a portfolio approach to determining impairment provisions for financial assets carried at amortised cost. More specifically, IAS 39 permits a collective evaluation of impairment for assets that are grouped on the basis of similar credit risk characteristics that are indicative of the debtors' ability to pay all amounts due according to the contractual terms (for example on the basis of a credit risk evaluation or grading process that considers asset type, industry, geographical location, collateral type, past-due status and other relevant factors). *[IAS 39.AG87].*

It is questionable whether an insurer's reinsurance assets would normally exhibit sufficiently similar credit risk characteristics to permit such an approach to determining impairment. That said, IAS 39 is clear that impairment losses recognised on a group basis represent an interim step pending the identification of impairment losses on individual assets in the group of financial assets that are collectively assessed for impairment. As soon as information is available that specifically identifies losses on individually impaired assets in a group, those assets are removed from the group. *[IAS 39.AG88].*

IFRS 9 does not contain any consequential amendments to IFRS 4 in respect of impairment of reinsurance assets. Therefore, if the new insurance accounting standard is not yet adopted when IFRS 9 is applied, insurers will continue to use an incurred loss impairment model for reinsurance assets notwithstanding the fact that an expected loss model will be used for financial assets within the scope of IFRS 9.

The revised ED proposes that a cedant should consider the risk of non-performance by the reinsurer, including the effects of collateral and losses from disputes within the fulfilment cash flows, on an expected present value basis.[18]

7.2.6   Accounting policy matters not addressed by IFRS 4

7.2.6.A   Derecognition of insurance and reinsurance assets

IFRS 4 does not address the derecognition of insurance or reinsurance assets. The IASB could identify no reason why the derecognition criteria for insurance assets should differ from those for financial assets accounted for under IAS 39 (or IFRS 9), but declined to address the issue 'because derecognition of financial assets is a controversial topic'. *[IFRS 4.BC105].* Consequently, derecognition of insurance assets should be dealt with under existing accounting practices which may differ from the requirements of IAS 39 (or IFRS 9).

AEGON discloses the following policy concerning the derecognition of reinsurance assets.

Extract 54.9: AEGON N.V. (2008)
Notes to the consolidated financial statements [extract]
Note 2.12   **Reinsurance assets** [extract]

Reinsurance assets are measured consistently with the amounts associated with the underlying insurance contracts and in accordance with the terms of each reinsurance contract. They are subject to impairment testing and are derecognized when the contractual rights are extinguished or expire or when the contract is transferred to another party.

The revised ED states that where an entity buys reinsurance, it should derecognise the underlying insurance contract or contracts if, and only if, the underlying insurance contract or contracts are extinguished.[19] It does not address derecognition of insurance assets.

7.2.6.B   Impairment of insurance assets

IFRS 4 is silent on the impairment model to be used for receivables arising under insurance contracts that are not reinsurance assets (discussed at 7.2.5 above). An example of these would be premium receivables due from policyholders. Insurers should therefore apply their existing accounting policies for determining impairment provisions for these assets, although an impairment model similar to that required by IAS 39 for financial assets would also appear to be appropriate. IFRS 9 changes the impairment model from an incurred loss model to an expected loss model (see Chapter 49).

The revised ED is also silent on impairment of insurance assets although, under the proposed model, premiums (including premium adjustments and instalment premiums) from policyholders and any additional cash flows that result from those premiums are included within the fulfilment cash flows.[20]

7.2.6.C   Gains and losses on buying reinsurance

Some local accounting requirements often define reinsurance contracts more strictly than direct insurance contracts to avoid income statement distortion caused by contracts that have the legal form of reinsurance but do not transfer significant insurance risk. Such contracts are sometimes described as financial reinsurance. One such source of distortion is caused because many local GAAPs do not require the discounting of non-life insurance claims liabilities. If the insurer buys reinsurance, the premium paid to the reinsurer reflects the present value of the underlying liability and is, therefore, potentially less than the existing carrying amount of the liability. This could result in a gain on the initial recognition of the reinsurance contract (a 'day 1' gain) where a reinsurance asset is recognised at an amount equivalent to the undiscounted liability and this is less than the premium payable for the reinsurance contract. This day 1 gain arises largely because of the inability to discount the underlying liability. Initial recognition of gains could also arise if the underlying insurance liability is measured with excessive prudence. [IFRS 4.BC110].

IFRS 4 defines a reinsurance contract using the same terms as an insurance contract. The IASB decided not to use the definition of a reinsurance contract to address the problems described above because it found no conceptual reason to define a reinsurance contract any differently to a direct insurance contract. It considered making a distinction for situations where significant distortions in reported profit were most likely to occur, such as retroactive contracts, but eventually considered that developing such a distinction would be time-consuming and difficult, and there would have been no guarantee of success. [IFRS 4.BC111, 113].

Consequently, IFRS 4 does not restrict the recognition of gains on entering into reinsurance contracts but instead requires specific disclosure of the gains and losses that arise (see 10.1.3 below).

Insurers are therefore permitted to continue applying their existing accounting policies to gains and losses on the purchase of reinsurance contracts (which may or may not prohibit gains on initial recognition) and are also permitted to change those accounting policies according to the criteria discussed at 8 below.

The revised ED proposes that day 1 gains or losses on the purchase of reinsurance contracts held are normally treated as a contractual service margin and not recognised immediately in profit or loss. However, day 1 losses are recognised in profit or loss as an expense if the reinsurance coverage relates to events that occurred before the purchase of the reinsurance contract.[21] In subsequent discussions, the IASB tentatively decided that, after inception, an entity should recognise in profit or loss any changes in estimates of fulfilment cash flows for a reinsurance contract that an entity holds when those changes arise as a result of changes in estimates of fulfilment cash flows for an underlying direct insurance contract that are recognised immediately in profit or loss.[22]

7.2.6.D   Acquisition costs

IFRS 4 is silent on how to account for the costs of acquiring insurance contracts. 'Acquisition costs' are not defined within the standard, although the Basis for Conclusions states that they are 'the costs that an insurer incurs to sell, underwrite and initiate a new insurance contract', [IFRS 4.BC116], a description that would appear to exclude costs associated with amending an existing contract.

IFRS 4 neither prohibits nor requires the deferral of acquisition costs, nor does it prescribe what acquisition costs should be deferred, the period and method of their amortisation, or whether an insurer should present deferred acquisition costs as an asset or as a reduction in insurance liabilities. [IFRS 4.BC116].

The IASB decided that the treatment of acquisition costs was an integral part of existing insurance models that could not easily be amended without a more fundamental review of these models in Phase II. [IFRS 4.BC116].

Insurers are therefore permitted to continue applying their existing accounting policies for deferring the costs of acquiring insurance contracts.

Zurich Financial Services and Generali provide examples of the diversity in practice regarding which acquisition costs are capitalised. Zurich apply US GAAP to their insurance contracts and only capitalise expenses that are directly related to and vary with the acquisition. Generali apply Italian GAAP to their insurance contracts and also capitalise indirect expenses.

Extract 54.10: Zurich Financial Services Group (2008)

Notes to the consolidated financial statements [extract]

Note 4   Critical accounting estimates and judgements [extract]

f) Deferred policy acquisition costs [extract]

Deferred policy acquisition costs generally consist of commissions, underwriting expenses and policy issuance costs. The amount of acquisition costs to be deferred is dependent on judgements as to which issuance costs are directly related to and vary with the acquisition. The related asset is amortized over the premium earning pattern for non-life and certain life products. For most life products, amortization is based on the estimated future profitability of the contract throughout its life. The estimation of profitability considers both historical and future experience as regards assumptions, such as lapse rates or investment income.

Extract 54.11: Assicurazioni Generali S.p.A. (2008)

Notes to the consolidated financial statements [extract]

Part D   Summary of significant accounting policies [extract]

6.2 – Deferred acquisition costs

In accordance with IFRS 4, deferred acquisition costs are accounted for in line with local GAAP. This item includes acquisition commissions and other expenses directly or indirectly attributable to the acquisition or renewal contracts and deferrable over the term of the contracts.

Both IAS 18 and IFRS 15 permit only incremental costs that are directly attributable to securing an investment management contract to be recognised as an asset. An incremental cost is one that would not have been incurred if the entity had not secured the investment management contract. *[IAS 18.IE14(b)(iii), IFRS 15.91-93]*. These criteria may be different from those applied to acquisition costs for insurance contracts under local GAAP.

The revised ED proposes that directly attributable acquisition costs that can be allocated on a rational and consistent basis to the individual portfolios of insurance contracts are included in the estimates of cash flows used to determine the fulfilment cash flows which form part of the initial measurement of an insurance contract. No distinction is made between the costs of successful acquisition efforts and unsuccessful efforts.[23]

7.2.6.E   Salvage and subrogation

Some insurance contracts permit the insurer to sell (usually damaged) property acquired in settling the claim (salvage). The insurer may also have the right to pursue third parties for payment of some or all costs (subrogation). IFRS 4 contains no guidance on whether potential salvage and subrogation recoveries should be presented as separate assets or netted against the related insurance liability. This will be considered in Phase II. *[IFRS 4.BC120]*.

Chapter 54

Royal & SunAlliance is an example of an entity which discloses that its insurance liabilities are stated net of anticipated salvage and subrogation.

Extract 54.12: Royal & SunAlliance Insurance Group plc (2008)

Significant accounting policies [extract]

Insurance liabilities [extract]

The provisions for claims outstanding, whether reported or not, comprise the estimated cost of claims incurred but not settled at the balance sheet date. It includes related expenses and a deduction for the expected value of salvage and other recoveries.

The revised ED proposes that potential recoveries (such as salvage and subrogation) on past and future claims should be included as part of the contractual cash flows to the extent that they do not qualify for recognition as separate assets.[24]

7.2.6.F   Policy loans

Some insurance contracts permit the policyholder to obtain a loan from the insurer with the insurance contract acting as collateral for the loan. IFRS 4 is silent on whether an insurer should treat such loans as a prepayment of the insurance liability or as a separate financial asset. This is because the IASB does not regard the issue as a priority. *[IFRS 4.BC122].*

Consequently, insurers can either present these loans either as separate assets or as a reduction of the related insurance liability depending on their local GAAP requirements.

The revised ED does not explicitly address policy loans but implies that these are part of the contractual cash flows and included within the overall insurance contract asset or liability.

7.2.6.G   Investments held in a fiduciary capacity

Insurers often make investments on behalf of policyholders as well as on behalf of shareholders. In some cases, this can result in the insurer holding an interest in an entity which, either on its own, or when combined with the interest of the policyholder, gives the insurer control of that entity (as defined by IFRS 10).

8   CHANGES IN ACCOUNTING POLICIES

IFRS 4 imposes a number of constraints that apply whenever an insurer wishes to change its accounting policies for insurance contracts. These requirements apply both to changes made by an insurer that already applies IFRS and to changes made by an insurer adopting IFRS for the first time. *[IFRS 4.21].*

They reflect the IASB's concern that insurers might change their existing policies to ones that are less relevant or reliable contrary to the requirements of IAS 8. One option would have been for the IASB to prohibit any changes in accounting policies to prevent lack of comparability (especially within a country) and management discretion to make arbitrary changes. However, it decided to permit changes in accounting policies for insurance contracts provided they can be justified, as is required for any change in accounting policy under IFRS. *[IFRS 4.BC123, 125].*

The general and specific requirements relating to changes in accounting policies are discussed below.

8.1 Criteria for accounting policy changes

An insurer may change its accounting policies for insurance contracts if, and only if, the change makes the financial statements more relevant to the economic decision-making needs of users and no less reliable, or more reliable and no less relevant to those needs. Relevance and reliability should be judged by the criteria in IAS 8. *[IFRS 4.22].*

Relevance relates to the economic decision-making needs of users and reliability, in reference to the financial statements, relates to faithful representation, the economic substance of transactions and not merely their legal form, freedom from bias, prudence and completion in all material respects. *[IAS 8.10].* In making judgements regarding relevance and reliability management should refer to the requirements in IFRSs dealing with similar and related issues and the definitions, recognition criteria and measurement concepts in the IASB *Framework*. Management may also consider the most recent pronouncements of other standard-setting bodies that use a similar conceptual framework to develop accounting standards, other accounting literature and accepted industry practices to the extent that they do not conflict with IFRS. *[IAS 8.11-12].*

The Board also considers that as its conclusions for Phase II develop they will give insurers further context for judgements about whether a change in accounting policy will make the financial statements more relevant and reliable. *[IFRS 4.BC123].* More specifically, the change should bring the insurer's financial statements closer to meeting the criteria in IAS 8, but need not achieve full compliance with those criteria. *[IFRS 4.23].*

IAS 8 requires changes in accounting policies for which there are no specific transitional provisions to be applied retrospectively. As IFRS 4 does not contain any transitional provisions for changes in accounting policies for insurance contracts, any such changes will have to be retrospective, unless impracticable. *[IAS 8.19].*

Chapter 54

Aviva's financial statements illustrate an example of a change in an accounting policy used for insurance contracts.

Extract 54.13: Aviva plc (2008)

Notes to the consolidated financial statements [extract]

Note 2   **Presentation changes** [extract]

(b) (i)   **Restatement for the change in accounting policy for latent reserves** [extract]

As part of the Company's aim to continuously improve the relevance and reliability of its financial reporting, Aviva undertook a review of the Group's general insurance reserving in 2008.

As part of this review, the Group concluded that estimating our latent claim provisions on an undiscounted basis, and discounting back to current values, represented an improvement to the existing estimation technique. This approach is in line with best practice for long-term liabilities and moves the measurement of latent claims onto a more economic basis, consistent with our internal model for economic capital and the measurement model being proposed for both IFRS Phase II and Solvency II. This approach also improves consistency with the reporting of other long-tail classes of business which are already discounted, namely certain London Market latent claims and our Dutch Permanent health and Injury Business.

The discount rate that has been applied is based on the relevant swap curve in the relevant currency at the reporting date, having due regard to the duration of the expected settlement of the claims. The discount rate is set at the start of the accounting period with any change in rates between the start and end of the accounting period being reflected below operating profit as an economic assumption change. The range of discount rates used is shown in note 38c and depends on the duration of the claim and the reporting date. We estimate that latent claims will be payable for around the next 35 to 40 years with an average duration of 15 years.

The application of discounting to our latent claims represents a change in accounting policy and has been applied retrospectively. The cumulative impact of discounting in our opening reserves as at 1 January 2007 is to reduce insurance liabilities by £214 million and reinsurance assets by £61 million, and to increase retained earnings by £153 million. These have been treated as prior year adjustments in these financial statements.

8.2   Specific issues

In addition to the more general criteria considered at 8.1 above, certain changes of accounting policy are specifically addressed in IFRS 4. The need for the IASB to establish requirements in respect of these issues perhaps indicates that the criteria above are not as clear-cut on certain matters as the IASB would like.

The following are discussed below:

- continuation of existing practices;
- current market interest rates;
- prudence; and
- future investment margins. *[IFRS 4.23]*.

Shadow accounting is discussed separately at 8.3 below.

8.2.1   *Continuation of existing practices*

An insurer may continue the following practices but the introduction of any of them after IFRS has been adopted is not permitted because the IASB believes that they do not satisfy the criteria discussed at 8.1 above. *[IFRS 4.25]*.

8.2.1.A Measuring insurance liabilities on an undiscounted basis

Under many bodies of local GAAP, non-life insurance liabilities are not discounted to reflect the time value of money. In the IASB's view, discounting of insurance liabilities results in financial statements that are more relevant and reliable. Hence, a change from a policy of discounting to not discounting liabilities is not permitted. *[IFRS 4.25(a)]*. The IASB decided against requiring insurance liabilities to be discounted in IFRS 4 because it had not addressed the issue of the discount rate(s) to be used and the basis for any risk adjustments which is being addressed in Phase II. *[IFRS 4.BC126]*.

8.2.1.B Measuring contractual rights to future investment management fees in excess of their fair value

It is not uncommon to find insurance contracts that give the insurer an entitlement to receive a periodic investment management fee. Some local GAAP accounting policies permit the insurer, in determining the value of its contractual rights and obligations under the insurance contract, to discount the estimated cash flows related to those fees at a discount rate that reflects the risks associated with the cash flows. This approach is found in some embedded value methodologies. *[IFRS 4.BC128]*.

In the IASB's opinion, however, this approach can lead to results that are not consistent with fair value measurement. The IASB considers that if the insurer's contractual asset management fee is in line with the fee charged by other insurers and asset managers for comparable asset management services, the fair value of the contractual right to that fee would be approximately equal to what it would cost insurers and asset managers to acquire similar contractual rights. This approach is considered by the IASB to be consistent with how to account for servicing rights and obligations in IAS 39 (or IFRS 9). Therefore, IFRS 4 does not permit an insurer to introduce an accounting policy that measures those contractual rights at more than their fair value as implied by fees charged by others for comparable services. *[IFRS 4.BC129]*.

The reasoning behind this requirement is that the fair value at inception of such contractual rights will equal the origination costs paid, unless future investment management fees and related costs are out of line with market comparables. *[IFRS 4.25(b)]*.

8.2.1.C Introducing non-uniform accounting policies for the insurance contracts of subsidiaries

IFRS 10 requires consolidated financial statements to be prepared using uniform accounting policies for like transactions. *[IFRS 10.19]*. However, under current local requirements, some insurers consolidate subsidiaries without using the parent company's accounting policies for the measurement of the subsidiaries' insurance liabilities (and related deferred acquisition costs and intangible assets) which continue to be measured under the relevant local GAAP applying in each jurisdiction. *[IFRS 4.BC131]*.

The use of non-uniform accounting policies in consolidated financial statements reduces the relevance and reliability of financial statements and is not permitted by IFRS 10. However, prohibiting this practice in IFRS 4 would have forced some insurers to change their accounting policies for the insurance liabilities for some of their subsidiaries, requiring systems changes now that might not be subsequently required following Phase II. Therefore, the IASB decided that an insurer could continue to use non-uniform accounting policies to account for insurance contracts. If those accounting policies are not uniform, an insurer may change them if the change does not make the accounting policies more diverse and also satisfies the criteria set out at 8.1 above. *[IFRS 4.25(c), BC132].*

There is one exception to this requirement which is discussed at 8.2.2 below.

Old Mutual is an example of a company that applies non-uniform accounting policies to the measurement of its insurance contract liabilities.

Extract 54.14: Old Mutual plc (2008)

Accounting policies [extract]
(d) Insurance and investment contracts [extract]
(v) Insurance contract provisions [extract]

Insurance contract provisions for African businesses have been computed using a gross premium valuation method. Provisions in respect of African business have been made in accordance with the Financial Soundness Valuation basis as set out in the guidelines issued by the Actuarial Society of South Africa in Professional Guidance Note (PGN) 104 (2001). Under this guideline provisions are valued using realistic expectations of future experience, with margins for prudence and deferral of profit emergence.

Provisions for investment contracts with a discretionary participating feature are also computed using the gross premium valuation method in accordance with the Financial Soundness Valuation basis. Surplus allocated to policyholders but not yet distributed (i.e. bonus smoothing reserve) related to these contracts is included as a provision.

For the US business, the insurance contract provisions are calculated using the net premium method, based on assumptions as to investment yields, mortality, withdrawals and policyholder dividends. For the term life products, the assumptions are set at the time the contracts are issued, whereas the assumptions are updated annually, based on the experience for the annuity products.

Universal life and deferred annuity reserves are computed on the retrospective deposit method, which produces reserves equal to the cash value of the contracts.

Reserves on immediate annuities and guaranteed payments are computed on the prospective deposit method, which produces reserves equal to the present value of future benefit payments.

For other territories, the valuation bases adopted are in accordance with local actuarial practices and methodologies.

8.2.2   *Current market interest rates*

An insurer is permitted, but not required, to change its accounting policies so that it remeasures designated insurance liabilities (including related deferred acquisition costs and related intangible assets) to reflect current market interest rates. Any changes in these rates would need to be recognised in profit or loss. At that time, it may also introduce accounting policies that require other current estimates and assumptions for the designated liabilities. An insurer may change its accounting policies for designated liabilities without applying those policies consistently to all similar liabilities as IAS 8 would otherwise require. If an insurer designates liabilities for this election, it should apply current market interest rates (and, if applicable, the other current estimates and assumptions) consistently in all periods to all those liabilities until they are extinguished. *[IFRS 4.24]*.

The purpose of this concession is to allow insurers to move, in whole or in part, towards the use of fair value-based measures for insurance contracts.

AXA is an example of an insurance group which has used this option for some of its insurance contracts.

Extract 54.15: AXA Group (2008)

Notes to the consolidated financial statements [extract]

1.13.2 Insurance contracts and investment contracts with discretionary participating features [extract]

Some guaranteed benefits such as Guaranteed Minimum Death or Income Benefits (GMDB or GMIB), or certain guarantees on return proposed by reinsurance treaties, are covered by a risk management program using derivative instruments. In order to minimize the accounting mismatch between liabilities and hedging derivatives, AXA has chosen to use the option allowed under IFRS 4.24 to re-measure its provisions: this revaluation is carried out at each accounts closing based on guarantee level projections and takes into account interest rates and other market assumptions. The liabilities revaluation impact in the current period is recognized through income, symmetrically with the impact of the change in value of hedging derivatives. This change in accounting principles was adopted on first time application of IFRS on January 1, 2004 for contracts portfolios covered by the risk management program at that date. Any additional contracts portfolios covered by the risk management program after that date are valued on the same terms as those applied on the date the program was first applied.

Our view is that, where an entity has elected to account for some, but not all, of its insurance products using current market interest rates, or other current estimates and assumptions, it cannot selectively disregard an input variable, such as a change in interest rates, to determine the value of those liabilities. The input variable must be used every time those insurance contracts are valued.

8.2.3   *Prudence*

In the IASB's opinion, insurers sometimes measure insurance liabilities on what is intended to be a highly prudent basis that lacks the neutrality required by the IASB's *Framework*. This may be particularly true for insurers who are required under local GAAP to measure their liabilities on a regulatory basis. However, IFRS 4 does not define how much prudence is 'sufficient' and therefore does not require the elimination of 'excessive prudence'. *[IFRS 4.BC133]*. As a result, insurers are not required under IFRS 4 to change their accounting policies to eliminate excessive prudence. However, if an insurer already measures its insurance contracts with sufficient prudence, it shall not introduce additional prudence. *[IFRS 4.26]*.

The liability adequacy test requirements discussed at 7.2.2 above address the converse issue of understated insurance liabilities.

8.2.4   *Future investment margins*

An insurer need not change its accounting policies for insurance contracts to eliminate the recognition of future investment margins (which may occur under some forms of embedded value accounting). However, IFRS 4 imposes a rebuttable presumption that an insurer's financial statements will become less relevant and reliable if it introduces an accounting policy that reflects future investment margins in the measurement of insurance contracts, unless those margins directly affect the contractual payments.

Two examples of accounting policies that reflect those margins are:

(a)   using a discount rate that reflects the estimated return on the insurer's assets; and

(b)   projecting the returns on those assets at an estimated rate of return, discounting those projected returns at a different rate and including the rate in the measurement of the liability. *[IFRS 4.27]*.

Such accounting policies are used in some embedded value methodologies. For example, the CFO Forum European Embedded Value (EEV) Principles state that the value of future cash flows from in-force covered business should be the present value of future shareholder cash flows projected to emerge from the assets backing the liabilities of the in-force covered business reduced by the value of financial options and guarantees.[25] The EEV methodology is considered to be an indirect method of measuring the insurance liability because the measurement of the liability is derived from the related asset. In contrast, direct methods measure the liability by discounting future cash flows arising from the book of insurance contracts only. If the same assumptions are made in both direct and indirect methods, they can produce the same results. *[IFRS 4.BC138]*.

The IASB appears to have been concerned that insurers might take advantage of the lack of specific accounting guidance for insurance contracts in IFRS 4 as an opportunity to change their accounting policies to an embedded value basis on the grounds that this was more relevant and no less reliable, or more reliable and no less relevant than their existing accounting policies (possibly prepared on an 'excessively prudent' regulatory basis). The use of embedded value measures by insurers is discussed at 1.3.3 above.

The IASB's view is that the cash flows arising from an asset are irrelevant for the measurement of a liability unless those cash flows affect (a) the cash flows arising from the liability or (b) the credit characteristics of the liability. Therefore, the IASB considers that the following two embedded value approaches involve practices that are incompatible with IFRS, namely:

- applying an asset discount rate to insurance liabilities; and

- measuring contractual rights to investment management fees at an amount that exceeds their fair value (see 8.2.1.B above).

However, the IASB concluded that it could not eliminate these practices, where they were existing accounting policies, until Phase II gives guidance on the appropriate discount rates and the basis for risk adjustments and therefore the use of asset-based discount rates for the measurement of insurance liabilities is not prohibited. *[IFRS 4.BC142]*.

In addition, where embedded values are generally determined on a single best estimate basis, the IASB considers that they do not reflect a full range of possible outcomes and do not generally adequately address liabilities arising from embedded guarantees and options. Further, the IASB believes that existing embedded value approaches are largely unregulated and there is diversity in their application. *[IFRS 4.BC141]*.

It is possible for insurers to introduce accounting policies that use an embedded value approach even if that involves the use of asset-based discount rates for liabilities if they can overcome the rebuttable presumption described above. This will be if, and only if, the other components of a change in accounting policies increase the relevance and reliability of its financial statements sufficiently to outweigh the decrease in relevance and reliability caused by the inclusion of future investment margins. For example, suppose an insurer's existing accounting policies for insurance contracts involves excessively prudent assumptions set at inception and a discount rate prescribed by a regulator without direct reference to market conditions, and the assumptions ignore some embedded options and guarantees. The insurer might make its financial statements more relevant and no less reliable by switching to a basis of accounting that is widely used and involves:

(a)   current estimates and assumptions;

(b)   a reasonable (but not excessively prudent) adjustment to reflect risk and uncertainty;

(c)   measurements that reflect both the intrinsic value and time value of embedded options and guarantees; and

(d)   a current market discount rate, even if that discount rate reflects the estimated return on the insurer's assets. *[IFRS 4.28]*.

In some measurement approaches, the discount rate is used to determine the present value of a future profit margin. That profit margin is then attributed to different periods using a formula. In those approaches, the discount rate affects the measurement of the liability only indirectly. In these circumstances, the IASB has concluded that the use of a less appropriate discount rate has a limited or no effect on the measurement of the liability at inception. However, in other approaches, the IASB considers that the discount rate determines the measurement of the liability directly. In the latter case, because the introduction of an asset-based discount rate has a more significant effect, the IASB believes that it is highly unlikely that an insurer could overcome the rebuttable presumption described above. *[IFRS 4.29]*.

The IASB believes that in most applications of embedded value the discount rate determines the measurement of the liability directly and therefore it is highly unlikely that an insurer could overcome the rebuttable presumption described above if it wanted to change its accounting policies for insurance contracts to an embedded value basis. *[IFRS 4.BC144]*.

8.3   Shadow accounting

IFRS 4 grants relief to insurers allowing them to mitigate an accounting mismatch occurring when unrealised gains or losses on assets backing insurance contracts affect the measurement of the insurance contracts. This relief, known as 'shadow accounting', ensures that all gains and losses on investments affect the measurement of the insurance assets and liabilities in the same way, regardless of whether they are realised or unrealised and regardless of whether the unrealised investment gains and losses are recognised in profit or loss or in other comprehensive income using a revaluation reserve. In particular, the relief permits certain gains or losses arising from remeasuring insurance contracts to be recognised in other comprehensive income whereas IFRS 4 otherwise requires all gains and losses arising from insurance contracts to be recognised in profit or loss. Normally, this change in accounting policy would be adopted upon transition to IFRS. Application of shadow accounting is always voluntary and in practice it is also applied selectively.

In many local GAAP accounting models, gains or losses on an insurer's assets have a direct effect on the measurement of some or all of its insurance liabilities, related deferred acquisition costs and related intangible assets. *[IFRS 4.30].* In some of these models, prior to the introduction of IFRS, the insurer's assets were measured at cost or amortised cost and unrealised fair value movements were not recognised. Under IFRS, most of an insurer's assets are likely to be held at either fair value through profit or loss or available-for-sale with unrealised fair value gains recognised in profit or loss or other comprehensive income respectively. If the unrealised gains on the insurance liabilities (or deferred acquisition costs and intangible assets) which the assets back were not also recognised there would be an accounting mismatch.

The IASB believe that, in principle, gains or losses on an asset should not influence the measurement of an insurance liability unless the gains or losses on the asset alter the amounts payable to policyholders. Nevertheless, this was a feature of some existing measurement models for insurance liabilities and the IASB decided that it was not feasible to eliminate this practice. The IASB also acknowledged that shadow accounting might mitigate volatility caused by differences between the measurement basis for assets and the measurement basis for insurance liabilities. However, that is a by-product of shadow accounting and not its primary purpose. *[IFRS 4.BC183].*

IFRS 4 permits, but does not require, a change in accounting policies so that a recognised but unrealised gain or loss on an asset affects the related insurance liabilities in the same way that a realised gain or loss does. In other words, a measurement adjustment to an insurance liability (or deferred acquisition cost or intangible asset) arising from the remeasurement of an asset would be recognised in other comprehensive income if, and only if, the unrealised gains or losses on the asset are also recognised in other comprehensive income. *[IFRS 4.30].*

Recognition of movements in insurance liabilities (or deferred acquisition costs or intangible assets) in other comprehensive income only applies when unrealised gains on assets are recognised in other comprehensive income such as for available-for-sale investments accounted for under IAS 39, debt securities classified at fair value through other comprehensive income under IFRS 9 or property, plant and equipment accounted for using the revaluation model under IAS 16. *[IFRS 4.IG10].*

Shadow accounting is not applicable for liabilities arising from investment contracts accounted for under IAS 39 (or IFRS 9). However, shadow accounting may be applicable for a DPF within an investment contract if the measurement of that feature depends on asset values or asset returns. *[IFRS 4.IG8].*

Further, shadow accounting may not be used if the measurement of an insurance liability is not driven by realised gains and losses on assets held, for example if the insurance liabilities are measured using a discount rate that reflects a current market rate but that measurement does not depend directly on the carrying amount of any assets held. *[IFRS 4.IG9]*.

The implementation guidance to IFRS 4 includes an illustrative example to show how shadow accounting through other comprehensive income might be applied. This example is reproduced in full below.

Example 54.31: Shadow accounting

Background

Under some national requirements for some insurance contracts, deferred acquisition costs (DAC) are amortised over the life of the contract as a constant proportion of estimated gross profits (EGP). EGP includes investment returns, including realised (but not unrealised) gains and losses. Interest is applied to both DAC and EGP, to preserve present value relationships. For simplicity, this example ignores interest and ignores re-estimation of EGP.

At the inception of a contract, insurer A has DAC of CU20 relating to that contract and the present value, at inception, of EGP is CU100. In other words, DAC is 20 per cent of EGP at inception. Thus, for each CU1 of realised gross profits, insurer A amortises DAC by CU0.20. For example, if insurer A sells assets and recognises a gain of CU10, insurer A amortises DAC by CU2 (20 per cent of CU10).

Before adopting IFRSs for the first time in 2013, insurer A measured financial assets on a cost basis. (Therefore, EGP under those national requirements considers only realised gains and losses.) However, under IFRSs, it does not apply IFRS 9 and classifies its financial assets as available for sale. Thus, insurer A measures the assets at fair value and recognises changes in their fair value directly in other comprehensive income. In 2013, insurer A recognises unrealised gains of CU10 on the assets backing the contract.

In 2014, insurer A sells the assets for an amount equal to their fair value at the end of 2013 and, to comply with IAS 39, transfers the now-realised gain of CU10 from other comprehensive income to profit or loss.

Application of paragraph 30 of IFRS 4

Paragraph 30 of IFRS 4 permits, but does not require, insurer A to adopt shadow accounting. If insurer A adopts shadow accounting, it amortises DAC in 2013 by an additional CU2 (20 per cent of CU10) as a result of the change in the fair value of the assets. Because insurer A recognised the change in the assets' fair value in other comprehensive income, it recognises the additional amortisation of CU2 directly in other comprehensive income.

When insurer A sells the assets in 2014, it makes no further adjustment to DAC, but transfers DAC amortisation of CU2 relating to the now-realised gain from other comprehensive income to profit or loss.

In summary, shadow accounting treats an unrealised gain in the same way as a realised gain, except that the unrealised gain and resulting DAC amortisation are (a) recognised in other comprehensive income rather than in profit or loss and (b) transferred to profit or loss when the gain on the asset becomes realised.

If insurer A does not adopt shadow accounting, unrealised gains on assets do not affect the amortisation of DAC (i.e. the CU2 of DAC amortisation would have been recognised in profit or loss in 2013). *[IFRS 4.IG10, IE4]*.

Chapter 54

Old Mutual is an example of an entity that applies shadow accounting.

Extract 54.16: Old Mutual plc (2008)

Accounting policies [extract]

(d) Insurance and investment contracts [extract]

(v) Insurance contract provisions [extract]

The group applies shadow accounting in relation to certain insurance contract provisions in the South Africa long-term business, and DAC and PVIF assets in the United States long-term business, in respect of owner occupied properties or available-for-sale financial assets, in order for recognised unrealised gains or losses on those assets to affect the measurement of the insurance contract provisions, DAC or PVIF assets in the same way that the recognised gains or losses do.

In respect of the South Africa long-term business, shadow accounting is applied to insurance contract provisions where the underlying measurement of the policyholder liability depends directly on the value of owner-occupied property and the unrealised gains and losses on such property, which are recognised in equity. The shadow accounting adjustment to insurance contract provisions is recognised in equity to the extent that the unrealised gains or losses on owner-occupied property backing insurance contract provisions are also directly recognised in equity.

In respect of the United States long-term business, shadow accounting adjustments are made to the amortisation of DAC and PVIF assets in respect of unrealised gains and losses on available-for-sale financial assets to the extent that those unrealised gains and losses would impact the calculation of DAC or PVIF amortisation were they recognised in income. The shadow DAC and PVIF amortisation charge is recognised in equity in line with the unrealised gains and losses on the relevant financial assets until such time as those assets are sold or otherwise disposed of, at which point the accumulated amortisation recognised in equity is recycled to the income statement in the same way as the unrealised gains or losses on those financial assets.

Shadow accounting relief can also be applied for insurance liabilities where the assets backing these liabilities are held at fair value through profit or loss.

IFRS 4 does not specifically address the interaction between shadow accounting and the liability adequacy test. We believe that shadow accounting is applied before the liability adequacy test and the implications of this are discussed at 7.2.2.D above.

The revised ED proposes that insurers should normally be required to present in OCI changes in the insurance liability arising from changes in the discount rate and to present in profit or loss interest expense using the discount rate locked in at inception of the insurance contract.[26] In subsequent discussions, the IASB tentatively decided that an entity should have an accounting policy choice at an insurance portfolio level whether to present the effect of changes in discount rates in profit or loss or in other comprehensive income. An entity should apply IAS 8 to changes in accounting policy relating to the presentation of the effect of changes in discount rate. For an entity that applies the premium-allocation approach, discounts the liability for incurred claims and chooses to present the effect of the changes in discount rates in OCI, the interest expense in profit or loss for the liability for incurred claims should be determined using the discount rate locked-in at the date the liability for incurred claims is recognised.[27]

8.4   Redesignation of financial assets

IAS 39 generally prohibits the reclassification of a financial asset into the 'fair value through profit or loss' category while it is held or issued. *[IAS 39.50].* IFRS 9 allows such reclassifications only when an entity changes its business model for financial assets. *[IFRS 9.4.4.1].* However, when an insurer changes its accounting policies for insurance liabilities, it is permitted, but not required, to reclassify some or all of its financial assets at fair value through profit or loss. This reclassification is permitted if an insurer changes its accounting policies when it first applies IFRS 4 and also if it makes a subsequent policy change permitted by IFRS 4. This reclassification is a change in accounting policy and the requirements of IAS 8 apply, i.e. it must be performed retrospectively unless impracticable. *[IFRS 4.45].*

The IASB decided to grant this exemption from IAS 39 (or IFRS 9) in order to allow an insurer to avoid an accounting mismatch when it improves its accounting policies for insurance contracts and to remove unnecessary barriers for insurers wishing to move to a measurement basis that reflects fair values. *[IFRS 4.BC145].*

This concession cannot be used to reclassify financial assets out of the fair value through profit or loss category. These remain subject to the normal IAS 39 (or IFRS 9) requirements.

The revised ED proposes that insurers would be permitted, but not required, upon adopting the new standard, to redesignate a financial asset as measured at fair value through profit or loss if doing so would eliminate or significantly reduce an inconsistency in measurement or recognition. In addition, insurers would be required to revoke previous designations of financial assets at fair value through profit or loss if the initial application of the new standard eliminates the accounting mismatch that led to the previous designation. Insurers that had adopted IFRS 9 previously would also be able to designate an investment in an equity instrument as at fair value through other comprehensive income or revoke a previous such designation.[28] In subsequent discussions, the IASB tentatively decided to confirm the transition relief proposals in the revised ED and to consider providing further relief to permit or require an entity to reassess the business model for financial assets at the date of initial application of the new insurance contracts standard.[29]

8.5 Practical issues

8.5.1 Changes to local GAAP

As most entities are applying some form of local GAAP for their insurance contracts under IFRS 4, a common issue is whether an entity is obliged to change its accounting policy when local GAAP changes or whether the decision to change accounting policy for IFRS purposes is one that remains solely with the insurer.

We believe that the decision to change an accounting policy established on the initial adoption of IFRS is at the discretion of the entity. Accordingly, any change in local GAAP for insurance contracts that was used as the basis for the initial adoption of IFRS does not oblige the insurer to change its accounting policies.

Although an entity is not required to change its policies when local GAAP changes, it can make voluntary changes provided the revised accounting policy makes the financial statements more relevant and no less reliable or more reliable and no less relevant, as discussed at 8.1 above.

When a local accounting standard is changed, it is likely that the change is made for a reason. Therefore, there would normally be a rebuttable presumption that any change in local GAAP is an improvement to the existing standard and so is more relevant and no less reliable or more reliable and no less relevant to users than the previous standard would have been.

The fact that an entity can decide whether or not to apply changes in local GAAP will inevitably, over time, lead to further diversity in practice and potentially encourage 'cherry picking' of accounting policies. This emphasises the need for a comprehensive recognition and measurement standard sooner rather than later.

The financial statements of AXA provide an example of a change in accounting policy caused by a change to local GAAP.

Extract 54.17: AXA Group (2007)

Notes to the consolidated financial statements of AXA Group [extract]

Note 1.12.2   Insurance contracts and investment contracts with discretionary participating features [extract]

Following the adoption of UK Financial Reporting standard FRS27, reserves relating to with-profit contracts and the FFA were subject to a change in accounting policies in 2006, that was applied retrospectively, consistently with what other UK insurance companies applied. Reserves were adjusted on a "realistic" basis, and related deferred acquisition costs and unearned revenues reserves were cancelled. These adjustments had no impact on net income or shareholders' equity. The presentational impact of applying this standard is detailed in note 14. This change in accounting principles only applied to the Group's UK with-profit contracts.

An entity should not state that it uses a particular local GAAP for insurance contracts if it no longer complies with that GAAP due to it not implementing a local GAAP accounting policy change.

9   INSURANCE CONTRACTS ACQUIRED IN BUSINESS COMBINATIONS AND PORTFOLIO TRANSFERS

9.1   Expanded presentation of insurance contracts

IFRS 3 requires most assets and liabilities, including insurance liabilities assumed and insurance assets acquired, in a business combination to be measured at fair value. *[IFRS 4.31]*. The IASB saw no compelling reason to exempt insurers from these requirements. *[IFRS 4.BC153]*.

However, an insurer is permitted, but not required, to use an expanded presentation that splits the fair value of acquired insurance contracts into two components:

(a)   a liability measured in accordance with the acquirer's accounting policies for insurance contracts that it issues; and

(b)   an intangible asset, representing the difference between (i) the fair value of the contractual insurance rights acquired and insurance obligations assumed and (ii) the amount described in (a). The subsequent measurement of this asset shall be consistent with the measurement of the related insurance liabilities. *[IFRS 4.31(a), (b)]*.

We note that technically this IFRS 4 intangible has no intrinsic value that can be actuarially calculated. It is no more than the balancing number between the purchase price allocated to the insurance liability and the amount recorded for the insurance liability by the purchaser under the purchaser's existing GAAP. The more prudent (higher) the basis of liability measurement, the higher the value of the intangible.

This alternative presentation had often been used in practice under many local GAAPs. Life insurers have variously described this intangible asset as the 'present value of in-force business' (PVIF), 'present value of future profits' (PVFP or PVP) or 'value of business acquired' (VOBA). Similar principles apply in non-life insurance, for example, if claims liabilities are not discounted. *[IFRS 4.BC147]*.

The IASB decided to let these existing practices continue because:

- they wished to avoid insurers making systems changes for Phase I that might need to be reversed in Phase II. In the IASB's opinion the disclosures about the intangible asset provide transparency for users;

- IFRS 4 gives no guidance on how to determine fair values (although IFRS 13 does not exclude insurance contracts from its scope – see 9.1.1.B below); and

- it might be difficult for insurers to integrate a fair value measurement at the date of a business combination into subsequent insurance contract accounting without requiring systems changes that could become obsolete in Phase II. *[IFRS 4.BC148]*.

An insurer acquiring a portfolio of insurance contracts (separate from a business combination) may also use the expanded presentation described above. *[IFRS 4.32]*.

An illustration of how a business combination might be accounted for using the expanded presentation is given below.

Example 54.32: Business combination under IFRS 4

Insurance entity A purchases an insurance business owned by Entity B for £10 million. Under A's existing accounting policies for insurance contracts the carrying value of the insurance contract liabilities held by B is £8 million. Entity A estimates the fair value of the insurance contract liabilities to be £6 million. The fair value of other net assets acquired, including intangible assets, after recognising any additional deferred tax, is £13 million. The tax rate is 25%.

This gives rise to the following journal entry to record the acquisition of B in A's consolidated financial statements:

	£m	£m
Cash		10.0
Present value of in-force (PVIF) business intangible (£8m less £6m)	2.0	
Carrying value of insurance liabilities (A's existing accounting policies)		8.0
Goodwill	3.5	
Other net assets acquired	13.0	
Deferred taxation on PVIF		0.5

The intangible asset described at (b) above is excluded from the scope of both IAS 36 and IAS 38; instead IFRS 4 requires its subsequent measurement to be consistent with the measurement of the related insurance liabilities. *[IFRS 4.33]*. As a result, it is generally amortised over the estimated life of the contracts. Some insurers use an interest method of amortisation, which the IASB considers is appropriate for an asset that essentially comprises the present value of a set of contractual cash flows. However, the IASB considers it doubtful whether IAS 38 would have permitted such a method, hence the scope exclusion from IAS 38. This intangible asset is included within the scope of the liability adequacy test discussed at 7.2.2 above which acts as a quasi-impairment test on its carrying amount and hence is also excluded from the scope of IAS 36. [IFRS 4.BC149].

Generali is one entity that uses the expanded presentation discussed above and its accounting policy for acquired insurance contracts is reproduced below.

Extract 54.18: Assicurazioni Generali S.p.A. (2008)

Notes to the consolidated financial statements [extract]
Part D   **Summary of significant accounting policies** [extract]
Note 1.2.1   **Insurance contracts acquired in a business combination or portfolio transfer** [extract]

In case of acquisition of non-life insurance contracts in a business combination or portfolio transfer, the group recognises an intangible asset, i.e. the value of the acquired contractual relationships (Value of Business Acquired).

The VOBA is the present value of the pre-tax future profit arising from the contracts in force at the purchase date, taking into account the probability of renewals of the one year contracts. The related deferred taxes are accounted for as liabilities in the consolidated balance sheet.

The VOBA is amortized over the effective life of the contracts acquired, by using an amortization pattern reflecting the expected future profit recognition. Assumptions used in the development of the VOBA amortization pattern are consistent with the ones applied in its initial measurement. The amortization pattern is reviewed on a yearly basis to assess its reliability and to verify the consistency with the assumptions used in the valuation of the corresponding insurance provisions.

The difference between the fair value of the insurance contracts acquired in a business combination or a portfolio transfer, and the insurance liabilities measured in accordance with the acquirer's accounting policies for the insurance contracts that it issues is recognised as intangible asset and amortized over the period in which the acquirer recognises the corresponding profits.

The Generali Group applies this accounting treatment to the insurance liabilities assumed in the acquisition of insurance portfolios. Therefore, the assumed insurance liabilities are recognized in the balance sheet according to the acquirer's accounting policies for the insurance contracts that it issues. The intangible assets are not in the scope of IAS 38 and IAS 36.

The future VOBA recoverable amount is tested on yearly basis.

Investment contracts within the scope of IAS 39 (or IFRS 9) are required to be measured at fair value when acquired in a business combination.

As discussed at 3.3 above, there should be no reassessment of the classification of contracts previously classified as insurance contracts under IFRS 4 which are acquired as a part of a business combination.

The revised ED proposes that an entity treats the consideration paid or received in a portfolio transfer (excluding any amounts received or paid for any other assets and liabilities acquired in the same transaction) as a pre-coverage cash flow. In accordance with the general requirements of the revised ED, the entity would measure the insurance contracts as the sum of the fulfilment cash flows and the contractual service margin, if any.[30] In subsequent discussions, the IASB tentatively decided to clarify that contracts acquired through a portfolio transfer or a business combination should be accounted for as if they had been issued by the entity at the date of the portfolio transfer or business combination.[31]

9.1.1 Practical issues

9.1.1.A The difference between a business combination and a portfolio transfer

When an entity acquires a portfolio of insurance contracts the main accounting consideration is to determine whether that acquisition meets the definition of a business. IFRS 3 defines a business as 'an integrated set of activities and assets that is capable of being conducted and managed for the purpose of providing a return in the form of dividends, lower costs or other economic benefits directly to investors, or other owners, members or participants'. *[IFRS 3 Appendix A].* The application guidance to IFRS 3 notes that a business consists of inputs and processes applied to those inputs that have the ability to create outputs. Although businesses usually have outputs they do not need to be present for an integrated set of assets and activities to be a business. *[IFRS 3.B7].* Where it is considered that a business is acquired, goodwill may need to be recognised as may deferred tax liabilities in respect of any acquired intangibles. For an isolated portfolio transfer, neither goodwill nor deferred tax should be recognised.

The determination of whether a portfolio of contracts or a business has been acquired will be a matter of judgement based on the facts and circumstances. Acquisitions of contracts that also include the acquisition of underwriting systems and/or the related organised workforce are more likely to meet the definition of a business than merely the acquisition of individual or multiple contracts.

Rights to issue or renew contracts in the future (as opposed to existing insurance contracts) are separate intangible assets and the accounting for the acquisition of such rights is discussed at 9.2 below.

9.1.1.B Fair value of an insurer's liabilities

IFRS 4 does not prescribe a method for determining the fair value of insurance liabilities. However, the definition of fair value in IFRS 4 is the same as that in IFRS 13 and insurance contracts are not excluded from the scope of IFRS 13. Therefore, any calculation of fair value must be consistent with IFRS 13's valuation principles.

Deferred acquisition costs (DAC) are generally considered to have no value in a business combination and are usually subsumed into the PVIF intangible. The fair value of any unearned premium reserve will include any unearned profit element as well as the present value of the claims obligation in respect of the unexpired policy period at the acquisition date which is likely to be different from the value under existing accounting policies.

9.1.1.C Deferred taxation

IAS 12 requires deferred tax to be recognised in respect of temporary differences arising in business combinations, for example if the tax base of the asset or liability remains at cost when the carrying amount is fair value. IFRS 4 contains no exemption from these requirements. Therefore, deferred tax will often arise on temporary differences created by the recognition of insurance liabilities at their fair value or on the related intangible asset. The deferred tax adjusts the amount of goodwill recognised as illustrated in Example 54.32 at 9.1 above. *[IAS 12.19].*

Chapter 54

9.1.1.D   *Negative intangible assets*

There are situations where the presentation described at 9.1 above may result in the creation of a negative intangible asset, at least in theory. This could arise, for example, where the acquirer's existing accounting policies are such that the contractual liabilities acquired are measured at an amount less than their fair value although this is likely to raise questions about whether the carrying value of the liabilities are adequate (see 7.2.2 above). IFRS 4 is silent on the subject of negative intangible assets but there appears to be no prohibition on their recognition.

9.2   Customer lists and relationships not connected to contractual insurance rights and obligations

The requirements discussed at 9.1 above apply only to contractual insurance rights and obligations that existed at the date of a business combination or portfolio transfer.

Therefore, they do not apply to customer lists and customer relationships reflecting the expectation of future contracts that are not part of the contractual insurance rights and contractual insurance obligations existing at the date of the transaction. *[IFRS 4.33].* IAS 36 and IAS 38 apply to such transactions as they apply to other intangible assets.

The following example deals with customer relationships acquired together with a portfolio of one-year motor insurance contracts.

Example 54.33:   Purchase of portfolio of one-year motor insurance contracts

Background

Parent A obtained control of insurer B in a business combination on 31 December 2014. B has a portfolio of one-year motor insurance contracts that are cancellable by policyholders.

Analysis

Because B establishes its relationships with policyholders through insurance contracts, the customer relationship with the policyholders meets the contractual-legal criterion for recognition as an intangible asset. IAS 36 and IAS 38 apply to the customer relationship intangible asset. *[IFRS 3.IE30(d)].*

10   DISCLOSURE

One of the two main objectives of IFRS 4 is to require entities issuing insurance contracts to disclose information about those contracts that identifies and explains the amounts in an insurer's financial statements arising from these contracts and helps users of those financial statements understand the amount, timing and uncertainty of future cash flows from those insurance contracts. *[IFRS 4.IN1].*

For many insurers, the disclosure requirements of the standard had a significant impact when IFRS 4 was applied for the first time because they significantly exceeded what were required under most local GAAP financial reporting frameworks.

In drafting the disclosure requirements, the main objective of the IASB appears to have been to impose similar requirements for insurance contracts as for financial assets and financial liabilities under IFRS 7.

The requirements in the standard itself are relatively high-level and contain little specific detail. For example, reconciliations of changes in insurance liabilities, reinsurance assets and, if any, related deferred acquisition costs are required but no details about the line items those reconciliations should contain are specified. By comparison, however, other standards such as IAS 16, provide details of items required to be included in similar reconciliations for other amounts in the statement of financial position.

The lack of specific disclosure requirements is probably attributable to the diversity of accounting practices permitted under IFRS 4. We suspect the IASB probably felt unable to give anything other than generic guidance within the standard to avoid the risk that local GAAP requirements may not fit in with more specific guidance.

However, the disclosure requirements outlined in the standard are supplemented by sixty nine paragraphs of related implementation guidance which explains how insurers may or might apply the standard. According to this guidance, an insurer should decide in the light of its circumstances how much emphasis to place on different aspects of the requirements and how information should be aggregated to display the overall picture without combining information that has materially different characteristics. Insurers should strike a balance so that important information is not obscured either by the inclusion of a large amount of insignificant detail or by the aggregation of items that have materially different characteristics. To satisfy the requirements of the standard an insurer would not typically need to disclose all the information suggested in the guidance. *[IFRS 4.IG12].*

The implementation guidance does not, however, create additional disclosure requirements. *[IFRS 4.IG12].* On the other hand, there is a reminder that IAS 1 requires additional disclosures when compliance with the specific requirements in IFRSs is insufficient to enable users to understand the impact of particular transactions, other events and conditions on the entity's financial position and financial performance. *[IFRS 4.IG13].* The guidance also draws attention to the definition and explanation of materiality in IAS 1. *[IFRS 4.IG15-16].*

The disclosure requirements are sub-divided into two main sections:

(a)   information that identifies and explains the amounts in the financial statements arising from insurance contracts; and

(b)   information that enables users of its financial statements to evaluate the nature and extent of risks arising from insurance contracts.

Each of these is discussed in detail below. They are accompanied by examples illustrating how some of disclosure requirements have been applied in practice.

As discussed at 2.2.2 above, disclosures for investment contracts with a DPF are within the scope of IFRS 7, not IFRS 4.

Chapter 54

10.1   Explanation of recognised amounts

The first disclosure principle established by the standard is that an insurer should identify and explain the amounts in its financial statements arising from insurance contracts. *[IFRS 4.36]*.

To comply with this principle an insurer should disclose:

(a)   its accounting policies for insurance contracts and related assets, liabilities, income and expense;

(b)   the recognised assets, liabilities, income and expense (and cash flows if its statement of cash flows is presented using the direct method) arising from insurance contracts. Furthermore, if the insurer is a cedant it should disclose:

   (i)   gains or losses recognised in profit or loss on buying reinsurance; and

   (ii)   if gains and losses on buying reinsurance are deferred and amortised, the amortisation for the period and the amounts remaining unamortised at the beginning and the end of the period;

(c)   the process used to determine the assumptions that have the greatest effect on the measurement of the recognised amounts described in (b). When practicable, quantified disclosure of these assumptions should be given;

(d)   the effect of changes in assumptions used to measure insurance assets and insurance liabilities, showing separately the effect of each change that has a material effect on the financial statements; and

(e)   reconciliations of changes in insurance liabilities, reinsurance assets and, if any, related deferred acquisitions costs. *[IFRS 4.37]*.

Each of these is discussed below.

10.1.1   *Disclosure of accounting policies*

As noted at 10.1 above, IFRS 4 requires an insurer's accounting policies for insurance contracts and related liabilities, income and expense to be disclosed. *[IFRS 4.37(a)]*. The implementation guidance suggests that an insurer might need to address the treatment of some or all of the following:

(a)   premiums (including the treatment of unearned premiums, renewals and lapses, premiums collected by agents and brokers but not passed on and premium taxes or other levies on premiums);

(b)   fees or other charges made to policyholders;

(c)   acquisition costs (including a description of their nature);

(d)   claims incurred (both reported and unreported), claims handling costs (including a description of their nature) and liability adequacy tests (including a description of the cash flows included in the test, whether and how the cash flows are discounted and the treatment of embedded options and guarantees in those tests – see 7.2.2 above). Disclosure of whether insurance liabilities are discounted might be given together with an explanation of the methodology used;

(e)   the objective of methods used to adjust insurance liabilities for risk and uncertainty (for example, in terms of a level of assurance or level of sufficiency), the nature of those models, and the source of information used in those models;

(f)   embedded options and guarantees including a description of whether:

    (i)   the measurement of insurance liabilities reflects the intrinsic value and time value of these items; and

    (ii)   their measurement is consistent with observed current market prices;

(g)   discretionary participation features (including an explanation of how the insurer classifies those features between liabilities and components of equity) and other features that permit policyholders to share in investment performance;

(h)   salvage, subrogation or other recoveries from third parties;

(i)   reinsurance held;

(j)   underwriting pools, coinsurance and guarantee fund arrangements;

(k)   insurance contracts acquired in business combinations and portfolio transfers, and the treatment of related intangible assets; and

(l)   the judgements, apart from those involving estimations, management has made in the process of applying the accounting policies that have the most significant effect on the amounts recognised in the financial statements as required by IAS 1. The classification of a DPF is an example of an accounting policy that might have a significant effect. *[IFRS 4.IG17].*

Because an insurer's accounting policies will normally be based on its previous local GAAP, the policies for such items will vary from entity to entity.

Set out below are the accounting policies for premiums and claims for Aviva. These are based on UK GAAP which has different requirements for recognition of premiums from life and general (non-life) insurance business.

Extract 54.19: Aviva plc (2008)

Accounting policies [extract]

(G) Premiums earned

Premiums on long-term insurance contracts and participating investment contracts as recognised as income when receivable, except for investment-linked premiums which are accounted for when the corresponding liabilities are recognised. For single premium business, this is the date from which the policy is effective. For regular premium contracts, receivables are taken at the date when payments are due. Premiums are shown before deduction of commission and before any sale-based taxes or duties. Where policies lapse due to non-receipt of premiums, then all related premium income accrued but not received from the date they are deemed to have lapsed is offset against premiums.

General insurance and health premiums written reflect direct business incepted during the year, and exclude any sales-based taxes or duties. Unearned premiums are those proportions of the premiums written in a year that relate to periods of risk after the balance sheet date. Unearned premiums are calculated on either a daily or monthly pro rata basis. Premiums collected by intermediaries, but not yet received, are assessed based on estimates from underwriting or past experience, and are included in premiums written.

Deposits collected under investment contracts without a discretionary participation feature (non-participating contracts) are not accounted for through the income statement, except for fee income (covered in policy H) and the investment income attributable to those contracts, but are accounted for directly through the balance sheet as an adjustment to the investment contract liability.

(K) Insurance and participating investment contract liabilities [extract]

Claims

Long-term business claims reflect the cost of all claims arising during the year, including claims handling costs, as well as policyholder bonuses accrued in anticipation of bonus declarations.

General insurance and health claims include all losses occurring during the year, whether reported or not, related handling costs, a reduction for the value of salvage and other recoveries, and any adjustments to claims outstanding from previous years.

Claims handling costs include internal and external costs incurred in connection with the negotiation and settlement of claims. Internal costs include all direct expenses of the claims department and any part of the general administrative costs directly attributable to the claims function.

Long-term business provision

Under current IFRS requirements, insurance and participating investment contract liabilities are measured under accounting policies consistent with those adopted previously under existing accounting practices, with the exception of liabilities remeasured to reflect current market interest rates and those relating to UK with-profit and non-profit contracts, to be consistent with the value of the backing assets. For liabilities relating to UK with-profit-contracts, the Group has adopted FRS 27, *Life Assurance*, which adds to the requirements of IFRS but does not vary them in any way. Further details are given in policy A above.

In the United States, shadow adjustments are made to the liabilities or related deferred acquisition costs and are recognised directly in equity. This means that the measurement of these items is adjusted for unrealised gains or losses on the backing assets such as AFS financial investments (see policy S), that are recognised directly in equity, in the same way as if those gains or losses had been realised.

The long-term business provisions are calculated separately for each life operation, based either on local regulatory requirements or existing local GAAP at the later of the date of transition to IFRS or the date of acquisition of the entity, and actuarial principles consistent with those applied in the UK. Each calculation represents a determination within a range of possible outcomes, where the assumptions used in the calculations depend on circumstances prevailing in each life operation. The principal assumptions are disclosed in note 38(b). For liabilities of the UK with-profit fund, FRS 27 requires liabilities to be calculated as the realistic basis liabilities as set out by the UK Financial Services Authority, adjusted to remove the shareholders' share of future bonuses. For UK non-profit insurance contracts, the Group applies the realistic regulatory basis as set out in the FSA Policy Statement 06/14, *Prudential Changes for Insurers*, where applicable.

General insurance and health provisions [extract]

(i) Outstanding claims provisions [extract]

General insurance and health outstanding claims provisions are based on the estimated ultimate cost of all claims incurred but not settled at the balance sheet date, whether reported or not, together with related claims handling costs. Significant delays are experienced in the notification and settlements of certain types of general insurance claims, particularly in respect of liability business, including environmental and potential exposures, the ultimate cost of which cannot be known with certainty at the balance sheet date. Provisions for certain claims are discounted, using rates having regard to the returns generated by the assets supporting the liabilities. Any estimate represents a determination within a range of possible outcomes. Further details of estimation techniques are given in note 38(c).

Provisions for latent claims are discounted, using rates based on the relevant swap curve, in the relevant currency at the reporting date, having due regard to the duration of the expected settlement date of the claims. The discount rate is set at the start of the accounting period with any change in rates between the start and end of the accounting period being reflected below operating profit as an economic assumption change. The range of discount rates used is described in note 38c. This is a change in accounting policy, the effects of which are given in note 2(b)(i).

(ii) Provision for unearned premiums

The proportion of written premiums, gross of commission payable to intermediaries, attributable to subsequent periods is deferred as a provision for unearned premiums. The change in this provision is taken to the income statement in order that revenue is recognised over the period of risk.

The following example from Allianz illustrates an accounting policy for reinsurance contracts based on US GAAP.

Extract 54.20: Allianz SE (2008)

Notes to the consolidated financial statements [extract]

2. Summary of significant accounting policies [extract]

Reinsurance contracts

The Allianz Group's consolidated financial statements reflect the effects of ceded and assumed reinsurance contracts. Assumed reinsurance refers to the acceptance of certain insurance risks by Allianz that other companies have underwritten. Ceded reinsurance refers to the transfer of insurance risk, along with the respective premiums, to one or more reinsurers who will share in the risks. When the reinsurance contracts do not transfer significant insurance risk according to SFAS 113, deposit accounting is applied as required under SOP 98-7.

Assumed reinsurance premiums, commissions and claim settlements, as well as the reinsurance element of technical provisions are accounted for in accordance with the conditions of the reinsurance contracts and with consideration of the original contracts for which the reinsurance was concluded.

Premiums ceded for reinsurance and reinsurance recoveries on benefits and claims incurred are deducted from premiums earned and insurance and investment contract benefits. Assets and liabilities related to reinsurance are reported on a gross basis. Amounts ceded to reinsurers from reserves for insurance and investment contracts are estimated in a manner consistent with the claim liability associated with the reinsured risks. Revenues and expenses related to reinsurance agreements are recognised in a manner consistent with the underlying risk of the business reinsured.

To the extent that the assuming reinsurers are unable to meet their obligations, the Group remains liable to its policyholders for the portion reinsured. Consequently, allowances are made for receivables on reinsurance contracts which are deemed uncollectible.

An example of an accounting policy showing a split of contracts with a DPF between liability and equity (AMP) is shown at 6.1 above.

An example of an accounting policy for a liability adequacy test (Allianz) is shown at 7.2.2 above.

Examples of accounting policies for deferred acquisition costs (Zurich Financial Services and Generali) are shown at 7.2.6.B above.

An example of an accounting policy for salvage and subrogation (Royal & SunAlliance) is shown at 7.2.6.C above.

If the financial statements disclose supplementary information, for example embedded value information, that is not prepared on the basis used for other measurements in the financial statements, it would be appropriate to explain the basis of preparation. Disclosures about embedded value methodology might include information similar to that described above, as well as disclosure of whether, and how, embedded values are affected by estimated returns from assets and by locked-in capital and how those effects are estimated. *[IFRS 4.IG18].*

10.1.2 Recognised assets, liabilities, income and expense

As noted at 10.1 above, IFRS 4 requires disclosure of the recognised assets, liabilities, income and expense (and cash flows if using the direct method) arising from insurance contracts. *[IFRS 4.37(b)].*

Chapter 54

10.1.2.A   Assets and liabilities

IAS 1 requires minimum disclosures on the face of the statement of financial position. *[IAS 1.54]*. In order to satisfy these requirements, an insurer may need to present separately on the face of its statement of financial position the following amounts arising from insurance contracts:

(a)   liabilities under insurance contracts and reinsurance contracts issued;

(b)   assets under insurance contracts and reinsurance contracts issued; and

(c)   assets under reinsurance contracts ceded which, as discussed at 7.2.4 above, should not be offset against the related insurance liabilities. *[IFRS 4.IG20]*.

Neither IAS 1 nor IFRS 4 prescribe the descriptions and ordering of the line items presented on the face of the statement of financial position. An insurer could amend the descriptions and ordering to suit the nature of its transactions. *[IFRS 4.IG21]*.

IAS 1 requires the presentation of current and non-current assets and liabilities as separate classifications on the face of the statement of financial position except where a presentation based on liquidity provides information that is reliable and more relevant. *[IAS 1.60]*. In practice, a current/non-current classification is not normally considered relevant for insurers, and they usually present their IFRS statements of financial position in broad order of liquidity.

IAS 1 permits disclosure, either on the face of the statement of financial position or in the notes, of sub-classifications of the line items presented, classified in a manner appropriate to the entity's operations. The appropriate sub-classifications of insurance liabilities will depend on the circumstances, but might include items such as:

(a)   unearned premiums;

(b)   claims reported by policyholders;

(c)   claims incurred but not reported (IBNR);

(d)   provisions arising from liability adequacy tests;

(e)   provisions for future non-participating benefits;

(f)   liabilities or components of equity relating to discretionary participating features. If these are classified as a component of equity IAS 1 requires disclosure of the nature and purpose of each reserve within equity;

(g)   receivables and payables related to insurance contracts (amounts currently due to and from agents, brokers and policyholders); and

(h)   non-insurance assets acquired by exercising rights to recoveries. *[IFRS 4.IG22]*.

Similar sub-classifications may also be appropriate for reinsurance assets, depending on their materiality and other relevant circumstances. For assets under insurance contracts and reinsurance contracts issued an insurer might need to distinguish:

(a)   deferred acquisition costs; and

(b)   intangible assets relating to insurance contracts acquired in business combinations or portfolio transfers. *[IFRS 4.IG23]*.

If non-uniform accounting policies for the insurance liabilities of subsidiaries are adopted, it might be necessary to disaggregate the disclosures about the amounts reported to give meaningful information about amounts determined using different accounting policies. *[IFRS 4.IG30].*

Munich Re's gross technical provisions on the face of the statement of financial position are illustrated below, together with some further detail shown in selected notes.

Extract 54.21: *Münchener Rückversicherungs – Gesellschaft Aktiengesellschaft (2008)*

Consolidated balance sheet as at 31 December 2008 [extract]
Equity and liabilities [extract]

	Notes	€m	€m	Prev. year €m	Change €m	balance sheet %
C. Gross technical provisions						
I. Unearned premiums	(19)	6,421		5,719	702	12.3
II. Provision for future policy benefits	(20)	98,738		94,933	3,805	4.0
III. Provision for outstanding claims	(21)	45,031		44,560	471	1.1
IV. Other technical provisions	(22)	9,292		10,536	−1,244	−11.8
Thereof:						
Provision for deferred premium refunds relating to disposal groups	(16)	–		−172	172	100.0
			159,482	155,748	3,734	2.4
D. Gross technical provisions for life insurance policies where the investment risk is borne by the policyholders	(23)		**2,940**	2,308	632	27.4

Note 20 Provision for future policy benefits [extract]

Gross provision for future policy benefits according to types of insurance cover

€m	31.12.2008	Prev. year
Life	77,638	74,882
Reinsurance	9,338	9,993
Primary insurance	68,300	64,889
Term life insurance	2,529	2,297
Other life insurance	40,772	40,544
Annuity insurance	23,956	21,026
Disability insurance	1,037	918
Contracts with combination of more than one risk	6	4
Health	20,503	19,037
Reinsurance	5	5
Primary insurance	20,498	19,032
Property-casualty	597	1,014
Reinsurance	299	748
Primary insurance	298	266
Total	**98,738**	**94,933**

Chapter 54

The provision for future policy benefits in life reinsurance largely involves contracts where the mortality or morbidity risk predominates. In reinsurance, annuity contracts have a significantly lower weight than in primary insurance.

In reinsurance, measurement is carried out partly individually for each risk and partly collectively for reinsured portfolios, using biometric actuarial assumptions based on the tables of the national actuarial associations. These are adjusted for the respective reinsured portfolio, in line with the probabilities observed for the occurrence of an insured event. A discount rate is chosen that is based on a conservative capital-market scenario.

In primary insurance, measurement is generally carried out individually for each risk. For German life and health primary insurance, to which approx. 87% of the provisions for future policy benefits are apportionable, biometric actuarial assumptions based on the tables of the German Association of Actuaries are used. We also largely use the tables of the national actuarial associations for the rest of the primary insurance business. The actuarial interest rate employed for discounting is limited by the respective maximum actuarial interest rate prescribed by the supervisory authorities.

Essentially the same actuarial assumptions have been used as in the previous year for measuring the provisions for future policy benefits for business in force.

Further information on the underwriting risks and discount rates can be found under (36) Risks from insurance contracts in the life and health segment and (37) Risks from insurance contracts in the property-casualty segment.

Note 21 Provision for outstanding claims [extract]
Gross provisions by type

€m	Reinsurance 31.12.2008	Prev. year	Primary insurance 31.12.2008	Prev. year	Total 31.12.2008	Prev. year
Life and health segment						
Disability claims provisions	1,470	1,537	897	860	2,367	2,397
Provision for other benefit cases	1,941	1,977	1,438	1,327	3,379	3,304
Property-casualty segment (claims reserve)						
Case reserve	17,668	17,602	3,908	3,801	21,576	21,403
IBNR reserve	16,455	16,342	1,254	1,114	17,709	17,456
Total	**37,534**	**37,458**	**7,497**	**7,102**	**45,031**	**44,560**

In the life and health segment, the provision for outstanding claims consists of a provision for disability cases and a provision for other benefit cases. The disability claims provision involves periodic payments and is usually due long term. It is calculated as the present value of the expected future payments. Discount rates are disclosed in Note (36) Risks from insurance contracts in the life and health segment. The biometric actuarial assumptions are selected using appropriate actuarial principles. The provision for other benefit cases is largely measured at face value and is usually due short term. This provision includes an IBNR reserve, whose amounts are estimated using actuarial methods.

In the property-casualty segment, the claims reserve consists of the case reserve and the IBNR reserve. The case reserve reflects the amount which is expected to be needed to settle claims which are known and reported at the balance sheet date. The major part of this provision is measured at face value. A smaller part refers to provisions for annuities in personal accident, liability and workers' compensation insurance. These are calculated as the present value of the expected future payments. The respective discount rates are disclosed in Note (37) Risks from insurance contracts in the property-casualty segment. The biometric actuarial assumptions are selected using appropriate actuarial principles. The IBNR reserve is calculated using actuarial methods on the basis of historical claims development data and taking into account foreseeable future trends.

CNP Assurances provided the following analysis of its insurance contract liabilities.

Extract 54.22: CNP Assurances (2008)

Notes to the financial statements [extract]

Note 10   **Insurance and financial liabilities** [extract]

Note 10.1   **Analysis of insurance and financial liabilities** [extract]

The following tables show the subclassifications of insurance liabilities that require separate disclosure under IFRS.

10.1.1   **Analysis of insurance and financial liabilities at 31 December 2008** [extract]

In € millions

	31/12/2008		
	Before reinsurance	Net of reinsurance	Reinsurance
Non-life technical reserves	**5,227.0**	**4,551.5**	**675.6**
Unearned premium reserves	184.4	168.1	16.3
Outstanding claims reserves	750.4	677.4	73.0
Bonuses and rebates (including claims equalisation reserve on group business maintained in liabilities)	56.5	53.6	3.0
Other technical reserves	4,235.7	3,652.4	583.3
Liability adequacy test reserves	0.0	0.0	0.0
Life technical reserves	**81,069.3**	**75,650.3**	**5,419.1**
Unearned premium reserves	79,590.2	74,215.6	5,374.6
Outstanding claims reserves	1,160.7	1,120.4	40.3
Policyholder surplus reserves	208.6	204.4	4.2
Other mathematical reserves	109.8	109.8	0.0
Liability adequacy test reserves	0.0	0.0	0.0
Financial instruments with DPF	**148,776.8**	**148,776.5**	**0.3**
Unearned premium reserves	145,111.0	145,110.7	0.3
Outstanding claims reserves	1,727.1	1,727.1	0.0
Policyholder surplus reserves	1,938.5	1,938.5	0.0
Other mathematical reserves	0.1	0.1	0.0
Liability adequacy test reserves	0.0	0.0	0.0
Financial instruments without DPF	**6,439.8**	**6,229.5**	**210.4**
Derivative instruments embedded in financial instruments with or without DPF	**0.0**	**0.0**	**0.0**
Deferred participation reserve	**356.7**	**356.7**	**0.0**
Total insurance and financial liabilities	**243,092.2**	**236,786.8**	**6,305.3**

IFRS 7 requires an entity to disclose the carrying amount of financial assets pledged as collateral for liabilities, the carrying amount of financial assets pledged as collateral for contingent liabilities, and any terms and conditions relating to assets pledged as collateral. *[IFRS 7.14-15]*. In complying with this requirement, it might be necessary to disclose segregation requirements that are intended to protect policyholders by restricting the use of some of the insurer's assets. *[IFRS 4.IG23A]*.

Chapter 54

Prudential makes the following disclosures in respect of the segregation of various of its assets and liabilities.

Extract 54.23: Prudential plc (2008)

Notes on the group financial statements [extract]
D5: Capital position statement for life assurance business[extract]
d Transferability of available capital

For PAC and all other UK long-term insurers, long-term business assets and liabilities must, by law, be maintained in funds separate from those for the assets and liabilities attributable to non-life insurance business or to shareholders. Only the 'established surplus' – the excess of assets over liabilities in the long-term fund determined through a formal valuation – may be transferred so as to be available for other purposes. Distributions from the with-profits sub-fund to shareholders reflect the shareholders' one-ninth share of the cost of declared policyholders' bonuses.

Accordingly, the excess of assets over liabilities of the PAC long-term fund is retained within that company. The retention of the capital enables it to support with-profits and other business of the fund by, for example, providing the benefits associated with smoothing and guarantees. It also provides investment flexibility for the fund's assets by meeting the regulatory capital requirements that demonstrate solvency and by absorbing the costs of significant events or fundamental changes in its long-term business without affecting the bonus and investment policies.

For other UK long-term business subsidiaries, the amounts retained within the companies are at levels which provide an appropriate level of capital strength in excess of the regulatory minimum.

For Jackson, capital retention is maintained at a level consistent with an appropriate rating by Standard & Poor's. Currently Jackson is rated AA. Jackson can pay dividends on its capital stock only out of earned surplus unless prior regulatory approval is obtained. Furthermore, dividends which exceed the greater of 10 per cent of Jackson's statutory surplus or statutory net gain from operations for the prior year require prior regulatory approval.

For Asian subsidiaries, the amounts retained within the companies are at levels that provide an appropriate level of capital strength in excess of the local regulatory minimum. For ring-fenced with-profits funds, the excess of assets over liabilities is retained with distribution tied to the shareholders' share of bonuses through declaration of actuarially determined surplus. The Singapore and Malaysian businesses may, in general, remit dividends to the UK, provided the statutory insurance fund meets the capital adequacy standard required under local statutory regulations.

Available capital of the non-insurance business units is transferable to the life assurance businesses after taking account of an appropriate level of operating capital, based on local regulatory solvency targets, over and above basis liabilities. The economic capital model described in section D1 (concentration of risks) takes into account restrictions on mobility of capital across the Group with capital transfers to and from business units triggered at a solvency level consistent with these targets. The model takes into account restrictions on the availability to the Group of the estate of the various with-profits funds throughout the Group.

10.1.2.B   Income and expense

IAS 1 lists minimum line items that an entity should present on the face of its income statement. It also requires the presentation of additional line items when this is necessary to present fairly the entity's financial performance. To satisfy these requirements, disclosure of the following amounts on the face of the income statement might be required:

(a)   revenue from insurance contracts issued (without any deduction for reinsurance held);

(b)   income from contracts with reinsurers;

(c)   expense for policyholder claims and benefits (without any reduction for reinsurance held); and

(d)   expenses arising from reinsurance held. *[IFRS 4.IG24].*

The extracts below show two alternative methods of presenting revenue and expense on the face of the income statement. Royal & SunAlliance presents subtotals of net premiums (premiums net of reinsurance premiums) and net claims (claims net of reinsurance claims) on the face of its income statement. AEGON presents reinsurance premiums within expenses and reinsurance claims within income on the face of its income statement.

Extract 54.24: Royal & SunAlliance Insurance Group plc (2008)

Consolidated income statement [extract]

For the year ended 31 December 2008

	Notes	2008 £m	2007 £m
Continuing operations			
Income			
Gross written premiums		**7,273**	6,596
Less: reinsurance premiums		**(811)**	(759)
Net written premiums		**6,462**	5,837
Change in the gross provision for unearned premiums		**(112)**	(235)
Less: change in provision for unearned premiums, reinsurers' share		**8**	5
Change in provision for unearned premiums		**(104)**	(230)
Net earned premiums		**6,358**	5,607
Net investment return	2	**681**	709
Other operating income	4	**104**	113
Total income		**7,143**	6,429
Expenses			
Gross claims incurred		**(4,205)**	(4,044)
Less: claims recoveries from reinsurers		**63**	387
Net claims and benefits	3	**(4,142)**	(3,657)
Underwriting and policy acquisition costs		**(1,925)**	(1,776)
Unwind of discount		**(92)**	(81)
Other operating expenses	4	**(117)**	(119)
Total expenses		**(6,276)**	(5,633)

Extract 54.25: AEGON N.V. (2008)

Consolidated Income Statement of AEGON Group For The Year Ended December 31 [extract]

Amount in EUR million (except per share data)	Note	2008	2007	2006
Income				
Premium income	31	22,409	26,900	24,570
Investment income	32	9,965	10,457	10,376
Fee and commission income	33	1,703	1,900	1,665
Other revenues	34	5	14	4
Total revenues		34,082	39,271	36,615
Income from reinsurance ceded	35	1,633	1,546	1,468
Results from financial transactions	36	(28,195)	4,545	9,397
Other income	37	6	214	11
TOTAL INCOME		7,526	45,576	47,491
Charges				
Premiums to reinsurers	31	1,571	1,606	1,671
Policyholder claims and benefits	38	(808)	34,135	35,267
Profit sharing and rebates	39	98	83	133
Commissions and expenses	40	6,109	5,939	6,085
Impairment charges/(reversals)	41	1,113	117	33
Interest charges and related fees	42	526	474	362
Other charges	43	2	181	1
TOTAL CHARGES		8,611	42,535	43,552

IAS 18 requires an entity to disclose the amount of each significant category of revenue recognised during the period, and specifically requires disclosure of revenue arising from the rendering of services. *[IAS 18.35(b)]*. Although revenue from insurance contracts is outside the scope of IAS 18, similar disclosures may be appropriate for insurance contracts. IFRS 4 does not prescribe a particular method for recognising revenue and recording expenses so a variety of models are used, the most common ones being:

- recognising premiums earned during the period as revenue and recognising claims arising during the period (including estimates of claims incurred but not reported) as an expense;

- recognising premiums received as revenue and at the same time recognising an expense representing the resulting increase in the insurance liability; and

- initially recognising premiums received as deposit receipts. Revenue will include charges for items such as mortality, and expenses will include the policyholder claims and benefits related to those charges. *[IFRS 4.IG25]*.

IAS 1 requires additional disclosures of various items of income and expense. To meet this requirement the following additional items might need to be disclosed, either on the face of the income statement or in the notes:

(a) acquisition costs (distinguishing those recognised as an expense immediately from the amortisation of deferred acquisition costs);

(b)   the effects of changes in estimates and assumptions (see 10.1.5 below);

(c)   losses recognised as a result of applying liability adequacy tests;

(d)   for insurance liabilities measured on a discounted basis:

(i)   accretion of interest to reflect the passage of time; and

(ii)   the effect of changes in discount rates; and

(e)   distributions or allocations to holders of contracts that contain a DPF. The portion of profit or loss that relates to any equity component of those contracts is an allocation of profit or loss, not expense or income (see 6.1 above). *[IFRS 4.IG26].*

These items should not be offset against income or expense arising from reinsurance held. *[IFRS 4.IG28].*

Some insurers present a detailed analysis of the sources of their earnings from insurance activities, either in the income statement, or in the notes. Such an analysis may provide useful information about both the income and expense of the current period and risk exposures faced during the period. *[IFRS 4.IG27].*

To the extent that gains or losses from insurance contracts are recognised in other comprehensive income, e.g. as a result of applying shadow accounting (see 8.3 above), similar considerations to those discussed above will apply.

If non-uniform accounting policies for the insurance liabilities of subsidiaries are adopted, it might be necessary to disaggregate the disclosures about the amounts reported to give meaningful information about amounts determined using different accounting policies. *[IFRS 4.IG30].*

10.1.2.C   Cash flows

If an insurer presents its cash flow statement using the direct method, IFRS 4 also requires it to disclose the cash flows that arise from insurance contracts although it does not require disclosure of the component cash flows associated with its insurance activity. *[IFRS 4.IG19].*

10.1.3   Gains or losses on buying reinsurance

Gains or losses on buying reinsurance may, using some measurement models, arise from imperfect measurements of the underlying direct insurance liability. Furthermore, some measurement models require a cedant to defer some of those gains and losses and amortise them over the period of the related risk exposures, or some other period. *[IFRS 4.IG29].*

Therefore, a cedant is required to provide specific disclosure about gains or losses on buying reinsurance as discussed at 7.2.6 and 10.1 above. In addition, if gains and losses on buying reinsurance are deferred and amortised, disclosure is required of the amortisation for the period and the amounts remaining unamortised at the beginning and end of the period. *[IFRS 4.37(b)(i)-(ii)].*

Chapter 54

Zurich Financial Services is one insurer that defers and amortises gains on buying reinsurance for 'retroactive' reinsurance contracts in accordance with its existing accounting policies, which are derived from US GAAP.

Extract 54.26: Zurich Financial Services Group (2008)

Consolidated financial statements [extract]

3. Summary of significant accounting policies [extract]

b) Insurance contracts and investment contracts with discretionary participating features (DPF) [extract]

Reinsurance [extract]

Premiums paid under the retroactive contracts are included in reinsurance recoverables in the balance sheet. If the amount of gross claims provisions reinsured is higher than the premium paid, reinsurance receivables are increased by the difference, and the gain is deferred and amortized over the period in which the underlying claims are paid.

10.1.4   *Process used to determine significant assumptions*

As noted at 10.1 above, IFRS 4 requires disclosure of the process used to determine the assumptions that have the greatest effect on the measurement of the recognised amounts. Where practicable, quantified disclosure of these assumptions should also be given. *[IFRS 4.37(c)].*

Some respondents to ED 5 expressed concern that information about assumptions and changes in assumptions (see 10.1.5 below) might be costly to prepare and of limited usefulness. They argued that there are many possible assumptions that could be disclosed and excessive aggregation would result in meaningless information, whereas excessive disaggregation could be costly, lead to information overload, and reveal commercially sensitive information. In response to these concerns, the IASB determined that disclosure about assumptions should focus on the process used to derive them. *[IFRS 4.BC212].* Further, the standard refers only to those assumptions 'that have the greatest effect on the measurement of' the recognised amounts.

IFRS 4 does not prescribe specific assumptions that should be disclosed, because different assumptions will be more significant for different types of contracts. *[IFRS 4.IG33].*

For some disclosures, such as discount rates or assumptions about future trends or general inflation, it may be relatively easy to disclose the assumptions used (aggregated at a reasonable but not excessive level, when necessary). For other assumptions, such as mortality rates derived from tables, it may not be practicable to disclose quantified assumptions because there are too many, in which case it is more important to describe the process used to generate the assumptions. *[IFRS 4.IG31].*

The description of the process used to describe assumptions might include a summary of the most significant of the following:

(a) the objective of the assumptions, for example, whether the assumptions are intended to be neutral estimates of the most likely or expected outcome ('best estimates') or to provide a given level of assurance or level of sufficiency. If they are intended to provide a quantitative or qualitative level of assurance that level could be disclosed;

(b) the source of data used as inputs for the assumptions that have the greatest effect, for example, whether the inputs are internal, external or a mixture of the two. For data derived from detailed studies that are not carried out annually, the criteria used to determine when the studies are updated and the date of the latest update could be disclosed;

(c) the extent to which the assumptions are consistent with observable market prices or other published information;

(d) a description of how past experience, current conditions and other relevant benchmarks are taken into account in developing estimates and assumptions. If a relationship would normally be expected between past experience and future results, the reasons for using assumptions that differ from past experience and an indication of the extent of the difference could be explained;

(e) a description of how assumptions about future trends, such as changes in mortality, healthcare costs or litigation awards were developed;

(f) an explanation of how correlations between different assumptions are identified;

(g) the policy in making allocations or distributions for contracts with discretionary participation features. In addition, the related assumptions that are reflected in the financial statements, the nature and extent of any significant uncertainty about the relative interests of policyholders and shareholders in the unallocated surplus associated with those contracts, and the effect on the financial statements of any changes during the period in that policy or those assumptions could be disclosed; and

(h) the nature and extent of uncertainties affecting specific assumptions. In addition, to comply with IAS 1, an insurer may need to disclose the assumptions it makes about the future, and other major sources of estimation uncertainty, that have a significant risk of resulting in a material adjustment to the carrying amounts of insurance assets and liabilities within the next financial year. *[IFRS 4.IG32].*

Chapter 54

Ping An disclose the following assumptions in relation to their insurance liabilities together with further detail about those assumptions.

Extract 54.27: Ping An Insurance (Group) Company of China Ltd (2008)

Notes to financial statements [extract]
4. Critical accounting estimates and judgements in applying accounting policies [extract]
(2) Estimates and assumptions [extract]

Life insurance contract liabilities

The liability for life insurance contracts (including investment contracts with DPF) is either based on current assumptions or on assumptions established at inception of the contract, reflecting the best estimate at the time increased with a margin for risk and adverse deviation. All contracts are subject to a liability adequacy test, which reflect management's best current estimate of future cash flows.

Certain acquisition costs related to the sale of new policies are recorded in deferred policy acquisition costs and are amortized to the income statement over time. If the assumptions relating to future profitability of these policies are not realized, the amortization of these costs could be accelerated and may require additional write-offs to the income statement.

The main assumptions used relate to mortality, morbidity, investment returns, expenses, lapses and surrender rates. The Group base mortality and morbidity tables on standard industry tables which reflect historical experiences, adjusted when appropriate to reflect the Group's unique risk exposure, product characteristics, target markets and own claims severity and frequency experiences.

Estimates are also made as to future investment income arising from the assets backing life insurance contracts. These estimates are based on current market returns as well as expectations about future economic and financial developments.

Assumptions on future expense are based on current expense levels, adjusted for expected expense inflation adjustments if appropriate.

Lapse and surrender rates depend on product features, policy duration and external circumstance, such as sale trends. Credible own experience is used in establishing these assumptions.

Property and casualty and short term life insurance contract liabilities

For property and casualty and short term life insurance contracts, estimates have to be made both for the expected ultimate cost of claims reported at the balance sheet date and for the expected ultimate cost of claims incurred but not yet reported at the balance sheet date ("IBNR"). It may take a significant period of time before the ultimate claims cost can be established with certainty and for some type of policies, IBNR claims form the majority of the balance sheet liability. The ultimate cost of outstanding claims is estimated by using a range of standard actuarial claims projection techniques, such as the Chain Ladder and Bornheutter-Ferguson methods.

The main assumption underlying these techniques is that a company's past claims development experience can be used to project future claims development and hence ultimate claims costs. As such, these methods extrapolate the development of paid and incurred losses, average costs per claim and claim numbers based on the observed development of earlier years and expected loss ratios. Historical claims development is mainly analyzed by accident year, but can also be further analyzed by geographical areas, as well as by significant business lines and claim types. Large claims are usually separately addressed, either by being reserved at the face value of loss adjustor estimates or separately projected in order to reflect their future development. In most cases, no explicit assumptions are made regarding future rates of claims inflation or loss ratios. Instead, the assumptions used are those implicit in the historic claims development data on which the projections are based. Additional qualitative judgment is used to assess the extent to which past trends may not apply in future (for example to reflect one-off occurrences, changes in external or maker factors such as public attitudes to claiming, economic conditions, levels of claims inflation, judicial decisions and legislation, as well as internal factors such as portfolio mix, policy conditions and claims handling procedures), so as to arrive at the estimated ultimate cost of claims that present the likely outcome from the range of possible outcomes, taking account of all the uncertainties involved.

41. Risk and capital management [extract]

1(a) Long term life insurance contracts and investment contracts with DPF [extract]

Assumptions

Material judgment is required in determining the liabilities and in the choice of assumptions relating to both long term life insurance contracts and investment contracts. Such assumptions are determined as appropriate and prudent estimates at the date of valuation.

The key assumptions to which the estimation of liabilities is particularly sensitive are as follows:

Mortality, morbidity and lapse rates

Mortality and morbidity rates, varying by age of the insured, and lapse rates, varying by contract type, are based upon expected experience at the date of contract issue plus, where applicable, a margin for adverse deviation. The mortality, morbidity and lapse assumptions are based on experience studies of the Group's actual experience.

For long term life insurance policies, increased mortality rates will lead to a larger number of claims and claims will occur sooner than anticipated, which will increase the expenditure and reduce profits for the shareholders.

For annuity contracts, a high mortality will decrease payments, thereby reducing expenditure and increase profits.

The impact of an increase in lapse rates at early duration of the policy would tend to reduce profits for the shareholders but lapse rates at later policy durations is broadly neutral in effect.

Investment return

Future investment return for non-investment-linked life insurance contracts has been changed to be 4.25% in 2009 and to increase by 0.25% every year to 5.5% by 2014 and thereafter. These rates have been derived by consideration of the current market condition and the Group's current and expected future asset allocation. They are the best estimate rates used in gross premium reserve valuation and liability adequacy test on a portfolio basis.

An increase in investment return assumption may lead to a decrease in policyholders' liabilities.

Expenses

Maintenance expenses assumptions reflect the projected costs of maintaining and servicing in force policies. The assumption for policy administration expenses is determined based on expected unit costs. Unit costs have been based on an analysis of actual experience.

Others

Other assumptions include taxation, future bonus rates, etc.

The assumptions used to estimate the liabilities of the Group's long term life insurance contracts and investment contracts with DPF require judgement and are subject to uncertainty.

Chapter 54

Some life insurers give details of the mortality tables used for measuring their insurance contract liabilities. AMP provide an example of the type of disclosures made.

Extract 54.28: AMP Limited (2008)

Notes to the financial statements [extract]

19. Life insurance contracts [extract]

(a) Assumptions and methodology applied in the valuation of life insurance contract liabilities [extract]

(ix) Mortality and morbidity [extract]

Standard mortality tables, based on national or industry wide data, are used (e.g. IA95-97 and IM(F)80 in Australia and New Zealand). These are then adjusted by factors that take account of AMP Life's own experience, primarily over the past three years. For annuity business, adjustment is also made for mortality improvements prior to and after the valuation date.

Rates of mortality assumed at 31 December 2008 are 1% to 6% lower than those assumed at 31 December 2007 in Australia and New Zealand. Rates of annuitant mortality in are unchanged.

Typical mortality assumptions, in aggregate, are as follows:

	Conventional – % of IA95-97		Term – % of IA95-97	
Risk products	Male	Female	Male	Female
Australia	80%	80%	63%	63%
New Zealand	78%	78%	63%	63%

	Male – % of IM80	Female – % of IF80
Annuities		
Australia	72%	61%

For disability income business, the claim assumptions are currently based on CIDA85, which is derived from North American experience. It is adjusted for AMP Life's experience, with the adjustment dependent on age, sex, waiting period, occupation, smoking status and claim duration. Incidence rates and termination rates are both unchanged as at 31 December 2008 compared to those at 31 December 2007.

For trauma cover, standard tables are not available and so assumptions are mostly based on Australian population statistics, with adjustment for smoking status as well as AMP Life's recent claim experience. Assumptions at 31 December 2008 are unchanged from those used at 31 December 2007.

The Actuarial tables used were:

IA95-97 – A mortality table developed by the Institute of Actuaries of Australia based on Australian insured lives experience from 1995-1997.

IM80* / IF80* – IM80 and IF80 are mortality tables developed by the Institute of Actuaries and the Faculty of Actuaries based on United Kingdom annuitant lives experience from 1979-1982. The tables refer to male and female lives, respectively, and incorporate factors that allow for mortality improvements since the date of the investigation. *IM80 and IF80 are these published tables amended for some specific AMP experience.

CIDA85 – A disability table developed by the Society of Actuaries based on North American disability income experience from 1973-1979.

Prudential provides the following disclosures about allocations and distributions in respect of contracts with a DPF.

Extract 54.29: Prudential plc (2008)

Notes on the financial statements [extract]
D: Life assurance business [extract]
D2: UK insurance operations [extract]

i With-profits products and PAC with-profits sub-fund

Within the balance sheet of UK insurance operations at 31 December 2008, as shown in note D2(a), there are policyholder liabilities and unallocated surplus of £72.1 billion (2007: £90.5 billion) that relate to the WPSF. These amounts include the liabilities and capital of Prudential Annuities Limited, a wholly owned subsidiary of the fund. The WPSF mainly contains with-profits business but it also contains some non-profit business (unit-linked, term assurances and annuities). The WPSF's profits are apportioned 90 per cent to its policyholders and 10 per cent to shareholders as surplus for distribution is determined via the annual actuarial valuation.

With-profits products provide returns to policyholders through bonuses that are 'smoothed'. There are two types of bonuses: 'annual' and 'final'. Annual bonuses are declared once a year, and once credited, are guaranteed in accordance with the terms of the particular product. Unlike annual bonuses, final bonuses are guaranteed only until the next bonus declaration.

When determining policy payouts, including final bonuses, Prudential considers policyholders' reasonable expectations, the need to smooth claim values and payments from year to year and competitive considerations, together with 'asset shares' for specimen policies. Asset shares broadly reflect the value of premiums paid plus the investment return on the assets notionally attributed to the policy, less the other items to be charged such as expenses and the cost of the life insurance cover.

For many years, UK with-profits product providers, such as Prudential, have been required by law and regulation to consider the reasonable expectations of policyholders in setting bonus levels. This concept is established by statute but is not defined. However, it is defined within the regulatory framework, which also more recently contains an explicit requirement to treat customers fairly.

The WPSF held a provision of £42 million at 31 December 2008 (2007: £45 million) to honour guarantees on a small amount of guaranteed annuity products. SAIF's exposure to guaranteed annuities is described below.

Beyond the generic guarantees described above, there are very few explicit options or guarantees such as minimum investment returns, surrender values or annuities at retirement and any granted have generally been at very low levels.

10.1.5 The effects of changes in assumptions

As noted at 10.1 above, IFRS 4 requires disclosure of the effects of changes in assumptions used to measure insurance assets and insurance liabilities, showing separately the effect of each change that has a material impact on the financial statements. *[IFRS 4.37(d)].* This requirement is consistent with IAS 8, which requires disclosure of the nature and amount of a change in an accounting estimate that has an effect in the current period or is expected to have an effect in future periods. *[IFRS 4.IG34].*

Assumptions are often interdependent. When this is the case, any analysis of changes by assumption may depend on the order in which the analysis is performed and may be arbitrary to some extent. Not surprisingly, IFRS 4 does not specify a rigid format or content for this analysis. This allows insurers to analyse the changes in a way that meets the objective of the disclosure requirement and is appropriate for their particular circumstances. If practicable, the impact of changes in different assumptions might be disclosed separately, particularly if changes in those assumptions have an adverse effect and others have a beneficial effect. The impact of interdependencies between assumptions and the resulting limitations of any analysis of the effect of changes in assumption might also be described. *[IFRS 4.IG35]*.

The effects of changes in assumptions both before and after reinsurance held might be disclosed, especially if a significant change in the nature or extent of an entity's reinsurance programme is expected or if an analysis before reinsurance is relevant for an analysis of the credit risk arising from reinsurance held. *[IFRS 4.IG36]*.

Old Mutual make the following disclosures in respect of the impact of changes in assumptions.

Extract 54.30: Old Mutual plc (2008)
Notes to the consolidated financial statements [extract]
23 Long term and general business policyholder liabilities [extract]
(v) Assumptions [extract]

Various assumption changes have been made which have resulted in a net increase in the value of insurance contract provisions of £11 million (2007: £22 million) on the Published basis. The reserve for investment guarantees which have been calculated on a market-consistent basis was increased by £27 million (including a discretionary margin), as a result of the reduction in swap yields and increases in volatilities. Lower economic assumptions also led to an increase in underlying policyholder liabilities of £8 million. The basis for terminations and alterations was strengthened leading to an increase in liabilities of £35 million. Lower expense and mortality assumptions reduced liabilities by £39 million and £13 million respectively. Methodology changes and error corrections reduced liabilities by £6 million.

Aviva disclose the impact of changes in assumptions for their insurance business in a tabular format.

Extract 54.31: Aviva plc (2008)
Consolidated financial statements [extract]
42 – Effects of changes in assumptions and estimates during the year [extract]

This disclosure only allows for the impact on liabilities and related assets, such as reinsurance, deferred acquisition costs and AVIF, and does not allow for offsetting movements in the value of backing financial assets.

	Effect on profit 2008 £m	Effect on profit 2007 £m
Assumptions		
Long term insurance business		
Interest rates	(521)	850
Expenses	24	(13)
Persistency rates	2	(2)
Mortality for assurance contracts	44	16
Mortality for annuity contracts	26	11
Tax and other assumptions	93	60

Investment contracts		
Interest rates	**(75)**	12
Expenses	**(27)**	5
Persistency	**2**	–
Tax and other assumptions	**36**	7
General insurance and health business		
Change in loss ratio assumptions	**(1)**	–
Change in discount rate assumptions	**(94)**	3
Change in expense ratio assumptions	**–**	(4)
Total	**(491)**	945

The impact of interest rates for long-term business relates primarily to the UK, Ireland and the Netherlands, driven by the market level of risk-free rates. Lower valuation interest rates in 2008 had the effect of increasing liabilities for traditional business and hence a negative impact on profit. This follows an increase in market interest rates in 2007 which had the reverse effect. The overall impact on profit also depends on movements in the value of assets baking the liabilities, which is not included in this disclosure.

Favourable impacts for expense and mortality assumption changes for insurance contracts relate mainly to the UK. Other assumption changes include further implementation of FSA Policy Statement PS06/14 for non-profit business and expense inflation adjustments in the UK, and reserve releases in Asia, partly offset by compensation for unit-linked policies in the Netherlands.

10.1.6   *Reconciliations of changes in insurance assets and liabilities*

As noted at 10.1 above, IFRS 4 requires reconciliations of changes in insurance liabilities, reinsurance assets and, if any, related deferred acquisition costs, although it does not prescribe the line items that should appear in the reconciliations. *[IFRS 4.37(e)].*

The changes need not be disaggregated into broad classes, but they might be if different forms of analysis are more relevant for different types of liability. For insurance liabilities the changes might include:

(a)   the carrying amount at the beginning and end of the period;

(b)   additional insurance liabilities arising during the period;

(c)   cash paid;

(d)   income and expense included in profit or loss;

(e)   liabilities acquired from, or transferred to, other insurers; and

(f)   net exchange differences arising on the translation of the financial statements into a different presentation currency, and on the translation of a foreign operation into the presentation currency of the reporting entity. *[IFRS 4.IG37].*

This reconciliation is also required for each period for which comparative information is presented. *[IFRS 4.IG38].*

Chapter 54

The reconciliations given by CNP Assurances for life insurance, non-life insurance and investment contracts with a DPF are shown below. In the tables the amounts are shown before and after the impact of reinsurance.

Extract 54.32: CNP Assurances (2008)

Notes to the financial statements [extract]
10. Insurance and financial liabilities [extract]
10.2 Change in technical reserves [extract]

This note presents changes in technical reserves by category, such as those arising from changes in the assumptions applied to measure insurance liabilities. Each change with a material impact on the consolidated financial statements is shown separately. Movements are presented before and after reinsurance.

10.2.1.1 Changes in mathematical reserves – life insurance – 2008 [extract]

In € millions	2008		
	Before reinsurance	Net of reinsurance	Reinsurance
Mathematical reserves at the beginning of the period	216,835.0	211,703.6	5,131.4
Premiums	24,530.7	24,049.3	481.4
Extinguished liabilities (benefit payments)	(17,456.2)	(17,238.7)	(217.5)
Locked-in gains	7,213.5	7,109.3	104.2
Change in value of unit-linked portfolios	(5,591.2)	(5,591.2)	0.0
Changes in scope (acquisitions/divestments)	(20.2)	(20.0)	(0.2)
Asset loading	(1,016.7)	(1,016.7)	0.0
Surpluses/deficits	0.0	0.0	0.0
Currency effect	(435.0)	(435.0)	0.0
Changes in assumptions	0.2	0.2	0.0
Consolidation of Marfin Insurance Holdings Ltd	467.1	467.1	0.0
Other	174.0	298.4	(124.4)
Mathematical reserves at the end of the period	224,701.2	219,326.3	5,374.9

10.2.2.1 Changes in mathematical reserves – non-life insurance – 2008 [extract]

In € millions	2008		
	Before reinsurance	Net of reinsurance	Reinsurance
Outstanding claims reserves at the beginning of the period	678.5	608.7	69.8
Claims expense for the period	1,416.1	1,275.3	140.8
Prior period surpluses/deficits	(3.3)	(1.0)	(2.3)
Total claims expenses	**1,412.8**	**1,274.3**	**138.5**
Current period claims settled during the period	(1,322.5)	(1,172.6)	(149.9)
Prior period claims settled during the period	(37.4)	(34.9)	(2.5)
Total paid claims	**(1,359.9)**	**(1,207.5)**	**(152.4)**
Changes in scope of consolidation and changes of method	0.0	0.0	0.0
Translation adjustment	(22.9)	(22.9)	0.0
Changes in scope of consolidation: Marfin Insurance Holding	42.0	24.9	17.1
Outstanding claims reserves at the end of the period	**750.4**	**677.4**	**73.0**

10.2.3 Changes in mathematical reserves – financial instruments with DPF [extract]

In € millions

	2008		
	Before reinsurance	Net of reinsurance	Reinsurance
Mathematical reserves at the beginning of the period	7,881.2	7,553.8	327.4
Premiums	795.0	768.8	26.2
Extinguished liabilities (benefit payments)	(961.8)	(935.0)	(26.8)
Locked-in gains	43.9	43.9	0.0
Change in value of unit-linked portfolios	(1,203.5)	(1,087.1)	(116.4)
Changes in scope (acquisitions/divestments)	(13.1)	(13.1)	0.0
Currency effect	(111.8)	(111.8)	0.0
Changes in scope of consolidation	0.0	0.0	0.0
Other	10.0	10.0	0.0
Mathematical reserves at the end of the period	6,439.9	6,229.5	210.4

A reconciliation of deferred acquisition costs might include:

(a)   the carrying amount at the beginning and end of the period;

(b)   the amounts incurred during the period;

(c)   the amortisation for the period;

(d)   impairment losses recognised during the period; and

(e)   other changes categorised by cause and type. *[IFRS 4.IG39].*

ING's reconciliation of deferred acquisition costs is illustrated below.

Extract 54.33: ING Group N.V. (2008)

Notes to the consolidated financial statements [extract]
10. Deferred acquisition costs

Changes in deferred acquisition costs

	Investment contracts		Life insurance		Non-Life insurance		Total	
	2008	2007	2008	2007	2008	2007	2008	2007
Opening balance	101	83	10,183	9,645	408	435	10,692	10,163
Capitalised	50	31	2,495	2,766	126	257	32,671	3,054
Amortisation and unlocking	−12	−12	−1,884	−1,294	−130	−274	−2,026	−1,580
Effect of unrealised revaluations in equity			1,523	43			1,523	43
Changes in the composition of the group	−34		−1,289		−104	−5	−1,427	−5
Exchange rate differences	−16	−1	461	−938	−35	10	410	−929
Disposal of portfolios				−39		−15		−54
Closing balance	89	101	11,489	10,183	265	408	11,843	10,692

For flexible life insurance contracts the growth rate assumption used to calculate the amortisation of the deferred acquisition costs for 2008 is 6.4% gross and 5.6% net of investment management fees (2007: 6.6% gross and 5.6% net of investment management fees).

In 2008, Changes in the composition of the group related for EUR 1,164 million to the sale of ING Life Taiwan.

An insurer may have intangible assets related to insurance contracts acquired in a business combination or portfolio transfer. IFRS 4 does not require any disclosures for intangible assets in addition to those required by IAS 38 (see 9.2 above). *[IFRS 4.IG40].*

10.2   Nature and extent of risks arising from insurance contracts

The second key disclosure principle established by IFRS 4 is that information should be disclosed to enable the users of the financial statements to evaluate the nature and extent of risks arising from insurance contracts. *[IFRS 4.38].*

To comply with this principle, an insurer needs to disclose:

(a)   its objectives, policies and processes for managing risks arising from insurance contracts and the methods used to manage those risks;

(b)   information about insurance risk (both before and after risk mitigation by reinsurance), including information about:

(i)   sensitivity to insurance risk;

(ii)   concentrations of insurance risk, including a description of how management determines concentrations and a description of the shared characteristic that identifies each concentration (e.g. type of insured event, geographical area or currency); and

(iii)   actual claims compared with previous estimates (i.e. claims development). This disclosure has to go back to the period when the earliest material claim arose for which there is still uncertainty about the amount and timing of the claims payments, but need not go back more than ten years. Information about claims for which uncertainty about the amount and timing of claims payments is typically resolved within one year need not be disclosed;

(c)   information about credit risk, liquidity risk and market risk that would be required by IFRS 7 if insurance contracts were within the scope of that standard. However:

(i)   an insurer need not provide the maturity analyses required by IFRS 7 if it discloses information about the estimated timing of the net cash outflows resulting from recognised insurance liabilities instead. This may take the form of an analysis, by estimated timing, of the amounts recognised in the statement of financial position rather than gross undiscounted cash flows; and

(ii)   if an alternative method to manage sensitivity to market conditions, such as an embedded value analysis is used, an insurer may use that sensitivity analysis to meet the requirements of IFRS 7. However, disclosures are still required explaining the methods used in preparing that alternative analysis, its main parameters and assumptions, and an explanation of the objectives of the method and of its limitations; and

(d)   information about exposures to market risk arising from embedded derivatives contained in a host insurance contract if the insurer is not required to, and does not, measure the embedded derivatives at fair value. *[IFRS 4.39].*

These disclosures are based on two foundations:

(a) there should be a balance between quantitative and qualitative disclosures, enabling users to understand the nature of risk exposures and their potential impact; and

(b) disclosures should be consistent with how management perceives its activities and risks, and the objectives, policies and processes that management uses to manage those risks so that they:

    (i) generate information that has more predictive value than information based on assumptions and methods that management does not use, for example, in considering the insurer's ability to react to adverse situations; and

    (ii) are more effective in adapting to the continuing change in risk measurement and management techniques and developments in the external environment over time. *[IFRS 4.IG41].*

In developing disclosures to satisfy the requirements, it might be useful to group insurance contracts into broad classes appropriate for the nature of the information to be disclosed, taking into account matters such as the risks covered, the characteristics of the contracts and the measurement basis applied. These broad classes may correspond to classes established for legal or regulatory purposes, but IFRS 4 does not require this. *[IFRS 4.IG42].*

Under IFRS 8 – *Operating Segments* – the identification of operating segments reflects the way in which management allocates resources and assesses performance. It might be useful to adopt a similar approach to identify broad classes of insurance contracts for disclosure purposes, although it might be appropriate to disaggregate disclosures down to the next level. For example, if life insurance is identified as an operating segment for IFRS 8, it might be appropriate to report separate information about, say, life insurance, annuities in the accumulation phase and annuities in the payout phase. *[IFRS 4.IG43].*

In identifying broad classes for separate disclosure, it is useful to consider how best to indicate the level of uncertainty associated with the risks underwritten, so as to inform users whether outcomes are likely to be within a wider or a narrower range. For example, an insurer might disclose information about exposures where there are significant amounts of provisions for claims incurred but not reported (IBNR) or where outcomes and risks are unusually difficult to assess, e.g. for asbestos-related claims. *[IFRS 4.IG45].*

It may also be useful to disclose sufficient information about the broad classes identified to permit a reconciliation to relevant line items on the statement of financial position. *[IFRS 4.IG46].*

Information about the nature and extent of risks arising from insurance contracts will be more useful if it highlights any relationship between classes of insurance contracts (and between insurance contracts and other items, such as financial instruments) that can affect those risks. If the effect of any relationship would not be apparent from disclosures required by IFRS 4, additional disclosure might be useful. *[IFRS 4.IG47].*

A more detailed analysis of risk disclosures made by insurers is discussed below.

Chapter 54

10.2.1 *Objectives, policies and processes for managing insurance contract risks*

As noted at 10.2 above, IFRS 4 requires an insurer to disclose its objectives, policies and processes for managing risks arising from insurance contracts and the methods used to manage those risks. *[IFRS 4.39(a)].*

Such disclosure provides an additional perspective that complements information about contracts outstanding at a particular time and might include information about:

(a) the structure and organisation of the entity's risk management function(s), including a discussion of independence and accountability;

(b) the scope and nature of its risk reporting or measurement systems, such as internal risk measurement models, sensitivity analyses, scenario analysis, and stress testing, and how these are integrated into the entity's operating activities. Useful disclosure might include a summary description of the approach used, associated assumptions and parameters (including confidence intervals, computation frequencies and historical observation periods) and strengths and limitations of the approach;

(c) the processes for accepting, measuring, monitoring and controlling insurance risks and the entity's underwriting strategy to ensure that there are appropriate risk classification and premium levels;

(d) the extent to which insurance risks are assessed and managed on an entity-wide basis;

(e) the methods employed to limit or transfer insurance risk exposures and avoid undue concentrations of risk, such as retention limits, inclusion of options in contracts, and reinsurance;

(f) asset and liability management (ALM) techniques; and

(g) the processes for managing, monitoring and controlling commitments received (or given) to accept (or contribute) additional debt or equity capital when specified events occur.

It might be useful to provide disclosures both for individual types of risks insured and overall. They might include a combination of narrative descriptions and specific quantified data, as appropriate to the nature of the contracts and their relative significance to the insurer. *[IFRS 4.IG48].*

The following extract from AMP provides an example of disclosures concerning the management of life insurance risks.

Extract 54.34: AMP Limited (2008)

Notes to the consolidated financial statements [extract]
19. Life insurance contracts [extract]
(h) Life insurance risk

The life insurance activities of AMP Life involve a number of non-financial risks concerned with the pricing, acceptance and management of the mortality, morbidity and longevity risks accepted from policyholders, often in conjunction with the provision of wealth management products. Financial risks involved in AMP Life are covered in Note 20.

The design of products carrying insurance risk is managed to ensure that policy wording and promotional materials are clear, unambiguous and do not leave AMP Life open to claims from causes that were not anticipated. Product prices are set through a process of financial analysis, including review of previous AMP Life and industry experience and specific product design features. The variability inherent in insurance risk is managed by having a large portfolio of individual risks, underwriting and the use of reinsurance.

Underwriting is managed through a dedicated underwriting department, with formal underwriting limits and appropriate training and development of underwriting staff. Individual policies carrying insurance risk are underwritten on their merits and are generally not issued without having been examined and underwritten individually. Individual policies which are transferred from a group scheme are generally issued without underwriting. Group risk insurance policies meeting certain criteria are underwritten on the merits of the employee group as a whole.

Claims are managed through a dedicated claims management team, with formal claims acceptance limits and appropriate training and development of staff to ensure payment of all genuine claims. Claims experience is assessed regularly and appropriate actuarial reserves are established to reflect up-to-date experience and any anticipated future events. This includes reserves for claims incurred but not yet reported.

AMP Life reinsures (cedes) to specialist reinsurance companies a proportion of its portfolio or certain types of insurance risk. This serves primarily to:

– reduce the net liability on large individual risks
– obtain greater diversification of insurance risks
– provide protection against large losses.

The specialist reinsurance companies are regulated by APRA or industry regulators in other jurisdictions and have strong credit ratings from A+ to AAA.

Chapter 54

This extract from Beazley Group illustrates the disclosure of non-life insurance and reinsurance risk policies and processes.

Extract 54.35: Beazley Group plc (2008)

Notes to the financial statements [extract]
2 Risk management [extract]
2.1 Insurance risk [extract]

The group's insurance business assumes the risk of loss from persons or organisations that are directly exposed to an underlying loss. Insurance risk arises from this risk transfer due to inherent uncertainties about the occurrence, amount and timing of insurance liabilities. The four key components of insurance risk are underwriting, reinsurance, claims management, reserving and ultimate reserves. Each element is considered below.

a) Underwriting risk [extract]

Underwriting risk comprises four elements that apply to all insurance products offered by the group:

• Cycle risk – the risk that business is written without full knowledge as to the (in)adequacy of rates, terms and conditions;

• Event risk – the risk that individual risk losses or catastrophes lead to claims that are higher than anticipated in plans and pricing;

• Pricing risk – the risk that the level of expected loss is understated in the pricing process; and

• Expense risk – the risk that the allowance for expenses and inflation in pricing is inadequate.

The group's underwriting strategy is to seek a diverse and balanced portfolio of risks in order to limit the variability of outcomes. This is achieved by accepting a spread of business over time, segmented between different products, geography and size.

The annual business plans for each underwriting team reflect the group's underwriting strategy, and set out the classes of business, the territories in which business is to be written and the industry sectors to which the group is prepared to expose itself. These plans are approved by the board and monitored by the monthly underwriting committee.

Our underwriters calculate premiums for risks written based on a range of criteria tailored specifically to each individual risk. These factors include but are not limited to the financial exposure, loss history, risk characteristics, limits, deductibles, terms and conditions and acquisition expenses.

The group also recognises that insurance events are, by their nature, random, and the actual number and size of events during any one year may vary from those estimated using established statistical techniques.

To address this, the group sets out the exposure that it is prepared to accept in certain territories to a range of events such as natural catastrophes and specific scenarios which may result in large industry losses. This is monitored through regular calculation of realistic disaster scenarios (RDS). The aggregate position is monitored at the time of underwriting a risk, and reports are regularly produced to highlight the key aggregations to which the group is exposed.

The group uses a number of modelling tools to monitor aggregation and to simulate catastrophe losses in order to measure the effectiveness of its reinsurance programmes. Stress and scenario tests are also run using these models. The range of scenarios considered include natural catastrophes, marine, liability, political, terrorism and war events.

One of the largest types of event exposure relates to natural catastrophe events such as flood damage, windstorm or earthquake. Where possible the group measures geographic accumulations and uses its knowledge of the business, historical loss behaviour and commercial catastrophe modelling software to assess the probable maximum loss (PML). Upon application of the reinsurance coverage purchased, the key gross and net exposures are calculated on the basis of extreme events at a range of return periods.

The group's high-level catastrophe risk appetite is set by the board and the business plans of each team are determined within these parameters. The board may adjust these limits over time as conditions change. Currently, the group operates to catastrophe risk appetite for a probabilistic 1 in 250 year US event of $340m net of reinsurance.

To manage underwriting exposures, the group has developed limits of authority and business plans which are binding upon all staff authorized to underwrite and are specific to underwriters, classes of business and industry. In 2008, the normal maximum gross PML line that any one underwriter could commit the managed syndicates to was $100m. In most cases, maximum lines for classes of business were much lower than this.

These authority limits are enforced through a comprehensive sign-off process for underwriting transactions including dual sign-off for all line underwriters and peer review for all risks exceeding individual underwriters' authority limits. Exception reports are also run regularly to monitor compliance.

All underwriters also have a right to refuse renewal or change the terms and conditions of insurance contracts upon renewal. Rate monitoring details, including limits, deductibles, exposures, terms and conditions and risk characteristics are also captured and the results are combined to monitor the rating environment for each class of business.

b) Reinsurance risk [extract]

Reinsurance risk to the group arises where reinsurance contracts put in place to reduce gross insurance risk do not perform as anticipated, result in coverage disputes or prove inadequate in terms of the vertical or horizontal limits purchased. Failure of a reinsurer to pay a valid claim is considered a credit risk which is detailed separately below.

The group's reinsurance programmes complement the underwriting team business plans and seek to protect group capital from an adverse volume or volatility of claims on both a per risk and per event basis. In some cases the group deems it more economic to hold capital than purchase reinsurance. These decisions are regularly reviewed as an integral part of the business planning and performance monitoring process.

The reinsurance security committee (RSC) examines and approves all reinsurers to ensure that they possess suitable security. The group's ceded reinsurance team ensures that these guidelines are followed, undertakes the administration of reinsurance contracts, monitors and instigates our responses to any erosion of the reinsurance programmes.

10.2.2 Insurance risk – general matters

As noted at 10.2 above, IFRS 4 requires disclosure about insurance risk (both before and after risk mitigation by reinsurance). *[IFRS 4.39(c)].*

These disclosures are intended to be consistent with the spirit of the disclosures required by financial instruments. The usefulness of particular disclosures about insurance risk depends on individual circumstances. Therefore, the requirements have been written in general terms to allow practice in this area to evolve. *[IFRS 4.BC217].*

Disclosures made to satisfy this requirement might build on the following foundations:

(a) information about insurance risk might be consistent with (though less detailed than) the information provided internally to the entity's key management personnel as defined in IAS 24 – *Related Party Disclosures* – so that users can assess the entity's financial position, performance and cash flows 'through the eyes of management';

(b) information about risk exposures might report exposures both gross and net of reinsurance (or other risk mitigating elements, such as catastrophe bonds issued or policyholder participation features). This is especially relevant if a significant change in the nature or extent of an entity's reinsurance programme is expected or if an analysis before reinsurance is relevant for an analysis of the credit risk arising from reinsurance held;

(c) in reporting quantitative information about insurance risk, disclosure of the strengths and limitations of those methods, the assumptions made, and the effect of reinsurance, policyholder participation and other mitigating elements might be useful;

(d) risk might be classified according to more than one dimension. For example, life insurers might classify contracts by both the level of mortality risk and the level of investment risk. It may sometimes be useful to display this information in a matrix format;

(e) if risk exposures at the reporting date are unrepresentative of exposures during the period, it might be useful to disclose that fact; and

(f) the following disclosures required by IFRS 4 might also be relevant:

(i) the sensitivity of profit or loss and equity to changes in variables that have a material effect on them (see 10.2.3 below);

(ii) concentrations of insurance risk (see 10.2.4 below); and

(iii) the development of prior year insurance liabilities (see 10.2.5 below). *[IFRS 4.IG51].*

Chapter 54

Disclosures about insurance risk might also include:

(a)   information about the nature of the risk covered, with a brief summary description of the class (such as annuities, pensions, other life insurance, motor, property and liability);

(b)   information about the general nature of participation features whereby policyholders share in the performance (and related risks) of individual contracts or pools of contracts or entities. This might include the general nature of any formula for the participation and the extent of any discretion held by the insurer; and

(c)   information about the terms of any obligation or contingent obligation for the insurer to contribute to government or other guarantee funds established by law which are within the scope of IAS 37 as illustrated by Example 54.16 at 3.8.2 above. *[IFRS 4.IG51A].*

Legal & General provide the following narrative disclosures about the type of life insurance contracts that it issues.

Extract 54.36: *Legal & General Group plc (2008)*

Notes to the financial statements [extract]
50. Risk management and control [extract]
Long term insurance risks [extract]

Protection business (individual and group)

The Group offers protection products which provide mortality or morbidity benefits. They may include health, disability, critical illness and accident benefits; these additional benefits are commonly provided as supplements to main life policies but can also be sold separately. The benefit amounts would usually be specified in the policy terms. Some sickness benefits cover the policyholder's mortgage repayments and are linked to the prevailing mortgage interest rates. In addition to these benefits, some contracts may guarantee premium rates, provide guaranteed insurability benefits and offer policyholders conversion options.

Life savings business

A range of contracts are offered in a variety of different forms to meet customers' long term savings objectives. Policyholders may choose to include a number of protection benefits within their savings contracts. Typically, any guarantees under the contract would only apply on maturity or earlier death. On certain older contracts there may be provisions guaranteeing surrender benefits. Savings contracts may or may not guarantee policyholders an investment return. Where the return is guaranteed, the Group may be exposed to interest rate risk with respect to the backing assets.

Pensions (individual and corporate)

These are long term savings contracts through which policyholders accumulate pension benefits. Some older contracts contain a basic guaranteed benefit expressed as an amount of pension payable or a guaranteed annuity option, which exposes the Group to interest rate and longevity risk. These guarantees become more costly during periods when interest rates are low or when annuitant mortality improves faster than expected. The ultimate cost will also depend on the take-up rate of any option and the final form of annuity selected by the policyholder.

Other options provided by these contracts include an open market option on maturity, early retirement and late retirement. The Group would generally have discretion over the terms on which these options are offered.

Annuities

Deferred and immediate annuity contracts are offered. Immediate annuities provide a regular income stream to the policyholder, purchased with a lump sum investment, where the income stream starts immediately after the purchase. The income stream from a deferred annuity is delayed until a specified future date. Bulk annuities are also offered, where the Group manages the assets and accepts the liabilities of a company pension scheme or a life fund.

Non-participating deferred annuities written by the Group do not contain guaranteed cash options.

Annuity products provide guaranteed income for a specified time, usually the life of the policyholder, in exchange for a lump sum capital payment. No surrender value is available under any of these products. The primary risks to the Group from annuity products are therefore mortality improvements and investment performance.

There is a block of immediate and deferred annuities within the UK non profit business with benefits linked to changes in the RPI, but with contractual maximum or minimum increases. In particular, most of these annuities have a provision that the annuity will not reduce if RPI falls. The total of such annuities in payment at 31 December 2008 was £226m (2007: £162m). Thus, 1% negative inflation, which was reversed in the following year, would result in a guarantee cost of approximately £2m (2007: £2m). Negative inflation sustained over a longer period would give rise to significantly greater guarantee costs. Some of these guarantee costs have been partially matched through the purchase of negative inflation hedges and limited price indexation bonds.

The following extract from the financial statements of Amlin illustrates a tabular presentation of insurance risk showing information about premiums and line sizes by class of business.

Extract 54.37: Amlin plc (2008)

Notes to the accounts [extract]
3. Risk disclosures [extract]
3.1 Underwriting risk [extract]
C. Marine risks [extract]
Marine classes

	2008 Gross premium	Current maximum line size	2008 Average line size
	£m	£m	£m
Hull	17	10	1.4
Cargo	32	17	3.5
Energy	39	20	3.3
War and terrorism	25	17	8.7
Specie	9	24	6.3
Bloodstock	21	4	0.6
Yacht (hull and liability)	30	4	1.0
Liability	21	57	4.3

Notes:
1) Limits are set in US dollars converted at a rate of exchange of £1 = US$1.5 and therefore currency rate of exchange changes may increase or reduce the sterling limits.
2) Maximum line size is after business written and ceded by specific proportional treaties to Amlin Bermuda Ltd.
3) Premium are stated net of acquisition costs.

The hull and cargo account is worldwide, covering property damage to ships and loss, or damage to a large variety of cargo or goods in transit. The hull account can include machinery breakdown and the account written is generally targeted towards lower value tonnage, smaller "brownwater" vessels and fishing boats. These accounts can be impacted by attritional claims of a small size as well as a single individual large claim. The cargo account in particular could also be involved in a major natural catastrophe loss. In an economic recession, it is expected that premium income will fall from these areas as trade reduces and hull values are impacted by reduced freight rates. It is also possible that claims frequency increases due to increased economic pressures affecting fraud and theft claims.

The energy portfolio is mainly offshore rig and construction policies which may be impacted by large individual claims from construction fault or property damage such as fire or explosion but is also exposed to severe catastrophe losses in the North Sea and Gulf of Mexico. The account includes control of well to limit loss of oil and avoid pollution and also some business interruption cover which indemnifies companies for loss of production.

War business includes aviation, marine and on land terrorism coverage and is exposed to single incidents or a series of losses arising from concerted action. A small amount of political risk, confiscation and contract frustration is written.

Chapter 54

Specie business consists of the insurance against damage or theft to fine art, the contents of vaults and other high value goods including jewellers' block and cash in transit. The fine art may be shown at exhibitions which have very high aggregate values at risk. The class is therefore exposed to the potential for a frequency of small claims and also large individual losses. Some specie is written in catastrophe zones e.g. California.

The bloodstock account protects for death, illness or injury to horses mainly in the UK but business from the USA, Australia and South Africa is also written. This covers racing and eventing horses or breeding studs. The average value insured is below £1 million but there is the potential for an aggregate loss such as a stable fire which could cause multiple claims.

Yacht business covers property damage and third party injury for small leisure boats and craft. The bulk of the account is smaller value yachts in the UK and Europe, although there are a number of binders written by coverholders elsewhere, such as Scandinavia, Canada and Australia. There is an expectation of a large number of small claims, as average values are low in comparison to other claims written in the Group. Third party liability yacht claims arise from injury or damage caused by one of our policyholders to third parties. There is also the potential for a large catastrophe loss such as a UK windstorm where there are large aggregate sums insured in coastal regions such as southern England.

The marine liability portfolio is written to protect ship-owners, harbours, charterers and energy companies against damage or injury to third parties. This includes the potential for pollution damage and clean up claims. The account could suffer a large catastrophe incident from a collision causing death of crew and passengers or an oil or chemical spill which could require large clean up costs.

10.2.3   Insurance risk – sensitivity information

As noted at 10.2 above, IFRS 4 requires disclosures about sensitivity to insurance risk. *[IFRS 4.39(c)(i)].*

To comply with this requirement, disclosure is required of either:

(a)   a sensitivity analysis that shows how profit or loss and equity would have been affected had changes in the relevant risk variable that were reasonably possible at the end of the reporting period occurred; the methods and assumptions used in preparing that sensitivity analysis; and any changes from the previous period in the methods and assumptions used. However, if an insurer uses an alternative method to manage sensitivity to market conditions, such as an embedded value analysis, it may meet this requirement by disclosing that alternative sensitivity analysis. Where this is done, the methods used in preparing that alternative analysis, its main parameters and assumptions, and its objectives and limitations should be explained; or

(b)   qualitative information about sensitivity, and information about those terms and conditions of insurance contracts that have a material effect on the amount, timing and uncertainty of future cash flows. *[IFRS 4.39A].*

Quantitative disclosures may be provided for some insurance risks and qualitative information about sensitivity and information about terms and conditions for other insurance risks. *[IFRS 4.IG52A].*

Although sensitivity tests can provide useful information, such tests have limitations. Disclosure of the strengths and limitations of the sensitivity analyses performed might be useful. *[IFRS 4.IG52].*

Insurers should avoid giving a misleading sensitivity analysis if there are significant non-linearities in sensitivities to variables that have a material effect. For example, if a change of 1% in a variable has a negligible effect, but a change of 1.1% has a material effect, it might be misleading to disclose the effect of a 1% change without further explanation. *[IFRS 4.IG53].*

Further, if a quantitative sensitivity analysis is disclosed and that sensitivity analysis does not reflect significant correlations between key variables, the effect of those correlations may need to be explained. *[IFRS 4.IG53A].*

If qualitative information about sensitivity is provided, disclosure of information about those terms and conditions of insurance contracts that have a material effect on the amount, timing and uncertainty of cash flows should be made. This might be achieved by disclosing the information discussed at 10.2.2 above and 10.2.6 below. An entity should decide in the light of its circumstances how best to aggregate information to display an overall picture without combining information with different characteristics. Qualitative information might need to be more disaggregated if it is not supplemented with quantitative information. *[IFRS 4.IG54A].*

QBE provide the following quantitative information about non-life insurance sensitivities in their financial statements:

Extract 54.38: QBE Insurance Group (2008)

Notes to the financial statements [extract]
3. Critical accounting estimates and judgements [extract]
(A) Ultimate liability arising from claims under insurance contracts [extract]
(vii) Impact of changes in key variables on the outstanding claims provision [extract]

The impact of changes in key outstanding claims variables is summarised in the table below. Each change has been calculated in isolation from the other changes and each change shows the after tax impact on profit and equity assuming that there is no change to:

- Any of the other variables – This is considered unlikely as, for example, an increase in interest rates is normally accompanied by an increase in the rate of inflation. As can be seen from the table below, the impact of a change in discount rates is largely offset by the impact of a change in the rate of inflation. The impact on financial assets of a change in interest rates is shown in note 5(A)(ii).

- The probability of adequacy – It is likely that if, for example, the central estimate was to increase by 5%, at least part of the increase would result in a decrease in the probability of adequacy, which is currently estimated to be 86.1%. Likewise, if the coefficient of variation were to increase by 1%, it is likely that the probability of adequacy would reduce from its current level and that the change would therefore impact the amount of risk margins held rather than net profit after income tax or equity.

	MOVEMENT IN VARIABLE %	FINANCIAL IMPACT (1)			
		PROFIT (LOSS) 2008 $M	EQUITY 2008 $M	PROFIT (LOSS) 2007 $M	EQUITY 2007 $M
Central estimate	+5	(524)	(524)	(430)	(430)
	–5	524	524	430	430
Inflation rate	+1	(283)	(283)	(248)	(248)
	–1	268	268	236	236
Discount rate	+1	265	265	251	251
	–1	(284)	(284)	(270)	(270)
Coefficient of variation	+1	(115)	(115)	(148)	(148)
	–1	113	113	137	137
Weighted average term to settlement	+10	68	68	123	123
	–10	(68)	(68)	(125)	(125)

(1) Determined at the consolidated entity level net of reinsurance and taxation at the prima facie rate of 30%.

> The consolidated entity has adopted government bond rates appropriate to the mean term and currency of the outstanding claims provision. This has resulted in a probability of adequacy of 86.1%. If the consolidated entity had applied swap rates appropriate to the mean term and currency of the outstanding claims provision, the probability of adequacy would have been 89.4%.

The following extract from Legal & General's financial statements shows sensitivity analysis on a European Embedded Value basis for life insurance liabilities.

Extract 54.39: Legal & General Group plc (2008)

Notes to the financial statements [extract]

50. Risk management and control [extract]

Sensitivity analysis [extract]

Table 6 below shows the effect of alternative assumptions on the long term embedded value, prepared in accordance with the guidance issued by the CFO Forum in October 2005. These sensitivities correspond to those contained within the Supplementary Financial Statements on page 172 of the Annual Report and Accounts.

Table 6 – Effect on embedded value [extract]

As at 31 December 2008	As published £m	1% lower risk discount rate £m	1% higher risk discount rate £m	1% lower interest rate £m	1% higher interest rate £m	1% higher equity/ property yields £m
UK	6,146	384	(336)	(73)	5	110
International	1,463	126	(109)	17	(23)	3
	7,609	**510**	**(445)**	**(56)**	**(18)**	**113**

As at 31 December 2008	As published £m	10% lower equity/ property values £m	10% lower maint-enance expenses £m	10% lower lapse rates £m	5% lower mortality (UK annuities) £m	5% lower mortality (other business) £m
UK	6,146	(248)	68	66	(111)	40
International	1,463	(6)	12	59	n/a	95
	7,609	**(254)**	**80**	**125**	**(111)**	**135**

Opposite sensitivities are broadly symmetrical.

The Group uses embedded value (EV) financial information to manage and monitor performance, and to manage interdependences between different aspects of financial risks, for example for market risk. This provides information about the value which is being created on the Group's long term insurance contracts.

EV information is calculated for the Group's life and pensions business (covered business). All other businesses are accounted for on the IFRS basis adopted in the primary financial statements.

The EV methodology requires assets of an insurance company, as reported in the primary financial statements, to be attributed between those supporting the covered business and the remainder. The method accounts for assets in the covered business on an EV basis and the remainder of the Group's assets on the IFRS basis adopted in the primary financial statements. Sensitivities have been presented for covered business only. In this context the non covered business is considered not to be material. Whilst EV sensitivities do not directly reflect the short term movements under IFRS, they more closely reflect the long term economic out turn.

Cash flow projections are determined using realistic assumptions for each component of cash flow and for each policy group. Future economic and investment return assumptions are based on conditions at the end of the financial year. Future investment returns are projected by one of two methods. The first method is based on an assumed investment return attributed to assets at their market value. The second, which is used in the US, where the investments of that subsidiary are substantially all fixed interest, projects the cash flows from the current portfolio of assets and assumes an investment return on reinvestment of surplus cash flows. The assumed discount and inflation rates are consistent with the investment return assumptions. The main assumptions are provided on page 161 in the Supplementary Financial Statements.

10.2.4 Insurance risk – concentrations of risk

As noted at 10.2 above, IFRS 4 requires disclosure of concentrations of insurance risk, including a description of how management determines concentrations and a description of the shared characteristic that identifies each type of concentration (e.g. type of insured event, geographical area, or currency). *[IFRS 4.39(c)(ii)].*

Such concentrations could arise from, for example:

(a) a single insurance contract, or a small number of related contracts, for example when an insurance contract covers low-frequency, high-severity risks such as earthquakes;

(b) single incidents that expose an insurer to risk under several different types of insurance contract. For example, a major terrorist incident could create exposure under life insurance contracts, property insurance contracts, business interruption and civil liability;

(c) exposure to unexpected changes in trends, for example unexpected changes in human mortality or in policyholder behaviour;

(d) exposure to possible major changes in financial market conditions that could cause options held by policyholders to come into the money. For example, when interest rates decline significantly, interest rate and annuity guarantees may result in significant losses;

(e) significant litigation or legislative risks that could cause a large single loss, or have a pervasive effect on many contracts;

(f) correlations and interdependencies between different risks;

(g) significant non-linearities, such as stop-loss or excess of loss features, especially if a key variable is close to a level that triggers a material change in future cash flows; and

(h) geographical and sectoral concentrations. *[IFRS 4.IG55].*

Disclosure of concentrations of insurance risk might include a description of the shared characteristic that identifies each concentration and an indication of the possible exposure, both before and after reinsurance held, associated with all insurance liabilities sharing that characteristic. *[IFRS 4.IG56].*

Disclosure about the historical performance of low-frequency, high-severity risks might be one way to help users assess cash flow uncertainty associated with those risks. For example, an insurance contract may cover an earthquake that is expected to happen, on average, once every 50 years. If the earthquake occurs during the current reporting period the insurer will report a large loss. If the earthquake does not occur during the current reporting period the insurer will report a profit. Without adequate disclosure of long-term historical performance, it could be misleading to report 49 years of large profits, followed by one large loss, because users may misinterpret the insurer's long-term ability to generate cash flows over the complete cycle of 50 years. Therefore, describing the extent of the exposure to risks of this kind and the estimated frequency of losses might be useful. If circumstances have not changed significantly, disclosure of the insurer's experience with this exposure may be one way to convey information about estimated frequencies. *[IFRS 4.IG57].* However, there is no specific requirement to disclose a probable maximum loss (PML) in the event of a catastrophe because there is no widely agreed definition of PML. *[IFRS 4.BC222].*

ING discloses its concentration to various industries and geographical areas in a tabular format.

Extract 54.40: ING Group N.V. (2008)

Notes to the consolidated annual accounts [extract]
Risk management [extract]

Risk concentration: ING insurance portfolio, by economic sector (1)

	Insurance Americas		Insurance Europe		Insurance Asia/Pacific		Total ING Insurance	
	2008	2007	**2008**	2007	**2008**	2007	**2008**	2007
Non-Bank Financial Institutions	**53.3%**	52.3%	**26.4%**	19.6%	**18.7%**	16.8%	**39.1%**	34.7%
Central governments	**3.2%**	1.7%	**33.7%**	35.8%	**22.7%**	38.1%	**16.6%**	20.1%
Commercial banks	**6.2%**	11.0%	**12.8%**	8.1%	**23.7%**	16.2%	**10.8%**	10.8%
Private Individuals	**3.5%**	3.5%	**10.5%**	13.9%	**11.8%**	7.8%	**7.1%**	7.9%
Real estate	**8.7%**	7.9%	**1.7%**	1.6%	**2.0%**	1.6%	**5.4%**	4.6%
Utilities	**4.0%**	4.0%	**1.7%**	1.4%	**4.0%**	2.9%	**3.2%**	2.9%
Natural Resources	**3.5%**	3.5%	**0.6%**	1.1%	**1.6%**	1.4%	**2.2%**	2.3%
Other	**17.6%**	16.1%	**12.6%**	18.5%	**15.5%**	14.6%	**15.6%**	16.7%
	100.0%	100.0%	**100.0%**	100.0%	**100.0%**	100.0%	**100.0%**	100.0%

(1) Based on credit risk measurement contained in lending, pre-settlement, money market and investment activities. The ratings reflect probabilities of default and does not take collateral into consideration.

Overall risk concentrations remained stable in 2008 for ING Insurance with a small shift towards Commercial Banks as a result of increased equity derivatives trading business at Insurance Europe. Private Individuals in Europe decreased, due to the sale of EUR 4.5 billion in residential mortgages to Retail Banking (Nationale Nederlanden Hypotheek Bedrijf). Food, Beverages and Personal Care accounted for 2.5% in 2007, but fell below the 2.0% threshold in 2008. All other industries not shown in the table above have less than 2.0% concentrations.

Largest economic exposures: ING Insurance portfolio by country (1,2)

amounts in billions of euros	Insurance Americas		Insurance Europe		Insurance Asia/Pacific		Total ING Insurance	
	2008	2007	**2008**	2007	**2008**	2007	**2008**	2007
United States	**58.6**	56.2	**2.0**	1.7	**1.1**	2.3	**61.7**	60.2
Netherlands	**0.8**	0.7	**14.6**	22.0	**0.2**	0.3	**15.6**	23.0
France	**0.3**	0.4	**6.8**	5.9	**0.1**	0.5	**7.2**	6.8
Italy	**0.3**	0.3	**5.9**	6.4	**0.2**	0.2	**6.4**	6.9
South Korea	**0.1**	0.1			**6.2**	6.6	**6.3**	6.7
United Kingdom	**1.8**	1.9	**3.5**	0.4	**0.4**	0.4	**5.7**	5.4
Germany	**0.3**	0.3	**5.3**	0.1	**0.1**	0.3	**5.7**	6.7
Canada	**5.5**	6.0	**0.1**				**5.6**	6.1

(1) Only covers total exposures in excess of EUR 5 billion, including intercompany exposure with ING Bank.

(2) Country is based on the country of residence of the obligor.

The portfolio in the Netherlands decreased principally due to the sale of residential mortgages to retail Banking (Nationale Nederlanden Hypotheek Bedrijf). There were no other significant shifts in the portfolio concentration.

Brit Insurance discloses the potential impact of modelled realistic disaster scenarios (estimated losses incurred from a hypothetical catastrophe).

Extract 54.41: Brit Insurance Holdings plc (2008)

Notes to the financial statements [extract]

4. Risk management policies [extract]

iv) Aggregate exposure management [extract]

As a further guide to the level of catastrophe exposure written by the Group, the table below shows hypothetical claims as at 1 January 2009 for various RDSs.

Event	Modelled industry claims US$m	Brit insurance gross claims £m	Brit Insurance net claims £m	Comments
Florida hurricane – Tampa bay	125,000	299	171	Category 4 storm on the SS Scale, landfalling in Tampa. Brit Insurance estimates include demand surge, flood associated with the hurricane, and non-property exposures.
Florida hurricane – Miami	125,000	257	129	Category 5 storm on the SS Scale, landfalling in Miami. Brit Insurance claim estimates include demand surge, flood associate with the hurricane, and non-property exposures.

Chapter 54

US north east coast hurricane	78,000	263	151	Category 4 storm on the SS Scale, landfalling in Suffolk County, New York State. Brit Insurance claim estimates include demand surge, flood associated with the hurricane, and non-property exposures.
California earthquake – Los Angeles	78,000	290	115	Magnitude 7.2 earthquake on the MMI scale, on the Elsinore fault in Los Angeles. Brit Insurance claim estimates include demand surge, fire following the earthquake, and non-property exposures.
California earthquake – San Francisco	78,000	300	120	Magnitude 7.4 earthquake on the MMI scale, on the San Andreas Fault in San Francisco. Brit Insurance claim estimates include demand surge, fire following the earthquake, and non-property exposures.
Europe windstorm	31,000	244	99	A winter storm with peak gusts in excess of 112mph resulting in a broad swath of damage across southern England, France, Belgium, Netherlands, Luxembourg, Germany and Denmark. Brit Insurance claim estimates include demand surge and UK coastal flood.
Japan earthquake	51,000	196	101	Based on a repeat of the Great Kanto event in 1923, a magnitude 7.9 earthquake in the Tokyo Metropolitan Area.

10.2.5   *Insurance risk – claims development information*

As noted at 10.2 above, IFRS 4 requires disclosure of actual claims compared with previous estimates (i.e. claims development). The disclosure about claims development should go back to the period when the earliest material claim arose for which there is still uncertainty about the amount and the timing of the claims payments, but need not go back more than ten years. Disclosure need not be provided for claims for which uncertainty about claims payments is typically resolved within one year. *[IFRS 4.39(c)(iii)].*

These requirements apply to all insurers, not only to property and casualty insurers. However, the IASB consider that because insurers need not disclose the information for claims for which uncertainty about the amount and timing of payments is typically resolved within a year, it is unlikely that many life insurers will need to give the disclosure. *[IFRS 4.IG60, BC220].* Additionally, the implementation guidance to IFRS 4 states that claims development disclosure should not normally be needed for annuity contracts because each periodic payment is regarded as a separate claim about which there is no uncertainty. *[IFRS 4.IG60]*.

It might also be informative to reconcile the claims development information to amounts reported in the statement of financial position and disclose unusual claims expenses or developments separately, allowing users to identify the underlying trends in performance. *[IFRS 4.IG59]*.

The implementation guidance to IFRS 4 provides an illustrative example of one possible format for presenting claims development which is reproduced in full below. From this it is clear that the IASB is expecting entities to present some form of claims development table. This example presents discounted claims development information by underwriting year. Other formats are permitted, including for example, presenting information by accident year or reporting period rather than underwriting year. *[IFRS 4.IG61]*.

Example 54.34: *Disclosure of claims development* *[IFRS 4.IG61 IE5]*

This example illustrates a possible format for a claims development table for a general insurer. The top half of the table shows how the insurer's estimates of total claims for each underwriting year develop over time. For example, at the end of 2010, the insurer estimated that it would pay claims of CU680 for insured events relating to insurance contracts underwritten in 2010. By the end of 2011, the insurer had revised the estimate of cumulative claims (both those paid and those still to be paid) to CU673.

The lower half of the table reconciles the cumulative claims to the amount appearing in the statement of financial position. First, the cumulative payments are deducted to give the cumulative unpaid claims for each year on an undiscounted basis. Second, if the claims liabilities are discounted, the effect of discounting is deducted to give the carrying amount in the statement of financial position.

Underwriting year	2010 CU	2011 CU	2012 CU	2013 CU	2014 CU	Total CU
Estimate of cumulative claims:						
At end of underwriting year	680	790	823	920	968	
One year later	673	785	840	903		
Two years later	692	776	845			
Three years later	697	771				
Four years later	702					
Estimate of cumulative claims	702	771	845	903	968	
Cumulative payments	(702)	(689)	(570)	(350)	(217)	
	–	82	275	553	751	1,661
Effect of discounting	–	(14)	(68)	(175)	(285)	(542)
Present value recognised in the statement of financial position	–	68	207	378	466	1,119

The example appears to be gross of reinsurance but IFRS 4 is silent on whether development information should be given on both a gross basis and a net basis. If the effect of reinsurance is significant it would seem appropriate to provide such information both gross and net of reinsurance.

The illustrative example also provides only five years of data although the standard itself requires ten (subject to the transitional relief upon first-time adoption). Given the long tail nature of many non-life insurance claims liabilities it is likely that many non-life insurers will still have claims outstanding at the reporting date that are more than ten years old and which will need to be included in a reconciliation of the development table to the statement of financial position.

IFRS 4 is also silent on the presentation of:

- exchange differences associated with insurance liabilities arising on retranslation;
- claims liabilities acquired in a business combination or portfolio transfer; and
- claims liabilities disposed of in a business combination or portfolio transfer.

As IFRS 4 is silent on these matters, a variety of treatments would appear to be permissible provided they are adequately explained to the users of the financial statements and consistently applied in each reporting period. For example, exchange rates could be fixed at the date the claims are incurred, the original reporting period dates or amounts could be retranslated at each reporting date. Claims liabilities acquired in a business combination or portfolio transfer could be reallocated to the prior reporting periods in which they were originally incurred by the acquiree or all liabilities could be allocated to the reporting period in which the acquisition/portfolio transfer occurred.

Aviva's loss (claims) development tables are shown below. These are presented on an accident year basis. Aviva discloses both gross and net insurance liabilities in this format.

Extract 54.42: Aviva plc (2007)

Notes to the consolidated financial statements [extract]
38   Insurance liabilities [extract]
(d)   Loss development tables
(i)   Description of tables

The tables that follow present the development of claim payments and the estimated ultimate cost of claims for the accident years 2001 to 2007. The upper half of the tables shows the cumulative amounts paid during successive years related to each accident year. For example, with respect to the accident year 2002, by the end of 2007 £5,618 million had actually been paid in settlement of claims. In addition, as reflected in the lower section of the table, the original estimated ultimate cost of claims of £6,250 million was re-estimated to be £6,122 million at 31 December 2007. This decrease from the original estimate is due to the combination of a number of factors. The original estimates will be increased or decreased, as more information becomes known about the individual claims and overall claim frequency and severity.

In 2005, the year of adoption of IFRS, only five years were required to be disclosed. This is being increased in each succeeding additional year, until ten years of information is included.

The Group aims to maintain strong reserves in respect of its non-life and health business in order to protect against adverse future claims experience and development. As claims develop and the ultimate cost of claims become more certain, the absence of adverse claims experience will then result in a release from earlier accident years as shown in the loss development tables. However, in order to maintain reserve adequacy, the Group transfers releases to current accident year (2007) reserves where the development of claims is less mature and there is much greater uncertainty attaching to the ultimate cost of claims. The release from prior accident year reserves during 2007 is also due to an improvement in the estimated ultimate cost of claims.

(ii)   Gross figures

Before the effect of reinsurance, the loss development table is:

Accident year	All prior years £m	2001 £m	2002 £m	2003 £m	2004 £m	2005 £m	2006 £m	2007 £m	**Total £m**
Gross cumulative claim payments									
At end of accident year		(3,029)	(2,952)	(2,819)	(2,971)	(3,345)	(3,653)	(4,393)	
One year later		(4,766)	(4,486)	(4,190)	(4,561)	(5,011)	(5,525)		
Two years later		(5,303)	(4,921)	(4,613)	(4,981)	(5,449)			
Three years later		(5,701)	(5,233)	(4,972)	(5,263)				
Four years later		(5,966)	(5,466)	(5,258)					
Five years later		(6,121)	(5,618)						
Six years later		(6,223)							
Estimate of gross ultimate claims									
At end of accident year		6,590	6,250	6,385	6,891	7,106	7,533	8,530	
One year later		6,770	6,372	6,172	6,557	6,938	7,318		
Two years later		6,775	6,287	6,124	6,371	6,813			
Three years later		6,798	6,257	6,036	6,178				
Four years later		6,754	6,205	5,932					
Five years later		6,679	6,122						
Six years later		6,630							
Estimate of gross ultimate claims		6,630	6,122	5,932	6,178	6,813	7,318	8,530	
Cumulative payments		(6,223)	(5,618)	(5,258)	(5,263)	(5,449)	(5,525)	(4,393)	
	3,201	407	504	674	915	1,364	1,793	4,137	**12,995**
Effect of discounting	(266)	(4)	(4)	(4)	(2)	(3)	(5)	(9)	**(297)**
Present value	2,935	403	500	670	913	1,361	1,788	4,128	**12,698**
Cumulative effect of foreign exchange movements	–	19	24	37	46	36	99	–	**261**
Effect of acquisitions	12	3	2	63	17	23	29	34	**183**
Present value recognised in the balance sheet	2,947	425	526	770	976	1,420	1,916	4,162	**13,142**

Chapter 54

(iii)   Net of reinsurance

After the effect of reinsurance, the loss development table is:

Accident year	All prior years £m	2001 £m	2002 £m	2003 £m	2004 £m	2005 £m	2006 £m	2007 £m	Total £m
Net cumulative claim payments									
At end of accident year		(2,970)	(2,913)	(2,819)	(2,870)	(3,281)	(3,612)	(4,317)	
One year later		(4,624)	(4,369)	(4,158)	(4,378)	(4,925)	(5,442)		
Two years later		(5,088)	(4,779)	(4,565)	(4,712)	(5,344)			
Three years later		(5,436)	(5,064)	(4,924)	(4,986)				
Four years later		(5,648)	(5,297)	(5,180)					
Five years later		(5,763)	(5,424)						
Six years later		(5,841)							
Estimate of net ultimate claims									
At end of accident year		6,186	6,037	6,218	6,602	6,982	7,430	8,363	
One year later		6,333	6,038	6,093	6,266	6,818	7,197		
Two years later		6,321	5,997	6,037	6,082	6,688			
Three years later		6,329	5,973	5,942	5,882				
Four years later		6,286	5,912	5,851					
Five years later		6,219	5,855						
Six years later		6,173							
Estimate of net ultimate claims		6,173	5,855	5,851	5,882	6,688	7,197	8,363	
Cumulative payments		(5,841)	(5,424)	(5,180)	(4,986)	(5,344)	(5,442)	(4,317)	
	1,634	332	431	671	896	1,344	1,755	4,046	**11,109**
Effect of discounting	(39)	(3)	(4)	(4)	(2)	(3)	(5)	(9)	**(69)**
Present value	1,595	329	427	667	894	1,341	1,750	4,037	**11,040**
Cumulative effect of foreign exchange movements	–	13	21	34	45	34	97	–	**244**
Effect of acquisitions	8	2	2	43	16	22	28	19	**140**
Present value recognised in the balance sheet	1,603	344	450	744	955	1,397	1,875	4,056	**11,424**

In the loss development tables shown above, the cumulative claim payments and estimates of cumulative claims for each accident year are translated into sterling at the exchange rates that applied at the end of that accident year. The impact of using varying exchange rates is shown at the bottom of each table. Disposals are dealt with by treating all outstanding and IBNR claims of the disposed entity as "paid" at the date of disposal. The loss development tables above include information on asbestos and environmental pollution claims provisions from business written before 2001. The claim provisions, net of reinsurance, in respect of this business at 31 December 2007 were £323 million (*2006: £312 million*). The movement in the year reflects strengthening of provisions by £20 million (*2006: £9 million*), foreign exchange rate movements and timing differences between claim payments and reinsurance recoveries.

10.2.6   *Credit risk, liquidity risk and market risk disclosures*

As noted at 10.2 above, IFRS 4 also requires disclosure of information about credit risk, liquidity risk and market risk that would be required by IFRS 7 if insurance contracts were within the scope of that standard. *[IFRS 4.39(d)].*

Such disclosure should include:

- summary quantitative data about exposure to those risks based on information provided internally to key management personnel; and

- to the extent not already covered by the disclosures discussed above, the information required by IFRS 7.

IFRS 7 allows disclosures about credit risk, liquidity risk and market risk to be either provided in the financial statements or incorporated by cross-reference to some other statement, such as a management commentary or risk report, that is available to users of the financial statements on the same terms as the financial statements and at the same time. This approach is also permitted for the equivalent disclosures about insurance contracts. *[IFRS 4.IG62].*

To be informative, the disclosure about credit risk, liquidity risk and market risk might include:

(a)   information about the extent to which features such as policyholder participation features might mitigate or compound those risks;

(b)   a summary of significant guarantees, and of the levels at which guarantees of market prices or interest rates are likely to alter cash flows; and

(c)   the basis for determining investment returns credited to policyholders, such as whether the returns are fixed, based contractually on the return of specified assets or partly or wholly subject to the insurer's discretion. *[IFRS 4.IG64].*

10.2.6.A   *Credit risk disclosures*

Credit risk is defined in IFRS 7 as 'the risk that one party to a financial instrument will fail to discharge an obligation and cause the other party to incur a financial loss'.

For a reinsurance contract, credit risk includes the risk that the insurer incurs a financial loss because a reinsurer defaults on its obligations under a reinsurance contract. Furthermore, disputes with reinsurers could lead to impairments of the cedant's reinsurance assets. The risk of such disputes may have an effect similar to credit risk. Thus, similar disclosure might be relevant. Balances due from agents or brokers may also be subject to credit risk. *[IFRS 4.IG64A].*

Chapter 54

The specific disclosure requirements about credit risk in IFRS 7 are:

(a)   an amount representing the maximum exposure to credit risk at the reporting date without taking account of any collateral held or other credit enhancements;

(b)   in respect of the amount above, a description of the collateral held as security and other credit enhancements;

(c)   information about the credit quality of financial assets that are neither past due nor impaired;

(d)   the carrying amount of financial assets that would otherwise be past due or impaired whose terms have been renegotiated;

(e)   for financial assets:

(i)   an analysis of the age of those that are past due at the reporting date but not impaired;

(ii)   an analysis of those that are individually determined to be impaired as at the reporting date, including the factors considered in determining that they are impaired; and

(iii)   for the amounts disclosed above a description of collateral held as security and other credit enhancements and, unless impracticable, an estimate of the fair value of this collateral or credit enhancement.

(f)   when financial or non financial assets held as security are taken possession of during the reporting period and such assets meet the recognition criteria in other IFRSs disclosure is required of:

(i)   the nature and carrying amount of the assets obtained; and

(ii)   when the assets are not readily convertible into cash, the entity's policies for disposing of such assets or for using them in its operations.

The disclosures in (a) to (e) above are to be given by class of financial instrument. *[IFRS 7.36-38].*

IFRS 7 also contains a requirement to disclose a reconciliation of an entity's allowance account for credit losses. However, this requirement does not apply to insurance contracts as the relevant paragraph in IFRS 7 is not specified in IFRS 4 as one of those that should be applied to insurance contracts. Nevertheless, this requirement does apply to financial assets held by insurers that are within the scope of IAS 39 (or IFRS 9), such as mortgages and other loans and receivables due from intermediaries which have a financing character or are due from those not acting in a fiduciary capacity.

Zurich Financial Services provides the following disclosures about the credit risk for reinsurance assets and insurance receivables.

Extract 54.43: Zurich Financial Services Group (2008)

Consolidated financial statements [extract]
Risk review [extract]
Credit risk relating to reinsurance assets [extract]

As part of our overall risk management strategy, the Group cedes insurance risk through proportional, non-proportional and specific risk reinsurance treaties. While these cessions mitigate insurance risk, the recoverables from reinsurers and receivables arising from ceded reinsurance expose the Group to credit risk.

Our Corporate Reinsurance Security Committee manages the credit quality of our cessions and reinsurance assets. The Group typically cedes new business to authorized reinsurers with a minimum rating of BBB. The premiums ceded to reinsurers that are below investment grade or not rated are to a large extent collateralized.

Reinsurance assets include reinsurance recoverables of USD 18,595 million and USD 26,970 million as of December 31, 2008 and 2007, respectively, which are the reinsurer's share of reserves for insurance contracts, and receivables arising from ceded reinsurance of USD 1,166 million and USD 1,372 million as of December 31, 2008 and 2007, respectively. Expected reserves for uncollectable amounts of reinsurance assets amount to USD 206 million and USD 239 million as of December 31, 2008 and 2007, respectively.

Reinsurance assets in the table below are shown before taking into account the fair value of credit default swaps, bought by the Group to mitigate credit risks of the reinsurance exposure, and other collateral such as cash or letters of credit from banks rated at least 'A', which can be converted into cash and deposits received under ceded reinsurance contracts. The decrease of reinsurance assets in 2008 compared with 2007 is mainly attributable to the sale of a pension annuity portfolio to the reinsurer, subsequent to the approval from the UK High Court, effective on June 30, 2008.

The weighted average credit quality of the reinsurance assets (including receivables, but after deduction of collateral) was 'A' as of December 31, 2008 and 2007, respectively. For credit risk assessment purposes collateral has been taken into account at nominal value as an approximation for fair value. For collateral we apply minimum requirements, such as a minimum rating for the issuers of letters of credit and guarantees, and for pledged assets a minimum coverage ratio of 100 per cent.

Table 10 – Reinsurance premiums ceded and reinsurance assets by rating of reinsurer

for the years ended December 31

	2008				2007			
	Premiums ceded		Reinsurance assets		Premiums ceded		Reinsurance assets	
	USD millions	% of total	USD millions	% of total	USD millions	% of total	USD millions	% of total
Rating								
AAA	189	3%	417	2%	234	2%	542	2%
AA	1,495	24%	9,106	47%	9,203	70%	18,149	65%
A	2,465	40%	6,368	33%	1,796	14%	5,956	21%
BBB	706	11%	1,291	7%	670	5%	1,320	5%
BB	172	3%	280	1%	215	2%	461	2%
B	70	1%	96	–	15	–	162	1%
Unrated	1,129	18%	1,996	10%	1,064	8%	1,513	5%
Total	**6,226**	**100%**	**19,554**	**100%**	**13,197**	**100%**	**28,103**	**100%**

Chapter 54

Credit risk relating to receivables

The Group's credit risk exposure to receivables from third party agents, brokers and other intermediaries arises where they collect premiums from customers to be paid to the Group or pay claims to customers on behalf of the Group. Receivables from ceded reinsurance form part of the reinsurance assets and are managed accordingly. The Group has policies and standards to manage and monitor credit risk from intermediaries with a focus in day-to-day monitoring of the largest positions. As part of these standards the Group requires that intermediaries maintain segregated cash accounts for policyholder money. Additionally, the Group requires intermediaries to satisfy minimum requirements in terms of their capitalization, reputation and experience as well as providing short-dated business credit terms. Past due but not impaired receivables should be regarded as unsecured, but some of these receivable positions may be offset by collateral.

10.2.6.B   Liquidity risk disclosures

Liquidity risk is defined in IFRS 7 as 'the risk that an entity will encounter difficulty in meeting obligations associated with financial liabilities that are settled by delivering cash or another financial asset'.

The specific disclosure requirements in IFRS 7 relating to liquidity risk are:

(a)   a maturity analysis for non-derivative financial liabilities (including issued financial guarantee contracts) that shows the remaining contractual maturities;

(b)   a maturity analysis for derivative financial liabilities. The maturity analysis should include the remaining contractual maturities for those derivative financial liabilities for which contractual maturities are essential for an understanding of the timing of cash flows; and

(c)   a description of how the liquidity risk inherent in (a) and (b) is managed. *[IFRS 7.39]*.

IFRS 7 also requires disclosure of a maturity analysis of financial assets an entity holds for managing liquidity risk (e.g. financial assets that are readily saleable or expected to generate cash inflows to meet cash outflows on financial liabilities) if that information is necessary to enable users of its financial statements to evaluate the nature and extent of liquidity risk. *[IFRS 7.B11E]*. As most insurers hold financial assets in order to manage liquidity risk (i.e. to pay claims) they are likely to have to provide such an analysis and, indeed, some insurers have historically provided such an analysis.

For financial liabilities within the scope of IFRS 7 the maturity analysis should present undiscounted contractual amounts. *[IFRS 7.B11D]*. However, an insurer need not present the maturity analyses of insurance liabilities using undiscounted contractual cash flows if it discloses information about the estimated timing of the net cash outflows resulting from recognised insurance liabilities instead. This may take the form of an analysis, by estimated timing, of the amounts recognised in the statement of financial position. *[IFRS 4.39(d)(i)]*. The guidance in respect of the maturity analysis for financial assets is silent as to whether such analysis should be on a contractual undiscounted basis or on the basis of the amounts recognised in the statement of financial position.

The reason for this concession is to avoid insurers having to disclose detailed cash flow estimates for insurance liabilities that are not required for measurement purposes. Because various accounting practices for insurance contracts are permitted, an insurer may not need to make detailed estimates of cash flows to determine the amounts recognised in the statement of financial position. *[IFRS 4.IG65B]*.

However, this concession is not available for investment contracts whether or not they contain a DPF. These contracts are within the scope of IFRS 7 not IFRS 4. Consequently, a maturity analysis of contractual undiscounted amounts is required for these liabilities.

An insurer might need to disclose a summary narrative description of how the flows in the maturity analysis (or analysis by estimated timing) could change if policyholders exercised lapse or surrender options in different ways. If lapse behaviour is likely to be sensitive to interest rates, that fact might be disclosed as well as whether the disclosures about market risk (see 10.2.6.C below) reflect that interdependence. *[IFRS 4.IG65C].*

Prudential's liability maturity analysis for its UK insurance operations is shown below. The disclosure is on a discounted basis and includes investment contracts although, as stated in a footnote to the table, an undiscounted maturity profile of those investment contracts is disclosed elsewhere in the financial statements.

Extract 54.44: Prudential plc (2008)

Notes on the group financial statements [extract]
D2. UK insurance operations [extract]
K. Duration of liabilities

With the exception of most unitised with-profit bonds and other whole of life contracts the majority of the contracts of the UK insurance operations have a contract term. However, in effect, the maturity term of contracts reflects the earlier of death, maturity, or lapsation. In addition, with-profit contract liabilities as noted in D2(g) above include projected future bonuses based on current investment values. The actual amounts payable will vary with future investment performance of SAIF and the WPSF.

The tables below show the carrying value of the policyholder liabilities. Separately, the Group uses cash flow projections of expected benefit payments as part of the determination of the value of in-force business when preparing EEV basis results. The tables below also show the maturity profile of the cash flows used for 2008 and 2007 for that purpose for insurance contracts, as defined by IFRS, i.e. those containing significant insurance risk, and investment contracts, which do not.

| | With-profits business | | | 2008 £m Annuity business (insurance contracts) | | | Other | | |
	Insurance contracts	Investment contracts	Total	PAL	PRIL	Total	Insurance contracts	Investment contracts	Total
Policyholder liabilities	39,010	23,367	62,377	11,477	12,513	23,990	9,756	11,584	21,340
				2008%					
Expected maturity:									
0 to 5 years	47	26	38	30	29	29	31	32	32
5 to 10 years	26	23	25	24	23	23	23	22	23
10 to 15 years	13	19	15	18	17	18	18	18	18
15 to 20 years	7	15	10	12	13	13	12	12	12
20 to 25 years	4	11	7	8	8	8	8	7	7
Over 25 years	3	6	5	8	10	9	8	9	8

Notes

i The cash flow projections of expected benefit payments used in the maturity profile table above are from value of in-force business and exclude the value of future new business, including vesting of internal pension contracts.

ii Benefit payments do not reflect the pattern of bonuses and shareholder transfers in respect of the with profits business.

iii Investment contracts under Other comprise certain unit-linked and similar contracts accounted for under IAS 39 and IAS 18.

iv For business with no maturity term included within the contracts, for example with-profits investment bonds such as Prudence Bond, an assumption is made as to likely duration based on prior experience.

v The maturity tables shown above have been prepared on a discounted basis. Details of undiscounted cash flow for investment contracts are shown in note G2.

10.2.6.C   Market risk disclosures

Market risk is defined in IFRS 7 as 'the risk that the fair value or future cash flows of a financial instrument will fluctuate because of changes in market prices'. Market risk comprises three types of risk: currency risk, interest rate risk and other price risk.

The specific disclosure requirements in respect of market risk are:

(a)   a sensitivity analysis for each type of market risk to which there is exposure at the reporting date, showing how profit or loss and equity would have been affected by changes in the relevant risk variable that were reasonably possible at that date;

(b)   the methods and assumptions used in preparing that sensitivity analysis; and

(c)   changes from the previous reporting period in the methods and assumptions used, and the reasons for such changes. *[IFRS 7.40]*.

These disclosures are required for insurance contracts. However, if an insurer uses an alternative method to manage sensitivity to market conditions, such as an embedded value analysis, it may use that sensitivity analysis to meet the requirements of IFRS 4. *[IFRS 4.39(d)(ii)]*. In addition, it should also disclose:

(a)   an explanation of the method used in preparing such a sensitivity analysis, and of the main parameters and assumptions underlying the data provided; and

(b)   an explanation of the objective of the method used and of limitations that may result in the information not fully reflecting the fair value of the assets and liabilities involved. *[IFRS 7.41]*.

Because two approaches are permitted, an insurer might use different approaches for different classes of business. *[IFRS 4.IG65G]*.

Where the sensitivity analysis disclosed is not representative of the risk inherent in the instrument (for example because the year-end exposure does not reflect the exposure during the year), that fact should be disclosed together with the reasons the sensitivity analyses are unrepresentative. *[IFRS 7.42]*.

If no reasonably possible change in a relevant risk variable would affect either profit or loss or equity, that fact should be disclosed. A reasonably possible change in the relevant risk variable might not affect profit or loss in the following examples:

- if a non-life insurance liability is not discounted, changes in market interest rates would not affect profit or loss; and

- some entities may use valuation factors that blend together the effect of various market and non-market assumptions that do not change unless there is an assessment that the recognised insurance liability is not adequate. In some cases a reasonably possible change in the relevant risk variable would not affect the adequacy of the recognised insurance liability. *[IFRS 4.IG65D].*

In some accounting models, a regulator may specify discount rates or other assumptions about market risk variables that are used in measuring insurance liabilities and the regulator may not amend those assumptions to reflect current market conditions at all times. In such cases, compliance with the requirements might be achieved by disclosing:

(a) the effect on profit or loss or equity of a reasonably possible change in the assumption set by the regulator; and

(b) the fact that the assumption set by the regulator would not necessarily change at the same time, by the same amount, or in the same direction, as changes in market prices, or market rates, would imply. *[IFRS 4.IG65E].*

An insurer might be able to take action to reduce the effect of changes in market conditions. For example, it may have discretion to change surrender values or maturity benefits, or to vary the amount or timing of policyholder benefits arising from discretionary participation features. There is no requirement for entities to consider the potential effect of future management actions that may offset the effect of the disclosed changes in any relevant risk variable. However, disclosure is required of the methods and assumptions used to prepare any sensitivity analysis. To comply with this requirement, disclosure of the extent of available management actions and their effect on the sensitivity analysis might be required. *[IFRS 4.IG65F].*

Because some insurers manage sensitivity to market conditions using alternative methods as discussed above, different sensitivity approaches may be used for different classes of insurance contracts. *[IFRS 4.IG65G].*

Some insurers combine their market risk disclosures with their other sensitivity disclosures. Extract 54.39 (Legal & General) at 10.2.3 above is an illustration of this.

Many life insurance contract liabilities are backed by matching assets. In these circumstances giving isolated disclosures about the variability of, say, interest rates on the valuation of the liabilities without linking this to the impact on the assets could be misleading to users of the financial statements. In these circumstances it may be useful to provide information as to the linkage of market risk sensitivities.

10.2.7   Exposures to market risk from embedded derivatives

As noted at 10.2 above, disclosure is required if there are exposures to market risk arising from embedded derivatives contained in a host insurance contract if the insurer is not required to, and does not, measure the embedded derivatives at fair value. *[IFRS 4.39(e)].*

Chapter 54

Fair value measurement is not required for derivatives embedded in an insurance contract if the embedded derivative is itself an insurance contract (see 4 above). Examples of these include guaranteed annuity options and guaranteed minimum death benefits as illustrated below. *[IFRS 4.IG66].*

Example 54.35:   Contract containing a guaranteed annuity option

An insurer issues a contract under which the policyholder pays a fixed monthly premium for thirty years. At maturity, the policyholder can elect to take either (a) a lump sum equal to the accumulated investment value or (b) a lifetime annuity at a rate guaranteed at inception (i.e. when the contract started). This is an example of a contract containing a guaranteed annuity option.

For policyholders electing to receive the annuity, the insurer could suffer a significant loss if interest rates decline substantially or if the policyholder lives much longer than the average. The insurer is exposed to both market risk and significant insurance risk (mortality risk) and the transfer of insurance risk occurs at inception of the contract because the insurer fixed the price for mortality risk at that date. Therefore, the contract is an insurance contract from inception. Moreover, the embedded guaranteed annuity option itself meets the definition of an insurance contract, and so separation is not required. *[IFRS 4.IG67].*

Example 54.36:   Contract containing minimum guaranteed death benefits

An insurer issues a contract under which the policyholder pays a monthly premium for 30 years. Most of the premiums are invested in a mutual fund. The rest is used to buy life cover and to cover expenses. On maturity or surrender, the insurer pays the value of the mutual fund units at that date. On death before final maturity, the insurer pays the greater of (a) the current unit value and (b) a fixed amount. This is an example of a contract containing minimum guaranteed death benefits. It is an insurance contract because the insurer is exposed to significant insurance risk as the fixed amount payable on death before maturity could be greater than the unit value.

It could be viewed as a hybrid contract comprising (a) a mutual fund investment and (b) an embedded life insurance contract that pays a death benefit equal to the fixed amount less the current unit value (but zero if the current unit value is more than the fixed amount). *[IFRS 4.IG68].*

Both of the examples of embedded derivatives above meet the definition of an insurance contract where the insurance risk is deemed significant. However, in both cases, market risk or interest rate risk may be much more significant than the mortality risk. So, if interest rates or equity markets fall substantially, these guarantees would have significant value. Given the long-term nature of the guarantees and the size of the exposures, an insurer might face extremely large losses in certain scenarios. Therefore, particular emphasis on disclosures about such exposures might be required. *[IFRS 4.IG69].*

To be informative, disclosures about such exposures may include:

• the sensitivity analysis discussed at 10.2.6.C above;

• information about the levels where these exposures start to have a material effect on the insurer's cash flows; and

• the fair value of the embedded derivative, although this is not a required disclosure. *[IFRS 4.IG70].*

An extract of Aviva's disclosures in respect of financial guarantees and options is shown below.

Extract 54.45: Aviva plc (2008)

Notes to the consolidated financial statements [extract]
Note 40 **Financial guarantees and options** [extract]

(iii) Ireland

Guaranteed annuity options

Products with similar GAO's to those offered in the UK have been issued in Ireland. The current net of reinsurance provision for such options is £180 million (2007: £160 million). This has been calculated on a deterministic basis, making conservative assumptions for the factors which influence the cost of the guarantee, principally annuitant mortality option take-up and long-term interest rates.

These GAOs are "in the money" at current interest rates but the exposure to interest rates under these contracts has been hedged through the use of reinsurance, using derivatives (swaptions). The swaptions effectively guarantee that an interest rate of 5% will be available at the vesting date of these benefits so there is reduced exposure to a further decrease in interest rates.

"No MVR" guarantees

Certain unitised with-profit policies containing "no MVR" guarantees, similar to those in the UK, have been sold in Ireland.

These guarantees are currently "in-the-money" by £16 million (2007: "out-of-the-money" by £53 million). This has been calculated on a deterministic basis as the excess of the current policy surrender value over the discounted value (excluding terminal bonus) of the guarantees. The value of these guarantees is sensitive to the performance of investments held in the with-profit fund. Amounts payable under these guarantees are determined by the bonuses declared on these policies. It is estimated that the guarantees would be "in-the-money" by £16 million (2007: "out-of-the-money" by £46 million) if yields were to increase by 1% per annum and by £16 million (2007: "out-of-the-money" by £29 million) if equity markets were to decline by 10% from year end 2008 levels. There is no sensitivity to either interest rates or equity markets since there is no longer any exposure to equity in those funds and a matching strategy has been implemented for bonds.

Return of premium guarantee

Until 2005, Hibernian Life wrote two tranches of linked bonds with a return of premium guarantee, or a price floor guarantee, after five or six years. The provision for these over and above unit and sterling reserves, at the end of 2008 is £18 million (2007: £0.1 million).

It is estimated that the provision would increase by £4 million (2007: £1 million) if equity markets were to decline by 10% from year end 2008 levels. However, the provision increase would be broadly off-set by an increase in the value of the hedging assets that were set up on sale of these policies. We would not expect any significant impact on this provision as a result of interest rate movements. It is estimated that the provision would increase by £2 million if property values were to decline by 10% from year end 2008 levels. This would be offset by an increase in the value of the hedging assets by £1 million, the difference reflecting the fact that only the second tranche was hedged for property exposure.

10.2.8 Other disclosure matters

10.2.8.A IAS 1 capital disclosures

Most insurance entities are exposed to externally imposed capital requirements and therefore the IAS 1 disclosures in respect of these requirements are likely to be applicable.

Where an entity is subject to externally imposed capital requirements, disclosures are required of the nature of these requirements and how these requirements are incorporated into the management of capital. Disclosure of whether these requirements have been complied with in the reporting period is also required and, where they have not been complied with, the consequences of such non-compliance. [IAS 1.135].

Many insurance entities operate in several jurisdictions. Where an aggregate disclosure of capital requirements and how capital is managed would not provide useful information or distorts a financial statement user's understanding of an entity's capital resources separate information should be disclosed for each capital requirement to which an entity is subject. [IAS 1.136].

Although there is no explicit requirement to disclose the amounts of the regulatory capital requirements, some insurers do so to assist users of the financial statements. Ping An is an example of an entity that discloses its externally imposed regulatory capital requirements.

Extract 54.46: Ping An Insurance (Group) Company of China Ltd (2008)

Notes to the financial statements [extract]
41. Risk and capital management [extract]
(6) Capital management [extract]

The Group's capital requirements are primarily dependent on the scale and the type of business that it underwrites, as well as the industry and geographic location in which it operates. The primary objectives of the Group's capital management are to ensure that the Group complies with externally imposed capital requirements and that the Group maintains healthy capital ratios in order to support its business and to maximize shareholders' value.

The Group manages its capital requirements by assessing shortfalls, if any, between the reported and the required capital levels on a regular basis. Adjustments to current capital levels are made in light of changes in economic conditions and risk characteristics of the Group's activities. In order to maintain or adjust the capital structure, the Group may adjust the amount of dividends paid, return capital to ordinary shareholders or issue capital securities.

The Group fully complied with the externally imposed capital requirements as at 31 December 2008 and no changes were made to its capital base, objectives, policies and processes from the previous year.

The table below summarizes the minimum regulatory capital for major insurance subsidiaries of the Group and the regulatory capital held against each of them.

	December 31, 2008			December 31, 2007		
(in RMB million)	Regulatory capital held	Minimum regulatory capital	Solvency margin ratio	Regulatory capital held	Minimum regulatory capital	Solvency margin ratio
The Group	**88,270**	**28,663**	**308.0%**	121,104	24,883	486.7%
Ping An life	**33,752**	**18,371**	**183.7%**	45,218	15,704	287.9%
Ping An Property & casualty	**5,047**	**3,293**	**153.3%**	4,895	2,695	181.6%

As discussed at 7.2.1 above, equalisation and catastrophe provisions are not liabilities but are a component of equity. Therefore, they are subject to the disclosure requirements in IAS 1 for equity. IAS 1 requires disclosure of a description of the nature and purpose of each reserve within equity. [IFRS 4.IG58].

10.2.8.B   Financial guarantee contracts

A financial guarantee contract reimburses a loss incurred by the holder because a specified debtor fails to make payment when due. The holder of such a contract is exposed to credit risk and is required by IFRS 7 to make disclosures about that credit risk. However, from the perspective of the issuer, the risk assumed by the issuer is insurance risk rather than credit risk. *[IFRS 4.IG64B]*.

As discussed at 2.2.3.D above, the issuer of a financial guarantee contract should provide disclosures complying with IFRS 7 if it applies IAS 39 (or IFRS 9) in recognising and measuring the contract. However, if the issuer elects, when permitted, to apply IFRS 4 in recognising and measuring the contract, it provides disclosures complying with IFRS 4. The main implications are as follows:

(a)   IFRS 4 requires disclosure about actual claims compared with previous estimates (claims development), but does not require disclosure of the fair value of the contract; and

(b)   IFRS 7 requires disclosure of the fair value of the contract, but does not require disclosure of claims development. *[IFRS 4.IG65A]*.

10.2.8.C   Fair value disclosures

Insurance contracts are not excluded from the scope of IFRS 13 and therefore any insurance contracts measured at fair value are also subject to the disclosures required by IFRS 13. However, insurance contracts are excluded from the scope of IFRS 7.

Disclosure of the fair value of investment contracts with a DPF is not required by IFRS 7 if the fair value of that feature cannot be measured reliably. *[IFRS 7.29(c)]*. However, IFRS 7 does require additional information about fair value in these circumstances including disclosure that fair value information has not been provided because fair value cannot be reliably measured, an explanation of why fair value cannot be reliably measured, information about the market for the instruments, information about whether and how the entity intends to dispose of the financial instruments and any gain or loss recognised on derecognition. *[IFRS 7.30]*.

For insurance contracts and investment contract liabilities with and without a DPF which are measured at fair value, disclosures required by IFRS 13 include the level in the fair value hierarchy in which the liabilities are categorised. *[IFRS 13.93]*. Very few insurance or investment contract liabilities are likely to have quoted prices (unadjusted) in active markets and are therefore likely to be Level 2 or Level 3 measurements under IFRS 13.

For investment contract liabilities without a DPF measured at amortised cost, disclosure of the fair value of those contracts is required as well as the assumptions applied in determining those fair values and the level of the fair value hierarchy in which those fair value measurements are categorised. *[IFRS 13.97]*.

When unit-linked investment liabilities are matched by associated financial assets some have argued that there is no fair value adjustment for credit risk as the liability is simply the value of the asset. However, there will be at least some risk, however small, of non-payment with regard to the liability. Therefore, it would be appropriate to provide some form of qualitative disclosure that credit risk was taken into account in assessing the fair value of the liability or why it was thought to be immaterial and/or relevant only in extreme situations.

10.2.8.D   Key performance indicators

IFRS 4 does not require disclosure of key performance indicators. However, such disclosures might be a useful way for an insurer to explain its financial performance during the period and to give an insight into the risks arising from insurance contracts. *[IFRS 4.IG71].*

11   FUTURE DEVELOPMENTS IN INSURANCE CONTRACT ACCOUNTING

11.1   The Phase II discussion paper

In May 2007 the IASB published a Discussion Paper (DP) – *Preliminary Views on Insurance Contracts.* The DP contained the IASB's preliminary views on various recognition and measurement issues to be considered in accounting for insurance contracts and set out the issues that were still under consideration.

The key proposal of the DP was that insurance contract liabilities would be measured at the amount that an insurer would expect to pay at the reporting date to transfer its remaining contractual rights and obligations immediately to another party. The IASB referred to this measurement model as 'current exit value'.

Nearly all of the respondents to the discussion paper had significant concerns about particular aspects of the building blocks proposed in the DP. As a result, at its June 2009 meeting, the IASB rejected the 'current exit value' model proposed by the DP.[32]

11.2   The Phase II Exposure Draft

In July 2010, the IASB published an Exposure Draft (2010 ED), ED 2010/8 – *Insurance Contracts.*

The 2010 ED proposed that an insurer should measure insurance liabilities using a model based on the 'present value of fulfilment cash flows' plus a residual margin when required to eliminate day 1 gains. The residual margin is set up at inception and recognised over the policy coverage period. It is not re-estimated. For most short-duration contracts a modified version of the measurement approach will apply. In the modified version, the fulfilment cash flows approach will be used only for events that have already occurred (incurred claims liability). During the contract period, the insurer would measure the contract using an allocation of the total premium for that period, on a basis similar to the unearned premium approach used in much existing practice.

The 2010 ED proposed that the modified method be mandatory for those contracts whose coverage period is approximately one year or less that do not contain significant embedded options or derivatives. Consequently, entities that write both short-term and long-term contracts would have two different measurements and two different sets of disclosure requirements.

The 'present value of fulfilment cash flows' approach uses the following building blocks:

- a current estimate of future cash flows;
- a discount rate that adjusts those cash flows for the time value of money; and
- an explicit risk adjustment.

An entity should incorporate, in an unbiased way, all available information about the amount, timing and uncertainty of all cash flows that will arise as the contract is fulfilled. Cash flows should also be remeasured at the end of each reporting period and any movements reported in profit or loss.

The discount rate should adjust the cash flows for the time value of money in a way that captures the characteristics of the liability. It is implied that the discount rate is based on the risk-free rate adjusted for the characteristics unique to the liability such as illiquidity. Own credit risk is specifically excluded. If the cash flows depend wholly, or in part, on the performance of specific assets then the measurement of the contract should reflect that fact.

The risk adjustment is intended to capture the effects of uncertainty associated with the cash flows arising from the contract. It should be the maximum amount that the insurer would rationally pay to be relieved of the risk that the ultimate fulfilment cash flows may exceed those expected. The risk adjustment should be determined for each separate portfolio of insurance contracts without any credit for diversification of risk between those portfolios.

A high-level summary of other matters addressed by the 2010 ED is as follows:

- financial investments with a DPF are included within the scope of the proposed standard only if they invest in the same pool of assets as insurance contracts;
- fixed-fee service contracts are excluded from the scope of the proposed standard;
- financial guarantee contracts are included within the scope of the proposed standard and not IAS 39 (or IFRS 9);
- an entity must recognise an insurance obligation at the earlier of when it is bound by the contract or first exposed to risk. Accordingly, an insurer may have to recognise a contract prior to the start of the coverage period;
- a contract boundary is defined as the point at which an insurer either: (a) is no longer required to provide coverage, or (b) has the right and practical ability to reassess the risk of a particular policyholder and, as a result, can set a price that fully reflects that risk;
- entities are required to unbundle components of contracts that are not closely related to the insurance coverage;
- reinsurance contracts are measured initially at the present value of the fulfilment cash flows including the risk of non-performance by the reinsurer. If the present value of the fulfilment cash flows for the reinsurance contract is greater than zero a gain is recognised in profit or loss. However, if the present value of the fulfilment cash flows is less than zero then the cedant should record the difference as a residual margin within the reinsurance asset;

Chapter 54

- acquisition costs can be included in the present value of fulfilment cash flows only to the extent that they are incremental at an individual contract level. These increase the present value of the fulfilment cash flows thereby decreasing the residual margin. Non incremental costs are expensed as incurred;

- all expected cash flows resulting from participating features should be included in the measurement of insurance contracts in the same way as any other contractual cash flow;

- insurance contracts acquired via business combinations must be measured at the higher of the fair value of the portfolio and the present value of the fulfilment cash flows. If the fair value is higher, the difference is recognised as a residual margin. If the fair value is lower, the difference is additional goodwill;

- insurance contracts acquired via portfolio transfers are initially measured at the higher of either the consideration received or the present value of the fulfilment cash flows. If the consideration is higher, then the difference is recognised as a residual margin. If the present value of fulfilment cash flows is higher, then a loss should be recognised immediately.

The 2010 ED proposed a presentation model that focused on margins and other key performance information. The presentation model required those contracts not using the simplified short-term model to treat all premiums as deposits and all claims and benefits as repayments to the policyholder. As a result, volume measures such as premiums and claims were not permitted to be shown on the face of the income statement. Instead, minimum disclosures included changes to the risk adjustment in the period, the release of the residual margin, changes in estimates and the interest on insurance liabilities. This was a major change from most existing models where premiums and claims are shown on the face of the income statement.

For those contracts accounted for using the alternative short-term model an insurer was permitted to present premium revenue and claims incurred on the face of the income statement.

The 2010 ED proposed a number of additional disclosures for insurers including a reconciliation of the opening and closing aggregate contract balances with minimum prescribed line items and disclosure of the equivalent confidence levels implied by the risk adjustment if the risk adjustment is determined under the conditional tail expectation or cost of capital techniques.

On transition, the proposals required portfolios of insurance contracts to be measured at the present value of the fulfilment cash flows, starting at the earliest period presented. There was no residual margin on transition. Any difference between the fulfilment value cash flows and previous GAAP carrying amounts, which include existing deferred acquisition costs and intangible assets arising from insurance contracts assumed in prior business combinations, was recognised in retained earnings. The lack of a residual margin on transition would result in different measurements and profit recognition for those contracts in existence on transition date compared with those arising after transition.

11.3   The revised Phase II Exposure Draft

In June 2013, the IASB published a revised Exposure Draft (revised ED), ED 2013/7 – *Insurance Contracts*. The revised ED took into account the re-deliberations by the IASB since the July 2010 ED.

The measurement principles for insurance contracts that are set out in the revised ED are similar to those of the 2010 ED, i.e. a current value measurement model comprising of the expected present value of future cash flows, a risk adjustment and a contractual service margin (referred to as a residual margin in the 2010 ED). One of the main criticisms of the 2010 ED was that the proposed model, especially for long duration contracts, would, in effect force insurers to measure both assets and liabilities on a current value basis with the effects of remeasurement reported through profit or loss. Many comment letters on the 2010 ED expressed significant concern about the earnings volatility that would ensue because changes in market conditions would usually have a different impact on financial assets and insurance liabilities. In the respondents' view, such fluctuations would highlight short-term market fluctuations rather than reflect the expected long-term performance of an insurer. Another key concern was the presentation model in the statement of comprehensive income, in particular the removal of volume information such as premiums and claims caused by the IASB's decision to focus on summarised margin information. The comment letters in response to the 2010 ED also raised many other issues such as which cash flows and acquisition expenses to include, unbundling, the application of the simplified model and the treatment of reinsurance contracts.

Consequently, the IASB took on the challenges raised in the comment letters as part of its re-deliberations and made changes to many areas of the proposals. Although the IASB decided that re-exposure of the draft standard was necessary, it wanted to avoid re-opening areas that in its view had already been deliberated sufficiently during past discussions. As a result, the IASB invited comment only on five areas where it believed significant changes had been made compared with the 2010 ED:

- adjusting the contractual service margin for differences between current and previous estimates of future cash flows related to future coverage and other future services provided the contractual service margin is sufficient to absorb any unfavourable changes (the 2010 ED proposed that the margin was not adjusted subsequently);

- measuring fulfilment cash flows for certain types of contracts with participating features that vary directly with returns on underlying items by reference to the carrying amount of the underlying items with changes to the liabilities presented in profit or loss or other comprehensive income on the same basis as changes in the value of the underlying items (the 2010 ED did not contain such specific measurement and presentation guidance for these contracts);

- presentation of insurance contract revenue and expenses in profit or loss (the 2010 ED proposed that entities would use a summarised margin approach);

- recognising in other comprehensive income the impact of measuring the current value of the insurance contract using the current discount rate compared with the discount rate at contract inception (the 2010 ED proposed that all effects of changes in discount rates should always be presented in profit or loss); and

- proposing that, on transition, an entity should apply the standard retrospectively in accordance with IAS 8 unless impracticable in which case simplified transition requirements would be applied (the 2010 ED proposed that an entity should recognise no contractual service margin for contracts in force at the beginning of the earliest period presented).

Although the IASB only invited comment on these five areas, a number of other important changes were made compared with the 2010 ED which include the following:

- in determining which cash flows are included within the model, the 2010 ED made reference to cash flows that are incremental at the portfolio level. The revised ED includes all cash flows that relate directly to the fulfilment of a portfolio of contracts, including an allocation of fixed and variable overheads that are directly attributable to fulfilling that portfolio;

- in determining which cash flows are included in the model, the 2010 ED used acquisition costs that are incremental at the individual contract level. The revised ED uses acquisition costs which are directly attributable at the portfolio level that can be allocated on a rational and consistent basis, for both successful and unsuccessful efforts;

- the revised ED clarifies that two approaches can be used to establish discount rates: a 'top-down' approach and a 'bottom-up' approach. Guidance is also included that requires an insurer to estimate the inputs necessary to determine the relevant rates to the extent observable information is not available;

- the revised ED eliminates the guidance included in the 2010 ED that permitted only three methods for estimating the risk adjustment. Instead, the application guidance now focuses on setting out the characteristics that the risk adjustment should meet;

- the revised ED states that the contractual service margin should be recognised systematically in profit or loss over the coverage period in a way that best reflects the transfer of services under the contract. The 2010 ED proposed that the margin would be recognised in profit or loss in a way that best reflects the exposure from providing insurance coverage;

- the simplified model (referred to as the modified approach in the 2010 ED) is optional (rather than mandatory as in the 2010 ED) for those contracts which would produce measurements that are a reasonable approximation to those that would be produced using the building block approach or the coverage period of the contract at initial recognition arising from all premiums within the contract boundary is one year or less;

- the revised ED proposes that a cedant records any difference between the future cash inflows plus the risk adjustment and the future cash outflows of an acquired insurance contract as a contractual service margin. This means that, in contrast to the model for underlying direct contracts, the contractual service margin can be both positive and negative. However, if a reinsurance contract reimburses a cedant for liabilities incurred as a result of past events a negative contractual service margin is recognised in profit or loss immediately;

- ceded premiums are presented net of ceding commissions;

- cash flows that affect either the amount of ceded premiums or ceding commissions that are contingent on claims or benefits experience should be recognised as claims or benefit cash flows rather than premiums;

- the revised ED retains the 2010 ED definition of an insurance contract but adds that a reinsurance contract is deemed to transfer significant insurance risk if substantially all of the insurance risk is assumed by the reinsurer;

- there are additional criteria for scope exclusions regarding fixed-fee service contracts but the existing scoping for financial guarantee contracts from IFRS 4 has now been retained so that those contracts previously regarded as insurance contracts by the issuer would be accounted for under the new standard rather than IAS 39 (or IFRS 9);

- the revised ED clarifies that the standard would apply to financial instruments with discretionary participation features by an entity that also issues insurance contracts but eliminates the additional requirement from the 2010 ED that such contracts participate in the same pool of assets as insurance contracts;

- the definition of a portfolio is changed compared with the 2010 ED by adding a requirement that a portfolio of insurance contracts is priced similarly commensurate to the risk taken;

- the term 'unbundling' is no longer used; instead the revised ED refers to 'separating components from an insurance contract'. The revised ED requires an insurer to separate from an insurance contract (i) embedded derivatives if they meet certain specified criteria; (ii) distinct investment components; and (iii) performance obligations to provide goods and services;

- the revised ED requires an insurer to exclude from the statement of comprehensive income insurance contract revenue and incurred claims in respect of investment components that have not been separated;

- the revised ED clarifies that an insurance contract should be recognised at the earliest of: the beginning of the coverage period; the date when payments from the policyholder become due; or when there is evidence that a portfolio of insurance contracts is onerous. The 2010 ED proposed that an insurer should recognise an insurance contract when it becomes party to an insurance contract;

- the revised ED introduces guidance on how to treat modifications to insurance contracts;

- the revised ED clarifies that the date of recognition for contracts acquired in a portfolio transfer or business combination is the date of the transfer or the business combination; and

- the revised ED requires extensive disclosures in respect of reconciliations from the opening to the closing balance of the aggregate carrying amounts of insurance contract liabilities and insurance contract assets.

Chapter 54

The revised ED does not propose an effective date but instead states that the effective date will be around three years after the issuance of the final standard.

Comments on the revised ED were due by 25 October 2013. In its subsequent discussions, the IASB has made the following major tentative decisions which result in a change from the proposals in the revised ED:

- an entity will be able to make an accounting policy choice at a portfolio level whether to present the effects of changes in discount rates in profit or loss or in other comprehensive income (the revised ED proposed that the effects of all changes in discount rates would be presented in other comprehensive income);

- subsequent changes in cash flow estimates of reinsurance contracts held should be recognised in profit or loss by the cedant when changes in the expected reinsured losses of the underlying direct contracts are recognised in profit or loss. This would occur when, for example, the underlying contracts have become onerous and the contractual service margin on those contracts has been reduced to zero;

- for non-participating contracts, the coverage period that best represents the transfer of service represented by the contractual service margin is insurance coverage that (i) is provided on the basis of the passage of time and (ii) reflects the expected number of contracts in force;

- the contractual service margin should not only be adjusted for subsequent changes in estimates of future cash flows but also for subsequent changes to the risk adjustment;

- for contracts acquired through a portfolio transfer or in a business combination such contracts should be accounted for as if they had been issued by the entity as at the date of the portfolio transfer or business combination;

- significant insurance risk occurs only when there is a possibility that an issuer will incur a loss on a present value basis;

- reconciliations should be required of opening and closing balances of the components of the insurance contract asset or liability, of premiums received in the period to insurance premium revenue, inputs used in determining the insurance contract revenue recognised in the period and the effect of insurance contracts that are initially recognised in the period on the amounts that are recognised in the statement of financial position; and

- on transition, several simplifications have to be applied if the full retrospective approach would be impracticable according to IAS 8.

The major issue which has not been fully resolved at the time of writing this publication is the accounting for participating contracts. The IASB has spent some time discussing an alternative to the measurement and presentation exception ('mirroring approach') proposed in the revised ED which was generally criticised by respondents.

At its June 2015 meeting, the IASB tentatively decided that, for insurance contracts with direct participation features, it would modify the general measurement model so that changes in the estimate of the fee that the entity expects to earn from the contract are adjusted in the contractual service margin (the 'variable fee' approach).

The fee that the entity expects to earn from the contract is equal to the entity's expected share of the returns on underlying items, less any expected cash flows that do not vary directly with the underlying item for participating contracts (e.g. guarantee minimum benefits and expenses). The IASB tentatively decided that contracts with direct participation features should be defined as contracts for which:

- the contractual terms specify that the policyholder participates in a share of a clearly identified pool of underlying items;

- the entity expects to pay to the policyholder a substantial share of the returns from the underlying items; and

- a substantial proportion of the cash flows that the entity expects to pay to the policyholder should be expected to vary with thee cash flows from the underlying items.

The IASB also tentatively decided that for all insurance contracts with participation features, an entity should recognise the contractual service margin in profit or loss on the basis of the passage of time (and reflecting the expected number of contracts in force).[33]

At its September 2015 meeting, the IASB made a number of further tentative decisions as follows:

- for all insurance contracts, an entity shall present changes in estimates of the amount of cash flows that result from changes in market variables consistently with the way that the effects of the changes in discount rates are presented. For example, if the changes in discount rates are presented in other comprehensive income, those cash flow effects should also be presented in other comprehensive income;

- the standard shall specify the objective for disaggregating changes in the carrying amount of insurance contracts arising from changes in market variables between profit or loss and other comprehensive income, but it will not specify detailed mechanics for the determination of the insurance investment expense (i.e. the expense for interest accretion on the insurance liability) using a cost measurement basis (i.e. an effective yield approach);

- for contracts i) that meet the scope of the variable fee approach and ii) for which the entity holds the underlying items, the insurance investment expense item is determined consistently with the accounting returns reflected in profit or loss for those underlying assets (this is referred to as 'the current period book yield approach');

- when an entity is required to change between the effective yield approach and the current period book yield approach (and vice versa) the standard will specify the mechanics of how this is to be implemented;

- the option to fully recognise the impact of changes in market variables in profit or loss as an accounting policy choice will be extended to contracts with participating features;

- a simplified approach for determining the insurance investment expense for contracts in which changes in market variables affects the amount of cash flows

will be permitted when retrospective application of the new standard is impracticable; and

- when an entity uses the variable fee approach to measure insurance contracts and uses a derivative measured at fair value through profit or loss to mitigate the financial risk from a guarantee embedded in the insurance contract, the entity would be permitted to recognise in profit or loss the changes in the value of the guarantee determined using fulfilment cash flows provided certain conditions are met including documentation of the entity's risk management objectives and strategy for using the derivative in this way;

At the time of writing this chapter, the IASB still has a number of technical decisions to make before a new standard can be issued.[34]

11.4   Mitigating the impact on insurers of applying IFRS 9 before IFRS 4 Phase II

It has become clear that the effective date of IFRS 4 Phase II is likely to be at least two years after the effective date of IFRS 9. Consequently, the IASB has been asked to address concerns arising from additional accounting mismatches and volatility that result from the different effective dates. Accounting mismatches could arise in profit or loss when insurance contract liabilities are measured based on a locked-in discount rate but changes in the fair value of assets are reported in profit or loss. This could be the case under both IAS 39 and IFRS 9 but effects may increase under IFRS 9 where financial assets that are currently held at amortised cost or AFS could be required to be reclassified at fair value through profit or loss. Further profit or loss volatility could arise from changes in the shareholder's interest in financial assets underlying participating contracts when such assets are carried at fair value through profit or loss. Such volatility is not expected to arise under IFRS 4 Phase II because of the variable fee approach (see 11.3 above) so this is viewed as temporary volatility (at least for those contracts that will qualify for the variable fee approach).

At its September 2015 meeting, the IASB agreed to produce an Exposure Draft (ED) to IFRS 9 of changes to IFRS 4. If adopted, these proposals will allow insurers the option to either (i) defer the implementation of IFRS 9 until the earlier of the effective date of a new standard for insurance contracts and accounting periods beginning on or after 1 January 2021 ('deferral approach') or (ii) account for financial instruments in accordance with IFRS 9 but with an option to exclude from profit and loss and recognise in other comprehensive income, the difference between amounts that would be recognised in profit or loss in accordance with IFRS 9, and the amounts recognised in profit or loss in accordance with IAS 39 ('overlay approach'). The overlay approach would therefore give insurers an option to remove from profit or loss some of the accounting mismatches and temporary volatility that could occur from applying IFRS 9 before the new standard for insurance contracts is implemented.

The deferral approach would apply only to reporting entities with a predominant part of their business devoted to the activity of issuing contracts within the scope of IFRS 4. This would be determined by reference to the proportion of total liabilities that are within the scope of IFRS 4. The IASB believe that 'predominant' should represent a high hurdle and the related IASB Staff Paper indicated that this was likely to mean an entity with two thirds of total liabilities within the scope of IFRS 4 would not qualify. The IASB decided not to propose a quantitative threshold but would provide an example specifying a threshold that is higher than the example in the Staff Paper. The assessment should be performed initially at the date when the entity would otherwise be required to apply IFRS 9, i.e. for periods commencing on or after 1 January 2018. If there is a subsequent demonstrable change in the corporate structure of the entity, for example an acquisition or disposal of a business, which could result in a change in the predominance of the entity's activities, the assessment should be reperformed.

The deferral option would apply at the reporting entity level and not below. So, for example, a conglomerate financial institution would assess its eligibility by reference to the consolidated financial statements for the entire group. Subsidiaries within the conglomerate that issue their own (separate or consolidated) financial statements would assess the eligibility criteria at their own level for the purpose of their own reporting.

The overlay approach would permit an entity to remove from profit or loss and recognise in other comprehensive income the difference between (i) the amounts that would be recognised in profit or loss in accordance with IFRS 9 and (ii) the amounts recognised in profit or loss in accordance with IAS 39 for specified assets. An entity would therefore apply IFRS 9 in full but make the adjustments described above in profit or loss and other comprehensive income. The approach will apply only to financial assets that are classified at fair value through profit or loss in accordance with IFRS 9 when they were previously measured at either amortised cost or AFS in accordance with IAS 39. Further, it will apply only to financial assets that are designated by an entity as relating to contracts that are within the scope of IFRS 4. Various disclosures will be required in order to understand and explain the overlay adjustment.

At the time of writing this publication, the IASB has still to discuss the comment period for the proposed ED for which publication is planned in late 2015.[35]

11.5   The road ahead

Currently, the IASB expects to issue a new standard in 2016 after the remaining technical decisions have been made. Considering the IASB's stated intent to set an effective date no earlier than three years after issuance of the final standard, if the standard is issued in 2016, it is unlikely to have an effective date before 2020.

References

1 *IASB Update*, May 2002.

2 www.cfoforum.nl

3 ED/2013/7, Insurance Contracts, IASB, June 2013, para. BCA154.

4 ED/2013/7, para. B19.

5 *Effect of board redeliberations on the 2013 Exposure Draft Insurance Contracts*, IASB, June 2015, p.50.

6 ED/2013/7, para. 7(e).

7 *Effect of board redeliberations on the 2013 Exposure Draft Insurance Contracts*, IASB, June 2015, p.5.

8 *IFRIC Update*, January 2008, p.3.

9 ED/2013/7, para. 10(a).

10 ED/2013/7, paras. 10(b) and B31-32.

11 *IFRIC Update*, November 2005, p.6.

12 *IFRIC Update*, January 2010, p.2.
13 ED/2013/7, paras. 3(c), Appendix A.
14 *Effect of board redeliberations on the 2013 Exposure Draft Insurance Contracts*, IASB, June 2015, p.42.
15 ED/2013/7, paras. 49-50.
16 ED/2013/7, paras. 54-55.
17 ED/2013/7, paras. 63 and 67.
18 ED/2013/7, para. 41(b)(iii).
19 ED/2013/7, para. 51.
20 ED/2013/7, para. B66(a).
21 ED/2013/7, para. 41(c).
22 *Effect of board redeliberations on the 2013 Exposure Draft Insurance Contracts*, IASB, June 2015, p.22-23.
23 ED/2013/7, para. B66(c).
24 ED/2013/7, para. B66(j).
25 *European Embedded Value Principles*, CFO Forum, May 2004, p.3.
26 ED/2013/7, paras. 60(h) and 64.
27 *Effect of board redeliberations on the 2013 Exposure Draft Insurance Contracts*, IASB, June 2015, p.30.
28 ED/2013/7, paras. C11-C12.
29 *Effect of board redeliberations on the 2013 Exposure Draft Insurance Contracts*, IASB, June 2015, pp.83-84.
30 ED/2013/7, paras. 44-46.
31 *Effect of board redeliberations on the 2013 Exposure Draft Insurance Contracts*, IASB, June 2015, p.24.
32 *IASB Update*, June 2009.
33 *IASB Update*, June 2015, pp.2-3.
34 *IASB Update*, September 2015, pp.8-12.
35 *IASB Update*, September 2015, pp.2-6.

Index of extracts from financial statements

Index of standards

IFRS 2

IFRS 3

IFRS 4

IFRS 1

IFRS 6

IFRS 7

IFRS 8

IFRS 10

IFRS 12

IFRS 14

IFRS 15

IFRS 28

IAS 1

IAS 12

IAS 16

IAS 17

IAS 18

IAS 20

IAS 21

IAS 23

IAS 24

IAS 27

IAS 33

IAS 34

IAS 37

IAS 39

IAS 40

IAS 41

IFRIC 1

Index

Notes

Notes

Notes

Notes

Notes